3600 Wilsher
(213) 281 - 7253

Ken Dakis

(how to establis the busness)
(or how to open the business)
Said to I am student LACC. and ms. Chang Stud

L 100

CONTEMPORARY BUSINESS

EIGHTH EDITION

CONTEMPORARY BUSINESS

EIGHTH EDITION

LOUIS E. BOONE

Ernest G. Cleverdon Chair of Business and Management
University of South Alabama

DAVID L. KURTZ

R. A. and Vivian Young Chair of Business Administration
University of Arkansas

THE DRYDEN PRESS
HARCOURT BRACE COLLEGE PUBLISHERS

Fort Worth Philadelphia San Diego New York Orlando Austin San Antonio
Toronto Montreal London Sydney Tokyo

EDITOR-IN-CHIEF *Lyn Maize*
ACQUISITIONS EDITOR *Daryl Fox*
DEVELOPMENTAL EDITOR *Stacey Sims*
PROJECT EDITOR *Amy Schmidt*
ART DIRECTOR *Melinda Welch*
PRODUCTION MANAGER *Ann Coburn*
PERMISSIONS AND PHOTO RESEARCH EDITOR *Adele Kraus*
PRODUCT MANAGER *Lisé Johnson*
DIRECTOR OF EDITING, DESIGN, & PRODUCTION *Diane Southworth*
PUBLISHER *Diana Farrell*

COPYEDITOR *David Talley*
INDEXER *Joyce Teague*
PRODUCTION AND EDITORIAL SERVICES *Seaside Publishing Services*
COMPOSITOR *GTS Graphics, Los Angeles*
TEXT TYPE *10 pt Times Roman*

Address for Editorial Correspondence
The Dryden Press, 301 Commerce Street, Suite 3700, Fort Worth, TX 76102

Address for Orders
The Dryden Press, 6277 Sea Harbor Drive, Orlando, FL 32887-6277
1-800-782-4479, or 1-800-433-0001 (in Florida)

Acknowledgments begin on page xxii, which constitutes a continuation of the copyright page.

ISBN: 0-03-010274-X

Printed in the United States of America
5 6 7 8 9 0 1 2 3 4 048 9 8 7 6 5 4 3 2 1

The Dryden Press
Harcourt Brace & Company

To the 2.5 million students
who began their business studies using
Contemporary Business *in their classes.*

THE DRYDEN PRESS SERIES IN MANAGEMENT

ANTHONY, PERREWÉ, AND KACMAR
Strategic Human Resource Management,
Second Edition

BARLETT
Cases in Strategic Management for Business

BEREMAN AND LENGNICK-HALL
Compensation Decision Making: A Computer-Based Approach

BOURGEOIS
Strategic Management From Concept to Implementation

BRACKER, MONTANARI, AND MORGAN
Cases in Strategic Management

BRECHNER
Contemporary Mathematics for Business and Consumers

CALVASINA AND BARTON
Chopstick Company: A Business Simulation

COSTIN
Readings in Total Quality Management

COSTIN
Managing in the Global Economy: The European Union

COSTIN
Management Development and Training: A TQM Approach

CZINKOTA, RONKAINEN, AND MOFFETT
International Business,
Fourth Edition

CZINKOTA, RONKAINEN, MOFFETT, AND MOYNIHAN
Global Business,
Fourth Edition

CZINKOTA, RONKAINEN, MOFFETT, AND MOYNIHAN
Global Business

DAFT
Management,
Third Edition

DAFT
Understanding Management

DESSLER
Managing Organizations in an Era of Change

FOEGEN
Business Plan Guidebook
Revised Edition

GATEWOOD AND FEILD
Human Resource Selection
Third Edition

GOLD
Exploring Organizational Behavior: Readings, Cases, Experiences

GREENHAUS
Career Management,
Second Edition

HARRIS AND DESIMONE
Human Resource Development

HIGGINS AND VINCZE
Strategic Management: Text and Cases
Fifth Edition

HILLS, BERGMANN, AND SCARPELLO
Compensation Decision Making,
Second Edition

HODGETTS
Management: Theory, Process, and Practice

HODGETTS
Modern Human Relations at Work,
Sixth Edition

HODGETTS AND KROECK
Personnel and Human Resource Management

HODGETTS AND KURATKO
Effective Small Business Management,
Fifth Edition

HOLLEY AND JENNINGS
The Labor Relations Process,
Fifth Edition

JAUCH AND COLTRIN
The Managerial Experience: Cases and Exercises
Sixth Edition

KEMPER
Experiencing Strategic Management

KINDLER AND GINSBURG
Transformational Change in Organizations

KIRKPATRICK AND LEWIS
Effective Supervision: Preparing for the Twenty-first Century

KUEHL AND LAMBING
Small Business: Planning and Management
Third Edition

KURATKO AND HODGETTS
Entrepreneurship: A Contemporary Approach
Third Edition

KURATKO AND WELSCH
Entrepreneurial Strategy: Text and Cases

LENGNICK-HALL AND HARTMAN
Experiencing Quality

LEWIS
Io Enterprises Simulation

LONG AND ARNOLD
The Power of Environmental Partnerships

MCMULLEN AND LONG
Developing New Ventures: The Entrepreneurial Option

MATSUURA
International Business: A New Era

MONTANARI, MORGAN, AND BRACKER
Strategic Management: A Choice Approach

MORGAN
Managing for Success

NORTHCRAFT AND NEALE
Organizational Behavior: A Management Challenge
Second Edition

PENDERGHAST
Entrepreneurial Simulation Program

RYAN, ECKERT, AND RAY
Small Business: An Entrepreneur's Plan
Fourth Edition

SANDBURG
Career Design Software

VECCHIO
Organizational Behavior
Third Edition

WALTON
Corporate Encounters: Law, Ethics, and the Business Environment

ZIKMUND
Business Research Methods
Fourth Edition

PREFACE

WINNER OF THE
1994 WILLIAM HOLMES MCGUFFEY AWARD FOR EXCELLENCE & LONGEVITY

***CONTEMPORARY BUSINESS*, BY BOONE AND KURTZ**

Contemporary Business was awarded the first William Homes McGuffey Award for Excellence and Longevity in 1994 by the Text Academic Authors Association, Inc. (TAA). The selection was made by a panel of judges who themselves are noted textbook authors in business. The award recognizes *Contemporary Business* as one of the best college textbooks published in the past half-century and the authors' contribution to the education of today's business leaders.

"How do you win the McGuffey Award?" This question brings to mind the old story of the first-time visitor to New York city who asked a passerby, "How do you get to Carnegie Hall?" The answer: Practice, practice, practice!

For the past two decades, we have worked unceasingly to make each new edition of *Contemporary Business* better than the previous one. First, we listen. We seek advice from colleagues throughout North America and from their students. We visit dozens of campuses each year, gathering feedback from instructors and students. Their suggestions and criticisms serve as focal points in discussions between the authors and publisher about ways to enhance the value of each new edition.

Next, we experiment. We try out ideas, new approaches, and new assignments in our own classes. As full-time classroom teachers of the first business course, we benefit from knowing firsthand just how effective a new assignment, a new chapter, or a new approach is. Our own students give us this feedback on a daily basis. This hands-on experience by the authors is lacking in most other introductory business texts, which are typically written by authors who teach in other disciplines.

Finally, we evaluate the results of our experiments, decide on the changes that should be made, and implement them in each new edition. Our guiding credo is, "First we will be best, then we will be first."

The result of this effort is a book that combines quality with customer satisfaction. We are gratified in knowing that our colleagues have made *Contemporary Business* the number-one choice by a margin of two to one over the second-place text. The book is

BUSINESS & MANAGEMENT
COORDINATOR: DR. LOUIS E. BROOKE, BMSB 5-D, 460-6009
UNDERGRADUATE

4593	BMS	150	1	INTRO TO BUSINESS & MGMT	4	MW	200 350	L. BOONE	BMSB 165

currently being translated into Russian to serve as the cornerstone of the nation's emerging business-education programs.

BOOK FEATURES

If imitation is truly the sincerest form of flattery, *Contemporary Business* has received a host of accolades. A quick review of newly-released competitive texts reveals how closely the text model established in previous editions is followed by other authors. The typical competing business text will contain a virtually identical listing of chapters and a text design that includes the successful innovations of our previous editions. Because of this "innovate, then watch others imitate" pattern, teachers of basic business courses anticipate each new edition of *Contemporary Business* as a model for future editions of other texts. The new Eighth Edition will not disappoint them.

The fundamental changes occurring in today's business world, changes that will affect our lives as we enter the new century, are thoroughly examined in the new edition. Terms appearing regularly in daily news reports are integrated with the business concepts in the text. Examples include:

- the Internet
- interactive media
- information superhighway
- empowerment
- outsourcing
- customer satisfaction
- integrated marketing communication
- strategic alliances
- workplace diversity
- critical thinking
- downsizing
- narrowcasting
- home-based work
- competitive benchmarking
- GATT and NAFTA
- on-line computer services
- technology
- cross-functional teams
- reinventing the corporation

Another feature of the new edition is currency. *Contemporary Business* is as up-to-date as today's publishing technology allows. The result is a finished product that offers examples as recent as:

- devaluation of the Mexican peso
- rumblings in the U.S.–Japan trade wars
- the Oklahoma City terrorist bombing
- impact of the O. J. Simpson case on the use of celebrity endorsers.
- danger of derivatives as an investment vehicle.

FEWER CHAPTERS AND FEWER TEXT PAGES

A continuing complaint from both students and instructors is that introductory business texts are simply too long. Over the past two editions, we have reduced the number of chapters from 24 to 20. We have also addressed the requests of professors for a more concise book by reducing the length of the new eighth edition by 100 pages.

The new 20-chapter text has been created by condensing materials in four chapters and adding two new chapters—for a new edition two chapters shorter than the previous one. The changes include the following:

- The Process of Management and The Internal Organization, formerly Chapters 7 and 8, are combined in a single chapter entitled Management and the Internal Organization.
- Chapter 19, Financial Management and Institutions, now covers the discussions previously divided into two chapters: financial management and money, banking, and financial institutions.

- The previous edition's chapter on risk and insurance is now condensed in Appendix B.
- Subjects previously covered in a separate chapter on human relations have been integrated into three chapters devoted to human resource management, teamwork and communication, and labor-management relations.

Two new chapters have been added to this eighth edition of *Contemporary Business:* Chapter 7, Total Quality Management, and Chapter 10, Teamwork and Communication. These subjects are vital to business today. Coverage includes approaches used by successful organizations in today's changing business environment.

NEW TOTAL QUALITY MANAGEMENT CHAPTER

Another first for this edition is a separate chapter on the role of quality in business success. Instead of a narrow conception of quality as affecting only production processes, this new chapter shows how total quality management can be applied throughout the organization, from human resource management and finance to marketing and information. The importance of employee involvement, empowerment, training, and teamwork in achieving world-class quality to provide customer satisfaction is examined as well. Current examples of quality programs and approaches in organizations are integrated thoroughly throughout the text.

NEW TEAMWORK AND COMMUNICATION CHAPTER

Another first in this new edition of *Contemporary Business* is the addition of an entire chapter devoted to two fundamental concerns of today's business executives: the shift of organizations to working in teams and the importance of effective communication. Coverage includes work teams and special-purpose problem-solving teams, cross-functional teams, team development, conflict resolution, oral and written communication, verbal and nonverbal communication, and communication technology.

NEW EMPHASIS ON TECHNOLOGY IN INFORMATION SYSTEMS

Chapter 17, Information for Business Decisions, has been completely revised to reflect the increasing number of innovations in the information industry. The Internet and online information services such as CompuServe, Prodigy, and America Online are common tools in daily operations, and their growth is expected to transform business as we know it by increasing communication between people and organizations throughout the world. Obviously, information and the technologies that bring it to us are a necessary part of any introductory business course today.

NEW CONCEPTUAL APPROACH TO THE ACCOUNTING CHAPTER

In direct response to reviewer requests, the chapter on accounting is written with an emphasis on the more contemporary conceptual approach as opposed to the traditional procedural approach. No longer do students memorize basic rules and procedures. The chapter has been completely rewritten to reflect the most modern teaching methods at colleges and universities across the country.

NEW INTERNATIONAL INDEX

Three years ago, *Contemporary Business* was the first text to place the international chapter early in the text and to thoroughly integrate international examples. Now it is the first to include a separate International Index at the end of the text. This index provides an easy way for students and instructors to locate specific international examples in the text. Chapter 3, Global Dimensions of Business, is still placed early in this eighth edition, and international examples are still thoroughly integrated throughout the text.

NEW FEATURE BOXES

Three new boxes, which focus on current issues and concepts in the chapters, appear throughout the text. Their titles reflect their topics:

- Strength in Diversity, which highlight *all* aspects of diversity, not just cultural, in the business world.
- A Broader Purpose, which spotlight current issues relating to ethics and social responsibility.
- Business in Action, which focus on current events in the business world.

NEW PEDAGOGY—MORE OUTCOME-BASED AND SKILL-ORIENTED

The pedagogy has been strengthened to focus on more outcome-based learning and on developing individual and team skills.

- *Achievement Check Summary:* This new feature, appearing at the end of each chapter, is an innovative approach to the traditional summary. Students are provided with a mini-quiz tied to the chapter learning goals. This question-and-answer format provides a more interactive and creative method for reviewing key chapter concepts than just reading a summary would.
- *Questions for Critical Thinking:* Each of the boxes ends with questions that force students to tie concepts discussed in the chapter to the story in the box. Critical thinking questions also help students develop analytical skills while considering specific business situations.
- *Team-Building Exercises:* These exercises appear at the end of each part and are designed to encourage students to work in teams to solve business issues or to complete business-related exercises. The Team-Building Exercises are also tied directly to specific content materials covered in each part to reinforce the concepts discussed therein. We extend special thanks to Stacey Sims, Hal Babson, Murray Brunton, John Bowen, and University Associates for their contributions to the development of this new feature.
- *Video Cases:* Many of the popular Video Cases are new to this edition; some have been entirely revised to reflect current changes in the organization and its environment. Each chapter ends with a video case that brings to life the material in the video itself.
- *Careers in Business* and *Career Design Exercises:* These features of *Contemporary Business* have proven themselves to be a valuable resource for business students and instructors alike. For this reason, they still appear at the end of each part to get students thinking about their future career choice and help them prepare for it.

NEW INFO-GRAPHIC DESIGN

An exciting and innovative new text design includes contemporary info-graphic artwork. These info-graphics are used in selected tables and figures to help students better visualize information. At least one info-graphic appears in each chapter and provides students with a more useful and creative way to understand and remember the information presented.

CAREER PREPARATION

Contemporary Business continues to integrate career information into the text in response to comments from students and instructors at dozens of colleges and universities. As the authors visited campuses during the past three years, students throughout the United States and Canada expressed their concerns about finding jobs after graduation. These concerns are important enough to deserve a major commitment to addressing them. This new edition includes career features from the previous edition as well as a new career exercise on CD-ROM.

Students of the late 1990s are pragmatic. They know how important it is to prepare early for a career, to match their individual abilities and interests to specific career alternatives, and to create an academic plan to help them secure that first job on their career path. But they need help in accomplishing this objective.

The first business course is a perfect setting in which to begin career preparation. As the student is exposed to many different aspects of the world of business throughout the course, he or she also can begin to consider which areas represent potential careers. In addition to a description of popular business careers in Appendix A, we have included profiles of recent graduates who have begun successful careers in different business disciplines. We also provide *Career Design Software,* which includes résumé and self-assessment tools. Eric Sandberg, a business professor for 12 years and current president of Career Design Software, designed this product and created special data sets for it based on extensive interviews with business executives.

The Career Design Exercises included in the software will help the student decide on a major; identify strong skills; determine whether starting a business may be the most appropriate career path; create custom résumés that will stand out from others; and develop communication skills by organizing thoughts through writing. These materials are fully integrated with the text, require no special preparation by the instructor, need no special equipment, and—best of all—are absolutely free with the purchase of a new copy of *Contemporary Business,* Eighth Edition.

INSTRUCTIONAL RESOURCE PACKAGE

The Dryden Press has spared no expense to make this the premier learning system on the market today. Many instructors with limited resources teach large classes. Supplementary materials provide a means of expanding and improving the students' learning experience. The teaching/learning package provided with the book is designed to meet the needs of instructors facing a variety of teaching conditions and to enhance students' experience in their first business course.

INSTRUCTOR'S RESOURCE MANUAL, VOLUMES I AND II

Over the past 20 years, the Instructor's Resource Manual has been transformed into one of the most relied-upon tools of the entire supplement package. Every effort has been made to produce a guide that not only follows the materials in each chapter, but also enhances teaching by providing real-world examples of the concepts therein. The following sections are included for each text chapter:

- Changes from previous edition
- Annotated Learning Goals
- Lecture Outline

- Lecture Illustration File
- Answers to Critical Thinking Questions
- Answers to Review Questions
- Answers to Discussion Questions
- Answers to Video Case Questions
- Supplemental Cases
- Instructor's Notes for Team-Building Exercises
- Controversial Issues
- Experiential Exercises
- Guest Speaker Suggestions
- Term Paper Suggestions

ELECTRONIC INSTRUCTOR'S LIBRARY

This new and innovative instructor resource system is comprised of electronic versions of the *Instructor's Resource Manual, Test Bank, Transparencies,* and *Learning Guide,* all on a disk in WordPerfect 5.1 format.

MEDIA INSTRUCTOR'S MANUAL

A separate *Media Instructor's Manual* with easy-to-use guidelines helps instructors incorporate the videos, laser disk, and LectureActive software into lectures and classroom presentations.

VIDEOS

Each new edition of *Contemporary Business* has incorporated the latest technological advances in teaching. Once again, we provide a new series of videos created, produced, filmed, and/or edited by the Center for Instructional Technology in Marketing (CITM), at Central Michigan University, in partnership with well-known companies. Since their inception, the focus of the *Contemporary Business* videos has been integration with concepts covered in the text. They contain real-world examples, on-location footage, special effects, and state-of-the-art graphics.

Business professors have guided the scripting and production of the videos specifically produced for this eighth edition of *Contemporary Business*. Twenty videos are included in the package, ranging from such giants as Marriott, Andersen Consulting, Whirlpool, and Harley-Davidson to lesser-known companies such as Kropf Orchards, Slazenger Golf, and The Delfield Company. They include international businesses, service firms, and organizations founded and managed by entrepreneurs, and they focus on quality, ethics, and diversity. The videos are approximately 8 to 10 minutes in length. Their titles are as follows:

Chapter 1: Marriott International
Chapter 2: Andersen Consulting
Chapter 3: Whirlpool Corporation
Chapter 4: The Detroit Zoo
Chapter 5: Danimation
Chapter 6: Slazenger Golf
Chapter 7: Wainwright Industries Inc.
Chapter 8: Kropf Orchards
Chapter 9: University National Bank
Chapter 10: Valassis Communications, Inc.
Chapter 11: Harley-Davidson
Chapter 12: The Delfield Company
Chapter 13: The Toronto Blue Jays
Chapter 14: Second Chance
Chapter 15: Next Door Foods
Chapter 16: Dayton-Hudson
Chapter 17: United Parcel Service
Chapter 18: Archway Cookies
Chapter 19: Firstbank Corporation
Chapter 20: Roney & Company

The Media Instructor's Manual provides the following materials for each video case: teaching objectives, a list of chapter concepts illustrated in the video, video warm-up questions and exercises, a detailed outline of the video, answers to in-text video case questions, video recap, experiential exercises, and a multiple-choice quiz. The superb instructional materials for the video cases were prepared by Norman Cregger of Central Michigan University Center for Instructional Technology in Marketing.

LASER DISK AND LECTUREACTIVE PRESENTATION SOFTWARE

The Dryden Press once again is shaping business education by including a laser disk in the instructor's supplementary materials. The disk contains graphic and textual elements from the textbook and support materials integrated with video and animation sequences to provide a dynamic, easy-to-use multimedia presentation of fundamental business concepts.

Specifically, the laser disk includes the 20 videos, 250 transparencies, all of the figures from the book, additional graphics, chapter learning goals, and a variety of other relevant text screens.

The LectureActive Presentation Software gives instructors the ability to preprogram lectures using the *Contemporary Business* laser disk. LectureActive allows the instructor to add and modify video captions and labels on the screen, add information to note cards, organize and reorganize lecture note cards, edit videos for length, and create text screens. The finished product is a unique and personalized lecture presentation.

TEST BANK

Over half of the 3,500 questions in the revised *Test Bank* are new to this edition. Questions are keyed to chapter learning goals, text page number, and type of question (knowledge or application). Questions include multiple-choice, true/false, and a short essay for each learning goal. Mini-cases with multiple-choice questions and critical thinking questions emphasize the importance of the concepts presented in each chapter. The *Test Bank* was prepared by E. George Stook, Roland D. Tollefson, and David A. Wiley, all of Anne Arundel Community College.

COMPUTERIZED TEST BANK AND REQUESTEST SERVICE

A computerized version of the printed test bank is available in Windows, IBM, and Macintosh formats. Instructors can edit test questions, add new questions, scramble questions, and create up to 99 versions of the same test. A phone-in test master service is also available with a 48-hour turnaround period.

TRANSPARENCY ACETATES, MASTERS, AND TEACHING NOTES

Approximately 250 full-color overhead transparency acetates are available. Each acetate illustrates key concepts discussed in the text. Many acetates are new to this edition and most are original, that is, they do not repeat text figures. Transparency masters highlight actual figures and graphics found in the text. A complete set of teaching notes is included for both the acetates and masters.

BUSINESS CAREER DESIGN SOFTWARE

This excellent software, created by Eric Sandberg, provides students with interactive exercises which are integrated with each of the text's end-of-part Career Design Exercises. After completing one or two questionnaires or activities, students can use the software program to measure their current capabilities and then to obtain personalized advice on improving skills. Exercises cover topics such as leadership style, entrepreneurial quotient, and setting goals, and incorporate real-world business articles and experiences. The new CD/ROM-based Discovering Your Business Career takes the student through an extensive questionnaire in which he or she rates a variety of job-related activities. The software also includes a custom résumé module. The Career Design software can be packaged free with each copy of the textbook.

COMPUTER SIMULATION

The *Chopsticks Simulation Game,* created by Professors Eugene J. Calvasina, James Leon Barton, Jr., Ava Honan, Richard Calvasina, and Gerald Calvasina of Auburn University, challenges students to develop and experience the business concepts presented int he text and to utilize frequently-used business decision-making tools. The game is accompanied by an instructor's manual that provides game instructions and student worksheets. The simulation game is available on disk for use with IBM and IBM-compatible PCs.

QUALITY, DIVERSITY AND BUSINESS MATH SUPPLEMENTAL MODULES

Modules on the subjects of quality, diversity assessment, and business math provide additional coverage for instructors who wish to further emphasize any of these areas.

ASSESSMENT MODULE

This unique module allows instructors to assess student mastery of text concepts. Organized by chapter, this assessment module includes chapter learning goals, review questions, essay questions and unique assessment exercises.

LEARNING GUIDE

The *Learning Guide* is invaluable in helping students master business concepts. Each chapter includes a brief outline, experiential exercises, a self-quiz, cases, and short-answer questions. Crossword puzzles included are at the end of each chapter. *Learning Guide* solutions appear at the end of the guide, rather than in the *Instructor's Resource Manual.* The *Learning Guide* was prepared by Joan Sepic-Mizis of St. Louis Community College at Florissant Valley and Kathy Daruty of Los Angeles Pierce College.

ALTERNATE LEARNING GUIDE

A unique alternate version of the *Learning Guide* is available with this eighth edition of *Contemporary Business.* Answers and solutions are not provided at the back of the guide, making this a tool that can be used to further challenge students. When required as a part of the course materials, instructors can assign homework from the *Alternate Learning Guide,* using it to evaluate how well students are retaining concepts covered in the text.

COMPUTER CASES SUPPLEMENT AND THE B&K BUSINESS DISK

These innovative components are designed to assist instructors who want to include analytical problems as homework assignments or to use such tools as the microcomputer in the basic business course. The computer cases supplement includes three to five business problems and solutions per chapter, focusing on concepts discussed therein. The business disk includes complete programs for the computer cases and the solutions to each case.

PORTFOLIO OF BUSINESS PAPERS

To help students understand the variety of official documents required in a modern business organization, a *Portfolio of Business Papers* has been assembled to accompany the text. Authentic business papers and complete teaching notes are available to professors who use *Contemporary Business* in their classes. The papers were edited by Nikki Paahana of the DeVry Institute of Technology, Columbus, Ohio.

ACKNOWLEDGMENTS

The authors gratefully acknowledge the following colleagues who reviewed all or part of the eighth edition and its ancillaries. We are extremely grateful for the insightful comments of the following people:

Robb Bay, Community College of Southern Nevada
Rowland Chidomere, Winston-Salem State University
Robert Cox, Salt Lake Community College
Jodson Faurer, Metropolitan State College at Denver
Milton Glisson, North Carolina AT&T State University
Don Gordon, Illinois Central College
Stephen Griffin, Tarrant County Junior College
Stephen Griffin, Tarrant County Junior College
Douglas Heeter, Ferris State University
Paul Hegele, Elgin Community College
Tom Heslin, Indiana University, Bloomington
Vince Howe, University of North Carolina, Wilmington
Geraldine Jolly, Barton College
Dave Jones, La Salle University
Kenneth Lacho, University of New Orleans
Thomas Lloyd, Westmoreland County Community College
Martin St. John, Westmoreland County Community College
Sheb True, Loyola Marymount University
Robert Ulbrich, Parkland College
W. J. Walters, Central Piedmont Community College
Tom Wiener, Iowa Central Community College
Joyce Wood, Northern Virginia Community College
Gregory Worosz, Schoolcraft College

Last, but not least, we want to thank our good friends at The Dryden Press and Seaside Publishing Services. Our acquisitions editor, Daryl Fox, our developmental editor, Stacey Sims, our project editor, Amy Schmidt, our designer, Melinda Welch, and our production managers, Lynne Bush and Ann Coburn, have been most supportive and helpful. Other key Dryden professionals who made this edition possible include Lyn Hastert Maize, Virginia Warren, Sam Stubblefield, and our product manager Lisé Johnson. Considerable contributions from Jeanne Lowe, Alice Fugate, Mary Howell and Wendy Caster also deserve mention.

Louis E. Boone
David L. Kurtz

ABOUT THE AUTHORS

LOUIS E. BOONE (Ph.D.) holds the Ernest G. Cleverdon Chair of Business and Management and serves as coordinator of the introductory business course at the University of South Alabama. He formerly chaired the Division of Management and Marketing at the University of Tulsa and has taught courses in management and marketing in Australia, Greece, and the United Kingdom.

Dr. Boone is a prolific researcher. In addition to authoring numerous marketing and business texts and computer simulation games, he is author of *Quotable Business,* published by Random House. His current research focuses on event and sports marketing. Dr. Boone's research has been published in such journals as the *Journal of Business Strategy, International Journal of Management, Journal of Business Research, Sports Marketing Quarterly, Journal of Psychology, Business Horizons, Journal of Marketing,* and the *Journal of Business of the University of Chicago.* He is recent recipient of the Phi Kappa Phi Outstanding Scholar Award from the University of South Alabama and is listed in *Who's Who in America.*

DAVID L. KURTZ (Ph.D.) holds the R. A. and Vivian Young Chair of Business Administration at the University of Arkansas. He previously held the Thomas F. Gleed Chair of Business and Finance at Seattle University and has also served as head of the Marketing Department at Eastern Michigan University.

Dr. Kurtz has authored or coauthored 26 books and more than 100 articles, cases, and papers. He has been the editor of two academic journals and has served as president of the Western Marketing Educators Association. He was co-chair of the 1995 World Marketing Congress in Melbourne, Australia. He has also been involved in consulting and training activities in business and has been the president of a small corporation.

CONTENTS IN BRIEF

CONTENTS

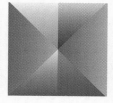

CONTEMPORARY BUSINESS

EIGHTH EDITION

CHAPTER 1
FOUNDATIONS OF BUSINESS

CHAPTER 2
ECONOMIC CHALLENGES FACING THE UNITED STATES

CHAPTER 3
GLOBAL DIMENSIONS OF BUSINESS

CHAPTER 4
SOCIAL RESPONSIBILITY AND BUSINESS ETHICS

PART I

CONTEMPORARY BUSINESS AND ITS ENVIRONMENT

CHAPTER 1

FOUNDATIONS OF BUSINESS

LEARNING GOALS

1. Explain what a business is and how it and a not-for-profit organization operate within the private enterprise system.

2. Define the role of the entrepreneur in the private enterprise system.

3. Outline the basic rights of the private enterprise system.

4. Discuss the factors of production and their factor payments.

5. Identify the possible degrees of competition in a private enterprise system.

6. Explain the concepts of gross domestic product and productivity.

7. Analyze how the historical development of the U.S. economy influences contemporary business.

8. Outline the factors that influence business in the late 1990s.

9. Identify the different types of economic systems.

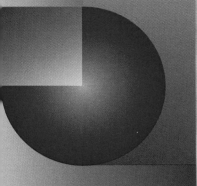

HONG KONG: BUSINESS IN TRANSITION Captain Charles Elliot of the Royal Navy claimed Hong Kong as a British colony in 1840. For his efforts, he was dismissed by Lord Palmerston, the British foreign secretary, who dismissed Hong Kong as just a "barren rock." ■ For years, Hong Kong was overshadowed by Shanghai as a major international business center. Things changed in 1949, however, when Mao Tse-tung led communist forces into the city. For the next few decades, Shanghai was limited by the stern yoke of China's communist government, which emphasizes shared ownership of property and profits. Foreign business people, vital cogs in Shanghai's economy, were driven away. Meanwhile, Hong Kong embraced the free enterprise system with its emphasis on competition; and businesses from all over the world began setting up shop there. ■ Today, Hong Kong is a thriving city-state of 6 million people. Its people, 98 percent of whom are Cantonese-speaking Chinese, live on just 400 square miles of land. Despite its small size, Hong Kong has achieved remarkable economic success. For instance, Hong Kong:

- Is among the world's richest nations (It ranked sixth at the beginning of the 1990s.)
- Has the 10th largest trading volume in the world
- Holds the world's 12th largest foreign exchange reserve
- Has the 8th largest stock market in the world
- Has an unemployment rate of just 2 percent

Hong Kong has always preserved close ties to mainland China. In fact, the People's Republic of China is Hong Kong's most important trading partner, accounting for a third of its total trade. Japan ranks second in trade with the British colony. China has invested approximately $20 billion in Hong Kong, more than the United States, Japan, and Britain. Similarly, Hong Kong accounts for two-thirds of China's foreign direct investment. In fact, companies based in Hong Kong employ more manufacturing employees in China than in the Crown colony itself. It is estimated that up to one-third of Hong Kong's currency is actually in China, a situation that may foreshadow what is to come. ■ June 30, 1997 marks one of the most important dates in Hong Kong history. On that day, the Union Jack will be hauled down and the Crown colony will become the Hong Kong Special Administrative Region of the People's Republic of China. Sino-British negotiations in the early 1980s resulted in a joint declaration in 1984 that decreed that Hong Kong would maintain its capitalist economy for at least 50 years beyond 1997. The Chinese also assured freedoms of the press, speech, association, and religion. In essence, Hong Kong would operate under the principle of "one country, two systems" after the Chinese takeover. Hong Kong was even permitted to retain its own currency system and government. ■ With its foreseeable future assured, Hong Kong returned to work. However, the Peking government immediately began to modify the deal that it had struck with the British. The mainland Chinese insisted upon what they called *convergence;* in other words, they wanted to influence any decisions Britain made before 1997. For example, Hong Kong's sorely needed new airport became a major controversy since the British needed Chinese cooperation to secure financing and issue contracts that would remain in effect after the 1997 takeover date. ■ The People's Republic of China also issued a constitution for the future Hong Kong Special Administrative Region. The so-called "Basic Law" diluted some of the Chinese promises in the joint declaration. For example, the bill of rights that guaranteed various personal freedoms was made subordinate to the Basic Law. China also reserved the right to declare states of emergency in Hong Kong at its sole discretion. Furthermore, China got the right to appoint the bulk of the Hong Kong legislature. ■ The Tiananmen Square massacre shook normally unconcerned Hong Kongers, and 1 million of them marched in protest. Many residents emigrated to other countries. The United States, Canada, Australia, and

Singapore were popular destinations for these emigrés. Still others went to Tonga, Fiji, Mauritius, and Jamaica. This wave of emigration deprived the Crown colony of some of its best educated and most skilled workers. This was a cruel twist of fate for a country that provided a safe haven for so many people who fled the communist armies in 1949. ■ With June 30, 1997 approaching quickly, it remains to be seen if China will honor its "one country, two systems" pledge. If it does, Hong Kong will certainly play a major role in the future economic development of mainland China. Conventional wisdom says that China clearly recognizes the benefits of a vibrant Hong Kong economy, but suppose that China's leaders decide to subvert the original joint declaration. Hong Kong could quickly find itself playing a secondary role to another Chinese city. Shanghai's 13 million residents are already seeing the effects of its capitalistic rebirth, and many foreign-based firms agree. Over 300 U.S. companies have already opened offices there. ■ Only time will reveal the eventual destiny of Hong Kong, but one thing remains certain—Hong Kong will still be a lot more than a barren rock.[1]

CHAPTER OVERVIEW

What image does the word *business* evoke? Some think of jobs, others of merchants whom they patronize as consumers, and still others of the millions of firms that make up the world's economy. This broad, all-inclusive term can apply to many kinds of enterprise. Business provides the bulk of people's employment as well as the products they enjoy.

business
All profit-seeking activities and enterprises that provide goods and services that an economic system needs.

Business consists of all profit-seeking activities and enterprises that provide goods and services that an economic system needs. Some businesses produce tangible goods such as automobiles, breakfast cereals, and computer chips. Others provide services such as insurance, car rentals, and lodging. Business is the economic pulse of a nation, the means through which society's standard of living improves. Profits are a primary mechanism for accomplishing the goals of business. Accountants and businesspeople define profit as the difference between a company's revenues (receipts) and expenses (expenditures). More formally, **profits** are the financial rewards received by successful businesspeople who take the risks involved in business. Profits provide incentives for people to start companies and expand them and to offer consistently high-quality, competitive goods and services.

profit
Reward for the businessperson who takes the risks involved in blending people, technology, and information in creating and marketing want-satisfying goods and services that provide customer satisfaction.

not-for-profit organization
Firm whose primary objective is something other than returning a profit to its owners.

Even though the earlier definition of *business* focuses on firms whose objectives include earning profits for their owners, the business concepts discussed in this text clearly apply also to **not-for-profit organizations**—firms with primary objectives other than returning profits to their owners. The 1.3 million not-for-profits that operate in the United States employ almost 11 million people (including volunteers) and generate an estimated $300 billion in revenues each year. This sector includes museums, libraries, religious and human service organizations, secondary schools, many health-care facilities, colleges and universities, symphony orchestras, fraternal organizations, and thousands of other groups such as government agencies, political parties, and labor unions.

Just as important as profits are the social and ethical responsibilities that successful business organizations must meet. To succeed in the long run, companies must deal responsibly with employees, consumers, suppliers, competitors, units of government, and the general public. Chapter 4 will discuss social responsibility and business ethics more fully. This chapter's study of business begins by describing the private enterprise system. The chapter then examines the issue of productivity, summarizes the history of U.S. business, and looks at the current business era. It concludes by exploring alternative economic systems.

PRIVATE ENTERPRISE SYSTEM

Most U.S. businesses, large and small, belong to the so-called **private enterprise system,** in which their success or failure depends on how well they match and counter the offerings of competitors. **Competition** is the battle among businesses for consumer acceptance. Sales and profits are the yardsticks by which businesses measure such acceptance.

private enterprise system
Economic system in which success or failure depends on how well firms match and counter the offerings of competitors.

competition
Battle among businesses for consumer acceptance.

Examples abound of firms that once enjoyed success, but that failed to continue satisfying consumer demands. Competition assures that, over the long run, companies that satisfy consumer demands will succeed and those that do not will fail.

In the private enterprise system, firms must continually adjust their strategies, product offerings, service standards, and operating procedures to prevent competitors from gaining larger shares of the industry's sales and profits. Consider that, at one time, Montgomery Ward was a major force in retailing, but Sears beat Montgomery Ward to take over a major share of the market. Today, Wal-Mart leads the U.S. retail sector. The Bentonville, Arkansas discounter is also expanding rapidly into Canada, Mexico, Argentina, Brazil, and even Hong Kong and the People's Republic of China. In the meantime, Sears is attempting to strengthen its competitiveness by eliminating unprofitable activities such as its catalog business and featuring new fashion items and well-known brands of electronic products and appliances.

Competition is the mechanism that guarantees that the private enterprise system will continue to offer the goods and services that provide high living standards and sophisticated lifestyles. Few business organizations escape the influence of competition. Even not-for-profit organizations, like the American Cancer Society, must compete for contributions with other not-for-profit groups such as the American Heart Association, the local symphony, or your own college. Similarly, the U.S. Postal Service competes with private employers to hire workers.

ROLE OF THE ENTREPRENEUR

An **entrepreneur** is a risk taker in the private enterprise system, someone who seeks a profitable opportunity and then devises a plan and forms an organization to earn those

entrepreneur
Risk taker in the private enterprise system.

Mexico's new TV Azteca invested $30 million in equipment from Harris Corporation in order to provide a high-quality signal to viewers of the World Cup soccer championships. As a newly privatized television network, TV Azteca needed the new equipment to attract customers–viewers. In order to meet the needs of its customer, TV Azteca, Harris Corporation had to provide the products and service quickly to get the system operating in time for the soccer championships. As part of the private enterprise system, companies like Harris and TV Azteca must continually adjust to meet the desires and expectations of their customers. Competition assures success for the businesses that best satisfy customers.

profits. Some entrepreneurs set up new companies and ventures; others revitalize already established firms. The entrepreneurial spirit lies at the heart of the private economic system. If no one would take risks, there would be no successful businesses, and the private enterprise system could not exist. Chapter 6 will discuss the role of the entrepreneur in more detail.

capitalism
Economic system founded on the principle that competition among businesses best serves society.

The private enterprise system, or **capitalism,** is founded on the principle that competition among firms best serves the needs of society. Adam Smith, often identified as the father of capitalism, first described this process in his book *The Wealth of Nations*, published in 1776. Smith asserted that an economy is best regulated by the invisible hand of competition. He believed that competition among companies would assure that consumers would receive the best possible products and prices because the less efficient producers would gradually be driven from the marketplace.

The invisible hand concept is a basic premise of the private enterprise system. In the United States, competition regulates economic life. In fact, U.S. citizens feel that competition is so vital that they have passed laws to strengthen its role. These laws, called *antitrust laws,* preserve the advantages of competition by prohibiting attempts to monopolize markets. The Sherman Antitrust Act (1890) and the Clayton Act (1914), discussed in Chapter 4, are the primary U.S. antitrust laws. Many other government regulations also influence firms' operations.

BASIC RIGHTS WITHIN THE PRIVATE ENTERPRISE SYSTEM

Citizens living in a private enterprise economy rely on certain rights that are critical to the operation of capitalism. As shown in Figure 1.1, these include the rights to private property, control of profits, freedom of choice, and fair competition.

private property
Property that can be owned, used, bought, sold, and bequeathed under the private enterprise system.

The private enterprise system guarantees people the right to own, use, buy, sell, and bequeath most forms of **private property,** including land, buildings, machinery, equipment, inventions, and various intangible properties. The right to private property is the most basic freedom under the private enterprise system. People living under a private enterprise system have the right to any property they buy and to all benefits resulting from such ownership.

The private enterprise system also guarantees a business owner the right to all profits (after taxes) earned by the firm. This implies no guarantee that the business will earn a profit, but if the firm prospers, the owner is legally and ethically entitled to enjoy the profits.

FIGURE 1.1 BASIC RIGHTS OF THE PRIVATE ENTERPRISE SYSTEM

Under a private enterprise system, citizens are free to choose their employments, purchases, and investments. This means that people can begin or terminate businesses with minimal government interference. They can change jobs, negotiate wages, and join labor unions if they so desire. Consumers can choose among different breads, pieces of furniture, television programs, magazines, and other goods and services.

Americans are so accustomed to this freedom of choice that they sometimes forget its importance. The private enterprise economy maximizes human welfare and happiness by providing alternatives. Other economic systems sometimes limit freedom of choice in order to accomplish government goals, such as increasing industrial production.

The private enterprise system also allows the public to set rules for competitive activity. This is why the U.S. government has passed laws to prohibit cutthroat competition, that is, excessively competitive practices designed to eliminate competitors. It has also established ground rules that outlaw price discrimination, fraud in financial markets, and deceptive practices in advertising and packaging.

FACTORS OF PRODUCTION

Capitalism, like other economic systems, requires certain inputs to operate effectively. Economists call these inputs the factors of production. The four **factors of production** are natural resources, human resources, capital, and entrepreneurship. Not all firms require the same combination of factors; each business has its own mix.

Natural resources encompass everything that is useful as a productive input in its natural state, including agricultural land, building sites, forests, and mineral deposits. Natural resources are the basic resources required in any economic system.

Human resources are critical inputs to an economic system. Human resources include anyone who works, from the chief executive officer of a huge corporation to a self-employed auto detailer.

Capital includes the resources that a business needs to finance its operations, such as money, machines, tools, and buildings. These funds can be provided in the form of investments, profits, or loans. Businesses use them to build factories, buy raw materials, and hire workers.

Entrepreneurship is the willingness to take risks to create and operate a business. As explained earlier, the entrepreneur is the risk taker in the private enterprise system. Sometimes the entrepreneur actively manages the business; in other cases, this responsibility is delegated to a salaried manager.

All four factors of production must receive financial returns to function in the private enterprise system. As shown in Table 1.1, these payments take the forms of rent, wages, profits, and interest. Specific factor payments vary among industries, but all businesses require all factors of production in some degree. If you were to decide to start your own business (entrepreneurship), for example, you could buy your raw materials

factors of production
Basic inputs into the private enterprise system, including natural resources, human resources, capital, and entrepreneurship.

natural resources
Everything that is useful as a production input in its natural state.

human resources
Organization's employees.

capital
Funds that finance the operations of a business.

entrepreneurship
Taking risks to set up and operate a business.

TABLE 1.1 FACTORS OF PRODUCTION AND THEIR FACTOR PAYMENTS

FACTOR OF PRODUCTION	CORRESPONDING FACTOR PAYMENT
Human resources	Wages
Entrepreneurship	Profits
Capital	Interest
Natural resources	Rent

(natural resources) from a supplier and get a loan (capital) to start the business by agreeing to pay interest to the lender. You would compensate your employees (human resources) by paying them wages.

TYPES OF COMPETITION

Four basic degrees of competition characterize a private enterprise system: pure competition, monopolistic competition, oligopoly, and monopoly. Analysts can classify firms on the basis of the relative competitiveness of their particular industries.

pure competition
Market situation that features many firms in an industry so none can individually influence market prices.

Pure competition is a market situation that features many firms in an industry that are close enough in size to prevent any single company from influencing the prices charged in the marketplace. Pure competition involves firms selling similar products that cannot be differentiated from those of competitors. Firms can enter or leave a purely competitive market relatively easily. Agriculture is probably the closest modern example of pure competition, although government price-support programs make it somewhat less competitive.

monopolistic competition
Market situation that features firms that differentiate their products from those of competitors.

Monopolistic competition is a market situation that features firms that can differentiate their products from those of competitors. You see monopolistic competition in action when you watch commercials that try to persuade you to choose one brand over another. Monopolistic competition gives a firm some power over the price it charges. Think about retail stores, where prices can vary among different brands of clothes, cosmetics, and other items.

oligopoly
Market situation that features few sellers and substantial entry restrictions.

Oligopoly is a market situation that features few sellers. In some oligopolies, such as the steel industry, the products are similar; in others, such as automobiles, they are different. The huge investments required to enter these markets tend to discourage new competitors. Still, the primary difference between oligopoly and the previously mentioned types of competition is that the limited number of sellers gives the oligopolist more control over price. In an oligopoly, the prices of competitive products are usually quite similar because substantial price competition would reduce every firm's profits. All competitors typically meet price cuts by one firm in the industry.

monopoly
Market situation that features no direct competitors.

Monopoly is a market situation that features a single firm with no competitors. Since the Sherman and Clayton Acts prohibit attempts to monopolize markets, nearly all monopolies in the United States are government-regulated monopolies, such as public utilities. Firms that sell electricity and natural gas are regulated by state agencies that administer many aspects of the regulated monopolies' operations, including pricing and profits. In a pure monopoly, a firm would have substantial control over pricing, but in a regulated monopoly, pricing is subject to rules imposed by the regulators. A regulated monopoly faces few directly competitive products, and entry into the industry is restricted by the government. In fact, in some states, a public utility must periodically seek voter approval to continue its service. Table 1.2 presents the features of each type of competition.

MEASURING THE PRODUCTIVITY OF AN ECONOMY

To compete in today's marketplace, a nation's economy must be productive. **Productivity** is the measure of efficiency. It can be defined as the relationship between the number of units of goods and services produced and the number of inputs of human and other resources necessary to produce them. This ratio of output to input can be calculated for a nation, an industry, or a single firm. When a set amount of inputs generate increased outputs, an increase in productivity has occurred. Total productivity considers all inputs necessary to produce a specific amount of outputs. Stated in equation form:

productivity
Measure of the efficiency of production.

$$\text{Total productivity} = \frac{\text{Output (goods or services produced)}}{\text{Input (human/natural resources, capital)}}$$

TABLE 1.2 TYPES OF COMPETITION

	TYPES OF COMPETITION			
CHARACTERISTICS	PURE COMPETITION	MONOPOLISTIC COMPETITION	OLIGOPOLY	MONOPOLY
Number of competitors	Many	Few to many	Few	No direct competitors
Ease of entry into industry by new firms	Easy	Somewhat difficult	Difficult	Regulated by government
Similarity of goods or services offered by competing firms	Similar	Different	Can be similar or different	No directly competing goods or services
Control over price by individual firms	None	Some	Some	Considerable in a pure monopoly; little in a regulated monopoly
Examples	Small-scale farmer in upstate New York	JCPenney	Boeing	Dominion Resources

A productivity ratio often focuses upon only one of the inputs of the equation, for example, labor productivity or output per worker hour. An increase in labor productivity means that the same amount of work produces more goods and services.

A popular measure of a nation's productivity is its gross domestic product. **Gross domestic product (GDP)** is the sum of all goods and services produced within a nation's boundaries. U.S. GDP includes everything made by foreign firms within the United States, but it excludes goods and services made abroad by U.S. firms.

gross domestic product (GDP) *Sum of all goods and services produced within a nation's boundaries.*

Productivity is a widely used method for measuring a company's efficiency; in turn, the total productivity of a nation's businesses is a measure of its economic strength. The first U.S. census, conducted in 1790, revealed that 50 percent of the labor

BMW now produces automobiles at its new plant in Spartanburg, South Carolina. The sum of these goods is included in the U.S. gross domestic product even though the owner of the plant is a foreign corporation. U.S. gross domestic product does not, however, include the sum of goods and services produced abroad by U.S.-owned companies.

force was engaged in agriculture to feed the nation. Today, less than 3 percent of the U.S. work force feeds the nation and generates surpluses for consumers throughout the world.

What is the current status of overall U.S. productivity? After a lapse of 8 years, during which Japan led the world in productivity, the United States again became the world leader in 1993. Figure 1.2 shows the steady rise in U.S. productivity.

Increased U.S. productivity has not benefited everyone equally, however. Consider that auto workers now earn $65,000 to $70,000 a year. In fact, electricians in some plants take in over $100,000 a year. The industry employs considerably fewer full-time auto workers than it has in the past, however, and those workers average 10 hours of overtime a week and six Saturday shifts a year. As a result, sick time has increased and the United Auto Workers have protested to management. One assembly line worker commented, "I never thought I'd see the day when I welcomed a strike for a few days off."

In addition to the trend toward overtime, the auto makers and other employers are using more part-time employees. The rationale is simple—employers do not have to pay benefits to part-time workers, and they can expand or contract their labor forces quickly. In fact, Stephen Roach, an economist with the Morgan Stanley investment firm, has described the current U.S. economy this way: "The leader in this recovery is not IBM, not Wal-Mart, not General Motors. It is Manpower, the company that offers you a job for a week without benefits, not knowing where you're going to be next Monday."[2]

Meanwhile, the focus of the U.S. economy is shifting to service-sector productivity. Over 70 percent of U.S. jobs are now in services, the largest share of any nation, though service jobs have been growing even faster overseas. The rapid growth in manufacturing productivity has reduced the share of the labor force needed in that sector and prompted workers worldwide to move into service industries. Fortunately, the United States appears to be even further ahead of the pack in service-sector productivity. A recent McKinsey & Co. comparison of U.S. productivity in information and four other service industries with productivity levels in Germany, Japan, France, and Britain con-

FIGURE 1.2 U.S. PRODUCTIVITY INDEX

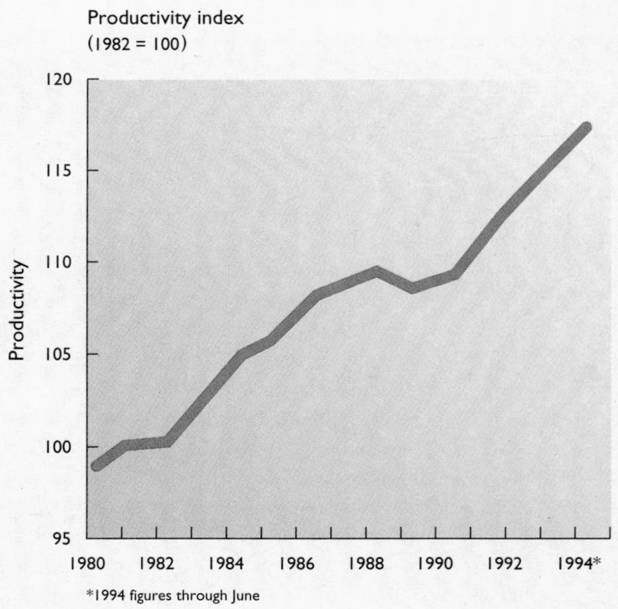

Temporary workers are trained in high-speed packing techniques by Norell Services, a temporary employment service, before being sent to work at Nike. Reliance on part-time and temporary labor continues to grow as companies like Nike choose to hire workers for the short term rather than the long term.

cluded that U.S. levels are substantially higher. A big reason for the lead is service companies' investments in computers, telecommunications networks, and other technologies that make their employees more productive.[3]

ECONOMIC HISTORY OF THE UNITED STATES

Business influences—and reflects—many aspects of a country's culture, its customs and politics, even its family life. This is true both in the United States and abroad. As business becomes more global, people must become increasingly sensitive to the business customs of other countries. For instance, many offices in the United States close at 5 p.m., a tradition that was begun in order to allow families to spend their evenings together. In France, however, the midday meal is traditionally a time for family togetherness. French businesses may give their employees two or even three hours off for lunch, but then stay open later in the evenings.

The United States has a fascinating business history. As this section will explain, the history of the American economy continues to influence how U.S. businesses operate today.

COLONIAL SOCIETY

Colonial society was primarily agricultural, built on the output of its farms and plantations. The young nation's prosperity depended on the success of its crops, and most people lived in rural areas. The cities were small compared to those of Europe and functioned as the marketplaces and residences of craft workers, traders, bankers, and government officials.

The real economic and political power of the nation was centered in rural areas, though. People were tied to the land socially as well as economically. The colonies looked to England for manufactured items and capital to finance infant industries. Even after the Revolutionary War (1776 to 1783), the United States maintained close economic relations with England. British investors provided much of the money to finance the developing business system, and this financial influence continued well into the nineteenth century.

INDUSTRIAL REVOLUTION

The industrial revolution began in England around 1750. The traditional manufacturing system of independent, skilled workers individually pursuing their specialties gave way to a factory system that mass-produced items by bringing together large numbers of semiskilled workers. The factory system profited from savings created by large-scale production. For example, bigger businesses could often purchase raw materials more cheaply in larger lots. Specialization of labor (each worker performing only one specific task or job) also improved production efficiency. With these innovations, the factory system revolutionized business.

Influenced by the events occurring in England, the United States began to industrialize rapidly. Agriculture became mechanized, and factories sprang up everywhere. Still, most business historians agree that real progress had to wait until railroads provided a fast, economical method of transporting the goods purchased and produced by businesses. The American industrial revolution was highlighted by the rapid construction of railroad systems during the 1840s and 1850s. Besides providing the necessary transportation system, railroads also created the need for greater quantities of lumber and steel, and they expedited land development.

AGE OF THE ENTREPRENEUR

During the nineteenth century, U.S. businesses made sizable advances. Eli Whitney introduced the concept of interchangeable parts, an idea that would later facilitate mass production. Peddlers, the salespeople of the day, operated throughout the country. Financiers became less dependent upon England, and the banking system became better established after some early problems. Inventors created a virtually endless array of commercially useful products.

People were encouraged to take risks and become entrepreneurs. Cornelius Vanderbilt, John D. Rockefeller, J. P. Morgan, and Andrew Carnegie all became wealthy because of their willingness to take business risks during this period. Admittedly, the speculation that characterized the economy during the 1800s hurt some people, but, on balance, the entrepreneurial spirit of the age did much to advance the U.S. business system and raise the overall standard of living.

PRODUCTION ERA

The early part of the twentieth century—the production era—was a period when businesspeople concentrated almost solely on production activities. Industries felt pressure to produce more and more goods to satisfy consumer demand and reduce shortages.

Work became increasingly specialized. Assembly lines, such as the one introduced by Henry Ford, became common. Owners turned over their responsibilities to a new class of managers who specialized in operating established companies rather than starting new ones.

Businesspeople tended to view marketing strictly as selling. They did not yet accept disciplines like consumer research. In other words, marketers were responsible solely for distributing products after they were produced. Business was oriented internally rather than toward the consumer.

MARKETING CONCEPT

The post-World War II era was influenced by an important new concept in management. The marketing concept became the prevalent business philosophy with its assertion that all activities and functions of the organization should be directed toward identifying and satisfying the wants and needs of consumers. A consumer orientation became the principal goal of companies.

Business organizations throughout the United States formed marketing research departments to analyze consumers' desires before actual production began. This approach represented a marked contrast to the earlier philosophy of making a product, then trying to sell it to the consumer. Advertising reached ever-larger numbers of consumers and increased the efficiency of firms' promotional efforts. Today, a firm must have a strong consumer orientation to remain competitive in the marketplace.

INFLUENCES ON BUSINESS IN THE LATE 1990S

Every period in history has posed particular challenges and obstacles to business, and the current era is no exception. The way that businesspeople respond to these issues today will have a significant impact on America and the world tomorrow.

GLOBALIZATION OF BUSINESS

Overseas sales account for 11 percent of the profits of U.S. corporations. Exports of goods and services now represent a bigger part of the U.S. economy than auto making and house building combined.[4] Clearly, doing business internationally is vital to a strong American economy. In fact, it is virtually impossible to travel outside the United States without observing the internationalization of business. Pizza Hut outlets, FedEx delivery trucks, and Coca-Cola are almost as familiar in Paris as in Los Angeles. Foreign firms build every videocassette player sold in America. Walkmans offer portable entertainment to music lovers from Tokyo to Philadelphia.

Global businesses such as Hewlett-Packard link their international operations to work on problems that affect their customers. When a Hewlett-Packard customer calls with a problem, the call is automatically routed to the most appropriate of the firm's four global customer-support centers, depending on time of day. In complex situations, time can often present an obstacle, but HP employees view finding a solution as an on-going project. At 6 p.m. California time, for instance, the assignment moves to the Australian staff and work continues without a hitch.[5]

The five largest U.S. exporters are Boeing, General Motors, General Electric, IBM, and Ford. Coca-Cola, sold in 195 different countries, is an excellent example of a global product. Over 80 percent of the firm's annual profits come from international sales.

Cola-Cola is produced in China for that country's growing soft-drink market. Coke is also sold in 194 other countries.

The United States is also an attractive market for foreign competitors. Its size and the standards of living enjoyed by American consumers have motivated such foreign companies as Mercedes-Benz, Sony, and Ikea to set up production and distribution facilities here. In addition, foreign firms have purchased such well-known U.S. companies as Saks Fifth Avenue, 7-Eleven convenience stores, Barnes & Noble, MCA Records, and Universal Studios.

PARTNERSHIPS AND STRATEGIC ALLIANCES

strategic alliance
Long-term partnership of firms designed to improve their overall competitiveness.

Traditionally, successful firms have been headed by visionaries who have bested competitors in the marketplace to build their organizations. In a growing trend of the late 1990s, firms often seek to improve their competitiveness by teaming up with other companies to create **strategic alliances,** partnerships formed to create competitive advantages. These long-run partnerships often cross national borders, and they can involve any size of company from the tiniest business to two or more industrial giants. Nowhere are strategic alliances more common than in the telecommunications industry, where U.S. competitors AT&T, MCI, and Sprint are forming alliances with national telephone companies throughout Europe, Central and South America, and Asia in the rush to achieve global dominance.

Many strategic alliances combine suppliers and business customers in partnering arrangements to develop mutually beneficial initiatives, such as designing new products or troubleshooting existing ones. For instance, Japan's Honda formed a strategic alliance with U.S.-based Donnelly Corporation to craft an improved type of exterior mirror for Honda cars. As a first step, Honda sent several engineers to work with Donnelly engineers to improve the efficiency of two Donnelly plants. The resulting savings reduced Donnelly's costs by 2 percent a year. The U.S. firm then built an entirely new factory, incorporating many of these improvements, and began making Honda's exterior mirrors. The partnership has grown from $5 million in sales the first year to an estimated $60 million in sales by 1997. Both companies plan to make their strategic alliance a permanent arrangement that will benefit each of them. As one Honda manager says, "To Honda, long term means forever—assuming you're doing the job."[6]

IMPROVING QUALITY

While U.S. businesses have invented many high-quality products through the years, lately other nations, such as Japan, have developed reputations for making outstanding products. Business leaders now emphasize the importance of total quality management, a commitment to quality as a crucial business goal for an entire company. It is vital for the U.S. firms to develop high-quality goods and services in order to attract new customers. It is also important to maintain quality over the long term to keep those customers coming back for more.

Motorola's strategic alliances, for example, pursue a strong emphasis on quality. First, the company looks for potential partners that share its corporate focus on quality. It then fosters this approach by requiring partners' employees to take classes in total quality management and customer satisfaction at Motorola University. Even after being chosen as partners, suppliers must maintain rigorous quality standards; Motorola teams tour their factories every 2 years and grade their quality and timeliness against those of competitors. In addition, Motorola managers rate suppliers every month on an index that combines cost and quality, and they compare suppliers' performance against competitors'.[7] Chapter 7 will take a closer look at the importance of quality in achieving business success.

BUSINESS IN ACTION

STARBUCKS: HOW TO GROW A COMPANY In some cities, Starbucks outlets are so common that they've become part of the landscape—in San Diego, two Starbucks stores separated by only two city blocks both thrive. As of this writing, Starbucks' 511 outlets serve some eight million customers each week. ■ Starbucks is predicated on a simple goal—serving a great cup of coffee—and its success seems almost inevitable. Yet in 1982, when Howard Schultz first came to Starbucks, it was a small, quietly profitable company with only 85 employees and low-key ambitions. ■ Starbucks was founded in the early 1970s by Jerry Baldwin, Zev Siegel, and Gordon Bowker. Located in Seattle's charming Pike Place Market, the first Starbucks sold coffee beans. Brewed coffee was only offered as a free sample of the wares. In 1982 Schultz joined Starbucks to improve the company's marketing strategies. On a trip to Italy, however, he was inspired by the number of coffee bars in Italy—and by their importance to Italian neighborhoods. Schultz then left Starbucks to open his own coffee houses. In 1987 he and several partners purchased Starbucks. At that point the company had only 11 stores. ■ Schultz's ambition was simple: He wanted customers to associate Starbucks with a first-rate cup of coffee. Producing an excellent product, however, was not enough. In addition, Schultz wanted everything about a customer's experience at Starbucks to be top-notch. Toward that goal, he instituted extensive training for Starbucks employees, along with a benefits package unparalleled in the retail industry. To attract and keep high-quality, loyal, and hard-working employees, Starbucks offers health care (even to part-timers), stock options, and, yes, free coffee. As a result, Starbucks employees stay with the company much longer (and steal much less while they're there) than the average retail employee. ■ Schultz also set up a Starbucks mail order business, giving consumers a chance to become acquainted with Starbucks coffee even before stores opened in their cities. In addition, Schultz instituted a distinctive advertising campaign for Starbucks, which included detailed explanations of the ingredients of various coffee drinks. The advertisements were later expanded into brochures available at Starbucks outlets. More recently, Schultz has focused on educating consumers to make better coffee at home with Starbucks-brand coffee by using coffee makers purchased from Starbucks. ■ While Schultz was savvy enough to grow the Starbuck chain from 11 stores to over 500 in only eight years, he is also pragmatic enough to realize that anyone can open a coffee house. "There's no secret sauce here," he has explained. "Anyone can do it." For years, Schultz has maintained an edge over actual and potential competitors through Starbucks' two main strengths: the quality of the product and the expertise and attitude of the employees. And now he has added a third: speed. Schultz plans to have around two thousand Starbucks outlets open and active by the year 2000. Sources: Telephone interview with public relations department, Starbucks, April 28, 1995; "Pulse Points," *U.S. News & World Report,* October 17, 1994, p. 18; Alice Z. Cuneo, "Starbucks' Word-of-Mouth Wonder," *Advertising Age,* March 7, 1994, p. 12; and Matt Rothman, "Into the Black," *Inc.,* January 1993, pp. 59–65.

QUESTIONS FOR CRITICAL THINKING

1. What are the dangers of establishing a business around a commodity such as coffee?
2. Do you think Starbucks is a fad business or is there long-term potential?
3. What do you think would happen to Starbucks if employee benefits were cut back to typical part-time retailing benefits?

ROLE OF TECHNOLOGY

technology
Business application of knowledge based on scientific discoveries, inventions, and innovations.

Technology involves the business application of knowledge based on scientific discoveries, inventions, and innovations. Technological breakthroughs such as videotelephones, orthoscopic surgery, and bullet trains result in new goods and services for consumers, better customer service, lower prices, and improved working conditions. Technology can make products obsolete, just as cassette tapes and CDs wiped out the market for vinyl record albums. It can also can open up new business opportunities.

Changes in technology can create whole new industries and new ways of doing business. Technological innovations ranging from voice recognition and scanners to advanced fiber optics and online services play critical roles in advancing a nation's standard of living in the late 1990s.

FOCUSING ON PEOPLE

An earlier section identified people as a crucial input to any economic system. Ironically, perhaps, the growing importance of technology makes it even more important for organizations to make effective use of human resources. Computer networks allow employees to work together directly and pool their collective knowledge. This tends to flatten the organizational hierarchy, creating a more informal organization.

More and more organizations are discovering the benefits of teamwork, in which employees work together on projects. At Lotus Development, software writers in Asia and Europe team up via computer networks with their American colleagues to develop new products. Once it took Lotus 3 to 4 months to create a Japanese version of a new English-language software package; thanks to international teamwork, it now takes three to four weeks.

Empowerment also requires employees to develop greater aptitude for analyzing situations and making their own decisions. Westin Hotels, for instance, has created a set of skill standards for recruiting, hiring, training, and retaining its 35,000 employees. Hotel managers identified 14 key characteristics that effective employees need, no matter what their organizational ranks. In addition to technical competence, these skills include the ability to show initiative, a commitment to quality, and good communication skills. Since Westin began screening employees for these skills and the ability to manage themselves, its turnover rate has fallen dramatically.

TREND TOWARD OUTSOURCING

outsourcing
Contracting of work to an outside firm.

Another trend influencing the business world of the late 1990s is **outsourcing,** in which a company farms out one or more of its in-house operations to a preferred vendor that can perform those tasks with a high quality level. Outsourcing can save money because a company does not have to hire additional staff to perform those functions, which may result in savings on salaries and benefits while freeing existing personnel to do other tasks. For example, a firm may outsource its warehousing, payroll, delivery services, or data processing operations. Eastman Kodak has outsourced its computer operations to IBM; large oil companies often outsource cleaning and maintenance work on oil refineries.[8] Outsourcing will be considered in a variety of contexts throughout this text.

ALTERNATIVE ECONOMIC SYSTEMS

Much of the world lives under economic systems other than capitalism. The number of countries that practice other systems makes it important to learn the primary features of these alternative economies. This text, *Contemporary Business,* does not concern itself with political questions, but rather with the economic aspects of communism, socialism, and mixed economies.

COMMUNISM

communism
Economic theory, developed by Karl Marx, that eliminates private property and provides for common ownership of the means of production.

The writings of Karl Marx in the mid-1800s formed the basis of communist theory. Marx wanted to abolish all private property. He believed that the upper classes exploited workers, leading to a class struggle that would make way for a new world order called **communism.** All property would be shared by the people of a community (hence the name *communism*), under the direction of a strong central government.

Marx felt that a nation's people should ultimately own all of the country's productive capacity, but he conceded that the central government would have to operate businesses until a classless society could evolve. Marx felt that this classless society would be based on the idea, "From each according to his abilities, to each according to his needs." This means that each individual should contribute what he or she can to society, but that the society's resources should be distributed to its citizens according to their needs rather than their contributions. As you can see, this represents a very different approach from the capitalist idea of paying people according to the work they perform. While such a system benefits those who are unable to work, it also takes away much of the incentive for workers to do their jobs well, since pay is not necessarily tied to performance. Under communism, the central government owns the means of production, and the people, in turn, work for state-owned enterprises. The government determines what people can buy because it dictates what factories produce.

Many nations adopted communist economic systems during this century in an effort to improve the quality of life for their citizens. In practice, however, communist governments often gave people little or no freedom of choice in selecting jobs, purchases, or investments. Continuing economic troubles led to the collapse of the communist governments in the former Soviet Union and eastern Europe. Today, communism remains entrenched in just a few countries like the People's Republic of China, North Korea, and Cuba.

Former Soviet Union Many formerly communist nations have gone through dramatic changes. Some of the most exciting changes have occurred in the republics that formerly comprised the Soviet Union. These new nations have restructured their economies by introducing Western-style capitalism and private enterprise. By decentralizing economic planning and providing more incentives for workers, they are shifting to market-driven systems.

Entrepreneurship and joint ventures have also emerged in Russia in recent years. Consider the case of Jeffrey Zieger, a twenty-something entrepreneur from Trenton, New Jersey. Zieger has launched a joint venture with a Russian partner, the Lenin District Food and Catering Trust, to open Tren-Mos, a western-style restaurant on Komsomolsky Street in central Moscow. Zieger pays a lot of personal attention to his customers, an uncommon practice in Russian restaurants. He also accepts both Russian rubles and hard currency. The rubles pay for many of the food ingredients bought at cheap, subsidized state prices. This allows Tren-Mos to earn a 65 percent profit margin on its dollar sales.[9]

Eastern Europe The breakup of the Soviet Union affected other communist governments, as well. As the USSR relinquished political control over eastern Europe, many countries in the region began experimenting with capitalism. As in the former USSR, the road to free enterprise has been bumpy. The withdrawal of government control exposed how uncompetitive eastern European industries had become under communism. Suddenly companies had to compete with Western firms for market share, and they found that their products were often substandard and their manufacturing processes out of date. Some eastern European companies have adjusted, though. OP Prostejov of the Czech Republic used to sell half of its output of coats and suits to Russia, but with the demise of this market, the firm found new customers in Germany, the Netherlands, Belgium, and Luxembourg.[10]

The Czech Republic and other eastern European countries have also provided fertile ground for aspiring American entrepreneurs and established U.S. companies. In fact, 30,000 Americans now live in the Czech Republic compared to only 100 just 5 years ago. The case of Lisa Frankenberg is typical. After graduating from college, Frankenberg went on a backpacking expedition through Europe. In Prague, the capital of Czech Republic, she met some people who used to work on her college newspaper, and the group started an English-language newspaper.

In a short period of time, Frankenberg discovered that the paper was appealing to the wrong group. "We were writing for backpackers, while our readers were the Arthur Andersen consultants and Coopers & Lybrand accountants." Frankenberg and a partner

STRENGTH IN DIVERSITY

FOUNDATIONS OF BUSINESS—RUSSIAN STYLE

In the years since the Soviet Union broke up and the Iron Curtain fell, many Americans have started to focus on Russia as a place to invest money and do business. After all, Russian stocks are reasonably priced, Russian labor is inexpensive, and the Russian market is enormous. That's the good news. ■ For the bad news, doing business in Russia can become a nightmare. Russia's decades-old state-owned economy is not yet set up for capitalism. Business laws are obscure—when any exist—and the courts are unprepared to deal with intricate financial matters. The entrenched Russian bureaucracy is like an impenetrable maze to outsiders. An American doing business in Russia may need dozens of signatures just to get started. Bribing bureaucrats to get those signatures is an accepted overhead cost in Russia. ■ Also, non-Russian companies in Russia must pay 20-plus different taxes which can change with little notice. Phibro Energy started pumping oil in Russia in 1990, pursuing immense potential profits. Over the next four years, however, Boris Yeltsin issued decrees that raised Phibro's taxes to 70 percent of its gross income and removed one of Phibro's drilling licenses. Gulf Canada, another energy company, complained that its tax bill exceeded its revenues! Many Russian taxes on foreign-owned businesses are set deliberately high to benefit local firms. ■ Americans who decide to invest in some of the thousands of privatized Russian companies also face myriad obstacles. Russian businesses often keep financial information secret or release misleading or dishonest balance sheets. It can be difficult even to find out at what price shares are trading; quotes in financial publications sometimes have little to do with reality. Once investors do manage to purchase equities, they often have difficulty registering the shares in their names. Stock funds are also risky in Russia's 60-plus unregulated stock markets; an investment may simply disappear along with the manager of the fund. ■ Yet these financial impediments seem insignificant compared with the actual life-and-death risks of doing business in Russia. Russian crime organizations demand chunks of businesses' incomes, and owners refuse at their peril. Bank presidents and other businesspeople are regularly murdered in Russia. Some business owners accept the need to pay one gang to protect them from others as part of life in Russia. ■ Obviously, business in Russia is not for the fainthearted, but many people still believe that Russia's newly opened markets offer enough potential to more than compensate for the risks. Time will tell. Sources: Alan Cooperman, "Moscow Headaches," *U.S. News & World Report,* October 10, 1994, p. 12; Peter Fuhrman, "What Boris Gives," *Forbes,* August 15, 1994, pp. 42–43; Melinda Liu and Betsy McKay, "The FBI versus Russia's Mob," *Newsweek,* July 25, 1994, p. 28; Patricia Kranz, "Russia's State Sell-Off: 'It's Sink-or-Swim Time,' " *Business Week,* July 4, 1994, pp. 46–47; Paul Klebnikov, "Russia—The Ultimate Emerging Market," *Forbes,* February 14, 1994, pp. 88–94; and Paul Klebnikov, "Go East, Young Man," *Forbes,* December 20, 1993, pp. 102–106.

QUESTIONS FOR CRITICAL THINKING

1. Would you invest your money in a Russian business? Why or why not?
2. What can local Russian businesses do to fight organized crime?
3. Is Russia a viable market for international businesses?

then started the business-oriented *Prague Post*. Today, the *Post* has a circulation of 15,000.[11]

SOCIALISM

socialism
Economic system that advocates government ownership and operation of all major industries.

Socialism, another major economic system, resembles communism in that the government owns and operates key industries that it considers vital to the public welfare, such as transportation, utilities, and medicine. However, it allows private ownership for industries that it considers less crucial, like shops and restaurants. Socialists believe that major industries are too important to be left in private hands and that government-owned businesses can operate more efficiently and serve the public better.

Lisa Frankenberg founded the *Prague Post*. American entrepreneurs like Frankenberg and established companies like Kmart have found business opportunities in eastern Europe.

The U.S. Commerce Department classifies Israel as a "democratic socialist economy."[12] Israel has about 170 government-owned enterprises, although it is currently going through a privatization effort. In addition, the national labor federation, Histradut, owns 25 percent of the nation's factories. Over one-sixth of the Israeli labor force works in Histradut enterprises, and virtually the entire labor force belongs to the labor federation.

MIXED ECONOMIES

In practice, many countries do not have pure economies that exemplify one type or another. Instead, they have **mixed economies** that combine government ownership and private ownership.

The proportions of private and public enterprise vary widely in mixed economies, and their mixes are always changing. Over 50 countries have converted government-owned companies into privately held firms in a trend known as **privatization.** Countries may privatize state-owned enterprises to improve their economies, believing that private corporations can manage and operate the businesses more cheaply and efficiently than government units can. Sometimes unloading these enterprises can raise badly needed cash for a government. In fact, privatization has raised $300 billion for national treasuries around the world. Great Britain, Mexico, and Chile are cited as countries that have benefited significantly from privatization.[13]

mixed economy
Economic system that mixes government ownership and private enterprise.

privatization
Trend to substitute private ownership for public ownership.

WHAT'S AHEAD

The study of business is an exciting, rewarding field that covers an ever-changing global landscape. Now that this chapter has introduced some basic terms and issues in the business world of the late 1990s, the next chapter will look at a few basic economic concepts, as well as some economic challenges facing society.

ACHIEVEMENT CHECK SUMMARY

Reread the learning goals that follow, and consider the questions for each goal. Answering these questions will reinforce the most important concepts in the chapter and allow you to check how well you have achieved these learning goals. Where a blank appears before a question, answer with *T* or *F*. Otherwise, circle the letter of the correct answer. An answer key to these questions is found at the end of this chapter.

LEARNING GOAL 1.1: Explain what a business is and how it and a not-for-profit organization operate within the private enterprise system.

1. ___ In the private enterprise system, businesses are the primary providers of the goods and services needed by society.
2. ___ Business and not-for-profit organizations both have as their primary objectives returning profits to owners.
3. ___ Over the long run, competition ensures that organizations that best satisfy customer demands will be more successful than those that do not.

LEARNING GOAL 1.2: Define the role of the entrepreneur in the private enterprise system.

1. ___ People who take the risks of pursuing business opportunities are called *entrepreneurs*.
2. ___ Profits represent both the reward and the incentive for risk taking.

LEARNING GOAL 1.3: Outline the basic rights of the private enterprise system.

1. Laws that prohibit price discrimination and deceptive advertising practices are included in the right to: (a) private property; (b) profits; (c) freedom of choice; (d) fair competition.
2. The most fundamental right of the private enterprise system is said to assure: (a) private property; (b) profits; (c) freedom of choice; (d) fair competition.
3. The right of the risk taker to retain his or her after-tax earnings is the right to: (a) private property; (b) profits; (c) freedom of choice; (d) fair competition.

LEARNING GOAL 1.4: Discuss the factors of production and their factor payments.

1. ___ Each factor of production generates a financial return.
2. ___ The factor payment for the use of capital is profit.

LEARNING GOAL 1.5: Identify the possible degrees of competition in a private enterprise system.

1. ___ The four basic degrees of competition in a private enterprise system are pure competition, monopolistic competition, oligopoly, and monopoly.
2. ___ An industry with monopolistic competition requires such large capital investment that very few producers can compete.
3. ___ The major difference between pure and monopolistic competition hinges on whether or not producers can differentiate their products.

LEARNING GOAL 1.6: Explain the concepts of gross domestic product and productivity.

1. ___ Productivity is a measure of efficiency found by dividing inputs into outputs.
2. ___ Gross domestic product equals the sum of all goods and services produced within a nation's boundaries.
3. ___ The nation with the most productive economy in the world is Japan.

LEARNING GOAL 1.7: Analyze how the historical development of the U.S. economy influences contemporary business.

1. ___ The colonial era was characterized by a factory system and the growth of large cities.
2. ___ The production era focused on mass production of standardized consumer goods.
3. ___ The marketing concept means that producers make what they can produce most effectively, and marketing amounts to simply selling that product.

LEARNING GOAL 1.8: Outline the factors that influence business in the late 1990s.

1. ___ Outsourcing refers to the increased globalization of business.
2. ___ Strategic alliances are long-run partnerships formed to improve competitiveness.
3. ___ While many U.S. firms are important exporters, the United States is rarely an attractive market for foreign competitors.

LEARNING GOAL 1.9: Identify the different types of economic systems.

1. ___ Socialism is an economic system in which the government owns all of a nation's productive capacity.
2. ___ It is safe to say that no society has a pure economic system today.

KEY TERMS

REVIEW QUESTIONS

1. Define *profit* and explain the role of profits in the private enterprise system.

2. What roles do entrepreneurs play in the private enterprise system? What type of people become entrepreneurs?

3. Why is Adam Smith identified as the father of capitalism? Discuss Smith's concept of the invisible hand of competition.

4. Discuss the basic rights that underlie the private enterprise system. How does each right contribute to the effective functioning of the private enterprise system?

5. Identify and describe the inputs required by the private enterprise system. What payments are made to each of these inputs?

6. The four basic degrees of competition are pure competition, monopolistic competition, oligopoly, and monopoly. Match these types with the businesses listed below:
   a. Texaco
   b. US West Communications
   c. Wal-Mart
   d. Fred and Susan Smith's 640-acre Iowa farm

7. What is meant by the term *productivity?* How is the concept of GDP related to productivity?

8. What factors or issues are expected to influence business in the late 1990s?

9. Identify the major eras in the historical development of the U.S. economy.

10. Differentiate among the private enterprise system, communism, socialism, and mixed economies. Discuss the current status of each of these economic systems.

DISCUSSION QUESTIONS

1. Kun-Hee-Lee, chairman of Korea-based Samsung Group, has commented, "Only organizations which contribute to mankind will last: those organizations which lack humanism and morality can never become premier companies and will not endure."[14] Do you agree with this comment?

2. Profit has sometimes been described as the regulator of the private enterprise system. Discuss the meaning of this comment.

3. Manufacturing workers in the United States now log 360 more hours of work each year than do their French counterparts. When compared to German workers, U.S. production personnel put in 430 more hours annually.[15] Do these statistics affect the productivity of the U.S., French, and German labor forces? Why are American workers putting in so much overtime? What are the long-term implications of this discrepancy in work hours?

4. The chapter presented a list of factors or issues that will influence business in the late 1990s. Rate the relative importance of these factors. Cite specific, real-world examples of each factor in action.

5. Pick a country other than the United States and analyze its economic system. How would you describe the country's economy? What trends do you see?

SOLUTIONS TO ACHIEVEMENT CHECK SUMMARY

L. G. 1.1: 1. T, 2. F, 3. T, **L. G. 1.2:** 1. T, 2. T, **L. G. 1.3:** 1. d, 2. a, 3. b, **L. G. 1.4:** 1. T, 2. F, **L. G. 1.5:** 1. T, 2. F, 3. T, **L. G. 1.6:** 1. T, 2. T, 3. F, **L. G. 1.7:** 1. F, 2. T, 3. F, **L. G. 1.8:** 1. F, 2. T, 3. F, **L. G. 1.9:** 1. F, 2. T.

VIDEO CASE

MARRIOTT INTERNATIONAL "If you can dream it, you can do it." Entertainment visionary Walt Disney's words might just as well have been written for another American entrepreneur. J. William Marriott's dream began in 1927 when he opened a nine-seat, root-beer stand called "The Hot Shoppe." From this humble beginning has risen one of the world's leading hospitality companies. By carefully blending the factors of production into a business attuned to customer needs, Marriott and his management team made the Marriott name a fixture in every state in America and in another 22 countries around the globe. Along the way, Marriott created jobs for 170,000 employees and generated revenues approaching $10 billion a year.

In serving the lodging market, Marriott management recognized that achieving customer satisfaction required the firm to adjust its service offerings to the needs of its different types of customers. For example, Marriott's Fairfield Inn properties target economy-minded travelers, Courtyard by Marriott facilities are aimed at the moderate-price market segment, and Marriott Hotels target travelers who are interested in quality lodgings with more amenities. Its line of Residence Inns aims to satisfy the needs of customers who stay five nights or more in the same facility. To appeal to the upscale market, the firm recently purchased the Ritz-Carlton chain, renowned throughout the world for its quality.

Even though lodging generates two-thirds of annual revenues, Marriott is not simply a hotel/motel chain. Serving the hospitality industry means businesses must provide value through packages of goods and services. At Marriott, this means spacious rooms, recreation facilities, and a swimming pool for lodgers; for its business market, it means food service and conference rooms.

Marriott has also successfully identified and responded to changes in the hospitality industry. A major lodging trend of the past two decades has been consolidation. As recently as 1980, 55 percent of lodging facilities in the United States were affiliated with chains. Today, two-thirds are, and the number continues to climb.

Although Marriott continues to be extremely successful in the $75 billion U.S. market, its management recognizes the huge opportunities that exist in the $150 billion-per-year international lodging market. Chains have made few inroads in the international lodging market so far, accounting for less than 17 percent of lodging revenues abroad. To capitalize on this opportunity, Marriott has decided to aggressively expand its presence in Europe, Latin America, the Caribbean, and in the Pacific Rim nations.

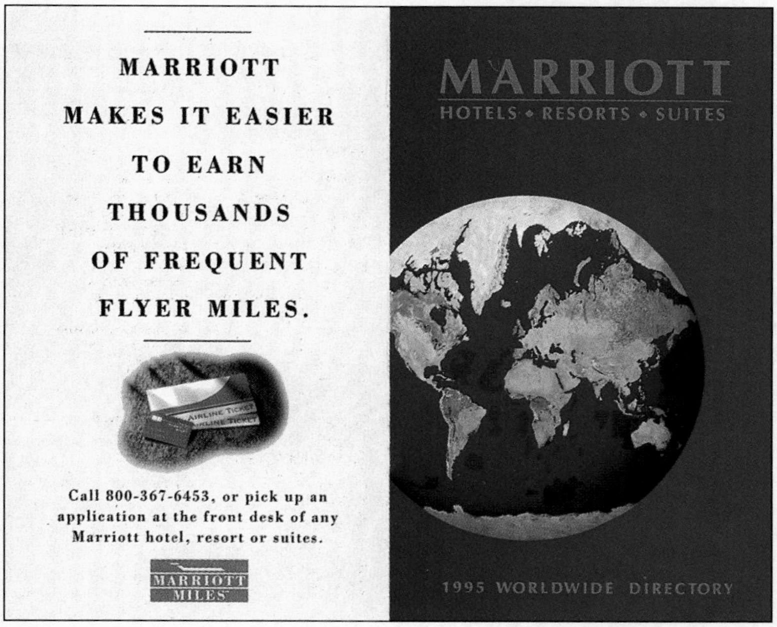

One of Marriott's early international facilities is the Warsaw Marriott, a world-class hotel in the former Soviet bloc nation of Poland. As Poland moved to a market-based economy in the late 1980s and 1990s, the Warsaw Marriott symbolized how a market-driven company can respond to customer needs. Business travelers to Poland gravitated to the hotel because they knew they would have access to the combination of services they required: interpreting and translating, photocopying and fax services, computer links, and secretarial services, in addition to comfortable rooms, a convenient location, and meeting facilities. Such "in-demand" services allow Marriott to ask a higher-than-average rate, but their Warsaw clientele are pleased with the added value they receive.

QUESTIONS

1.
J. Willard Marriott opened a nine-seat root-beer stand in 1927. As an entrepreneur, what was his role and what were his rewards?

2.
In what type of competition does Marriott engage (refer to Table 1.2)? Defend your answer using each characteristic described in the table.

3.
Explain the importance of international events to Marriott's decision makers as they plan expansion strategies.

4.
Explain how Marriott International blends each of the factors of production to create a successful business. What types of payment are received by each factor of production?

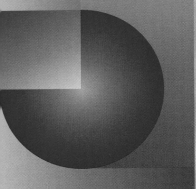

LEARNING GOALS

1. Differentiate between microeconomics and macroeconomics.

2. Show how supply and demand determine the equilibrium price.

3. Discuss important issues in macroeconomics, including inflation, recession, unemployment, and economic growth.

4. Distinguish between monetary policy and fiscal policy, and discuss how they help government to combat inflation and unemployment.

5. Explain what is meant by a service economy.

6. Discuss how American business can maintain global competitiveness.

CHAPTER 2

ECONOMIC CHALLENGES FACING THE UNITED STATES

RESPONDING EFFECTIVELY TO ECONOMIC CHALLENGES AT GM In 1992, General Motors (GM) lost $23.5 billion; its North American division alone lost more than $500 million a month. The auto maker's costs were the highest in its industry, its factories were the least efficient, and its cars averaged twice as many defects as those of Japanese competitor Toyota. ■ Enter Jack Smith, former head of GM Europe. When Smith took over as president and CEO of General Motors, he knew it was time to make some fundamental changes. He took a hard look at GM's operations and decided to overhaul many of its longstanding business practices. ■ Smith's major task was to change the company's corporate culture. Without strong, centralized management, each GM division had operated almost independently of the others, setting up its own computer systems, vehicle designs, and engineering procedures. Each division purchased its own supplies through widely dispersed, poorly coordinated offices. The company was organized into numerous profit centers which competed with each other for resources. Managers devoted much of their time to allocating overhead and calculating transfer prices, since these numbers had a big impact on a profit center's profitability; the Chevrolet division actually earned more from making Pontiac Firebirds and selling them to Pontiac than it did from selling Chevrolet Camaros to its own dealers. ■ To encourage the divisions to stop competing and start cooperating with each other, Smith created a strategy board to manage the North American car and truck business. The 14-member group gathered the top executives from manufacturing, engineering, finance, personnel, sales and marketing, purchasing, communications, and logistics to look at problems and issues from several functional viewpoints and to involve all business functions in resolving them. Explained G. Richard Wagoner, president of operations, "You figure out where the big holes are—where your costs are out of line or where you are weak in the marketplace. That suggests where you ought to dig. So you get some data together, present them to the board, and kick them around. It is changing the way we run the company. It's also fun. You can sit around and crack a joke or two." ■ One "big hole" that required immediate attention was the wide disparity between the processes, components, and products of GM's various divisions, which had resulted in incompatible systems. GM manufacturing plants had to allow for a total of 12 basic car platforms, which meant bigger factories, larger engineering staffs, and more inventory. Says Smith, "We didn't need 12 platforms. That's when you go broke." He reduced that number to 5 basic platforms that allow the car maker to produce distinctive models that still would share underlying mechanical components. ■ Smith also overhauled GM's product development process. The company consistently budgeted up to $2 billion a year to develop new models and then put the new designs on hold if it couldn't afford to produce them. Since 3-year delays were not uncommon, says Executive Vice President William Hoglund, "We had a whole design staff working to create new products that we couldn't afford, so we put them back on the shelf. When we finally came out with them, they were not particularly fresh." ■ Along the way, Smith eliminated several practices that looked good on paper but actually sabotaged sales. Fleet sales was one, in which GM sold 800,000 cars every year to rental-car companies. While this kept factories running and sustained market-share statistics, it ultimately hurt the auto maker because, after renting the vehicles for several months, the rental-car companies sold them as used cars. Customers quickly realized that they could buy a slightly used Cadillac DeVille with a few thousand miles for almost the same price as a new Buick Park Avenue; not sur-

prisingly, Buick sales suffered. GM management cut fleet sales by 50 percent. Says Smith, "It looks like an easy decision today, but when we made it, we said 'gulp.' After all, we lost two plants' worth of sales." In the long run, however, the move saved GM $400 million. ■ This chapter will discuss several key economic challenges confronting GM and other American companies, including developing better products, improving quality and competitiveness, and becoming more flexible. Clearly, GM has made progress toward meeting these goals. Over the past 4 years, U.S. car and truck sales have risen from 12.5 million to 15.3 million units. The company has gone from a $23.5 billion loss to a $2.5 billion profit, and its earnings continue to rise. After laying off 74,000 workers in North America, GM is hiring again for some plants and technical jobs. Enthuses Executive Vice President Harry Pearce, "There is more excitement around here than we've had in a long time. It is more than morale; it is a real feeling that people can make a difference." ■ At the same time, however, more improvements are needed. The company's return on sales averages 2.7 percent—better than before, but still below Smith's long-term goal of 5.0 percent. Layoffs have left the firm with an older work force (average age 46), a huge unfunded pension liability, and rising costs for retirees' health care. The biggest challenge lies ahead: to continue, and expand upon, the progress that has already been made. Says Executive Vice President Pearce, "I constantly worry that we will slip back into the complacency that got us into trouble in the past."[1]

CHAPTER OVERVIEW

Chapter 1 looked at economic concepts such as competition, factors of production and their corresponding factor payments, gross domestic product, productivity, degrees of competition, and comparative economic systems. This material provides some basic foundations of contemporary business.

This chapter will give you more background in economic theory and the economic challenges that face international business today. As we move into the final decade of the century, global competitiveness has become a key issue for U.S. businesses. The chapter will examine several competitiveness issues that the United States faces in an increasingly global economy. These issues include researching and developing better products, improving quality and service levels, improving the competitiveness of the work force, and improving organizational flexibility.

BASIC CONCEPTS IN ECONOMICS

economics
Social science of allocating scarce resources.

microeconomics
Study of the economic activities of a firm or individual.

Economics is the social science that seeks to understand the choices people make in using scarce resources.[2] The term *social science* means that economics is, above all, a study of people and their behavior. After all, resources become scarce only because people want more of them; soft drinks become scarce only if you want one and your friend has just bought the last can from the vending machine. Time is a scarce resource because you have so many different things you would like to do with it. Everyone makes economic choices every day when they decide what goods to buy, what services to use, and what activities will fit into their schedules.

The study of economics has two sides: microeconomics and macroeconomics. **Microeconomics** deals with the study of small economic units such as individuals, families, and companies. It is important to remember that, although these economic units may be small, their economic choices may be international in scope. Even though you are just one person, you involve yourself in international trade when you decide to buy a product made in another country. International trade is thus also part of the study of microeconomics.

The other branch of economics, **macroeconomics,** deals with bigger issues such as the overall operation of a country's economy. (*Macro* means "large.") Macroeconomics addresses several critical questions: How does an economy maintain adequate supplies of the resources that people want? What happens if the demand for scarce resources exceeds the supply? What government policies will be most effective in improving people's standard of living over time?

macroeconomics
Study of the overall operation of an economy.

This section will look in more detail at the branches of economics and the issues involved. Remember, though, that microeconomics and macroeconomics are interrelated; the big issues of macroeconomics reflect the small decisions made every day by microeconomic units like you.

SUPPLY AND DEMAND

Two important concepts in economics are supply and demand. **Supply** refers to sellers' willingness and ability to provide goods and services for sale in a market. **Demand** refers to buyers' willingness and ability to purchase these goods and services. The relationship between supply and demand determines price. Figure 2.1 shows that as the price of a particular product increases, the quantity supplied rises; but as the price increases, quantity demanded falls. The law of supply and demand states that prices (*P*) in a market are set by the intersection of these supply (*S*) and demand (*D*) curves. The point where the curves meet identifies the **equilibrium price** (*E*), the prevailing market price at which you can buy that item.

supply
Sellers' willingness and ability to provide products.

demand
Buyers' willingness and ability to purchase products.

equilibrium price
Price at which quantity supplied equals quantity demanded.

If the actual market price differs from the equilibrium price, people tend to make economic choices that return the prevailing price to the equilibrium amount. For instance, if sellers lower their prices below equilibrium, buyers are likely to snap up all of the available supply quickly. As sellers get more of the item, they are likely to mark up the price so they can increase their profits. On the other hand, if merchants mark their prices

FIGURE 2.1 LAW OF SUPPLY AND DEMAND

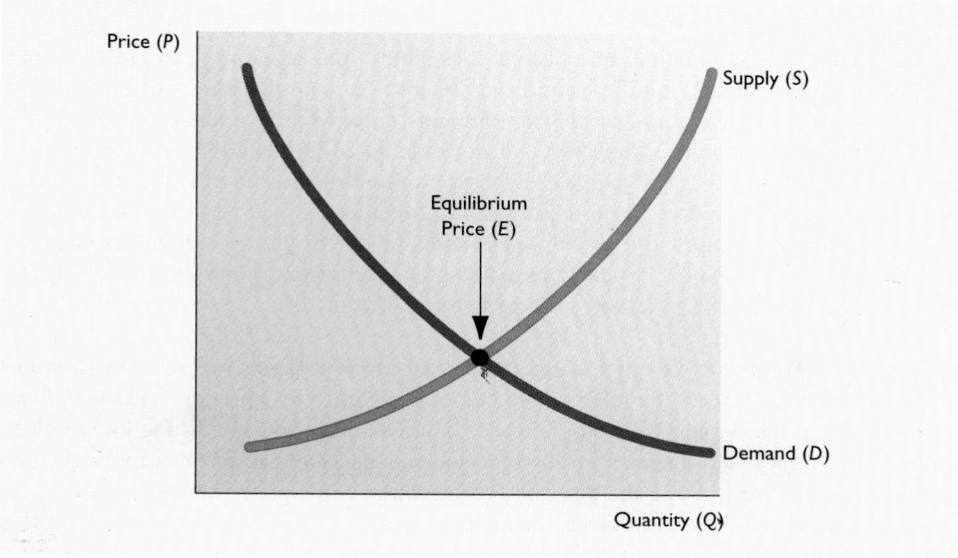

A BROADER PURPOSE

BREAKING THE LAWS OF SUPPLY AND DEMAND Fishing has always been a lucrative industry in Alaska. Fishermen prospered with net incomes of $100,000 and more in good years. Limited numbers of government fishing permits have sold for up to $300,000. Alaskan salmon has commanded some of the highest prices ever at market. When the salmon and herring ran, the fishing industry thrived. ■ It thrived, that is, until March 24, 1989. On that day, the *Exxon Valdez,* a mammoth oil tanker, spilled 11 million gallons of crude oil into the waters of the Prince William Sound. On that day, Alaska's fishing industry changed. ■ Reports showing the damage to wildlife and the environment were dramatic and upsetting. Clean-up crews found the carcasses of tens of thousands of fish, seals, and otters. Crews recovered the oily remains of some 36,000 birds with up to another 300,000 presumed dead. About 1,300 miles of the beautiful Alaskan coastline became an oily mess. These were the visible results; who could predict the long-range effects of such a disaster? ■ Today, Alaska's fishing industry is in a shambles, not because of any direct impact of the oil on the environment, but rather due to the ensuing legal case against the tanker's owner, Exxon. The battle lines were drawn between Exxon and the 12,000 Alaskan citizens affected by the spill. ■ At the crux of the issue is the supply of fish. Fishermen claim that the spill ruined their livelihoods. A year's catch of herring would usually be valued at about $10 million. In 1993 and 1994, though, the herring never came. In the 2 years following the spill, however, the supply of pink salmon reached record levels. In 1991, salmon were so plentiful that the excess was canned, financed by a $2 million donation from Exxon, and given to Russia. In 1992 and 1993, the supply of salmon then fell sharply. Exxon consultants maintain, supported by fishing records, that the size and value of the catch have al-

too high, buyers will purchase less of the product. Sellers then end up competing with each other for customers by lowering their prices to the point at which they sell all of their supply, which is the equilibrium price.

MICROECONOMICS: HOW DO SUPPLY AND DEMAND INTERACT?

As the earlier definition noted, microeconomics studies the economic activities of small units such as individuals, families, and firms. People's economic actions determine both the prices of goods and services and the amounts sold. Microeconomic information is vital for businesses because their survival depends on selling enough of their products at prices high enough to pay expenses and earn profits. It is also important to consumers, whose well-being may depend on the availability of these goods and services and their costs. The law of supply and demand is a dynamic concept, that is, it involves changes. The equilibrium price of a product does not remain constant. Changes in supply and demand force the market price of a product to rise or fall.

demand curve
Graph of the relationship between different prices and the quantity demanded at each price.

Changes in Demand versus Changes in Quantity Demanded The **demand curve** in Figure 2.1 shows the relationship between the price of a product and the amount of that product that buyers will purchase. Economists make a clear distinction between changes in demand and changes in quantity demanded. A change in quantity demanded is simply a movement along the demand curve, while a change in demand results in an entirely new demand curve. In the demand curve in Figure 2.1, note that when the price falls, the amount that customers demand rises. On the other hand, when the price rises, quantity demanded falls. In general, demand curves slope downward due to the inverse ways fluctuated greatly from year to year, regardless of any man-made disaster. Fishermen blame the slow years on the oil spill, however. The more abundant years would have been even better, they say, if not for the spill. Fishermen are claiming to be close to bankruptcy. ■ The demand for Alaskan salmon has also been affected. Lawyers for the fishermen say that the image of the product has been tarnished by the oil spill. Japanese buyers, who purchase approximately 60 percent of Alaskan salmon, refuse to pay the asking price and, thus, have driven prices downward. In 1988, pink salmon and sockeye brought a high of \$0.72 and \$2.26 per pound, respectively; in 1991, prices had dropped to \$0.12 and \$0.76 per pound. ■ Gunnar Knapp, a professor of economics at the University of Alaska and director of Salmon Market Information Services, feels that although the oil spill played a role in the drop in salmon prices, it cannot be held entirely responsible for the size and value of the annual catch. He argues that salmon prices rose in the late 1980s because the world salmon supply was low and the Japanese yen was high. From 1988 to 1991, the world's salmon supply was up significantly, causing a drop in prices. ■ Despite the legal case, Alaska is on the mend. The coastline now shows no signs of the oil spill. Jeff Wheelwright, who spent 5 years studying the effects of the oil spill, says that nature heals itself in time and the extent of the damages was "grossly exaggerated." ■ Everyone agrees that the oil spill did damage. The extent of the damage stirs a major difference of opinions between Exxon executives and Alaskan fishermen. Many view the fishermen's efforts as a greedy attempt to take advantage of Exxon's deep pockets. Others feel that the fishermen are justified in getting as much as they can. To date, Exxon has paid dearly for the spill: \$3.4 billion in clean-up and restoration costs, \$1 billion in government restitution payments, \$286 million in compensatory damages, and \$5 billion in punitive damages to the people of Alaska whose livelihoods were directly affected by the spill. The *Exxon Valdez* oil spill has proven to be an economic challenge facing the fishermen and government of Alaska as well as Exxon. Sources: Nina Munk, "We're Partying Hearty!" *Forbes*, October 24, 1994, p. 84; "Jury Awards \$286 Million to Fishermen over Losses from *Exxon Valdez* Accident," *BNA International Environment Daily*, August 30, 1994, p. 24; Jeff Wheelwright, "Exxon Is Right. Alas." *New York Times*, July 31, 1994, p. 31; and Natalie Phillips, "No Herring. Care for a Lawyer?" *Time*, May 9, 1994, p. 17.

QUESTIONS FOR CRITICAL THINKING

1. Do you think that Exxon has paid enough for its mistake? Why or why not?
2. What can the Alaskan government do to improve the state's economy?
3. What are the pros and cons of a resource-based economy?

relationship between the price of a product and the quantity of it that buyers will purchase.

What, then, is a change in demand? An answer to this question requires examination of the factors that combine to determine demand for a good or service. These include customer preferences and incomes, the prices of substitute and competing products, the number of buyers in a market, and their degree of optimism regarding the future. Changes in any of these factors will produce a new demand curve. In which direction will the new curve move? Table 2.1 supplies the answers.

Take a change in income as an example. If consumers' incomes rise, firms can sell more products at every price. This creates a whole new demand curve to the right of the old one. Figure 2.2 shows the difference between the old demand curve (labeled D_1) and the new demand curve (D_2). As you can see, every time demand shifts, it defines a new intersection with the supply curve (S) and a new market price (E). Of course, if consumers' incomes fall, the demand curve will shift to the left as demand declines at every possible price.

Changes in Supply versus Changes in Quantity Supplied The same reasoning applies to **supply curves.** A change in quantity supplied appears as a movement along a supply curve, reflecting suppliers' willingness to offer more goods and services at higher prices than at lower ones. By contrast, a change in supply results in a new supply curve.

supply curve
Graph of the relationship between different prices and the quantity supplied at each price.

The supply curve in Figure 2.1 illustrates the relationship between different prices and the quantity of a product supplied at each price. Like the demand curve, the supply curve can be affected by many different factors. Chapter 1 described four factors of production that help capitalism to operate effectively (natural resources, human resources,

TABLE 2.1 SHIFTS IN DEMAND CURVES

FACTOR	DEMAND CURVE SHIFTS TO THE RIGHT IF	DEMAND CURVE SHIFTS TO THE LEFT IF
Customer preferences	Increase	Decrease
Buyers' incomes	Increase	Decrease
Prices of substitute goods	Increase	Decrease
Prices of competing goods	Decrease	Increase
Number of buyers	Increases	Decreases
Buyers' optimism	Increases	Decreases

capital, and entrepreneurship). A change in the cost of any of these inputs can shift the supply curve. For instance, if the cost of raw materials (natural resources) rises, this change could reduce the supply of products that firms make from those raw materials. Figure 2.3 shows that this would shift the supply curve to the left (S_2) and raise the equilibrium price (E_2); since firms offer fewer products, those that they do make will command a higher price (P_2). This curve shows that, other things being equal, as prices rise, the quantity of a product that is supplied also rises.

On the other hand, if a newly discovered source increases the amount of raw materials that firms find available, the change reduces the cost of the raw materials and increases the supply of products, shifting the supply curve to the right. Other factors that can shift the supply curve include the cost of the technology necessary to make products, taxes, and the number of suppliers in a market. Table 2.2 summarizes how each of these factors affects the supply curve.

FIGURE 2.2 SHIFTS IN THE DEMAND CURVE

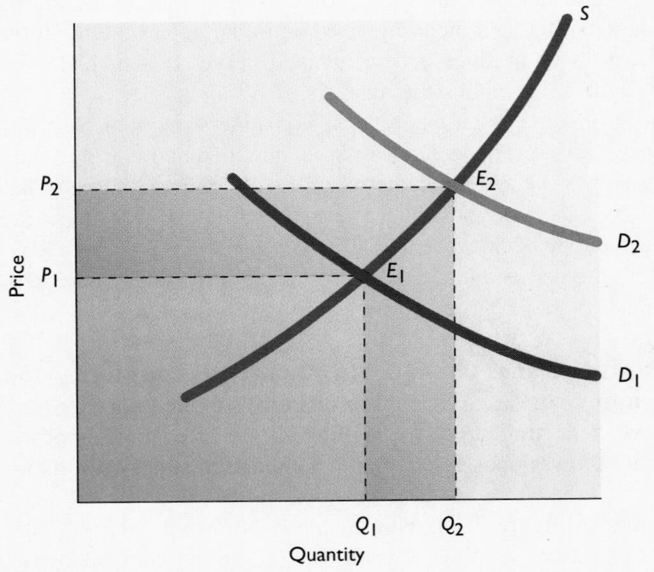

FIGURE 2.3 SHIFTS IN THE SUPPLY CURVE

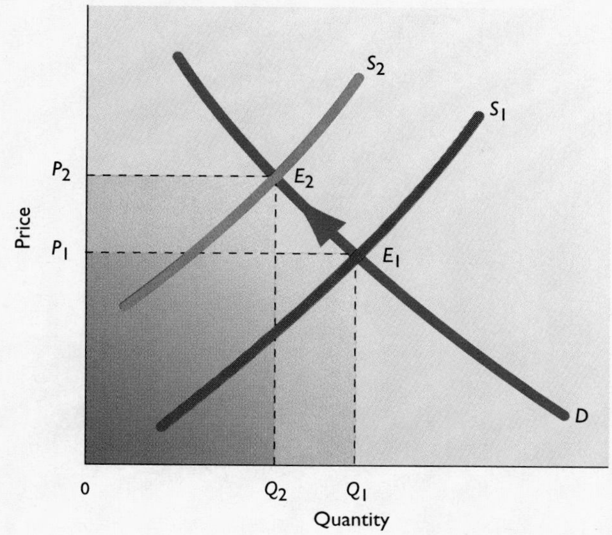

Changes in Both Supply and Demand Individual shifts in supply or demand have obvious effects on prices and the availability of products. In the real world, however, changes that affect supply and demand do not take turns. Several factors often change at the same time, and they keep on changing.

Sometimes such changes in multiple factors cause contradictory pressures on prices and quantities. In other cases, the final direction of prices and quantities reflects the factor that has changed the most.

MACROECONOMICS: DEALING WITH ECONOMY-WIDE ISSUES

Macroeconomics studies large-scale economic issues. Four issues that are especially important in macroeconomics are inflation, recession, unemployment, and economic growth.

TABLE 2.2 SHIFTS IN SUPPLY CURVES

FACTOR	SUPPLY CURVE SHIFTS TO THE RIGHT IF	SUPPLY CURVE SHIFTS TO THE LEFT IF
Costs of inputs	Decrease	Increase
Costs of technologies	Decrease	Increase
Taxes	Decrease	Increase
Number of suppliers	Increases	Decreases

Southeast Paper Manufacturing Co., owned by Knight-Ridder, is the world's largest manufacturer of newsprint made of 100 percent de-inked fiber. Between 1989 and 1994, demand for newsprint lagged and prices were depressed as newspaper advertising dwindled and newspapers printed fewer pages. In 1995, however, some paper mills closed and others left the business. This reduction in supply, along with an increase in newspaper advertising that boosted demand, and price increases due to environmental regulations, fiber content, and labor costs, sent newsprint prices rising. They are expected to reach $635 a metric ton, $200 a ton more than 1992 prices.

inflation
Sustained price increases for all goods and services.

Inflation A sustained increase in the prices of all goods and services is **inflation.** Inflation can be caused by many factors; two of the most important are costs and demand.

Cost-push inflation occurs when prices rise due to increases in costs for the various factors of production. Increases in the prices of natural resources or human resources, for instance, could push up the price of a final product.

Demand-pull inflation results when buyers want to buy more goods and services than the market actually offers. As the last section showed, when demand rises, so do prices. The overall demand for goods and services is linked to the amount of money in circulation; if the supply of money grows faster than the production of goods and services, demand-pull inflation can result.

Economic Growth Besides inflation, macroeconomics also studies economic growth in a country. A country's economy tends to follow a pattern of repeated expansion and contraction in economic activity. Its gross domestic product (GDP) may reach a peak, and then enter a period of contraction during which it falls. After a period of time, the economy again begins to expand and the GDP begins to grow until economic activity reaches another peak, and the cycle begins all over again.

recession
Cyclical economic contraction.

Recession A **recession** is a cyclical economic contraction that lasts 6 months or more. The challenge for macroeconomics is to find ways to encourage economic expansion while dealing most effectively with any recession or other economic contraction.

The most recent recession in the United States occurred during the early 1990s. While blue-collar, manufacturing workers have traditionally suffered more than other groups in economic contractions, the 1990s recession affected many white-collar workers, too. One survey done at the time found that almost half of 870 large U.S. companies had laid off white-collar employees in order to trim costs and become more competitive.[3]

unemployment
Joblessness of people who are looking for work.

Unemployment Still another issue in macroeconomics focuses on the effort to maintain economic conditions in which people who want jobs can find and keep them. **Unemployment** is defined as joblessness of people who are actively looking for work.

Recently, the U.S. Department of Labor revised its method for calculating the unemployment rate. Figure 2.4 compares unemployment under the old estimating approach to the results of the new method, which includes people who hold more than one job and so-called "discouraged workers" who want to work but have given up looking.

U.S. Department of Labor officials believe that the new method more accurately reflects Americans' employment status; in Figure 2.4, it results in a total unemployment rate of 7.3 percent, compared to older estimates of 6.8 percent.[4] Economists expect that the unemployment rate will fall slightly as the current economic expansion continues.[5]

In financial terms, of course, unemployment is undesirable because it accompanies lower production and less money being channeled into the economy. More important, perhaps, are the psychological costs of unemployment, since many people identify emotionally with their jobs.

Economists classify unemployment in four types: frictional, seasonal, cyclical, and structural unemployment. Frictional unemployment applies to members of the labor force who are temporarily not working, but are looking for jobs. This includes new graduates, people who have left one job for any reason and are looking for another, and former workers who have decided to return to the labor force. Seasonal unemployment is joblessness of workers in a seasonal industry. Construction workers, farm laborers, and retail clerks often suffer from seasonal unemployment. Cyclical unemployment includes people who are out of work due to a cyclical contraction in the economy, as discussed above. During periods of economic expansion, the unemployment rate may fall below normal, but during economic slowdowns, unemployment rises. At such times, even workers with good job skills may find themselves temporarily unemployed. Structural unemployment applies to people who remain unemployed for long periods of time, often with little hope of finding new jobs. This may occur because they lack the necessary skills for available jobs, or because the skills they have are no longer in demand.

MONETARY AND FISCAL POLICIES

The government can use monetary or fiscal policy, or both, to combat inflation and unemployment. Both have significant impacts on business. **Monetary policy** refers to gov-

monetary policy
Government policies and actions to regulate the nation's money supply.

FIGURE 2.4 COMPARISON OF UNEMPLOYMENT RATES CALCULATED BY TWO DIFFERENT METHODS

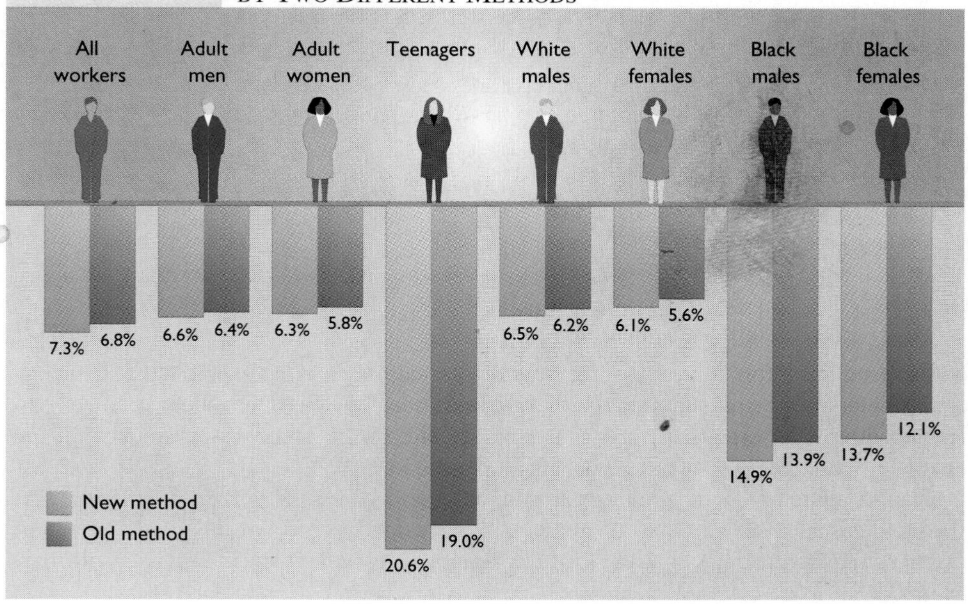

BUSINESS IN ACTION

FLAT TAX: TRUE TAX REFORM The federal income tax began in 1913 when a new law required the "rich" to pay 2 percent of their annual incomes to the federal government. Since then, the tax code has grown exponentially to a 10,000-page document consisting of 1,300 sections of confusing and complex rules. The U.S. tax system keeps a multitude of lawyers and accountants in business. Individual taxpayers spend $5 billion each year just for professional assistance in completing their tax forms. American companies spend approximately $100 billion each year complying with tax codes. ■ Today, the system may face significant change. Representative Dick Armey of Texas has introduced a bill entitled "Freedom and Fairness Restoration Act: A Comprehensive Plan to Shrink the Government and Grow the Economy." As a major component, the bill imposes a flat tax of 17 percent on all income, eliminating deductions as people now know them. A married couple would not be required to pay taxes on their first $26,200 of income. All income above that level would be subject to the 17 percent tax. Each dependent would add $5,300 to the exemption. A family of four, therefore, would pay taxes only on income in excess of $36,800. ■ The flat tax proposal promises many benefits. The most obvious is the simplification of the tax system. Most taxpayers would be able to fill out their income tax statements on postcards, and a majority of Americans would no longer require the services of professionals to prepare their tax statements. ■ The number of tax returns would decline dramatically as a result of the flat tax. Those Americans who earned less than the standard exemptions, including millions of moderate- to low-income families, would not be required to file returns. Businesses that file as many as 800 separate tax returns every year would see a major reduction in paperwork. ■ Most importantly, the flat tax would have a positive effect on the economy. Individuals would pay less in taxes, so they could spend and invest more. Since interest would no longer be taxed, individuals would save more, too. Eliminating taxes on capital gains, another feature of the bill, would send the stock market soaring and increase new business investment. Employment would rise and the quality of life would improve. ■ The authors of the bill estimate that the flat tax reform would remove a $200 billion burden on the economy—$100 billion spent to comply with the tax code and $100 billion thrown away on investments made for tax purposes rather than for economic gain. The greatest benefit of all would come in boosts to productivity. All of the time and effort spent by individuals and businesses to interpret, calculate, and avoid taxes could be turned to more positive purposes. ■ However, many groups perceive the proposed flat tax as unfavorable to them while favorable for others. Homeowners, for instance, may oppose the bill since mortgage interest would no longer be deductible. Charitable groups would be unhappy with the likely decrease in their donations since charitable contributions would no longer be deductible. The lower and middle classes may view the bill as an attempt by people in the upper class to reduce their own tax bracket. Sources: "A Tax Debate Worth Having," *Arkansas Business,* October 17, 1994, p. 6; Malcolm S. Forbes, "Happy Days Will Be Here Again," *Forbes,* July 18, 1994, p. 23; Malcolm S. Forbes, "How to Win the Tax Issue: Flatten It," *Forbes,* September 13, 1993, p. 38; and Howard Gleckman and Nancy Peacock, "They Don't Call It a Tax 'Code' for Nothing," *Business Week,* April 19, 1993, p. 82.

QUESTIONS FOR CRITICAL THINKING

1. What do you think would happen to the housing market if the flat tax were enacted and the deduction for mortgage interest eliminated?
2. What income bracket would benefit most from the flat tax?
3. How could the flat tax bill be amended to ensure a greater level of savings and investment by individuals?

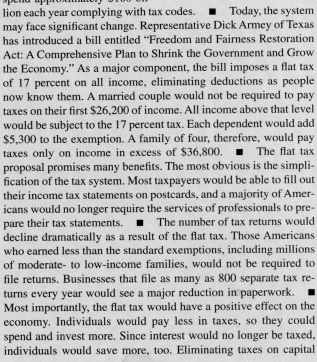

ernment policy efforts to control the size of the nation's money supply. An expansionary monetary policy puts more money into circulation. Business borrowing becomes easier and often less expensive; as businesses expand, hiring reduces unemployment. For example, bank interest rates fell during the recession of the early 1990s. By contrast, restrictive monetary policy reduces the money supply and helps reduce inflation. The specific methods used in monetary policy are discussed in Part 6 of this book. To a large extent, monetary policy is the work of the Federal Reserve, which is discussed in Chapter 19.

Fiscal policy concerns government revenues and expenditures. Increased government spending can increase economic activity and reduce unemployment. For example, the government may spend more on highway construction during a recession. By contrast, a tax increase lowers people's income and spending if government spending does not also increase, which can slow inflation.

fiscal policy
Government actions to set levels of revenues and expenditures.

SHIFT TOWARD A SERVICE ECONOMY

In a service economy, services make up a large share of economic activity, while manufacturing of physical products becomes less important economically. **Services** are intangible tasks that satisfy consumers' and business users' needs. They differ from physical goods in five important ways. One is intangibility; they cannot be seen, heard, tasted, touched, or smelled. Second, services are inseparable from providers; consumers essentially buy a promise when they purchase a service, and their choice obviously depends on who makes the promise. Third, services are perishable and their usefulness depends on timing; if an airplane flies with empty seats or a hotel has empty rooms for the night, the owners cannot recover the lost revenue. Fourth, services are hard to standardize; how they are performed depends on both the service provider and the consumer. Last, consumers often play roles in service development and distribution. Hairstylists listen to their clients' suggestions and overall desires and work to satisfy them; patrons of salad bars put together their own meals (with restaurants providing both services and goods). These are just two examples of the close interaction between customer and service provider.

services
Intangible tasks that satisfy consumers' and business users' needs.

GLOBAL COMPETITIVENESS

Chapter 1 noted that the world economy is becoming increasingly global. As an example, consider the number of international telephone calls placed annually to and from the United States; over the past decade, this number has soared from 500 million to almost 2.5 billion each year.[6] This shift toward globalization changes the competitive environment for business, both in the United States and in other countries. While a company may be an economic powerhouse at home, in this expanded worldwide setting, it becomes less significant. The big challenge for U.S. businesses in the late twentieth century focuses on developing their ability to compete in global markets.

Traditionally, a firm's competitiveness depended on its ability to keep costs down. If it could produce something more cheaply than competitors, then it could price prod-

British Airways provides its first-class trans-Atlantic passengers arrival services that allow them to check in more quickly than other passengers thanks to a special data network system. They also provide dressing rooms, showers, and staff to iron clothes.

ucts lower and outsell its rivals. A company's competitiveness was also linked to the resources that it could find in its particular geographic location. Today, however, competition based solely on costs has given way to competition based on many factors, including product design, product development, and efficient use of technology. Today's firms succeed or fail based on the quality and customer service that they provide. Improvements in technology and transportation have made companies independent of their locations. They can pass information around the world; workers in Ireland or the Bahamas can process data gathered in Asia, for instance, and transmit it to the United States.

The remaining sections of this chapter will examine several economic issues that U.S. businesses face in their quest to remain competitive in an increasingly global economy. Figure 2.5 summarizes these issues: researching and developing better products, improving quality and service, improving the competitiveness of the work force, improving organizational flexibility, and creating long-term global strategies.

RESEARCH AND DEVELOPMENT FOR BETTER PRODUCTS

research and development
Scientific process of developing new commercial products.

About 60 miles west of Osaka, Japan, workers are lining up 904 magnets in a huge underground ring nearly four-fifths of a mile in circumference. The Super Photon Ring, as it is called, will open in 1998 as the world's largest facility for short-wavelength radiation. It will store X-ray radiation to power microscopes for molecular research.

While the Photon Ring may sound like science fiction, actually it is part of a very practical policy for boosting Japan's long-term economic competitiveness. Scientific advances like this "are the only way to prepare for the future," says Tohru Amano, a research director at Japan's Science and Technology Agency. Many of Japan's largest companies are funding research and development projects that will take 10 to 20 years to yield profitable products. Research into new semiconductors, superconducting materials, and optoelectronics will eventually pay off in tiny, superfast devices based on the movements of individual electrons.[7]

The Super Photon Ring is an example of **research and development**, the scientific process of developing new commercial products. R&D, as it is often called, can create

FIGURE 2.5 REMAINING COMPETITIVE IN A GLOBAL ECONOMY

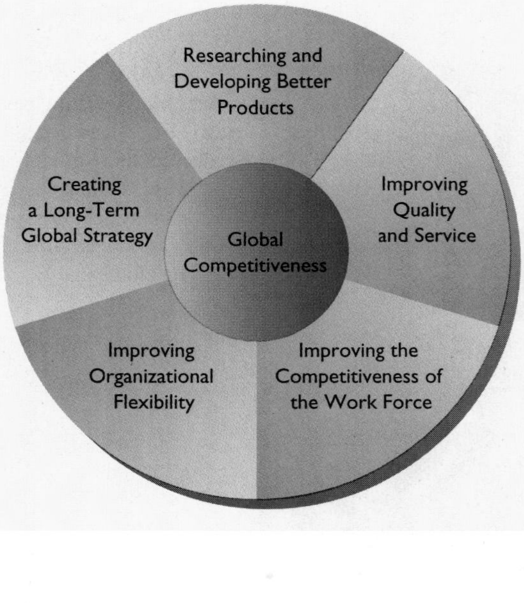

Research and development at Interval Research takes the form of role playing future scenarios, here in a kitchen and living room of the future. Founded by Microsoft cofounder Paul Allen, Interval's mission is to identify the electronics-related and information-related products that may interest consumers. Company researchers study real people and how the information age affects them. Already researchers have identified five prospective products.

totally new industries (as it created the airplane and automobile industries in an earlier day), and it can dramatically change existing industries. (Think about how computers have transformed so many people's jobs.)

Designing and developing a winning new product is not easy. Only one of every 20 to 25 ideas ever leads to a new product, and out of every 10 or 15 new products, only one becomes a commercial hit. However, companies that invest wisely in R&D often develop new products efficiently, before competitors beat them to market. Chrysler, for instance, developed its affordable Neon car in 31 months at a cost of $1.3 billion, which is low by industry standards.[8]

Failure to invest in R&D can put a company—and an entire country—at a severe disadvantage in global competition. For instance, U.S. electric-car makers lag far behind the electric-car industries of Europe and Japan, largely because other countries have spent more to develop innovative lithium and nickel-metal-hydride batteries. "Japan now has a big lead on us," admits Brian Barnett, director of battery industries studies at Arthur D. Little Inc. "We haven't made the investment, so we shouldn't be crying about the results," notes Elton Cairns, director of the Energy and Environment division at the Energy Department's Lawrence Berkeley Laboratory. Recently, the U.S. government formed a consortium with auto makers to fund further research and development in this area; the consortium has spent $260 million over the past 4 years to develop powerful, affordable batteries. Many government scientists, however, feel that this effort is still not enough. "We're just playing around," says one. "If we really wanted an electric-car business, we need to spend a billion dollars per year."[9]

IMPROVING QUALITY AND SERVICE

Also vital to global competitiveness are improvements in product quality and customer service. Says Jack Welch, chief executive officer of General Electric, "If you can't meet a world standard of quality at the world's best price, you're not even in the game." M. A. Hanna, a polymer maker with $1.3 billion in annual sales, invested in new, computerized systems to speed up the company's production process, reduce inventory, and cut the amount of scrap produced in its factories. These improvements have paid off;

Many companies see customer service as crucial to their businesses. Service representatives at Norfolk Southern Railway's National Customer Service Center in Atlanta use technology to provide information to customers and answer their questions. Representatives handle approximately 1,600 calls daily.

over the past four years, the firm has reduced by one-third the amount of working capital it needs to earn a dollar of sales. Lexus and Infiniti have stolen market share from German and American luxury cars by offering better quality at prices that average 40 percent less.

customer service
Aspect of a competitive strategy that defines how a firm treats its customers.

Customer service is the crucial aspect of a competitive strategy that defines how a firm treats its customers. Competitive firms make it as easy as possible for customers to order and receive their products. Notes Robert Immerman, founder of Ohio-based InterDesign, which sells small plastic items to retailers, "In the Seventies we went to the Post Office to pick up our orders. In the early Eighties we put in an 800 number. Late Eighties, we got a fax machine. In 1991 . . . we added electronic data interchange." These days, InterDesign receives more than half of its customers' orders via computer links, and errors in order entry and shipping have become relatively rare. As the error rate falls, however, customers' expectations rise. Immerman comments, "We had 50 weeks perfect with a big chain. Then one week we missed part of the order for one item on a long list—and they're on the phone wondering what's wrong."[10]

IMPROVING THE COMPETITIVENESS OF THE WORK FORCE

More and more, human resources are replacing factories and machines as a decisive competitive factor. "The only way we can beat the competition is with people," notes Robert Eaton, CEO of Chrysler. "That's the only thing anybody has. Your culture and how you motivate and empower and educate your people is what makes the difference." It is important for a company to create a culture that encourages employees to innovate and follow up on new ideas. Companies must then create systems to move new ideas through development and into the marketplace quickly.

Just adding new equipment is not enough; workers must use it effectively. Employees must have the skills to control, combine, and supervise work operations, and they must be motivated to provide the best quality and customer service possible. The skills that business demands of the U.S. work force are changing. Effective workers in a global economy must ask questions, define problems, combine information from many different sources, and deal with topics that stretch across disciplines and cultures.[11]

The best way for Americans to prepare for a global economy is to become as well-trained as possible and to continue educating themselves throughout their lives. Nynex, for instance, offers its employees an option to continue their studies by taking two years off from work and receiving $10,000 a year toward tuition or by working four days a week and attending classes for the fifth day. Says the company's CEO, "It costs in the short term, but I believe we'll build shareholder value in the future by doing this."

Another important skill is the ability to work in teams. According to Philip Condit, president of aircraft maker Boeing, "Your competitiveness is your ability to use the skills and knowledge of people most effectively, and teams are the best way to do that." Effective employee teams can bring a wide range of individuals' skills and work backgrounds to projects, delivering better-quality results. While developing Boeing's 777 passenger jet, for instance, team members discovered that designers had accidentally located the passengers' oxygen system in the same place as the gasper (the nozzle that directs fresh air toward passengers). Before Boeing organized its workers as teams, the conflict probably would not have been noticed until the plane was actually in production. Boeing's teams solved the problem in a mere three hours, however, by designing an innovative clamp that holds both systems.[12]

IMPROVING ORGANIZATIONAL FLEXIBILITY

"Management today has to think like a fighter pilot," says consultant Fred Wiersema. "When things move so fast, you can't always make the right decision—so you have to learn to adjust, to correct more quickly." This is true even for a venerable company like General Electric Lighting, founded in 1878. For years GE viewed fellow U.S. company Westinghouse as its principal rival, until Westinghouse sold its lamp division to Dutch firm Philips Electronics. As John Opie, GE Lighting's chief executive officer, recalls, "Suddenly we have bigger, stronger competition. They're coming to our market, but we're not in theirs. So we're on the defensive."

Opie reacted quickly by purchasing European firms such as Hungary's Tungsram and Britain's Thorn EMI. Today GE holds 18 percent of Europe's lighting market and is moving into Asia through a joint venture with Hitachi. GE Lighting made less than 20 percent of its sales outside the United States 5 years ago; today more than 40 percent of its sales come from abroad, and Opie predicts that this figure will rise above 50 percent in 1996.[13]

CREATING A LONG-TERM GLOBAL STRATEGIC POLICY

As the discussion of research and development explained, Japanese companies are pouring money into long-term research projects that could pay off in highly competitive new products. At the same time, U.S. industry has cut long-term research budgets by 15 percent over the past decade. Many businesspeople feel that these budget cuts represent short-range views that could hurt America's economic competitiveness in the long run.[14]

Prince Corporation, on the other hand, takes a long-term view of its business. An auto-parts supplier headquartered in Holland, Michigan, Prince designs and manufactures armrests, sun visors, vanity mirrors, cup holders, headliners, and other components for car interiors. To stay on top of its industry, Prince managers stay in close touch with auto makers and consumers. Says President John Spoelhof, "We need to understand what car buyers will want in 1999 so that when we sit down with the auto companies, we can figure out together what will surprise and delight the customers. Our motto is to be fast, flexible, and frugal."

Spoelhof's long-term goal is to become the first auto-parts supplier to provide an entire car interior, including instrument panel and roof, door, and floor trimmings. This strategy has the potential to win big profits, since supplying more parts per car could boost annual sales from $400 million to $1 billion. It also carries risks, as A. T. Kear-

Prince Corporation workers make mirrored visors for Cadillac DeVille automobiles. The company moved toward its long-term goal of being the first auto supplier to provide an entire car interior by providing door panels, floor console, visors, and grab handles for the 1995 Lincoln Continental.

ney consultant James Mateyka notes: "You increase your overhead and basic cost structure, and that leaves you vulnerable to piece suppliers."

To meet its goal, Prince is expanding rapidly. Its factories now run six days a week, up to 24 hours per day, and it is starting new operations in Mexico and England. Its employees emphasize quality as well as speed; to improve precision, they make three-dimensional prototypes and computer-aided-design printouts for every new design. The company's ambitious strategy appears to be working; it took a major step by supplying an unusually wide range of components—door panels, floor console, and overhead system—for the Lincoln Continental. Predicts Spoelhof, "By the year 2000 we will be doing a lot more things in different places."[15]

ACHIEVEMENT CHECK SUMMARY

Reread the learning goals that follow, and consider the questions for each goal. Answering these questions will reinforce the most important concepts in the chapter and allow you to check how well you have achieved these learning goals. Where a blank appears before a question, answer with *T* or *F.* Otherwise, circle the letter of the correct answer. An answer key to these questions is found at the end of this chapter.

LEARNING GOAL 2.1: Differentiate between microeconomics and macroeconomics.

1. ___ Macroeconomics deals with large issues that affect a country's overall economy.
2. ___ Microeconomics is concerned with the economic activities of an individual or a firm.
3. ___ Government policy that affects the overall economy is a good example of a microeconomic issue.

LEARNING GOAL 2.2: Show how supply and demand determine the equilibrium price.

1. ___ The demand schedule shows how many units people will purchase at different price levels.
2. ___ Changes in supply and demand will force the market price of a product or service to increase or decline.

LEARNING GOAL 2.3: Discuss important issues in macroeconomics, including inflation, recession, unemployment, and economic growth.

1. ___ A general decline in the prices of goods and services is known as inflation.
2. ___ A recession is a decline in the gross domestic product that lasts 6 months or more.
3. ___ Unemployment usually declines during a recession.

LEARNING GOAL 2.4: Distinguish between monetary policy and fiscal policy, and discuss how they help government to combat inflation and unemployment.

1. ___ A restrictive monetary policy helps to reduce inflation.
2. ___ Fiscal policy deals with government taxation and expenditures, while monetary policy affects the amount of money in circulation.

LEARNING GOAL 2.5: Explain what is meant by a service economy.

1. Compared to manufacturing, the service economy is: (a) increasing in size; (b) remaining stable; (c) decreasing in size; (d) disappearing rapidly.
2. Services are: (a) intangible; (b) inseparable from service providers; (c) highly perishable; (d) all of the above.

LEARNING GOAL 2.6: Discuss how American business can maintain global competitiveness.

1. ___ So long as U.S. industry is succeeding at home, it need not be concerned with global competition.
2. ___ Global competition focuses exclusively on controlling costs.
3. ___ Global competition depends increasingly on improving worker skills and will require American workers to engage in life-long learning.

KEY TERMS

economics 26
microeconomics 26
macroeconomics 27
supply 27
demand 27
equilibrium price 27
demand curve 28
supply curve 29
inflation 30
recession 30
unemployment 30
monetary policy 33
fiscal policy 35
services 35
research and development 36
customer service 38

REVIEW QUESTIONS

1. Distinguish between microeconomics and macroeconomics. Describe some issues involved in each.

2. What will happen to the equilibrium price and quantity of a certain product like doughnuts if government imposes a tax on its production? Can you cite an example?

3. What will happen to the equilibrium price and quantity of doughnuts if the following changes occur simultaneously?
   a. Consumers' incomes decline.
   b. Price of flour falls.

4. What is inflation? Explain the difference between cost-push inflation and demand-pull inflation.

5. Match the following descriptions with the correct type of unemployment: (a) frictional, (b) seasonal, (c) cyclical, and (d) structural unemployment.

   A factory worker suffers temporary layoff because of slow sales. b

   A steelworker loses a job when a mill closes permanently. c

   An agricultural worker remains unemployed between crops. d

   A recent graduate searches for employment. a

6. Distinguish between monetary policy and fiscal policy. How does each operate to regulate the economy? Cite specific examples.

7. Explain the importance of R&D in global competitiveness. How does the United States rate in regard to R&D expenditures?

8. Explain the importance of quality and customer service. Cite examples of roles of each in global competitiveness.

9. How can U.S. firms improve organizational flexibility and the competitiveness of their work forces?

10. Discuss the importance of developing a long-term global strategy.

DISCUSSION QUESTIONS

1. Economics has been called the "dismal science." Refute this characterization.

2. What is inflation? What can cause it? Suppose that you are the president, and your economic advisors warn that the United States appears to be entering a period of inflation. What could you do to combat this trend?

3. What is a recession? Describe some causes of a recession, and how it affects a nation's economy. If you were the president during a recession, what would you do?

4. Based on what you have read in this chapter, describe specific steps you can take to make yourself a more competitive employee in a global economy. What classes would you like to take? In what areas would you like to get more experience? Share your opinions with the class.

5. Last year the Japanese government spent $26 billion on research and development. While this was much less than the U.S. government spent ($68 billion), American funding for R&D is levelling off while Japanese funding rises almost 8 percent every year. The Japanese government is funding at least nine separate R&D projects in just one technology, quantum devices; several Japanese firms, including Fujitsu and Hitachi, have drawn on this research to create marketable products.[16] Discuss the implications of this trend. Do you feel that the U.S. government should take a similarly active role in R&D, or does this represent too much government interference in business? Explain your answer.

SOLUTIONS TO ACHIEVEMENT CHECK SUMMARY

L. G. 2.1: 1. T, 2. T, 3. F. **L. G. 2.2:** 1. T, 2. T. **L. G. 2.3:** 1. F, 2. T, 3. F. **L. G. 2.4:** 1. T, 2. T. **L. G. 2.5:** 1. a, 2. d. **L. G. 2.6:** 1. F, 2. F, 3. T.

VIDEO CASE

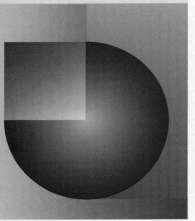

ANDERSEN CONSULTING Perhaps the biggest challenge facing businesses in the United States is responding to change in a globally competitive environment. However, many firms that recognize the need to change don't have the resources to make the required decisions on their own. They may have down-sized so that they no longer have the in-house expertise; they may have a one-time project that doesn't justify hiring someone on a permanent basis; or they may need to expand their business into regions of the globe in which they have no experience. In situations like these, companies turn to Andersen Consulting, which is in the $17 billion a year service industry of giving advice.

One of the company's major areas of expertise is technology. Andersen Consulting spent much of the last half of 1994 and well into 1995 helping companies prepare for the new Windows '95 software announced by Microsoft. The new software meant that businesspeople could operate a number of applications at the same time and share data between them, allowing for greater efficiency, less downtime, and fewer demands on company technical support—all for the relatively minor cost of purchasing the software itself. However, Windows '95 required that many companies make an additional investment in hardware upgrades to run the new program. Andersen Consulting helped companies evaluate their need for the product versus its costs and prepared them for making the transition.

Work with any one of Andersen's clients may encompass all aspects of the business: strategy, operations, organization, as well as technology. More often than ever before, Andersen Consulting provides the service of rethinking and re-engineering an organization. Whereas once consultants would visit a company, observe, and give their advice on specific problems in a relatively short amount of time, many of Andersen's projects are now taking 18–24 months, as consultants work with executives to build teams to analyze problems and develop solutions on an ongoing basis.

It is clear that a company that specializes in managing change for others must do the same for itself. Andersen Consulting has responded to changes in its business environment in a number of ways. For example, the company is now prepared to deliver its services around the globe. As managing partner George T. Shaheen states, "Serving . . . clients means providing a consistent level of quality service regardless of where they are." To achieve this, Andersen Consulting spends $40 million annually to transport its teams of consultants where they are needed. This rapid movement not only quickly spreads the latest management wisdom to the corners of the earth but also expedites the transfer of technology.

To maintain a level of flexibility in its own workforce, Andersen Consulting is taking advantage of some of the same technologies it recommends for its clients. The company provides its consultants with powerful notebook computers that serve as "virtual offices"

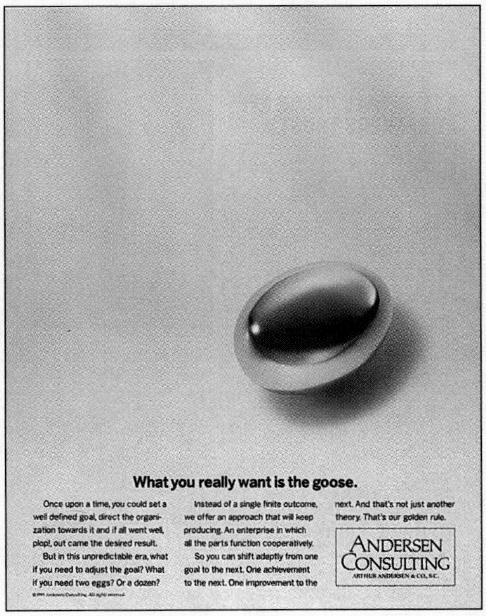

while they are on assignment. Consultants can perform most of their office tasks by using their handy notebook while on the road.

Also facilitating this go anywhere, do anything, employee-empowering attitude is Andersen's concept of Just-in-Time (JIT) learning and training. Roger Schank, head of Northwestern's Institute for Learning Services, argues that children and adults learn best when they receive information at the moment they need it. To implement this concept, Andersen Consulting has developed multimedia learning modules which deal with topics such as business practices, cultural differences, and new developments in technology. Employees can access the modules when they need them most—for example, just before starting a new assignment.

The company seems to have developed a winning combination of strategies to help businesses perform competitively in the global economy. Currently, Andersen Consulting derives 51 percent of its revenues outside the United States. It operates 150 offices in 46 countries—the hottest region being the Asian and Pacific Rim countries—and boasts total revenues of about $3 billion.

QUESTIONS

1.
What are the different implications of changing technology as in the case of Windows '95?

2.
Graphically show what you would expect to happen to the supply and demand curves for RAM, hard drives, and floppy disks because of the release of Windows '95.

3.
In what ways do services differ from goods? Relate your answer to Andersen Consulting's service of giving advice to businesses.

4.
How does Andersen Consulting help American businesses maintain global competitiveness?

CHAPTER 3

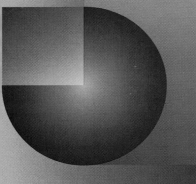

GLOBAL DIMENSIONS OF BUSINESS

LEARNING GOALS

1. Explain the importance of international business.

2. Discuss the basic concepts that underlie international business.

3. Explain why nations tend to specialize in certain goods.

4. Name the different levels of involvement in global business.

5. Explain countertrade.

6. Identify the main obstacles that confront global business.

7. Explain multinational economic integration.

8. Distinguish between a global strategy and a multinational strategy.

CANADIAN FOOTBALL INVADES THE UNITED STATES Larry Smith knew that he faced a major business problem in his new job. Smith's unique résumé included a season as a running back with the Montreal Alouettes football team. At the same time, he worked on a law degree at McGill University. Smith spent most of his post-football career in charge of Labatt's frozen food subsidiary before taking his new job as commissioner of the Canadian Football League (CFL). Smith became the only major league sports commissioner who had played the sport at the professional level. ■ The CFL represented over 100 years of professional football in Canada. The league's rules made its games an exciting entertainment option, at least when compared to the U.S. National Football League (NFL). CFL games are played with 12 men on a field longer and wider than those in the NFL. For instance, a CFL field is 110 yards long compared to the 100-yard length of its U.S. cousins. CFL teams also must make first downs in three plays rather than four. Moreover, CFL teams can take only 20 seconds between plays compared to the NFL's 40-second rule. As a result, passing plays dominate CFL games, which usually end up with high scores. ■ While Larry Smith inherited a fast-paced, interesting game, he also faced a gloomy financial picture. Attendance among the eight CFL teams was at a 20-year low. Only two of the CFL teams were profitable. In fact, Smith's former team, the Montreal Alouettes, had folded earlier. ■ Smith knew that expansion into the huge U.S. market was the only answer for the CFL. He noted, "Our league was in a position where if we didn't expand we were going to go the way of the dinosaurs." The CFL owners voted 7 to 1 in favor of Smith's plan. Only the Winnipeg Blue Bombers held out for the league's Canadian tradition. ■ The expansion plan that Smith developed sought to avoid head-to-head competition with the NFL. Smith hoped that this would also avoid the fate of the former United States Football League (USFL) which had teams in NFL cities like New York and Pittsburgh. ■ Commissioner Smith put it this way: ". . . we can get involved in cities where we'd never be a threat to the NFL, where it would never expand into, but where the fans still want to watch pro football at a high level. We can be a niche player." ■ In addition to picking non-NFL locations for expansion, the CFL also plays its games on Friday nights to avoid competition with college teams and the NFL. In addition, the CFL's season begins 2 months earlier than the NFL's season. ■ The CFL's first U.S. expansion team was the Sacramento Gold Miners. The Gold Miners' owner, Fred Anderson, had owned the Surge in the recently defunct World Leagues, so he had a football organization already in place. Anderson's coach and his star quarterback both made the transition to the CFL. ■ Sacramento was followed by the Las Vegas Posse and the Shreveport, Louisiana Pirates. The CFL also added Baltimore to the league. Baltimore had lost its beloved NFL Colts to Indianapolis when the team's owner moved out in the middle of the night. A decade later, the NFL passed over Baltimore's bid for an expansion team in favor of Charlotte and Jacksonville. The Baltimore CFL team, which is still unnamed because of pending litigation, sold 26,000 season tickets and led the CFL in attendance. ■ Despite a poor first season, the Shreveport Pirates were also well received. Jim Garner, the Pirates' vice president of administration, commented, "Our fans discovered quickly that CFL football was the same, yet different, so to speak. The 12-man teams, three downs rather than four, plus a longer and wider playing field provide for a novelty brand of football. American fans like action, and the CFL game is more fast-paced and higher scoring as a whole. I believe this difference is why there is a great opportunity for Canadian football in the States, whereas other leagues (USFL, World League) have failed because they were just another blend of American

11-man ball." ■ As the NBA had done in basketball, Commissioner Smith set a $2 million salary cap for his teams. Two dozen NFL stars each made more than the cap allowed for an entire CFL franchise. Each CFL team is allowed one marquee player, with the approval of the commissioner. The marquee player can receive up to $750,000 which is not counted against the cap. As a result of the cap, most CFL players earn about $50,000 annually, compared to the NFL average of $500,000. ■ The rosters of the U.S.–based CFL teams provide another interesting twist to this global business story. All of their players are American, unlike the Canadian-based teams. Since 1936, the CFL has limited each 37-man roster to 14 non-Canadian players. This action was taken in order to promote football in Canada, where just 23 universities field teams. The U.S. franchises are exempt from this CFL provision since it is contrary to U.S. law. Some of the Canadian franchises believe that U.S.–based teams have an unfair advantage since they can readily pick up NFL castoffs as replacement players. ■ The CFL has clearly been successful in its effort to expand abroad. What does the future hold for CFL expansion? Cities like Orlando; San Antonio; Birmingham; Milwaukee; Memphis; Nashville; Portland, Oregon; Oakland; Worcester, Massachusetts; and St. Louis are mentioned as future expansion sites. Smith hopes to have 10 to 12 U.S. teams in the CFL by 1997. He has also expressed confidence in his global business strategy by hiking the league's $3 million franchise fee to $6 million.[1]

CHAPTER OVERVIEW

Benjamin Franklin once said, "No nation was ever ruined by trade." Today, most businesspeople would agree with the 18th-century statesman. At one time, the international aspects of business mattered to only a few U.S. firms; most found all they needed in the domestic market. Today, though, foreign sales are essential to U.S. industries. As Figure 3.1 shows, foreign sales account for 29 percent of total sales for all industries. For some industries, foreign sales are even more important.

exporting *Selling domestic goods and services abroad.*

importing *Buying foreign goods, raw materials, and services.*

foreign production *Making goods and supplying services in a foreign country for sale there or in other countries.*

Analysts divide international business into three major activities. **Exporting** involves selling domestic goods and services abroad. **Importing** is purchasing foreign goods, raw materials, and services. **Foreign production** describes making goods and supplying services in a foreign country for sale there or in other countries.

Exporting goods and services accounts for 70 percent of the U.S. economy's growth. It is estimated that U.S. exports will amount to $1.2 trillion in 2000, largely as a result

FIGURE 3.1 FOREIGN SALES OF SELECTED U.S. INDUSTRIES

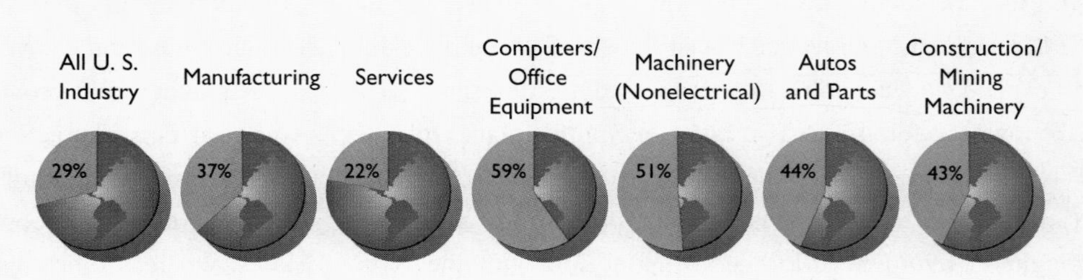

of an immense increase in trade with Mexico and Canada. More important to the typical American, export-related jobs pay 13 percent more than the average U.S. wage.[2]

CONCEPTS OF INTERNATIONAL BUSINESS

The main patterns of international business result from a combination of economic and political factors. To understand trade and world business, first review such concepts as the balance of trade, the balance of payments, and exchange rates.

BALANCE OF TRADE

A country's **balance of trade** is the relationship between its exports and imports. If a country exports more than it imports, it has a favorable balance of trade, called a *trade surplus*. If it imports more than it exports, it has an unfavorable balance of trade, called a *trade deficit*. The United States has run a trade deficit for several years. Despite being the world's top exporter, its citizens demand even more imports. Recently, the trade deficit reduced the U.S. economy's growth figure by two percent, a significant sum.[3]

balance of trade
Relationship between a country's exports and imports.

BALANCE OF PAYMENTS

A nation's balance of trade plays a central role in determining its **balance of payments**—the overall flow of money into or out of a country. Other factors affect the balance of payments, including overseas loans and borrowing, international investments, profits from such investments, and foreign aid. A favorable balance of payments, or a balance of payments surplus, means that more money is coming into a country from abroad than is leaving it. An unfavorable balance of payments, or balance of payments deficit, means that more money is leaving the country than entering it.

balance of payments
Flow of money into and out of a country.

EXCHANGE RATES

A nation's **exchange rate** is the rate at which its currency can be exchanged for the currencies of other nations. A currency's exchange rate is usually quoted in terms of another important currency. Recently, the U.S. dollar bought about 84 Japanese yen and 1.4 German marks, while the Canadian dollar was worth about 72 U.S. cents.

exchange rate
Rate at which a country's currency can be exchanged for other currencies.

At this Motorola, Inc. plant in northern Illinois, workers produce cellular telephones both for export and for the domestic market. The trade surplus that Motorola generates helps lower the overall U.S. trade deficit.

BUSINESS IN ACTION

WHY THE PESO WENT SOUTH The Mexican people enjoyed a taste of prosperity in recent years as inflation fell from 159 percent to just under 10 percent annually. The North American Free Trade Agreement (NAFTA) signed by the governments of the United States, Canada, and Mexico promised more exports, more jobs, and a higher standard of living to the citizenry. Prospects have faded as the recent devaluation of the peso, stock market crash, and skyrocketing interest rates have halted what progress the country made in establishing itself as a stable member of the international business community. Today, the Mexican economy is struggling to survive. How could this happen when it seemed that the country had finally overcome its reputation for political and economic turmoil? ■ The Mexican economy's collapse can be attributed to several factors. Carlos Salinas de Gortari, the president of Mexico until December 1, 1994, aligned the peso to the U.S. dollar to bring down inflation. At the same time, the country's leaders tried to encourage economic growth, which required major capital investment in equipment and facilities. With few or no sources of Mexican capital, foreign investments were sought. Since Mexico is considered a poor country, investors lent money only with short terms and high rates. Interest rates in the range of 20 percent attracted foreign investors, who poured $50 billion into the economy. Foreign money strengthened the peso further. In Spring 1994, a decline in foreign investments threatened the peso. Being an election year, Salinas hesitated to take any action that would be viewed negatively by the voters. Inflation would increase if the peso were allowed to slide. On the other hand, interest rates would increase if the peso were maintained at its current level. ■ Salinas chose, instead, to buy up pesos with some of the country's $30 billion in foreign-currency reserves. Ernesto Zedillo inherited the problem when he took office. The reserve pool quickly diminished to under $10 billion before Zedillo announced that 3.5 pesos no longer were worth $1. The peso immediately decreased in value by 70 percent. Overnight, Mexicans' buying power was cut by nearly one-third. Interest rates skyrocketed and the stock market crashed. ■ The events in Mexico adversely affected many people. The lower peso pre-

The exchange rate can have a major impact on a nation's economy. Changes in this variable can quickly wipe out or create a competitive advantage, so they dictate much of the decision whether or not to invest abroad. If the dollar rises in price relative to the yen, for instance, a dollar will buy more yen. This makes Japanese products less expensive, so Japanese imports increase and U.S. firms face greater competition.

devaluation
Reduction in value of a country's currency.

Devaluation describes a fall in a currency's value relative to other currencies or to a fixed standard. Sometimes nations take deliberate action to devalue their currency in an effort to increase exports. Devaluation of the dollar makes U.S. goods sell for less abroad and lowers costs for vacationing foreigners. If the dollar buys fewer yen, the price that U.S. consumers pay for Japanese products rises and competition for domestic firms loses strength. Devaluation also makes it more expensive for American companies to buy assets abroad, but less expensive for foreign firms to purchase U.S. assets.[4]

International exchange rates are based on a system called *floating exchange rates,* in which currency traders create a market for the world's currencies based on countries' relative trade and investment prospects. In theory, this leaves exchange rates free to fluctuate, or float, according to supply and demand. In practice, exchange rates do not float in total freedom. National governments often intervene to adjust their own exchange rates. Also, nations form currency blocs by linking their exchange rates to each other, and many governments practice protectionist policies that seek to guard their economies against trade imbalances.

vented the Mexican government from repaying billions in short-term debt it had accumulated. Foreign investors who pumped money into the economy because of NAFTA suffered major losses. American exporters will also see a major decline in business since a lower peso will prevent Mexicans from buying as many U.S. products as before. Mexicans had been buying about $50 billion of U.S. products. The high interest rates resulting from the devaluation of the peso will put many smaller Mexican companies out of business. Larger businesses are in for hard times, too, if they're paying off their dollar debts with lower pesos. Most importantly, the Mexican people will suffer. Their wages, buying power, standard of living, and hopes are slashed as they face many lean years in recovery. ■ Since NAFTA has formally linked the Mexican and United States governments, President Clinton took action before the economy collapsed totally. Faced with congressional opposition to a Mexican bailout, Clinton abandoned a plan for $40 billion in loan guarantees in favor of an internationally supported effort. The president is allowed to draw from the Exchange Stabilization Fund, currently valued at $37.5 billion, without congressional approval. Clinton thus promised Mexico a $20 billion package of loans and loan guarantees. The International Monetary Fund will provide $17.8 billion while the Bank for International Settlements, Canada, and several Latin American countries will contribute $29.8 billion for a total of $49.8 billion. The Mexican economy responded immediately to the news of the loan package. The stock market had its biggest one-day gain in seven years while the peso gained 55 centavos to close at 5.80. ■ Without this aid package, the Mexican government would probably have defaulted on its loans, causing several other Latin American countries to do the same. Instead, Mexico will be able to exchange its short-term debts for loans with longer maturities. ■ The crisis could also have affected the United States. If the Mexican economy had failed, thousands of Americans would lose jobs that depend on exports to Mexico. The number of illegal immigrants would have increased as Mexicans would have come to the United States in search of a better life. The crisis has been averted and for now Mexico faces a tough rebuilding process. Sources: James Gerstenzang and John M. Broder, "Clinton Offers New Mexican Aid Plan, Bypasses Congress," *Los Angeles Times,* February 1, 1995, p. 1; Juanita Darling, "Back from the Brink," *Los Angeles Times,* February 1, 1995, p. D1; Geri Smith, Elisabeth Malkin, Dean Foust, and Stanley Reed, "Surveying the Wreckage," *Business Week,* January 23, 1995, p. 58; Marc Levinson, Tim Padgett, and David Schrieberg, "Mexico's Wake-Up Call," *Newsweek,* January 9, 1995, p. 52; and James Flanigan, "The Peso's Plunge; A Case of Deja Vu," *Los Angeles Times,* January 8, 1995, p. 1.

QUESTIONS FOR CRITICAL THINKING

1. Should the United States continue to help the Mexican government as it has in the past? Why or why not?
2. What other enticements can the Mexican government use to lure foreign investors other than high interest rates?
3. If you were a Mexican citizen facing exorbitant interest rates, lower wages, and a lower standard of living, what would you do?

A disadvantage of the floating rate system is that exchange rates are highly sensitive to any new information that could affect business. For the most part, however, the floating rate system works well, and it will continue as the global basis for determining exchange rates.

SPECIALIZATION AMONG NATIONS

Nations usually benefit if they specialize in producing certain goods or services. By doing what they do best, they can exchange surplus domestic output for more of the foreign-made products that they need. This allows higher standards of living than these countries could achieve by producing everything themselves.

However, specialization can become dangerous if taken to an extreme. Many less-developed countries depend on exports of one or two primary commodities, such as sugar cane and copper, to earn foreign currency to pay for imported goods. If the price of a main good declines, the nation faces much more difficulty importing needed goods and services. Other problems can occur when a country depends on foreign nations to supply an input that is critical to its economy. For instance, oil is vital to the U.S. economy as fuel for cars and machinery. Much of this oil comes from Middle Eastern countries, so wars and political unrest in that area of the world endanger the essential U.S. oil supply.

ABSOLUTE ADVANTAGE

A country has an absolute advantage in marketing a product if it has a monopolistic position or it can produce the product at the lowest cost. Examples of absolute advantage are rare because few countries are sole suppliers and because rapidly changing economic conditions can wipe out advantages in production costs.

South Africa has traditionally had an absolute advantage in gem-quality diamonds, for instance, since it had a rare domestic source of these gems. However, discoveries of diamond deposits in other areas of the world, such as Canada, have removed South Africa's absolute advantage.

COMPARATIVE ADVANTAGE

A more practical approach to international specialization seeks to develop comparative advantage. A country has a comparative advantage in a product if it can supply that product more efficiently and at a lower cost than it can supply other goods, compared to other nations. For example, if Country A can produce a certain good three times as efficiently as Country B while it produces a second good only twice as efficiently as Country B, then Country A has a comparative advantage in the first good. Country B has a comparative advantage in the second good, even though it produces the good less efficiently than Country A does, because it produces that good relatively more efficiently than the other. Worldwide, the greatest supply of both products will result when each country specializes in producing the good for which it has a comparative advantage, that is, when Country A produces the first good and Country B produces the second.

Countries tend to follow this pattern of specialization. A tropical nation such as Costa Rica may specialize in agriculture to take advantage of its climate and inexpensive labor. U.S. exports, on the other hand, reflect America's comparative advantages as a highly industrialized country with rich natural and agricultural resources. The United States tends to export manufactured items (aircraft parts, electrical machinery), food products (grain and soybeans), and some natural resources (coal).

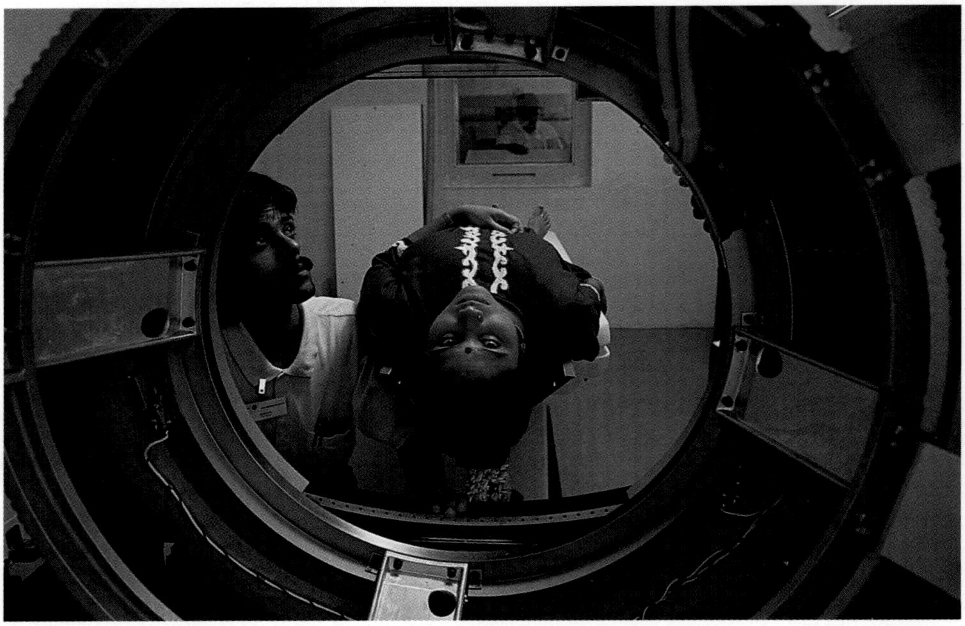

In a Bangalore, India plant jointly operated by General Electric and its Indian partner, Godrej, a technician tests a CT scanner. India's low wage structure, rising middle class, and comparatively well-educated work force give it a comparative advantage in labor-intensive work. Until 1991, the country pursued a policy of self-sufficiency, discouraging direct foreign investment. Since then, tariffs have fallen from 200 percent to 65 percent and corporate and income tax rates also have dropped significantly in order to encourage foreign investment and economic growth.

SELF-SUFFICIENCY

Some countries prefer to be self-sufficient rather than to specialize and trade. Many Central American nations have tried to remain self-sufficient, although this pattern is changing. Other countries seek self-sufficiency only in commodities that they regard as important strategic resources for their long-run development, such as energy in the United States. A few—Israel, for example—try to be self-sufficient in many national defense resources. These countries view the noneconomic advantages of self-sufficiency as more important to their national welfare than the economic advantages of specialization.

APPROACHES TO DOING BUSINESS ABROAD

Many firms pursue global business in an evolving process. For example, a small company might start exporting on a limited scale, then expand its overseas efforts as management gains experience and confidence in its ability to operate effectively abroad. The company may later seek even greater degrees of global involvement.

Four levels of involvement in global business include direct and indirect exporting, foreign licensing, overseas marketing, and international production and marketing. As a firm becomes more active internationally, both the risks and the degree of control over its marketing effort increase. This concept is illustrated in Figure 3.2.

DIRECT AND INDIRECT EXPORTING

Exporting firms produce goods at home and sell them abroad. Many companies engage in indirect exporting, often without realizing it, when their products become part of another good that is exported. Electronic components are a common example.

When a firm actually seeks export business, it engages in direct exporting, the most common form of international business. The company must devote both capital and managerial resources to this effort. Frequently, a firm will assign an in-house export manager to coordinate its export operation, or it may hire an outside company that specializes in export promotion. Table 3.1 lists the top ten U.S. exports and exporters.

While the exporters shown in Table 3.1 are large corporations, a firm need not be big in order to become a successful global exporter. The Commerce Department estimates that firms with fewer than 20 employees account for 12 percent of total U.S. exports.[5] Some of these exports originate in interesting ways. Take the case of Anders Dege from Norway. He learned about a unique smoke-protection device that was

FIGURE 3.2 LEVELS OF INVOLVEMENT IN GLOBAL BUSINESS

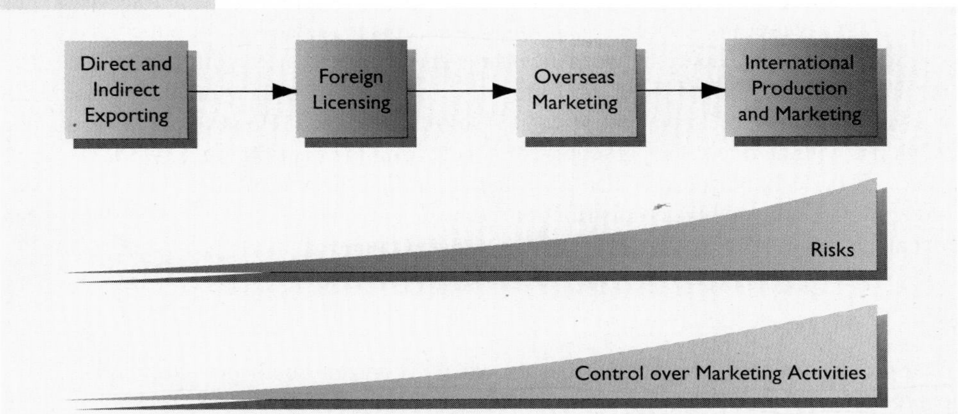

TABLE 3.1 TOP TEN U.S. EXPORTS AND EXPORTERS

Exporter	Major Export Product	Amount ($ billions)	Export	Amount ($ billions)
Boeing	Commercial aircraft	$17.5	Agricultural products	$42.2
General Motors	Motor vehicles and parts	14.0	Computers and office equipment	27.0
General Electric	Jet engines and turbines	8.2	Aircraft	26.3
IBM	Computers	7.5	Electrical machinery	32.2
Ford	Motor vehicles and parts	7.2	General industrial machinery	18.5
Chrysler	Motor vehicles and parts	7.0	Power-generating machinery	18.0
McDonnell-Douglas	Aerospace products	4.9	Motor vehicle parts	16.8
Philip Morris	Tobacco, beverages, and food products	3.8	Specialized industrial machinery	16.7
			Scientific instruments	14.4
Hewlett-Packard	Computers	3.7	Coal and other fuels	11.3
DuPont	Specialty chemicals	3.5		

invented by a man in Missouri and was produced in California. Someone in Dege's position might have tried to become the authorized Norwegian representative for the product. Instead, Dege moved to Colorado and became a distributor for the device. Once he had become established as a U.S.–based distributor, Dege began to sell the product in Norway via fax and telephone, thus adding to U.S. exports.[6]

FOREIGN LICENSING

Foreign licensing results from a contract in which a firm allows a foreign company to produce and distribute its products or use its trademark, patent, or processes in a specific geographic area. This gives firms a low-cost way to enter new markets. Licensing avoids protectionist barriers while providing access to local marketing research information and distribution channels.

OVERSEAS MARKETING

To begin overseas marketing, a firm establishes a foreign sales office. The parent company directly controls all foreign marketing, even though the goods and services may come from a variety of sources, such as domestic plants, licensees, or subcontractors.

Sometimes the choice between licensing and overseas marketing can be a critical one. PepsiCo first entered India via foreign licensing. At first, the strategy worked well; in 3 years, Pepsi won 25 percent of India's soft-drink market. However, arch rival Coke countered with an overseas marketing coup, acquiring the distribution network and sales offices of Parle Exports, an Indian firm that controlled 60 percent of the country's beverage market. An established distribution network gave The Coca-Cola Company a big advantage in covering the large, heavily populated country.[7]

INTERNATIONAL PRODUCTION

Total global business involvement occurs when a company both produces and markets its products abroad. A firm may enter foreign markets in this way by starting a subsidiary or acquiring an existing firm in the country where it wants to expand. Sometimes, too,

Value Club stores are retail/wholesale, cash and carry, warehouse stores similar to Sam's Clubs in the United States. Wal-Mart, owner of Sam's Clubs, formed a joint venture with Ek Chor Distribution System to create the shops in Hong Kong.

a company will enter into a **joint venture** with a local firm or government, sharing the operation's costs, risks, management, and profits with its local partner.

joint venture
Sharing a foreign operation's costs, risks, and management with a foreign firm or government.

The way in which a company enters a new market may depend on political forces. For instance, many American firms waited until the United States renewed China's most-favored-nation trading status before entering its market. Caterpillar Inc. quickly formed a joint venture to build hydraulic excavators in China, and the company expects the Chinese market to bring in $2 billion by 2000.[8]

A **multinational corporation** is a firm with significant operations outside its home country. America's largest multinationals include oil, auto, and chemical companies. These firms engage in extensive foreign direct investment, or ownership of assets abroad. The United States is now a net debtor nation because foreigners' holdings in the United States exceed U.S. holdings abroad. Japan is the largest holder of foreign direct investments in the United States.[9]

multinational corporation
Corporation with extensive international operations.

Contracting for production by outside firms is known as outsourcing (see Chapter 1). Outside suppliers are often foreign-based firms. For example, U.S. shoe manufacturer Nike contracts much of its production to suppliers in Asia.

COUNTERTRADE

Sometimes it is difficult to tell who is selling and who is buying in international trade when complications arise due to the practice of **countertrade,** or international bartering agreements in which exporters must buy something in order to sell something. Countertrade is involved to some degree in an estimated 15 to 30 percent of all international trade.

countertrade
International bartering agreement.

Countertrade usually arises when the buyer has limited foreign currency and must pay by exchanging other goods. On occasion, however, the buyer pays for some goods and the seller agrees to purchase other merchandise from the buyer or find a customer for the products. Countertrade may offer a firm's only opportunity to enter a particular market. Many developing countries simply cannot obtain enough credit or financial assistance to afford the imports that their people want. Countries with heavy debt burdens also resort to countertrade. Still other nations, such as China, may restrict imports. Under such circumstances countertrade can be a good way for companies to distribute their products to new markets in the hope of attracting future cash business.

BARRIERS TO GLOBAL BUSINESS

Various barriers complicate effective global business. Some minor barriers are easily overcome; others are nearly impossible to breach. In any case, business executives must expect and learn to handle multitudes of problems in their attempt to reach world markets. Figure 3.3 classifies the barriers to global business as cultural and physical barriers, tariffs and trade restrictions, and political and legal obstacles.

CULTURAL BARRIERS

To succeed in a foreign market, a firm must understand cultural factors such as language, education, social values, religious attitudes, and consumer habits. Many Asian cultures strongly emphasize personal relationships as crucial to doing business. This helps to explain, for example, why Japan has been so successful in forming business ties with Pacific Rim nations.

Cultural factors also help to explain why Euro Disneyland, Disney's huge theme park near Paris, has been less successful than its counterparts in the United States and Japan. Disney's management expected European tourists to behave like American families, who might spend up to a week in Florida's Disney World hotels. However, Europeans' per-capita income is lower than that of Japanese and American tourists, and they prefer to spend their money on long vacations. Many Euro Disney visitors were day-trippers who made brief stops and returned to Paris hotels the same evenings. For another problem, unlike snack-happy Americans, Europeans like to eat their meals at set times; long lines formed in front of park restaurants when everyone stopped for lunch at 12:30. Once the tourists got inside, they were less than pleased to discover that the eateries did not serve beer or wine. To complicate the situation further, French employees resented Disney's U.S.-style rules forbidding facial hair, makeup, and fingernails longer than 0.2 inches.[10]

PHYSICAL BARRIERS

A variety of physical barriers can also affect world trade. For one, location can make a big difference. Japan can do business with Pacific Rim nations more easily than the United States can because Japan is much closer geographically. For the same reason, many American businesses are investing money and moving operations to Mexico rather than to Asia. While investment opportunities in Latin America are tremendous, U.S. companies may face other physical barriers there, such as poor roads, mountainous terrain, and uncertain transportation systems.

Other, less visible barriers to trade may still have important effects. For instance, American electrical devices run on a different type of electric current than those in Europe. Different time zones can also make it difficult to do business with other coun-

FIGURE 3.3 BARRIERS TO GLOBAL BUSINESS

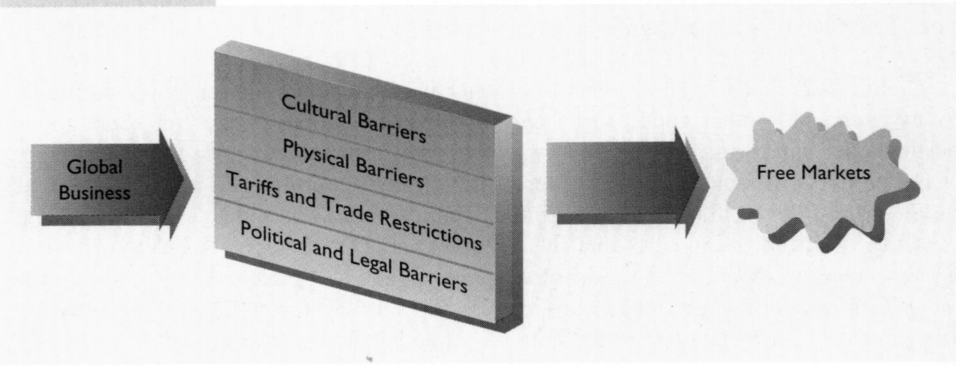

tries. U.S. stock brokers who deal with foreign stock exchanges often have to start work early and work late to accommodate worldwide business hours.

TARIFFS AND TRADE RESTRICTIONS

Tariffs and related trade restrictions also impede global commerce. These restrictions include import quotas, embargoes, and exchange controls.

Tariffs A **tariff** is a tax levied on products imported from abroad. Governments set some tariffs as amounts per pound, gallon, or other unit; they figure others based on the values of the goods. Tariffs can be classified as either revenue or protective tariffs. A revenue tariff is designed to raise funds for the government. Revenue tariffs were a major source of U.S. government revenue until the early 20th century. A protective tariff, which is usually set higher than a revenue tariff, is designed to raise the retail prices of imported items and improve the competitiveness of domestically made goods. Countries sometimes protect designated infant industries, and their related jobs, by imposing tariffs to bar foreign-made competitors.

tariff
Tax levied against imported products.

Trade Restrictions Governments can restrict trade in other ways besides imposing tariffs. An import quota sets a limit on the number of units of a certain product that can be imported. Such a quota seeks to protect domestic industries and their employees or to preserve foreign currency stocks.

The ultimate quota is the **embargo,** a total ban on imports or exports of products. Embargoes typically serve political rather than economic purposes. Until recently, U.S. businesses could not do business in Vietnam due to the U.S. government's trade embargo against that country. When the embargo ended, a market of 73 million people opened to U.S. firms. The Coca-Cola Company lined up two joint ventures, for example, and Mobil Oil teamed up with three Japanese partners to begin drilling in the South China Sea.[11]

embargo
Ban on imports or exports of certain products.

Foreign Trade Zones Many countries designate special areas where foreign goods may be held or processed and then re-exported without incurring further tariffs or other duties. These foreign trade zones are often located at major ports of entry or near impor-

A sign in Hanoi, Vietnam, welcomes American trade delegations. American companies were forbidden to conduct business in Vietnam because of a 19-year trade embargo dating back to the Vietnam war.

tant production facilities inland. Such a zone benefits both the government that maintains it and the foreign firms that use it. For foreign companies, the trade zone offers a convenient location near a major market without all of the costs normally associated with exporting products. They can import their merchandise, store it in the zone, and process, change, test, or demonstrate it without paying duties. The exporters pay duties only if they actually move goods outside the foreign trade zone. For the host country, the zone provides jobs for the people who process the merchandise in that area.[12]

Exchange Controls Foreign trade can also be regulated by exchange controls, under which firms can buy and sell only through a country's central bank or another designated government agency. The government can then allocate, expand, or restrict access to foreign currency for trading in accord with national policy.

Exchange controls can also be used selectively to reduce imports of specific products or operations of particular companies. (Sometimes countries impose exchange controls to restrict inflows of luxury or nonessential items.) Such regulations can create problems for firms because they can affect free trade in components or supplies for other products or for overseas production. Often a company must negotiate with government officials to agree on what can and cannot be brought into the country.[13]

Exchange controls are more common in less-developed countries, but they appear in the developed world as well. Britain, for example, had some form of exchange controls from World War II until the early 1980s.

GATT AND THE URUGUAY ROUND

General Agreement on Tariffs and Trade (GATT) *International accord that has sponsored a series of negotiations on tariffs and trade restrictions.*

While trade restrictions and tariffs continue to affect the flow of global commerce, the overall trend has moved the world toward free trade. The **General Agreement on Tariffs and Trade (GATT)** is an international trade accord that has sponsored a series of negotiations that have reduced worldwide tariff levels. The most recent negotiations, the so-called *Uruguay Round,* produced a new agreement after seven years. The pact covers global trade among 124 nations.

The Uruguay Round cut average tariffs by one-third or in excess of $700 billion. It reduced farm subsidies, which opened markets for U.S. agricultural exports. The agreement also improved protection for copyright and patent holders. In addition, international trading rules now apply to various service industries, with specific details to be set later. Finally, the new agreement set up the World Trade Organization to regulate future trade issues.

A government official estimates that the new GATT will create 2 million U.S. jobs and increase the gross domestic product of the United States by as much as $1 trillion over the next decade. Still, the trade agreement did not address many trade issues. For instance, France continues to limit imports of U.S. TV shows and movies in what it claims is an effort to protect French culture.[14]

POLITICAL AND LEGAL BARRIERS

Firms that operate abroad are often hindered by local politics and laws. Indonesia's government, for example, prohibits foreign firms from creating their own wholesale or retail distribution channels, which forces outside companies to use Indonesian distributors. Brazilian laws require foreign-owned manufacturers to buy most of their supplies from local vendors. Clearly, managers involved in international business must be well-versed in legislation that affects their industries if they want to compete in today's world marketplace.

America's trading relations with other nations may vary according to whether it grants these countries most-favored-nation (MFN) status, which subjects these countries to a single set of relatively low import duties. For example, trade with Vietnam is still

Hollywood films are popular in Paris. The French government held up the GATT agreement in order to limit imports of American films into the country, and more recently proposed a requirement that the majority of television programs shown in Europe be European produced.

restricted because the U.S. government has not granted most-favored-nation status to Hanoi.[15]

As mentioned earlier, many U.S. firms have started doing business in China since that nation's MFN status was renewed. The renewal has opened up new markets to AT&T, for example, since the Chinese government plans to spend $41.4 billion on telecommunications, and AT&T is competing against European and Japanese rivals for several contracts. William Warwick, CEO of AT&T China, believes that the MFN renewal gives AT&T an advantage. "By removing the uncertainty, it strengthens our position," he says. A U.S. official in Hong Kong agrees: "There was a subtle resistance to having a long-term supplier relationship with the U.S. firms. That's going to disappear."[16]

LEGAL FRAMEWORK FOR GLOBAL BUSINESS

The legal environment for U.S. firms operating abroad has three dimensions: U.S. law, host country law, and international requirements. All firms that operate in the United States must comply with comprehensive business legislation. In addition, their international operations are also subject to various trade regulations, tax laws, and import-export requirements.

MAJOR U.S. LEGISLATION

Three laws require special attention from U.S. firms: the Webb-Pomerene Export Act (1918), the Export Trading Companies Act (1982), and the Foreign Corrupt Practices Act (1978). The Webb-Pomerene Export Act creates an exemption from antitrust laws for certain combinations of U.S. firms that act together to develop export markets. The intent is to give U.S. industry economic power equal to that possessed by a *cartel,* a monopolistic organization of foreign firms. This is important because foreign firms frequently cooperate with each other in ways that would be illegal for U.S. firms under domestic antitrust law. Companies that operate under the Webb-Pomerene Act must not reduce competition within the United States and must not use unfair methods of competition.

The Export Trading Companies Act was designed to encourage formation of export trading companies by eliminating some antitrust barriers and allowing banks to partici-

BUSINESS IN ACTION

WHAT IS "MADE IN AMERICA"? A movement to "buy American" has been growing in the United States over the past decade. Many consumers check labels and try to buy only domestic products. Similarly, marketers such as giant mass merchandiser, Wal-Mart, feature and advertise consumer goods made in the United States. What about automobiles, though? Most Americans assume that any car manufactured by a U.S.–based company is made in America and that any car manufactured by a foreign company is made outside the United States. These consumers don't realize that the Ford they just bought may have been built in Mexico using Japanese parts. The Volvo they test-drove was made in Canada using parts made in the United States. What about the new Toyota Avalon? It was manufactured in Kentucky. What exactly is an American car? ■ The American Automobile Labeling Act of 1992 supposedly answers this question. Every automobile, truck, and minivan must now feature a parts content label telling consumers where the vehicle was assembled and where its component parts originated. The label is displayed on the vehicle in a manner similar to the fuel-economy label. ■ This label disclosing "domestic content" should clear up everything for consumers, shouldn't it? *Wrong!* ■ The labels favor American companies while stacking the deck against foreign manufacturers. Many European producers aren't as concerned about the regulation, as BMWs, Jaguars, and Mercedes have appeals of their own. Consumers who want foreign cars will buy them, whatever their domestic content. Japanese car makers, however feel that the new labeling rule will adversely affect their 23 percent market share. ■ The rule does not paint an accurate picture of all automobile production. In calculating domestic content, the rule omits labor costs from the final assembly process. For American makers that use many domestic parts, this omission makes little difference. Japanese makers who build cars in the United States tell a different story. Since Japanese makers use large amounts of imported parts in their United States facilities, they depend on the value of the labor of their U.S. workers—about $1,000 per car—to increase the amount of U.S. content they can claim. Excluding

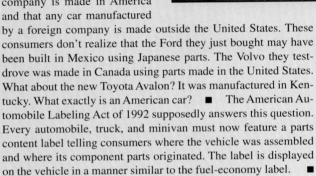

pate in such enterprises. An export trading company is any type of organization that seeks to expand exports.

Another important U.S. law, the Foreign Corrupt Practices Act, forbids U.S. firms from bribing foreigners to buy those firms' goods and services. Enacted in the wake of news reports of companies doing just that, the law also requires businesses to set up adequate accounting controls to monitor internal compliance. The law provides for penalties against both companies and officials. Firms can face fines up to $1 million for violations, while individuals can face $10,000 fines and up to 5 years in jail.

INTERNATIONAL TRADE REQUIREMENTS

International requirements emerge from the various agreements that nations have created. The United States has many friendship, commerce, and navigation (FCN) treaties with other nations. Such treaties address many aspects of international business relations, including the right to conduct business in the treaty partner's domestic market. Other international business agreements concern product standards, patents, trademarks, reciprocal tax treaties, export controls, international air travel, and international communications.

Originally set up to coordinate international financial relations, the International Monetary Fund (IMF) lends money to countries that require short-term assistance to conduct international trade. The IMF has played a major role in overseeing agreements between debtor countries and their lenders to renew loans while ensuring repayment. The World Bank was established to make long-term loans for economic development proj-

these labor costs reduces the domestic content of Japanese autos. ■ The calculation is also affected by the definition of final assembly. When Chrysler buys an already-assembled, American-made dashboard for its Concorde model, the entire cost including parts and labor count toward domestic content. However, when Honda assembles its own dashboards in its Ohio factory, it cannot include the labor costs since they're considered part of final assembly. As a result, the Japanese companies operating in the United States are penalized for their efficiencies. ■ Japanese companies that produce autos in both Japan and the United States face further disadvantages due to the line average aspect of the rule. Toyota, for example, produces the Camry in Japan and in California. Even if Toyota uses all American parts in the Camry cars it produces in California, the domestic content label for these vehicles must display the average of all Toyota Camry cars it produces worldwide. Under the new regulation, the domestic content of the Camry is expected to drop from 75 percent to about 30 percent because of line averaging. ■ Finally, 70 percent or more of a part must be made in the United States or Canada to count the part as domestic production, unless the company owns the supplier. If Toyota buys a battery or shock absorber from Delco, for instance, Toyota cannot count the 65 percent domestic content. General Motors can count the part, though, since it owns Delco. This puts Japanese companies who own fewer U.S. or Canadian parts manufacturers at a disadvantage to American companies. ■ Japanese car makers attempted to impress U.S. consumers with the jobs that their automobile factories provide to American citizens and to publicize models they actually produced in this country before the new regulation took effect. When Mitsubishi introduced its new Eclipse earlier in the year, for instance, the company advertised the vehicle as "'imported' from Illinois" where it was built. Once the rule took effect, though, many imported vehicles look even more foreign than before, and many domestic models look more American than before. Ford's Crown Victoria includes enough foreign parts to actually be classified as an import, but it is now considered a domestic car under the new rule. "It's a blatant appeal to pocketbook patriotism through phony math," says Nissan lobbyist Tim MacCarthy. What does he expect—the rule was made in the USA. Sources: Steven D. Kaye, "Want to Buy American?" *U.S. News & World Report,* October 10, 1994, p. 104; James R. Healy, "New Auto-Content Labels Ignite Controversy," *USA Today,* September 2, 1994, p. 3B; and James R. Healy, "Rules Re-Define Origin," *USA Today,* June 29, 1994, p. 2B.

QUESTIONS FOR CRITICAL THINKING

1. What factors might motivate consumers to buy a foreign car rather than an American car in spite of the new legislation?
2. If you were a marketing manager for a foreign auto maker, how would you market your products in light of this law?
3. Do you think consumers will actually choose whether or not to buy a vehicle because of the information provided on this new label?

ects. In addition, the Export-Import Bank of the United States helps U.S. businesses meet financing conditions necessary for exporting overseas. All of these financial institutions help to facilitate international business activity.

The legal requirements of host nations strongly affect international marketers. Japan, for example, is often cited as a nation with complex import requirements. Other nations, such as Mexico, put various restrictions on foreign ownership of domestic businesses. Most international businesspeople realize the importance of obeying the laws and regulations of the countries within which they operate. Violations of these legal requirements constitute setbacks for international business as a whole and should be carefully avoided.

DUMPING

Many countries prohibit **dumping,** or selling goods abroad at prices lower than those charged in domestic markets. U.S. law requires firms to sell imported items for at least production costs plus 10 percent overhead and a minimum 8 percent profit margin. If dumping is proved, punitive trade restrictions may be assigned to the dumped products.

dumping
Selling goods abroad at prices lower than those charged in domestic markets.

Firms dump products for a variety of reasons, usually to increase market share. This resembles predatory pricing in the domestic market since dumping undersells rivals and can force them out of business. Also, when a country's domestic market is too small to support an efficient level of production, the large U.S. market becomes a tempting target for dumping. Alternatively, a firm might dump surplus goods or technologically obsolete products overseas.

Dumping has become a controversial issue in the global marketplace. Since the mid-1980s, over 40 nations have created antidumping laws, many of them modeled on U.S. legislation. Many economists feel that U.S. laws make it too easy to prove dumping; indeed, the Commerce Department confirms claims of dumping in over 90 percent of all cases it investigates.[17]

MULTINATIONAL ECONOMIC COMMUNITIES

free trade area
Form of economic integration in which participants agree to trade among themselves without tariffs or trade restrictions.

customs union
Form of economic integration in which member nations establish a free trade area and impose a uniform tariff structure for trade with nonmember nations.

common market
Form of economic integration that maintains a customs union and seeks to bring all trade rules into agreement.

Since World War II, the world has seen a trend toward multinational economic integration by various means. In the simplest approach, countries may establish a **free trade area** in which they trade freely among themselves without tariffs or trade restrictions. Each maintains its own tariffs for trade outside this area. A **customs union** sets up a free trade area and specifies a uniform tariff structure for members' trade with nonmember nations. In a **common market,** or economic union, members go beyond a customs union to try to bring all members' government trade rules into agreement. These partnerships succeed in varying degrees. The following sections discuss three such efforts: NAFTA, FTAA, and the European Union.

NAFTA

The North American Free Trade Agreement (NAFTA) became effective in 1994 and created a free trade zone with the United States, Canada, and Mexico. By eliminating all trade barriers and investment restrictions between the three nations over the next 15 years, NAFTA opens up a market of 360 million people. Negotiations are now under way to add Chile as a NAFTA partner.

NAFTA has already had a significant effect on the trading partners. Consider U.S.–Mexico trade. In the first year of operation, NAFTA increased American trade with Mexico by about $16 billion. Most experts see this as only a beginning. In fact, some Mexicans have watched the rapid expansion of McDonald's and other U.S. companies and joked that *NAFTA* really means "North American Franchise Trade Agreement."

NAFTA has also made trade easier for small businesses. For instance, Linda McLaughlin of Houston opened a restaurant in the Mexican village of San Miguel de Allande in 6 months. Without NAFTA, the process would have taken several years and required a Mexican partner. U.S. business with Canada has also benefited. In fact, Canada remains the leading trade partner of the United States, buying over $100 billion of U.S. products annually. As a way to assess the economic impact of U.S. trade with Mexico and Canada, it is often noted that each $1 billion of additional exports creates 15,000 to 20,000 new jobs in the United States.[18]

FTAA

In late 1994, a Summit of the Americas was held in Miami, the first such meeting since 1967. The leaders of 34 democracies in North and South America agreed to set up the Free Trade Area of the Americas (FTAA) to eliminate trade restrictions like tariffs and import quotas by 2005. Much of this work is expected to be done before the end of the decade, a date that Argentina and other nations had advocated.

FTAA will define a single market of 850 million people who spend $13 trillion annually on goods and services, the world's largest free trade zone. Chile's proposed membership in NAFTA is one of the first steps toward the establishment of FTAA.

The hemisphere's leaders also agreed to address related environmental policies and workers' rights issues. In addition, the summit dealt with over 100 other international agenda items. These issues ranged from education and health care to efforts to halt money laundering in the narcotics trade.[19]

EUROPEAN UNION

Perhaps the best-known example of a common market is the European Union. The European Union covers 12 countries and 335 million people. It is expected to add another 10 nations, including several countries from the former Soviet bloc, like Slovakia and the Czech Republic.

To achieve its goal of a borderless Europe, the European Union is working to erase barriers to free trade among its members. This highly complex process involves standardizing business regulations and requirements, standardizing import duties and value-added taxes, eliminating customs checks, and creating a standardized currency known as the European Currency Unit (ECU). Europe's economic borders technically dissolved on December 31, 1992, although true economic integration will not take place for several more years.

Consider the difficulty of standardizing a currency in the face of large differences between the strengths of the members' various economies. Another problem derives from the persistence of centuries-old cultural traditions. For example, Belgium is a small country, but it contains three distinct cultures: Dutch consumers in the north, French speakers in the south (who view themselves as Wallonians rather than Belgians), and a small German community in the southeast.[20]

global strategy
Pursuing a standardized, worldwide product and marketing strategy.

DEVELOPING A GLOBAL BUSINESS STRATEGY

In developing a framework in which to conduct international business, managers can choose from either a global strategy or a multinational strategy. A **global strategy** specifies a standardized, worldwide product and marketing strategy. The firm sells the same product in essentially the same manner throughout the world. In Ford's global strategy, it merges its U.S., European, Asian, and Latin American operations into one huge organization with the goal of creating cars in standardized categories to be sold worldwide. Ford management hopes to reduce the company's costs dramatically by engineering products only once, rather than multiple times for different markets.[21]

Ford Meter Box Company's water valves, repair clamps, and other equipment for water utilities arrive in Miami for shipment to Panama. Ford Meter Box pursued a multinational business strategy when it decided to enter the Japanese market in the late 1980s. Unusual size and material specifications in Japan have forced the company to redesign the products it sells there. The strategy is paying off in rising Japanese sales.

multinational strategy
Strategy that treats each national market differently.

Under a **multinational strategy,** the firm treats each national market differently. It develops products and marketing strategies that appeal to the customs, tastes, and buying habits of particular national markets. Software maker Microsoft pursues a multinational strategy by creating products for specific markets, such as software that can read Japanese characters. Microsoft also staffs its overseas sales and distribution operations with local workers. "The local employees understand the bureaucracy and how to get through the red tape, which is usually much worse than in this country," explains Charles Stevens, general manager for worldwide business strategy. "They also understand the customer." Over the past 5 years, Microsoft's international sales have risen from 45 percent to 55 percent of the company's annual revenues.[22]

ACHIEVEMENT CHECK SUMMARY

Reread the learning goals that follow, and consider the questions for each goal. Answering these questions will reinforce the most important concepts in the chapter and allow you to check how well you have achieved these learning goals. Where a blank appears before a questions, answer with *T* or *F*. Otherwise, circle the letter of the correct answer. An answer key to these questions is found at the end of this chapter.

LEARNING GOAL 3.1: Explain the importance of international business.

1. ___ Overall, foreign sales account for less than 10 percent of American industry's sales.
2. ___ American companies can export or engage in foreign production to generate sales abroad.
3. ___ Exports account for more than one-half of U.S. economic growth.

LEARNING GOAL 3.2: Discuss the basic concepts that underlie international business.

1. ___ If imports exceed exports, a country has a favorable balance of trade.
2. ___ An unfavorable balance of trade results in a trade deficit.
3. ___ A strong dollar helps the United States create a favorable balance of trade.

LEARNING GOAL 3.3: Explain why nations tend to specialize in certain goods.

1. If a nation has the ability to produce a product more cheaply and efficiently than it can supply other products, that nation has: (a) an absolute advantage; (b) a comparative advantage; (c) a monopoly; (d) an excellent work force; (e) none of the above.
2. A country that is the sole producer of an item or that can produce it for less than any other nation has: (a) an absolute advantage; (b) a comparative advantage; (c) an oligopoly; (d) a slight advantage; (e) luck.

LEARNING GOAL 3.4: Name the different levels of involvement in global business.

1. ___ A country that produces goods at home and sells them abroad is engaged in exporting.
2. ___ Contracting with a foreign manufacturer to produce a product rather than exporting it is foreign licensing.
3. ___ Overseas marketing rarely involves foreign sales offices.

LEARNING GOAL 3.5: Explain countertrade.

1. ___ Countertrade is defined as international barter agreements.
2. ___ Countertrade often allows firms to enter markets of developing nations that lack the credit or currency to buy the imports they want.
3. ___ Countertrade decreases the dollar value of a nation's exports.

LEARNING GOAL 3.6: Identify the main obstacles that confront global business.

1. Language differences, education, social values, religious attitudes, and consumer habits are all examples of: (a) cultural barriers; (b) physical barriers; (c) tariffs and trade restrictions; (d) political and legal barriers.
2. Obstacles to international trade that occur due to uncertain transportation systems, differences in time zones, or long distances are examples of: (a) cultural barriers; (b) physical barriers; (c) tariffs and trade restrictions; (d) political and legal barriers.
3. Taxes on imports, quotas, and embargoes are all examples of: (a) cultural barriers; (b) physical barriers; (c) tariffs and trade restrictions; (d) political and legal barriers.

LEARNING GOAL 3.7: Explain multinational economic integration.

1. ___ Where obstacles still hamper multinational economic integration, the trend is toward greater freedom of trade.
2. ___ The European Union (EU) has the goal of erasing trade barriers throughout Europe.
3. ___ The General Agreement on Tariffs and Trade (GATT) is expected to eliminate 2 million American jobs.

LEARNING GOAL 3.8: Distinguish between a global strategy and a multinational strategy.

1. ___ A company that produces one standard product to sell worldwide has adopted a global strategy.
2. ___ A multinational strategy designs a unique product and/or marketing strategy for each foreign market.
3. ___ A multinational strategy greatly reduces the costs and risks of selling in different markets.

KEY TERMS

exporting 46	tariff 55
importing 46	embargo 55
foreign production 46	General Agreement on Tariffs and Trade (GATT) 56
balance of trade 47	dumping 59
balance of payments 47	free trade area 60
exchange rate 47	customs union 60
devaluation 48	common market 60
joint venture 53	global strategy 61
multinational corporation 53	multinational strategy 62
countertrade 53	

REVIEW QUESTIONS

1. Can a nation have a favorable balance of trade and an unfavorable balance of payments? Defend your answer.

2. Explain how exchange rates are established. What factors can affect them?

3. Distinguish between the concepts of absolute advantage and comparative advantage. Cite examples of both.

4. Identify the levels of involvement in international business and give an example of each.

5. Explain the trend toward outsourcing. Cite an example.

6. What is countertrade? Why do you think this has become such an important part of international business?

7. How does a firm that follows a multinational strategy operate in the global marketplace?

8. Describe three types of barriers that firms may face in international business. Give an example of each.

9. Explain the difference between a revenue tariff and a protective tariff. What type of tariff most concerns the United States today? Why?

10. Describe the three basic formats for multinational economic integration.

DISCUSSION QUESTIONS

1. The history of global business is full of embarrassing incidents. When Wal-Mart entered the Quebec market, it sent out an advertising flier in English, a definite mistake in the French-speaking province. The company quickly issued an apology in French. Along the same lines, McDonald's ran a World Cup promotion that featured the flags of the competitors on throwaway food bags. Unfortunately, the company did not realize that the Saudi Arabian flag contains sacred scripture from the Koran. Muslims were offended that this scripture would end up in trash bags. McDonald's quickly retreated.[23]

Can you identify any other global business mistakes similar to these incidents? What can businesspeople learn from these embarrassing moments? How can companies avoid offending cultural and religious sensitivities?

2. Several major league baseball teams are actively seeking fans outside the United States and Canada. The Florida Marlins target baseball fans from the Caribbean as well as Latin American countries. The Texas Rangers and Houston Astros have organized player visits to Monterrey and Mexico City. Similarly, the San Diego Padres, whose games are broadcast in Spanish, recruit players in Veracruz and play exhibition games in Tabasco.[24]

Why are foreign markets important to major league baseball? Can you think of any other ways to promote baseball abroad? Do other professional sports organizations engage in global business?

3. When the Japanese government was forced to import rice because of a poor harvest, it set up a policy to release the imported rice only as needed. The objective of the program was to protect Japanese rice growers, who carry considerable political clout. Surprisingly, some Japanese developed a taste for the imported rice, and it now sells on the black market for twice what the Japanese government paid for it.[25]

Relate this situation to the material in Chapter 3. Why do you think some Japanese developed a preference for the imported rice? Discuss.

4. Gallup China, the first foreign marketing research firm to operate in the People's Republic of China, did a study for the U.S. confectionery industry. Among its findings, the study discovered that people in southern China preferred a sweet flavor, while those in the north favored a more sour taste.[26] Relate this incident to the discussion of trade barriers. Also, how would this finding affect the strategy employed by a marketer of candy bars? Discuss.

5. Some 158 U.S. companies have direct investments in South Africa.[27] Discuss the opportunities and risks of doing business in a changing South Africa.

SOLUTIONS TO ACHIEVEMENT CHECK SUMMARY

L.G. 3.1: 1. F, 2. T, 3. T. **L.G. 3.2:** 1. F, 2. T, 3. F. **L.G. 3.3:** 1. b, 2. a, **L.G. 3.4:** 1. T, 2. T, 3. F. **L.G. 3.5:** 1. T, 2. T, 3. F. **L.G. 3.6:** 1. a, 2. b, 3. c. **L.G. 3.7:** 1. T, 2. T, 3. F. **L.G. 3.8:** 1. T, 2. T, 3. F.

VIDEO CASE

WHIRLPOOL Whirlpool Corporation is the world's leading manufacturer of major home appliances. Headquartered in Benton Harbor, Michigan, the company manufactures in 12 countries and markets products under 10 major brand names in more than 120 countries. Total overseas sales account for 40 percent of company revenues and are growing.

Sustainable growth in unit volume and profitability for Whirlpool depend on worldwide production and sales. Currently, Europe produces about 30 percent of worldwide sales. In contrast, the national markets of Latin America are relatively young, but growing. Collectively, they present far too much opportunity for long-term value creation to be ignored by Whirlpool Corporation. This region, which Whirlpool defines as the Caribbean and Central and South America, is expected to grow by four to six percent annually through the 1990s and into the next decade, a rate much higher than those projected for North America or Europe.

Yet another region of the world in which Whirlpool intends to be a major player is Asia, which has the potential to become Whirlpool's largest market. Currently, only about 10 percent of Asian households own a refrigerator. It is the fastest growing and second largest home appliance market in the world.

As Whirlpool chairman David Whitwam recalls, "I never managed a global company until January 1, 1989, when I woke up and we had a $2.2 billion business in Europe. When we bought that business, there weren't a dozen people in Whirlpool who had a passport." Whirlpool had just purchased the N.V. Philips European appliance division. European consumers spend twice as many days of household income for appliances than do consumers in the United States. At the same time, industry profit margins are traditionally much lower than those of North American manufacturers. Historically, the European appliance industry was set up to do business in individual, national markets. This produced inefficiencies since different designs, different parts, and different promotions were used in each country. As the European Union became a reality, Whirlpool saw a chance to eliminate some of those inefficiencies by consolidating Philips' scattered assets. As part of a program to slash $400 million in annual costs, Whirlpool closed a plant in Barcelona and trimmed 36 warehouses to eight in 1995. It also centralized inventory control, cutting the number of suppliers used in Europe in half—from 16,000 to 8,000. Where Philips bought refrigerator power cords from 17 suppliers, Whirlpool now buys from two. Measures like these allowed Whirlpool to cut inventory costs by one-third.

In Asia, Whirlpool has taken a deliberate multi-year approach. Consumer wants, needs, and expectations are very different in this market. The design requirements for a refrigerator change dramatically when it's to be placed in the living room—typical in many Asian countries because of both space limitations and the social status attached to owning

such an appliance. To minimize initial risk and investment, Whirlpool used sales subsidiaries, distributors, and sold product kits to be assembled by licensees.

National markets throughout Asia are expected to expand at rates of 8 to 12 percent annually after the year 2000. Widening Whirlpool's opening into Asia is the fragmented nature of the market. The current market-share leader holds a share that is less than one-half of Whirlpool's market share in North America. However, the same fragmentation that makes this market so attractive to Whirlpool also makes it more difficult to enter. Whirlpool can't enter the region by buying a single large manufacturer as it did when it bought N.V. Philips. Instead, the company will most likely assemble an integrated system of wholly-owned operations and strategic alliances. Right now, about half of the products sold by Whirlpool Asia are built to its specifications by other regional manufacturers. The remaining units come from company locations in Europe and North America. Asia is clearly a land of growth and opportunity for the balance of this decade and into the next. Only time will tell if Whirlpool is successful in tapping this immense market.

QUESTIONS

1.
How important is global business to Whirlpool?

2.
What approaches to international business are exhibited by Whirlpool? Is the level the same in each of the markets in which it participates?

3.
What problems confronted Whirlpool in Europe? In Asia?

4.
Why is the Asian market so important to Whirlpool?

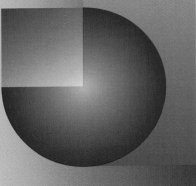

LEARNING GOALS

1. Explain the concepts of social responsibility and business ethics.
2. Describe the relationship between self-regulation and government regulation.
3. Explain how government regulates business.
4. Discuss the impact of deregulation.
5. Understand how to evaluate social performance.
6. Outline the responsibilities of business to the general public.
7. Identify the responsibilities of business to customers.
8. Describe the responsibilities of business to employees.
9. Explain the responsibilities of business to investors and the financial community.

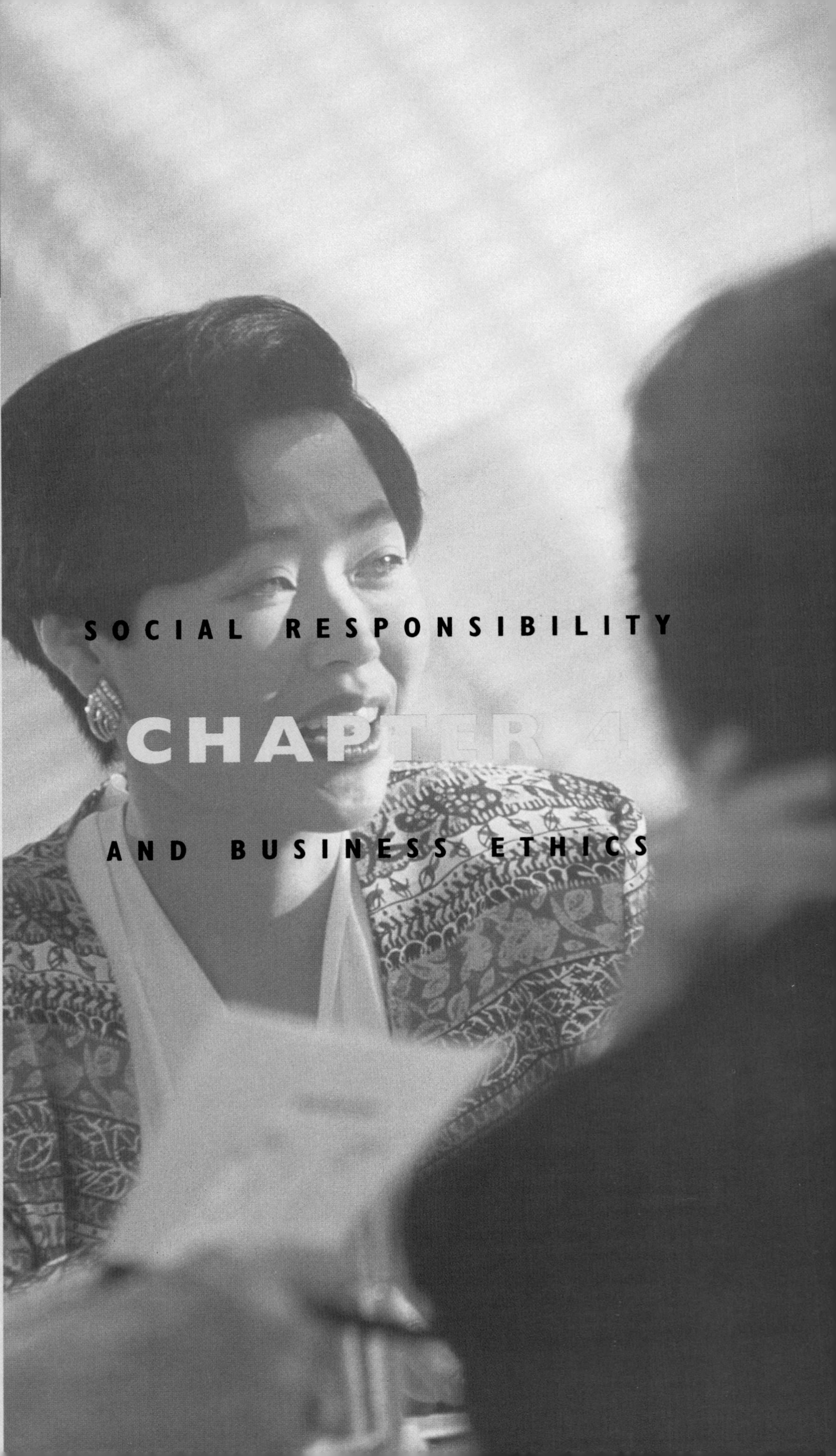

CHAPTER 4

SOCIAL RESPONSIBILITY AND BUSINESS ETHICS

THE BATTLE OVER DISNEY'S AMERICA The area around Manassas, Virginia had already seen two major conflicts. In 1861, Stonewall Jackson's Confederate army defeated the Union forces there in the Civil War Battle of Bull Run. A year later, the Confederates won a second Battle of Bull Run, this time under Robert E. Lee. ■ More recently, a third battle took place on this rolling stretch of Virginia Piedmont land, 35 miles southwest of Washington, D.C. This time, however, the Walt Disney Company was on one side, and the opposing army was a diverse mix of historians, environmentalists, and property owners. ■ At issue was Disney's latest project, a 3,000-acre theme park called "Disney's America." Designs for the complex called for 1,340 hotel rooms, 2,300 homes, 1.96 million square feet of retail and commercial space, and an historical park that would provide a panoramic view of America's past. The project would take 4 years and $650 million to build. ■ Disney's America was controversial from the start. Historians banded together to protest the park's theme. "The Disney people," said historian Shelby Foote, "will do to American history what they have already done to the animal kingdom—sentimentalize it out of recognition." Princeton history professor James McPherson worried that Disney would "trivialize" its subjects. The Black History Action Coalition threatened to boycott the park unless it excluded exhibits related to the Civil War and slavery. ■ Meanwhile, environmentalists argued that the park would ruin the unique character of the region of more than 20 historic towns, historic districts, and Civil War battlefields. The Piedmont Environmental Council, a coalition of 70 organizations and 5,000 families from the area, sued Disney, claiming that the park would bring overcrowding, pollution, and road congestion. "Disney will destroy the countryside," said one resident. Author David McCullough cited the urban sprawl that envelopes the company's existing U.S. parks, California's Disneyland and Florida's Disneyworld. He warned of a pending "commercial blitzkrieg" of motels, fast-food restaurants, and souvenir shops. ■ Disney executives, however, insisted that the benefits of the proposed park would far outweigh its drawbacks. Disney Chairman Michael Eisner promised that the project would bring the region 2,700 new jobs, while indirectly creating another 19,000. He also promised to give $169 million to the county over the first 10 years after the park opened and almost $2 billion to the state of Virginia over the first 30 years of the park's operation. Jody Powell, Disney's public relations consultant, portrayed the conflict as an attempt by wealthy Piedmont landowners to retain control of the scenic Manassas region: "It's their buffer zone. They don't own it, but they need to control it." ■ A few historians did support Disney's America. James Oliver Horton, an historian at George Washington University, described the park as "an opportunity to teach people who would never come to our classrooms or read our books." ■ The controversy symbolizes the difficult ethical decisions that businesspeople confront. Where, exactly, does the Disney Company's responsibility lie in a situation like this? Some might say that a business has the right to develop legally purchased land in order to make better returns for its stockholders. (Incidentally, the land had previ-

ously belonged to another corporate owner, Exxon.) Others might say that too many scenic areas and historic sites like Manassas have already been developed, and those that remain are precious public resources that should not be sacrificed. ■ The third Battle of Bull Run ended in defeat for Disney, which decided to give up its option on the Piedmont site. Executives vowed, however, that they had not abandoned the Disney's America concept entirely. "We are now in the site location business," said John Cooke, president of the Disney Channel and chairman of Disney's America. "We are starting afresh and are reaching out to historians who have opposed us to make sure our portrayal of the American experience is responsible." ■ Business analysts, for their part, question whether the United States needs another theme park at all. While Disney's operating income from theme parks is flat, its income from other sources—films, entertainment, and consumer products—has jumped. "I'm real happy Disney isn't building [the park]," says analyst David Londoner of Wertheim Schroder. He recommends that the company "take the equivalent amount of money and put it in software or into Disneyland and Disneyworld."[1]

CHAPTER OVERVIEW

social responsibility
Management philosophy that highlights the social and economic effects of managers' decisions.

Most of us would agree that business should operate in an ethical and socially responsible manner. As you can see from the opening example, many business decisions can involve questions about what a company owes to society. **Social responsibility** is management's consideration of the social and economic effects of its decisions. Figure 4.1 summarizes business's social responsibilities.

A wide range of social issues affect business, including substance abuse, ethnic and gender discrimination, and pollution. Some social problems affect the quality of a firm's most valuable asset, its work force. Drug abuse and alcoholism can make workers less productive; discrimination may restrict the employment opportunities of minority workers. Any steps that a firm can take to resolve social problems can help its employees—and improve its bottom line. Perhaps Jim Casey, founder of United Parcel Service (UPS), said it best nearly 50 years ago: "Are we working for money alone? If so, there is no surer way not to get it."[2]

FIGURE 4.1 THE SOCIAL RESPONSIBILITIES OF BUSINESS

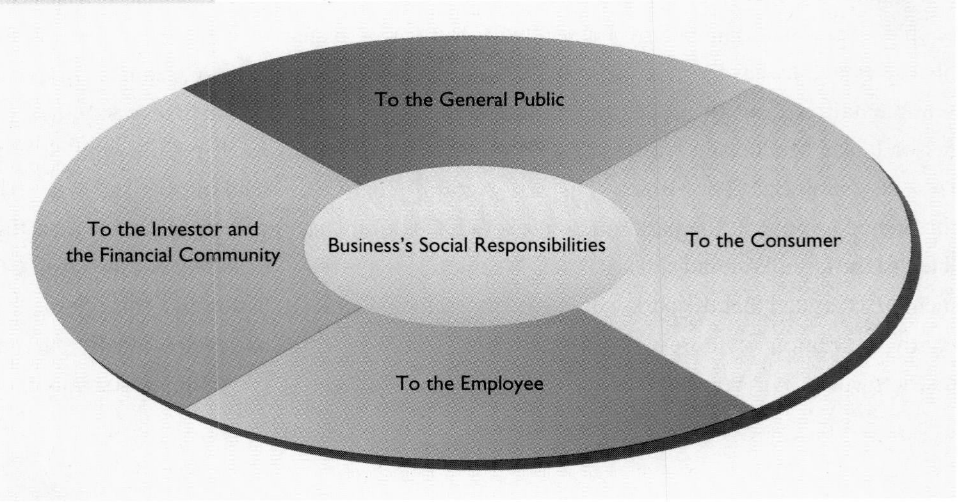

In addition to dealing with broad social issues, businesspeople may be required to resolve specific ethical questions. **Business ethics** deals with the right and wrong actions that arise in any work environment. Sometimes a conflict arises between an ideal decision and one that is practical under certain conditions, but it is no less important for companies to evaluate their ethical responsibilities in decision making.

business ethics *Standards of business conduct and moral values.*

Many firms find value in ethics training. After being investigated for fraud and mismanagement, aerospace and defense contractor Martin Marietta instituted a companywide program of ethics training. Training for senior executives focuses on the challenges of ethical decision making and balancing multiple responsibilities and priorities. Training for all employees includes access to an "ethics network" through which workers can report their concerns anonymously. Executives believe that the ethics program has improved Martin Marietta's relations with the government and with auditors. They also feel that publicity about the program has helped the company to win more contracts.[3]

SELF-REGULATION OR GOVERNMENT REGULATION?

Corporations frequently have problems regulating themselves. Look at food labels. When consumers became concerned about fat and cholesterol in their food, many food companies started advertising their products with magic words such as *light, low-cholesterol,* and *low-fat.* Some made health-related claims for their products without any scientific basis. To keep calorie counts on labels low, some companies listed unrealistically small serving sizes.

The Food and Drug Administration (FDA) finally stepped in and issued new guidelines to determine what could and could not appear on food labels. The new labels are easier to read and provide more information about nutrition. Under the new rules, for instance, a product labeled *low fat* must contain no more than 3 grams of fat per serving.[4]

Businesses that fail to regulate themselves may face severe penalties; recently consumers and attorney generals in over 40 states accused Sears automotive centers of misleading customers and selling them unnecessary parts and services. While the company denied any intent to defraud customers, CEO Edward Brennan admitted that its compensation systems and lack of monitoring could have "created an environment in which mistakes did occur."[5] Sears ended up refunding customers' money and offering coupons to those who had purchased certain auto services during a 2-year period. The total cost of the settlement was estimated at $60 million.

CURRENT STATUS OF SOCIAL RESPONSIBILITY AND ETHICS IN U.S. INDUSTRY

In a recent survey, California ethicist Michael Josephson found that ethical lapses are common in American business. About 30 percent of managers, for instance, admit to filing deceptive internal reports. Other examples of common corporate misconduct include stealing from employers, shorting shipments to customers, giving false data to vendors, and bribing foreign customs officials.[6]

Top-level executives make most ethical decisions, and they play crucial roles in shaping organizational climates that encourage ethical behavior. Ethical lapses in organizations rarely result from the actions of individuals; most reflect the values of corporate cultures, as established by top managers. It is important for employees to know that ethics and social responsibility are priorities for the firm.

Generally, organizations with ethical corporate cultures share the following traits:

- Ethical guidelines are clearly stated and communicated to employees.
- Managers are personally committed to these values, and are willing to base actions on them.

- Normal decision making and business practices reflect ethical values.
- The company's organizational structure and practices reinforce these values.
- Managers at all levels receive training and encouragement to make ethically sound decisions.[7]

GOVERNMENT REGULATION OF BUSINESS

Government regulates competition and competitors, as well as specific business practices. The next section reviews the requirements and practices of business regulation. A later section looks at how government regulation influences contemporary business.

REGULATIONS THAT AFFECT COMPETITION

Effective and ongoing competition is the cornerstone of the private enterprise economy. The *laissez-faire* ("hands off") doctrine that guided regulation during the United States' first 100 years was ideal for promoting the rapid growth of the nation geographically, politically, and economically.

As the country matured, however, too much economic power became concentrated in too few companies. This led to monopolies in certain basic industries. Mergers further concentrated economic power and caused problems that led to government intervention.

regulated industry
Industry in which competition is either limited or eliminated, and government monitoring substitutes for market controls.

Approaches to Regulating Competition When government regulation of competition and other commercial activity came about in the late 1800s, it took two broad forms: regulation of industry and enactment of statutes concerning competition. In a **regulated industry,** competition is either limited or eliminated, substituting close government control for free competition. Examples of regulated industries are found in public utilities and other industries closely tied to the public interest where competition would be wasteful or excessive. For example, only one electrical power company can serve a given market. The large capital investment required to construct a pipeline or electric transmission line or to build and operate a nuclear power plant makes this type of regulation appropriate. The lack of competition can sometimes cause deterioration in services and performance, though.

The second form of government regulation, enactment of statutes, has led to both state and federal laws that affect competition and various commercial practices. Table

Electric companies and other public utilities are regulated by government. Competing companies would duplicate power generation and distribution systems, causing great expense for consumers.

4.1 lists major federal laws and summarizes their effects on different aspects of American business.

Both state and federal statutes affect competition and various commercial practices. The first effort by the federal government to regulate competition was the Sherman Antitrust Act of 1890. This act prohibits any contract or conspiracy that tends toward restraint of trade. It also declares illegal any action that monopolizes or attempts to monopolize any part of commerce.

Additional Competitiveness Legislation Another major federal law, the Clayton Act of 1914, forbids such trade restraints as tying contracts, interlocking directorates, and certain anticompetitive stock acquisitions. A tying contract requires the exclusive dealer for a manufacturer's products to carry other products of the manufacturer in inventory. The legality of a tying contract depends on whether it restricts competitors from major markets. In interlocking directorates, competing companies have identical or overlapping boards of directors. The Clayton Act also forbids any purchase of another company's stock that reduces competition.

The Clayton Act is enforced by the Antitrust Division of the U.S. Department of Justice. Violators are subject not only to criminal fines or imprisonment, but also to civil damage suits by competitors or other parties. In some cases, the government allows the accused firm to enter into a consent order, under which it agrees voluntarily to cease the conduct that the government alleges is inappropriate. The Celler-Kefauver Antimerger Act (1950) amended the Clayton Act to prohibit major asset purchases that decrease competition in an industry.

REGULATION OF SPECIFIC BUSINESS PRACTICES

Besides competitive conditions, the government also regulates specific business practices. The Federal Trade Commission Act of 1914 banned unfair competitive practices and set up the Federal Trade Commission (FTC) to administer various statutes that apply to business. The powers and investigative capacities of the FTC have grown rapidly over the years; today it is the major federal regulatory and enforcement agency to oversee competitive practices. The FTC can sue violators or enter into consent orders with those that agree to cease questionable practices. The FTC Improvement Act of 1980 gives Congress 90 days to veto any FTC ruling with which it disagrees.

This text covers many other specific business practices regulated by government in other sections and in Appendix C, "Business Law."

EFFECTS OF DEREGULATION ON THE BUSINESS ENVIRONMENT

Deregulation, the movement toward eliminating legal restraints on competition in various industries, may significantly reshape the legal environment for business. The trend started in 1978 with the Airline Deregulation Act, which encouraged competition among airlines by allowing them to set their own rates and to add or abandon routes based on profitability. Several other industries have been deregulated, including railroads and trucking.

deregulation
Elimination of legal restraints on competition.

Deregulation can have a substantial impact on business. For example, the Airline Deregulation Act has led to mergers or acquisitions of several airlines. Because airlines can now freely select their routes, many have pulled out of smaller markets. As a result, commuter airlines have grown significantly. Commuter airlines such as Britt, Hensen, and Horizon now serve as passenger feeders to major airlines that operate out of large airports.

TABLE 4.1 MAJOR FEDERAL LAWS THAT AFFECT BUSINESS

DATE	LAW	DESCRIPTION
A. LAWS TO MAINTAIN A COMPETITIVE ENVIRONMENT		
1890	Sherman Antitrust Act	Prohibits restraint of trade and monopolization; delineates a competitive marketing system as national policy.
1914	Clayton Act	Strengthens the Sherman Act by restricting such practices as price discrimination, exclusive dealing, tying contracts, and interlocking boards of directors where the effect "may be to substantially lessen competition or tend to create a monopoly."
1914	Federal Trade Commission Act	Prohibits unfair methods of competition; established the Federal Trade Commission, an administrative agency that investigates business practices and enforces the FTC Act.
1938	Wheeler-Lea Act	Amended the FTC Act to further outlaw unfair practices and give FTC jurisdiction over false and misleading advertising.
1950	Celler-Kefauver Antimerger Act	Amended the Clayton Act to include major asset purchases that decrease competition in an industry.
1975	Consumer Goods Pricing Act	Prohibits pricing maintenance agreements among manufacturers and resellers in interstate commerce.
1980	FTC Improvement Act	Gives the Senate and House of Representatives joint veto power over FTC trade regulations; limits FTC power to regulate unfairness issues.
1992	American Automobile Labeling Act	Requires vehicle manufacturers to provide a label informing consumers of where the vehicle was assembled and where its components originated.
B. LAWS TO REGULATE COMPETITION		
1936	Robinson-Patman Act	Prohibits price discrimination in sales to wholesalers, retailers, or other producers; prohibits selling at unreasonably low prices to eliminate competition.
1937	Miller-Tydings Resale Price Maintenance Act	Exempts interstate fair trade contracts from compliance with antitrust requirements.
1993	North American Free Trade Agreement (NAFTA)	International trade agreement between Canada, Mexico, and the United States designed to facilitate trade by removing tariffs and other trade barriers among the three nations.
C. LAWS TO PROTECT CONSUMERS		
1906	Federal Food and Drug Act	Prohibits adulteration and misbranding of foods and drugs involved in interstate commerce; strengthened by the Food, Drug, and Cosmetic Act (1938) and the Kefauver-Harris Drug Amendment (1962).
1939	Wool Products Labeling Act	Requires identification of the type and percentage of wool used in products.
1951	Fur Products Labeling Act	Requires identification of the animal from which a fur product was derived.

TABLE 4.1 MAJOR FEDERAL LAWS THAT AFFECT BUSINESS (CONT.)

DATE	LAW	DESCRIPTION
C. LAWS TO PROTECT CONSUMERS (CONT.)		
1953	Flammable Fabrics Act	Prohibits interstate sale of flammable fabrics.
1958	National Traffic and Safety Act	Provides for the creation of safety standards for automobiles and tires.
1958	Automobile Information Disclosure Act	Prohibits automobile dealers from inflating factory prices of new cars.
1966	Child Protection Act	Outlaws sales of hazardous toys; 1969 amendment added products posing electrical, mechanical, or thermal hazards.
1966	Fair Packaging and Labeling Act	Requires disclosure of product identification, name and address of manufacturer or distributor, and information on the quality of contents.
1967	Federal Cigarette Labeling and Advertising Act	Requires written health warnings on cigarette packages.
1968	Consumer Credit Protection Act	Truth-in-lending law requiring disclosure of annual interest rates on loans and credit purchases.
1970	Fair Credit Reporting Act	Gives individuals access to their credit records and allows them to change incorrect information.
1970	National Environmental Policy Act	Established the Environmental Protection Agency to deal with various types of pollution and organizations that create pollution.
1971	Public Health Cigarette Smoking Act	Prohibits tobacco advertising on radio and television.
1972	Consumer Product Safety Act	Created the Consumer Product Safety Commission with authority to specify safety standards for most products.
1975, 1977	Equal Credit Opportunity Act	Bans discrimination in lending practices based on sex and marital status (as of 1975) and race, national origin, religion, age, or receipt of payments from public assistance programs (as of 1977).
1990	Nutrition Labeling and Education Act	Requires food manufacturers and processors to provide detailed nutritional information on the labels of most foods.
1990	Children's Television Act	Limits the amount of advertising to be shown during children's television programs to no more than 10.5 minutes per hour on weekends and not more than 12.0 minutes per hour on weekdays.
1991	Americans with Disabilities Act (ADA)	Protects the rights of people with disabilities; makes discrimination against the disabled illegal in public accommodations, transportation, and telecommunications.
1993	Brady Law	Imposes a five-day waiting period and a background check before a gun purchaser can take possession of the gun.
D. LAWS TO DEREGULATE SPECIFIC INDUSTRIES		
1978	Airline Deregulation Act	Grants considerable freedom to commercial airlines in setting fares and choosing new routes.
1980	Motor Carrier Act and Staggers Rail Act	Significantly deregulates trucking and railroad industries by permitting them to negotiate rates and services.

Critics of deregulation often point out negative effects of the trend. Some say that deregulation may lead to higher prices as competitors are eliminated. Others suggest that firms may sacrifice safety in the name of competition. All of these issues are legitimate concerns.

HOW CAN BUSINESSPEOPLE EVALUATE SOCIAL PERFORMANCE?

Historically, a company's social performance has been measured by its contribution to the U.S. economy and the employment opportunities it has provided. Variables such as wage payments often served to indicate social performance. While profits and employment remain important, today many factors contribute to an assessment of a firm's social performance. These include providing equal employment opportunities; respecting the cultural diversity of its employees; responding to environmental concerns; providing a safe, healthy workplace; and producing safe, high-quality products.

A business is also judged by its interactions with the community. Many corporations highlight charitable contributions and community service in their annual reports to demonstrate their social responsibility.

CONDUCTING A SOCIAL AUDIT

social audit
Formal examination of a firm's social responsibility performance.

Some firms measure social performance with a **social audit,** a formal procedure that identifies and evaluates all company activities that relate to social issues such as employment practices, environmental protection, conservation, and philanthropy. The social audit informs management about what the company is doing and how well it is performing. Based on this information, management may take steps to revise current programs or develop new ones.

Managers at NovaCare Inc., which provides rehabilitation services to nursing homes and hospitals, conducted a social audit when employee turnover reached a staggering 57 percent annually. CEO John Foster brought in consultants to interview and conduct focus groups with the company's employees, managers, and customers. An employee task force reviewed the results and drafted a vision statement that summarized the firm's goals and laid out a new framework for making decisions and setting policies.

Managers reorganized the company according to the results of the social audit. They gave field managers and clinicians greater authority to use resources and make decisions, and the company hired more managers with health-care backgrounds to emphasize its renewed focus on service quality and clinical issues. Within 4 years, NovaCare's turnover

Volunteers from Abbott Laboratories work on a house being built by Habitat for Humanity. Habitat constructs homes for low-income families who purchase the homes from the organization. Abbott employees volunteer more than 500 hours a year to Habitat projects. The company also donates cash for the cost of materials.

rate had fallen to 27 percent. Many NovaCare employees believe that the audit played an important role in creating a new corporate culture at the firm.[8]

EXTERNAL EVALUATIONS OF SOCIAL RESPONSIBILITY

Outside groups may conduct their own evaluations of business. Various environmental, church, and public-interest groups have created standards of corporate performance. Shoe manufacturer Stride Rite Corporation has received public-service awards from several such groups, including the National Women's Political Caucus and the Northeast Human Resources Association.[9]

Reports on many of these evaluations are available to the general public. The Council on Economic Priorities produces publications such as *The Better World Investment Guide,* which recommends basing investment decisions on companies' track records on various social issues, including environmental impact, nuclear weapons contracts, community outreach, and advancement of women and minorities. The council also issues reports that analyze the environmental records of various firms. "Companies with substandard environmental records must be held responsible for their air, water, and soil pollution," says Alice Tepper Marlin, executive director of the council.[10]

OTHER SIGNS OF SOCIAL RESPONSIBILITY

Many firms find that consumers evaluate their social track records in financial decisions, that is, by either buying or not buying the firms' goods and services. One holiday season, for example, American Express promised to donate 2 cents from every purchase made with its card to programs to fight hunger. Managers estimate that the campaign increased AmEx's U.S. sales by 9.4 percent that business quarter and raised $5 million for charity.[11]

Public opinion can be powerful. The Interfaith Council on Corporate Responsibility, a group of shareholders in various companies, meets with corporate managers to discuss social responsibility issues. Recently, the group met with executives at Time Warner to discuss tobacco advertising in the company's publications. While these ads bring in $62 million of revenue for Time Warner each year, the company is considering banning or restricting them in response to public pressure.[12]

FOCUSES OF SOCIAL RESPONSIBILITY

Just what does business owe to society? After all, a company must make money in order to survive in the marketplace. If it goes bankrupt, many people could suffer, including employees, customers, and their families. What happens when a company does things that could be considered harmful in order to stay in business?

The social responsibilities of business can be classified according to its relationships to the general public, customers, employees, and investors and the financial community. Many of these relationships stretch beyond national borders. The rest of the chapter looks at responsibilities in each of these categories.

RESPONSIBILITIES TO THE GENERAL PUBLIC

The responsibilities of business to the general public include dealing with public-health issues, protecting the environment, and developing the quality of the work force. Figure 4.2 summarizes these responsibilities. These responsibilities are discussed in the sections that follow.

Public-Health Issues Public-health concerns include—but are not limited to—issues such as smoking and secondhand smoke, substance abuse, and AIDS.

FIGURE 4.2 BUSINESS'S RESPONSIBILITIES TO THE GENERAL PUBLIC

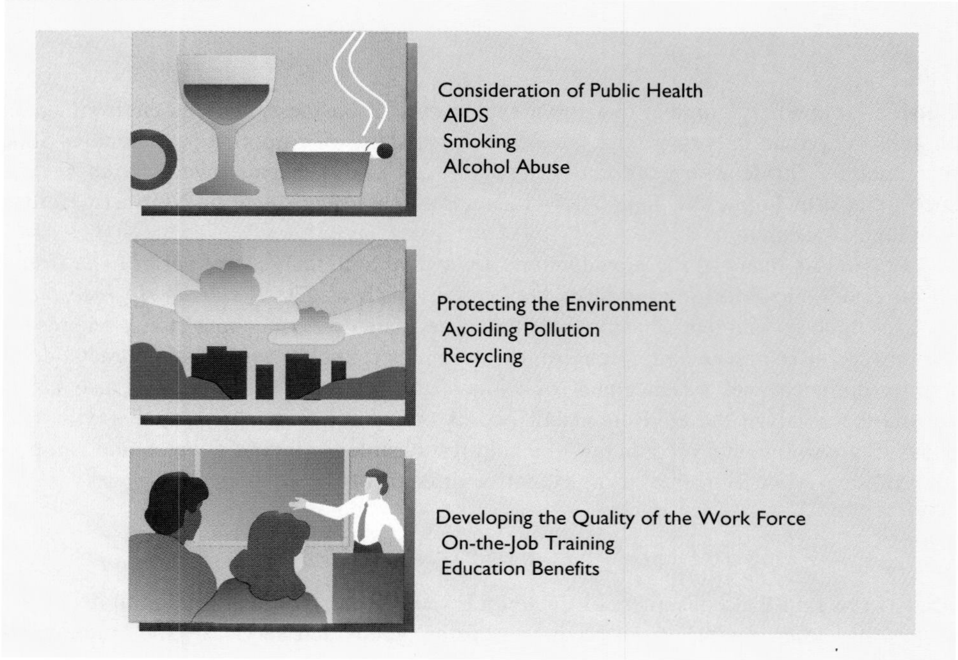

Consideration of Public Health
AIDS
Smoking
Alcohol Abuse
Protecting the Environment
Avoiding Pollution
Recycling
Developing the Quality of the Work Force
On-the-Job Training
Education Benefits

Smoking is a major health risk, since it is one of the top three risk factors for heart disease and stroke.[13] Furthermore, spouses and co-workers of smokers share this danger, since their exposure to so-called "secondhand smoke" increases their risks for cancer, asthma, and respiratory infections. As a result, many employers have banned smoking from the workplace.

Substance abuse, including alcohol abuse, is a serious public-health problem in the United States. Motor vehicle accidents are a major killer, and drunk drivers cause many serious crashes. Alcohol abuse has also been linked to serious diseases such as cirrhosis of the liver. For these reasons, public opposition to alcohol advertising is steadily growing. Many consumers view both alcohol and tobacco advertising as socially irresponsible. Some brewers have tried to counter these views by sponsoring advertising campaigns that promote moderation.

AIDS represents a different type of challenge to business firms when dealing with the consequences of this terrible disease. AIDS (acquired immunodeficiency syndrome) is a fatal disease that breaks down the body's ability to defend itself against illness and infection. AIDS is especially dangerous because a long time (typically five years) elapses between someone's first exposure to the AIDS virus and actual development of the disease. During this period, people may not show any symptoms of AIDS, and they probably don't even know they have it, but they are still carriers who can give the disease to others. This large pool of unknown carriers accounts for the rapid spread of the disease. In 1982, only 1,013 cases of AIDS were reported; today the victims number over 200,000.[14]

The rapid spread of AIDS has forced companies to educate their employees about it and to deal with employees who have the deadly disease. Health care for AIDS patients can be incredibly expensive, straining the ability of a small company to pay for health-care coverage. Do companies have the right to test potential employees for the AIDS virus? Some people feel that this would violate the rights of job applicants; others feel that a firm has a responsibility not to place AIDS patients in jobs where they could infect members of the general public. These are difficult questions; in resolving them, a business must balance the rights of individuals against the rights of society in general.

Protecting the Environment Ecology and environmental issues continue to become more important to the public. **Ecology**—the study of the relationships between living things and their environments—is now a legal as well as a societal issue for managers to consider.

ecology
Study of the relationships between living things and their environments.

Pollution **Pollution**—tainting or destroying a natural environment—is the major ecological problem today. Pollution can come from many sources. Burning fossil fuels such as coal and oil for energy introduces carbon dioxide and sulfur into the earth's atmosphere. Both of these chemicals cause environmental problems. The extra carbon dioxide collects in the atmosphere and traps heat, leading to the greenhouse effect, which keeps the earth's temperature warm enough to support life. However, during this century the amount of carbon dioxide in the atmosphere has soared as people have burned increasing amounts of fossil fuels. Many scientists fear that this could result in global warming, with disastrous results.

pollution
Tainting or destroying a natural environment.

Meanwhile, the sulfur from fossil fuels combines with water vapor in the air to form sulfuric acid. The acid rain that results kills fish and trees, and it can pollute the groundwater. In the northeastern United States, acid levels in rain and snow are now about 100 times the normal levels. Acid rain is also dangerous because wind can carry the sulfur all over the world. Sulfur from factories in the United States is damaging Canadian forests, and pollution from London smokestacks is destroying the forests and lakes of Scandinavia.[15]

Recycling as a Solution Every time someone throws away a plastic box, a newspaper, or a glass bottle, the act adds to the world's trash problem. Garbage just never seems to die; it stays intact in landfills for years, and places to put it are running short.

An important solution is **recycling**—reprocessing used materials for reuse. Recycling could provide much of the raw material that manufacturers need, but people must recycle much more waste. Some 40 percent of the garbage produced by a typical

recycling
Reprocessing of used materials for reuse.

Knight-Ridder, Inc.'s corporate director of environmental affairs works with all Knight-Ridder companies to ensure that they get the information they need to comply with environmental and safety regulations. One of the company's goals is to use 100 percent recycled newsprint with an average content of 40 percent recycled fiber by 2000.

The Herman Miller workers shown here are remaking old office panels, which would otherwise end up in landfills, so that they can be sold and used again.

American household consists of paper; just recycling your daily newspaper could save four trees every year.[16]

Recycling is not enough by itself. A full solution requires development of ways to reuse recycled material. For instance, 95 percent of German households participate in the Green Dot program, a not-for-profit recycling project. While the project collects 400,000 tons of sorted trash each year, it can recycle only 125,000 tons; the rest is stored in warehouses, farm fields, and abandoned airplane hangars. Some of it even ends up being shipped to other countries, such as Indonesia, which makes Germany the world's biggest trash exporter.[17]

conservation
Preservation of declining energy resources.

Analysts divide the complex topic of energy into short-term and long-term issues. In the short run, the problem focuses on **conservation**—preserving declining energy resources. Since burning fossil fuels damages the environment, and since supplies of these fuels are limited and will eventually run out, conservation presents an attractive solution. In addition to conserving current energy sources, long-term solutions must involve alternative energy sources. Nuclear power, wind, sun, synthetic fuels, and even garbage and other waste products have all been suggested as substitutes for fossil fuels.

Car makers, for instance, are developing electric cars that they hope will eventually replace standard, fossil-fuel-burning vehicles. California regulators have mandated that by 1998, 2 percent of the vehicles sold in the state must run on electricity. New York and Massachusetts will require electric vehicles the year after that, and ten other states, plus the District of Columbia, are considering similar laws. Ted Morgan, president of U.S. Electricar Inc., is working to develop engineless electric cars, but not for consumers. "That's the market the Big Three [auto makers] will go after," he says. Instead, Morgan plans to develop fleets of electric cars for utilities and the U.S. Postal Service.[18]

Developing the Quality of the Work Force In the past, a nation's wealth has often been thought to consist of its money, production equipment, and natural resources. A country's true wealth, however, lies in its people; an educated, skilled work force is a nation's most valuable asset. It is becoming increasingly clear that in order to remain competitive, American business must assume more responsibility for developing the quality of its work force.

Most new jobs require college-educated workers. Many professions will demand 10 years of study beyond high school, and even the least-skilled jobs will require certain levels of reading, computing, and thinking abilities. Business must encourage students to stay in school, continue their educations, and develop their skills. Companies must also encourage employees to learn new skills and remain competitive.

Companies also face social responsibilities to integrate women, members of various cultural groups, and the disabled fully into the economy. A recent survey by the National Organization on Disability, for instance, shows that two-thirds of disabled Americans between the ages of 16 and 64 are not working, even though the overwhelming majority of them want employment. Private employers can often provide cost-effective training programs that can play key roles in expanding these workers' employment opportunities. Marriott International sponsors a program called "Bridges . . . from school to work" that helps young people with disabilities make this transition. Marriott offers paid internships for special education students in the last year of high school. Approximately 500 students enroll in these internships every year; more than 80 percent of those who complete the internships receive offers of permanent jobs.[19]

By developing a culturally diverse work force, a company can create a significant competitive advantage. Consider Daniel's Jewelers, a 33-store chain based in California. "We have stores in neighborhoods that are predominantly Hispanic or African-American," says Co-President Howard Sherwood. "We hire salespeople from the neighborhood and they already have an understanding of the culture and the customer. When we have district manager meetings, we really listen to what our people are telling us because they know what the customer wants. . . . They tell me about Mexican Mother's Day and Quince Años (the Spanish celebration of a girl's 15th birthday) and other holidays and celebrations that are important to our customers."[20]

RESPONSIBILITIES TO CUSTOMERS

Consumer demands create another social responsibility issue for business. **Consumerism**—public demands that business consider consumer wants and needs in making its decisions—is a major social and economic movement. Ralph Nader is a leading force in this trend.

consumerism
Public demand for business to consider consumer wants and needs in making its decisions.

Consumerism and much consumer-protection legislation are based on the belief that consumers have certain rights. President Kennedy identified these as the right to be safe, the right to be informed, the right to choose, and the right to be heard. Many companies exert considerable effort to ensure full hearings for consumer complaints. Ford Motor Company, for example, has set up a consumer appeals board to resolve service complaints. The opening story to this chapter reported how complaints from over 60 consumer groups caused Walt Disney Company executives to change their minds about a proposed theme park in Virginia.[21]

Since consumerism began to emerge a few decades ago, consumer groups have sprung up throughout the country. Some have concentrated on specific situations, such as rate hikes by local public utilities, while others have attacked broader issues. As a net effect, this activity has promoted passage of numerous consumer-protection laws. Few doubt that more such laws will be passed in the years ahead and that they will have a big impact on business.

RESPONSIBILITIES TO EMPLOYEES

Business must meet wide-ranging responsibilities to its employees. Related issues include family leave, equal employment opportunities, multicultural diversity, sexual harassment, and sexism.

A BROADER PURPOSE

MEETING THE CHALLENGE OF SOCIAL RESPONSIBILITY AT COORS Beer makers are desperately hanging on during tough market conditions. Sales of Budweiser, Anheuser Busch's $4+ billion brand, and Miller Lite, Miller Brewing's big gun, were down 9 percent and 16 percent, respectively, over a recent three-year period. Coors is pursuing a survival strategy to keep its number three status in this volatile market. The family run company saw its flagship brand, Coors, decline to less than one-third of its market in the mid-1980s. It may seem safe to assume that Coors is focusing all of its efforts and money on this marketing dilemma, but it is not. Coors still devotes its time and resources to being a socially responsible company. ■ Coors' emphasis on social responsibility has made it a leader in corporate volunteering. In 1985, Coors created V.I.C.E. (Volunteers in Community Enrichment) and A.D.V.I.C.E. (Additional Duties Volunteers in Community Enrichment) to support community activities. Current and retired employees help senior and disabled citizens to live independently, collect and distribute food for those in need, preserve the environment with tree planting and recycling programs, and encourage reading and learning among young children. Since 1985, Coors volunteers have logged more than 220,000 hours through 686 community projects. ■ Coors is also actively involved in fighting illiteracy. The firm's award-winning "Literacy. Pass It On." program represents a long-term commitment to raise public awareness, recruit volunteers, support a toll-free hot line, and generate funds to reduce illiteracy. To date, the program has helped more than 420,000 nonreading adults and has raised over $5 million in donations to local, regional, and national literacy organizations. ■ Coors also acts in a socially responsible manner toward the environment. Since water is a main ingredient in beer, Coors is acting to preserve, protect, and clean up the water resources in the United States. The firm established its "Pure Water 2000" program in 1990 to fund more than 700 grassroots water resource projects across the country with more than

family leave
Giving employees leaves of absence from work in order to deal with family matters.

Family Leave As more families include two wage-earning parents, employees' responsibilities at home may clash with those at work. Some employees may care for elderly parents or relatives, while others find themselves juggling child-care problems or other family crises with the demands of their jobs. **Family leave**—giving employees leaves of absence from work in order to deal with family matters—has become an important issue for many workers.

The Family and Medical Leave Act of 1993 requires every business with 50 or more employees to provide up to 12 weeks of unpaid leave annually for an employee who has a child, who is adopting a child or becoming a foster parent, who is caring for a seriously ill relative or spouse, or who is seriously ill himself or herself. Workers must meet certain eligibility requirements. Employers must continue to provide health benefits during the leave and guarantee that employees will return to equivalent jobs.[22]

Equal Employment Opportunity Commission (EEOC)
Federal commission created to increase job opportunities for women and minorities and to help eliminate job discrimination.

affirmative action program
Program set up by a business firm to increase employment opportunities for women and minorities.

Ensuring Equal Employment Opportunities The Civil Rights Act (1964) ruled that discriminatory practices are illegal, and Title VII of the act specifically prohibits discrimination in employment. The **Equal Employment Opportunity Commission (EEOC)** was created to increase job opportunities for women and minorities and to help end discrimination based on race, color, religion, sex, or national origin in any personnel action. The EEOC defines minorities to include African Americans (not of Hispanic origin), Hispanics, Asians or Pacific islanders, and Native Americans or Alaskan natives.

The EEOC can help an employer to set up an **affirmative action program** to increase job opportunities for women, minorities, the disabled, and people in other pro-

$2 million. The program is administered by Coors local distributors, who select conservation efforts to support and match funds that Coors provides. The project has a consumer aspect, as well. Store displays educate consumers about water issues and problems, inform them about relevant local water projects, and provide information about conservation organizations with which consumers can get involved. Other Coors projects include introducing the aluminum beverage can, initiating buy-back recycling centers, maintaining the highest recycled content in containers, running fuel-efficient plants, and reusing and composting waste. ■ Coors also runs socially responsible advertising to promote safe and responsible drinking. Television and print ads have featured such themes as "Gimme the Keys" and "Now, Not Now" showing both appropriate and inappropriate times to drink Coors products. Coors' current television ads encourage consumers under the age of 21 to wait until they reach legal age to drink alcohol. Point-of-sale materials and public service announcements also promote safe and healthy decisions about responsible drinking. The "Drink Safely" logo appears on all of Coors' secondary packaging and in most of its advertising. ■ Finally, Coors is socially responsible in regards to its employees. Coors offers a number of programs addressing issues and problems affecting workers, including well-child referral services, mammogram services, and an on-site Wellness Center. Coors was one of the first companies to publish a policy to treat AIDS as any other serious illness. Afflicted employees are guaranteed full benefits, additional resources, and management support to remain productive within the organization. ■ These are only a few of the many programs and groups that Coors helps. Peter Coors, the company's CEO, sees social responsibility as a dependable path to profitability. Pollution and waste are things that a company produces but can't sell. Reducing these by-products will make a company more efficient and thus more profitable. Also, responsibility toward people affected by Coors' actions—referred to by Coors as *stakeholders*—is a vital part of the process. Sources: Alex Berenson, "Nature Conservancy Recruits Colorado Backers," *Denver Post,* July 19, 1994, p. C1; "Coors Stars in Ad Competition," *New York Times,* April 6, 1994, p. D20; Peter Coors, "The New Corporate Environmentalism," *Newsweek,* June 14, 1993, p. S3; and *1993 Annual Report,* Coors Brewing.

QUESTIONS FOR CRITICAL THINKING

1. What effect do you think the "Drink Safely" logo in advertising and on packaging has on consumers?
2. What can Coors do to prevent or discourage underage drinking of alcohol?
3. What other current social causes might be appropriate for Coors' involvement?

tected categories. Such programs include analyzing the present work force and setting specific hiring and promotion goals (with target dates) in areas where women, minorities, and others are underutilized. Businesses can also face penalties for violations.

The work of the EEOC receives reinforcement from the Equal Pay Act (1963), the Age Discrimination in Employment Act (1967), the Equal Employment Opportunity Act (1972), the Pregnancy Discrimination Act (1978), the Civil Rights Act of 1991, and numerous executive orders. The Americans with Disabilities Act (1991) protects the rights of disabled people. The Vietnam Era Veterans Readjustment Assistance Act (1974) protects the employment of both disabled and able-bodied veterans of the Vietnam war. Table 4.2 outlines the basic provisions of these laws.

Multicultural Diversity The American workplace is changing. By 2000, women will make up about 47 percent of all workers, while minorities and immigrants will hold 26 percent of all jobs. By the end of the decade, white males will account for only 32 percent of those entering the work force.

The racial and cultural blend within a society is called **multicultural diversity.** Diversity has always been part of American culture, as new immigrants have entered and become part of U.S. society. The challenge for U.S. business is to learn how to manage this diversity creatively to benefit from the different viewpoints, experiences, and talents of the various cultures in society.

multicultural diversity
Racial and cultural blend within a society.

To deal with a culturally diverse work force, managers must understand what motivates employees and how they function best. Developing a better understanding of people's cultures and behaviors will help businesspeople to manage culturally diverse staffs

TABLE 4.2 LAWS TO ENSURE EQUAL OPPORTUNITY

LAW	KEY PROVISIONS
Title VII of the Civil Rights Act of 1964 (as amended by the Equal Employment Opportunity Act of 1972)	Prohibits discrimination in hiring, promotion, compensation, training, or dismissal on the basis of race, color, religion, sex, or national origin.
Age Discrimination in Employment Act of 1968 (as amended)	Prohibits discrimination in employment against anyone aged 40 or over in hiring, promotion, compensation, training, or dismissal.
Equal Pay Act of 1963	Requires equal pay for men and women working for the same firm in jobs that require equal skill, effort, and responsibility.
Vocational Rehabilitation Act of 1973	Requires government contractors and subcontractors to take affirmative action to employ and promote qualified disabled workers. Coverage now extends to all federal employees. Coverage has been broadened by the passage of similar laws in more than 20 states and through court rulings to include persons with communicable diseases, including AIDS.
Vietnam Era Veterans Readjustment Assistance Act of 1974	Requires government contractors and subcontractors to take affirmative action to employ and retain disabled veterans. Coverage now extends to all federal employees and has been broadened by the passage of similar laws in over 20 states.
Pregnancy Discrimination Act of 1978	Requires employers to treat pregnant women and new mothers the same as other employees for all employment-related purposes, including receipt of benefits under company benefit programs.
Americans with Disabilities Act (1990)	Enables victims of employment discrimination to collect punitive damages. Stiffens employer penalties for intentional discrimination on the basis of an employee's disability. Also covers on-the-job problems.
Civil Rights Act of 1991	Makes it easier for workers to sue their employers for alleged discrimination. Enables victims of sexual discrimination to collect punitive damages; includes employment decisions and on-the-job issues such as sexual harassment, unfair promotions, and unfair dismissal. The employer must prove that it did not engage in discrimination.
Family Leave and Medical Act of 1993	Requires all businesses with 50 or more employees to provide up to 12 weeks of unpaid leave annually to employees who have had a child, are adopting a child or are becoming foster parents, who are caring for a seriously ill relative or spouse, or who are themselves seriously ill. Workers must meet certain eligibility requirements.

more effectively. Respecting employees' cultural differences is a vital part of management in the 1990s.

Employees at Seafirst Bank in Seattle take one-day seminars on multicultural diversity that help them to understand themselves and their customers better. Each seminar includes a self-awareness exercise with the following questions:

1. If you had to define yourself in four words or less, what would you say?
2. Describe an experience or moment at which you were aware of being those four words.
3. Describe something that makes you feel proud about those words.
4. Describe what is difficult about being those four words.

"Diversity awareness starts with self-examination and how you perceive yourself and how that could be different from how others perceive you," explains Ruby Okada, a Seafirst vice president. "People describe themselves in many ways but they share common experiences. This exercise helps them see that and teaches them to value differences."

A diverse work force can be a valuable resource for a company that deals with a diverse customer base. When David Bland, vice president and manager of ethnic marketing at Wells Fargo, decided to target Asian-American customers, he first consulted the bank's Asian-American employees. Bland surveyed 29 Asian staffers and used the information he gathered to create an extensive set of guidelines for marketing to Asian consumers. "We had people in our company who had dealt with these segments or came from these segments," he says. "We wanted to capitalize on their understanding of the culture. We wanted to do research before targeting the community."[23]

sexual harassment
Inappropriate actions of a sexual nature.

Sexual Harassment **Sexual harassment** refers to inappropriate actions of a sexual nature. The law defines two categories of sexual harassment: (1) unwelcome advances and requests for sexual favors that affect promotions and raises, and (2) a "hostile" work environment in which an employee feels hassled or degraded because of unwelcome flirting, lewd comments, or obscene jokes. The courts have ruled that allowing sexually oriented materials like pinup calendars and pornographic magazines at the workplace can create a hostile atmosphere that interferes with an employee's ability to do the job.

Sexual harassment is a major problem for business. Over 10,000 complaints are filed with the Equal Employment Opportunity Commission every year—double the number of 5 years ago. Research shows that 90 percent of *Fortune* 500 firms have dealt with complaints about sexual harassment. More than one-third of them have been sued at least once; a quarter of them have been sued repeatedly. Sexual harassment is estimated to cost the average large corporation $6.7 million a year in investigation costs, legal fees, and the like.

The Civil Rights Act of 1991 helped more employees to fight sexual harassment. For the first time, women (and men) could win damages for intentional sexual harassment. The law also allowed judges to force losing parties to pay fees for winners' expert witnesses, an often crucial but expensive component of winning a complex harassment case.

It is important for employers to resolve sexual harassment problems in-house, avoiding lawsuits if possible. Many firms have established antiharassment policies and employee-education programs. A recent survey of 600 major companies found that 50 percent of them planned to offer more sexual harassment training to managers and employees. An effective harassment prevention program would include (1) issuing a specific policy statement prohibiting sexual harassment, (2) developing a complaint procedure for employees to follow, (3) creating a work atmosphere that encourages sexually harassed staffers to come forward, and (4) investigating and resolving complaints immediately, taking disciplinary action against harassers.[24]

sexism
Discrimination against members of either sex (primarily a problem for women).

Sexism Sexual harassment is often part of the broader problem of sexism. **Sexism** refers to discrimination against members of either sex, but it primarily affects women. Some examples of sexism are blatant, as when a woman earns less than a male colleague to perform the same job or a male employee gains a promotion over a better-qualified female. Other instances are more subtle; the only female in a work group may not be introduced to a client or may not get a work assignment when a manager assigns tasks.

Sexism is a global issue. A United Nations study found that women, who account for one-half of the earth's population, do two-thirds of the world's work, earn one-tenth of the world's income, and own one-hundredth of the world's property. A U.N. Human Development Report concluded that no country offers its female citizens opportunities comparable to those enjoyed by males.

One important sexism issue concerns equal pay for equal work. As Figure 4.3 shows, median weekly wages for women in the United States amount to 76 percent of those for male workers. This actually represents an improvement; in 1980, women's wages aver-

A BROADER PURPOSE

60S-STYLE MANAGEMENT MEETS THE 90S AT BEN & JERRY'S In 1978, Ben Cohen and Jerry Greenfield invested $5 in a correspondence course to learn how to make ice cream. The childhood friends started their business in a converted gas station using an old Volkswagen squareback as the delivery van. The correspondence course paid off; today, Ben & Jerry's owns almost 40 percent of the $277 million superpremium ice cream market. ■ The company is unconventional, to say the least. Ben and Jerry, two ex-hippies, choose T-shirts and jeans over pin-striped suits as businesswear. They are known to surprise their employees with foot massages. They host Elvis Presley Days at their headquarters. They name new flavors of ice cream after rock-n-roll idols like Cherry Garcia for Jerry Garcia of the Grateful Dead. ■ Their unconventional ways have earned them recognition as leaders in the socially responsible business movement. The company's mission statement links product, economic, and social goals. The company developed the concept of the "double bottom line"—earning a profit while taking care of employees, customers, business partners, shareholders, and the planet in general. ■ Ben and Jerry's political and social views are the basis for their philosophy of "caring capitalism," using their business as a means of promoting social change. The firm donates 7½ percent of pretax earnings, approximately $500,000 each year, to causes such as saving the rain forest, the campaign against bovine growth hormone, and aiding the homeless. The company buys milk from a cooperative of Vermont family farmers. It created blueberry-flavored ice cream to help support a tribe of Maine Indians whose economy depended on blueberries. Ben and Jerry locate plants in areas with high unemployment. They have kept 1960s culture and values alive and well in the 1990s. ■ Recently, however, the company has been criticized for losing track of its unusual approach to business. Reports have surfaced that employees at the company suffer high rates of on-the-job injuries. The company points out that the rates are being reduced. Several small distributors claim that Ben & Jerry's has allowed its biggest distributor, Dreyer's Grand Ice Cream Inc., to bully its way into their territories. Other small competitors and franchisees feel they were mistreated by the

aged 64 percent of men's. The gap is closing only partly because of gains in women's salaries; the rest is due to a decline in men's earnings. Female high-school graduates still earn less than men who quit school before the ninth grade.[25]

In industrialized nations worldwide, women's pay averages just two-thirds that of men. Many women find their routes to corporate success blocked by glass ceilings of discrimination. Among several reasons for this, one is that many corporate jobs rely on recruitment by word of mouth and networking, which tends to exclude women and minorities. Women often have less access to training and development programs. Managers' stereotypes can make things worse; managers may assume that a woman with children would not be interested in transfers or promotions that would require longer hours. Executive search firms compound the problem by focusing on white males.[26]

RESPONSIBILITIES TO INVESTORS AND THE FINANCIAL COMMUNITY

Probably in no area does the public expect a higher level of business ethics than in financial transactions. Just because a business practice is legal doesn't mean that it is also ethical. When business evaluates its responsibilities to investors and the financial com-

company. Several lawsuits have been filed against the company by disgruntled distributors, competitors, and franchisees. Many within the industry claim that Ben & Jerry's has grown into a hard-nosed big business. ■ Perhaps the most telling sign that things have changed at Ben & Jerry's surfaced in early 1995. Ben Cohen decided to step down as chief executive of the company. Profits were down, sales slowed, and the stock price declined. Ben & Jerry decided to bring an executive on board who had experience in directing and growing a company of their firm's size while maintaining a commitment to social issues. "We need somebody who's been down the pike before," says Cohen. "I don't have the skills to lead and manage a company this size. I'm really stretched right now." In their quest for a new leader, they used the conventional approach of an executive search firm. The partners also used a rather unconventional approach of running a contest asking entrants to write 100-word essays on why they should get the job. ■ Ben and Jerry ran into one stumbling block in their search. They had established a company rule that the top executive could not be paid more than seven times the pay of the lowest-paid worker (approximately $140,000). The partners quickly found that this rule was preventing them from attracting qualified candidates. Despite this fact, Ben and Jerry still intended to maintain the policy of "salary compression." ■ After a 7-month search, Ben and Jerry hired Robert Holland, Jr. as chief executive of the company. Since the executive search firm found Holland, he was not required to write the 100-word essay. However, he did create the poem "Time, Values, and Ice Cream" for the owners. Holland will receive 12½ times the pay of the company's lowest-paid worker—$250,000—with a $125,000 bonus and a potential to make $180,000 in stock options. At a press conference at their headquarters, Ben Cohen removed his hat shaped like a pint of Ben & Jerry's ice cream and placed it on Holland's head as a ceremonial gesture. ■ Employees and stockholders are wondering if this change in policy indicates greater changes ahead. Are the populist values and caring capitalism that had formed the foundation of the company a thing of the past? A computer engineer at Ben & Jerry's said, "You wonder if this is the first step toward becoming a stereotypical bigger company."

Sources: Jesus Sanchez, "Cone Head Ben & Jerry's Ends Its Unusual Search for New Chief Executive," *Los Angeles Times,* February 2, 1995, p. D1; Doron P. Levin, "Fat Times Are Over for Premium Ice Cream Makers," *New York Times,* July 31, 1994, pp. 3–5; Robert Manor, "Ben, Jerry Aren't Above Making a Profit," *St. Louis Post-Dispatch,* July 5, 1994, p. 6B; and Maria Shao, "Ben & Jerry's Grows Up; Has 'Caring Capitalism' Become a Casualty of Big-Company Reality?" *Boston Globe,* July 3, 1994, p. 65.

QUESTIONS FOR CRITICAL THINKING

1. Are Ben and Jerry's unconventional business practices realistic in today's business world?
2. Was the company rule regarding the top executive's pay realistic for the 1990s?
3. What should be more important, maintaining the original business philosophy that helped build the company or changing to maximize profits?

FIGURE 4.3 THE PAY GAP

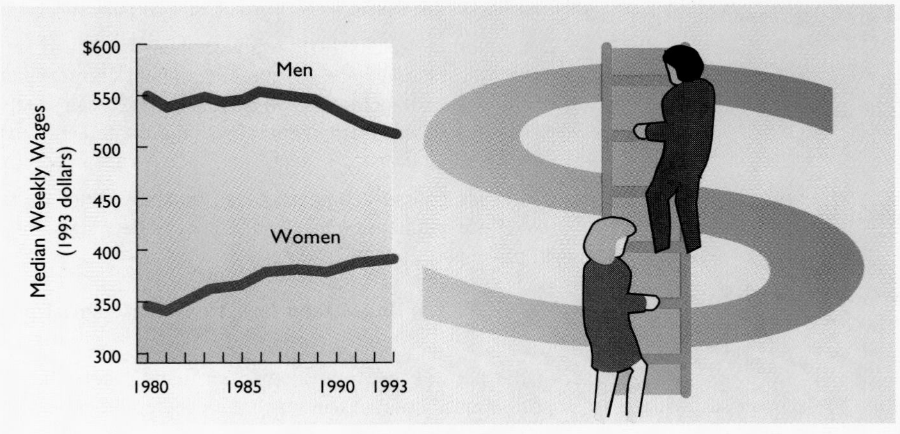

munity, it must recognize that the public expects behavior that is both legal and ethical. Ethical business behavior is not just something that sounds good on paper. A business firm that fails to meet its social responsibilities can hurt hundreds or even thousands of people.

Unethical securities trading practices can injure people who lose their investments or their jobs. Irresponsible investments can hurt millions of consumers. By the 1990s, failure rates of banks and savings and loan institutions (S&Ls) were the highest they had been since the 1930s depression. All too often, these problems resulted from too many high-risk investments. The banks used their deposits to finance real estate developers, third-world governments, and corporate leveraged buyouts. When these borrowers could not repay the loans, the banks failed.

So far, the federal government has covered all depositors' losses at failed banks and S&Ls. However, this has cost billions of dollars, and the government agencies that cover the debts are running out of money. Ultimately, taxpayers will end up paying for these unwise investments.

Sometimes investors strike back. Disgruntled former clients of brokerage firm Smith Barney (now Smith Barney Shearson) have filed a $28 million lawsuit against the company, claiming that it misled them when it sold expensive limited partnerships in four Long Island car dealerships. Soon after the transaction, three of the dealerships were in poor financial shape, and New York state officials closed the highest-volume dealership, alleging illegal sales practices. The investors' suit claims that Smith Barney concealed the true nature of the dealerships' management and has not compensated them appropriately for their losses. The average investment was $90,000. Smith Barney managers, for their part, have consistently denied any wrongdoing.[27]

ACHIEVEMENT CHECK SUMMARY

Reread the learning goals that follow, and consider the questions for each goal. Answering these questions will reinforce the most important concepts in the chapter and allow you to check how well you have achieved these learning goals. Where a blank appears before a question, answer with *T* or *F*. Otherwise, circle the letter of the correct answer. An answer key to these questions is found at the end of this chapter.

LEARNING GOAL 4.1: Explain the concepts of social responsibility and business ethics.

1. ___ Social responsibility is management's consideration of both the social and economic effects of its decisions.
2. ___ Business ethics are standards of conduct and moral values applied in business decision making.
3. ___ Social responsibility and ethical conduct generally cost more than they create in business value.

LEARNING GOAL 4.2: Describe the relationship between self-regulation and government regulation.

1. ___ Self-regulation means merely complying with the law.
2. ___ Management should realize that failure to self-regulate will lead the government to take steps to correct any abuses.
3. ___ Top management plays a crucial role in developing an organizational culture that encourages ethical behavior.

LEARNING GOAL 4.3: Explain how government regulates business.

1. ___ The earliest government regulations of business were enacted to maintain competition.
2. ___ In a free market economy, the law affects very few facets of business.

LEARNING GOAL 4.4: Discuss the impact of deregulation.

1. Deregulation means: (a) the government begins to set the price a firm can charge; (b) the government eliminates legal restraints on competition; (c) the firms involved can jointly set prices; (d) state governments rather than the federal government regulate firms.
2. Critics argue that deregulation can: (a) lead to higher prices; (b) reduce competition; (c) lead to lower safety standards; (d) all of the above.

LEARNING GOAL 4.5: Understand how to evaluate social performance.

1. ___ Social performance is evaluated on many criteria besides a firm's contribution to national output and employment opportunities.

2. ___ Social responsibility deals with a firm's relationships with customers, employees, and the general public, but not with a firm's responsibilities to investors.

LEARNING GOAL 4.6: Outline the responsibilities of business to the general public.

1. ___ Environmental protection, avoiding pollution, and promoting recycling are the responsibility of government, not the business community.
2. ___ American firms have found a significant competitive advantage in developing a culturally diverse and highly skilled work force.

LEARNING GOAL 4.7: Identify the responsibilities of business to customers.

1. John F. Kennedy described consumer rights as: (a) the right to safety; (b) the right to be informed; (c) the right to choose; (d) the right to be heard; (e) all of the above.
2. The demand that businesses respond to consumer needs and wants is: (a) increasing; (b) declining; (c) about the same as it was 50 years ago; (d) outlawed.

LEARNING GOAL 4.8: Describe the responsibilities of business to employees.

1. ___ The EEOC was created to increase job opportunities for all members of society and to help end discriminatory practices in employment.
2. ___ Since we are all Americans, business managers need not be concerned with the cultural diversity of their employees.
3. ___ Family leave is a benefit that companies may choose to offer, but no American firm is legally required to provide family leave.

LEARNING GOAL 4.9: Explain the responsibilities of business to investors and the financial community.

1. ___ Since investors are risk takers, managers face no ethical requirements to protect investor interests.
2. ___ If a business practice is legal, it is surely ethical.
3. ___ Investors who believe that managers have not dealt honestly with them have legal recourse.

KEY TERMS

social responsibility 68
business ethics 69
regulated industry 70
deregulation 71
social audit 74
ecology 77
pollution 77
recycling 77
conservation 78
consumerism 79
family leave 80
Equal Employment Opportunity Commission (EEOC) 80
affirmative action program 80
multicultural diversity 81
sexual harassment 83
sexism 83

REVIEW QUESTIONS

1. What do the terms *social responsibility* and *business ethics* mean? Cite an example of each. Discuss the current status of social responsibility and business ethics practices in U.S. industry.

2. Does self-regulation deter government regulation in matters of social responsibility and business ethics? Why or why not?

3. How does government regulate both competition and specific business practices? Describe specific regulations with which businesspeople should be familiar.

4. What is deregulation? What are its advantages and disadvantages?

5. Explain the need for internal and external social performance measures in business. What standards can businesspeople use for these purposes?

6. What are the responsibilities of business to the general public? Cite specific examples.

7. What basic consumer rights does the consumerism movement try to assure? How has consumerism improved the contemporary business environment?

8. What is meant by multicultural diversity?

9. Distinguish between sexual harassment and sexism. Cite examples of each. How can firms avoid these problems?

10. What are a firm's responsibilities to its investors and the financial community? What can happen when a firm fails to meet these responsibilities?

DISCUSSION QUESTIONS

1. The chapter described a self-awareness exercise completed by employees at Seafirst Bank in Seattle that helped them to understand themselves and their customers better. (See the section on page 82.[28]) Answer the four questions that the text listed for this exercise. Your instructor may want you to compare your answers with those of your classmates. Discuss what you have learned from this exercise.

2. Noted economist Milton Friedman believes that social responsibility is not really the concern of business. He says, "There is one and only one social responsibility of business—to use its resources and engage in activities designed to increase its profits so long as it stays within the rules of the game, which is to say, engages in open and free competition, without deception or fraud."[29] Other business scholars argue that companies have the obligation to address social responsibility issues such as those discussed in this chapter. What is your opinion? What arguments do you feel either support or disprove Friedman's position? Explain your answer.

3. Suppose that you own a small company with 12 employees. One of them tells you in confidence that he has just found out he has AIDS. You know that health-care costs for AIDS patients can be disastrously high, and this could drastically raise the health insurance

premiums that your other employees must pay. What are your responsibilities to this employee? To the rest of your staff? Explain.

4. Describe the major social and ethical issues facing the following firms:
   a. Automobile manufacturers
   b. Real estate developers
   c. Detergent manufacturers
   d. Drug companies that sell AIDS treatments
   e. Managers of stock brokerage firms

5. In recent years, corporations have been criticized for overpaying their top executives. While many executives do enjoy generous compensation packages, professional baseball players now average salaries over $1 million annually. Is top management overpaid? Underpaid? What factors should determine what a person earns?

SOLUTIONS TO ACHIEVEMENT CHECK SUMMARY

L. G. 4.1: 1. T, 2. T, 3. F. **L. G. 4.2:** 1. F, 2. T, 3 T. **L. G. 4.3:** 1. T, 2. F. **L. G. 4.4:** 1. b, 2. d. **L. G. 4.5:** 1. T, 2. F. **L. G. 4.6:** 1. F, 2. T. **L. G. 4.7:** 1. e, 2. a. **L. G. 4.8:** 1. T, 2. F, 3. F. **L. G. 4.9:** 1. F, 2. F, 3. T.

TEAM-BUILDING EXERCISE

This exercise introduces students to the concept of team-building, one of the challenges facing businesses as they seek to improve productivity of their employees and the quality of their product in order to remain competitive in a global business environment.

In this exercise, you will explore the various roles that naturally evolve out of the team environment and their impact on group decision-making. Some of those roles include:

- **Information Seeker** Asks questions, raises issues before reaching decision
- **Tension Reliever** Changes the subject, makes a joke, diverts attention from any conflict that might arise between team members
- **Clarifier** Links and integrates information
- **Gatekeeper** Maintains rules and discipline, making sure no one gets cut off and that everyone has a chance to speak
- **Initiator** Sets the process in motion and establishes the working style of the group
- **Follower** Provides support and encouragement
- **Information Giver** Answer questions and supplies data
- **Harmonizer** Seeks to smooth over any differences between group members and encourages compromise

Your instructor will divide the class into groups of 7 to 10 people and distribute a packet of instructions to each group. When your instructor gives the signal, open the packet and follow the directions you will find inside. This is a three-phase exercise.

Adapted from *A Handbook of Structured Experience for Human Relations Training,* vol. I, by J. W. Pfeiffer and J. E. Jones, eds. Copy © 1974 by Pfeiffer & Company. Used with permission.

VIDEO CASE

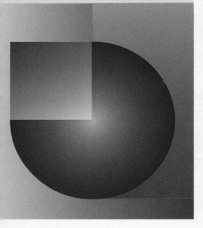

THE DETROIT ZOO Most companies recognize the importance of conducting business in a socially responsible and ethical way. Addressing important social problems is better for their employees and better for their business overall. Some companies, however, have a corporate culture that requires an additional commitment to social responsibility beyond the work they do as a matter of course. In the case of W. B. Doner & Company, that commitment involves taking on *pro bono* (without pay) work for certain non-profit organizations.

W. B. Doner, co-headquartered in Baltimore, Maryland and Southfield, Michigan, has become the 45th largest advertising agency in the world, primarily on the strength of its creative work. Clients include such well-known names as British Petroleum, National Car Rental, Chiquita International, Red Roof Inns, and B. F. Goodrich, among others. If the company preferred, it could restrict its work to paying customers, but instead it pursues its founder's vision of community involvement. As Alan Kalter, W. B. Doner president and CEO says, an ad agency may not be able to donate cash like its clients can, but it can, and should, donate its thinking and time. In accordance with this direction, W. B. Doner conducted a self-administered social audit and selected a variety of community-based programs to which they donate their services. One of the programs they identified for their services was the Detroit Zoo.

In 1992, the Zoo was going through a difficult transition period. The director retired, the Zoo was hit with state funding cuts of $1 million, and attendance was in decline. W. B. Doner assessed these problems for the Zoo just as they would have for a regular paying customer and developed a plan of action. They knew that other zoos around the country had successfully staged dinosaur exhibits, so they thought this strategy might work for the Detroit Zoo.

The objective for the summer of 1993 was to bring more people to the Zoo during the warm-weather season, when admissions and concessions would naturally increase, in the hopes of covering some of the state funding shortfall. Both parties agreed that an ambitious, yet realistic, goal would be 20 percent increase at the gate.

Presented with the challenge of having to do something spectacular to get the message through to the public, Doner had to call upon various members of the media and convince them to donate their services to the Zoo as well. In this effort, Doner contacted the number one television station in town, showed them what the Zoo was faced with, and convinced them to help. Doner also contacted local radio stations, as well as print advertisers, asking them to donate media time to the effort.

The decision to go ahead with a dinosaur exhibit was made in February of 1992. By a stroke of luck, *Jurassic Park* was released just before the dinosaur exhibit opened. The actual increase at the gate ended up being 33 percent, which translated into $800,000 more

than the previous year, almost replacing the lost state funding. In addition to the increase at the gate, sales of souvenirs and concessions ended up grossing $1.7 million, which provided a permanent endowment of $200,000 for the Zoo. The benefits of this campaign were much greater than what Doner could have given in a cash donation. Not only did attendance improve for the Summer season, many people rediscovered the Zoo, leading to increased attendance and revenues even after the "Dinosauria" exhibit ended.

As far as W. B. Doner is concerned, the only difference between the work they do for their *pro bono* clients and their paying ones is the latitude they're given. As Patricia Simpson, vice president and director of public relations for W. B. Doner, commented, "On one hand there is no difference, at least not from our end. The goal of the work that's created is to make it the best it can possibly be. The strategies used are usually a little simpler, not having a product to sell at a certain price lets you produce a more image-oriented piece which leaves more flexibility in terms of creativity. You have to work hard not to do something wonderful for a client like that."

QUESTIONS

1.
Why is the pro bono work done by W. B. Doner & Company an example of the company's social responsibility rather than its ethics?

2.
Were the results attained by this pro bono campaign beneficial to the general public? How?

3.
Were the results attained by the campaign beneficial to W. B. Doner? In what way?

4.
What aspects of corporate culture might prevent other companies from pursuing similar projects? What results of the W. B. Doner example might lead such companies to reconsider?

INTRODUCTION TO CAREERS IN BUSINESS

Contemporary Business offers the most complete career information package of any college business text in use today. This comprehensive package is comprised of four components: Career Profile, Career Job Descriptions, Career Design Exercises, and Appendix B, Your Career in Business.

The first component, *Career Profile,* introduces successful businesspeople who have recently completed business courses and/or earned degrees. They share their experiences and offer advice.

Career Job Descriptions, the second component, presents a broad range of business careers. It emphasizes employment in the fields discussed in each part. In many cases, Bureau of Labor Statistics employment projections to the year 2000 are also included. These descriptions can serve as a starting point in evaluating your career plans.

The third component, *Career Design Exercises,* is based on the work of John C. Crystal, a major contributor to the best-selling career book of all time—*What Color Is Your Parachute?* The exercises are designed to help you:

- Decide on a major
- Identify your best skills
- Discover what career direction to pursue
- Find out if starting a business may be the appropriate career path
- Determine your key preferences for co-workers and working conditions
- Make personal contacts leading to job interviews
- Create a custom résumé that will stand out from others
- Handle yourself in a professional manner during an interview
- Locate employers who are eager to hire people with your skills but do not recruit on campus and do not advertise their job opportunities
- Develop communications skills by organizing your thoughts in writing.

Appendix B, *Your Career in Business,* the final component of this career information package, is located at the end of the text. This appendix contains a wealth of information to help you identify and secure a job. Included are self-assessment tests for career development, job search guidelines, employment sources, tips on résumé writing and interviewing, and a discussion of special issues facing nontraditional students.

CAREER PROFILE: ELIZABETH GRIFFIN It didn't take Elizabeth Griffin long to realize the limitations that the lack of a college degree places on one's career opportunities. Griffin decided to begin working full-time as soon as she graduated from high school, and she found a job as a waitress at a local restaurant. Although the experience was useful in sharpening her interpersonal skills and gave her confidence in interacting with customers, it was also physically demanding, with irregular work hours and relatively poor pay. Most disturbing to Griffin was the lack of opportunities for promotion. After carefully evaluating her situation, she decided to continue her education and earn a degree at Westmoreland Community College. ■ She also decided to apply the skills she was acquiring in her business classes at Westmoreland by working as office manager in her family's resort-home construction business, Griffin Construction Company. The position gave her invaluable experience in handling administrative tasks such as working on bid proposals, handling payrolls, and being responsible for paying outstanding bills as they came due. ■ Griffin has continued her work as office manager, and credits her education with giving her the knowledge to enhance office efficiency.

During her first months on the job, she worked with huge invoice files and piles of paperwork, stacked all over the office. After she completed several computer classes, she was able to convert these files to databases and use spreadsheets and other computer programs to organize and maintain company records. Courses in human resource management and small business management also help her handle many day-to-day problems that arise. ■ Griffin's days and nights are hectic, as she continues the activities related to raising her four children. She still finds time to volunteer for the Special Olympics and for Wildlife Works, a Pennsylvania Game Commission-sponsored program. After earning her associate's degree at Westmoreland, she plans to transfer to St. Vincent's College in Lake Tahoe to pursue a degree in Environmental Administration. Once she achieves her educational goal, she hopes to combine her love of the outdoors and her experience in resort development with a career in environmental administration. Her advice to high school and college students: "Stay in school and get your degree. An education is essential for developing your abilities and achieving your goals."

CAREER JOB DESCRIPTIONS

Some specific jobs related to Part 1 of the text are discussed here. The Bureau of Labor Statistics estimates that demand for managers and statisticians will grow about as fast as the average for all occupations, while the demand for economists of all kinds will grow faster than average, primarily in business rather than in academic settings.

ECONOMISTS

Economists often conduct research to assist managerial decision making. They are employed in the private, public, and not-for-profit sectors. Academic preparation in economic theory and research methodology is necessary. Recent employment was 51,000.

Job Description Economists study the ways a society uses scarce resources (land, labor, raw materials, machinery) to produce goods and services. They research subjects such as comparative wage rates, the impact of economic factors on consumer demand, and the balance of trade. Their findings are reported to the management of corporations, banks, trade associations, labor unions, government departments, and others.

Career Path Junior-level economists assist senior-level personnel in their research. Advancement to the ranks of top management is possible.

Salary The average starting salary in private business for an economics graduate is about $25,200. The median base salary for a business economist is $65,000. The average salary in the federal government is $53,500.

INSPECTORS AND COMPLIANCE OFFICERS

Inspectors and compliance officers are responsible for enforcing the rules and regulations that protect the public in such matters as health, safety, trade, and immigration. Recently 155,000 people were employed as inspectors and compliance officers.

Job Description Health inspectors work in the areas of consumer safety, food, agricultural quarantine, and environmental health. Regulatory officers work in the area of immigration; customs; postal service; aviation safety; railroads; motor vehicles; occupational safety and health; mines; wage and hour compliance; and alcohol, tobacco, and firearms. Agricultural quarantine officers inspect shipments and people entering the country in order to protect U.S. farming industries. Immigration officers examine those seeking to enter the United States. Customs officers enforce the various laws and taxes dealing with exports and imports.

Career Path Because their functions are so diverse, qualifications for these jobs differ greatly. A qualifying exam is generally required. Successful candidates receive on-the-job training. A career ladder with regular promotions is available to all employees.

Salary Entry-level salaries vary according to the activity involved. The national median salary is $32,760; the federal average varies greatly, from $24,800 to $59,300.

INDUSTRIAL DEVELOPMENT SPECIALISTS

Most industrial development specialists are state government employees, but a few industrial development specialists also work for utility companies. The aim of industrial development is to create jobs and increase the tax base of a state.

Job Description These specialists work with businesses in an attempt to persuade them to locate within a state. They work with the state's tax department to provide corporate tax incentives and with other government agencies to provide adequate facilities for offices and plants. Industrial development specialists, especially in high-tech companies, also seek the cooperation of educational institutions, which can offer businesses qualified employees.

Career Path Industrial development specialists often gain experience working in state commerce department offices. They must have strong backgrounds in finance as well as strong negotiating skills.

Salary Salaries vary from state to state and with levels of experience.

INTERNATIONAL TRADE ECONOMISTS

International trade economists study the various economic aspects of trade with foreign nations. They work in the private, public, and educational sectors.

Job Description International trade economists must meet all the job requirements of other economists. In addition, they must be experts in international trade.

Career Path The career path depends upon whether the person is employed in the private, public, or educational sector.

Salary Salaries for international trade economists vary according to whether the person is employed in the private, public, or educational sector.

INTERNATIONAL BANKING OFFICERS

International banking officers must be knowledgeable about foreign financial systems and the trade relations between nations. They represent banks in all international dealings.

Job Description International banking officers are involved in decision-making roles in international banking divisions. They monitor existing business and accounts, and they must be experts in foreign banking practices and procedures.

Career Path Entry-level persons are usually assistants to an experienced international banking executive. Promotion to a senior position is possible. An eventual goal of many in this field is the top-level position of the international banking officer.

Salary Middle-level international banking officers generally earn between $60,000 and $80,000 a year.

IMPORT-EXPORT SPECIALISTS

Import-export specialists plan and supervise the flow of products to and from other nations. They make important contributions to international business.

Job Description Import-export specialists deal with various aspects of international trade; domestic customers and shippers, such as international freight haulers; and shipping, receiving, and billing activities. They are also responsible for compliance with the various legal requirements of international trade.

Career Path Entry-level employees assist import-export managers in performing their functions. Import-export managers usually hold middle-management positions reporting to an international manager.

Salary Salaries for import-export specialists vary according to the responsibilities of specific positions and among companies and industries. Average starting salaries fall between $20,000 and $25,000 with experienced managers earning over $37,000.

INTERNATIONAL EXECUTIVES

Companies often set up separate international units to handle their overseas affairs. International executives manage such a unit and oversee its operations.

Job Description The exact job requirements for international management positions vary from firm to firm. These people perform all the tasks expected of other managers at their particular levels.

Career Path International managers can be drawn from any department in an organization. They must be knowledgeable in international marketing, finance, law, and production. There are various levels of international management, usually ranging from middle management to top management. Many companies believe that all candidates for top management slots should have international experience.

Salary Salaries of international managers vary by company and industry.

LOBBYISTS

Large firms with important interests in local, state, or federal laws hire lobbyists to represent their positions. Lobbyists are typically attorneys or have backgrounds in public relations.

Job Description Lobbyists must monitor legal developments and legislative developments that affect their clients. Most of their work is done when the relevant legislative body is in session. They keep legislators up-to-date on their clients' interests and needs and provide them with information to justify positions, such as studies and research reports. They have formal and informal contacts with legislators and work to build relationships with those most important to their clients' interests.

Career Path Many lobbyists start with public relations firms, which handle the public affairs of a number of firms. Others are attorneys with law firms that represent clients with interests in pending legislation. They begin by doing research or handling smaller issues. With experience, they take on larger and more important clients. Top lobbyists often start their own firms.

Salary Earnings vary widely according to the size and number of clients.

STATISTICIANS

Statisticians collect, analyze, and present statistical data in order to provide managers with information for making better decisions. They work in both private and public sectors. There were 16,000 statisticians in the United States in a recent year.

Job Description Statisticians work in all phases of business and marketing research. They study the problems related to these issues, supervise data collection, and analyze results. The statistician's conclusions are then presented to management for action.

Career Path Entry-level personnel are often assigned to collect data or other basic tasks under the supervision of experienced statisticians. Senior-level personnel have increased responsibilities and may eventually be selected for supervisory or management positions.

Salary Beginning salaries in a federal government job for a college graduate with no experience may range from $15,700 to $19,500; with a master's degree, from $23,800 to $28,900, with a Ph.D. $28,900 to $34,600. Median salary for a government statistician was $51,893.

DISCOVERING YOUR BUSINESS CAREER: CAREER DESIGN EXERCISES

INTERESTS AND FASCINATIONS

This is the first and one of the most important exercises in this course, although it may not seem that way now. You will discover as the course progresses that anything that interests you is an important clue about your career direction.

When you are asked to list your interests, take the program's advice and type in as many of your interests as you can, regardless of whether or not you think they are job related. Since this introductory course provides a unique opportunity to discover what areas of business fascinate you, start this exercise by reviewing the chapters you have completed so far and write down any topics that interest you. Then add these to your "Interests and Fascinations" list on the computer.

THIS EXERCISE WILL HELP YOU TO

- Discover and keep track of your interests throughout the course.
- Understand that choosing a career that interests you can result in better pay and job satisfaction.
- Get a start in finding out what major to choose.

HOW TO LOCATE THE EXERCISE

When you see the main menu for the Career Design, select "What Do I Want?" Then select "Interests and Fascinations" to begin this exercise.

BUSINESS ADVENTURE

Now that you have completed the "Interests and Fascinations" exercise, here is another one that will help you discover even more about what you want. This exercise will stimulate your imagination about the things you would like to do in the field of business. The more you write, the better.

THIS EXERCISE WILL HELP YOU TO

- Discover some of your interests in the business world.
- Feel encouraged to actively pursue your dreams.
- Clarify your goals and determine what areas of life are important to you.
- Stimulate your thinking about what you want to accomplish in your life.

HOW TO LOCATE THE EXERCISE

When you see the main menu for Career Design, select "What Do I Want?" Then select "Business Adventure" to begin this exercise.

CHAPTER 5

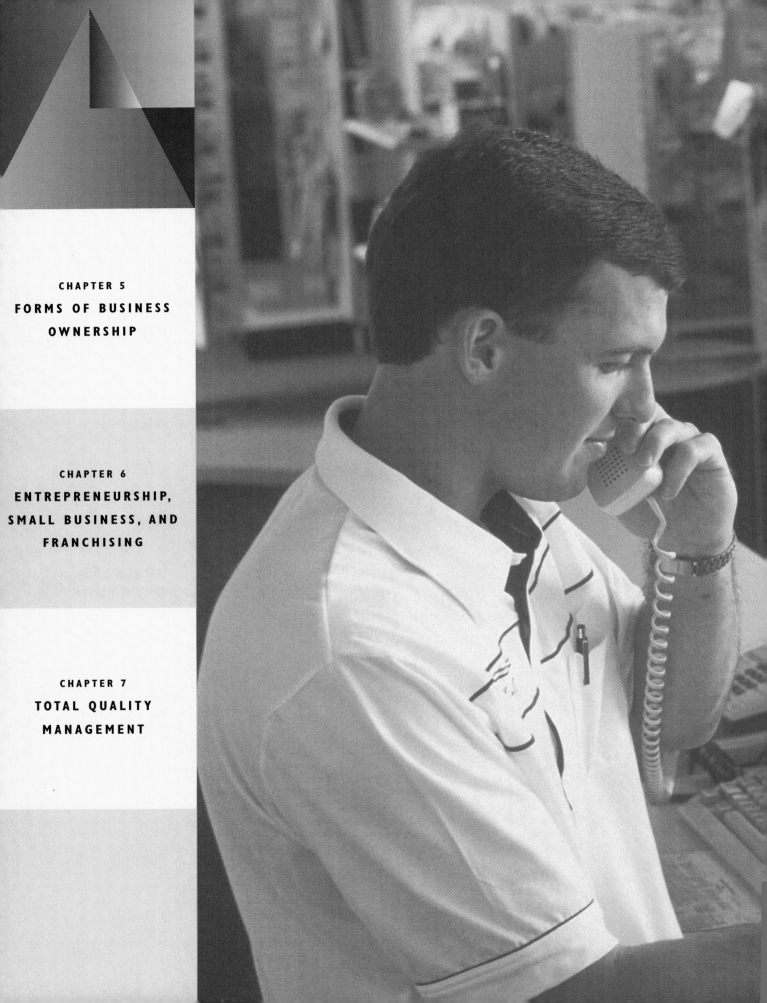

FORMS OF BUSINESS OWNERSHIP

CHAPTER 6

ENTREPRENEURSHIP, SMALL BUSINESS, AND FRANCHISING

CHAPTER 7

TOTAL QUALITY MANAGEMENT

PART II
THE STRUCTURE OF AMERICAN BUSINESS

CHAPTER 5

FORMS OF BUSINESS OWNERSHIP

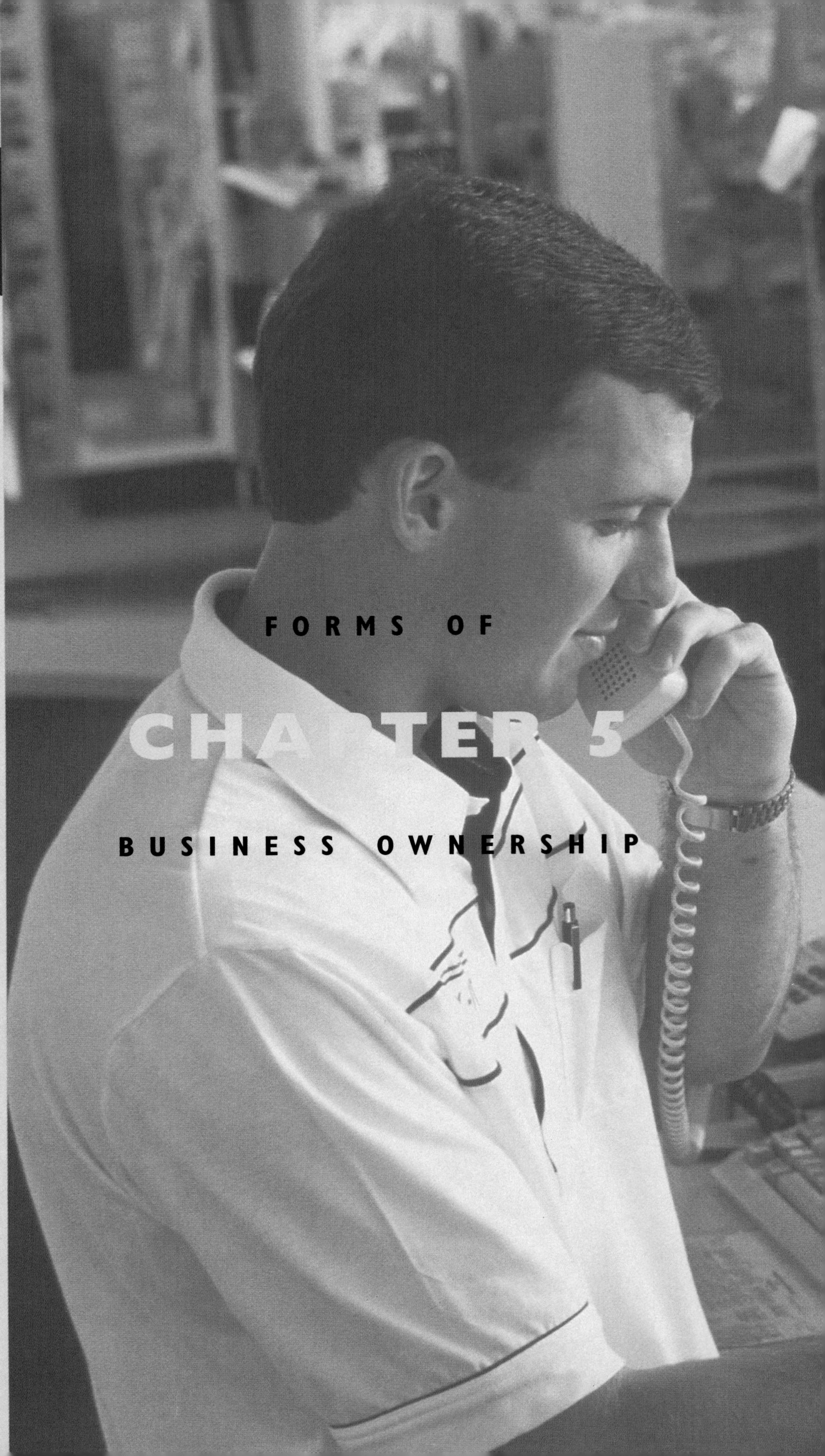

LEARNING GOALS

1. Identify and explain the three basic forms of business ownership.

2. Outline the advantages and disadvantages of sole proprietorships.

3. Compare the advantages and disadvantages of partnerships.

4. Outline the advantages and disadvantages of corporations.

5. Discuss how a corporation is organized and operated.

6. Identify the levels of corporate management.

7. Describe recent trends in corporate ownership.

8. Explain how private ownership, public ownership, and collective ownership (cooperatives) differ.

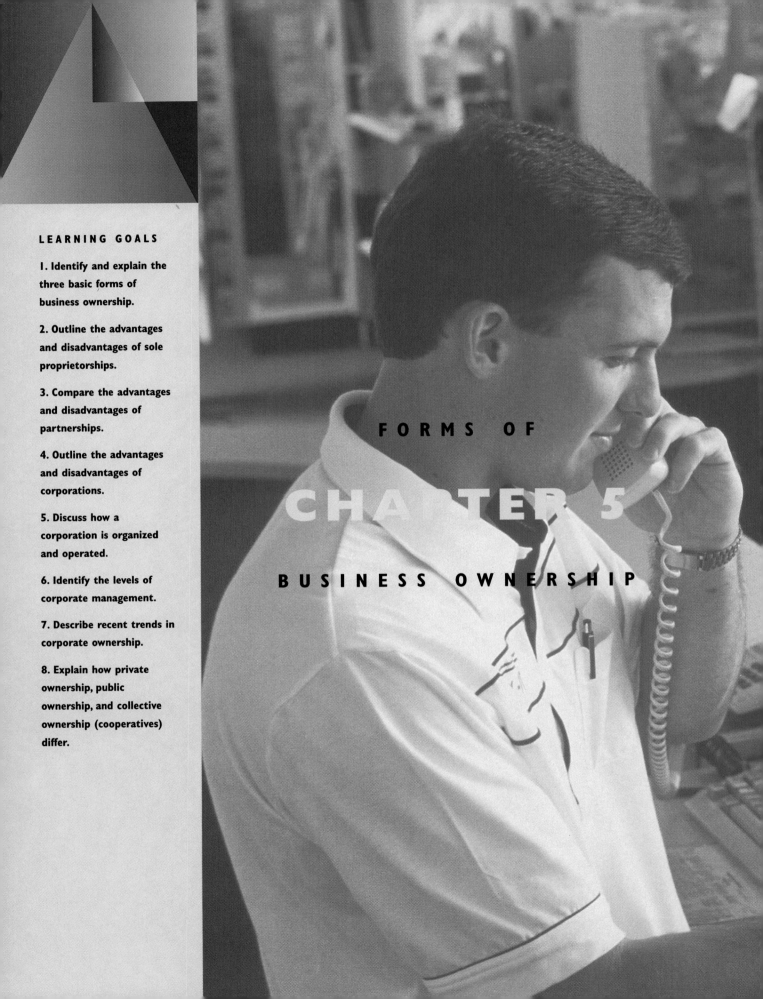

NESTLÉ—A WORLD-WIDE ORGANIZATION Nestlé has always been known for its coffee, chocolate, and milk products. Today, the Swiss firm is the largest branded food company in Mexico, Brazil, Thailand, and Chile, and it is rapidly growing in Vietnam and China, as well. Nestlé is the market leader in instant coffee in Australia, France, Japan, and Mexico. It controls the powdered milk markets in the Philippines and Brazil. In Chile, it has 73 percent of the cookie market and 70 percent of soups and sauces. ■ How does Nestlé manage so many successful ventures around the world? Its global strategy involves taking one of two paths, depending on whether the market is developed or still developing. ■ In developed markets, like Europe and the United States, Nestlé expands through acquisitions. In the last decade alone, it has spent nearly $18 billion to buy brands like Perrier, Carnation, Hills Brothers, and Stouffer's. Today the firm owns almost 8,000 brands worldwide. ■ In developing markets, Nestlé grows by adapting its ingredients and processing technologies to the area. Consider its approach to organizing a new powdered milk and baby cereal plant in the Chinese province of Heilongjiang (formerly Manchuria). ■ Since the local trains were unreliable, Nestlé plant managers in Heilongjiang decided to create their own distribution network, which area residents soon nicknamed "milk roads." The milk roads led to a system of central collection points where farmers could come to sell their milk. To increase production, Nestlé managers introduced a deceptively simple innovation—unlike China's government milk buyers, they paid the farmers immediately. Says Mike Garret, head of Nestlé's Asia/Pacific region, "Suddenly the farmers had an incentive to produce milk." Many farmers bought second cows; in 18 months, the number of cows in the district rose from 6,000 to 9,000. Managers organized a fleet of delivery vans to handle the increased volume of milk, and they hired retired teachers, government workers, and animal husbandry experts as farm agents to train the farmers in animal health and hygiene. Each agent was assigned to a village, and each received a commission on all sales to the company. ■ The result? In its first year, the Heilongjiang plant produced 316 tons of powdered milk and baby formula; 4 years later, it delivered 10,000 tons. Nestlé's sales in China are now about $200 million, and are expected to climb to $700 million by 2000. Says market analyst David Sheridan, "I haven't found another company willing to pour resources into China like this. The big payoff is still to come, but you can bet it will be solid and long-lasting." ■ Nestlé relies on talented regional managers who have extensive experience in their local markets. An example is Att Senasarn, general manager of Nestlé Thailand; born in Austria as Alfred Senhauser and now a naturalized Thai, Senasarn has worked for Nestlé's Thailand division for 30 years. Within Asia and Latin America, managers transfer from one country to another every 4 or 5 years, broadening their knowledge of the over-all region. Notes Andreas Schlapfer, managing director of Nestlé Thailand, "Unlike most American companies, managers in Nestlé can make their career away from the head office. U.S. managers usually come here on 2- to 3-year contracts." ■ The result is a big multinational corporation with annual sales of $43 billion. Les Pugh, an analyst with Salomon Brothers, believes that "Nestlé is the best-positioned food company in the world." Says Watinee Khutrakul, a director at Thai market research firm Deemar Survey Research, "As long as big competitors remain tentative about this part of the world, Nestlé can sweep up the market in any product category it chooses." ■ Nestlé managers readily admit that their competitors are becoming more aggressive. One threat comes from the rise of store brands. In Malaysia, a local company introduced its own brand of ketchup to sell for 25 percent less than Nestlé's Maggi brand; Nestlé managers promptly slashed prices throughout the country. Another threat comes from the growth of U.S.-style supermarkets in Thailand and Taiwan. These stores have started to demand volume discounts. ■ As developing

countries turn into developed markets, Nestlé introduces Western marketing techniques. In Thailand, for example, it has recruited a sales team of college graduates. Dubbed the Red Hot Sales Force, these men and women routinely jet to Australia, Hong Kong, and Europe for training in the latest marketing techniques and inventory control tools. Back home, they share this information with retailers and work closely with them to build stronger businesses. Nestlé's goal is to preempt its rivals by creating partnerships with local retailers before more competitors arrive. ■ So far, few of those rivals have come from the United States. Marvels Schlapfer, "One of the great mysteries of my life is, where is the American competition out here?"[1]

CHAPTER OVERVIEW

Every business, be it Microsoft or the neighborhood Mexican restaurant, must choose the type of legal ownership that best meets its needs. Several variables affect the choice of the right way to organize your business:

- How easy is it to form this type of organization?
- How much financial liability can you afford?
- What financial resources do you have?
- Will you be able to raise more money if you need it?
- What are the strengths and weaknesses of other people who are involved in this business?
- What are your own strengths and weaknesses? What kind of management style suits you best?

This chapter will look at the advantages and disadvantages of the three major forms of private business ownership—sole proprietorships, partnerships, and corporations—and discuss alternative forms of private and public ownership. It will also discuss ways to organize and operate a corporation and examine major trends in corporate ownership, both in the United States and abroad.

FORMS OF PRIVATE OWNERSHIP

Firms exhibit three major forms of private business ownership: sole proprietorships, partnerships, and corporations. Picking one of these options is sometimes referred to as a "choice of entity."[2] As Figure 5.1 shows, sole proprietorships, the most common form, account for 73 percent of all U.S. businesses. Partnerships make up 8 percent of U.S. firms, and corporations comprise the remaining 19 percent.

Each form of private ownership has unique advantages and disadvantages, which are summarized in Table 5.1. Anyone forming a new business should weigh these advantages and disadvantages very carefully. Miscalculations or oversights can have serious consequences, as actor Burt Reynolds discovered. A failure to incorporate on a restaurant deal left him personally liable for $28 million worth of debt on equipment and long-term leases when the project floundered.[3]

SOLE PROPRIETORSHIPS

sole proprietorship *Ownership and, usually, operation of an organization by one person.*

The most common form of business ownership, the **sole proprietorship,** is also the oldest and the simplest because no legal distinction separates the sole proprietor's role as an individual from his or her role as a business owner. Assets, earnings, and debts of the business are those of the owner. Although sole proprietorships are common in a variety of industries, they are concentrated primarily among small businesses such as repair shops, small retail outlets, and service organizations.

FIGURE 5.1 OWNERSHIP STRUCTURE OF U.S. BUSINESS

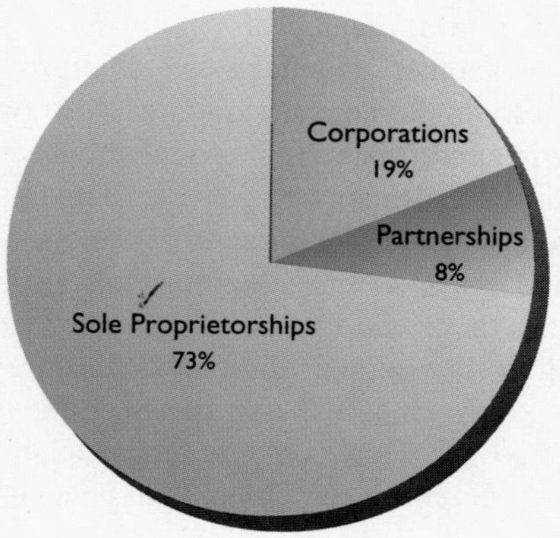

Sole proprietorships offer advantages that other business entities cannot. For one, they are easy to form and dissolve. (Partnerships are also easy to form, but difficult to dissolve.) Sole proprietorships give owners flexibility and the right to retain all profits, except what goes to the government for personal income taxes. Retention of all profits and responsibility for all losses give sole proprietors the incentive to operate as efficiently as possible.

Minimal legal requirements simplify entering and exiting a sole proprietorship. Usually the owner must meet only a few legal requirements for starting one, including registering the business or trade name at the county courthouse (to guarantee that two firms do not use the same name) and taking out any necessary licenses. (Restaurants, motels, retail stores, and many repair shops require certain kinds of licenses.) Some occupational licenses require a firm to carry specific types of insurance, such as liability coverage.

TABLE 5.1 ADVANTAGES AND DISADVANTAGES OF EACH FORM OF PRIVATE OWNERSHIP

FORM OF OWNERSHIP	ADVANTAGES	DISADVANTAGES
Sole proprietorship	1. Owner retains all profits 2. Easy to form and dissolve 3. Owner has flexibility	1. Unlimited financial liability 2. Financing limitations 3. Management deficiencies 4. Lack of continuity
Partnership	1. Easy to form 2. Can benefit from complementary management skills 3. Expanded financial capacity	1. Unlimited financial liability 2. Interpersonal conflicts 3. Lack of continuity 4. Difficult to dissolve
Corporation	1. Limited financial liability 2. Specialized management skills 3. Expanded financial capacity 4. Economies of larger-scale operation	1. Difficult and costly to form and dissolve 2. Tax advantage 3. Legal restrictions

The ease of dissolving a business set up as a sole proprietorship is an attractive feature for certain types of enterprises. This is particularly true for temporary businesses that involve just a few transactions. For example, someone could create a business to organize a single concert at a local arena.

Ownership flexibility is another advantage of a sole proprietorship. The owner can make management decisions without consulting others, take prompt action when needed, and keep trade secrets where appropriate. You've probably heard people say, "I like being my own boss." This flexibility leads many business owners to prefer sole proprietorships.

A disadvantage of the sole proprietorship comes from the owner's financial liability for all debts of the business. Also, its financial resources are limited to the owner's personal funds and money that he or she can borrow. Such financing limitations can keep the business from expanding. For another disadvantage, the owner must handle a wide range of management and operational tasks; as the firm grows, the owner may not perform all duties equally effectively. Finally, a sole proprietorship lacks long-term continuity, since death, bankruptcy, retirement, or a change in personal interests can terminate it.

PARTNERSHIPS

partnership
Business operated by two or more people as co-owners.

Another option for organizing a business is forming a **partnership.** The Uniform Partnership Act, which regulates this choice of entity in most states, defines a partnership as an association of two or more persons who operate a business as co-owners by voluntary legal agreement. Partnerships have been a traditional form of ownership for professionals offering services, such as physicians, lawyers, and dentists.

Partnerships are easy to form; as with sole proprietorships, the legal requirements involve merely registering the business name and taking out the necessary licenses. Another advantage is the opportunity for professionals to combine complementary skills. Partnerships also offer expanded financial capabilities when each of the partners invests money. They also usually give greater access to borrowed funds than do sole proprietorships.

Like sole proprietorships, most partnerships have the disadvantage of unlimited financial liability. Each partner bears full responsibility for the debts of the firm, and each is legally liable for the actions of the other partners. Partners must pay the partnership's debts from their personal funds if those debts exceed the partnership's assets. It is also much harder to break up a partnership than to dissolve a sole proprietorship. Rather than simply withdrawing funds from the bank, the partner who wants out must find someone to buy his or her interest in the firm.[4]

Partnerships are also vulnerable to interpersonal conflicts. Personal disagreements may quickly escalate into business battles. Good communication is the key to resolving conflicts before they destroy the partnership. Table 5.2 presents several crucial issues that partners should discuss before going into business together.

joint venture
Partnership formed for a specific undertaking.

Owners can choose from several different types of partnerships. A **joint venture** is a partnership formed for a specific undertaking. Johnson & Johnson entered the Korean market for baby-care products via Johnson & Johnson Korea, a joint venture with Korean firm Dong-A Pharmaceuticals. In a general partnership, all partners operate the business as co-owners and are equally liable for its debts. Some states also permit limited partnerships composed of both general partners and limited partners; a limited partner's liability cannot exceed the amount of capital contributed by that partner, provided the person plays no active role in the business. A third category of partnership, the master limited partnership (MLP), functions like a corporation and publicly trades shares on the major securities exchanges.

CORPORATIONS

corporation
Legal entity with authority to act and incur liability separate from its owners.

A **corporation** is a legal organization whose assets and liabilities are separate from those of its owner(s). Its formation requires the approval of the appropriate state agency. A

TABLE 5.2 HOW TO MAKE A PARTNERSHIP WORK

WRITE A BUSINESS PLAN

- What are our goals for a 1-year, 5-year, and longer time horizon?
- Who will do what?
- How will we structure ownership?
- How will we measure the company's success?

ASSEMBLE A BOARD OF ADVISORS

- What outside skills will complement ours?
- How often should the board meet?
- What influence will the board have on the partners?

TAKE A RETREAT

- What do we expect from each other?
- Does the partnership meet our needs?
- How can we improve it?

stockholder is someone who acquires shares of stock in a corporation, thereby becoming a part-owner of the business. When all or a majority of a corporation's stock is owned by another corporation, it is a **subsidiary** of that corporation, which is called the **parent company.**

Corporate ownership offers considerable advantages. First, because corporations have the status of separate legal entities, the stockholders take only limited financial risk; if the firm fails, they lose only the amounts they have invested. The limited risk of corporate ownership is clearly reflected in the names of such firms throughout the world. *Incorporated* or *Inc.* forms part of corporate names in the United States; *Limited* or *Ltd.* is common in Canada and the United Kingdom; *Proprietary Limited* or *Pty. Ltd.* appears in Australia; *Aktie Bolag* or *stock company* is the equivalent in Scandinavia.

Corporations offer other advantages. They can draw on the specialized skills of many employees, unlike sole proprietorships and partnerships where managerial skills are usually confined to the abilities of the owners. Expanded financial capability results because people outside the business may invest in it by buying shares of stock.

The larger-scale operation permitted by corporate ownership has several advantages. Employees can specialize in the work activities they perform best. Large firms can internally finance many projects by transferring money from one part of the corporation to another. Longer manufacturing runs usually make production more efficient and allow the firm to charge lower prices and attract more customers. Table 5.3 lists the nation's largest industrial corporations.

One disadvantage of corporations derives from their status as separate legal entities. They are subject to federal and state income taxes on their profits and, in addition, stockholders must pay taxes on any **dividends**—payments to stockholders from profits. Corporate ownership also involves some legal problems that sole proprietorships and partnerships do not encounter. The number of laws and regulations that affect corporations has increased dramatically in recent years.[5]

Corporations can find some tax relief if they meet certain size and stock ownership requirements to be recognized as *S corporations* or *Subchapter S* corporations. These corporations can elect to pay federal taxes as partnerships while retaining the advantages

stockholder
Person who acquires shares of stock in, and therefore owns part of, a corporation.

subsidiary
Corporation with all or a majority of its stock owned by another corporation.

parent company
Corporation that owns all or a majority of the stock in another corporation (called a subsidiary*).*

dividend
Payment to stockholders from a corporation's profits.

STRENGTH IN DIVERSITY

NATIVE AMERICAN BUSINESS SOARS Many Native Americans are exchanging their traditional dress for business suits and ties as they own a growing number of businesses. Since the late 1980s, the number of Native American-owned businesses has increased from 150 to 250 in a variety of industries such as oil, office supplies, ad specialties, trucking, construction, radio, and plastics. ■ One business that exemplifies the growth of Native American industry is SOAR (Sound of America Records) Corporation. Tom Bee, the president and CEO of SOAR, formed the corporation in 1988. "My goal in founding the label was to introduce the world to Native American music," says Bee. "I wanted to make people realize that Native Americans aren't just a myth or a part of history—that we're very much alive and have our own music." When he had trouble raising interest among major labels, Bee sold cassettes out of the back of his truck to trading posts, book stores, gift stores, and art galleries in the Four Corners region where Arizona, New Mexico, Colorado, and Utah meet, and where a large population of Indians live. In 1991, Bee struck a deal with Koch International to distribute SOAR releases to major record retailers. ■ Today, SOAR Corporation has expanded to form the SOAR Music Group with four specialty labels. The SOAR label features traditional and contemporary Native American music. Warrior focuses on rock and rap. Instrumentals and New Age recordings carry the Natural Visions label, and recordings of the spoken word and children's music can be found on the Dakotah label. Each of SOAR's releases has sold at least 10,000 copies, and several have reached the 25,000 mark. SOAR recently increased its menu of services by opening its own 24-track digital recording studio, where it plans to record its own artists and do outside work. ■ The company is constantly signing and releasing new acts on each of its labels. Some of its projects include "Once upon a Genocide" by rapper Julian B., "Beloved Tribal Woman" by Lisa LaRie, and a recording by a new singer, Jake Al Ream, whom Bee compares to Bruce Springsteen. ■ While Koch distributes to national retailers such as Best Buy, Sound Warehouse, Hastings, Tower Records, and Musicland, SOAR handles its own distribution to alternative outlets such as trading posts, galleries, arts and crafts stores, book stores, and powwow vendors. The company's distribution network also carries selected releases for other labels that fit into its area of expertise. SOAR recently became the independent distributor for Silverwave, Earthbeat, Music for Little People, and Rykodisc. ■ SOAR products are also now available through a mail-order catalog distributed to a approximately 25,000 consumers. Customers are encouraged to place orders through an 800 number. Many of the names on the mailing list have come from comment cards the company places in all of its products. Sources: Trudi Miller Roseblum, "Native American Label SOAR Lets Four Subsidiaries Take Flight," *Billboard,* July 16, 1994, p. 55; Tricia Serju, "Native American Firms Gain Visibility," *Detroit News,* October 3, 1993, p. 1; Marlene Mielhaff, "Tribal Entrepreneurship Soars," *Journal of Business Spokane,* May 13, 1993, p. 1; and Trudi Miller, "Native American Label Soars into Its Fifth Year," *Billboard,* March 27, 1993, p. 8.

QUESTIONS FOR CRITICAL THINKING

1. What other nontraditional methods of distribution might SOAR utilize?
2. Can SOAR find a market for its products outside the Native American community? Why or why not?
3. How might SOAR build awareness for its musical acts outside the Native American community?

of corporations. An S corporation can have no more than 35 corporate shareholders (70 including spouses), and a shareholder must hold at least 50 percent of the stock to change the company's corporate status.

limited liability company (LLC) *Company governed by an operating agreement similar to a partnership agreement, with the advantage of limited liability.*

In 47 states, a business owner can gain tax relief by organizing as a **limited liability company (LLC),** which combines the corporate advantage of limited liability with the favorable tax treatment of a partnership. An LLC is governed by an operating agreement that resembles a partnership agreement, but it reduces each partner's liability for the actions of the others.[6]

TABLE 5.3 THE 10 LARGEST U.S. INDUSTRIAL CORPORATIONS

RANK 1993		LOCATION	SALES ($ MILLIONS)	PROFITS ($ MILLIONS)	ASSETS ($ MILLIONS)
1	General Motors	Detroit, Mich.	133,621.9	2,465.8	188,200.9
2	Ford Motor	Dearborn, Mich.	108,521.0	2,529.0	198,938.0
3	Exxon	Irving, Texas	97,825.0	5,280.0	84,145.0
4	Intl. Business Machines	Armonk, N.Y.	62,716.0	(8,101.0)	81,113.0
5	General Electric	Fairfield, Conn.	60,823.0	4,315.0	251,506.0
6	Mobil	Fairfax, Va.	56,576.0	2,084.0	40,585.0
7	Philip Morris	New York, N.Y.	50,621.0	3,091.0	51,205.0
8	Chrysler	Highland Park, Mich.	43,600.0	(2,551.0)	43,830.0
9	Texaco	White Plains, N.Y.	34,359.0	1,068.0	26,626.0
10	E.I. Du Pont De Nemours	Wilmington, Del.	32,621.0	555.0	37,053.0

ORGANIZING AND OPERATING A CORPORATION

Suppose that you decide to start a business, and you believe that the corporate form offers the best way to organize it. How would you go about creating your business? This section considers the options and procedures involved in incorporating a business.

TYPES OF CORPORATIONS

Corporations can be classified as domestic, foreign, or alien corporations. Your firm is considered a **domestic corporation** in the state where it is incorporated. If you expect to do business in states other than the state of incorporation, you would register as a **foreign corporation** in each of those states. A firm incorporated in one nation that operates in another is known as an **alien corporation** where it operates.

domestic corporation
Corporation that operates in the state in which it is incorporated.

foreign corporation
Corporation that operates in a state other than the one in which it is incorporated.

alien corporation
Corporation organized in one country that operates in another.

Johnson Products Inc., a maker of personal-care products for African Americans, operates as a domestic, foreign, and alien corporation. The company is incorporated in Delaware, where it is a domestic corporation, but its headquarters are in Chicago, where it operates a large plant as a foreign corporation. The firm also operates overseas as an alien corporation, with sales and distribution centers in Europe and Great Britain.

PROCEDURES FOR INCORPORATION

A state typically designates a certain official or state agency, usually the secretary of state, to administer corporations. This official can supply blank articles of incorporation, corporate charters, or incorporation certificates (depending on the terminology used in a particular state). To create your corporation, you must complete this paperwork and file it with the appropriate state agency.

Various states usually require similar information in corporate charters. In Michigan, articles of incorporation must show the corporate name, corporate purpose, number of authorized shares of stock, registered office and agent, and name of the incorporator. In New York, a certificate of incorporation shows the name of the proposed corporation, its purposes, its location, the number of shares of stock it will have the authority to issue, the address to which any legal notice should be sent, and the incorporator's name. Texas requires applicants to draw up their own articles of incorporation that provide the corporate name and purpose; the names of the initial board of directors, the registered agent,

A worker at Nucor Corporation's Hickman, Arkansas sheet mill samples molten steel. Nucor formed a joint venture with US Steel and Praxair Inc. to create and refine a new method for making steel.

and the incorporator; the number of authorized shares and their par value; and the corporate duration.

STOCKHOLDERS

As this chapter mentioned earlier, stockholders are the owners of a corporation. Relatively few stockholders own some corporations, such as family businesses, and the stock is generally unavailable to outsiders. In such a firm, known as a *closed corporation* or *closely held corporation,* the stockholders also control and manage the corporation's activities. In contrast, an *open corporation* sells stock to the general public. Such a firm has diversified ownership, and often it is larger than a closely held corporation.

AT&T, for example, has about 2.34 million stockholders. These individuals obviously have little control over giant AT&T, but they will find a ready market for their shares if they decide to sell. The individual stockholder can sell stock in a large corporation more easily than shares in a small corporation with no public market for its stock.

Corporations usually hold annual stockholders' meetings, during which managers report on corporate activities and stockholders vote on any decisions that require their approval. Elections of certain directors and choices of independent public accountants are two matters that require votes at nearly all stockholders' meetings.

preferred stock
Stock that gives the owners first claim to the corporation's assets after it pays all debts.

common stock
Stock that gives its owners only residual claims to the firm's assets, along with voting rights in corporate decisions.

Shares are usually classified as common or preferred stock. Owners of **preferred stock** have the first claim to the corporation's assets after it has paid all debts. However, they usually do not have voting rights at stockholders' meetings. Owners of **common stock** have only residual claims on the firm's assets (receiving any money that remains after everyone else has been paid), but they do have voting rights. In such a vote, each share of common stock is worth one vote. A person who owns 100 shares may cast 100 votes. People who cannot attend the stockholders' meeting can give their proxies to authorize someone else to vote the shares. Many corporate boards can vote as they choose if the proxies are not returned, thus perpetuating the existing directors' positions.

Small stockholders generally have little influence on corporate management. A holder of 200,000 shares has 200,000 votes for each director, while the holder of 100 shares has only 100 votes. As a result, *cumulative voting*, which allows smaller stockholders to combine their votes to achieve more influence on the selection of directors,

Rebecca Matthias started Mothers Work, Inc. as a mail-order maternity clothes business. In order to help her company to expand, Matthias and her husband sold shares in their privately held business. Their initial stock offering brought in $16 million, which allowed the company to double its number of stores in less than one year.

has been proposed at many stockholders' meetings. If three director positions are open, cumulative voting allows the holder of 100 shares to cast 300 votes (100 × 3) for one person rather than 100 votes each for all three positions.

CORPORATE MANAGEMENT

Figure 5.2 illustrates the levels of management in a corporation. The stockholders elect a **board of directors,** which becomes the governing authority for the corporation. Members of the board may be academicians, retired politicians, community activists, or high-ranking executives from other companies. The board sets overall policy, authorizes major transactions involving the corporation, and hires the chief executive officer (CEO).

board of directors
Governing body of a corporation whose members are elected by the stockholders.

Most boards include both inside directors (corporate executives) and outside directors, people who are not employed by the organization. Sometimes the corporation's top executive also chairs the board. Generally, outside directors own shares of company stock.

The CEO and other members of top management, such as the chief operating officer (COO) and chief financial officer (CFO), set corporate policy, make most major corporate decisions, and manage the overall direction of the company. Managers at the next level, middle management, handle the operational functions of the company. At the bottom tier of management, supervisory personnel coordinate the day-to-day operations of the firm, assign specific tasks to employees, and often evaluate workers' job performance.[7]

Many people believe that U.S. corporations would benefit if outside directors had greater power. It is argued that this arrangement would make a company's management more accountable to stockholders. Recently, for instance, outside directors at General Motors outlined a new code for the auto maker's board of directors. Among its points, it stated that:

- Most board members should be outside directors.
- The board of directors, not GM's CEO, selects new board members and invites them to join, thus keeping them loyal to the board and not to GM's current management.
- A "Director Affairs Committee" will assess skills lacking in current board members and evaluate the board's performance in an annual report.
- Outside directors should meet alone regularly to discuss their own concerns.
- Board members should have "complete access" to the company's management.

FIGURE 5.2 LEVELS OF CORPORATE MANAGEMENT

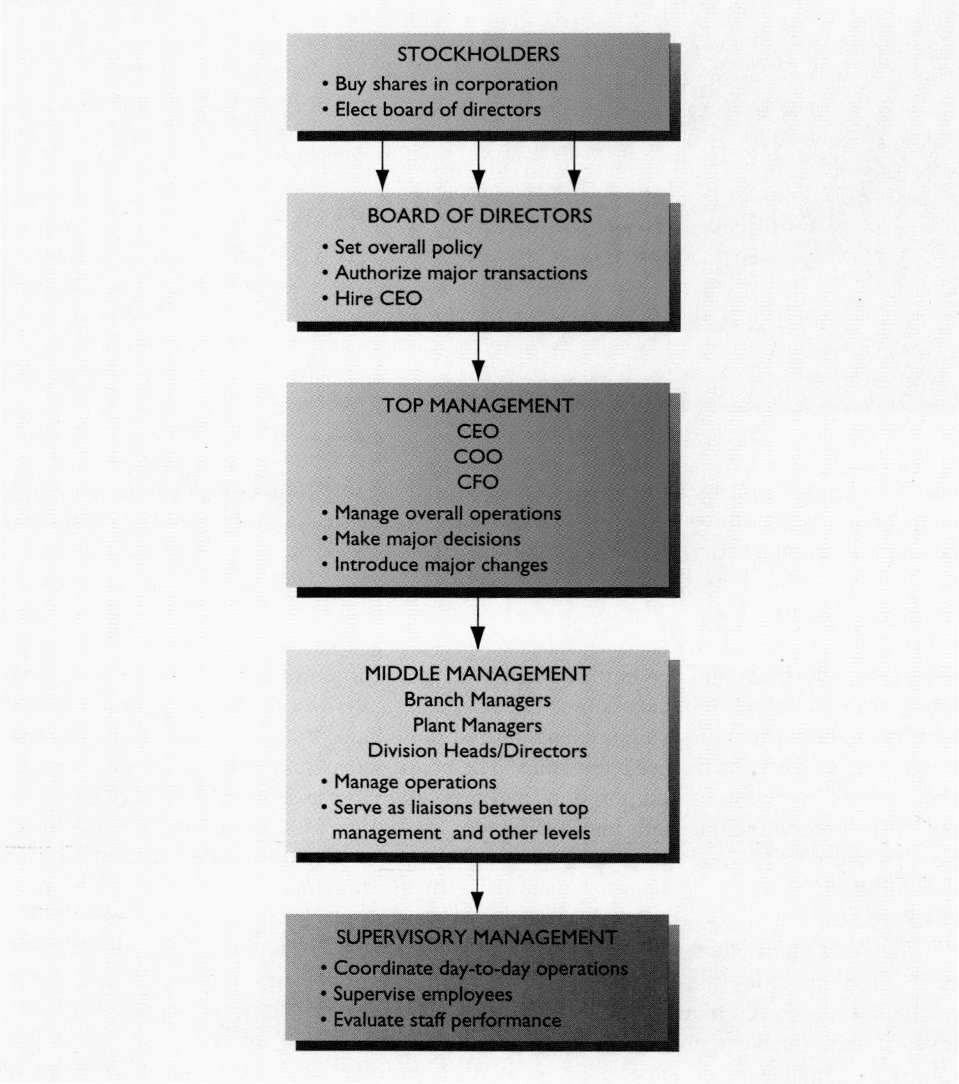

merger
Combination of two or more firms to form one company.

acquisition
Procedure in which one firm acquires the property and assumes the obligations of another.

- The CEO should report annually to the board on succession plans and management-development programs.

Says attorney Ira Millstein, who advises GM's board, "If every board in the country operated this way, the U.S. would be much more competitive."[8]

TRENDS IN CORPORATE OWNERSHIP

Corporate ownership has been in a state of flux in recent years. Many well-known firms have changed owners, become parts of other corporations, or split into smaller units. Trends in corporate ownership include mergers and acquisitions, divestitures, taking firms private, and employee ownership.

MERGERS AND ACQUISITIONS

In a **merger,** two or more firms combine to form one company. In an **acquisition,** one firm purchases the property and assumes the obligations of another company. Many mergers and acquisitions cross national borders.

In France a Pioneer Hi-Bred International agronomist (right) discusses the benefits of Pioneer seed with a French farmer. Pioneer took sole ownership of the company's distribution activities in France and created a new subsidiary.

The number of mergers and acquisitions fell during the early 1990s, but has recently risen again. Many of these deals are driven by managers' attempts to enter new markets and make their companies more competitive.[9]

Mergers can be classified as vertical, horizontal, or conglomerate mergers. A vertical merger occurs between firms at different levels in a channel of distribution. The primary reasons for a vertical merger are (1) to assure adequate raw materials and supplies for products or (2) to increase available distribution outlets for them. In a backward vertical merger, a firm joins with a supplier; in a forward vertical merger, a producer buys a firm that distributes its products. For instance, several Hollywood movie studios have acquired video rental companies in order to profit from that lucrative distribution outlet.

A horizontal merger joins firms in the same industry that wish to diversify and offer a more complete product line. For example, two banks might combine to offer expanded services to a larger customer base.

A conglomerate merger combines unrelated firms. The most common reasons for a conglomerate merger are to diversify, to spur sales growth, or to spend a cash surplus that might otherwise make the holder a tempting target for a takeover effort. Conglomerate mergers may involve firms in totally unrelated industries. Consider Metromedia International Group Inc., a venture that combines movie maker Orion Pictures, several eastern European telecommunications companies, and Actava Group, the maker of Snapper lawn mowers.[10]

Most mergers are friendly mergers, in which both parties agree to the new organizational structure because each feels that it will benefit from the change. For instance, Novell, which makes computer networking software, acquired WordPerfect Corporation, which makes word processing software, in order to offer a broader product line.[11]

However, some merger offers are unsolicited and unwanted, leading to a so-called *unfriendly merger*. When he heard that American Cyanamid Corporation was seeking a friendly merger with SmithKline Beecham, John Stafford, CEO of American Home Products Corporation, immediately countered by making his own unfriendly takeover bid worth $8.5 billion. Stafford reasoned that the merger would help American Home Products to expand its product line and cut costs by paring duplications in sales and administrative staffs.[12]

People cite arguments on both sides of the question of the value of unfriendly takeovers. Raiders claim that managers are more interested in protecting their own jobs than in benefiting stockholders, who will receive more than the market price for the firm's stock in an acquisition. Managers, on the other hand, may argue that corporate raiders are more concerned with short-term stock gains than with the long-term success of the company.

DIVESTITURES

divestiture
Selling off a corporation's divisions or units.

In a **divestiture,** a firm sells some of its divisions or units in order to raise cash, to trim units that are unrelated to the firm's other businesses, or to cut operating losses. Sometimes a firm may sell off divisions that it acquired in a merger because they turn out to be unprofitable or too difficult to manage. Sometimes divested units are converted into independent, private firms or acquired by their employees.

TAKING FIRMS PRIVATE

Management or a group of major stockholders might offer to buy all of a firm's stock. A successful bid would make the firm's stock privately held and remove it from public trading. This arrangement is known as "taking a firm private." Levi Strauss is an example of a firm that has gone private. Sometimes, a firm goes private and then sells a part ownership to the general public through a new stock issue. RJR-Nabisco and Safeway exemplify this situation.

EMPLOYEE OWNERSHIP

Another trend involves employee ownership, in which workers buy shares of stock in their employer. In this case, the corporate organization stays the same, but many of the

In the desert, vibrator trucks gather seismic data. Western Atlas Inc. is the world's largest provider of seismic data to the oil industry. The company was created when Litton Corporation spun off its commercial businesses from its defense businesses. This transaction provided Litton stockholders with one share of Western Atlas stock for each share of Litton stock held.

FIGURE 5.3 TOP EMPLOYEE-OWNED FIRMS

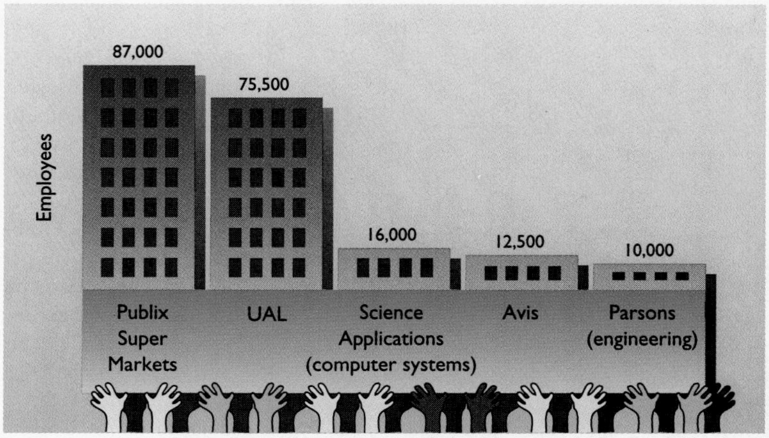

stockholders are now the employees. Employee ownership is growing in many industries; U.S. workers now control almost $60 billion in corporate stock. Figure 5.3 compares the stakes of employee shareholders in the nation's top five employee-owned firms.

Employee ownership is especially common in the airline industry. United Airlines employees took control of 55 percent of the company's stock, making it the second-largest employee-owned firm in the country.[13] Employees own 45 percent of TWA, and up to 37.5 percent of Northwest Airlines will be employee-owned within 10 years. Employees own 5 percent to 15 percent of the stock in Alaska, Delta, Southwest, USAir, and Hawaiian airlines, as well.[14]

PUBLIC AND COLLECTIVE OWNERSHIP

While most business organizations are owned privately by individuals or groups of individuals, municipal, state, or national governments own some, and groups of people own some collectively. Public, or collective, ownership is common in many industries in the United States and abroad.

PUBLIC OWNERSHIP

One alternative to private ownership is some form of **public ownership,** in which a unit or agency of government owns and operates an organization. In the United States, local governments often own parking structures and water systems. The Pennsylvania Turnpike Authority operates a vital highway link across the Keystone state. The federal government established the Tennessee Valley Authority to provide electricity in that region, and the Federal Deposit Insurance Corporation insures bank accounts.

public ownership
Enterprise owned and operated by a unit or agency of government.

Sometimes public ownership results when private investors are unwilling to invest, fearing a high probability of failure. As an example of this situation, consider the 1930s rural electrification program that significantly expanded utility lines in sparsely populated areas. At other times, public ownership has replaced private ownership of failed organizations. Certain functions, such as municipal water systems, are sometimes considered so important to the public welfare that only public ownership can protect people. Finally, some nations have used public ownership to foster competition by operating public companies as competitive business enterprises. In Bogota, Colombia, the government runs a TV and radio network, Instituto Nacional de Radio y Television

BUSINESS IN ACTION

OUTBACK STEAKHOUSE: AN INNOVATIVE FORM OF BUSINESS OWNERSHIP Fast food is fading and casual dining is growing in the 1990s. Consumers, say industry analysts, want familiar food at moderate prices with full-service, sit-down dining. Restaurants offering Mexican, Italian, seafood, or homestyle menus are finding success. Chains including Red Lobster, Olive Garden, Friday's, and Applebee's are thriving in suburban locations all over the country. ■ One chain that is showing extraordinary growth in the industry is the Outback Steakhouse. Owners Chris Sullivan, Robert Basham, and Timothy Gannon spent most of their careers in the restaurant business with various chains such as Steak & Ale and Chili's Grill & Bar. Their experience taught them a lot about the business, including the principle that good food, good service, and committed managers are necessary for success and growth. New restaurants constantly open their doors when a trend catches on and then close their doors when the trend subsides. To achieve long-term success, a restaurant must offer something truly different from the competition. The Outback Steakhouse is different. ■ Superior food separates the Outback from many of its competitors. The chain offers large portions at reasonable prices. The average guest tab, including the bar bill, is $15.60. For most restaurants, the cost of food rarely exceeds 36 percent of sales. At the Outback, the cost of food is 39 percent of sales. The chain purchases high-quality meats from Bruss Company of Chicago. Committing to purchases a year in advance allows the chain to lock in prices. The firm buys produce directly from growers and every restaurant serves fresh chicken. ■ The chain's hours of operation also make it different from its competitors. Most restaurants are open for lunch and dinner. Outback Steakhouses open only for dinner. To profit from lunch business, a restaurant needs a prime location near a high concentration of workplaces since patrons have less time for lunch than for dinner. Customers are willing to travel farther to dinner since "dinner is more of a destination location" says Naomi Talish, an analyst at Morgan Stanley. As a result, Outback leases or buys cheaper locations than restaurants that serve lunch. "Their real estate is in 'A' markets, but 'B' locations," says Talish. ■ Perhaps the

(INRAVISION), which broadcasts both educational and commercial programs. Public ownership remains common abroad, despite a general trend toward privatization.

Trend toward Privatization In recent years, a prevailing trend toward privatization has emerged as privately owned firms have taken over functions formerly performed by publicly owned companies. Today, private companies may provide some public services such as prisons and fire protection. Proposals also have sought to turn over publicly owned enterprises like the Bonneville Power Administration to private investors. Several states have subcontracted with private firms to operate state-owned nursing homes for military veterans.

Privatization is a definite international trend, as well. Under communist rule, state-owned companies employed more than 90 percent of Russia's workers; since the collapse of the Soviet Union, most of Russian industry has been privatized. While China still operates 100,000 state-owned companies, privatization is a growing trend there, as well.[15]

biggest point of differentiation is in the ownership of the restaurants. The chain's owners created a plan to offer ownership equity to individual restaurant managers. In return for a five-year contract and $25,000, the manager buys 10 percent of the restaurant's cash flow. Based on an average Outback outlet's sales of $3.2 million, cash flow is around $736,000. The restaurant's manager earns $73,600 in addition to the base salary of $45,000. The manager also receives stock options for around 4,000 shares that become vested in five years. To build long-term sales, the manager is given another incentive. A manager who decides to leave after five years receives 10 percent of the restaurant's last two years' cash flow averaged out and multiplied by five. Managers have been known to get payouts of over $300,000. A manager who chooses to stay for another five years must invest another $25,000. ■ Outback also offers equity positions to joint-venture partners (JVPs) who manage franchise groups. The JVP invests $50,000 in return for a $50,000 base salary plus about 9 percent of the cash flow generated by the restaurants in the group. A JVP of a group of ten Outback restaurants has the potential to earn more than $500,000 per year. ■ This unique form of ownership attracts solid managers who are veterans of the business, like Larry Siegel, who spent 10 years with Steak & Ale. "This was a chance to make a little money and end up with something in my pocket at the end of five years. After all that time with Steak & Ale, I got squat. I thought this was as close as I'd get to working for myself." ■ The ownership incentives also keep turnover to a minimum. In an industry where annual management turnover rates run 30 percent and higher, the Outback's turnover was only 5.4 percent in a recent year. This leads to consistency in food and service chainwide. Says Outback Chief Financial Officer Bob Merritt, "The better your staff knows their jobs, the more experience they have working as a team, the better you're going to execute." ■ How can the owners give up 20 percent of their annual cash flow? Owner Chris Sullivan explains, "It seems so foreign to people for a company to give up 20 percent of the deal when we're putting up the capital. But I look at it as sweat equity. It's hard work, the managers put heart and soul into it, the results are incredible, and we all benefit." The formula is very successful. The Outback Steakhouse chain has 210 units generating $544 million in sales. By 1996, the company hopes to have 350 restaurants generating $956 million in sales. Sources: Jay Finegan, "Unconventional Wisdom," *Inc.*, December 1994, p. 33; and Fred Faust, "Boomers Fueling Casual Dining Boom," *St. Louis Post-Dispatch,* May 16, 1994, p. BP15.

QUESTIONS FOR CRITICAL THINKING

1. What do you think would happen to the Outback Steakhouse's sales and profits if it changed strategies and opened in prime locations?
2. Do you think it would be realistic to offer a percentage of profits to employees in ranks lower than the restaurant managers?
3. Why is the initial individual manager's investment of $25,000 critical to the success of the restaurant?

COOPERATIVES

Another alternative to private ownership is collective ownership of a production, storage, transportation, and/or marketing organization. Such collective ownership occurs in a **cooperative,** an organization whose owners band together to collectively operate all or part of their industry. In a typical cooperative, owners control their organization by electing a board of directors from the cooperative's members. Well-known cooperatives include Sunkist Growers, Blue Diamond Growers, Associated Mills Producers, Gold Kist, CF Industries, Ocean Spray, Group Terminal Association, and Recreational Equipment Inc., the nation's largest consumer cooperative.

cooperative
Organization operated collectively by its owners.

Large numbers of small producers often create cooperatives to become more competitive in the marketplace. Italian olive growers, for example, have long banded together to form cooperatives. Recently, more than 40,000 of these small groups combined to form the Association of Italian Olive Oil Cooperatives. Membership in this large group gives growers an 8 percent share of the Italian market and a stake in several popular brands of olive oil, including Oliveta, Terre Verdi, Natura, and Antico Frantoio.[16]

A climbing wall at Recreational Equipment Inc. (REI) store allows people to test equipment. REI is owned by its approximately 1 million customers, and the cooperative expects to double in size by 2000.

ACHIEVEMENT CHECK SUMMARY

Reread the learning goals that follow, and consider the questions for each goal. Answering these questions will reinforce the most important concepts in the chapter and allow you to check how well you have achieved these learning goals. Where a blank appears before a question, answer with *T* or *F*. Otherwise, circle the letter of the correct answer. An answer key to these questions is found at the end of this chapter.

LEARNING GOAL 5.1: Identify and explain the three basic forms of business ownership.

1. In which of the three forms of business ownership are co-owners usually active in management? (a) a general partnership; (b) a sole proprietorship; (c) a corporation; (d) a limited partnership.
2. The most common form of business ownership is a: (a) general partnership; (b) sole proprietorship; (c) corporation; (d) limited partnership.
3. Additional capital is most easily obtained by a: (a) general partnership; (b) sole proprietorship: (c) corporation; (d) limited partnership.

LEARNING GOAL 5.2: Outline the advantages and disadvantages of sole proprietorships.

1. ___ Sole proprietorships offer ease of formation and dissolution, maximum flexibility, and the chance to retain all after-tax profits.
2. ___ Sole proprietorships suffer from financial limitations, unlimited financial liability, and lack of continuity.

LEARNING GOAL 5.3: Compare the advantages and disadvantages of partnerships.

1. ___ Like sole proprietorships, partnerships are easy to form and dissolve.
2. ___ The partnership form of ownership offers major advantages including complementary management skills and expanded financial capability.

LEARNING GOAL 5.4: Outline the advantages and disadvantages of corporations.

1. Which of the following describes a class of advantages of a corporation? (a) tax advantages; (b) legal restrictions; (c) limited financial liability; (d) ease of formation; (e) ease of dissolution.
2. Which of the following describes a class of disadvantages of a corporation: (a) financial obligations of owners; (b) economies of large-scale operation; (c) managerial skills; (d) attracting employees; (e) legal restrictions.

LEARNING GOAL 5.5: Discuss how a corporation is organized and operated.

1. ___ The owners of corporations are known as *partners.*
2. ___ A corporation is governed by a board of directors, who authorize major transactions and hire the CEO.
3. ___ A corporation that operates in the United States with a charter in another country is known as a *foreign corporation.*

LEARNING GOAL 5.6: Identify the levels of corporate management.

1. ___ Top managers include job titles like CEO, CFO, president, mayor or governor.
2. ___ Top managers are responsible for the functional operations of the firm.
3. ___ Managers who directly supervise employees and coordinate day-to-day operations of the firm are known as *supervisory managers*.

LEARNING GOAL 5.7: Describe recent trends in corporate ownership.

1. When two or more firms combine to form one company, the firms have: (a) become divested; (b) been taken private; (c) become a cooperative; (d) merged.
2. When one firm purchases the property and assumes the liabilities of another firm, there has been: (a) a vertical merger; (b) a horizontal merger; (c) an acquisition; (d) a divestiture.
3. If a sporting goods manufacturer purchases several sporting goods retailers, this would be an example of: (a) a vertical merger; (b) a horizontal merger; (c) a conglomerate merger; (d) an employee-ownership arrangement.

LEARNING GOAL 5.8: Explain how private ownership, public ownership, and collective ownership (cooperatives) differ.

1. When a group of wheat farmers collectively purchase a grain elevator, this is an example of: (a) private ownership; (b) public ownership; (c) collective ownership.
2. If the city of Los Angeles owns a parking garage, the garage is said to be: (a) privately owned; (b) publicly owned; (c) collectively owned.
3. In recent years, the prevailing trend in ownership has led toward: (a) creating collectives; (b) privatizing functions formerly performed by publicly owned organizations; (c) turning privately owned businesses over to the government to manage.

KEY TERMS

sole proprietorship 100
partnership 102
joint venture 102
corporation 102
stockholder 103
subsidiary 103
parent company 103
dividend 103
limited liability company (LLC) 104
domestic corporation 105
foreign corporation 105
alien corporation 105
preferred stock 106
common stock 106
board of directors 107
merger 108
acquisition 108
divestiture 110
public ownership 111
cooperative 112

REVIEW QUESTIONS

1. Outline the possible ownership structures in U.S. business.
2. What is a sole proprietorship? Why is this the most popular form of business ownership? Does this form of business ownership suffer from any disadvantages?
3. What is a partnership? What advantages and disadvantages characterize this form of business ownership?
4. Distinguish between a joint venture, a general partnership, a limited partnership, and a master limited partnership.
5. How would you define the term *corporation?* What is the primary advantage of the corporate form of business ownership?
6. Differentiate between a domestic corporation, foreign corporation, and alien corporation. Cite an example of each.
7. How does a corporation operate? What roles do the board of directors, top management, middle management, and supervisory management play?
8. Discuss the different types of mergers. Why would a firm's management decide to merge with another company?
9. What do people mean when they talk about privatization? Why is business showing a trend toward privatization today? Cite examples.
10. What is a cooperative? How does it differ from other business entities?

DISCUSSION QUESTIONS

1. What factors would determine your choice of a form of business ownership for a new enterprise? Why?
2. Assume that you are involved in establishing the following businesses. What form of ownership would you propose for each?
   a. Carolina Panthers professional football team
   b. Dry cleaning franchise in Fresno, California
   c. Philadelphia-based management consulting firm
   d. Small foundry in Warren, Michigan
3. Look at the listing of the nation's largest industrial corporations in Table 5.3 and compare it to similar lists published in the last 10 years. What changes have occurred? Can you make any generalizations about these changes?
4. What steps are necessary to set up a corporation in your state or locality? Do these procedures differ from requirements elsewhere? If so, how?
5. Secure announcements of future stockholders' meetings of corporations located in your area. Analyze the types of issues scheduled for debate at these meetings. Can you make any generalizations about them?

SOLUTIONS TO ACHIEVEMENT CHECK SUMMARY

L.G. 5.1: 1. a, 2. b, 3. c **L.G. 5.2:** 1. T, 2. T **L.G. 5.3:** 1. F, 2. T, **L.G. 5.4:** 1. c, 2. e **L.G. 5.5:** 1. F, 2. T, 3. F **L.G. 5.6:** 1. T, 2. F, 3. T **L.G. 5.7:** 1. d, 2. c, 3. a **L.G. 5.8:** 1. c, 2. b, 3. b.

VIDEO CASE

DANIMATION Many new start-up companies begin with a single talented person who has a great idea. In the rapidly growing field of multimedia development, Darjon Brittner fits this profile. Brittner began his business by doing freelance graphics work out of his home. Brittner soon realized that the area of multimedia presentations was growing rapidly. In order to take advantage of this growth, Brittner started Danimation. His entrepreneurial venture now provides businesses with the information they need to create graphics and 3-D animations for sales and marketing presentations and other communications needs.

In the early years, Brittner found that the concept of multimedia was so new that he had to spend much of his time explaining it. Potential customers did not understand how multimedia could benefit them. Desktop multimedia projects vary dramatically in organization, approach, and content. Most, however, share three basic characteristics that define them as multimedia projects.

- They integrate two or more media effects (text, graphics, sound, video, and animation) to convey a message or tell a story.
- They are designed to be viewed and interacted with on a computer.
- They let the presenter cover the material in any order and allow the audience to browse through on-line information in any sequence.

Desktop multimedia borrows much of its terminology from the entertainment industry. For example, multimedia projects are generally referred to as titles and the person who manages the development process is usually called the producer. In the case of a small, new company like Danimation, the producer would be responsible for the entire sequence of events in developing a title. Later, as the company's capabilities expand, the producer would probably be in charge of a development team.

Creating a multimedia title is a three-step process: planning and designing the title, developing the media effects, and authoring or producing the final product. In Danimation's case, a storyboard is created after initial interviews with a prospective client. This lays out the plan for the project. The storyboard then serves as the focal point for other meetings with the client to make sure that the project meets everyone's expectations. This work is done before the development of any graphics or animations, ensuring that all parties are comfortable with the project before any needless effort or expenses are incurred.

The ways in which a business might use multimedia extends well beyond entertainment. It can be used to accelerate and reinforce learning. In fact, today's CD-ROM technology, which can store a vast amount of information in the form of video, sound, data, graphics, and animation, has been referred to as Just-In-Time (JIT) learning. Studies have shown that a person's ability to learn and retain information is greatest if that information is made available to the learner when he or she has a need for it. Basically, having the in-

formation readily available results in faster learning with greater retention. Employees see an immediate need for the information and, therefore, have greater motivation to learn. Traditional unfocused training programs are less successful.

As Brittner became successful, he realized that structural changes would have to take place in his company if Danimation were to continue growing. No longer was a sole proprietorship the best fit for his company. Although a sole proprietorship is easy to form and allowed Brittner great flexibility in his hours and activities, other considerations became more important. For example, he discovered that his expanding client base required more complex and expensive services. Many of these clients expected Danimation to have a more professional office environment.

To resolve these roadblocks to growth, Brittner incorporated Danimation and set up shop in the Dallas Info-Mart, an address synonymous with corporate clout. Many technology companies, such as IBM and Compaq Computer, have offices there. These changes helped give the fledgling company greater credibility with potential clients. Danimation is now poised for growth in the years to come.

QUESTIONS

1.
What form of business ownership did Danimation begin with? Why did it make sense to start that way?

2.
What business service does Danimation provide? What is it used for?

3.
Why was it necessary to make a change in the form of business ownership?

4.
What were the advantages and disadvantages of the two different forms of business ownership?

CHAPTER 6

ENTREPRENEURSHIP, SMALL BUSINESS, AND FRANCHISING

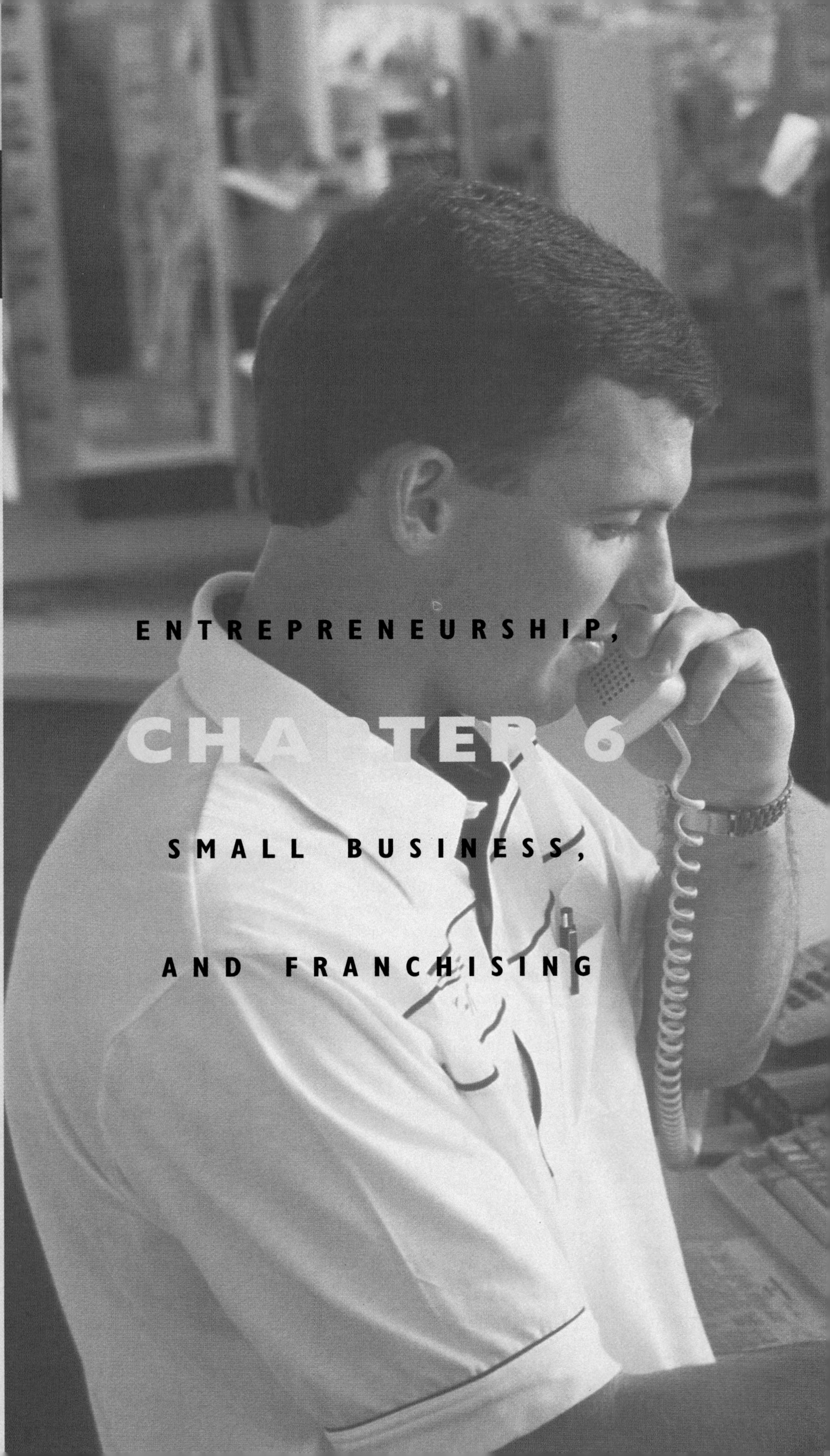

LEARNING GOALS

1. Explain the vital role that entrepreneurs and small businesses play in the global economy.

2. Define entrepreneurship, and describe how entrepreneurs differ from other businesspeople.

3. Define small business, and identify the industries in which most small firms are established.

4. Compare the advantages and disadvantages of small business.

5. Analyze the small business opportunities for women and minorities and the special challenges that face these entrepreneurs.

6. Describe how the Small Business Administration functions.

7. Outline the role of franchising in the U.S. economy, and list its advantages and disadvantages.

8. Outline the popular methods of small business operation in the global market.

9. Outline the components of a business plan.

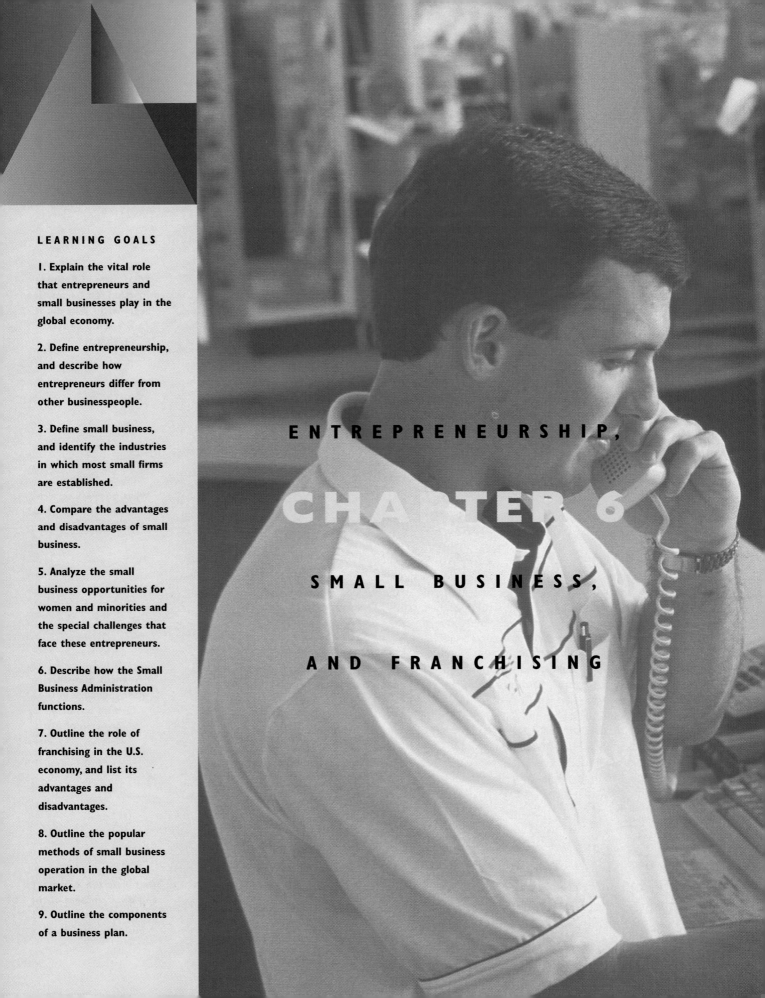

HOMELAND FASHIONS Sidewalk vendors, jazz festivals, and Black Entertainment Television's home shopping show: what do they have in common? All contribute to the rapid development of small businesses that link the United States and Africa. ■ Commerce has been an important part of African life for centuries. Consider Senegal, which in ancient times was part of the prosperous empire of Ghana. By the 17th century, Senegal's Goree Island was a thriving warehouse district for French businesses. After 300 more years, Goree Island had become a bustling tourist center. Senegalese entrepreneurs crafted and sold souvenirs—cowrie-shell bracelets, ebony carvings, boubou dresses—to American visitors. ■ Senegalese entrepreneurs soon realized that they could make even greater profits if they were to export their goods. An ebony carving that sold for $5 in Dakar could fetch $20 in Detroit. U.S.–bound shipments of African wares increased, and new companies arose to handle this trade. ■ One of the most successful is Homeland Fashions, a New York–based manufacturer of Afrocentric products. Homeland Fashions was founded by Mohamed Diop, a Senegalese who earned a bachelor's degree from Roosevelt University in Chicago, worked for Citicorp in West Africa, and returned to the United States to start his own firm. He imported cloth from Senegal and Ghana, and hired immigrant tailors to create clothing inspired by African styles. ■ Demand for Homeland's products increased rapidly, fueled by black Americans' growing interest in their African heritage and the arrival of more African immigrants in the United States. At first, Diop sold his merchandise mainly through catalogs and sidewalk vendors. African immigrants often set up informal shops on city streets to market Afrocentric goods, including Homeland Fashions items. ■ Soon, however, Diop and other entrepreneurs began exploring a new distribution channel for their products. Nationwide, the number of black-oriented craft shows, music festivals, and cultural events is rising. For instance, Detroit's African World Festival attracts more than 1 million visitors annually. At the same time, it draws over 100 Senegalese vendors, who sell their attractive wares both to consumers and to retailers who resell them through stores. "It's big business," says James Wyatt of the Museum of African American History, the festival sponsor. "I've heard of peddlers clearing $15,000 in a single weekend." ■ These days, Homeland Fashions manufactures over 300 items, from $8 *kente* baseball caps to $200 business suits. Over the past 2 years, annual sales have grown from $4 million to $6 million. In addition to marketing at events, Diop continues to sell his merchandise by catalog to wholesalers, retailers, and consumers. ■ Diop is also exploring another distribution outlet—home shopping. Black Entertainment Television and Home Shopping Network are developing BET Shop, a home-shopping service targeting African Americans. The Black Entertainment Television network reaches almost 40 million households nationwide, and Diop is excited about its market potential. In its first year of operation, BET's direct-marketing division, which sells music and skin-care products, generated close to $2 million in sales. ■ Homeland Fashions' success reflects the growing bond between the United States and Senegal. While Senegal's exports to the United States are increasing, so are U.S. exports to Senegal, which now top $6.5 billion. The Senegalese government has established the Dakar Industrial Free Zone, a state-owned free trade district, to encourage investment by foreign and domestic companies. Additional trade zones are planned. ■ Back in the United States, the market for Afrocentric products is likely to expand still further. An estimated 10,000 to 20,000 Senegalese now live in New York, Chicago, Atlanta, and Philadelphia. Many of them are self-employed businesspeople who are working their way through college. Typical of these entrepreneurs is Makhtar Ndoye, who drove a cab to finance his degree at New York University. Today, he manages the Horizon 96 insurance agency in Harlem's Little Senegal district, where he sells insurance to French- and Wolof-

speaking clients. In recent years, more than a dozen Senegalese entrepreneurs have joined him in the area, including grocery stores, hair-braiding salons, and specialty butchers who supply *halal* (kosher) meat to Muslim customers. Says Ndoye, "New York has become the promised land for Senegalese."[1]

CHAPTER OVERVIEW

Entrepreneurship and a strong small-business sector have always formed the backbone of every private enterprise system. They provide the competitive zeal that keeps the system effective. Numerous government actions have encouraged the development and continuity of these firms. Antitrust legislation, for example, was designed to maintain the competitive environment in which such companies thrive. A federal agency, the Small Business Administration, was set up in 1953 to assist small firms.

Entrepreneurship is more popular now than ever before; people launched 2 million businesses last year alone. In 1987, only about 3 percent of people who left corporate jobs started their own firms; today that number has tripled.[2] Professor Paul Reynolds of Marquette University estimates that about 4 percent of American adults are actively trying to start new companies. "At any given moment more people are trying to start a business than are getting married or having children," Reynolds notes.[3]

These statistics suggest the vital role that entrepreneurs and small-business owners play in contemporary business. Aside from the many services they provide to consumers, these organizations also help other businesses to function more efficiently. Many small firms serve as suppliers to large corporations; AT&T, for example, buys $1.5 billion of goods and services from more than 100,000 small companies every year. "The small companies have advantages," says Patricia Cox, AT&T's director of global procurement. "They have lower costs, lower overhead, and they tend to be specialists."[4]

business incubator
Facility that houses start-up firms.

Business incubators are an important part of small business today. **Business incubators** are organizations that provide low-cost, shared facilities to small, start-up ventures. A typical incubator might section off space in an abandoned plant and rent it to various small firms. Tenants often share secretaries and other business services.

About 500 business incubators now operate nationwide. Some are operated by industrial development authorities, others by not-for-profit organizations, colleges and universities, or private investors. Entrepreneurs who use these facilities have access to management support services and valuable management advice from in-house mentors. For instance, Vally Nance, owner of Alabama-based drug-trial company SORRA, Inc., benefited from advice in locating funding, a lawyer, and an accountant to help her growing business move from her home to a clinic office.[5]

ENTREPRENEURSHIP

As we learned in Chapter 1, an *entrepreneur* is a risk taker in the private enterprise system, a person who seeks a profitable opportunity and takes the necessary risks to set up and operate a business. Today, more and more people are choosing to take these risks. Many of them want to work for themselves rather than for others. They enjoy the feeling of controlling their own economic destinies. Women and members of minority groups often start their own businesses because they see limited opportunities within existing organizations. Still other entrepreneurs start home-based businesses because they want to spend more time with their families.

Many entrepreneurs, according to economist Kathryn Stafford, are professionals and managers who either lost their jobs or left voluntarily when corporations downsized. For people who have been through corporate restructuring, notes Stafford, "being in control of their own fate, being their own boss, begins to hold even more appeal than it might otherwise."[6]

Successful entrepreneurs tend to be a well-educated group. Nearly half of the entrepreneurs in the *Inc.* 500 list of the 500 fastest-growing small U.S. companies hold bachelor's degrees, and more than a third have advanced degrees.[7]

FORMS OF ENTREPRENEURSHIP

The Center for Entrepreneurial Leadership in the School of Management at the State University of New York at Buffalo defines distinct categories of entrepreneurs: classic entrepreneurs, intrapreneurs, and change agents.[8] A classic entrepreneur identifies a business opportunity and allocates available resources to tap that market. An intrapreneurs is an entrepreneurially oriented person who seeks to develop new products, ideas, and commercial ventures within the context of a large organization. (Chapter 9 will discuss intrapreneurs further.) By contrast, change agents are managers who seek to revitalize established concerns in order to keep their competitiveness in the modern marketplace. These individuals are described in various sections throughout this text.

ENTREPRENEURS AS A DIFFERENT BREED

Are entrepreneurs different from most people? Apparently they are. Research has identified roughly 40 personality characteristics that are associated with entrepreneurship. Figure 6.1 illustrates six traits that appear to be especially important for successful entrepreneurs:

- Internal locus of control. People with this trait believe that they can control their own fates, that the difference between success and failure depends on them.
- High energy level. No doubt about it, it takes a lot of work to start and build a successful business. Entrepreneurs must be willing and able to work long hours.
- Need to achieve. Successful entrepreneurs like to set their own goals and are motivated by the opportunity to achieve them.
- Tolerance for ambiguity. Starting a new company is risky, so entrepreneurs must tolerate ambiguous, uncertain situations.
- Awareness of passing time. Entrepreneurs tend to be impatient people who like to stay active; they rarely procrastinate.
- Self-confidence. Running a business requires the ability to make decisions and manage numerous details. Entrepreneurs need to have confidence that they can handle these challenges, not to mention other challenges that will arise in the future.[9]

FIGURE 6.1 CHARACTERISTICS OF ENTREPRENEURS

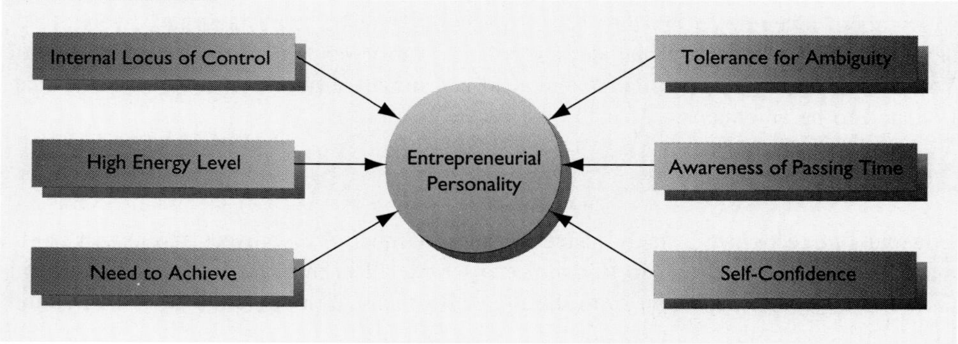

A BROADER PURPOSE

DEVELOPING FUTURE ENTREPRENEURS Melinda McMullen and Sandra Sowell-Scott may live on different coasts, but the two share the same philosophy: if students in the inner city have opportunities to learn in real-life business situations at early ages, they are more likely to succeed in life. What sets these women apart from the countless others who offer solutions for inner city problems is that they both practice what they preach—and they're getting results. ■ Melinda McMullen, a former advertising executive, along with Tammy Bird, a biology instructor, are using an entrepreneurial venture as a self-help program for inner-city kids in Los Angeles. Bird converted a weed-infested plot of land behind Crenshaw High School into a garden of cabbage, lettuce, broccoli, and various herbs. She hoped that the garden would keep a handful of interested students off the streets after school and on weekends. The group of six students who started the garden quickly attracted others. Many of the students immersed themselves in the project as they researched how to grow the herbs and vegetables without chemicals and pesticides. As students became more engrossed in the project, their overall grades improved. At the end of the year, the students sold their crops for $1,500 at local farmers' markets and donated 25 percent of their profits to the homeless. The balance of the funds helped to pay tuition bills for three graduating students. ■ The venture soon grew into "Food From the 'Hood." The Crenshaw students created and test marketed a 12-ounce bottle of salad dressing using ingredients grown in their garden. Luther, Young & Small, a local investment banking company, helped the students to structure the company with divisions for marketing, product, sales, community relations, and corporate-giving. The students designed their own logo and contracted with a local food manufacturer to make the product. Under the guidance of McMullen and Bird, the students

Differences between Entrepreneurs and Managers Although managers who leave corporate jobs sometimes start their own businesses, the skills that make a good manager are not necessarily those needed to launch a business, and vice versa. Consultants estimate that roughly 50 percent of corporate managers who start their own companies actually enjoy self-employment.

Robert Bogart, a former senior vice president at Primerica, started a fax-service business, All the Fax, when he was laid off after a merger. "Business was good," recalls Bogart, "but after a year I decided it wasn't for me." Why not? "As an executive in a large company, the issues are strategic," he explains. "You're implementing programs that affect thousands of people. In a small business, the issues are less complex. There's no administration. No maintenance. There's no executive secretary because you can't afford the $40,000 [cost]. You miss the seminars, the lunches, the trade groups. You worry about inventory every day, because you may not be in business next week if you have negative cash flow." What surprised Bogart most was "how much you have to sell. You're always out selling to companies and law offices. I didn't want to be a salesman. I wanted to be an executive."[10]

small business
Business that is independently owned and operated, is not dominant in its field, and meets certain size standards for its income or number of employees.

WHAT IS SMALL BUSINESS?

How can one recognize a small business? Sales, number of employees, assets, net worth, market share, and relationship to competitors have all been used to make this determination. The official definition from the Small Business Administration says that a **small business** is a firm that is independently owned and operated, is not dominant in its field, did all of the work. The salad dressing is distributed through numerous stores in southern California, including outlets of all of the big chains. ■ The students hope to raise $100,000 annually with Food From the 'Hood. The funds will pay for scholarships for students to attend college. McMullen and Bird insist that students must maintain their grades to stay in the program. So far, grades don't seem to be a problem as the involved students are enthusiastically participating and bettering their grade point averages. ■ On the other side of the country, Sandra Sowell-Scott created the after-school Entrepreneurial Training Program (YETP) at Temple University's Small Business Development Center in 1990. Sowell-Scott administers the program and teaches both the students and their instructors. The 14-week program emphasizes "real-world" entrepreneurship including reading business periodicals, visiting local businesses, and budgeting individual $300 stipends. Simulated and actual business endeavors are also presented to the aspiring entrepreneurs. She teaches students how to evaluate opportunities, determine consumer needs, develop products to meet those needs, and create structures for businesses including necessary funding and licensing. Sowell-Scott encourages the students to think for themselves and always to consider how they can improve conditions in their neighborhoods and communities. ■ More than 700 students have attended YETP. Several graduates of the program have launched successful businesses in the last 2 years including a snack counter, a florist/gift shop, and a T shirt silk screener. For her efforts, Sowell-Scott was named *Inc.* Magazine's Entrepreneurship Educator of the Year. ■ Both McMullen and Sowell-Scott are entrepreneurs themselves, in that they are risk takers who are seeking profitable opportunities. The profit they are seeking comes from the improvement in the quality of life for inner-city high school students. By teaching entrepreneurship, they are giving hope to people who might not otherwise have it. Their dedication to helping high school students is also helping the country. Says Sowell-Scott, "If we don't train kids from an early age, we can't expect to have good businesspeople in the future." Sources: Alessandra Bianchi, "Head of the Class," *Inc.*, December, 1994, p. 87; and Ron Harris, "A Path to College Paved with Salad Dressing," *Los Angeles Times,* October 22, 1993, p. B2.

QUESTIONS FOR CRITICAL THINKING

1. If you were in charge of either entrepreneurial program, who would you approach for funding?
2. If you were a local business in either Los Angeles or Philadelphia, what type of assistance could you offer these programs?
3. How might Sandra Sowell-Scott or Melinda McMullen package their programs for use in other cities?

and meets certain size standards for its income or number of employees.[11] Some standards apply only for loan programs, others for procurement, and still others for various special programs. In general, a small business has the following characteristics:

- Independently owned
- Independently operated and managed
- Only a minor player in its industry
- Fewer than 400 employees
- Limited capital resources

Small businesses are more common than one might think. In fact, 95 percent of all enterprises in the United States employ fewer than 50 people each. Further, 20 percent of the companies started last year are one- and two-person operations. Consider that 47,000 consultancies in the United States hire three or fewer people; the number of such firms has doubled in the last 2 years alone.[12] Small companies operate in nearly every industry, including farming, retailing, services, and high technology.

TYPICAL SMALL BUSINESS VENTURES

Small businesses compete against some of the world's largest organizations and against a multitude of other small companies. Retailing and service establishments are the most common nonfarming small businesses, and new-technology companies often start as small organizations.

Most farming is still the work of small businesses. The family farm is a classic example of a small business operation that is independently owned and operated, with relatively few employees, but with a substantial amount of unpaid family labor.

General-merchandise giants like Wal-Mart, K mart, and Sears may be the best known retailing firms, but small, privately owned retail enterprises outnumber them. Small businesses run retail outlets for shoes, jewelry, office supplies and stationery, apparel, flowers, drugs, convenience foods, and thousands of other products.

Other small business ventures include service-oriented industries and individuals such as restaurants, funeral homes, banking establishments, movie theaters, dry cleaners, carpet cleaners, shoe repairers, attorneys, insurance agents, automobile repair shops, public accountants, dentists, and physicians. Small companies often succeed in service industries because they are flexible enough to take on challenges that large service providers overlook. Consider San Diego–based Acucobol, which helps companies to transfer important programs written in the computer language COBOL to newer software. COBOL is an old language in computer terms—it's been around since the early 1960s. Many American firms still have enormous backlogs of vital business applications in COBOL, such as payroll and invoicing programs.

Enter Pamela Coker, who started Acucobol to make these programs compatible with newer computer languages. Coker has succeeded in a market that many software firms have bypassed; she actually has fewer competitors now than when she started the company. "Everybody thinks COBOL's dead," she says cheerfully. "The negative press has provided this hidden, secret market for us."[13] She points out that, in many areas of the world, COBOL remains the dominant language of business computing; 50 percent of Acucobol's revenues come from outside the United States.

Many new-technology firms, those that strive to produce and market scientific innovations, start as small businesses. Many great inventors have launched companies in barns, garages, warehouses, and attics. Small business is often the best (or only) option available to someone seeking to transform a technical idea into a commercial reality.

While most new businesses operate in industries that impose limited capital requirements, some technical firms require substantial capital to get off the ground. Sometimes larger, established corporations provide funding that enables these start-ups to pursue

Teenager Steve Lovett of Reston, Virginia, runs Lovett Enterprises, a service company that does yard work, automobile detailing, and odd jobs for local customers. He began at age 11 by washing cars; at 16 he'd franchised his business to four other teenagers.

research and develop new products. For instance, several large pharmaceutical companies have formed joint ventures with small biotech firms to identify and market commercial applications of genetic research. SmithKline Beecham invested $125 million in Human Genome Sciences, a Maryland-based start-up that is working to decipher the functions of specific human genes. While Human Genome Sciences has not yet developed any commercial products, its managers plan to patent their discoveries and use the information to develop marketable applications. SmithKline Beecham's investment gives it product rights and a 7 percent stake in future profits.[14]

ADVANTAGES OF A SMALL BUSINESS

Small businesses are not simply smaller versions of large corporations. Their legal forms of organization, market positions, staff capabilities, managerial styles and organization structures, and financial resources generally differ from those of bigger companies. These differences give them some unique advantages.

INNOVATION

Small firms are often the first to offer new products to the marketplace; Federal Express and Apple Computer are classic success stories. A more recent success is Specialty Silicone Products, a start-up company that makes high-tech rubber products. The firm's best sellers are seals for gas chromatographs, computerized devices used in drug testing and blood analysis. Specialty Silicone makes high-quality stoppers from Teflon-coated silicone that can take up to 150 punctures from hypodermic needles and still block out foreign contaminants that could affect test results. The little company ships $6 million worth of products every year, 17.5 percent of them to overseas markets. Says CEO Daniel Natarelli, "Anybody doing analysis uses these machines—every laboratory, hospital, police lab, and university, even high schools. The world is exploding with gas chromatographs."[15]

BETTER CUSTOMER SERVICE

A small firm can often operate more flexibly than a large corporation, allowing it to tailor its product line and services to the needs of its customers. As television broadcasts reach all over the globe, for example, more people are demanding specific products. Pooyransh Saini's store in the remote village of Kotputli in northwestern India may measure only 8 feet by 6 feet, but he is the sole retailer in his area to offer the Western brands that are becoming popular with his neighbors. His customers can choose between brand 555, a locally made detergent, and Surf, a detergent made by Unilever subsidiary Hindustan Lever. Notes Saini, "If you don't stock what people see on television, you lose customers."[16]

LOWER COSTS

Small firms can often provide products more cheaply than large firms can. Small firms usually have fewer overhead costs—costs not directly related to providing specific goods and services—and can earn profits on lower prices than large companies can offer.

A typical small business has a lean organization with a small staff and few support personnel. The lower overhead costs due to a smaller permanent staff can provide a distinct advantage to a small business. Such a firm tends to hire outside consultants or specialists, such as attorneys and accountants, only as needed. By contrast, larger organizations often keep such specialists as permanent staff members. As a rule, all growing organizations add staff personnel faster than line (or operating) personnel.

Consider the Brockton, Massachusetts area, where a growing population of immigrants have come to live from the west African republic of Cape Verde. When businesspeople need a translator to help them communicate with this expanding market, they can call on Chrissy Correia. This 15-year-old girl, who has been confined to a wheelchair since being shot at age 3, started her translation business after attending an entrepreneurship conference at Babson College. Her low overhead—the company is headquartered in her bedroom—allows her to charge less than a large translation firm could. Correia is also starting another venture, Crazy Creations, to sell hand-decorated baskets and watches with an African theme. "I'm taking orders. I hope to build my own business," says Correia. Her family supports her entrepreneurial goals. "They see I'm getting my life together. I'll make something of myself."[17]

Small businesses such as Correia's often have the benefit of unpaid labor. Entrepreneurs themselves are usually willing to work long hours with no overtime or holiday pay. In addition, family members contribute significant unpaid labor as bookkeepers, laborers, receptionists, delivery personnel, and the like.

To keep costs as low as possible, many entrepreneurs start their companies in their homes. This can be a good idea or a disaster, depending on the nature of the business and the nature of the entrepreneur. Some lines of work are better adapted to a home setting than others. Table 6.1 lists 10 professions in which a significant number of entrepreneurs earn six-figure annual incomes from their homes.

Business writers recommend the following guidelines for those who want to work at home:

- Love your work. Many people want to work at home because they love being home, not because they are passionate about what they're doing. However, working at home means no boss and no co-workers to get you motivated, so the motivation must stem from the work itself. "The work must be at least a 7 on a scale of your interests ranked from 1 to 10," notes business author Paul Edwards, not "something that makes you bury your head under the covers in the morning and go back to sleep."

TABLE 6.1 PROFITABLE HOME-BASED BUSINESSES

Business Activity	Estimated Annual Income	Estimated Start-Up Cost (Maximum)
Bill auditing	$50,000–$200,000	$ 7,400
Business broker	Up to $100,000	6,500
Business-plan writer	$24,000–$100,000	10,500
Advertising/marketing copywriter	$20,000–$175,000	6,200
Desktop video producer	$35,000–$150,000	22,000
Executive search	Average $123,000	9,400
Export agent	$60,000–$100,000	10,500
Home inspector	Average $100,000	9,300
Management consultant	Average $110,000	8,800
Professional-practice consultant	$90,000–$187,500	9,800

[a] Home-based businesses in which a significant number of entrepreneurs earn six-figure annual incomes

Todd Holmes and Louis Amoroso founded Beer Across America after discussing the success of a wine-of-the-month club. Their business created and filled a niche as a supplier of a monthly six-pack of beer from small, obscure breweries to Beer Across America members.

- Research the market and the field. Talk to business owners in the field to see if they enjoy working from home. Make sure there's a demand for the business.
- Stay flexible. Sometimes what you want to do isn't necessarily what customers want from you. When Ernest Fine left IBM after 28 years to start his own business, he planned to provide long-term strategic planning help for clients. He changed his focus, however, when he discovered that what customers really wanted was someone to help them solve computer problems quickly.
- Respect your neighborhood. Neighbors may complain, and even force a business owner to move to an office, if a home-based company creates too much traffic or noise in a residential area. "The best businesses to do from home are very silent ones," notes Coralee Kern, executive director of the National Association for the Cottage Industry.[18]

FILLING ISOLATED NICHES

The size of a big business excludes it from some markets. High overhead costs force it to set minimum sizes for targets at which to direct competitive efforts. Some large publishers, for example, identify minimum acceptable sales figures that reflect their overhead costs. Editorial and production expenses for a certain type of book may not be justified unless the publisher can sell, say, 7,000 copies. This situation provides substantial opportunities for smaller publishers with lower overhead costs.

In addition, certain types of businesses lend themselves better to smaller firms. Many service businesses illustrate this point. Finally, economic and organizational factors may dictate that an industry consist essentially of small firms. Upscale restaurants are an example.

Clark Childers, a 16-year-old boy who lives in Corpus Christi, Texas, founded a successful business by focusing on a niche market: sailboat owners. While Childers loved sailing, he hated the cover that protected his boat because it was so hard to position. "It was like trying to slip a straw back into its paper covering," he says. So Childers designed a simple nylon cover with an elastic band that fit over the boat as easily as a hairnet, taking only 60 seconds to install. Childers decided to market it. Christened QuikSkins, his cover is manufactured in Mexico and distributed through a Rhode Island dealer. To date, Childers has sold 300 units at $100 apiece, and he is developing other sailing-related products.

Childers' mother helps out during peak periods; one recent evening, they worked together from 5 P.M. to midnight to pack QuikSkins for shipping. "Mom loves this," says Childers. "She considers herself my promotional manager."[19]

DISADVANTAGES OF A SMALL BUSINESS

Small firms also have a variety of disadvantages, including a potential for poor management, a risk of inadequate financing, and government regulation. A small firm can be more vulnerable than a large, diversified corporation during a recession, since it probably has fewer resources to cushion a fall. Figure 6.2 shows the survival rate of new businesses in a variety of industries; on average, nearly 62 percent of all businesses dissolve within the first six years of operation. While small business owners can overcome these problems, it is important to think carefully about all of these issues before starting a company.

POOR MANAGEMENT

Poor management is a common reason why small businesses fail. Frequently, people go into business with little, if any, business training. Someone may launch an enterprise based on a great idea for a good or service, assuming that knowledge about business matters will come as the firm operates. Bankruptcy is often the result. Heed a word of caution: If you want to start a business, learn the basics of business first. It is also important to recognize your limitations; few business owners possess the specialized knowledge of an attorney or an accountant, for instance. Successful business owners know when to call on outside professionals for help.

Moreover, small business owners sometimes let their entrepreneurial optimism run wild. Full of excitement about projects and their potential, they may forget about details like paperwork. They may also neglect to "do their homework" before starting the small business. The belief that others will see a product as unique or better than that of the competition should be verified by marketing research. Entrepreneurs should ask themselves whether a market exists for what they want to sell and whether they can convince the public that they offer an advantage over the competition. Published sources, surveys, in-depth interviews, competitive analyses, observation, or a number of other research techniques can provide the answers to those questions.

Economist Kathryn Stafford notes that successful entrepreneurs who work at home tend to use professional practices in their business. These practices include using an answering machine or answering service to handle phone calls when no one is available;

FIGURE 6.2 SURVIVAL RATES OF BUSINESSES

Survival Rate of Businesses (shown as %)	Years of Survival <2	2–4	4–6
Total, All Industries	76.1	47.9	37.8
Construction	77.1	45.6	35.2
Manufacturing	78.7	56.2	46.2
Transportation, Communication, Public Utilities	75.7	46.2	37.0
Retail Trade	75.6	48.1	37.0
Finance, Insurance, Real Estate	74.2	46.2	36.0
Services	75.4	46.5	37.3

hiring an accountant and attorney for specialized advice; borrowing money from a bank, rather than a family member or friend, to finance the business; advertising in the Yellow Pages; and reserving space at home exclusively for business use.[20]

Perhaps the most important professional practice is to create a written business plan before starting a business; many entrepreneurs who go into business without one end up regretting it. A later section of this chapter will discuss guidelines for creating an effective business plan.

INADEQUATE FINANCING

Inadequate financing is another leading cause of small business problems. Many businesses start with inadequate capital and soon run short of funds. They often lack the resources to survive rough periods or to expand if they are successful. Figure 6.3 illustrates the financial obstacles that most often confront small businesses. The biggest problem is uneven cash flow; finding funds to pay taxes and employees ranks second.

Most financing for a typical small business comes from the entrepreneur's own resources. Banks provide relatively little funding for small companies. Home-based entrepreneurs may find it especially difficult to qualify for bank loans. "Conventional financing for most home-based businesses is minimal," says Gene Fairbrother, a consultant with the National Association for the Self-Employed.

Entrepreneurs may turn to venture capitalists for funding. **Venture capitalists** are business organizations or groups of private individuals that invest in promising new firms. Sometimes venture capitalists lend money to businesses; other times they become part-owners of new or struggling companies.

venture capitalist
Business organization or a group of private individuals that invest in new firms.

The Small Business Administration offers a variety of loan programs for small businesses, primarily through banks. Firms use these loans to finance construction, conversion, or expansion; for purchasing equipment, facilities, machinery, materials, and supplies; and for operating funds.[21]

GOVERNMENT REGULATION

Small business owners complain bitterly of excessive government regulation and red tape. The Small Business Administration estimates that government paperwork costs

FIGURE 6.3 GREATEST FINANCIAL OBSTACLES OF SMALL BUSINESSES

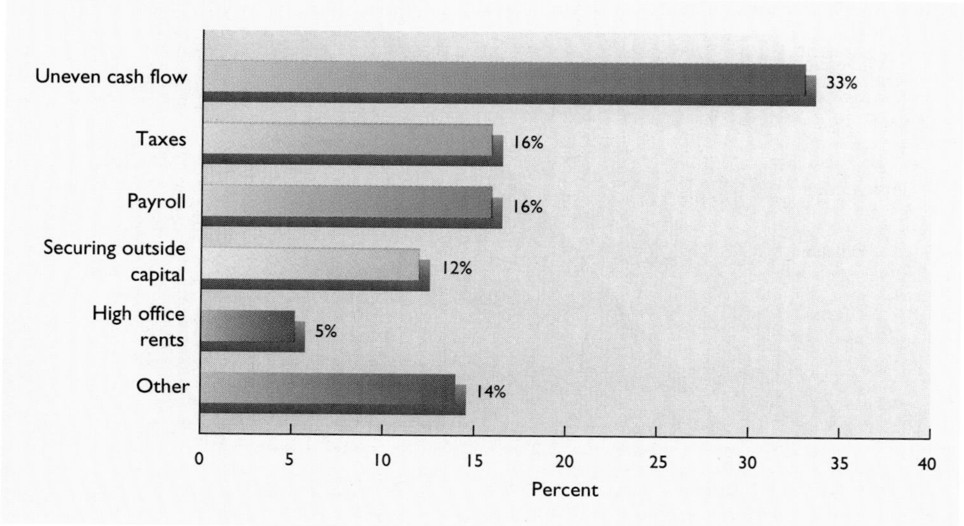

small firms billions of dollars each year. A larger firm with a substantial staff can usually cope better with the required forms and reports. Many experts within and outside government recognize a need to reduce the paperwork required of small businesses, since they are simply not equipped to handle the burden. Some small firms close down for this reason alone.

SMALL BUSINESS OPPORTUNITIES FOR WOMEN AND MINORITIES

Members of minority groups and women start many small businesses, possibly because they see better opportunities working for themselves than working for somebody else could provide. Figure 6.4 shows a breakdown of the types of businesses owned by women, African Americans, Hispanics, and other minorities. Clearly, service and retail firms are the most common types of small businesses for each group.

WOMEN-OWNED BUSINESSES

Each year, more than 7 million Americans participate in starting some type of new business. Women make up a substantial portion—roughly one-third—of these entrepreneurs. The Small Business Administration estimates that, by the end of the decade, women will head almost 40 percent of all small firms.[22]

Together, these companies have a tremendous economic impact. For example, businesses owned by women employ more of the U.S. population than all of the companies in the *Fortune* 500. The U.S. Census identifies 49 metropolitan areas where women-owned businesses have sales of more than $1 billion a year.[23]

More women are starting their own companies for several reasons. Some may leave large corporations when they feel blocked from opportunities for advancement, that is, when they hit the so-called *glass ceiling*. Other women may want more flexible work-

FIGURE 6.4 TYPES OF BUSINESSES OWNED BY MINORITIES AND WOMEN

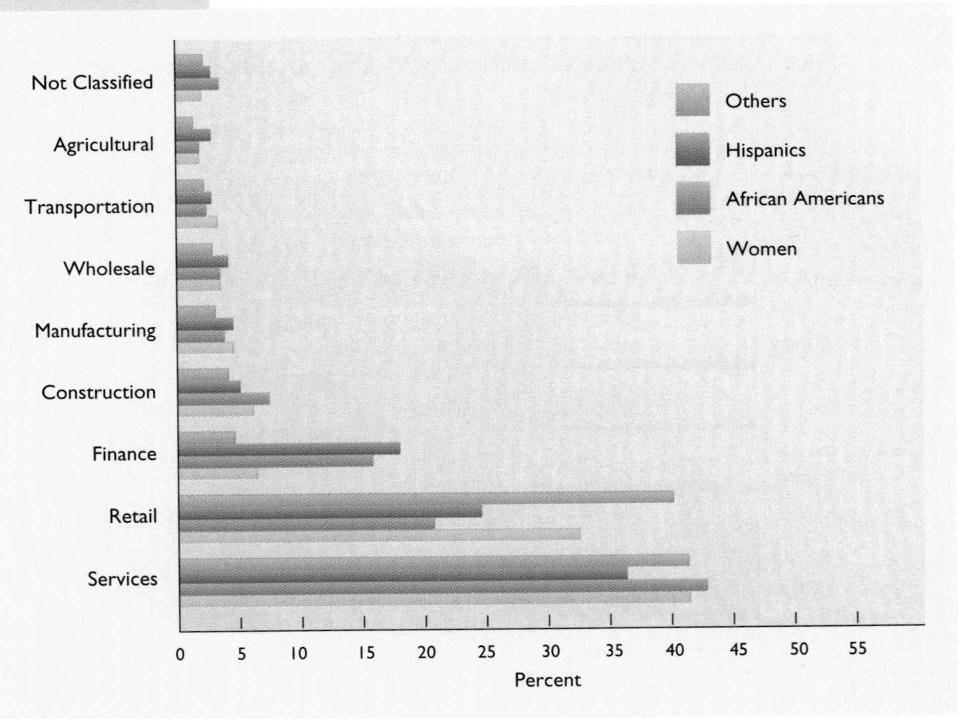

ing hours so they can spend more time with their families. Still others may have lost their jobs when their employers downsized, or left because they became frustrated with the bureaucracies in large companies.

Consider Natalie Stiles, CEO of Florida-based OCS Consulting Services. "Since I was a little kid," says Stiles, "I've always had something going—shining shoes, washing cars. And I always wanted to own a business." Stiles didn't pursue her dream, however, until after she became frustrated with working for large firms, including General Electric. Stiles found GE's hierarchical corporate culture stifling. "It took days to make decisions," she recalls. "There was no room at the top for mavericks. You were supposed to do what you were told and make your numbers."

Finally, she left to form her own business; many of her GE customers were so satisfied with her work that they followed her. Today, Stiles's company employs 40 people and generates annual revenues of $2.4 million. Stiles relishes her new-found independence to make decisions. "There were a lot of cash constraints at GE," she says. "I didn't have a fax machine there because our office was trying to save money. Now I'll invest money where I think it's going to bring a return." Recently, she experienced what might be the ultimate compliment: her former employer became one of her biggest clients.[24]

HISPANIC-OWNED BUSINESSES

Hispanics are the nation's largest group of minority business owners. During the past 10 years, the U.S. Hispanic population has grown by 53 percent and the number of Hispanic-owned firms has doubled.[25] Many economists foresee more growth ahead for Hispanic-owned businesses, especially as trade between the United States and Latin America increases with the implementation of NAFTA.

Despite their progress, Hispanic entrepreneurs, like other minority business owners, still face some obstacles. Minority entrepreneurs tend to start businesses on a smaller scale and have more difficulty finding investors. For instance, some industry analysts believe that minority entrepreneurs have more trouble buying franchises. At the beginning of the decade, minorities owned only 2.5 percent of U.S. franchises; today, while the number of minority-owned franchises has risen, it is still only 5 percent of the total. Franchise companies have started programs to boost minority participation, but some question remains about their effectiveness. "Some of these in-house initiatives are nothing but smoke and mirrors," claims Susan Kezios, president of Women in Franchising, a Chicago-based association that provides services for women and minorities who are interested in franchising. Minority groups, says Kezios, are "the last markets on franchisors' list of priorities."[26]

San Garza (center) is CEO and majority owner of Counter Technology Inc., a Washington, D.C.–based company that engineers and designs security systems for the aviation industry. According to census data, more than 115,000 U.S. businesses are owned by Hispanic women, but only 14 percent of those have full-time employees. Garza's firm employs 213 and earned $10 million in 1993. Garza's brother, Manuel Ray Garza (left), and her son, Trenton Higareda (right), both work for the business.

BUSINESSES OWNED BY AFRICAN AMERICANS AND OTHER MINORITIES

Over the past decade, the number of companies owned by African Americans has grown by 38 percent, and the total revenue of these firms has risen by 106 percent. This compares to a revenue increase of 55 percent for all U.S. businesses.[27]

The opening story to this chapter described how Homeland Fashions has prospered from a growing interest in African styles. Two other African-American entrepreneurs, T. J. Walker and Carl Jones, have built a business to create urban American fashions.

Walker and Jones decided to go into retailing when they heard friends talking about starting ethnic-clothing stores. The two friends traveled to New York and walked around Brooklyn and Queens to see what urban kids were wearing. Walker toted a sketchpad and jotted down ideas. They pooled their savings to start Threads 4 Life, which designs and sells $70 million worth of colorful, urban-inspired clothes each year. While the company's primary market is young, American blacks, many white teenagers buy the clothes, too. Sales are taking off in Europe and Japan, as well. As Jones says, "Black kids are setting the trends in fashion."[28]

SMALL BUSINESS ADMINISTRATION (SBA)

The **Small Business Administration (SBA)** is the principal government agency concerned with small U.S. firms. It is the advocate for small business within the federal government. The SBA has about 4,000 employees in its Washington headquarters and its various regional and field offices. Its primary operating functions include providing financial assistance, aiding in government procurement matters, and providing management training and consulting.

Small Business Administration (SBA)
Principal government agency concerned with small U.S. firms.

FINANCIAL ASSISTANCE FROM THE SBA

The SBA maintains two basic types of loan programs to help small business: guaranteeing loans made by private lenders and loaning money directly to small firms. The SBA guarantees loans made by private lenders, banks, or other institutions up to 90 per-

Larry and Anna Jo Darnell, co-owners of Momma Jo's and Zeno's Pizza in Wichita Falls, Texas, are recipients of two SBA-backed loans. Their first, in 1979, funded repairs to their restaurant after a tornado. They recently received their second loan to buy new equipment and expand the business to operate cafeterias in three local factories.

cent. Direct SBA loans are available only to applicants that cannot obtain private financing from SBA-guaranteed or participation loans.

The SBA also offers loans for special groups such as disadvantaged or disabled businesspeople, firms involved in energy conservation endeavors, development companies involved in helping small businesses in urban and rural communities, and small companies that are working to develop international markets. The SBA's Green-Line program guarantees 75 percent of a small company's revolving credit lines, up to $750,000.[29]

The SBA also offers "microloans" of less than $25,000 to very small firms. These loans are available from more than 100 sources throughout the United States, most of them not-for-profit business-development groups. Other federal agencies offer microloans, including the federal Economic Development Administration, some state governments, and some private lenders, such as credit unions and community-development groups.[30]

A Small Business Investment Company (SBIC) is an investment group that funds small businesses under an SBA license. An SBIC is set up with private funds. If the Small Business Administration licenses an SBIC, it can borrow up to 400 percent of its capitalization from the government. SBICs provide equity capital as well as fixed-rate loans with 3-year to 10-year durations.

Small Business Investment Company (SBIC)
An investment group that funds small businesses under an SBA license.

OTHER SBA SERVICES

In addition to financial assistance and advice, the SBA provides a variety of other services and publications. It maintains toll-free telephone numbers and on-line computer programs to answer questions. It offers hundreds of publications at little or no cost, and its conferences and seminars are widely available.

The SBA assists small firms in obtaining shares of government contracts. Current legislation requires that small companies receive some government procurement contracts. The **set-aside program** meets this requirement by specifying that only small businesses are eligible for selected government contracts. Any federal agency with buying authority must have an Office of Small and Disadvantaged Business Utilization to assure that these firms receive a reasonable portion of its procurement contracts.

In addition to the regular set-aside program for small firms, the SBA's 8(a) program allows companies owned by "socially and economically disadvantaged individuals" to negotiate government contracts outside the standard competitive bidding procedure. Nearly 4,000 minority-owned firms participate in this program, over 450 of them female-owned. Companies can remain in this program for nine years.

Another valuable SBA service involves providing management training and consulting through a variety of programs. The **Small Business Institute (SBI)** offers the services of business students as consultants on small-business problems at no cost to the firms that request help; the SBI program operates under faculty supervision at hundreds of colleges and universities. **Small Business Development Centers (SBDCs)** help small companies through research and consulting activities, charging fees to offset the costs. The Women's Network for Entrepreneurial Training matches fledgling entrepreneurs with experienced business owners who give advice and help. The **Service Corps of Retired Executives (SCORE)** and the **Active Corps of Executives (ACE)** offer volunteer management consultants who assist people with small business problems.

set-aside program
Legislation that specifies certain government contracts to allot to small businesses.

Small Business Institute (SBI)
SBA program in which business students offer consulting services to small businesses.

Small Business Development Center (SBDC)
SBA program in which college faculty members and others assist small businesses through research and consulting activities, charging fees to offset costs.

Service Corps of Retired Executives (SCORE)
SBA program in which retired executives volunteer as consultants to assist small businesses.

Active Corps of Executives (ACE)
SBA program in which volunteer consultants assist people in small business.

franchising
Agreement that specifies the methods by which a dealer can produce and market a supplier's good or service.

FRANCHISING

The franchising concept has played a major role in the growth of small business. **Franchising** is a contractual business arrangement between a manufacturer or another supplier and a dealer. The contract specifies the methods by which the dealer markets the good or service of the supplier. Franchises can involve both goods and services; some of the best known are Domino's, McDonald's, and Subway.

Starting a small, independent company can be a risky, time-consuming endeavor, but franchising can reduce the amount of time and effort needed to expand. For instance, Ken Rosenthal knew he wanted to start a bakery, but he also knew he wanted to avoid the long hours that this service-oriented industry frequently requires. "I'll never forget one story," he recalls. "This guy was working around the clock. He'd come home, get in the shower, turn on the water, and sit on the floor to rest. And when the hot water ran out and the shower ran cold, it was time to go back to work." When Rosenthal opened a bakery/cafe called the Saint Louis Bread Company, he planned from the beginning to franchise his concept. With a franchise, comments the company's CEO David Hutkin, "You give away a big percentage, and you don't make as much money, but it's a cheaper way to grow."

Thanks to franchising, the Saint Louis Bread Company has grown from one cafe in 1987 to more than 17 today. Rosenthal has two large notebooks filled with inquiries from 400 potential franchisees. Notes Myron Klevens, one of Rosenthal's partners. "We'd like to be kind of the itsy-bitsy spider—here's St. Louis, and here's someplace else, here's someplace else, and sort of link them all up."[31]

FRANCHISING SECTOR

Franchising started just after the Civil War when the Singer Company began to franchise sewing-machine outlets. The concept became increasingly popular after 1900 within the automobile industry. Automobile travel led to demands for gasoline, oil, and tires; makers of all of these commodities employed franchising. Soft-drink and lodging firms offered additional popular franchises.

The concept is growing rapidly. Total U.S. sales from franchising are expected to top $1 trillion by 2000. Franchising is also popular overseas. Franchise sales in Australia, for example, currently amount to $32 billion a year, and are expected to hit $50 billion to $60 billion by the end of the decade.[32] Business format franchises account for 74 percent of the industry, including employment services, quick printing shops, janitorial services, fast-food outlets, and real-estate sales offices.[33]

FRANCHISING AGREEMENTS

franchisee
Small business owner who contracts for the right to sell the goods or services of the supplier (franchisor) in exchange for some payment.

franchisor
Supplier of a franchise that provides various services in exchange for payments by the franchisee.

The two principals in a franchising agreement are the franchisee and the franchisor. The dealer is the **franchisee,** a small business owner who contracts to sell the good or service of the supplier, or **franchisor,** in exchange for some payment (usually a flat fee plus future royalties or commissions). The franchisor typically provides building plans, site selection help, managerial and accounting systems, and other services to assist the franchisee. The franchisor also provides name recognition for the small business owner who becomes a franchisee. This public image is created by advertising campaigns, to which the franchisee typically contributes.

The franchisee purchases both tangible and intangible items from the franchisor. A franchisor may charge a management fee in addition to its initial franchise fee and a percentage of sales or profits. Another may require contributions to a promotional fund. Total costs can vary widely. Start-up costs for a Wendy's fast-food restaurant can run anywhere from $805,000 to $1.3 million. By contrast, start-up costs for a Coverall cleaning service franchise average $2,500.[34]

Many franchisors provide some type of training for new franchisees and franchise employees. The Saint Louis Bread Company, for example, offers 56 training modules on topics such as "Espresso Standards" and "Product Packaging"; different positions within a franchise require workers to complete different combinations of modules. Says Hutkin, "New hires spend 10 hours paid time with a manager getting cross-trained in how to run the register, how to make sandwiches, how to make cappuccino."[35]

BENEFITS AND PROBLEMS OF FRANCHISING

As for any other business property, the buyer of a franchise bears the responsibility to know what he or she is buying. Poorly financed or poorly managed franchise systems are no better than poorly financed or poorly managed independent businesses. Thousands of franchise businesses close each year, and estimates of franchise failure rates range from 30 percent to 50 percent.[36] The franchising concept does not eliminate the risks of a potential small business investment; it merely adds alternatives.

Advantages of franchises include the availability of a performance record, a recognizable company name, a tested management program, and business training. An existing franchise has a performance record on which the prospective buyer can make comparisons and judgments. Earlier results can indicate the likelihood of success in a proposed venture. In addition, a widely recognized name gives the franchisee a tremendous advantage; car dealers, for instance, know that their brand-name products will attract given clienteles. A tested management program usually allows the prospective franchisee to avoid worrying about setting up an accounting system, establishing quality control standards, or designing employment application forms. In addition, some franchisors offer valuable business training. McDonald's, for instance, teaches franchise basics at its Hamburger University in Oak Brook, Illinois.

On the negative side, franchise fees and future payments can be very expensive. Good franchises with tested management systems, proven performance records, and widely recognized names usually sell for more than those without such benefits. Prospective franchisees must decide whether the franchise offers a product worth the expenses involved.

For another potential drawback, the franchisee is judged by the actions of his or her peers. A successful franchise unit can lose customers if other units of the same franchise fail. A strong, effective program of managerial control is essential to offset any bad impressions created by unsuccessful franchises.

Finally, someone who is considering buying a franchise must think first about whether he or she has the right personality for the endeavor. Earlier, this chapter mentioned that the skills that make a good entrepreneur are not necessarily the same as the skills that make a good business owner. Along with the franchise, a franchisee buys the corporate culture and procedures of the larger firm. A highly independent, entrepreneurial person may find this frustrating and prefer to operate independently. However, many people have found franchising to offer a great mix, with some of the benefits of independent business ownership, but without some of the risks.

SMALL BUSINESS GOES GLOBAL

Small businesses used to ignore overseas markets. However, with exports becoming ever more important to the U.S. economy, and with the development of a worldwide economy, more small firms are going global.

PROBLEMS IN FINANCING GLOBAL EXPANSION

Small companies may face more difficulty than large firms in entering international markets. Lack of funding creates a big barrier; small companies are less likely to qualify for loans from banks and other traditional lenders. "There's supposedly billions of dollars in capital out there, but not much is going the way of small businesses that have sales of less than $2 million and need a $500,000 loan," says Miles Spencer, a principal with investment bank Norwalk Associates. A Federal Reserve survey of loan officers shows that only 6 out of 57 banks have eased credit standards for small company borrowers.[37]

Rather than searching for sources of private funds, some small business owners look for lower-risk ways to enter international markets. Licensing, franchising, and exporting through intermediaries offer three possible strategies.

STRENGTH IN DIVERSITY

RENEWED COMMITMENT TO DIVERSITY AT BURGER KING In 1983, Burger King made a commitment to Operation PUSH that it would create more opportunities for minorities. Still, the company has been criticized for its lack of progress in this area. Lawrence Otis Graham, a black former Wall Street lawyer, cited Burger King as having one of the lowest rates of minority participation in management. In his book *The Best Companies for Minorities,* Graham claimed that Burger King had filled less than 5 percent of its management positions with minorities. The company's Atlanta office also faces a pending racial discrimination suit. ■ Burger King has now taken positive steps to encourage and help minorities with new business opportunities. The company unveiled its "Eight-Point Plan" backed by a commitment of $100 million to support ethnic franchisees and suppliers over a five-year period. The company is also devoting $500,000 to underwrite and sponsor minority community events. The plan targets minority groups like African Americans, Asians, Hispanics, and Native Americans. ■ Burger King has allocated $50 million toward start-up capital for suppliers. Minority suppliers will be offered loan guarantees and, in some cases, actual loans in return for shares of their profits. The other $50 million will be used to help minority franchisees buy or develop restaurant sites. Funds will go for loan guarantees, leasing, and capital restructuring costs. The program will be overseen by Burger King's Diversity Action Council, a group of four Burger King executives and ten minority community leaders and business owners. Reverend Willie T. Barrow, a member of the committee and chairperson of Operation PUSH, says, "We will closely monitor the company's processes and progress in franchising, procurement, banking, marketing, advertising, employment, and nonprofit giving. We want to make sure that Burger King's customer base—40 percent minority—is

LICENSING AND FRANCHISING

Chapter 3 introduced the concept of licensing. This represents the most limited way to enter a foreign market. Under a licensing agreement, one firm allows another to use its intellectual property in exchange for compensation in the form of royalties. Examples of intellectual property include trademarks, patents, copyrights, and technical know-how. For instance, a firm that has developed a new type of packaging might license the process to other companies abroad.

Licensing can give a firm access to a foreign market that is closed to more direct forms of exporting and investment. It also allows a firm to enter a new market with a proven concept. Licensing does not guarantee future expansion, though. In fact, the licensing company may end up creating its own competitor in that market![38]

Franchising, another way for small firms to enter foreign markets, is actually a type of licensing in which the franchisor grants the franchisee the right to do business in a prescribed manner. Worldwide, franchising is growing 2.5 percent a year compared to an overall global business growth rate of 2.3 percent. About 15 to 20 percent of U.S. franchisors have overseas outlets. Canada is the biggest market for U.S. franchises, followed by Japan, continental Europe, Australia, and the United Kingdom.[39] Some franchises that have become popular in the United States actually started in other countries. Today, 2,000 to 3,000 foreign companies in 60 industries have franchises in the United States.

A franchise owner may establish a presence in a new market by taking up permanent residence there. David West, a former investment banker, has no plans to return to his native New York. West is now general manager of Tower Records' Mexican sub-

reflected in terms of franchises and suppliers." ■ Burger King has received over 1,200 inquiries about the program. Stephen B. Singletary, a Burger King franchisee who owns 15 restaurants in four states, saw the program as an opportunity and took advantage of it. Burger King and Hudson Foods, Inc., one of the country's largest producers of poultry products, are backing the creation of Diversity Food Processing LLC in Petersburg, Virginia. As president and CEO, Singletary will own 62 percent of the company while Burger King and Hudson will divide the remaining shares. ■ Diversity Food Processing will be one of the largest black-owned companies in the United States. Restaurant Services Inc. in Miami helped to make the deal possible. RSI's agreement to purchase beef products from Diversity allowed the new company to obtain financing. Diversity expects sales to reach $125 million annually by supplying beef products to Burger King restaurants and to grocery stores. ■ Burger King pledged to Operation PUSH 10 years ago that 15 percent of its restaurants would be owned by minorities. Burger King is close to fulfilling its promise since minorities now own 14 percent of its 6,200 U.S. outlets. African Americans own 3.5 percent. Burger King is hoping that its new program will increase these numbers. The company is looking for businesspeople who can own and manage multiple restaurants for Burger King. Scott Colabuono, Burger King's chief financial officer and Diversity Action Council chairperson, says, "We are growing the field with seed money but our goal is to get African-American franchise owners to expand in terms of multiple units and locations." Burger King is also considering nontraditional locations anchored by other businesses and institutions such as convenience stores, toll-road stops, and college campuses. One such example is the Burger King restaurant that recently opened at Xavier University in New Orleans. The owner is Cedric Smith, a black owner of four other Burger Kings. The company will target historically black colleges as part of its program. Sources: Mark Lowery, "Burger King's Black Meat Processing Plant," *Black Enterprise,* November, 1994, p. 26; Carolyn M. Brown, "More than Just Window Dressing?" *Black Enterprise,* September, 1994, p. 103; David Poppe, "Minorities Say Burger King's Actions Thwarted Their Success as Franchisees," *Miami Daily Business Review,* January 7, 1994, p. A6; and "Burger King Pledges $100M to Help Boost Minority Participation," *Jet,* December 27, 1993, p. 46.

QUESTIONS FOR CRITICAL THINKING

1. What other types of programs should Burger King create in support of minorities?
2. If you were supervising Burger King's "Eight-Point Plan," how and to whom would you advertise the program?
3. What other nontraditional means of distribution might Burger King consider to promote minority ownership?

sidiary, which operates several franchises. His perks include weekends at the nearby mountain resort of Cuernavaca. In Mexico, he notes, "There's more free time for my wife and myself."[40]

EXPORTING THROUGH INTERMEDIARIES

Sometimes a small firm can achieve export success by teaming up with another firm that can provide services that the small company could not afford on its own. An **export management company** is a domestic firm that specializes in performing international marketing services as a commissioned representative or distributor for other companies. For another option, a small firm might work with an **export trading company,** a general trading firm that plays varied roles in world commerce by importing, exporting, countertrading, investing, and manufacturing.

export management company *Firm that performs international marketing services as a commissioned representative or distributor for other companies.*

export trading company *Trading firm involved in importing, exporting, countertrading, investing, and manufacturing.*

Some companies may play both roles. New Jersey–based Medical International Inc. helps over 70 U.S. manufacturers to market their health-care equipment and supplies abroad. Medical International's export services include researching markets, establishing foreign sales outlets, promoting products, handling correspondence, arranging for financing and payment, shipping merchandise, and representing clients at international trade shows. Says Export Manager Carol Myers, "Small- and medium-sized U.S. companies think it's great to have our expertise selling their products. Many of them wouldn't export at all on their own. Some get an unsolicited foreign order, and it sits on their desks for a long time and ends up in the trash can. The smaller companies don't know about such matters as letters of credit. They just don't feel comfortable with international marketing."[41] By its third year of operation, Medical International was selling more than $800,000 worth of products in Asia, Latin American, Europe, Africa, and the Middle East.

CREATING A BUSINESS PLAN

business plan
A written document that provides an orderly statement of a company's goals, how it intends to achieve its goals, and the standards by which it will measure achievements.

Creating a business plan represents perhaps the most important task that an entrepreneur faces. An effective business plan can make the difference between a company that succeeds and one that fails. A **business plan** is a written document that provides an orderly statement of a company's goals, how it intends to achieve those goals, and the standards by which it will measure achievements. Notes Raymond Boggs, an economist at business research firm BIS Strategic Decisions, "Whether the plan calls for fast growth or slow doesn't matter much. When you do a business plan, you're forced to make your assumptions explicit and to challenge them."[42]

Planning usually works best if the whole organization participates. Planning can combine ideas and communicate information while making everyone a part of the team.

The small business owner must follow no one format for a business plan, but almost all plans detail time frames for achieving specific goals, flows of money (both income and expenses), and units of achievement (in subjective and numerical terms). A business plan should also cover the methods by which the firm will achieve goals, procedures it will follow, and values that it holds important. Perhaps most importantly, the plan should always be open to revision.

Before writing a plan, the business owner should answer some questions. How would you explain your idea to a friend? What purpose does your business serve? How does your idea differ from existing businesses? What is the state of the industry you are entering? Who does your customer or client base include? How will you market the firm's goods or services? How much will you charge? How will you finance your business? What qualifies you to run this business?

Give special attention to the name of your business. Does the name reflect the firm's goals? Is it already registered by someone else? Does it have any hidden meanings to other people? What does it mean phonetically in other languages? Is it offensive to any religious or ethnic group?

Juan Faxas' business, Glomar, Inc., makes professional-quality baseball bats. The Major League Baseball strike of 1994 cost Glomar 94 percent of its market, but the company's business plan provided it with direction and alternatives; the company pursued retailing and achieved significant sales at sporting goods stores and batting-cage parks.

Be sure to do adequate research. Trade journals are excellent sources of industry-related information. The Small Business Administration and the local library can also assist you with research. It helps to talk to suppliers in the industry and to local licensing authorities. How many similar businesses have succeeded? How many have failed? Why? What risks are specific to your industry? What markups are typical? What are common levels of expenses and profit percentages?

Components of a business plan might include:

- An executive summary that answers the who, what, why, when, where, and how questions for the business in brief. (Although the summary appears early in the plan, it probably should be written last.)
- An introduction that gives a general statement of the concept, purpose, and objectives of the proposed business, along with an overview of the industry. It should include a brief description of the owner's education, experience, and training and should refer to a résumé included later in the plan.
- A section on marketing that describes the firm's target market, its anticipated competitors, and plans for distribution, advertising, pricing, and location of facilities. This section should cover the background of the industry and industry trends as well as the potential of the new venture. It should also point out any unique or distinctive features of the business and explain the reasons for a particular start-up date.
- Other topics to be included in the marketing section include rental, leasing, or purchase costs, and the influences of traffic volume, neighboring businesses, demographics, parking, accessibility, and visibility. Further discussion should review labor costs, utility access and rates, police and fire protection, zoning restrictions, and other government rules and regulations.
- A section that details an operating plan forecast, a plan for obtaining capital, and a description of plans for spending funds.
- A section that estimates assets and liabilities and analyzes when the break-even point will occur.
- Plans written to obtain funding should include résumés of the principals of the business.

A business plan should cover some other topics, including whether the firm will be a sole proprietorship, partnership, or corporation; when it will need to hire employees and what job descriptions will guide their work; the lines of authority in the business; a risk management plan, including detailed information on insurance; a list of suppliers and methods for assessing their reliability and competence; and a policy for extending credit to customers.

The financial part of the business plan requires particular attention to detail. If the plan becomes part of a request for financing, the banker will look at the owner's management skills and experience, the risk of the enterprise, collateral, and the ability to repay the loan. In reviewing a plan for venture capital, however, the venture capitalist will look at the potential for profits and growth and not so much at downside risks.

If certain assumptions underlie the body of the plan, tie them into the financial section. A plan for two outlets, for example, should provide cash flow projections that show how the firm will pay for them. Deal with both significant and insignificant variables. The bankers or investors who analyze a plan may not know whether it will cost $250 or $25,000 to install an exotic, high-tech part, but they will know that a telephone system for 50 people will cost more than $250 per month. Carelessness with seemingly insignificant variables can undercut credibility.

Itemize monthly expenses rather than simply projecting annual amounts. A firm with $100,000 in annual costs may not spend $8,000 each month. It must pay some expenses monthly and some annually. An owner who must cover a lot of annual payments up front will be running back to financiers in the first month to explain problems with the cash flow projection. This is not a good way to start.

A plan must state all assumptions it makes about the conditions under which the firm will operate. Besides cash flow projections, it should also project a detailed profit-and-loss statement.

The assembled plan should offer a table of contents so that readers can turn directly to those parts of the plan that interest them most. Make sure that the plan is presented in an attractive and professional format.[43]

ACHIEVEMENT CHECK SUMMARY

Reread the learning goals that follow, and consider the questions for each goal. Answering these questions will reinforce the most important concepts in the chapter and allow you to check how well you have achieved these learning goals. Where a blank appears before a question, answer with *T* or *F*. Otherwise, circle the letter of the correct answer. An answer key to these questions is found at the end of this chapter.

LEARNING GOAL 6.1: Explain the vital role that entrepreneurs and small businesses play in the global economy.

1. ___ It is fair to say that a strong small business sector is the backbone of the private enterprise system.
2. ___ In the United States, the number of small businesses is declining.
3. ___ Small businesses annually create very few new jobs.

LEARNING GOAL 6.2: Define entrepreneurship, and describe how entrepreneurs differ from other businesspeople.

1. ___ An entrepreneur is a risk taker.
2. ___ Successful entrepreneurs rarely have college degrees.
3. ___ An entrepreneur generally has several defining characteristics, including a high tolerance for ambiguity, a high need for achievement, and a high energy level.

LEARNING GOAL 6.3: Define small business, and identify the industries in which most small firms are established.

1. The Small Business Administration defines a small business as one that: (a) is independently owned and managed; (b) represents a small part of its industry; (c) obtains capital from a limited number of people; (d) all of the above.
2. Many small businesses are found in: (a) retailing; (b) farming; (c) high-tech; (d) services; (e) all of the above.

LEARNING GOAL 6.4: Compare the advantages and disadvantages of small business.

1. ___ Small businesses bring innovation to the economy and fill isolated market niches.
2. ___ Inadequate management skill and limited access to financing are leading causes of small business failures.

LEARNING GOAL 6.5: Analyze the small business opportunities for women and minorities and the special challenges that face these entrepreneurs.

1. ___ The number of women-owned and minority-owned businesses is increasing.
2. ___ Of the minority groups, Hispanics own the largest number of small businesses.
3. ___ Women-owned and minority-owned businesses tend to be less vulnerable than other entrepreneurs during downswings in the economy.

LEARNING GOAL 6.6: Describe how the Small Business Administration functions.

1. The Small Business Administration (SBA): (a) is the federal agency that serves as a small-business advocate; (b) is a private, not-for-profit organization that serves as a small-business advocate; (c) is headquartered in New York; (d) takes over failed businesses.
2. The major function of the SBA is to: (a) provide financial assistance to small business; (b) aid small businesses in government procurement matters; (c) provide management training and consulting; (d) all of the above.

LEARNING GOAL 6.7: Outline the role of franchising in the U.S. economy, and list its advantages and disadvantages.

1. ___ A franchise is a contract between a manufacturer or supplier and a dealer that specifies the methods by which to market a good or service.
2. ___ A well-established franchise is cheaper to open than an independent small business.

LEARNING GOAL 6.8: Outline the popular methods of small business operation in the global market.

1. ___ Franchising is a widely used method to enter international markets.
2. ___ Foreign licensing can help a firm enter a foreign market that is otherwise closed to more direct forms of exporting.
3. ___ It is illegal for small businesses to use export management companies or export trading companies in their efforts to penetrate foreign markets.

LEARNING GOAL 6.9: Outline the components of a business plan.

1. A good business plan should spell out: (a) an evaluation of the business owner and the industry; (b) a marketing plan; (c) a financial plan; (d) all of the above.
2. The purpose of a business plan should be to: (a) clarify and challenge the entrepreneur's ideas for a business; (b) create a

document to inform potential investors, lenders, or suppliers; (c) decide upon the business's organization and structure; (d) all of the above.

KEY TERMS

business incubator 120
small business 122
venture capitalist 129
Small Business Administration (SBA) 132
Small Business Investment Company (SBIC) 133
set-aside program 133
Small Business Institute (SBI) 133
Small Business Development Center (SBDC) 133
Service Corps of Retired Executives (SCORE) 133
Active Corps of Executives (ACE) 133
franchising 133
franchisee 134
franchisor 134
export management company 137
export trading company 137
business plan 138

REVIEW QUESTIONS

1. Define the terms *entrepreneurship* and *small business.* Why are entrepreneurs so important to private enterprise?

2. How does entrepreneurship differ from other kinds of management? Cite some examples.

3. In what sectors of the U.S. economy is small business most important? To what do you credit its strengths in these areas?

4. Outline the advantages that small firms have over larger ones. Cite an example of each advantage.

5. Why is financing such a major problem for a small business? Explain how to overcome this disadvantage.

6. Describe the current status of women in small business. Discuss the reasons for this situation.

7. What is the current status of minorities in small business?

8. Explain the primary functions of the Small Business Administration. How does it perform these functions?

9. What is franchising? Why is it such a vital element of the small business sector?

10. The chapter notes that a written business plan can make the difference between success and failure in an entrepreneurial venture. Why do you think this is so?

DISCUSSION QUESTIONS

1. Choose an entrepreneur or small business owner in your area and interview him or her about the experience of owning one's own business. What advice would this person give about starting a business? What mistakes do new business owners commonly make? Share your findings with the class.

2. Chapter 6 discussed the skills that an entrepreneur, a manager, and a franchise owner need. Which of these occupations would best suit your skills and personality? Explain honestly.

3. Choose a franchise company that operates outlets both in the United States and in other countries. Compare the operations of the U.S. outlets with those of outlets in at least two foreign countries. Are they different, and if so, in what ways? (For instance, you could compare the menu of an American fast-food franchise with its menus in other nations.) If you find differences, explain why you think they exist.

4. Why don't more small U.S. firms export their products? What do you think would encourage them to do so?

5. Suppose that you have decided to start your own company. Write a brief business plan for your business. Include the major components described in this chapter.

SOLUTIONS TO ACHIEVEMENT CHECK SUMMARY

L.G. 6.1: 1. T, 2. F, 3. F **L.G. 6.2:** 1. T, 2. F, 3. T **L.G. 6.3:** 1. d, 2. e **L.G. 6.4:** 1. T, 2. T **L.G. 6.5:** 1. T, 2. T, 3. F **L.G. 6.6:** 1. a, 2. d **L.G. 6.7:** 1. T, 2. F **L.G. 6.8:** 1. T, 2. T, 3. F **L.G. 6.9:** 1. d, 2. d.

VIDEO CASE

SLAZENGER GOLF Entrepreneurs and small business owners play a vital role in today's economy, and more people than ever seem to be willing to accept the risks of small business ownership in order to work for themselves. But contemporary business is highly competitive and often international in scope, and entrepreneurs have to plan carefully in order to succeed. That was the challenge facing David R. Branon and Geoffrey W. Gorman when they founded David•Geoffrey and Associates in 1987.

David•Geoffrey and Associates produces golf balls, golf clubs, golf accessories and apparel for a market loaded with big name brands and where high volume, but low margin sales are the norm. Branon and Gorman knew that they had to find an innovative way to reach golfers if they were going to succeed. Since they weren't a large organization with huge overhead costs, they knew they could be profitable selling smaller numbers of golf balls and equipment than their competitors. With that in mind, their competitive strategy involved selecting those segments of the market where price was not of prime importance and then finding a way to gain an advantage.

First, Branon and Gorman realized they needed to target a segment of the golfing market that had a high level of discretionary income, that played primarily at private country clubs, and that played a higher than average number of rounds of golf in any given year. Looking closely at marketing research, the partners realized that the players who fit these requirements were generally men in their fifties with an average income of almost $80,000.[44] These players, dubbed the "Country Club Traditionals," were likely to spend more for apparel, merchandise, and other course items than any of the other six groups surveyed. In fact, they outspent the other groups by several thousand dollars.

Once Branon and Gorman had identified their target market, they needed an innovative strategy for reaching it. They knew that a successful strategy would have to enlist the aid of local golf pros across the country, since the pros had the greatest influence on the purchasing patterns of the target group. They decided to license the rights to their brand name, Slazenger, in a way that would benefit the pros. In order to do this, they instituted two restrictions which they refused to waive under any circumstance. First, in order to sell Slazenger equipment and apparel, the pro shop had to be an "on course" shop; second, the Slazenger products could not be sold to anyone who intended to resell them elsewhere. In essence, this authorized account agreement grants exclusive channels of distribution to on course pro golf shops, allowing sellers of Slazenger products to maintain higher prices and better profit margins, since they are not competing with high-volume discount stores.

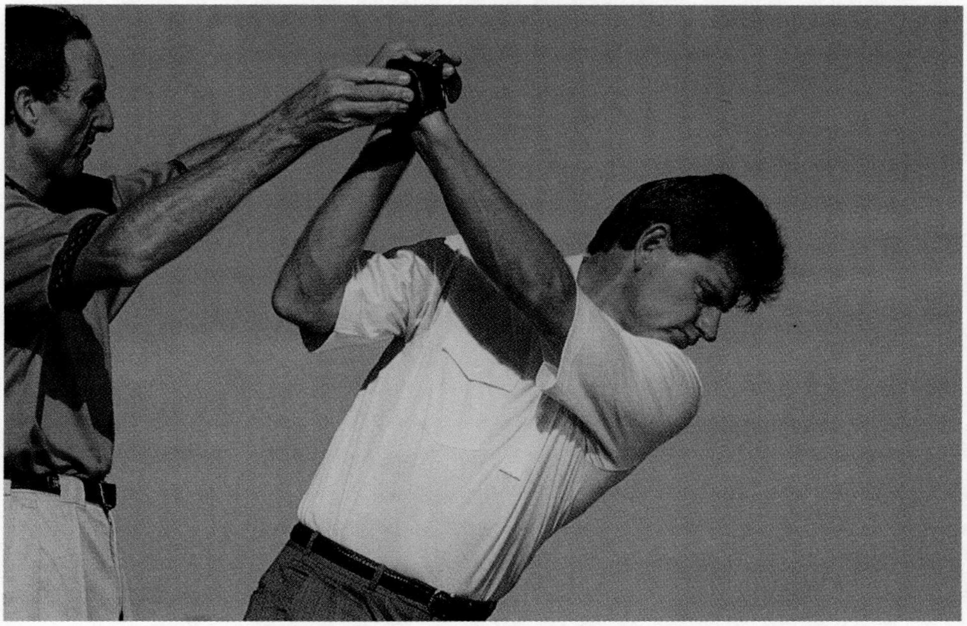

In case that wasn't enough, David•Geoffrey and Associates also developed a "Slazenger Founders' Club" program for golf professionals. Once a golf shop reaches a qualifying level of $5,000 in annual sales, the company contributes predetermined amounts of money against each invoice into a tax-sheltered retirement/annuity plan in the professional's name. The golf pros automatically add to a nest egg for their future with every sale—an arrangement that provides an additional incentive for supporting the Slazenger line.

These innovative strategies have paid off for David•Geoffrey and Associates. Sales in a recent year were slightly over $43 million. Their example should provide encouragement for other entrepreneurs who need to develop a successful marketing strategy of their own.

1.
What are the advantages and disadvantages of being a relatively small company in the golf equipment and apparel market in the United States?

2.
What special problems might a small company like Slazenger face if it wanted to expand its market to include golf enthusiasts besides the country-club set?

3.
Develop an ongoing business plan for Slazenger. Where do you think they should direct their efforts in the future?

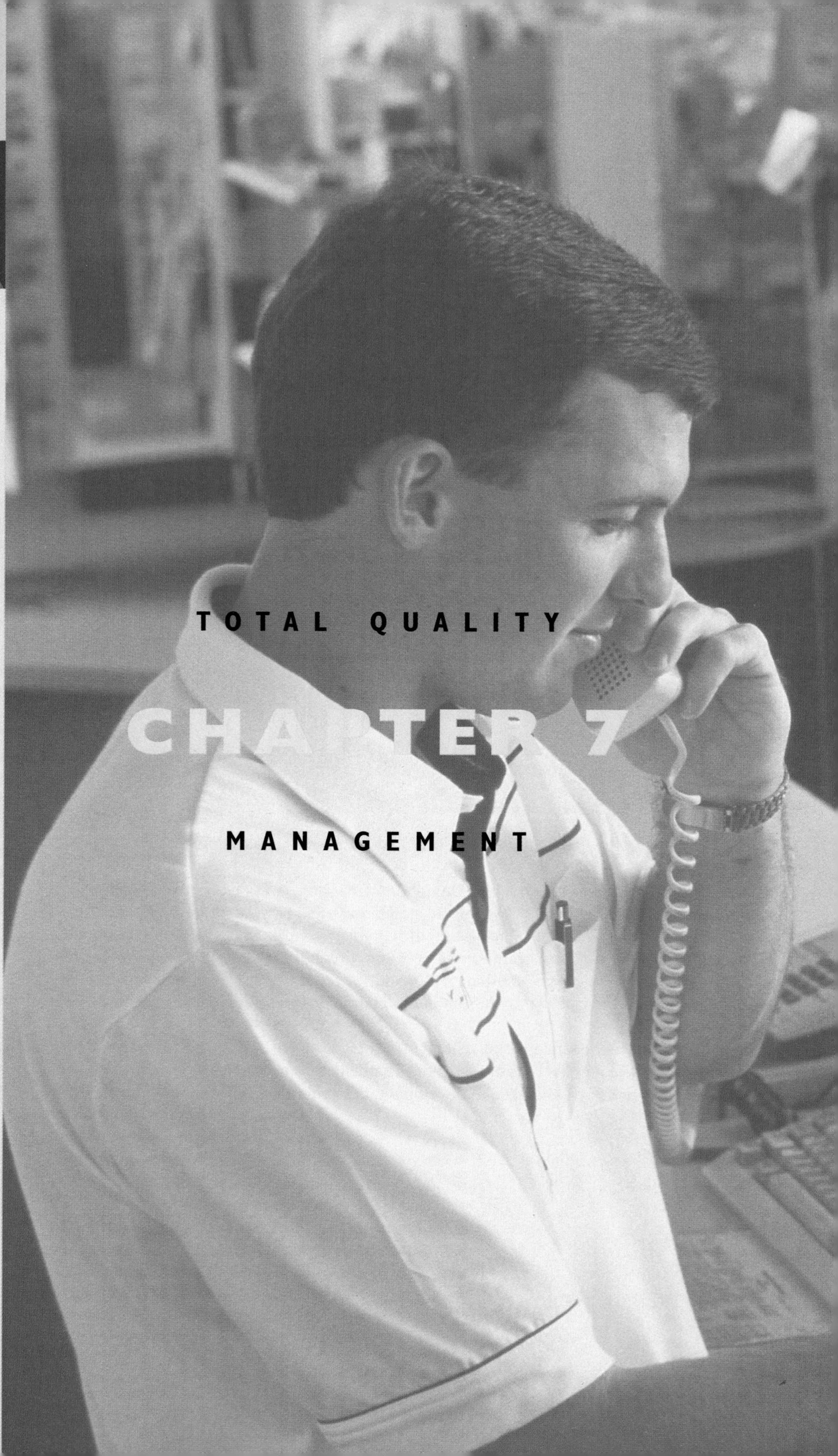

CHAPTER 7

TOTAL QUALITY MANAGEMENT

LEARNING GOALS

1. Explain the importance of quality and customer satisfaction in achieving a competitive advantage.

2. Summarize the status of quality programs in the United States, Japan, and Europe.

3. Discuss the role of top management in applying total quality management (TQM) to an organization.

4. Relate TQM to various functions within an organization, including production, human resource management, marketing, information processing, and financial management.

5. Identify the major methods of securing feedback from customers, employees, and suppliers.

6. Describe how an organization can work toward continuous process improvement.

7. Define benchmarking and explain its contributions to quality and customer satisfaction.

8. Identify the components of employee involvement and their impact on quality and customer satisfaction.

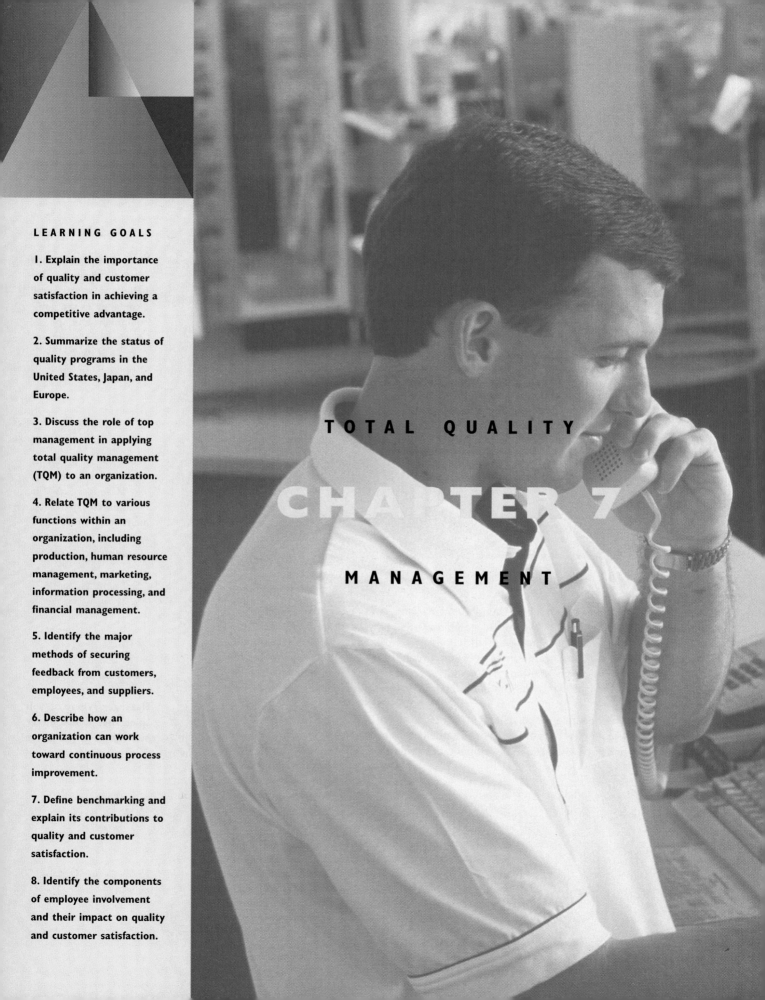

AT&T SWEEPS QUALITY AWARDS

The competition for the 1994 Malcolm Baldrige National Quality Award, America's top prize for organizational quality, involved 71 companies. Only 3 of them won. GTE Directories and Wainwright Industries were first-time winners, while AT&T captured an unprecedented third Baldrige Award. The U.S. telecommunications giant went on to accomplish another first that same year when it became a double award winner by capturing the highest quality award presented by the Japanese, the Deming Prize. Says AT&T CEO Robert Allen, "I feel like we won both the World Series and the World Cup on the same day!" ■ The primary function of AT&T Consumer Communications Services, the division that received one of the Baldrige awards, is to provide long-distance service to the residential market. Its alternative long-distance calling plans—True Rewards, True USA, and True World Savings—attracted 25 million customers in just 9 months. By contrast, MCI's Friends and Family program took 3 years to get just 10 million customers. ■ Under the leadership of Joseph Nacchio, AT&T Consumer Communications Services has undergone a major transformation that culminated in its receipt of the Deming Prize. In an era of competition from MCI, Sprint, and dozens of smaller companies, Nacchio has brought on board new managers from firms as far afield from the telecommunications industry as Revlon. Although these managers lack communications industry experience, they know how to respond adeptly to customer needs and changing competitive environments. They are also experienced in using market research to find new customers. ■ The division's managers run it much differently than the way it ran a decade ago. AT&T's new emphasis on empowering employees has resulted in many of the improvements that positioned it to receive the national quality awards. Nacchio describes the changes this way: "It's night and day, black and white." ■ Other divisions are also benefiting from these corporate changes. Since implementing quality programs in its 2,400-employee Texas plant, AT&T Power Systems has increased its customer base sixfold, cut inventories in half, and is now recycling 98 percent of its reusable materials. This AT&T division, which makes electrical power systems for telecommunications equipment, has accomplished all of this by shifting decision-making power from managers to front-line employees. At any one time, the division has 250 to 300 employee groups working to improve operations. ■ AT&T top managers encourage quality initiatives, provided they meet strict company criteria. Any new quality program must first demonstrate that it can yield at least a 30 percent reduction in defects and a 10 percent return on funds invested in the program. "It isn't the old 'Give me money and I'll fix it' stuff," explains one corporate quality officer. "We're taking the cost out of making our system better." ■ Quality has become one of the most important issues in today's business environment. A company reaps more than financial rewards when it makes quality improvement an integral part of its operations; employee morale soars when the collective efforts of a work force are recognized in the form of a national award. As one quality consultant points out, aiming for the Steuben-designed Baldrige Award or the Deming Prize "gives people focus and reasons to do all the things they should be doing anyway."[1]

The Sound Of Your Voice Helped Us Win This Award.
1994 Malcolm Baldrige National Quality Award
October 1994. AT&T Consumer Long Distance wins nation's highest quality award.
Providing you with superb long distance service doesn't just mean giving you the best sound quality. It also means listening and learning exactly what you want and need. That's how quality is achieved; and that's just what the *Malcolm Baldrige National Quality Award* is all about. You see, true quality doesn't just happen. It takes the commitment of every man and woman who works here. All 44,000 of us. And to have that commitment recognized makes us all feel pretty good. *1 800-896-8600.*
AT&T. Your True Voice.℠
AT&T
AT&T Consumer Long Distance is the business of AT&T Consumer Communications Services.

CHAPTER OVERVIEW

Managing for quality to provide complete customer satisfaction is essential for a firm to survive and thrive in today's competitive global marketplace. Like AT&T, many U.S. companies have learned the hard-won lesson that their long-term success depends on delivering superior quality goods and services at good value. Quality-conscious companies such as AT&T involve employees from finance, production, marketing, and every other business function in understanding and satisfying customer needs and wants. In fact, a company that commits itself to quality becomes so customer-focused that it manages its operations according to its customers' definitions of quality. Stew Leonard's, the Norwalk, Connecticut-based supermarket, has this philosophy statement etched on a large boulder at the store's front entrance: "Rule 1: The customer is always right," says the motto. "Rule 2: When the customer is wrong, reread Rule 1."

quality
Degree of excellence or superiority of an organization's goods and services.

customer satisfaction
Concept of a good or service pleasing buyers because it meets their emotional needs and quality expectations.

This chapter discusses the role of customer-focused quality in building competitive advantage. To help you understand why the issue of quality is a critical challenge facing U.S. firms, as well as their foreign competitors, the chapter begins by examining the importance of quality and customer satisfaction and looking at quality programs in the United States, Japan, and Europe. It then discusses ways to apply total quality management to each function of the organization and ways to obtain feedback. Finally, it examines the critical quality issues of continuous process improvement, benchmarking, and employee involvement.

IMPORTANCE OF QUALITY AND CUSTOMER SATISFACTION

Quality describes the degree of excellence or superiority of an organization's goods and services. The term *quality* has a broad meaning that encompasses both the tangible and intangible characteristics of a good or service. Tangible characteristics include such physical traits as durability and reliability. The overall definition of quality also includes the intangible component of **customer satisfaction,** the concept of a good or service pleasing buyers because it meets their emotional needs and quality expectations. The true measure of quality is whether a firm satisfies its customers.

The Coca-Cola Company faces the task of providing consistent product quality in more than 195 countries around the world. In addition, it must provide vigorous customer service to the 8 million retail outlets that sell Coca-Cola products. As the advertising headline in Figure 7.1 states, the firm's commitment to quality is judged millions

FIGURE 7.1

COCA-COLA: CUSTOMER SATISFACTION BASED ON PRODUCT QUALITY AND SERVICE.

of times every day—each time someone enjoys a Coke. As author and consultant A. V. Feigenbaum notes, "Quality is what your customers say it is—not what you say it is."[2]

Organizations throughout the world are working to offer high-quality goods and services that create customer satisfaction through **total quality management (TQM),** an approach that involves a commitment to quality in achieving world-class performance and customer satisfaction as a crucial strategic objective for an entire company. In a total quality organization, marketers develop products that people want to buy, engineers design products to work the way customers want to use them, production workers build quality into every product they make, salespeople deliver what they promise to customers, information systems specialists use technology to ensure that the firm fills customer orders correctly and on time, and financial managers help to determine prices that give value to customers.

total quality management (TQM) *Companywide commitment to quality in achieving world-class performance and customer satisfaction as a crucial strategic objective.*

As Ray Stata, CEO of integrated-circuit maker Analog Devices, puts it, "Total quality essentially involves attention to process, commitment to the customer, involvement of employees, and benchmarking of best practices. It is hard to believe you cannot benefit from that."[3]

Does quality pay? Absolutely! Studies show that quality programs can boost company revenues by as much as 40 percent while decreasing production costs 20 to 50 percent, saving 40 percent on space and inventory, cutting production time by as much as 70 percent, and building strong customer loyalty.

As TQM grows, a growing number of quality-conscious organizations are stressing the return on quality investments. Companies focus their efforts to improve quality on measures that produce tangible customer benefits while lowering costs or increasing sales.[4] For example:

- When GTE set up a program to encourage questions and suggestions, it found that customers who called and complained were also more likely to drop cellular service. GTE upgraded its system to stop complaints in the first place.

Analog Devices CEO Ray Stata not only believes in TQM, he is convinced that top management must get personally involved to make his company's quality drive work.

BUSINESS IN ACTION

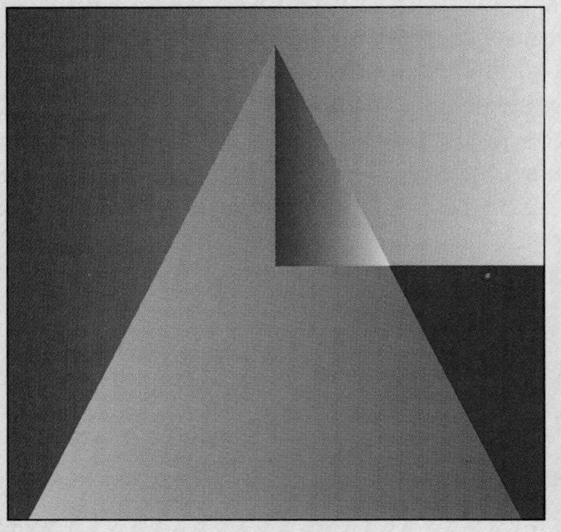

WEGMANS Ask typical Rochester, New York, residents the name of the firm they're most proud of and chances are you won't get Eastman Kodak or Xerox for an answer. Instead, you are likely to hear the name of the local grocery chain. Even though people outside New York have probably never heard of the firm, Wegmans Food Markets is a powerhouse of quality and overall excellence in the grocery business. The 90-year-old chain of about 50 outlets controls over half of the Rochester market and is rapidly making headway across the state. The stores are big, the freshness and quality of the products are unsurpassed, and the profits are soaring—an estimated four times as high as those of competing supermarkets. ■ Perhaps the most important factor in Wegmans' success is product quality. With the stores' enormous sales volume, workers restock food categories like produce as often as 12 times a day. Local suppliers bypass warehouses and deliver produce directly to individual stores. New York apple growers have even developed special fruit boxes for Wegmans that go directly onto a store display. This direct movement from supplier to Wegmans store shelves slashes shipping and handling costs, while also providing shoppers the freshest produce possible. ■ Wegmans' attention to quality also prevents substandard products from ever appearing on the store shelves. Some suppliers have learned this the hard way. "Once you turn down a few loads of pears or strawberries, whether it's from Chile, California, or Mexico, people don't waste their time, money, or effort to send produce we'll reject," says CEO Robert Wegman. ■ Customer service is an indispensable factor in the Wegmans' success formula. Store inventories are modified to reflect differences in food preferences in different geographic areas. Individual stores stock Polish or Jewish specialty products to reflect food-purchasing patterns of different neighborhoods. ■ Wegmans also goes out of its way to stock produce from local growers, featuring the growers by name and region. As Daniel Wegman, son of the firm's CEO, puts it, "As years went on, we realized people liked home-grown products." ■ A high-quality work force of 23,000 employees also contributes to Wegmans' success. Employees receive competitive wages and benefits and participate in a companywide profit-sharing program. The work force, attention to customers, and the commitment to provide high-quality, competitively priced products combine to make Wegmans the Nordstrom's of the supermarket industry. As one industry consultant put it, "We consider them the best chain in the country, maybe in the world. They have created something that gets the customer beyond price." Source: Quotations from Wendy Bounds, "As Big as Kodak Is in Rochester, N.Y., It Still Isn't Wegmans," *The Wall Street Journal,* December 27, 1994, pp. A1, A6.

QUESTIONS FOR CRITICAL THINKING

1. What do you think would happen to sales and profits if Wegmans offered a lower quality grade of produce?
2. What would be the pros and cons of having produce delivered to a Wegmans' warehouse rather than to individual stores?
3. What would be the results if Wegmans only restocked six times per day rather than 12?

- Instead of stressing prompt delivery at any cost, UPS is scheduling free time for drivers to talk with customers. The objective is to produce millions in additional sales by improving customer relations and developing new sales leads.
- Rather than just pushing workers to meet strict package-sorting goals, Federal Express is investing in sorting equipment to cut down on misdirected packages, which can cost the company $50 each.

In addition to generating financial returns from reduced costs, increased satisfaction, and added sales, quality-improvement programs are essential if firms are to keep up with their competitors. As more companies worldwide apply the principles of total quality management, standards rise. Chey Jong-Hyon, chairman of Korean petroleum products maker Sunkyong Group, notes, "If we merely try to be excellent, our gap with the world's top companies will remain because they keep improving. Only by seeking super-excellence can we reach their level or overtake them." Or, to quote Ram Charan, quality consultant to many of the world's largest companies: "If you're not *better* than the best on a worldwide basis, you're not going to make a living."[5]

NATIONAL QUALITY PROGRAMS

During the past decade, a quality revolution has spread throughout business. More and more firms around the world are realizing that quality programs directly affect company profitability. In fact, they are crucial to an organization's continued existence: A company that fails to provide the same level of quality as its competitors will not stay in business very long.

QUALITY PROGRAMS IN THE UNITED STATES

One response to the inroads Japanese and European competitors made in both U.S. and international markets during the 1980s was the creation of the Malcolm Baldrige National Quality Award. Widespread concerns that the quality levels of imported products exceeded U.S.-made products led Congress to establish this prize in 1987 as part of a national quality improvement effort. Named after the late secretary of commerce, the Baldrige Award represents the highest level of national recognition for quality that a U.S. company can achieve. Its purposes are to promote quality awareness, to recognize quality achievements of U.S. companies, and to publicize successful quality strategies. Each year, only two awards can be given in each of three categories: manufacturing, services, and small business. Applicants scoring more than 600 points undergo on-site evaluations for compliance with the award's standards. Award winners may publicize and advertise their receipt of the award, as long as they agree to share information about their quality strategies with other U.S. organizations.

The Baldrige Award has become a successful motivator for American industry by giving companies a goal to focus their efforts. At DuPont, in fact, so many divisions want to apply that some will have to wait until after 2000 to take their turns. Recent winners include Xerox Business Products and Systems (manufacturing), Federal Express (services), and a relatively unknown small business, Globe Metallurgical. As the opening story described, three AT&T divisions have won the award—credit cards, consumer long-distance service, and network systems. Criteria used in selecting Baldrige Award winners are described in Figure 7.2.

Since the first Baldrige Award, U.S. firms have made steady improvements in their operations. Average defects per vehicle manufactured by U.S. car makers have fallen from 7.3 to 1.5. A decade ago, 8 percent of the steel products made in the United States contained defects, and almost 3,000 U.S.-made computer chips failed for every billion hours of computer usage. Today, defect rates have plummeted to 1 percent of steel products and fewer than 100 chips.[6]

QUALITY PROGRAMS IN JAPAN

In an effort to rebuild their country's industrial base after World War II, Japanese business and industry leaders studied the work of American quality advocates, especially W. Edwards Deming. By the 1970s, the Japanese had emerged as formidable global competitors. They had achieved a worldwide reputation for producing goods and services of high, yet affordable quality.[7]

To show their appreciation for Deming's role in the rebirth of Japan as an economic superpower, the Japanese government created the Deming Prize in 1951. This award recognizes companies and individuals who achieve the most significant gains in quality. It is awarded annually in a ceremony broadcast on national television in Japan. To this day, the Deming Prize remains Japan's most coveted industrial award.

FIGURE 7.2 WINNING THE BALDRIGE AWARD

Baldrige Award Criterion	Description	Relative Weight
Customer focus and satisfaction	Effectiveness of systems to determine customer requirements and demonstrated success in meeting them	30%
Quality and operational results	Results in quality achievement and quality improvement, demonstrated through quantitative measures	18
Human resource development and management	Success of efforts to develop and realize the full potential of the work force for quality	15
Management of process quality	Effectiveness of systems and processes for assuring the quality of all operations	14
Leadership	Senior executives' success in creating and sustaining a quality culture	10
Information and analysis	Effectiveness of information collection and analysis for quality improvement and planning	7
Strategic quality planning	Effectiveness of integrating quality requirements into business plans	6

QUALITY PROGRAMS IN EUROPE

ISO 9000
International standards for quality management and quality assurance.

The nations that comprise the European Union represent not only formidable competitors to U.S. firms, but also a sizable export market for goods with quality levels that match EU standards. The European Union has contributed to the worldwide interest in quality in the late 1990s with its **ISO 9000** standards, international standards for quality management and quality assurance. Developed by the International Standards Organization (ISO) to ensure consistent quality among the products manufactured and sold throughout the EU nations, ISO 9000 creates a widely recognized quality model. Many European companies now require suppliers to become ISO-certified as a condition of doing business with them.

To receive certification, a company must undergo an on-site audit to ensure that it has documented quality procedures in place and that all employees understand and follow those procedures. Meeting ISO requirements is an ongoing process; companies are audited briefly once every 6 months and must complete recertification every three years. ISO 9000 companies are required to limit their purchases to ISO 9000 certified suppliers. Roughly 40,000 companies worldwide are ISO certified. This number includes only about 400 U.S. firms and just 48 firms in Japan.

Like Japan and the United States, the European Union has created its own quality award, the European Quality Award. The application and assessment process resembles that of the Baldrige Award, with a focus on customer satisfaction, human resource management, and leadership. Applicants are also assessed on their quality management of resources and their firms' impact on the environment.

As additional countries join the European Union, trade barriers among EU member nations are falling, and firms are phasing in new rules governing production processes. These regulations can be highly detailed—specifications for the electrical systems of washing machines, for instance, fill more than 100 typed pages—and U.S. exporters must be aware of them.[8]

An Allen-Bradley facility in Milwaukee, Wisconsin, produces printed circuit boards on an automated production line. Allen-Bradley has received ISO 9000 certification for more than 17 plants in the United States, Canada, and Great Britain.

APPLYING TQM THROUGHOUT THE ORGANIZATION

Organizations today recognize improving quality as a critical strategy for building competitive advantage. As Figure 7.3 shows, quality improvements affect an organization both internally and externally. Within the organization, higher quality leads to increased productivity and lower costs. Externally, quality improvements increase customer satisfaction and reduce prices, both of which in turn boost market share. Ultimately, a successful commitment to total quality should result in increased earnings and profitability.

TQM is often viewed as an effort that primarily affects production by increasing efficiency on the shop floor. This section corrects this narrow view by examining the application of TQM to all business functions, including production, human resource management, marketing, information processing, and financial management. Creation of a total quality organization begins with commitment and involvement by top management.

TOP MANAGEMENT INVOLVEMENT

An effective TQM program begins with the involvement of top managers who believe that the success of their firm depends on quality and customer satisfaction. As Charles Aubrey, president of the American Society for Quality Control, puts it, top managers "must take a strategic view of quality: setting priorities, identifying what's most critical to the success of the enterprise, and focusing improvement efforts on the customer. These are decisions that only top management can make."[9]

The remarkable turnaround achieved by the U.S. automobile industry following two decades of declining market share testifies to the effectiveness of commitments to world-class quality by workers and managers at every level, including top management. U.S. auto makers faced sagging sales, huge financial losses, and widely held perceptions of auto buyers that their models could not match the quality of European and Japanese cars and other Asian brands. Top managers at Ford, General Motors, and Chrysler responded by making the needed commitments to offer products and customer satisfaction second to none. The tangible results of these commitments are clear, as the mid-1990s have seen the U.S. Big Three auto makers regain market share, earn soaring profit levels, and move to the top of Car of the Year and the J. D. Power & Associates award lists. The auto companies' quality commitment is reflected in the Ford Mustang advertisement shown in Figure 7.4.

FIGURE 7.3 HOW QUALITY IMPROVEMENTS BENEFIT AN ORGANIZATION

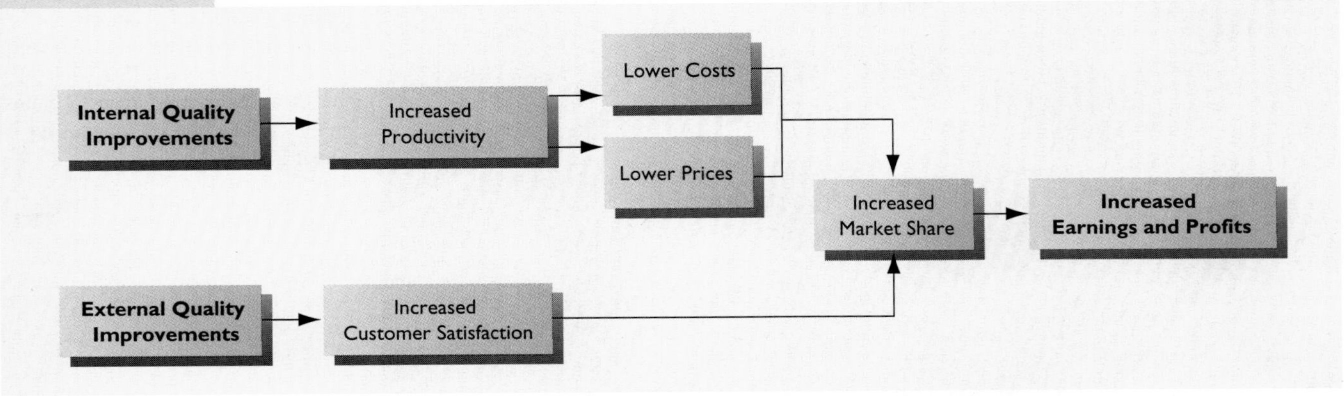

Quality advocate W. Edwards Deming created a classic set of guidelines, listed in Figure 7.5, for top managers. His "14 Points for Quality" encourage managers to view their organizations as systems that use the knowledge and skills of all employees to improve quality. Managers are responsible for communicating the goals of total quality management to all staff members and for encouraging them to improve themselves and take pride in their work. Research determines customers' needs and wants. Using this information, the firm then designs and redesigns functional, dependable goods and services; removes defects by reducing variations; and builds relationships of loyalty and trust with suppliers to improve incoming materials and to decrease costs.

Lee Kun Hee, chairman of Korea's Samsung Corp., motivates his management team to improve quality by applying what he calls "shock therapy." To alert managers to the need for TQM, he issued surprise orders for senior executives to fly to Los Angeles and visit local dealers of Samsung's electronic products. Lee had already talked with these dealers and knew that they would barrage his staff with numerous complaints about product defects and customer service shortcomings. By moving the managers out of their offices and onto the firing line, Lee hoped to produce a jolt of reality that would il-

FIGURE 7.4

TOP MANAGEMENT'S COMMITMENT TO QUALITY AT FORD MOTOR

FIGURE 7.5 DEMING'S 14 POINTS FOR QUALITY IMPROVEMENT

Deming's 14 Points for Quality

1. Drive out fear.
2. Eliminate quotas and numerical goals.
3. Break down all barriers between departments.
4. Eliminate inspection by building products right the first time.
5. Institute a vigorous education program.
6. Remove barriers that rob workers of their right to pride of workmanship.
7. Institute leadership with the aim of helping people do a better job.
8. Eliminate slogans, exhortations, and production targets.
9. Adopt a new philosophy to awaken managers to the challenge, to learn responsibilities, and to take on leadership.
10. End practice of awarding business based on the price tag. Move toward single supplier and base long-term relationship on loyalty and trust.
11. Improve constantly and forever the system of production, marketing, and service.
12. Put everyone to work to accomplish this transformation.
13. Institute job training.
14. Create constancy of purpose toward the improvement of goods and services to become competitive, stay in business, and to provide jobs.

luminate the firm's quality problems. After all, Samsung, the largest non-Japanese conglomerate in Asia, had seen its earnings drop to $600 million on global sales of $54 billion.[10]

TQM AND PRODUCTION

Early efforts to improve quality within the production process focused mostly on end-of-the-line inspections. Workers were positioned at the ends of assembly lines to weed out finished products that failed to meet quality specifications. While end-of-the-line inspections are still used today, it is increasingly viewed as an approach that is designed backwards. It does nothing to correct the manufacturing errors that created the problems in the first place. In addition, inspecting finished goods can be time-consuming and ineffective, since inspectors do not always catch defective products. Finally, it is expensive. Samsung's Chairman Lee estimates that every year, 6,000 of his firm's 36,000 employees spend their time identifying and then repairing an average of 20,000 defective products.

The quality movement began as an attempt to improve product quality by improving the production process itself. An early approach still used today, **statistical quality control** is a system that employs statistical procedures to gather and analyze data to pinpoint and correct problem areas. It involves developing control charts to detect variations in the manufacturing process that could produce defective products. By controlling these variations, statistical quality control builds quality into the production process rather than relying on inspection to find defective products.

statistical quality control
System of locating and measuring quality problems in production processes.

Organizations that seek to improve their own production systems will also demand better quality and quicker response times from their suppliers. This effort often leads them to slash the number of suppliers with whom they do business. Xerox bought equipment from 5,000 suppliers 10 years ago; today, it buys from 500 firms, a 90 percent reduction. Motorola has trimmed its supplier ranks by 70 percent, Digital Equipment by 67 percent, and General Motors by 45 percent. Since Xerox pared its supplier list, it has also reduced its reject rate on parts by a factor of 13.

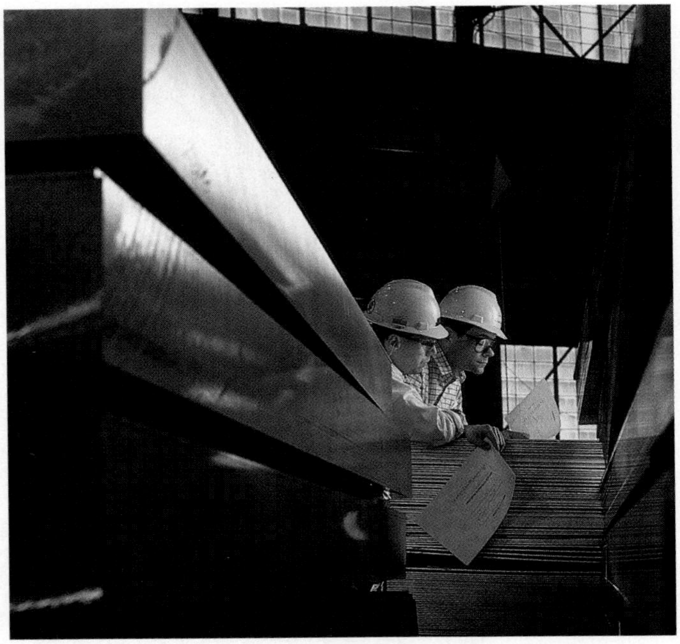

Alcoa workers pore over statistical quality-control charts to ensure zero defects in the Boeing 777 wings.

When Boeing began planning its new 777 aircraft, it selected Alcoa to supply special aluminum alloys for the new plane's wings and outer skin. Alcoa relied on statistical quality control charts to monitor key steps in producing these components to make sure that the new alloy did not vary at any time from the original design specifications.

ISO 9000 certification is rapidly becoming a prerequisite for firms to do business in Europe and for their suppliers. The U.S. chemical giant DuPont learned the importance of these standards recently when it lost a major European order for polyester film to an ISO-certified British firm. That same year, DuPont revised its internal standards to meet ISO requirements.[11]

TQM AND HUMAN RESOURCE MANAGEMENT

An organization cannot be any better than its employees allow it to be. Indeed, Baldrige Award recipients often win praise for the quality of their human resource management practices. AT&T's Universal Card Services division certifies local day-care centers for employees' offspring, helps parents find qualified care providers for mildly ill children, and offers employees and their families free use of the company health club. Employees who need auto financing can take advantage of low interest rates offered by AT&T's credit union.

What is the best way to motivate employees to improve quality? When psychologists at the American Quality Foundation studied worker attitudes and behavior, they found key differences between U.S. and Japanese workers. While the Japanese enjoy working toward incremental, step-by-step improvements, Americans tend to get impatient and look for ways to achieve single breakthroughs. Japanese employees are likely to search more methodically for quality improvements, while U.S. workers tend to react more emotionally. Thus, the foundation recommends that managers of American workers motivate them by focusing on major changes rather than small ones and by encouraging each worker to feel a sense of individual achievement and personal reward.

external customer
Person or organization that buys or uses another firm's good or service.

Another effective motivational technique involves the concepts of internal and external customers. So far, this chapter has discussed customer satisfaction in terms of **external customers**—people or organizations who buy or use another firm's good or service.

However, TQM also emphasizes the importance of **internal customers**—individual employees or entire departments within an organization who depend on the work of other people or departments to perform their jobs. For example, a Dell Computer employee who processes an order for a new PC is the internal customer of the Dell salesperson who completed the sale, just as the person who bought the product is the salesperson's external customer. When employees view their colleagues as internal customers, they feel motivated to deliver higher-quality goods and services to their co-workers. They accept responsibility for helping fellow employees to do their jobs better and to add further value to the production and marketing processes.[12]

internal customer
Employee or department within an organization that depends on the work of other people or departments to perform a job.

Any department that in some way adds value to the end user's product is, in fact, an internal customer who needs information. Consider how clearly the product design engineer at a firm such as Texas Instruments must understand a product's end users and their needs. In such a case, the design engineer becomes one of the marketing department's internal customers. If the marketing department does not clearly identify the target customer to the design engineer, it fails to deliver satisfactory customer service.[13]

TQM AND MARKETING

TQM identifies customer satisfaction as the primary goal of marketing. As Sam Walton, founder of America's largest retailer Wal-Mart, once said, "An improvement's not an improvement until your customer knows about it."[14] TQM must focus first and foremost on the customer; quality in marketing means customer-driven marketing. This fact is evident from the criteria for the Baldrige Award, for which the customer satisfaction score accounts for 300 of 1,000 total points.

Total quality management influences the marketing function in several ways. One is product design; quality product decisions involve selecting the tangible and intangible characteristics that allow a good or service to meet customer needs. Firms must design products with changing customer values in mind. Singapore Airlines, for instance, addresses the needs of busy travelers by offering over-ocean fax transmission as a standard passenger service. Its Boeing 747 jets have facsimile machines in the front and rear cabins. A jet's transmitter sends the fax message to a satellite that beams it to ground

On the Dell Computer Corporation production line, a worker installs a motherboard and the computer's serial number. This worker is the internal customer of the Dell salesperson who sold the computer. Since each Dell computer is made specifically for its owner, the salesperson must take down complete and accurate information to ensure that internal customers—the line workers who build the machine—produce the proper product.

stations in Singapore, Norway, or England. From these stations, messages travel via telephone lines to their destinations.

Audi marketers emphasize the quality of their Audi 100 TDI sedan to British car buyers by focusing on fuel economy. Advertising messages like the one in Figure 7.6 feature the headline "A Thousand Miles on One Tankful" to grab the attention of English consumers who spend up to $3 per gallon for gasoline. The fuel economy message is driven home by the photo of the camel with text that reads, "The new Audi TDI recently traveled 1,338 miles on a single tank of diesel, averaging 76 miles per gallon and taking the world record into the bargain. Which makes it the perfect car for those who can't choose between luxury and economy."

TQM also challenges an organization to increase the speed and efficiency with which it delivers goods and services so that a customer receives the right amount, at the right place, and at the right time. Such a customer-focused distribution strategy boosts customer satisfaction. This is why California-based Granite Rock, a supplier of crushed rock and concrete, developed GraniteXpress, a 24-hour automated system for dispensing rock from its quarry. Customers drive their trucks up to a concrete-loading facility and insert magnetic cards to place orders and charge them to their accounts. In less than 10 minutes, the correct amount of rock slides down a chute into a waiting truck. President Bruce Woolpert got the idea from watching people use automatic teller machines: "We thought if they can dispense $20 bills accurately, then we can do that with rock."[15]

TQM also affects an organization's advertising and personal selling efforts. Advertising for United Parcel Service (UPS) communicates the firm's slogan, "tightest ship in the shipping business," by focusing on speed and dependability. Through ads, news features, and sales presentations, UPS customers learn about the efficiency of the firm's 62,000 neatly dressed delivery people. At each stop, the UPS driver sheds the seat belt, toots the horn, and cuts the engine as the truck brakes to a stop. In a single motion, up goes the emergency brake and the shifter moves into first gear, ready for takeoff after delivery. A clipboard goes under the right arm and a package under the left. The keys, teeth up, are on the middle finger of the driver's right hand. The representative of the world's largest overnight shipping company then trots to the office or house at the prescribed 3 feet per second.

A customer-oriented marketing strategy often includes a guarantee of customer satisfaction. L. L. Bean has built a successful business based on the guarantee it states in

FIGURE 7.6

MATCHING TQM EFFORTS TO CUSTOMER NEEDS

The image of L. L. Bean apparel is greatly enhanced by the mail-order firm's promise of complete satisfaction or a "no questions asked" replacement or refund.

every apparel catalog: "Our products are guaranteed to give 100 percent satisfaction in every way. Return anything purchased from us at any time if it proves otherwise." Oakley Millwork, Inc., an Illinois-based seller of building supplies, offers an extraordinary guarantee. If a customer orders a product that is out of stock and must be back-ordered, the company provides it free of charge. Clients in the building industry were thrilled with the guarantee. "I directly attribute a 20 percent increase in our sales to that guarantee the year it came out," says owner Glen Johnson.[16]

TQM AND INFORMATION PROCESSING

Effective information systems can support TQM programs by improving customer service and boosting employees' productivity. This encourages U.S. companies to spend more than $1 billion a year on computers and related technologies as tools for customer-service departments. In a recent survey of 782 large American and European companies, 70 percent of the respondents identified customer service as the major focus of their investments in technology.[17]

For years, clerks at American Express had to laboriously type handwritten numbers on every charge slip—900,000 slips a day—into the company's computer system. Inevitable clerical errors led to billing errors and angry customers. AmEx responded by purchasing handwriting-recognition computer systems that can read and process legibly written numbers. The firm's error rate has plummeted, and so has processing time. While the system cost more than $10 million, it is expected to pay for itself within 4 years. Says Cliff Dodd, senior vice president, "It is critically important to us."[18]

Whirlpool Corporation's computer system recently generated an alert when its information system reported several complaints about a new washing machine model developing annoying leaks after just a few washloads. Not only did the computer system warn management about the problem, it also provided repair centers with a list of people who had purchased the model. Whirlpool quickly dispatched mechanics to make the necessary repairs and keep customers happy.[19]

While information technologies can improve customer service, they can also detract from it if badly planned. Voice mail began as a communication medium for people within an organization, but it has evolved into a virtual receptionist for many companies. Such a system can save time and money, but poorly designed voice mail can frustrate callers and alienate potential customers, who may decide to call competitors instead. Telecommunications consultant Tom Hunse says, "These days, the [primary] user of voice mail is the [out-of-office] caller. It's not the way you want to treat a customer or client when they call." Hunse suggests the following guidelines for a high-quality voice mail system:[20]

- Offer callers the option of talking to a human operator at any time during the message.
- Change the message daily to reflect the specifics of your schedule.
- Ask callers to leave detailed messages to help assemble the necessary information when returning their calls.
- Check for messages regularly, at least three times a day. Return all calls within 24 hours.

TQM AND FINANCIAL MANAGEMENT

Applying TQM to financial management means establishing clear quality goals and linking them to employee compensation and financial returns for the company. An employee-owned company like United Airlines links high-quality customer service directly to the firm's profits—and to long-term returns for its owner-employees. Consequently, as Figure 7.7 indicates, the promise of a financial payoff is likely to prompt a United employee to work harder to serve customers in dozens of different locations around the world.

Despite the relationship of quality and financial success, a study by the American Quality Foundation and accounting giant Ernst & Young found that quality performance

FIGURE 7.7

UNITED AIRLINES: OWNER-EMPLOYEES' FINANCIAL PAYOFFS FOR WORKING HARDER measures played no role in determining senior managers' compensation at 80 percent of American companies. Lack of clear, quality-oriented financial objectives can derail projects and waste precious funds.

When Mike Walsh took over as CEO of Tenneco, the giant gas pipeline firm and automobile parts manufacturer was posting annual losses of $732 million despite generating over $1.3 billion in annual revenues. Walsh immediately instituted financial management measures that revealed a linkage between Tenneco's losses and specific quality problems. These problems included unscheduled downtime due to equipment failures, growing numbers of warranty claims due to defects, insufficient project planning, and inadequate testing and inspection procedures. Dana Mead, Tenneco president, explains, "We used total quality as an integral part of addressing the crisis. We burned cost-of-quality objectives into the goals for every operating unit." Walsh also changed Tenneco's compensation scheme to link a significant portion of every senior manager's bonus to meeting those objectives. Within 3 years, Tenneco had reversed its downward spiral and was earning $215 million in operating income annually.[21]

IMPORTANCE OF FEEDBACK TO QUALITY

As a first step in improving quality, a company must compile feedback against which to measure its present performance. *Feedback* consists of messages returned by an audience to a sender that may cause the sender to alter or cancel an original message. Feedback can be obtained from three primary sources: customers, employees, and suppliers.

CUSTOMER FEEDBACK

The task of choosing the best way to obtain and measure customer feedback can often challenge management since *gaps*—differences between actual and perceived quality of goods and services—may disrupt the message. Xerox CEO Paul A. Allaire described such a gap found a few years ago at the headquarters of the firm that invented the photocopier market: "We were fairly arrogant, until we realized the Japanese were selling quality products for what it cost us to make them."[22]

Managers sometimes receive positive surprises when they learn about favorable gaps, that is, when their products perform better than expected. To avoid unfavorable gaps, firms must go beyond traditional performance measures and explore what drives customer behavior. They must then formulate their mission statements, goals, and performance standards to reflect customer perceptions.

Many companies measure customer satisfaction by monitoring purchasing behavior over time and surveying customers periodically regarding their experiences with company products and service personnel. Red Lobster has long appreciated feedback it receives from diners. The seafood restaurant chain offers the brief questionnaire shown in Figure 7.8 to allow guests to report their satisfaction levels and specific problem areas. By surveying diners over an extended period, Red Lobster management can both spot trends in diner expectations and identify and correct specific problems in individual restaurants.

Toll-free telephone lines can serve as an effective customer feedback system. More than two-thirds of U.S. manufacturers maintain toll-free numbers, compared to just 40 percent a decade ago. Firms install these lines and print the numbers on packages, for one reason, because consumers often associate the promotion of toll-free numbers with high-quality goods and services. In addition, talking to customers yields valuable information. "We get immediate feedback on our products," explains a spokesperson for Starkist Foods. Toll-free phone lines are "a wonderful research tool," according to Pillsbury CEO Paul Walsh. "If we have a problem with a product, we want to be the first to hear about it."[23] Chapter 13 discusses customer feedback and customer satisfaction measurement in more detail.

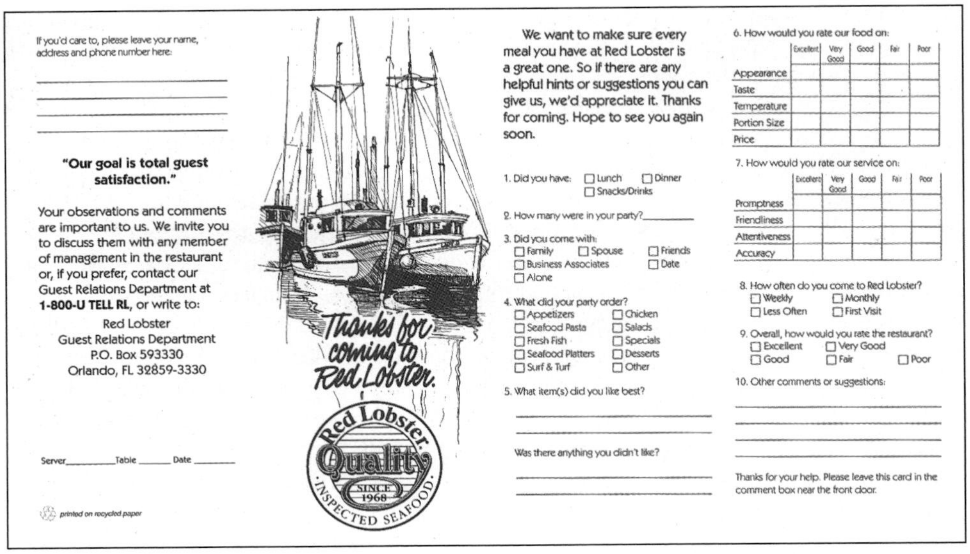

If you'd care to, please leave your name, address and phone number here:

"Our goal is total guest satisfaction."

Your observations and comments are important to us. We invite you to discuss them with any member of management in the restaurant or, if you prefer, contact our Guest Relations Department at **1-800-U TELL RL**, or write to:

Red Lobster
Guest Relations Department
P.O. Box 593330
Orlando, FL 32859-3330

Server______ Table ______ Date ______

printed on recycled paper

Thanks for coming to Red Lobster.

Red Lobster. Quality · Since 1968 · Inspected Seafood ·

We want to make sure every meal you have at Red Lobster is a great one. So if there are any helpful hints or suggestions you can give us, we'd appreciate it. Thanks for coming. Hope to see you again soon.

1. Did you have: ☐ Lunch ☐ Dinner ☐ Snacks/Drinks

2. How many were in your party?______

3. Did you come with:
☐ Family ☐ Spouse ☐ Friends
☐ Business Associates ☐ Date
☐ Alone

4. What did your party order?
☐ Appetizers ☐ Chicken
☐ Seafood Pasta ☐ Salads
☐ Fresh Fish ☐ Specials
☐ Seafood Platters ☐ Desserts
☐ Surf & Turf ☐ Other

5. What item(s) did you like best?

Was there anything you didn't like?

6. How would you rate our food on:

	Excellent	Very Good	Good	Fair	Poor
Appearance					
Taste					
Temperature					
Portion Size					
Price					

7. How would you rate our service on:

	Excellent	Very Good	Good	Fair	Poor
Promptness					
Friendliness					
Attentiveness					
Accuracy					

8. How often do you come to Red Lobster?
☐ Weekly ☐ Monthly
☐ Less Often ☐ First Visit

9. Overall, how would you rate the restaurant?
☐ Excellent ☐ Very Good
☐ Good ☐ Fair ☐ Poor

10. Other comments or suggestions:

Thanks for your help. Please leave this card in the comment box near the front door.

FIGURE 7.8

RED LOBSTER'S SOURCE OF FEEDBACK

EMPLOYEE FEEDBACK

Federal Express CEO Frederick Smith points out that, "Customer satisfaction begins with employee satisfaction." Effective managers take time to solicit and respond to employee feedback. Sam Walton used to ride with Wal-Mart truck drivers and visit stores early in the morning to talk with employees. Thousands of firms ask employees to complete standardized surveys. As another method, for decades U.S. and Japanese companies have actively solicited ideas from employees and then rewarded individuals and teams for their suggestions.

The Ritz-Carlton's employee feedback programs helped the chain to become the first hotel to win the Baldrige Award. Every Ritz-Carlton employee receives more than 100 hours of quality training, double the amount offered by most U.S. companies. The hotel's 13-member quality management team meets weekly to address quality problems identified by employees. A new hire is interviewed on the 21st day on the job and again on the 30th day in order to answer questions and review the new employee's progress. These reviews help management to evaluate quality performance.[24]

Quality researcher Kathryn Troy suggests that an organization should develop a recognition program to honor skilled employees and give them a chance to tell other employees what they do. "It sounds hokey, but it's successful," Troy explains. "Almost all of the total quality graybeards who have been at it for years have well-established recognition programs. Corning, Xerox, Motorola, and Milliken—they all have them."[25]

SUPPLIER FEEDBACK

Another element of total quality management involves giving feedback to and receiving it from suppliers. This forces managers to think in terms of customer/supplier partnerships that require members to consider each other as customers. For example, a manufacturer orders its parts from another company, the supplier, and the two form a partnership. The manufacturer becomes the supplier's customer. In recent years, companies have started to demand higher levels of quality from their suppliers, and suppliers have faced pressure to comply in order to maintain business relationships.

Livingston, New Jersey's St. Barnabas Medical Center is one of a growing number of health-care providers that asks all patients to complete questionnaires on employees, the quality of hospital food, and overall cleanliness. One respondent to the survey shown

Mary Kay Cosmetics recognizes and rewards sales representatives with diamonds and pink Cadillacs. Such company recognition can motivate employees to provide high-quality goods and services.

in Figure 7.9 was pop singer Whitney Houston, who had a baby there. Feedback from Houston and other, less-famous patients helps the medical center to track the performance of Seiler Corp., the contract-services firm that provides dietary and housekeeping services for St. Barnabas and other hospitals. The feedback also directly affects Seiler's profits, since its fees are tied to quarterly survey scores. Seiler executives view the arrangement with St. Barnabas as a true partnership, and they have invested $1.2 million to update the hospital's kitchen. As Ronald Del Mauro, president of St. Barnabas, comments, "If we're successful, they're successful."[26]

CONTINUOUS PROCESS IMPROVEMENT

In recent years, Japanese quality programs have migrated across the Pacific to be implemented throughout America and Europe. **Continuous process improvement,** *kaizen* in Japanese, is the process of constantly studying and making changes in work activities to improve their quality, timeliness, efficiency, and effectiveness. Continuous improvement keeps a firm producing value-added goods and services that meet customer needs and generating innovations that exceed customer expectations. This requires an ongoing process, since customers' needs, wants, and expectations are always changing.

continuous process improvement *Constantly studying and adjusting work activities to improve their quality, timeliness, efficiency, and effectiveness.*

The quality of work processes determines, to a large extent, the quality of the resulting goods and services. Quality processes can even give the organization a competitive advantage. Continuous process improvement efforts focus on three objectives: reducing cycle time, reducing variation, and eliminating waste.

REDUCING CYCLE TIME

Cycle time is the time required to complete a work process or activity from beginning to end. For example, cycle time can measure the time it takes to design a conveyor system, handle a customer inquiry, or create an employee training video. In each case, a firm can reduce cycle time through several means. It might simplify work processes, eliminate steps that do not add value to the product, and bring individuals from several departments together to work out production inefficiencies that add to cycle time. Cycle time reductions accomplish two important objectives:

cycle time *Time required to complete a work process or activity.*

FIGURE 7.9 CUSTOMER FEEDBACK TO EVALUATE SUPPLIER PERFORMANCE

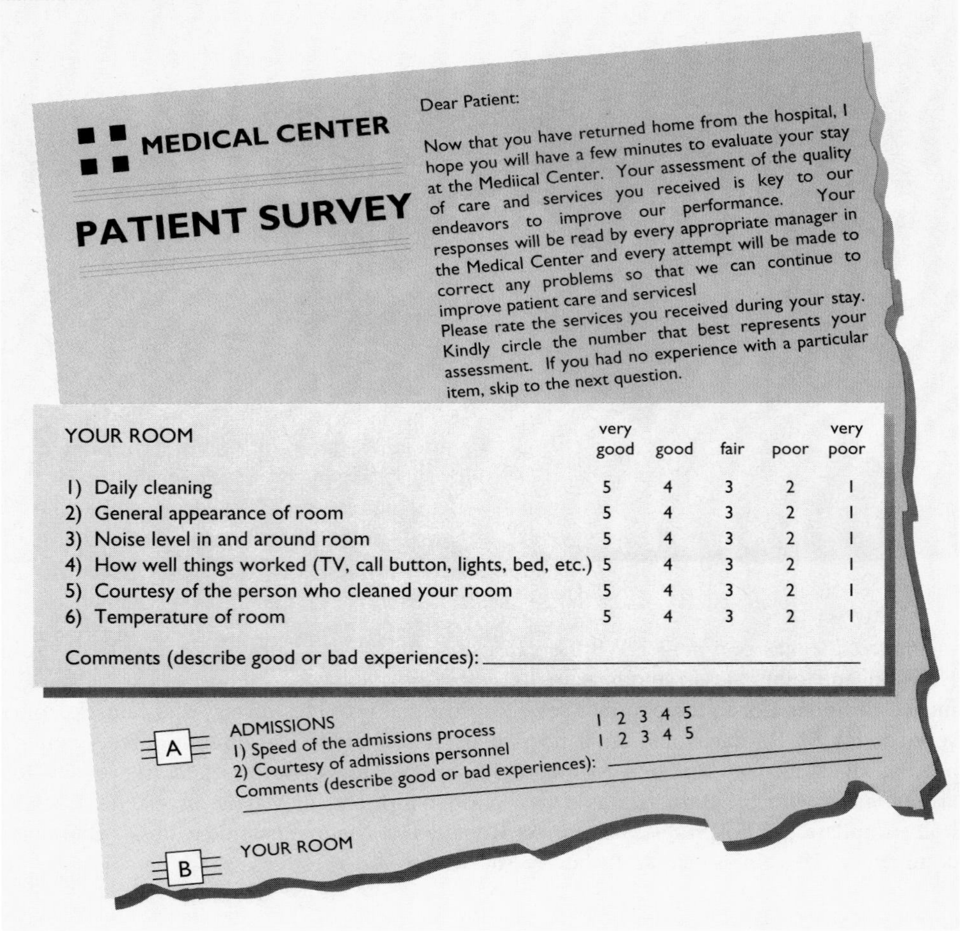

MEDICAL CENTER

PATIENT SURVEY

Dear Patient:

Now that you have returned home from the hospital, I hope you will have a few minutes to evaluate your stay at the Mediical Center. Your assessment of the quality of care and services you received is key to our endeavors to improve our performance. Your responses will be read by every appropriate manager in the Medical Center and every attempt will be made to correct any problems so that we can continue to improve patient care and servicesl

Please rate the services you received during your stay. Kindly circle the number that best represents your assessment. If you had no experience with a particular item, skip to the next question.

YOUR ROOM	very good	good	fair	poor	very poor
1) Daily cleaning	5	4	3	2	1
2) General appearance of room	5	4	3	2	1
3) Noise level in and around room	5	4	3	2	1
4) How well things worked (TV, call button, lights, bed, etc.)	5	4	3	2	1
5) Courtesy of the person who cleaned your room	5	4	3	2	1
6) Temperature of room	5	4	3	2	1

Comments (describe good or bad experiences): ______

A ADMISSIONS

1) Speed of the admissions process 1 2 3 4 5

2) Courtesy of admissions personnel 1 2 3 4 5

Comments (describe good or bad experiences): ______

B YOUR ROOM

- Reducing the time required to bring new products to the marketplace
- Permitting the firm to produce and deliver customer orders more quickly

L. L. Bean, the Freeport, Maine mail-order firm, is a recognized leader in cycle time control. Workers use flowcharts to track movements involved in filling customer orders to help them eliminate wasted movements. The warehouse stores frequently ordered merchandise closer to the packing station, for example. Such improvements result in 99.9 percent error-free shipments for orders filled within a few hours after receipt.[27]

reengineering
Mapping out existing delivery-chain processes in detail and applying technology to key steps to reduce cycle time or errors.

The concept of cycle time is closely associated with a term that has become a business buzz-word of the late 1990s: **reengineering,** or the process of mapping out delivery-chain processes in detail to identify potential reductions in cycle time or process errors through applying technology to those key steps. When a company reengineers a process, it carefully evaluates and then modifies management systems, job designs, and work flows in an effort to improve efficiency and reduce cycle time. Ford Motor Company's vendor-payment system kept 400 accounting department employees awash in a sea of paperwork. When top managers learned that rival Mazda performed the same work with only five workers in its accounts payable division, they realized that reengineering was needed. Computers now match receipt records, purchase orders, and invoices and then prepare checks automatically. Today, only 100 Ford employees handle the same work, and company vendors receive payments immediately upon receipt of shipments.[28]

FIGURE 7.10 PDCA CYCLE

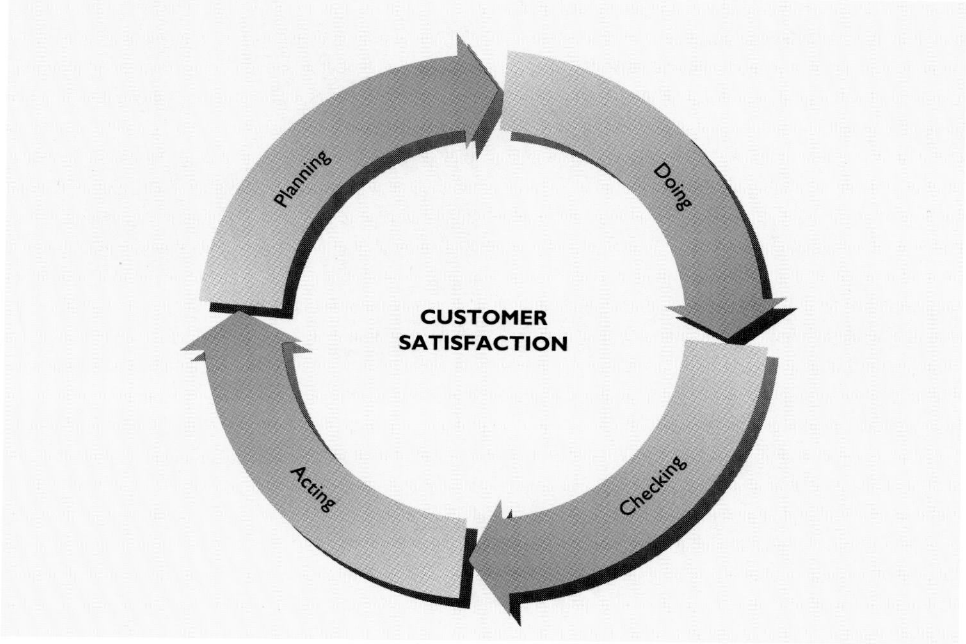

Wal-Mart's new computer and telecommunications technologies have allowed the discount retail giant to reduce dramatically the time lag between ordering products from its vendors and delivery of merchandise to its retail stores. The shorter cycle time that this reengineering produced allowed Wal-Mart to cut its inventory carrying costs and to pass on the savings to customers in the form of lower prices. The result was a significant competitive advantage for the Bentonville, Arkansas-based firm.

One approach by which a firm can map out cycle time and find areas for improvement is the **PDCA cycle,** a step-by-step process of **p**lanning, **d**oing, **c**hecking, and **act**ing. In the planning step, shown at the top of Figure 7.10, employees analyze their work and determine what changes might improve it. In the doing step, they implement these changes. During the checking step, they observe the effects of the change. Acting, the final step, changes work activities to bring about improvement. Throughout the cycle, employees examine their own jobs and their contributions to customer satisfaction.

PDCA cycle
Step-by-step process to reduce cycle time by ***p****lanning,* ***d****oing,* ***c****hecking, and* ***a****cting.*

Total quality organizations apply the PDCA cycle to all business processes, from planning long-term strategies to adjusting short-term details of customer service routines. A recent patient survey by administrators at Orlando's Florida Hospital Medical Center identified food service as an important determinant of patients' attitudes toward hospitals. The survey also revealed that 12 percent of the firm's patients had complained about its food. Managers used the following PDCA cycle to help resolve the problem:[29]

- *Planning.* Staffers analyzed the hospital's food service operations and found that the inefficient tray-line layout sometimes led to food mixups. A patient on a restricted diet might receive a tray intended for one on a regular diet, and vice versa.
- *Doing.* The staff experimented with ways to reorganize the tray lines to reduce the chances of error.
- *Checking.* Measuring the results of the change, the staff found that complaints about food fell from 12 percent to 2 percent. Overall patient satis-

In this ad, Rockwell highlights its use of continuous process improvement to cut the cost of Space Shuttle operations and main-engine production by more than 20 percent.

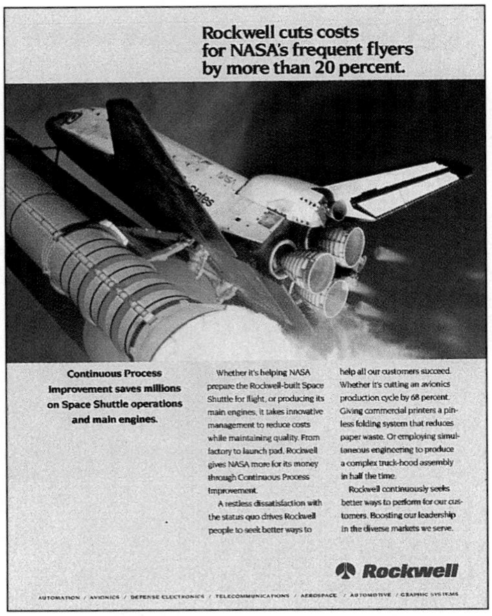

faction with the food increased, even though the meals themselves tasted the same as they always had.

- *Acting*. The hospital adopted the new tray-line setup as a permanent arrangement.

REDUCING VARIATION

All work processes, goods, and services show some degree of variation. This can result from such factors as poor market research, faulty machinery or outdated technology, inadequately trained employees, inefficient work procedures, and defective parts and materials from suppliers.

Product variation in the creation and marketing of services changes substantially for equipment-based or people-based services. Firms can standardize these intangible products more simply in equipment-based service industries like computer time sharing, motion picture theaters, automated car washes, and dry cleaners. Eliminating product variation is much more difficult for people-based service providers such as lawn-care firms, plumbing and appliance repair firms, recruiting agencies, lawyers, and accountants. In fact, it is sometimes difficult even to assure consistency in the services provided by different employees of the same firm.

Both goods producers and service providers institute quality programs to train employees to use statistical controls and problem-solving methods to reduce variations. The goal is to reach the highest possible performance standard so customers can depend on consistently high quality each time they purchase a good or service.

Effective work processes build quality into a product by reducing variations in production that could cause errors. Clothing manufacturer Health-Tex combines well-trained employees, state-of-the-art production machinery, and high-quality materials to produce its long-lasting, fashionable lines of infant and children's wear, as shown in Figure 7.11. Incorporating high quality levels from the beginning of the production line is much more cost effective than inspecting finished products to spot defects and correct problems.

L. L. Bean workers can fill orders rapidly because the company controls its cycle time. By reducing wasted movement and carefully organizing the warehouse, L. L. Bean can ship orders within a few hours of receiving them.

ELIMINATING WASTE

To economically produce and market goods and services that satisfy customers, quality companies concentrate on eliminating waste. Waste includes any work activity that does not add value for the customer.

Wasted time and resources cost companies enormous amounts of money. The costs associated with poor-quality products and production processes, such as scrap, rework, and loss of customers, are called the **costs of quality.** These costs have internal and exter-

costs of quality
Costs associated with poor quality, such as scrap, rework, and loss of customers.

It won't be long before he's a teenager in ripped jeans, wrinkled shirts and unlaced shoes. Dress him cute while you can.
Healthtex

FIGURE 7.11

ENSURING PRODUCT CONSISTENCY THROUGH HIGH-QUALITY PRODUCTION AND DISTRIBUTION PROCESSES

STRENGTH IN DIVERSITY

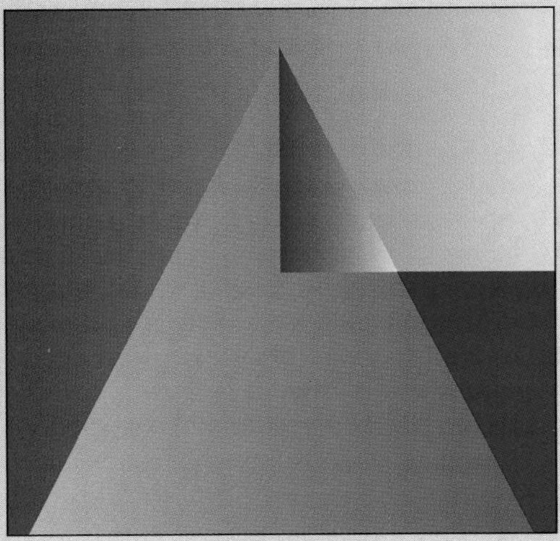

MARCOPOLO, S.A. How did such a small company tucked away in the largely Italian city of Caxias do Sul in southern Brazil become such a success in the globally competitive business of bus manufacturing? The 47-year-old company makes bus bodies, then assembles them on chassis made by Mercedes, Saab, and other major automotive companies. They are then sold as airport shuttles to firms like Hertz and National as well as to private and municipal bus lines in over 40 countries. Half of each year's production is sold outside Brazil. Marcopolo customers give the firm high marks for meeting customer needs through a combination of quality products, fair prices, and service. ■ The firm was born in 1949 when Paulo Bellini and six other young mechanics pooled their savings to start the business. It was a lofty objective, given the founders' lack of experience and the lack of any automotive production industry in Brazil at that time. Marcopolo's first order came from a local commuter line, but production was painfully slow; the young firm took 90 days to handcraft each bus. After 10 years, production had improved enough that the plant could turn out two buses a month. By the 1980s, production capacity had increased to ten buses per day. ■ Marcopolo thrived on offering customized solutions to problems faced by different types of users. The firm would make special seats, give the customer a bigger or smaller luggage rack, or even build fruit racks for buses in farm towns. ■ The company's major quality breakthroughs came when Bellini and production chief Claudio Gomes went to Japan on a research mission. They visited a dozen factories and learned the values of production teams, just-in-time systems, and other elements of efficient Japanese manufacturing. The travelers brought the ideas back to Brazil and implemented them in their factory. They held seminars for workers to explain the improved manufacturing methods. Nothing was overlooked from cleanliness of the factory floors to employees' quality of worklife, and the results are apparent. Today each production team posts reports on everything from the number of days running without accident or other work stoppage to how many liters-per-bus of paint the finishing operation consumes. ■ Inventory controls have also been tightened. Using computer systems, parts are ordered and shipped as soon as a contract is entered into the computer, keeping the production line on track or ahead of schedule. The progress of every window is carefully charted, from ordering glass to installing window units in a bus. The same procedure tracks seats, railings, accordion doors, and fiberglass dashboards. Gomes estimates that the company has cut the average time between parts procurement and installation from 2 weeks to 3 days for most of the roughly 100,000 regular components, and his goal is to cut that time to a matter of hours. ■ Becoming an international company has meant modernizing facilities and processes to meet customer demands of quality and price. Says Bellini confidently, "Evolving to perfection is our goal." Source: Quotations from Joel Millman, "Evolving to Perfection," *Forbes*, November 7, 1994, pp. 298, 299.

QUESTIONS FOR CRITICAL THINKING

1. What do you think would happen if Marcopolo stopped customizing vehicles and only produced a standardized product?
2. What would be the pros and cons of moving their production facility closer to the chassis manufacturers' facilities?
3. What are the benefits of getting employees involved in the manufacturing process through production teams?

nal dimensions. Most internal quality costs are measurable; examples include discarding unusable parts, reworking defective parts, inspecting and discarding faulty goods, redesigning inferior products, and retraining employees. External costs are more difficult to measure. They include lost sales, missed marketing opportunities, frequent repairs, negative word-of-mouth advertising, bad publicity, and loss of customers to competitors.

Continuous process improvement must go beyond making the production line more efficient. Five years ago, Motorola accountants spent 11 days of every month completing paperwork and financial statements for the previous month's work. By reducing cycle time through streamlining the department's procedures, the same work now takes 2 days. Not only does the new system free Motorola accountants to perform other tasks, but it also reduces dramatically the time required for outside auditors to inspect the company's records, saving Motorola 50 percent in external accounting charges.[30]

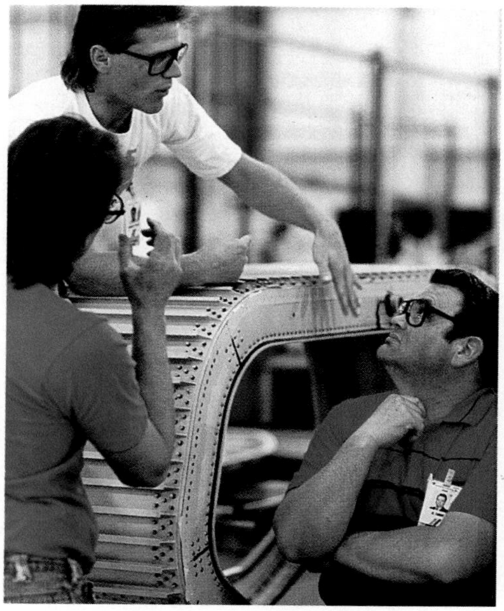

McDonnell-Douglas Corporation teammates work out a more efficient way to apply sealant to the MD-80 aircraft's fuel tank module. By implementing quality-improvement techniques, the company achieved dramatic reductions in internal quality costs in one year. For instance, the rejection rate for delivered parts was cut by more than 50 percent, and the total cost of processing and working around rejected parts was similarly reduced.

BENCHMARKING

What specifically does *high quality* mean? Is 99 percent defect-free performance satisfactory? Firms in some industries pursue zero defects as a very real goal. Even a 99.9 percent error-free performance standard would mean that 18 commercial air carriers would crash every day in the United States, the U.S. Postal Service would lose 17,000 pieces of mail each hour, doctors would perform 500 incorrect surgical operations each week, and financial institutions would deduct $24.8 million from the wrong accounts every hour.[31]

Most quality-conscious organizations rely on an important tool called **benchmarking** to set performance standards. This approach to creating a world-class organization consists of identifying how business leaders achieve superior performance levels in their industries and continuously comparing and measuring one's own firm's performance against these outstanding performers.[32] Benchmarking involves learning how the world's best goods and services are designed, produced, and marketed, and then using the information to help improve the company's own operations. The purpose of benchmarking is to achieve superior performance that creates a competitive advantage in the marketplace.

benchmarking
Setting performance standards by continuously comparing and measuring one's own firm against business leaders.

As Figure 7.12 shows, the five-phase benchmarking process begins with planning. In this phase, participants select the companies they want to benchmark and determine how to collect the needed data. Next, in the analysis phase, evaluation team members study their own company's practices and compare them with those of firms that they consider the best in their industries. The third step, integration, begins with communicating the results of this comparison to the members of the organization. Goals and action plans are then developed to incorporate the superior practices. The fourth phase, action, involves implementing these plans and monitoring their progress. The evaluators measure the new processes against the benchmarks, which they replace as needed. In the final stage, maturity, the organization achieves a leadership position in its industry by integrating the best industry practices into all organizational functions.[33]

PLANNING AND ANALYSIS

A firm should focus its benchmarking project on **critical success factors,** activities and functions that it considers most important in gaining competitive advantage and achieving long-term success. These factors vary between organizations. One firm might iden-

critical success factors
Factors that a firm considers most important in gaining competitive advantage and achieving long-term success.

FIGURE 7.12 BENCHMARKING PROCESS

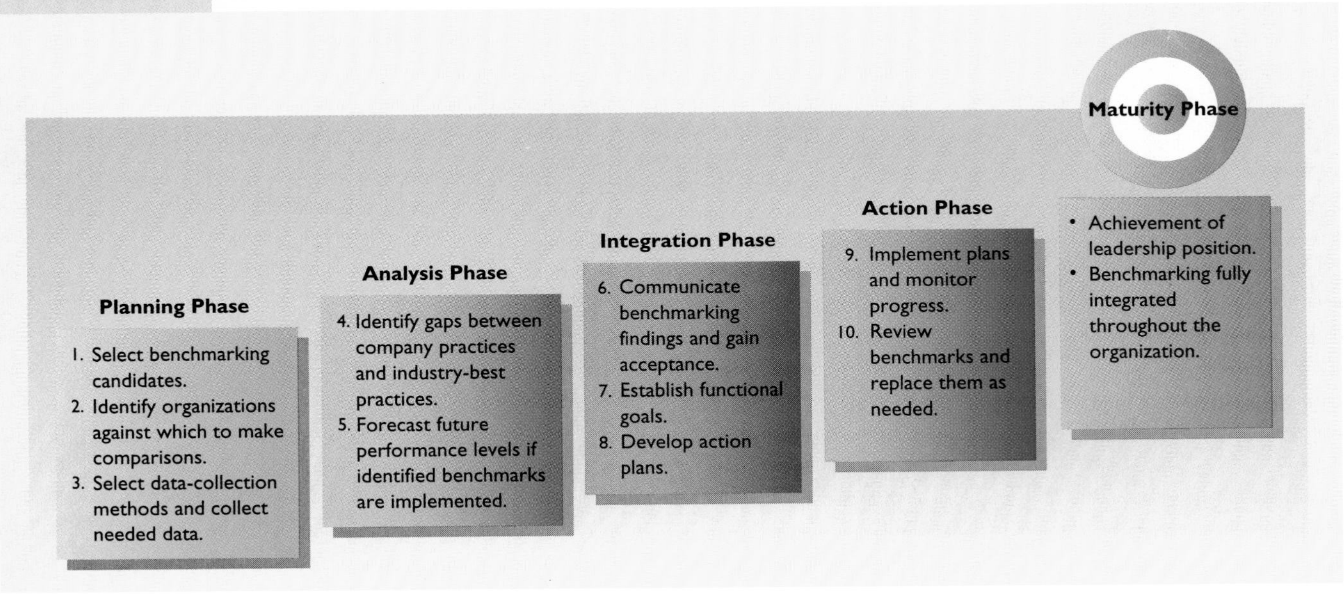

Planning Phase
1. Select benchmarking candidates.
2. Identify organizations against which to make comparisons.
3. Select data-collection methods and collect needed data.
Analysis Phase
4. Identify gaps between company practices and industry-best practices.
5. Forecast future performance levels if identified benchmarks are implemented.
Integration Phase
6. Communicate benchmarking findings and gain acceptance.
7. Establish functional goals.
8. Develop action plans.
Action Phase
9. Implement plans and monitor progress.
10. Review benchmarks and replace them as needed.
Maturity Phase
• Achievement of leadership position.
• Benchmarking fully integrated throughout the organization.

tify a critical factor as satisfying customers with excellent service; another might target bringing products to the marketplace faster.

After deciding what to benchmark, a firm must identify other organizations that are recognized performance leaders. In identifying leaders, a benchmarking company may look internally, to competitors, or to firms in other industries. *Internal benchmarking* requires comparisons between similar functions performed in different departments or divisions within a firm. *Competitive benchmarking* involves comparisons with direct product competitors. Reports in magazines such as *Consumer Reports* publicize well-known competitive benchmarks when they compare competing brands of products such as stereos or coffee makers. The J. D. Power consumer satisfaction rankings compare initial quality assessments of auto purchasers. In *functional benchmarking*, a firm compares its own functions with those of firms in different industries. Benchmarking pioneer Xerox Corp. has benchmarked organizations as diverse as Florida Power & Light (quality programs), American Express (billing and collections), and Mary Kay Cosmetics (warehousing and distribution operations).

INTEGRATION, ACTION, AND MATURITY

Firms use the findings of benchmarking to implement improvements such as setting new performance goals, changing current processes by adapting the best practices of benchmark partners, and measuring the progress of the new work practices. Managers should communicate benchmarking results to employees so they understand the reasons for changes, the opportunities for improvement, how they can help implement changes, and the effects of changes on the organization's overall business strategy.

For instance, a recent benchmarking project at Xerox concerned the company's cost centers. Management wanted to reorganize them into money-making profit centers. Employees at the Business Systems Group's logistics and distribution cost center established benchmarks by gathering data on how to operate a successful profit center. Information sources included vendors, other companies with similar cost centers, and noncompeting firms in various industries. Using this information, staff established market

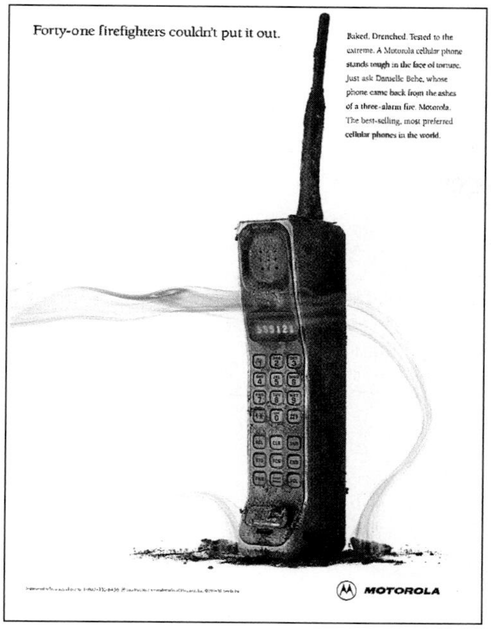

Forty-one firefighters couldn't put it out.
Baked. Drenched. Tested to the extreme. A Motorola cellular phone stands tough in the face of torture. Just ask Danielle Behe, whose phone came back from the ashes of a three-alarm fire. Motorola. The best-selling, most preferred cellular phones in the world.
MOTOROLA

Motorola maintains its world leadership in wireless communications, semiconductor technology, and advanced electronics through a commitment to quality and a recognition that it must lead its industries through superiority over competitors in every important dimension.

values for the functions that their center's employees performed. Based on these values, the staff negotiated service levels with managers of Xerox departments who used the services of their center, and then they developed level-of-service targets. Finally, the center began marketing its services to outsiders. Within 2 years, this external business began generating a profit.

Many firms strive for a *zero defects* standard as a performance goal. H. J. Heinz production facilities target an error-free standard of 99.9997 percent, which translates to 3.4 defects per million units. Xerox sets a standard of one mistake per 1,000 transactions recorded by its accounting department, and it is working toward a goal of one mistake per 1 million transactions.

Today, benchmarking is a major component of most firms' quality programs. AT&T, Metropolitan Life, IBM, Marriott, and thousands of other large and small firms use benchmarking as a standard tool for measuring quality. Increased interest in benchmarking has spawned a number of associations, councils, and specialized consulting firms. The American Productivity and Quality Center has organized an International Benchmarking Clearinghouse that offers benchmarking training, a database of best practices, and conferences to help members share information.[34]

employee involvement
Practices that motivate employees to perform their jobs better through empowerment, training, and teamwork.

ENCOURAGING EMPLOYEE INVOLVEMENT

Any effort to boost customer satisfaction and promote companywide quality usually depends on **employee involvement,** practices that motivate employees to perform their jobs better through empowerment, training, and teamwork. Employee involvement seeks to unleash the energy, creativity, and talents of all employees. Bringing out workers' best qualities makes them feel better about themselves and their work. It also helps them to feel a sense of ownership and thus take greater pride in their work. As Figure 7.13 illustrates, firms encourage employee involvement through three practices: empowerment, training, and teamwork.

FIGURE 7.13 ENCOURAGING EMPLOYEE INVOLVEMENT

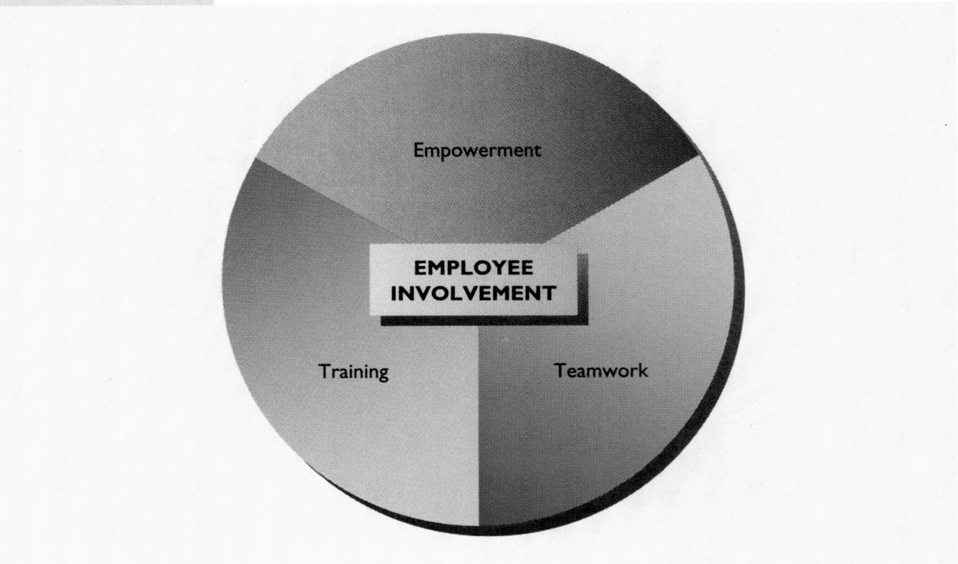

EMPOWERMENT

empowerment
Practice of giving employees the authority to make decisions about their work without supervisory approval.

Empowerment is the practice of giving employees authority to make decisions about their work without supervisory approval. Empowered employees have increased responsibility for implementing an organization's vision and strategy. For example, in the production process, empowered assembly-line workers can stop the process when they detect a problem and then find a solution.

Empowerment taps the brain power of all employees to find better ways of doing their jobs and executing their ideas. Some quality analysts believe that empowering employees may give U.S. firms an opportunity to pass the Japanese in quality by unleashing American workers' potential to innovate. Organizations that empower employees nurture their capacity to improve and create. John Wilesmith of Rank Xerox summarizes the major benefit of empowerment as, "getting more from your work force, tapping the wisdom and knowledge of every employee, believing that with every pair of hands you hire, you get a free brain."

Empowerment can make a highly effective contribution to marketing strategy. Customers appreciate dealing with an employee who has the authority to handle a transaction or complaint efficiently, without having to check with a supervisor. Superior service leaves a lasting impression and personally ties the customer to the company. Hotel chain Ritz-Carlton empowers its front-desk personnel to waive charges from guests' bills if they perceive a problem; housekeepers have the authority to order a new washing machine if they feel that the hotel needs one.

Empowerment can also become a powerful competitive weapon. By empowering employees, AT&T's Universal Card Service division gains a value-added competitive advantage in the marketplace. The company gives its telephone representatives, who handle up to 40,000 calls a day, the authority to raise customers' credit limits, investigate complaints, and issue new cards without prior approval of their supervisors. As a result, representatives resolve 95 percent of customer concerns in one phone call. Universal Card staffers can also meet on their own to devise solutions for persistent problems.

Empowerment keeps both external and internal customers happy. Each month, Universal Card Services garners more than 2,000 commendations, either letters or complimentary phone calls, from external customers. Meanwhile, telephone reps view their

At Rockwell International's Newark, Ohio plant, workers examine heavy-duty truck front axle spindles. Employee empowerment programs launched by Rockwell have produced an array of results throughout the company: faster warranty claim disposition, less absenteeism, reduced engineering response time, improved customer response and service, and continued improvements in safety and environmental matters.

work as important. The company rewards quality work by tying quarterly bonuses and pay raises to how well employees reach their performance goals. The turnover for service reps is exceptionally low—8 percent a year, compared to up to 50 percent in other companies.[35]

TRAINING

To become involved in a job on even the most basic level, an employee needs a thorough understanding of the job or process. Employee training provides workers with a wide range of learning experiences, beginning with management sharing knowledge about the organization's visions, values, and strategies. To help them identify with the purpose of their work, employees should be able to answer these questions:

- Who are our major competitors?
- What are our company's strengths and weaknesses compared to our competitors?
- How are we performing in measures such as sales, profits, and market share?
- Who are our target customers?
- What are our customers' needs and expectations?
- How satisfied are our customers with our goods and services?

Teaching employees the technical skills needed to measure and monitor the quality of their work is another aspect of training. Technical training varies depending on employees' jobs, but it can involve learning how to use quality management tools, such as statistical quality control and problem-solving methods, as well as learning more about customers' needs.

"The training program is one of the reasons that I joined Eastman Chemical," comments Tom Weaver, a market development representative. All Eastman sales reps go through an extensive six-month to nine-month training program, including experience in the technical services labs where they learn to operate the same equipment that their customers use to process Eastman products. "When they go to call on a company they can talk to the technical person or a lab person and not just walk in and say 'This is what I've got, let's see if it fits,'" explains Ridley Ruth, Eastman's training supervisor.[36]

The importance of quality training is underscored by the huge investments that organizations make in educating and developing employees. TQM training alone can cost anywhere from $300,000 for a company with fewer than 3,000 employees to $12 million at a corporation with 13,000 workers.[37]

TEAMWORK

team
Small group of people with complementary skills who are committed to a common purpose, approach, and set of performance goals.

The final component of employee involvement is teamwork. A **team** is a small group of people with complementary skills who are committed to a common purpose, approach, and set of performance goals. They all hold themselves mutually responsible and accountable for accomplishing their objectives. Quality organizations group employees into teams and teach them team-building skills. By working collectively, teams of employees produce higher performance levels, respond more quickly, and work more flexibly to meet customer needs.

quality circle
Small group of employees from one work area or department who meet regularly to identify and solve problems.

Three types of employee involvement teams include quality circles, cross-functional teams, and self-managed teams. The **quality circle** idea originated in Japan, where firms gathered small groups of employees from common work areas or departments to meet regularly to identify and solve problems. A quality circle in one city's police department redesigned the layout of the headquarters to provide a private area in which detectives could conduct interviews. An employee group for camping-equipment maker Coleman Co. suggested design improvements to a propane lamp valve that now saves the company $50,000 a year.

cross-functional team
Group of employees from different departments who work on a specific project, such as developing a new product or solving a particular problem.

The second type of employee involvement team, the **cross-functional team,** gathers employees from different departments to work on a specific project, such as developing a new product or solving a complex problem. When Colgate decided to develop a new automatic dishwashing detergent to sell throughout the world, it assembled a team with representatives from research and development, manufacturing, product management, and Colgate's European Coordination Group. The cross-functional team's efforts led to the introduction of Galaxy Automatic detergent in the 12 countries that account for 95 percent of worldwide dishwasher detergent sales.

self-managed team
Group of employees who work with little or no supervision.

The **self-managed team,** the final type of employee involvement team, is a group of employees who work with little or no supervision. Team members schedule their own work, complete training to do other employees' jobs, and accept responsibility for the quality of their work and accountability for performance results.

Depending on the objective of the task, teams can range in size from several employees in one work area to hundreds of employees from different company locations around the world. Chapter 10 discusses teamwork in greater detail.

ACHIEVEMENT CHECK SUMMARY

Reread the learning goals that follow, and consider the questions for each goal. Answering these questions will reinforce the most important concepts in the chapter and allow you to check how well you have achieved these learning goals. Where a blank appears before a question, answer with *T* or *F*. Otherwise, circle the letter of the correct answer. An answer key to these questions is found at the end of this chapter.

LEARNING GOAL 7.1: Explain the importance of quality and customer satisfaction in achieving a competitive advantage.

1. ___ Customer satisfaction is defined as the degree of excellence or superiority of an organization's goods and services.
2. ___ The true measure of quality is whether the organization is satisfying its customers.
3. ___ Total quality management (TQM) focuses on design and production, but does not apply to distribution, sales, or pricing activities.

LEARNING GOAL 7.2: Summarize the status of quality programs in the United States, Japan, and Europe.

1. ___ The Malcolm Baldrige National Quality Award was created by Congress to recognize and promote excellence of American-made goods and services.
2. ___ The Deming Prize, the most prestigious award for quality in Japan, is named after an American.
3. ___ The European Union's ISO 9000 standards were created to help ensure consistent quality among the products manufactured and sold throughout the European Union.

LEARNING GOAL 7.3: Discuss the role of top management in applying total quality management (TQM) to an organization.

1. Effective TQM programs begin with strategies developed by: (a) top management; (b) middle management; (c) supervisory management; (d) consultants who eliminate the need for management in organizations that use TQM.
2. Deming's 14 Points for Quality: (a) ask managers to view their organizations as integrated systems; (b) depend upon the knowledge and skill of all employees to reach quality objectives; (c) require that the design and production of goods and services be based on research into customer needs and wants; (d) all of the above.

LEARNING GOAL 7.4: Relate TQM to various functions within an organization, including production, human resource management, marketing, information processing, and financial management.

1. ___ Statistical quality control attempts to build quality into the production process rather than relying on after-production inspections to find defects.
2. ___ Organizations trying to improve their own quality generally rely on ever-increasing numbers of suppliers.
3. ___ Motivating workers and offering helpful employee services has little to do with achieving TQM goals.
4. ___ Applying TQM to financial means setting clear quality goals and linking them to financial returns and employee compensation.

LEARNING GOAL 7.5: Identify the major methods of securing feedback from customers, employees, and suppliers.

1. ___ More than two-thirds of U.S. manufacturers offer toll-free numbers to get customer feedback.
2. ___ Quality-oriented firms should establish programs to recognize good employees.
3. ___ Firms generally find that dealing with suppliers as business partners over the long term is costlier than shopping between competing bidders for each major purchase.

LEARNING GOAL 7.6: Describe how an organization can work toward continuous process improvement.

1. ___ Once a TQM program is in place it rarely needs revision.
2. ___ Continuous process improvement programs focus on reducing cycle time, reducing variations, and eliminating waste.

LEARNING GOAL 7.7: Define benchmarking and explain its contributions to quality and customer satisfaction.

1. Benchmarking: (a) is a single-step process done at the design stage of a product; (b) compares a company to other American producers, but not to foreign producers in the same industry; (c) compares an organization's performance to standards maintained by other superior performers in the same industry; (d) should focus on issues other than critical success factors; (e) all of the above.
2. A firm that achieves a leadership position in its industry has reached the stage in the benchmarking process known as: (a) planning; (b) analysis; (c) integration; (d) action; (e) maturity.

LEARNING GOAL 7.8: Identify the components of employee involvement and their impact on quality and customer satisfaction.

1. Employee involvement in TQM requires; (a) employee empowerment; (b) employee training in an organization's values and strategies as well as in technical skills; (c) teamwork; (d) all of the above.
2. A self-managed team: (a) meets regularly to identify and solve quality problems; (b) brings workers from different departments together to solve complex problems; (c) is a work group of relatively unsupervised workers who are responsible and held accountable for quality results; (d) all of the above.

KEY TERMS

quality 146
customer satisfaction 146
total quality management (TQM) 147
ISO 9000 150
statistical quality control 153
external customer 154
internal customer 155
continuous process improvement 161
cycle time 161
reengineering 162
PDCA cycle 163
costs of quality 165
benchmarking 167
critical success factors 167
employee involvement 169
empowerment 170
team 172
quality circle 172
cross-functional team 172
self-managed team 172

REVIEW QUESTIONS

1. Define the concepts of quality and customer satisfaction.
2. How does total quality management help an organization to compete more effectively?
3. Compare the Baldrige Award, the Deming Prize, and the European Quality Award. How are they alike? How do they differ?
4. Why is it important for senior management to support a quality program?
5. Distinguish between external customers and internal customers.
6. How can a firm determine whether it is satisfying its customers?
7. What is a customer/supplier partnership?

8. What are the goals of continuous process improvement?

9. What criteria might a firm use to choose a suitable benchmark partner?

10. How can managers encourage employee involvement?

DISCUSSION QUESTIONS

1. Apply continuous process improvement to a service or procedure at your college or university. At the present time, does this service satisfy customers as much as it could? If not, why not? How might you analyze and resolve any problems?

2. During the 1980s, sales of catalog retailer L. L. Bean grew 20 percent a year. More recently, the firm's sales growth has slowed to 3 percent a year or less. Meanwhile, returns that once averaged 5 percent of sales have risen to 14 percent. To cut costs, CEO Leon Gorman has cut inventory levels and slowed spending on automation, preferring instead to hire seasonal workers, who now comprise 40 percent of the company's total work force. Despite this effort, competitors such as Land's End are gaining market share. Unlike L. L. Bean, Land's End is investing $5 million in new computer systems and warehouse equipment.

Develop a quality program that might help L. L. Bean.

3. Identify an organization in your city or state that you consider to be a world-class competitor measured by quality and customer satisfaction. Defend your choice.

4. In designing its Aurora model, Oldsmobile attempted a new approach to product development. It created assembly-line "stop stations" where groups of five employees work at their own pace to bolt the Aurora body together. The 3-year development process received help from a rotating group of 50 hourly workers and engineers. In the final stages, Oldsmobile formed another group composed of employees from marketing, public relations, engineering, and manufacturing, as well as several Oldsmobile dealers. This group developed a dealer training program and an advertising campaign for the Aurora.

Relate the Aurora product development process to the chapter's discussion of benchmarking, empowerment, training, and teamwork.

5. Choose two companies that have active total quality management programs. (Possibilities include such firms as Motorola, Xerox, AT&T, and DuPont.) Compare the various initiatives in each company's programs. How are they alike? How do they differ?

SOLUTIONS TO ACHIEVEMENT CHECK SUMMARY

L.G. 7.1: 1. F, 2. T, 3. F. **L.G. 7.2:** 1. T, 2. T, 3. T. **L.G. 7.3:** 1. a, 2. d. **L.G. 7.4:** 1. T, 2. F, 3. F, 4. T. **L.G. 7.5:** 1. T, 2. T, 3. F. **L.G. 7.6:** 1. F, 2. T. **L.G. 7.7:** 1. c, 2. e. **L.G. 7.8:** 1. d, 2. c.

TEAM-BUILDING EXERCISE

In the following exercise, your team will explore some of the issues involved in starting a business and deciding on a form of business ownership.

1. The instructor will divide the class into groups of three to five and assign each team a form of business ownership.

2. Decide on the specific business your team wishes to consider, keeping in mind that it should reflect the characteristics of the form of business ownership that you have been assigned. You can be as creative as you wish in selecting your imaginary business, choosing a type of business your team members have had personal experience with or simply one you would like to have experience with in the future.

3. Start-up: Develop a partial business plan for your proposed business, focusing on points one and two of the guidelines on pages 138–140 of your text. Be sure to indicate the specific form of business you select and how you plan to finance the start-up.

4. Total Quality Management: You recognize the importance of customer satisfaction to the success of your new business and decide to implement a quality program. Identify the internal and external customers of your imaginary business. What do you think their major quality requirements will be? What measures will you need to implement to satisfy those specific needs? What competitor provides the benchmark for your industry and what can you do to reach its standard of performance?

5. Present your business to the class and explain the decisions you've made in developing your business plan and quality program.

VIDEO CASE

WAINWRIGHT INDUSTRIES, INC. Quality has become the key ingredient to business success for hundreds of firms in the late 1990s. Quality programs permeate every industry, company, and department of the most competitive firms today. At Wainwright Industries, Inc., quality concepts are key factors in this parts manufacturer's relationship with its employees, suppliers, and customers.

Wainwright's commitment to quality has involved an ongoing search for ways to improve the organization as a whole. Ideas from inside and outside the firm have resulted in streamlined processes and reductions in delivery times. Training programs have become more effective, and employee empowerment has produced a rich source of ideas. In fact, each Wainwright associate—a term preferred over employee—averages one implemented improvement each week.

Wainwright is a major supplier of stamped and machined parts to American and foreign customers in the automobile, aerospace, home-security, and information processing industries. By continuously improving production operations and employee and business relationships, the firm generates some $30 million in annual sales.

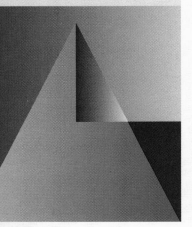

As a supplier to so many different industries, Wainwright must ensure its products meet a variety of customer specifications. The supplier certification requirements that exist in some industries are welcomed by Wainwright management as an opportunity to improve customer satisfaction. Quality efforts have earned Wainwright the enviable status of preferred supplier to a growing number of quality-conscious customers. The company also leverages the strengths of its own suppliers, tapping their expertise and capabilities. In search of better ways of doing business, Wainwright benchmarked acknowledged world-class performers in the electronics, textile, and other industries. From these visits, Wainwright managers learned new processes and programs that, when implemented, enhanced the quality objectives of the firm.

Milliken & Co., a recent Baldrige Award winner, was one of the companies whose operations Wainwright decided to study. This led Wainwright to implement a continuous improvement process designed to elicit suggestions from associates and engage them fully in quality efforts. After some fine-tuning of the process, the flow of suggestions has increased dramatically. A key to the program's success has been providing quick feedback on every suggestion. Every suggestion has been acted upon by management within 24 hours of its receipt, and many are implemented immediately.

Rising levels of customer satisfaction and steadily increasing business are indications that Wainwright is putting good ideas into practice. Since 1992, overall customer satisfaction has risen to 95 percent. At the same time, defect and scrap rates, manufacturing cycle time, and quality costs have all declined, attesting to improved levels of operational efficiency. Internally, quality improvements have directly benefitted associates in the forms of increased profit sharing and improved work place safety. For Wainwright, the benefits include fewer accidents and an 86 percent decline in workers' compensation costs, and absenteeism has been slashed to 1 percent. These improvements also add up to a high level of job satisfaction among Wainwright associates.

Wainwright aims for total customer satisfaction, a moving target that the company tracks through extensive sets of quality measures. Drawing from all levels of the organization, chairman Arthur D. Wainwright and the company's senior management team lead a planning process that sets company goals, develops underlying implementation strategies, and sets key quality requirements for goods, services, and operational performance. Responsibility and authority for accomplishing goals and meeting customer requirements are entrusted to the company's associates, who work in teams to design and implement improvements. They even have the power to make purchasing decisions.

Associates are recognized as the company's most important resource. Beginning with their first day on the job and almost every day thereafter, associates are fully engaged in Wainwright's quality efforts. During new associate orientation, senior managers explain the importance of quality and customer satisfaction and outline the company's approaches

Malcolm Baldrige
National Quality Award
1994 Winner

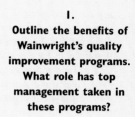

to continuous improvement. Two follow-up sessions are held after associates have been on the job 24 and 72 days. Continuity is assured through semiannual appraisals, during which each associate's performance is coupled with quality measures for each of the company's five strategic indicators. To ensure that associates have the knowledge and skills necessary to accomplish quality and performance objectives, the company invests in training programs on such topics as quality values, communication techniques, problem solving, statistical process control, and synchronous manufacturing—a systematic method for identifying and evaluating opportunities to simplify processes and reduce waste. Wainwright encourages associates to pursue promotions, and provides full reimbursement for courses taken for professional and personal development.

The status of Wainwright's continuous improvement efforts is tracked by the company's information and analysis center. Trends for quality and performance indicators are identified and each customer is assigned a monthly satisfaction index score. In addition, the center sets targets for exceeding customer expectations and provides weekly customer feedback reports. A green flag next to a customer's satisfaction rating indicates that Wainwright is on track in meeting its goals; a red flag warns of problems that could prevent the company from accomplishing its goals. For every red flag, an action team is formed to work with the customer, study the problem, and identify and implement corrective actions.

At the division level, quality trends and satisfaction ratings for both internal and external customers are formally reviewed by all division associates on a weekly basis. Monthly reviews are also conducted by senior management. To keep quality foremost in the minds of Wainwright associates, a meeting area has been designated for all in-house training, staff meetings, and presentations to customers and suppliers.

Continuous improvement efforts are credited for building the strength of the company, from helping it leverage investments in computer-aided design and manufacturing equipment (such as part-sequencing and just-in-time delivery service) to streamlining requisition procedures that today allow 95 percent of all purchase orders to be processed within 24 hours of receipt. At the production end, process reengineering and simplification have enabled Wainwright to cut the lead time for making one of its main products from 9 days to 15 minutes, and defect rates have declined tenfold. For customers, this means an on-time delivery rate of 100 percent, as compared with the former rate of 75 percent.

The pursuit of quality has made Wainwright a formidable competitor in its field. Since initiating its continuous improvement process in 1991, the company reports a steadily growing market share, productivity gains above industry averages, and increased profit margins, all of which is proof that quality pays.

QUESTIONS

1.
Outline the benefits of Wainwright's quality improvement programs. What role has top management taken in these programs?

2.
Relate Wainwright's benchmarking experiences to the steps in the benchmarking process discussed in this chapter. Why do you think the firm chose to benchmark firms from different industries?

3.
Discuss the roles played by teams in Wainwright's total quality management efforts. Why does the firm place so much emphasis on employee training? How does the company encourage its associates to become involved in its continuous improvement efforts?

4.
How might Wainwright secure feedback from its internal customers, external customers, and suppliers?

CAREERS IN BUSINESS

CAREER PROFILE: TOM PATTON For as long as he can remember, Tom Patton has possessed a driving passion for business and, especially, for entrepreneurship. But he pushed his dreams of starting his own business into the background following his graduation from Oregon State University when he received a job offer from John Deere Co. that was too good to turn down. His evaluation of the job proved correct, and Patton spent 16 successful years with Deere, first as a sales representative and later as a sales manager. When the firm announced a bonus program for senior employees as part of a volunteer workforce reduction, Patton saw a chance to fulfill his dormant, but not forgotten, dream of entrepreneurship. He took the early retirement offer from Deere and moved his family back to their native Pacific Northwest. ■ Even though he had managed to accumulate a financial nest egg, Patton decided to move cautiously. Following discussions with former OSU business professors, his alumni association, and the Agricultural Trade Association, he landed a position with the Tri City Industrial Development and Economic Council (TRIDEC), an organization responsible for attracting industry to the tri-city area of Pasco, Kennewick, and Richland, Washington. After identifying companies interested in expanding or relocating, Patton plays host to company representatives and demonstrates what the communities can offer in terms of a quality work force, business infrastructure, and overall quality of life. He uses his sales and interpersonal skills to match the needs of each business to the needs of the community to their mutual benefit. Patton's abilities were rewarded by his 1995 promotion to senior vice president of commerce and industry. ■ Patton has also managed to find time to pursue his entrepreneurial dream. The idea for a new venture came during the telecast of an exceptionally exciting basketball game. At one point in the game, the crowd was so loud that the commentator mentioned it. Tom and his friend thought it would be great to actually measure the crowd noise level. After researching the technology involved, they developed a prototype for a Crowd Noise Scoreboard that would measure and display the level of noise a crowd produced. Tom realized that he didn't have the resources or experience to produce or market the idea, so he presented it to the major players in the industry and found a taker. He licensed the idea of the Crowd Noise Scoreboard and now receives a royalty on all sales. Tom recommends licensing to any entrepreneur who doesn't have the funds or the experience to thoroughly develop an idea alone. He is currently developing another idea involving interactive media.

Small business is a crucial part of the U.S. economy, since it creates two-thirds of the nation's GDP. Retail stores, service firms, and high technology companies are among the most common small businesses. Franchising, an important aspect of small business, employs millions of people working in businesses that range from muffler repair shops to dental offices and from fast-food restaurants to employment agencies.

This section will investigate some specific jobs in small business and franchising, including small business owners, small business consultants, franchise directors, franchisees, venture capitalists, and travel agents, as well as the attorneys and legal assistants who help people set up businesses.

SMALL BUSINESS OWNERS

Small business owners are usually involved in the conception, financing, and day-to-day operations of their enterprises.

Job Description Many small business owners are people who saw consumer needs for specific goods or services and decided to go into business to fill those needs. Judging the marketability of a product involves conducting market research into such areas as location and pricing. Small business owners must also find ways to finance their enterprises, which often involves working with banks, setting up partnerships, and submitting business plans to the SBA. The day-to-day operation of a business entails keeping records, managing employees, advertising, and dealing with customers.

Career Path Many owners gained their experience working in other small businesses. Others worked for large corporations and decided they would rather work for themselves.

Salary The earnings of small business owners vary widely.

SMALL BUSINESS CONSULTANTS

Many small business owners employ consultants to help them put their businesses on a sound footing.

Job Description Small business consultants help firms to develop financial plans to attract investors or secure business loans. They also set up marketing plans and accounting systems to meet day-to-day financial needs. In addition, consultants work with owners to establish employee benefit packages or provide needed advice on management techniques.

Career Path Many people in this field are employed by large consulting firms, while others operate their own consulting firms. Most business consultants have degrees in business. Many gain experience and develop networks of business contacts working for established firms before becoming consultants.

Salary Earnings vary widely, depending upon personal efforts and levels of experience and contacts.

FRANCHISE DIRECTORS

Franchise directors, also known as *franchisors,* run franchise operations on a local, state, or national level. They work with franchisees, who sell their goods or services to the public.

Job Description Franchisors provide franchisees with proven products, management and marketing know-how, training, ongoing assistance, standardized operating procedures, and common identities. Franchise directors need sound backgrounds in finance and marketing. They must also be able to work with state and local governments to ensure that franchise operations comply with applicable disclosure requirements.

Career Path Many franchise directors gain experience in the franchise field by first working for other franchisors. Others start successful small businesses that have the potential for growth. They believe the best way to achieve this growth is through franchising.

Salary The earnings of franchise directors are often tied to the up-front fees collected by their franchises when franchisees buy into the operation, ongoing royalties, and fees for various authorized parts and services. Their incomes typically depend on the number of franchises in operation and their business success.

FRANCHISEES

Franchisees buy into ongoing franchise operations, which become their own small businesses.

Job Description Franchisees are independent businesspeople who finance and manage their own firms. Because buying into an established franchise chain is often costly, franchisees must be prepared to work with banks and financiers to raise funds. Once the business is in operation, they face the same responsibilities as other small business owners. They must also establish effective working relationships with franchisors.

Career Path Franchisees share similar backgrounds with those engaged in other small businesses. One major difference is that the franchisee buys into an established business whose products are often already known to the public, while the small business owner goes into business without the same benefit.

Salary Earnings vary depending on the success of the franchise.

VENTURE CAPITALISTS

Venture capitalists provide an essential financing service to small business owners.

Job Description Entrepreneurs in need of start-up money often turn to venture capitalists for funds. Venture capitalists see ideas that might turn into profitable businesses and decide to back the entrepreneur with needed financing in exchange for a percentage of the business. Venture capitalists work closely with banks and other financing sources. They also work closely with entrepreneurs, who present financial and business plans for review.

Career Path Venture capitalists must have strong backgrounds in finance. Many have worked in the finance functions of large corporations.

Salary Earnings depend on the number of businesses venture capitalists finance and the success of these enterprises.

TRAVEL AGENTS

Travel agencies are a rapidly growing type of small business that make travel arrangements for both business and individual clients. The Bureau of Labor Statistics expects faster than average growth in this employment field in the years ahead.

Job Description Travel agents provide an important service to their clients, saving both time and money in planning and arranging their trips. Travel agents must be very detail oriented and able to work on a number of projects at once. Travel agencies use computer reservation systems to obtain airline tickets and hotel rooms. Agents also take phone calls from clients to determine their needs and contact vendors to work on special arrangements.

Career Path Beginning travel agents might work directly for airlines as reservation agents or in travel agencies handling relatively uncomplicated bookings. Their responsibilities increase with experience and ability. At the top of the ladder, travel agents set up their own agencies.

Salary In a recent year experienced travel agents earned, on average, $25,007. The average starting salary was $12,428.

PRIVATE PRACTICE ATTORNEYS

Businesses have many legal needs that are primarily filled by attorneys specializing in corporate law. In a recent year 626,000 lawyers were in the work force, with much faster than average growth forecast until 2000.

Job Description About four-fifths of all attorneys go into private practice to represent small businesspeople and other firms that require their assistance. Their practices often cover a range of commercial law.

Career Path New law school graduates do research for experienced attorneys and handle small cases. As they gain experience, they take on increased responsibility. A law firm partnership is the ultimate career step for attorneys in private practice.

Salary Annual salaries of beginning lawyers in private industry average $36,600, while experienced lawyers average about $134,000.

LEGAL ASSISTANTS

Legal assistants, or paralegals, work with attorneys to provide legal services to individuals and businesses, including many small businesses. Currently, about 95,000 people are employed as legal assistants throughout the United States.

Job Description Paralegals are supervised by attorneys. Most of their work involves legal research, but they also file court papers, help to develop legal arguments, and assist with affidavits. Legal assistants working directly for firms assist attorneys with their specific areas of responsibility, such as financing.

Career Path Beginning paralegals are given routine tasks and are closely monitored. As they acquire experience, they are assigned more challenging responsibilities. Some paralegals become office managers and supervise other staff.

Salary The average starting salary for legal assistants in a recent year was $21,540. The average salary was $28,300.

CORPORATE ATTORNEYS

Businesses have many legal needs that are primarily filled by in-house or hired attorneys specializing in corporate law.

Job Description Depending on the size of the firm, the corporate attorney may be a generalist or a specialist in a type of law, such as tax law or labor law. The corporate attorney meets with top officials of the firm to discuss strategy and give legal advice. A great deal of time is spent preparing for negotiations or trials.

Career Path New hires work for experienced attorneys and handle small cases. As they gain experience, they take on increased responsibility. Many CEOs have started in firms' legal departments.

Salary Size of the company and location play a role in determining salaries. Corporate attorneys receive pay increases as they take on more responsibility. The average starting salary for a corporate attorney in a recent year was $41,300.

DISCOVERING YOUR BUSINESS CAREER: CAREER DESIGN EXERCISES

SKILLS

At the end of Part I, you learned that your interests are very important in choosing a career. You may have thought that there were many things that interested you but that you were not capable of doing. This exercise will help you discover your skills and talents, and you will be surprised at the number of skills you possess. In fact, it is not unusual for students to uncover 50 or more of their skills in this exercise.

By the way, this is not a time to be modest. If you think you have a skill, type it in. Your professor may help you to verify if you truly possess the skills you listed.

THIS EXERCISE WILL HELP YOU TO

- Identify many of your skills and talents.
- Discover you possess far more skills than you realize.
- Improve your awareness of your value to a potential employer.

HOW TO LOCATE THE EXERCISE

When you see the main menu for Career Design, select "Who Am I?" Then select "Skills."

ENTREPRENEURIAL QUOTIENT

Have you ever thought that you might want to start your own business some day? This exercise will help you determine whether you have what it takes to become an entrepreneur. Your professor may also follow up with some important things to consider in deciding if a new business idea is worth pursuing.

THIS EXERCISE WILL HELP YOU TO

- Develop a realistic picture of what it takes to become an entrepreneur.
- Gain some personal insights into your inclination toward starting your own business.

HOW TO LOCATE THE EXERCISE

When you see the main menu for Career Design, select "Who Am I?" Then select "Entrepreneurial Quotient."

CHAPTER 8

MANAGEMENT AND THE INTERNAL ORGANIZATION

CHAPTER 9

MANAGEMENT OF HUMAN RESOURCES

CHAPTER 10

TEAMWORK AND COMMUNICATION

CHAPTER 11

LABOR–MANAGEMENT RELATIONS

CHAPTER 12

PRODUCTION AND OPERATIONS MANAGEMENT

PART III

MANAGEMENT: ORGANIZATION, PEOPLE, AND PRODUCTION

CHAPTER 8

MANAGEMENT AND THE INTERNAL ORGANIZATION

LEARNING GOALS

1. Distinguish between a firm's mission statement and its corporate objectives.
2. Explain the concept of competitive differentiation and identify the primary methods used to create it.
3. Explain SWOT analysis and how it is used in corporate planning.
4. Differentiate between the various methods of quantitative and qualitative forecasting.
5. Discuss the need for organizational structure, and evaluate each of the four basic forms of organization.
6. Identify the skills required for managerial success.
7. Explain the concept of leadership, and identify the three basic leadership styles.
8. List the steps in the decision-making process, and contrast programmed and nonprogrammed decisions.
9. Discuss qualities that characterize successful global managers.

SEGA "Welcome to the next level"—The slogan says it all. Since its birth in 1954, Sega Enterprises Ltd. has beaten its competitors by offering its customers the next wave in technology. ■ Although Sega's headquarters are located in Japan, the company was actually founded by Brooklyn native David Rosen. At 29, Rosen returned to Tokyo after a tour of duty there in the U.S. Air Force. His first business venture took market share from darkroom services by providing photo booths where customers could have their pictures taken and developed within minutes. Next, he created coin-operated mechanical games, which became popular on American military bases. In fact, the name *Sega* is derived from the first two letters of *Service Games,* the labels stamped on the game boxes. ■ During the 1960s, Sega achieved global recognition with its game Periscope, which became a worldwide hit. Recalls Rosen, "We got letters saying Sega had saved the industry." In 1989, Sega attacked video-game market leader Nintendo by introducing its sophisticated Genesis system, with 16-bit processing power. Since then, Nintendo's share of the 16-bit market has fallen from 60 percent to 37 percent, with Sega picking up the slack. ■ Competition in the video game industry can be as bloody as any video game itself, though. Game players quickly tire of yesterday's hit and seek tomorrow's sensation, and manufacturers are competing for ever larger market shares. These days, Sega, Nintendo, Sony, Atari, and 3DO are fighting to win the video game war. Price wars in Europe slashed Sega's profits by 63 percent in a single year, and overstocked inventories continue to hold down earnings. ■ Sega's plans involve a two-pronged management strategy based on product innovation. Every year, the firm invests $200 million in researching and developing new video games. Its latest innovation, code-named *Saturn,* utilizes state-of-the-art computing technology to play both compact disks and cartridges. Major competitor Nintendo's Project Reality machine will handle only cartridges at this time. ■ Sega CEO Hayao Nakayama realizes that his company must move beyond its core video game industry. He predicts that Sega will quickly evolve into an entertainment empire of unprecedented scale. "I see us as a new form of entertainment company," says Thomas Kalinske, CEO of Sega of America. "I don't think we should be happy until there are more people using our products than sitting down to watch *Melrose Place* or *Beverly Hills 90210.*" ■ Toward this end, the firm is forming strategic alliances with a wide range of corporate partners, including AT&T, Hitachi, Yamaha, and JVC. Many of these alliances involve exploring opportunities along the information superhighway. A joint venture with Catapult Entertainment allows Genesis enthusiasts in selected cities to compete over telephone lines via Catapult's XBAND modem and network service. Another venture with AT&T lets customers with Edge 16 modems play video games over phone lines. And then there's the Sega Channel, a pay-to-play cable channel sponsored by Sega, Time Warner, and Tele-Communications Inc. Sega executives now see their company in a position to help design the look and feel of the information superhighway. ■ Sega's most ambitious new venture is another entirely new form of entertainment: the virtual reality theme park. Visitors step inside stationary, windowless, truck-sized capsules, where computer-generated graphics create sensations of adventure in three dimensions. Customers drive race cars, steer space ships, and fight off alien invaders. ■ Sega has opened three virtual reality parks so far, with plans to open 50 by 1997. While the current parks are all in Japan, the company hopes to bring the concept to the United States within a year. Despite their high-tech computers, these parks are relatively inexpensive to build and operate. They require only about 3 percent of the land area consumed by Florida's Disney World, and they do away with the need for costly rides. Joypolis, the Yokohama theme park, earned almost $37 million during its first year alone. ■ Despite its success so far, not everyone believes that Sega can easily make the transition from manufacturing games to providing entertainment. Expansion has already sent Sega's costs

soaring; the firm now employs 5,200 workers, three times as many as in 1992. Some industry analysts express another concern that consumer reaction against the violence in Sega's products will hurt the company. "Sega has gotten to where they are with more violent and harder-edged concepts," comments Dan Acuff, president of Youth Market Systems in Glendale, California. "Nintendo has stayed softer, but I wouldn't suggest they leave the higher ground. There could be more moral backlash that could fall in the favor of Nintendo." Pressure from Congress and children's advocacy groups has forced Sega to pull its Night Trap game off of store shelves. ■ Rosen and other Sega execs remain confident, however, that customers will accompany them to the next level, whatever it may be. Each generation of technology, Rosen believes, inevitably burns itself out, but, he adds, "From those ashes, we have always had a stronger industry emerge."[1]

CHAPTER OVERVIEW

The governor of the state of California, the head coach of the New England Patriots, the chairman of The Gap chain of retail stores—these are all examples of managers. Other managers preside over organizations as diverse as Illinois State University, the Mayo Clinic, and a nearby Burger King.

The importance of effective management to organizational success cannot be overstated. Analyses of business failures usually list poor management as one of the leading causes. Says Al Dunlap, a consultant who has engineered turnarounds for many failing companies, "The problems all start at the top, with the senior people going through the motions and the board accepting the status quo. They hire consultants and draw up plan after plan—but somebody's got to execute, somebody's got to manage."[2]

Despite its challenges, a management career still appeals to many students in introductory business courses. When asked about their professional objectives, many students reply, "I want to be a manager."

This chapter will examine the meaning of the word *management* and its universal applications. First, it will look at how a company can create competitive differentiation. It will then examine the importance of mission statements and corporate objectives. It will discuss how managers use different types of planning and forecasting techniques to meet these objectives and look at different types of organizational structures, the skills required for managerial success, and the process of managerial decision making. Finally, it will examine international management issues and discuss new career opportunities for displaced managers.

UNIVERSAL MANAGEMENT PRINCIPLES

management
Achievement of organizational objectives through people and other resources.

Management is the achievement of organizational objectives through people and other resources. The manager's job is to combine human and technical resources in the best way possible to achieve the organization's objectives. Managers are not directly involved in production, that is, they do not produce finished products. Instead, they direct the efforts of others toward the company's goals.

The management principles and concepts presented in this chapter apply to not-for-profit organizations as well as profit-seeking firms. The local library administrator, the head of the Salvation Army, and a Boy Scout troop leader all perform managerial functions similar to those performed by their counterparts in industry. Service-oriented agencies benefit from effective management as much as profit-oriented ones do.

NEED FOR A VISION

An important managerial quality is **vision,** the ability to perceive marketplace needs and methods by which an organization can satisfy them. Thomas Edison, the famed inventor of thousands of products ranging from the electric light bulb to the phonograph and motion picture, was such a person. Not only did he have the ability to make great technological breakthroughs, but he also never forgot to focus on *salable solutions* to very real problems. As he put it, "Anything that won't sell, I don't want to invent. Its sales is proof of utility and utility is success."[3] Other well-known visionaries include:

vision
Ability to perceive marketplace needs and methods by which an organization can satisfy them.

- Fred Smith, who conceived of a nationwide overnight package delivery service with a sorting hub in Memphis, called Federal Express
- Anita Roddick, whose natural skin products and cosmetics, produced and packaged in an environmentally conscious manner, are the basis of The Body Shop global chain of retail outlets
- Wally Amos, a pioneer in producing and marketing premium-priced, high-quality gourmet cookies in the United States and abroad

Few businesspeople can match the vision of entrepreneur Edward Tuck. An electrical engineer who flies planes as a hobby, Tuck recently conceived the idea of building a network of hundreds of low-orbiting satellites to facilitate global communication. He sees a huge potential market, since 50 percent of the world's people live at least two hours away from a phone.

Tuck has been joined by two other entrepreneurs who are also known for their vision: William Gates, who started software manufacturer Microsoft, and Craig McCaw, who founded McCaw Cellular. The three plan to build a huge system of 840 low-orbit satellites—almost three times the number of satellites currently orbiting the earth. The system, called *Teledesic,* will provide videoconferencing, interactive media, and other information services to subscribers around the world.

Although Teledesic will cost $9 billion to build, it offers a totally new level of service to subscribers. Teledesic customers will be able to send and receive an almost unlimited amount of voice, data, and video information.[4]

DEVELOPING THE ORGANIZATION'S MISSION STATEMENT AND OBJECTIVES

Before managers formulate plans and strategies, they need to determine their company's larger purpose. In developing a mission statement and organizational objectives, a company defines its general goals and lays out a plan for achieving them. The **mission statement,** a written explanation of a company's aims, may include information about what goods or services the firm will offer and what market it will serve, as well as information on the company's belief system or morals and its treatment of employees. The three mission statements shown in Figure 8.1 illustrate these companies' expressions of their individual aims and beliefs.

Mission statements generally seek to guide the work of people within a company, but they can also inform customers of a company's point of view. Office furniture manufacturer Haworth, Inc., of Holland, Michigan, has developed a long mission statement that discusses principles ("Haworth competes enthusiastically in a free enterprise system."), customer satisfaction ("We listen to our customers and understand their changing needs."), human resources ("Our corporate culture offers a participative environment that supports teams and individuals."), and dedication to quality ("At Haworth, we combine smart thinking with hard work to eliminate wasted time, effort, and materials.").[5]

mission statement
Written explanation of a company's aims.

objectives
Guideposts by which managers define standards that the organization should accomplish in such areas as profitability, customer service, and employee satisfaction.

Objectives set guideposts by which managers define standards that the organization should accomplish in such areas as profitability, customer service, and employee satisfaction. While the mission statement delineates the company's goals in general terms,

FIGURE 8.1 MISSION STATEMENTS

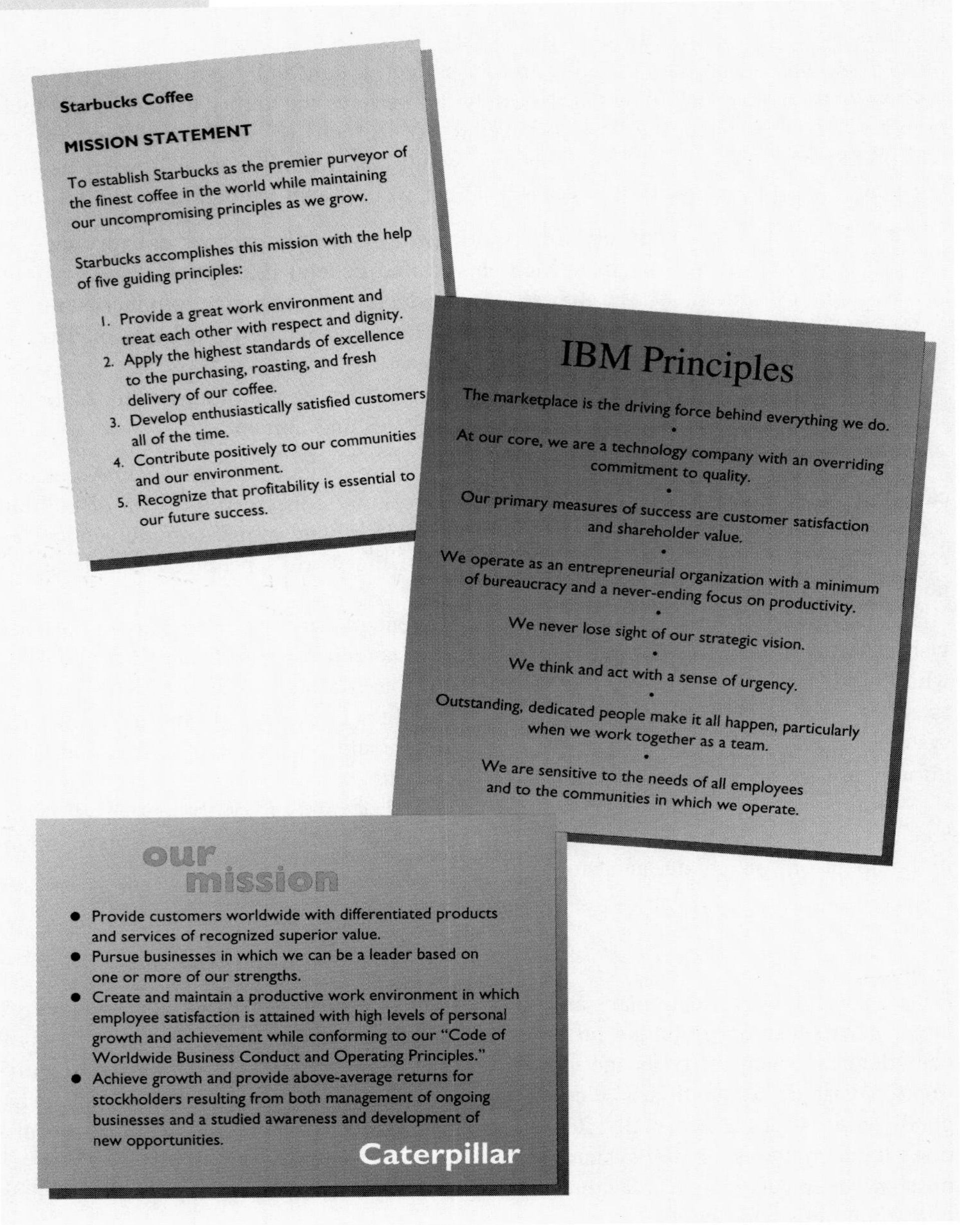

Starbucks Coffee
MISSION STATEMENT
To establish Starbucks as the premier purveyor of the finest coffee in the world while maintaining our uncompromising principles as we grow.
Starbucks accomplishes this mission with the help of five guiding principles:
1. Provide a great work environment and treat each other with respect and dignity.
2. Apply the highest standards of excellence to the purchasing, roasting, and fresh delivery of our coffee.
3. Develop enthusiastically satisfied customers all of the time.
4. Contribute positively to our communities and our environment.
5. Recognize that profitability is essential to our future success.
IBM Principles
The marketplace is the driving force behind everything we do.
At our core, we are a technology company with an overriding commitment to quality.
Our primary measures of success are customer satisfaction and shareholder value.
We operate as an entrepreneurial organization with a minimum of bureaucracy and a never-ending focus on productivity.
We never lose sight of our strategic vision.
We think and act with a sense of urgency.
Outstanding, dedicated people make it all happen, particularly when we work together as a team.
We are sensitive to the needs of all employees and to the communities in which we operate.
our mission
Provide customers worldwide with differentiated products and services of recognized superior value.
Pursue businesses in which we can be a leader based on one or more of our strengths.
Create and maintain a productive work environment in which employee satisfaction is attained with high levels of personal growth and achievement while conforming to our "Code of Worldwide Business Conduct and Operating Principles."
Achieve growth and provide above-average returns for stockholders resulting from both management of ongoing businesses and a studied awareness and development of new opportunities.
Caterpillar

objectives are more concrete. More and more businesses are setting objectives in terms other than profitability. As public concern about environmental issues mounts, many firms find that operating in an environmentally responsible manner pays off with customers. Others channel some of their profits into socially responsible causes, such as funding educational programs and scholarships.

Objectives serve three important functions. First, by specifying end goals for the organization, objectives direct the efforts of managers. For example, General Electric identified the "need for speed" as a primary objective for its effort to stay competitive in a rapidly changing marketplace. Figure 8.2 illustrates the factors that GE identified as essential to meeting this goal. The company started with meetings called *Work-Out* ses-

FIGURE 8.2 IDENTIFYING PRIMARY OBJECTIVES AT GENERAL ELECTRIC

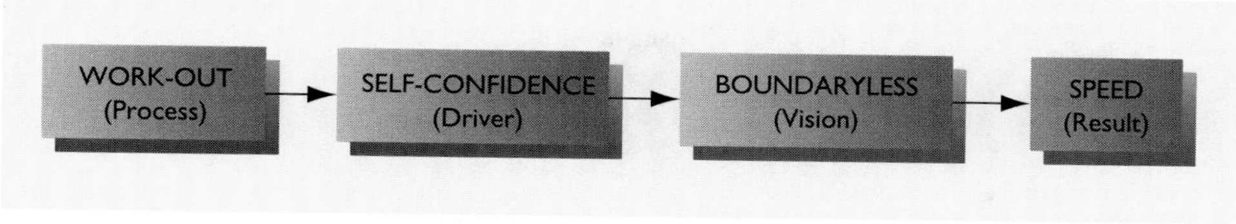

sions attended by employees from all areas and levels of the company. Employees were encouraged to pinpoint problems, bring up ideas, and suggest solutions. This process improved self-confidence for all workers, leading to GE's vision of a company without boundaries in which departments work together rather than independently of each other.

For a second important function, objectives provide standards or tangible benchmarks against which to evaluate organizational performance. Without such standards, the manager has no means of deciding whether work succeeds or fails. If performance appears unsatisfactory, management can refocus the organization in the direction of its objectives.

Finally, objectives encourage managers and workers to do their best. A certain percentage of defect-free products, for example, might be set as a goal, and the firm might link bonuses, profit sharing, or other incentives to accomplishing it.

CREATING COMPETITIVE DIFFERENTIATION

Once a company has developed a mission statement and set objectives, it still faces the challenge of competing with other companies that pursue similar missions and objectives. **Competitive differentiation** refers to any aspect of a company or its performance that makes it more successful than its competitors. Figure 8.3 illustrates methods of creating competitive differentiation, such as improving management of human resources, implementing a total quality management program, developing innovative products, improving logistics within the company through just-in-time techniques, utilizing up-to-date technology, and reducing overhead and prices. Many firms combine several of these techniques in achieving competitive differentiation.

competitive differentiation
Any aspect of a company or its performance that makes it more successful than its competitors.

HUMAN RESOURCES

Howard Schultz, president and CEO of coffee retailer Starbucks, has never forgotten what it was like to be financially insecure. "My dad was a blue-collar worker," he explains. "He didn't have health insurance or benefits, and I saw firsthand the debilitating effect that had on him and on our family." Schultz determined never to treat workers the way his father was treated. This determination motivated Schultz to provide Starbucks employees with a benefits plan that is unprecedented in the retail service industry, with many part-time workers and traditionally high turnover. Starbucks employees who work more than 20 hours a week receive health insurance, including preventive medical, vision, and dental coverage, plus stock options and, of course, coffee.

Says Schultz, "More than half of our retail sales force is part-time workers. That tells me that the majority of our customers are coming into contact with part-timers. How we treat our people is directly related to how we treat our customers and to the quality of our product. It's unarguable that our part-timers are key to the company's success."

Employee turnover at Starbucks is less than 50 percent annually. For food retailers, the usual rate is over 100 percent. Since Starbucks provides extensive training for each worker, says Schultz, "the longer an employee stays with us, the more we save." In addition, employee pilfering is low.

FIGURE 8.3 SOURCES OF COMPETITIVE DIFFERENTIATION

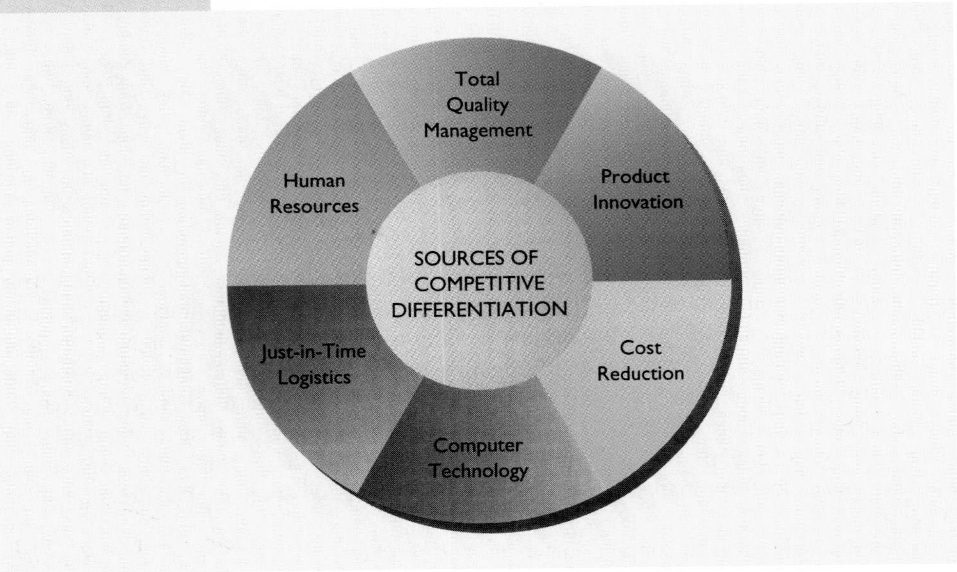

Schultz identifies employee loyalty as one of Starbucks' main strengths. He says that, when the workers became stockholders, "All kinds of employees started coming up with ways to save money and improve productivity." He adds, "Our only sustainable competitive advantage is the quality of our work force. We're building a national retail company by creating pride in—and a stake in—the outcome of our labor."[6]

TOTAL QUALITY MANAGEMENT

As Chapter 7 explained, total quality management (TQM) is an approach to competition based on pursuing quality as a strategic objective and viewing the organization as an entire system in which all members contribute to its final results. A TQM system trains workers to be more assertive and knowledgeable. TQM makes quality part of the process from start to finish. This includes investing money up front to make products correctly the first time.

Some companies have found TQM to be expensive and ineffective. Without sufficient guidance and support from the highest levels of a business, different divisions and individuals may pursue the same goal by taking different actions, actions that may actually conflict with each other.[7] Although TQM programs require additional funding initially, ultimately they save money for companies by reducing expenses related to poor quality, such as downtime, repairs, rework, and employee attrition, not to mention angry customers.

Mail-order company L. L. Bean overcame these limitations and developed a successful TQM system by relying heavily on employee commitment. After executives discovered that employees wanted to provide quality service, but lacked the authority to make it happen, they decided to "maximize customer satisfaction in the most efficient and effective way by totally involving people in improving the way work is done." Managed mostly by the human resources department, L. L. Bean's TQM program focuses on changing the ways in which employees and management interact, with managers trading the role of experts for that of coaches and developers. The results? Increased profits, happier customers, better employee performance, fewer accidents, and higher efficiency.[8]

PRODUCT INNOVATION

The chapter's opening story reported how Sega Enterprises uses constant product innovation to stay competitive in the fast-changing entertainment industry. Life Fitness, an Illinois maker of exercise equipment, adapts technology from Sega's rival, Nintendo, to add competitive differentiation to its own products.

Not many people enjoy riding a stationary bicycle. Life Fitness's Exertainment system attempts to make the exercise more interesting by combining it with Nintendo's Mountain Bike Rally video game. Interactive software lets the rider's speed and steering and the bike's resistance respond directly to events in the game. Exercisers can select from eight characters, eight bike models, and eight types of terrain to program their own customized workouts. Oil slicks, bumpy roads, and other hazards make the course more challenging. In addition, the software monitors the rider's heart rate, tracks workouts, and charts progress over time. Life Fitness plans to add Nintendo games to stair climbers and other exercise equipment to create an entire line of Exertainment products.[9]

JUST-IN-TIME LOGISTICS

Just-in-time (JIT) logistics is a method of streamlining the operations of a manufacturer or service provider by eliminating wasted time and space. By reducing "nonvalue-added time" (for instance, the time during which a partially assembled product sits on a table awaiting a missing part or a finished product sits in a warehouse) and boosting "value-added time," JIT decreases overhead and increases profits.

Although JIT may sound appropriate only to large manufacturing companies, it can be helpful for the smallest service business, as well. For instance, a self-employed electrician can benefit from the JIT approach by limiting the parts kept on hand, arranging appointments with no wasted time, or nonvalue-added time, between them, and striving to do a perfect job the first time. In this way, the electrician will improve his or her income through JIT methods.[10] Chapter 12 will discuss JIT further.

COMPUTER TECHNOLOGY

Every industry can benefit from advances in computer technology. Mail-order companies keep databases on people's buying habits to target their mailings to the most responsive audiences. Bookstores track inventory and determine instantly which distributor has the book that a customer seeks. A retailer checks in seconds whether a buyer's credit card is valid.

The developing technology of videoconferencing allows employees to talk and work together through their personal computers. Videoconferencing systems can transmit video images, sounds, and graphics through computers equipped with microphones and tiny cameras. Rich Martin, an engineer at air conditioner manufacturer Carrier Corp., uses a videoconferencing system to teach Carrier service technicians how to repair the company's new products. While Martin repairs air conditioners on camera at Carrier's North American headquarters in Syracuse, New York, his students watch and learn on computer screens located across the country. In addition to cutting travel expenses, videoconferencing demonstrations help employees to learn new techniques more quickly and to work together more easily.[11] Chapter 17 will discuss in more detail the roles that computer technologies play in making companies more competitive.

COST REDUCTION

One method of creating competitive differentiation is as old-fashioned and simple as it could be: charge less for the product. This tactic challenges the firm to offer low prices, yet still make a profit. Retailer Wal-Mart solved this problem by insisting on the lowest

A BROADER PURPOSE

TECHNOLOGY SAVES JOBS AT CATERPILLAR

The impact of downsizing, farming out functions that previously were performed by company employees, and developing leaner, more competitive operations often affects more than a firm's profitability. These increasingly common changes in business operations during the late 1990s also show up in a shrinking list of employees. News reports of such downsizing typically include estimates of numbers of employees who will be laid off as a result of the cutbacks, but Caterpillar management has used technology to ensure that its ongoing corporate restructuring saves jobs along with the firm's standing as a profitable company. ■ For decades, the manufacturer of giant earth-moving, construction, and materials-handling heavy equipment had been one of America's corporate legends, praised for its high-quality products and its service-oriented competitiveness. It also made a strong contribution to export sales, generating 60 percent of its $10 billion sales abroad. The firm continued to remain competitive in the world market against such international rivals as Japan's Komatsu despite its labor-management difficulties of the late 1980s and early 1990s. ■ Aging, inefficient factories and an increasingly dated management structure began to catch up with the Peoria, Illinois-based firm, however, and CAT managers found themselves scrambling to recover from a 10 percent sales decline and annual losses approaching the $1 billion mark by the early 1990s. Turning the company around would require redesigning operations, moving to a more computer-based manufacturing system, and cutting layers of management. Realizing that such fundamental changes to a firm's internal structure are typically accompanied by massive job layoffs, CAT employees braced themselves to fight against foreseen job losses.

possible prices from suppliers. Its guarantee of everyday low pricing (EDLP) enticed people into the store, and as consumer loyalty grew, Wal-Mart eliminated expensive advertising campaigns. This combination of techniques made Wal-Mart a giant in discount retailing.

However, retailing is a competitive field, and other stores also adopted EDLP policies. In addition to longtime competitor Target, specialty retailers such as The Limited and catalog companies like Spiegel have lowered their prices to compete. "I think everybody prices off of Wal-Mart," says Wal-Mart Stores Division President Bill Fields. "You've got The Limited reaching levels we'd thought they'd never get to."[12] Wal-Mart is fighting back by building huge supermarket/discount stores and by expanding into Mexico and Canada.

PLANNING PROCESS

planning
Anticipating the future and determining the best courses of action to achieve organizational objectives.

With the mission statement developed, the objectives defined, and the method of achieving competitive differentiation determined, managers must plan the actions that will allow the company to anticipate the future and achieve its objectives. **Planning** involves making decisions about what activities the organization should perform; how big it should become; what production, marketing, and financial strategies it should set; and what resources it will need. In other words, planning answers the questions what should be done, by whom, where, when, and how.

Planning is a perpetual process. At start-up of a business, the owners and/or managers may focus the majority of their time on planning. Later, as business conditions and laws change, the business will need to change, as well. Therefore, companies must frequently monitor their operations and make necessary adjustments to their plans.

■ Caterpillar management chose to use the new information technologies of the 1990s to save jobs, however, not to eliminate them. Employee retraining played a major role in accomplishing this goal. In the past decade, the company has retrained employees whenever possible to perform the new tasks required in implementing modern, computer-based technologies. In 1993, some 30,000 employees were taught new skills and learned how to refine their old ones. Mike Walters, a 20-year veteran of the firm, is glad that CAT is taking advantage of new processes and methods. At the East Peoria, Illinois factory, Walters now operates a newly automated work cell, complete with its own state-of-the-art robot. Walters and tens of thousands of other CAT employees thank information technology for saving their jobs. If Caterpillar had not reengineered its manufacturing processes when it did, the company might not have survived in its highly competitive industry. In just one year following reorganization, the company reduced in-process inventories by more than 60 percent and cut the average time it took to process a part from 25 days to 6 days. ■ Many employees have also been retrained in CAT's second major restructuring effort: customer satisfaction. In 1990, the corporate structure was decentralized, pushing decision making into 13 profit centers and 4 service centers. Today, the company is sharply focused on customers' needs. It responds to customer requirements for new and updated products faster than ever before. Emphasis on product support and distribution has also played a major role in CAT's comeback. It now controls its highest level of global market share ever. ■ Statistics bear out Caterpillar's commitment to protecting the jobs of its work force. In 1993, the company increased the size of its hourly work force by 725 and reduced management and salaried employment by 224. Overall, worldwide employment ended the year at 51,250—an increase of 501 over the previous year. As CAT continues implementing state-of-the-art technologies, improving its work environment, expanding product lines and services, and pursing new business opportunities, it continues to reorganize and to preserve its commitment to the people who make it happen. Sources: Doug Bartholomew, "Caterpillar Digs In," *Information Week*, June 7, 1993, p. 21; and Caterpillar's *1993 Annual Report*.

QUESTIONS FOR CRITICAL THINKING

1. What are the dangers of cutting management and salaried personnel?
2. What are the advantages and disadvantages of utilizing multiple profit centers?
3. When is retraining not possible in restructuring?

Ongoing analysis and comparisons of actual performance with company objectives enable managers to adjust plans before problems become crises. Accomplishing other managerial functions also depends on sound, continual planning.

TYPES OF PLANNING

Analysts classify planning based on its scope. Types of planning, as shown in Table 8.1, include strategic, tactical, operational, adaptive, and contingency planning.

The most far-reaching type of planning is **strategic planning,** the process of determining the primary objectives of an organization, adopting courses of action, and allocating the resources necessary to achieve objectives. The strategic planning process is reflected in the firm's mission statement. For example, Kansas Gas and Electric Company defines its mission simply: "Provide excellent service to customers and a profit to shareholders." Strategic plans tend to be both broad and long-range, focusing on organizational objectives that will have major impacts on the organization over several years.

strategic planning
Process of determining the primary objectives of an organization, adopting courses of action, and allocating the resources necessary to achieve objectives.

Tactical planning involves implementing the activities specified by strategic plans. Tactical planning tends to focus on current and near-term activities required to implement overall strategies. Although strategic and tactical planning have different time frames, both must be integrated into an overall system designed to achieve organizational objectives.

tactical planning
Planning for short-term implementation of current activities and related resource allocations.

Operational planning creates the work standards that guide implementation of tactical plans. This involves choosing specific work targets and the right employees to carry out plans. Operational plans often state quotas, standards, or schedules. For example, the management of a major publishing house expects its sales representatives to make 20 customer contacts per day, with the first one at 8 A.M. or earlier.

operational planning
Work standards that guide implementation of tactical plans.

TABLE 8.1 TYPES OF PLANNING

TYPE	DESCRIPTION	EXAMPLE
Strategic planning	Establish overall objectives, position the organization in its environment; can be short-term or long-term	British Petroleum's plans to achieve its growth objectives through mergers and market expansions
Tactical planning	Implement activities and resource allocations; typically short-term	B. Dalton's Christmas gift book selection mailing
Operational planning	Set quotas, standards, or schedules to implement tactical plans	Standards for handling grievances within 48 hours of receipt
Adaptive planning	Ensure flexibility for responding to changes in the business environment by developing scenarios to take advantage of potential opportunities or problems	Nike's investigation of moving its athletic shoe production from Asia to Mexico following the passage of NAFTA
Contingency planning	Planning for emergencies	American Airlines' replacement of ATR commuter planes following a series of crashes

adaptive planning
Focusing and building on the strengths of the company while remaining flexible to develop opportunities.

contingency planning
Planning to cover problems resulting from a crisis to enable the company to resume operations as quickly and smoothly as possible.

Planning at the strategic, tactical, and operational levels needs to be fluid enough and forward-looking enough to adapt to changes in the situation and environment that surround a business. Therefore, to succeed in the volatile business world, companies must emphasize focus and flexibility in making plans; that is, companies must practice **adaptive planning.** In emphasizing focus, managers identify and then build on what the company does best. To emphasize flexibility they develop scenarios of future activities to prepare the firm to take advantage of opportunities when they occur. For example, a company that serves international markets must plan for changes in the strength of the dollar versus other currencies.

One of the more contemporary aspects of planning, **contingency planning,** seeks to resume operations as quickly and as smoothly as possible after a crisis while fully communicating what happened to the public. This process involves two components: business continuation and public communication. Many firms have developed management strategies to speed recovery from accidents such as airline crashes, factory fires, chemical leaks, oil spills, product tampering, and product failure. Contingency planning is more important than ever today. Over half of the worst industrial accidents in this century have taken place since 1977.

The 1994 Major League Baseball strike and the management lockout that delayed the beginning of the National Hockey League's 1995 season affected more people than athletes and fans. Together, they devastated the sales expectations of The Topps Company, a New York-based maker of sports trading cards. Revenues dropped by 66 percent within the first quarter following the stoppages of play and management was faced with the need for sales alternatives in the wake of sagging buyer interest.[13]

Many firms designate crisis managers to handle emergencies that may arise and to create effective crisis-prevention programs. Such a program would include providing special training to keep workers alert to dangers, delegating decision making and authority in a crisis to those who run the operation, improving internal communication systems, avoiding overworking employees, and ensuring that technology does not take away workers' ability to evaluate a situation.

Intel Corp.'s image as the world's premiere chip maker was threatened recently as word spread of mathematical glitches in its highly regarded Pentium microprocessor.

In contingency planning, companies prepare possible management strategies for swiftly resuming operations and communication with the public in the wake of unexpected crises like the bombing of this federal building in Oklahoma City.

After weeks of deliberation, the firm's crisis management team decided to replace any of the 3 million plus chips for any buyers who requested it. The offer, shown in Figure 8.4, could cost the giant chip maker over $600 million.[14]

INTEGRATING PLANNING WITH OTHER MANAGERIAL FUNCTIONS

Each step in planning gets more specific. From the global mission statement to general objectives to individual plans, each phase must fit into a comprehensive planning framework. The framework must also include small functional plans aimed at individual employees and relevant to individual tasks; these must fit within the overall framework to allow the firm to reach its objectives and achieve its mission. To ensure these results, the planning function must be integrated with the other three managerial functions of organizing, leading, and controlling.

Once plans have been developed, the manager's next step typically is organizing. **Organizing,** the second of the managerial functions shown in Figure 8.5, is the means by which management blends human and material resources through a formal structure of tasks and authority. It involves classifying and dividing work into manageable units by determining the specific work activities necessary to accomplish organizational objectives, grouping work activities into a logical pattern or structure, and assigning activities to specific positions and people.

organizing
Management function of blending human and material resources through a formal structure of tasks and authority.

The organizing function encompasses the important steps of staffing the organization with competent employees capable of performing the necessary activities and assigning authority and responsibility to these individuals. Chapter 9 discusses staffing in more detail.

After formulating plans and creating and staffing an organization, the manager's task centers on **leading,** which is guiding and motivating employees to accomplish organizational objectives. This work includes explaining procedures, issuing orders, and seeing that mistakes are corrected. The leading function is important at every level in the organization. To get things done through people, supervisors must be effective leaders.

leading
Guiding and motivating employees to accomplish organizational objectives.

FIGURE 8.4

IMPLEMENTING A CRISIS PLAN

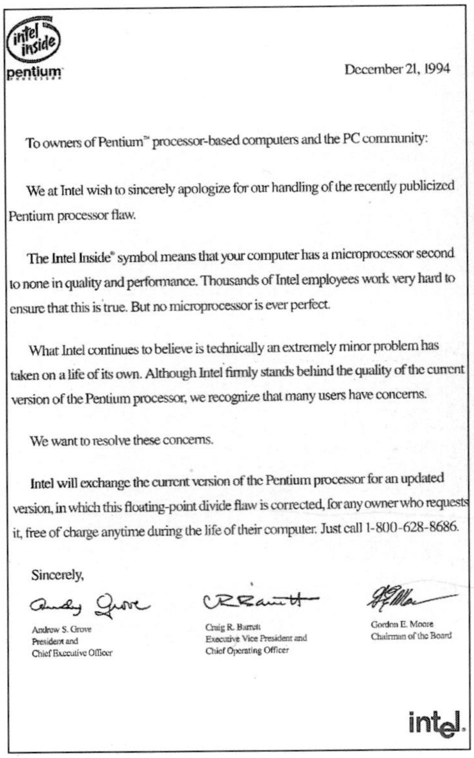

intel inside pentium

December 21, 1994

To owners of Pentium™ processor-based computers and the PC community:

We at Intel wish to sincerely apologize for our handling of the recently publicized Pentium processor flaw.

The Intel Inside® symbol means that your computer has a microprocessor second to none in quality and performance. Thousands of Intel employees work very hard to ensure that this is true. But no microprocessor is ever perfect.

What Intel continues to believe is technically an extremely minor problem has taken on a life of its own. Although Intel firmly stands behind the quality of the current version of the Pentium processor, we recognize that many users have concerns.

We want to resolve these concerns.

Intel will exchange the current version of the Pentium processor for an updated version, in which this floating-point divide flaw is corrected, for any owner who requests it, free of charge anytime during the life of their computer. Just call 1-800-628-8686.

Sincerely,

Andrew S. Grove
President and
Chief Executive Officer

Craig R. Barrett
Executive Vice President and
Chief Operating Officer

Gordon E. Moore
Chairman of the Board

intel.

However, middle and top managers must also be good leaders and motivators, and they must create an environment that fosters such leadership.

controlling
Evaluating the organization's performance to determine whether it is accomplishing its objectives.

Controlling is the management function of evaluating the organization's performance to determine whether it is accomplishing its objectives. The basic purpose of controlling is to evaluate the success of the planning function. The four basic steps in controlling are to establish performance standards, monitor actual performance, compare it to established standards, and, if performance does not meet standards, determine why and take corrective action.

PLANNING AND THE MANAGEMENT PYRAMID

top management
Highest level of the management hierarchy, staffed by executives who develop long-range plans and interact with the public and outside entities.

middle management
Level of management responsible for developing detailed plans and procedures to implement the general plans devised by top management.

supervisory management
First-line management responsible for the details of assigning workers to specific jobs and evaluating performance.

Chapter 5 divided a firm's management into three categories: top, middle, and supervisory management. The pyramid-shaped Transamerica headquarters building shown in Figure 8.6 is both a familiar part of the San Francisco landscape and a symbol of the shape of the traditional organizational structure found in most companies.

Although all three categories represent groups of managers, each level stresses different activities and different scopes of planning. **Top management,** the highest level of the management hierarchy, is staffed by executives who develop long-range plans and interact with the public and outside entities such as government. **Middle management** is more involved than top management in specific operations within the organization. Middle managers must develop detailed plans procedures to implement the general plans devised by top management. **Supervisory management,** or *first-line management,* includes people who are directly responsible for the details of assigning workers to specific jobs and evaluating performance daily or even hourly. Most people obtain their first managerial experience at the supervisory management level. They may have such job titles as supervisor, chairperson, department head, group leader, or section chief. In each case, the position involves coordinating the work of operating employees to accomplish tasks assigned by middle management.

FIGURE 8.5 FOUR MANAGEMENT FUNCTIONS

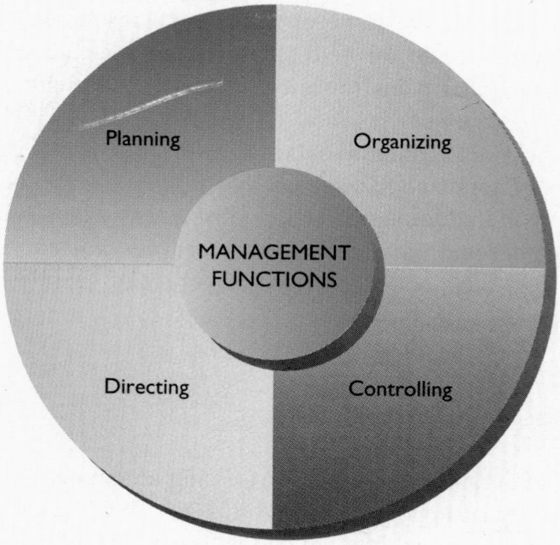

In general, members of top management, including the board of directors and the chief executive officer, spend a great deal of time on long-range strategic planning. Middle managers and supervisors focus on shorter-term tactical and operational planning. All managers should practice adaptive planning and contingency planning as these tasks relate to their particular areas of responsibility.

At any level, managers need the ability to lead and motivate other people, the ability to work in teams, the skill to formulate and carry out long-range plans, the courage to take risks, and the ability to relate to others. The lack of some of these abilities often prevents people from moving up the managerial ladder.

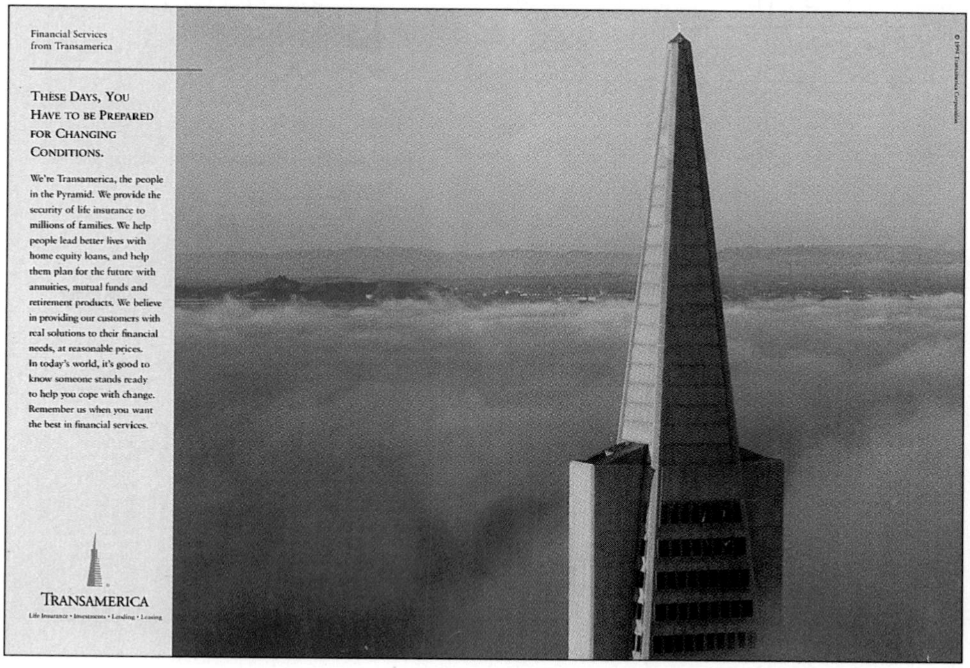

FIGURE 8.6

MANAGEMENT PYRAMID

ASSESSMENT AND EVALUATION

Throughout the planning process, managers must continually assess organizational resources and evaluate risks and opportunities, since developmental and marketing plans can depend on both internal and external pressures. Production, marketing, finance, technology, and employee talents are some of the internal resources that managers need to monitor frequently and evaluate for both strengths and weaknesses. They can then orient objectives and functional plans toward a company's strengths, aiming other objectives at overcoming weaknesses.

Organizations must also monitor outside factors, including environmental legislation, technological developments, successes and failures of competing companies, and changing social trends. In addition, managers must assess changes in uncontrollable factors, such as the weather and the value of the American dollar relative to other currencies, and the effects of these factors on the availability of supplies and the accessibility of foreign markets.

SWOT ANALYSIS

SWOT analysis
Organized method of assessing a company's internal strengths and weaknesses, and external opportunities and threats.

SWOT analysis is an organized method of assessing a company's internal strengths and weaknesses and its external opportunities and threats. SWOT analysis relies on the basic premise that developing a critical internal and external view of reality will lead the manager to select the appropriate strategy for accomplishing the organization's mission. As Figure 8.7 reveals, SWOT analysis allows managers to formulate a practical approach to planning based on a realistic assessment of a company's situation. Any company can be assessed through SWOT analysis at any point in its history.

When strengths and opportunities mesh, a company has *leverage* in the marketplace. As a hypothetical example, take a skin-products manufacturer with an extensive inventory of high-strength sunscreen products when TV weather reports start announcing UV

FIGURE 8.7 SWOT ANALYSIS

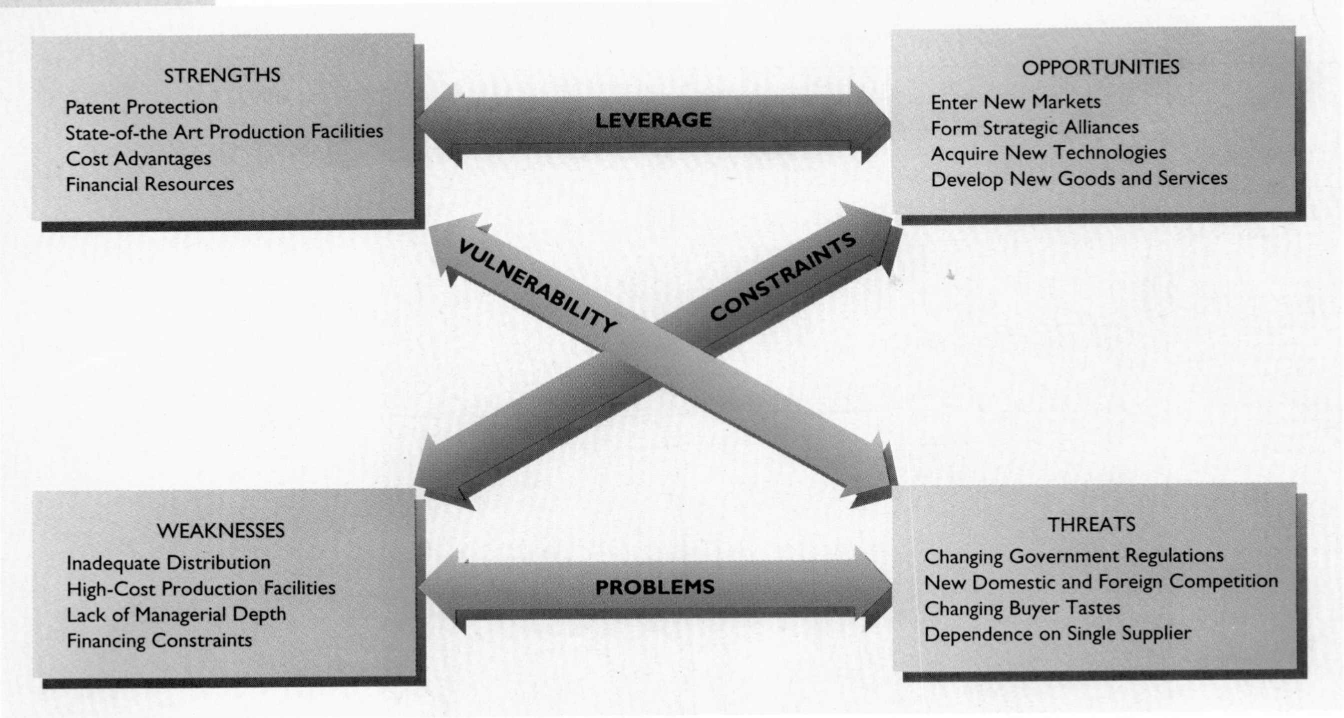

ratings regularly. On the other hand, when external threats assail a company's weaknesses, the company has a *problem* to address. This would occur if, when weather reports began to publicize UV ratings, the manufacturer had already decided to focus on suntan products rather than sunscreen products. In this case, the regular UV ratings would constitute a *threat* rather than an *opportunity*.

In cases where opportunity knocks but a company's weaknesses render it unable to answer, a *constraint* exists. In such a case, the manufacturer's focus on sun-protection products might limit its options if it were to lack inventory and cash while UV ratings were motivating more consumers to purchase sunscreen.

The combination of an outside threat with an inside strength is called a *vulnerability*. This might occur if the manufacturer of the top-selling sunscreen were to become the focus of false rumors that its products contained carcinogens.

STRATEGIC BUSINESS UNITS

As a company grows, it can produce more goods and services. A publishing company may issue multiple lines of books ranging from medical journals to literary fiction to photography to high school textbooks. How can such a large organization continuously evaluate and assess the present success and future plans of each segment of its business?

One technique is to break the company down into **strategic business units (SBUs).** Each SBU becomes an individual organization with its own executives, workers, objectives, and products—and its own planning. This configuration gives the overall company more flexibility since smaller divisions can respond more quickly to changes in the marketplace and each SBU can make decisions independent of the needs and limitations of other parts of the company. While the literary fiction division of the publishing company focuses on quick delivery of products to avid readers, the photography book SBU could investigate cutting-edge, four-color printing technology.

strategic business units (SBUs) *Related product groupings of businesses within a multiproduct firm with specific managers, resources, objectives, and competitors.*

Units of software manufacturer Microsoft, for instance, pursue expansive and varied goals. Therefore, the SBU approach is a logical way to divide up the work of the huge company. Microsoft's advanced technology division seeks to supply the software

Asea Brown Boveri (ABB) is a global engineering company headquartered in Zurich but with factories world-wide, including this one in Hungary. The company operates as 1,300 strategic business units, each with its own executives, workers, objective, and products.

for TV-top boxes that plug users into thousands of digitized movies and TV shows and for computers so small that they can be worn like wristwatches. The consumer software division focuses on consumer-oriented "edutainment" CD-ROM titles. The basic research division concentrates on such challenges as developing natural language programs that understand English commands.[15]

FORECASTING

Developing plans requires managers to make predictions regarding future events. Before placing orders for raw materials and component parts at an auto assembly plant, procurement specialists require an estimate of the number of vehicles that the firm plans to produce during the following few months. A manager may have to answer the question, "Do we have enough funds on hand to get us through the holiday season?" The answer depends on the amount of funds that management expects to receive and distribute over this time period. If managers base these plans on faulty estimates, significant problems are likely to arise. Consequently, forecasts are important management tools.

forecasting
Estimation or prediction of a company's future sales or income over the short term, intermediate term, or long term.

Forecasting is the estimation or prediction of a company's future sales, income, or market share. Forecasts can focus on the short term (under 1 year), the intermediate term (1 to 5 years), or the long term (over 5 years). They may also be qualitative (subjective) or quantitative (based on historical data and mathematical methods). In fact, firms often combine these approaches in developing future estimates. Table 8.2 summarizes the benefits and limitations of various types of qualitative and quantitative forecasting methods.

TABLE 8.2 BENEFITS AND LIMITATIONS OF VARIOUS FORECASTING TECHNIQUES

TECHNIQUE	BENEFITS	LIMITATIONS
QUALITATIVE METHODS		
Sales force composite	Salespeople have expert customer, product, and competitor knowledge; quick, inexpensive	Inaccurate forecasts may result from low estimates of salespeople concerned about their influence on quotas
Jury of executive opinion	Opinions come from executives in many different departments; quick, inexpensive	Managers may lack sufficient knowledge and experience to make meaningful predictions
Delphi technique	Group of experts can accurately predict long-term events such as technological breakthroughs	Time consuming, expensive
Survey of buyer intentions	Useful in predicting short-term and intermediate-term sales for a firm that has only a few customers	Intention to buy may not result in actual purchase; time consuming, expensive
QUANTITATIVE METHODS		
Test markets	Provides realistic information on actual purchases rather than on intent to buy	Alerts competitors to new-product plans; time consuming, expensive
Trend analysis	Quick, inexpensive; effective when customer demand and environmental factors are stable	Assumes the future is a continuation of the past; ignores environmental changes
Exponential smoothing	Same benefits as trend analysis, but emphasizes more recent data	Same limitations as trend analysis, but not as severe due to emphasis on recent data

Forecasts are important because they guide the planning process and support decision making. On the other hand, they are also problematical, as they can become outdated and incorrect due to changes in consumer spending habits, extreme weather conditions, unexpected moves by competitors, and other wild cards.

QUALITATIVE FORECASTING TECHNIQUES

Managers employ a number of qualitative forecasting techniques. The most common approaches are the sales force composite, the jury of executive opinion, the Delphi technique, and buyer surveys.

The sales force composite calls for salespeople to forecast short-term sales based on their extensive knowledge of their territories. Results are compiled by district, by region, and nationwide. The sales force composite produces useful but limited forecasts. Although salespeople may be savvy about customers and competitors, they are likely to focus on their sales quotas. Because of these limitations, the sales force composite is best used in tandem with other forecasting methods.

The jury of executive opinion bypasses the weaknesses of reliance on managers' opinions by compiling and averaging forecasts of top executives from all divisions. This technique works better with input from experienced managers who are well informed about sales and changing trends. The jury of executive opinion is particularly well suited to short-term forecasting, and it is useful in the development of new products.

The Delphi technique resembles the jury of executive opinion, but it consults a jury made up of experts from outside the company. The firm sends a questionnaire to each expert and compiles and averages answers. Instead of just using that data, it sends another questionnaire, adjusted to account for the first set of answers, to each expert. The technique is not considered complete until the experts reach a consensus. Although an expensive and lengthy process, the Delphi technique can forecast technological advances and long-term company success.

Another form of forecasting relies on information culled from buyer surveys, based on mailed questionnaires and/or telephone and personal interviews. This expensive technique has some serious limitations; people may not reveal their true buying habits, for one, and even if they honestly plan to make certain purchases, they may not ultimately do so. Buyer surveys work best for short-term or intermediate-term forecasting for companies with few customers.

QUANTITATIVE FORECASTING TECHNIQUES

Quantitative forecasting methods include test markets, trend analysis, and exponential smoothing.

Companies sometimes distribute new products in limited test markets to assess likely success. Through this realistic testing, businesses can identify the best prices, promotional strategies, and packaging for their wares. The success of a product in a few areas can often be extrapolated to a larger region or the whole country. Test marketing is expensive and risks tipping off competitors about a company's plans, but it provides pragmatically useful data.

Trend analysis is a mathematical approach to forecasting based on the assumption that the trends of the past will continue in the future. If, for instance, sales of a particular item have been increasing at 10 percent each year, trend analysis assumes that the 10 percent growth will continue. This method has two major limitations: it requires extensive historical data and any change in market stability will make forecasts based on this technique useless.

Exponential smoothing is a form of trend analysis that tries to paint a more realistic picture of future sales. By counting recent historical data as more important than less recent information, exponential smoothing bases its forecasts on the more relevant information.

ORGANIZATIONAL STRUCTURE

organization
Structured grouping of people working together to achieve organizational objectives.

An **organization,** the result of the organizing process, can be defined as a structured grouping of people working together to achieve organizational objectives. An organization features three key elements: human interaction, goal-directed activities, and structure. As Figure 8.8 suggests, the organizing process should result in an overall structure that permits interactions among individuals and departments needed to accomplish overall company objectives.

For a small business, the organizing process is relatively simple. The owner–manager of the local dry-cleaning firm employs a few people to sell, launder, and dry-clean clothing and to make deliveries. The owner usually handles purchasing tasks. The owner also assigns jobs to employees and personally directs business operations in pursuit of profits and growth. The tasks of coordinating work schedules and training new employees are relatively uncomplicated. Should one employee prove less effective in operating the check-out terminal, he or she can be reassigned to one of the cleaning tasks.

As a company grows, however, the need for organization increases. With increased size comes specialization and more employees. Rather than a single salesperson, the manager employs a sales force, rather than one bookkeeper, an entire accounting department. The large number of personnel and accompanying specialization make it impossible for one person to supervise all operations. Some type of formal organization becomes necessary.

Although a small firm experiences fewer organizational problems than a large one, both must have a formal structure to ensure that people perform tasks designed to accomplish company objectives. In a dry-cleaning company, for example, specific duties are assigned to wrappers, pressers, and other personnel.

DEPARTMENTALIZATION

departmentalization
Subdivision of work activities into units within the organization.

Departmentalization is the subdivision of work activities into units within the organization. This lets individuals specialize in certain jobs and thus perform them efficiently. A marketing department, perhaps headed by a marketing vice president, may include

FIGURE 8.8

CREATING AN EFFECTIVE ORGANIZATIONAL STRUCTURE

sales, advertising, and marketing research. A human resource department may include recruitment, training, employee benefits, and industrial relations.

Five major forms of departmentalization subdivide work by products, geographic areas, customers, functions, and processes. As Figure 8.9 illustrates, departmentalization on several different bases can appear in a single company. The figure shows departments organized according to functions performed, geographic regions covered, and types of customers served. Deciding which bases should underlie departmentalization involves balancing the advantages and disadvantages of each. The experience and judgment of top management come into play in such decisions.

The organizational structure of Procter & Gamble, the Cincinnati-based manufacturer of household goods ranging from Pringle's potato chips and Crest toothpaste to Tide detergent, exhibits product departmentalization. Each product-based division—food products, toiletries, paper products, packaged soaps and detergents, coffee, and industrial goods—is headed by a vice president.

Dillard's organizes its department stores in a geographic departmentalization scheme, as do railroads, gas and oil distributors, and other retailers. Many sporting goods stores subdivide in customer departmentalization schemes, with a wholesale operation serving school systems and retail divisions serving other customers.

Petroleum firms like Mobil and Texaco sometimes divide their operations on the basis of functional departmentalization, with exploration, production, refining, marketing, and finance departments. Finally, many manufacturers utilize process departmentalization, setting up separate departments to cut material, heat-treat it, form it into its final shape, and paint it.

ORGANIZATION CHARTS

As the organization grows, the manager must assign part of his or her activities to subordinates in order to have time to devote to managerial functions. The act of assigning activities to subordinates is called **delegation.** Subordinates to whom managers assign tasks thus receive responsibility, or obligations to perform those tasks. Along with responsibility go both authority, the power to make decisions and to act on them in carrying out responsibilities, and accountability, or responsibility for the results of their per-

delegation
Act of assigning activities to subordinates.

FIGURE 8.9 VARIOUS FORMS OF DEPARTMENTALIZATION IN ONE COMPANY

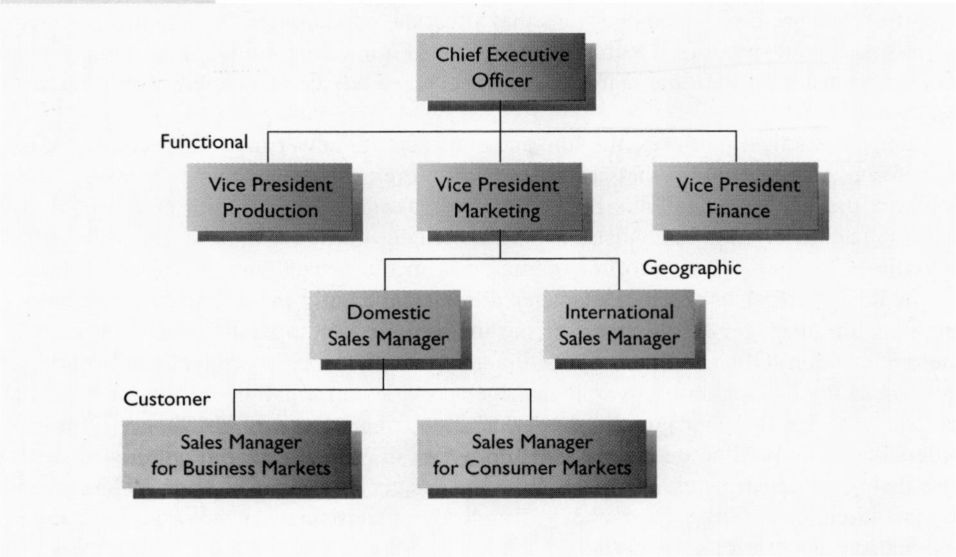

203 to

formance. However, the final accountability for employees' performance rests with their managers, who are accountable in turn to their bosses.

organization chart
Representation of the authority and responsibility relationships in an organization.

Most organizations depict their authority and responsibility relationships in **organization charts.** In organizations as diverse as Major League Baseball's California Angels and the California Highway Patrol, these diagrams represent blueprints that show the division of work, chain of command, and departmentalization of activities. They provide all employees with visual statements of these relationships, enabling them to see how their work efforts relate to the overall operation of their companies and to whom they report.

TYPES OF ORGANIZATIONAL STRUCTURES

Organizations can be classified into four main types according to the nature of their internal authority relationships: line, line-and-staff, committee, and matrix organizations. These categories are not mutually exclusive. In fact, most of today's business organizations combine elements of different types of organizational structures.

LINE ORGANIZATIONS

line organization
Structure with a direct flow of authority from the chief executive to subordinates.

chain of command
Set of relationships that indicates who gives direction to whom and who reports to whom.

A **line organization,** the oldest and simplest organizational structure, is based on a direct flow of authority from the chief executive to subordinates. The line organization defines a simple, clear **chain of command**—the set of relationships that indicates who gives direction to whom and who reports to whom. This makes buck-passing extremely difficult. Decisions can be made quickly because the manager can act without consulting anyone other than an immediate supervisor. Line organizations share an obvious defect, though. Each manager has complete responsibility for a number of activities and cannot possibly be an expert in all of them. Thus, the line organization is ineffective in any but the smallest organization. Hair salons, "mom-and-pop" grocery stores, and small law firms can operate effectively with simple line structures. Ford, General Electric, and Boeing cannot.

LINE-AND-STAFF ORGANIZATIONS

line-and-staff organization
Structure that combines the direct flow of authority of a line organization with staff departments that serve, advise, and support the line departments.

The **line-and-staff organization** combines the direct flow of authority of a line organization with staff departments that serve, advise, and support the line departments. Line departments work directly on decisions that affect the operation of the organization. Staff departments lend specialized technical support. As Figure 8.10 shows, employees receive daily supervision from a line manager and specialized advice and suggestions from staff personnel.

For all practical purposes, the line-and-staff and the newer matrix structures are the only forms of organization that can meet the requirements of modern businesses. They combine the line organization's rapid decision-making capability with effective, direct communication of staff specialists' expert knowledge to direct diverse and widespread activities. The line-and-staff form is common in medium-sized and large-sized firms.

A line manager and a staff manager differ significantly in their authority relationships. A line manager forms a part of the main line of authority that flows throughout the organization. Often, line managers directly perform the critical functions of production, financing, or marketing. A staff manager provides information, advice, or technical assistance to aid line managers in their work. Staff managers lack the authority to give orders or to compel line managers to act, although they do have line authority to supervise their own departments. Examples of staff managers in medium-sized and large-sized organizations include the director of research, the advertising manager, the legal counsel, and the director of engineering.

FIGURE 8.10 LINE-AND-STAFF ORGANIZATION

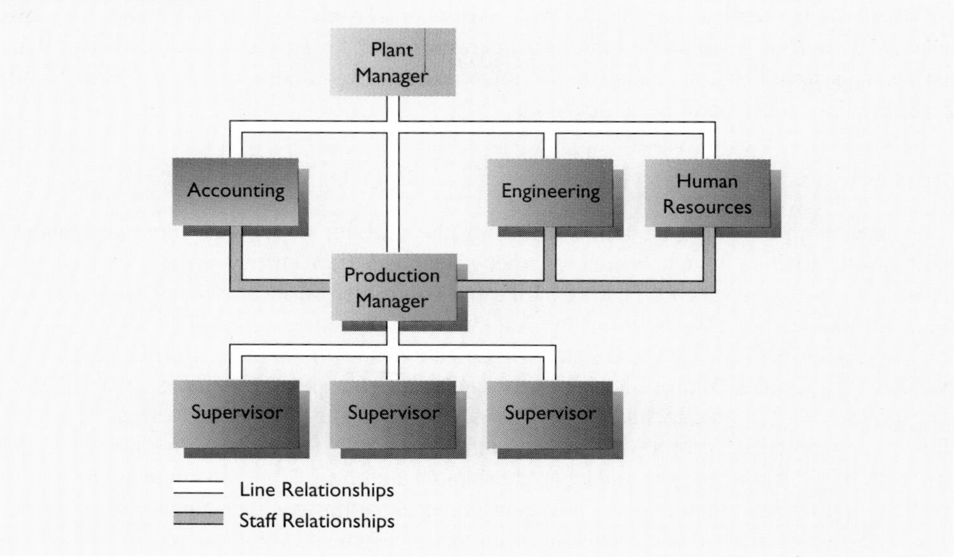

COMMITTEE ORGANIZATIONS

committee organization *Structure in which groups of individuals jointly hold authority and responsibility.*

In a **committee organization,** groups of individuals jointly hold authority and responsibility rather than concentrating them in a single manager. This structure typically forms part of a regular line-and-staff structure.

Examples of the committee structure appear throughout organizations. For example, various firms have used the concept of an office of the CEO, in which two or more executives share the duties of the chief executive officer. Committees also work in other areas such as new-product development. The new-product committee may include managers from such areas as accounting, engineering, finance, manufacturing, marketing, and research. Involving representatives from all critical areas in developing new products

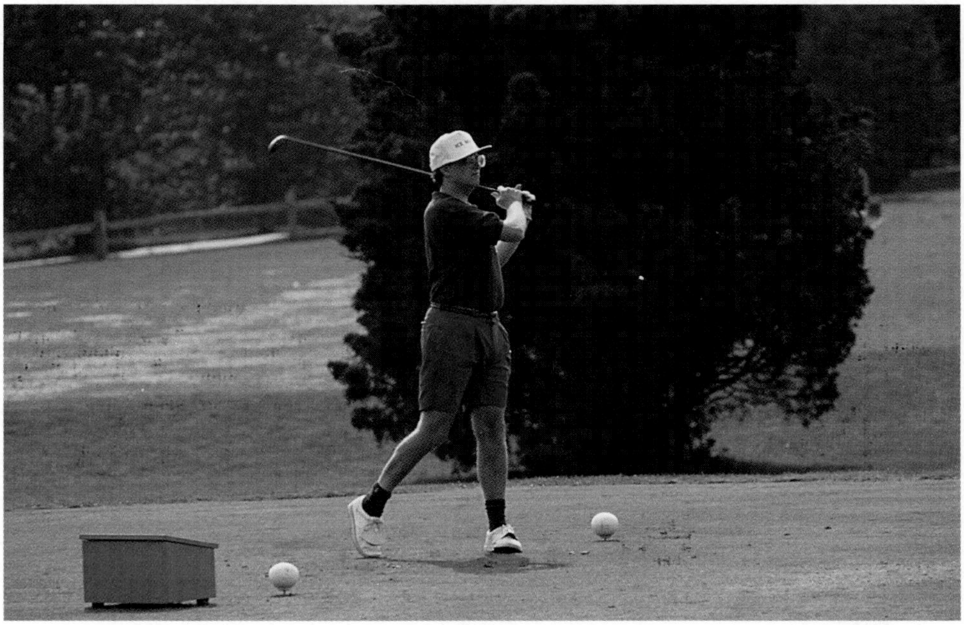

Microsoft Corporation's Bill Gates takes time for golf from his duties as chief executive officer. Microsoft's Office of the President includes Gates plus the chief operating officer, the executive vice president for sales and support, and the executive vice president for products. This arrangement allows each of the committee to handle a portion of the day-to-day operations.

generally improves planning and company morale because diverse perspectives—production, marketing, and finance—create a broader view.

Committees tend to act slowly and conservatively, and they often make decisions through compromise among conflicting interests rather than by choosing the best alternative. The definition of a camel as "a horse designed by a committee" provides an apt description of some committee decisions.

MATRIX ORGANIZATIONS

matrix, or project management, organization
Structure that brings together specialists from different parts of the organization to work on specific projects.

A growing number of organizations are using the **matrix,** or **project management, organization** structure which brings together specialists from different parts of the organization to work on specific projects. Like the committee form, the matrix organization typically defines a subform within the line-and-staff structure.

As Figure 8.11 shows, the matrix organization is built around specific projects or problems. It gathers employees with different areas of expertise to focus on these specific problems or unique technical issues. As an identifying feature of such an organization, some members report to two superiors instead of one. Project team members receive instructions from the project manager (horizontal authority), but maintain membership in their permanent functional departments (vertical authority). The term *matrix* comes from the intersection of the horizontal authority-responsibility flow with the vertical

FIGURE 8.11 MATRIX ORGANIZATION

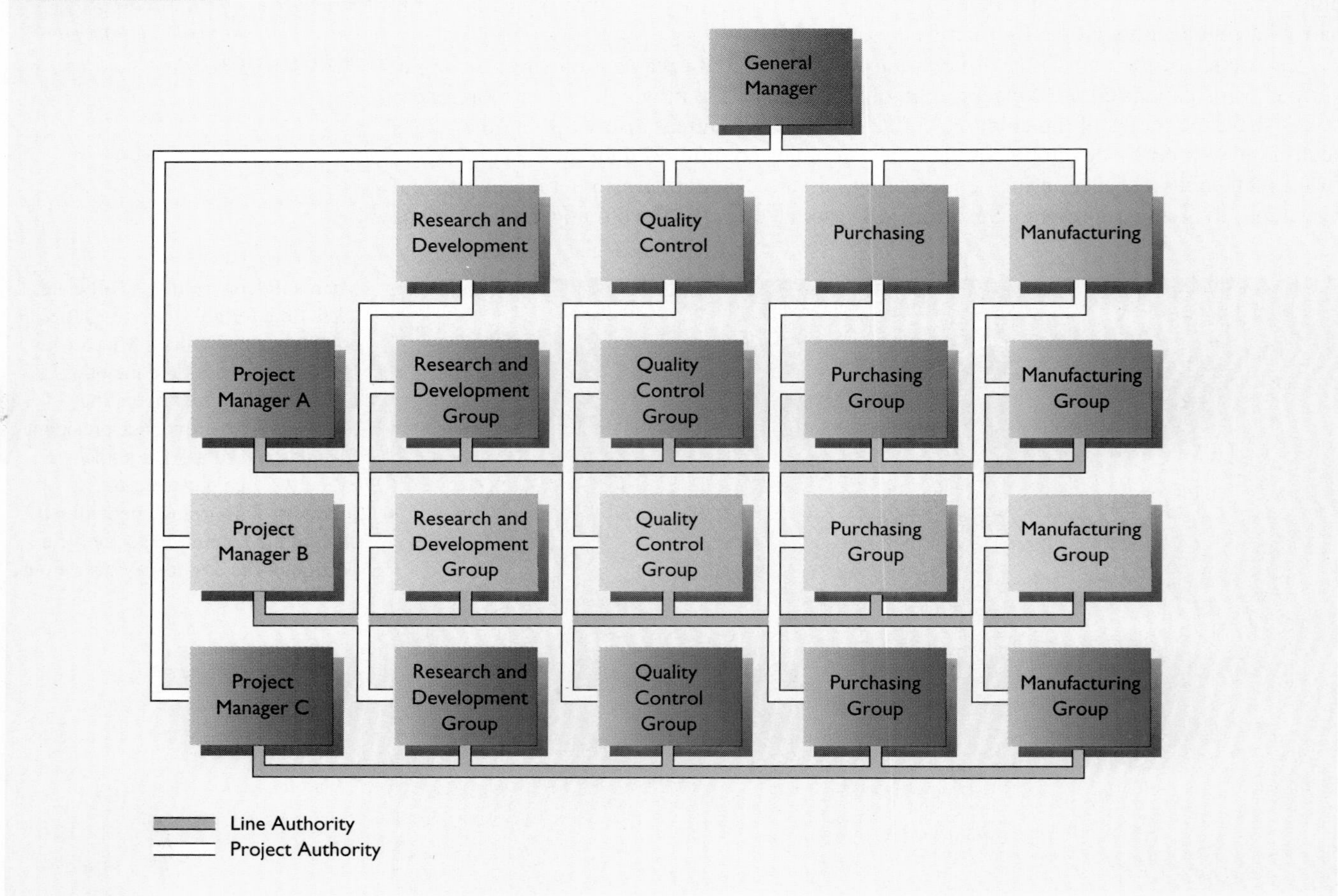

flows of the traditional line-and-staff organization. This type of organization has been used in organizations as diverse as Dow Chemical, Chase Manhattan Bank, Procter & Gamble, Lockheed Aircraft, and the Harvard Business School.

The major benefits of the matrix structure come from its flexibility and its capability to focus resources on major problems or products. However, it challenges the project manager to mold individuals from diverse parts of the organization into an integrated team. Also, team members must be comfortable working for more than one boss.

Many high-tech companies use the matrix structure to adapt quickly to fast-changing markets and apply the expertise of various specialists to short-term projects. Recently, for example, staffers from several departments at microprocessor maker Intel Corp., including marketing and legal experts, formed a project team to create a new $80 million marketing campaign. After rolling out the campaign, team members disbanded to join other project teams. Intel CEO Andy Grove likens a manager in the company's matrix structure to "a node in a not-so-crisply defined network" of people.[16]

COMPARING THE FOUR FORMS OF ORGANIZATION

Table 8.3 summarizes the advantages and disadvantages of each form of organization. Although most large companies are organized as line-and-staff structures, the line organization is usually the best form for a smaller business. The committee form appears in limited applications in major corporations. The matrix approach is increasingly common in both medium-sized companies and large, multiproduct firms to focus diverse organizational resources on specific problems or projects.

TABLE 8.3 COMPARING THE FOUR FORMS OF ORGANIZATION

FORM OF ORGANIZATION	ADVANTAGES	DISADVANTAGES
Line	Simple and easy for both managers and subordinates to understand Clear delegation of authority and responsibility for each area Quick decisions Direct communication	No specialization Overburdening of top executives with administrative details
Line-and-staff	Specialists to advise line managers Employees reporting to one superior	Conflict between line and staff unless relationships are clear Staff managers making only recommendations to line managers
Committee	Combined judgment of several executives in diverse areas Improved morale through participation in decision making	Committees slow in making decisions Decisions are the result of compromises rather than a choice of the best alternative
Matrix	Flexibility Provides method for focusing strongly on specific major problems or unique technical issues Provides means of innovation without disrupting regular organizational structure	Problems may result from employees being accountable to more than one boss Project manager may encounter difficulty in developing a cohesive team from diverse individuals recruited from various parts of the organization Conflict may arise between project managers and other department managers

SKILLS REQUIRED FOR MANAGERIAL SUCCESS

Face facts: You have agonized several times in the past about whether you have what it takes to be a good manager. Certainly, you have many strengths, but do they form the right combination to make you successful, happy, and productive as a manager or should you focus your education more toward acquiring narrower skills that would make you a valued specialist rather than a corporate leader?

Figure 8.12 shows an evaluation form that has served such business giants as Ford, TRW, Xerox, and Boeing in their quest to find out how people operate in certain areas, such as teamwork, communications, and embracing technology. It is designed to be completed by managers, their bosses, and co-workers, but simply completing it without input from others should offer some insight into how you might rate as a manager.[17]

FIGURE 8.12 How Good a Boss Are You?

HOW GOOD A BOSS ARE YOU?

Ask the people who work with and for you—as well as your boss—to answer these questions about you. Questions are taken from *The Profilor,* an assessment developed by Personnel Decisions of Minneapolis. Ratings are on a scale of 1 to 5. A 5 means you exhibit a behavior "to a very great extent"; a 1 means "not at all."

The manager:

Develops strategies to help make the organization successful.

☐ 5 To a very great extent
☐ 4 To a great extent
☐ 3 To some extent
☐ 2 To a little extent
☐ 1 Not at all
☐ NA Does not apply

Recognizes broad implications of issues.
☐ 5 ☐ 4 ☐ 3 ☐ 2 ☐ 1 ☐ NA

Understands complex concepts and relationships.
☐ 5 ☐ 4 ☐ 3 ☐ 2 ☐ 1 ☐ NA

Analyzes problems from different points of view.
☐ 5 ☐ 4 ☐ 3 ☐ 2 ☐ 1 ☐ NA

Makes decisions in the face of uncertainty.
☐ 5 ☐ 4 ☐ 3 ☐ 2 ☐ 1 ☐ NA

Makes sound decisions based on adequate information.
☐ 5 ☐ 4 ☐ 3 ☐ 2 ☐ 1 ☐ NA

Integrates planning across work units.
☐ 5 ☐ 4 ☐ 3 ☐ 2 ☐ 1 ☐ NA

Translates business strategies into clear objectives and tactics.
☐ 5 ☐ 4 ☐ 3 ☐ 2 ☐ 1 ☐ NA

Provides clear direction and defines priorities for the team.
☐ 5 ☐ 4 ☐ 3 ☐ 2 ☐ 1 ☐ NA

Fosters the development of a common vision.
☐ 5 ☐ 4 ☐ 3 ☐ 2 ☐ 1 ☐ NA

Acts decisively.
☐ 5 ☐ 4 ☐ 3 ☐ 2 ☐ 1 ☐ NA

Takes a stand and resolves important issues.
☐ 5 ☐ 4 ☐ 3 ☐ 2 ☐ 1 ☐ NA

Wins support from others.
☐ 5 ☐ 4 ☐ 3 ☐ 2 ☐ 1 ☐ NA

Gets others to take action.
☐ 5 ☐ 4 ☐ 3 ☐ 2 ☐ 1 ☐ NA

Champions new initiatives within and beyond the scope of the job.
☐ 5 ☐ 4 ☐ 3 ☐ 2 ☐ 1 ☐ NA

Involves others in the change process.
☐ 5 ☐ 4 ☐ 3 ☐ 2 ☐ 1 ☐ NA

Has the confidence and trust of others.
☐ 5 ☐ 4 ☐ 3 ☐ 2 ☐ 1 ☐ NA

Shows consistency between words and actions.
☐ 5 ☐ 4 ☐ 3 ☐ 2 ☐ 1 ☐ NA

Persists in the face of obstacles.
☐ 5 ☐ 4 ☐ 3 ☐ 2 ☐ 1 ☐ NA

Puts a top priority on getting results.
☐ 5 ☐ 4 ☐ 3 ☐ 2 ☐ 1 ☐ NA

How you rate

If you score all 4s and 5s, you are viewed as competent. Focus on fine-tuning and making the most of those strengths.

If you score 3 on any item, determine how important the skill or behavior is to your job. If it's important, try to improve.

If you score below 3, it's fix-it time. Target those areas for development.

STRENGTH IN DIVERSITY

MATRIX ESSENTIALS, INC. Back in the early 1960s, Sydell Miller didn't let the tiny percentage of female senior managers in American businesses dissuade her from striving for her dream. She did something about it. Today, she is a classic success story of a housewife-hairdresser who rose to head a multimillion-dollar company generating sales in over 20 different countries. ■ Matrix Essentials posts annual sales of over $200 million, making it the nation's largest professional hair-care company. The business that would grow to this level had a modest beginning as a jointly managed partnership between Miller and her hair-stylist husband, Arnie. While Arnie handled the production end of the salon, Sydell applied her managerial abilities to expanding the services that it offered its clientele. As a result, the salon was among the first in the nation to offer facials, nail care, retail sales of beauty and hair-care products, and an in-house clothing boutique. Within a few years, Arnie had 54 other operators in the fast-growing salon. Sydell decided it was time to expand into manufacturing and to seek additional outlets for the salon's well-received products. Operating out of the Miller basement, Sydell also took on the marketing challenges of the expanded venture. At first, she made most of the sales calls to buyers at drugstores, discount stores, and other salons. Later, she recruited and trained a sales force to handle these sales and service calls. ■ The 1970s were down years for the entire hair-care industry, especially for salons. As Sydell recalls, "People simply didn't feel good about being hairdressers. The whole industry needed a boost." Instead of reducing the company's risk exposure by cutting operations, Sydell had the vision to spot an exciting opportunity. Matrix Essentials moved out of the basement and work began immediately on a series of new products. ■ Luck boosted the fledgling company as several of the new products became immediate hits. For example, So Color could be applied the same day as a permanent, saving time for both hairdressers and their customers. The product also blended nicely with the changing American lifestyles of the early 1980s. As Sydell explains, "Lifestyles became busier, people didn't have time to keep coming back to the salon. With new synergistic products, women could get more treatments without making more trips." ■ The stream of new Matrix products, each attuned to the changing hair-care needs of the marketplace, was an important factor in Matrix's success. The second—and equally important—component was the educational programs that Sydell developed to educate both customers and professional hair stylists about these products. This was Sydell's key to changing the industry. She opened the Matrix Institute of Professional Development to provide hairdressers, salon owners, cosmetologists, and sales reps with the technical skills necessary to compete in a rapidly changing industry. Says Sydell, "We were committed not to just selling products, but to helping the entire industry. Education became a major part of our business." Through seminars and conferences held at the institute, attendees learn everything from styling techniques to promotional strategies and salon psychology. ■ Sydell remembers the hard work and perseverance of the early years. "We started this business in a recession. It was tough, but we saw signs all along that told us if we could hang in there financially, we had the right idea." After Arnie died, Sydell continued to lead the company in its biggest growth years, introducing Systeme Biolage and expanding product lines to include lipstick, nail polish, and other cosmetics. Her combination of vision, managerial talents, and perseverance are key ingredients in the success of Matrix. Source: Gayle Sato Stodder, "Tressed for Success," *Entrepreneur*, December 1994, pp. 136–141.

QUESTIONS FOR CRITICAL THINKING

1. What are the pros and cons of expanding operations at a time when an industry as a whole is down?
2. What are some potential areas of expansion for Matrix?
3. What is Sydell Miller's leadership style and why is it so successful?

Every manager at every level in the organization must possess skills in three basic areas: technical, human relations, and conceptual skills. Although the importance of each type of skill varies at different levels, managers use all three at some time during their careers.

Technical skills reflect the manager's ability to understand and use techniques, knowledge, and tools of a specific discipline or company department. An employee in the human resource department, for instance, must understand the technical details of workplace laws. Technical skills are particularly important for first-line managers, who frequently deal with production employees who operate machinery, for salespeople who must explain technical details of their firms' products, and for computer programmers who work on complicated software development assignments.

Human relations skills are people skills that involve the manager's ability to work effectively with and through people. Human relations skills include communicating, leading, and motivating workers to accomplish assigned activities. Good communications skills are critical for effective managers. In addition, the ability to interact with superiors and people outside one's immediate department or work area become important. The ability to create a work environment that encourages organization members to contribute their best efforts is a crucial managerial skill at every level.

Conceptual skills reflect the ability to see the organization as a unified whole and to understand how each part of the overall organization interacts with other parts. These skills involve a manager's ability to see the big picture by acquiring, analyzing, and interpreting information. Such skills are especially important for top-level managers, who must develop long-range plans for the future direction of the organization.

Tommye Jo Daves, manager of a North Carolina Levi Strauss sewing plant, is an example of someone who possesses all three types of skills. Daves certainly has technical skills. She joined the company in 1959 and worked her way up from seamstress to supervisor to plant manager. In her current position, she has plenty of opportunity to practice her human relations skills, especially since the plant adopted a matrix organization in which teams of workers participate in running the factory. Admits Daves, "Sometimes it's real hard for me not to push back and say, 'You do this, you do that, and you do this.' Now I have to say, 'How do you want to do this?' I have to realize that their ideas may not be the way to go, but I have to let them learn that for themselves." Along the way, Daves has also developed conceptual skills. Her advice to would-be managers: "You can't lead a team by just barking orders, and you have to have a vision in your head of what you're trying to do."[18]

Like Daves, all managers within an organization need to possess technical, human relations, and conceptual skills. However, the relative importance of each skill differs for each level of management. Supervisory managers, who spend much of their time dealing with operating workers, must show strong technical and human relations skills. Top managers, on the other hand, need strong conceptual skills and human relations abilities, but they spend little time dealing with technical matters. Middle managers require a blend of all three types of skills.

LEADERSHIP STYLES

leadership
Act of motivating or causing others to perform activities designed to achieve specific objectives.

Leadership, a critical management function and the most visible component of a manager's responsibilities, was defined earlier in this chapter as the act of motivating or causing others to perform activities designed to achieve specific objectives. A recent survey revealed that the most important reason that causes employed people to look for new jobs is dislike for their bosses. The feeling of being underutilized on the job was the second most common reason, followed by money complaints.[19]

As important as effective leadership is to organizational success, no one should be surprised that a great deal of research has focused on the characteristics of a good leader. Great leaders do not all share the same qualities, but three traits are often mentioned: empathy (the ability to place oneself in another's position), self-awareness, and objectivity in dealing with others.

Research on leadership focuses on different styles of leadership and circumstances under which each style might prove successful. This approach to leadership, known as the *contingency theory,* argues that managers should adjust their leadership styles to match the situations at hand.

WHICH LEADERSHIP STYLE IS BEST?

Leadership involves exercising power—the ability of one person to influence the behavior of another. The way in which a leader uses available power to lead others is referred to as *leadership style.*

People display a continuum of leadership styles, within which analysts identify three basic styles. At one end of the continuum, autocratic leaders make decisions on their own without consulting others. The autocratic leader reaches a decision, communicates it to subordinates, and requires them to implement it. Democratic leaders, by contrast, involve their subordinates in making decisions. A democratic sales manager, for example, allows sales personnel to participate in setting sales quotas, while an autocratic sales manager simply assigns a quota for each salesperson. The most democratic style belongs to free-rein leaders, who believe in minimal supervision and leave most decisions to their subordinates.

The appropriate leadership style depends on the leader, the subordinates, and the situation. In short, the best leadership style is one that adapts to the circumstances at hand. Some leaders are uncomfortable in situations that invite active participation of subordinates in decision making. Some followers lack the ability or the desire to assume such responsibility. Furthermore, the specific situation helps to determine which style will be most effective. Managers may have to handle problems that require immediate solutions without consulting subordinates. Under less intense time pressure, participative decision making may work best.

In general, the current trend is leading businesses toward democratic and free-rein leadership. As U.S. companies eliminate layers of management, lines of authority become shorter and the contributions of individual employees become more valuable. Says consultant and author Peter Senge, "People working together with integrity and authenticity and collective intelligence are profoundly more effective as a business than people living together based on politics, game playing, and narrow self-interest."

Robert Cushman, CEO of GS Technologies, which makes steel for mining equipment and mattress coils, decided to try a more democratic leadership style when hate mail from his employees became a daily occurrence. The company's market share was shrinking, the number of worker grievances was rising, and in 10 years the firm had been forced to lay off 80 percent of its workers. Cushman called a two-day meeting of 35 managers and union leaders to solicit ideas for turning the company around. At first, the meeting exploded in name-calling, but it eventually turned into a constructive session in which managers and employees worked out mutual solutions to productivity problems. Since implementing these solutions, GST's sales and profits have risen dramatically.[20]

CORPORATE CULTURE

The most appropriate leadership style for a particular company depends greatly on its **corporate culture,** the value system of an organization. Managerial philosophies, workplace practices, and communication networks all form part of the concept of corporate culture. Tyson Foods' corporate culture is reflected in workers' dress: everyone—even CEO Don Tyson—wears tan work clothes on the job.

corporate culture
Value system of an organization.

A corporate culture is typically shaped by the leaders who founded and developed the company and by those who have succeeded them. One generation of employees passes on a corporate culture to newer employees. Sometimes this is part of formal training. New managers who attend McDonald's Hamburger University may learn skills in management, but they also acquire the basics of the organization's corporate culture. Employees can absorb corporate culture through informal contacts, as well, by talking with other workers and through their experiences on the job.

Corporate culture has a major impact on the success of an organization. Everyone knows and supports the objectives of an organization with a strong culture. In an organization with a weak culture, no clear sense of purpose guides actions.

MANAGERIAL DECISION MAKING

decision making
Recognizing a problem, identifying it, evaluating alternatives, selecting and implementing an alternative, and following up.

The most important task of a leader is decision making. Managers earn their salaries by making decisions that enable their firms to solve problems that arise. In addition, managers work continually to anticipate and prevent problems.

The decision-making process can be broken down into five steps. In a narrow sense, it can amount simply to choosing among two or more alternatives, the chosen alternative being the decision. In a broader sense, however, **decision making** involves recognizing a problem or opportunity, identifying it, evaluating alternatives, selecting and implementing an alternative, and following up to collect feedback on the effectiveness of the decision. Whether for a routine decision or a unique one (such as a decision to construct a major new manufacturing facility), the systematic, step-by-step approach will be effective.

TYPES OF DECISIONS

Managers can classify decisions by their relative uniqueness. A programmed decision involves simple, common, frequently occurring problems for which solutions have already been determined. Examples of programmed decisions include choosing the starting salary for a computer programmer, determining reorder points for raw materials used in production, and selecting price discounts to offer for large-quantity purchases. Organizations develop rules, policies, and detailed procedures for making such decisions consistently, quickly, and inexpensively. Since such solutions eliminate the time-consuming process of identifying and evaluating alternatives and making new decisions each time a situation occurs, they free managers to devote time to more complex problems.

A nonprogrammed decision involves complex, important, and nonroutine problems or opportunities. Because nonprogrammed decisions typically accompany situations that have not occurred before, identifying alternatives, evaluating them, and implementing the best ones become critical tasks.

Managers often succeed or fail based on their ability to make nonprogrammed decisions. Bill Gates, chairman of Microsoft Corp., has created a hugely successful software company with annual revenues in excess of $4.5 billion by being willing to make plenty of these decisions. Gates is funding a variety of research projects to explore risky new opportunities in technology, including speech recognition systems, interactive TV services, satellite networks, biotechnology initiatives, and multimedia programs. While the outlay is tremendous, so is the potential. Says Gates, "Companies in this business have often lost their way. We will not fall short for not having an expansive view of how technology can be used."[21]

MANAGING ACROSS BORDERS

Many firms face an important common decision: choosing and training managers to oversee international operations and foreign-based offices. Placing a manager overseas can be expensive and difficult, both for the company and the manager, so firms select carefully. AT&T hires psychologists to help pick managers who seem most suited to the challenges of working in different countries. Candidates for such transfers must take a written test and go through management interviews. General Electric offers classes in foreign languages and cultural customs to its middle-level engineers and managers. American Express regularly transfers managers to overseas offices to help them gain cross-cultural experience. PepsiCo, General Motors, and Raychem all offer global management training programs.

Managers with international experience stress the importance of teamwork and communication skills. "We tend to look for people who can work in teams and understand the value of cooperation and consensus," notes a Unilever executive. Successful managers also realize that many cultures do not share American attitudes toward work.[22]

NEW OPPORTUNITIES FOR MANAGERS

Clearly, business organizations are undergoing a revolution in structure. The tasks and responsibilities expected of managers within these organizations are also changing as they manage diverse groups of employees and flexible work teams, assume broader spans of control, and encourage intrapreneurship. Also, the reduced managerial ranks resulting from downsizing adds to the number of employees each surviving manager must supervise, placing even more pressure on those who remain.

While traditional supervisory and middle-management positions might be getting more scarce, other opportunities will present themselves to those with good management skills. Some middle managers leave large corporations for smaller firms. Another option is to become a contract manager, working for an organization on a temporary appointment. Temporary management is growing fast in the United States and Europe, where a manager may contract with an employer to work for a specified period of time.

An increasing number of managers are deciding to start their own companies. In fact, the number of people who start their own businesses after losing their jobs has tripled since 1987. One example is Monica Castaneda, a former defense contract administrator at TRW. After a layoff, Castaneda opened a sewing business to make flame-retardant suits for test pilots and embroidered uniforms for race-car drivers. "I thought I'd spend all my time sewing," she says. However, as her business grows, she finds herself delegating the stitchery to others and returning to the skills she honed at TRW. "What I'm really good at is administration and taking care of contracts."[23]

Managers, and all employees, need to remain flexible and develop new skills. Consider Jim Dettore, who left his long-time employer to start the Brand Institute, a New York City consultancy that develops brand names for new goods and services. First, Dettore taught himself to use a computer, then he used the computer to teach himself to write a business plan. He spends many weekends in the library, researching existing brand names. Dettore finds that self-employment demands much greater flexibility than his old job did. "I have to know everything and do everything," he says. "I'm much more involved in the details. I've talked to consumers, I've done original research. My presentations to clients are more authentic, and that helps when I make sales calls." Dettore has named products for AT&T, Johnson & Johnson, and American Cyanamid, and his list of clients continues to grow. He enjoys his work and, as he puts it, the decision to start his own firm "was the best thing that ever happened to me."[24]

Monica Castaneda moved from a job as a contract administrator at TRW to managing her own uniform-embroidering business. Many managers put skills they developed while working for others to good use in their own businesses.

ACHIEVEMENT CHECK SUMMARY

Reread the learning goals that follow, and consider the questions for each goal. Answering these questions will reinforce the most important concepts in the chapter and allow you to check how well you have achieved these learning goals. Where a blank appears before a question, answer with *T* or *F*. Otherwise, circle the letter of the correct answer. An answer key to these questions is found at the end of this chapter.

LEARNING GOAL 8.1: Distinguish between a firm's mission statement and its corporate objectives.

1. ___ A mission statement makes explicit a firm's purpose and aims.
2. ___ A firm sets specific objectives only for financial variables such as sales or profits.

LEARNING GOAL 8.2: Explain the concept of competitive differentiation and identify the primary methods used to create it.

1. ___ *Competitive differentiation* refers to any aspect of a firm or its performance that makes it succeed over its competitors.
2. ___ Since competition is always based on price, keeping overhead costs and prices down is the only critical focus of competitive differentiation programs.

LEARNING GOAL 8.3: Explain SWOT analysis and how it is used in corporate planning.

1. SWOT analysis requires management to consider: (a) internal strengths and weaknesses along with external opportunities and threats; (b) suppliers, workers, other competitors, and time; (c) strategic planning, working plans, operational plans, and time frames; (d) sales, work force, organizational structure, and technologies.
2. When a firm's strengths and opportunities mesh, it has: (a) a problem in the marketplace: (b) leverage in the marketplace; (c) vulnerability in the marketplace; (d) a constraint to overcome.

LEARNING GOAL 8.4: Differentiate between the various methods of quantitative and qualitative forecasting.

1. ___ Forecasts are estimates or predictions of a firm's future sales, income, or market share.
2. ___ Sales force composites, executive opinion, buyer surveys, and the Delphi technique are good examples of qualitative forecasting techniques.
3. ___ Quantitative forecasting techniques rely on historical data and mathematical methods.

LEARNING GOAL 8.5: Discuss the need for organizational structure, and evaluate each of the four basic forms of organization.

1. ___ An organization's structure groups people and activities to permit more complete and more efficient attainment of organizational objectives.
2. ___ The line-and-staff organization is the oldest and simplest organization structure.
3. ___ As an organization grows larger, its need for organization structure diminishes.

LEARNING GOAL 8.6: Identify the skills required for managerial success.

1. To be successful, a manager must develop: (a) technical skills; (b) human-relations skills; (c) conceptual skills; (d) all of the above.
2. If a person can see the big picture and understand how parts of the organization relate to the whole, that person is said to have good: (a) technical skills; (b) human-relations skills; (c) conceptual skills; (d) administrative skills.

LEARNING GOAL 8.7: Explain the concept of leadership, and identify the three basic leadership styles.

1. ___ *Leadership* can be defined as motivating others to perform the activities needed to reach an organization's objectives.
2. ___ Contingency leadership is the idea that one leadership style works best regardless of the circumstances at hand.
3. ___ With free-rein leadership, managers have lost control of their subordinates and operations will suffer.

LEARNING GOAL 8.8: List the steps in the decision-making process, and contrast programmed and nonprogrammed decisions.

1. ___ The first step in the decision-making process is to propose alternative solutions.
2. ___ A situation for which a procedure exists to evaluate alternatives and reach a decision is known as a *programmed decision*.
3. ___ When a situation is unique, complex, or entirely new, a manager will probably have to make a nonprogrammed decision.

LEARNING GOAL 8.9: Discuss qualities that characterize successful global managers.

1. ___ Successful global managers should realize that everyone wishes they could be like Americans, and that American work values and consumer tastes apply anywhere.
2. ___ Successful global managers are good at working cooperatively in teams, building consensus, and communicating with people from different cultures.

KEY TERMS

management 186
vision 187
mission statement 187
objectives 187
competitive differentiation 189
planning 192
strategic planning 193
tactical planning 193
operational planning 193
adaptive planning 194
contingency planning 194
organizing 195
leading 195
controlling 196
top management 196
middle management 196
supervisory management 196
SWOT analysis 198
strategic business unit (SBU) 199

forecasting 200
organization 202
departmentalization 203
delegation 203
organization chart 204
line organization 204
chain of command 204
line-and-staff organization 204
committee organization 205
matrix, or project management, organization 206
leadership 210
corporate culture 211
decision making 212

REVIEW QUESTIONS

1. Explain this statement: "Management principles are universal." Do you agree or disagree?

2. Distinguish between strategic and tactical planning. Give an example of each.

3. What is competitive differentiation? How do firms achieve it?

4. Explain the concepts of leverage, problems, constraints, and vulnerabilities as they relate to SWOT analysis.

5. Outline the major forecasting techniques. Define each of these methods.

6. What level of the management pyramid would each of the following persons occupy?
   a. Department head
   b. Chief operating officer
   c. Supervisor
   d. Branch manager
   e. Army major
   f. Dean

7. Summarize the major strengths and weaknesses of each type of formal organizational structure.

8. Classify each of the following as either a programmed or nonprogrammed decision. Defend your answers.
   a. Registrar's office system for processing student requests to drop or add courses
   b. Retail store manager's decision about the number of men's dress shirts to order
   c. Hospital's procedure for admitting new patients
   d. Management's decision to relocate corporate headquarters from Detroit to Dallas

9. Identify and briefly explain the three skills required for managerial success. Which skills are relatively more important for top management? Which are more important for first-line managers?

10. Describe some traits that would make a manager a good candidate for a foreign transfer. Would you be a good candidate for such a post? Why or why not?

DISCUSSION QUESTIONS

1. You have decided to start one of the following businesses:
   a. Import/export firm
   b. Music store
   c. Delivery service
   d. Supermarket
   e. Clothing store

   Choose one and write a mission statement for your business. How might your company create competitive differentiation?

2. How might SWOT analysis and SBUs help your business?

3. As the owner of the business selected above, what forms of forecasting would you use?

4. The typical professional sports team is owned by wealthy individuals who enjoy being involved with a particular sport. The owners usually make major policy decisions, but a hired general manager handles other managerial duties. The general manager oversees facilities, equipment, vendors, and personnel matters. He or she may also have responsibility for player personnel decisions such as trades, new-player drafts, and assignment of players to minor leagues. The field manager or head coach takes charge of the team's actual performance. This person assists the general manager in matters concerning players. Other personnel employed by a professional team include team physicians, assistant coaches, trainers, equipment managers, secretaries, scouts, and ticket sales personnel. Draw an organization chart for a professional sports team. Discuss the strengths and weaknesses of this organizational structure.

5. Describe the skills that you think someone working in a matrix organization would need. What can you do to prepare yourself for a successful career in such a company? Be specific.

SOLUTIONS TO ACHIEVEMENT CHECK SUMMARY

L. G. 8.1: 1. T, 2. F. **L. G. 8.2:** 1. T, 2. F. **L. G. 8.3:** 1. a, 2. b. **L. G. 8.4:** 1. T, 2. T, 3. T. **L. G. 8.5:** 1. T, 2. F, 3. F. **L. G. 8.6:** 1. d, 2. c. **L. G. 8.7:** 1. T, 2. F, 3. F. **L. G. 8.8:** 1. F, 2. T, 3. T. **L. G. 8.9:** 1. F, 2. T.

VIDEO CASE

KROPF ORCHARDS Most apple buyers give little thought to the planning that goes into getting them to the produce section of the grocery, but managers at Kropf Orchards know all too well the importance of planning, organizing, and controlling such an operation. To do this effectively, Kropf has turned to SWOT analysis—a planning technique that involves assessing a company's strengths, weaknesses, opportunities, and threats—in order to recognize opportunities and problems and to create leverage for the firm.

For years, Kropf Orchards has been a successful operation. But its management realized that success is the end result of careful planning—and of the implementation of those plans. In 1993, the firm conducted several strategic planning meetings to determine what needed to be done to maintain its position in the future. Management knew that the family-owned business would have to make significant changes in order to remain competitive in the rapidly changing and increasingly demanding marketplace and still provide maximum returns to growers. In fact, the company even lacked a formal mission statement. Instead, it was operating under the basic tenets expressed by the founders 90 years earlier; that is, to give customers "premium quality for a value!"

Several objectives were decided upon during these early planning meetings. Management knew they had to respond to a changing market, one in which firms were consolidating to achieve the economies of scale needed to lower costs of fruit packing while continuing to meet customers' expectations. One consideration in these meetings was retaining employees. For Kropf and many other family-owned businesses, that meant creating an environment in which younger employees have job security and opportunities for advancement. From a production standpoint, other changes included installing a modern, temperature-controlled storage and packing facility to ensure a premium-quality product.

In addition to these objectives, Kropf felt it was time to take a close look at itself. With this in mind, management performed a SWOT analysis to determine the firm's current position and its best direction for the future, and found the following:

- *Strengths* included a strong production base consisting of 4,000 acres of orchards belonging to independent growers in addition to its own 1,000 acres. Kropf also enjoys a favorable reputation in the fruit-packing industry for providing high-quality products and (although its facility was far from new) the most technologically advanced packing plant east of the Rockies.
- *Weaknesses* identified in the analysis included the inability to supply the large quantities involved in a typical supermarket chain contract and in the growing export market. Kropf also lacked equipment for sorting a wider range of sizes and grades, preventing the firm from maximizing the return on its investment. Many of the orchards were still operating under old-style layouts and growing less popular varieties of apples. Finally, installing temperature-controlled storage was a necessity for prolonging the life of the fruit.

- *Opportunities* were plentiful, as Kropf management discovered. New packing equipment could remedy many of the firm's production weaknesses, by increasing the potential volume for larger contracts and by offering greater flexibility in sorting and grading. Providing greater storage space would allow Kropf to utilize its investment in capital equipment more efficiently. Expanding Kropf's base of independent growers could enable the firm to attract more business. By expanding their own packing capacity, Kropf could control more of the market and reduce the likelihood of new competition. Fruit exporting also offered new opportunities, allowing Kropf a chance to increase sales by as much as 20 percent.
- *Threats* to Kropf were mainly present in the form of competition from other types of fruit for market share. Just 20 years ago, such exotic fruits as kiwi and mango were available only in season and even then not everywhere in America. Today, they can be found in the produce section of most supermarkets and fruit stands.

. . . Kropf has turned to SWOT analysis . . . in order to recognize opportunities and problems and to create leverage for the firm.

After reaching agreement of their objectives and assessing the results of the SWOT analysis, Kropf's management team decided that the company had a strategic window of opportunity to expand operations. By combining their strengths with opportunities for expanding their production base and sales, they could achieve leverage in the marketplace. To capitalize on this leverage, Kropf invested $3 million to construct a 67,000-square-foot state-of-the-art packing and storage facility. A $250,000 computer monitors temperature, humidity, and carbon dioxide levels in the controlled storage areas every three minutes. Apples stored in these controlled-atmosphere rooms maintain their freshness and crispness for months, allowing the fruit to be held in inventory until apple prices begin to rise, rather than having to sell the fruit when it is picked, regardless of market prices. Fresh apples are now found year-round across the United States, as well as in most export markets.

Yet another outcome of this analysis is the changeover from old-style orchards with 150 trees per acre to high-density orchards containing 500 to 600 dwarf and semi-dwarf trees per acre. With increasing productivity, quality, and packing capabilities, the future looks bright for Kropf Orchards, allowing the current generation of family managers to continue to strive toward the founder's goal of "premium quality for a value."

QUESTIONS

1.
Explain the relationship between a firm's mission statement and its objectives. Is the company motto of "premium quality for a value" a mission statement? A corporate objective? Defend your answer.

2.
Which components of the SWOT analysis conducted by Kropf managers represent internal factors? Which are external factors? Explain why some factors are labeled problems, others constraints, and still others are called vulnerabilities.

3.
After conducting a SWOT analysis, Kropf managers were delighted to discover that their firm possessed leverage in the marketplace. What factors created this leverage?

4.
If the new-style orchards succeed in increasing apple output threefold and U.S. demand continues to grow at a much smaller pace, what is likely to happen to the price fruit packers like Kropf receive for their product?

CHAPTER 9

MANAGEMENT OF HUMAN RESOURCES

LEARNING GOALS

1. Explain the importance of human resource management and the responsibilities of a human resource department.

2. List the needs in Maslow's hierarchy.

3. Distinguish between Theory X, Theory Y, and Theory Z managers.

4. Explain how recruitment, selection, orientation, training, and evaluation contribute to placing the right person in a job.

5. Outline the different forms of compensation.

6. Explain the concept of job enrichment and how it can motivate employees.

7. Explain the impact of downsizing and outsourcing on today's organizations.

8. Describe the role of intrapreneurship in a modern organization.

9. Discuss the importance of time management.

10. Identify and briefly describe each of the major human resource concerns for the 21st century.

H-P EMPOWERS EMPLOYEES

In 1938, David Packard and William Hewlett decided to start a company. They had no products to sell—they lacked even ideas for products. They did, however, have a vision: They wanted to bring people together and create products with technology that would make a difference. ■ The two Stanford University graduate students launched their enterprise out of a garage in Palo Alto, California. After first calling it The Engineering Company, they decided to use their own names. They flipped a coin to see whose would appear first. ■ Their humble start-up prospered, and then it plateaued in the 1980s. Though Hewlett-Packard remained a respected manufacturer of calculators, computers, and scientific and medical instruments, the company became bureaucratic and slow-moving. It missed out on several promising new markets, while focusing on products that customers didn't always need or buy. Eventually, new products came to account for only 30 percent of H-P's annual sales, and the firm fell to seventh place among U.S. computer makers. ■ Lewis Platt, H-P's chief executive officer, realized that the firm needed to transform itself from a stodgy, multilayered corporation into a nimble, fast-moving company that could respond quickly to changes in the marketplace. As an important first step in the rethinking process, H-P moved to empower employees by giving them additional decision-making authority and responsibility. Platt reorganized the 96,000-employee corporation into a conglomerate of smaller ventures, each responsible for its own success. H-P managers gained the authority to develop their own market strategies and to reinvest the capital that their ventures generated. As Jim Olson, manager for video products, put it, "We don't feel an allegiance to any other part of H-P. We feel an allegiance to the customer." ■ Empowerment extends to nonmanagement employees, as well. At H-P's customer service center, for example, workers organized into independent teams are encouraged to choose their own supervisors. "In the H-P environment, you really can't order people to do anything," says Platt. "As CEO, my job is to encourage people to work together, to experiment, to try things, but I can't order them to do it. We've picked people who are high-energy self-starters. You can't tell them what to do. The best I can do is sort of bring people together and hope they mate." ■ H-P also encourages employees to practice entrepreneurship within the corporate structure. This gives workers of a small company the freedom to innovate, while providing a large company's financial support and expertise. The combination can be highly successful, as Olson's video products division has proved. ■ A few years ago, Olson and other managers realized that the TV and communications industry was growing rapidly and H-P wasn't part of it. Olson set out to convert the Stanford Park division, which made microwave devices for the shrinking defense market, into a supplier for the booming $14 billion video industry. He faced just one problem: H-P knew nothing about video. Olson set to work to change this. "We did no formal training. We bought people airline tickets and books and sent them out to spend a lot of time with customers. They left as microwave engineers and came back as video engineers." ■ The video team returned to H-P, plunged into research and design, and created 14 new products within 9 months. The VidJet Pro allows video images to be filed with a videotape so customers can see what's on a tape without having to watch it. Another new product monitors the quality of video signals, and still another innovation is a video server that feeds movies into interactive TV systems. When Pacific Bell announced plans for its movies-on-demand service to California homes, Olson's division competed against industry giants IBM and DEC for the contract—and won. "We're street fighters here," says Olson. ■ Thanks to innovations like these, H-P's profits are growing by 30 percent a year. New products now account for 70 percent of its orders, and H-P has risen from seventh to second

place among U.S. computer makers. Despite his undeniable success so far, however, Platt is far from complacent: "Most companies our size that have been very successful got themselves in deep difficulty—IBM, DEC, General Motors, Sears Roebuck. The only mistake they made is that they did whatever it was that made them leaders a little too long. I worry every morning that I, too, will be party to hanging on too long." ■ Industry analysts, not to mention H-P employees, are more optimistic. "It's the way a business should be run—with a tremendous amount of modesty and an interest in what the future should hold," says analyst John Logan.[1]

CHAPTER OVERVIEW

The importance of people to the success of any organization is stressed in the very definition of *management:* the use of people and other resources to accomplish organizational objectives. This chapter addresses the critical issue of human resource management. It examines the way an organization recruits, trains, and motivates people. It also discusses employee training, development, and counseling. Finally, the chapter takes a look at human resource concerns of the next century, including opportunities and challenges in managing older workers, two-career and nonfamily households, contingency workers, elder-care issues, and an increasingly diverse work force.

HUMAN RESOURCE MANAGEMENT: A VITAL MANAGERIAL FUNCTION

human resource management *Process of acquiring, training, developing, motivating, and appraising a sufficient quantity of qualified employees to perform necessary organizational activities, and developing activities and an organizational climate to generate maximum efficiency and worker satisfaction.*

This chapter emphasizes people—the human element—and their importance in accomplishing an organization's goals. Most organizations devote considerable attention to **human resource management,** which can be defined as (1) the process of acquiring, training, developing, motivating, and appraising a sufficient quantity of qualified employees to perform the activities necessary to accomplish organizational objectives, and (2) developing specific activities and an overall organizational climate to generate maximum worker satisfaction and employee efficiency.

While the owner-managers of small organizations usually assume complete responsibility for human resource management, larger organizations designate company specialists called *human resource managers* to perform these activities in a systematic manner. The position is becoming increasingly important as competition increases, use of outsourcing and part-time workers grows, cost control receives new emphasis, wage and benefit programs become more complex, and the characteristics of the work force change. These human resource managers assume primary responsibility for forecasting personnel needs, recruiting, and aiding in selection of new employees. They also assist in training and evaluation and administer compensation, employee benefits, and safety programs.

Businesspeople can view human resource management in two ways. In a narrow sense, it includes the functions and operations of a single department in a firm: the human resource, or personnel, department. Most firms with 200 or more employees establish such departments. In a broader sense, though, human resource management involves the entire organization, even when a special staff department exists. After all, general managers also work to train and develop workers, evaluate their performance, and motivate them to perform as efficiently as possible.

The core responsibilities of human resource management include planning for human resource needs, recruitment and selection, training/management development, performance appraisal, and compensation and employee benefits. Trained specialists from the human resource department typically work to carry out each of these responsibilities. However, they usually share such responsibilities with line managers, ranging from the company president (who is involved in overall planning) to first-line supervisors (who may play roles in preliminary interviews with applicants and in employee training). In

A century ago, companies hired workers by posting a notice outside the gate, stating that a certain number of workers would be hired the following day. The notice might list skills, such as welding or carpentry, or it might simply list the number of workers needed. The next morning, people would appear at the front gate—a small number in prosperous times, large crowds in periods of high unemployment—and the workers would be selected. The choices were often arbitrary; the company might hire the first four in line or the four people who looked the strongest or healthiest. Workers operated under a precise set of strict rules. This is one turn-of-the-century example of such a list.

RULES FOR CLERKS, 1900

1. This store must be opened at sunrise. No mistake. Open at 6:00 A.M. summer and winter. Close about 8:30 or 9 P.M. the year round.
2. Store must be swept and dusted, doors and windows opened, lamps filled and trimmed, chimneys cleaned, counters, base shelves, and showcases dusted, pens made, a pail of water and the coal must be brought in before breakfast, if there is time to do it and attend to all the customers who call.
3. The store is not to be opened on the Sabbath day unless absolutely necessary and then only for a few minutes.
4. Should the store be opened on Sunday the clerks must go in alone and get tobacco for customers in need.
5. Clerks who are in the habit of smoking Spanish cigars, being shaved at the barber's, going to dancing parties and other places of amusement, and being out late at night will assuredly give the employer reason to be overly suspicious of employee integrity and honesty.
6. Clerks are allowed to smoke in the store provided they do not wait on women while smoking a "stogie."
7. Each store clerk must pay not less than $5.00 per year to the church and must attend Sunday school regularly.
8. Men clerks are given one evening a week off for courting and two if they go to the prayer meeting.
9. After the 14 hours in the store, leisure hours should be spent mostly in reading.

a company that practices worker empowerment, human resource staffers share responsibilities even with operative employees on the shop floor. By accomplishing these tasks, the human resource department achieves its overall objectives of (1) providing qualified, well-trained employees for the organization, (2) maximizing employee effectiveness in the organization, and (3) satisfying individual employee needs through monetary compensation, employee benefits, advancement opportunities, and job satisfaction.

HOW NEEDS MOTIVATE PEOPLE

From his examination of 20 top American firms, Robert Leering, author of *A Great Place to Work*, concludes that any manager can turn a bad workplace into a good one through what he calls "the three *R*s." In the first of these, the firm grants workers more and more *responsibility* for their jobs. The second *R* involves sharing the *rewards* of the enterprise as equitably as possible. The third *R* is ensuring that employees have *rights*. These include some kind of grievance procedure, access to corporate records, and the right to confront those in authority without fearing reprisals.

Building the three *R*s into an organization should contribute to employee morale. **Morale,** the mental attitude of employees toward their employers and jobs, involves a sense of common purpose with respect to the other members of the work group and to the organization as a whole. High morale is a sign of a well-managed organization because workers' attitudes toward their jobs affect the quality of the work they do. One of the most obvious signs of poor manager-worker relations is poor morale. It lurks behind absenteeism, employee turnover, slowdowns, and wildcat strikes. It shows up in lower productivity, employee grievances, and transfers.

morale
Mental attitude of employees toward their employers and jobs.

Burnout, a byword in business today, shows up in low morale and fatigue. Burnout has recognizable symptoms, according to Dr. Donald Rosen, a psychiatrist who directs the Professionals in Crisis program at the Menninger Clinic: "Victims are lethargic, feel empty, no longer able to take satisfaction in what they once enjoyed. They have a deep questioning of the value of the tasks they perform."[2] The most likely burnout candidates are those workers who care most about their jobs and the company. Such employees may experience burnout upon feeling a sense of futility and a lack of accomplishment. Kenneth Pelletier, a stress management consultant and psychiatrist, believes that a manager can inspire workers and prevent burnout by showing appreciation for effort. Appreciation is, according to Pelletier, "the most underestimated benefit."[3]

What factors lead to high employee morale? Interestingly, managers and employees give different answers. In one classic study, summarized in Figure 9.1, managers thought that the most important factors involved satisfying basic needs for money and job security. Employees, however, wanted to be appreciated, to be treated sympathetically, and to feel like part of a team.

Other studies support these results. Madelyn Hochstein, head of opinion polling company DYG, notes that many people leave corporate jobs and start their own firms seeking quality of life and more interesting careers rather than higher pay. "There's a sense that you won't make a lot of money, but you're part of the action," says Hochstein.[4]

need
Lack of something useful; discrepancy between a desired state and an actual state.

motive
Inner state that directs an individual toward the goal of satisfying a felt need.

Maintaining high employee morale requires more than just keeping employees happy. A two-day workweek, longer vacations, or almost continual work breaks could easily produce happy employees, but truly high morale results from an organization's understanding of human needs and its success at satisfying those needs in ways that reinforce organizational goals.

Each person is motivated to take actions designed to satisfy needs. A **need** is simply the lack of something useful. It reflects a gap between an individual's actual state and his or her desired state. A **motive** is the inner state that directs a person toward the goal of satisfying a felt need. Once the need—the gap between where a person is now

FIGURE 9.1 SOURCES OF HIGH MORALE

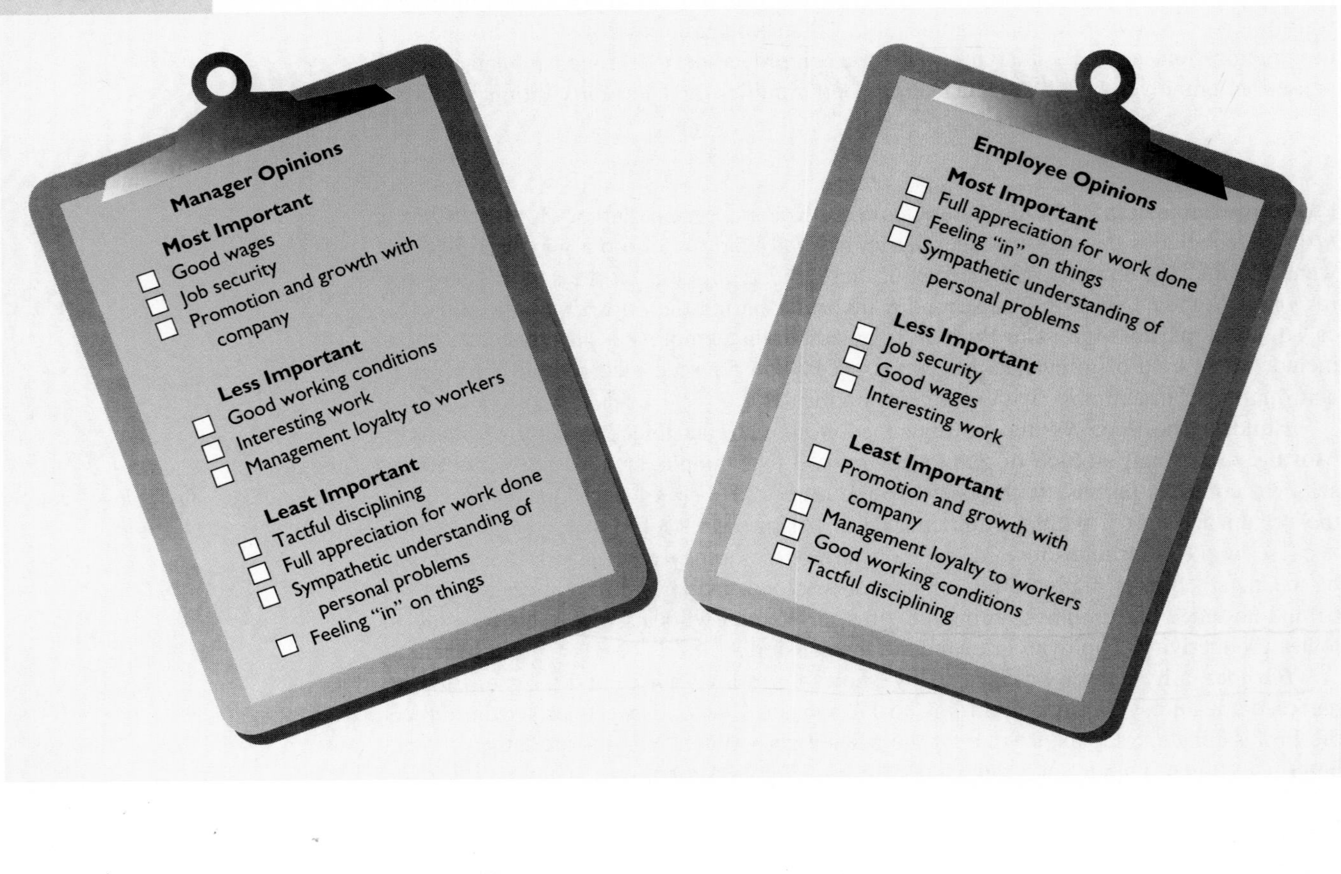

and where he or she wants to be—becomes important enough, it produces tension and the individual is *moved* (the root word for *motive*) to reduce this tension and return to a condition of equilibrium.

Consider an example. If you have been in class or worked at your job until 1:00 P.M., food may represent your immediate need. Your lack of lunch is reflected in the motive of hunger, so you move—literally—to address your need by walking to a nearby restaurant where you buy the $2.69 special (hamburger, fries, and soft drink). By 1:20 P.M. you have satisfied your need for lunch. Now you are ready to satisfy your next need: getting to your 2:00 P.M. class on time! Figure 9.2 depicts the principle behind this process. A need produces a motivation, which leads to goal-directed behavior, resulting in need satisfaction.

MASLOW'S NEEDS HIERARCHY

Psychologist Abraham H. Maslow developed a widely accepted list of human needs based on these important assumptions:

- People are wanting animals whose needs depend on what they already possess.
- A satisfied need is not a motivator; only those needs that have not been satisfied can influence behavior.
- People's needs are arranged in a hierarchy of importance; once they satisfy one need, at least partially, another emerges and demands satisfaction.

need

FIGURE 9.2 PROCESS OF MOTIVATION

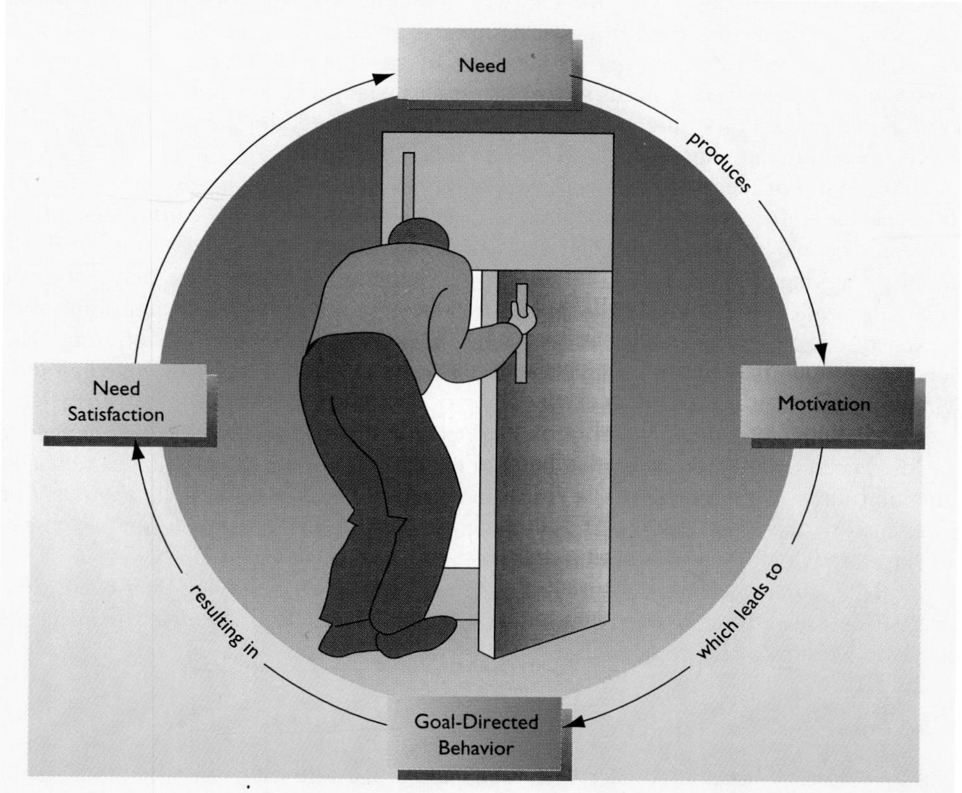

Mary Kay cosmetics sales representatives who excel at sales or recruiting are crowned queen at the company's yearly seminar. Such company recognition helps to fulfill individuals' esteem needs, making it a powerful motivator.

Everyone has needs that they must satisfy before they can consider higher-order needs. On the bottom level, Maslow's hierarchy of needs places *physiological needs*—the most basic needs, such as the desire for food, shelter, and clothing. Since most people in industrialized nations today can afford to satisfy these basic needs, higher-order needs are likely to play greater roles in worker motivation. These include *safety needs* (job security, protection from physical harm, and avoidance of the unexpected); *social needs* (the desire to be accepted by members of the family and other individuals and groups); and *esteem needs* (needs to feel accomplishment, achievement, and respect from others). The competitive urge to excel, to improve on the performance of others, is an esteem need and an almost universal human trait.

At the top of the hierarchy, Maslow placed *self-actualization needs*—needs for fulfillment, for realizing one's own potential, for using one's talents and capabilities in full. Different people may have different self-actualization needs. One person may feel fulfilled by writing a poem, another by running a marathon. Someone else may not attain self-actualization until listed in the *Guinness Book of World Records*. Organizations seek to satisfy employees' self-actualization needs, whatever they may be, by offering challenging and creative work assignments and opportunities for advancement based on individual merit.

As a major contribution, the needs hierarchy concept states that, for most people, a satisfied need is no longer a motivator. Once the individual satisfies physiological needs, attention turns to higher-order needs. Sometimes such an individual will obviously be motivated by the need to relieve thirst or hunger, but interest most often focuses on satisfying safety, belongingness, and the other needs on the ladder.

Effective managers seek ways to motivate employees by satisfying their needs. Figure 9.3 describes how various individuals and companies have attempted to meet the needs in Maslow's hierarchy.

THEORIES X, Y, AND Z

Maslow's theory became popular with managers because it seems to accommodate the facts relatively simply. After all, few people care about self-actualization when they're

FIGURE 9.3 MASLOW'S HIERARCHY OF NEEDS

Self-Actualization Needs
Accomplishment, opportunities for advancement, growth, and creativity

As a young man, Sid Craig wrote his goals on his bathroom mirror every morning (a frequent entry: "Become the owner of the company"). After a career that included teaching ballroom dancing and owning five Arthur Murray franchises, Craig and his wife Jenny built the enormously successful chain of Jenny Craig diet clinics in the United States and Australia. Craig not only realized his dream of building and running a successful business, but his and his wife's ownership shares are now worth almost $500 million.

Esteem Needs
Recognition, approval of others, status, increased responsibilities

When Union Carbide's CEO asked for volunteers to develop new business ideas, 10 percent of the 2,000-member specialty chemicals staff signed up. Some 66 new-venture ideas dreamed up by these volunteers are being studied by Union Carbide.

Social (Belongingness) Needs
Acceptance, affection, affiliation with work groups, family, friends, co-workers, and supervisors

Auto workers at the Fremont, California assembly plant operated as a joint venture between GM and Toyota are referred to as *team members.* Team members rotate jobs and work together in an atmosphere of "mutual trust." They produce almost defect-free cars.

Safety Needs
Protection from harm, employee benefits, job security

IBM, AT&T, Xerox, and Johnson & Johnson have created stress-management programs for employees that include everthing from exercise and meditation to counseling and referrals.

Physiological Needs
Food, water, and shelter

In the early 1900s, Henry Ford aided his employees in satisfying physiological needs by paying them $5 a day—twice the going wage.

starving. Business organizations have been extremely successful in satisfying people's lower-order physiological and safety needs. The traditional view of workers as ingredients in the production process—as machines like lathes, drill presses, and other equipment—led management to try to motivate them with money. Today's managers have been forced to reconsider their assumptions about employees and how best to motivate them.

Psychologist Douglas McGregor, a student of Maslow, proposed the concepts of Theory X and Theory Y as labels for the assumptions that different managers make about worker behavior and how these assumptions affect management styles. **Theory X** assumes that employees dislike work and managers must coerce, control, or threaten them to motivate them to work. Managers who accept this view feel that the average human being prefers direction, wishes to avoid responsibility, has relatively little ambition, and wants security above all. Such managers are likely to direct their subordinates through close and constant observation, continually holding over them the threat of disciplinary action, and demanding that they adhere closely to company policies and procedures.

Theory X
Managerial assumption that workers dislike work and must be coerced, controlled, or threatened to motivate them to work.

If people actually behave in the manner described by Theory X, this may be because the organization satisfies only their lower-order needs. If the organization enables them to satisfy their social, esteem, and self-actualization needs as well, employees may start to behave differently. McGregor labeled this thinking **Theory Y,** an assumption that workers like work and, under proper conditions, accept and seek out responsibilities to fulfill their social, esteem, and self-actualization needs. The Theory Y manager consid-

Theory Y
Managerial assumption that workers like work and, under proper conditions, accept and seek out responsibilities to fulfill their social, esteem, and self-actualization needs.

ers the expenditure of physical and mental effort in work as natural as play or rest. Unlike the traditional management philosophy that relies on external control and constant supervision, Theory Y emphasizes self-control and direction. Implementation requires a different managerial strategy that includes worker participation in major and minor decisions that Theory X would reserve for management.

Theory Z
Management approach emphasizing employee participation as the key to increased productivity and improved quality of work life.

The trend toward downsizing, empowering, and increasing employee participation in decision making has led to a third set of management assumptions labeled **Theory Z.** This approach views involved workers as the key to increased productivity for the company and improved quality of work life for employees. Theory Z organizations blend Theory Y assumptions with Japanese management practices. Long-term employment for employees and shared responsibility for making and implementing decisions characterize such organizations. Evaluations and promotions occur relatively slowly, and promotions are tied to individual progress rather than to the calendar. Employees receive varied, nonspecialized experience to broaden their career paths.

The move toward Theory Z's participative management style is dramatically reshaping U.S. corporations. As the last chapter described, many companies are adopting the matrix organizational structure to reap the benefits of teamwork to solve problems. Increasingly, managers are asking workers how to improve their jobs and then giving them the authority to do it.

This is exactly what Bob Woods, head of Zeneca Agricultural Products, did when profits at the agrochemicals firm dropped dramatically. Woods turned first to his senior managers and then to the employees who reported to these executives. He formed a cross-functional team of middle managers from various departments and gave them authority to solve the cash crisis. The employees reorganized the company according to customer groups rather than product lines. They also dismantled key business processes, such as product development and order processing, and made them more efficient. Throughout this difficult period, Woods was careful to show employees that he supported their efforts. He spent most of his time visiting with team members and encouraging them to "Take a chance. Get out of the box. Don't give me back what I've already got." These days, profits at Zeneca are up by 68 percent, and a newly energized work force is implementing still more improvements.[5]

HERZBERG'S MAINTENANCE VERSUS MOTIVATIONAL FACTORS

Maslow's distinctions between lower- and higher-order needs were supported by research conducted three decades ago by psychologist Frederick Herzberg. His study, focusing on various job factors that might prove to be sources of satisfaction or dissatisfaction, identified two main categories: maintenance and motivational. *Maintenance factors*, such as salary, working conditions, and job security, must be present to prevent worker dissatisfaction, but they are not strong motivators. *Motivational factors* are job-centered factors, such as recognition, responsibility, advancement, and growth potential, that are strong sources of employee motivation.

If maintenance factors are absent or inadequate, they are likely to serve as *dissatisfiers*, so for this reason they are important. For example, since most industrial firms make free parking available for their employees, a large employee parking lot is a maintenance factor. During the late 1980s, a General Motors Corporation decision to encourage employee purchases of GM cars by banning Fords, Hondas, Toyotas, and other competitive models from salaried employees' parking lots proved to be a major dissatisfier. This policy started GM employees sniping at each other, and many complaints were registered before the restrictions were removed by GM management.

Key motivational factors, however, are related to the job itself. The supervisor motivates the worker with greater job involvement.

BUILDING THE TEAM

Given the importance of a well-trained, high-quality employee team to an organization's success, it is not surprising that human resource management becomes such an important function. The entertainment industry visionary Walt Disney expressed it this way: "You can dream, create, design, and build the most wonderful place in the world, but it requires people to make the dream a reality." Not just people, but well-trained, well-motivated people are required. The recruitment and selection process plays a major role in convincing such people to join an organization. Writer Leo Rosten observed that, "First-rate people hire first-rate people. Second-rate people hire third-rate people."

Recruitment is expensive. The process can include interviews, tests, medical examinations, and training. The human resource manager must carefully recruit potential employees who have the necessary qualifications for a job, since an employee who leaves the firm after a few months can cost a company up to $75,000 in lost productivity, training costs, and employee morale. A poor employee who stays with the company can cost even more.

To ensure that potential employees offer both the necessary qualifications for a job and needed future skills, or the capability to learn them, most firms use a six-step approach to recruitment and selection, as shown in Figure 9.4. Rejection of an applicant may occur at any of these steps.

Businesses search through both internal and external sources to find candidates for specific jobs. Most firms follow policies that encourage hiring from within, that is, considering their own employees first for job openings. If no qualified internal candidates present themselves, managers must look for people outside the organization. Outside sources for potential job applicants include colleges, advertisements in newspapers and professional journals, public employment agencies (such as state employment services), unsolicited applications, and recommendations by current employees.

Career-advice author Carol Kleiman notes that firms can find promising applicants by networking in unlikely places, such as escalators, doctors' offices, stores, bathrooms, and even church pews. One hair salon in Pittsburgh even introduces clients to each other and lets them leave résumés there. The best places to network, however, are professional-association meetings, which often attract recruiters.[6]

Chapter 2 detailed a number of federal and state laws enacted over the last three decades to prohibit discrimination in hiring practices. Failure to meet these legal requirements may prevent the firm from profiting from the strengths of a diverse work force, in addition to stiff penalties and bad publicity that can result. In addition to these laws, employers must observe various other legal restrictions governing hiring practices.[7] For instance, some firms try to screen out high-risk employees by requiring drug testing for job applicants, particularly in industries where employees are responsible for public safety, such as airline firms and public transportation companies. Drug testing is controversial, however, due to concerns about privacy. Furthermore, positive test results may be inaccurate; traces of legal drugs, such as prescribed medications, may chemically resemble traces of illegal substances. Several states have passed laws restricting drug tests.

FIGURE 9.4 STEPS IN THE RECRUITMENT AND SELECTION PROCESS

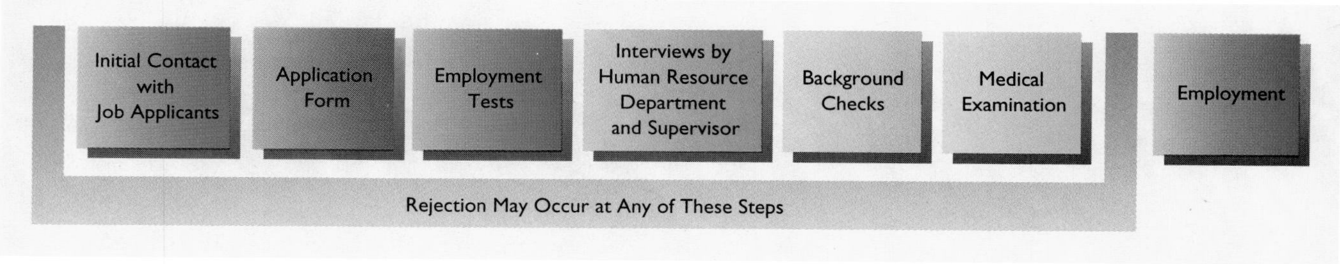

The law prohibits the use of polygraph (lie detector) tests in almost all pre-hiring decisions, as well as in random testing of current employees. The only organizations exempt from this law are federal, state, and county governments; firms that do sensitive work under contract to the Defense Department, FBI, or CIA; pharmaceutical companies that handle controlled substances; and security guard services.

Employees, for their part, must recognize legal restrictions that govern their own behavior. For instance, a growing number of communities have banned smoking in workplaces and public areas. Many employers have policies against hiring smokers, and some penalize current employees who smoke by charging higher premiums for health insurance and other benefits.

ORIENTATION, TRAINING, AND EVALUATION

A newly hired employee usually completes an orientation program, which is administered jointly by the human resource department and the department in which the person will work. As another major function, the human resource department works to develop and maintain a well-trained, productive labor force. Firms should view employee training as an ongoing process throughout each employee's tenure with the company. **On-the-job training,** one popular instructional method, trains employees for job tasks by allowing them to perform the tasks under the guidance of experienced employees.

on-the-job training
Training employees for job tasks by allowing them to perform the tasks under the guidance of experienced employees.

In a variation of this approach, apprenticeship training, an employee learns a job by serving as an assistant to a trained worker for a relatively long time period. Apprenticeship programs are much more common in Europe than in the United States. While American apprenticeships usually focus on blue-collar trades, many white-collar professions in Europe involve apprenticeships. Employees at German department stores, for exam-

When these government office workers want to smoke, they must go to a designated smoking area. An increasing number of businesses, including large corporations such as General Motors, Heinz USA, and Texas Instruments, are creating smoke-free work environments. Recent findings on the adverse effects of second-hand smoke will only accelerate the trend. Employers say smokers are expensive: They cost money in sick leave, insurance premiums, legal liability, and building maintenance.

ple, frequently serve apprenticeships of two to three years. Such a worker's training includes three days a week working in the store and two days in classes learning accounting methods and product information. Even store managers go through three-year apprenticeship programs.[8]

Off-the-job training involves some form of classroom training, which uses classroom techniques—lectures, conferences, audiovisual aids, programmed instruction, or special machines—to teach employees difficult, high-skill jobs. A **management development program** provides training designed to improve the skills and broaden the knowledge of current and potential managers. Such a program is often conducted off of a company's premises. General Motors, Holiday Inn, McDonald's, and Xerox are among the dozens of giant companies that have established college-like institutes that offer specific programs for current and potential managers.

management development program
Training designed to improve the skills and broaden the knowledge of current and potential managers.

Management development training can exert a powerful force to shape a company's corporate culture, for good or ill. When Jack Welch became CEO of General Electric, he found an organization hampered by slow decision making, numerous political struggles between managers, and an overall lack of innovation. Many GE executives had completed the management development program outlined in the company's antiquated training guides, known as the *Blue Books*. Welch promptly called his managers together and announced that they could find no more textbook answers to GE's problems. He had the Blue Books burned on the spot. He then revamped the firm's training center and brought in consultants to retrain executives in new management techniques. Welch sees training as so vital, in fact, that he continues to visit the center every two weeks, where he supervises GE's overall training curriculum and drops in on classes.[9]

Another important human resource management activity, **performance appraisal,** is the evaluation of an individual's job performance by comparing actual performance with desired performance. Based on this information, managers make objective decisions about compensation, promotion, additional training needs, transfers, or terminations. Such appraisals are not confined to business; professors appraise student performance through assignments and examinations, while students appraise instructors by completing written evaluations.

performance appraisal
Defining acceptable employee performance levels, evaluating them, then comparing actual and desired performance of individuals to aid in decisions about training, compensation, promotion, transfers, or terminations.

EMPLOYEE COMPENSATION

In one of its most difficult functions, human resource management works to develop an equitable compensation and benefits system. Because labor costs represent a sizable percentage of any firm's total product costs, excessively high wages may make products too expensive to compete effectively in the marketplace. Inadequate wages lead, however, to high employee turnover, poor morale, and inefficient production.

The terms wages and salary are often used interchangeably, but they do have slightly different meanings. *Wages* represent compensation based on the number of hours worked or the amount of output produced. Firms generally pay wages to production employees, retail salespeople, and maintenance workers. *Salaries* are employee compensation calculated as weekly, monthly, or annual amounts. White-collar workers such as office personnel, executives, and professional employees usually receive salaries.

An effective compensation program should attract well-qualified workers, keep them satisfied in their jobs, and inspire them to produce. Most companies base their compensation policies on five factors: (1) salaries and wages paid by other companies that compete for the same personnel, (2) government legislation, (3) the cost of living, (4) their own ability to pay, and (5) workers' productivity.

Many employers seek to reward superior performance and motivate employees to excel by offering some type of incentive compensation in addition to salaries or wages, as rewards for exceptional performance. Figure 9.5 compares the four major forms of incentive compensation: profit sharing, gain sharing, lump-sum bonuses, and pay for knowledge.

FIGURE 9.5 FOUR FORMS OF INCENTIVE COMPENSATION

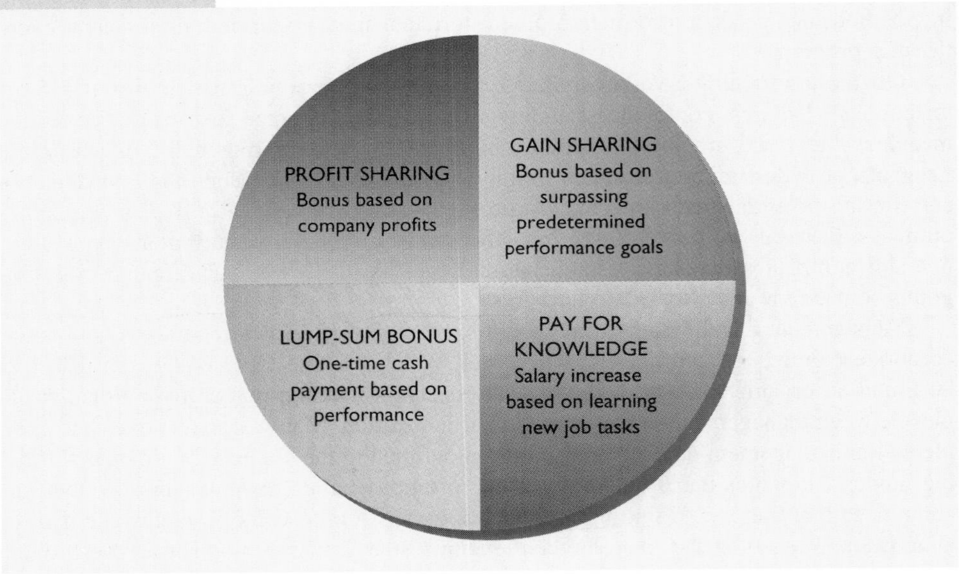

Managers often earn incentive compensation based on their subordinates' performance. Managers of operating divisions at food wholesaler Sysco Corp. receive bonuses only if their units' pretax profits exceed 4 percent of revenues and the units' return on capital figures exceed 12 percent. Executives receive bonuses only if the company's return on equity is 14 percent or more and if its earnings per share grow by 10 percent. Says CEO John Woodhouse, "A good president will make 50 percent of his compensation in bonus." Last year Woodhouse earned a base salary of $562,500 and received almost as much—$470,900—in incentive compensation.[10]

EMPLOYEE BENEFITS

employee benefits
Employee rewards such as pension plans, insurance, sick-leave pay, and tuition reimbursement that an organization gives, entirely or in part, at its own expense.

The typical organization furnishes many benefits to employees and their families in addition to wages and salaries. **Employee benefits** are rewards such as pension plans, insurance, sick leave, child care, and tuition reimbursement that an organization gives, entirely or in part, at its own expense. Some benefits are required by law; most employers must contribute to each employee's federal Social Security account. In addition, they make payments to state employment insurance programs that assist laid-off workers and to workers' compensation programs that provide compensation to workers who suffer job-related injuries or illnesses.

One desirable employee benefit is job protection for workers who need emergency time off to care for dependents or for themselves if they become too ill to perform their work. The Family and Medical Leave Act of 1993 requires covered employers to offer up to 12 weeks of unpaid, job-protected leave to eligible employees. The law applies to all public agencies, including state, local, and federal employers and schools.[11]

Other benefits may be provided voluntarily. Examples include health insurance, pensions and retirement programs, paid vacations and leave time, and employee services such as tuition-reimbursement facilities.

Employee benefits represent a large and rapidly growing component of human resource costs. Wages account for only 61 percent of the typical employee's earnings; employee benefits determine the other 39 percent. Benefit costs have risen faster than wages and salaries during the past 10 years, and one reason is the soaring cost of med-

FIGURE 9.6 WHERE THE EMPLOYEE BENEFIT DOLLAR GOES

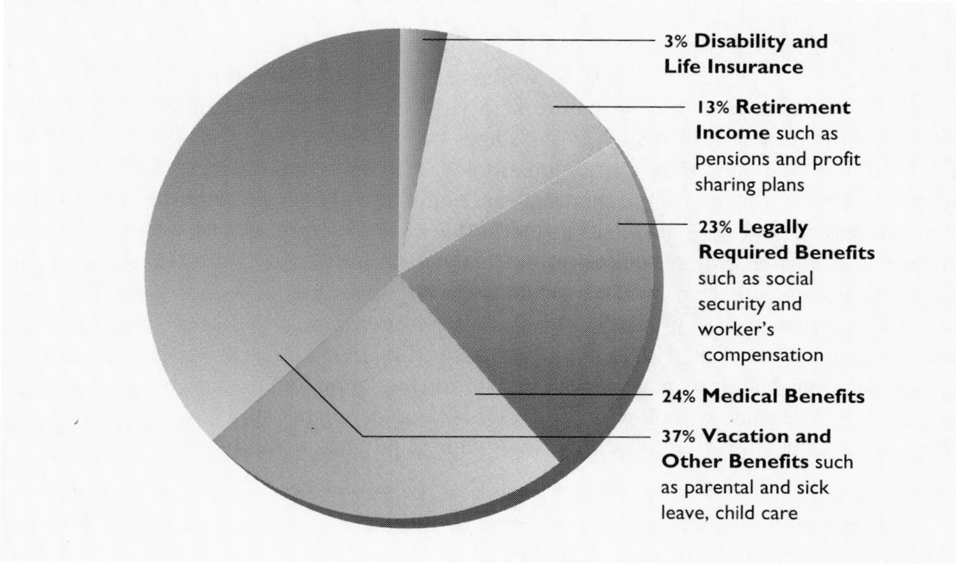

ical benefits. Even though employees' vacations and leaves of absence currently take the biggest chunk of a company's benefits budget, medical costs are increasing much more rapidly. Figure 9.6 outlines the relative allocation of employee benefits.

Employee benefits are even more costly in Europe, where a worker enjoys a guaranteed 37-hour work week with six weeks of vacation annually and a yearly bonus of an extra month's pay. Employees are also entitled to generous maternity and paternity leaves, with parents' jobs protected for up to three years. These generous benefits come at a price, however. High costs have forced some European firms to move their operations to other, cheaper countries, and European unemployment rates are rising. Some politicians, in fact, are calling for a shorter work week of 32 hours, which would cut each worker's pay by about 6 percent.[12]

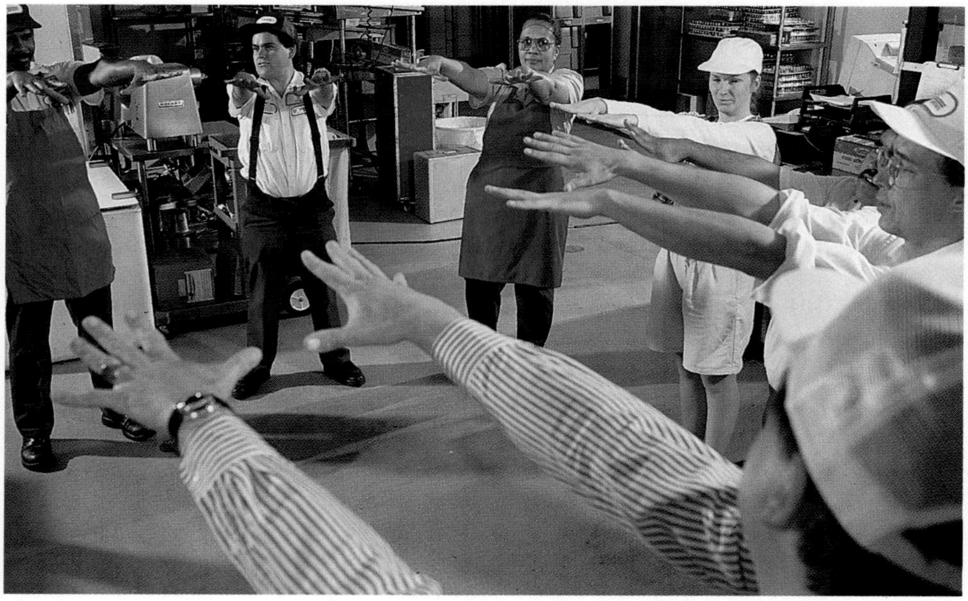

Employees at LSG/Sky Chef's El Paso kitchen begin each morning with stretching exercises to reduce back injuries. This is part of Sky Chef's effort to prevent worker injury. The company provides training covering health and safety topics like proper lifting techniques, handling of kitchen tools, and working in refrigerated rooms. It also provides incentive pay to employees who carry out their duties in exemplary ways.

flexible benefit plan *System of variable benefits that provides each employee with a specific dollar amount of benefits that the worker can allocate to selected areas of coverage.*

In an increasingly common method of controlling benefits costs, many firms offer **flexible benefit plans.** Also called *cafeteria plans,* these systems set up flexible benefits packages that give employees specific dollar amounts of benefits that they can allocate to selected areas of coverage. These plans suit two-income households well, in their desire to avoid duplicate coverage, as well as single people, who do not need expensive family plans. Also, the flexible nature of a cafeteria plan permits employees to adjust their benefits packages through various stages of their life cycles.

Safe working conditions are a vital employee benefit for all workers. All employees deserve safe workplaces, but every year an estimated 10,000 workers die from on-the-job injuries—about 30 a day. Another 70,000 are permanently disabled from job-related injuries or illnesses. Some of the most dangerous industries are steel making, ship building, logging, construction, and food processing.[13]

Recognition of the importance of a safe work environment led to the creation of the Occupational Safety and Health Administration (OSHA), a federal agency that tries to assure safe and healthful working conditions for the labor force. Employers are responsible for knowing and complying with all OSHA standards that apply to their workplaces. They must also inform employees of their rights and responsibilities under the law.

JOB ENRICHMENT

job enrichment *Redesigning work to give employees more authority in planning their tasks, deciding how to complete their work, and allowing them to learn related skills or to trade jobs.*

In their search for ways to improve employee productivity and morale, a growing number of firms are focusing on the motivational aspects of the job itself. Rather than simplifying the tasks involved in a job, they seek to enrich the job by making it more satisfying and meaningful. **Job enrichment** involves redesigning work to give employees more authority in planning their tasks, deciding how to complete their work, and allowing them to learn related skills or to trade jobs with others.

A recent survey of 77 major companies found that job enrichment played a crucial role in determining which new products succeeded and which did not. Successful product development teams enjoyed full support from top management and had authority to manage their projects themselves. Boeing, for example, encourages its product development teams to take the initiative in solving a problem. "We have the no-messenger rule," says Henry Shomber, a Boeing chief engineer. "Team members must make decisions on the spot. They can't run back to their supervisors for permission." This approach helped the aircraft manufacturer to create its new 777 passenger jet with less than half as many design problems as had plagued earlier models.[14]

The term *job enlargement* is sometimes used interchangeably with job enrichment, but it differs in that it merely expands a worker's assignments to include additional, smaller tasks. Rather than performing two tasks, a worker might complete four similar tasks. Enlarging a job might lead to job enrichment, but not necessarily. Job enrichment occurs only when the new tasks give an employee greater authority and responsibility for the end result. Enrichment offers employees more opportunity to be creative and to set their own paces within the limits of an overall schedule.

FLEXIBLE WORK SCHEDULES

flextime *Scheduling system that allows employees to set work hours within constraints specified by the firm.*

According to a recent study of 7,437 employees ranging from clerks to managers, the primary stress factor for U.S. workers is time pressure.[15] When American Express surveyed its employees about what they wanted most, the answer was clear: free time.[16] This helps explain why flexible work schedules help companies to attract and motivate talented employees and enrich their jobs. Firms achieve flexible schedules through flextime, compressed workweeks, job sharing, and home-based work.

A scheduling system that allows employees to set work hours within constraints specified by the firm is called **flextime.** Most employers that offer flextime designate certain core hours when employees must be on the job, perhaps between 9 A.M. and 3 P.M.[17]

Technology in such forms as computers, E-mail, fax machines, and online data retrieval services has accelerated the growth of home-based work. AT&T's Integrated Services Digital Network offers telecommunicators combined voice, data, and video transmission services previously available only in businesses. All of these features are available without having to rewire the home or use a modem.

Meetings are typically scheduled during these core hours. In general, flextime is more common in insurance, finance, retailing, and government positions than in manufacturing jobs. It is also more widespread in Europe than in the United States; an estimated 40 percent of the Swiss work force and 25 percent of German workers have flexible schedules, compared to roughly 12 percent of workers in the United States. Other alternative work-scheduling practices include compressed workweeks—where employees work the same number of hours in fewer than the typical five days, and job sharing, which divides one job assignment between two or more employees.

More and more companies now offer employees a fourth option of **home-based work,** in which they do the same jobs working at home instead of in the office. Home-based workers are sometimes called *telecommuters* because many "commute" to work electronically by hooking up via home computers to their companies' computer systems. Technologies such as personal computers, electronic mail, and facsimile machines make working at home easier than ever before.

home-based work
Program in which employees work at home, sometimes linked to their employers by terminals that access central computers.

The number of company employees who work at home rose 15 percent last year to reach 7.6 million. While most home-based workers like the arrangement, some people adapt better than others. Successful telecommuters need to be self-disciplined, reliable, and computer literate; they must also produce work with minimal supervision. These people need bosses who are comfortable with setting goals and managing from afar.[18]

Some companies allow their workers to choose among these flexible options. At American Express, for example, customer service agents and credit analysts are free to set their own hours. Many of the company's travel agents now work from home. Despite the variety of work schedules, employee productivity remains as high as ever.[19]

DOWNSIZING REVOLUTION

Traditionally, as companies have grown larger, they have become *tall organizations*, with many levels in the management hierarchy. During the 1970s, many organizations grew progressively taller as the number of middle-management positions increased dramatically. The progression from supervisory to middle to top management became a recognized career path for many managers.

downsizing
Management decision to eliminate layers from the management hierarchy in an effort to reduce costs and improve efficiency.

More recently, however, organizations have begun **downsizing,** in which management decides to eliminate layers from the management hierarchy in efforts to reduce costs and improve efficiency. This creates a *flat organization*, with many positions at the same level in the hierarchy.

After World War II, big organizations made sense as companies grew rapidly. Technology, for the most part, was limited to typewriters and slide rules. Markets were regulated and largely domestic, and the work force consisted primarily of low-skilled or semiskilled employees. However, firms can no longer sustain these cumbersome organizational structures in today's globalized, high-tech environment.

In recent years, the United States and every other industrialized country have begun to see the effects of a management revolution. Reports of layoffs and plant closings have filled the headlines. Surveys by the American Management Association show that, since 1988, 33 percent to 50 percent of large and midsized U.S. companies have cut the sizes of their work forces. Over a 6-year period, *Fortune* 500 companies have eliminated 4.7 million jobs—a quarter of their employees.[20] Furthermore, two-thirds of the firms that downsize in one year continue to downsize in the following year.[21]

Downsizing affects all levels of employees, including hourly workers, professionals, and managers. America's largest corporations are reshaping their traditional, vertical management hierarchies into leaner, faster, and more efficient structures. During the 1990s, a new horizontal management style is clearly emerging in corporate America.

As Figure 9.7 reveals, companies downsize for many reasons. The two most common objectives are to reduce costs by cutting overhead and streamlining the organizational structure and to increase customer satisfaction. Other reasons include reducing purchasing and logistics costs, improving employee satisfaction, facilitating introductions of new products or technologies, speeding up product development, improving market share and competitiveness, and improving financial performance.

Downsizing can pay off. Many companies that suffered deep cuts in the early stages of restructuring would have suffered even worse if they had not reduced costs. Most firms find that downsizing can improve productivity, enhance quality and customer ser-

FIGURE 9.7 TOP OBJECTIVES FOR CHANGE: WHY DOWNSIZING OCCURS

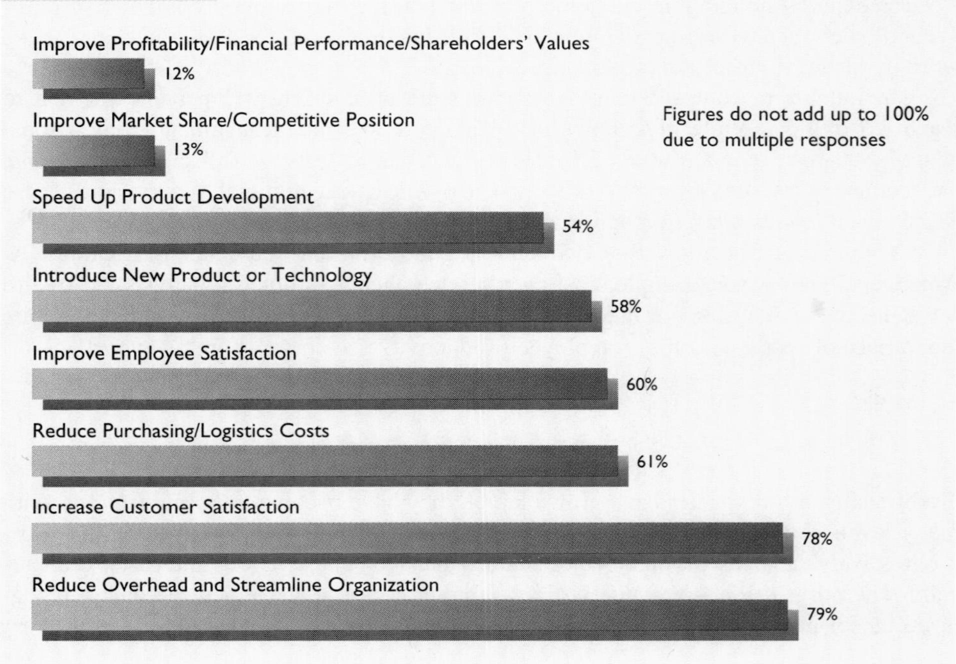

vice, and make employees more willing to take risks. Research shows that effective downsizing usually takes the form of selective reorganization rather than sweeping layoffs.[22] Honeywell has restructured its operations by selling off its defense operations and computer business, and by cutting its work force by 30 percent. It recently reported steady earnings and plans to increase annual sales from $6 billion to $10 billion by the end of the decade.[23]

COSTS OF DOWNSIZING

Despite these advantages, downsizing remains controversial. Some managers see it as a fad that cuts costs relatively quickly without having to correct inefficient ways of doing business. Others insist that downsizing is a painful but necessary step to remain competitive in a global economy.

Some economic experts question whether job cuts always bring improved productivity. A financial analysis of 140,000 factories revealed that, while 55 percent of productivity gains came from downsized companies, 45 percent came from companies that were hiring more workers.

In addition, management must consider how downsizing affects the workloads of remaining employees.[24] Another recent survey found that 68 percent of executives who downsized experienced unanticipated problems. Any time employees lose their jobs, no matter the number, significant emotional and financial factors cloud the picture. "If you keep making sizable job cuts," says Alfred Dunlap, CEO of Scott Paper Company, "you destroy morale and you paralyze the company."[25] As business author Robert Tomakso points out, "You've got a lot of shell-shocked survivors, and now you're forcing them into task forces to reengineer how the work is done. Come on—there's tremendous unreality to that."[26]

Downsizing doesn't always cause layoffs. Many companies have cut their work forces by offering early retirement plans, voluntary severance programs, and reassignments. Managers need to remember that the decision to downsize must join with a commitment to quality and growth, not just a reduction in costs. Two important components of successful downsizing are employee empowerment and outsourcing. As Chapter 1 discussed, empowerment ensures that employees can carry on the operations of the firm. Outsourcing allows experts outside the firm to perform functions that in-house staff previously performed.

EMPOWERING EMPLOYEES

As an organization downsizes, remaining workers must take on new tasks and responsibilities. Entire management levels often vanish, and remaining managers must assume control of more employees than ever before.

Empowering employees—giving them additional decision-making authority and responsibility—helps the organization to deal with these changes. It frees managers from hands-on control of subordinates and motivates workers by making their jobs more interesting. Too many traditionally tall organizations have discouraged employees by eliminating much of their power to make decisions that affect their jobs. Management today faces the challenge of finding ways to encourage creativity and innovation.

empowering
Giving employees additional decision-making authority and responsibilities.

Honeywell, for example, makes empowerment an important part of its strategy. While Honeywell executives plan further restructuring—they want to combine three sales forces into one and consolidate 176 U.S. field offices into 136—they empower workers to make most decisions about how to restructure jobs. At each field location, task forces of employees, none of them managers, are responsible for reorganizing work procedures. Most of the people who lose their jobs move to other positions with Honeywell. Says one employee, "In the past it was all top-down. There were no voices and no choices. Now the company is listening."[27]

OUTSOURCING

outsourcing
Relying on outside specialists to perform functions previously performed by company employees.

Another important development has accompanied the corporate downsizing trend: **outsourcing,** or relying on outside specialists to perform functions previously performed by company employees. Outsourcing began on a small scale, as firms typically began by contracting services such as maintenance, cleaning, and delivery. Today, outsourcing has expanded to include outside contracting of many fundamental tasks. Figure 9.8 shows the services that firms outsource most often. While housekeeping and maintenance still appear on the list, so do other functions such as architectural design, food service, security, construction management, space planning, reprographics, and office relocations. Some companies outsource such functions as production of one or more items in their product lines, accounting and legal services, and warehousing and transporting finished goods.

Outsourcing complements downsizing in a variety of ways. It reduces the need for employees to perform certain tasks. It allows a firm to continue performing the functions it does best, while hiring other firms to do tasks that they can handle more competently. Another benefit of outsourcing is the firm's ability to negotiate the best price from among

FIGURE 9.8 SERVICES MOST OFTEN OUTSOURCED

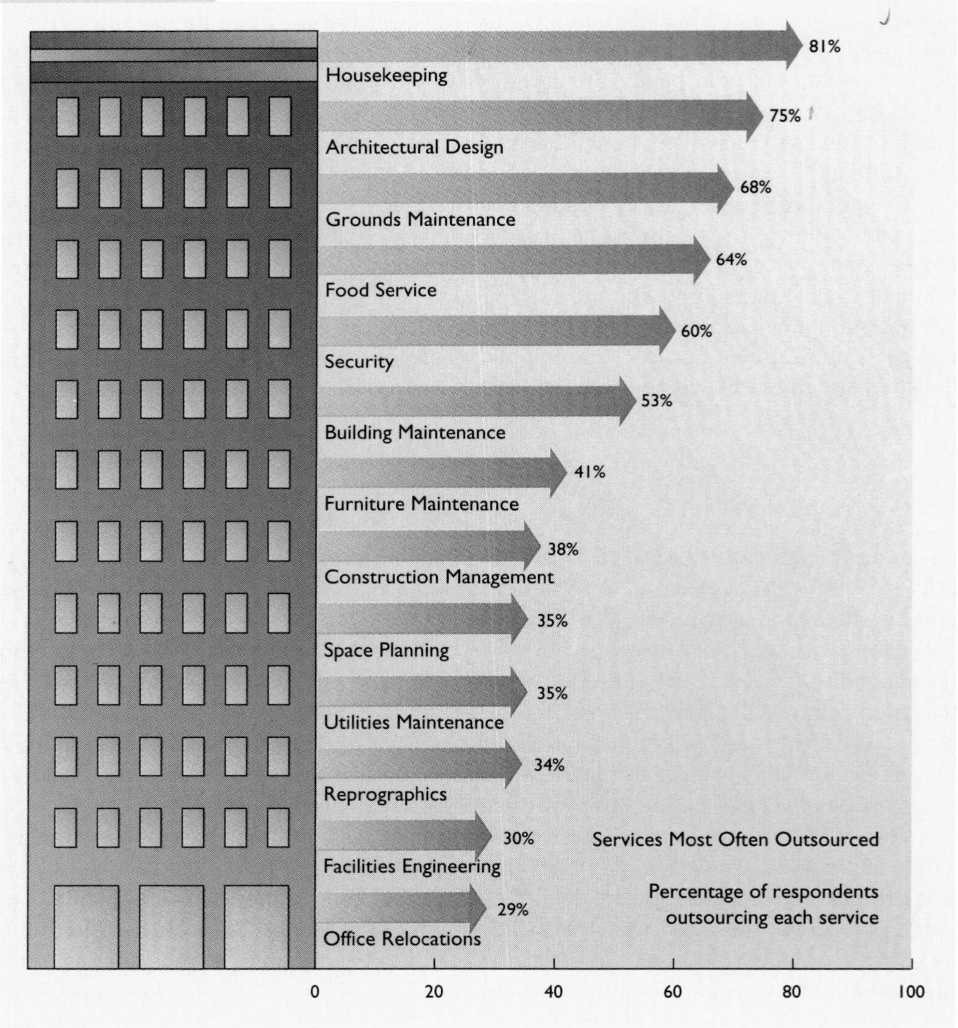

competing bidders and the chance to avoid the long-term human resource costs associated with in-house operations. Firms that outsource also have the flexibility to change suppliers at the end of a contract.

Outsourcing has become important in the competitive strategies of both U.S. and international firms. When computer-equipment maker Fujitsu Personal Systems, a California-based subsidiary of the Japanese multinational corporation Fujitsu, entered the European market, distribution became a major problem. Italy was especially difficult, since customs officials delayed, and sometimes even lost, incoming shipments. Fujitsu deliveries to Italy were arriving in from two weeks to never, so the company outsourced its delivery function to United Parcel Service. These days, all European orders pass through UPS's warehouse in the Netherlands, and Italian orders arrive an average of four days after placement.[28]

The key to success in outsourcing is a 100 percent commitment by both parties. Outsourcing is a partnership in the purest sense of the word.[29]

INTRAPRENEURSHIP

A major human resource management concern plagues managers at many giant U.S. and foreign corporations as they struggle to retain the entrepreneurial spirit of small business within their huge, multilayered organizations staffed by hundreds, or even thousands, of employees. Major innovations have often emerged from the domain of small business. Many small firms begin when entrepreneurs take risks to set up and operate new businesses. From Thomas Edison's development of the phonograph to the birth of the Apple computer in Steven P. Jobs's garage, the U.S. entrepreneurial sector has given birth to dozens of major industries. Entrepreneurs have given the world such popular consumer products as ball-point pens, fiberglass skis, Velcro fasteners, and Big Mac hamburgers.

Today, many corporations are encouraging **intrapreneurship,** entrepreneurial activity within the corporate structure. Although the intrapreneur may begin by assembling a special task force and/or working within the confines of a matrix structure, a successful project may result in an entirely new subsidiary of the corporation. In some cases, a separate company is formed at the outset. While this approach shares the disadvantages described in an earlier chapter for the matrix organization, the advantages lie in the avail-

intrapreneurship
Entrepreneurial activity within the corporate structure.

QuadMark Ltd. executives test the company's single-sheet copier. Organizations like Xerox Technology Venture foster intrapreneurship by encouraging and funding the development of employees' ideas into viable products and companies such as QuadMark.

able financing and necessary manufacturing and marketing expertise already in place in a large company. In addition, the intrapreneuring option may permit a firm to retain valuable, entrepreneurially oriented employees who might otherwise leave the company and start their own businesses.

Xerox Corp. fosters intrapreneurship by setting up a separate division, Xerox Technology Ventures, solely to identify, fund, and organize companies based on employees' ideas. One Xerox intrapreneur is engineer Denis Stemmle, a 26-year company veteran who conceived the idea of a portable, battery-powered, plain-paper copier. Funding from Xerox Technology Ventures enabled Stemmle to form his own firm, Quixote Products Limited, and begin marketing his QuadMark copier. Intrapreneurship benefits both employer and employee. As part owner of Stemmle's business, Xerox can explore a new market and share the profits from QuadMark sales. Stemmle, in turn, benefits from having access to Xerox's expertise and equipment. Recently, the company allowed him to borrow a $100,000 microscope for several days.[30]

TIME MANAGEMENT

time management
Effective allocation of one's time among different tasks.

"If it weren't for the last minute, nothing would ever get done." Everyone could name at least one person who could adopt this statement as a personal philosophy. Benjamin Franklin's admonition that "time is money" applies equally well almost 250 years since he included the maxim in his *Poor Richard's Almanac*. Human resource costs constitute a major expense item for most firms, and both managers and operating employees who wisely manage time generate productivity boosts every working day. **Time management,** effective allocation of one's time among different tasks, is a key element of managerial success in the late 1990s.

TIME MANAGEMENT GUIDELINES

Numerous time management guidelines have been suggested over the years. Some of the best-known include always leave at least a quarter of your time unscheduled; assign priorities to tasks; break big jobs into smaller ones; and, when taking on something new, give up something old.

The following paragraphs discuss some other generally accepted time management ideas with examples of how some successful top executives implement them.

Establish Goals and Set Priorities Make a list of long-term and short-term projects. Look at the list regularly and revise it as needed. Arrange the items on the list in order of importance and then divide them into specific tasks, then start at the top of the list and get to work. Do not get upset if your priorities change by the hour—just revise your list and get on with the work. Schedule your daily activities on an hour-by-hour appointment calendar.

Charles J. Conroy, an international law specialist with the New York law firm Baker & McKenzie, travels extensively for his job. A typical trip involves meeting with clients in five Asian and European cities in 10 days. Conroy plans his travel schedule to allow as much time as possible with his family by grouping his trips in two-week marathons every 6 weeks. He also takes advantage of free time when he can; he may go to the office at 5:30 A.M. so he can spend a few hours that afternoon with his daughter before hopping an evening plane to Europe.[31]

Learn to Delegate Work Part of setting priorities is deciding whether you really need to do a task yourself. One management professor lists only six things that a top manager should always do: plan, select the team, monitor their efforts, motivate, evaluate, and reward them. The manager should consider delegating any other tasks, that is, assigning them to a subordinate.

Some questions should guide the decision about what to delegate. Is this project truly necessary? (Will anyone really read this report you're struggling to produce?) Would this project benefit a subordinate? (An employee may be eager for the experience and opportunity to try something new.) Is this what superiors think the manager should spend time doing? (If not, can someone else do it instead?)

After deciding what to delegate, the manager should follow this procedure to get desired results: give clear instructions on what to do, make sure workers understand instructions, set deadlines, and allow enough time to correct mistakes.

Concentrate on the Most Important Activities Learn the Pareto principle of time management: You can achieve 80 percent of your goals in only 20 percent of your time if you work on tasks that are critical to the completion of the overall project and avoid those that contribute little to the outcome.

Do the Most Important Work When You Are Most Alert Work on high-priority items when you are mentally alert and on low-priority items when your energy has ebbed. Business professor Donald Van Eynde points out, "As you become more and more tired, you achieve less. The typical response is to work harder and longer. Overbooked, overstressed, you forget you had that meeting scheduled. You start to get angry with other people, along the lines of 'I know I said I would do this, but I really resent it.' "[32]

Group Activities Together Set aside a period of time to read all of your mail and answer all of your phone calls. This will help you make the most efficient use of your time.

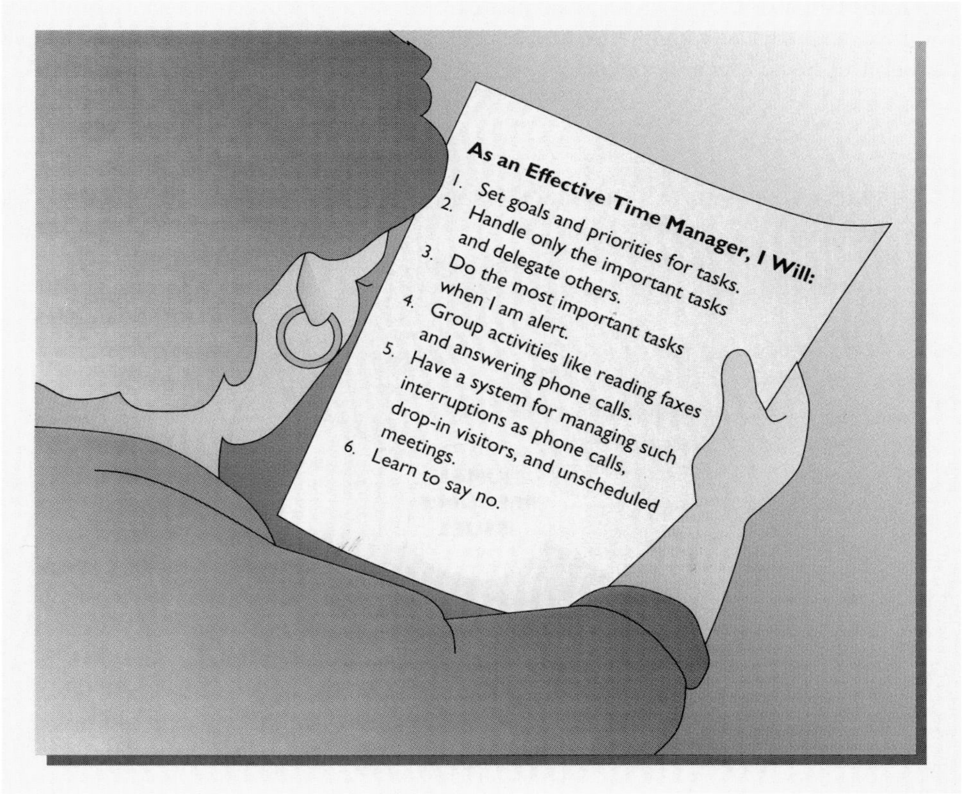

As an Effective Time Manager, I Will:
1. Set goals and priorities for tasks.
2. Handle only the important tasks and delegate others.
3. Do the most important tasks when I am alert.
4. Group activities like reading faxes and answering phone calls.
5. Have a system for managing such interruptions as phone calls, drop-in visitors, and unscheduled meetings.
6. Learn to say no.

Learn How to Handle Interruptions Incoming phone calls, unscheduled visitors, and even the mail can play havoc with a schedule. Control these interruptions by having a secretary handle all but essential calls when you are working on an important task, by working in another office where no one will find and interrupt you, by setting times when subordinates can talk to you and times when they cannot except for emergencies, and by learning how to deal with long-winded callers. Interrupting yourself also wastes time. Instead of getting yet another cup of coffee or walking down the hall to chat with a friend, try to finish what you are doing, even if the job is difficult or unpleasant. Just think how good you will feel when it's done!

HUMAN RESOURCE CONCERNS FOR THE NEW CENTURY

As business approaches the 21st century, it must adjust current policies and develop new strategies to address pressing human resource concerns. Figure 9.9 identifies these issues as an aging work force, the growth of two-career and nonfamily households, the need to break through the so-called *glass ceiling*, the rise of contingency workers, the increasing need for elder-care services, and the continuing trend toward a culturally diverse work force.

OLDER WORKERS

As the U.S. population ages, so does the work force. The 1960s counterculture slogan "Never trust anyone over 30" seems increasingly out of place as the median age approaches 31 and people over 65 represent the fastest-growing segment of the population. Federal and state laws prohibit mandatory retirement for most workers, so attempts to reduce company payrolls by eliminating the typically above-average wages and salaries of older, more experienced workers usually involve financial incentives to encourage voluntary retirement. These **worker buyout** plans typically include financial packages that include cash bonuses, continuation of such employee benefits as insurance coverage, and unusually high retirement benefits to cover the gap between retirement and the onset of Social Security payments.

worker buyout
Financial incentive designed to encourage older employees to voluntarily retire.

FIGURE 9.9 HUMAN RESOURCE ISSUES FOR THE NEW CENTURY

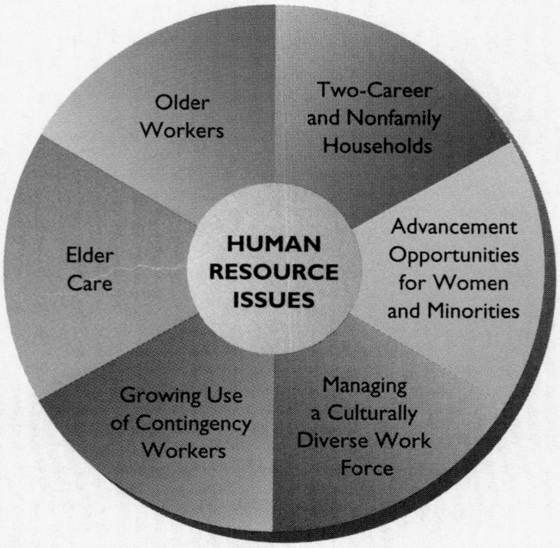

A BROADER PURPOSE

OLDER WORKERS: AN UNTAPPED HUMAN RESOURCE GOLD MINE Somehow in the discussion of environmental concerns, the need for recycling, and the emphasis on the fact that Spaceship Earth has only a finite amount of water, topsoil, minerals, and other natural resources, people have overlooked the effect of the same concerns on human resources. After all, at any one moment in time, only a limited number of qualified people are available to perform the work of business, and business continues to clamor for more. ■ At the same time, a curious phenomenon is occurring. Relatively youthful, highly qualified people are choosing to retire though they are likely to enjoy another decade or more of continued health and vitality. Since 1960, the median retirement age for men has fallen from 67 to 61. Over the past two decades, the number of workers between 55 and 65 has declined by 273,000. This trend is particularly striking in light of the passage of the Age Discrimination in Employment Act, which prohibits mandatory retirement in almost every job category. These decisions to retire early have been voluntary choices on the part of employer and employee, frequently stimulated by early retirement incentive bonuses offered by companies wishing to downsize and reduce the number of their more experienced—and usually higher-paid—employees. ■ However, most employers would agree with these conclusions about the older segment of the U.S. work force: Older workers are very dependable, seldom late, and have low rates of absenteeism. ■ These workers typically are highly trained and have many years of on-the-job experience. ■ They are conscientious workers who add a sense of caring to coworkers and customers alike. ■ Still, many employers are reluctant to hire older workers, seeing only the prospects of higher medical costs, higher wages, and higher insurance premiums than younger workers would bring. Also, they see a higher price tag on the services of older workers than for younger, less experienced employees. ■ Although many older Americans would like to rejoin the work force, they don't necessarily want to rejoin the rigid, often stress-filled jobs of their youths. They also don't want many of the stereotypical jobs for elderly persons, such as low-pay, low-prestige service-sector jobs. ■ Surveys have found that many retirees would have preferred to continue working with their former employers on job-sharing, part-time, or flextime schedules. Jill Quadagno, a Florida State University gerontologist, offers another suggestion: "Older workers would be ideally suited for short-term jobs, part-time jobs, yet we don't see much of that happening. We don't see employers moving toward flexible labor forces using older workers." ■ One small but notable exception is United Security, based in Defuniak Springs, Florida, where every employee is a part-time retiree. The company payroll lists former police officers, teachers, and military personnel. The company, owned by a 64-year-old retired auto worker, prefers retirees over younger workers for their dedication and reliability. As the owner puts it, "They show up for work, they do a good job, and they don't sit around watching the clock." Source: Quadagno quotation from Jeff Kunerth, "There Is a Boom These Days in Older Workers," *Mobile Register,* October 23, 1994, p. 13E.

QUESTIONS FOR CRITICAL THINKING

1. How does the older workers' work ethic differ from the younger generation's work ethic?
2. If you were director of personnel for a company hiring older workers, how would you find potential employees?
3. What are some businesses that could utilize older workers?

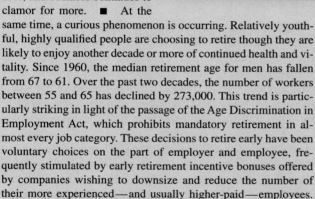

In addition to reducing company payrolls, worker buyouts may improve the morale of remaining workers who see tangible evidence of management's attempts to maintain job security by resorting to a buyout rather than a layoff. Also, unclogging job and promotion opportunities improves the upward mobility of younger employees.

However, business pays a price when it loses older workers. These employees are often the most experienced and knowledgeable, and many employers find that they simply perform more effectively than less experienced workers. Don McDermott, who heads a human resource consulting firm in New Jersey, notes that many companies replace older workers with novices and then find that the newcomers often can't handle the jobs as well.

Some companies reward and retain experienced employees by switching them into new positions if their old jobs become obsolete or less important. AT&T holds longtime employees responsible for keeping their skills up to date and remaining valuable to the company. Says one electrical engineer, a 20-year veteran of Bell Labs, "They don't expect me to see 15 years into the future. But they expect me to recognize that the box I'm working on now will be a microchip in a year, with ten times as much software, and I have to be ready." Says Hal Burlingame, AT&T's executive vice president for human resources, "People will have very long careers here. It just won't be static."[33]

TWO-CAREER AND NONFAMILY HOUSEHOLDS

In 1970, women held only 22 percent of nonclerical, white-collar jobs in the United States; today they hold 46 percent. This statistic reflects the increase in two-career households. In addition, it indicates the growth of nonfamily households, which usually consist of someone living alone or a single parent living with children. Over the past year, the number of family households rose 0.5 percent, but the number of nonfamily households grew at more than twice that rate—1.3 percent. Women head many of these nonfamily households.[34]

Both two-career and nonfamily household arrangements have specific job-related needs that demand responses from employers. These issues may arise, for instance, when a firm hires a manager, professional staff member, or highly skilled employee from another geographic area. If this person is a member of a two-career household, the firm must frequently offer relocation services for the spouse to attract the new employee. For example, IBM reimburses spouses for up to $500 in job-search expenses. Other firms aid by providing employment leads and financial assistance until the spouse locates a job in the new city.

As often happens, social trends create entrepreneurial opportunities. Rosemary Jordano started an emergency child-care service after realizing how many working parents needed someplace to bring their kids if they couldn't rely on their regular baby-sitters. Her business, Children First, is funded by various corporations, including Gillette and Bankers Trust Company, which offer the service as a benefit to employees who might otherwise have to miss work. Operating through six centers in three states, Children First offers backup day care for employees at 29 companies, and Jordano plans to open four more centers soon.[35]

GLASS CEILING

A U.S. Department of Labor study concluded that women and minorities find it difficult to advance beyond a certain level within many business organizations. Where this level falls in the corporate hierarchy varies from company to company. It has been called the **glass ceiling,** however, because it is an invisible barrier that resists the efforts of women and minorities to pass. "The corporate culture is more important than policy," says human resource consultant Rose Jones. "If the culture doesn't change, nothing will change for women."[36]

glass ceiling
Invisible barrier that keeps women and minorities from advancing to top management.

The glass ceiling remains surprisingly strong at many firms. Despite the rising number of women in professional positions, a recent study shows that women hold less than one-third of all managerial jobs, and even fewer—less than 5 percent—reach the corporate vice president level.[37] Human resource experts estimate that only a small percentage, perhaps 3 to 5 percent, of American companies have been effective in adding women and minorities to their work forces. A recent survey of 1,405 corporations by the Hay Group found that only 5 percent of them felt they were doing a "very good job" of removing the glass ceiling.[38]

STRENGTH IN DIVERSITY

EXABYTE In 1989, Exabyte, a Boulder, Colorado, manufacturer of computer storage tape drives, hired Mike Kirchner, who is deaf, to work on its assembly plant. Any fears the company had about Kirchner's abilities were quickly dispelled. Says human resources manager Dan Peters: "We became interested in hiring someone else like Mike, not because he was deaf, but because he had great organizational skills." ■ Exabyte had the jobs. Founded in 1985 and run by Peter Behrendt, an IBM manager for 26 years, it was growing fast. In 1989 sales tripled to $90 million. So two months after Kirchner signed on, he urged a deaf friend from high school, John Martinez, to apply for a job. He got it. ■ Four more deaf employees have come abroad since, accounting for 0.5 percent of the work force, twice the U.S. average. Exabyte also scores as a hirer of nonwhites, who make up 12 percent of 1,150 employees versus 6 percent of the local population. ■ Today, Kirchner helps coordinate production and Martinez supervises five "hearing" workers, who have learned the hand signs for "Good!" and even for "Put on your antistatic jacket." ■ The company thinks diversity is worth the cost, which includes hiring a translator for meetings and offering sign language classes to other staffers. Says human resources boss Richard Shinton: "The accommodations are things you'd have to be a Scrooge not to do. And other employees know that if they have an issue, they'll be treated fairly. It's a morale booster all around." ■ So it is. Says Martinez, 32, talking through a translator: "Exabyte's done a lot more for me than other places." Adds Monte Way, who has worked under him: "We used to communicate by notes, but my spelling's terrible, so I learned to sign. It didn't slow us down at all." Source: Jennifer Reese, "If You Can Read This, You Can Get a Job," *Fortune*, July 12, 1993, p. 11.

QUESTIONS FOR CRITICAL THINKING

1. How much of an investment should a company make to accommodate an employee with special needs?
2. How might the work ethic of an employee with special needs differ from the work ethic of other employees?
3. How can Exabyte educate the community on hiring employees with special needs?

A recent report by the Labor Department indicates that the glass ceiling may be harder to break through for African-American and Hispanic women than for white women. While 14 percent of white women say they have lost jobs or promotions because of their gender, about 23 percent of Hispanic females and 28 percent of African-American women believe that their job opportunities have been limited by their gender.[39]

The ceiling can be broken, however, as shown by the experience of Sara Lee Corp. "We are the largest company in the world named for a woman, a distinction we are proud of," says John Bryan, the firm's chairman. "It gives us a little bit of responsibility to be ahead of the curve on women's issues." Since many of the company's customers are women, Bryan notes, he didn't want to have "a bunch of old men sitting around trying to figure out the business." Instead, he set specific targets for hiring women into high-level positions and held managers accountable for meeting those goals. Sara Lee began hiring female managers during the 1980s and has one of the highest percentages of women executives in its industry. Currently, 17 percent of Sara Lee's top 500 managers and 11 percent of its division presidents are women, but Bryan has set new targets. By 2000, he wants to raise those figures to 30 percent and 20 percent, respectively. The women in these positions serve as role models for other employees, according to Judy Sprieser, president of Sara Lee's bakery division. When she tours the company's plants, she says, "Invariably, a woman on the plant line will pull me aside and say, 'We're so excited you're up there.'"[40]

GROWING USE OF CONTINGENCY WORKERS

One result of increased automation and downsizing during the 1990s is the growth in employment of so-called *contingency workers*, sometimes referred to as *just-in-time employees*. Contingency workers are employees who work part-time, temporarily, or on limited contracts. As Figure 9.10 illustrates, this sector of the U.S. work force has grown significantly in the past 20 years and now comprises roughly one-quarter of all employees. The number of Americans working part-time has risen by 2.2 million people during this same time period.[41] As the Kelly Services ad on the right side of Figure 9.10 explains, this leading supplier of temporary employees now assists employers in a cost-effective method of screening workers who may become full-time employees. The Kelly Select Program allows the potential employer to evaluate would-be employees' actual on-the-job performance before making an employment decision.

Many of today's contingency jobs have been created as companies have outsourced certain operations, such as legal, auditing, and mail-room services, hiring these workers only as needed. Part-time work has resulted from such management trends as compressed workweeks, job sharing, flextime, and home-based work programs. The needs of two-career households, nonfamily households, and a more flexible labor force have also contributed to the number of part-time workers. Finally, a temporary assignment often serves as a starting point for many jobs, from secretaries and assembly-line workers to professionals.

Temporary-help services employ an average of 1.9 million U.S. workers a day, nearly double the number five years ago, yet only one-half of the expected flexible work force by 2005.[42] Nationally, the average part-time worker is a 30-year-old woman.

Contingency workers can be economical for a company, since, while they may earn compensation comparable to that of full-time employees, they typically receive fewer

FIGURE 9.10 GROWTH IN PART-TIME, CONTRACT, AND SELF-EMPLOYED WORKERS

Employers are pushing more people than ever into the organizational fringes. Part-time, contract, and self-employed workers are rising as a percent of total employment.

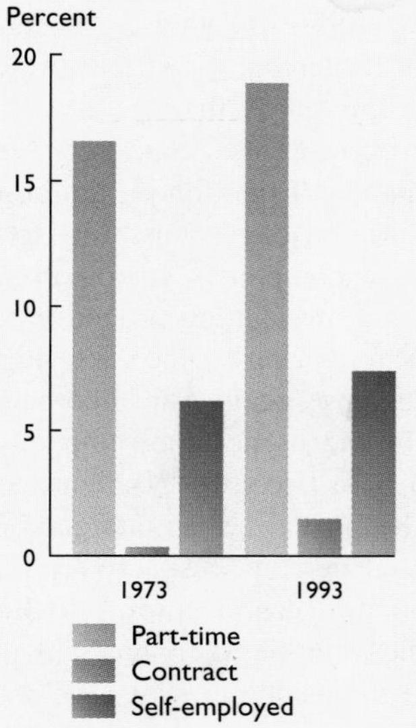

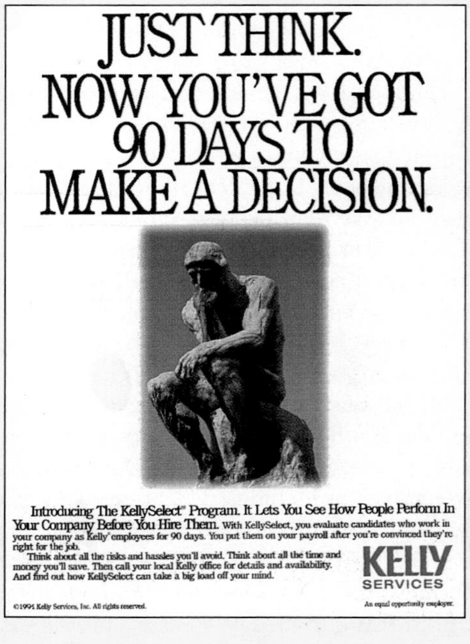

benefits. Part-time wage rates often amount to only 60 percent of full-time wages, allowing firms to reduce their human resource costs even more. A contingency work force is also more flexible, since it can be eliminated easily if business declines. For example, Blue Cross/Blue Shield of Rhode Island reduced its work force by 40 percent over a five-year period simply by laying off part-time and contract workers, sacrificing no full-time positions.[43]

The short-term savings from using contingency employees may have negative long-term implications, however. Overreliance on contingency workers may leave the company without an experienced, well-trained work force, especially in a downsized organization. Furthermore, many contingency workers must juggle more than one job. Harvard University economist Juliet Schor estimates that American workers average four more weeks of work per year than they did 20 years ago. Inevitably, this takes a toll on families. "Unfortunately, the reality and logistics of being a working mother—or involved father, for that matter—have not become any easier," comments Aimee McCrory, president of a Houston investment management firm and mother of two children. "I mean, most parents work, and yet the P.T.A. meetings are still at 10 A.M."[44]

ELDER CARE

Consider just one workplace: U.S. West Communications in Omaha, Nebraska. Over the past year, several of this office's 12 software designers have been forced to miss work in order to care for aging relatives. One took time off to help her father move from his farm to a nearby town; another rushed to a different state when her father suffered a stroke. Other U.S. West employees missed work to help hospitalized relatives recover or to care for them in their homes. Says one worker, "Elder care is the biggest personal issue we face in maintaining productivity from day to day."

These workers are not alone. Roughly 15 to 16 percent of American workers already have some type of elder-care responsibility, and about 22 percent of workers expect to assume these responsibilities over the next 4 years. The number of Americans aged 86 years or older will almost double by 2030 and more than triple by 2050, according to the Census Bureau. Families will provide most of the long-term care for these people. "In the coming years, elder care will have a greater impact on the workplace than child care," says Sally Coberly, a specialist on aging with the Washington Business Group on Health. "As the baby boom moves deeper into middle age, the need for elder-care services will simply explode."

Elder care presents a challenge for employers as well as for workers and their relatives. One study found that, when managers fail to give employees enough flexibility to deal with elder-care responsibilities, 3.3 percent of these employees quit altogether, 8.3 percent change jobs, 14.0 percent reduce their work hours, and 15.0 percent change their schedules. Andrew Scharlach, a professor of aging at the University of California, Berkeley, estimates that absenteeism and turnover due to elder-care issues cost U.S. companies $17 billion annually.

Several companies are developing strategies to help employees cope more effectively. Surveys show that workers value flexible scheduling because it allows them to arrange elder-care solutions without falling behind at work. Continental Corp. encourages managers to follow a "rule of flexibility" that allows employees to experiment with different schedules. Some companies hire consultants to teach employees about elder-care issues. Boston-based Work/Family Directions Inc. gave 575 such seminars last year—an increase of 27 percent over the year before. Still other employers offer referrals to hot lines and consulting services. Working Solutions, an Oregon consulting firm, provides case managers who work one-on-one to help clients' employees with legal questions and financial planning.[45]

MANAGING A CULTURALLY DIVERSE WORK FORCE

Comparing the current ethnic makeup of the U.S. work force with projections for 2050 reveals that the European-American segment of the labor force will decline from 75 percent today to 53 percent by the mid-21st century. The Hispanic population is the fastest-growing segment of the labor force. Over the past year alone, the number of U.S. households headed by African Americans grew by 0.8 percent, while those headed by Hispanics rose 11.1 percent.[46]

Unfortunately, companies' hiring practices do not always reflect the demographic realities of the U.S. population. Studies show that some whites feel a lingering, perhaps even unconscious, reluctance to hire members of other cultural groups. According to Arthur Brief, a professor of organizational behavior at Tulane University, this reluctance may stem from a belief shared by some managers that "most of our work force is white . . . so we ought to be careful about putting someone different into the job." He adds, "They don't appreciate that they act on that discomfort in making decisions."[47]

Clearly, successful companies will find effective ways to manage and empower increasingly diverse groups of workers. Chemical company Hoechst Celanese conducts periodic salary reviews to pinpoint any salary disparities that are not related to seniority or job performance. The first such review did reveal differences between the compensation levels of white male employees and their female and nonwhite peers, which Hoechst promptly remedied. "It caused a little commotion when we made salary adjustments," recalls CEO Ernest Drew. "Some people didn't realize they were underpaid."

Hoechst also encourages managers to identify and coach employees who show high potential, no matter what their cultural backgrounds. When engineer Adrienne Brown, who happens to be African American, joined the company, her supervisor, who happens to be white and male, encouraged her to articulate her professional goals. Says Brown, "I wrote down my goals plus all the things I needed to do, like seminars to attend, to get where I wanted to be. I asked my manager if I was on a reasonable track." Brown has consistently met her own goals, and she has been promoted twice in three years. "This company is making a real effort," she says enthusiastically. "My peers at other companies have not been exposed to similar diversity practices."[48]

The growing diversity of the work force is evidenced in many forms: gender, ethnic/cultural backgrounds, and age. By the year 2010, half of the nation's work force will be made up of people aged 40 and older.

ACHIEVEMENT CHECK SUMMARY

Reread the learning goals that follow, and consider the questions for each goal. Answering these questions will reinforce the most important concepts in the chapter and allow you to check how well you have achieved these learning goals. Where a blank appears before a question, answer with *T* or *F*. Otherwise, circle the letter of the correct answer. An answer key to these questions is found at the end of this chapter.

LEARNING GOAL 9.1: Explain the importance of human resource management and the responsibilities of a human resource department.

1. ___ As technology has advanced, the need for human resource management has declined.
2. ___ Human resource management includes finding, training, motivating, compensating, and appraising enough qualified employees to accomplish organizational objectives.
3. ___ Managers outside the human resource department rarely have human resource management responsibilities.

LEARNING GOAL 9.2: List the needs in Maslow's hierarchy.

1. According to Maslow: (a) a fully satisfied need is the best motivator; (b) needs arise in a hierarchy; (c) safety-actualization needs are the most fundamental and arise first; (d) all of the above.
2. Actions taken to avoid danger and the unexpected generally represent responses to: (a) physiological needs; (b) safety and security needs; (c) social needs; (d) esteem needs; (e) self-actualization needs.
3. Gaining respect from others or recognition for a job well done helps to satisfy: (a) physiological needs; (b) safety and security needs; (c) social needs; (d) esteem needs; (e) self-actualization needs.

LEARNING GOAL 9.3: Distinguish among Theory X, Theory Y, and Theory Z managers.

1. A manager who thinks that workers are lazy, dislike work, and need constant and close supervision is characterized as: (a) Theory X; (b) Theory Y; (c) Theory Z.
2. Managers who realize that workers want to meet their higher level needs at work are characterized as: (a) Theory X; (b) Theory Y; (c) Theory Z.
3. Theory Z organizations: (a) blend Theory Y with Japanese management practices; (b) rely on worker empowerment and participative management styles; (c) may not evaluate and promote workers as frequently as more traditional organizations; (d) all of the above.

LEARNING GOAL 9.4: Explain how recruitment, selection, orientation, training, and evaluation contribute to placing the right person in a job.

1. ___ The recruitment and selection process includes finding and evaluating job applicants.
2. ___ Employee training should be viewed as an ongoing process throughout a worker's tenure with a company.
3. ___ While operating workers require training, few organizations have programs aimed at developing the skills of managers.

LEARNING GOAL 9.5: Outline the different forms of compensation.

1. Payments to workers calculated on a weekly, monthly, or annual basis are known as: (a) wages; (b) salary; (c) benefits; (d) incentive compensation.
2. Most employers base their compensation policies upon: (a) compensation offered by competitors for labor in the same area; (b) government legislation and the cost of living; (c) the company's ability to pay and worker productivity; (d) all of the above.
3. Benefit programs: (a) include benefits required by law such as Social Security; (b) include pension plans, insurance, paid vacation, sick leave, and family leave; (c) account for 39 percent of a typical employee's earnings; (d) all of the above.

LEARNING GOAL 9.6: Explain the concept of job enrichment and how it can motivate employees.

1. ___ Learning new skills, rotating jobs with others, and having more authority to plan and execute one's own job are all examples of job enrichment.
2. ___ While job enrichment can make for greater job satisfaction, there is no evidence that it leads to greater productivity or organizational success.

LEARNING GOAL 9.7: Explain the impact of downsizing and outsourcing on today's organizations.

1. Downsizing: (a) reduces the number of workers within an organization; (b) often eliminates whole levels of management, resulting in flatter organizational structures; (c) generally requires greater empowerment of remaining workers; (d) all of the above.
2. Outsourcing: (a) relies on outside specialists to perform functions previously performed by the firm's employees; (b) adds flexibility while reducing costs; (c) allows a company to focus on what it does best; (d) all of the above.

LEARNING GOAL 9.8: Describe the role of intrapreneurship in a modern organization.

1. ___ *Intrapreneurship* refers to various attempts to make a large organization achieve the innovative dynamics of a smaller firm.
2. ___ Intrapreneurship units in large organizations allow new operations the freedom of small businesses, while providing these units the benefits of the financial, manufacturing, and marketing expertise of the larger organization.

LEARNING GOAL 9.9: Discuss the importance of time management.

1. ___ Time management is important only for top managers.
2. ___ A manager should do the most important tasks at the time of day when he or she performs best.

LEARNING GOAL 9.10: Identify and briefly describe each of the major human resource concerns for the 21st century.

1. ___ Older workers can be forced to retire at age 65.
2. ___ The trend toward two-career households and single-parent households creates challenges that employers will have to address.
3. ___ Modern management must ensure equal opportunity for an increasingly diverse work force.

KEY TERMS

human resource management 220
morale 221
need 222
motive 222
Theory X 225
Theory Y 225
Theory Z 226
on-the-job training 228
management development program 229
performance appraisal 229
employee benefits 230
flexible benefit plan 232
job enrichment 232
flextime 232
home-based work 233
downsizing 234
empowering 235
outsourcing 236
intrapreneurship 237
time management 238
worker buyout 240
glass ceiling 242

REVIEW QUESTIONS

1. Explain the primary functions of a human resource department. Which of these responsibilities are most likely to be shared with line departments?

2. Which needs in Maslow's hierarchy of human needs do the following statements address?
   a. "The new Eastman Kodak labor agreement will guarantee the jobs of at least 80 percent of all Kodak workers through 2005."
   b. "This is an entry-level job here at Gomex Clothiers, and we pay minimum wage for the first six months."
   c. "We have just organized a company field hockey team. Why don't you try out Thursday afternoon right after work?"
   d. "Judy won our Employee of the Month award this month due to her exceptional performance."
   e. "We pay a 20 percent bonus for employees who work the midnight shift."

3. Write a brief job scenario for each of three people employed in organizations with Theory X, Theory Y, and Theory Z management. Relate each of these employees to Maslow's needs hierarchy and list ways that managers might try to motivate each employee.

4. Identify several methods of work structuring that should result in job enrichment. Can you think of situations where job enrichment programs would not be effective? List these situations and explain your reasoning.

5. Why do many firms follow policies of hiring from within? What problems does such a policy raise?

6. Compare and contrast the various types of employee training programs.

7. Distinguish among the major pay-for-performance compensation plans.

8. Explain why so many organizations have been downsizing and outsourcing during the 1990s.

9. Describe specific ways in which a company might empower its employees.

10. Why are more firms using contingency workers? Is this trend beneficial or detrimental to U.S. business? Explain your answer.

DISCUSSION QUESTIONS

1. What does Frederick Herzberg mean by dissatisfiers? How do they relate to Maslow's hierarchy of human needs?

2. Consider your most recent or current job supervisor. Would you describe this person as a Theory X, Theory Y, or Theory Z manager? Why do you think your boss has adopted this management approach?

3. Discuss the type of compensation plan you would recommend for each of the following:
   a. Lawn mower repair technician
   b. Retail salesperson
   c. Assembly line worker in an electronics factory
   d. Professional athlete

4. One common belief holds that corporate downsizing in recent years has eroded many workers' feelings of commitment to their employers. Do you believe that businesses have a social responsibility to employees? Is downsizing a justifiable business strategy? Defend your answer.

5. A survey of 2,010 workers performing 23 different jobs conducted by the Institute of Social Research of the University of Michigan gave "Most Boring" awards to the following jobs: assembly-line worker, forklift-truck driver, machine tender, and monitor of continuous-flow production. By contrast, these jobs were ranked on the bottom of the scale as least boring: physician, professor, air traffic controller, and police officer. Identify some common characteristics of each group of jobs that appear to explain their rankings.

SOLUTIONS TO ACHIEVEMENT CHECK SUMMARY

L. G. 9.1: 1. F, 2. T, 3. F. **L. G. 9.2:** 1. b, 2. b, 3. d. **L. G. 9.3:** 1. a, 2. b, 3. d. **L. G. 9.4:** 1. T, 2. T, 3. F. **L. G. 9.5:** 1. b, 2. d, 3. d. **L. G. 9.6:** 1. T, 2. F. **L. G. 9.7:** 1. d, 2. d. **L. G. 9.8:** 1. T, 2. T. **L. G. 9.9:** 1. F, 2. T. **L. G. 9.10:** 1. F, 2. T, 3. T.

VIDEO CASE

UNIVERSITY NATIONAL BANK Customer satisfaction surveys consistently rank banks at the bottom of the list in comparison with other types of firms with which people do business. Only airlines generate more complaints. And policies like the one recently announced by First Chicago Bank—charging customers $3 for the privilege of transacting their business through a live teller rather than an ATM—haven't helped the situation any.

Carl J. Schmitt of University National Bank and Trust Company (UNB) of Palo Alto, California, vowed that his bank would achieve its growth and profitability goals by making customer satisfaction a part of every bank employee's responsibility. Since the banking industry offers intangible services to its clients, employees are critical in the creation of these services. Consequently, a key prerequisite to attracting and retaining satisfied customers is effective human resource management.

Schmitt decided to demonstrate to the bank's employees the kind of service they should provide to customers by providing the same type of service to each of them. Today, each staff member's birthday is recognized with a card containing a crisp fifty-dollar bill. Bank officers make sure a red rose appears on everyone's desk for Valentine's Day. For Thanksgiving, every employee receives a bottle of wine; for Christmas, an 8-pound honey-baked ham; and for New Year's Eve, a bottle of champagne. The bank building itself has been designed with the employees in mind. Instead of placing the air conditioning units in their typical location on the roof of the building, the architects were instructed to create a roof garden that could be used by employees as a place to relax, have lunch, and hold special functions.

Schmitt also enriched the jobs of UNB employees by giving them more authority, responsibility, and a sense of ownership over the tasks they perform. Rather than setting up a special human resource management staff, he gave each line manager the responsibility and authority to recruit, hire, train, develop, motivate, and evaluate staff in his or her department.

This policy of empowering employees and managers means that the company structure is flatter than most in the industry. As a result, Schmitt often finds himself working as support for loan officers and sometimes even pitching in for tellers when things get busy. The flatter structure pays off in lower overhead for the company and in higher compensation for the employees than the industry norm—another factor affecting employee commitment to the job and, ultimately, to the customer. Schmitt sees another benefit accruing from above-average salaries for members of the UNB work force. Employees don't have to worry about going someplace else within the industry to improve their incomes.

The result of Schmitt's human resource management strategy is a bank that delivers

customer satisfaction through people who excel at their jobs, not because they have to, but because they want to. Banking hours at University National Bank are longer than normal, and customers who cannot make it to the bank during regular hours can phone for special appointments. Standard customer service includes everything from a free shoe shine in the lobby to a fleet of four vans that pick up deposits from business owners, sparing them a trip to the bank. This is neither a typical banking service nor a typical bank van. The van windows are painted with scenes of bank robbers being captured and counterfeiters at work. Teller service is outstanding; if more than three people are waiting at a teller window, the nearest available bank employee opens an additional window to minimize waiting.

Greeting customers with a smile is considered to be one of the services the bank provides and is included as such in the company's annual report. As Ann Sonnenberg, UNB's marketing vice-president, says, "Being nice is neither difficult nor expensive." And it gets results. Bank assets have more than quadrupled with the new emphasis on employee and customer satisfaction.

QUESTIONS

1.
How does University National Bank go about performing the function of human resource management? Why?

2.
Explain how University National Bank provides for the various levels of Maslow's needs hierarchy.

3.
What potential problems are created by the lack of a separate human resource management department? Suggest methods UNB officials could use to minimize the occurrence of such problems.

4.
Would you classify the management style of UNB as fitting Theory X, Theory Y, or Theory Z? Explain your choice.

CHAPTER 10

TEAMWORK AND COMMUNICATION

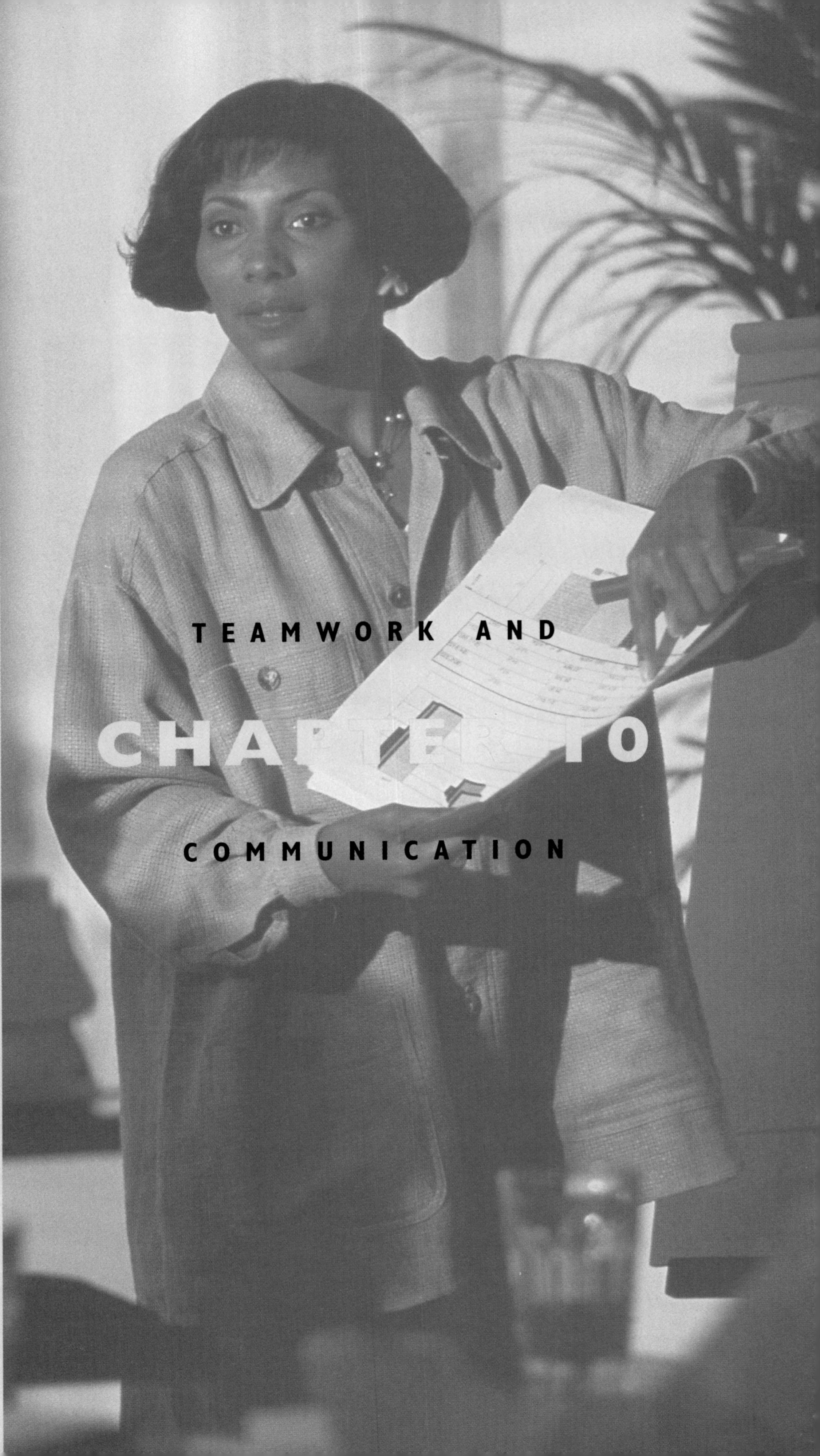

LEARNING GOALS

1. Distinguish between the two major types of teams in organizations.

2. Identify the characteristics of an effective team and the different roles played by team members.

3. List the stages of team development.

4. Relate team cohesiveness and norms to effective team performance.

5. Identify each of the factors that can cause conflict in teams, and discuss conflict resolution styles.

6. Explain the importance of effective communication skills in business.

7. Compare the different types of communication.

8. Identify and explain several important considerations in international business communication.

9. Summarize important developments in communication technology and how they affect business communication.

LIFESTYLE TEAM PLOTS NEW DIRECTION FOR THERMOS

Monte Peterson knew that he faced the business challenge of his life even before he accepted the job as CEO of Thermos in 1990. He had to, in his words, "totally reinvent the company." The Schaumburg, Illinois company, famous for its Thermos bottle and lunch boxes, had moved into the gas and electric cookout grill market. However, the competitive climate in this market was far different from the near monopoly Thermos enjoyed in the beverage container field. Well-known, entrenched competitors like Sunbeam, Char-Broil, and Weber limited Thermos's growth potential. Even worse, the entire product category was becoming a commodity product as department stores began selling look-alike products under their own brands. To grow in this market, Peterson knew that Thermos needed a breakthrough new product to offer customers in the value-conscious 1990s. ■ The new CEO realized that the firm's traditional organizational structure built around marketing, manufacturing, and finance functions was not appropriate for the tasks he had in mind. To revitalize the stagnant barbeque-grill market and avoid introducing just one more humdrum, me-too product, he needed to build an interdisciplinary team based on markets rather than business functions. The result was the creation of a self-managed team that included employees from engineering, marketing, manufacturing, and finance. Team managers took full control of the project, christened themselves the *Lifestyle team,* and went out into the field to study consumers' cookout habits. They focused first on customer needs, and then they moved on to design a new product to meet those needs. Input from outside suppliers included suggestions regarding design alternatives that would cook faster and cleaner. ■ Team leadership rotated according to priority. When market research was most important, the marketing department representative supervised the group; when the time came to work out the technical design aspects, team leadership shifted to research and development employees. ■ The eight-member team's efforts culminated in development of the Thermos Thermal Electric Grill, a sleek, ecologically sound cookout grill that one writer described as "looking like something the Jetsons might use." In addition to running cleaner and more cheaply than coal or gas units, the electric grill won four design awards for its beauty and utility. Created in a span of less than 24 months, the new grill has been a major marketplace success. Its striking design and ease of use, requiring no cleanup and no heavy propane tanks, combined with a barbeque taste produced by a new heating technology. These benefits made such Thermos dealers as Kmart and Target repeat purchasers. ■ Peterson is so pleased with the success of his team-oriented new-product development program that he has teams currently at work developing improved gas-grill designs. He feels that the firm's share of the market will increase tenfold from the 2 percent it held in 1990 to 20 percent by the end of the decade, and he credits the team approach for this success. In his words, "We needed to reinvent our product lines, and teamwork is doing it for us."[1]

CHAPTER OVERVIEW

Chapter 1 first introduced teamwork as one of the major business opportunities and challenges of the late 1990s. Chapter 7 discussed teamwork as an important component of employee involvement and a means of helping to motivate employees to perform their jobs better.

Chapter 7 also discussed the contributions of quality circles, groups of employees from the same work area who meet regularly to identify and solve quality-related problems in their areas. Chapter 8 described the matrix organizational structure, a means of blending the expertise of managers and operating employees from finance, engineering, marketing, and other functions to work on specific projects.

This chapter examines the characteristics of successful teams, discusses sources of team conflict, and explores ways to resolve disagreements that might arise among team members or between teams. It also examines the importance of communication in promoting teamwork and discusses the factors that facilitate effective communication, both inside and outside an organization. Finally, the chapter considers some guidelines for effective international communication and looks at the latest developments in communications technology, including the Internet, virtual reality, and interactive media.

TEAMWORK

Participating in a team sport is an important part of growing up. Most of us have joined some type of team in school—a soccer team, scouts, a debate team, or a drama club. In each case, the purpose of the team was either to perform a certain function or solve a particular problem. Headlines in the two ads shown in Figure 10.1 emphasize performance: winning a race and creating a multiple-person structure using teams of highly trained athletes.

The same concepts drive teams in business; business teams are either work teams or problem-solving teams. The Thermos electric-grill project illustrates the growing trend toward employee teams in business, and the ability to work effectively in teams is more important than ever before. A recent survey of the nation's 500 largest corporations found that teamwork is the topic taught most frequently in today's employee training programs.

FIGURE 10.1

ACHIEVING PERFORMANCE OBJECTIVES THROUGH TEAMWORK

Some teams, like the management and work teams at Thermos, work together over extended periods of time. Others collaborate for much shorter periods. For example, CEO Joseph Day of the German-Japanese joint venture Freudenberg-NOK asks each of his employees to serve on special problem-solving task forces called *GROWTTH* (Get Rid of Waste through Team Harmony) *teams.* Each GROWTTH team spends no more than 3 days at one of the company's 14 U.S. plants to analyze work processes and recommend improvements. In a typical year, about 40 different teams visit each factory.

Every visit results in development and implementation of several practical suggestions. Although many changes deal with relatively small issues, their combined impact is significant cost savings and improvements in quality. Says Day, "What we are doing is what any company will have to do to survive a decade from now."[2]

WHAT IS A TEAM?

As Chapter 7 discussed, a **team** is a small group of people with complementary skills who are committed to a common purpose, approach, and set of performance goals. All team members hold themselves mutually responsible and accountable for accomplishing the team's objectives. Consider some well-known industry examples:

team
Small group of people with complementary skills who are committed to a common purpose, approach, and set of performance goals.

- Xerox develops new products through multidisciplinary teams that work in a single process, instead of vertical functions or departments.
- Lexmark International, a former IBM division, replaced 60 percent of its managers worldwide in manufacturing and support with cross-functional teams.
- Eastman Chemical, a Kodak unit, replaced its senior vice presidents for administration, manufacturing, and R&D with over 1,000 self-directed teams.
- Motorola's Government Electronics group redesigned its supply management organization as a process with external customers at the end; team members conduct peer evaluations.[3]

Teams can be as small as two people or as large as 75. In practice, however, most teams have fewer than 15 members. The important characteristic comes from team members' common goal and their combined effort to achieve it.

The benefits of teamwork, coupled with the downsizing of traditional organizational structures, have produced a virtual rainbow of forms, as shown in Figure 10.2: problem-solving teams, product-development teams, management teams, work teams, and quality circles; firms even form virtual teams with geographically separated members who interact via computer systems. The most popular types of teams today represent two species: work teams, which include high-performance or self-managed teams, and special-purpose, problem-solving teams.

WORK TEAMS AND PROBLEM-SOLVING TEAMS

The trend in U.S. business toward developing teams began in the 1980s when American managers began to address quality concerns in a variety of ways. One method, forming quality circles, brought together groups of workers to meet weekly or monthly to discuss ways to improve quality. This concept spread like wildfire as such teams demonstrated their ability to help companies cut defects and reduce rework burdens. By 1987, two-thirds of America's 1,000 largest corporations used quality circles. By the mid-1990s, the percentage of major firms using quality circles to solve minor quality problems had declined, primarily due to typically modest increases in productivity as a result of limitations on the scope of these groups' activities.

The current focus on teams and teamwork has evolved into two basic forms of teams. **Work teams** have become relatively permanent fixtures in about two-thirds of U.S. com-

work team
Mid-1990s style of work in which a small group of people with complementary skills perform the day-to-day work of an organization.

THE FIVE SPECIES OF TEAMS
The kingdom of teams can be confusing. Here's a rundown of the most common types.
Virtual Teams
A characteristic of this new type of work team: members talk by computer flying in and out as needed and take turns as leader.
Management Teams
Consisting mainly of managers from various functions, like sales and production, this species coordinates work among teams.
Quality Circles
In danger of extinction, this type, typically made of workers and supervisors, meets intermittently to air work-place problems.
Problem-Solving Teams
This most popular of types comprises knowledge workers who gather to solve specific problems and then disband.
Work Teams
An increasingly popular species, work teams do just that—the daily work. When empowered, they are self-managed teams.

FIGURE 10.2

FIVE SPECIES OF TEAMS

panies. They represent a mid-1990s style of work in which small groups of people with complementary skills perform the day-to-day work of an organization. A work team of Procter & Gamble design engineers might tackle the task of producing a series of new products. A work team empowered with the authority to make decisions about how to complete its daily work is properly described as a *self-managed team*. Common tests for a self-managed team asks questions like these: Can it change the order of tasks? Does it have a budget?

Self-managed teams work most effectively when they combine employees with varying skills and functions. Members are cross-trained to perform each other's jobs as needed. Empowering these teams with the decision-making authority they need to perform their organizational roles usually means permitting them to select fellow team members, spend money, solve problems, evaluate results, and plan future projects.[4]

The people at Boeing, the world's largest aircraft manufacturer and one of America's leading exporters, are true believers in the virtues of teamwork. After all, teamwork to develop the new 777 passenger jet cut the number of engineering hangups by more than half. As Boeing President Philip Condit put it, "Your competitiveness is your ability to use the skills and knowledge of people most effectively, and teams are the best way to do that."[5]

Boeing empowers team members to encourage them to work together and develop initiative. When the Seattle-based giant set out to design the 777, a massive project involving 10,000 employees and more than 500 suppliers, it created a hierarchy of teams. Designed to pull all of the Boeing work teams together, the 777 team structure had three layers. At the top, a management team of 5 or 6 top managers accepted responsibility for the plane being built correctly and on time. In the middle, a large group of 50 or so leaders organized in 2-person teams oversaw the 200-plus work teams, each responsible for a specific part of the plane. These work teams were typically cross-functional groups of 5 to 15 workers. Work team examples included the wing team, the flap team, and the tail team.

problem-solving team
Temporary combination of workers who gather to solve a specific problem and then disband.

A **problem-solving team,** in contrast to a work team, creates a temporary combination of workers who gather to solve a specific problem and then disband. Boeing calls

Boeing set up 238 teams to carry designs from their initial concepts through the design and manufacturing phases of Boeing 777 production. The teams included employees from across the company, as well as representatives from key suppliers and customers.

these teams *airplane integration teams* and often sets them up as negotiators and arbitrators to reduce conflicts that sometimes arise among work teams. A few months ago, a Boeing problem-solving team was asked to resolve such a conflict after one work team had designed the passenger oxygen system to mount at the same spot where a second team had planned to install the gasper, a tiny nozzle that directs fresh air toward the passenger. Within 3 hours, the three teams had brainstormed an ingenious solution: a special clamp to hold both systems. At the old Boeing, a problem like that probably would have been caught only when the plan reached the manufacturing stage.

Special-purpose, problem-solving teams differ from quality circles in important ways. Where quality circles are permanent committees designed to handle any workplace problems that may arise, problem-solving teams have specific missions that can range from broad (find out why customers are not satisfied) to narrow (solve the overheating problem in generator No. 4). After completing the task, the problem-solving team usually disbands. Over 90 percent of America's 1,000 largest companies use problem-solving teams, one-third more than just 7 years ago.

Although the *cross-functional team* concept is typically associated with problem-solving teams, individuals from diverse functional backgrounds can also serve as members of more permanent work teams. Such teams made major contributions to the development of Boeing's 777. Boeing engineers, marketers, and mechanics worked with representatives from key suppliers and customers to ensure that the final product provided optimum value and customer satisfaction. This practical input from Boeing employees, suppliers, and potential purchasers resulted in creation of an airplane with unprecedented ease of operation, repair, and maintenance.[6]

TEAM CHARACTERISTICS

Teams can increase productivity, raise morale, and nurture innovation, but only if the right type of team works on a particular task. Companies such as DEC (America's second-largest computer maker), Nynex (the Baby Bell supplier for New York and New England), and Boeing (the world's largest aircraft manufacturer) have all used teams successfully. Besides matching the right type of team to a job, managers must assemble the right people for a team. It is important to note that, while 680 of the nation's 1,000 largest companies currently use work teams, only 10 percent of the people who work at these firms serve on such teams.

Teams consume time, energy, and money. They must, therefore, be formed carefully with several factors in mind. The most important of these factors is to choose the right type of team to accomplish an objective. To work effectively, team members should receive training support, strong communication links, and specific information about the jobs they must perform. Many team-oriented companies stumble on one major pitfall when they create teams that are not really needed. Some people work better alone, and individuals can better accomplish some tasks. Before forming a team, managers should analyze the work to be done, decide whether a team approach suits that work, and then select the best type of team.

Effective teams share a number of characteristics. Three of the most important are the size of the team, the roles played by its members, and its diversity.

TEAM SIZE

Should some ideal size guide formation of a team? Effective teams can have anywhere from 5 to 12 members, but many proponents of teams believe that the ideal size is about 7 people. A group of this size is big enough to benefit from a variety of diverse skills, yet small enough that members can communicate easily and feel part of a close-knit entity.

Rubbermaid organizes workers in its home products division into teams of 5 to 7 people, one each from manufacturing, research and development, finance, marketing, and other departments. Each team focuses on a particular product line, such as bathroom accessories. The team approach works so well that Rubbermaid introduces new products at an average rate of one a day, and 90 percent of these products achieve their sales targets.[7]

While teams smaller and larger than this optimum size can also be effective, they create certain challenges for team leaders. Participants in a small team of two to four members want to get along with each other; they tend to interact informally, discuss more personal topics, and make fewer demands on team leaders. A large group of more than 12 members presents a greater challenge for a team leader since decision making becomes more centralized and participants may feel less committed to team goals. Large teams also tend to suffer more disagreements, absenteeism, and membership turnover. Subgroups may form, leading to possible conflicts among factions. As a general rule, teams of more than 20 people should divide into subteams, each with its own members and goals.

TEAM ROLES

task specialist role
Role played by team members who devote time and energy to helping the team accomplish its goals.

socio-emotional role
Role played by team members who devote time and energy to providing support for group members' emotional needs and social unity.

Over time, team members tend to play certain roles, which can be classified as task specialist roles or socio-emotional roles. As Figure 10.3 points out, someone who assumes a **task specialist role** devotes time and energy to helping the team accomplish its goals. This group member actively proposes new solutions, evaluates the suggestions of others, and asks for more information. This person may bring up new ideas, summarize the progress of the discussion, and attempt to energize the group when interest drops. A team member who plays a **socio-emotional role** devotes time and energy to providing support for group members' emotional needs and social unity. This person encourages others to contribute ideas and may change personal opinions in order to maintain team harmony. Such a group member attempts to reduce group tensions and reconcile conflicts.

Some team members may play dual roles, contributing to the team's task and supporting members' emotional needs at the same time. Those who can assume dual roles may become team leaders because they satisfy both types of needs. Finally, a team mem-

FIGURE 10.3 TEAM MEMBER ROLES

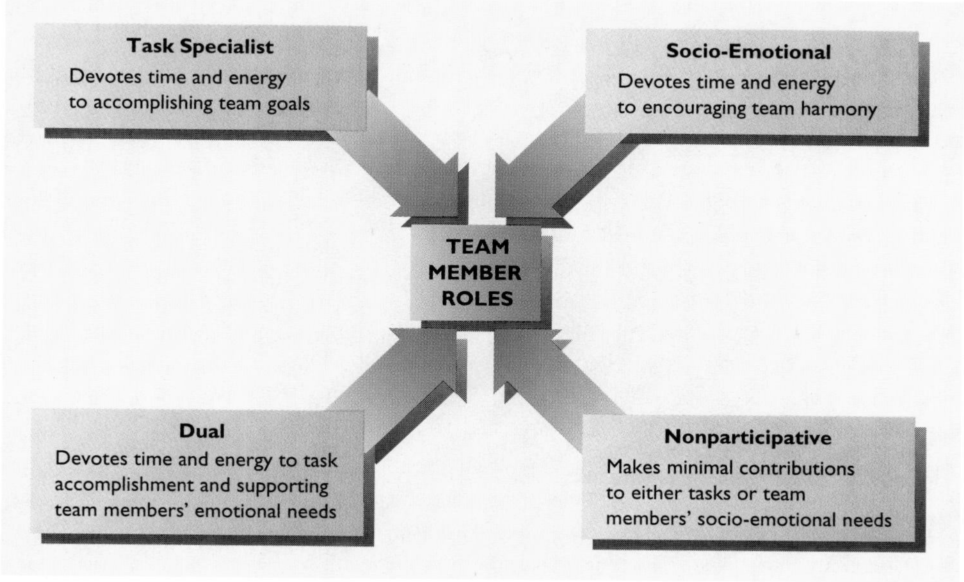

ber may fall into a nonparticipator role, contributing little to either the task or members' socio-emotional needs.

Teams challenge managers to ensure balance between members capable of performing each type of role. Both the task specialist and socio-emotional roles are important, and too many members playing either can impair a group's ability to function. Teams filled with task specialists may be productive in the short term but fail to satisfy expectations over a longer time period, since team members may become unsupportive and not convey enough personal concern for each other. Teams filled with socio-emotional members can be satisfying but unproductive, since participants may hesitate to disagree or criticize each other.[8]

VALUE OF DIVERSITY

Several years ago, CEO Ernest Drew of chemical giant Hoechst Celanese organized a conference to analyze the company's corporate culture and suggest ways to change it to improve performance. The firm's top 125 officers attended the conference, most of them white males, along with 50 women and minorities from the ranks of middle management. The group divided into small problem-solving teams, some mixed by race and gender and others almost entirely Caucasian males. When the teams presented their findings, says Drew, "It was so obvious that the diverse teams had the broader solutions. They had ideas I hadn't even thought of. For the first time, we realized that diversity is a strength as it relates to problem solving. Now we knew we needed diversity at every level of the company where decisions are made."[9]

Several research studies have confirmed Drew's conclusion. Research at the University of North Texas, for example, compared the work of culturally diverse teams of business students to that of all-white teams over a period of 17 weeks. By the end of the study, the heterogeneous teams displayed a broader range of viewpoints and produced more innovative solutions to problems.

Since its conference, Hoechst has intensified efforts to hire and train qualified employees regardless of their cultural characteristics. The chemical giant's polyester tex-

STRENGTH IN DIVERSITY

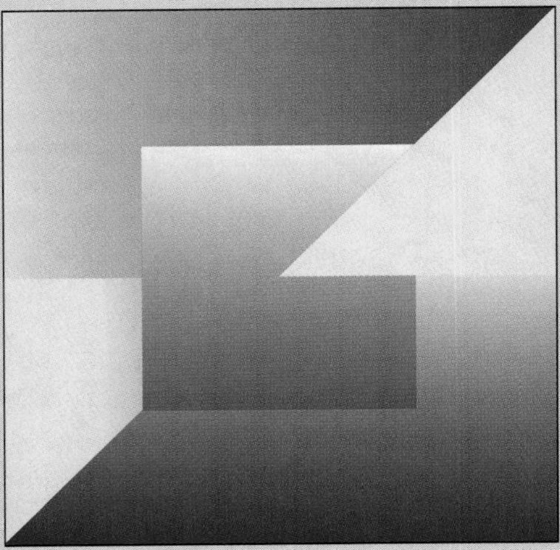

JULIA GARCIA: PROUD POTATO-CHIP PACKER Ask factory worker Julia Garcia about her potato-chip-packing job and she will tell you, "It used to be it was just the same-ol'-same-ol', but now that teams have replaced supervisors, there are more things happening. It's more fun." So what makes this Frito Lay employee so happy after 13 years? Teamwork. ■ Teamwork typically involves exchanging supervisory personnel for worker empowerment. Since Garcia became a member of one of Frito Lay's 22 nationwide teams, she has been trained to perform a number of different jobs. In addition to her regular chip-packing job, Garcia is now qualified to run the potato slicing machine, determine crew scheduling, interview new hires, and act as a quality-control technician to monitor the spices on the chips. ■ Garcia had worked in a factory environment before joining Frito Lay. Once a supervisor in a Levi Strauss & Co. factory, she was not sure how she would perform in the Frito Lay team environment. "It kind of frightened me at first," she recalls. "I thought, 'I'm not going to be able to decide anything.' " What Garcia has discovered is that she and the nine other members of her team are responsible for everything from potato processing to equipment maintenance. ■ Frito Lay, like many other companies that implement the team concept, has discovered that teams and employee empowerment bring rewards. Since 1990, the firm's Lubbock plant has reduced management ranks from 38 to 13 and increased its hourly work force by 20 percent to 220. Cost reductions have been significant, and quality has improved so much that the Lubbock plant has moved from 20th to 6th among 48 Frito Lay plants. Garcia's team has been credited with major contributions to these improvements. ■ In the past five years as a Frito Lay team member, Garcia has learned a lot about teams and what makes them successful. She will tell you that the ability to communicate and a positive attitude are essential skills for members of a team. Working in a team means praising and criticizing the work of others. "You might be doing something that can be improved, but you can't see that yourself. Maybe somebody else can." That's what makes positive communication skills so important. ■ Before Frito Lay formed its teams, Garcia and her co-workers went to work, punched a time clock, did their jobs, and went home. No one talked about quality, production rates, waste, or process improvements. Today, everyone works together in a collective effort to make the Lubbock plant the most efficient Frito Lay factory in the nation. Thanks to teams, Garcia now talks about her job as if it were her family, and she's proud of it. "This is my job," she says. "This is where I spend half of my life and I want it to be a good place to work." Source: Quotations from Wendy Zellner, "Team Player: No More Same-Ol'-Same-Ol'," *Business Week,* October 17, 1994, pp. 95–96.

QUESTIONS FOR CRITICAL THINKING

1. What are the advantages and disadvantages of training hourly personnel in a number of jobs?
2. What types of personalities will be successful in a team environment? What types of personalities will not be successful in a team environment?
3. What are some ways team members can communicate on the job?

tile filament division illustrates team success. The division had lost money for 18 years straight until, in desperation, Drew placed it under the control of a diverse group of managers. Previously, the division had concentrated on commodity production, but the new management team decided to target niche markets such as automotive upholstery shops. They also found ways to improve quality while cutting costs. These days, the division is highly profitable, as William Harris, head of worldwide fibers, points out: "We tried everything for so many years, but the business did not perform better until we had a diverse management group."[10]

TEAM PROCESSES

The earlier discussion may have created the impression that all companies should organize their employees as teams. Actually, however, not all firms suit the team format. Furthermore, while some departments within an organization may thrive using the team concept, others may not. "Teams are great, but some work needs to be accomplished solo," says Kathleen Emery, vice president of the consulting firm Designed Learning Inc. "Be selective. When work makes sense to be done in teams, then do it; when it doesn't, don't. Teams aren't the answer to every situation."[11]

A study of 45 team projects at a dozen major U.S. companies found that certain types of teams work more effectively than others, depending on the goal of a particular project. A cross-functional team can effectively develop an entirely new good or service. However, a vertical team from a single department such as product engineering may do a better job on reaching a simple goal like modifying an existing product. Members of cross-functional teams need time to establish their roles and begin working together productively, and such delays could allow a competitor's modifications to reach the market faster.

If management decides to use a team approach, it should implement the decision systematically. As Figure 10.4 shows, the first step should be to agree on precisely what the team should accomplish. The focus should then move to customer needs and the best ways to achieve customer satisfaction. Managers should meet with all employees who are associated with a particular facet of the project to discuss team goals and the best ways to do the work. This may involve restructuring some jobs and cross-training employees to perform more than one task.[12]

Managers can increase the likelihood of forming effective work teams by working systematically. The team-formation process begins with analysis of successful teams in other organizations, and it involves team members in planning and implementation accompanied by built-in flexibility and a willingness to modify plans when necessary. Note that in the final step, managers determine an appropriate compensation plan for team members. This can be difficult, since compensation must motivate individual team members while still encouraging them to act as a team. Managers should devote considerable time to selecting the best ways to reward individual achievements and added responsibilities.

Organizations frequently allow team members to provide input on these issues and perhaps make the final decision themselves. Management should avoid individual incentive programs such as contests and personal bonuses, since they foster competition rather than cooperation within groups. "Don't set up a reward system that acknowledges individual achievement at the expense of the team," suggests consultant Ron Johnson.[13]

A team of Pitney Bowes workers meets with a company trainer. When Pitney Bowes implemented team organizations, the company provided more than 27,000 hours of training over 3 years to workers, enabling them to move from single-skilled, assembly line work to work in self-directed teams.

FIGURE 10.4 NINE STEPS TO BETTER WORK TEAMS

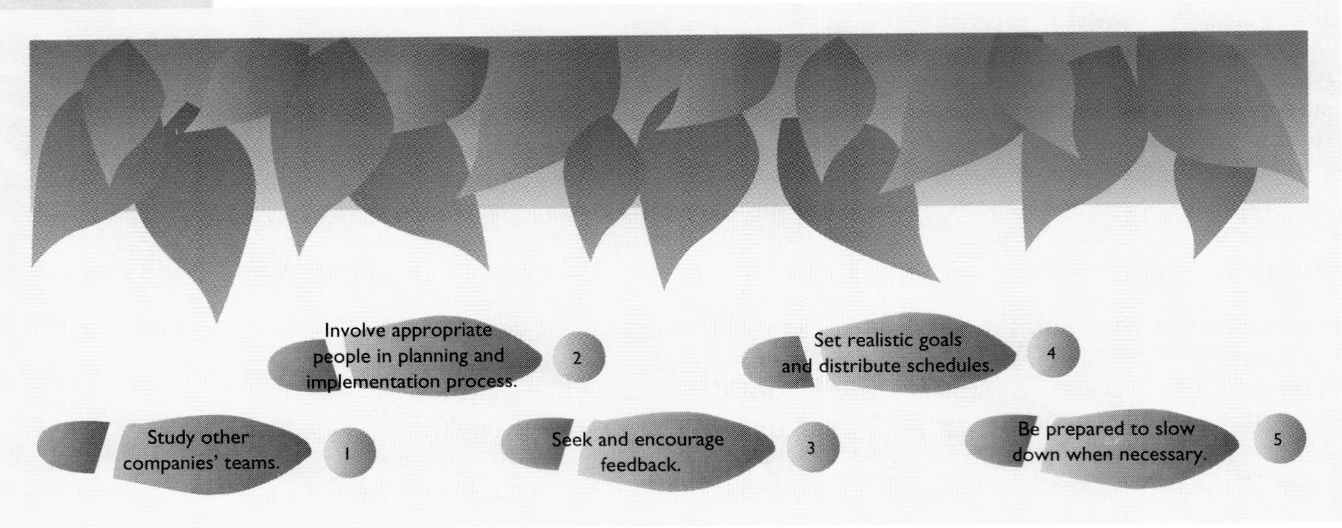

STAGES OF TEAM DEVELOPMENT

Once a manager has formed a team, the group goes through five stages of development: forming, storming, norming, performing, and adjourning. These stages are shown in Figure 10.5.

The *forming* stage is an orientation period during which team members get to know each other and find out which behaviors the group finds acceptable. During this early phase, team members are curious about what is expected of them and whether they will fit in with the group. An effective team leader provides time for participants to become acquainted and converse informally.

During the next phase, *storming*, participants' individual personalities begin to emerge as they clarify their roles and expectations. Conflicts may arise as people disagree over the team's mission and jockey for position and control of the group. Subgroups may form based on common interests or concerns. At this stage, the team leader should encourage everyone to participate, allowing people to work through their uncertainties and conflicts. A team must move beyond this stage in order to become truly productive.

As a team passes beyond storming, it enters the *norming* stage. Members resolve initial differences, accept each other, and reach consensus about the roles of the team leader and other participants. The norming stage is usually brief, and the team leader should use this time to emphasize the team's unity and the importance of its objectives.

Next comes the *performing* stage, characterized by problem solving and a focus on task accomplishment. At this point, team members interact frequently and handle any conflicts constructively. The team leader focuses on high task performance and encourages both socio-emotional team members and task specialists to contribute.

The *adjourning* stage occurs as the group disbands following completion of its task. This phase focuses on wrapping up and summarizing the team's experience and accomplishments. The team leader may recognize participants' contributions with some type of ritual, perhaps by handing out plaques or awards.[14]

team cohesiveness *Extent to which team members feel attracted to the team and motivated to remain a part of it.*

TEAM COHESIVENESS

Teams tend to be most productive when they are highly cohesive. **Team cohesiveness** is the extent to which team members feel attracted to the team and motivated to remain

FIGURE 10.4

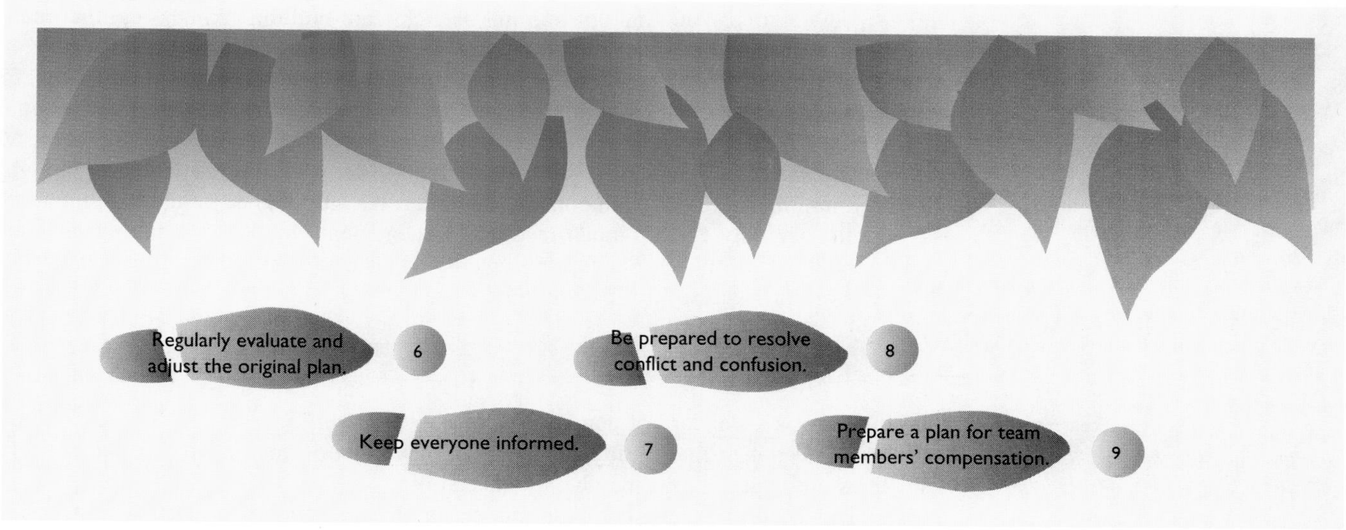

Regularly evaluate and adjust the original plan.
6
Keep everyone informed.
7
Be prepared to resolve conflict and confusion.
8
Prepare a plan for team members' compensation.
9

a part of it. This cohesiveness typically increases when members interact frequently, share common attitudes and goals, and enjoy being together. Low team cohesiveness erodes morale.

Managers at GM's Saturn Corp. are learning first-hand the importance of team cohesiveness. Teams of Saturn workers handle a variety of tasks and enjoy an unusual level of control over operations at the firm's Spring Hill, Tennessee assembly plant. When the Saturn program first began, these teams were highly cohesive. One reason was that many

FIGURE 10.5 FIVE STAGES OF TEAM DEVELOPMENT

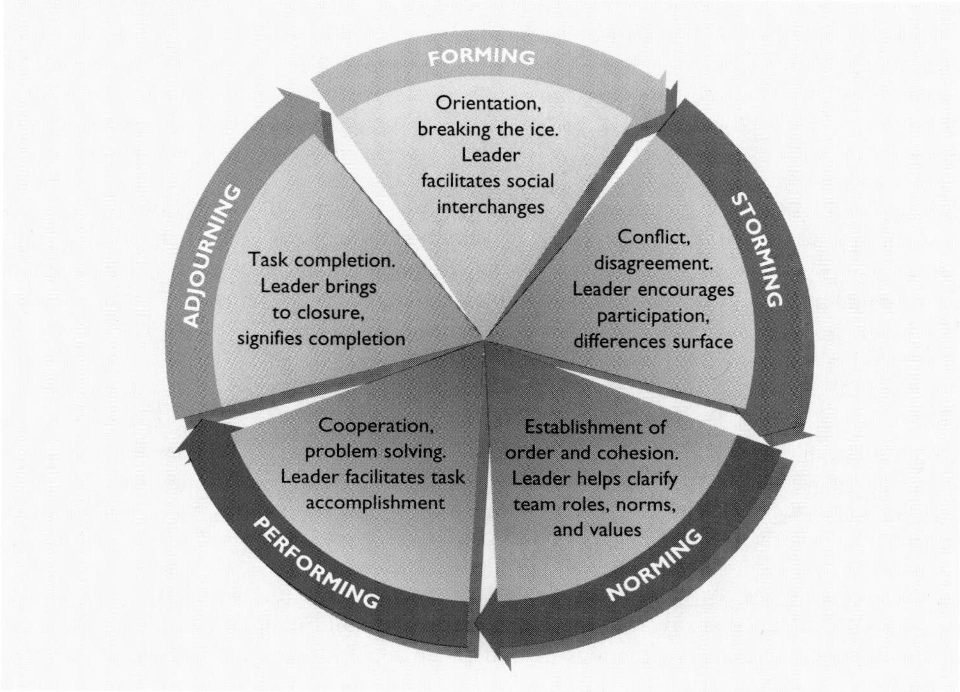

Orientation, breaking the ice. Leader facilitates social interchanges

Establishment of order and cohesion. Leader helps clarify team roles, norms, and values

Task completion. Leader brings to closure, signifies completion

new hires shared a common interest in becoming part of the Saturn experiment. Another reason for cohesiveness was the company's extensive training program. Every new worker received up to 700 hours of training in such team-building skills as conflict management and communication.

Recently, in an effort to cut costs, managers reduced new-employee training to 175 hours and refocused the training emphasis on job-specific tasks rather than interpersonal skills. Further, a new union agreement committed management to limit new hires to GM workers who had been laid off from other plants. Many of these applicants brought weaker commitments to the team concept. "These folks are tougher to integrate into Saturn," admits Timothy Epps, human resource management chief. The resulting tensions have sparked occasional conflicts among employees and their union representatives, which in turn have led to lower team cohesiveness.[15]

TEAM NORMS

team norm
Standard of conduct shared by team members that guides their behavior.

A **team norm** is a standard of conduct shared by team members that guides their behavior. Norms are not formal, written guidelines; they are informal standards that identify key values and clarify team members' expectations.

In GM's Saturn project, conflicts among employees reflected differing norms. The original Saturn workers joined the firm, attracted by the promise of greater cooperation with management and a larger role in running the factory. Many of them share a view of Saturn as a great experiment in labor-management relations. As one assembly worker put it, "We are the future of the American car industry, if it has a future."[16] Opposing this norm, some new hires who had been laid off at other GM plants believe that Saturn's labor leaders are too closely allied with its management. While most Saturn employees continue to support the company's innovative labor system, a growing minority—29 percent in a recent election—support a shift to a more traditional relationship.

TEAM CONFLICT

conflict
Antagonistic interaction in which one party attempts to thwart the intentions or goals of another.

Among all of a team leader's skills, none is more important than the ability to manage conflict. **Conflict** is an antagonistic interaction in which one party attempts to thwart the intentions or goals of another. A certain amount of conflict is inevitable in teams, but too much can impair the ability of team members to exchange ideas, cooperate with each other, and produce results.

CAUSES OF CONFLICT

Conflict can stem from many sources. It frequently results from competition for scarce resources, such as information, money, or supplies. In addition, team members' personalities may clash, or their ideas about what the team should accomplish may conflict. Poor communication can also cause misunderstandings and resentments. Finally, conflict can result from unclear job responsibilities or team roles.

STYLES OF CONFLICT RESOLUTION

Conflict resolution styles represent a continuum, from assertive to cooperative styles. Team members can rely on no one best way to manage conflict. The most effective resolution style varies according to the particular situation. Different tactics define several choices:

- *Competing style.* A decisive, assertive approach that might be expressed as, "We'll do this my way." While it does not build team rapport, the competing style suits situations of unpopular decisions or emergencies.

- *Avoiding style.* Neither assertive nor cooperative, the avoiding style is most effective when conflict results from some trivial cause or creates a no-win situation, when more information is needed, or when open conflict would be harmful.
- *Compromising style.* Blending moderate degrees of both assertiveness and cooperation, this approach works well when two opposing goals are equally important, when combatants are equally powerful, or when the team feels pressure to achieve some sort of immediate solution.
- *Accommodating style.* Emphasizing a high degree of cooperation, this style can help to maintain team harmony. A team member may choose to back down if an issue is more important to others in the group.
- *Collaborating style.* High assertiveness and cooperation characterize the collaborating style. While this frequently time-consuming approach can require lengthy negotiation, it can achieve a win-win situation. It is useful when consensus from all parties is important or when the team must merge the viewpoints of all participants into a mutually acceptable solution.

A team leader can reduce the disruptive impact of conflict by focusing team members on broad goals that go beyond the immediate source of a disagreement. When Thermos CEO Monte Peterson first organized the electric-grill group, some participants resisted the idea of working in teams. Peterson dealt with their objections by emphasizing the importance of the project to Thermos' long-term success. "Like a politician, you provide a platform for change and then paint a picture of the difference between winning and losing," he says. "After that, the old barriers break down, and teamwork becomes infectious."[17]

When conflict results from ambiguous or overlapping responsibilities, a team leader can handle it by clarifying participants' respective tasks and areas of authority. The leader may encourage the opponents to negotiate an agreement. This works well if they can deal with the situation in a businesslike, unemotional way. Antagonists may turn over stubborn disagreements to a mediator, an outside party who will discuss the situation with both sides and make a decision. As Chapter 8 described, mediation often resolves disputes between labor unions and management.

Thermos CEO Peterson had to act as an informal mediator several times during the development of the electric grill. At one point, the team reached an impasse over price. While the team members from finance and research and development insisted on a price of $299, members from the marketing department argued that this was too expensive to sell at discount chains like Kmart and Target. Finally, Peterson settled the argument by saying, "Give me a reason why you *can't* sell it at that price level." When the dissenters were unable to come up with a reason, the $299 price became official.[18]

Perhaps the team leader's most important contribution to conflict resolution is to facilitate good communication. Ongoing communication ensures that team members perceive each other accurately, understand what the team expects of them, and obtain information that they need. Better communication improves the likelihood that members will work cooperatively as a team. The remainder of this chapter discusses the importance of effective communication and looks at how good communication skills promote success, both inside and outside the organization.

IMPORTANCE OF EFFECTIVE COMMUNICATION

Communication, defined as meaningful exchanges of information through messages, is essential to business. Managers, for example, spend 80 percent of their time in direct communication with others, whether on the phone, in meetings, or in conversation. They spend the other 20 percent on desk work, much of which is also communication in the form of writing and reading.

communication
Meaningful exchanges of information through messages.

Communication skills are just as important for other businesspeople, as well. Consider a few examples. Communication with the marketplace, in the form of market research, helps a company to learn what products customers want and what changes they would prefer in existing goods and services. Communication among engineers, marketers, and production workers enables a company to create products that provide customer satisfaction, while communication through advertising and personal sales presentations creates a favorable image for the company and persuades customers to buy.

Every communication follows a step-by-step process that resembles an interaction among six elements: sender, message, channel, audience, feedback, and context. As Figure 10.6 shows, the process begins when the *sender* composes the *message* and sends it through a communication carrier, or *channel. Encoding* describes the translation of a message into understandable terms and a form capable of being transmitted through the communication medium selected by the sender. The sender chooses from many channels, including written messages, face-to-face conversations, and electronic mail. The *audience* consists of the person or persons who receive the message and interpret its meaning. *Decoding* occurs when the receiver interprets the message. *Feedback* from the audience—a response to the sender's communication—helps the sender to determine whether the message was interpreted correctly.

Every communication takes place in some sort of situational and cultural *context.* Context can exert a powerful influence on how well the communication process works. A conversation between two people in a quiet room, for example, may be a very different experience from the same conversation held outdoors on a freezing cold day next to a noisy construction site.

A sender needs to pay attention to audience feedback, even to solicit feedback if the audience volunteers none, since this response clarifies whether the message was perceived as intended. Even with the best intentions, sender and audience can misunderstand each other. A major aircraft company announced a 10 percent pay reduction by means of individual letters to its employees signed by the president, but the immediate effect was surprising. Employees greeted the message with amusement rather than disappointment because it arrived at each employee's desk on April Fool's Day! Unfortunately, the company had to provide official verification to establish the true meaning—a pay cut.

BASIC FORMS OF COMMUNICATION

People communicate in many different ways. Some of them—calling a meeting of team members or writing a formal mission statement—are obvious. Other, less obvious methods range from gestures and facial expressions during a conversation to leaning forward when speaking to someone; still, these subtle methods can significantly affect the mes-

FIGURE 10.6 COMMUNICATION PROCESS

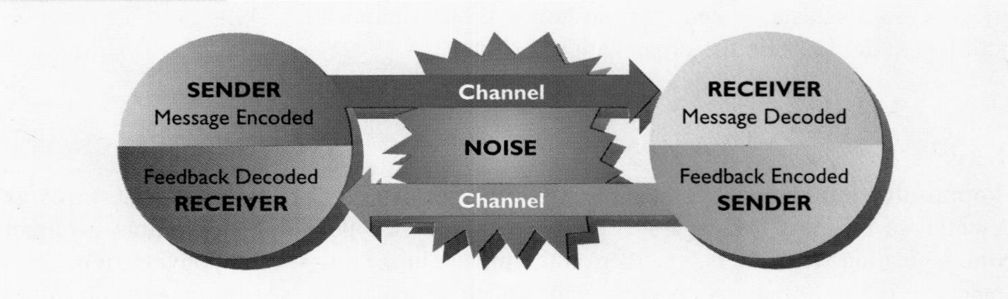

sage that is communicated. It is convenient to discuss communication based on the forms shown in Table 10.1: oral and written, formal and informal, verbal and nonverbal communication.

Oral Communication As mentioned earlier, managers spend a great deal of their time communicating orally, whether in person or on the phone. Some businesspeople prefer to communicate this way, feeling that oral channels allow them to convey their true messages most accurately. A vital component of oral communication is **listening,** the skill of receiving a message and interpreting its genuine meaning by accurately grasping the facts and feelings it conveys. While listening is the first communication skill that people learn in life and the one they use the most often, it is also the one in which they receive the least formal training.

listening
Skill of receiving a message and interpreting its genuine meaning by accurately grasping the facts and feelings it conveys.

It is tempting to think that listening is easy—after all, it seems to require no effort. This appearance is deceptive, however. While the average person talks at a rate of roughly 150 words per minute, the brain can handle up to 400 words per minute. This discrepancy can lead to boredom, inattention, and misinterpretation. In fact, immediately after listening to a message, the average person can recall only half of it. Several days later, the recall percentage falls to 25 percent or less.

Noise, interference with messages during transmission, can occur as a result of physical factors like poor reception of a radio message or inability to hear a conversation with a co-worker. In other instances, misinterpretations produce faulty communications. Insurance companies such as Metropolitan study accident-claim data in an attempt to spot problem areas and adjust coverage costs accordingly. Most such data report expected reasons for accidents like excessive speed, alcohol, equipment malfunction, and inattentiveness, among others. As the bulletin board in Figure 10.7 reveals, however, some explanations are bizarre.

TABLE 10.1 FORMS OF COMMUNICATION

FORM	DESCRIPTION	EXAMPLE
Oral communication	Communication transmitted through speech	Personal conversations, speeches, meetings, voice mail, telephone conversations, videoconferences
Written communication	Communication transmitted through writing	Letters, memos, formal reports, news releases, e-mail, faxes
Formal communication	Communication transmitted through the chain of command within an organization to other members or to people outside the organization	Internal—memos, reports, meetings, written proposals, oral presentations, meeting minutes; external—letters, written proposals, oral presentations, speeches, news releases, press conferences
Informal communication	Communication transmitted outside formally authorized channels without regard for the organization's hierarchy of authority	Rumors spread through the grapevine
Verbal communication	Transmission of messages in the form of words	Meetings, telephone calls, voice mail, videoconferences
Nonverbal communication	Communication transmitted through actions and behaviors rather than through words	Gestures, facial expressions, posture, body language, dress, makeup

FIGURE 10.7

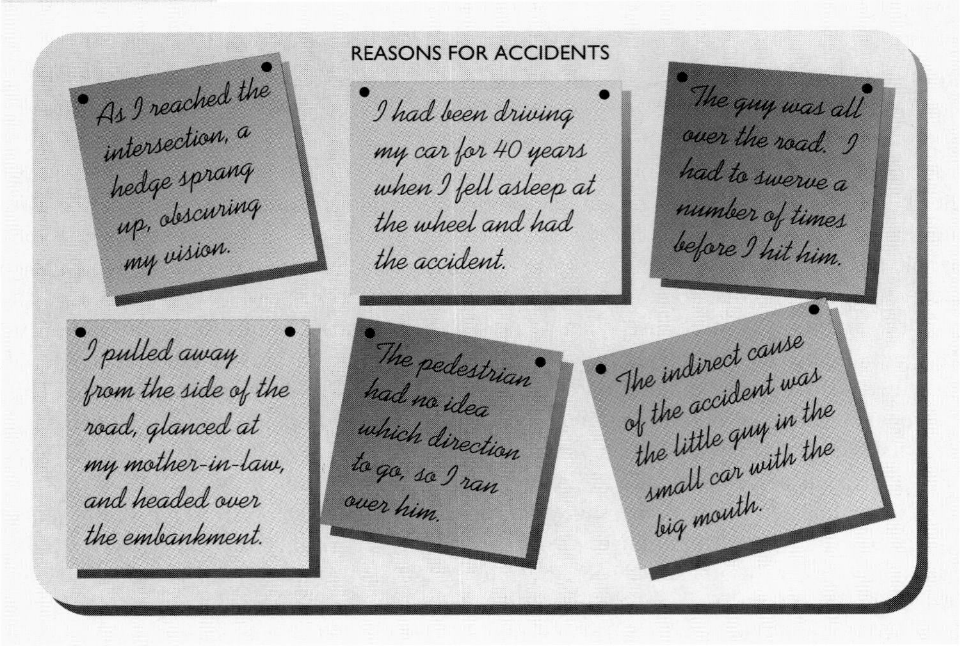

REASONS FOR ACCIDENTS
As I reached the intersection, a hedge sprang up, obscuring my vision.
I had been driving my car for 40 years when I fell asleep at the wheel and had the accident.
The guy was all over the road. I had to swerve a number of times before I hit him.
I pulled away from the side of the road, glanced at my mother-in-law, and headed over the embankment.
The pedestrian had no idea which direction to go, so I ran over him.
The indirect cause of the accident was the little guy in the small car with the big mouth.

Written Communication Effective written communication accommodates its audience, the channel of communications, and the appropriate degree of formality. When writing a formal business document such as a complex report or an important letter, the author should plan in advance and construct the document carefully. The process of writing a formal document can be divided into five stages: planning, research, organization, composition and design, and revision.[19]

Electronic mail and computer networks may call for a less formal writing style than other written communication. "The medium favors the terse," says Crawford Kilian, a writing teacher at Canada's Capilano College. "Short paragraphs, bulleted lists, and one-liners are the units of thought here." Electronic writers often communicate through a combination of words, acronyms, and *emoticons,* little faces (also called *smileys*) constructed with punctuation marks to convey emotional content. The emoticons in Figure 10.8 resemble faces when you look at them sideways. While electronic mail may be more informal than a letter, it is still important to write well. "It's so competitive that you have to work on your style if you want to make any impact," says software designer Jorn Barger.[20]

formal communication channel *Path for messages that flow within the chain of command or task responsibility structure defined by an organization.*

informal communication channel *Path for communication outside formally authorized channels without regard for the organization's hierarchy of authority.*

Formal Communication Communication that follows links in a company's official organization chart reflects a **formal communication channel,** a path for messages that flow within the chain of command or task responsibility structure defined by an organization. The most familiar example of this form of communication is probably *downward communication,* which occurs when someone who holds a senior position in the organization communicates with subordinates. Managers, for example, may communicate downward via electronic mail, formal presentations, policy manuals, notices posted on bulletin boards, and reports printed in company newsletters.

Informal Communication **Informal communication channels** carry messages outside formally authorized channels without regard for the organization's hierarchy of

FIGURE 10.8 EMOTICONS: ADDING INFORMALITY TO FORMAL COMMUNICATIONS

:-)	Sarcastic; "Don't hit me for what I just said."
:-(	Depressed or upset by a remark
:-I	Indifferent
;-)	Winking at a suggestive remark
:-/	Skeptical
:-P	Sticking out tongue
:-D	Laughing at someone
:-@	Screaming
:[)	Drunk
8-)	Wearing sunglasses
::-)	Wearing normal glasses
(-:	Left-handed

authority. A familiar example of an informal channel is the **grapevine,** an internal information channel that conducts information through unofficial, independent sources. Research shows that many employees cite the grapevine as their most frequent source of information. Grapevines disseminate information rapidly. While a message sent through formal channels may take days to reach its audience, messages that travel via the grapevine can arrive within hours. Grapevines are also surprisingly reliable, carrying accurate information 75 to 96 percent of the time. However, even a tiny inaccuracy can distort an entire message.

grapevine
Internal channel that transmits information through unofficial, independent sources.

At Quantum Health Resources, which provides medicines and services for people with chronic diseases, CEO Douglas Tickney uses informal communication channels to foster creativity. Tickney encourages employees to brainstorm during casual, impromptu get-togethers. "It's those Monday mornings or Friday afternoons—that's when you really need to create an atmosphere where people can say, 'Why aren't we thinking about going into thrombosis?' An idea like that might not come out during a formal planning meeting."[21]

Verbal and Nonverbal Communication So far, this section has considered different forms of verbal communication, or communication that conveys meaning through words. **Nonverbal communication,** communication transmitted through actions and behaviors, may carry equal weight, though. Gestures, posture, eye contact, tone of voice, even clothing choices—all of these send nonverbal communication cues. Nonverbal cues become important during oral communication since they can distort the intended meaning of a message.

nonverbal communication
Communication transmitted through actions and behaviors.

Nonverbal cues can have a far greater impact on people's ability to communicate than they realize. One study, for instance, divided face-to-face conversations into three sources of communication cues: verbal (the actual words spoken), vocal (pitch, tone, and timbre of a person's voice), and facial expressions. The researchers evaluated relative weights of these factors in message interpretation as follows: verbal (7 percent), vocal (38 percent), and facial expressions (55 percent).[22]

FIGURE 10.9 COMMUNICATION VARIATIONS IN DIFFERENT ZONES OF PERSONAL SPACE

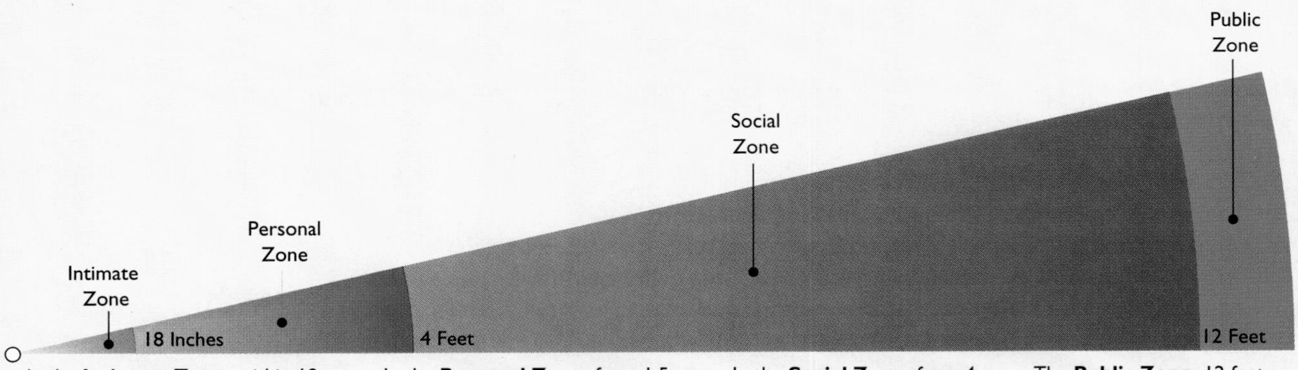

- In the **Intimate Zone,** within 18 inches of each other, good friends and family members engage in activities like comforting, lovers make love, and competitors in sports events wrestle and tackle. Not only can partners touch and hug each other, but they are aware of each other's body heat and body odor. If people whisper, they can be heard.
- In the **Personal Zone,** from 1.5 to 4 feet, less intense exchanges are allowed. Touch is more limited, and body heat and odor are unnoticeable (unless odor is strong). Speech becomes louder, and looking becomes more important than in the intimate zone. Not only is it easier to focus, but you can also see more of the other person.
- In the **Social Zone,** from 4 to 12 feet, exchanges are more formal. Typical are those between business associates. They can touch at the closer end of the range, and then only if one or both lean toward the other. Visual cues become more important, and voices become louder.
- The **Public Zone,** 12 feet and more, is characteristic of brief standing exchanges, such as calling to a friend across a street, or formal exchanges between a speaker (perhaps teacher or minister) and an audience. Voices have to be loud, and it is impossible to see much facial expression detail.

Even personal space—the physical distance between people who are communicating—can convey powerful messages. Figure 10.9 illustrates a continuum of personal space and social interaction with four zones: intimate, personal, social, and public zones. In the United States, most business conversations occur within the social zone, roughly between 4 and 12 feet apart. If one person tries to approach closer than that, the other is likely to feel uncomfortable or threatened.

Interpreting nonverbal cues from people with unfamiliar cultural backgrounds can be especially challenging. Concepts of appropriate personal space can differ substantially, to name just one example. Latin Americans insist on conducting business while standing too close for the comfort of most Americans and northern Europeans, who back away to preserve their personal space, causing the Latin Americans to perceive them as cold and unfriendly. To protect themselves from such feelings of personal threat, experienced Americans use desks or tables to separate themselves from their Latin American counterparts. "The result," explains cultural anthropologist Edward T. Hall, "is that the Latin American may even climb over the obstacles until he has achieved a distance at which he can comfortably talk."[23]

People are usually sending nonverbal messages, even when they try consciously not to do so. Sometimes nonverbal cues may reveal a person's hidden attitudes and thoughts. A discrepancy between verbal and nonverbal messages may indicate that someone is not being truthful. Generally, when verbal and nonverbal cues conflict, audiences tend to believe the nonverbal indicators. Consider what happened when several employees at manufacturing firm Refuse Compactor told their plant manager, George Miller, that they wanted a pay raise, an extra week of vacation, and another paid holiday. Miller told them to put the request in writing so he could show it to company president Art Nevill. However, his nonverbal cues apparently did not fit his verbal message, since the employees interpreted this remark as a rejection. Shortly thereafter, they voted to join a union and went on strike.[24]

COMMUNICATION WITHIN THE ORGANIZATION

internal communication
System of communication through channels within an organization.

Internal communication involves communication through channels within an organization. Examples include memos, meetings, speeches, phone conversations, even a simple conversation over lunch. Internal communication may be relatively simple in a small organization since it often occurs face to face. Unclear instructions can be remedied by further conversation. Communication problems increase as the organization grows, however. Messages, many transmitted in writing, often pass through several layers in the formal organization. The distortion of the original message as it flows through several intermediaries is illustrated by the following sequence:

Memo from Colonel to Executive Officer

Tomorrow evening at approximately 2000 hours Halley's Comet will be visible in this area, an event which occurs only once every 76 years. Have the troops fall out in the battalion area in fatigues, and I will explain this rare phenomenon to them. In case of rain, we will not be able to see anything, so assemble them in the theater and I will show them films of the comet.

Executive Officer to Company Commander

By order of the colonel, tomorrow at 2000 hours, Halley's Comet will appear above the battalion area. If it rains, fall the troops out in fatigues, then march to the theater where this rare phenomenon will take place, something which occurs only once every 76 years.

Company Commander to Lieutenant

By order of the colonel, be in fatigues at 2000 hours tomorrow. The phenomenal Halley's Comet will appear in the theater. In case of rain, in the battalion area, the colonel will give another order, something which occurs once every 76 years.

Lieutenant to Sergeant

Tomorrow at 2000 hours, the colonel will appear in the theater with Halley's Comet, something which happens every 76 years. If it rains, the colonel will order the comet into the battalion area.

Sergeant to Squad

When it rains tomorrow at 2000 hours, the phenomenal 76-year-old General Halley, accompanied by the colonel, will drive his comet through the battalion area in fatigues.

The sender of the message must continually consider the recipient's reaction and make certain that the message is both clearly written and likely to be interpreted correctly.

Computers and electronic mail, or e-mail, can facilitate internal communications within large organizations; these methods may even make companies less formal. "Businesses that have pervasive use of electronic mail operate differently," says Intel CEO Andrew Grove. "It squeezes all the slack out of the system."[25] It also removes time and geography constraints, improves the accuracy of exchanged information, and can effectively promote customer relationships by maintaining customer-supplier contacts and supplying such information as product modifications and price changes. These benefits explain why North American businesses sent almost 6 billion e-mail messages last year. If each message included 50 words, this traffic would amount to sending 1,000 manuscripts the length of *War and Peace* every day.[26]

Certainly, electronic mail speeds up internal communications at Boston Chicken, the fast-growing restaurant chain. Managers use networking software to collaborate on team projects, develop menus, solve distribution problems, and plan the chain's expansion. Online records of sales and cost breakdowns help them to monitor the business. Presi-

A BROADER PURPOSE

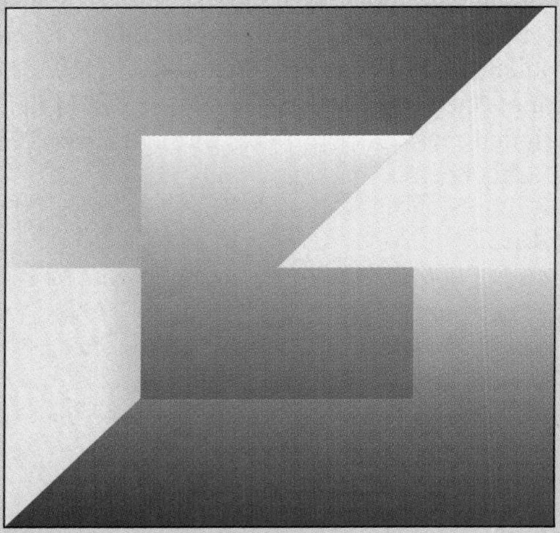

COMMUNICATING WITHOUT OFFENDING As more businesses operate globally, they can encounter enormous problems communicating with customers, employees, and the general public in diverse locales with different languages and cultures. Wide variations change the meanings of words and phrases, even among nations whose people speak the same language.

- Helene Curtis had to change the name of its Every Night shampoo line to Every Day when the firm expanded sales to Sweden because Swedes usually wash their hair in the morning.
- Hoover is such a well-known brand in the United Kingdom that the British use *hoover* as a verb for vacuuming.
- Americans call facial tissues *kleenex.*

Examples abound of embarrassing, often costly mistakes that have occurred in international business due to faulty communication resulting from failure to understand these communication differences. Here are several examples of communication failures involving oral and written messages as well as different meanings conveyed by gestures and other forms of body language.

- Puerto Rican Chevy dealers complained about the name chosen for a new GM model: the Nova. Although the word literally means stars, it sounds like the Spanish phrase *no va,* which means "It doesn't go." GM wisely called the model the *Caribe* in Latin America.
- In India and Bulgaria, shaking your head sideways means yes and nodding means no.
- The thumb and forefinger circle okay sign used in the United States signifies money in Japan, zero in France, and is a vulgar gesture in Latin America.
- A Flemish translation of the phrase "Body by Fisher" from the General Motors logo came out "Corpse by Fisher."
- The Chinese characters that phonetically represented the brand name on the Coca-Cola bottle in China during the 1920s translated as a perplexing message: "bite the wax tadpole." Today, the new characters translate as "happiness in the mouth."
- Conducting personal interviews in Belgium or Switzerland requires the ability to speak four different languages.
- In Japan, Ronald McDonald is called "Donald McDonald" because it is easier to pronounce.
- Chinese marketers have made several unfortunate brand-name choices for products intended for sale in the United States. At the top of the list of "What Not to Name a Product" are White Elephant batteries and Fang Fang lipstick.
- In South America, Parker Pen Co. once unwittingly indicated that its product would prevent unwanted pregnancies.

Awareness of the possibility of different interpretations is the starting point for minimizing their occurrence. To protect written messages, all messages intended for communication to individuals and mass markets in different cultures should be carefully reviewed by local experts who can spot such miscommunications before they occur. Taking this step would have prevented Kellogg's from being remembered as the firm whose advertisements urged Swedish consumers to buy Burned Farmers—the translation of the name of their Bran Buds cereal!

QUESTIONS FOR CRITICAL THINKING

1. What other areas of business might pose interpretation problems for businesses operating internationally?
2. How can a company ensure that its intended message is correctly communicated or translated in foreign markets?
3. How can a company whose message has been miscommunicated in a foreign market overcome the negative impact of the mistake? Use one of the examples mentioned above in your analysis.

dent Bruce Harreld, along with other managers, pays particular attention to the database of customer gripes, which can be sorted by region or type of complaint. "We look for patterns," says Harreld. "The messages go back to the regional level and, as of this fall, back to the store itself electronically, so that everyone sees."[27]

COMMUNICATING IN TEAMS

Communications networks within teams can be divided into two broad categories: centralized and decentralized. In a **centralized network,** team members communicate through a single person to solve problems or make decisions. In a **decentralized network,** members communicate freely among themselves and arrive at decisions together.

centralized network
Communication by team members through a single person to solve problems or make decisions.

decentralized network
System in which team members communicate freely among themselves and arrive at decisions together.

Which type of network is more effective? It depends on the nature of the team's problem or decision. Research has shown that centralized networks usually solve simple problems more quickly and accurately. Members simply pass information along to the central decision maker. However, for complex problems, a decentralized network actually works faster and comes up with more accurate answers. Team members pool their data, provide greater input into decisions, and emerge with higher-quality solutions. This research indicates that organizations should use centralized team networks to deal with simple problems, but should set up decentralized teams to handle more complex issues. Members of decentralized teams should be encouraged to share information with each other and generate as much input into the solution as possible.[28]

Decentralized teams handle the complex process of new product development well. The decentralized structure of Thermos' Lifestyle team allowed team members to catch several design flaws in the Thermal Electric Grill before they resulted in manufacturing glitches. The first design for the grill featured custom-made, tapered legs that would have required an expensive, time-consuming production process. In a centralized team, representatives from the manufacturing division might not have seen the design until late in the development process. However, the problem surfaced early, during informal discussions between designers and production staff, and the designers promptly replaced the first version with a new, straight-legged style. Says Frederick Mather, director of research and development, "If that mistake hadn't been caught, we would have lost three to four months doing rework on the design."[29]

ProShare, a division of Intel Corp., produces computer-based videoconferencing products that facilitate this sort of information sharing by allowing team members to view pictures of each other on their desktop computer screens as they work together on documents, spreadsheets, and other applications. One satisfied customer is the airline sys-

Videoconferencing is a high-tech communication tool that is rapidly changing the way firms work.

FIGURE 10.10 VIDEOCONFERENCING: A HIGH-TECH BUSINESS COMMUNICATION TOOL

- **Now:** Companies hold videoconferences when people in different locations need to see and talk to one another.
- **What they use:** Most systems sold now are room-size setups that cost $15,000 to $100,000.
- **What's ahead:** New desktop systems that cost less than $6,000 are making videoconference technology more convenient and affordable.

BUYERS ARE HOOKED
Sales of videoconference systems — including desktop systems — are expected to increase sharply.
Systems shipped:

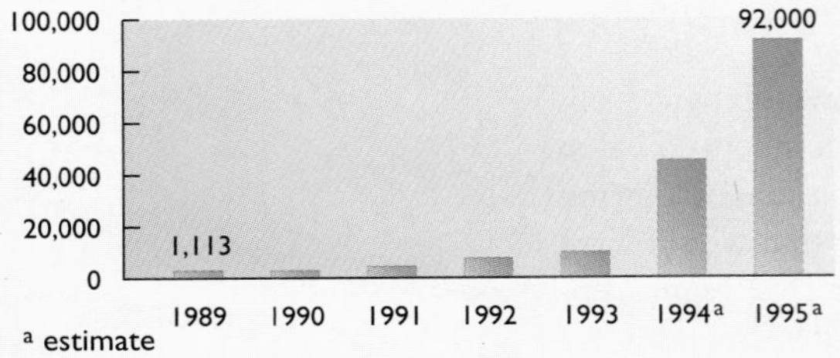

tems division of Unisys, which sells computers and software to airlines. "Each time we go to the video, we'll probably save from $75 to $100," says Gary Hart, director of sales and marketing. "It's the kind of sale where a lot of people are involved—program managers, project managers, legal, marketing, as well as myself and the sales rep. The savings [from videoconferencing] will come from eliminating overnight couriers when preparing proposals for an airline."[30] PictureTel CEO Norman Gaut, shown in Figure 10.10, demonstrates one of the company's desktop videoconference systems. The PictureTel PCS 100 computer allows people to work on text together.

COMMUNICATION WITH AUDIENCES OUTSIDE THE FIRM

external communication
Meaningful exchange of information through messages between an organization and its major audiences.

External communication is a meaningful exchange of information through messages between an organization and its major audiences, such as customers, suppliers, other firms, the general public, and government officials. Businesses use external communication to keep their operations functioning and to maintain their positions in the marketplace.

The central focus of a company's external communication, of course, is the customer, since creating goods and services that provide customer satisfaction is the ultimate purpose of business. Every interaction with customers—for sales presentations, order fulfillment, routine dealings, or one-time transactions—should create goodwill and contribute to customer satisfaction.

Figure 10.11 provides a good illustration of external communication between McIlhenny Co. of Avery Island, Louisiana and its current and prospective customers. The reader can almost feel the aroma and heat of the baked potato in the striking photo. The brief headline emphasizes the unique characteristics of the firm's Tabasco brand pepper sauce and its ability to enhance the flavor of food. The ad creates the possibility of two-way communication by including an 800-number through which readers can request additional information.

FIGURE 10.11

ADVERTISING: MAJOR FORM OF EXTERNAL COMMUNICATION WITH A FIRM'S MARKET

Effective communication can help a firm to win back lost customers. When KFC Japan experienced a 10 percent decline in business in a single year, Toshiki Nakata, its deputy general manager, commissioned a market survey to find out why. A surprising number of respondents stated that, while they liked KFC's food, they thought that it was very expensive. Nakata promptly announced a value strategy that targeted the chain's largest customer group in Japan: people 18 to 26 years old who buy from urban outlets near railway and subway stations. KFC lowered the price on its biggest-selling meal by 16.8 percent to ¥500 at city stores. "We call it our one-coin price," says Nakata. KFC regained 10 percent of its lost customers within a few months after the one-coin price took effect.[31]

Just as personal computer-based videoconferencing facilitates internal communication, it also offers similar benefits for communication outside the firm. Market Strategies, a small market research company in Portland, Oregon, contacts major customers through its videoconferencing system to discuss new bids and current projects and to resolve any complaints before they can jeopardize a project. Says Michael Malone, the firm's president, "The major benefit is the avoidance of misunderstanding. I can watch a customer and see how he or she is reacting to the material we're discussing."[32]

INTERNATIONAL BUSINESS COMMUNICATION

In an effort to build sales in China, PepsiCo marketers created a promotional campaign based on the theme, "Come Alive with Pepsi." Poor sales surprised them until they discovered that the direct Chinese translation of their slogan was "Bring your ancestors back from the dead." Managers ordered a hasty rewrite.

As this example shows, businesspeople who want to succeed in the international marketplace must keep their communications linguistically and culturally appropriate. This principle should also guide efforts to market products to subcultures within the United States as Tropicana managers discovered when they tried to sell their orange juice to Miami's Cuban population. The juice was already popular in Puerto Rico under the label *Jugo de China*. Tropicana put the same packages on Miami shelves, only to be surprised by poor sales. Managers discovered that, while *China* meant "orange" to Puerto Ricans, it only meant "China" to Cubans, who had no desire to buy Chinese juice.[33]

Communication snafus occur even among English-speaking countries. Most Americans know that the British refuse to call trucks *trucks;* they insist on calling them *lorries.* They call the hood of the car a *bonnet* and the garage attendant will search your back seat looking for a trunk. Translate *trunk* to *boot.* Windshields are *windscreens, tire* is spelled *tyre,* and the elevator is simply a *lift.* It is little wonder that playwright George Bernard Shaw referred to the United States and Great Britain as "two countries separated by a common language."

It is helpful to understand the cultural context that surrounds and influences every attempt at international business communication. Anthropologists divide cultures into two basic types, low-context and high-context cultures. Communication in **low-context cultures** tends to rely on explicit written and verbal messages; examples include Switzerland, Germany, Scandinavia, and the United States. Communication in **high-context cultures,** however, is more likely to depend not only on the message itself, but also on everything that surrounds it, such as nonverbal cues and the personal relationship between the communicators.

low-context culture *Communication based on explicit written and verbal messages.*

high-context culture *Communication based not only on the message itself, but also on everything that surrounds it.*

Western businesspeople must carefully temper their low-context styles to the expectations of colleagues and clients in high-context settings. While Americans tend to prefer direct action, wanting to "get down to business" soon after shaking hands or sitting down to a meal, businesspeople in Mexico or the Near East prefer to become acquainted first. It is wise to allow time for relaxed meals during which conversations avoid business-related topics. Instead, effective businesspeople engage in small talk and discuss their families and countries. Parties may meet several times before actually transacting any business.

The ability to communicate cross-culturally is becoming more and more important in business. This may explain why immigrant CEOs manage so many successful American companies. Roberto Goizeuta, head of Coca-Cola, hails from Cuba; 3M's Livio DeSimone comes from Canada; Wolfgang Schmitt, CEO of Rubbermaid, was born in Germany. An international viewpoint definitely leads to business success. As DeSimone says, "Two-thirds of our top 100 managers have spent more than three years outside the United States. They are comfortable anywhere." Schmitt notes another advantage: "It gives you a certain empathy for minorities, because you've been one."[34]

COMMUNICATIONS TECHNOLOGY

This chapter has already illustrated how various communications technologies—computers, videoconferencing, e-mail, and networks—can influence the communication process. Some numbers can confirm the recognition by business of their contributions. Since 1983, 25 million computers have been installed in U.S. offices; over 10 million fax machines and 26 million U.S. e-mail addresses have been added since 1987; 11.9 billion messages were left on voice-mail boxes last year.[35] As Figure 10.12 illustrates, communications giants like AT&T are investing billions in new technologies aimed at making the process of exchanging information even simpler in the future.

Technological developments like networks provide three major benefits for organizations. First, they speed up business operations by allowing people to exchange information and make decisions much more quickly. Second, they bypass functional boundaries allowing people in different departments to communicate directly rather than going through formal channels. Finally, computer networks allow people with diverse skills to work together. "To develop complex products, you need lots of people with specialized knowledge, working together in a little virtual department," says John Manzo, vice president of engineering at Pitney Bowes.[36]

Changes in technology can create whole new industries and new ways of doing business. Technological innovations, ranging from voice recognition and scanners to advanced fiber optics and online services play an important role in advancing a nation's

FIGURE 10.12

SHAPE OF COMMUNICATION IN THE FUTURE

standard of living. The next few sections consider three recent technological developments: interactive media, virtual reality, and the Internet.

INTERACTIVE MEDIA

interactive media
Program applications that allow users to interact with computers to perform several different functions at the same time.

Interactive media are program applications that allow users to interact with computers to perform several different functions at the same time. Imagine shopping for an apartment by computer. Want to see the living room? The screen shifts to that room, allowing you to look around; it then displays the kitchen, and then the bedroom, even the insides of the closets. Want to go to the mall without leaving home? Simply key in the name of the store where you want to shop and control the simulated travel up and down the aisles, pausing to examine specific items, determine their sizes and prices, and even place orders. Industry analysts predict that this kind of interactive media soon will become a major player in businesses that together generate more than $300 billion annually in the United States alone. These industries include video games, videotape rentals, cable TV, catalog shopping, TV shopping, and books and periodicals.

Interactive media are likely to affect the future of advertising, too. The SoftAd Group, located in Mill Valley, California, creates interactive marketing materials for clients such as Ford, Abbott Laboratories, and glass manufacturer PPG Industries. SoftAd has developed two programs, one to help viewers learn more about Ford vehicles and one to explain the advantages of windows made from PPG glass. Interactive ads like these allow customers to experiment with colors and styles, explore different options, and ask for more information.[37]

VIRTUAL REALITY

Your business is thriving, so you hire an architect and an ergonomical engineer and set out to make the perfect work space. During the first office walk-through, you are delighted with the gigantic windows flooding natural light into the drafting room. You are also pleased with the assorted colors and varied heights of cubical dividers that keep the clerical area from looking too regimented. You are disappointed, however, that the

A shopper experiments with short hair using a Styles on Video computer imaging system. Technological innovations like this interactive media system create new ways of doing business and take some of the guess work out of shopping.

dark walls in your office overwhelm the simple furniture you prefer. No problem—just ask the architect to change the computer program. What you have been experiencing is a walk through virtual reality.

For another possibility, perhaps you are being trained to assemble computer parts in a sterile room. The protective clothing and gloves you wear are unfamiliar, and you drop an expensive component on the floor. Rather, you drop an expensive *virtual* component; with no harm done, you continue practicing your new skills.

Virtual reality quickly has matured from its start as a clumsy entertainment curiosity. Early virtual-reality systems forced the user to don a large mask or helmet that provided images and sound and a cumbersome, sensor-heavy data glove. The systems provided changing points of view and some sensory feedback as the user moved head and hand, but the grainy images changed slowly and awkwardly. New technology, however, includes advanced liquid-crystal displays and the Cyber Finger, a wristband that actually responds to the electrical signals sent out by muscles in the user's hand and fingers.

The potential of virtual and enhanced reality grows as technology advances. Colt Virtual Reality Ltd. has developed Vegas 2 with a library of virtual people. Together with software from Dimension Ltd., it allows the user to model emergencies. With this system, an engineer can examine where best to put the exits in a department store, based on the behaviors of virtual shoppers with their virtual children and even virtual wheelchairs, after a virtual fire breaks out.

Enhanced reality allows the user wearing special glasses to see both real surroundings and the enhanced reality image, which might be a pattern or instructions to follow. A surgeon can have a patient's magnetic resonance imaging scan projected onto the patient's shaved head, displaying the exact location of a tumor. Virtual and enhanced reality can provide flying lessons on the ground, wind-tunnel testing for computer-generated airplane models, and a way to explore the inside of a molecule.

Internet
All-purpose global network composed of some 48,000 different networks around the globe that, within limits, lets anyone with access to a personal computer send and receive images and data anywhere.

INTERNET

The **Internet** is the world's first digital-information utility—an all-purpose global network composed of some 48,000 different networks around the globe that, within limits, lets anyone with access to a personal computer send and receive images and data anywhere. Online service companies such as American Online, CompuServe, and Prodigy Services are finding new and better ways for their subscribers to access the Internet's vast resources. Personal computer manufacturers are now working on new models that come with Internet access software already installed.

The list of Internet subscribers has grown to include more than 6 million organizations around the world; in just the past 5 years, the Internet's population has jumped from an estimated 1 million individuals to more than 32 million, with 1 million new "Netizens" each month. Today, the network provides full service in 75 countries, and computer owners in 77 more countries are able to send and receive simple e-mail via the Internet.

With so many users and a strong potential for even more, the industry is seeking ways to make it easier for subscribers to reach this key access point to the information superhighway. The World Wide Web is an Internet service group of over 7,000 independently owned computers that work together as one. Access to these computers, called *Web servers,* is facilitated by new software programs that even a novice can understand and use.

One such software tool, Mosaic, allows the user to browse from one Web computer to another. As Figure 10.13 shows, it also allows users to transform the Internet's text-only format with colorful pictures. Users can see everything from paintings in the Louvre and photos taken by NASA's Hubble telescope to movie clips from current Hollywood movies or merchandise in virtual malls. James H. Clark, Mosaic Communications chairman, predicts that such software programs "will blend into the future era of interactive television."[38]

No one owns the Internet. It is the result of technical, social, and commercial innovation and teamwork. It took root in 1969 when the Pentagon funded the Arpanet, which initially linked four research labs for the purpose of testing networking. During the 1970s, Arpanet expanded to reach dozens of universities and corporations. Soon it offered e-mail, access to remote databases, and electronic bulletin boards. Finally, it evolved into the Internet Protocol, which allows any number of computer networks to link up and act

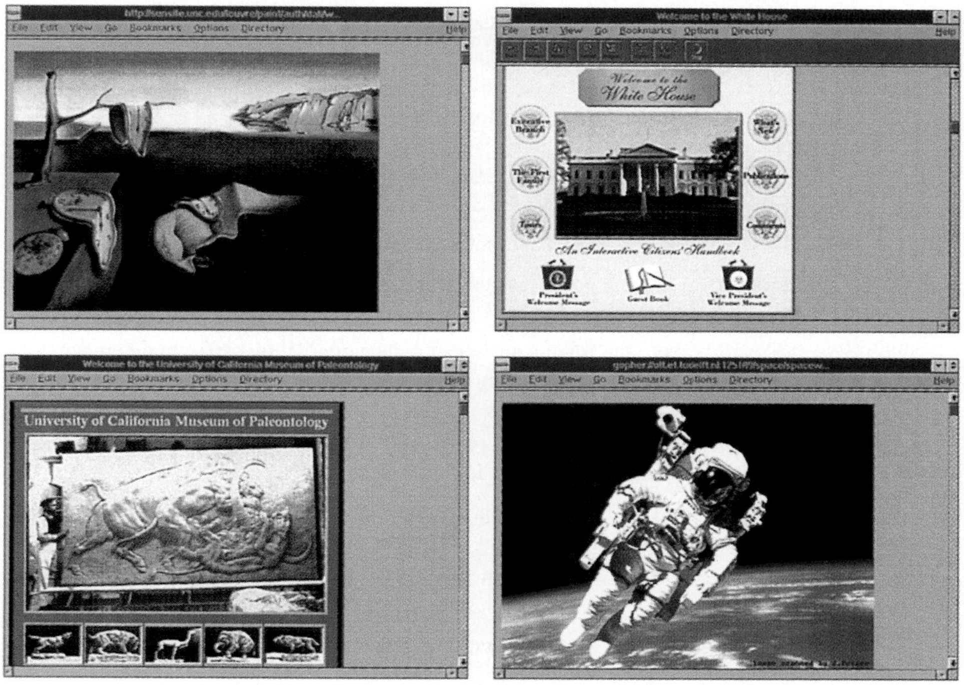

FIGURE 10.13

INTERNET: PICTURES AND INFORMATION FROM AROUND THE GLOBE

as one. The system works just like a global mail system in which dozens of independent authorities collaborate to move and deliver one another's letters. By the 1980s, millions of computers and thousands of networks were using the Internet. Industry researchers refer to the Internet as the Wild West of technology, where the rules and regulations are just now being written.

The Internet offers endless opportunities. It could become one of the most efficient marketing, sales, and customer support tools of this century. GE maintains one of 21,000 commercial Internet addresses to provide technical data to help customers use its resins. Xerox Corp. allows customers to try out software across the Internet. Volvo and Alfa Romeo are using the Web to send photos and information about new cars to virtual car buyers. J. P. Morgan & Co. offers clients access to its risk-management database. Hyatt Hotels Corp. promotes its hotels and resorts, and it gives discounts to customers who say they saw it on the Net.

Chapter 17 will further explore the roles of these and other communications technologies in business.

ACHIEVEMENT CHECK SUMMARY

Reread the learning goals that follow, and consider the questions for each goal. Answering these questions will reinforce the most important concepts in the chapter and allow you to check how well you have achieved these learning goals. Where a blank appears before a question, answer with *T* or *F*. Otherwise, circle the letter of the correct answer. An answer key to these questions is found at the end of this chapter.

LEARNING GOAL 10.1: Distinguish between the two major types of teams in organizations.

1. ___ Work teams are permanent, small groups of people with complementary skills who handle the ongoing, day-to-day operations of the organization.
2. ___ Problem-solving teams are temporarily assembled to solve specific problems and then disbanded.

LEARNING GOAL 10.2: Identify the characteristics of an effective team and the different roles played by team members.

1. Effective teams: (a) generally have 30 or more members; (b) typically have between 5 and 12 members; (c) always have fewer than 7 members; (d) are more innovative if everyone has a common background.
2. Effective teams require their members to fill all of the following roles, *except:* (a) task specialist roles, (b) socio-emotional roles; (c) dual roles; (d) nonparticipant roles.

LEARNING GOAL 10.3: List the stages of team development.

1. The first stage of team development, in which members get acquainted and oriented, is known as: (a) forming; (b) storming; (c) norming; (d) performing; (e) adjourning.
2. As teams develop, members may differ as they try to clarify expectations and roles in the stage of group development known as: (a) forming; (b) storming; (c) norming; (d) performing; (e) adjourning.
3. When team members resolve differences and reach a consensus about the roles of the team leader and other participants, the group has reached the stage known as: (a) forming; (b) storming; (c) norming; (d) performing; (e) adjourning.

LEARNING GOAL 10.4: Relate team cohesiveness and norms to effective team performance.

1. ___ When team cohesiveness is low, productivity improves.
2. ___ Team norms are shared values and expectations of team members.
3. ___ Team cohesiveness is high when members are attracted to the team and motivated to remain in it.

LEARNING GOAL 10.5: Identify each of the factors that can cause conflict in teams, and discuss conflict resolution styles.

1. ___ Team conflict is generally reduced when resources are scarce.
2. ___ Vague assignments and roles are common causes of team conflict.
3. ___ Team leaders can reduce conflict by clarifying member tasks and focusing the members on broad, common goals.

LEARNING GOAL 10.6: Explain the importance of effective communication skills in business.

1. ___ Most managers spend 80 percent of their time in direct communication with others.
2. ___ People with reasonably good English skills need not solicit feedback to ensure clear communication.
3. ___ As organizations grow, communication problems tend to decline.

LEARNING GOAL 10.7: Compare the different types of communication.

1. ___ Formal communication channels within the organization generally follow the chain of command.
2. ___ In general, when verbal and nonverbal communication cues conflict, a communicator tends to believe the verbal cues.
3. ___ The grapevine moves information more rapidly than formal communication channels and is surprisingly reliable.

LEARNING GOAL 10.8: Identify and explain several important considerations in international business communication.

1. ___ Businesspeople all over the world rely equally on explicit written and oral messages to transmit information.
2. ___ In a high-context culture, communication depends more on nonverbal cues and the relationship between the communicators.

LEARNING GOAL 10.9: Summarize important developments in communication technology and how they affect business communication.

1. Modern communication technologies such as computers, videoconferencing, electronic mail, and networks: (a) make it more difficult to create, organize, and distribute messages; (b) make it easier to create, organize, and distribute messages; (c) have little use in international transactions; (d) have little impact on the efficiency of communication.
2. The Internet: (a) is an all-purpose global network; (b) is composed of more than 48,000 different networks around the world; (c) allows users of personal computers to send and receive images and data anywhere; (d) all of the above.

KEY TERMS

team 255
work team 255
problem-solving team 256
task specialist role 258
socio-emotional role 258
team cohesiveness 262
team norm 264
conflict 264
communication 265
listening 267
formal communication channel 268
informal communication channel 268
grapevine 269
nonverbal communication 269
internal communication 271
centralized network 273
decentralized network 273
external communication 274
low-context culture 276
high-context culture 276
interactive media 277
Internet 278

REVIEW QUESTIONS

1. Distinguish among work teams, problem-solving teams, and cross-functional teams.

2. Is there an optimal size for a team? Identify the problems that often occur with large teams.

3. Which team roles are most important to achieving the goals of a team? Which role would you be most likely to assume in a team?

4. Describe each of the five stages of team development. What happens during each stage?

5. List the factors that can lead to team conflict. What resolution styles does the chapter identify?

6. Draw a diagram of the communication process and label each element. Explain the concept of noise.

7. Compare the different types of communication discussed in the chapter, including oral, written, formal, informal, and nonverbal communication.

8. Explain why businesspeople need to be effective communicators.

9. Describe the roles of computers and related technologies in business communication.

10. Discuss the principles that should guide businesspeople's international communications.

DISCUSSION QUESTIONS

1. Suppose that you have been asked to create a training program to help employees at a local company improve their teamwork and communication skills. Develop a plan that describes your program.

2. Interview someone from another nation who is visiting or living in the United States. What are this person's most vivid impressions of America and Americans? How do American work practices and communication styles differ from those in this person's homeland? Write a summary of the interview.

3. Think back to your most recent experience as part of a team at work or school. Analyze the team's development. Can you recall specific examples of each stage of development? What were the norms of this group? How would you assess its degree of cohesiveness? How did this cohesiveness influence the team's effectiveness?

4. Keep a record of your communications for one day. Include phone conversations, personal conversations, and mail. Write a two-page report that summarizes your findings and include a description of your personal communication style and patterns.

5. More and more businesspeople are communicating with foreign customers, colleagues, and vendors via fax machines and electronic mail. Discuss the advantages and disadvantages of using these channels for international communication.

SOLUTIONS TO ACHIEVEMENT CHECK SUMMARY

L. G. 10.1: 1. T, 2. T. **L. G. 10.2:** 1. b, 2. d. **L. G. 10.3:** 1. a, 2. b, 3. c. **L. G. 10.4:** 1. F, 2. T, 3. T. **L. G. 10.5:** 1. F, 2. T, 3. T. **L. G. 10.6:** 1. T, 2. F, 3. F. **L. G. 10.7:** 1. T, 2. F, 3. T. **L. G. 10.8:** 1. F, 2. T. **L. G. 10.9:** 1. b, 2. d.

VIDEO CASE

VALASSIS COMMUNICATIONS, INC. For many Americans, the Sunday newspaper is the most traditional communications medium in existence. People buy the Sunday paper for a variety of reasons: comics, sports, more in-depth coverage of current events, the arts, and, yes, the coupons. Current TV ads show young couples drinking coffee and cutting out coupons—many of them created by Valassis Communications, Inc.

Valassis began in 1969 as a broker for printing companies, but, two years later, management realized that profits could be enhanced by adding commercial printing capabilities to the firm's service offerings. Knowledgeable Valassis managers with innovative ideas introduced a new product in the coupon industry—the glossy, multi-page, color-coupon supplements placed in the middle of every Sunday newspaper and often in daily papers across the United States. These supplements, known as free-standing inserts (FSIs), contain coupons and promotional advertising for America's top packaged-goods companies. Today, two-thirds of the *Fortune 500* business giants are Valassis clients.

Clients receive their money's worth when they use Valassis' FSIs in their marketing programs, since they provide high-quality color reproduction, can be targeted to specific cities or regions, and are cost efficient compared to other methods of coupon distribution. The best part is that consumers love to receive them. In fact, newspaper readership surveys show that Valassis coupon supplements are second only to the front-page news in popularity. Each week, over 55 million coupon supplements, averaging 28 pages each, are distributed to some 400 newspapers nationwide.

Employees will be the first to tell you about Valassis' unique corporate culture, one that fosters teamwork and new ideas and emphasizes customer satisfaction. Work teams continually exceed all expectations. When faced with the challenge of a new competitor in 1994, Valassis printing press crews ran the presses faster and more efficiently, surpassing production objectives and lowering printing costs for the fourth consecutive year. In less than 12 months, the new competitor was no longer in business. The paper purchasing team members set their own goals for 1994. Their aim was high, but since they set the goals themselves, they had the commitment to follow through. The result was a reduction in a major cost component for Valassis.

Valassis' customer service team also illustrates the importance of working together—with both coworkers and customers. This team developed "flexible closing dates" by working with customers to accommodate their scheduling needs. The turnaround time on contracts was shortened by several days by empowering sales teams to handle customer contracts directly. This task was handled before by contract coordinators (one of whom recommended that her job be eliminated to increase efficiency). Since then, the other contract coordinators have been assigned to other departments.

In addition to adopting the team approach, Valassis integrated new computer technology into its printing processes. The firm's VI-Link program enables customers to transmit details of their promotion via computer disk or modem, eliminating unnecessary phone calls and paperwork while ensuring the accuracy of the customer's promotion.

All of Valassis' efforts are monitored by a cross-functional team made up of representatives from different business functions within the company. This team, called "On the M.O.V.E." (Motivate Our Valassis Employees), researches and implements programs like flextime, job sharing, and suggestion review systems, as well as planning a variety of events designed to enhance employee morale.

Recognizing the importance of people, both inside and outside the company, has been the major key to Valassis' success. Over the last 25 years, teamwork has supported the company's internal growth and has allowed Valassis to make major acquisitions. This success allowed Valassis to add several items to its product line. The following are a few of their current offerings:

- *C&C County Inserts* FSIs that are distributed to over 400 newspapers in small, rural communities with key retail locations. This program allows marketers to reach consumers in outlying areas with a four-color coupon vehicle, while promoting traffic in local stores.
- *Valassis ROP Solutions* Run-of-press (ROP) coupon programs that place clients' coupons and other promotional advertising directly on the pages of over 7,000 newspapers nationwide, thereby offering efficient pricing and total flexibility.
- *Valassis Impact Printing* Specialty print promotions that carry the message of one company, rather than several companies, including brochures, catalogue, and magazine inserts.
- *Valassis In-Store Marketing* A network of over-the-aisle electronic signs in over 5,000 U.S. supermarkets, featuring promotional/advertising messages from manufacturers and retailers.

Work teams, such as the Valassis printing press crews, exceeded all expectations when they were faced with the challenge of a new competitor. . . .

In addition to these various goods and services, Valassis has been entering into joint ventures and making acquisitions around the globe. In 1994, Valassis Communications entered into a joint agreement with a Mexican firm to form Valassis de Mexico. Valassis has also acquired an 80 percent interest in the French firm *Groupement des Agents de Presse et de Publicite* (GAPP). In 1995, Valassis purchased McIntyre & Dodd, an established leader in consumer sales promotion and direct response merchandise marketing in Canada.

Valassis has been able to achieve its position in a highly competitive industry through its ability to communicate both with employees on the inside and clients on the outside. Next Sunday, when you read the paper, think of Valassis and the numerous people working together to bring you—and millions like you around the globe—that colorful coupon supplement.

QUESTIONS

1.
How important are effective communication skills to a firm like Valassis, whose business is promoting other businesses? What difficulties can you imagine arising from poor communications with a client in this industry?

2.
What different types of teams are used at Valassis?

3.
How has Valassis utilized technology to better communicate with its clients? With its clients' customers?

4.
What developments in communication technology might change the way companies such as Valassis promote products to consumers in the future?

LEARNING GOALS

1. Summarize the history of labor unions and list their primary goals.

2. Identify the major federal laws that affect labor unions and explain the key provisions of each law.

3. Explain how collective bargaining agreements are established and the roles played by arbitrators and mediators.

4. Outline the sources of power, or "weapons," of labor and management.

5. Discuss the future of organized labor.

CHAPTER 11

LABOR-MANAGEMENT RELATIONS

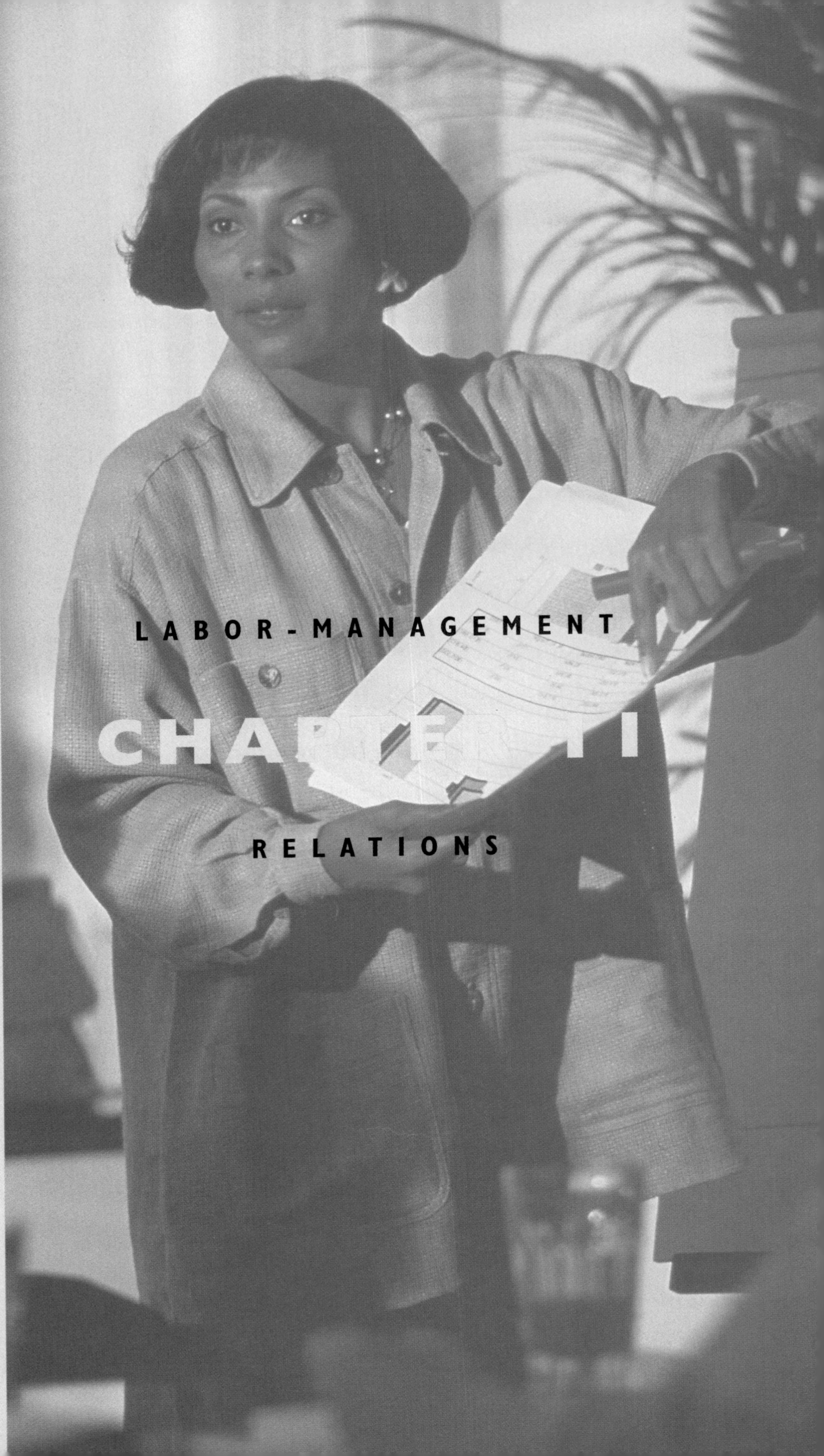

TEAM BUILDING AT JEEP In 1986, American Motors' Jeep plant in Toledo, Ohio enjoyed a dubious distinction. *Forbes* magazine singled it out as a prime example of poor manufacturing practices and destructive labor-management relations. Relations had deteriorated so badly at the plant that the magazine confidently predicted it would "soon join the industrial scrap heap." ■ A decade later, the Toledo plant is back in *Forbes*—but this time the story is quite different. Far from joining the scrap heap, the factory is setting new standards for cooperation between labor and management. It is also, not coincidentally, setting new standards for quality. "An impressive turnaround," notes the magazine. ■ At first glance, the Toledo facility seems an unlikely site for a successful experiment in state-of-the-art industrial relations. The elderly complex, dating back to 1903, is a maze of 60 buildings with 22 elevators. Repeated efforts to improve its product quality had been frustrated by persistent labor-management disputes. ■ What happened to change this story? First, Chrysler bought American Motors and updated the plant. The auto maker then established its companywide "product quality improvement" program that brings employees and management together in self-guided teams to work to cut costs and improve manufacturing techniques. Initially, the program spurred resistance from both sides. "Union members never said, 'My company.' It was always *that* company or *their* company," comments John Miller, President of United Auto Workers (UAW) Local 412. "Our task was to reach our members and make them part of the company." Managers were even more reluctant to buy into the idea. ■ Chrysler's product quality improvement program has been especially successful at the Toledo facility, where the union contract allows assembly workers to work with management to set work rules without regard to rules in place at other plants. In return for a pay raise and a 5-year contract, the Toledo UAW members agreed to flexible work rules that reduced the number of job classifications from 130 to 19. The work force, both hourly and salaried, split into teams to explore various initiatives for saving money and boosting quality. Union representatives and plant managers met regularly to discuss the teams' progress and to review new ideas for further cost savings and quality enhancements. ■ As an example of the new, cooperative spirit at Toledo, consider its innovative recycling program, a brainchild of the plant's Jeep Wrangler quality team. The team of hourly workers and managers negotiate with waste haulers, select recyclers, and determine what to recycle and how to do it. As team member Jim Walters points out, "We must research companies and make sure they are going to do what they say they are going to do." Colleague Tony Zglinski sums it up more succinctly: "We did the research so no vendor could B.S. us," he smiles. ■ Team members take their mission seriously. They have been known to rummage through trash bins to ensure separation of recyclable and nonrecoverable materials. Sometimes they spot-check haulers' trucks to make certain the trucks carry full loads. An employee who fails to recycle a component is likely to get a stern reminder. ■ Since the program began, it has been responsible for recycling 430 tons of plastic, paper, and light metal, and it reclaims 18 tons of copper every year. In just 2 years, it has saved the plant $2 million—savings that will multiply if the Jeep Wrangler team's system is adopted companywide, which seems likely. ■ The recycling program is just one of many ongoing, cooperative projects that are paying off at the plant. This year, plant

There's Only One Jeep®...
A Division of the Chrysler Corporation.
Jeep
Eagle
To learn about Jeep products and how you can participate in a Jeep Jamboree, please call 1-800-925-JEEP.
Always wear your seat belt. Jeep is a registered trademark of Chrysler Corporation.

output will total 284,000 Jeeps and Dodge Dakota pickup trucks—24 percent more than a decade ago—with 4 percent fewer workers. The Toledo facility has received Ohio's Excellence in Exporting award in recognition of its success in building the Jeep Comanche and Jeep Cherokee, Chrysler's top-selling vehicles overseas. The plant also builds right-hand-drive Cherokees for several foreign markets, making Chrysler the first American car company to mass-produce right-hand-drive vehicles for export. ■ At Toledo, managers and union workers prize the plant's current spirit of cooperation. As recently as a decade ago, 1,500 worker grievances were pending at one time; today only 20 await resolution. UAW members now display a new sense of involvement. As one Jeep Wrangler product quality improvement facilitator puts it, "If this was a management-only thing, it would probably fall apart. Instead, this is a whole plant effort. It's a total package, a new philosophy of work."[1]

CHAPTER OVERVIEW

Every society and culture develops some kind of a system of industrial relations. The people who head the organizations that provide necessary goods and services, the people who do the work, and the government organizations that maintain the society define the various industrial relationships. This chapter focuses on the relationships between labor and management.

The chapter begins by exploring reasons for the emergence of labor unions and a brief history of their operations in the United States. Next it focuses on legislation that affects labor-management relations. The process of collective bargaining is then discussed, along with an examination of union and management weapons. The chapter concludes with a look at the future of labor-management relations.

EMERGENCE OF LABOR UNIONS

Organized labor is not indigenous to the United States. For hundreds of years, organizations of craft workers have existed in Europe and Asia. Over the years, they have developed into powerful workers' organizations. Today, with the growing interdependence among nations around the world and the increasing number of multinational corporations, understanding labor-management relations becomes imperative for business students.

While membership roles of unions in the United States and many other countries have declined, unionized workers still constitute a significant percentage of some nations' labor forces, including 46 percent of workers in the United Kingdom, 47 percent of those in Italy, and 39 percent of those in Germany.[2] The basic, underlying purpose of unions—to protect and provide for workers—is a consistent characteristic of every organized labor union throughout the world.

NEED FOR LABOR UNIONS

The Industrial Revolution brought advantages of specialization and division of labor. These changes increased efficiency because each worker could specialize in some aspect of the production process and become proficient at it. Bringing together numerous workers also increased output as compared to traditional handicraft methods of production. The factory system converted the jack-of-all-trades into a specialist.

The Industrial Revolution also produced a more sinister impact on the lives of workers in the 19th and early 20th centuries, though. Specialization made them dependent on the factory for their livelihoods. In prosperous times, they could count on employment,

Breaker boys pick slate and rock as coal runs down a chute. By 1906 the national Child Labor Committee reported there were some 10,000 boys under age 14 working in the anthracite coal fields of northeastern Pennsylvania. Throughout the first decades of the twentieth century unions and reformers won state requirements gradually raising the minimum age for employment. In 1941 the United Mine Workers won contractual language requiring that workers be 19 years old to work in the mine.

but periodic depressions threw them out of work. Unemployment insurance was a subject for dreamers, and the image of the poorhouse represented reality for unemployed workers.

Working conditions were often bad. Jobs in many factories required long workdays with no protective safety standards. At the beginning of the 19th century, young children worked for a few pennies a day to help their families. In Boston in 1830, children comprised two-fifths of the labor force. The labor of young women drove the entire cotton and woolen industries. Work hours lasted from daybreak to dark, and wages were low. In the spinning and weaving mills of New Jersey, children earned an average of a little more than $1 a week.

By the end of the nineteenth century, the typical workweek ran to 60 hours, but in some industries, such as steel, 72 or even 84 hours was common. That breaks down to seven 12-hour days a week. Working conditions still frequently remained unsafe, and child labor remained common.

Workers gradually learned that bargaining as a unified group could bring them improvements in job security, wages, and working conditions. The organized efforts of Philadelphia printers in 1786 resulted in the first U.S. minimum wage—$1 a day. After 100 more years, New York City streetcar conductors banded together in successful negotiations that reduced their workday from 17 to 12 hours. The sweeping changes in labor-management relations over the past century produced profound changes in wages, hours of work, and working conditions. The increased number of labor union officials and employee-designated directors on corporate boards represents visible signs of success.

HISTORY OF U.S. LABOR UNIONS

Although the history of trade unionism in the United States begins before the Declaration of Independence, early unions were loose-knit, local organizations that served primarily as friendship groups or benevolent societies to help fellow workers in need. Such unions were typically short-lived, growing during prosperous times and suffering severely during depressions.

EARLY LABOR ORGANIZATIONS

For more than 200 years, individual workers have sought methods of improving their living standards, working conditions, and job security. Over time, as workers began to unite, they realized that collectively, they often grew sufficiently strong to elicit responses

labor union
Group of workers who have banded together to achieve common goals in the key areas of wages, hours, and working conditions.

to their demands. This inspired the birth of labor unions. A **labor union** is a group of workers who have banded together to achieve common goals in the key areas of wages, hours, and working conditions.

Two types of labor unions exist in the United States: craft unions and industrial unions. A *craft union* joins skilled workers in a specific craft or trade, such as carpenters, painters, printers, and heavy-equipment operators. An *industrial union* combines all workers in a given industry, regardless of their occupations or skill levels. Industrial unions include the United Steelworkers, the United Auto Workers, the Amalgamated Clothing Workers, and the United Transportation Union.

The first truly national union was the Knights of Labor, founded in 1869. By 1886, its membership exceeded 700,000 workers, but it soon split into factions. One faction promoted revolutionary aims, wanting the government to take over production. The second faction wanted the union to continue focusing on the economic well-being of union members and opposed the socialist tendencies of some members. This faction merged with a group of unaffiliated craft unions in 1886 to form the **American Federation of Labor (AFL),** which became a national union of affiliated, individual craft unions.

American Federation of Labor (AFL)
National union made up of affiliated, individual craft unions.

The AFL's first president was Samuel Gompers, a dynamic man who believed that labor unions should operate within the framework of the existing economic system and who vehemently opposed socialism. Gompers' bread-and-butter concept of unionism kept the labor movement focused on the critical objectives of wages, hours, and working conditions. The AFL grew rapidly, and by 1920, three out of four organized workers were AFL members.

Unions grew slowly between 1920 and 1935, though. The philosophy of organizing labor along craft lines had spurred the AFL's 40-year growth record, but it encountered difficulties as few nonunion, skilled craft workers remained for it to organize. Several unions in the AFL began to organize workers in the mass-production automobile and steel industries. Successes in organizing the communications, mining, newspaper, steel, rubber, and automobile industries resulted in the formation of a new group, the **Congress of Industrial Organizations (CIO)**—a national union of affiliated, individual industrial unions. This new technique of organizing entire industries rather than individual crafts was so successful that the CIO soon rivaled the AFL in size.

Congress of Industrial Organizations (CIO)
National union made up of affiliated, individual industrial unions.

By 1945, total union membership had passed 14 million workers, 35.5 percent of the labor force in the United States. In 1955, the AFL and CIO united under the presidency of George Meany. The only major national union not affiliated with the AFL–CIO today is the National Education Association. Of more than 200 separate unions in the United States, approximately half are affiliated with the AFL–CIO.

Currently, almost 17 million U.S. workers, 15.8 percent of the nation's full-time labor force, belong to labor unions. Of these, 11 percent work in private industry, while the rest are government employees. This represents the lowest level of union membership since the Depression of the 1930s. Although the traditional strength of unions focused on blue-collar industries, the organized sector has become increasingly white-collar and female as the U.S. economy has evolved from a manufacturing basis to a more service-based system. In fact, labor has found its most success over the past two decades in efforts to recruit government employees and professionals such as health-care workers.[3]

LOCAL, NATIONAL, AND INTERNATIONAL UNIONS

Like the formal structure of a large organization, labor unions typically forge links to form a hierarchy. A **national union** joins together many local unions, which make up the entire union organizational structure. The **local union** operates as a branch of a national union, representing union members in a given geographic area. For instance, Local 837 is an 800-member union that represents workers at the A. E. Staley plant in Decatur, Illinois, a division of British sweetener manufacturer Tate & Lyle. Local 837 is a branch of a large national union, the Allied Industrial Workers of America.[4]

Local craft unions represent workers such as carpenters or plumbers in a particular area. The local union receives its charter from the national union and operates under the national union's constitution, bylaws, and rules. Most organized workers identify closely with their local unions and are acquainted with local union officers, even though they seldom attend regular union meetings except for those that deal with important issues such as contract negotiations, strike votes, or union elections. An estimated 5 to 10 percent of unionized workers regularly attend local union meetings.

national union
Large labor organization composed of numerous local unions.

local union
Branch of a national union representing members in a specific area.

Large national and international unions in the Untied States include the National Education Association, Teamsters, International Brotherhood of Electrical Workers, International Association of Machinists and Aerospace Workers, United Steelworkers of America, and the American Federation of Teachers. Almost half of U.S. union members belong to one of these giant organizations.

In such industries as automobiles, steel, and electrical products, collective bargaining over major issues occurs at the national level with representatives of various local unions present. An **international union** is a union with members outside the United States, usually in Canada. Some such unions choose names to reflect their international status, such as the International Union of Operating Engineers.

international union
National union with members outside the United States.

While local unions form the base of the union structure, federations such as the AFL–CIO occupy the top. A **federation** brings together many national and international unions to serve mediation and political functions. As one major function, a federation mediates disputes between affiliated unions. In addition, it performs a political function, representing organized labor in world affairs and in contacts with unions in other nations. Federation representatives frequently speak before Congress and other branches of government, and they assist in coordinating efforts to organize nonunion workers.

federation
Association of numerous national and international unions to serve mediation and political functions.

However, some unions, such as the National Education Association, do not belong to the major U.S. federation, the AFL–CIO. In 1989, the AFL–CIO readmitted the nation's second-largest union, the Teamsters, 30 years after expelling it for refusing to answer charges of corruption.

LABOR LEGISLATION

Government attitudes toward unions have varied considerably during the past century. These shifting attitudes appear clearly in Table 11.1, which summarizes major pieces of legislation enacted during this period.

UNION SECURITY PROVISIONS

Since unions focus their efforts on improving the incomes and working conditions of all workers, their belief that every employee should join a union should not seem surprising. A **closed shop** is a business with an employment agreement that prohibits management from hiring nonunion workers. To get a job at such a firm, a worker must join the union, and remaining a union member is a condition of continued employment. Unions have considered the closed shop an essential ingredient of security, giving them unquestioned power in demands for wages and working conditions. Unions argue in favor of the closed shop because all employees enjoy the benefits of union contracts, they claim, so all should support the union.

closed shop
Illegal employment policy requiring a firm to hire only current union members.

Employers have argued, however, that forcing people to join an organization as a condition of employment violates a fundamental principle of freedom. Moreover, if an employer can hire only union members, it might have to pass over the best, most qualified workers. Finally, employers have claimed that a guaranteed membership may make union leaders irresponsible and lead them to deal dishonestly with their members. Congress showed its support for these arguments by passing the Taft-Hartley Act, which prohibits the closed shop.

TABLE 11.1 LABOR LEGISLATION

1932 NORRIS-LA GUARDIA ACT

Early federal legislation that protects unions by greatly reducing management's ability to obtain court injunctions to halt union activities. Before this act, employers could easily obtain court decrees forbidding strikes, peaceful picketing, and even membership drives. Such an injunction automatically made the union a wrongdoer in the eyes of the law if it continued the activities.

1935 NATIONAL LABOR RELATIONS ACT (WAGNER ACT)

Legislation that legalized collective bargaining and required employers to negotiate with elected representatives of their employees. It established the National Labor Relations Board (NLRB) to supervise union elections and prohibit unfair labor practices such as firing workers for joining unions, refusing to hire union sympathizers, threatening to close if workers unionize, interfering with or dominating the administration of a union, and refusing to bargain with a union.

1938 FAIR LABOR STANDARDS ACT

Continuing the wave of pro-union legislation, it set a federal minimum wage and maximum basic workweek for workers employed in industries engaged in interstate commerce. It also outlawed child labor. The first minimum wage was set at $0.25 an hour, with exceptions for farm workers and retail employees.

1947 TAFT-HARTLEY ACT (LABOR-MANAGEMENT RELATIONS ACT OR LMRA)

As unions continued to grow, legislation began focusing on unfair practices of unions as well as employers. The Taft-Hartley Act limited unions' power by prohibiting such practices as coercing employees to join unions; coercing employers to discriminate against employees who are not union members, except for failure to pay union dues under union shop agreements; discrimination against nonunion employees; picketing or conducting secondary boycotts or strikes for illegal purposes; featherbedding; and excessive initiation fees under union shop agreements.

1959 LANDRUM-GRIFFIN ACT (LABOR-MANAGEMENT REPORTING AND DISCLOSURE ACT)

Legislation that amended the Taft-Hartley Act to promote honesty and democracy in running unions' internal affairs. It requires a union to set a constitution and bylaws and to hold regularly scheduled elections of union officers by secret ballot, and it sets forth a bill of rights for members. The act also requires unions to submit certain financial reports to the U.S. Secretary of Labor.

1988 PLANT-CLOSING NOTIFICATION ACT

Legislation that requires employers with more than 100 employees to give workers and local elected officials 60 days' warning of a shutdown or mass layoff. It also created the Worker Readjustment Program to assist displaced workers.

union shop
Employment policy requiring nonunion workers to join a union that represents a firm's workers within a specified period.

agency shop
Employment policy allowing workers to reject union membership, but requiring them to pay fees equal to union dues.

Under a modification of the closed shop, the **union shop,** all current employees must join the union as soon as an election certifies it as their legitimate bargaining agent. New employees must join the union within a specified period, normally 30 days. The majority of all union contracts specify union shop requirements.

An **agency shop** is a business with an employment agreement that allows it to hire all qualified employees, but nonunion workers must pay the union a fee equal to union dues. This agreement eliminates what the unions have labeled *free riders*, nonmembers who might benefit from union negotiations without supporting the union financially.

The **open shop,** the opposite of the closed shop, makes union membership voluntary for all existing and new employees. Individuals who choose not to join a union are not required to pay union dues or fees.

The Taft-Hartley Act permits states to pass **right-to-work laws** that prohibit union shops and outlaw compulsory union membership. Located mainly in the South and the Great Plains areas, Figure 11.1 identifies the 21 right-to-work states.

open shop
Employment policy making union membership and dues voluntary for all workers.

right-to-work laws
State laws that prohibit compulsory union membership.

OTHER UNFAIR LABOR PRACTICES

The Taft-Hartley Act outlaws unfair practices of unions, as well as employers, such as refusal to bargain with the employer, striking without 60 days' notice, most secondary boycotts, and featherbedding, or demanding pay for workers who do no work. Most writers cite the second brakeman on a diesel locomotive as a good current example of featherbedding. In one classic example, the British civil service created a job in 1803 for a worker to stand on the Cliffs of Dover with a spyglass and ring a bell if Napoleon approached. The job was abolished in 1945.

One of unions' most powerful weapons is the **boycott,** an attempt to prevent people from purchasing a firm's goods or services. The law identifies two kinds of boycotts: primary and secondary boycotts. In a *primary boycott,* union members urge people not to patronize a firm directly involved in a labor dispute. In contrast, a *secondary boycott* is intended to force an employer to stop dealing with another firm involved in a labor dispute. The union pressures an otherwise uninvolved party in order to force its real adversary into capitulating. The Taft-Hartley Act outlaws secondary boycotts deemed by the courts to be coercive.

boycott
Attempt to keep people from purchasing goods or services from a company as part of a labor dispute.

Taft-Hartley also allows employers to sue unions for breach of contract and to engage in antiunion activities as long as they do not become coercive. Unions must make financial reports to their members and disclose their officers' salaries; they cannot use dues to fund political contributions or charge excessive initiation fees. The act also provides for a cooling-off period—an 80-day suspension of threatened strikes that the president of the United States and the courts find "imperil the national health and safety." During this period, employees must return to work or continue working. At the end of the 80 days, union members must vote by secret ballot on the latest company offer.

FIGURE 11.1 STATES WITH RIGHT-TO-WORK LAWS

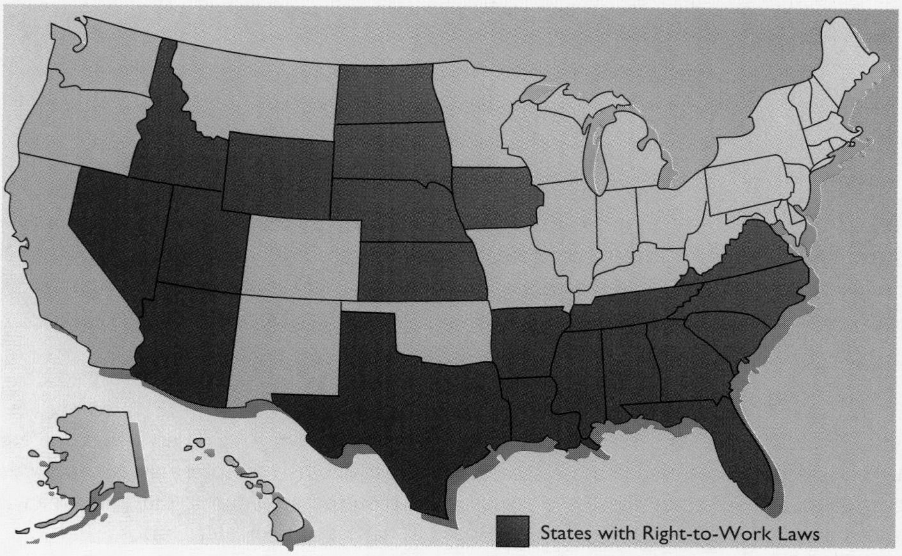

A BROADER PURPOSE

PURGING UNION ACTIVISTS

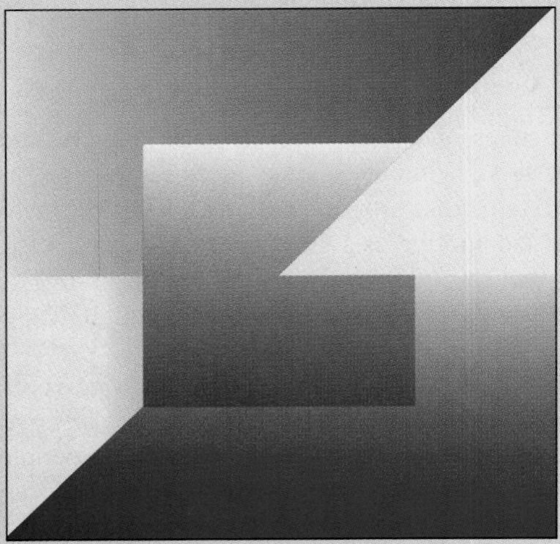

The wording of the 1935 Wagner Act, commonly regarded as organized labor's Magna Carta, seems clear: it is illegal to fire someone for exercising the legal right to "form, join, or assist" a labor union. The law failed to prevent Garney Morris from expressing his displeasure, however, when the International Brotherhood of Electrical Workers began an organizing drive among his employees. ■ Morris, a Bucks County, Pennsylvania electrical contractor, repeatedly threatened to close his business and even fired five electricians who supported the union. One National Labor Relations Board judge described Morris as running "a campaign of wholesale intimidation and coercion." In nearby Reading, Pennsylvania, Yerger Trucking owner Ronald Yerger faces charges of giving union supporters inferior equipment and undesirable routes and schedules. He prevented one employee from getting a mortgage by telling the lender that the driver was about to lose his job. Yerger even closed his company and reopened 12 days later under a different name. ■ Morris and Yerger's actions are not isolated events. Data collected by the Commission on the Future of Worker-Management Relations reveals that unlawful dismissals occur in 25 percent of all union drives and that firms illegally discharge at least 2,000 workers each year for participating in union campaigns. ■ How can apparently clear-cut violations of a 60-year-old federal law continue? The problem is that an employer found to have violated the Wagner Act faces no fines or criminal penalties. The law requires only that the firm rehire the worker with back pay minus any other income the worker may have earned during the time the case moves toward court. Additionally, the worker cannot sue for damages. As Teamster lawyer Walt DeTreux points out, "It's actually beneficial to the employer to discharge somebody. The organizing drive goes down the tubes. And then 2 years, 3 years later, the guy gets reinstated. The employer has to pay him back pay. But he's beaten the organizing drive." NLRB officials agree: "Experience has shown that a reinstatement-and-back-pay remedy is not an effective disincentive." ■ In spite of legislation and agencies like the NLRB, an increasing number of companies are determined to stay nonunion by any means necessary. With the rise in the number of firings resulting from organizing attempts, many unions are changing their approach to organizing activities. Teamsters Local 107 in Philadelphia no longer holds its campaigns in the open; no one is encouraged to wear hats, T-shirts, or buttons. Says William Hamilton, the chief organizer for the local, "We found out that secrecy and quickness are the way to go."

Source: Quotations from "American Businesses Still Purging Union Activists," *Mobile Register,* September 4, 1994, pp. 1F, 2F.

QUESTIONS FOR CRITICAL THINKING

1. What penalties do you think would make the Wagner Act more effective?
2. How do you think the law should be changed to better protect workers?
3. How might non-union companies discourage unionization without firing employees?

COLLECTIVE BARGAINING PROCESS

As its primary objective, a labor union seeks to improve wages, hours, and working conditions for its members. It works to achieve this goal primarily through **collective bargaining,** a process of negotiation between management and union representatives for the purpose of arriving at mutually acceptable terms for employees' wages and working conditions.

HOW EMPLOYEES FORM A UNION

collective bargaining
Negotiation between management and union representatives concerning wages and working conditions.

Before workers can form a union, they must conduct an organizing drive to collect the signatures of at least 30 percent of their fellow employees on special authorization cards. These cards designate the union as the employees' exclusive representative in bargaining with management. If the drive secures the required signatures, the union can then petition the National Labor Relations Board (NLRB) for an election. As Figure 11.2 describes, if more than 50 percent of the employees vote in favor of union representation, the union is certified.

FIGURE 11.2 STEPS TO START A UNION

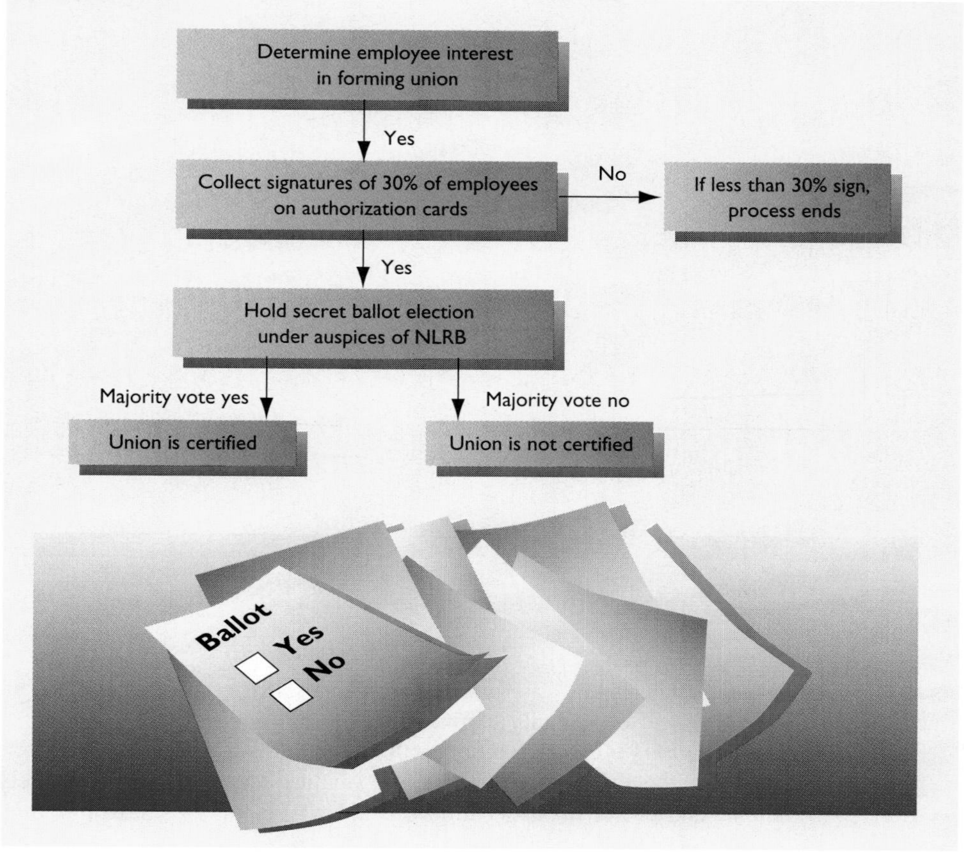

Once a majority of a firm's workers accept a union as their representative, the National Labor Relations Board certifies the union and the firm's management must recognize it as the legal collective bargaining agent for all employees. This sets the stage for union representatives and management to meet formally at the bargaining table to work out a collective bargaining agreement.

BARGAINING PATTERNS

Bargaining patterns and the number of unions and employers involved vary for different industries and occupational categories. Most collective bargaining involves *single-plant, single-employer agreements*. On the other hand, a *multiplant, single-employer agreement* applies to all plants operated by an employer. For example, terms and conditions approved in the bargaining agreement between Westinghouse Electric and the International Brotherhood of Electrical Workers apply to all Westinghouse plants. *Coalition bargaining* involves negotiations between a coalition of several unions that represent the employees of one company. In *industrywide bargaining,* a single national union engages in collective bargaining with several employers in a particular industry.

Disagreements between Caterpillar Tractor Co. and its 17,000 unionized employees over industrywide bargaining led to a long strike during the mid-1990s. Caterpillar opposed the United Auto Workers' attempt to apply industrywide bargaining agreements, arguing that its international operations forced it to compete in dozens of different countries around the globe, and this required a unique agreement between management and

United Auto Workers union strikers jeer workers who cross their picket line at a Caterpillar, Inc. manufacturing facility. Caterpillar has faced nearly continuous labor unrest since 1992 when the company objected to the UAW's attempt to negotiate a contract based on one in place at Deere & Co.

its employees. Says the chairman of Caterpillar, Donald Fites, "Is it worth signing a contract that won't allow you to be globally competitive?"[5]

In general, manufacturers prefer to bargain with one individual local union at a time rather than dealing with a coalition of several unions. Smaller, separate unions are likely to exert less influence and power than a coalition would wield.

BARGAINING ZONE

Issues covered in bargaining agreements include wages, work hours, benefits, union activities and responsibilities, grievance procedures and arbitration, and employee rights and seniority. As in all types of negotiations, the collective bargaining process features volleys of demands, proposals, and counterproposals that ultimately result in compromise and agreement. Figure 11.3 illustrates a contract negotiation focused on a single wage issue and two security issues, a union-shop provision and a seniority rule. The horizontal line represents a continuum of outcomes for union and management. The union's initial demand—its best outcome—is a 10 percent wage increase (based on productivity increases and increases in the cost of living) along with the addition of a union-shop provision. Management initially offers a 2 percent wage increase and elimination of current security rules. The initial demands represent merely starting points in the negotiations; they rarely, if ever, become final agreements.

As the figure reveals, each party identifies a final offer beyond which it will not bargain. In this case, if the union does not accept management's final offer of a 4 percent pay increase and no union shop, the union will strike. Likewise, if management rejects the union's final offer of an 8 percent increase and retention of the seniority rule, management will close the plant, move its operations, or bring new employees into its existing facility rather than agree to a settlement that would make it unprofitable.

bargaining zone
Range of collective bargaining that defines when a union will strike and when management will close the plant.

Between each party's initial and final offers, however, lies the **bargaining zone,** a gray area of possibility within which both parties will likely come to agreement. The final agreement depends on the negotiating skills and relative power of management and union representatives.

FIGURE 11.3 BARGAINING ZONE

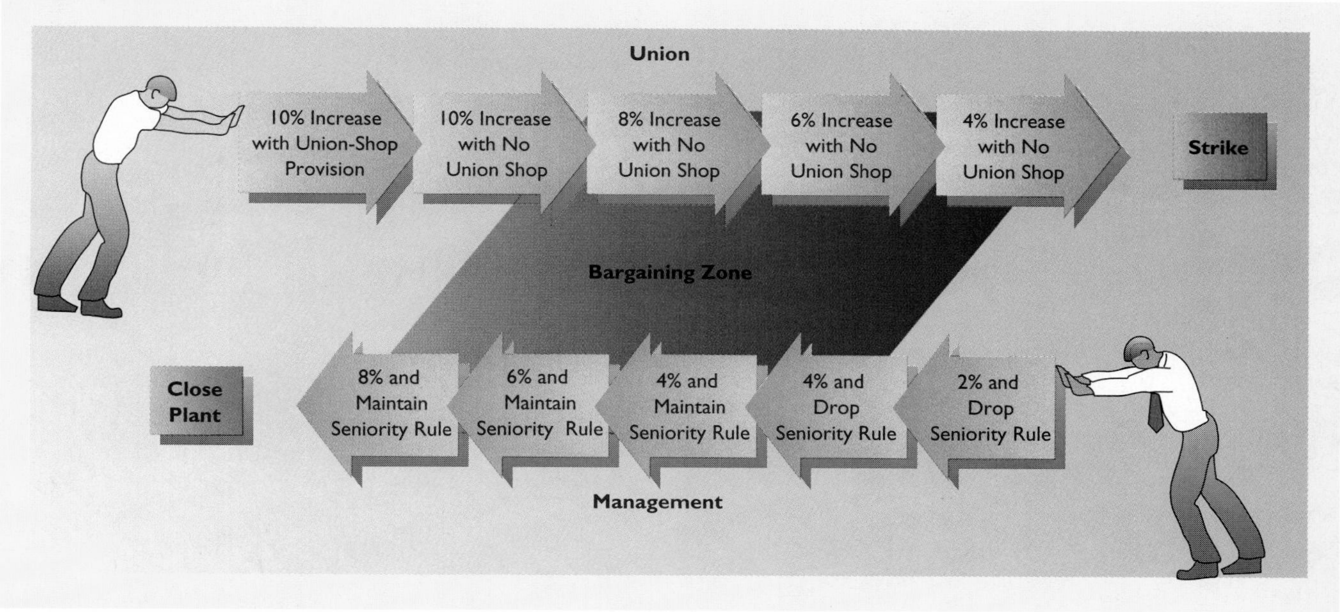

UNION CONTRACTS

A union contract typically covers a 2-year or 3-year period. Such an agreement often represents days and even weeks of discussion, disagreement, compromise, and eventual agreement. Once the negotiators reach agreement, union members must vote to accept or reject the contract. If they reject the contract, union representatives may resume the bargaining process with management representatives, or the union members may strike to try to obtain their demands.

Once ratified by the union membership, the contract becomes a legally binding agreement that governs all labor-management relations during the period specified. Union contracts typically cover such areas as wages, industrial relations, and the methods for settlement of labor-management disputes. Some fill only a few pages, while others run more than 200 pages. Figure 11.4 indicates topics typically included in a union contract.

In the mid-1990s, workers at United Parcel Service (UPS) waged the company's first-ever nationwide strike to protest changes in work rules that they felt violated the principles of their union contract. In recent years, new technologies and global competition have pushed UPS to become more productive. The company lost significant market share to Federal Express after FedEx established a computer network that could track and locate a package at any point during the delivery cycle. Price competition from nonunion rivals such as Roadway Package Services (RPS) forced UPS to add services without raising its rates.

The productivity push angered some UPS employees, who felt the company was starting to expect too much. In a recent bid to compete against Federal Express, for example, UPS expanded its guarantee of delivery by 10:30 A.M. to cover most of the country. Some drivers complained that the new policy forced them to deliver air packages first and then double back to make their regular deliveries. They contended that the rise in the volume of package deliveries by 30 to 60 packages daily forced them to drive faster, work more overtime, and skimp on safety checks. Said driver Mario Rojas of Kansas City, Missouri, "The heavy day used to be Wednesday. Now it's all week."

FIGURE 11.4 TYPICAL PROVISIONS IN A UNION CONTRACT

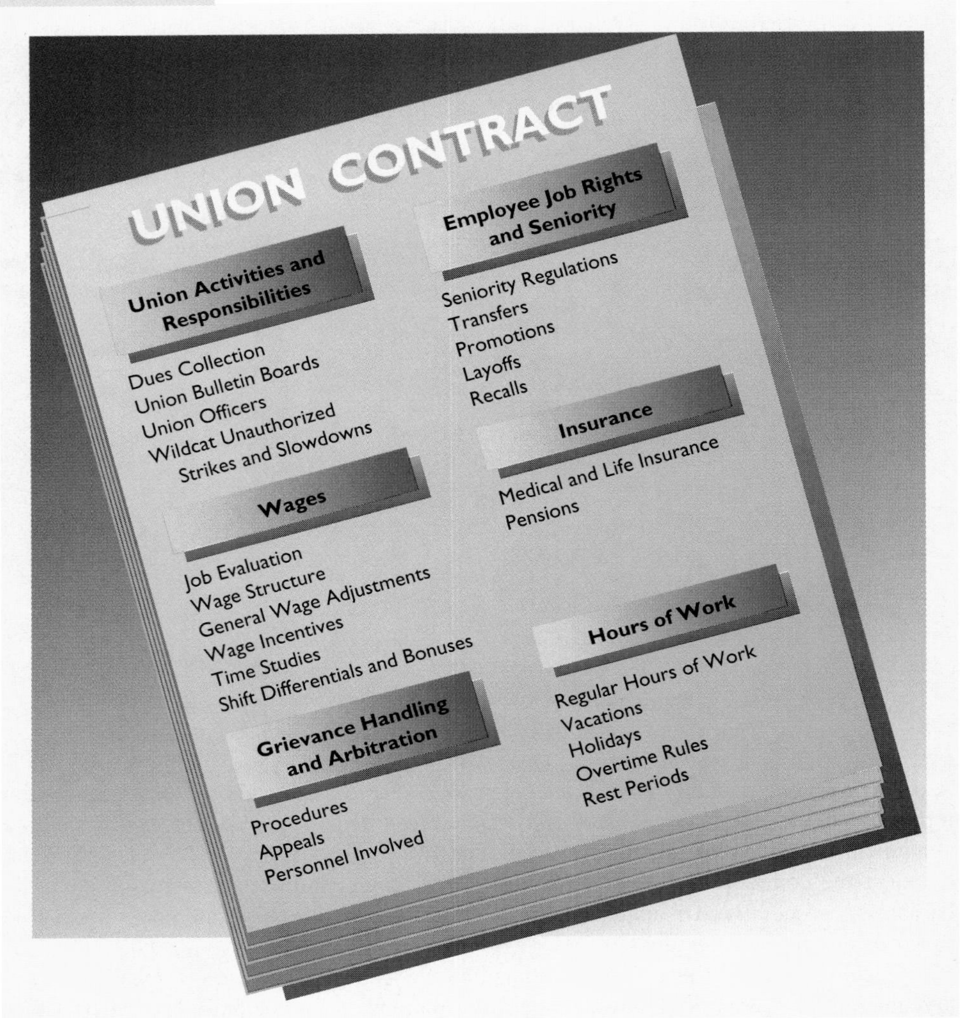

More conflicts ignited when management tried to expand UPS's share of the light trucking market by raising its maximum package weight from 70 pounds to 150 pounds. Drivers and sorters, concerned that the new guidelines would lead to back injuries, complained to the federal Occupational Safety and Health Administration (OSHA). OSHA investigated and cited the UPS hub in Columbus for a safety violation.

While UPS managers admitted asking more from employees, they insisted that the company needed to change to remain competitive. Workers acknowledged the competitive pressures facing the company, but worried about how many more changes they would be asked to make. "The issues at UPS are going to become more common as companies enter the productivity race," says William Morin, chairman of consulting firm Drake Beam Morin. "It's a very tough balancing act."[6]

WAGE ADJUSTMENTS IN LABOR CONTRACTS

In addition to setting wages during contract negotiations, labor and management often agree to provisions for wage adjustments during the life of the contract. Some adjustments, such as cost-of-living adjustments (COLAs) and wage reopeners, can benefit employees; others, such as givebacks, can benefit the organization.

During periods of rising prices, unions support rising wage demands by arguing that an increase in the cost of living without an offsetting wage increase amounts to a cut in real wages and a drop in purchasing power. Consequently, unions and management must agree on an indicator for the cost of living. Usually, they settle on the *consumer price index (CPI)* as determined by the Bureau of Labor Statistics. The CPI tracks the costs of such items as housing, clothing, food, and automobiles. The union and management must negotiate the base period, the starting date, and the CPI most appropriate for the contract's calculations. Management receives nothing in return for this wage increase since it does not reflect a change in employees' productivity.

Approximately 30 percent of all organized workers are currently covered by contracts with **cost-of-living adjustment (COLA) clauses,** also called *escalator clauses.* Such clauses are designed to protect the real incomes of workers during periods of inflation by increasing wages in proportion to increases in the CPI. A low inflation rate during the past few years has diminished the importance of COLA clauses in labor contracts. COLA provisions are becoming more common, not only in labor agreements, but also outside the collective bargaining arena. For example, benefits for 31 million Social Security recipients and 2.5 million military and civil service retirees now rise automatically with inflation. An estimated 50 million U.S. citizens now have their incomes adjusted by some automatic COLA.

cost-of-living adjustment (COLA) clause
Clause in a union contract that protects workers' real income by adjusting wages to reflect changes in the consumer price index; also called an escalator clause.

Wage reopener clauses, another method of achieving wage adjustments, allow contract parties to re-negotiate wages at a predetermined date during the life of the contract. Reopener clauses are written into almost 10 percent of all labor contracts.

Attention of both union and nonunion employees in recent years has focused sharply on the nation's balance of trade deficit and how well U.S. companies compete in world markets. As one tangible response, unions in many major industries have allowed **givebacks**—wage and employee-benefit concessions to help employers to remain competitive and to continue to provide jobs for union members.

giveback
Wage or fringe benefit concession by union members to help an employer to remain competitive.

Givebacks have become common in industries fighting off competition from abroad including autos, rubber manufacturing, steel mills, cement, agricultural and construction equipment, and meatpacking. They have also occurred in such industries as airlines, trucking, and telecommunications, where deregulation forced firms to become more cost-conscious to remain competitive.

Wage adjustments and givebacks raise controversy in other countries, too. Through the years, Germany's powerful unions have negotiated generous wage increases, and German workers are now the highest-paid employees in the world. Figure 11.5 compares industrial labor costs for Germany, the United States, France, Japan, and Great Britain.

FIGURE 11.5 WELL-PAID GERMAN WORKERS

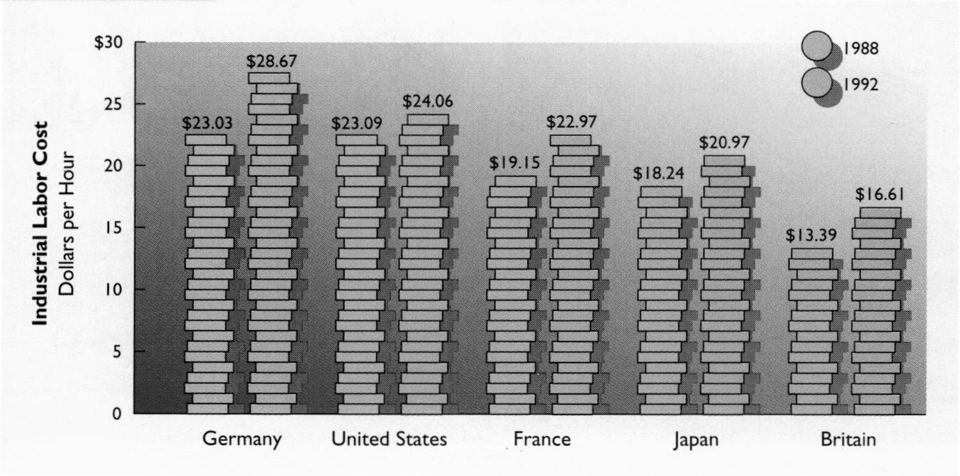

I.G. Metall, Germany's largest labor union, recently voted to pursue a 26 percent wage increase for members in eastern Germany to bring their pay more into line with that of western German workers. Employers, for their part, asked union members for givebacks that would lower the raises to 9 percent, just enough to cover inflation in that part of the country.[7]

SETTLING UNION-MANAGEMENT DISPUTES

Although strikes make newspaper headlines, 95 percent of all union-management negotiations result in signed agreements without work stoppages. Approximately 140,000 union contracts are currently in force in the United States. Of these, 133,000 emerged from successful negotiations with no work stoppages. The courts are the most visible and familiar vehicle for dispute settlement, but negotiation settles most labor disputes. Both sides feel real motivation to make a negotiation work, since each invests so much time, money, and personnel costs in court settlements. Other dispute resolution mechanisms such as mediation, fact-finding, and arbitration are quicker, cheaper, less complicated procedurally, and generate less publicity.

MEDIATION

mediation
Process of settling union-management disputes through recommendations of an impartial third party.

When negotiations break down between union and management, they sometimes resort to a voluntary negotiation process to settle disputes. This **mediation** process brings in a third party, called a *mediator,* to make recommendations for the settlement of differences. In 1994, W. J. Usery served as a mediator in an effort to reach an agreement between major league baseball team owners and striking players.

The Taft-Hartley Act requires union representatives and management to notify each other of desired changes in a union contract 60 days before it expires. They must also notify a special agency, the Federal Mediation and Conciliation Service, within 30 days

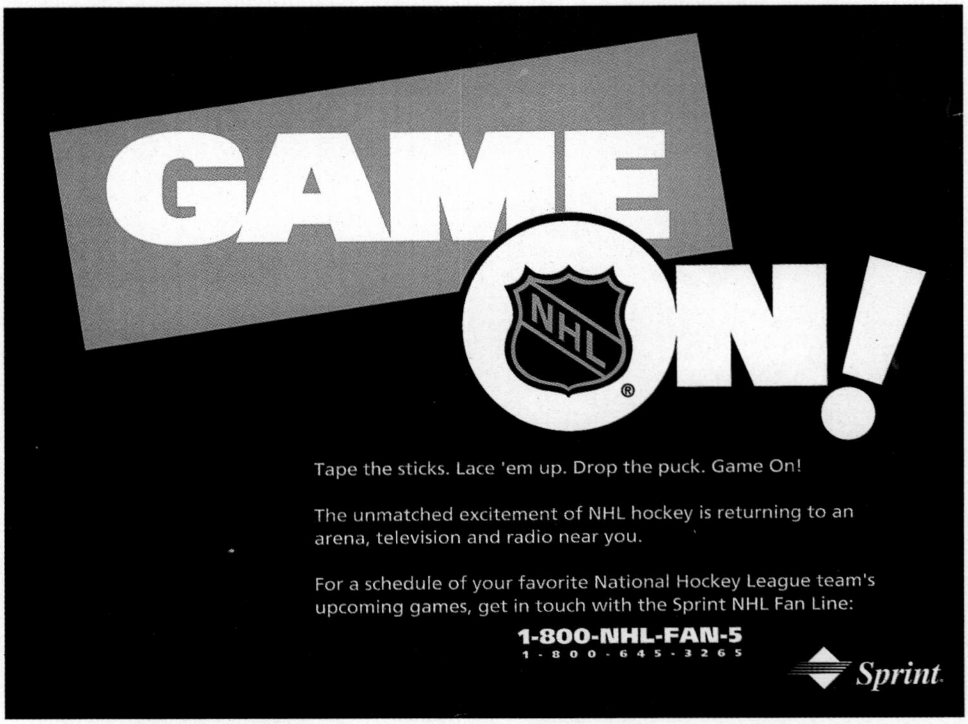

At the end of the National Hockey League dispute that shortened the 1994–95 season, Sprint ran this ad proclaiming the sport's return and providing fans with the Sprint NHL telephone number for schedule information. After a three-and-a-half month lockout, players accepted salary limits for rookies, limits on free agency, and reduced arbitration rights. Team owners, in turn, gave up demands for a cap on salaries and a luxury tax on payrolls.

after that time if workers have not accepted a new contract. The agency's staff of several hundred mediators assists in settling union-management disagreements that affect interstate commerce. In addition, some states, among them New York, Pennsylvania, and California, operate their own mediation agencies.

Although the mediator does not serve as a decision maker, he or she can assist union and management representatives in reaching an agreement by offering suggestions, advice, and compromise solutions. Because both sides must give their confidence and trust to the mediator, that person's impartiality is essential. Community social or political leaders, attorneys, professors, and distinguished national figures often serve as mediators.

ARBITRATION

When parties cannot resolve disputes voluntarily through mediation, they begin the process of **arbitration**—bringing in an impartial third party called an *arbitrator* to render a binding decision in the dispute. Both the union and management must approve the impartial third party, and his or her decision is legally enforceable. In essence, the arbitrator acts as a judge, making a decision after listening to both sides of the argument. In *voluntary arbitration*, both union and management representatives decide to present their unresolved issues to an impartial third party. Arbitration provisions appear in 90 percent of all union contracts to resolve issues on which union and management representatives fail to agree.

arbitration
Process of bringing an impartial third party into a union-management dispute to render a legally binding decision.

Occasionally, a third party, usually the federal government, will require management and labor to submit to *compulsory arbitration*. Although it remains rare in the United States, considerable interest focuses on compulsory arbitration as a means of eliminating prolonged strikes in major industries that threaten to disrupt the economy.

Arbitrators have often resolved disputes between professional baseball players and team owners. In 1975, pitcher Andy Messersmith challenged the game's longstanding reserve system, which reserved rights to an athlete's services as one team's exclusive property. Messersmith refused to sign his contract, insisting that he should be able to

American Airlines flight attendants, members of the Association of Professional Flight Attendants, celebrate the end of their Thanksgiving 1993 strike. The strike ended when President Clinton persuaded American Airlines chairman Robert L. Crandall to accept binding arbitration.

play for any ball club, and the players' union supported him. The dispute came before an arbitrator who agreed with Messersmith; this ruling made baseball players with specified years of major league experience free agents.

Another baseball dispute came up for arbitration during the 1980s when team owners attempted to control soaring player salaries by agreeing not to hire those who asked for high fees. Union leaders complained that the owners were violating the labor contract by acting in collusion. Again, an arbitrator agreed and awarded affected players $280 million in damages.

Recent salary disagreements in the sports arena have created still more business for mediators and arbitrators. Players cite fierce competition and short professional careers and insist that they are entitled to salaries that reflect these facts. Says Bret Boone, second baseman for the Cincinnati Reds, "I believe that if you're the best at something in the world you should be paid accordingly."[8] Team owners worry, however, that sports revenues are likely to taper off, and they view players' demands as unrealistic. Baseball players and team owners continued to reject each other's offers during the 1994 season until finally the players went on strike.

GRIEVANCE PROCEDURES

A union contract guides relations between the firm's management and its employees and states the rights of each party. No contract, regardless of how detailed it is, can eliminate the possibility of later disagreement, though.

Differences of opinion may arise, for example, on how to interpret a particular clause in the contract. Management may interpret a contract's layoff policy as based on seniority for each work shift. The union may see it as based on the seniority of all employees. Over half of the contract disagreements that occur each year involve employee suspensions, transfers, and terminations; seniority; and vacation and work schedules.

grievance
Employee or union complaint that management is violating some provision of the union contract.

Such a difference can generate a **grievance,** a complaint, by a single worker or the entire union, that management is violating some provision of the union contract. Because grievance handling is the primary source of contact between union officials and management between contract negotiations, the resolution of grievances plays a major role in the parties' relationship.

Since grievances are likely to arise over such matters as transfers, work assignments, and seniority, almost all union contracts require that workers submit these complaints to formal grievance procedures. Figure 11.6 shows the five steps in a typical grievance procedure. The employee first submits the grievance to the immediate supervisor through the shop steward, the union's representative in the organization. If the supervisor solves the problem, it goes no further. If this first step produces no satisfactory agreement, however, a higher union official may take the grievance to a higher manager. If the highest company officer cannot settle the grievance, an outside arbitrator makes a final, binding decision.

WEAPONS OF UNIONS AND MANAGEMENT

Although labor and management settle most differences through the collective bargaining process or through formal grievance procedures, both unions and management occasionally resort to weapons of power to make their demands known.

UNION WEAPONS

strike
Employees' temporary work stoppage until a dispute is settled or a contract signed.

The chief weapons of unions are strikes, picketing, and boycotts. In a **strike** or *walkout,* one of the most effective tools of the labor union, employees precipitate a temporary work stoppage until a dispute has been settled or a contract signed. Since a company does not pay striking workers, the union generally establishes a fund to provide workers' wages, allowing them to continue striking without financial hardship.

FIGURE 11.6 STEPS IN THE GRIEVANCE PROCEDURE

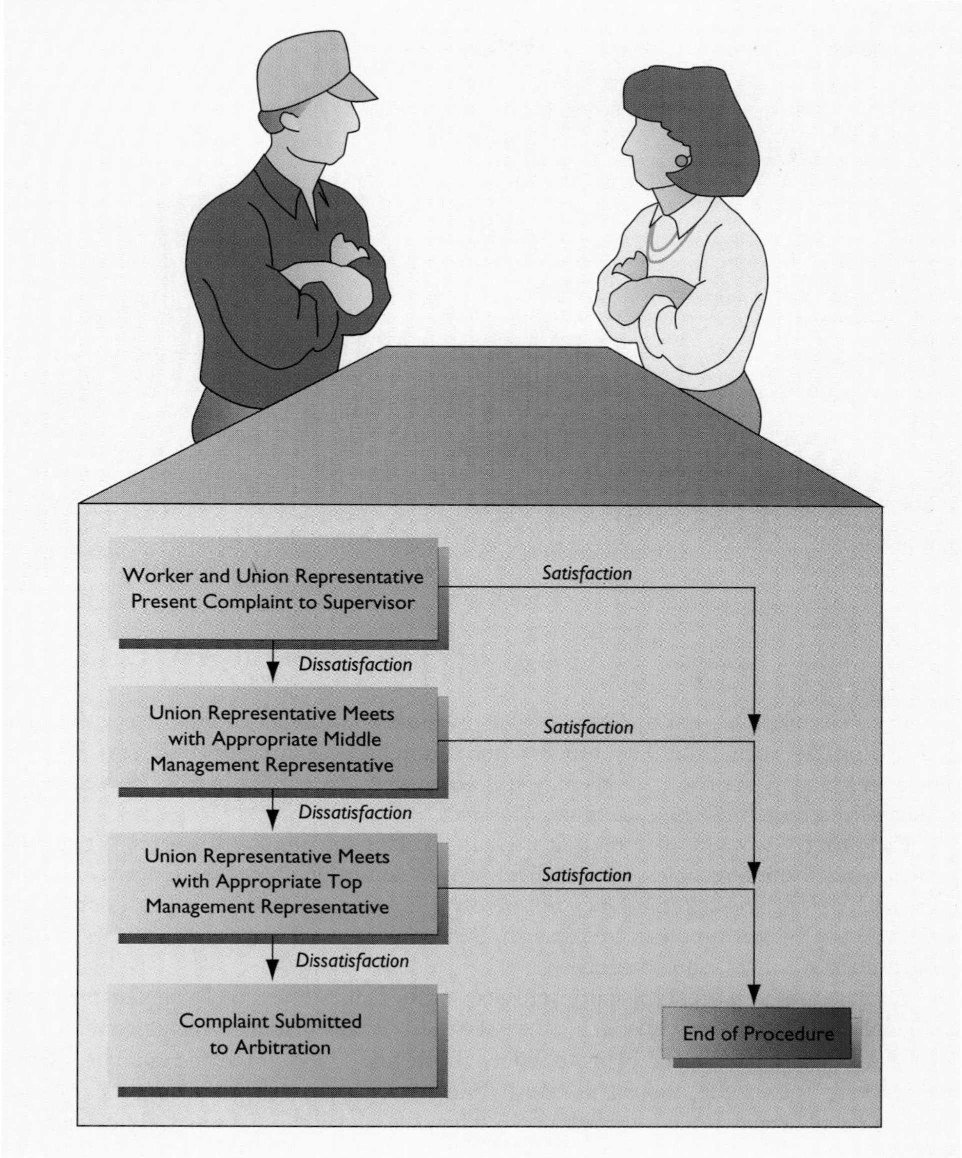

Although the power to strike represents unions' ultimate weapon, they do not wield it lightly. The UPS strike described earlier was the company's first walkout in its 90-year history. While the strike lasted only 1 day, it was expensive. UPS estimates that it cost the company more than $100 million in lost business and added expenses.[9]

Not all union members can resort to strikes or threats of strikes. Even though federal employees have been permitted to join unions and bargain collectively since 1962, they are not allowed to strike. Each federal civilian employee takes a no-strike pledge when hired. A decade ago, the nation's air traffic controllers went on strike to reinforce their contract demands, and President Ronald Reagan dismissed them. His decision was based on arguments shown on the right side of Figure 11.7. By contrast, those who believe that all employees deserve the right to strike voice the arguments shown on the left side of the table.

FIGURE 11.7 PUBLIC EMPLOYEES AND THE RIGHT TO STRIKE

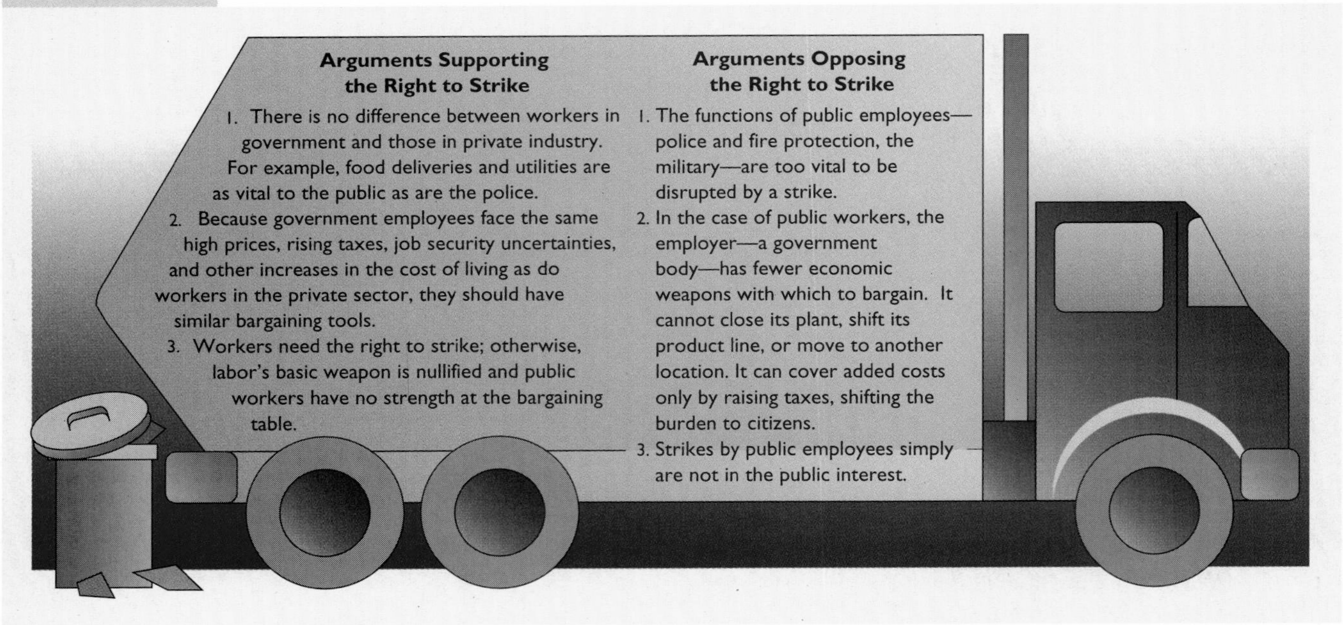

Arguments Supporting the Right to Strike
1. There is no difference between workers in government and those in private industry. For example, food deliveries and utilities are as vital to the public as are the police.
2. Because government employees face the same high prices, rising taxes, job security uncertainties, and other increases in the cost of living as do workers in the private sector, they should have similar bargaining tools.
3. Workers need the right to strike; otherwise, labor's basic weapon is nullified and public workers have no strength at the bargaining table.
Arguments Opposing the Right to Strike
1. The functions of public employees—police and fire protection, the military—are too vital to be disrupted by a strike.
2. In the case of public workers, the employer—a government body—has fewer economic weapons with which to bargain. It cannot close its plant, shift its product line, or move to another location. It can cover added costs only by raising taxes, shifting the burden to citizens.
3. Strikes by public employees simply are not in the public interest.

In some instances, laws prohibit strikes by state and municipal employees. In these cases, workers such as police officers and firefighters, sanitation workers, hospital employees, and even prison guards may still go on strike by calling in sick. Hence, police strikes have come to be known as the *blue flu.*

picketing
Workers marching at a plant entrance to protest some management practice.

Picketing—workers marching at the entrances of the employer's plant as a public protest against some management practice—gives unions another effective way to apply pressure. As long as picketing does not involve violence or intimidation, it is protected under the U.S. Constitution as free speech. Picketing may accompany a strike, or it may protest alleged unfair labor practices.

Because union workers usually refuse to cross picket lines, the picketed firm may be unable to obtain deliveries and other services. When management at government-owned Air France announced plans to reduce the airline's work force and cut some workers' wages, for example, thousands of Air France employees picketed airports in Paris. The government was forced to back down when the picketing disrupted flights and airport operations.[10]

As defined earlier, a boycott is an organized attempt to keep the public from purchasing the goods or services of a firm. Some unions have organized remarkably successful boycotts, and some unions even fine members who defy primary boycotts.

Although the Taft-Hartley Act outlaws coercive secondary boycotts, Supreme Court rulings have significantly expanded the rights of unions to use this weapon. Although they cannot picket a firm to force it to stop dealing with another company involved in a labor dispute, the court protected other forms of expression, such as distributing handbills at the site of the first firm.

MANAGEMENT WEAPONS

lockout
Management shutdown of a firm to pressure union members.

Management has its own weapons for dealing with organized labor. In the past, firms have used the **lockout**—in effect, a management strike to bring pressure on union members by closing the firm. Firms rarely lock out workers today unless a union strike has partially shut down a plant. In 1994, National Hockey League team owners resorted to a lockout to pressure NHL players into signing a new bargaining agreement. The result was similar to the major league baseball strike—a suspension of part of the 1994–1995 playing season before NHL owners and players reached an agreement in early 1995 and play resumed.

In recent years, managers at organizations ranging from International Paper Company to the National Football League have resorted to replacing striking workers with **strikebreakers,** nonunion workers who cross picket lines to fill the jobs of striking workers. Firms find it less difficult to recruit strikebreakers in high-status fields such as professional football and in high-paying industries located in areas of high unemployment. Nevertheless, even in favorable conditions, management frequently encounters difficulties in securing sufficient numbers of replacement workers with required skills. Some employers have resorted to reassigning supervisory personnel and other nonunion employees to continue operations during strikes.

strikebreaker
Nonunion worker hired to replace a striking worker.

Attempts to bust unions can backfire on management, so a recent trend has led toward cooperative relationships between labor and management. After Japan's NKK Corp. bought 70 percent of U.S. steel maker National Steel Corp., for instance, the company set up a cooperative relationship with its union workers. Managers established a no-layoff policy for all 9,500 union members who had at least 1 year's seniority, and they moved hourly workers into supervisory positions. Company managers also shared data on earnings and market conditions with union workers. This unusual level of cooperation paid off in higher productivity; in 6 years, the number of hours necessary to make a ton of steel at National's plants fell by 33 percent. These days, National Steel's ads proclaim, "We're partners with labor because we can't imagine a future without them."[11]

Management sometimes obtains an **injunction**—a court order prohibiting some practice—to prevent excessive picketing or certain unfair union practices. Before passage of the Norris-La Guardia Act, firms frequently used injunctions to prohibit all types of strikes. Since then, court orders have been limited to restraining violence, restricting picketing, and preventing damage to company property.

injunction
Court order prohibiting some union or management practice.

Some employers have formed **employers' associations** to cooperate in their efforts and present a united front in dealing with labor unions. Employers' associations may even act as negotiators for individual employers that want to reach agreements with labor unions. An industry characterized by many, small firms and a single, large union may follow an increasing tendency for industrywide bargaining between the union and a single representative of the industry employers. Building contractors may bargain as a group with construction unions, for example. Although they do not negotiate contracts, the National Association of Manufacturers and the United States Chamber of Commerce are examples of employers' associations. Both groups promote the views of their members on key issues.

employers' association
Organization that encourages cooperative efforts by employers to present a united front in dealing with labor unions.

LABOR-MANAGEMENT RELATIONS IN NONUNIONIZED ORGANIZATIONS

Although unionization is an implicit assumption in almost any discussion of labor-management relations, unions represent less than one in six U.S. workers. A very small business may employ only a handful of nonunion workers. Another portion of the nonunionized segment of the U.S. labor force consists of managerial employees. Other nonunion employees work in industries where unions have never become strong. Still other nonunion employees have simply rejected attempts to establish unions in their workplaces.

Management often chooses to offer a compensation and benefit structure comparable to those of unionized firms in the area. Willingness to offer comparable wages and working conditions coupled with effective communications, emphasis on promotions from within, and employee participation in goal setting and grievance handling may help an employer to avert unionization by convincing workers that they would receive few additional benefits for the union dues they would have to pay. In fact, many argue that the threat of joining a union gives nonunion employees an effective tool in securing desired wages, benefits, and working conditions.

EMPLOYEE GRIEVANCES IN NONUNION FIRMS

peer-review board
Committee of peer workers and management representatives with the power to make binding decisions to resolve disputes over promotion decisions, dismissals, and other disciplinary actions.

Employee grievance systems in nonunion companies typically follow the same step-by-step approach as those in unionized firms. To ensure that employees receive fair treatment in disputes over firings, promotions, and disciplinary actions, a growing number of firms are instituting **peer-review boards** to resolve these disputes. Major companies such as Federal Express, Digital Equipment, General Electric, Citicorp, and Borg-Warner rely on peer boards, typically consisting of three worker peers and two management representatives.

An effective grievance procedure generally includes the following elements:

- The grievance procedure should follow written policies and procedures, and every employee should receive a copy.
- Grievances should be settled at the lowest possible organizational level, preferably between the employee and the supervisor.
- The grievance procedure should follow a series of distinct steps; each stage should exhaust all possible solutions before progressing to the next step.

If a dispute moves through all the steps of the grievance procedure without resolution, it should go to an arbitrator or a peer-review board.[12] Peer-review boards side with management's position in an estimated 60 to 70 percent of all cases. Still, they contribute valuable input toward building an open, trusting atmosphere. They can help management to deter union organizing and, perhaps most importantly, stem the rising number of costly legal claims for wrongful discharge and discrimination.

The need for worker protection provided by labor unions diminishes considerably in a firm where management and employees cooperate to build a Theory Z-type organi-

At National Steel Corporation, the United Steelworkers union represents employees. Company and union cooperation led to job guarantees for workers and the expansion of worker teams and empowerment systems to improve productivity.

zation. Delta Airlines is an excellent example of more than 100 major U.S. corporations that have worked to cement good labor-management relations by eliminating layoffs. Other well-known firms with programs to protect employees against layoffs include Federal Express, S. C. Johnson, Lincoln Electric, and Digital Equipment. Motorola's no-layoff policy applies to employees with at least 10 years' service.

JOB SECURITY IN NONUNION COMPANIES

Security has always been a primary motivation for workers to form labor unions. Common security clauses in bargaining agreements protect seniority rights. Also, pension programs are important benefits of union affiliation.

In recent years, Japanese management styles have made countless headlines. Numerous articles and books have extolled various Japanese policies, among them the practice of guaranteeing lifetime security for workers. The stories have not presented the total picture, though; only about 20 percent of Japanese employees actually enjoy lifetime job security, and the recent recession has endangered even their jobs.

Japan Airlines (JAL), for instance, plans to reduce its work force by about 4,300 full-time employees over the next 4 years—roughly 20 percent of its work force. The airline's managers are trying to avoid layoffs by offering workers as much as $600,000 each to quit. Many of these Japanese workers will probably lose their places to foreign employees who will earn as much as 50 percent less than their remaining Japanese coworkers. The airline began hiring non-Japanese flight attendants, for instance, 2 years ago, and managers estimate that by 1988, 28 percent of flight attendants will come from outside Japan. Wage costs on flights that include foreign staffers average an economical 4 percent of total costs, compared to a stiff 12 percent for all-Japanese crews.

JAL is not alone in its attempt to cut staff. A recent survey notes that about half of the companies listed on the Tokyo Stock Exchange have reduced their payrolls. Some units of Toshiba, Sanyo, NEC, and Matsushita have laid off workers. Only 2 percent of Japanese merchant ships still have completely Japanese staffs. For every two Japanese sailors, these ships employ three Koreans or Filipinos.[13]

In the United States, the 1990s have witnessed declining job security for both white-collar and blue-collar employees. Among many reasons, employment has declined due to competition, reorganization, elimination of unnecessary management layers, and installation of labor-saving technology. Only a relative handful of companies with more than 1,000 employees, such as S. C. Johnson and Lincoln Electric, still maintain no-layoff policies. For more than a century, U.S. employers have responded to declining sales and profit margins by cutting what they considered an expendable resource—labor. Even though many U.S. managers believe that job security can improve productivity, few have acted to implement job security policies.

A notable exception is Lincoln Electric Co. in Euclid, Ohio, which has not laid off a single employee since 1951. The no-layoff policy protects all full-time workers who have been with the firm 3 years or more. When a sales slump idles workers, the firm transfers them internally to other positions, for which the company trains them. During one recession, for example, 15 percent of Lincoln's employees made internal transfers.[14]

Instead of no-layoff guarantees, firms may offer incentives for early retirement and resignation. These reductions in the work force have separated hundreds of thousands of workers over the past few years, allowing companies to cut staff without resorting to layoffs. Although such a program may cost the employer some of its most highly qualified and experienced workers, the change often replaces older workers with younger employees who receive lower wages. At the same time, rewarding senior employees with early retirement bonuses is likely to enhance overall employee morale, in contrast to the destructive effects of a decision to lay off workers.

STRENGTH IN DIVERSITY

SIGNS OF LIFE IN UNIONS AROUND THE GLOBE Cheap imports have devastated the U.S. steel industry and membership in the United Steelworkers union fell by 600,000. German heavy manufacturing industries have the highest labor costs in the world today. The North American Free Trade Agreement has cost jobs in the Canadian paper industry. French electronics workers are losing jobs as domestic manufacturers relocate to low-wage nations, and the Italian computer industry is suffering from high labor costs, as well. ■ In spite of all these factors—and the widespread belief among many that organized labor is rapidly becoming a dinosaur—unions have begun to revamp their basic organizational goals to better serve their members. Even in Europe, where unions have traditionally been strong, they are addressing new issues that reflect dynamic economic and social changes. ■ In 1994, U.S. labor unions received good news: the first annual membership growth in 14 years. Union membership increased by over 200,000 workers in spite of downsizing, international competition, and free trade agreements. Says U.S. Labor Secretary Robert Reich, "Organized labor's goals—that is, more jobs and better jobs and health care and safer working conditions—are exactly the same goals as working Americans have generally." ■ Around the globe, union reports are not as bright. In Argentina, labor leaders have traditionally been respected for, if nothing else, their power. Today, however, most Argentineans see union officials as corrupt and inept. Says one political analyst who studies organized labor, "They've lost their power and their credibility, and it's hard to imagine they'll get it back." Of the country's 14-million-member work force, the General Confederation of Workers claimed 4 million members just 2 decades ago. Today, the GCW has split into three factions, losing over 1 million members. ■ Labor unions and leaders in European Union nations face similar problems. They no longer exercise the immense control over business negotiations that they once did. Labor leaders in the world's most industrialized nations are struggling to save jobs. One-half billion new workers will enter the world's labor pool during this decade, 90 percent of them in nations such as China and Mexico where wages are low and unions are scarce. ■ Global competition has affected the traditional work forces of many nations. Almost one-quarter of American and European workers are employed by multinational corporations that can move their operations anywhere. The problem, as one expert points out, is that "Capital can go anywhere. Labor cannot. Labor has been outmaneuvered." ■ One of the greatest strengths of organized labor in the world's richest countries is the ability to raise the productivity of union workers by keeping them trained with the newest technology and by redesigning work processes. A highly trained and highly paid union worker is more valuable to a company in the long-run than a poorly trained and poorly paid worker. Sources: "Unions Showing Signs of Bouncing Back," *Mobile Press Register,* September 5, 1994. p. 7B; "Unions Lose Power, Respect in Argentina," *Mobile Press Register,* March 23, 1994, p. 2E; and David Hage, "Unions Feel the Heat," *U.S. News & World Report,* January 24, 1994, pp. 57–62..

QUESTIONS FOR CRITICAL THINKING

1. Why do you think membership in unions declined for so many years?
2. Assume you are operating your own business that requires a factory for manufacturing. Would you encourage unionization? Why or why not?
3. What would happen to countries such as Mexico and China if their labor forces became unionized?

WORKER OWNERSHIP OF COMPANIES

As the ultimate step in convincing employees of their stake in the continuing prosperity of the firm, worker ownership gives them a financial share in their employer. During the past decade, more than 9,000 *employee stock ownership plans (ESOPs)* have emerged across the nation. ESOPs have helped to save failing businesses and to motivate employees in healthy firms to increase their productivity.

While ESOP programs have been most popular with small companies, they have also appeared in some large firms, such as JCPenney, Avis, United Airlines, and Procter & Gamble. Many companies that establish ESOPs find that they boost employee morale and productivity; employees feel motivated to work harder because, as part owners of the business, they share in its gains and losses.

One of the largest employee-owned firms is Science Applications International, a high-tech research and engineering company in which 9,500 of its 15,000 employees own stock. When a company does well, an ESOP program can prove highly profitable for employee shareholders; one Science Applications technician recently retired with stock worth $300,000.[15]

However, a worker takeover does not guarantee success. Employees own 45 percent of TWA, but the airline continues to struggle with failing cash reserves and a long-term debt of $1.8 billion. Employee owners have seen the value of their TWA stock decline 37 percent in 10 months. Still, managers worry that TWA's employee owners will refuse to lay off fellow workers in order to pare costs. "There is a reluctance to furlough at an employee-owned airline," says Glenn Zander, a former vice chairman. "People think they bought their jobs, and they don't want to find out differently." Some business analysts believe that it is unfair to judge employee ownership based on TWA's example. They feel that TWA's financial troubles reflect unwise management decisions made before the employee buyout.[16]

FUTURE OF ORGANIZED LABOR

Despite their valuable contributions to business, the future role of labor unions is unclear. As noted earlier, unions represent less than one U.S. worker in six—roughly 17 million people. As shown in Figure 11.8, this represents a huge decline since 1977, when 26.2 percent of the labor force was unionized. Union membership has declined 6 percent over the past decade alone, and labor experts predict that it will fall still further during the first decades of the 21st century.[17]

A number of forces have contributed to the decline in unions. They include the shift from a manufacturing economy to a service economy, changes in organizational practices, a shift in favor of free-market ideologies, and labor legislation.

The United States has rapidly advanced beyond the large, unionized work forces of manufacturing industries into new, high-tech industries characterized by many competing firms, each with fewer employees than the manufacturing giants and more difficult to unionize. The blue-collar ranks, the source of union membership strength in the past, have suffered from company decisions to lower wage rates and from moves to automate production facilities, both in the United States and abroad.

KFC Corporation managers check stock in the cafeteria of Puerto Rico's Universidad Metropolitana. KFC, part of PepsiCo, manages the cafeteria. All PepsiCo Inc. employees can participate in the company's employee stock option plan (ESOP). Many companies have found ESOPs an effective way to reward employees and improve productivity.

FIGURE 11.8 DECLINE OF UNIONS AND WAGES

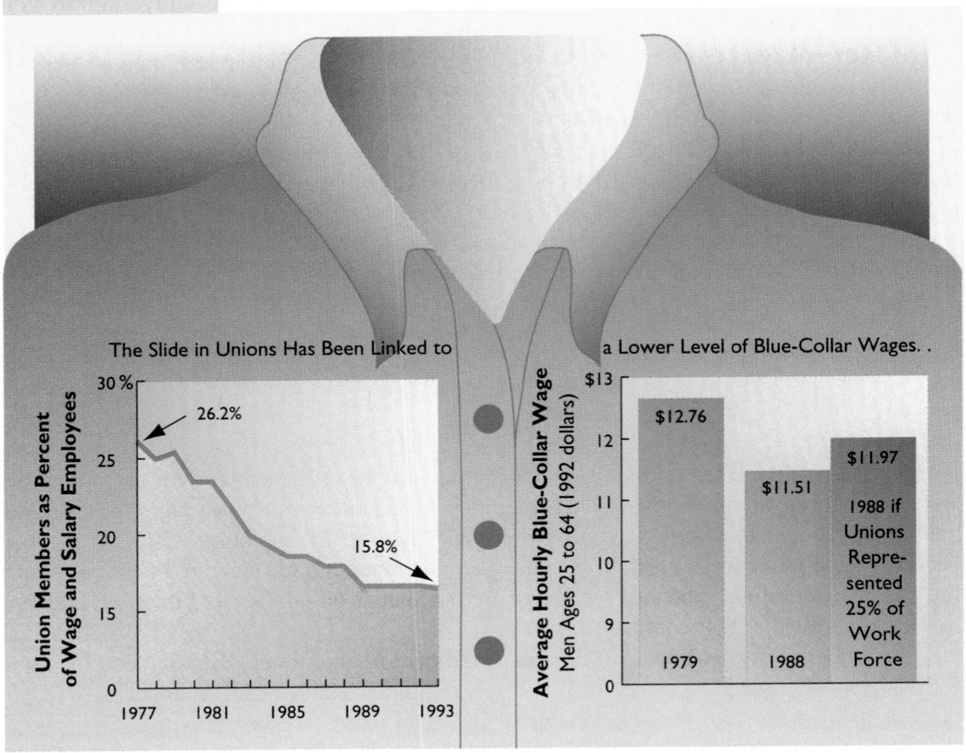

Unions outside the United States also face declining membership. Unions' share of the work force has dropped from 56 percent to 46 percent in the United Kingdom, from 19 percent to 11 percent in France, and from 31 percent to 25 percent in Japan.[18]

Many experts see labor in a cooperative relationship with management in the future. Strikes are as infrequent in Great Britain as they have been in over a century. Union workers at Dutch steel maker Hoogovens reached a compromise with managers by agreeing to a wage freeze and early retirement for 600 workers in return for job guarantees for the rest. Union workers at an AT&T facility in Atlanta helped managers design a work-team system that improved phone-repair and quality-control procedures. The new system proved so cost-effective that AT&T moved 100 jobs back to Atlanta from Mexico.[19]

ACHIEVEMENT CHECK SUMMARY

Reread the learning goals that follow, and consider the questions for each goal. Answering these questions will reinforce the most important concepts in the chapter and allow you to check how well you have achieved these learning goals. Where a blank appears before a question, answer with *T* or *F*. Otherwise, circle the letter of the correct answer. An answer key to these questions is found at the end of this chapter.

LEARNING GOAL 11.1: Summarize the history of labor unions and list their primary goals.

1. ___ A labor union is a group of workers who unite to achieve common goals in the areas of compensation, job security, and work conditions.
2. ___ The first union in the United States was the AFL–CIO.
3. ___ Today, more than 50 percent of American workers belong to unions.

LEARNING GOAL 11.2: Identify the major federal laws that affect labor unions and explain the key provisions of each law.

1. The 1938 act that set a federal minimum wage and maximum basic working hours, outlawed child labor, and provided for overtime pay is the: (a) Fair Labor Standards Act; (b) Norris-La Guardia Act; (c) Wagner Act; (d) Taft-Hartley Act; (e) Landrum-Griffin Act.
2. The 1947 act that was designed to curb unfair labor practices and to balance the power of unions and management by prohibiting closed shops, featherbedding, discriminatory activi-

ties of unions, and secondary boycotts is the: (a) Fair Labor Standards Act; (b) Norris-La Guardia Act; (c) Wagner Act; (d) Taft-Hartley Act; (e) Landrum-Griffin Act.

LEARNING GOAL 11.3: Explain how collective bargaining agreements are established and the roles played by arbitrators and mediators.

1. ___ The collective bargaining process is aimed at producing a contract between management and workers.
2. ___ A mediator is an impartial third party brought into a union-management dispute to render a legally binding decision.
3. ___ Most collective bargaining processes end in strikes before the parties can reach new agreements.

LEARNING GOAL 11.4: Outline the sources of power, or "weapons," of labor and management.

1. A charge that management is in violation of the union contract is a: (a) grievance; (b) strike; (c) lockout; (d) boycott.
2. Which of the following represent weapons that management can use against organized labor? (a) hiring strikebreakers; (b) injunctions; (c) lockouts; (d) employers' associations; (e) all of the above.
3. Which of the following represent weapons that unions can use against management? (a) threat of a strike; (b) a walkout or strike; (c) a boycott; (d) picketing; (e) all of the above.

LEARNING GOAL 11.5: Discuss the future of organized labor.

1. ___ Union membership has increased dramatically in the past 20 years and is expected to continue growing.
2. ___ It is illegal for service workers to unionize.
3. ___ With new management practices like peer review and employee empowerment, most workers feel they need unions more than ever.

KEY TERMS

labor union 288
American Federation of Labor (AFL) 288
Congress of Industrial Organizations (CIO) 288
national union 288
local union 288
international union 289
federation 289
closed shop 289
union shop 290
agency shop 290
open shop 291
right-to-work laws 291
boycott 291
collective bargaining 292
bargaining zone 294
cost-of-living adjustment (COLA) clause 297
giveback 297
mediation 298
arbitration 299
grievance 300
strike 300
picketing 302
lockout 302
strikebreaker 303
injunction 303
employers' association 303
peer-review board 304

REVIEW QUESTIONS

1. Trace the development of labor unions in industrialized society. Briefly outline the history of the union movement in the United States.

2. Distinguish among local unions, national unions, international unions, and labor federations. Categorize the AFL–CIO and identify its primary function.

3. Trace the development of labor legislation in the United States.

4. Discuss right-to-work laws and their impact on business and labor.

5. Describe the collective bargaining process and relate it to the concept of bargaining zones.

6. Differentiate between a closed shop, union shop, agency shop, and open shop. Which of these is directly affected by the Taft-Hartley Act?

7. Distinguish between mediation and arbitration.

8. Outline the steps in the grievance procedure. What role does the shop steward play in a typical grievance?

9. Explain the major weapons of unions and management. Describe instances in which each might be used.

10. Explain why so many ESOPs have been formed in recent years. What are the major advantages and disadvantages of worker ownership?

DISCUSSION QUESTIONS

1. In 1977, the American Federation of Government Employees revised its constitution to permit membership of military personnel. To date, however, it has made no attempt to organize the 2 million men and women in the U.S. armed forces. A survey of union members showed general opposition to seeking new members from the uniformed military. Prepare a list of the advantages and disadvantages to the military of allowing soldiers to join labor unions.

2. What is the purpose of the cooling-off period that the president of the United States may order under the Taft-Hartley Act? Which party in a labor dispute is likely to benefit more from this provision of the act?

3. Explain why major firms such as IBM, Sears, Eastman Kodak, and Texas Instruments operate without unions. Do efforts to protect job security eliminate the need for unions? Explain your answer.

4. Secure a copy of a collective bargaining agreement from a firm. Develop a scenario of a management-labor bargaining session for the next contract.

5. Discuss the likely changes in union operations and objectives that may result from the role of the baby-boom generation in the labor force.

SOLUTIONS TO ACHIEVEMENT CHECK SUMMARY

L.G. 11.1: 1. T, 2. F, 3. F, **L.G. 11.2:** 1. a, 2. d, **L.G. 11.3:** 1. T, 2. F, 3. F, **L.G. 11.4:** 1. a, 2. e, 3. e, **L.G. 11.5:** 1. F, 2. F, 3. F

VIDEO CASE

HARLEY-DAVIDSON It has been said that Harley-Davidson is the best-loved brand name in the United States. Oh, sure, Ford and Coke and Nike are all well-respected brand names. But you don't see people tattooing those logos on their bodies!

Harley motorcycles enjoy such global popularity that it is nearly impossible to walk into a dealership and drive out on a new model—even if you have the financial resources to plunk down as much as $20,000 cash for a two-wheeler. Demand far outstrips production, so would-be owners place deposits with their orders and wait at least several months for delivery.

A casual observer viewing Harley-Davidson's enviable position in the marketplace would be shocked to learn how close the company came to bankruptcy a few years ago. The Milwaukee-based firm was a traditional manufacturer with a reputation for high-quality products and an antagonistic relationship with its unionized work force. Despite poor union-management relations, the Harley name and image allowed the firm to survive recessions, a depression, two world wars, and increasingly intense competition from rapidly improving products offered by German and Japanese motorcycle manufacturers.

When Harley-Davidson first set up shop, over 150 U.S. motorcycle manufacturers were operating. By the 1970s, it was the sole survivor. But it was an ailing company, one that many observers expected to fail. In fact, temporary government protection against foreign imports was necessary to stave off bankruptcy. An alliance between Harley-Davidson managers and the firm's unionized employees, however, transformed the firm into one of America's most visible manufacturing successes in one of the best turnaround stories of the past two decades.

The old Harley-Davidson production system had been created in the scientific management era, with its focus on optimal job design as fundamental to optimal performance. However, scientific management philosophy frequently assumes—explicitly or implicitly—that *money* is the primary motivating factor for workers. Differing assumptions on employee motivation by management and operative employees often leads to the formation of unions on the part of employees, and stringent work rules on the part of management, creating a divisive atmosphere.

Fortunately for Harley-Davidson management and shareholders, extensive analysis of competitive production practices, particularly of their Japanese competitors, led the firm to revise its assumptions about employee motivation. Recognizing that Harley employees would ultimately determine the fate of the company, they initiated fundamental changes in union-management relationships. Management decided that the company would not be successful unless Harley employees believed that their actions were good for the organization. More importantly, employees had to believe that what was good for Harley-Davidson was good for the individual. Involving production employees in decision making and problem solving allowed them to feel like an important part of the organization. Using employee knowledge to restructure tasks, improve production processes, and even redesign products not only made the process better, but also acted as a motivator for everyone involved.

The transformation that has occurred in the past two decades at Harley-Davidson is nothing short of phenomenal. Today, employees regularly make day-to-day decisions af-

Just released. The Harley-Davidson Bad Boy.

fecting their jobs. Union representatives participate as partners in making major decisions affecting the firm's future, decisions that previously would have remained exclusively in the hands of management. Management and unionized employees work hand in hand in seeking the best possible solutions to problems that affect them all. The old adversarial relationship has been transformed by Harley-Davidson's new operating philosophy.

Other tangible evidence of the benefits accruing from this management-employee alliance exists. Harley-Davidson was one of the first U.S. manufacturers to design and implement employee involvement programs. They also pioneered the use of quality circles in the United States. Union representatives now participate in meetings once opened exclusively to management. They make recommendations on capital expenditures and evaluate system and design changes aimed at enhancing quality or reducing costs. As a result, morale is at an all-time high, grievance filings have been cut in half, and absenteeism is down by 44 percent.

The current success of Harley-Davidson has caught the attention of the highest office in the nation. Former president Ronald Reagan summed it up this way: "The Harley-Davidson example makes a very strong statement about how government can help the best and brightest in American management and labor come together in ways that will create new jobs, new growth, and new prosperity."

QUESTIONS

1.
Relate the events in this case to the development of labor unions in the United States. Why do you think Harley-Davidson employees decided to form a union?

2.
Discuss the changes that have occurred in Harley-Davidson's relationship with its employees since the 1970s. What benefits have Harley employees received from these changes? What potential problems do employees face as a result of these changes?

3.
In what ways has management benefitted from the decision to share decision-making authority with its employees?

4.
Although the Harley-Davidson work force continues to be unionized, some people argue that it is no longer a necessary part of the organization. Do you agree or disagree? Defend your position.

CHAPTER 12

PRODUCTION AND OPERATIONS MANAGEMENT

LEARNING GOALS

1. Explain the strategic importance of production and operations management to a firm.

2. Discuss the role in production of computers and technologies such as robots, CAD/CAM, FMS, CIM, MRP, and MRP II.

3. Outline the major factors involved in selecting the most appropriate plant location.

4. Describe the major tasks of production and operations managers.

5. Compare alternative designs for production facilities.

6. List the steps in the purchasing process.

7. Compare the advantages and disadvantages of maintaining large inventories.

8. Identify the steps in the production control process.

9. Discuss the benefits of quality control.

ACER Stan Shih didn't exactly grow up with money. As a boy, he learned basic business principles by helping his mother sell duck eggs in rural Taiwan. He did not buy his first pair of shoes until he entered high school. ■ Shih could, however, recognize potential when he saw it. While studying electrical engineering at Taiwan's National Chiao-tung University, he read about America's burgeoning computer industry and quickly realized that microprocessors had the power to revolutionize business. In 1976, he and several unemployed friends pooled their savings to start their own technology company, Acer Inc. ■ At first, Acer designed handheld electronic games, but Shih convinced his partners to aim for a more lofty goal: building Acer into a computer manufacturer of worldwide scope. This ambitious task would force Acer to compete against well-established, respected global brands such as IBM and Compaq. Many Western customers saw the label "Made in Taiwan" as a signal of a low-cost, poor-quality product. Indeed, many Taiwanese computer makers earned this reputation by building low-end clones of Western machines. ■ To distinguish Acer from its Taiwanese competitors, Shih reasoned, it would have to produce high-quality computers that could compete technologically with brands that enjoyed much greater name recognition. At the same time, however, Shih knew that he had to keep production costs low enough to compete on price. Cost considerations constantly challenge computer manufacturers. While faster and cheaper computer power is a boon for consumers, it can bankrupt computer makers that try to recoup money invested in rapidly aging designs. As one Taiwanese manager put it, "It's like selling melting ice." ■ First, Shih addressed the quality challenge. Acer engineers designed an innovative mix of interchangeable components, including a standard housing that workers could snap together, without screws, in a record 30 seconds. The firm could plug components together in different combinations to meet customers' varying needs. Engineers also developed the OOBE (Out of Box Experience) program, a design that vastly simplifies the process of setting up a newly purchased Acer computer. "Right now, the technology is a little complex for the average user," says Ronald Chwang, Acer America president. "Acer is leading the PC industry with OOBE, [which is] aimed at ensuring customer satisfaction. We are empowering the user to have a pleasant experience." Brags Michael Culver, senior director of product marketing, "In our focus-group testing, it took beginners only 6 minutes to get their systems out of the box, plugged in, and powered up." ■ Next, Shih tackled the cost issue by adopting an operations strategy that he calls "the fast-food business model"—a just-in-time system that eliminates waste by providing the right part at the right price at the right time. Rather than assembling whole computers in Taiwan, the company ships components to roughly 60 distributors around the world. The distributors assemble computers on a just-in-time basis as orders arrive. ■ The fast-food model allows Acer to cut costs by reducing inventories. In the past 2 years alone, it has halved supply levels to a scant 45-day backlog. Notes Shih, "We turn over our inventory ten times a year." The just-in-time system lets the company wait to install expensive components, such as microprocessors, until the last minute, thus giving their prices time to fall. Acer distributors also buy many components locally to avoid import delays and charges. In the American market, for example, Acer saves 4 percent on tariffs by shipping computers without microprocessors, which it buys in the United States from Intel. ■ These days, Acer has acquired a reputation for introducing computers with more features at lower prices than comparable IBM models. Acer was the first computer maker to sell a machine based on Intel's latest microprocessor, the 90-MHz Pentium. Acer's engineers are now readying a videoconferencing system, complete with camera, that will allow users to hold full-screen, full-color videoconferences. ■ Shih achieved Acer's original goal of becoming a global player long ago. His firm is now the biggest computer manufacturer in Taiwan, the

top-selling computer brand in Southeast Asia, and the second-ranked brand in Latin America. Acer's small market share in the United States is growing; the company recently moved up to tenth-largest in sales, and it won't stay there long if Shih can help it. "Being in the top ten, according to my calculation, means that you survive," he notes with characteristic resolve. "Being among the top five means that you can make a profit."[1]

CHAPTER OVERVIEW

Society allows businesses to operate only as long as they contribute. By producing and marketing desired goods and services, businesses satisfy this commitment. They create what economists call *utility*—the want satisfying power of a good or service. The four basic kinds of utility are time, place, ownership, and form utility. Firms create time, place, and ownership utility through their marketing functions by offering goods and services to consumers at convenient locations when they want to buy them and at facilities where title to them can be transferred at the time of purchase.

Firms create *form utility* by converting raw materials and other inputs into finished goods or services. For example, Levi's converts fabric, thread, and zippers into jeans. The firm's production function creates form utility.

production
Application of resources like people and machinery to convert materials into finished goods or services.

production and operations management
Managing people and machinery used in converting materials and resources into finished goods and services.

Production applies resources like people and machinery to convert materials into finished goods or services. The task of **production and operations management** is to manage the application of people and machinery in converting materials and resources into finished goods and services. Figure 12.1 illustrates the production process.

Note that, while the term *production* is sometimes used interchangeably with *manufacturing,* this ignores an important difference. *Production* is a broader term that spans both manufacturing and nonmanufacturing industries. For instance, extractive industries (such as fishing, lumber, and mining) undertake production, as do creators of services. Services are intangible outputs of the production system. They include outputs as diverse as trash hauling, education, haircuts, tax accounting, health-delivery systems, mail services, transportation, and lodging. Figure 12.2 lists five examples of production systems for a variety of goods and services.

Whether the production process results in a tangible product or an intangible service, it always converts inputs into outputs. In this conversion process, it may make major changes in raw materials or combine finished parts. A butcher performs a production function by reducing a side of beef to ground beef, steaks, and roasts. A subway system combines rails, trains, and employees to create its output: the service of carrying you where you want to go. Both of these processes create form utility.

This chapter describes the process of producing goods and services. It looks at the importance of production and operations management to a business and discusses new technologies that are transforming the production function. It then discusses the tasks of the production and operations manager, the importance of quality, and the impact of production on the environment.

STRATEGIC IMPORTANCE OF THE PRODUCTION FUNCTION

Like marketing, accounting, or human resource management, the production process is a vital business function. Indeed, without production, none of the other functions would exist. Without a good or service, a company cannot create profits. Without profits, the firm quickly fails. The production process is just as crucial in a not-for-profit organization, since its good or service justifies the organization's existence.

In short, the production function adds value to a company's inputs by converting them into marketable outputs. This added value comes from turning the outputs into

FIGURE 12.1 PRODUCTION PROCESS

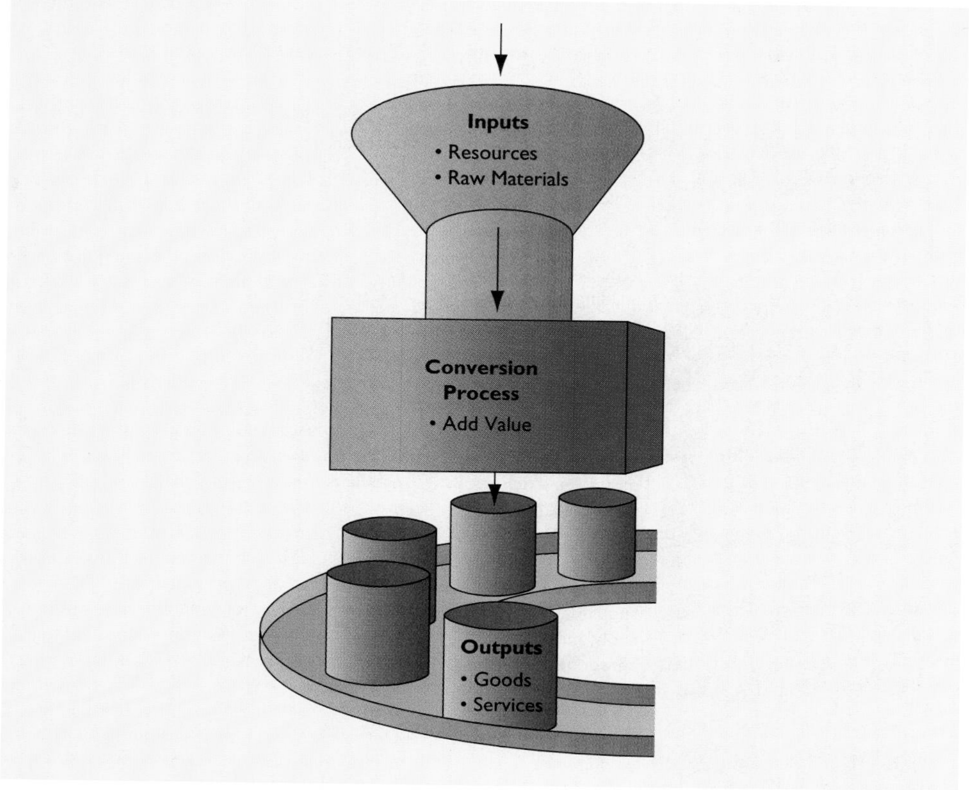

something for which customers will pay. Developing nations such as China have come to recognize the economic importance of effective production. Indeed, the Chinese government has purchased several U.S. factories to disassemble and move them to China, where they will be reconstructed to begin operations anew. Purchases include a microchip facility from Pennsylvania, an auto-engine assembly line from Michigan, and a steel mill from California. "China could build a new steel mill like this one," explains Wang Shengli, who is supervising that move. "We bought this one because we can have it operating sooner than if we built our own."[2]

Thus, production and operations management plays an important strategic role. Effective management can lower the costs of production, boost the quality of goods and services, and allow the firm to respond dependably to customers' demands. It can also help the company to stay flexible, so that it can respond more quickly when customers' demands change.

MASS PRODUCTION

The United States began as a colonial supplier of raw materials to Europe and evolved into an industrial giant. Much of this remarkable change resulted from **mass production,** manufacturing products in large amounts through effective combinations of specialized labor, mechanization, and standardization. Mass production makes large quantities of products available at lower prices than would be possible for individually crafted products.

mass production
Manufacturing goods in large quantities as a result of standardization, specialized labor, and mechanization.

FIGURE 12.2 TYPICAL PRODUCTION SYSTEMS

Example	Primary Inputs	Transformation	Outputs
Pet Food Factory 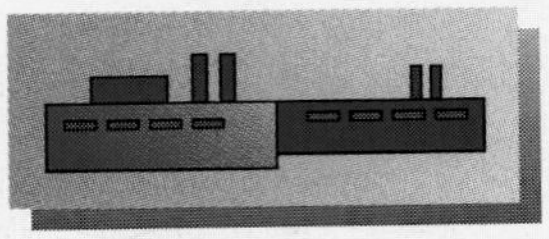	Grain, water, fish meal, personnel, tools, machines, paper bags, cans, buildings, utilities	Converts raw materials into finished goods	Pet food products
Trucking Firm 	Trucks, personnel, buildings, fuel, goods to be shipped, packaging supplies, truck parts, utilities	Packages and transports goods from sources to destinations	Delivered goods
Department Store 	Buildings, displays, shopping carts, machines, stock goods, personnel, supplies, utilities	Attracts customers, stores goods, sells products	Marketed goods
Automobile Body Shop 	Damaged autos, paints, supplies, machines, tools, buildings, personnel, utilities	Transforms damaged auto bodies into facsimiles of the originals	Repaired automobile bodies
County Sheriff's Department 	Supplies, personnel, equipment, automobiles, office furniture, buildings, utilities	Detects crimes, brings criminals to justice, keeps the peace	Acceptable crime rates and peaceful communities

Mass production begins with *specialization,* dividing work into its simplest components so that each worker can concentrate on performing one task. Once they separate jobs into smaller tasks, managers can increase productivity through *mechanization,* making machines perform work previously done by people.

The third component of mass production—*standardization*—involves producing uniform, interchangeable goods and parts. Standardized parts make it easier to replace defective or worn-out components. If your car's windshield wiper blades wear out, for instance, you can buy replacements at any auto supply store. Just think how long it would take—and how much more it would cost—if you had to have the replacements specially crafted!

assembly line
Manufacturing technique that carries the product past several work stations where workers perform specialized tasks.

A logical extension of specialization, mechanization, and standardization leads to the **assembly line.** This manufacturing technique places the product on a conveyor belt that carries it past a number of work stations where workers perform specialized tasks such as welding, painting, installing individual parts, or tightening bolts. Henry Ford revolutionized the auto assembly process with this approach. Ford's innovation generated phenomenal results. Before implementing the assembly line, Ford's workers assembled Model Ts at the rate of one for each 12-hour workday. The assembly-line technique slashed the number of work hours required to 1.5. Not surprisingly, dozens of other industries whose production functions assembled complex products quickly adopted the assembly-line technique.

Mass production, popular among manufacturers in countries around the globe, typically involves assembly lines such as this one in a GE light bulb factory in Budapest, Hungary.

NEW APPROACHES TO PRODUCTION

Although mass production brings advantages for a firm, it imposes limitations, too. It is a highly efficient method of producing large numbers of similar products. However, mass production becomes less efficient when a firm makes small batches of different items. Companies may focus on efficient production methods rather than on what customers really want. Furthermore, specialization can make workers' jobs boring since they do the same task repeatedly. To become more competitive, many firms are adopting newer, more flexible production systems, such as flexible production, customer-driven production, and the team concept. Mass production and such new techniques are not mutually exclusive, however. Many firms retain their mass-production systems, but improve them by applying newer production techniques.

FLEXIBLE PRODUCTION

Flexible production is an important goal at Caterpillar, which has spent $1.8 billion over the past 10 years to modernize and automate its factories. In many Caterpillar plants, sophisticated new tools allow fewer workers to perform production work faster than just a few years ago. At the company's Montgomery, Illinois factory, 39 riderless vehicles, guided by lasers, slide quietly down factory aisles carrying parts to the assembly line as needed.[3]

Like Caterpillar, many companies now recognize the advantages of flexible, so-called *lean production methods* that require fewer workers and less inventory. Figure 12.3 compares traditional mass production with newer, more flexible methods. As you can see, while mass production makes large batches of similar items most efficiently, flexible production can be cost-effective with smaller batches, too. Flexible production methods also require new arrangements for customer contact, inventory, design, and engineering.

CUSTOMER-DRIVEN PRODUCTION

With customer-driven production, customers' demands determine what stores stock and, in turn, what manufacturers make. Japanese firms have implemented this approach in

FIGURE 12.3 FLEXIBLE PRODUCTION VERSUS MASS PRODUCTION

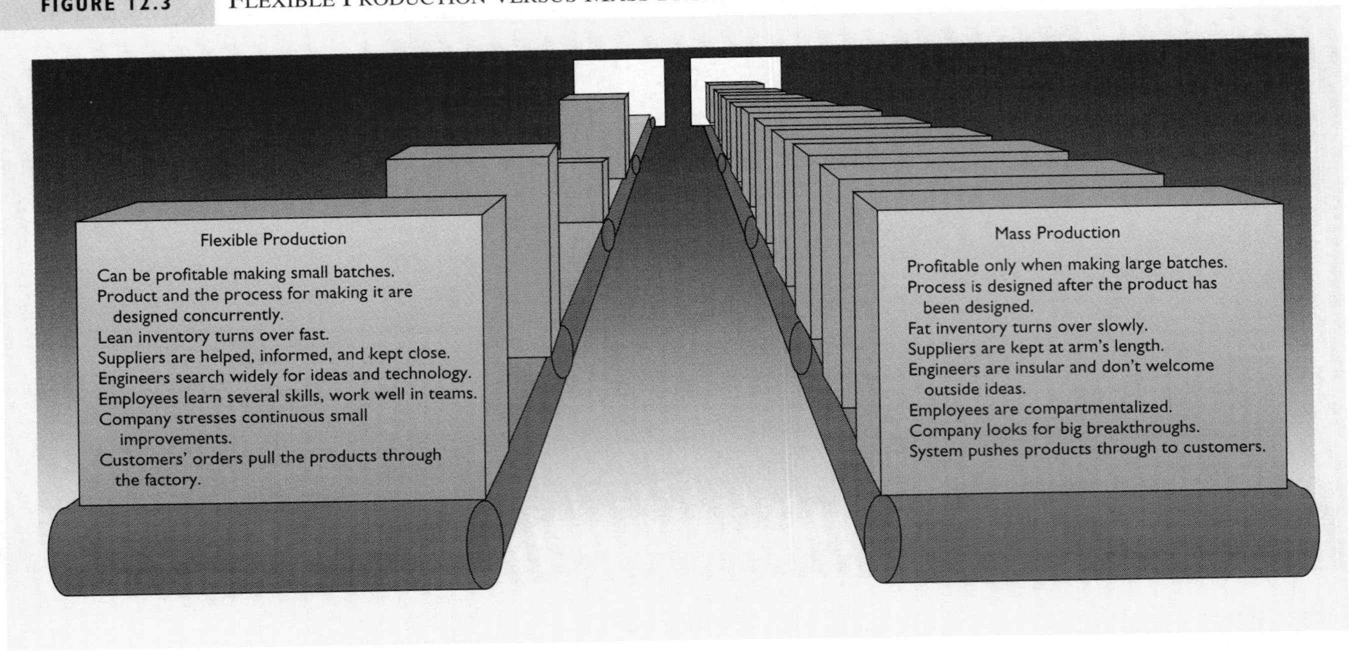
Flexible Production
Can be profitable making small batches.
Product and the process for making it are designed concurrently.
Lean inventory turns over fast.
Suppliers are helped, informed, and kept close.
Engineers search widely for ideas and technology.
Employees learn several skills, work well in teams.
Company stresses continuous small improvements.
Customers' orders pull the products through the factory.
Mass Production
Profitable only when making large batches.
Process is designed after the product has been designed.
Fat inventory turns over slowly.
Suppliers are kept at arm's length.
Engineers are insular and don't welcome outside ideas.
Employees are compartmentalized.
Company looks for big breakthroughs.
System pushes products through to customers.

many of their factories, with notable success. Several U.S. companies are testing computer links between their factories and retailers that will allow them to base production on retail sales.

TEAM CONCEPT

Some production methods challenge mass production with its emphasis on specialized workers performing repetitive tasks. The team concept, discussed in an earlier chapter, combines employees from various departments and functions such as design, manufacturing, finance, and maintenance to work together on designing and building products. The teams may also include people from outside the firm, such as suppliers and customers. This kind of teamwork is sometimes called *concurrent engineering,* since the team completes engineering concurrently with design, production, and other functions.

General Electric Motors was ready to close its plant in Fort Wayne, Indiana 2 years ago. The factory had been losing money for years, and the cost of producing motors there continued to rise. Dick Krause, the plant's new manager, decided to apply the team concept by grouping employees into teams that followed the progress of individual parts from start to finish. Krause also began sharing facts and statistics about GE competitors and customers, and he arranged for all workers to take classes in group dynamics. Today, the cost of producing a motor at the Fort Wayne plant has fallen by 16 percent, elapsed time from order to shipment has shrunk from 55 days to 16, and quality has improved from 2,300 rejects per million to only 150 per million. Employees overwhelmingly support Krause's commitment to the team concept. Says one, "Krause doesn't think management is necessary in manufacturing, he thinks we can do it."[4]

CLASSIFYING PRODUCTION PROCESSES

The methods by which firms produce goods and services can be classified according to the means they employ and the time they require. A good or service results from either an analytic or a synthetic system involving either a continuous or an intermittent process. An *analytic system* reduces a raw material to its component parts in order to extract one

A BROADER PURPOSE

PRODUCTION VERSUS PRIVACY Productivity. The word seems to be on every manager's lips. As companies strive to compete in a global marketplace, they seek ways to excel by combining technology and human resources to squeeze more output from the same quantities of inputs. New technologies also enable managers to measure and compare worker performance in detail that they could never achieve before. ■ Thousands of firms, ranging from insurance companies and collection agencies to catalog firms and other telemarketers, set up computers and surveillance devices like video cameras to count the number and length of calls employees make. Based on this information, managers then calculate a standard against which to compare each worker's performance. An estimated 26 million workers perform such repetitive tasks as making airline reservations, providing customer service, and conducting telephone marketing work under the unblinking electronic eyes of phones, computers, and cameras. ■ Critics of employee monitoring, such as unions and privacy-advocacy groups, label such firms "electronic sweatshops," complaining that constant, invasive monitoring denies employees' rights to privacy and may create stress-related health problems. As one union official puts it, "You can trespass outrageously on the privacy rights of workers. Too many employers practice the credo, 'In God We Trust; on employees and customers, we spy.' " ■ Employers see electronic monitoring in a different light, defending the practice as a valuable tool for assessing, improving, and rewarding on-the-job performance and assuring quality. Since today's technologies allow managers to count computer keystrokes and videotape individual work stations, they can provide detailed feedback to identify and reward superior performance and take steps to improve inadequate work activities. ■ Such monitoring is a simple, inexpensive practice for any firm with a computer network. One U.S. employer in five currently searches employees' computer files and voice mail, e-mail, or network messages. Only about a third of these firms give their workers advance notice of such monitoring. Not only is this monitoring completely legal, employers need not even inform employees about the practice. As privacy expert Alan Westin points out, "You're on the employer's premises, using the employer's tools, engaging in conversations with the employer's customers." ■ Some forms of monitoring extend beyond the office. With soaring costs for health insurance, many firms offer incentives to workers not to smoke, either at work or at home, and to enroll in fitness programs. At-home and at-work personal behavior begins to merge in such cases, blurring many privacy distinctions. ■ Concerns over employee privacy have reached the U.S. Congress, which is considering legislation to limit electronic monitoring. In addition, a growing number of firms are questioning whether concerns for privacy may actually hurt performance rather than boost productivity. Recent research indicates that companies must use monitoring fairly to get employees to accept it as an efficient, objective evaluator of on-the-job performance. Many advisors urge employers to explain to employees how supervisors look and listen in on production workers, why they do so, and what limits they observe.

Sources: Lini S. Kadaba, "Employers' Eavesdropping Proves Stressful for Workers," *Mobile Register,* October 1, 1994, pp. D1, D3; and Lee Smith, "What the Boss Knows about You," *Fortune,* August 9, 1993, p. 89.

QUESTIONS FOR CRITICAL THINKING

1. How else might a company measure and compare worker on-the-job performance?
2. Do you think today's workers need to be constantly monitored? Why or why not?
3. Draft a law with remedies protecting privacy of workers as might be proposed by Congress.

or more products. Petroleum refining breaks down crude oil into gasoline, wax, fuel oil, kerosene, tar, and other products. A meat-packing plant slaughters cattle to produce various cuts of meat, glue from the horns and hooves, and leather from the hides.

A *synthetic system* reverses the method of an analytic system. It combines a number of raw materials or parts into a finished product or changes raw materials into completely different finished products. An assembly line produces an automobile by combining thousands of individual parts. Synthetic systems produce drugs, chemicals, and stainless steel.

Production by *continuous process* generates finished products over a period of days, months, or even years in long production runs. The steel industry provides a classic example. Its blast furnaces never completely shut down except for malfunctions. Petroleum refineries, chemical plants, and nuclear power facilities also represent continuous process production. A shutdown can ruin such equipment and prove extremely costly.

Intermittent process production generates products in short production runs, shutting down machines frequently or changing them in order to produce different products. Most services result from intermittent production systems. Standardization of services provided by accountants, plumbers, electricians, and dentists has traditionally been considered impossible because each service provider confronts different problems that require individual approaches or production systems. This thinking has encountered challenges in recent years, however, as service providers have sought to enhance productivity. The move to industrialize the service sector is illustrated by Jiffy Lube auto service, giant vision-products retailers such as Lens Crafters, the Olive Garden restaurant chain, Terminix pest control services, home-cleaning services such as The Maids, and the growing number of dental chains located in regional shopping centers. Movement toward a continuous-flow production system, once thought impossible for services, is revolutionizing the service sector.

TECHNOLOGY AND THE PRODUCTION PROCESS

Like other business functions, production has changed dramatically as computers and related technologies have developed. In addition to making the production process more efficient, automation allows companies to redesign their current methods to make production more flexible. This change allows a company to design and create new products faster, modify them more rapidly, and meet customers' changing needs more effectively. Important production technologies include robots, computer-aided design, computer-aided manufacturing, flexible manufacturing systems, and computer-integrated manufacturing.

ROBOTS

robot
Reprogrammable machine capable of performing numerous tasks that require programmed manipulations of materials and tools.

To free people from boring, sometimes dangerous assignments, many production managers have replaced blue-collar workers with steel-collar workers: robots. A **robot** is a reprogrammable machine capable of performing a variety of tasks that require programmed manipulations of materials and tools. Robots can repeat the same tasks over and over without varying their movements.

Initially, robots were most common in the automotive and electronics fields, but more industries are adding them to production lines as technology continues to make them less expensive and more flexible. Firms operate many different types of robots. The simplest kind, a pick-and-place robot, moves in only two or three directions as it picks up something from one spot and places it in another. Field robots assist human workers in nonmanufacturing, often hazardous, environments such as nuclear power plants, space stations, and battlefields.

COMPUTER-AIDED DESIGN AND COMPUTER-AIDED MANUFACTURING

computer-aided design (CAD)
Interaction between a designer and a computer to conceive a product, facility, or part that meets predetermined specifications.

A process called **computer-aided design (CAD)** enables engineers to design parts and buildings on computer screens faster and with fewer mistakes than they could produce in traditional drafting systems. Using a special electronic pen, engineers can sketch three-dimensional designs on an electronic drafting board or directly on the screen. The computer then allows them to make major and minor design changes and to analyze the

At Ford Motor Company's facility in Dearborn, Michigan, designers using CAD workstations display potential vehicles on screens big enough to show a life-size Lincoln Continental. Ford's CAD system transmits the design data to Ford facilities around the world, where the data are used to create a computer model for simulated crash testing, calculate weight and aerodynamic properties, create full-size Styrofoam mock-ups, and print out high-quality computer-generated images to test customer interest.

design for certain characteristics or problems. Through a computer simulation, engineers can put a new car design through an on-screen road test to see how it performs. If they find a problem with weight distribution, for example, they can make the necessary changes on a computer terminal. Only when they satisfy themselves with all of the structural characteristics of their design will they manufacture an actual car model. In a similar manner, aircraft designers can analyze the shape and strength of a proposed aircraft fuselage and wings under various conditions.

The process of **computer-aided manufacturing (CAM)** picks up where CAD leaves off. Special-design computers enable manufacturers to analyze the steps that a machine must take to produce a needed product or part. Electronic signals transmitted to the production processing equipment instruct it to perform the appropriate production steps in the correct order.

computer-aided manufacturing (CAM)
Computer analysis of CAD output to determine necessary steps to implement the design and electronic transmission of instructions to production equipment to produce the part or product.

Three-dimensional design software has changed the way companies design and create new products. Figure 12.4 compares the traditional method of product design with the new, computer-based method by which Timex created its B-29 wristwatch, shown in the middle of the figure. The traditional method involves more steps. Further, even as late as Step 4, the firm can discover errors that require it to begin the whole process all over again. Computer-aided design, however, allows designers to test ideas and change them if necessary before products become physical realities.

FLEXIBLE MANUFACTURING SYSTEMS

A **flexible manufacturing system (FMS)** is a facility that workers can modify quickly to manufacture different products. The typical system consists of computer-controlled machining centers to produce metal parts, robots to handle the parts, and remote-controlled carts to deliver materials. All components are linked by electronic controls that dictate what will happen at each stage of the manufacturing sequence, even automatically replacing broken or worn-out drill bits and other implements.

flexible manufacturing system (FMS)
Facility that allows production methods to be modified quickly when different products are manufactured.

General Motors is reorganizing its global operations based on flexible manufacturing systems that can customize cars for different markets. According to Lou Hughes, who heads GM's Opel and Vauxhall divisions in Europe, "We're learning to take a car

DOING PRODUCT DESIGN BY HAND...
1 SKETCHING Using pencil and paper, the designer draws the idea
2 RENDERING The idea is drawn or painted on paper to give a more detailed idea of the product
3 MODELING A skilled craftsman makes a three-dimensional model of the product from wood or clay for evaluation by marketing and engineering
4 ENGINEERING/MANUFACTURING Engineers decide how to build the product. For the first time, the design is fed into a computer. Engineers, designers, and marketers make revisions. The design is then fed electronically into a CAD/CAM system and later manufactured
IMAGE OF A TIMEX B-29 GENERATED BY ALIAS
...AND BY 3-D COMPUTER SOFTWARE
1 SKETCHING, RENDERING, AND COMPUTER MODELING Using a workstation, the designer sketches an idea, then fleshes it out using rendering software. The computer generates a realistic 3-D model of the product on the screen. Because it's electronic, the design can be tweaked easily and cheaply. A physical mock-up can be made by transferring the design electronically to computerized milling equipment. But this entire step can often be skipped
2 ENGINEERING/MANUFACTURING Once all revisions have been made, data describing the computer-generated 3-D model are transferred directly to a CAD/CAM system and produced
DATA: BW

FIGURE 12.4

TRADITIONAL MANUFACTURING VERSUS COMPUTER-AIDED MANUFACTURING

platform and wrap stuff around it that lets us be very responsive to individual markets without going through all the reengineering of heating systems and body structure."[5] The FMS approach allows GM to adapt the basic platform of its Opel Astra, a popular subcompact in Europe, to create American models such as the Chevy Cavalier and Saturn. The system begins with a larger platform, such as GM Europe's Opel Omega, and fits a new grille and other custom parts to create an American Cadillac.

As Figure 12.5 indicates, Japanese manufacturers place much more importance on flexibility than U.S. firms by targeting variety, innovation, and technological superiority. U.S. manufacturers emphasize customer service and reliability. Note how narrow these gaps are compared to Japanese attitudes.

COMPUTER-INTEGRATED MANUFACTURING

computer-integrated manufacturing (CIM)
Production system in which computers help workers to design products, control machines, handle materials, and control the production function in an integrated fashion.

Combining robots, CAD/CAM, FMS, computers, and other technologies leads to **computer-integrated manufacturing (CIM),** a production system in which computers help workers to design products, control machines, handle materials, and control the production function in an integrated fashion. CIM does not necessarily imply more automation and fewer people. It does involve a different type of automation organized around the computer. The key to CIM is a centralized computer system that integrates and controls various separate processes and functions.

Russell Corp. is an old company, founded 91 years ago, but its factories are anything but old-fashioned. The firm has spent over $500 million in the last 5 years to install computer-integrated manufacturing systems that have turned it into the nation's largest supplier of athletic uniforms. In its textile mills, seeing-eye computers sort fabrics by color, lasers cut the fabrics, robots sew seams, and automated, remotely guided vehicles carry materials from one part of the plant to another. Since 1983, Russell's profits have more than tripled to reach $82 million. At the same time, its production costs have fallen from 69 percent of sales to 66 percent.[6]

CHOOSING THE BEST LOCATION

One of a firm's major decisions focuses on choosing the right place to build a production facility. As Figure 12.6 shows, factors that characterize the best location fall into three categories: transportation, physical, and human factors.

Transportation factors include proximity to markets and raw materials along with availability of transportation alternatives. Physical variables involve such issues as water

FIGURE 12.5 COMPARING FLEXIBILITY IN U.S. AND JAPANESE MANUFACTURING STRATEGIES

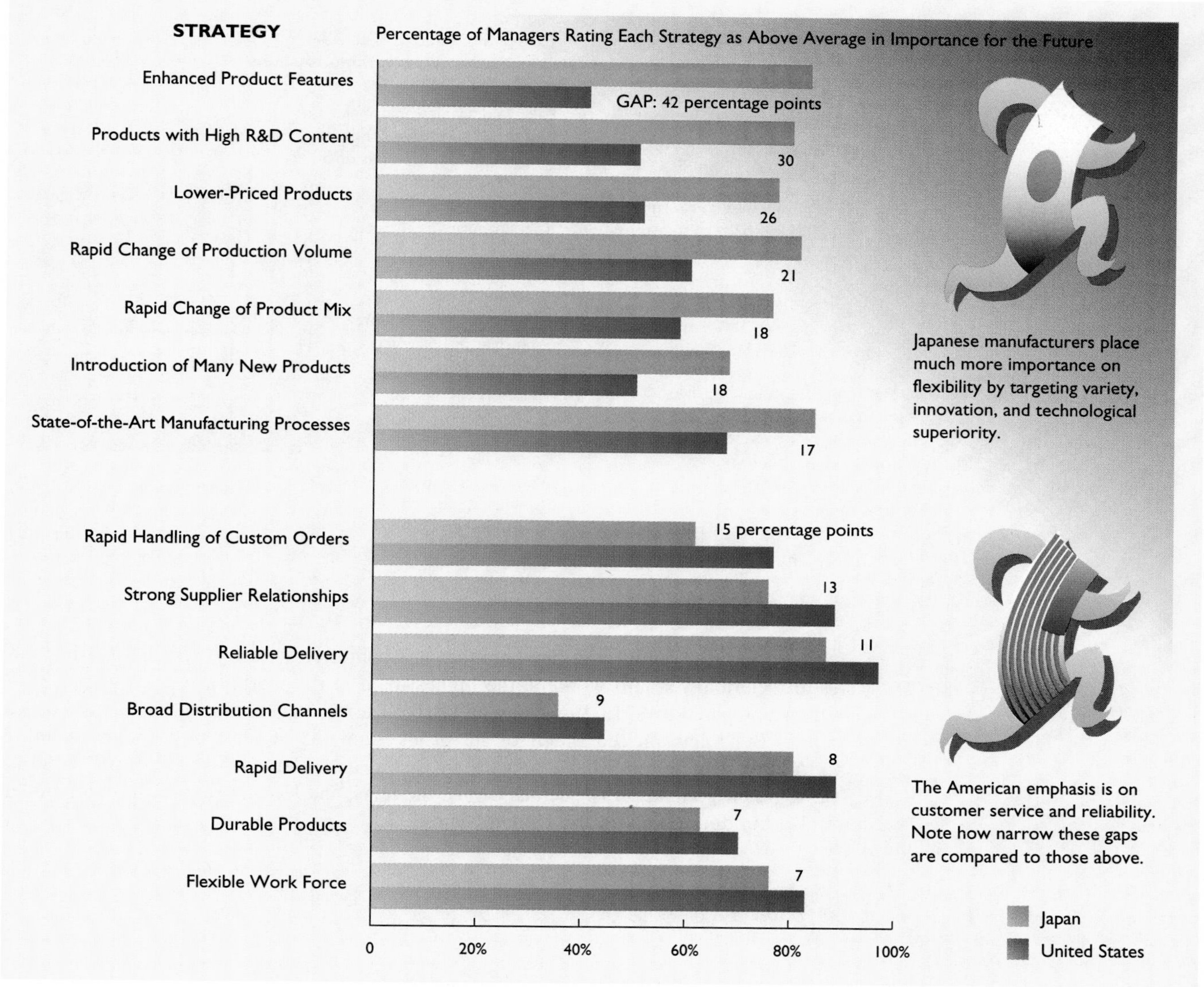

supply, available energy, and options for disposing of hazardous wastes. Human factors include the area's labor supply, local regulations, and living conditions.

Many communities require firms that want to locate there to prepare **environmental impact studies** that analyze how proposed plants would affect the quality of life in surrounding areas. Regulatory agencies typically require such studies to cover topics like the impact on transportation facilities; energy requirements; water and sewage treatment needs; effect on natural plant life and wildlife; and water, air, and noise pollution.

environmental impact study *Analysis of the impact of a proposed plant location on the quality of life in the surrounding area.*

Labor costs and the availability of a qualified labor force raise important issues, as well. Many electronics firms, for example, locate facilities in the San Jose, California and Boston areas, both of which offer high concentrations of skilled technicians. Other industries, however, are moving their production operations to countries with low labor costs. As Figure 12.7 shows, Germany ranks highest among industrialized nations in average hourly labor costs, and the country is losing an estimated 100,000 jobs a year. Many of these jobs are migrating to areas with lower labor costs such as Spain, Portugal, eastern Europe, and the United States.

FIGURE 12.6 FACTORS IN THE LOCATION DECISION

Location Factor	Examples of Affected Businesses
Transportation	
Proximity to markets	Baking companies or manufacturers of other perishable products, dry cleaners and hotels or other services for profit
Proximity to raw materials	Mining companies
Availability of transportation alternatives	Brick manufacturers, retail stores
Human Factors	
Labor supply	Auto manufacturers, hotels
Local regulations	Explosives manufacturers, welding shops
Community living conditions	All businesses
Physical Factors	
Water Supply	Paper mills
Energy	Aluminum, chemical, and fertilizer manufacturers
Hazardous wastes	All businesses

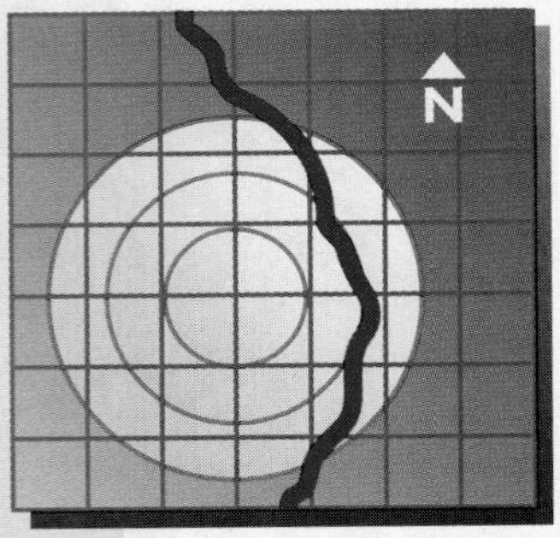

As a case in point, consider Germany's automotive industry, which is losing jobs steadily. Germany's auto workers, the highest-paid in the world, average a high $25.80 an hour compared to $21.64 in Japan and $16.64 for U.S. workers.[7] German auto maker Daimler-Benz has moved much of its production out of Germany and now builds sport/utility vehicles in Alabama, vans in Spain, and Mercedes-style sedans in South Korea. Other German firms, such as BMW, Siemens, and Helima Helvetian International, are also building plants in the United States.[8]

FIGURE 12.7 AVERAGE HOURLY LABOR COSTS FOR DIFFERENT COUNTRIES

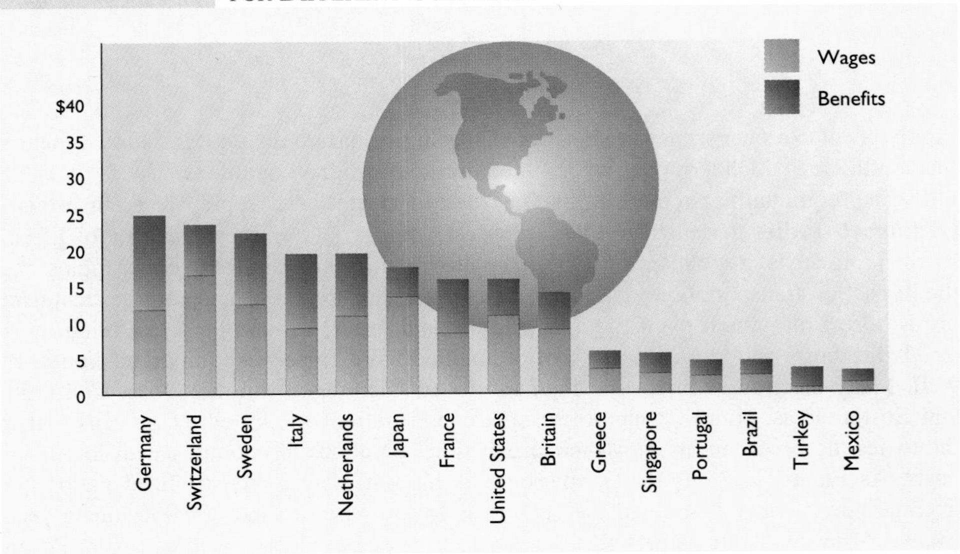

TASKS OF PRODUCTION MANAGERS

Production and operations managers oversee the work of people and machinery to convert inputs (materials and resources) into finished goods and services. As Figure 12.8 shows, these managers perform four major tasks. First, they plan the overall production process. Next, they determine the best layout for the production facilities and implement the production plan. Finally, they control the production process to maintain the highest possible quality. Part of the control process involves continually evaluating results. If problems occur, managers should return to the first step and adjust the production process, if necessary.

PLANNING THE PRODUCTION PROCESS

A firm's total planning process begins with its choice of the goods or services to offer its customers. This is the essence of the firm's reason for existence. Other decisions such as machinery purchases, pricing decisions, and selection of retail outlets all grow out of product planning.

Market research studies elicit consumer reactions to proposed products, test prototypes of new products, and estimate their potential sales and profitability levels. The production department concerns itself primarily with (1) converting the original product concept into the final product and (2) designing production facilities to produce this new product as efficiently as possible. The new item or service must not only win acceptance from consumers, it must also make possible economical production to assure an acceptable return on company funds invested in the project.

Traditionally, product planning was confined to the production and marketing departments. Today, however, many firms are adopting the team concept to involve other company personnel, and even customers and suppliers, in product design and development. General Electric, for example, encourages employees from many divisions, including assembly workers, to develop ideas for new products and ways to produce them more efficiently. At GE Power Systems, which makes electrical generating equipment,

FIGURE 12.8 TASKS OF PRODUCTION MANAGERS

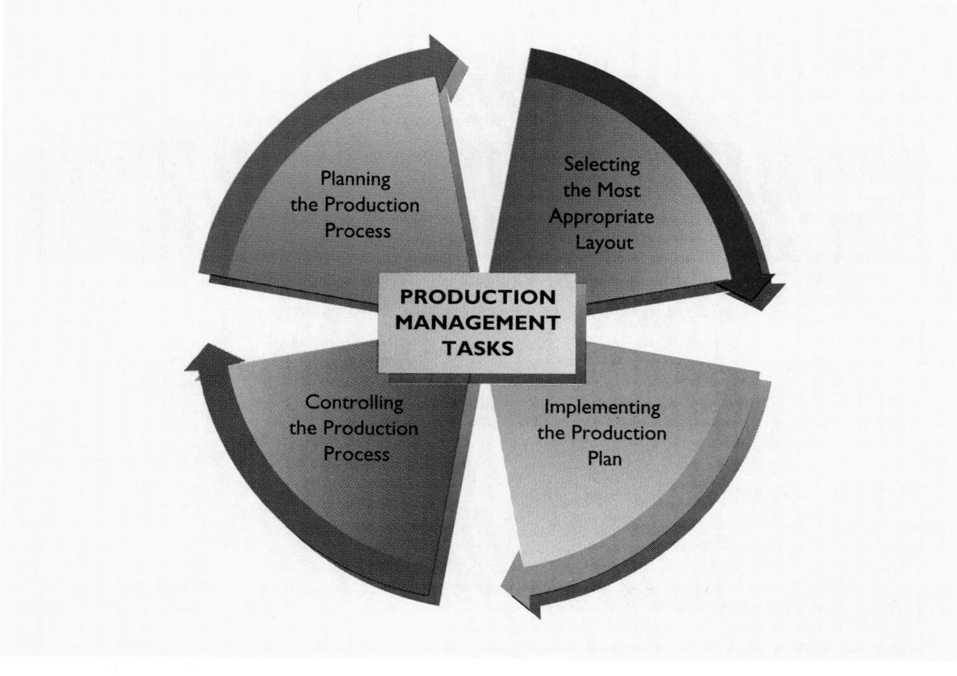

employee-initiated changes in production techniques have reduced inventory costs by from $90 million to $100 million a year. "All of the good ideas—all of them—come from the hourly workers," says Gary Reiner, GE's vice president for business development.[9]

DETERMINING THE FACILITY LAYOUT

Once managers have established the production process, they can determine the best layout for the facility. This requires them to consider all phases of production and the necessary inputs at each step. Figure 12.9 shows three common layout designs: process, product, and fixed-position layouts. It also shows a customer-oriented layout that typically characterizes service providers.

A *process layout* groups machinery and equipment according to their functions. The goods in process move around the plant to reach work stations. A process layout often facilitates production of a variety of nonstandard items in relatively small batches.

A *product layout* sets up all machines along a product-flow line, and the goods in process move along this line past work stations. This type of layout efficiently produces large numbers of similar products, but it may prove inflexible and able to accommodate only a few product variations.

A *fixed-position layout* places the product in one spot, and workers, materials, and machines come to it. This approach suits a product that is very large, bulky, heavy, or fragile. Examples include building a bridge, assembling a large airplane, or constructing a missile.

A service organization must also decide on an appropriate layout design. The firm should arrange its facilities to enhance the interactions between customers and its services. A hospital, for instance, lays out various departments, each specializing in a different function such as radiology, intensive care, or surgery. Patients move to different departments depending on their needs. If you think of patients as the inputs, which of the layouts described earlier does the hospital follow? If you guessed process layout, you are right.

FIGURE 12.9 BASIC TYPES OF FACILITY LAYOUTS

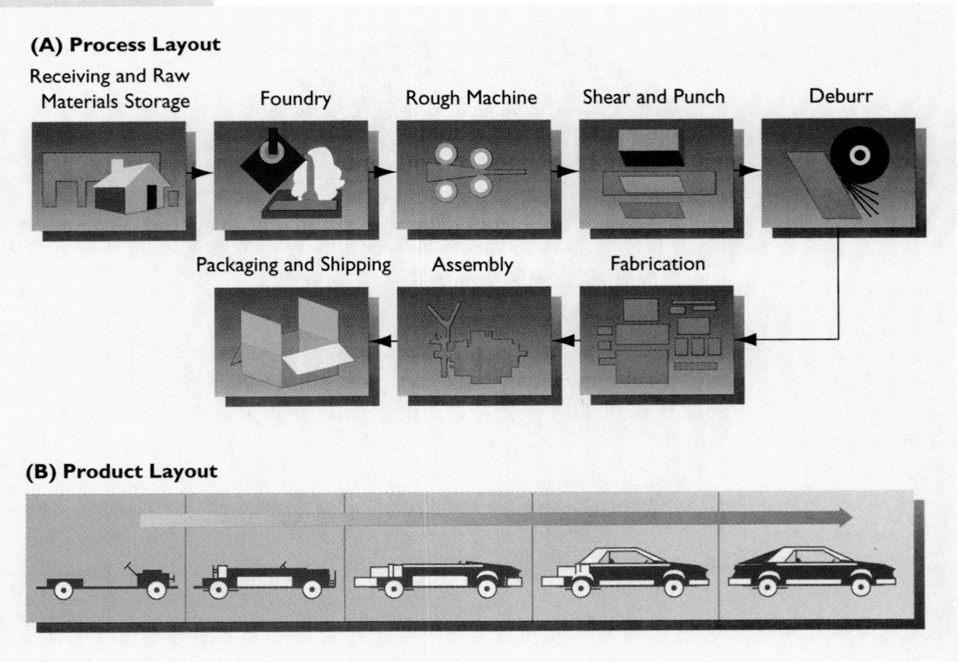

FIGURE 12.9 BASIC TYPES OF FACILITY LAYOUTS

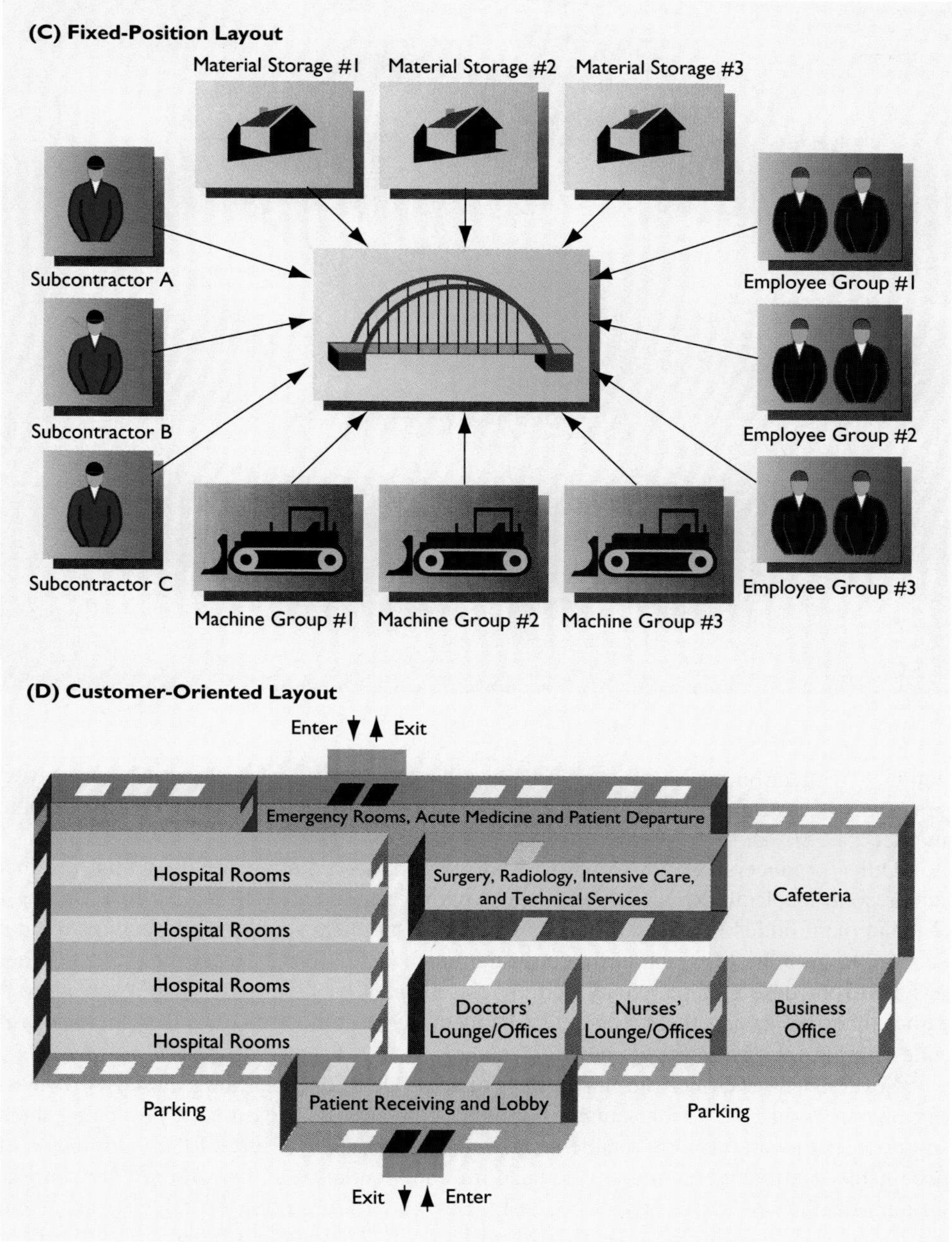

make, buy, or lease decision *Firm's choice among manufacturing, purchasing, or leasing a needed product, component, or material.*

IMPLEMENTING THE PRODUCTION PLAN

Now that managers have planned the production process and determined the best layout, their next task requires them to implement the production plan. This involves (1) deciding whether to make, buy, or lease components; (2) selecting the best suppliers for materials; and (3) controlling inventory to keep enough, but not too much, on hand.

MAKE, BUY, OR LEASE DECISION

One of the fundamental issues facing every producer is the **make, buy, or lease decision**—whether to manufacture a needed product or component, to purchase it from an outside supplier, or to lease it. Some firms actually subcontract all production to outside

Technicians at Martin Marietta's Denver plant assemble Titan IV rockets. Because of the rocket's size, a fixed-position layout is used in the assembly area.

suppliers. Solectron makes the Apple Power PC, Coosa Baking produces General Mills' granola bars, and various local bottlers make Snapple beverages for different geographic markets.[10]

Other producers rely on supplier firms to produce components of a final product under contract. Rolls-Royce provides the engines for the Boeing 757, while Boeing's Wichita plant builds the nose, and another outside supplier, Vought, manufactures the tail section. Regardless of which airline buys the finished 757, it may lease the plane to other airlines from time to time. Many commercial airlines, in fact, lease all of their aircraft rather than purchasing them. Figure 12.10 identifies a number of outside firms that provide components for Boeing's new 777 plane.

Several factors affect the make, buy, or lease decision, including the costs of leasing or purchasing parts from outside suppliers compared to the costs of producing them in-house, the availability of outside suppliers and the dependability of their shipments of acceptable quality and quantities, the need for confidentiality, and whether the firm needs an item for the short term or the long term. Because airlines often experience equipment shortages, they may arrange for short-term leases of engines and other aircraft components to meet immediate operating needs.

Even when the firm decides to purchase from outside suppliers, managers should maintain more than one supply source. An alternative supplier assures that the firm can obtain needed materials despite strikes, quality assurance problems, or other situations that may affect suppliers.

SELECTING THE RIGHT SUPPLIER

Once a company decides what to purchase, it must choose the best suppliers for its needs. To make this choice, managers compare the quality, prices, availability, and services offered by competing companies. Different suppliers may offer virtually identical qual-

FIGURE 12.10 OUTSIDE SUPPLIERS OF BOEING 777 COMPONENTS

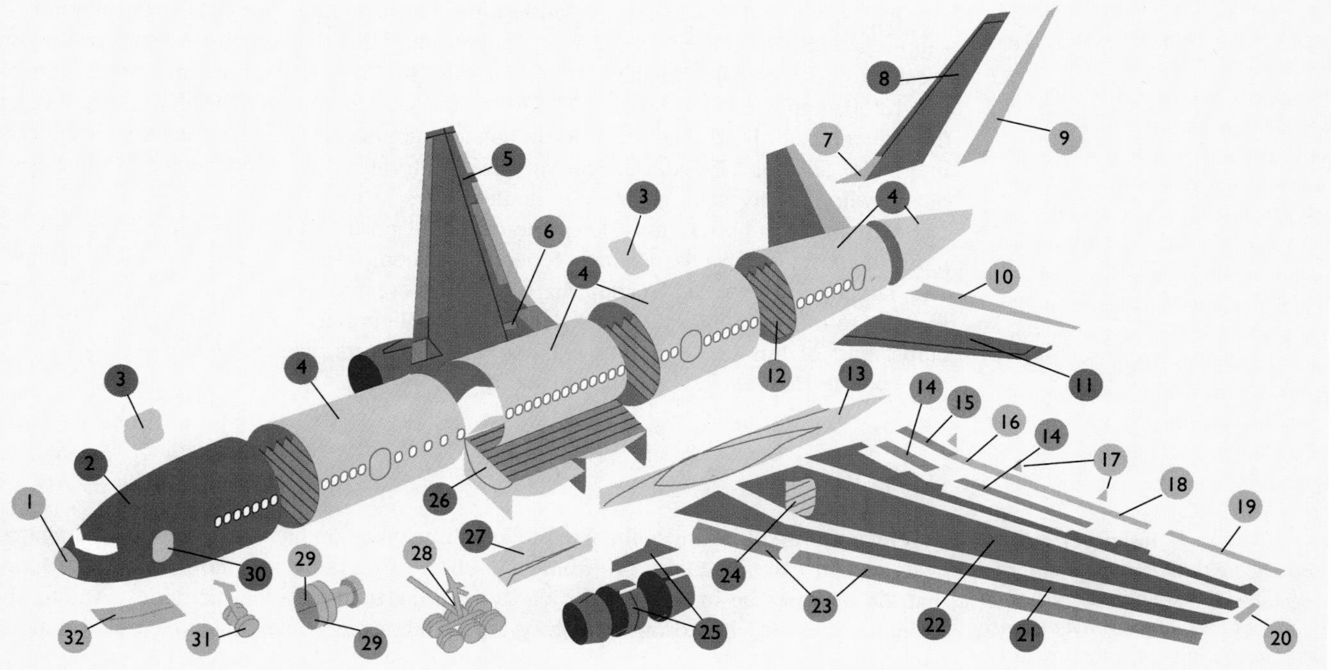

Boeing
- 2 Nose Section
- 5 Trailing Edge Panels
- 8 Vertical Fin
- 11 Horizontal Stabilizer
- 21 Fixed Leading Edge
- 22 Wing Box
- 25 Nacelles, Struts, and Fairings

International Suppliers
- 1 Radome
- 7 Dorsal Fin
- 9 Rudder
- 10 Elevator
- 16 Flaperon
- 17 Flap Support Fairings
- 18 Outboard Flap
- 19 Aileron
- 20 Wing Tip Assembly
- 28 Main Landing Gear
- 29 Engine
- 31 Nose Landing Gear
- 32 Nose Landing Gear Doors

Japanese Suppliers
- 3 Cargo Doors
- 4 Fuselage Panels
- 13 Wing-to-Body Fairing
- 24 In-Spar Ribs
- 26 Wing Center Section
- 27 Main Landing Gear Doors
- 30 Passenger Doors

U.S. Suppliers
- 6 Fixed Trailing Edge
- 12 Floor Beams
- 14 Spoilers
- 15 Inboard Flaps
- 23 Leading Edge Slats
- 29 Engine

ity and price, and choices often hinge on factors such as the firm's previous experience with each supplier, speed of delivery, warranties on purchases, and other services.

For a major purchase, negotiations between the purchaser and potential suppliers may stretch over several weeks or even months, and the buying decision may rest with a number of persons in the firm. The choice of a supplier for an industrial drill press, for example, may require a joint decision by the production, engineering, and maintenance departments, as well as by the purchasing agent. These departments must reconcile their different views before they can make a purchasing decision.

Firms often purchase raw materials and component parts on long-term contracts. If a manufacturer requires a continuous supply of materials, a 1-year or 2-year contract with a supplier ensures availability.

As firms build longer-term relationships with suppliers, they slash the number of suppliers with whom they do business. At the same time, they call upon suppliers to play greater roles in product design and engineering. In 1984, European auto maker Renault had 1,850 suppliers; today it has 800. During the same period, Renault has also increased the percentage of parts that it buys from outside suppliers rather than manufacturing them internally. Says one Renault executive, "We are trying to give more sales to fewer suppliers, who can invest in our new programs."[11]

Remaining suppliers must keep their favored positions by providing higher-quality parts. A recent survey found that 76 percent of companies had stopped doing business with suppliers who failed to adopt higher quality-control standards. In this environment, in order to meet producers' stricter demands, suppliers must raise their own quality standards. Part of this task involves making sure that parts meet manufacturers' specifications before they leave a supplier's factory.

INVENTORY CONTROL

inventory control
Balancing the costs of holding raw materials, component parts, and finished inventory (which increase with the addition of more inventory) and order-processing costs (which decrease as the quantity ordered increases).

perpetual inventory
Continuously updated listing of items in inventory.

Inventory control balances the need to keep inventory on hand to meet demand against costs to carry the inventory. The financial costs of carrying inventory reflect the funds that the firm ties up in stocks, so it cannot use the funds in other activities. Among the expenses involved in storing inventory are warehousing, taxes, insurance, and maintenance.

Holding too much inventory wastes money, but a shortage of raw materials, parts, or goods for sale often delays production, and delays in production mean unhappy customers if they cause late deliveries. Firms lose business when they consistently fail to meet promised delivery dates or when they offer only empty shelves to patrons. The firm must balance this against the cost of holding inventory to set acceptable inventory levels.

Effective inventory control can save a great deal of money. As one common technique for monitoring the amount and location of inventory, many firms maintain **per-**

Federal-Mogul's oil seal plant in Mexico City lowered inventory levels by shortening lead times for replenishing supplies and learning to manufacture in smaller lot sizes. Four storage racks, eliminated through inventory reductions, provided space to expand the plant's trim and finish department.

petual inventory systems. Such an inventory-control system typically relies on computers, and many systems automatically determine orders and print purchase orders at the appropriate times. Many supermarkets link their scanning devices to perpetual inventory systems which reorder needed merchandise. As the system records a shopper's purchase, it subtracts the item from inventory data stored in the computer. Once inventory on hand drops to a predetermined level, the system automatically reorders the merchandise.

Some companies save still more money by handing over their inventory control to other firms. Owens & Minor, a hospital supply company based in Richmond, Virginia, buys and manages hospitals' inventories. Its hospital clients pay for supplies only as they use them. Owens & Minor employees take daily inventory counts at each hospital using handheld, radio-frequency computers that communicate with the hospital's own computer system. When the inventory level for a particular item falls to a certain amount, the computer automatically transmits an order electronically to Owens & Minor's Los Angeles warehouse. The supplier keeps its own inventory levels low by sending daily sales information and reordering automatically from manufacturers.[12]

JUST-IN-TIME SYSTEMS

A **just-in-time (JIT) system** represents a broad management philosophy that reaches beyond the narrow activity of inventory control to influence the entire system of production and operations management. A JIT system seeks to eliminate all sources of waste—anything that does not add value in operations activities—by providing the right part at the right place at the right time. This results in less inventory, lower costs, and better-quality goods and services than traditional production.

just-in-time (JIT) system
Management philosophy aimed at improving profits and return on investment by involving workers in the operations process and eliminating waste through cost reductions, inventory reductions, and quality improvements.

The inventory control function in a JIT system supplies parts to a production line or a company as needed. This lowers factory inventory levels and inventory control costs. The JIT system also lets firms respond quickly to changes in the market, retaining only the most essential personnel to maintain inventory.

JIT production shifts much of the responsibility for carrying inventory to suppliers, which operate on forecasts, since they must keep more on hand to respond to manufacturers' needs. Suppliers who cannot keep enough high-quality parts on hand often lose customers to suppliers who can.

The JIT philosophy can apply to service industries as well as manufacturers. For example, remember Owens & Minor's inventory control service. The average hospital, according to Robert Anderson, Owens & Minor planning director, has a 9-month backlog of supplies. When Owens & Minor took over South Miami Homestead Hospital, for instance, the institution's inventory included old baby formula with expired dates and almost a year's supply of catheters. The excess inventory translated into excess costs; hospital employees spent valuable time monitoring inventory levels, ordering fresh supplies, and tossing out old products. Owens & Minor's computerized ordering system allowed the hospital to reduce its inventory levels from 9 months' worth to 1 month's worth. The inventory, which used to consume an annual budget of $250,000, now costs just $50,000 a year.[13]

Manufacturers in many industries have adopted JIT methods. Figure 12.11 illustrates the ratio of inventories to final sales in nonfarm businesses. Thanks in part to JIT, the ratio has steadily fallen since 1979. Economist Michael K. Evans estimates that U.S. inventories now average a mere 2 percent to 3 percent above optimum levels, which saves American industry billions of dollars over past practices. This benefits the economy, since firms can invest this money, spend it on new product development, or return it to shareholders as dividends. Says Alan Dawes, who heads operations at General Motors' auto components group, "There's absolutely no way we're going away from just-in-time."[14]

FIGURE 12.11 RATIO OF INVENTORY TO SALES

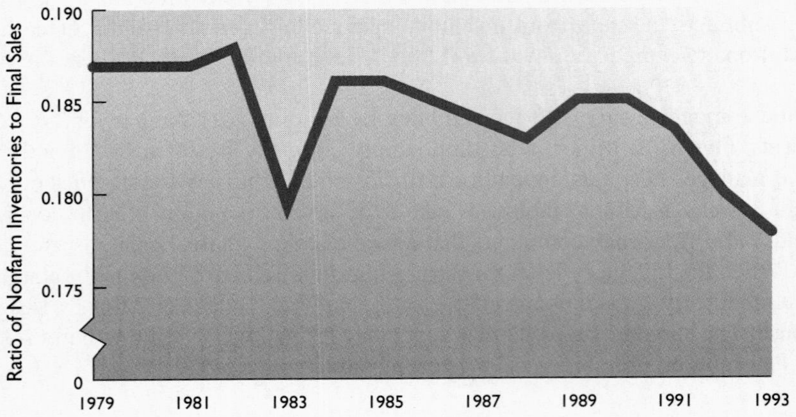

MATERIALS REQUIREMENT PLANNING

materials requirement planning (MRP)
Computer-based production planning system by which a firm can ensure that it has needed parts and materials available at the right time and place in the correct amounts.

Clearly, effective inventory control requires careful planning to make sure the firm has everything it needs to make its products. How do production and operations managers coordinate all of this information? They rely on **materials requirement planning (MRP),** a computer-based production planning system that allows a firm to ensure that it has all parts and materials it needs to produce its products and services at the right time and place and in the right amounts.

Managers use special computer programs to create schedules that identify specific parts and materials required to produce an item, the exact quantities required of each, and the dates on which to release orders to suppliers and to receive delivery for the best timing within the production cycle.

A small company might get by without an MRP system. If a firm makes a simple product with few components, a telephone call may ensure overnight delivery of crucial parts. For a complex product, however, such as a car or a B-1 bomber, MRP becomes invaluable. For instance, Boeing buys subassemblies for its 777 from more than 30 major subcontractors scattered throughout the United States and ten other nations. Some components originate as far away as Singapore and Australia. Just imagine what a headache it would be to keep track of all these components and schedules! Through MRP, managers can coordinate the deadlines for individual subassemblies with deadlines for the overall assembly.[15]

CONTROLLING THE PRODUCTION PROCESS

So far this chapter has discussed three basic tasks of production and operations managers: planning the overall production process, determining the plant layout, and implementing the production plan. That leaves the final task, and perhaps the most important one of all: controlling the production process to maintain the highest possible quality.

production control
Well-defined set of procedures for coordinating people, materials, and machinery to provide maximum production efficiency.

Production control creates a well-defined set of procedures for coordinating people, materials, and machinery to provide maximum production efficiency. Suppose that a watch factory must produce 800,000 watches during October. Production-control executives break this total down into a daily production assignment of 40,000 watches for each of the month's 20 working days. Next, they determine the number of workers, raw materials, parts, and machines the plant needs to meet the production schedule.

Similarly, a service business such as a restaurant must estimate how many meals it will serve each day and then determine the number of people it needs to prepare and

BUSINESS IN ACTION

MORE THAN JUST A SUPPLIER

Perhaps more than ever before, the manager of the late 1990s recognizes the importance of the firm's suppliers to achieving output and cost targets. Firms' reductions in numbers of suppliers and their shifts to JIT systems have combined to create strategic alliances of suppliers and customers aimed at producing competitive advantages for both. Today, however, this working relationship is beginning to revolutionize the product-development process as suppliers play ever larger roles in the creation of new products and product components. ■ Traditionally, a manufacturer provided detailed specifications of needed parts and suppliers bid against one another to win contracts. The supplier with the lowest bid that could achieve specified quality levels and turn out the number of needed items on the schedule dictated by the manufacturer got the contract. Today, however, manufacturers are asking these same suppliers to develop new and better parts. ■ When Whirlpool Corp. decided to introduce a new gas range, it farmed out design and production of the gas burner system to Eaton Corp., a supplier that already makes gas valves and regulators for other appliance manufacturers. While Eaton enjoyed the benefits of adding a new client, Whirlpool expected to get its new range to market several months sooner than it could achieve on its own. ■ In a similar move, McDonnell-Douglas Corp. is saving $300 million of the $500 million cost of developing its new 100-seat jetliner. Suppliers, in turn, subcontract tooling and assembly of the plane. Chrysler managers have carefully chosen a group of suppliers to design everything from car seats to drive shafts. This subcontracting is credited with the auto maker's strong comeback in the mid-1990s. ■ In retrospect, the benefits of such arrangements seem obvious. The supplier of a part can design it more cheaply than the customer primarily because it can exploit economies of scale, spreading engineering costs much more efficiently than a single assembler can. Moreover, the practice of relying on fewer suppliers enhances their relationships with purchasers. As Thomas Stallkamp, Chrysler's purchasing chief, points out, "In the future, [the new alliances] will remain the most important thing." No longer must suppliers bid against each other on regular intervals; instead, the firm makes longer-term commitments to individual suppliers. ■ This trend toward long-term manufacturer-supplier relationships is expected to increase American companies' international competitiveness. However, a lingering concern of companies engaged in these new alliances is that there will be fewer secrets as more manufacturers share industrial knowledge with suppliers, and vice versa. Partners must share sensitive information about pricing strategies, profit margins, and market strategies from the outset, creating a risk for manufacturers. Many industry experts counsel companies to give serious consideration before turning to suppliers for engineering help. Says Tom Slaight, an A. T. Kearney efficiency expert, "If you give it all away, you pretty much have no edge in the marketplace." Source: Neal Templin and Jeff Cole, "Manufacturers Use Suppliers to Help Them Develop New Products," *The Wall Street Journal,* December 19, 1994, pp. A1, A8.

General Motors.
"When I hear people talking about our cars, they're talking about me, too."
Chuck Camilleri worked on the production line at General Motors' Livonia Engine Plant even before there was a production line. Chuck and about eighty other workers sat down with suppliers and engineers to plan it from the ground up. It wasn't easy. Sometimes it was a real battle. But the more people got involved, the more they cared. And the Livonia plant turned into a model of safety, efficiency and quality. After all that work, Chuck can be sensitive about the reputation of the cars he helps build. It's only natural. He puts a bit of himself into every one of them.

QUESTIONS FOR CRITICAL THINKING

1. What additional pressures are put on suppliers who are involved in the design process versus those who merely supply parts?
2. Assume a supplier invests a large sum to design a part for a manufacturer. For how long should a company be required to buy parts from this supplier?
3. What are the disadvantages of relying on fewer suppliers?

serve the food, as well as how much food to purchase and how often. For example, the restaurant manager may need to buy meat, fish, and fresh vegetables every day or every other day to ensure freshness, while buying canned and frozen foods less often, depending on storage space.

MANUFACTURING RESOURCE PLANNING

While an MRP system controls inventory, a more advanced computer-based system controls all of a firm's resources. Called **manufacturing resource planning,** or **MRP II,** the system integrates planning data from individual departments—marketing, production, engineering, and finance—to produce a master business plan for the entire organization. MRP II then translates the business plan into marketing forecasts; requirements for inventory, materials handling, and personnel; and production schedules. All managers have access to this information. With MRP II, a change in a marketing forecast automatically

manufacturing resource planning (MRP II)
System that integrates planning data from individual departments to produce a master business plan.

produces an adjustment in production scheduling. Some MRP II software can even advise managers on solutions to manufacturing and other production problems.

FIVE STEPS IN PRODUCTION CONTROL

Figure 12.12 illustrates production control as a five-step process composed of planning, routing, scheduling, dispatching, and follow-up. These steps are part of the firm's overall emphasis on total quality management.

production planning
Phase of production control process that determines the amount of resources needed to produce a certain amount of goods or services.

Production Planning The phase of production control called **production planning** determines the amount of resources (including raw materials and other components) needed to produce a certain amount of goods or services. The production planning process develops a bill of materials that lists all parts and materials the firm needs to produce a good or service. Comparing information about needed parts and materials with the firm's perpetual inventory data allows the purchasing department to identify necessary additional purchases. The MRP system establishes delivery schedules to ensure that needed parts and materials arrive at regular intervals as required during the production process. Similar analysis ensures that the necessary machines and workers are available when needed. Although material inputs contribute to service-producing systems, such systems tend to depend more on personnel than on materials.

routing
Phase of production control process that determines the sequence of work throughout the facility.

scheduling
Phase of production control process that develops timetables that specify how long each operation in the production process should take and when to perform it.

Routing The phase of production control that determines the sequence of work throughout the facility, called **routing,** specifies who will perform each aspect of production at what location. Routing depends on two factors: the nature of the good or service and the facility layouts discussed earlier—product, process, or fixed-position layouts.

Scheduling In another phase of production control, **scheduling,** managers develop timetables that specify how long each operation in the production process takes and when workers should perform it. Efficient scheduling ensures that production meets delivery schedules and uses resources efficiently.

FIGURE 12.12 FIVE STEPS IN PRODUCTION CONTROL

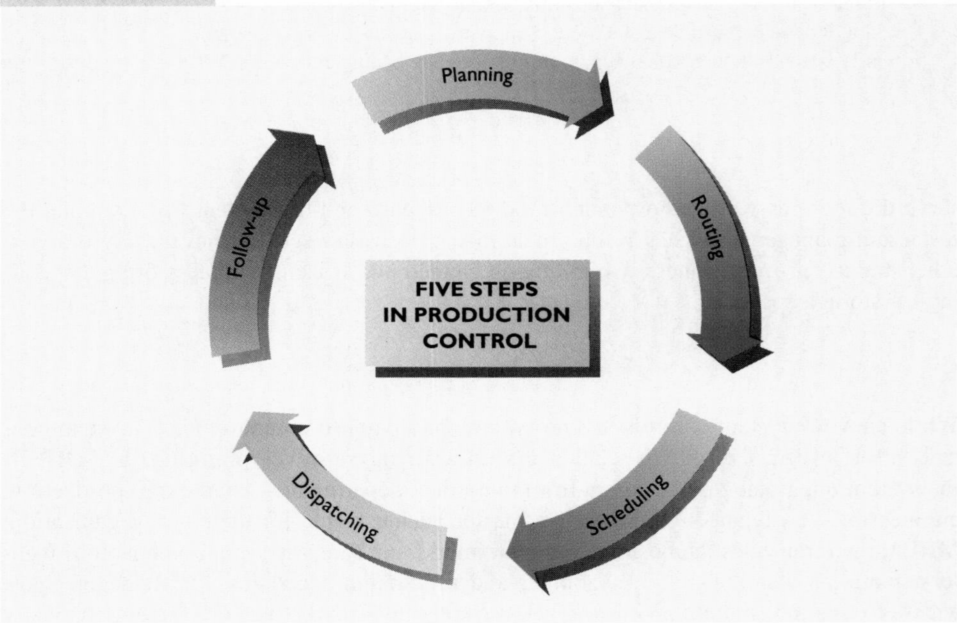

Scheduling is extremely important for a manufacturer of a complex product with many parts or production stages. A watch, for example, contains dozens of component parts, and scheduling must make each available in the right place, at the right time, and in the right amounts to keep the production process functioning smoothly.

Scheduling practices vary considerably in service-related organizations. Small service firms such as local trucking companies or doctors' offices may use relatively unsophisticated scheduling systems and resort to such devices as "first come, first served" rules, appointment schedules, or take-a-number systems. They may rely on part-time workers and standby equipment to handle demand fluctuations. On the other hand, hospitals typically implement sophisticated scheduling systems similar to those of manufacturers.

Managers look to a number of analytical methods for help with scheduling. One of the oldest methods, the *Gantt chart,* tracks projected and actual work progress over time. Gantt charts like the one in Figure 12.13 remain popular because they show a manager at a glance the status of a particular project. However, they are most effective for scheduling relatively simple projects.

A complex project might require a **PERT (Program Evaluation and Review Technique)** chart, which seeks to minimize delays by coordinating all aspects of the production process. First developed for the military, PERT has been modified for industry. Consider, for example, a simplified PERT diagram for construction of a house in Figure 12.14. The red line indicates the **critical path**—the sequence of operations that requires the longest time for completion. Operations outside the critical path have some slack time and can be performed earlier or delayed until later in the production process. Managers can assign some workers and machinery to critical-path tasks early in the process, then reassign them to noncritical operations as needed.

PERT (Program Evaluation and Review Technique)
Scheduling technique to minimize production delays by coordinating all aspects of the process.

critical path
Sequence of operations in a PERT diagram that requires the longest time for completion.

In practice, a PERT network may consist of thousands of events and cover months of time. Complex computer programs help managers to develop the network and find the critical path among the maze of events and activities.

Dispatching The phase of production control in which the manager instructs each department on what work to do and the time allowed for its completion is called **dispatching.** The dispatcher authorizes performance, provides instructions, and lists job priorities.

dispatching
Phase of production control process in which managers instruct each department on what work to do and the time allowed for its completion.

Follow-Up Because even the best plans sometimes go awry, firms need some way to keep management aware of problems as they arise. **Follow-up** is the phase of production control in which managers spot problems in the production process and determine needed adjustments. Problems take many forms; machinery malfunctions, delayed shipments, and employee absenteeism can all affect production. The production control system must report these delays to managers so they can adjust production schedules.

follow-up
Phase of production control process that spots production problems and informs managers of needed adjustments.

FIGURE 12.13 GANTT CHART

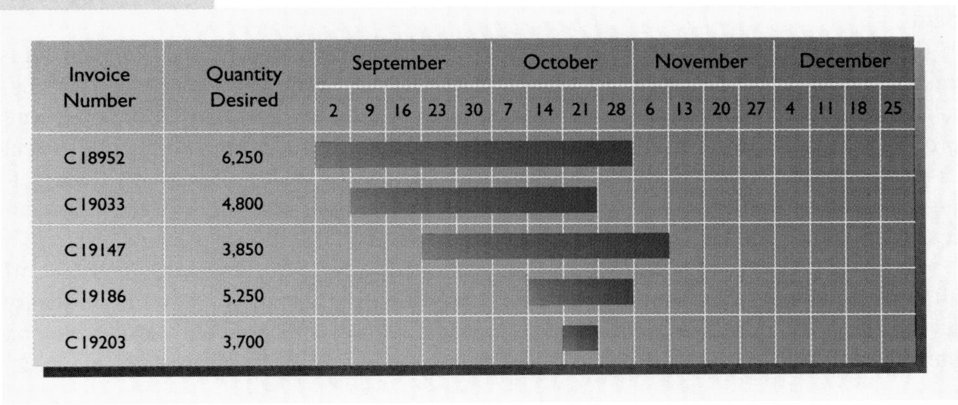

Invoice Number
Quantity Desired
September
October
November
December
2 9 16 23 30 7 14 21 28 6 13 20 27 4 11 18 25
C18952
6,250
C19033
4,800
C19147
3,850
C19186
5,250
C19203
3,700

FIGURE 12.14 PERT DIAGRAM FOR BUILDING A HOME

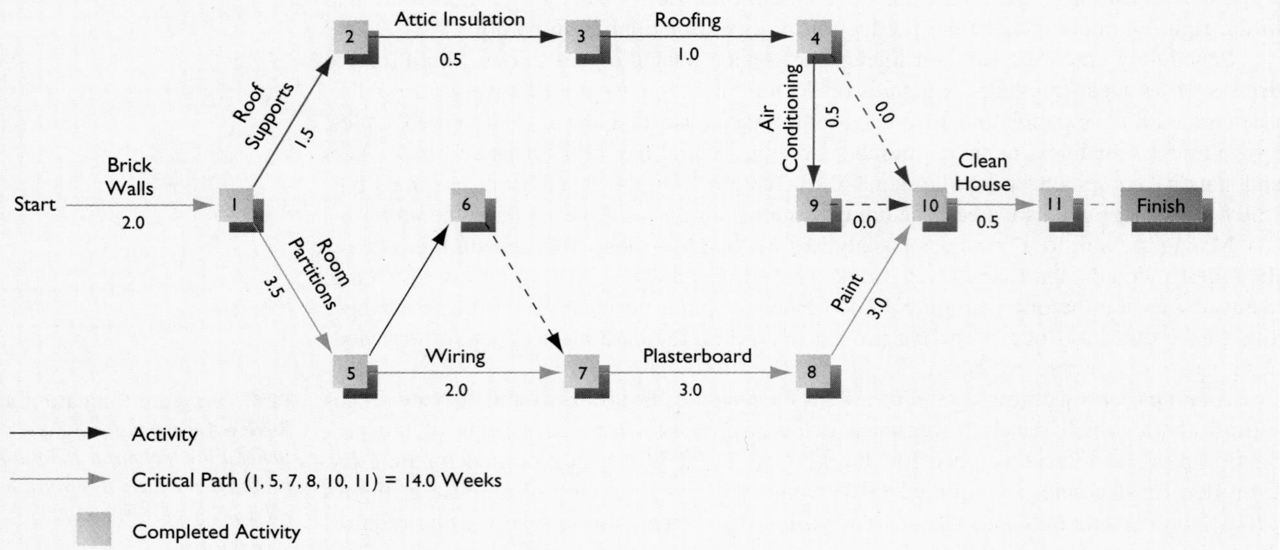

IMPORTANCE OF QUALITY

Quality, as discussed in Chapter 7, is just as vital in the product development and production functions as in other areas of business. More companies are realizing that, by building quality into product designs from the very beginning, they are more likely to produce quality products. Investing more money up front in quality design and development ultimately decreases the cost of quality, or costs that result from failure to make the good or service right the first time. These costs average at least 20 percent of the sales revenues for most companies. Some typical costs of quality include downtime, repair costs, rework, and employee turnover. Production and operations managers must set up systems to track and reduce such costs. If managers concentrate on producing a quality product that satisfies the needs of customers, they will reduce costs of quality as a byproduct.

quality control
Measurement of goods and services against established quality standards.

Quality control involves measuring goods and services against established quality standards. Firms need such checks to spot defective products and to prevent inferior shipments to customers. Devices for monitoring quality levels of a firm's output include visual inspection, electronic sensors, robots, and X-rays. A high rejection rate on products or components sends a danger signal that production is not achieving quality standards.

Of course, a company cannot rely solely on inspections to achieve quality. A typical American factory can spend up to half of its operating budget to identify and fix mistakes. This is both costly and time-consuming. A company must instead identify all processes involved in producing goods and services and work to make them as efficient as possible. This requires finding the causes of problems in the processes and eliminating those causes. If a company concentrates its efforts on improving processes, a quality product will result.

A few years ago, the Cummins Engine Company shut down its factory and laid off all of its employees in Columbus, Indiana, citing the plant's high costs and poor quality levels. Recently, the factory got a second chance and Columbus employees are making the most of their new opportunity. To head off quality problems from the beginning,

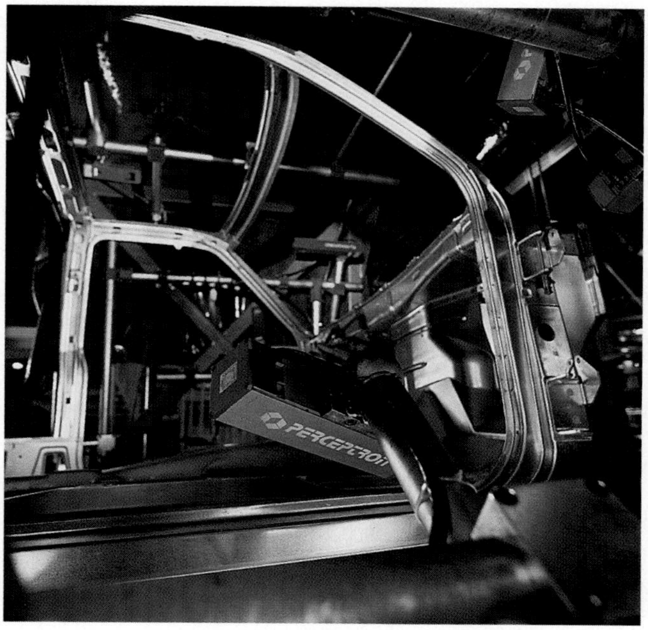

Perceptron computer-operated red-laser cameras take pictures of a General Motors' truck frame before it is welded. Computers convert the images to measurements and compare those measurements with perfect measurements stored in memory. If a part is mis-aligned, the system can sound an alarm and shut down the line until workers can adjust the part. Systems like Perceptron's help users like GM, Ford and Chrysler control quality in the production process and save rework and repair costs.

Cummins tested all job applicants' math ability and interviewed them extensively to look for teamwork skills. Hirees received 250 hours of training in quality control, engine mechanics, and mathematics. The plant makes quality control an ongoing process, as workers and managers meet regularly to review product defects found during inspections and devise solutions to the problems that caused the defects. As quality has improved, so has the plant's production rate, from 150 engines a day in 1993 to 180 today. This new attention to quality, says Tim Solso, executive vice president for operations, has enabled the plant to "beat every single target since the day it opened." Production worker Randy Acton puts it simply: "We work smarter."[16]

ACHIEVEMENT CHECK SUMMARY

Reread the learning goals that follow, and consider the questions for each goal. Answering these questions will reinforce the most important concepts in the chapter and allow you to check how well you have achieved these learning goals. Where a blank appears before a question, answer with *T* or *F*. Otherwise, circle the letter of the correct answer. An answer key to these questions is found at the end of this chapter.

LEARNING GOAL 12.1: Explain the strategic importance of production and operations management to a firm.

1. ___ Production and operations managers oversee the conversion of inputs (labor, materials, machines) into outputs (goods and services).
2. ___ Production and operations managers are needed by businesses, but are rare in the not-for-profit sector.

LEARNING GOAL 12.2: Discuss the role in production of computers and technologies such as robots, CAD/CAM, FMS, CIM, MRP, and MRP II in production.

1. ___ Computer-integrated manufacturing (CIM) can integrate production through a centralized computer system that designs products, controls machines, and handles materials.
2. ___ When a facility has short manufacturing runs and must make rapid modifications, a flexible manufacturing system (FMS) drastically reduces changeover times.
3. ___ Materials requirement planning (MRP) integrates data from a variety of departments to produce a master business plan for the whole organization.

LEARNING GOAL 12.3: Outline the major factors involved in selecting the most appropriate plant location.

1. ___ Production managers should consider proximity to markets, labor, and suppliers when selecting a location.

2. ___ Firms should always seek to locate in areas with the fewest government regulations and taxes.

LEARNING GOAL 12.4: Describe the major tasks of production and operations managers.

1. Managers of the production function are responsible for: (a) planning overall production processes; (b) determining the best layouts for production facilities; (c) implementing production plans; (d) maintaining quality control standards in production; (e) all of the above.
2. Today, product planning: (a) is confined to the production department; (b) involves the production and marketing departments; (c) increasingly utilizes the team concept; (d) never includes customer or supplier input; (e) excludes evaluation of production processes.

LEARNING GOAL 12.5: Compare the alternative designs for production facilities.

1. ___ Process layouts are used for nonstandard products produced in relatively small batches.
2. ___ When interaction between providers and customers of services is important, the product layout is often employed.

LEARNING GOAL 12.6: List the steps in the purchasing process.

1. ___ Producers must first determine if they will make their own products and components or buy or lease them from outside vendors.
2. ___ The major objective of the purchasing process is to have the right materials in the right amounts available at the right times and places.

LEARNING GOAL 12.7: Compare the advantages and disadvantages of maintaining large inventories.

1. ___ Inventory control balances the need to have inventory on hand with the costs of carrying that inventory.
2. ___ Extra inventory is more costly than inadequate inventory.
3. ___ JIT systems try to maximize inventory on hand to guard against production delays.

LEARNING GOAL 12.8: Identify the steps in the production control process.

1. ___ The phase in which managers spot problems in the production process and inform others of needed adjustments is called *production planning*.
2. ___ Gantt charts and PERT networks are commonly used production scheduling techniques.

LEARNING GOAL 12.9: Discuss the benefits of quality control.

1. ___ Investing more money up front in quality design and development ultimately lowers the costs of maintaining high quality.
2. ___ The most efficient way to control quality is to spot check output and fix any mistakes.

KEY TERMS

production 314
production and operations management 314
mass production 315
assembly line 316
robot 320
computer-aided design (CAD) 320
computer-aided manufacturing (CAM) 321
flexible manufacturing system (FMS) 321
computer-integrated manufacturing (CIM) 322
environmental impact study 323
make, buy, or lease decision 327
inventory control 330
perpetual inventory 330
just-in-time (JIT) system 331
materials requirement planning (MRP) 332
production control 332
manufacturing resource planning (MRP II) 333
production planning 334
routing 334
scheduling 334
PERT (Program Evaluation and Review Technique) 335
critical path 335
dispatching 335
follow-up 335
quality control 336

REVIEW QUESTIONS

1. Give two examples of production facilities in your city or region that use each of the following manufacturing methods:
   a. analytic process
   b. synthetic process
   c. continuous process
   d. intermittent process

2. Suggest types of form utility that the following firms might produce:
   a. lawn care service
   b. oil refinery
   c. commercial bus line
   d. family planning center

3. Explain why effective production and operations management can provide a strategic advantage for a firm.

4. Distinguish between MRP and MRP II. What business purpose does each serve?

5. Explain the concept of a flexible manufacturing system.

6. Assign a facility layout to each of the businesses listed and explain the reasons behind your selection: (1) process layout, (2) production layout, (3) fixed-position layout.
   a. watch repair shop
   b. medical examination room
   c. sporting event
   d. one-hour dry cleaner
   e. retail gift shop

7. Describe the technological improvements transforming the production function.

8. What factors are likely to be most important in the make, buy, or lease decision? List instances when make, buy, or lease decisions might be made for the following types of firms:

a. tropical plant store
b. concrete company
c. bridal service
d. antique furniture refinishing shop

9. Relate the tasks of production and operations managers to each of the following. Give specific examples of each component.
a. major league sports facility in the Savannah area
b. locally owned drug store
c. meat packing house
d. VCR assembly plant

10. Distinguish among CAD, CAM, and CIM.

DISCUSSION QUESTIONS

1. Evaluate your city or county as a prospective industrial site and suggest organizations that would suit the location.

2. Choose a service organization in your community, perhaps a restaurant or an office at your school, and evaluate its production process. How efficient is it? Does the resulting service meet your standards? Can you suggest any changes in quality control standards?

3. A successful production plan provides sufficient manufactured, purchased, or leased materials; efficient production schedules; and a controlled inventory. Draw a proposed production plan, including make, buy, or lease decisions, for a small business in your area.

4. Assess the effect on inventory control resulting from the various inventory systems discussed in the chapter.

5. What is quality control? Suggest ways in which each of the following firms could practice it:
a. local finance company
b. city parks department
c. state-owned golf course
d. shoe manufacturer that exports 50 percent of its goods abroad

SOLUTIONS TO ACHIEVEMENT CHECK SUMMARY

L.G. 12.1: 1. T, 2. F. **L.G. 12.2:** 1. T, 2. T, 3. F. **L.G. 12.3:** 1. T, 2. F. **L.G. 12.4:** 1. e, 2. c. **L.G. 12.5:** 1. T, 2. F. **L.G. 12.6:** 1. T, 2. T. **L.G. 12.7:** 1. T, 2. F, 3. F. **L.G. 12.8:** 1. F, 2. T. **L.G. 12.9:** 1. T, 2. F.

TEAM-BUILDING EXERCISE

The following exercise will dramatize the three forms of leadership, increase awareness of how different styles of leadership can affect the performance of subordinates, and examine the phenomenon of competition among teams.

1. Your instructor will divide the class into teams of at least six participants. Extra team members will assist the observer. Each group will need a package of drinking straws and straight pins, one leader instruction sheet, one observer worksheet, and one copy of the discussion worksheet for each participant.

2. Each group must designate a leader and at least one observer. The leader, and only the leader, will read the leader instruction sheet. The leader must follow the instructions explicitly.

3. When your instructor tells you to start, you will have 15 minutes to build a structure out of pins and straws. The structures will be judged on three equal criteria: height, strength, and beauty.

4. At the end of the construction phase, you will rate your team experience on three factors, using a five-point scale (five is high). The factors are:
a. Satisfaction with the leader.
b. Satisfaction with your participation.
c. Satisfaction with the group's product.
Each team calculates its members' average for each of the three factors to arrive at an official team rating.

5. The instructor calls for the average ratings of each team and posts them on a chart for all to see, then directs the evaluation of the final structures in the three categories by a show of hands, followed by a class discussion of the results.

6. The observers share their responses on the observer worksheet with the rest of the team. Team members complete the discussion sheet from the instructor.

Adapted from *A Handbook of Structured Experience for Human Relations Training,* vol. V, by J. W. Pfeiffer and J. E. Jones (eds.).

VIDEO CASE

THE DELFIELD COMPANY Look behind the counters in the compact, yet amazingly efficient, kitchens of fast-food chains such as Taco Bell, Arby's, Burger King, and KFC and you will see commercial equipment made by The Delfield Company. Schools, hotels, grocery stores, and military installations are also Delfield customers. The company, one of the three largest manufacturers of refrigerated holding cabinets and commercial kitchen equipment in the United States, saw its 1995 sales increase by 13 percent over the previous year to $120 million. Although a number of factors contributed to Delfield's marketplace success, none is more important than management's decisions regarding facility layouts for the firm's production plants.

When Delfield decided to open a new production facility in Covington, Tennessee, management considered all of the plant location factors discussed in this chapter. They were well aware of Tennessee's popularity as a production facility location for both American and foreign firms because of the state's convenient location to both suppliers of component parts and to customers. In addition, the state enjoys excellent transportation facilities, utilities, and a skilled labor force.

Once the location was chosen, Delfield production planners decided to use a product layout design. This design is well-suited for the Covington plant, an assembly-line, mass-production facility built to produce large numbers of standardized products. It also permits Delfield to use robots in the production process to perform monotonous and potentially dangerous tasks, such as feeding stainless steel sheets into cutting and bending machines.

Delfield production planners do not rely solely on the product layout approach to plant layout. Their Mt. Pleasant, Michigan production facility is set up on a process layout design. This approach satisfies the plant manager's need for the flexibility to fill orders involving small numbers of custom-designed products. The design allows Delfield to tap the niche market for custom-designed commercial kitchen equipment. The availability of different layout designs in the two facilities makes it possible for Delfield to serve different types of customers with a quality product at a competitive price.

Product-design engineers used the newest technologies in designing kitchen equipment at both production facilities. Computer-aided design (CAD) makes it easy and fast to change product specifications during the design phase. The specifications are compiled in a database of instructions for computer-aided manufacturing (CAM) operations, such as cutting and bending steel. CAD/CAM has given Delfield a competitive advantage by reducing the time required to deliver a custom product by as much as several weeks.

Delfield's success has grown out of its recognition of the value of people to the firm—employees, customers, and suppliers alike. President Kevin McCrone outlines the strategic focus of the company with five points:

1. Stay very close to the customer
2. Make sure your people have the skills and tools to build a quality product.
3. Invest in the resources that allow your people to provide excellent service to your customers.
4. Use speed and flexibility as competitive weapons.
5. Have suppliers that you can depend on so that your customers can depend on you.

Suppliers today play an important strategic role in the production and operations of most firms. Delfield relies on its suppliers to provide quality parts when and where they are needed. The firm's production facilities depend on materials requirement planning (MRP)

to control the production process and maintain efficient inventories. Anita Moffat, director of purchasing, explains the importance of suppliers this way: "In selecting a supplier to be a Delfield supplier, we look at a number of factors: Can they provide the technology background and services we need? Are they large enough to meet our needs? Are they capable of growing along with us? Is their quality up to our standards? At some point we look at their price. Does it remain relatively stable or does it increase over time?"

Generally, it takes a considerable amount of time to become a Delfield supplier. In fact, the process is more like becoming a partner, with both parties involved in helping Delfield grow. If a potential supplier meets the requirements stated above, the firm might receive an initial small order which is carefully tested and inspected for quality. If the order meets Delfield's standards, additional orders will be placed and may involve more products within a supplier's product line. In the case of Washington Specialty Metals, a supplier of stainless steel flat sheets, this relationship took four years to fully develop. It is now Delfield's sole supply source for stainless steel sheets. Washington Specialty Metals views the relationship as a partnership, where both share gains during good times and losses during economic downturns.

The partnership between Delfield and Washington Specialty Metals requires the use of a just-in-time (JIT) system in the production process. The risks and costs of keeping higher levels of inventory on hand is transferred from Delfield to Washington Specialty Metals. However, as Jack Bigham, vice president of sales, points out, the sheet steel supplier receives many benefits. "We have an entire wall of inventory of the types of stainless flat sheet that Delfield requires dedicated just to Delfield. When Anita calls, the product is loaded on the truck and delivered the next day. Delfield gets what they need, when they need it. At the same time, it gives us a competitive advantage our competition can't touch. that's what partnering is about in the '90s."

QUESTIONS

1.
Relate Delfield's decision to locate its new facility in Tennessee to the plant location factors listed in Figure 12.6. Make any assumptions necessary.

2.
What are the benefits of JIT inventory for Delfield? Are there any benefits to the supplier? Added costs?

3.
Defend the plant layout decisions made by Delfield for its Tennessee and Michigan production facilities. Refer to the factors listed in Figure 12.9 in your answer.

4.
Explain the contributions of current production technologies to Delfield's success in achieving production efficiency and customer satisfaction.

CAREERS IN BUSINESS

CAREER PROFILE: FRED VERTREES Like many business professionals, Fred Vertrees began planning his career early in college. As an undergraduate at Indiana University, he knew he was interested in educating and training people. He didn't know quite what direction he wanted to take, however, until he entered the Instructional Systems Technology Department in graduate school. There he learned the essential skills and methodologies necessary for corporate training and development. His first job out of school was with Andersen Consulting, working in their new Change Management department. It was a good job, but not as satisfying as he had hoped. ■ A year later, Vertrees left Andersen Consulting for his current job with American Airlines. As an instructional design specialist, he and two others are involved in company-wide employee development and training. Vertrees helps managers develop plans for achieving their business goals. This involves interviewing members of a department to assess their current skills and competencies, identifying areas requiring new skills or new staff, and recommending any additional equipment or training that might be necessary to achieve set objectives. ■ American Airlines managers work directly with Vertrees, who then develops training programs to teach the specific skills needed to accomplish the tasks managers have identified. The managers share their knowledge of operations and Vertrees determines the most efficient way to accomplish the operation. All three design specialists offer basic management training courses for American Airlines personnel on subjects ranging from conducting performance reviews and improving supervisory skills to coaching and counseling. ■ His job at American Airlines allows Vertrees to enjoy his work and use his potential to the fullest. He advises students interested in training and education to "be flexible, be willing to change belief systems, and be willing to learn."

Management careers are available in all types of organizations: business firms, government, and not-for-profit organizations. Managers plan, organize, direct, and control tasks performed by other people to accomplish organizational objectives.

Some specific jobs in management and production are city manager, hotel manager, health services manager, retail manager, accounting manager, sales manager, purchasing agent, and first-line supervisor. The Bureau of Labor Statistics' outlook through the 1990s forecasts that job opportunities for hotel managers, health service administrators, and accounting managers will grow faster than the average for all occupations, and that opportunities for purchasing agents will grow as fast as the average.

CITY MANAGERS

City managers are administrators who oversee the operations of cities or other units of government such as counties. They report to the elected representatives of the communities they serve.

Job Description City managers provide overall direction for the various departments of city government. The heads of such departments as planning, water and sewers, streets, recreation, and public safety report to the city manager. One of the biggest tasks a city manager faces is preparing periodic budget requests for the city council. A background in government accounting and public finance is desirable. In addition, a city manager must be actively involved in the community and must keep in close contact with the public.

Career Path The starting point in this career path is a job as an assistant city manager. Once a person acquires sufficient expertise in municipal management, he or she may apply for a city manager position. This usually necessitates a move to another town. There are only 11,000 city managers in the United States.

Salary Salaries vary according to city; managers for larger cities generally earn much more than those in smaller towns. In a recent year, the salaries of city managers for cities with populations under 2,500 averaged $35,000. For cities with populations over 1 million, the average salary was $127,000. The average salary of all city managers was $60,000.

HOTEL MANAGERS

Hotel managers work at the executive level of the hotel and motel industry. They make the daily decisions required to keep a hotel operating efficiently. More than 99,000 hotel managers and assistant managers are employed in the United States.

Job Description Hotel managers and assistants supervise the various activities necessary in lodging establishments: registration and checkout, housekeeping, accounting, maintenance, food service, entertainment, and security. Hotel managers report to higher-level management or to the hotel's owners or board of directors. They are responsible for the overall profitable operation of their units.

Career Path Many motel and hotel chains have management training programs. Successful completion of such a program may result in promotion to a department head in a large hotel or to manager of a motel. The next step is a general management position.

Salary Salaries vary widely. General managers in large, prestigious hotels may earn much more than a resident manager of a small hotel. The average salary of hotel managers in a recent year was $59,100. Their income is sometimes supplemented with bonuses based on profitability. For hotels with 150 rooms or less the average salary was $44,900. For hotels with 350 rooms or more, the average salary was $86,700.

HEALTH SERVICES MANAGERS

Health services managers work at the business management level of the health-care industry. They work in hospitals, health maintenance organizations, clinics, public health departments, nursing homes, and other health-oriented units. The chief administrator typically reports to the board of directors or trustees of the unit. Currently, 302,000 health services managers are employed in the United States.

Job Description Health services managers direct the full range of activities of a health-care facility. The professional medical staff makes treatment decisions concerning patients, but most of the operational decisions for a facility are made by its administrator. Health services managers are also involved in budgeting, fund-raising, planning, and interacting with the public served by the unit. It should also be noted that individuals in the fields of long-term care or nursing homes must pass licensing examinations.

Career Path Trainee and assistant administrator positions are available. Promotion comes with experience and effective performance.

Salary In a recent year the median starting salary for a health services manager with a master's degree was $30,524. For hospital CEOs, salaries ranged from $77,000 to $223,600.

RETAIL MANAGERS

The retail sector involves a wide variety of store types: department stores, discounters, specialty shops, and so on. Thousands of managers are needed to operate these stores.

Job Description Store managers must perform a variety of tasks. They supervise personnel, plan work schedules, oversee merchandising, make pricing decisions, and design promotions. They often work long hours and sometimes have to make decisions in sensitive personnel matters.

Career Path Retail managers often begin as assistant managers, handling one department in a larger store. They can move up into areas such as merchandising or into managing an entire store or a number of stores.

Salary Retail salaries vary widely, depending on the size of the retailer and the responsibilities held. In a recent year beginning salaries for college graduates at large stores typically fell between $18,400 and $23,700, while managers at smaller stores earned less. Supermarket managers earned between $13,000 and $30,000.

ACCOUNTING MANAGERS

Accounting managers, sometimes called *chief accountants,* are experienced accountants or auditors who have been promoted to supervisory and managerial positions in this functional area. They are key members of their organizations' management teams.

Job Description Accounting managers direct the activities of accounting and related clerical personnel. They analyze and approve the information and reports generated by the accounting unit. Accounting managers interact with other financial executives and top management.

Career Path Accounting managers are usually promoted from within firms' accounting departments, so the entry-level position is accounting trainee. Advancement to senior-level positions is possible with experience.

Salary Accounting managers' salaries in a recent year averaged $55,100.

SALES MANAGERS

A sales manager supervises all or part of a company's sales force. Sales managers exist in every firm that requires a sales force and at all levels in the distribution channel: producer, wholesaler, and retailer.

Job Description Sales managers recruit, hire, train, organize, supervise, and control sales organizations. They report to top marketing executives or to general management. They work to produce a company's revenue. Effective interaction with sales personnel and customers is an important aspect of the job.

Career Path Sales managers begin as sales representatives. Successful experience may lead to being designated a senior salesperson or sales supervisor. Upon promotion to district or division manager, the individual breaks away from selling per se and becomes a manager. It is possible to be promoted to even higher levels of sales management with additional responsibilities. A vice president of sales or national sales manager heads an entire sales organization.

Salary Sales managers' salaries in a recent year ranged from below $25,000 to more than $250,000, with a median salary of $39,000. Salaries between $75,000 and $100,000 are not uncommon, and many sales managers also earn bonuses. Regional sales managers' salaries averaged $64,000.

PURCHASING AGENTS

The purchasing agent, sometimes called an *industrial buyer* or *procurement manager,* secures the raw materials, component parts, and supplies needed by a firm. Purchasing agents are employed in the private, public, and not-for-profit sectors. More than 624,000 purchasing agents are employed in the United States.

Job Description Purchasing agents must be knowledgeable about the various vendors and their offerings. They must acquire the best possible deals for their employers in terms of price, quality, delivery, and payment. Agents in large enterprises sometimes specialize in certain types of purchases.

Career Path Once a person understands an organization's operations, he or she is given purchasing responsibilities. An assistant purchasing manager usually oversees the work of several agents. Career advancements include the position of director of procurement, director of purchasing, vice president for purchasing, or vice president for materials management.

Salary In a recent year the salary range was $13,959 to $56,581 in the private sector; in government, beginning salaries averaged $24,400. The median salary for purchasing agents was $33,067.

FIRST-LINE SUPERVISORS

Supervisory positions are the first level of management. First-line supervisors direct operating employees in manufacturing, construction, transportation, and distribution. Currently, about 1.8 million first-line supervisors are at work in the United States.

Job Description The primary task of first-line supervisors is to meet company goals and schedules. They are responsible for motivating and leading operating employees to accomplish organization objectives. They also deal with interpersonal relations and conflict, labor-management issues, and on-the-job health and safety matters.

Career Path Some trainee positions are available. A first-line supervisor may be promoted to department head and then to general manager.

Salary Earnings vary greatly depending on the industry. Recently, the median annual income for all first-line supervisors was a little over $30,680.

Many students may eventually select careers in human relations, human resource management, and labor relations. Jobs available in these fields include arbitrators, labor relations specialists, employee benefits specialists, training specialists, college recruiters, industrial psychologists, and employment counselors.

The Bureau of Labor Statistics, which has projected the employment outlook through 2000, forecasts that job opportunities for psychologists will grow faster than the average for all occupations and that opportunities for personnel and labor relations workers will grow about as fast as the average. Some 422,000 people worked in personnel, training, and labor relations positions in a recent year.

ARBITRATORS

Arbitrators use their knowledge of the law and common sense to mediate and settle a variety of disputed issues.

Job Description Many arbitrators specialize in labor relations, providing an alternative to costly lawsuits as a means of solving disputes for businesses, unions, and other parties. They analyze the information submitted to them by their clients (both parties in a dispute) and render judgments on proper settlements.

Career Path Arbitrators often have backgrounds in law. They generally begin with simple cases and, as they gain experience, graduate to more complicated ones.

Salary Earnings vary with experience and the types of cases decided.

LABOR RELATIONS SPECIALISTS

These specialists deal with all aspects of labor-management relations. They assist operating management in contract negotiations with labor unions.

Job Description Labor relations specialists must be knowledgeable in labor law, collective bargaining, and administration of collective bargaining contracts. They assist managers in conducting negotiations and are responsible for administering the organization's labor contracts.

Career Path Beginning labor relations specialists deal with routine matters such as grievances. Their duties expand as they broaden their experience in the field. The director of labor relations, who often heads management teams during labor negotiations, holds the top position in this field.

Salary In a recent year the median annual salary for labor relations managers was $70,000. In the federal government the average annual salary was $50,400.

EMPLOYEE BENEFITS SPECIALISTS

Employee benefits specialists play a key role in the human resource department. They are responsible for designing and administering the company's employee benefits package, which includes insurance and pension plans.

Job Description Employee benefits specialists develop and administer various programs for employees, such as life, health, dental, and disability insurance; pension coverage; profit sharing; and stock options. The job of the specialist in designing and administering these programs has become increasingly complex because of government regulations and the desire of most firms to reduce the cost of employee benefits.

Career Path Beginning employee benefits specialists must familiarize themselves with the details of their company's benefits package. Until they gain experience, their work is closely supervised by senior staff members. With experience, workers take on more design and planning responsibilities.

Salary In a recent year employee benefits managers earned a median salary of $47,300.

TRAINING SPECIALISTS

Training specialists are in charge of the various training and employee education programs that a company offers.

Job Description Training specialists are involved in all phases of company training programs, from assessing the needs for these programs to creating and implementing them to determining their effectiveness. Much of the training specialist's work involves conducting orientation and on-the-job training sessions for new employees. They also help experienced employees to polish their existing skills and learn new ones.

Career Path To learn required skills, training specialists often rotate from department to department within the company or assess training techniques used by other employers. A background in education, instructional technology, or psychology is useful. Training specialists are generally supervised by a training manager.

Salary In a recent year training specialists earned a median salary of $49,400. Corporate training directors earned an average of $63,900.

COLLEGE RECRUITERS

College recruiters visit college campuses and search for qualified job applicants.

Job Description Recruiters travel to campuses with a list of job openings for their companies and the qualifications needed for each job. Recruiters talk with students about job openings, analyze their resumes, interview those who are qualified, and arrange for further interviews at the company's offices for promising candidates.

Salary Salaries vary widely depending on the size and location of the firm and its type of business. The median salary in a recent year was $30,000.

INDUSTRIAL PSYCHOLOGISTS

Industrial and organizational psychologists apply psychological techniques to managerial problems. They may be involved in personnel screening, training, counseling, and other areas.

Job Description Industrial psychologists require comprehensive education in the field of psychology. A psychologist's assistance can be useful in a variety of business situations. The work of an individual psychologist varies in accordance with the assigned activity. For example, he or she may work with management to develop better training programs and to improve worker productivity.

Career Path Educational attainment is very important in this career. At least a master's degree is needed for career progress, and often only those with Ph.D. degrees are eligible for top-level jobs.

Salary The median annual income of doctoral-level psychologists working in business is approximately $76,000.

EMPLOYMENT COUNSELORS

State employment offices employ the bulk of the nation's employment counselors. These people evaluate and place job applicants.

Job Description Employment counselors use interviews and various tests to assess a person's capabilities for the job market. They then try to match these people to available jobs. Sometimes employment counselors get involved in career planning and counseling. They may also work with other agencies or educational institutions to improve a person's job skills.

Career Path Most beginning counselors undergo a training period before taking on a caseload of job applicants. Supervisory and management positions are also available.

Salary In a recent year, salaries of employment counselors with state agencies averaged between $17,000 and $25,000. Those in private industry generally earned more.

CAREER DESIGN EXERCISES

SURVEYING

Before making any decisions about something important—such as choosing a major or deciding on a career—you first need to gather a lot of information. That way, you will feel more confident that your choice is a good one.

To make an informed decision, it is necessary not only that you read about your topic of interest, but that you talk with people who are personally involved. For example, you could uncover many facts about a career interest in the *Occupational Outlook Handbook*. However, to get an idea about what it is really like on the job, you need to visit with people who actually do the work. This process is called "surveying."

In your survey of an important topic, you will complete three sections: "Preparing a Plan," "Conducting Survey," and "Evaluating Results."

THIS EXERCISE WILL HELP YOU TO

- Get the exact information you need to make good decisions.
- Learn how to research any topic of interest.
- Discover a method for making valuable contacts, such as potential employers.
- Verify that you have enough information before you make decisions.

HOW TO LOCATE THE EXERCISE

When you see the main menu for Career Design, select "How Do I Get There?" Then select "Surveying."

LEADERSHIP STYLE

As you have learned, the best leaders vary their style according to what the situation requires. If they are managing a group of unmotivated employees who work only for the paycheck, they would closely supervise the group. By contrast, they might give a highly educated, self-motivated group much more freedom in their work.

Even though your style of leadership may need to change according to the circumstances, it is helpful to know your leadership tendencies. That way, you can determine if a given situation already matches your "natural" leadership style or requires you to change it.

THE EXERCISE WILL HELP YOU TO

- Learn what approaches you like to use in leading others.
- Determine under what circumstances your current leadership style works best.

HOW TO LOCATE THE EXERCISE

When you see the main menu for Career Design, select "Who Am I?" Then select "Leadership Style."

CHAPTER 13

MARKETING MANAGEMENT AND CUSTOMER SATISFACTION

CHAPTER 14

PRODUCT AND PRICING STRATEGIES

CHAPTER 15

DISTRIBUTION STRATEGY

CHAPTER 16

PROMOTIONAL STRATEGY

MARKETING PART MANAGEMENT

CHAPTER

MARKETING MANAGEMENT AND CUSTOMER SATISFACTION

LEARNING GOALS

1. Explain how marketing creates utility, and list the major functions of marketing.
2. Identify the components of a market.
3. Explain the marketing concept.
4. Outline the basic steps in developing a marketing strategy.
5. Identify the components of the marketing environment.
6. Describe the marketing research function.
7. Identify the methods for segmenting consumer and business markets.
8. Differentiate between buyer behavior and consumer behavior, and outline the determinants of both.
9. Describe relationship marketing and how firms use the technique.

MARKETING RESEARCH RENOVATES BUSINESS FOR HYATT

The early years of this decade brought tough times for the hotel industry with losses averaging $1,200 per room in a typical year. Along with such cost-saving measures as cutting 1,000 middle-management jobs and providing fewer towels in hotel room bathrooms, Hyatt's management responded to the losses by refiguring its corporate structure and attitude. Among the many changes, Darryl Hartley-Leonard, Hyatt president, appointed Jim Evans as senior vice president of both marketing and sales. ■ Evans understood that the future of the hotel industry depended on attention to two areas: marketing and customer satisfaction. A focus on meeting customer needs would be crucial. Evans developed cross-functional teams that included members of the operations and finance departments as well as people from sales and marketing to serve each target market. To enhance cooperation within the teams, members underwent cross-training, which helped them to understand the demands of other people's jobs. For 1 day each year, "Hyatt in Touch Day," employees even performed one another's jobs. For example, Evans spent 1 day as a bellhop, carrying guests' luggage. ■ Market research quickly revealed many ways in which Hyatt could improve its customer service. Evans developed the Hyatt Business Plan after market research among business travelers revealed that most of them work harder on the road than ever before. President Hartley-Leonard noted, "A business traveler needs a fax machine and paper clips more than . . . a shower cap or a mint on the pillow at night." ■ Other customer-oriented Hyatt programs include Destination Hyatt and Meeting Connection for business meeting coordinators, Camp Hyatt for families traveling with children, and Gold Passport for frequent guests. In cities where Hyatt competes with larger, newer hotels, the firm focuses on weekend travelers and small groups. ■ Hyatt directs part of its marketing effort toward informing travelers about the various Hyatt programs. Toward this end, the company developed a publicity campaign called "We've Thought of Everything," which supplemented print and TV advertising with direct mail. Whereas Hyatt had aimed earlier campaigns at people who were traveling for fun, this campaign concentrated on travelers in general and on Hyatt's different target markets specifically. Explained Evans, "We're trying to find ways to distinguish ourselves."[1]

WHOEVER SAID THERE'S NO SUCH THING AS OVERNIGHT SUCCESS NEVER STAYED AT A HYATT.
Hyatt Business Plan.
No Phone Access Charges • In-Room Fax • Printers and Copiers • Express Breakfast
At Hyatt, overnight success stories are business as usual—thanks to Hyatt Business Plan. You can take advantage of a personal work space and desk phone with no phone access charges,* in-room fax,** and 24-hour access to photocopiers and printers on your floor. As well as express breakfast and a morning newspaper. A terrific value considering Business Plan is just $15 over the regular room rate. After all, nothing makes you feel better in the morning than a good night's work. Call your travel planner or Hyatt at 1-800-233-1234.
HYATT
HOTELS & RESORTS
We've Thought Of Everything.
Hyatt Hotels and Resorts are managed by two separate groups of companies—companies associated with Hyatt Hotels Corp. and companies associated with Hyatt International Corp. © 1994 Hyatt Corp. *No phone access charges for 800#'s, local calls, and credit card calls. **Fax machine charged per usage.

CHAPTER OVERVIEW

Every organization, profit-oriented or not-for-profit, must serve consumer needs to succeed. J. C. Penney succinctly warned his store managers, "Either you or your replacement will greet the customer within the first 60 seconds." Marketing links the organization and the consumer by determining and analyzing consumer needs and informing consumers that the organization can meet those needs.

In addition to selling goods and services, marketing can advocate ideas or viewpoints and educate people. California's antismoking campaign uses TV commercials and billboards to educate people about the habit's dangers and urge them to stop smoking.

marketing
Planning and executing the conception, pricing, promotion, and distribution of ideas, goods, and services to create exchanges that satisfy individual and organizational objectives.

The American Marketing Association defines **marketing** as planning and executing the conception, pricing, promotion, and distribution of ideas, goods, and services to create exchanges that satisfy individual and organizational objectives. Simply put, the ultimate goal of marketing is customer satisfaction.

This chapter will examine the role of marketing in business and describe how an organization develops a marketing strategy. In addition, the chapter discusses consumer behavior and decision making, and the roles of employees and quality in achieving customer satisfaction.

EXCHANGE PROCESS

exchange process
Process by which two or more parties trade things of value so that each feels better off after the trade.

Marketing activity begins when the exchange process becomes important to society. The **exchange process** occurs when two or more parties trade things of value (goods such as food and clothing or services such as health care and legal advice) so that each party feels better off after the trade. For example, a consumer may trade a check for $15.95 to Barnes & Noble in exchange for a new novel.

Where does marketing fit in the exchange process? Consider a hypothetical island society consisting of two groups, each of which produces its own food and clothing. One of the groups is particularly skilled at sewing and weaving; the other has developed advanced agricultural techniques. The exchange process allows each group to concentrate on what it does best by trading the products of its labor beyond what the group consumes. This specialization and division of work increases total production and raises the standards of living of both groups. The exchange process could not occur, however, if each group did not market its products. This example shows that marketing is a prime determinant of society's overall standard of living.

CREATING UTILITY

utility
Want-satisfying power of a good or service.

Utility has been defined as the want-satisfying power of a good or service. Production creates form utility by converting raw materials and other components into finished goods and services, as when Warner Bros. gathers together actors, a script, a director, scenery, film stock, and a crew to produce a movie. This chapter focuses on the other three types of utility—time, place, and ownership utility, all of which depend on marketing.

A firm creates time utility by offering a good or service when the consumer wants to purchase it. Supermarkets stay open 24 hours a day, allowing customers to shop at their convenience, to offer time utility.

A firm creates place utility by offering a good or service in the right place. Veterinarians who make house calls to examine sick pets provide place utility.

Arranging for an orderly transfer of ownership creates ownership utility. Retailers create ownership utility by accepting cash, checks, or credit cards in payment, making it easier for customers to purchase merchandise. Similarly, Damark International sells computers, furniture, VCRs, tools, and other products via catalogs and an 800 number that customers can call at any time, day or night. Transfer of ownership is only a phone call away.

FUNCTIONS OF MARKETING AS APPLIED TO THE EXCHANGE PROCESS

Marketing is more than just selling; this complex activity affects all aspects of an organization and its dealings with consumers. Marketing adds to the want-satisfying power of goods and services (that is, their utility) by performing eight basic functions: buying, selling, transporting, storing, standardizing and grading, financing, risk taking, and collecting market information. Manufacturers, wholesalers, and retailers can perform these functions.

WHAT IS A MARKET?

A **market** consists of people who have purchasing power along with the ability and authority to buy. You might love to own a Miata convertible, but that does not necessarily mean you can buy one! If not, you are not part of the Miata market.

As one of the first rules, a successful salesperson learns to determine which person in a firm has the authority to make purchasing decisions. Otherwise, the salesperson can waste hours convincing a department head to switch to a particular product, only to discover that the ultimate buying decision rests with the purchasing director.

market
People with both purchasing power and the ability and authority to buy.

CONSUMER AND INDUSTRIAL MARKETS

Markets can be classified by the types of products they handle into two major categories: markets for consumer products and markets for business products. **Consumer products** are goods and services purchased by ultimate consumers for their own use. Most of the products you buy, including clothing, shampoo, and CDs, are consumer goods. **Business products,** sometimes called *organizational* or *industrial products,* are goods and services purchased as inputs, either directly or indirectly, to the production of other goods for resale. The plastic that Epson buys to build its printers is an industrial product.

consumer product
Good or service purchased by the ultimate consumer for his or her own use.

business product
Good or service purchased as an input, either directly or indirectly, to production of other goods for resale.

A good can be a consumer product or a business product, depending on who buys it and why. The computer you buy for use at home is a consumer product; if a company buys that same computer for office use, it becomes a business product. Similarly, the car radio you purchase and install in your car is a consumer product, but an original equipment radio bought and installed by Chrysler is a business product.

Marketers must understand a market's buying patterns and individuals' purchasing behavior. This knowledge is critical whether a marketer deals with consumer or business goods and services.

MARKETING CONCEPT

The **marketing concept** leads a firm to adopt a consumer orientation in order to achieve long-term success. In other words, a business should gear all of its efforts toward satisfying consumer needs. Both profit-oriented and not-for-profit organizations can apply the marketing concept.

Initially, most organizations focus on production. They concern themselves primarily with supplying their product. This situation is common in a **seller's market,** one characterized by shortages. The Mighty Morphin' Power Rangers fad caused the action dolls to fly out of stores as soon as they were delivered, a situation that epitomizes a seller's market. A **buyer's market** is characterized by adequate or even excess supplies. The proliferation of stores that sell discounted computers illustrates a buyer's market. Marketing is crucial in a buyer's market.

The marketing concept evolved with the post–World War II shift from producing wartime supplies to making consumer goods. General Electric's 1952 annual report included a comment that is now considered a classic description of the marketing concept:

marketing concept
Consumer orientation intended to achieve long-term success.

seller's market
Market situation characterized by product shortages.

buyer's market
Market situation characterized by adequate or even excess supplies.

> *(The concept) introduces . . . marketing . . . at the beginning rather than at the end of the production cycle, and integrates marketing into each phase of the business. Thus, marketing, through its studies and research, will establish for the engineer, the design and manufacturing [departments], what the consumer wants in a given product, what price he [or she] is willing to pay, and where and when it will be wanted. Marketing will have authority in product planning, production, scheduling, and inventory control, as well as in sales, distribution, and servicing of the product.*[2]

Implementing the marketing concept can lead to some unexpected destinations. Consider the case of United Parcel Service, a firm that traditionally emphasized punctuality as its primary marketing goal. UPS was determined to deliver all overnight packages by 10:30 a.m.; toward that end, the company performed detailed efficiency studies. It examined such specifics as the speed of elevators and the exact amount of time it took a customer to come to the door; the company even redesigned the seats of delivery vans so that drivers could get in and out more quickly.

However, when UPS surveyed customers to ask how to improve service, the responses were unexpected. Customers didn't focus on punctual delivery; instead, they wanted more access to the people making the deliveries. Mostly, they wanted time to ask questions and get advice about shipping.

UPS took these findings very seriously. Drivers now have 30 minutes a day to spend with customers. Drivers who make sales while interacting with customers receive commissions. Responding to consumer preferences has not been inexpensive for UPS, which has had to hire more drivers. However, listening to customers has been lucrative, and UPS estimates that its new interpretation of the marketing concept has produced millions of dollars in income.[3]

MARKETING IN NOT-FOR-PROFIT ORGANIZATIONS

The marketing concept is also important to not-for-profit organizations. Regis College in Denver, for instance, had university staff conduct marketing studies to assess what potential students—that is, adults in the area—wanted from the school. Today Regis offers numerous off-campus classes so that busy full-time workers can conveniently attend

A UPS driver prepares to make a delivery. UPS management revised its interpretation of the marketing concept when it learned customers wanted not only punctual delivery, but also time to ask questions of and get advice from drivers. Drivers now have thirty minutes per day to interact with customers, and the new interpretation has produced millions of dollars in income.

evening sessions. The school even delivers books and registration materials to those who cannot go to the central campus. An accelerated degree program allows full-time workers to complete their junior and senior years in 2 years of evening classes. The school has also started a franchising business by offering its successful adult education program to other colleges. Says Father David M. Clarke, Regis president, "We're not-for-profit, but we're not for loss either."[4]

The not-for-profit sector includes organizations such as museums, colleges and universities, symphony orchestras, religious and human services organizations, government agencies, political parties, and labor unions. Not-for-profit groups can be classified as either public or private groups. San Diego State University is a public, not-for-profit organization operated by the state of California, while the University of San Diego, a Catholic institution, is a private, not-for-profit organization open to the public. Like a profit-seeking firm, a not-for-profit organization may market a tangible good or an intangible service, or both. The U.S. Postal Service, for example, offers watches and clocks that feature artwork from stamps (tangible goods) as well as mail delivery (an intangible service).

Five types of not-for-profit marketing include person marketing, place marketing, cause marketing, event marketing, and organization marketing. Person marketing efforts seek to attract the attention, interest, and preference of voters toward a specific individual. In marketing by a political candidate, for one example, campaign managers conduct market research to identify voters and financial supporters and then design promotions such as advertising, fund-raising events, and political rallies to reach those voters and donors.

Place marketing attempts to attract people to a particular area such as a city, state, or nation. In addition to marketing their regions as vacation destinations or possible factory locations, representatives of some areas advertise to specific market segments. For instance, Las Vegas, once known solely as a gambling center, now advertises itself as a family destination.

Cause marketing promotes a cause or social issue. Cause marketing examples cover a wide range of issues, including gun control, birth defects, child abuse, physical fitness, overeating, and alcoholism. For-profit organizations may work with not-for-profit organizations in cause marketing, as when Chevron includes an environmental message in its advertising.

Event marketing involves marketing or sponsoring short-term events such as athletic competitions and cultural and charitable performances. Like cause marketing, event marketing often forges partnerships between not-for-profit and for-profit organizations. As an example, rock stars offer concerts to raise money for not-for-profit organizations or charities.

Organization marketing attempts to influence consumers to accept the goals of, receive the services of, or contribute in some way to an organization. The Smithsonian Institution in Washington, D.C., tries to attract new members by offering free 3-month trial memberships. Temporary members receive complimentary issues of *Smithsonian* magazine and qualify for discounts on special tours and items sold through museum gift shops.

DEVELOPING A MARKETING STRATEGY

Every organization, whether it operates for profit or not, needs to develop a **marketing strategy** to effectively reach consumers. The two-step process for developing such a strategy involves (1) studying, analyzing, and selecting a firm's target market and (2) developing a marketing mix to satisfy that market. Figure 13.1 illustrates this process.

Often a company will compose a written marketing plan outlining its marketing strategy. A marketing plan includes information about the target market, sales and revenue goals, the marketing budget, and the timing for implementing the marketing mix.

FIGURE 13.1 A Marketing Mix Reaches a Selected Target Market

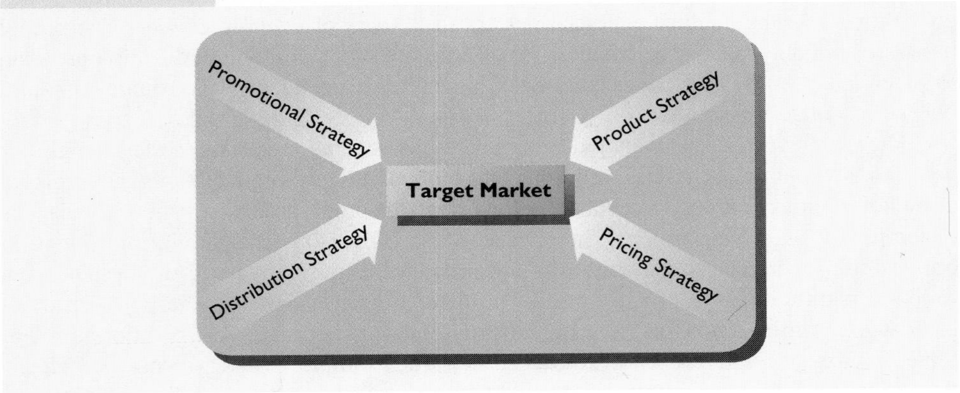

SELECTING A TARGET MARKET

marketing strategy
Studying, analyzing, and selecting a firm's target market and developing a marketing mix to satisfy that market.

target market
Group of consumers toward which an organization directs its marketing efforts.

Consumer needs and wants vary considerably, and no single organization has the resources to satisfy everyone. This fact forces a first decision in developing a marketing strategy: to select a **target market**—the group of consumers toward which an organization will direct its marketing efforts. Consider the following examples.

Sega targets teenagers by pushing a constant flow of exciting new videogames into the market. According to Edward Volkwein, senior vice president of marketing, "Kids' No. 1 desire is to be up on new stuff all the time."[5]

Naxos produces inexpensive classical music CDs; by focusing on the pieces themselves rather than hiring famous (and expensive) musicians, Naxos targets a worldwide audience of people who love music but cannot or choose not to pay up to $20 for a com-

Bausch & Lomb's research showed that by age 65 more than 60 percent of the population experiences significant but correctable hearing loss. Research into the demographics of industrialized countries showed rapid growth of the over-55 age group. This led Bausch & Lomb to target hearing, vision, and dental products to the senior market.

pact disc. Naxos markets its $5.99 CDs (which cost slightly more outside the United States) on its own racks in music stores.[6]

Sometimes an organization aims a good or service at several target markets. A college or university might select several target markets for its fund-raising campaign, including alumni, wealthy benefactors, foundations, and local businesses. Target marketing requires considerable research and analysis, as later sections of the chapter dicuss.

DEVELOPING A MARKETING MIX

Organizations must create a marketing mix to satisfy the needs of their target markets. The **marketing mix** combines the firm's product, pricing, distribution, and promotion strategies. The marketing mix allows the organization to match consumer needs with product offerings.

marketing mix
Organization's combined product, pricing, distribution, and promotion strategies.

Product strategy includes decisions about a firm's package designs, brand names, trademarks, warranty, product life cycle, and new-product developments; Chapter 14 examines this subject in depth. Pricing strategy, also discussed in Chapter 14, is one of the most difficult questions in marketing decision making. Distribution strategy, examined in Chapter 15, involves physical distribution of goods, selection of distribution channels, and organization of wholesaling intermediaries and retailers who distribute the firm's products. Promotional strategy, explored in Chapter 16, involves personal selling, advertising, sales-promotion tools, and public relations. The organization must carefully blend these elements to produce effective communication between the firm and the marketplace.

To illustrate how to combine marketing-mix elements to satisfy the needs of a target market, consider Steven Spielberg's record-breaking movie *Jurassic Park.* The movie needed a particularly strong marketing mix since the target market included virtually everyone on earth.

The marketing of *Jurassic Park* started when Spielberg signed on to the project. Because of his fame and track record in movies like *E.T.* and *Close Encounters of the Third Kind,* many magazines, newspapers, and TV shows immediately started covering the movie (promotion). Spielberg used state-of-the-art special effects and his own considerable skills to make an exciting, crowd-pleasing movie (product). In addition, MCA, the movie studio that released *Jurassic Park,* contracted with over 100 licensees, including McDonald's and Toys R Us, to produce more than 1,000 related products; each licensee publicized the movie as it publicized its own product (promotion and product).

Tickets for *Jurassic Park* went on sale 3 weeks before the movie opened, and people who charged their tickets by phone were entered into the "*Jurassic Park* Journey of a Lifetime" sweepstakes (distribution and promotion). In addition, the movie opened in other countries soon after the U.S. opening, so the U.S. publicity served as a launching point for international publicity (distribution and promotion).

The marketing mix for *Jurassic Park* succeeded so well that the movie took in some $900 million, and MCA and Amblin Entertainment (Spielberg's company) were jointly named *Advertising Age*'s Promotional Marketer of the Year. Still, the development of the marketing mix for *Jurassic Park* had only begun!

When MCA released *Jurassic Park* on video, it teamed with distributor Universal Home Video for a second round of promotions. Tie-ins with McDonald's and Jell-O guaranteed that the familiar *Jurassic Park* logo would fill TV screens and print ads (promotion). In addition, the video was released internationally soon after the U.S. release (distribution). To complete the marketing mix, the *Jurassic Park* video carried a reasonable price of $24.98, with discount coupons available with purchases of tie-in products from McDonald's and Jell-O (price). *Jurassic Park*'s hard-hitting marketing mix may well make it the most financially successful movie in the history of film.[7]

STRENGTH IN DIVERSITY

TARGET MARKET: GAY AND LESBIAN AMERICA Marketers have been reluctant to advertise directly to gays and lesbians for years. Would advertising to gays alienate a company's straight customers? Would a company advertising to gays be viewed as supporting the gay lifestyle? Would a marketer running an ad in a gay publication be associated with any sexually explicit pictures known to appear in the issues? All of these concerns and more have caused mainstream marketers to ignore the gay segment. ■ Several factors have caused marketers to reevaluate the segment, though. One factor, the recession, made many companies tighten purse strings, diminishing their advertising budgets. As a result, marketers are focusing their advertising dollars on current product users and segments with highly desirable demographics. Another factor is the availability of media. Many marketers have saturated conventional media vehicles with their advertisements. Finally, other marketers are promoting products with declining market shares. These marketers are looking for new segments to target. ■ The gay segment, which accounts for about 6 percent of the population, is very desirable for advertisers. The spending power of the gay and lesbian market is estimated to be approximately $500 billion annually. The segment is affluent; the average annual income of a gay household is over $51,000 while the annual income of a lesbian household is around $43,000. These consumers are well-educated, brand-loyal, and image-conscious, especially in regard to luxury and fashion products. Gay and lesbian households often have high levels of disposable income. ■ Some marketers recognized the viability of the segment long ago. Miller Beer has been targeting gays since 1989. The company recently signed on as the first national sponsor of the International Gay Rodeo Association's 15 events. Philip Morris has been pursuing the segment because of its desirable demographics. A company representative said, "We included *Genre* because we're targeting young adult smokers in their mid-20s, with a somewhat affluent background. It wasn't the fact that the publication reached the gay market. It reached young adult males." ■ The appealing demographics have attracted many new national advertisers such as Ikea, Saab, American Express, AT&T, Philip Morris, Virgin Atlantic Airways, Benetton, and Hiram Walker & Sons to promote to gays. Some of these advertisers run their usual ads in gay publications. Others customize ads for the segment. American Express, for example, advertises traveler's checks with the signatures of two men and two women. Ikea came under criticism for running a television spot featuring two gay men shopping for furniture in one of its stores. AT&T used a direct-mail brochure featuring

STANDARDIZATION VERSUS ADAPTATION IN GLOBAL MARKETS

Marketing a good or service overseas involves an important choice: does the organization sell the same product to everyone (standardization), or does it modify the product to fit each market (adaptation)? This choice translates into four basic marketing alternatives: selling the existing product in the international marketplace, modifying the product for different countries or regions, designing new products for foreign markets, or incorporating all of the various national differences into one product design and introducing a global product.

The advantages of standardizing include lower costs. This approach works best with business goods, such as steel, chemicals, and farm equipment, and other products whose acceptance tends not to depend on national cultures.

Adaptation, on the other hand, lets companies deal more effectively with local competitors, consumer behavior patterns, and government regulations. Consumer goods generally require adaptation because their popularity tends to depend more on culture than that of business products.

Different companies are trying different approaches to the daunting task of convincing British consumers to try iced tea. Hot tea is a staple of the British diet, but iced tea was alien to the British Isles until recently. Snapple is betting on standardization by three couples—two men, two women, and a man and a woman—all in affectionate poses with the slogan "Let Your True Voice Be Heard." ■ Until recently, the *Advocate* was the only publication through which advertisers could reach gays. With its controversial political views, sexually explicit pictures, and phone-sex ads, however, advertisers shied away. To attract advertisers, though, the *Advocate* has shifted these features to a separate publication called *The Advocate Classifieds,* making the *Advocate* more advertiser friendly. Many other opportunities now give access to the gay and lesbian segment. Publications such as *Genre* and *Out* are more lifestyle oriented rather than politically oriented, making them appealing to the advertising community. Gay events such as the Gay Games and Cultural Festival in New York attract 500,000 visitors who are estimated to spend $111 million during the week of the events. Corporate sponsorships range from $50,000 to $500,000 for the games. Since Miller Beer signed on as a sponsor last year, other marketers have followed suit. ■ Opportunities also exist to coordinate promotions to reach the gay and lesbian market. At a recent march in Washington, D.C., a marketer hired 350 people to hand out 500,000 event packs that included promotions and ads for a range of products from gay-oriented travel packages to books to health clubs to health foods. Epic, a major recording label, distributed several thousand copies of cassettes with samples of releases from gay-friendly acts such as the Indigo Girls and Basia. The company hopes to increase consumer interest in the bands and their recordings. ■ Another, more discreet means of reaching gays is through Direct Male, a direct-mail vehicle sent to households with gay men. The packets are mailed to 50,000 households three times a year. Philip Morris and Ramada Inn have both advertised in Direct Male and were happy with the response. Philip Morris included a smoker's survey in the pack promising a free lighter to consumers who participated in the survey. A company representative said, "It was an inexpensive way to reach adult males—with a high response rate." ■ Advertising to gays can be very lucrative for a company. Says Rick Dean of Overlooked Opinions, a marketing research firm specializing in the gay market, "Companies that market directly to gays tend to get the stranglehold for that product in the gay market." However, marketers must be aware of segments within the gay market. Robert Bray of the National Gay and Lesbian Task Force warns, "I would caution marketers who think there is only one way to reach gays. It's very different trying to reach gay men in West Hollywood than, say, lesbians in Columbus, Ohio." Sources: "More Companies Aim Ads at Gays." *Mobile Register,* October 9, 1994, p. 7-F; Larry Flick, "Major Labels Courting Gay, Lesbian Market," *Billboard,* July 30, 1994, p. 1; Riccardo A. Davis, "Marketers Game for Gay Events," *Advertising Age,* May 30, 1994, p. S-1; and Gary Levin, "Mainstream's Domino Effect," *Advertising Age,* May 30, 1994, p. 30.

QUESTIONS FOR CRITICAL THINKING

1. Which do you think is more effective: running current ads in gay media or customizing ads for the segment?
2. If you were in charge of public relations for a company, how would you respond to complaints from customers who oppose the strategy of advertising to the gay segment?
3. Should the gay market be handled or approached any differently than any other segment? Why or why not?

attempting to win British customers over with noncarbonated fruit drinks; the company hopes that they will enjoy Snapple products enough to give its flavored iced teas a chance. Unilever's Brooke Bond Foods Ltd. and PepsiCo produce Liptonice, a carbonated iced tea; they hope that this adaptation will make the product attractive to the unenthusiastic Britons. The third major iced tea maker, Nestea, has chosen a third road by focusing on other European markets and skipping the United Kingdom altogether.[8]

MARKETING ENVIRONMENT

In selecting a target market and developing a marketing mix, marketers must consider the competitive, political and legal, economic, technological, and social and cultural environments in which they work. These five external forces, outlined in Figure 13.2, provide a framework for planning product, pricing, distribution, and promotional strategies aimed at a target market.

COMPETITIVE ENVIRONMENT

Marketers must continually monitor the activities of their firm's competitors in order to devise a strategy that will give them a marketing edge. This can be a very difficult goal, as the competitive environment may change day by day. For example, Goodyear devel-

FIGURE 13.2 COMPONENTS OF THE MARKETING ENVIRONMENT

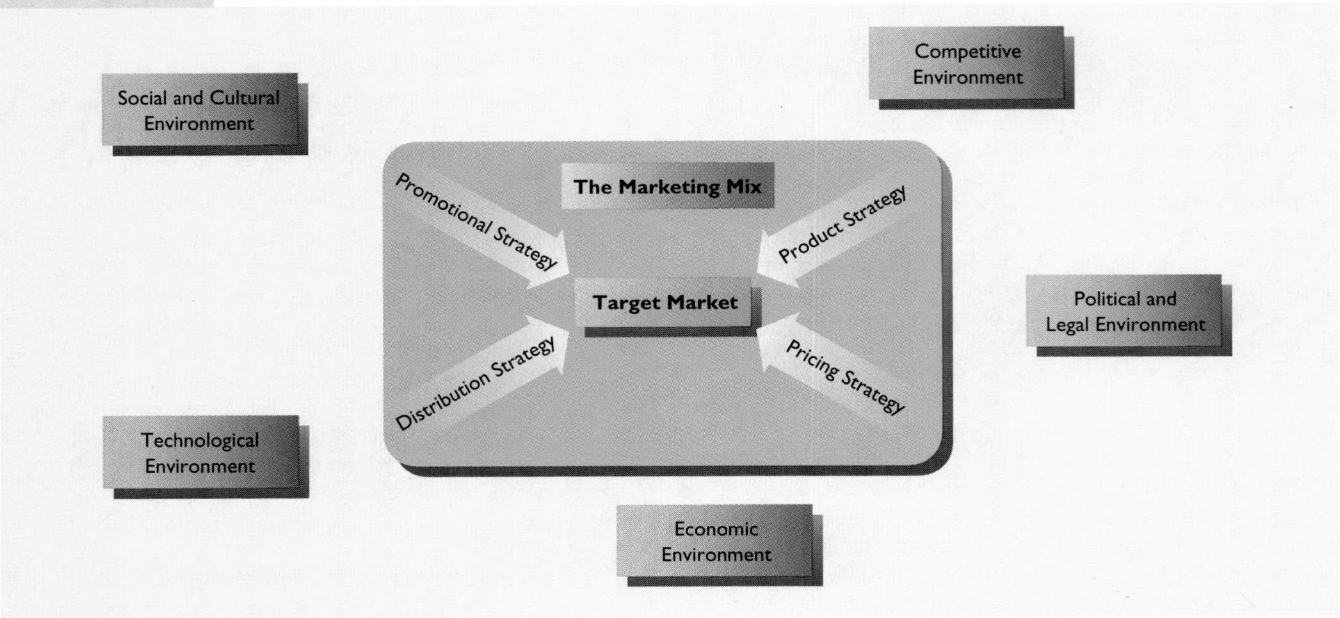

oped a tire, the Aquatred, that offers extra safety by pushing water away from itself. Almost immediately, Goodyear's competitors produced similar tires.[9]

POLITICAL AND LEGAL ENVIRONMENT

Federal, state, and local laws regulate many marketing activities, ranging from package labeling to product safety decisions. These laws are designed to maintain a competitive environment and protect consumers; noncompliance can expose the firm to fines, bad publicity, and lawsuits. Furthermore, the legal environment can change enormously from year to year. For example, the automotive industry has had to adapt to laws specifying emission limits and the cigarette industry is battling antismoking laws across the entire country.

One change in the political and legal environment may have far-reaching ramifications. Some states have begun to try to tax out-of-state companies that license logos or products or in some way profit from commerce related to intangible assets in those states. The trendsetter, South Carolina, has succeeded in forcing New Jersey–based Toys R Us to pay South Carolina state taxes because Toys R Us collects royalties on use of its Geoffrey mascot in that state. If more states succeed in taxing out-of-state organizations, banks, publishers, software companies, trademark holders, and celebrities (who often license use of their names and likenesses) will see smaller bottom lines, and they may have to change the way they do business.[10]

ECONOMIC ENVIRONMENT

Economic forces such as inflation, unemployment, and business cycles influence how much consumers are willing and able to spend as well as what they buy. For example, interest rate hikes by the Federal Reserve slowed the housing market in late 1994. Understanding how economic forces influence consumer buying behavior allows marketers to adjust their marketing-mix strategies.

During a recession, consumers more willingly buy basic products with low prices; marketers might respond to such a trend by lowering prices and increasing promotional spending to stimulate demand. Different strategies succeed during prosperous times, when consumers decide to purchase higher-priced goods and services. Marketers might then consider raising prices, expanding distribution, and multiplying product lines.

TECHNOLOGICAL ENVIRONMENT

Changes in technology have significant effects on how marketers design, produce, price, distribute, and promote their goods and services. New technology can make a product obsolete. Just as carbon paper gave way to copying machines and vinyl records lost the music market to compact discs, today's state-of-the-art technology may some day be eclipsed. Therefore, organizations must keep looking ahead for technological advances with which to gain competitive advantage and create new marketing opportunities.

SOCIAL AND CULTURAL ENVIRONMENT

Consumer values change, and marketers must keep abreast of these changes to keep their marketing strategies on target. One recent social change, discussed in more detail in Chapter 16, is consumer emphasis on recycling and limiting wasteful packaging. Hewlett-Packard has responded to this consumer trend by packaging its fax machines in boxes labeled "For a better environment, this container was not bleached white. All printing was done using water-based inks. All packaging materials were manufactured without CFCs."

To some extent, all organizations feel the effects on external forces in the marketing environment. Marketers must monitor these forces; assess the impact they will have on goods, services, and marketing practices; and then adjust their marketing strategies accordingly.

MARKETING RESEARCH

Marketing research collects and evaluates information to help make marketing decisions. It links the marketer to the marketplace by providing data about potential target markets to design effective marketing mixes. Marketers conduct research to identify marketing problems and opportunities, to analyze competitors' strategies, to evaluate and predict consumer behavior, to gauge the performance of existing products and package designs and assess the potential of new ones, and to develop price, promotion, and distribution plans.

marketing research
Collection and evaluation of information to help make marketing decisions.

Marketing research involves more than just collecting information. Researchers must decide how to collect the information, interpret the results, and communicate the results to managers to support their decision making.

DATA COLLECTION PROCESS

Marketing researchers look for both internal data and external data. An organization generates internal data within its own operations. Researchers can find a tremendous amount of useful information from financial records about such variables as changes in accounts receivable, inventory levels, customers, product lines, profitability of particular divisions, and sales volumes by territories, salespeople, customers, or product lines.

Researchers can find external data, information generated outside the firm, from various sources. Trade associations, for example, publish reports on activities in particular industries. Advertising agencies collect information on the audiences reached by various media. National marketing research firms offer information to organizations by subscription.

A group of doctors blows bubbles before being surveyed by a marketing research firm. The firm believes that playing games encourages participants to relax. Relaxed subjects may speak more openly and reveal their true feelings and attitudes, giving researchers more valid information.

Federal, state, and local government publications are important data sources. Researchers most frequently rely on government statistics for census data on population characteristics such as age, sex, race, education level, household size and composition, occupation, employment status, and income. This information helps marketers to assess the buying behavior of certain segments of the population, anticipate changes in their markets, and identify markets with growth potential.

In addition to reviewing published data, market researchers also gather information by conducting observational studies and surveys. In observational studies, researchers view the actions of the respondents, either directly or through mechanical devices. Traffic counts can determine the best location for a new fast-food restaurant. People meters (electronic, remote-control devices that record the viewing habits of each household member) monitor television audience viewership to provide a basis for setting advertising rates.

Simple observation cannot supply some information. When researchers need information about attitudes, opinions, and motives, they often conduct surveys. Survey methods include:

1. Telephone interviews
2. Mail surveys
3. Personal interviews
4. Focus groups

A focus group interview brings together 8 to 12 people in one location to discuss a particular topic. Ideas generated during focus group interviews are especially helpful to marketers in developing new products, improving existing products, and creating effective advertising campaigns.

The information collected by researchers becomes valuable only when it can support decisions within the framework of the organization's strategic plan. When researchers collect more accurate information, more effective marketing strategies result.

DATABASE MARKETING RESEARCH

database
Collections of data accessible by computer.

Like most businesspeople, marketing researchers have benefited greatly from widespread access to computers. Data collections that are accessible by computer are known as **data-**

bases. Some companies keep their own databases, perhaps including customers' names and addresses, frequency of purchases, favored products, family sizes and makeups, and places of employment. Firms gather some data in conventional ways, such as telephone interviewing and group surveys, and then input the data into the database. They gather other data directly by computer systems, as when a customer places a phone order and the salesperson keyboards all relevant data.

Marketing Information Systems Using a **marketing information system (MIS),** market researchers can manage an overwhelming flood of information by having a computer organize data in a logical and accessible manner. An MIS combines internal and external data, stores and classifies the data, analyzes and retrieves data according to decision makers' needs, and produces information that matches users' needs. Through the MIS, a company can monitor its marketing strategies and identify any problems.

marketing information system (MIS)
System that combines internal and external data, stores and classifies the data, analyzes and retrieves the data according to decision makers' needs, and produces information that matches users' needs.

Marketing Decision Support Systems A **marketing decision support system (MDSS),** part of an MIS, displays information in useful visual and graphic forms. As with the MIS, the database forms the foundation of the MDSS. The user accesses the database through interactive instructions and displays. Through graphics, spreadsheet, and modeling software, the user can then assess the current condition of the market, forecast future market conditions, and simulate the results of various marketing strategies. Other uses of an MDSS include sales analyses and forecasts and analyses of customer behavior. The MDSS turns data into usable tools for marketers.

marketing decision support system (MDSS)
Part of an MIS that displays information in useful visual and graphic forms.

Using an MIS and MDSS Through an MIS, a marketer might retrieve the exact number of cans of chicken noodle soup sold each day in a particular supermarket chain over the last year, then use the MDSS to turn that data into a graph. By adding information about the timing of advertising campaigns, the marketer could trace the effect of advertising on the sale of chicken noodle soup. This information could then guide decisions about future advertising.

Cindy Lay, director of marketing research for Proffitt's Inc., a department store chain in Tennessee, used her customer database to examine in detail the buying habits of women who purchased Liz Claiborne and Anne Klein dresses. After discovering that many waited until the dresses had been marked down twice before buying them, Lay responded by notifying these customers of a special two-day sale, turning the marketing of slightly discounted dresses into a special event. Dress sales increased by 97 percent, and Proffitt's made up to $75 more per dress.[11]

Marketers also use commercial online services, such as CompuServe, America Online, NEXIS, and Dow Jones News/Retrieval Service. Through these services, market researchers can find databases about specific target markets; search through magazines, newspapers, and trade journals; peruse industry forecasts; and research companies on the New York and American Stock Exchanges.

MARKET SEGMENTATION

Identifying target markets for a product is crucial to marketing success. **Market segmentation,** the process of dividing a total market into several relatively homogeneous groups, is a way to identify target markets. Both profit-oriented and not-for-profit organizations practice market segmentation to help define their target markets.

Firms can segment markets in a variety of ways. Consumer marketers practice demographic, geographic, psychographic, and product-related segmentation. Business marketers rely on geographic, customer-based, and end-use segmentation.

Market segmentation works best when it can quantify the segment in terms of both size and spending power. Once they identify a target market segment, marketers can create an appropriate marketing strategy.

market segmentation
Process of dividing a total market into several relatively homogeneous groups.

A company must plan to defend a targeted segment against inroads by a competitor. Does another company have a better way of reaching the target segment, of keeping the targeted customers happy, or of offering better prices or service? Is another company developing a new technology that can lure away the market segment? By answering these questions, a company can improve its own market segmentation and prepare ways to defend its market segment from competitors.[12]

Market segmentation allows concentrated, or niche, marketing, in which the marketer aims only at a particular segment of a total market. For instance, to reach owners of pickup trucks, a marketer would place advertisements in vehicle-related magazines rather than in *People* or *Newsweek.* Micromarketing takes this concept one step further by targeting people in a particular neighborhood or who hold a particular job. Both concentrated marketing and micromarketing allow efficient application of the advertising dollar, with strategies aimed directly at the target market. Both approaches also rely on sales to a few customers with the risk that changes in consumer buying habits will have large negative impacts.

SEGMENTING CONSUMER MARKETS

The most common basis for segmenting consumer markets sets divisions that reflect demographics. Firms have practiced geographic segmentation for centuries, and more recently marketers have turned to psychographic and product-related segmentation, as well.

GEOGRAPHIC SEGMENTATION

Geographic segmentation, one of the oldest segmentation methods, can be extremely useful when consumer preferences and purchase patterns for a good or service differ between regions. However, contemporary marketers face the problem that marketplaces keep shifting. For instance, the U.S. population has shown a decided movement to the Sunbelt and coastal areas and westward.

Perhaps as a result of these movements, research on geographic preferences can provide surprising results. Cold remedies sell particularly well in San Antonio while Wonder Bread is a hit in New York. The people of Salt Lake City chew a lot of bubble gum, and Chicagoans are quite fond of Twinkies.[13]

Sometimes geographic segmentation succeeds not by catering to the habits or preferences of the people of a certain region, but rather because a product, or a way of marketing it, is new to that region. Managers of the small company PageNet knew they had to develop a strong and specific marketing strategy to compete with corporate giants Southwestern Bell and Pacific Telesis. As one of its first steps, PageNet targeted the geographic segments of Ohio and Texas. PageNet managers believed that in each state, charging consistently low prices could win PageNet a chunk of the market. After succeeding in these markets, PageNet branched out, geographic segment by geographic segment.[14]

DEMOGRAPHIC SEGMENTATION

Demographic segmentation, the most common segmentation approach, divides markets on the basis of demographic or socioeconomic characteristics such as sex, income, age, occupation, household size, education, family life-cycle stage, and ethnic group. For example, PageNet extended its market segmentation strategy to include the demographic facet of occupation. PageNet managers judged that members of the several professions would most likely use pagers, including salespeople, messengers, doctors, and lawyers.[15]

Avon attempts to reach readers of the magazine *Hispanic* with this Spanish-language ad. Survey results showed Hispanic consumers are more inclined to buy products with Spanish-language ads, so many marketers are using this strategy to woo this demographic segment.

Ethnic group marketing also relies on demographic segmentation. However, with "minorities" predicted to account for 33 percent of consumers by the turn of the century, these efforts amount to a lot more than niche marketing. Although more than 50 percent of companies in the *Fortune* 500 embrace ethnic marketing, many companies seem reluctant to target ethnic groups, often because they don't know how. As Geri Duncan Jones of the American Health and Beauty Aids Institute remarked, "Ethnic consumers are not simply white consumers with different-colored skin." Maintaining customer satisfaction is the key here, just as in the majority market.

When market research revealed that Hispanics consume more smoked sausage than the American population in general, Hillshire Farms & Kahn's, a subsidiary of Sara Lee Corp., developed radio advertisements, recipes, and coupons in Spanish. "Disfrute el sabor de lo mejor," they all say. "Enjoy the taste of the best."

Sometimes companies generate new products specifically for ethnic markets. For example, Tyco Toys has developed Ana, La Quinceanera, a doll that celebrates turning 15 years old—a special birthday for Hispanic girls with backgrounds in certain countries.

Because ethnic groups are so large and varied, marketing to them requires complex analysis. According to the U.S. Census Bureau, Asian Americans come from 16 separate countries of origin; Hispanic Americans come from more than 25. Nevertheless, certain marketing strategies and tactics have proven successful. More than half of Hispanic consumers responding to a survey said that they were more inclined to buy products with Spanish-language ads. Over 60 percent of African Americans named equal treatment as one of their main criteria in choosing where to shop. Lafayette Jones of Segmented Marketing Services Inc. says that marketers "must maintain respect and understanding for [ethnic] differences. That, in a nutshell, is what effective ethnic marketing is all about."[16]

PSYCHOGRAPHIC SEGMENTATION

Psychographic segmentation segments markets based on behavioral and lifestyle profiles. Lifestyle is the summation of a consumer's needs, preferences, motives, attitudes, family, job, social habits, and cultural background. Psychographic analysis evaluates these facets of people's lives to define various groups of individuals within society, enabling a firm to tailor its marketing approach to a carefully chosen market segment.

SRI International, a market research firm, has identified a set of lifestyle categories that have helped marketers to segment markets. The VALS 2 (Values and Lifestyles) Program classifies consumers according to resources (income, education, self-confidence, health, eagerness to buy, intelligence, and energy level) and self-orientation (principle-oriented, status-oriented, and action-oriented). The VALS 2 program is illustrated in Figure 13.3.

Principle-oriented consumers have set views. They include fulfillers (mature, home-oriented, well-educated professionals who like value and welcome new ideas) and believers (family-oriented and community-oriented people who are brand loyal and favor American-made products). The status-oriented groups consist of achievers (work-oriented, successful types who like their jobs, respect authority, and favor the status quo) and strivers (lower-income workers with values similar to those of achievers). Action-oriented consumers include experiencers (people who engage in active physical and social activities and avidly consume new products) and makers (self-sufficient people with little interest in material possessions). The two final VALS 2 categories are strugglers, who have few resources, but who remain brand loyal to the extent possible, and actualizers, who have high incomes and high self-esteem and tend to indulge their self-orientations in a variety of ways.

FIGURE 13.3 VALS 2 GROUPINGS

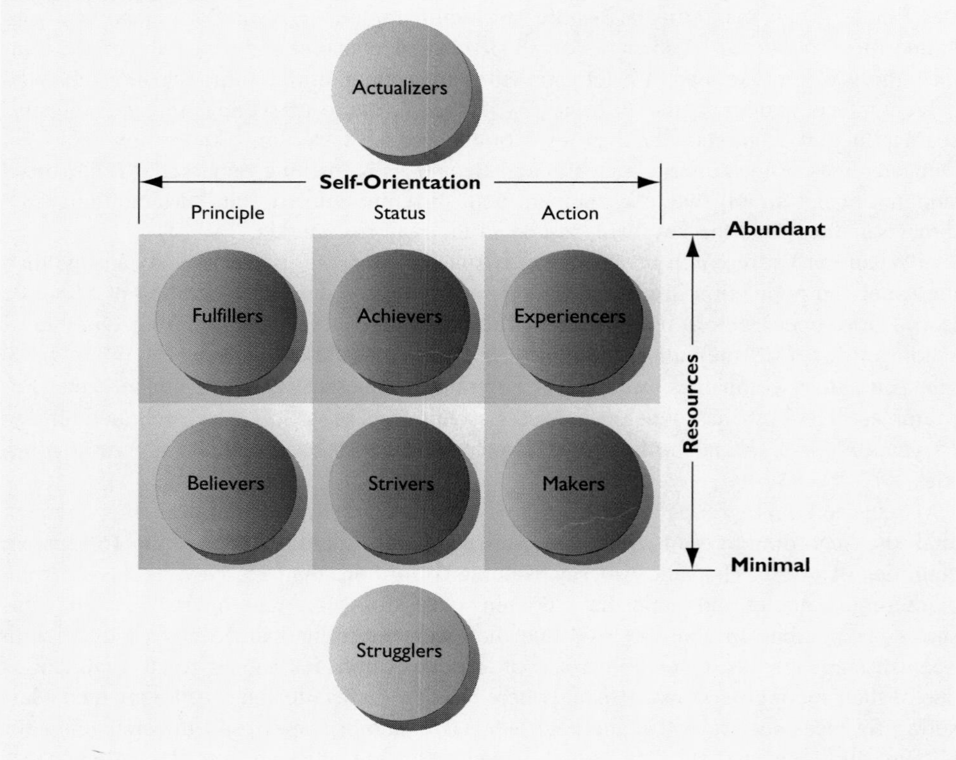

The VALS 2 system allows marketers to identify consumers who are likely to desire their firm's goods and services. SRI analyzes research data and characterizes respondents according to the eight VALS 2 groups for marketers who subscribe to its service.[17]

PageNet used a simple form of psychographic segmentation, focusing on people who might see their lifestyles enhanced by its pagers. Among these people were families with an older relative who might want or need to contact a family member.[18]

PRODUCT-RELATED SEGMENTATION

Product-related segmentation classifies consumers according to their relationships to the good or service. This segmentation approach can take three forms: (1) segmenting by the benefits buyers derive from a good or service, (2) segmenting by usage rates for a product, and (3) segmenting by degree of brand loyalty.

To illustrate product-related segmentation, Canon Computer Systems targeted owners of its color printer as the potential audience for a color scanner; as a result, 50 percent of the printer users who received direct mail offers from Canon requested more information, a very high response rate. As a bonus, Canon offered purchasers of the new scanner four free printer ink cartridges.[19]

Segmenting a target audience according to product usage rate usually breaks that audience into heavy-user, medium-user, and light-user segments. The heavy-user segment, often estimated at 20 percent of a product's audience, can often account for 80 percent of its sales, leading to the so-called *80/20 principle.* Airlines reward their loyal heavy-user segments by awarding frequent flyer miles. A marketer trying to win over a competitor's heavy-user segment would take a different tack. A firm can often reach light-users and nonusers more easily than a competitor's best customers since it need not overcome preexisting habits.

Another form of product-related segmentation focuses on customers' degrees of brand loyalty. Reaching out to people who drink six cans of cola each day requires a different marketing strategy than approaching people who drink six cans of Mandarin Orange Slice each day. Once a company has identified its brand loyal audience, it can cater to that audience by offering special coupons or giveaway items like T-shirts.

SEGMENTING BUSINESS MARKETS

Market segmentation also helps firms to target business (or organizational or industrial) marketing. Business segmentation employs geographic segmentation, customer-based segmentation, or end-use segmentation.

Vendors in geographically concentrated industries such as aircraft manufacturing, automobiles, and oil field equipment find geographic segmentation useful since they can assign salespeople to areas that serve specific industries.

Customer-based segmentation designs a business good or service to suit a specific organizational market. Clothing makers who specialize in police uniforms practice customer-based segmentation.

The exact way the customer will use a product, the end-use application, determines the third method of segmenting business markets. For instance, a variety of suppliers have designed software packages that connect retailers with their vendors by computer. This linkage is referred to as *electronic data interchange,* or *EDI.*

BUYER BEHAVIOR

After breaking down a total market, marketers must consider the behavior of consumers and business users in various market segments. **Buyer behavior** refers to the process by which buyers make purchase decisions. Buyer behavior is a broad term that covers both ultimate consumers and business buyers. By contrast, the term **consumer behavior** refers

buyer behavior
Process by which consumers and business buyers make purchase decisions.

consumer behavior
Buyer behavior of ultimate consumers.

to the buying behavior of ultimate consumers only. By studying buyer behavior, marketers can identify attitudes toward their products and how customers use the products. This information helps marketers to develop more effective marketing strategies.

INFLUENCES ON CONSUMER BEHAVIOR

Both personal and interpersonal factors influence the behavior of an ultimate consumer. Personal influences on consumer behavior include a person's needs and motives, perceptions, attitudes, learned experiences, and self-concept. Marketers frequently apply psychological techniques to understand what motivates people to buy and to study consumers' emotional reactions to goods and services.

Managers at Ford Motor Company decided that the 45 percent industry average of people who bought the same brand of car a second time was too low, so they looked for services they could provide to influence consumers to view Ford positively. Ford discovered almost 100 ways to please customers, including providing transportation while their cars were being fixed and providing "a pleasant, nonpressured purchase experience."[20] Ford then developed specific service and sales standards by which Ford dealers could measure their success in dealing with customers.

The interpersonal determinants of consumer behavior include cultural influences, social influences, and family influences. For example, retailers of ethnic health and beauty care products have found that carrying these goods causes ethnic customers to develop greater store loyalty.[21]

INFLUENCES ON BUSINESS BUYING BEHAVIOR

Business purchasers face a variety of organizational influences, since many people can play roles in such purchases. A design engineer may help to set the specifications that potential vendors must satisfy. A procurement manager may invite selected companies to bid on a purchase. A production supervisor may evaluate the operational aspects of the proposals that the firm receives, and the vice president of manufacturing may make the final decision.

CONSUMER DECISION-MAKING PROCESS

Consumer decision making follows the sequential process outlined in Figure 13.4. This process begins when the consumer recognizes a problem or opportunity. If someone needs a new pair of shoes, that becomes a problem to solve. If someone wins $5,000 in the New Jersey state lottery, that becomes an opportunity to enjoy.

To solve the problem or take advantage of the opportunity, the consumer seeks out information about the intended purchase and evaluates alternatives, such as available brands. The goal is to find the best response to the perceived problem or opportunity.

Eventually the consumer reaches a decision and completes the transaction (the purchase act). Later, he or she will evaluate the experience with the purchase (postpurchase evaluation). Feelings about the experience will influence future purchase decisions (feedback). Both interpersonal and personal determinants of consumer behavior affect the various steps in the sequence.

RELATIONSHIP MARKETING

The concept of relationship marketing displays close links to both market segmentation and buyer behavior. **Relationship marketing** refers to situations where a company develops long-term, cost-effective links with individual customers for the mutual benefit of both. These relationships with customers can become vital strategic tools for a firm. As discussed earlier, preexisting customers often make the best customers, and main-

FIGURE 13.4 STEPS IN CONSUMER DECISION MAKING

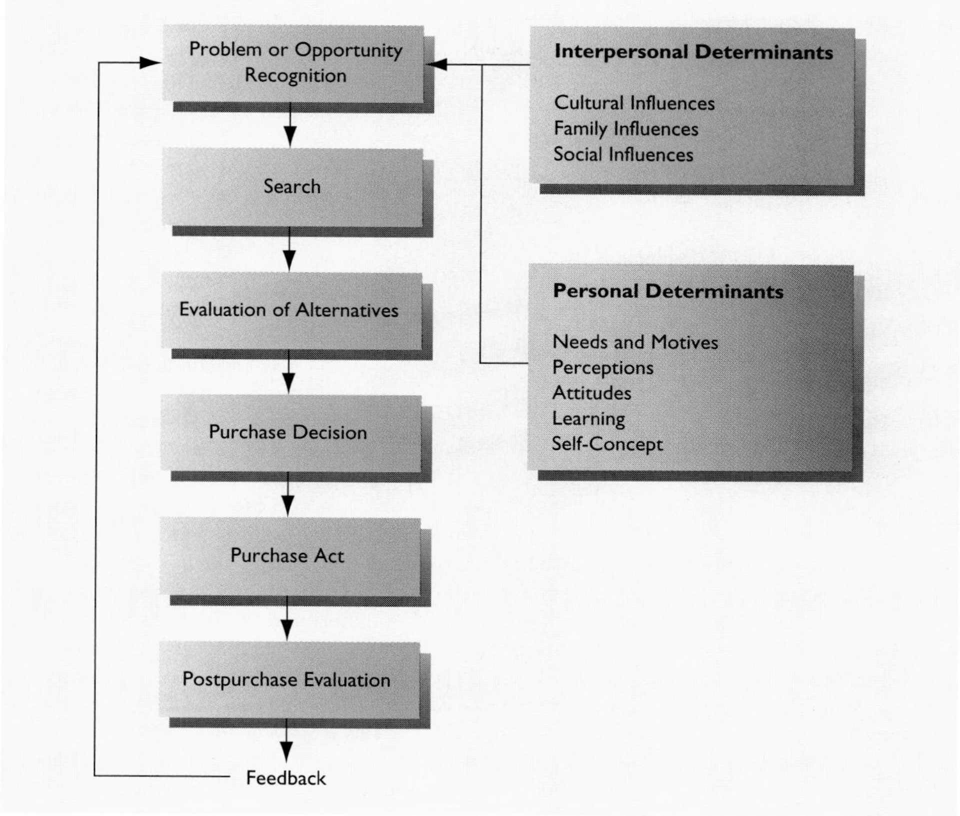

taining a positive and personal relationship with them can anchor a strong and successful marketing strategy. Examples of relationship marketing include giving special offers to particular customers, personalizing direct mail to them, and otherwise treating customers as individuals rather than as parts of a group.

relationship marketing
Program by a company to develop long-term, cost-effective links with customers.

Consider Nestlé's relationship marketing efforts in France. The marketers at Nestlé Baby Food of France call their version of relationship marketing *individualized marketing.* In an early step in this marketing approach, Nestlé sought to improve the vacations of French families by setting up rest stops alongside various highways. Each rest stop, or *Le Relais Bébé,* is a small blue and white structure with pictures of cartoon teddy bear Ptipo, the emblem of Nestlé baby food, painted on the sides. Hostesses at these rest stops give away baby food and disposable diapers, and the sites offer high chairs and changing tables. This service encourages French families to become more familiar with Nestlé products. Says Fabienne Petit, marketing director for Nestlé, "At the key moment of the baby's meal, Nestlé through its hostesses finds itself in direct contact with the mothers in a consumer/brand relationship that is quite unusual." Nestlé also interacts with customers by providing a toll-free number for information about infants' nutritional requirements.

Nestlé's relationship marketing effort centers on a 220,000-item database that stores names and addresses of new mothers and their babies; Nestlé gathers this information from French maternity records. Nestlé sends each mother a mailing including a reply card on which the recipient can agree to receive more mailings. When the baby reaches 3 months old, the mother receives a package that mentions the baby's name and includes samples, coupons, and information on infant development. Further packages arrive when

BUSINESS IN ACTION

WOMEN: A MAJOR FORCE IN CAR BUYING When it considered car buying, Detroit didn't take women seriously for years. Advertisements showed women as passengers in their husbands' cars or applauding their husbands' choices. Occasionally, a mom would be shown loading and unloading kids and groceries from a family car. The Big Three auto makers—General Motors, Ford, and Chrysler—virtually ignored the segment and pursued only the male market. ■ While Detroit ignored women, Japanese auto makers focused on them. In the 1980s, Honda and others researched the American market to identify marketing opportunities. The Japanese introduced a number of compact cars with more standard equipment, better quality, and lower prices than U.S.–made vehicles. To appeal to all consumers, ads for the Japanese cars focused on the cars themselves, and not on who was driving them. This strategy proved successful; the Honda Accord became the best-selling car in the United States in 1989 with women purchasing more than half of the vehicles. ■ After years of losing sales and market share to imports, domestic auto makers finally woke up and discovered that the female segment of the population is a major force behind car buying. Women buy almost half of all vehicles sold in the United States. Industry experts predict that by 2000, women will buy 60 percent of all vehicles sold. Furthermore, women influence between 80 and 85 percent of all new-car purchases. Women drive about half of all cars on the road and 90 percent of all minivans. ■ The demographics of the female segment are most attractive to auto companies today. The U.S. market includes approximately 23 million single adult women. Women represent half of the U.S. work force. More than 6.5 million women earn $75,000 or more a year. Women buy a majority of the cars priced under $20,000. They purchase about 22 percent of light trucks and 39 percent of sport utility vehicles. ■ In response to these facts, Detroit's Big Three changed their marketing strategies. All three corporations created women's advisory committees to ensure attention for women's needs and motives in designs of both products and advertisements. What motivates a

the baby reaches 6 months, 9 months, 1 year, 18 months, and 2 years old. Nestlé even arranges to have the mother receive a rose on Mother's Day, with a card "signed" by her baby.

Petit points to four components in the success of Nestlé's approach: a personal touch, careful timing, providing help instead of just pushing merchandise, and developing a form of friendship with the customer. As a result of this relationship marketing approach, Nestlé's share of the French baby food market has grown from 19 percent to 43 percent in a mere 7 years.[22]

customer satisfaction *Ability of a good or service to meet or exceed a customer's needs and expectations.*

As its ultimate goal, relationship marketing seeks to achieve customer satisfaction, the basis of all successful marketing. Chapter 13 concludes with a discussion of this vital concept.

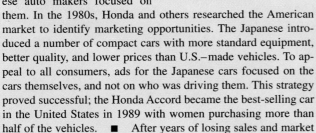

CUSTOMER SATISFACTION

Customer satisfaction is the ability of a good or service to meet or exceed a customer's needs and expectations. It is important because satisfied consumers become long-term customers who account for a big percentage of a company's business. (Remember the 80/20 principle?)

EMPLOYEES AND CUSTOMER SATISFACTION

Employees must become deeply involved in promoting customer satisfaction. A salesperson can gain a customer's loyalty by providing excellent service. An assembly line woman in purchasing a car is quite different from what motivates a man. Women are more interested in dependability, low price, and safety. Men are more interested in prestige, appearance, styling, horsepower, and acceleration. ■ The input from these advisory committees receives serious consideration from auto makers. Many changes have been made in product designs to accommodate the needs of women. Fortunately for the car companies, most of the changes benefit other segments also. Front seats used to be benches adjusted only by drivers. Now, front seats are split and adjusted independently by passengers and drivers. The lumbar support built into seat backs was actually designed for pregnant women, but the feature relieves back strain for men also. Women needed more space between buttons on the dashboard to accommodate longer finger nails, although men with larger fingers appreciate the extra space, too. Power steering was originally created for women since they have less upper body strength. Seniors and others also find this feature beneficial. ■ Listening to the female segment is paying off for this industry. Bruce Gorden, a marketing manager at Ford, says, "We used a lot of women's input in the design development of the Explorer. We put in features we knew would appeal to women, like touch drive that puts it into four-wheel, and touch windows and locks." As a result, women buy 32 percent of all Explorers. Ford hopes to translate the same success to its luxury line. ■ Car advertisements are portraying women differently. Female spokespersons, such as Lindsay Wagner, are being used, and more women are seen driving cars in either business situations or athletic settings, reflecting changes in the social environment. ■ Car dealers are also recognizing that women buy cars differently than men. Most women have sought out information about their purchases and evaluated alternatives. They have reached their decisions and know how much they want to spend when they enter dealerships. They are not interested in playing the negotiating game. Men prefer to negotiate and are willing to spend a great deal of time with the salesperson dickering over price. As a result, they have seemed more comfortable dealing with men than women in the car-buying process. This bias costs the female consumer; a recent study found that black women paid $450 more and white women $200 more for new cars than white men. Dealers are responding by hiring more women sales reps and, in general, salespeople with more education and sophistication to appeal to both genders. Some dealerships even offer sensitivity instruction as part of their sales training programs. Sources: Diana T. Kurylko, "Ford Cultivates Women's Advice on European Cars," *Advertising Age,* September 5, 1994, p. 27; Tim Triplett, "Automakers Recognizing Value of Women's Market," *Marketing News,* April 11, 1994, p. 1; and Lucy Danziger, "Driving Force," *Working Woman,* April, 1993, p. 60.

QUESTIONS FOR CRITICAL THINKING

1. For what other products might marketers overlook women as potential buyers?
2. How should auto makers market cars to women?
3. How might car dealers make women feel more comfortable in their dealerships?

worker can develop a less expensive way to make a product. On the other hand, a sullen salesperson or an inattentive assembly line worker can easily hurt customer satisfaction. Employees with 10 years' experience have been shown to be three times more productive than new employees.[23]

Managers can foster employee enthusiasm and commitment through internal marketing, employee empowerment, employee training, and teamwork. These concepts were discussed in detail earlier in Chapter 7. However, it is important to recognize that they can also enhance the marketing concept.

Internal marketing, marketing efforts aimed at internal customers, treats each link between employees as a marketing opportunity. When a marketing manager asks a database operator for information, the manager becomes the operator's customer. This view of company relationships motivates employees to raise their standards to match those for dealing with external customers.

Employee empowerment gives the worker authority to make decisions and take responsibility for his or her work. For example, if a customer is dissatisfied with a rental car, an empowered desk clerk would have the authority to offer a discount on the spot rather than waiting for a manager to make that decision. Some companies encourage employees to submit ideas for new products. An AT&T Universal employee suggested that, instead of transferring Spanish-speaking callers to a Spanish-language line, AT&T should set up a direct 800 number for Spanish speakers. The employee's suggestion both improved service for Hispanics and saved money for AT&T.[24]

Employee training improves workers' skills and increases their loyalty. Some companies also teach their employees how to do other employees' jobs. This helps workers

A British Airways passenger is alerted to his freshly pressed suit. To create high customer satisfaction among its first-class trans-Atlantic passengers, British Airways provides arrival services such as dressing rooms, showers, and staff to iron clothes.

to understand the needs of their co-workers, or internal customers, and to understand where their own work fits into the larger picture.

Teamwork motivates employees because they work together and rely on one another. Workers often achieve higher goals in teams than working separately. Quality circles are small teams, usually from a single area or department, that meet to identify and solve problems. Cross-functional teams made up of workers from various areas often work together toward a particular goal such as developing a new product. Self-managed teams work with little supervision, making their own schedules and procedures and taking responsibility for the quality of the results. GE and Southern California Edison, which uses GE equipment, set up cross-company teams that succeeded in limiting the time it took to repair GE equipment used by Southern California Edison.[25]

QUALITY AND CUSTOMER SATISFACTION

Quality, another concept that was explained in Chapter 7, has close links to customer satisfaction. Quality can reflect concrete factors, such as the reliability of a car, or less tangible factors, such as whether a customer likes the purchasing experience. It could be said that the level of customer satisfaction is the report card of quality.

British Airways provides a quality travel experience by offering first-class travelers dinner in the airport so they needn't be disturbed on the airplane, pajamas and comfy pillows and blankets on board, and access to dressing rooms and showers on landing.[26]

CUSTOMER SATISFACTION IN THE GLOBAL MARKETPLACE

Achieving customer satisfaction in the global marketplace requires the same efforts as achieving customer satisfaction in the United States. Global firms must pay particular attention to the competitive, political and legal, economic, technological, and social and cultural environments. All may differ substantially from comparable conditions in the United States—and from those in the country next door.

Latin America, where most countries share Spanish as the primary language, is considered an easier market to enter than Asia, where businesspeople encounter literally thousands of languages and cultures. Mexico is the Latin American country most like the United States, but it still differs enough to require a different marketing approach. Mexico imposes strict restrictions on pricing and packaging, and Mexicans sometimes prefer different products than Americans do. Also, most of the Mexican population is quite poor compared to the U.S. population. However, an estimated 15 million people have incomes high enough to form a strong customer base in Mexico. The first step is to find out what the Mexican consumers want.[27]

ACHIEVEMENT CHECK SUMMARY

Reread the learning goals that follow, and consider the questions for each goal. Answering these questions will reinforce the most important concepts in the chapter and allow you to check how well you have achieved these learning goals. Where a blank appears before a question, answer with *T* or *F*. Otherwise, circle the letter of the correct answer. An answer key to these questions is found at the end of this chapter.

LEARNING GOAL 13.1: Explain how marketing creates utility, and list the major functions of marketing.

1. ___ Utility in marketing is defined as want-satisfying power.
2. ___ Retailers create ownership utility when they accept credit cards as a method of payment.
3. ___ Risk taking by intermediaries, financing inventory, and collecting market information are all functions of marketing.

LEARNING GOAL 13.2: Identify the components of a market.

1. ___ A market consists of people with needs and wants, money to spend, and the willingness and authority to spend.
2. ___ When you buy a personal computer for business use you have made a purchase in the consumer market.
3. ___ The consumer and industrial markets are distinguished by the buyer's intended use of the product or service purchased.

LEARNING GOAL 13.3: Explain the marketing concept.

1. ___ In a buyer's market, supply exceeds demand.
2. ___ The marketing concept requires organizations to orient all of their activities toward the customer.
3. ___ The marketing concept has little application in a not-for-profit organization.

LEARNING GOAL 13.4: Outline the basic steps in developing a marketing strategy.

1. The first step in developing a marketing strategy is to: (a) create a product to sell; (b) select a target market; (c) develop a price strategy; (d) develop a distribution strategy; (e) plan a promotional campaign.
2. Package design, branding, labeling, and product life cycle management are all components of: (a) product strategy; (b) price strategy; (c) distribution strategy; (d) promotional strategy; (e) all of the above.

LEARNING GOAL 13.5: Identify the components of the marketing environment.

1. Federal, state, and local laws and regulations are components of the: (a) social/cultural environment; (b) economic environment; (c) technological environment; (d) competitive environment; (e) political/legal environment.
2. When organizations respond to changes in consumer values they are responding to the: (a) social/cultural environment; (b) economic environment; (c) technological environment; (d) competitive environment; (e) political/legal environment.

LEARNING GOAL 13.6: Describe the marketing research function.

1. ___ Marketing research requires the collection and interpretation of data to support marketing decisions.
2. ___ Marketing research focuses exclusively on external data.
3. ___ The U.S. government provides little if any useful information to private firms doing marketing research.

LEARNING GOAL 13.7 Identify the methods for segmenting consumer and business markets.

1. Market segmentation: (a) combines different groups into one mass market; (b) divides the varied total market into groups with similar characteristics; (c) has little application in defining target markets; (d) is done for the consumer market, but not for the business market.
2. Segmenting markets on the basis of age, race, gender, occupation, household type, or ethnic group is: (a) demographic segmentation; (b) geographic segmentation; (c) psychographic segmentation; (d) product-related segmentation.

LEARNING GOAL 13.8: Differentiate between buyer behavior and consumer behavior, and outline the determinants of both.

1. ___ While consumer behavior refers to the behavior of ultimate consumers, buyer behavior concerns the behavior of consumers and business users in the various market segments.
2. ___ Cultural, social, and family influences are considered personal determinants of consumer behavior.

3. ___ Like consumer purchases, industrial purchases tend to hinge on the purchase decisions of single buyers.

LEARNING GOAL 13.9: Describe relationship marketing and how firms use the technique.

1. ___ Preexisting customers are important to a successful marketing strategy.
2. ___ The goal of relationship marketing is to achieve customer satisfaction.
3. ___ The products and customer service standards that a firm must maintain are identical anywhere in the world.

KEY TERMS

marketing 352
exchangeprocess 352
utility 352
market 353
consumer product 353
business product 353
marketing concept 353
seller's market 353
buyer's market 353
marketing strategy 355
target market 356
marketing mix 357
marketing research 361
database 362
marketing information system (MIS) 363
marketing decision support system (MDSS) 363
market segmentation 363
buyer behavior 367
consumer behavior 367
relationship marketing 368
customer satisfaction 370

REVIEW QUESTIONS

1. What type of utility do the following marketing efforts create?
   a. Kinko's copying stores' policy of staying open 24 hours a day
   b. L. L. Bean's 800 number
   c. Pizza Hut's pizza delivery
   d. Chrysler's manufacturing plant

2. List examples of marketers who perform each of the eight basic functions of marketing. What, if anything, does this list suggest?

3. What is a market? Distinguish between consumer and business markets.

4. What is the marketing concept? How successfully do you think the following organizations have adopted the marketing concept?
   a. Your college
   b. Barnes & Noble
   c. Major league baseball
   d. NBC

5. Outline the types of not-for-profit marketing. Cite examples of each.

6. Identify the probable target markets of each of the following organizations and products:
   a. Chicago Bulls
   b. Entenmann's line of fat-free food
   c. Pampers
   d. Manufacturers of cellular phones
   e. Infiniti

7. Explain the meaning of the term *marketing mix*. What are its components? What decisions must marketers make to define a marketing mix?

8. Define the term *marketing research*. How does research support business decision making? Also, identify the acronyms *MIS* and *MDSS*.

9. Differentiate between buyer behavior and consumer behavior. What are the steps in the consumer decision-making process?

10. Match the segmentation variables below with the following market segmentation methods: (1) geographic segmentation, (2) demographic segmentation, (3) psychographic segmentation, and (4) product-related segmentation.
    a. Ethnic group
    b. Lifestyle
    c. Urban, suburban, or rural background
    d. Cholesterol-free products

DISCUSSION QUESTIONS

1. Develop a marketing mix for a firm in your community. Also identify the firm's target market and marketing research needs.

2. Wrigley has retained its chunk of the U.S. chewing gum market by keeping prices low at five sticks for $0.25. Wrigley's gum is also well entrenched in over 100 foreign markets, including England, Australia, and China.[28] What changes in the competitive, political and legal, economic, technological, and social and cultural environments here and abroad might hurt sales of Wrigley's gum? What changes might help? How can Wrigley anticipate and prepare for these changes?

3. Blockbuster Entertainment Corp. has developed a database with information on 40 million customers that helps the firm to target direct mail campaigns. One promotion of video games to families with children had an impressive 30 percent response rate. How might Blockbuster continue to add names to its database? Recently, Blockbuster has started managing amphitheaters (with Sony Music Corp. and Pace Entertainment Corp.). How might Blockbuster utilize its database to reach the potential audience for rock concerts at those amphitheaters? For classical music performances? Blockbuster is also getting involved in movie making. How might Blockbuster use its database to help decide what sorts of movies to make?[29]

4. In research on the spending habits of wealthy individuals, defined as those with household incomes over $100,000, the survey company Roper Starch Worldwide found four subgroups: the adventurous consumer (who likes luxurious and trendy products), the stylish consumer (who is very brand loyal), the utilitarian consumer (who is more interested in price than luxury), and the conservative consumer (who responds well to catalogs).[30] How do these categories compare with VALS 2 categories? How would you market a new luxury car to people in each of these groups?

5. The Mighty Morphin' Power Rangers craze has swept the United States with astonishing force. Stores can't keep up with the demand for Power Ranger books, plastic weapons, action dolls, and clothing; some have even rationed the toys, selling only one per family. The Power Rangers TV show, put together by combining fresh footage

with clips from the Japanese show *Zyu Rangers,* is a huge hit, millions of Power Ranger novellas have sold, and a movie is due in mid-1995.[31] Discuss how various influences on consumer behavior may have affected the Power Rangers fad and how marketers might keep the fad going. Would relationship marketing be appropriate here? Why or why not?

SOLUTIONS TO ACHIEVEMENT CHECK SUMMARY

L. G. 13.1: 1. T, 2. T, 3. T. **L. G. 13.2:** 1. T, 2. F, 3. T. **L. G. 13.3:** 1. T, 2. T, 3. F. **L. G. 13.4:** 1. b, 2. a. **L. G. 13.5:** 1. e, 2. a. **L. G. 13.6:** 1. T, 2. F, 3. F. **L. G. 13.7:** 1. b, 2. a. **L. G. 13.8:** 1. T, 2. F, 3. F. **L. G. 13.9:** 1. T, 2. T, 3. F.

VIDEO CASE

THE TORONTO BLUE JAYS The Toronto Blue Jays are firm believers in the concepts of marketing management and customer satisfaction. Before the 1994 strike, they attracted more than 4 million fans annually, even though the price for a pair of Blue Jays tickets was one of the highest in professional baseball. Now they, like all other major-league clubs, are working to bring the fans back.

The Toronto Blue Jays have long realized that they are not merely in the business of selling baseball. What they really sell is entertainment, and they must take into consideration a multitude of consumer needs and wants. These wants and needs are known collectively as the marketing concept. If the product they sell is considered to be "Toronto Blue Jays baseball" in its rawest form, the only place to buy the product would be at their ballpark, creating a seller's market. In reality, they are in competition for the fan's dollar with all other forms of entertainment. This means they must satisfy the needs and wants of their target market better than the local symphony, movie houses, theatrical performances, or other leisure activities can. In this broader competitive context, one can see that the Blue Jays sell their product in a buyer's market.

Marketing success requires accurate information about the intended market. The Blue Jays have multiple target markets. Fans come from an area which extends well beyond the Toronto city limits and encompasses southwest Ontario, as well as northern New York state. In addition to the 4 to 4½ million people within a two-hour drive of the stadium, the Blue Jays have fans following them on television and in the sports page of their local newspapers.

In order to more effectively satisfy the needs of the organization's target market, the Blue Jays have created a marketing mix consisting of the following strategies:

- *Product Strategy* The Blue Jays emphasize wholesome family entertainment, Canadian pride, emotion, and plain old good fun. The Sky Dome itself is an asset, garnering rave reviews from the fans. They are enthusiastic about its levels, its architecture, how easy it is to get around inside, the big-screen TV for instant replays and close-ups, the facilities for the disabled, and, as one fan commented, "the greatest thing is the restrooms, twice as many as the law requires, you never have to wait in line."
- *Pricing Strategy* The Blue Jays' payroll is one of the highest in major league baseball, and Sky Dome operating expenses are high. This translates into high ticket costs (two adults can expect to spend $60 to $70 to see a game), but most fans agree that it is worth the price.
- *Distribution Strategy* The Blue Jays' decision to locate the Sky Dome in downtown Toronto helped keep the downtown area vibrant and alive and utilized the mass transportation infrastructure already in place. The Blue Jays also had to devise an equitable way to distribute tickets, using a computerized database of previous season ticket holders and waiting list for tickets.
- *Promotional Strategy* Many different components make up the Blue Jays' overall promotional strategy, including:
  Mass Media—TV, radio, and print
  Person marketing—promoting specific players as role models
  Place marketing—the city of Toronto promotes the Blue Jays and the Sky Dome as tourist attractions

QUESTIONS

Cause marketing—players participate in charity benefits for causes such as children's hospitals
Event marketing—promoting special events such as World Series games
Relationship marketing—promotional giveaways (free bats, free sandwiches) to Blue Jays fans promote other businesses as well

How do the Blue Jays gather information on their customers in order to more effectively utilize these various strategies? The Blue Jays organization conducts a series of comprehensive marketing surveys, selecting 200 fans at each of ten mid-season games. These fans then fill out a survey seeking reactions to various components of the total "Blue Jays experience," from the availability of tickets and parking to the game itself. The survey also covers aspects related to the general entertainment experience, such as food, drinks, and souvenirs. Once the responses are collected and compiled, consumer satisfaction rates are calculated. The organization has found that customers give the Blue Jays a 90 percent or better satisfaction rate in most categories. Survey responses are distributed to all key staff to aid them in continually improving the customer's game experience.

As Paul Markle, director of marketing for the Toronto Blue Jays says, "To be able to sell something, you have to know what the customer's needs are." This sentiment is echoed by Pat Gillick, executive vice president, "Of the 4 million fans, if we can make a majority feel satisfied when they go home, they got good value for their money, that they've seen a good product on the field, and want to come back here, that's when I feel satisfied." The Blue Jays have had a winning customer satisfaction combination in the past, however, customer satisfaction in the current season is crucial to their future success.

1.
Do professional sports teams operate in a buyer's or a seller's market? Defend your answer.

2.
What group(s) comprise the Blue Jays' target market?

3.
What strategies do the Blue Jays use to tailor their offering to the target market?

4.
How do the Blue Jays go about collecting information that might be useful in better serving their customers? Can you think of other ways to gather useful input?

PRODUCT AND PRICING STRATEGIES

CHAPTER

LEARNING GOALS

1. Explain what a product is and list the components of product strategy.
2. Identify the classifications of consumer goods, business goods, and services.
3. Discuss the product mix and product lines.
4. Identify and describe the stages of the product life cycle.
5. List the stages of new-product development.
6. Explain how firms identify their products.
7. Outline the different types of pricing objectives.
8. Discuss how firms set prices in the marketplace.
9. Explain how to use breakeven analysis in pricing strategy.
10. Differentiate between skimming and penetration pricing strategies.

A NEW PRICING STRATEGY AT GENERAL MILLS Coupons are common marketing tools in the $8.7 billion breakfast cereal industry. Almost two-thirds of all cereal purchases are made with coupons or other promotions. The five largest cereal manufacturers scattered 25.5 billion coupons last year at a cost of $610 million to lure consumers to their brands. Why then would General Mills, the second-largest cereal manufacturer with a 29 percent share of the market, announce that it was cutting back on coupons? Consider that out of the roughly 100 coupons distributed per person by cereal companies, only two were actually redeemed at a cost of $1.22 per redemption. ■ Instead of issuing coupons, General Mills has taken an unprecedented step in consumer products marketing—a price reduction. The company has announced that it will cut spending on inefficient couponing and price promotion by more than $175 million and cut prices on a variety of brands by an average of 11 percent. The General Mills brands affected include Cheerios, Wheaties, Whole Grain Total, Golden Grahams, Lucky Charms, and Trix. The average retail price of a 15-ounce box of Cheerios, for example, will drop from $3.30 to $2.90. ■ The price reduction came at a time when consumers were questioning the high prices of cereal. How can a 14-ounce box of wheat cereal cost 2 to 3 times as much as a 24-ounce loaf of wheat bread? If the cereal is so costly to produce, how can companies afford to issue coupons with face values up to $1.00? ■ General Mills' new pricing strategy addresses these consumer concerns. The company is attempting to provide consumers with consistent values at the retail level. Coupons can give a brand a temporary boost in sales immediately after their distribution, but coupons encourage consumers to shop for the best deal available on a certain brand. This strategy does not build brand loyalty. The strategy of everyday low pricing does. ■ General Mills is not abandoning coupons altogether. It will just reduce the number and value of coupons that it offers, as it looks for new ways to reach consumers efficiently with offers such as on-pack peel-off coupons and other in-store couponing techniques. In the meantime, General Mills hopes that everyday low prices will attract new users and build brand loyalty. Other cereal manufacturers have not followed suit. Market leader Kellogg's even raised the prices of its products 2.6 percent. Only time will tell if consumers truly want everyday low prices or if they have come to expect volumes of high-value coupons.[1]

CHAPTER OVERVIEW

This chapter will deal with the first two components of the marketing mix: product strategy and pricing strategy. Marketers broadly define a **product** as a bundle of physical, service, and symbolic attributes designed to satisfy consumer wants. Therefore, product strategy involves considerably more than just producing a good or service. It also includes decisions about package designs, brand names, trademarks, warranties, product images, and new-product development. Think, for instance, about your favorite soft drink. Do you like it for its taste alone, or do other attributes such as clever ads, attractive packaging, and overall image also attract you? The other attributes may influence you more than you realize; a recent *Consumer Reports* study of coffees found that many brands such as Eight O'Clock 100 percent Colombian and other lesser-known brands actually taste better than Maxwell House and Folgers, but these two continue to lead the market—a reflection of their successful product strategies.[2]

product
Bundle of physical, service, and symbolic attributes designed to satisfy consumer wants.

The second element of the marketing mix is pricing strategy. **Price** is the exchange value of a good or service. An item is worth only what someone else is willing to pay for it. In preindustrial societies, people determine exchange value by trading products for other products; a horse may be worth two goats, and six apples may be worth two loaves of bread. Modern societies use money for exchange. In either case, the price of a good or service is its exchange value. Pricing strategy deals with the multitude of factors that influence a price.

price
Exchange value of a good or service.

The chapter begins by describing the classification of goods and services, the product mix, and the product life cycle. It then discusses how firms develop, identify, and package products and how they identify the service attributes of products. The second part of the chapter focuses on the details of setting prices.

CLASSIFYING GOODS AND SERVICES

Marketers have found it useful to classify goods and services as either consumer or business products, depending on who purchases the particular item. These classifications can be further subdivided, and each type requires a different competitive strategy.

CLASSIFYING CONSUMER GOODS

A variety of classifications have been suggested for consumer goods, but the most typical categories are convenience, shopping, and specialty goods. This system, based on consumer buying habits, has been used for about 70 years.

Convenience goods are items that consumers seek to purchase frequently, immediately, and with little effort. Vending machines, 7-Eleven stores, and local newsstands usually stock convenience products. Examples include newspapers, chewing gum, magazines, milk, beer, and bread.

Shopping goods are those that consumers typically purchase only after comparing competing products in competing stores on bases such as price, quality, style, and color. Someone intent on buying a new automobile may visit many dealers, examine dozens of cars, and spend days making the final decision.

Specialty goods are those that purchasers are willing to make special efforts to obtain. Such a purchaser is already familiar with the item and sees no reasonable substitute for it. Alumni are known to buy a variety of products featuring the logos from their alma maters. Oak Grove International has tapped this loyal alumni market by offering a truly unique specialty product—custom-designed funeral caskets featuring school colors and athletic symbols.[3]

Note that a shopping good for one person may be a convenience item for someone else. Majority buying patterns determine a particular product's classification.

MARKETING STRATEGY IMPLICATIONS FOR CONSUMER GOODS

The consumer product classification system is a useful tool in marketing strategy. For example, once they classify a new lawn edger as a shopping good, marketers have a better idea of its promotion, pricing, and distribution needs. Figure 14.1 details the impact of the consumer products classification on various aspects of marketing strategy.

CLASSIFYING BUSINESS GOODS

The five main categories of business goods (also known as *industrial* or *organizational goods*) are installations, accessory equipment, component parts and materials, raw materials, and supplies. While marketers classify consumer products by buying habits, they classify industrial products based on how customers use them and by their basic characteristics. Long-lived products whose sales usually involve large sums of money are called *capital items.* Less costly products that users consume within a year are referred to as *expense items.*

Installations are major capital products such as new factories, heavy equipment and machinery, and custom-made equipment. Buyers typically use installations for production of other items. For example, General Motors purchased an automated monorail system from Litton Industries to transport cars on the GM assembly line. Installations are expensive and often involve buyer and seller negotiations that may last several years before actual purchases.

Accessory equipment includes capital items that are usually less expensive and shorter-lived than installations. Examples are hand tools and fax machines. Buyers use some accessory equipment, such as portable drills, to produce other goods and services, while other equipment, such as a personal computer, performs important administrative and operating functions.

FIGURE 14.1 RELATIONSHIP BETWEEN CONSUMER GOODS CLASSIFICATION AND MARKETING STRATEGY

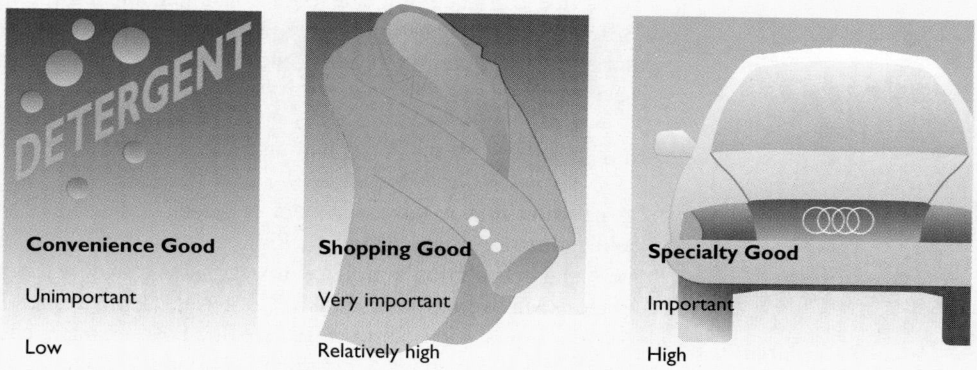

Marketing Strategy Factor	Convenience Good	Shopping Good	Specialty Good
Store image	Unimportant	Very important	Important
Price	Low	Relatively high	High
Promotion	By manufacturer	By manufacturer and retailers	By manufacturer and retailers
Distribution channel	Many wholesalers and retailers	Relatively few wholesalers and retailers	Very few wholesalers and retailers
Number of retail outlets	Many	Few	Very small number; often one per market area

Component parts and materials are business goods that become part of final products. Some component parts become visible in finished goods, such as Goodyear tires on Dodge Caravans and many other brands of automobiles. Other component parts and materials are not readily seen. For example, the Nutrasweet Company manufactures its famous artificial sweetener and sells it to other manufacturers to produce soft drinks, jams, ice cream, candies, and canned fruits.

Raw materials are similar to component parts and materials because they become inputs to the production of final products. These include farm products such as cotton, wheat, cattle, and milk and natural materials such as iron ore, lumber, and coal. Grading of most raw materials assures buyers of standardized products of uniform quality.

Supplies are expense items used in a firm's daily operation that do not become part of final products. Supplies include paper clips, cleaning supplies, light bulbs, and copy paper. Buyers purchase these goods regularly and spend little time on these purchase decisions.

MARKETING STRATEGY IMPLICATIONS FOR BUSINESS GOODS

Each group of business goods requires a different marketing strategy. Because manufacturers market most installations and many component parts directly to buyers, their promotional efforts emphasize personal selling rather than advertising. By contrast, marketers of supplies and accessory equipment rely more on advertising since they often sell their products through intermediaries such as wholesalers. Producers of installations and component parts may involve their customers in new-product development, especially for custom-made business products. Finally, firms that market supplies and accessory equipment place greater emphasis on competitive pricing strategies than do other business products marketers, who concentrate on product quality and servicing.

CLASSIFYING SERVICES

Services can be classified as either consumer or business products. Child-care centers and shoe repair shops provide services for consumers, while ADP's payroll services and AppleOne's temporary office workers are examples of business services. In some cases, a service can accommodate both consumer and business markets. For example, when ServiceMaster cleans upholstery in a home, it performs a consumer service, but when it spruces up the painting system and robots in a manufacturing plant, it acts as a business service.

PRODUCT MIX

product mix
Assortment of products offered by a firm.

product line
Series of related products offered by a firm.

A **product mix** is the assortment of goods and services that a firm offers to consumers and industrial users. Although Philip Morris may be best-known for its tobacco products, the corporation's product mix includes a wide variety of product lines such as beverages (Maxwell House, Sanka, Kool-Aid, Capri, Miller Beer), processed meats (Oscar Mayer, Louis Rich), breakfast cereals (Post brands), cheeses (Kraft), desserts (Jell-O Gelatin), bakery goods (Entenmann's, Lender's Bagels), dinners (Budget Gourmet, Kraft Macaroni and Cheese), and other grocery lines (Log Cabin, Shake 'n' Bake, Stove Top, salad dressings, Tombstone Pizza).

The product mix is a combination of product lines and individual offerings that make up the product line. A **product line** is a series of related products. Kraft's product line of cheeses, for example, includes Kraft Singles, Kraft Shredded, Kraft Crackerbarrel, Philadelphia Cream Cheese, Velveeta, and Cheese Whiz.

Marketers must continually assess their firm's product mix to ensure company growth, to satisfy changing consumer needs and wants, and to adjust to competitors'

Coca-Cola has expanded its product line in recent years with the addition of Cherry Coke and caffeine-free Diet Coke. An unsuccessful new product introduction, New Coke, led to a repackaging of the original formula as Coca-Cola Classic.

offerings. Consumers' concerns about health, for instance, have prompted Philip Morris to introduce reduced-fat versions of Philadelphia Cream Cheese, Jell-O, Entenmann's, Kraft Mayonnaise, and Oscar Mayer luncheon meats. Being socially responsible and sensitive to the environment, the corporation contributed over $1 million to initiatives in environmental education, water conservation, improvement of farming and agricultural methods, and solid-waste reduction. Looking for continued growth internationally, the corporation has acquired food businesses in Scandinavia, the United Kingdom, Canada, the United States, Brazil, Argentina, Costa Rica, Lithuania, Poland, the Czech Republic, Bulgaria, Turkey, and China.[4]

Clearly, successful product mixes and product lines undergo constant change. To remain competitive, marketers look for gaps in their firm's assortment and fill them with new products or modified versions of existing ones. A helpful tool that marketers use in making product decisions is the product life cycle.

PRODUCT LIFE CYCLE

Once a product is actually on the market, it often goes through a series of four stages known as the **product life cycle.** These four stages progress from introduction through growth, maturity, and decline. Figure 14.2 shows these steps, along with typical industry sales and profits and current examples of products at the various life-cycle stages. Can you think of other examples?

product life cycle
Four stages through which a successful product passes: introduction, growth, maturity, and decline.

Product life cycles are not set in stone; not all products follow this progression precisely, and different products may spend different periods of time in each stage. A fad product may pass through its entire life cycle in a very brief period. Time is ticking for sales of the President Bill Clinton wristwatch. Sales for the watch, which runs backward, will probably dry up when Clinton leaves office. By contrast, the automobile has been in the maturity stage for over 30 years. Increasing competition and rapid improvements in technology compress many products' life cycles.

The concept of the product life cycle helps the marketer to anticipate developments throughout the various stages of a product's life. Profits assume a predictable pattern through the stages, and promotional emphasis must shift from product information in the early stages to heavy brand promotion in the later ones. Since marketing programs will

FIGURE 14.2 STAGES IN THE PRODUCT LIFE CYCLE

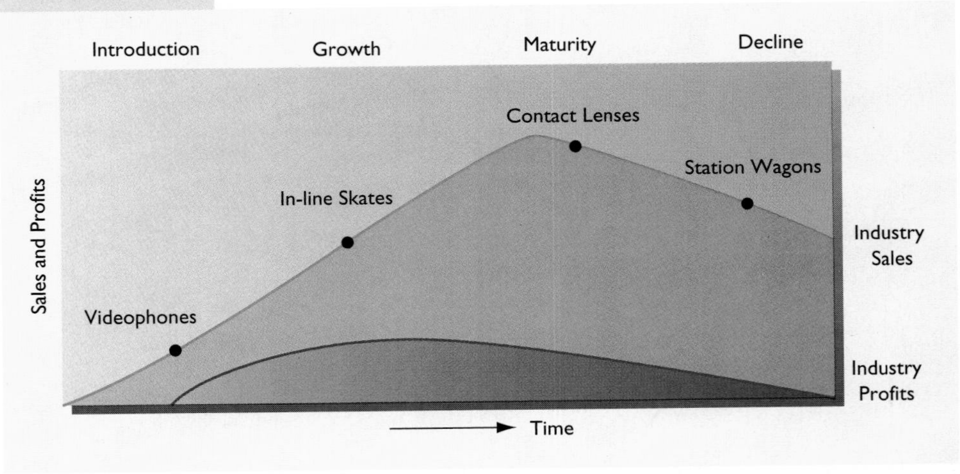

change at each stage in the life cycle, it is important to understand the characteristics of all four stages of the product life cycle.

INTRODUCTION

Early in the product life cycle, the firm tries to built demand for its new offering. Because neither consumers nor distributors may be aware of the product, marketers must use promotional programs to inform the market about the item and explain its features, uses, and benefits. PepsiCo is hoping to reverse the 5-year trend of declining market shares for both regular and diet colas by introducing Pepsi Max, a 53-calorie drink sweetened with part sugar, part NutraSweet. Pepsi Max is targeted to teens and young adults who don't want a lot of sugar, but dislike the taste of diet soft drinks.[5]

New-product development and introductory promotional campaigns, though important, are expensive and commonly lead to financial losses in the first stage of the product life cycle. A new product can cost a staggering $40 million to introduce, but such expenditures are necessary to allow the firm to profit later.[6]

GROWTH

Sales climb quickly during the product's growth stage as new customers join the early users who are now repurchasing the item. Person-to-person referrals and continued advertising by the firm induce others to make trial purchases. The company also begins to earn profits on the new product. Unfortunately, this encourages competitors to enter the field with similar offerings. Appearances can deceive, though. Any marketer would classify a brand that's been in existence for about 60 years as in the mature stage. Although Spam generated stagnant sales for years, the brand has recently enjoyed an impressive 26 percent sales increase in 2 years, placing it in the growth stage once again. Joel Johnson, the man responsible for Spam's resurgence and the Spamburger campaign, says, "I do not believe in the terminology of mature brands. If a business is not growing, it's not healthy."[7] Price competition appears in the growth stage, and total industry profits peak in the later part of this stage.

To gain a larger share of a growing market, firms may develop different versions of a product to target specific segments. Kellogg's introduced Frosted Mini-Wheats, a bite-size variety of a popular brand, in 1988. An aggressive investment in marketing initiatives including the "Kid in you" advertising campaign has catapulted the brand to the nation's third-largest cereal brand behind Frosted Flakes and Cheerios in the $9 billion cereal category.[8]

MATURITY

As shown in Figure 14.2, industry sales increase early in the maturity stage, but eventually they reach a saturation level that makes further expansion difficult. Competition also intensifies, increasing the availability of the product. Firms concentrate on capturing competitors' customers, often dropping prices to enhance their own products' appeal. Sales volume fades late in the maturity stage, and some of the weaker competitors leave the market.

Firms promote mature products aggressively to protect their market shares and to distinguish their products from those of competitors. Even though Listerine has dominated the mouthwash category for most of its 115-year history, it has recently lost share in a declining market to both its own Cool Mint and to private-label brands. In an effort to regain share and attract new users, Warner-Lambert has redesigned the package and replaced its signature glass bottle with a more modern, plastic bottle. The company hopes a new flavor, Fresh Burst, will also breathe new life into the brand.[9]

DECLINE

Sales continue to fall in the decline stage of the product life cycle. Profits also decline and may become losses as further price-cutting characterizes the reduced market. The decline stage is usually caused by a product innovation or a shift in consumer preferences. Competing in pricing wars can harm a firm's own product. In 1987, Dial Corporation introduced Lunch Buckets, a line of single-serve, microwaveable meals in cups. The category quickly grew to $300 million as Hormel, Chef Boyardee, Campbell's, and others launched competing products. A fierce price war developed as a host of competitors fought for limited shelf space. Sale prices of two-for-$1.00 became the norm for products that had retailed for $1.29 each. Lunch Bucket's sales peaked at $50 million, and the product posted sales of only $13.4 million for the recent fiscal year. The entire category has declined to $172 million. Lunch Bucket is an example of a product that may have grown too quickly for its own good.[10]

EXTENDING THE PRODUCT LIFE CYCLE

Sometimes it is possible to extend a product's life cycle by one of several strategies:

Increase Frequency of Use For example, MCI increased the use of collect calls by simplifying the service. Consumers now need only dial 1-800-COLLECT to place a collect call.

Add New Users Introducing a product to new markets abroad might add new users. Straight Arrow, a Pennsylvania-based animal-care product company, found through research that its Mane N Tail horse shampoo was actually being used on people. The company then decided to pursue the human market. Today, after repackaging and label changes, the product is distributed in hair salons and drugstores. Sales for Straight Arrow have skyrocketed from $500,000 5 years ago to $30 million last year since the firm discovered a new segment of users for its product.[11]

Find New Uses for the Product Arm & Hammer baking soda is a classic example; the company has expanded its original use in baking to include newer uses as a toothpaste, refrigerator freshener, flame extinguisher, first-aid remedy, denture cleaner, cleaning agent, and pool pH adjuster. Since the antacid Tum's began featuring a secondary use as a calcium supplement in its advertising, the brand has bypassed market-leader Rolaids in 4 years to lead the market with a 21.2 percent share.[12]

Arm & Hammer has successfully extended its product life cycle by promoting new uses for its baking soda.

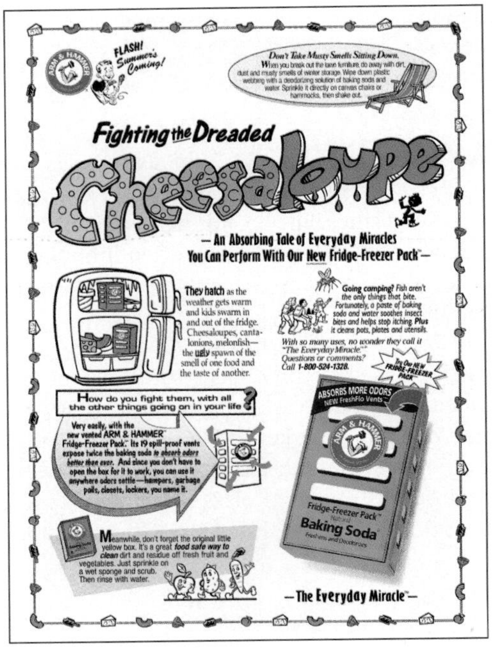

Change Package Sizes, Labels, and Product Designs Campbell's recently redesigned the labels for its soup line, the first packaging change in the product line's 100-year history. Campbell's added pictures of each soup to the red and white cans in an effort to differentiate the varieties better on the shelf. Whether the change has turned off loyal consumers who were used to the classic look remains to be seen.[13]

The marketer works to extend a product's life cycle as long as the item remains profitable. Indeed, some products can be highly profitable during the later stages of their life cycles, since the makers have already recovered all of their initial development costs.

MARKETING STRATEGY IMPLICATIONS OF THE PRODUCT LIFE CYCLE

The product life cycle helps marketers to design a marketing strategy flexible enough to accommodate changing marketplace characteristics. For instance, knowing that advertising emphasis will change from informative to persuasive messages as the product faces new competitors during its growth stage helps the marketer to anticipate competitors' actions and make necessary adjustments. These competitive moves may include product variations and changes in pricing and distribution.

Product Variations As mentioned earlier, Warner-Lambert hopes to attract new users in a shrinking mouthwash category by introducing a new flavor, Fresh Burst, to the Listerine line. The company also changed its signature glass bottle to plastic. The updated image is intended to make the brand seem more contemporary.[14]

Price Changes Procter & Gamble recently dropped prices from 5 to 15 percent on some brands to protect its higher-priced brands and put pressure on competitors, especially store brands. The brands affected include: Joy, Era, Luvs, and Camay.[15]

Changes in Distribution Avon has found an abundance of new users by selling its products in a most unlikely place—the Amazon. Avon's sales force of 400,000 generated $70 million in sales last year in Brazil alone. Brazil is now Avon's second-largest market behind only the United States.[16]

NEW-PRODUCT DEVELOPMENT

The creation of new products is the lifeblood of an organization. Products do not remain economically viable forever, so a firm must develop new ones to assure its survival. For many firms, new products account for a sizable part of sales and profits.

Black & Decker attributes part of its significant growth and market leadership to new-product introductions over the past several years. The company introduced the DeWalt line of 33 tools 3 years ago; it added 37 products to the line the following year, and a third wave of new products is scheduled. Black & Decker also launched its Quantum line of tools targeted to 20 million or more do-it-yourselfers and introduced 18 basic consumer power tools under its own name. These new product introductions helped to solidify Black & Decker's market leadership in the $2 billion North American power-tools market.[17]

Each year, firms introduce thousands of new products. Some, such as DAT (digital audiotape), represent major technological breakthroughs. Others are improvements or variations of existing products. For example, marketers made use of the unused space on all compact discs by adding song lyrics and artist biographies that users can display on a television screen.

New-product development is expensive, time-consuming, and risky, since only about one-third of new products inspire marketing success stories. Products can fail for many reasons. Some are not properly developed and tested, some are poorly packaged, and others lack adequate promotional support or distribution; a product may fail simply because it does not satisfy a consumer need or want. Consider the case of Crystal Pepsi.

Pepsi and Coke have dominated the soft-drink market for decades. For the past few years, though, both products have lost sales and market share to new beverages like Snapple and Clearly Canadian that appeal to more health-conscious consumers.

In an attempt to capture a piece of this growing market, Pepsi introduced Crystal Pepsi, a clear, caffeine-free soft drink with all natural flavorings. The product offered low sodium, sugar, and calories and had no preservatives. The new product's performance was most disappointing, though. The clear cola captured only about 1 percent of the $48 billion U.S. soft-drink market despite a major spending campaign, and some of this share probably came at the expense of other Pepsi products. Consumers apparently did not buy the concept of a clear cola. PepsiCo is giving it one last try before giving up completely on the brand by launching a new ad campaign that touts the new taste and packaging.[18]

Firms aim most newly developed products today at satisfying specific customer needs or wants. New-product development is becoming increasingly efficient and cost-effective because marketers use systematic methods.

STAGES IN NEW-PRODUCT DEVELOPMENT

The new-product development process has six stages: (1) generating new-product ideas, (2) screening, (3) business analysis, (4) product development, (5) test marketing, and (6) commercialization. Each stage requires a "go/no go" decision by management.

GENERATING NEW-PRODUCT IDEAS

The new-product development process starts with generating ideas for new offerings. Ideas come from many sources, including customers, suppliers, employees, research scientists, market researchers, inventors outside the firm, and competitors' products. The most successful ideas work directly to satisfy customer needs or resolve consumer complaints.

Consumers have complained about cable television for years. Reception at times is poor. Outages occur during crucial times in major sporting events. Regional games from some areas of the country are not available in other time zones. Digital Satellite Systems is offering an alternative for the disgruntled cable subscriber: a programming ser-

STRENGTH IN DIVERSITY

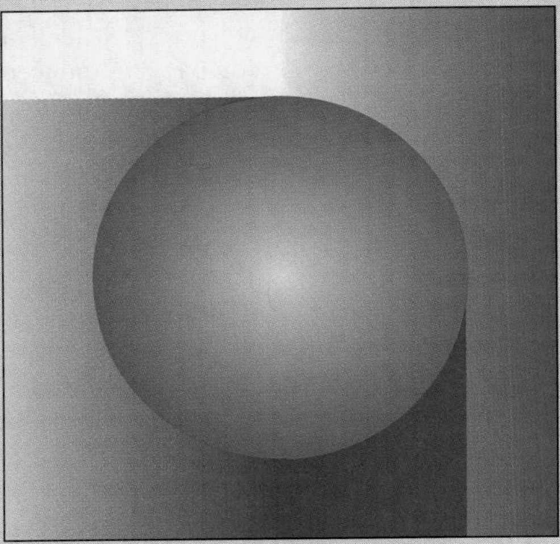

NEW COMPUTER PRODUCTS ASSIST THE DISABLED In the United States today there are approximately 43 million people with disabilities. Between 70 and 80 percent of disabled Americans are unemployed. New products on the market can help reduce this number and give many disabled individuals the chance to work. Some 12,000 to 15,000 products are now available to help disabled people overcome many impairments. One of these products, the computer, has proven itself useful in many situations. In fact, computer technology is responsible for providing more opportunities for the disabled than any other technology. ■ A product as simple as a software program that enlarges letters on the screen or makes them bolder allows slightly visually-impaired people to perform tasks on the computer as efficiently as sighted individuals. For those with no sight, a screen reader, special software which interacts with a voice synthesizer, reads aloud whatever appears on the computer screen. If a scanner is hooked up to the screen reader, a blind person can access any written document, including company reports, memos, books, and newspapers. In the past accessing information has been a barrier for disabled persons both in the workplace and in the world at large. Richard Ring, a sightless editor of a computer magazine for the blind, sums up the importance of this. "If I have access to any information you do, and I can use it in the same way that you do, then I can do the job that you do." ■ For mobility-impaired people, a host of new software programs are available that change the way the keyboard and computer interact. For example, Stickykeys is a program that allows a combination of keys to be typed using only one finger. Word-predictive software reduces the number of keys one needs to type to get a desired word by providing a list of words each time a letter or combination of letters

vice that beams 150 channels directly into the home. Thomson Consumer Electronics, Inc. produces the personal satellite dish, which is about the size of a large plate. Subscribers to the service will receive 50 pay-per-view movie channels and 30 commercial-free music channels along with CNN, MTV, Nickelodeon, ESPN, HBO, and Cinemax. Backers of the project are spending $90 million on an ad campaign to attract subscribers.

The service is expected to cut into cable television's market. Price, though, may deter some prospective subscribers. The satellite dish costs about $1,000.00. In addition, the monthly subscription fees range from $7.95 to $64.90.[19]

SCREENING

This stage eliminates ideas that do not mesh with overall company objectives or that the firm cannot develop given its resources. Some firms sponsor open discussions of new-product ideas among representatives of different functional areas. Spectrum Control Inc., a producer of electronic filters and other specialty electronic products, holds such meetings an average of once every 2 weeks, during which product managers, company scientists, and other managers evaluate new-product ideas.[20]

BUSINESS ANALYSIS

Further screening at this stage evaluates whether an idea fits with the company's product, distribution, and promotional resources. The analysis also involves assessing the new product's potential sales, profits, growth rate, and competitive strengths.

Sometimes this stage includes concept testing, or market research designed to solicit initial consumer reactions to new-product ideas before the products are developed. Today, Campbell Soup Company conducts concept testing using a grid designed to match comis typed. Head pointers, switches, and modified keyboards are also helpful. For those with more serious mobility problems, voice-recognition systems may be the answer. When a user speaks into the computer's microphone, his or her words appear on the screen. Another new product uses an infrared beam bounced off the cornea to control the keyboard. Simple eye movements access a menu of activities or "eye-type" words. No hand movements are required to input information. ■ Today's computers can be equipped to enable people with just about any kind of disability to function efficiently in the workplace. But these solutions can be expensive, with some costing several thousand dollars. The Americans with Disabilities Act of 1990 requires that companies make a reasonable accommodation for people with disabilities, but is a several thousand dollar expenditure reasonable? Fortunately, financial help is available through state vocational and rehabilitation departments. Medicaid may also pay for adaptive equipment if a physician writes a prescription for the device. ■ It is critical that the disabled person research the special equipment he or she will need to perform a job. Offices such as the Technical Act Center and the Alliance for Technology Access, located in almost every state, have product-demonstration showrooms or can provide information and referrals. ■ With the aid of these new computer products, more and more disabled people are becoming members of the workforce. Says Barbara Sistak of Don Johnston, a Chicago-based company, "If you have control of one muscle somewhere, then you can have access to a computer and then the rest of the world." Studies have shown that disabled workers are highly loyal and productive employees who are rarely absent. Companies that focus on a person's abilities rather than disabilities may find a wealth of potential talent in disabled people. Sources: Helen J. Mosquera, "Technological Considerations for Physically Challenged Telemarketing Employees," *Telemarketing,* November 1994, p. 5; Eric Minton, "The Great Equalizer: Computer Communication Devices for the Handicapped," *Independent Living,* November 1994, p. 7; Joseph J. Lazzaro, "Computers for the Disabled," *Byte,* June 1993, p. 7; and Bob Filipczak, "Adaptive Technology for the Disabled," *Training,* March 1993, p. 3.

QUESTIONS FOR CRITICAL THINKING

1. Who do you think should pay for the necessary specialized products for a disabled person's job: the employer, the government, or the disabled person?
2. How should these specialized products be marketed?
3. How would these goods be classified and what type of pricing strategy should the manufacturers use for retail sale?

binations of flavors and brands to consumer preferences. Campbell's latest success, Cream of Broccoli soup, was born from this grid. An older version of the flavor, developed in 1985 before Campbell's used the grid, sold poorly. The grid test showed why: the match was wrong, since most consumers did not eat the product as soup, but instead cooked with it. The company relaunched Cream of Broccoli as a cooking soup, sponsored recipe contests, and lowered the price. Today, Cream of Broccoli is Campbell's first new soup since 1947 to make the firm's top 10 list.[21]

PRODUCT DEVELOPMENT

At this stage the firm creates an actual product, subjects it to a series of tests, and revises it. Tests measure both the product's actual features and how consumers perceive it. Inadequate testing during the development stage can doom a product, and even a company, to failure. Federal Express learned this lesson the hard way. In the early 1990s, FedEx introduced Zap Mail, a new system of delivering correspondence within hours rather than overnight. FedEx advertised the service via full-page print ads explaining the complex technology in detail. After only 1 year, FedEx discontinued the service which customers never really understood. If FedEx had involved customers in the development of the product, Zap Mail might be alive and well today.[22]

TEST MARKETING

The firm actually sells a new product in a limited area during **test marketing.** The company examines both the product and the marketing effort proposed to support it during this phase. Marketers select cities or television coverage areas that are typical of the targeted market segments for such tests. Test market results help managers to determine the

test marketing
Stage in the new-product development process at which the firm sells a product in a limited area.

product's likely performance in a full-scale introduction. Gatorade, Quaker Oats' sports-drink unit, is currently testing Sun Bolt in the relatively untapped morning-beverage market. Sun Bolt, with 58 grams of caffeine, is the first caffeinated beverage positioned as a morning igniter for adults.[23]

Some firms choose to skip test marketing and move directly from product development to commercialization. These companies cite four main problems with using test marketing:

1. Test marketing can be expensive.
2. Competitors who learn about a test market project may try to skew results by lowering their prices, distributing coupons, or running special promotions.
3. Long-lived durable goods (dishwashers, compact disc players) are seldom test marketed due to the major financial investment required to develop and launch them.
4. Test marketing can alert competitors to future plans.

In general, test marketing should be skipped only for a product that is highly likely to succeed.[24]

COMMERCIALIZATION

This is the stage at which the firm offers its new product in the general marketplace. Sometimes it is referred to as a *product launch.* Considerable planning goes into activities at this stage, since the firm must gear its promotional, distribution, and pricing strategies to support the new product offering.

PRODUCT IDENTIFICATION

brand
Name, term, sign, symbol, or design that identifies the goods or services of a firm.

brand name
Words or letters that identify a firm's offerings.

trademark
Brand with legal protection exclusive to its owner.

Product identification is another vital aspect of marketing strategy. Firms identify their products by brands, brand names, and trademarks. A **brand** is a name, term, sign, symbol, design, or some combination of these elements that helps to identify the products of one firm and to differentiate them from competitors' offerings. Pepsi, Mountain Dew, and Slice are all soft drinks made by PepsiCo, but a unique combination of name, symbol, and package design distinguishes each brand from the others.

A **brand name** is the part of a brand composed of words or letters included in a name that identifies and distinguishes a firm's offerings from those of competitors. A brand name is the part of a brand that can be vocalized. Many brand names, such as Coca-Cola, McDonald's, American Express, and IBM, are famous around the world.

A **trademark** is a brand with legal protection granted solely to the brand's owner. Trademark protection includes not only the brand name, but also pictorial designs, slogans, packaging elements, and product features such as color and shape. Rolls-Royce Motor Cars Inc. has received trademark protection not only for the Rolls-Royce brand name, mascot, and badge, but also for the automobile's radiator grille.

Brands are important in developing a product's image. If consumers are aware of a particular brand, its appearance becomes advertising for the firm. The RCA trademark of the dog at the phonograph, for example, provides instant advertising to shoppers who spot it in a store. Successful branding also helps a firm to escape some price competition, since well-known brands often sell at considerable price premiums over their competitors.

SELECTING AN EFFECTIVE BRAND NAME

Good brand names are easy to pronounce, recognize, and remember; Crest, Visa, and Avis are examples. Global firms face real problems in selecting brand names since an excellent brand name in one country may prove disastrous in another. Most languages have a short *a* sound, so *Coca-Cola* and *Texaco* are pronounceable almost anywhere. An advertising campaign for E-Z washing machines failed in the United Kingdom, however, because the British pronounce *z* as *zed.* Bimbo is an effective brand name for a line of high-quality bakery products marketed by Anheuser-Busch in Spain, but the name would be a disaster in the United States, where Anheuser-Busch uses the Earth Grains brand name for its premium bakery goods.

A brand name should project the right image to the buyer. Accutron suggests the quality of a high-priced, accurate timepiece. Airborne Express suggests a fast delivery service with a broad geographic reach. Sometimes changes in the market environment require changes to a brand name. Dep Corporation changed the brand name of Ayds diet candy to Diet Ayds because they were concerned that the old name would remind consumers of the AIDS virus.

Brand names must also be legally protectable. Trademark law states that brand names cannot contain words in general use, such as *television* or *automobile.* No organization can claim exclusive use of generic words—words that describe a type of product. On the other hand, if a brand name becomes so popular that it passes into common language and turns into a generic word, the company can no longer protect it as a brand name. At one time, aspirin and linoleum were exclusive brand names, but today they have become generic terms and are no longer legally protectable. See Appendix C for more information on trademark law.

The task of selecting an effective and legally protectable brand name is becoming more difficult as the number of new-product introductions increases each year. In a recent year, marketers introduced 17,571 new products in the food and drug areas alone, an increase of 4.6 percent over the previous year.[25]

Many firms hire professional brand name consultants to create new product names. United Airlines turned to CKS Partners of San Francisco to create its new shuttle service's brand identity. The consultants developed a new United Shuttle logo featuring the word *shuttle* in a swooping script. The logo is intended to convey the fast, last-minute efficiency that customers expect in a shuttle service.[26]

BRAND CATEGORIES

A brand offered and promoted by a manufacturer is known as a **national brand** or a *manufacturer's brand.* Examples are Tide, Jockey, Gatorade, Swatch, and DoveBar. Not all brand names belong to manufacturers, though. Some are the property of retailers or distributors. A **private brand** (often known as a *house, distributor,* or *retailer brand*) identifies a product that is not linked to the manufacturer, but instead carries a wholesaler's or retailer's label. Sears' line of DieHard batteries and The Limited's Forenza label are examples. Private brands represent high profits for retailers and a threat to branded products. As noted in Table 14.1, private-label products are no longer limited to canned vegetables and detergents. As private-label sales grow, so do the number and variety of private-label products on the market.

national brand
Brand offered and promoted by a manufacturer.

private brand
Brand owned by a wholesaler or retailer.

Increases in private-brand sales represent an international trend. In the United Kingdom, half of the sales of J. Sainsbury and Tesco, the leading supermarkets, come from their private brands.[27]

Many retailers offer a third option to manufacturers' and private brands: **generic products.** These items feature plain packaging, minimal labeling, and little if any advertising, and they meet only minimum quality standards. Generic products sell at consid-

generic product
Nonbranded item with plain packaging and little or no advertising support.

TABLE 14.1 LEADING PRIVATE-LABEL CATEGORIES AND TOP GAINERS IN UNIT VOLUME

Top Ten Private-Label Categories (Dollar Volume, $ Millions)		Top Ten Gainers in Unit Volume
1. Milk	$5,600	1. Ready-to-drink tea
2. Fresh bread/rolls	1,700	2. Baby formula
3. Cheese	1,500	3. Miscellaneous remedy tablets
4. Fresh eggs	1,300	4. Meat pies
5. Ice cream	1,000	5. Shelf-stable drinks
6. Carbonated beverages	777	6. Cigarettes
7. Frozen, plain vegetables	757	7. Adult-incontinence products
8. Sugar	638	8. Frozen poultry
9. Shelf-stable vegetables	605	9. Miscellaneous health tablets
10. Refrigerated juices	578	10. Refrigerated pasta

erable discounts from manufacturers' and private brands. Many consumer goods are available as generic products, such as paper towels, toilet paper, breakfast cereal, and pasta.

DEGREES OF BRAND LOYALTY

Although branding is very important to a marketer, the degree of brand loyalty among consumers varies widely according to the type of product. A golfer, for example, may buy only Ping clubs. Many consumers, however, might readily accept a generic type of paper towel. Brand recognition, brand preference, and brand insistence are three degrees of brand loyalty.

brand recognition
Degree of brand acceptance at which the consumer is aware of the brand.

Brand recognition means simply that the consumer is familiar with the good or service. Marketers often distribute free samples and discount coupons to build this familiarity, since consumers purchase recognized brands more frequently than unknown ones.

brand preference
Degree of brand acceptance at which the consumer selects one brand over competing brands if the preferred brand is available.

Brand preference is the degree of brand loyalty at which the consumer will purchase loyally if the brand is available. Many consumer products, such as potato chips and soft drinks, fall into this category. A considerable portion of all marketing expenditures go to build brand preference.

brand insistence
Degree of brand acceptance at which the consumer will accept no substitute.

Brand insistence is the degree of brand loyalty at which a consumer will accept no substitute for a preferred brand. If it is not readily available locally, the consumer will drive to an area where it is available, special order it from a factory, or turn to mail order or telephone buying. Brand insistence is the ultimate degree of brand loyalty, and few brands reach this pinnacle. Cosmetics are an example of a product that might inspire this degree of brand loyalty.

FAMILY BRANDS AND INDIVIDUAL BRANDS

family brand
Brand name for several related products or an entire product mix.

Another branding decision marketers must make is the choice between a family branding strategy or an individual branding strategy. A **family brand** is a single brand name for several related products. KitchenAid, Johnson & Johnson, Xerox, and Hunt's use family brand names for their entire product lines. When a firm that practices family branding introduces a new product, both customers and retailers recognize the familiar brand name. Promotion of individual products in a line benefits all of the products within the well-known family brand.

Other firms create **individual brands** by giving products within a line different brand names. For example, Procter & Gamble has individual brand names for its different laundry detergents—Tide, Cheer, Dash, and Oxydol. Each brand targets a unique market segment. Consumers who want a cold-water detergent can buy Cheer rather than Tide or Oxydol instead of a competitor's brand. Individual branding builds competition within a firm and enables the company to increase overall sales.

individual brand
Separate brand name for each product in a line.

PACKAGES AND LABELS

Except for generic products, packaging also plays an important role in product strategy. The original purpose of packaging was to protect against damage, spoilage, and theft. Over the years, however, packaging has also acquired a marketing objective.

Perrier, "Earth's first soft drink," was the leading bottled water and favorite drink of yuppies in the 1980s, but an influx of waters and new-age beverages combined with a benzene scare in the early 1990s to send Perrier's sales plummeting to a low of $50 million. Perrier is making a mighty comeback using a package redesign as the focal point of a $7 million marketing campaign. The new Perrier bottles sold in restaurants feature the art of four up-and-coming artists printed on translucent shrink-wrap. The "art of refreshment" ad theme touts the bottle art as collector's items. Perrier views the redesign as a way to create "a refreshing new personality for the '90s."[28]

Consumers' increasing desire for convenience has also increased the importance of packaging. For decades, bakers have struggled to use Crisco shortening. The greasy product was difficult to measure and nearly impossible to clean out of measuring cups and utensils. Procter & Gamble recently repackaged the product in measured sticks just like butter and margarine. Now, Crisco is more convenient to use because the new packaging makes it easy to measure and easy to clean.

PACKAGING

Packaging also offers a means for a company to differentiate its product from competitors. Innovative packaging has accounted for the successful introduction of Goldschlager

"Quick. Name a soft drink." Just outside of Austin, Texas, a billboard heralds the return of Coca-Cola's unmistakable contour bottle to the United States. The contour bottle sign, recognized all over the world, differentiates Coke from its competitors.

Schnapps premium liqueur. The clear, bell-shaped decanter displays shiny, 24-carat gold flakes that are dispersed throughout the liqueur. The bottle resembles a snow dome when shaken. The product has found a niche with the under-30 crowd, especially in bars and restaurants where it is imbibed as a shooter or after-dinner cordial.[29]

Packaging is responsible for one of the biggest components of cost in many consumer products. This makes cost-effective packaging one of industry's greatest needs.

Choosing the right package is especially crucial in international marketing, since marketers must be aware of many variables. One variable is cultural preference. Consumers in African nations, for instance, often prefer bold colors, but they may either prefer (or frown upon) national flag colors, and they often associate red with death or witchcraft. Package sizes can vary according to the purchasing patterns and market conditions of a country. In countries with little refrigeration, people may want to buy their beverages one at a time rather than in six-packs. Package weight is another important issue, since the cost of shipping is often based on weight. In some areas, customs duties are also assessed according to the gross weight of the shipment, including the packaging.[30]

LABELING

Labeling is often an integral part of the packaging process. Soft drinks, frozen vegetables, milk, and snack foods are examples. Product labels must meet federal requirements set forth in the Fair Packaging and Labeling Act (1966). The law intends to provide adequate information about package contents so consumers can make value comparisons among competing products. The FDA recently updated labeling regulations. Now, most food labels must list clearly exact amounts of fat, cholesterol, calories, and vitamins in each serving of the products. Food manufacturers must also follow stricter rules when describing their products. The FDA intends these new regulations to prevent food manufacturers from using terms such as *healthy, low fat,* and *lite* where they do not apply.

Some food makers, however, have found a loophole that exempts them from the sweeping label changes. Since the FDA lacks the authority to force a company to change the size of its package, the agency must overlook the labels on packages that are considered too small or too round to accommodate the new labels. According to the "Lifesaver rule," any package whose label area matches the height or width of an ordinary package of Lifesavers candies is exempt. These labels need only supply a telephone number or address where consumers can contact the company for nutritional information. Products such as bear-shaped honey bottles, specially shaped condiment jars, and some milk containers meet these requirements.[31]

Marketers who ship products to other countries have to comply with labeling requirements in those nations. Typical questions facing international marketers include: Should they print labels in more than one language? Should labels specify ingredients? Do labels give enough information about the product to meet government standards?[32]

Universal Product Code (UPC)
Bar code read by optical scanner in systems that print the name and price of each item on a receipt.

Another important influence on packaging and labeling comes from the **Universal Product Code (UPC),** the bar code read by optical scanners in systems that print the name of each item and its price on a receipt. You are probably familiar with the UPC bar codes on groceries and other merchandise. Many retailers rely on these identifiers not just for packaging and labeling, but also for input to evaluate customers' purchases and control inventory. These bar codes are also making their way into other industries. United Parcel Service uses Maxicode, a bar code about the size of a postage stamp that holds 100 characters of data. UPS will be using Maxicode to carry destination and tracking information on the 3 billion packages it processes each year.[33]

PRICING STRATEGY

After developing, identifying, and packaging a good or service, the firm must set its price. This is the second aspect of the marketing mix. As an earlier section noted, price is the exchange value of a good or service. Pricing strategy has become one of the most important features of modern marketing.

All goods and services offer some utility or want-satisfying power. Individual preferences determine how much utility a consumer will associate with a particular good or service. One person may value leisure-time hobbies while another focuses more on buying property, cars, or furniture. Consumers face an allocation problem, though; they have limited amounts of money and endless ways to spend it. The price system helps them to make allocation decisions. You might prefer to spend your money on a vacation rather than on a personal computer, but if air fares rise, you might decide to allocate funds to the computer instead. You also might prefer a Lexus over other cars, but if you cannot afford a Lexus, chances are you will choose another car.

Prices help to direct the overall economic system. A firm uses various factors of production, such as natural resources, labor, and capital, based on their relative prices. High wage rates may cause a firm to install labor-saving machinery, and high interest rates may lead management to decide against a new capital expenditure. Prices and volume sold determine the revenue a firm receives and influence its profits.

PRICING OBJECTIVES

Marketers attempt to accomplish certain objectives through their pricing decisions. Research has shown that pricing objectives vary from firm to firm, and that many companies pursue multiple pricing objectives. Some companies try to improve their profits by pricing their offerings high, while others set low prices to attract new business. The three basic categories of pricing objectives are (1) profitability, (2) volume, and (3) other objectives, including social and ethical considerations, status quo objectives, and image goals.

PROFITABILITY OBJECTIVES

Some type of profitability objectives guides the pricing strategies of most firms. Marketers know that:

$$\text{Profit} = \text{Revenue} - \text{Expenses}$$

and that revenue is a result of the selling price times the quantity sold:

$$\text{Total revenue} = \text{Price} \times \text{Quantity sold}$$

Some firms try to maximize profits by increasing prices to the point where they sell fewer units. This approach may or may not work. A 10 percent price hike that reduces volume by only 8 percent increases profitability, but a 5 percent hike that reduces volume by 6 percent is less profitable. In fact, a small reduction in price can result in a major reduction in profits, as is illustrated in Figure 14.3.

Profit maximization forms the basis of much of economic theory, yet it is often difficult to apply in practice. Many firms have turned to a simpler profitability objective—the *target-return goal.* Most target-return pricing goals state desired profitability levels in terms of returns on either sales or investment. For example, a company might specify a goal of a 9 percent return on sales or a 20 percent return on investment.

profit maximization
Pricing strategy in which managers set an increasing level of profitability as an objective.

VOLUME OBJECTIVES

In another approach to pricing strategy, **sales maximization,** managers set an acceptable minimum level of profitability and then try to maximize sales. This strategy views sales

sales maximization
Pricing strategy under which managers set an acceptable minimum level of profitability and then try to maximize sales.

FIGURE 14.3 PERILS OF A PRICE CUT

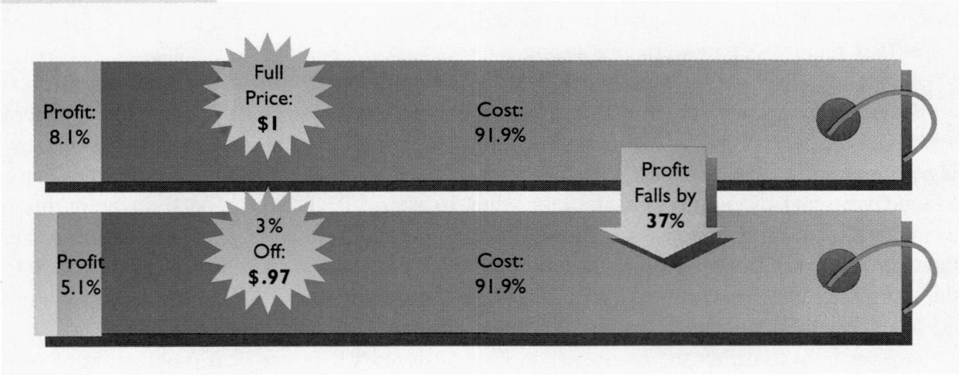

expansion as more important than short-run profits to the firm's long-term competitive position. In order to attract customers, stores may advertise certain products called *loss leaders* at or below cost. When a grocery store advertises milk or other items at extremely low prices, the store hopes that you will buy not just the loss leaders, but other products, as well.

market share
Percentage of a market controlled by a certain company or product.

A second volume objective bases decisions on **market share**—the percentage of a market controlled by a certain company or product. One firm may seek to achieve a 25 percent market share in a certain industry. Another may want to maintain or expand its market share for particular products or product lines.

Many marketers follow value-pricing principles to attract consumers who want more quality for their money. Nestlé's Chase & Sanborn, one of the oldest brand names in the coffee market, has maintained a low-price strategy for years, and value pricing is paying off for the brand. Bad weather in Brazil has forced coffee prices upward, making Chase & Sanborn an even better buy. Market share is up and Chase & Sanborn has been one of the few brands to increase sales and market share within the coffee market, thanks to value pricing.[34]

Market share objectives have become popular for several reasons. One of the most important is the ease with which market share statistics can serve as yardsticks for measuring managerial and corporate performance. Another is that increased sales may lead to lower production costs and higher profits. On a per-unit basis, a firm can produce 100,000 pens more cheaply than just a few dozen.

OTHER PRICING OBJECTIVES

Social and ethical considerations play important roles in some pricing situations. For example, prices may depend on what the target market can pay; some unions base dues on the incomes of members.

Many firms have status quo pricing objectives; that is, they are inclined to follow their markets' leaders. These companies seek stable prices that allow them to put their competitive efforts into other areas, such as product design or promotion. This situation is most common in oligopolistic markets, which were discussed in Chapter 1.

Image goals often affect pricing strategy, too. Upscale stores such as Saks Fifth Avenue set price structures to reflect the high quality levels of their merchandise. Discounters like Kmart and Target, however, try to project images of good value at low prices. A firm's pricing strategy may be an integral part of the overall image it wishes to convey.

This ad for the Lassale line of Seiko watches carries no price; instead it creates an image for the watches, which are finished in 22 karat gold. Because consumers generally believe that higher priced goods are of better quality, pricing can be an important factor in promoting the quality of goods.

PRICE DETERMINATION

While pricing is usually regarded as a function of marketing, it also requires considerable input from other areas of the company. Accounting and financial managers have always played major roles in pricing by providing sales and cost data necessary for good decision making. Production and industrial engineering personnel play similarly important roles. Computer analysts, for example, ensure that the firm's information system provides up-to-date information needed in pricing. It is essential for managers at all levels to realize the importance of pricing and the contributions of different departments to choosing the right price.

Price determination can be viewed from two perspectives. Economic theory provides an overall viewpoint, while cost-based pricing looks at the decision as a practical, hands-on problem.

ECONOMIC THEORY

Economic theory, as discussed in Chapter 1, assumes a profit maximization objective. It dictates that managers set a market price at the point where the amount of a product desired at a given price equals the amount that suppliers will provide at that price. In other words, this is the point where the amount demanded and the amount supplied are in equilibrium. The demand curve is a schedule of amounts that consumers demand at different price levels. At \$3 per pound, they might buy 5,000 pounds of an industrial chemical. A price increase to \$4 per pound might reduce sales to 3,200 pounds, and a \$5 per pound price might result in sales of only 2,000 pounds, as some potential customers would decide to accept less expensive substitutes or to wait for the price to fall. Correspondingly, the supply curve is a schedule that shows the amounts that firms will offer in the market at certain prices. The intersection of these schedules is the equilibrium price in the marketplace for a particular good or service.

COST-BASED PRICING

Although economic theory leads to correct decisions regarding the overall market for a product, managers face the problem of setting the prices of individual brands based on limited information. Anticipating how much of a product they will sell at a certain price is difficult, so businesses tend to adopt cost-based pricing formulas. Although these are simpler and easier to use than economic theory, executives have to apply them flexibly in each situation.

Marketers begin the process of cost-based pricing by totaling all costs associated with offering a product in the market, including production, transportation, and marketing expenses. They then add an amount to cover any unexpected or overlooked expenses and ensure a profit. The total becomes the price.

Obviously, with cost-based pricing, high costs can mean high prices. Japanese consumers pay a lot for food, a reflection of the high costs incurred by transportation, marketing intermediaries, and markups. Most of these transactions are controlled by Nokyo, a huge group of cooperatives and other businesses. Nokyo imports raw materials for agricultural products—fertilizer, for example—into Japan. It sells the raw ingredients to fertilizer producers, then buys the finished fertilizer and sells it to distributors, who in turn sell it to cooperatives where farmers can buy it. These costs add up to food prices that average 25 percent of a Japanese family's disposable income, compared to 17 percent spent by an American family.[35]

breakeven analysis
Method of determining the minimum sales volume needed at a certain price to cover all costs.

variable cost
Cost that changes with the production level, such as the costs of labor and raw materials.

fixed cost
Cost that remains stable regardless of the production level.

breakeven point
Level of sales that will cover all of the company's costs, including both fixed and variable costs.

Breakeven Analysis: A Tool in Cost-Based Pricing Marketers often use **breakeven analysis** as a method to determine the minimum sales volume a product must generate at a certain price level to cover all costs. This involves a consideration of various costs and total revenue. Total cost *(TC)* is composed of total variable costs *(TVC)* and total fixed costs *(TFC)*. **Variable costs** change with the level of production (such as labor and raw materials), while **fixed costs** remain stable regardless of the production level (such as the firm's insurance premiums). Total revenue is determined by multiplying price by the number of units sold.

The **breakeven point** is the level of sales that will cover all of the company's costs, including both fixed and variable costs. It is the point at which total revenue just equals total costs. Sales beyond the breakeven point will generate profits; sales volume below the breakeven amount will result in losses. The following formula gives the breakeven point in units:

$$\text{Breakeven point (in units)} = \frac{\text{Total fixed costs}}{\text{Contribution to fixed costs per unit}}$$

A product selling for \$20 with a variable cost of \$14 per item produces a \$6 per-unit contribution to fixed costs. If the firm has total fixed costs of \$42,000, then it must sell 7,000 units to break even. The calculation of the breakeven point in units is:

$$\text{Breakeven point} = \frac{\$42{,}000}{\$20 - \$14} = \frac{\$42{,}000}{\$6} = 7{,}000 \text{ units}$$

Figure 14.4 illustrates this breakeven point graphically. Marketers can use breakeven analysis to determine the profits or losses that would result from several different proposed prices. Since different prices will produce different breakeven points, marketers could compare the calculations of sales necessary to break even with sales estimates from market research studies. This comparison can identify the best price, one that would attract enough customers to exceed the breakeven point and earn profits for the firm.

TYPES OF PRICING STRATEGIES

Pricing is an important and risky decision for a firm. Selecting the right price for a new product is difficult, since a price tag that is too high can definitely hurt sales. The U.S. lodging industry recently learned this the hard way when firms tried to cash in on one

FIGURE 14.4 BREAKEVEN ANALYSIS

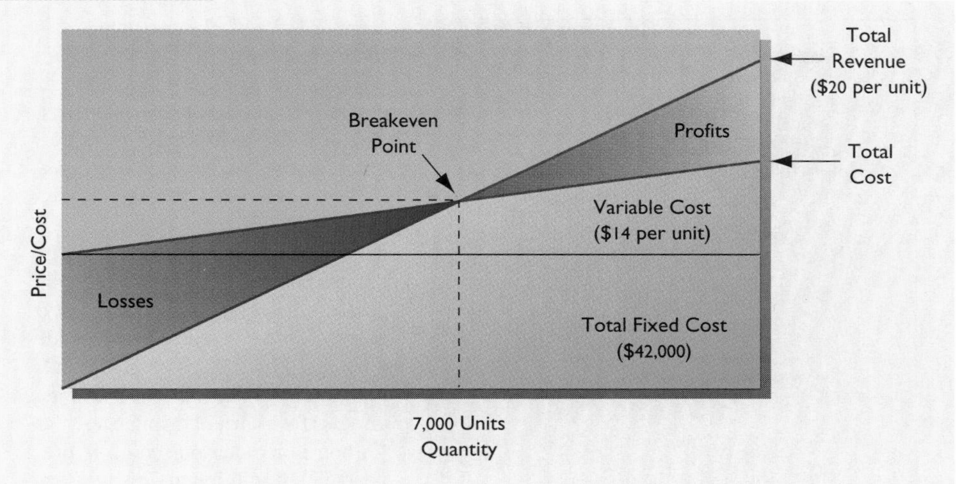

of the world's most popular events, the World Cup. Prices for some hotel rooms were up to double the normal rates. As a result, fans booked only one-half of the 1 million room nights estimated for the event. Roland Baumann, general manager of the Hyatt Regency in Washington, D.C., recognized this as a blown opportunity. "With rates more reasonable, we at least would have had a chance at more business."[36]

Because pricing decisions are so risky, it is usually best to field test alternative prices with sample groups of consumers. Once a product is launched, it is difficult to change prices during the introductory period.

Pricing involves important decisions for the firm. One option is to price the product competitively, that is, to match a competitor's price. A marketer that selects a competitive pricing strategy is attempting to succeed through nonprice competition. In other words, the marketer seeks to compete on the basis of advertising, better distribution, and similar methods, rather than on price. Two primary pricing strategies are skimming pricing and penetration pricing.

Skimming Pricing The strategy of *skimming pricing* sets the price of a product relatively high compared to similar goods and then gradually lowers it. This strategy works best when the market is segmented by price, that is, where some people may buy the product if it is priced at $10.00, a larger group may buy it at $7.50, and a still larger group may buy it at $6.00. It is also effective in situations where a firm has a substantial lead on competitors with a new product. The skimming strategy has been effective when some products have been first introduced, such as color televisions, calculators, personal computers, and VCRs.

A skimming strategy allows the firm to recover its cost rapidly by maximizing revenue. This becomes a disadvantage, however, if early profits tend to attract competitors, putting pressure on prices. For example, most ballpoint pens now sell for less than $1, but when the product was first introduced after World War II, it sold for about $20.

Penetration Pricing The second type of pricing strategy, *penetration pricing*, involves pricing the product relatively low compared to similar goods in the hope that it will secure wide market acceptance that will allow the company to raise its price. Firms often introduce soaps and toothpastes this way. Penetration pricing discourages competition because of its low profits. Firms often follow this method when they expect rapid

BUSINESS IN ACTION

FIRST ALERT: STAYING FIRST IN A MANDATED MARKET

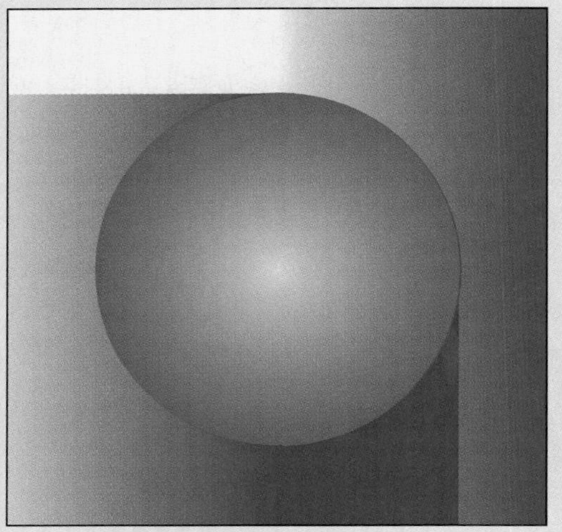

Manufacturers must work hard to sell most products in today's marketplace. Marketers spend millions of dollars to encourage consumers to buy their products. Rarely will products sell without some minimal level of marketing support. ■ The carbon monoxide detector is that rare product that sells with little or no marketing support. Why? Because a new law mandates that Chicago, Illinois residents must have the product in their homes. The recent ordinance requires that carbon monoxide detectors be installed within 40 feet of all bedrooms in homes and apartments heated by coal, kerosene, natural gas, oil, wood, and propane. Other major U.S. cities such as Pittsburgh are considering similar ordinances. The Consumer Product Safety Commission has also proposed a requirement to install detectors in new homes nationwide. ■ Carbon monoxide is a silent killer. The odorless, colorless, and poisonous gas is a byproduct of burning oils, natural gas, and other fuels. In the past, people were alerted to a carbon monoxide problem because impurities in fuel would give off a scent or leave black soot, but today's fuels leave no trace. Also, modern, well-insulated homes exclude air that might normally dilute the gas. The gas goes unnoticed and is quickly absorbed by the body causing symptoms such as nausea, dizziness, and headaches. Too much carbon monoxide is lethal. The elderly, unborn babies, and infants are at the greatest risk. Over 200 deaths a year are attributed to carbon monoxide poisoning from inefficient or malfunctioning furnaces, space heaters, or other fuel-burning appliances. ■ Carbon monoxide poisoning is preventable. In addition to Chicago's ordinance and other legislation, the demand for detectors has soared due to the highly publicized death of tennis great Vitas Gerulaitis, who died in his sleep as a malfunctioning pool heater vented into his cottage. ■ BRK Brands, Inc. has been manufacturing the First Alert carbon monoxide detector since 1993. In 1994, the company sold 300,000 units at a wholesale cost of $30 each. Sales in 1995 are expected to reach 1.5 million. First Alert is the market leader with about a 75 percent market share. ■ A law requiring con-

In Brazil, Procter & Gamble sells Pampers Uni, a less expensive version of its Pampers disposable diaper. Because most of the growth of consumer goods is in developing countries like Brazil, P&G developed Pampers Uni based on what consumers in Brazil could afford. Procter & Gamble will introduce its regular version of Pampers as incomes grow and customers wish for better products.

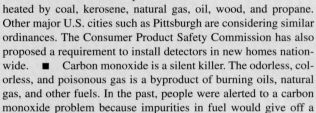

sumers to buy a product does not guarantee financial success for the producer, though. First Alert came under fire when a weather condition known as a *thermal inversion* descended on Chicago and set off carbon monoxide detectors throughout the city. The city's fire department responded to over 1,800 calls from residents whose detectors registered unsafe levels of carbon monoxide. About 85 percent of the detectors involved in these calls were made by First Alert. In the first 3 months after the ordinance went into effect, the fire department investigated 12,990 carbon monoxide-related calls. Only 68 victims were taken to hospitals. The number of these victims actually diagnosed with carbon monoxide poisoning was unknown. ■ City officials criticized the First Alert detector as being too sensitive. The detector's alarm sounds at very low levels of carbon monoxide. Once set off, the detector must be placed in an environment free of carbon monoxide above 40°F for up to 48 hours. ■ BRK Brands responded to the problem by offering refunds to owners of First Alert detectors. Consumers who phone a toll-free number and send their detectors back to the company will receive full refunds. The offer was expected to cost the company millions of dollars. Even though it offered the refund, the company still denied city officials' accusations that the detectors are too sensitive for use by the general population. ■ Chicago will not repeal the ordinance, despite the controversy surrounding the nuisance calls. The city will, however, rely on design changes recommended by Underwriters Laboratories, an independent firm, to address the issues presented by the new ordinance. In the meantime, BRK Brands has developed an improved, less sensitive version of its detector with a fast reset button. Sources: Susan Chandler, "Red Alert at First Alert," *Business Week,* January 9, 1995, p. 44; Al Podgorski, "Council to Keep Detectors in Place," *Chicago Sun-Times,* January 5, 1995, p. 16; Jeffrey D. Zbar, "Detector Woes Flare in Chicago," *Advertising Age,* January 2, 1995, p. 23; Fran Spielman, "Fire Department Again Responding to All Calls," *Chicago Sun-Times,* December 24, 1994, p. 4; Jeffrey D. Zbar, "First Alert Rings Up Huge Market Share with Carbon Monoxide Detector," *Advertising Age,* November 7, 1994, p. 12; Jeffrey Steele, "How to Detect which Product Is Best for You," *Chicago Tribune,* October 31, 1994, p. 5; and Barbara Kantrowitz, Adam Rogers, and Gregory Beals, "Colorless, Odorless, and Deadly," *Newsweek,* October 3, 1994, p. 60.

QUESTIONS FOR CRITICAL THINKING

1. Are marketing activities (i.e., advertising, promotion) necessary for these products?
2. How could the problems with carbon monoxide detectors have been avoided?
3. What would be the pros and cons of the government endorsing certain brands of carbon monoxide detectors?

competition from similar products and when large-scale production and marketing will substantially reduce overall costs.

Sometimes pricing strategies shift. Nissan recently announced a change in pricing strategy on its flagship sedan, the Maxima. The new base sticker price of just under $20,000 represents a $2,500 drop from the previous year's model. At a time when most other car companies are increasing prices, how can Nissan afford to lower its price? It also reduced cost by switching some of last year's standard features—security system, alloy wheels, and automatic transmission—into options. It also reduced the costs of some parts by substituting less expensive alternatives. Nissan is hoping that the lower-priced Maxima will maintain its market share against rivals Toyota Camry, Chrysler Eagle Vision, and Dodge Intrepid.[37]

PRODUCT LINE PRICING

Under the strategy of **product line pricing,** a seller offers merchandise at a limited number of prices rather than setting an individual price for each item. For instance, a boutique might offer lines of women's sweaters priced at $50, $80, and $120. Product line pricing is a common marketing practice among retailers. The original 5-and-10-cent stores are an example of its early use. Today, the 99¢ Stores offer a variety of household and personal care products that are all priced at $0.99—nothing in the store is over this price point.

product line pricing
Offering groups of merchandise at a limited number of prices instead of pricing each item individually.

Product line pricing simplifies the pricing function, but marketers must clearly identify the market segments to which they want to appeal. Three high-priced lines might not be appropriate for a store located in a low-to-middle-income area.

One disadvantage of product line pricing is that it is sometimes difficult to alter the price ranges once they have been set. If costs go up, the firm must either raise the price of the line or reduce its quality. Consumers may resist these alternatives. While product line pricing can be useful, its implementation must be considered carefully.

CONSUMER PERCEPTION OF PRICES

Marketers consider how consumers perceive prices. If a buyer views a price as too high or too low, the marketer must correct the situation. Price–quality relationships and psychological pricing are important in this regard.

PRICE–QUALITY RELATIONSHIP

Research shows that the consumer's perception of product quality is related closely to an item's price; a higher price raises perceptions of quality. Most marketers believe that this perceived price–quality relationship exists over a relatively wide range of prices, although consumers may view extreme prices as either too expensive or too cheap. Marketing managers need to study and experiment with prices because the price–quality relationship can be critically important to a firm's pricing strategy.

Most of the big car makers expect high sticker prices for the electric cars they are mandated to sell in California by the late 1990s. Renaissance Cars, Inc. of Florida sees things differently. The firm is betting that consumers will buy more cars if they offer high quality priced right. The firm is introducing its Tropica, a two-seat electric vehicle with a maximum speed of 62 mph that meets all freeway safety requirements, in California and Florida. The convertible is targeted to commuters, retirees, and college-age consumers who want dependable, yet affordable transportation. Renaissance has priced the Tropica at least $10,000 below the preliminary guesstimates for comparable models from the big auto makers.[38]

PSYCHOLOGICAL PRICING

Many marketers believe that consumers find certain prices more psychologically appealing than others. The image pricing goals mentioned earlier are an example of psychological pricing, which is used throughout the world.

Have you ever wondered why retailers set prices like $39.95, $19.98, or $9.99 instead of $40.00, $20.00, or $10.00? Before the age of cash registers and sales taxes, retailers followed this practice of *odd pricing* to force clerks to make correct change as part of cash control efforts. It is now a common practice in retail pricing because many believe that consumers are more attracted to uneven amounts. In fact, some stores use prices ending in 1, 2, 3, 4, 6, or 7 to avoid the look of more common prices like $5.95, $10.98, and $19.99. Their prices are more likely to be $1.11, $3.22, $3.86, $4.53, $5.74, or $9.97.

ACHIEVEMENT CHECK SUMMARY

Reread the learning goals that follow, and consider the questions for each goal. Answering these questions will reinforce the most important concepts in the chapter and allow you to check how well you have achieved these learning goals. Where a blank appears before a question, answer with *T* or *F*. Otherwise, circle the letter of the correct answer. An answer key to these questions is found at the end of this chapter.

LEARNING GOAL 14.1: Explain what a product is and list the components of product strategy.

1. ___ A product is defined as a bundle of symbolic, service, and physical attributes designed to satisfy consumer wants.
2. ___ Product strategy does not include warranties or customer service.
3. ___ New-product development is an important part of product strategy.

LEARNING GOAL 14.2: Identify the classifications of consumer goods, business goods, and services.

1. A manager can divide consumer goods into convenience, shopping, and specialty categories based upon: (a) what consumer needs the goods meet; (b) when the products are used; (c) the buying habits of consumers; (d) the types of production processes used.
2. Products that consumers purchase quickly and with minimum effort are called: (a) shopping goods; (b) brand goods; (c) convenience goods; (d) specialty goods; (e) quick goods.
3. A new airplane purchased by an airline is classified as a(n): (a) raw material; (b) accessory equipment; (c) component part; (d) supply; (e) installation.

LEARNING GOAL 14.3: Discuss the product mix and product lines.

1. ___ The assortment of goods and services a firm offers its customers is called its *product line*.
2. ___ In order to ensure company growth, marketers should continually assess their product mixes and adjust their offerings.
3. ___ If a firm develops and markets a unique product for an industrial customer, it has expanded its product mix.

LEARNING GOAL 14.4: Identify and describe the stages of the product life cycle.

1. The product life cycle stage in which sales climb rapidly, the producer begins to earn a profit, and competitors begin to enter the field is known as: (a) introduction; (b) growth; (c) maturity; (d) decline.
2. During what stage of the product life cycle will industry sales reach a saturation level because of intense competition and price cutting? (a) introduction; (b) growth; (c) maturity; (d) decline.
3. Strategies to extend the product life cycle include: (a) increasing the frequency of use; (b) finding new users; (c) changing the product; (d) all of the above.

LEARNING GOAL 14.5: List the stages of new-product development.

1. ___ Only about one-third of new products are commercial successes.
2. ___ During the initial screening stage, a new product is evaluated on its prospects for financial success.
3. ___ Selling a product on a trial basis in a limited area is called *test marketing*.

LEARNING GOAL 14.6: Explain how firms identify their products.

1. ___ A good brand name should be easy to spell, pronounce, and remember.
2. ___ A private brand carries the manufacturer's name.
3. ___ The only important consideration in packaging is how well it protects the product.

LEARNING GOAL 14.7 Outline the different types of pricing objectives.

1. Pricing objectives expressed as a percentage return on investment or sales are termed: (a) volume objectives; (b) sales maximization objectives; (c) target return goals; (d) market-share objectives; (e) profit maximization objectives.
2. If marketers attempt to increase the percentage of industry sales their products will attract, they are using: (a) breakeven analysis; (b) sales maximization objectives; (c) market-share objectives; (d) return-on-sales objectives; (e) cost–benefit analysis.

LEARNING GOAL 14.8: Discuss how firms set prices in the marketplace.

1. ___ In cost-based pricing, marketers total all costs associated with offering a product and add an amount to cover unexpected expenses and profit.
2. ___ A change in price level typically brings about a change in the amount of product demanded.

LEARNING GOAL 14.9: Explain how to use breakeven analysis in pricing strategy.

1. Breakeven analysis identified the breakeven point in units by: (a) dividing total costs by the number of units sold; (b) dividing fixed costs by the unit contribution to fixed costs; (c) dividing sales revenue by variable cost per unit; (d) dividing sales price by variable costs.
2. If a company has fixed costs of $60,000, a selling price of $10 per unit, and variable costs per unit of $4, how many units must it sell to break even? (a) 5,000; (b) 10,000; (c) 15,000; (d) 20,000.

LEARNING GOAL 14.10: Differentiate between skimming and penetration pricing strategies.

1. ___ A penetration pricing policy is used by firms attempting to earn the largest possible profit at the introduction of the product.
2. ___ The skimming pricing strategy involves starting out at a high price, then gradually lowering the price.

KEY TERMS

product 380
price 380
product mix 382
product line 382
product life cycle 383
test marketing 389
brand 390
brand name 390
trademark 390
national brand 391
private brand 391
generic product 391
brand recognition 392
brand preference 392
brand insistence 392
family brand 392
individual brand 393
Universal Product Code (UPC) 394
profit maximization 395
sales maximization 395
market share 396
breakeven analysis 398
variable cost 398
fixed cost 398
breakeven point 398
product line pricing 400

REVIEW QUESTIONS

1. How do marketers define the term *product?* What is included in marketers' concept of product?

2. Differentiate among the following categories of consumer goods, business goods, and services:
   a. Convenience, shopping, and specialty goods
   b. Installations, accessory equipment, component parts and materials, raw materials, and supplies
   c. Consumer and business services

3. Can a product be both a consumer good and a business good? Give an example.

4. What is a product mix? Identify its primary components.

5. Suggest products with which you are familiar that represent each of the stages in the product life cycle. Why did you classify these products as you did?

6. Identify and explain the stages in new-product development. Illustrate each stage with a hypothetical example.

7. Differentiate among brand, brand name, and trademark. Cite examples of each.

8. List and identify the various pricing objectives of companies. Which ones do you think are most important to marketers? Why?

9. Assume that a product selling for $10 has a variable cost of $6 per unit. If total fixed costs for this product are $36,000, how many units must the firm sell to break even?

10. Contrast the skimming and penetration pricing strategies. What types of products or market situations best suit each strategy?

DISCUSSION QUESTIONS

1. Mountain Valley Spring Water Company bottles drinking water from a spring 10 miles north of Hot Springs, Arkansas. The water, highly regarded for its purity, is consumed by the king of Saudi Arabia and has been served in the White House since the administration of Calvin Coolidge. Classify Mountain Valley Spring Water as a consumer good. Discuss why you classified it as you did.

2. Cardiologist Marvin Wayne developed his image of the perfect cookie while experimenting in a military mess in Vietnam. Now marketed as Dr. Cookie, the cookies are high in fiber and complex carbohydrates, low in salt and cholesterol, and contain no sulfites, preservatives, or artificial ingredients. The Bothell, Washington firm sells Dr. Cookie to consumers via mail order. It also sells directly to airlines such as United and Horizon as a snack and directly to companies for use during business meetings. The company also sells Dr. Cookie dough through a few selected retailers. How would you classify Dr. Cookie?[39]

3. Suggest a brand name for each of the following new products and explain why you chose each name:
   a. Development of exclusive homesites
   b. Low-price, term life insurance policy sold by mail
   c. Airline's improved business-class service on Asian routes
   d. Lawn edger that is more durable than its competitors

4. Collect four advertisements for the same product in different countries. (Possibilities might be Coca-Cola, Pepsi, or McDonald's.) Assess the packaging, product designs, trademarks, and images shown in the ads; are they different or similar? If they differ, explain in what ways. What product strategy or strategies is the company using for each market?

5. In the escalating fast-food war, most fast-food restaurants now offer value menus with reduced prices for some popular items. For example, McDonald's sells a 59¢ hamburger, Burger King sells a 99¢ Whopper, and Taco Bell sells a 59¢ taco. Discuss the dangers in lowering everyday prices.

SOLUTIONS TO ACHIEVEMENT CHECK SUMMARY

L. G. 14.1: 1. T, 2. F, 3. T. **L. G. 14.2:** 1. c, 2. c, 3. e. **L. G. 14.3:** 1. F, 2. T, 3. T. **L. G. 14.4:** 1. b, 2. c, 3. d. **L. G. 14.5:** 1. T, 2. F, 3. T. **L. G. 14.6:** 1. T, 2. F, 3. F. **L. G. 14.7:** 1. c, 2. c. **L. G. 14.8:** 1. T, 2. T. **L. G. 14.9:** 1. b, 2. b. **L. G. 14.10:** 1. F, 2. T.

VIDEO CASE

SECOND CHANCE Richard Davis knew that careful product and pricing strategies would be critical to the successful marketing of the product he had invented and patented. Davis had his work cut out for him. His company, Second Chance, produces a product that most people will never need, buy, or wear, and yet he expected to charge anywhere from $200 to well over $1,000 for it. Davis had invented a new type of soft body armor or "bullet proof" vest.

In the introductory stage of the product life cycle, Davis' goal was simply to inform potential customers that his product existed and that it worked. In 1972, he had himself filmed as he shot himself in the chest with a handgun. The idea was perhaps a bit melodramatic, but it worked. Davis has since been shot 172 times to help prove the effectiveness of his product. In fact, he holds the Guinness record for being shot the greatest number of times and surviving.

Once Davis had gotten the word out about his body armor, he needed to refine his product strategy. Since he was and is actively involved in the development of the product he sells, he knew that he had to demonstrate superiority to competing products in two important areas: effectiveness and comfort. Davis had already shown in his films and demonstrations that the product was effective against the kinds of bullets most law enforcement officers were likely to encounter. Emphasizing the relative comfort of his body armor was his next goal. While it is possible to manufacture body armor that will stop even the so-called "Cop Killer" bullet, today's patrol officer won't buy it if it's not comfortable. No matter how good a vest is, if it's not worn, it's not working.

To emphasize the comfort of his product, advertisements for Davis' newest body armor show it being crumpled up into a ball with a caption making the challenge, "Can you do this with a panel from your concealable soft body armor?" This advertisement visually demonstrates the thinness and flexibility of the product, allowing the potential customer to imagine the ease and comfort of wearing this newest version, thereby differentiating it from the competition.

Davis' next problem was settling on the right price for his product. Each vest has to be custom fitted for optimum performance and to ensure that it is soft and comfortable enough to be worn for long periods of time. The company must offer a range of options in length, width, thickness, color, and shape to closely match the product with customers' needs and desires. They've even fitted dogs. The need to customize body armor results in literally thousands of product variations. These variations are grouped into product lines with different price ranges. The basic vest starts at around $200. The middle of the road product is known as the Superfeatherlite™ and sells for $500 to $600. The top of the line is the Monarch,™ which goes for $800 to $1,000. They all work, but the Monarch™ is the thinnest and most comfortable.

As a result of developing effective product and pricing strategies, Second Chance leads its industry in units sold and in the number of lives saved annually.

Even though this industry is only about 23 years old, the product technology's obsolescence cycles are getting shorter and shorter. Second Chance has always excelled at applying the newest technology base available at the time that a product is manufactured. First generation products were made from ballistic nylon; second generation from Kevlar 29®; and third generation from Kevlar 129.® The current fourth generation is made of Araflex™ IV—a technology that Second Chance helped develop. This newest material has enabled Second Chance to introduce a product that is thinner, lighter, and more flexible than anything available before.

As a result of developing effective product and pricing strategies, Second Chance leads its industry in units sold and in the number of lives saved annually. Currently, more than 550 law enforcement officers have been saved by the technology Second Chance developed and produced. Statistics like this have brought Second Chance high levels of brand recognition, preference, and even insistence by their marketplace—all of which will help Second Chance remain an industry leader well into the future.

QUESTIONS

1.
What stage of the product life cycle would you say Second Chance body armor is in? What factors have combined to extend its product life cycle?

2.
Is soft body armor a consumer good or a business good? Why?

3.
Would you classify this product as a convenience, shopping, or a specialty product? Explain your answer.

4.
Give likely descriptions of consumers displaying each of the different degrees of brand loyalty (brand recognition, brand loyalty, brand insistence).

DISTRIBUTION STRATEGY

CHAPTER

LEARNING GOALS

1. Explain the value created by the distribution function.

2. Identify the major components of a distribution strategy.

3. Outline the various types of distribution channels, and discuss the factors that influence channel selection.

4. Explain how a vertical marketing system (VMS) differs from a traditional distribution channel.

5. Describe the different degrees of market coverage.

6. Identify the various types of wholesaling intermediaries.

7. Outline the primary categories of retailers.

8. Explain the role of the physical distribution function.

MEETING NEW CHALLENGES AT SUPERVALU Food wholesaling is a tough business these days. Supermarket chains buy directly from manufacturers. Warehouse stores bypass intermediaries. Both supermarkets and warehouse stores offer such low retail prices that they are forcing many independent grocers, whose prices are higher, out of business. As the independents are squeezed, so are the wholesalers. Does this mean the end for the food wholesaling business? ■ Not if you talk to Supervalu, a wholesaler now considered the largest in the world. Since 1978, Supervalu's revenues have gone from $2.5 billion to $16 billion and earnings have grown from almost $26 million to a whopping $185 million. ■ In a business with a declining survival rate for wholesalers, how has Supervalu achieved such success? It has recognized trends in the retailing business and adapted to them. Supervalu realized that it would need a larger customer base to increase its sales volume, which in turn would support larger warehouse facilities. All of these factors would contribute to more efficient operations. Supervalu responded by increasing its base of grocery retailers. By purchasing 12 major wholesale operations and picking up customers from other wholesalers that had gone out of business, the company came to service 4,350 retailers in 47 states. ■ Supervalu maintains its customer base and attracts new business by offering superior customer service. The company supports its independent-market customers in the areas of financing, computer services, training, and store designs. Supervalu's top priority is to increase the sales and profits of its customers, regardless of size. The company knows that increasing customers' sales and profits will also increase its own. ■ Supervalu realized, however, that it could not tie its future growth to independent grocers alone. As a result, Supervalu expanded into retail. By purchasing fellow wholesaler Wetterau, Supervalu added Shop 'n Save, Sav-A-Lot, and Laneco to its fold, which already included Cub Foods, County Market, and other supercenter, discount, and club stores. Supervalu has also increased its presence in New England and Texas by purchasing retail chains there. To date, Supervalu has 258 company-owned stores generating about $4 billion in sales. ■ The move into retail has strengthened Supervalu in two ways. Retail sales generate higher margins than wholesale sales, thus boosting profits. Also, by servicing its own stores, Supervalu acts as a wholesaler to increase its wholesale volume. As a result, Supervalu's margins are 25 percent higher than other wholesalers in a business where every penny counts. ■ Supervalu plans to continue its market dominance through forward integration and is looking to acquire other retail chains. It also sees opportunities in the international market. Supervalu must pursue this strategy carefully, though. By expanding into retailing, Supervalu risks putting its own original customers—the independents—out of business. By maintaining close relationships with its customers and continuing to provide superior service, however, Supervalu is expected to continue its growth and dominance in the wholesale market.[1]

CHAPTER OVERVIEW

After firms produce and price products, they must distribute the products to the marketplace. All organizations perform some distribution function. Del Monte distributes its products to you by placing them in supermarkets and convenience stores. Public libraries use bookmobiles to distribute their services to people in outlying areas.

Economists often use the terms *place, time,* and *ownership utility* to describe the value of distribution. The marketer adds to a product's value by getting it to the right place at the time the consumer wants to buy it and by making it possible to transfer ownership. A good distribution strategy increases a company's competitiveness substantially. Indeed, firms without good distribution strategies usually fail. Think about the last time you could not find something you wanted in a store; did you go to a competing store and buy it there instead? This is one reason why Wal-Mart has been so successful. Founder Sam Walton always tied store locations to the locations of warehouses to make products easily and quickly available when consumers want them.

Distribution also provides jobs. Salespeople, warehouse managers, truck drivers, and forklift operators all work in distribution. Other workers service the products that flow through a distribution network. Most people who work in distribution are classified as service personnel. In other words, they provide services to other sectors of the economy.

This chapter will look at the two major components of an organization's distribution strategy: distribution channels and physical distribution. **Distribution channels** are the paths through which products—and title to them—flow from producer to consumer. They are the means by which all organizations distribute their goods and services.

distribution channel
Path through which goods and services, and title to them, flow from producer to consumer.

physical distribution
Movement of goods from producer to user.

The second major component of distribution strategy, **physical distribution,** is the actual movement of products from producers to users. Physical distribution covers a broad range of activities, including customer service, transportation, inventory control, materials handling, order processing, and warehousing.

DISTRIBUTION CHANNELS

Distribution channels consist of **marketing intermediaries** (also called *middlemen*), the people or firms that operate between the producer and the consumer or industrial user. The two main categories of marketing intermediaries are wholesalers and retailers.

marketing intermediary
Channel member that operates between the producer and the consumer or business purchaser.

wholesaling intermediary
Channel member that sells goods primarily to retailers, other wholesalers, or business users.

retailer
Channel member that sells goods and services to individuals for their own use rather than for resale.

Wholesaling intermediaries are persons or firms that sell mainly to retailers and other wholesalers or industrial users. Usually they do not sell products to people for their own use. Sysco, the largest marketer and distributor of food-service products in the United States, buys more than 185,000 food products from manufacturers and resells them to some 245,000 restaurants, hotels, schools, health-care facilities, and other institutions in the United States and Canada.[2]

Retailers, by contrast, are persons or firms that sell goods and services to individuals for their own use rather than for resale. As a consumer, you are probably most familiar with retailers among all marketing intermediaries. Consumers usually buy their food, clothing, shampoo, furniture, and appliances from some type of retailer. The supermarket where you buy your groceries may have bought some of its stock from Sysco and then resold it to you.

FUNCTIONS OF MARKETING INTERMEDIARIES

Marketing intermediaries perform various functions that help the distribution channel to operate smoothly, including buying, selling, storing, and transporting products. Some intermediaries also sort and grade bulky items. Wholesalers of fresh produce, for example, receive bulk shipments of fruits and vegetables from growers; sort the produce according to size, color, and ripeness; and then repack it in smaller boxes for customers such as restaurants and grocery stores.

As another important service, marketing intermediaries provide information to other channel members. Many wholesalers and retailers use scanners and computer technology to measure who buys producers' goods, how much they buy, and how often.

By buying a manufacturer's output, intermediaries provide the necessary cash flow for the producer to pay workers and buy new equipment. By selling, they provide consumers or other intermediaries with desired goods and services. The buying/selling function of intermediaries makes the distribution channel more efficient. It facilitates the exchange process because it reduces the number of transactions needed between the producer and the consumer. Think about this exchange process. If each of four manufacturers were to sell directly to four consumers, this would require 16 separate transactions; an intermediary cuts the number of necessary transactions to eight, as illustrated in Figure 15.1.

Marketing intermediaries enter a channel of distribution because they can perform some activities more efficiently or less expensively than manufacturers or other channel members. Sometimes their efficiency wanes and others must replace them, but someone in the channel must perform vital distribution functions.

TYPES OF DISTRIBUTION CHANNELS

Manufacturing and service industries distribute their output through hundreds of channels. Canned foods usually pass through the hands of wholesalers and retailers before they reach your cart in the grocery store. Producers may sell some vacuum cleaners and encyclopedias directly to you at your home. No one channel is right for every product. The best channel depends on the circumstances of the market and on consumer needs, and the choice may change over time. In order to stay competitive, marketers must keep their distribution methods up to date.

Austin, Texas–based Dell Computers built its $3 billion business through direct sales and mail-order marketing. About 4 years ago, the computer giant changed its distribution strategy in hopes of reaching a larger market and entered the retail market selling its products through CompUSA, PC World, Best Buy, Sam's Club, and Price/Costco. Recently, however, Dell decided to change its strategy again since retail sales accounted

FIGURE 15.1 MARKETING INTERMEDIARIES TO REDUCE TRANSACTIONS

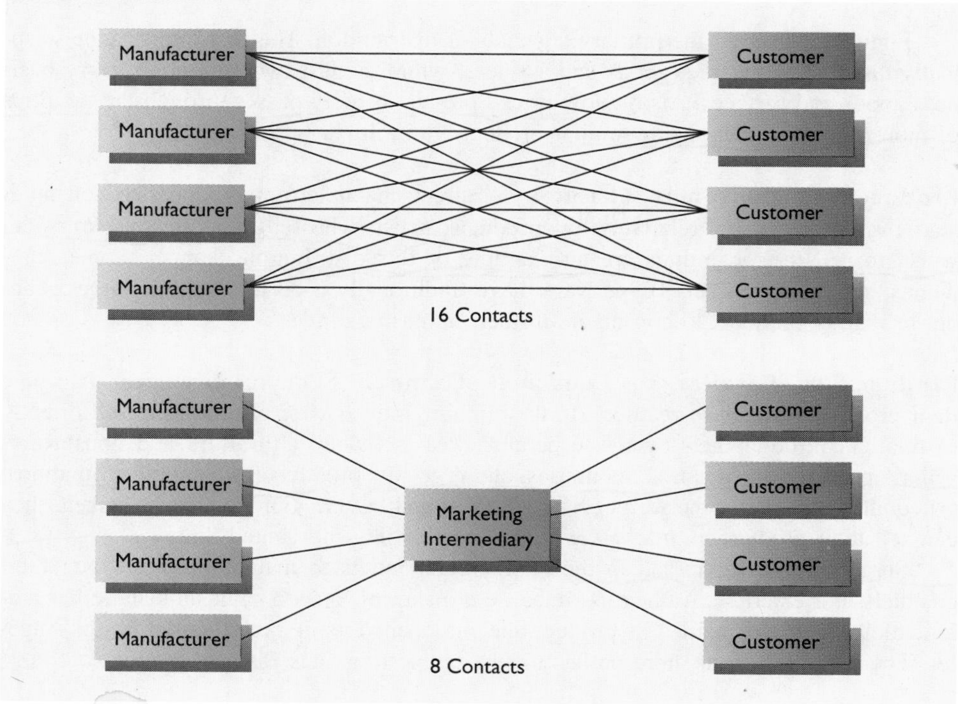

BUSINESS IN ACTION

NEW DISTRIBUTION STRATEGY PAYS OFF FOR TCBY

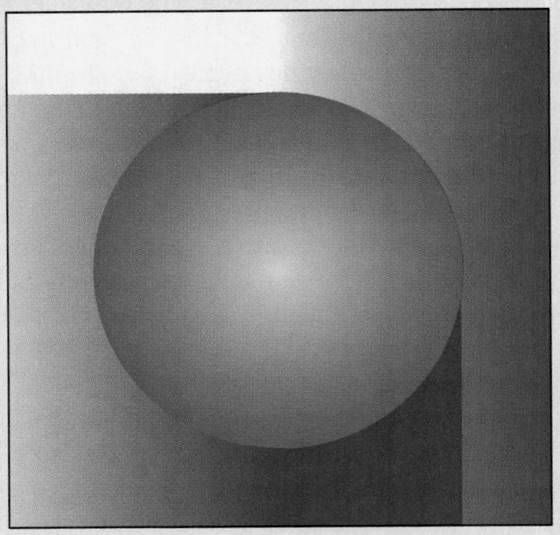

Frozen yogurt was a hot product in the 1980s when consumers were ready for a low-fat alternative to calorie-laden ice cream. Frank Hickingbotham, a former Baptist minister, benefited from the product's popularity when he opened a yogurt shop called TCBY, The Country's Best Yogurt, featuring several flavors of frozen yogurt. When the fad caught on, Hickingbotham opened more stores, as fast as one each day in the mid-1980s. Sales soared from $6.1 million in 1984 to $135 million in 1990. TCBY stores quickly achieved international success with outlets in such faraway locations as Nassau and Singapore. ■ The increase in demand and sales attracted tough competition. Other chains such as Penguin's opened their doors to this lucrative market, and even Baskin-Robbins shed its image as an exclusive retailer of ice cream, changing its name to Baskin-Robbins Ice Cream and Frozen Yogurt to increase sales. By 1990, the frozen yogurt market had become saturated. ■ TCBY's sales declined and the company was forced to close 200 of its stores in a slump that continued for 2 years. TCBY had to rethink its marketing strategy, including efforts to expand its product line and increase distribution, to reverse the sales decline. ■ In the first step toward rebuilding the company, TCBY is testing "TCBY Treats" in 12 company stores in the Dallas area. These stores feature 14 flavors of ice cream, a variety of hand-dipped yogurt flavors, frozen custard, and 41 flavors of shaved ice in addition to its traditional frozen yogurt menu. The variety of products will appeal to families in which different members have different tastes. TCBY is also testing the TCBY Cafe, a cafe featuring salads, soups, and low-fat sandwiches in an outdoor or indoor setting in downtown Little Rock. ■ In the second step toward rebuilding, TCBY is pursuing nontraditional sites to increase distribution. The company recently placed carts or kiosks in 804 new sites in airports, stadiums, hospitals, and other locations that represent new markets for TCBY. ■ In considering nontraditional sites, TCBY recog-

for only 2 percent of its overall business. The company has withdrawn its products from retail channels and is refocusing on the source of its success—direct sales and mail-order marketing. Dell will test other methods of reaching consumers such as retail kiosks and on-line services.[3]

Figure 15.2 shows the primary channels of distribution. The first four channels typically distribute consumer goods and services, while the last two commonly carry business goods and services. Also, a low-priced product usually passes through the facilities of more intermediaries than a similar product with a higher price tag.

Producer to Consumer Channel A direct channel from producer to consumer suits most services, but relatively few products. Artists who set up booths on Paris sidewalks to sell their paintings are an example of this distribution channel. Some companies, such as Avon and Tupperware, have traditionally used this kind of direct channel to market products to consumers in their homes or offices.

Producer to Retailer to Consumer Channel Some manufacturers distribute their products directly to retailers. In the clothing industry, many producers sell directly to retailers through their own salespeople. Ikea, a Swedish furniture and housewares seller, operates 90 stores in 22 countries, and it gets its products from suppliers in almost 50 countries, many in the former Soviet Union and eastern Europe. Through Ikea, they can sell their products in markets worldwide, including the United States.[4]

Some manufacturers set up their own retail outlets to maintain control over their channels. For example, Authentic Fitness, the maker of Speedo swimsuits and other athletic clothing, has expanded its product line and opened its first retail outlet in Los Angeles. The firm plans four more outlets to serve as testing sites for new products.[5]

nized that the company and frozen yogurt have penetrated most major cities. Although it sees opportunities in smaller towns, sales generated in these areas probably would not support full store operations. TCBY further increased its distribution and sales potential by introducing TCBY Express, a 20-foot-by-8-foot mobile frozen yogurt truck to serve these areas. The company hopes to capitalize on the same strategy that made Wal-Mart the biggest retailer in the country—targeting small towns. ■ The marketing strategy for TCBY Express targets "hometown USA." Units are currently being franchised in southeastern Arkansas with onboard refrigerators, freezers, yogurt dispensers, and service counters. TCBY Express will offer a more varied menu than company stores, including hot dogs, chili dogs, shaved ice, and ice cream in addition to frozen yogurt, since the units will serve areas with fewer competitors. ■ The Express mobile units are all owned by the company. A 5-year TCBY Express franchise costs only $5,000, much less than the $20,000 fee for a 10-year store franchise. Also, a store franchisee must pay for the construction of the store itself along with equipment and inventory. TCBY Express franchisees simply lease trucks from the company for $950 per month. ■ TCBY Express offers a very versatile retailing system. "The mobility of this unit gives you an opportunity to test market a site and determine whether or not it will justify a larger type unit later," says Hickingbotham. The unit can also make appearances at special events such as concerts and fairs to take advantage of the crowds. Once a site is chosen, the Express truck can simply be connected to utility lines. Some store franchisees lease Express trucks to start businesses while their stores are being built. TCBY plans on placing 200 Express units in the first year. ■ TCBY's new marketing strategies are paying off. The company recently posted its first sales increase in 3 years. By remaining flexible, increasing the product line, and improving distribution, TCBY hopes to continue posting sales increases. International expansion will contribute to the bottom line with three new franchises opening in the Middle East. New stores are also planned for Egypt, Bahrain, Kuwait, Qatar, Saudi Arabia, and the United Arab Emirates by 1998. Sources: Leroy Donald, "TCBY Tries Something Old: Ice Cream," *Arkansas Democrat-Gazette,* August 6, 1994, p. 1D; Leroy Donald, "Small Towns Get a Taste of TCBY," *Arkansas Democrat-Gazette,* March 21, 1994, p. D1; and David Hage, "Sweet Taste of Success," *U. S. News and World Report,* March 7, 1994, p. 54.

QUESTIONS FOR CRITICAL THINKING

1. What are the pitfalls of basing a business on a single product like frozen yogurt?
2. What other types of nontraditional sites might increase distribution for TCBY?
3. What are the pros and cons of expanding a product line to reverse a sales decline?

Producer to Wholesaler to Retailer to Consumer Channel Thousands of manufacturers rely on the traditional channel for consumer goods, distribution through wholesalers, because it is more efficient than maintaining large sales forces of their own to reach retailers. Supervalu, as mentioned at the beginning of this chapter, buys thousands of products from manufacturers and resells them to over 4,350 independent grocery stores in 47 states. By selling their products to Supervalu, suppliers avoid having to hire a large sales staff, yet they still get their products into stores nationwide.[6]

Producer to Wholesaler to Wholesaler to Retailer to Consumer Channel Commonly, more than one wholesaler participates in the distribution of agricultural products (canned and frozen foods) and petroleum products (oil and gasoline). An extra wholesaling level is required to divide, sort, and distribute bulky items. Large, multinational oil companies such as Royal Dutch/Shell Group and British Petroleum Co. follow this pattern.

Producer to Industrial User Channel The direct channel from producer to user most commonly distributes business goods and services. This channel carries nearly all business products except accessory equipment and operating supplies. In Japan, for instance, IBM sells many of its large, mainframe computers directly to corporations.

Producer to Wholesaler to Industrial User Channel Some industrial products flow through indirect channels from producer to wholesaler to user, as do small accessory equipment and operating supplies that are produced in large lots but sold in small amounts. For example, Wal-Mart's Sam's Club opens early on Tuesdays and Thursdays to serve business card holders, the firm's commercial accounts, and then opens to retail customers at 12 P.M.

FIGURE 15.2 Primary Channels of Distribution

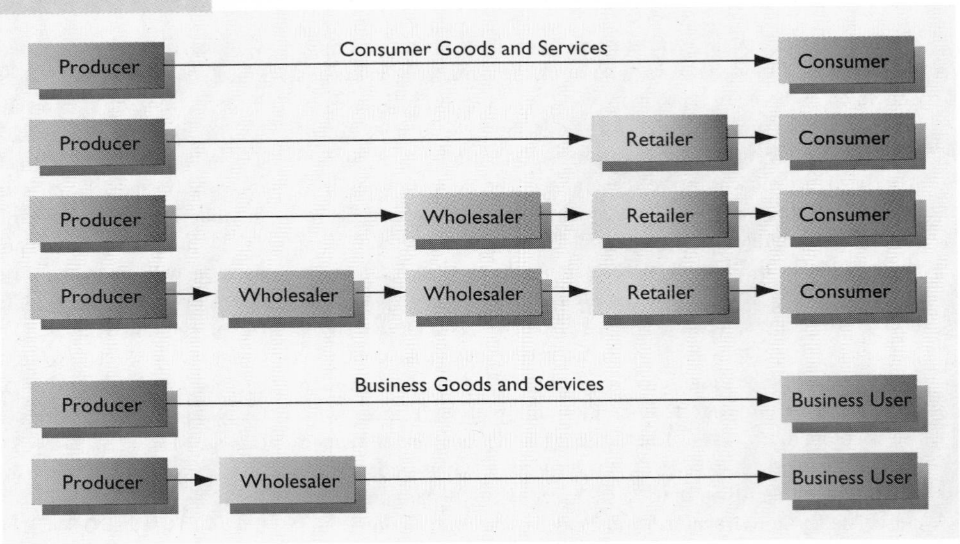

SELECTING A DISTRIBUTION CHANNEL

The choice of a distribution channel depends on several factors: the market, the product, the producer, and the competition. These factors are often interrelated.

Market Factors As a producer, your most important consideration in choosing a distribution channel is the market segment that you want to reach. Consider the case of Beer Across America.

Beer Across America works on the same premise as a book-of-the-month or wine-of-the-month club. Each month, the company ships two 6-packs of beer directly to members' homes from different microbreweries around the country. Members pay $15 per month plus shipping and handling for the service. The firm solicits members through direct-response radio ads and mailings to groups like Beer Drinkers of America, whose membership tops 185,000. Today, the company's sales are almost $16 million.

Beer Across America is a good example of the convenience that distribution channels offer to both producers and consumers. Microbreweries cooperate eagerly with BAA since many of these smaller breweries sell only about 10,000 cases of product each year. Beer Across America will order 30,000 cases itself from a microbrewery whose product it carries. Consumers are willing to pay for the convenience of having unique products delivered to their doors each month.[7]

To sell a product to more than one market segment, a producer may need more than one distribution channel. In fact, some companies are finding that multiple distribution channels simply help them to sell more. Some firms sell their products through both retail outlets and mail order, for example.

A new technology is creating an additional distribution channel. Videotex is an online computer service that offers news, information, and mail-order shopping for various products to subscribers. Orlando cable viewers can now access ShopperVision, a grocery and drug product videotex home shopping system. On the two-way interactive system, consumers view a 3D diagram of a supermarket. They push their simulated carts up and down the aisles and fill them with all of the products that regular supermarkets offer. A local order fulfillment company delivers the products at a cost of $5 to $10 per order. Grocers are excited about this new distribution channel since home-delivery purchases average $111 versus an average in-store purchase of $23.[8]

Product Factors In general, shorter distribution channels carry products that are complex, expensive, custom-made, or perishable. McDonnell-Douglas sells its MD11 and DC10 aircraft directly to airlines, including both domestic customers like American and Delta and foreign airlines such as China Airline. Inexpensive or standardized products are typically sold through longer channels. Examples include office furniture and plumbing fixtures.

Producer Factors A producer that offers a broad product line and that has the financial and marketing resources to distribute and promote its products is more likely to choose a shorter channel of distribution. For example, Gerber's 600-person sales force sells direct to over 35,000 retail outlets including grocery, drug, mass merchandising, and convenience stores. The company offers a full line of baby products including baby foods, formula, apparel, and accessories. Gerber recently gave each salesperson a laptop computer to process information. Sales reps input data and messages after each sales call; a host computer at headquarters surveys the laptops every night, accumulates the data, analyzes it, and prepares reports for both reps and management. Gerber's management feels that its direct sales force helps the firm to respond more effectively to retail customers' needs, and thus to provide better service, than intermediaries could offer. The changeover to electronic communications has given sales reps and account managers an additional 8 hours of selling time each week, and management is putting this extra time to good use. Gerber is acting as the broker for baby formula products of Mead Johnson and paper products of Scott Paper.[9]

Competitive Factors Performance is a key consideration when choosing a distribution channel. A producer loses customers if its intermediary fails to promote or deliver its products effectively.

Sometimes a producer may switch channels if distribution becomes too difficult or complex. The confusing variety of customs procedures and postal systems in different countries—distribution channels for products sold abroad—has created a market opportunity for Intertrans, an Irvine, Texas-based shipper. Suppose that you want to send products from a factory in the United States to one in Singapore. An Intertrans representative in Singapore will receive the shipment, deal with the red tape of customs, export documentation, and licensing, and deliver your packages to their final destination. The company has become so attractive, in fact, that it was recently acquired by Fritz Company in San Francisco as a means to expand that company's base of operations.[10]

VERTICAL MARKETING SYSTEMS

Some companies have developed **vertical marketing systems (VMSs),** or planned networks of distribution channels designed to reduce conflict among channel members and other distribution problems. In the past, most distribution channels developed as unplanned systems that changed to meet consumer needs. The three types of vertical marketing systems are corporate, administered, and contractual VMSs.

vertical marketing system (VMS) *Planned distribution channel organized to reduce channel conflict and improve distribution efficiency.*

CORPORATE VMS

In a corporate vertical marketing system, one enterprise owns all channel members. Standard Brands, for example, manufactures home-improvement products and paints. Standard Brands produces the merchandise and then sells it through its corporate-owned retail outlets.

ADMINISTERED VMS

An administered vertical marketing system is a distribution system dominated by one channel member, often called the *channel captain.* A manufacturer, a wholesaler, or a retailer can play this role. Traditionally, the channel captain has been the manufacturer that provides the promotional budget to support a brand. In recent years, however, an increasing number of retailers and wholesalers have assumed roles as channel captains.

In Japan, businesses traditionally have formed alliances often dominated by one channel member. Toyota, for instance, heads a vertically integrated alliance that includes 175 primary suppliers and 4,000 secondary suppliers. Such distribution systems, known as *keiretsu,* have a strong influence on Japanese business. The Japanese firm NEC is one of few companies worldwide with completely vertically integrated operations.[11] Retailers in Japan often serve simply as showrooms for individual manufacturers or wholesalers; even their employees may work for manufacturers and their salaries depend on bonuses received from that firm.

CONTRACTUAL VMS

Contractual vertical marketing systems have had the greatest impact on distribution strategy of all types of VMS. Such a system binds members through a contractual agreement. Franchises such as Pizza Hut and Subway are contractual VMSs. Franchises were discussed in detail in Chapter 6.

Another contractual system is the wholesaler-sponsored voluntary chain of retail stores. Under this kind of agreement, a wholesaler provides marketing programs, merchandise selection, and other services to independent retailers that agree to purchase the wholesaler's products. McKesson Corporation, the nation's largest wholesale distributor of pharmaceuticals, sells about 31,000 products to 19,500 pharmacies, chain stores, and drugstores. McKesson teamed up with Medis Health and Pharmaceutical Services, Canada's only nationwide drug distributor, to create the first integrated, international distribution organization for pharmaceuticals. McKesson also recently acquired a minority interest in Nadro S.A. de C.V., Mexico's leading drug distributor. With this acquisition, McKesson has expanded its marketplace to include 365 million consumers—the entire North American continent.[12] Another wholesaler-sponsored chain is IGA Food Stores. This system helps independent retailers to compete with mass merchandisers and retail chains.

A third type of contractual VMS is the retail cooperative, in which retailers set up their own common wholesaling operation. The retailers agree to buy a certain amount of merchandise from the wholesaling operation, but they may also choose a common store name and develop a private-label line of goods. Retail cooperatives, such as Associated Grocers, are common in the grocery industry. Like the wholesaler-sponsored system, retail cooperatives help independent retailers to compete with mass merchandisers and large retail chains.

MARKET COVERAGE

Any distribution strategy decision must consider market coverage. For example, probably only one Nissan dealer serves your immediate area, but several retail outlets may sell General Electric products. Coca-Cola can be found everywhere—in supermarkets, neighborhood convenience stores, service stations, vending machines, restaurants, and coffee shops. Different types of products require different kinds of distribution coverage. Three categories of marketing coverage include intensive, exclusive, and selective distribution.

INTENSIVE DISTRIBUTION

In an **intensive distribution** strategy, a marketer tries to place a product in nearly every available outlet. Chewing gum, newspapers, soft drinks, popular magazines, and other low-priced, convenience products are available in many convenient locations. This kind of saturation of the market requires distribution through wholesalers to achieve maximum market coverage.

intensive distribution
Market coverage strategy that tries to place a product in every available outlet.

USA Today practices intensive distribution. The national daily newspaper is sold at thousands of newsstands, newspaper vending machines, and retail outlets throughout the country to saturate the market and provide maximum convenience for the paper's nearly 6 million readers. The ultimate form of convenience, direct delivery to the consumer's home, provides both time and place utility.

EXCLUSIVE DISTRIBUTION

In the opposite of intensive distribution, **exclusive distribution,** a manufacturer gives a retailer or wholesaler the exclusive right to sell its products in a specific geographic area. Automobile companies practice a familiar form of exclusive distribution. Expensive jewelry items reach customers through another exclusive distribution system.

exclusive distribution
Market coverage strategy that gives a retailer or wholesaler exclusive rights to sell products in a specific geographic area.

An exclusive distribution contract allows the retailer to carry enough inventory and provide services that it might not if it had to contend with competing dealers nearby. Because the dealer has a guaranteed sales area, it is likely to make expensive investments in the business. In return, the manufacturer helps the dealer to develop a quality image and promote its products effectively.

SELECTIVE DISTRIBUTION

Somewhere between the extremes of intensive and exclusive distribution lies **selective distribution,** in which a manufacturer selects a limited number of retailers to distribute its product lines. Television sets and electrical appliances are often handled in this man-

selective distribution
Market coverage strategy that selects a limited number of retailers to distribute products.

Wrigley's products are available in 109 international markets, including shops like this one in China. Wrigley's gum, Coca-Cola, and Pepsi are found around the world because each company has chosen an intensive distribution strategy.

ner. A manufacturer hopes to develop close working relationships with dealers and often splits advertising expenses with them. Many manufacturers maintain extensive servicing and training facilities to help retailers distribute their products more effectively.

Step 2, an Ohio-based toy company, has chosen not to distribute its products through mass merchandisers and warehouse clubs. Manufacturers have little to no control over the enormous discounts at which these retailers sell products. These deep discounts hurt independent retailers and condition consumers to buy only when stores mark down goods. Instead, Step 2 distributes through independent stores and cooperatives so both the manufacturer and retailer can control retail price points and earn higher profits.[13]

WHOLESALING

industrial distributor
Wholesaling intermediary that sells products to business users.

Wholesaling is a crucial part of the distribution channels for many products, particularly consumer goods. As defined earlier, wholesalers are marketing intermediaries that sell to retailers, business purchasers, and other wholesalers, but not directly to the ultimate consumer. The traditional customer of the wholesaling intermediary is the retailer. Still, some wholesaling intermediaries, referred to as **industrial distributors,** sell to business users, while others sell to other wholesalers.

Wholesaling intermediaries can be classified on the basis of ownership. Manufacturers own some, retailers own others, and still others operate as independent organizations. Figure 15.3 outlines the various categories of wholesaling intermediaries.

MANUFACTURER-OWNED WHOLESALING INTERMEDIARIES

A manufacturer may decide to market its products through company-owned sales branches and sales offices for a number of reasons. A producer of perishable products may operate its own distribution centers to speed delivery directly to retailers. Company-owned channels often carry complex products that require installation and servicing and intensely competitive items that require a lot of promotion.

sales branch
Manufacturer-owned marketing intermediary that stocks a manufacturer's products and processes orders from inventory.

Sales branches stock the products they distribute and process orders from their inventory. These wholesalers are common in the chemical, petroleum products, motor vehicle, and machine and equipment industries. Snap-On Tool Corporation has 54 sales branches to warehouse hand tools and other equipment that its dealers sell to professional mechanics. Snap-On also maintains five large distribution centers that supply products to sales branches, as well as a National Outside Warehouse (NOW) that can purchase and distribute commonly requested products not available at the firm's other warehouses.[14]

sales office
Manufacturer-owned office for salespeople that encourages close local contacts for regular and potential customers.

A **sales office** is exactly what the name implies, an office for salespeople. Unlike sales branches, sales offices do not perform storage functions or warehouse any inventory. Manufacturers set up sales offices in various regions to provide localized selling

FIGURE 15.3 CATEGORIES OF WHOLESALING INTERMEDIARIES

Manufacturer-Owned
- Sales Branches
- Sales Offices

Independent
- Merchant Wholesalers (full-function, limited-function, rack jobbers)
- Agents and Brokers

Retailer-Owned
- Buying Groups
- Cooperatives

efforts and to improve customer service. For example, some manufacturers of kitchen and bathroom fixtures maintain showrooms to display products in sample room arrangements. Here salespeople can discuss the products and builders can get an idea of how the items would look in a home. However, when a builder actually places an order, the merchandise is delivered from a separate warehouse.

INDEPENDENT WHOLESALING INTERMEDIARIES

Most U.S. wholesalers are independent wholesalers. They account for about two-thirds of all wholesale trade. Independent wholesalers can be classified as either merchant wholesalers or agents and brokers.

Merchant Wholesalers The various types of **merchant wholesalers** take legal title to the products they handle. A merchant wholesaler that provides a complete assortment of services for retailers or industrial buyers is known as a **full-function merchant wholesaler.** An example is Fleming, a food wholesaler that offers both food and a range of support services to over 10,000 stores, including 3,700 supermarkets and 340 company-owned stores. Fleming processes orders from stores; provides shipping, receiving, and accounting services for various product lines; and distributes the products.[15]

Another type of full-function merchant wholesaler, a **rack jobber,** sets up and services a particular section of a retail store, such as paperback books, magazines, toys, or records. A rack jobber supplies racks, sets up displays, stocks and prices merchandise, and completely services space that it rents from the retailer on a commission basis.

A **limited-function merchant wholesaler** takes legal title to the products it handles, but provides fewer services. It may, for example, warehouse products, but not deliver them to customers, or it may warehouse and deliver products, but not provide financing. The ultimate example of a limited-function merchant wholesaler, a **drop shipper,** forwards orders directly to producers for shipment to customers. Drop shippers operate in industries like lumber and coal, never physically handling products, although they do hold legal title.

Agents and Brokers In contrast to merchant wholesalers, **agents and brokers** never take title to the products they handle, although they may or may not take possession of those products. These intermediaries bring buyers and sellers together and generally perform fewer services than merchant wholesalers. You are probably familiar with real estate agents, who act as intermediaries between people who want to sell their houses and people who want to buy. A real estate agent never takes title or possession of a seller's property, but provides time and ownership utility by making the transaction easier and more convenient for both seller and buyer. Similarly, stockbrokers match up people who want to sell stock with potential buyers. Other agent wholesalers include sales agents of various types; manufacturers' agents, who sell noncompeting lines of several producers on a commission basis; commission merchants, who sell agricultural products for farmers; and auction houses.

merchant wholesaler
Independent wholesaler that takes legal title to the goods it distributes.

full-function merchant wholesaler
Merchant wholesaler that performs many services in addition to taking legal title to goods it distributes.

rack jobber
Full-function merchant wholesaler that sets up and services a particular section of a retail store.

limited-function merchant wholesaler
Merchant wholesaler that takes legal title to the goods it distributes, but provides few services.

drop shipper
Limited-function merchant wholesaler that takes legal title to the goods it distributes, but never physically handles them.

agents and brokers
Independent wholesalers that never take title to the goods they distribute, but may or may not take possession of those goods.

RETAILER-OWNED WHOLESALING INTERMEDIARIES

Sometimes, retailers band together to form their own wholesaling organizations in the form of either a buying group or a cooperative. The retailers seek to reduce costs or to provide some special service that they do not find readily available in the marketplace. To achieve cost savings through quantity purchases, independent retailers may form a buying group. Others may form a cooperative, which, as described earlier, is a contractual vertical marketing system.

PARTNERING BETWEEN WHOLESALERS AND RETAILERS

In the past, wholesalers and retailers coexisted, each group attempting to maximize its own profits. With manufacturers cutting costs, customers seeking lower prices, and the growth of discount and warehouse stores that bypass intermediaries, wholesalers and distributors have been forced to redefine their roles in the marketplace to survive.

Today's successful wholesalers work in partnership with retailers. Wholesalers can succeed by offering valuable services that promote increased retail sales, retail training, joint planning and forecasting, and effective communications. If a wholesaler sets a top priority of increasing the retailer's sales, then the wholesaler's own sales will increase, too. Wholesalers that choose not to adapt to the demands of the current marketplace will lose customers and sales.

RETAILING

Retailers are the final link in the distribution channel. Since they are often the only channel members that deal directly with final consumers, they must remain constantly alert to customers' needs. They must also keep pace with developments in the fast-changing business environment. Within their dynamic business setting, retailers have to stay on their toes in order to remain competitive. Table 15.1 lists the six largest retailers in the United States.

WHEEL OF RETAILING

wheel of retailing
Concept of retailing evolution in which new types of retailers gain competitive footholds by emphasizing low prices in exchange for limited services.

The table illustrates the constant change in retailing as new stores replace older establishments. In a process called the **wheel of retailing,** new retailers enter the market by offering lower prices than existing competitors made possible through reductions in service. Supermarkets and discount houses, for example, gained their initial market footholds through low-price, limited-service appeals. These new entries gradually add services as they grow. Ultimately, they become targets for competitive assault by new retailers that enter the industry. For instance, today's attractive Wal-Mart stores, while still part of a discount chain, offer more conveniences than the chain's initial outlets offered, such as good lighting, wide aisles, big parking lots, and credit-card purchasing. They do not resemble early discounters that often operated from shacks set up on unpaved lots in dreary factory districts.

The wheel of retailing shows how the "survival of the fittest" principle determines business success. Retailers that fail to change fail to survive.

TABLE 15.1 AMERICA'S SIX LARGEST RETAILERS

RANK	COMPANY	SALES
1	Wal-Mart Stores	67.3 billion
2	Sears, Roebuck	54.9 billion
3	Kmart	34.1 billion
4	Kroger	22.4 billion
5	JCPenney	19.6 billion
6	Dayton Hudson	19.2 billion

TYPES OF RETAILERS

While stores account for most retailing activity, about 10 percent of total retail sales occur in nonstore environments. This breakdown suggests grouping retailers into two broad categories: store and nonstore retailers. The major types of store retailers include department stores, specialty shops, variety stores, convenience stores, discount outlets, off-price stores, factory outlets, catalog stores, supermarkets, hypermarkets, and warehouse clubs. Table 15.2 describes these retailers. The major types of nonstore retailing include direct selling, direct-response retailing, and automatic merchandising.

Direct selling brings the seller into direct contact with the buyer. For years, direct-selling retailers such as Avon, Amway, and Tupperware have sold their products in customers' homes. Because women, the traditional target market of these firms, have entered the work force in record numbers, however, many of these retailers now sell their merchandise in offices and factories. Avon has also expanded its operations outside the United States. Of Avon's 1.7 million independent representatives, 1.3 million are now located outside the United States. Avon's products are now available in 120 countries on six continents. Today more than 60 percent of Avon's sales come from outside the United States.[16]

Direct-response retailers sell products through mail or telephone orders of catalog merchandise or through telephone orders of merchandise advertised on television. Mail-

TABLE 15.2 TYPES OF STORE RETAILERS

TYPE OF RETAILER	DESCRIPTION	EXAMPLES
Variety store	Offers a variety of low-priced merchandise	F. W. Woolworth, Ben Franklin
Department store	Offers a wide variety of merchandise in departmentalized sections (furniture, cosmetics, clothing) and many customer services	Dillard's, Bon Marche, Marshall Field's, JCPenney
Specialty store	Offers a complete selection in a narrow range of merchandise	Shoe stores, camera shops, jewelry stores
Convenience store	Offers staple convenience goods, long store hours, rapid checkouts, adequate parking facilities, and convenient locations	7-Eleven, Circle K, Dairy Mart, gasoline stations
Discount store	Offers a wide selection of merchandise at low prices and few services	Kmart, Target, Wal-Mart
Off-price store	Offers designer or brand-name merchandise of many manufacturers at discount prices	T. J. Maxx, Marshall's, Loehmann's
Factory outlet	Manufacturer-owned store selling seconds, production overruns, or discontinued lines	Nike outlet store
Catalog store	Offers discounted merchandise from showrooms that display samples of products detailed in catalogs mailed to consumers	Service Merchandise, Zales, Gordon Jewelry
Supermarket	Large, self-service store offering a wide selection of food and nonfood merchandise	Winn-Dixie, Kroger, Lucky, Safeway, Super Fresh, Albertson's
Hypermarket	Giant store (at least three times the size of the average supermarket) offering food and general merchandise at discount prices	Hypermart USA, Bigg's, Meijer, Carrefour, Fred Meyer, Omni
Warehouse club	Large, warehouse-style store that sells food and general merchandise at discount prices to people who are part of its associated membership group	Sam's Club

In the Amazon region of Brazil, an Avon representative demonstrates a product for Tembe tribesmen. Direct selling continues to be Avon's primary sales method.

order selling began with a Montgomery Ward catalog in 1872. Today, mail-order houses range from Land's End (family clothing, white goods, and the like) to Williams-Sonoma ("A Catalog for Cooks") to Hammacher Schlemmer (upscale gift items) to Smith & Hawken (home and garden products). The fastest-growing area of direct-response retailing, home shopping services, use cable television networks to sell merchandise through telephone orders. This mode of nonstore selling is generating big dollars. For example, Joan Rivers sold a line of jewelry on the QVC Shopping Network that generated $30 million in sales.[17] Another type of home shopping exploits videotex technology to advertise and distribute products through personal computer subscription services. As discussed earlier, videotex can help a retailer reach more customers without building more stores.

Automatic merchandising through vending machines is an excellent method of retailing various types of consumer goods. Candy, soft drinks, ice, fruit, ice cream, chewing gum, sandwiches, coffee, milk, hot chocolate, and soup are all available through vending machines. You can even buy film-inspired CDs and T-shirts from vending machines in movie theater lobbies.

HOW RETAILERS COMPETE

Retailers compete with each other in many ways. Nonstore retailers focus on making the shopping experience as convenient for consumers as possible; Home Shopping Network allows them to shop while watching TV at home. Discount houses and warehouse clubs such as Sam's Club compete by offering shoppers a wide range of merchandise at low prices, but with little atmosphere. At the other extreme, a specialty shop such as The Nature Company offers customers maximum atmosphere (soothing background music) as they shop for environmentally oriented products, all of which are available for demonstration (telescopes, globes, minerals, and books).[18]

scrambled merchandising
Practice in which retailers carry dissimilar product lines to appeal to consumers seeking one-stop shopping.

Many retailers try to increase sales by diversifying their product lines, a practice known as **scrambled merchandising.** Original drugstores just sold medicines. They added soda fountains and newspapers, and now they sell cameras, small appliances, greeting cards, cosmetics, and toys. Grocery stores used to be just that; now many supermarkets rent videotapes, fill prescriptions, and sell nonfood items such as clothing and flowers in addition to groceries. Fry's, primarily a consumer electronics retailer, offers a variety of beverages and snack foods such as potato chips, candy, and bakery products in a section near checkout lines.

DEVELOPING A RETAILING STRATEGY

A retailer faces a unique marketing environment as the channel member that has direct contact with final consumers. It must develop a marketing strategy that satisfies its particular target market. The products offered, the prices, the store's location, its promotion method, and its atmosphere must all work together to project an image that appeals to a well-defined market segment.

Target Market Developing a retailing strategy begins with identifying the target market. For instance, Gottschalks, a department store chain headquartered in California, targets middle-income families in small to medium-sized towns. Dollar General, a discount chain based in Kentucky, targets low-income customers who live in rural towns with populations below 25,000.[19]

Product Strategy After identifying a target market, the retailer must plan how best to satisfy that market. This decision must specify general product categories, product lines, prices, and how much variety to offer. To suit its customers, Dollar General sells a variety of products—clothes, housewares, and health and beauty aids—pricing everything at $25 or less.

The recent growth trends of specialty retailers and discount houses have forced some retailers to change their product strategies. **Category killers,** discount chains that sell only one category of products, can be stiff competition for a store that stocks a smaller range of those products. Thus, many department stores no longer sell toys (thanks to category killer Toys R Us) or consumer electronics (due to competition from Best Buy Superstores and Circuit City).

category killer
A discount chain that sells only one category of products.

The Flower Warehouse in Costa Mesa, California is a category killer specializing in do-it-yourself flower arrangements. While other warehouse stores, mass merchandisers, and supermarket chains sell small selections of precut flowers, the Flower Warehouse is a self-service operation that offers deep discounts. Customers wander among barrels of products, select their flowers, and arrange them themselves or under the guidance of warehouse employees. Flower Warehouse keeps prices low since it purchases flowers directly from growers rather than through higher-priced wholesalers. Customers like buying fresh flowers and having a hand in arranging them. The Flower Warehouse has four locations, with three more expected to open soon.[20]

Customer-Service Strategy How can a department store or specialty boutique compete with category killers since it cannot offer as wide a selection? As one competitive move, it might offer a high level of customer service instead of low prices and wide selection. Since services add to the retailer's operating costs, discount stores tend to offer very few. Thus, a competing retailer may provide a full range of services, including gift wrapping, alterations, and delivery.

Some upscale retailers, such as Nordstrom's, have been very successful in attracting customers by offering enhanced services. At Nordstrom's, you do not have to remember what size you wear or what colors you prefer; clerks keep notebooks on what you like so they can advise you better. If you get worn out from shopping, you can get your shoes shined while a musician serenades you on a grand piano. In London, Harrod's offers visitors a wide range of services, including the option of ordering any product they want that the store does not carry. You can do your banking at Harrod's or take a $320 tour of London in the store's own vintage Rolls-Royce.[21]

Some companies have found that education is one of the best services they can offer. Dollar General Stores defied the odds and opened a retail store in a Nashville housing project. As part of its commitment to make the store successful, Dollar General worked with local agencies to create an educational program to help reduce the neighborhood's unemployment problem. Graduates of the program are eligible to work in the store. Both the program and the store are doing very well. Says Cabot Pyle, corporate communications director, "What we have found is the key to success is inviting the neighborhood to be part of the store . . . that they take a figurative ownership in the store."[22]

Convenience is another customer service that can pay off well. Consumers always welcome ways to save time. Futuredontics has created a niche for itself with its 1-800-DENTIST service. Consumers in need of dentists' services can dial 1-800-DENTIST to get listings of dentists in their areas. Futuredontics provides the list, the dentists' qualifications, and their specialties. The 1-800-DENTIST service saves consumers the time and effort of shopping for a dentist by consolidating information.[23]

Pricing Strategy Retailers are the channel members that determine the prices that consumers pay for goods and services. They base their prices on the cost of their own purchases of merchandise from other channel members. Discount retailers buy in large volumes so they can offer merchandise at lower prices.

A retailer's prices can influence customers' perceptions of the store. Saks Fifth Avenue advertises that it carries Joy by Jean Patou, a perfume that bills itself as "the costliest fragrance in the world." (Would you believe $300 an ounce?) By associating itself with such prices and products, Saks creates and maintains an upscale image for its stores.[24]

Location/Distribution Strategy Location represents every retailer's primary distribution decision. Will the store locate in a downtown business district, an outlying area, or a neighborhood or regional shopping center? A good location often makes the difference between success and failure in retailing.

The location decision depends on the retailer's size, financial resources, product offerings, and target market. When populations shifted from urban to suburban areas in the 1950s, department stores augmented their traditional locations in downtown districts with branches in suburban shopping malls to provide convenient locations for their target customers.

A recent trend is the specialty store shopping center. In contrast to a shopping mall, which offers a wide variety of stores, a specialty center targets a more defined market segment by offering an assortment of similar stores. Some specialty centers attract price-conscious consumers by gathering factory outlets and discount stores; others target big spenders by placing several high-fashion clothing and accessory stores together.

Promotional Strategy A retailer designs advertisements and develops other promotions to provide information about their store's location, merchandise offering, prices, and hours. A retailer also uses promotions to project a certain image that will attract its target market. Wal-Mart's advertising focuses on the theme of "everyday low prices" to attract cost-conscious consumers. Compare this to the image communicated by ads for Piaget with the message "Why watch connoisseurs the world over say there is only one Piaget." The ads go on to describe the features that have earned Piaget "its place as the timepiece of perfection."[25]

atmospherics
Physical characteristics and amenities that attract customers and help to satisfy their shopping needs.

Store Atmosphere Besides price and promotion, consumers' perceptions of a retailer are also shaped by **atmospherics,** the physical characteristics of a store and its amenities. A store's exterior should draw customers inside, and the interior should induce shop-

This ad for Piaget reflects the promotional strategy for this product. It encourages buyers to regard their purchase as a high-quality item worth the expense.

pers to buy. All interior elements—store layout, merchandise presentation, lighting, color scheme—should appeal to the target market.

Philadelphia's Center City John Wanamaker department store is a city landmark that has long been famous for tradition and quality merchandise. The store offers Roman arches, white marble columns, and a white-gloved doorman, not to mention the world's largest functioning pipe organ, played twice a day by a full-time organist. During the Christmas season Wanamaker's presents an hourly holiday extravaganza: a five-story light show with more than 100,000 lights, a 60-foot Christmas tree, dancing waters, and computerized figures that create a fairyland of color.[26]

PHYSICAL DISTRIBUTION

The second of the two major components of distribution strategy, physical distribution involves the actual movement of goods from producer to user. This covers a broad range of activities, including customer service, transportation, warehousing, materials handling, inventory control, and order processing.

Physical distribution is important for two reasons. First, such activities account for, on average, one-fifth of the cost of a manufactured product. In the past, businesses focused narrowly on making production more efficient to lower product costs. More recently, however, managers have begun to realize that reducing the cost of physical distribution offers another key tactic to improve productivity and become more competitive. Physical distribution is important, as well, because much of customer satisfaction depends on reliable movements of goods.

The objective of physical distribution is to provide a specified level of customer service at the lowest possible overall cost. The costs of the different factors involved are often interrelated. Low inventory levels, for example, may reduce warehousing costs, but they can lead to higher transportation and order-processing costs. Physical distribution strategy must take into account how all of these different costs relate to each other. Manufacturers, wholesalers, and retailers have reduced the costs of physical distribution through computer links that let channel members share information, speed up order processing and delivery, and reduce inventory on hand.

CUSTOMER SERVICE STANDARDS

customer service standards *Specifications for the quality of service that a firm will provide for its customers.*

Customer service standards specify the quality of service that a firm provides for its customers. Managers frequently set quantitative guidelines, for example, requiring that all orders be processed within 24 hours after they are received.

National Semiconductor, the world's 13th-largest microchip maker, recently overhauled its worldwide distribution network. The company produces chips at six plants—four U.S. plants and one each in Britain and Israel. National used to transport the chips to seven Southeast Asian assembly plants. From there, it shipped finished products around the world to various customers such as IBM, Ford, Toshiba, and Compaq. The chips travelled on 20,000 different routes flown by 12 different airlines making stops at 10 different warehouses along the way. The system was an inventory manager's nightmare.

After finding that most products generated little or no profit because of high distribution costs, the company cut the number of products it sells by 45 percent. All finished chips go to a central facility in Asia where FedEx stores, sorts, and ships them to customers. As a result, National has increased its sales by $584 million in 2 years. National can also now deliver products from the factory to customers in 4 days or less. Still, the company is not satisfied with these results; it intends to meet its goal of a 72-hour delivery time soon.[27]

TRANSPORTATION

The form of transportation by which a firm ships its products depends primarily on the kinds of products, the distances, and the costs. The physical distribution manager can choose among a number of companies and modes of transportation.

Transportation Companies Transportation firms can be classified into four basic types: common carriers, contract carriers, private carriers, and freight forwarders. A *common carrier* offers to perform transportation services within a particular line of business for the general public. One example is a truck line operating in an area where general merchandise is handled. The truck line will serve anyone in the area who offers it general merchandise to haul, although it may not handle some specialized items such as liquid petroleum gas or aviation gas. Examples of common carriers are United Airlines and Consolidated Freightways.

Contract carriers transport goods for hire by individual contract or agreement. They do not perform services for the general public; instead, they usually offer specialized services that meet the individual needs of their customers. Contract carriers are often owner/operator motor carriers. Usually they solicit large shipments from a particular shipper to a particular recipient. On a smaller scale, independent truckers sometimes contract with timber companies to move logs.

Private carriers transport their own property in their own vehicles. Shell has its own fleet of oceangoing crude-oil tanker ships. Similarly, Wal-Mart operates an extensive trucking operation.

Freight forwarders differ from the other kinds of carriers in that they do not own any of the equipment used in intercity transportation of freight. They are common carriers that lease or contract bulk space from other carriers, such as airlines and railroads, and resell this space to small-volume shippers. The freight forwarder picks up the merchandise from the shipper, loads it into the equipment of another carrier, delivers it to its destination, and takes care of all billing involved. For instance, Flagship Express Services Inc. leases three DC-8-71 cargo jet aircraft in order to provide nightly air freight service between New York, Chicago, Los Angeles, and San Francisco. Flagship Express markets this service to (1) express carriers that want to divert traffic from crowded hub airports, (2) international airlines that need to move freight into and out of their U.S.

gateways, (3) courier companies, and (4) other freight forwarders that want to be more competitive in the overnight express market.[28]

Freight forwarders provide shippers the advantage of better, less expensive service, and they save the carriers the trouble of handling and billing for many small shipments. As a further advantage of freight forwarding, the forwarder knows at all times the location of each piece of freight while it is in transit. This intermediary saves money and improves service for everyone.

Modes of Transportation The five major modes of transportation are railroads, trucks, water carriers, pipelines, and air freight. The faster methods typically cost more than the slower ones. Table 15.3 compares speed, reliability of delivery, shipment frequency, location availability, handling flexibility, and cost for the five modes of transportation.

Railroads Trains carry about 37 percent of all domestic intercity freight, mostly as services of common carriers.[29] Intercity freight is measured by the ton-mile, the movement of 1 ton of freight for a distance of 1 mile. None of the nation's railroads acts as a contract carrier, and only a few (owned and operated by mining companies, lumbering operations, and very large manufacturers like steel mills) are private carriers.

Carload freight is the kind of transportation service railroads generally handle. Shippers provide loaded cars to be delivered to someone who will unload the cars. This type of freight costs less because railroad workers need not do the loading and unloading. Companion services to carload freight are containerization and trailer-on-flatcar (piggyback) services. Railroads also offer trainload services to shippers of bulk commodities like coal and iron ore. Some trains of this type never stop; they run constantly using continuous loading and unloading equipment.

In an effort to improve service standards and capture more of the market, railroads are offering services such as run-through trains, which bypass congested terminals, and unit trains, which serve individual customers, who pay lower rates for each shipment.

Trucks Highway transportation accounts for about 28 percent of domestic freight shipping. The principal advantage of highway transportation over other modes comes from flexibility. A truck carrier can operate wherever it can find a road, whereas trains depend on rails and planes require airports. A number of transcontinental highway carriers move freight coast to coast. However, highway carriers are most efficient for distances up to about 300 to 400 miles. For longer distances, railroads offer more advantages.

TABLE 15.3 MODES OF TRANSPORTATION

		Factor				
Mode	Percent of Domestic Intercity Volume	Speed	Dependability in Meeting Schedules	Frequency of Shipments	Availability in Different Locations	Cost
Rail	37.00%	Average	Average	Low	High	Medium
Water	15.00	Very slow	Average	Very low	Low	Very low
Truck	28.00	Fast	High	High	Very high	High
Pipeline	19.00	Slow	High	High	Very low	Low
Air	0.33	Very fast	High	Average	Average	Very high

Trains are monitored electronically from Union Pacific Railroad Company's underground dispatch center in Omaha. In an effort to improve customer service, individual railroads, through the Association of American Railroads, are equipping all freight cars with radio-activated identification tags. These tags permit continuous monitoring of freight cars on a railroad's tracks, thereby allowing railroads to immediately alert customers to delays, efficiently plan the makeup of trains, and improve schedules.

Products most often handled by motor carriers are clothing, furniture and fixtures, food, leather products, and machinery. Highway carriers are divided into common carriers, contract carriers, and private carriers.

The typical highway common carrier uses its own equipment to pick up freight at the shipper's door and deliver it to a freight terminal where it is loaded into larger trucks for delivery to a terminal in another city. There it is unloaded and delivered by smaller vehicles. Contract highway carriers can frequently offer lower rates than common carriers because they serve limited numbers of customers, deal in volume shipments, and operate only when they have profitable loads. Wholesale grocery companies, supermarket chains, department stores, manufacturing firms, and mining companies often maintain private-carrier operations.

Water Carriers Water transportation, though slow, is one of the least expensive of all modes of transportation. The two basic types of water carriers are inland or barge lines and oceangoing, deepwater ships. Oceangoing ships operate on the Great Lakes, between U.S. port cities, and in international commerce.

About 15 percent of the volume of U.S. intercity freight travels through the inland waterways. This system of waterways includes the Mississippi, Arkansas, Ohio, Tennessee, and other rivers; inland canals; and the Great Lakes. Much of this freight, especially on the rivers and canals, moves on barges pushed by mammoth tugs. Great Lakes traffic is handled by specially built ships, some of them 1,000 feet long. This low-cost type of transportation lends itself mainly to hauling bulk commodities such as fuel, oil and petroleum products, coal, chemicals, minerals, and farm products.

Pipelines Pipelines carry 19 percent of intercity freight, especially petroleum products ranging from crude oil to highly refined products and natural gas. Some successful experiments have been made in handling other bulk commodities, such as coal, this way. These commodities are ground into small pieces and mixed with water to form a slurry, which is then pumped through the pipelines. Pipelines can transport many liquids and gases more cheaply and quickly than other modes of transportation.

Air Freight While still dwarfed by other transportation modes, carrying only about one-third of 1 percent of all freight, domestic air freight has become increasingly important in recent years. Air freight is usually limited to valuable products such as furs or perishable items such as flowers and live lobsters.

Most of the U.S. certificated airlines are common carriers. Some of them (as well as a group of firms known as *supplemental carriers*) engage in charter work, which is a form of contract carriage. Many business organizations own or lease aircraft to transport their personnel or, in some cases, their freight; this is defined as *private carriage.* For example, Wal-Mart aviation operates a fleet of planes to transport its executives and buyers to stores, markets, and various meetings.

WAREHOUSING

Warehousing is the part of physical distribution that involves storing products. Intermediaries operate two types of warehouses: storage and distribution warehouses. A *storage warehouse* keeps goods for relatively long periods of time. Most often, this involves items with seasonal supply or demand, such as farm products.

warehousing
Storage of goods.

A *distribution warehouse* gathers and redistributes products. Companies try to keep items there the shortest times possible. Distribution warehouses are mainly used by manufacturers that serve several small customers in various, distant locations or by firms that have several suppliers in one area.

MATERIALS HANDLING

Materials handling is the physical distribution activity of moving items within plants, warehouses, transportation terminals, and stores. Firms handle goods with equipment such as forklift trucks, conveyor belts, and trucks. Materials handling has been improved in many firms by unitization—combining as many packages as possible into one load to be handled by a forklift truck—sometimes with steel bands or shrink packaging. Containerization—putting packages, usually several unitized loads, into a compact form that is relatively easy to transfer—has significantly reduced transportation costs for many products by cutting materials handling time, theft, insurance costs, damage, and scheduling problems.

materials handling
Movement of goods within a firm's warehouse, terminal, factory, or store.

INVENTORY CONTROL

Inventory control involves managing inventory costs such as storage facilities, insurance, taxes, and handling. Inventory is expensive; holding $1,000 worth of inventory for just 1 year can cost a company $250. To reduce costs, many firms use computerized inventory control management systems. Wetterau, a food-service wholesaler, installed online inventory control systems in its distribution centers to make its warehousing and transportation operations more efficient and to provide retail customers with information to support their buying decisions.

inventory control
Function of controlling all costs associated with inventory.

Chapter 12 discussed another method of controlling inventory, the just-in-time (JIT) inventory system. JIT reduces inventory control costs, giving a company a big competitive advantage over other suppliers that are unable to do this.

Many grocers are now experimenting with different forms of JIT and other inventory control systems. The 87-store supermarket chain Shaw's utilizes its *supervised reorder (SRO),* system to control inventory. SRO combines scanner data, perpetual inventories, and regular shelf audits to ensure that the right amount of products arrive on store shelves at the right time. SRO reduces labor and handling costs, out-of-stock conditions, and overstock conditions. Industry analysts estimate that SRO has saved Shaw's at least 0.5 percent of its total sales.[30]

BUSINESS IN ACTION

ROLLING INVENTORIES: INNOVATIONS IN DISTRIBUTION STRATEGY AT SATURN The status of the U.S. economy is judged by many factors. One such factor is warehouse inventories. Inventory buildups often signal economic growth. Inventories increase as demands for products increase. However, a recent trend in distribution is distorting the picture. Demand for products is increasing, yet inventories remain low. The cause of this discrepancy traces to so-called *rolling inventories*. As more manufacturers implement just-in-time inventory systems, trucks and railcars are functioning as miniature warehouses on wheels. New technology allows trucking companies and their customers to track the progress of a shipment and pinpoint its exact delivery time. If the truck experiences mechanical difficulties, a replacement can be sent to ensure that the shipment arrives on time. ■ Because some shipments now bypass warehouses and proceed directly to production lines, trucking companies must meet strict delivery schedules. Larry Mulkey, president of Ryder Dedicated Logistics Inc., says, "There are sometimes less than 10-minute lag times." This can be a problem since so many outside factors—weather, road construction, breakdowns—affect delivery schedules. ■ Saturn, a division of General Motors, relies heavily on rolling inventories as its warehouse system. The company maintains almost no inventory of component parts at its manufacturing facility. A central computer coordinates deliveries of presorted and preinspected parts at docks 21 hours a day, 6 days each week. This is truly a massive job since Saturn buys components from suppliers in 39 states at an average distance of 550 miles from the Spring Hill, Tennessee plant. ■ Saturn relies on Ryder System, the largest logistics management company in the United States, to coordinate deliveries. Ryder has set up its command post 2 miles from the Saturn plant. Trucks pulling trailers that average 90 percent full arrive each day at the Ryder facility. The trailers carry large, reusable plastic bins full of parts. Each bin has a barcode to identify the parts. The trailers move by shuttle tractor to the plant as they are needed. ■ The truckers who deliver their loads at the Ryder facility immediately hitch up trailers full of empty bins and return them to suppliers. The trailers also include boxes of service parts for Saturn dealers. Each driver receives a plastic key that contains electronic data. The driver plugs the key into an onboard computer and a detailed itinerary appears on the screen including routes to follow and a timetable. ■ Reordering parts from suppliers is another enormous task. The old system relied on computer programs to forecast future needs. Today, Saturn and its suppliers are linked electronically. Every time a new Saturn automobile is produced, the system automatically reorders parts used in the car. This is known as the *pull system* of replenishment. Saturn's director of materials flow and transportation says of the system, "We had systems so complex they bordered on artificial intelligence. Now, when we use a part, we pay for it, and then we order another one." ■ By using rolling inventories, companies like Saturn cut handling and warehouse costs while dramatically improving efficiency. However, these firms face risks in relying on trucks for precise deliveries. The General Motors/Toyota facility in Fremont, California was forced to shut down its production line when a rolling inventory truck experienced mechanical problems on the road. This cost the joint venture thousands of dollars in down time. When the system works, though, it works well. Saturn boasts an inventory turn rate of 300 times a year thanks to its system of rolling inventories. Sources: Ronald Henkoff, "Delivering the Goods," *Fortune,* November 28, 1994, p. 64; and Lucinda Harper, "Trucks Keep Inventories Rolling Past Warehouses to Production Lines," *The Wall Street Journal,* February 7, 1994, p. A5A.

QUESTIONS FOR CRITICAL THINKING

1. How do rolling inventories affect suppliers?
2. What are the dangers in relying on rolling inventories?
3. What are the pros and cons of utilizing an outside logistics firm to coordinate a company's inventory delivery system versus establishing a department within the company to handle the task?

ORDER PROCESSING

order processing
Preparation of an order for shipment.

The physical distribution activity of **order processing** includes preparing orders for shipment and receiving orders when shipments arrive. Like the other aspects of physical distribution, efficient order processing can make a company more competitive.

Purchases of Tide by Kroger customers are monitored by the check-out counter's scanning system. The scanned data is transferred directly to Procter & Gamble's computers and automatically triggers Tide orders and deliveries to the store. This inventory control system allows Procter & Gamble's factories to run more efficiently, cuts Kroger's warehouse costs, and minimizes mistakes.

Compaq, with sales of almost $10 billion, recently surpassed both IBM and Apple to become the world's biggest PC maker. Still, the company had a major problem: only 40 percent of its computers reached its more than 31,000 customers on time. Each computer was spending an average of 4 weeks in Compaq's Houston distribution center. Compaq overhauled its system so that, today, sophisticated software matches customer orders with on-hand inventory daily. Radio signals carry the ordering information to drivers of trucks that run between shelves in the distribution center. Workers take the products from shelves, sort them onto pallets, and load them into waiting trucks, in a system known as *cross-docking*. Under the new system, a computer's average time in the distribution center has fallen by half. Soon, Compaq will no longer be producing computers on speculation, hoping that supply and demand will balance out its output. Compaq will manufacture every product in this build-to-order system for a specific order.[31]

Order processing and the other physical distribution activities performed by channel members ensure that customers receive the right products at the right times and the right places. In the next chapter, you will learn how channel members tell customers about their goods and services in order to persuade them to buy.

ACHIEVEMENT CHECK SUMMARY

Reread the learning goals that follow, and consider the questions for each goal. Answering these questions will reinforce the most important concepts in the chapter and allow you to check how well you have achieved these learning goals. Where a blank appears before the question, answer with *T* or *F*. Otherwise, circle the letter of the correct answer. An answer key to these questions is found at the end of this chapter.

LEARNING GOAL 15.1: Explain the value created by the distribution function.

1. ___ Distribution policy is not a basis upon which companies compete.
2. ___ Distribution is the marketing activity most involved in the creation of time, place, and ownership utility.
3. ___ A retailer who accepts credit cards has helped to create ownership utility.

LEARNING GOAL 15.2: Identify the major components of a distribution strategy.

1. ___ Physical distribution includes transportation and warehousing.
2. ___ A retailer is classified as an intermediary or middleman.
3. ___ Distribution channels are the paths that goods and services (and title to them) follow from producer to consumer.

LEARNING GOAL 15.3: Outline the various types of distribution channels and discuss the factors that influence channel selection.

1. ___ Distribution channels should be chosen on the basis of the type of product, the markets served, the costs involved, and competitive factors.
2. ___ Each manufacturer should select the one best channel for distributing its output and stick to that channel.

LEARNING GOAL 15.4: Explain how a vertical marketing system (VMS) differs from a traditional distribution channel.

1. ___ In a corporate VMS, the channel members are owned by one enterprise.
2. ___ An administered VMS is dominated by one channel member.
3. ___ Most franchises are examples of a contractual VMS.

LEARNING GOAL 15.5: Describe the different degrees of market coverage.

1. ___ Consumer convenience goods are usually intensively distributed.
2. ___ Automobile manufacturers would most likely use selective distribution.
3. ___ Exclusive distribution is used by a manufacturer that favors a limited number of retailers handling its products.

LEARNING GOAL 15.6: Identify the various types of wholesaling intermediaries.

1. ___ Some manufacturers own their own wholesaling intermediaries.
2. ___ Merchant wholesalers do not take title to the goods they handle.
3. ___ Retailers never own wholesalers.

LEARNING GOAL 15.7: Outline the primary categories of retailers.

1. ___ Retailers fall into two main categories: store and nonstore retailers.
2. ___ Since companies like Amway, Tupperware, and Avon sell their products in customers' homes, they are not considered retailers.
3. ___ Teleshopping is a good example of store retailing.

LEARNING GOAL 15.8: Explain the role of the physical distribution function.

1. The primary objective of physical distribution is to: (a) cut transportation costs; (b) minimize inventory; (c) eliminate warehouses; (d) maximize the level of customer service at the lowest possible total cost.
2. The physical distribution function of marketing includes: (a) choosing the mode of transport and the appropriate carrier; (b) processing customer orders; (c) warehousing, inventory control, and materials handling; (d) all of the above.

KEY TERMS

distribution channel 410
physical distribution 410
marketing intermediary 410
wholesaling intermediary 410
retailer 410
vertical marketing system (VMS) 415
intensive distribution 417
exclusive distribution 417
selective distribution 417
industrial distributor 418
sales branch 418
sales office 418
merchant wholesaler 419
full-function merchant wholesaler 419
rack jobber 419
limited-function merchant wholesaler 419
drop shipper 419
agents and brokers 419
wheel of retailing 420
scrambled merchandising 422
category killer 423
atmospherics 424
customer service standards 426
warehousing 429
materials handling 429
inventory control 429
order processing 430

REVIEW QUESTIONS

1. Draw and explain the distribution channels for consumer products and for business products. How does a marketer select a specific channel?

2. What is a vertical marketing system? What are the major types of vertical marketing systems?

3. Differentiate among intensive, exclusive, and selective distribution strategies. Cite examples of each.

4. Explain how independent wholesaling intermediaries differ from both (a) manufacturer-owned wholesaling intermediaries and (b) retailer-owned wholesaling intermediaries.

5. What is the wheel of retailing? Give an example that illustrates this concept.

6. Cite local examples, if you can, of a variety store, department store, specialty store, convenience store, discount store, off-price store, factory outlet, catalog store, supermarket, hypermarket, warehouse club, and category killer.

7. How do retailers compete? What strategies must retailers develop?

8. What is scrambled merchandising? Why have so many retailers adopted this strategy?

9. Differentiate among a common carrier, contract carrier, private carrier, and freight forwarder. Cite examples of each.

10. Outline the various modes of transportation. Compare them on the basis of speed, dependability in meeting schedules, frequency of shipments, availability in different locations, flexibility in handling, and cost.

DISCUSSION QUESTIONS

1. The most expensive meat in the world is Wagyu, a type of beef that comes from a strain of Japanese black cattle raised on

beer and grain soaked with sake, or rice wine. (No, this is not a joke.) Most of these cattle are raised on small, family-owned farms throughout Japan, and are brought to the Kobe area of Japan for finishing and processing. Wagyu meat is exported to the United States and sold through a single butcher in New York City for $109 a pound.[32] Describe the importance of distribution strategy in the Wagyu industry. What product and market factors are involved?

2. Make a list of all the items you might buy in a typical visit to the supermarket. Now suppose that no supermarket was available to serve as an intermediary in these transactions. Describe how you would locate and buy each of these products. Relate this to the concepts of place, time, and ownership utility.

3. Which distribution channel would you select for the following products:
   a. Car seat for infants
   b. Income tax preparation service
   c. Forklift truck
   d. Pears

4. Which type of market coverage would best suit the following products?
   a. Rolls-Royce automobiles
   b. Bubble gum
   c. Men's cologne
   d. Bulldozers and other earth-moving equipment

5. Which transportation mode would you suggest for the following products:
   a. Sheet steel
   b. Natural gas
   c. Live lobsters
   d. Breakfast cereal

SOLUTIONS TO ACHIEVEMENT CHECK SUMMARY

L.G. 15.1: 1. F, 2. T, 3. T. **L.G. 15.2:** 1. T, 2. T, 3. T. **L.G. 15.3:** 1. T, 2. F. **L.G. 15.4:** 1. T, 2. T, 3. T. **L.G. 15.5:** 1. T, 2. F, 3. T. **L.G. 15.6:** 1. T, 2. F, 3. F. **L.G. 15.7:** 1. T, 2. F, 3. F. **L.G. 15.8:** 1. d, 2. d.

VIDEO CASE

NEXT DOOR FOODS Glen Johnson founded the Imperial Oil/Next Door Foods company in 1926 with only a pedal-operated truck, a five gallon bucket, and a nearby bulk plant. Back then, the company was known as Johnson Oil, and the owner himself delivered White Star brand oil directly to the fields where farmers needed it for their equipment. Since then, the company has modified its distribution strategy a number of times in response to a changing business environment.

The first major change occurred as Johnson's business took off, and he expanded his company by buying his father's Philips 66 gasoline station. By the 1950s the company had grown to include 52 service stations serving central, western, and northern Michigan, and it sold its own brand of oil—Imperial Oil—that Johnson registered and trademarked for use in the state.

That growth, however, took place in an era of full-service gasoline stations, and by the time Dave Johnson, Glen's grandson, assumed control of the business in the early 1980s, times had changed. Johnson decided to refocus the firm by combining the gasoline stations with convenience stores. He closed some existing service stations, remodeled others, constructed new stations from the ground up, and acquired existing convenience outlets, including Royal Food Stores and Rebel Food Stores. When Johnson's initial efforts were complete, the company had 18 locations at its command, making it the second largest independent owner–operator of convenience stores in Michigan.

With this change in focus also came a few changes in the company's distribution strategy. In the past, the company operated a private fleet of trucks to supply its own gas stations. It has now switched to private contract carriers. And Dave Johnson turned his attention to the development of the Next Door Food Store concept.

Changing to a hybrid gas station/convenience store has complicated the company's distribution strategy. Imperial Oil has two supply sources for gasoline, Total and Marathon Oil. Imperial uses two suppliers to protect against possible product shortages and price increases. At the same time, concentrating its business with only two suppliers qualifies Imperial Oil for quantity discounts which keep the price of gas to the company—and to the consumer—competitive.

In contrast, Next Door Food Stores use a number of different independent wholesaling intermediaries. For the most part, the kinds of products carried in a convenience store require intensive distribution. Many items, such as magazines, newspapers, snack foods, and chips, are supplied by rack jobbers who come into the store regularly to check the existing inventory of their product, bring in a fresh supply from their truck, and rotate and stock the merchandise. Products such as Coca-Cola and Pepsi are distributed directly by local bottling plants.

Moving to a hybrid convenience store/gas station arrangement has complicated the company's distribution strategy.

Grocery items are delivered by a full-function merchant wholesaler, who delivers hundreds of different products in relatively small quantities, since space for on-site warehousing of product is very limited. Next Door Food Stores use a "build-to" system to determine what quantities of each item should be ordered. The wholesaler prepares a chart showing the quantity needed of each item to make it from one delivery to the next, based on the product mix and sales trends for each individual store. The manager simply counts the stock physically on hand, subtracts that number from the quantity listed on the build-to sheet, and orders the difference. This inventory control system helps keep inventory to a minimum and reduces carrying costs.

Another idea that Next Door Food Stores are implementing is that of branded food concepts within the convenience store itself. They have allocated a portion of each store's floor space to a Subway Sandwich Shop. Customers can pick up a sandwich when they stop to fill their tanks or to buy milk or bread. All of these offerings are intended to save time and effort for the on-the-go consumer—the convenience store's target market.

QUESTIONS

1.
How is value created for the customer by a gas station/convenience store?

2.
In which category of market coverage do most of the products sold by Next Door Food Stores fall? Why?

3.
What role does Imperial Oil/Next Door Food Stores play in the physical distribution of its products?

4.
What is meant by the "branded food concept?" Cite examples other than those contained in the case.

PROMOTIONAL

CHAPTER

STRATEGY

LEARNING GOALS

1. List the objectives of promotion.
2. Explain the concept of a promotional mix.
3. Describe the various personal selling tasks.
4. Identify the steps in the sales process.
5. Describe the different types of advertising.
6. Identify the various advertising media.
7. Explain the roles of sales promotion and public relations in promotional strategy.
8. Identify the factors that influence the selection of a promotional mix.
9. Contrast pushing and pulling promotional strategies.
10. Discuss factors that influence international promotion.

THE PROMOTIONAL POSSIBILITIES OF INTERACTIVE MEDIA For years, advertising industry soothsayers have predicted the coming of interactive media. Their crystal balls showed a world where consumers could respond immediately to ads through their television sets or computers. The concept seemed unbelievable, something out of a science fiction movie. Unbelievable as it seemed, it is here—interactive media has arrived. ■ Imagine watching a basketball game on television. During a break in the action, you view a beer commercial while your next-door neighbor sees a pizza commercial. ■ Imagine driving in your car on a freeway and viewing advertisements beamed to a small screen on the dashboard. Different ads appear depending on your location. ■ Imagine having your own personal shopper who explores cyberspace looking for products and information that appeals to you. ■ Imagine watching a television commercial featuring a product that appeals to you such as a compact disk player. By pressing a button on your remote control, you are able to see more detailed information, including how disks fit in the player, and even test the sound quality of the machine. ■ All of these examples are no longer concepts; these forms of interactive media are actually undergoing testing. The age of interactivity has come. Winn-Dixie and Eckerd Drugs are participating in an interactive shopping program on a television network in Orlando. Consumers who tune in will have the choice of shopping for groceries at Winn-Dixie or health and beauty aids at Eckerd by pushing buttons on their remote controls. A shopper can first browse through electronic ads, coupons, and weekly special bulletins. The shopper then chooses a product category. The products appear on a simulated shelf, just as they do in the supermarket. Using the remote control, the shopper can pick up any product and look at the ingredient label or nutritional content. If the shopper wants to purchase the product, it goes in the simulated cart. When the shopper finishes, the system tallies the bill and charges it to a credit card or adds it to the shopper's cable bill. Shoppers Express delivers the products to the buyer's home. Eckerd purchases are delivered free, while Winn-Dixie charges $9.95 per delivery. ■ Ford Motor Company tested interactive television as the sole sponsor of the interactive telecast in Quebec of the Lillehammer Olympics. Ford launched its new Windstar minivan interactively at this time. Viewers could select one of four advertisements and respond to on-screen messages. A viewer who answered a question correctly at the end of the commercial received an Olympic sweatshirt. Although a survey conducted after the Olympics found that only 25 percent of the viewers watched the commercials interactively, Ford is continuing its efforts by advertising on a next-generation interactive TV system being introduced in 34,000 homes in northern Quebec. ■ Marketers are still trying to determine the place of advertising in interactive media. A recent survey of 1,000 adults found that although 31.4 percent were aware of the term *interactive media,* only 29.1 percent said that interactive services at home should include advertising. Almost half of all respondents said that advertising on home interactive services is not at all acceptable. This may discourage some marketers, but other major marketers such as Nestlé and IBM continue to test interactive media.[1]

CHAPTER OVERVIEW

This chapter completes the discussion of marketing strategy by focusing on promotion, the final marketing mix element. **Promotional strategy** is the function of informing, persuading, and influencing a consumer decision. It is as important to a not-for-profit organization such as the American Heart Association as for a profit-oriented company like Colgate-Palmolive.

promotional strategy
Function of informing, persuading, and influencing a consumer decision.

Some promotional strategies try to develop primary demand, or consumer desire for a general product category. America's Pork Producers attempted to overcome the negative image of the meat while stimulating demand for the product category with its "Pork—The Other White Meat" campaign on television and in print. Most promotional strategies, however, seek to create selective demand, or the desire for a particular product. When American Express advertises "Don't Leave Home without It," it wants you to use its own credit card, and not Visa or MasterCard.

This chapter will first look at the objectives of promotion. Next, it will discuss the components of the promotional mix—personal selling, advertising, sales promotion, and public relations. Finally, it will talk about the factors that influence marketers' decisions in selecting a promotional mix.

OBJECTIVES OF PROMOTIONAL STRATEGY

Promotional strategy objectives vary among organizations. Some use promotion to expand their markets, others to hold their current positions, still others to present corporate viewpoints on public issues. Promotional strategies can also help firms to reach selected markets. As Table 16.1 illustrates, objectives include providing information, differentiating a product, increasing sales, stabilizing sales, and accentuating a product's value.

An organization may pursue more than one promotional objective. Gerber Products Company, the category leader in the baby food market, is using a new promotional vehicle to reach consumers. The firm mailed its "Gerber Little Baby Book" to 300,000 households with infants under 3 months old. As one objective, the book intended to provide valuable information about feeding and caring for babies in an effort to educate new parents. Another objective was to encourage purchases of Gerber products. The booklet

The National Pork Producers Council, in cooperation with the National Pork Board, runs a print and television advertising campaign for "Pork—The Other White Meat." This promotional strategy includes recipes and serving suggestions designed to inform, persuade, and influence consumer decisions about purchasing pork.

TABLE 16.1 OBJECTIVES OF PROMOTIONAL STRATEGY

PROVIDING INFORMATION	DIFFERENTIATING A PRODUCT	INCREASING SALES	STABILIZING SALES	ACCENTUATING A PRODUCT'S VALUE
A customer must know what your product is and where to find it.	Show how your product is the right one for the target customer.	Successful promotion can make you the market leader.	Evening out the cycle makes your operations smoother.	Tell the customer how you offer more for the money.

included advertisements and coupons for an assortment of Gerber baby products and for products of other companies like Kodak and Duracell that wished to be involved. The Gerber booklet was so successful that the firm recently rolled it out nationally, and Gerber plans to distribute an updated version quarterly. The company also plans to add separate versions for families with older infants and toddlers.[2]

PROVIDING INFORMATION

In the early days of promotional campaigns, when many items were often in short supply, most advertisements were designed to tell the public where they could find products. Today, a major portion of U.S. advertising still plays an informational role. Large sections in Wednesday and Thursday editions of daily newspapers consist of advertising that tells shoppers which products are featured by stores and at what prices. Health insurance advertisements in Sunday newspaper supplements emphasize information about rising hospital costs. Field salespeople keep buyers aware of the latest technological advances in a particular field. Fashion retailers advertise to keep consumers abreast of current styles.

Promotional campaigns designed to inform often target specific market segments. Ralston Foods, for example, found in focus group research that children's choices account for 38 percent of Chex cereal sales. However, when asked, mothers said they didn't think their kids liked Chex cereal. Based on this information, Ralston redesigned their packages and launched an ad campaign to reach these mothers. New packaging and television ads send out the message "Eight out of 10 kids like Chex!" In the past, Ralston tried to appeal to kids by introducing line extensions such as Junior Chex and Graham Chex. Now the company is realizing how much its flagship products appeal to kids. The company has furthered this appeal as one of the marketing partners for the video release of Disney's *The Lion King.* Ralston is hoping to increase its 3.1 percent share of the $9 billion cereal market by targeting kids.[3]

DIFFERENTIATING A PRODUCT

Marketers often develop a promotional strategy to differentiate their firm's good or service from those of competitors. Called **positioning,** the idea is to communicate to consumers meaningful distinctions about the attributes, price, quality, or usage of a good or service. Market research is a valuable tool for positioning since it helps to identify what consumers want and what attributes they consider important. Pedialyte, a beverage intended to replenish the body's supply of potassium and other important electrolytes, is essentially Gatorade for babies. However, instead of promoting the product for use by adults after a tough workout, Ross/Abbot Laboratories has positioned Pedialyte for use

positioning
Promotional strategy intended to differentiate a good or service from those of competitors in the mind of a prospective buyer.

by children and infants dehydrated because of illness. Television ads inform viewers that Pedialyte is the only electrolyte solution scientifically developed for use by children, and grocery stores typically stock the product with baby-care products rather than with other beverages. The packaging itself announces that Pedialyte is "Pediatrician recommended."

INCREASING SALES

Increasing sales volume is the most common objective of a promotional strategy. As noted earlier, some strategies concentrate on stimulating primary demand while others work on selective demand.

Philip Morris is taking a most unusual approach in introducing its newest cigarette brand. Instead of adding another brand to its stable of tobacco products, Philip Morris is disguising the brand as a small-town entry trying to compete against the big city, corporate brands. Although Philip Morris manufactures the product, the label lists "Dave's Tobacco Company, Concord, North Carolina" as the proprietor. An on-pack promotional flyer recounts how the company began: "Dave was fed up with cheap, fast-burning smokes. Instead of just getting mad, he did something about it. . . . Dave's tobacco company was born." The firm also sent sales brochures to retailers supporting the small-town premise and advising them not to display Dave's products near other Philip Morris products with a story that started, "Down in Concord, N.C., there's a guy named Dave. He lives in the heart of tobacco farmland. . . . Dave's homegrown smokes don't mix with the 'corporate' cigarettes."

Although Philip Morris is giving the impression that Dave's is a small company, the largest tobacco marketer is backing the brand with a corporate-sized advertising campaign in newspapers, magazines, and billboards. Dave's is hoping to generate sales from the Generation X market.[4]

STABILIZING SALES

Sales stabilization is another goal of promotional strategy. Firms often promote sales contests during slack periods to motivate sales personnel by offering prizes such as vacation trips, televisions, and scholarships to those who meet certain goals. Companies distribute sales promotion materials—calendars, pens, and the like—to customers to stimulate sales during off-periods.

Advertising is another tool that can stabilize sales. A common problem in the hotel industry occurs when hotels, crowded on weekdays with business travelers, sit relatively empty between Friday and Monday. Many hotels promote weekend packages with lower rates in order to attract tourists and vacationers. Marriott, for instance, offers a "Two for Breakfast Weekend" that includes a room at a reduced price for a Thursday, Friday, Saturday, or Sunday night, plus a free breakfast for two the next morning.

A stable sales pattern has several advantages. It evens out the production cycle, reduces some management and production costs, and simplifies financial, purchasing, and market planning. An effective promotional strategy can contribute to accomplishing these goals.

ACCENTUATING THE PRODUCT'S VALUE

Some promotional strategies are intended to enhance products' value, such as warranty programs and repair services. Lexus, Toyota's luxury car line, promotes its generous service guarantee as well as the car's features. If your Lexus breaks down within the first 4 years, the company promises roadside assistance regardless of mileage. Toyota will pay you up to $200 a day for food and lodging if the breakdown occurs more than 100 miles from home, and it will fly parts to the repair shop located closest to you. The Lexus warranty covers repairs up to 4 years or 50,000 miles with no deductible at all.[5]

COMPONENTS OF THE PROMOTIONAL MIX

Promotion consists of two components: personal selling and nonpersonal selling. Personal selling is a person-to-person promotional presentation to a potential buyer. Nonpersonal selling consists of advertising, sales promotion, and public relations. A firm's **promotional mix** is its combination of personal selling and nonpersonal selling. Marketers attempt to develop a promotional mix for their firm that effectively and efficiently communicates its message to target customers. A relatively new approach, known as **integrated marketing communications (IMC),** ties together all promotional activities into one coordinated strategy.[6] The unified, customer-focused promotional message frequently results in a competitive advantage.

promotional mix
Combination of personal and nonpersonal selling designed to achieve promotional objectives.

PERSONAL SELLING

Many companies consider **personal selling**—a person-to-person promotional presentation to a potential buyer—as the key to marketing effectiveness. Today, sales and sales-related jobs employ about 14 million Americans.[7]

The sales functions of most companies are changing rapidly. Some changes have been only cosmetic, such as changing the job title *salesperson* to *account representative* while the job itself stays the same. Many firms are making more significant changes in their sales forces, though. Sales duties have been expanded, and in some instances, the job itself has changed. Today's salespeople often act as consultants to their customers. They focus not just on getting a sale, but on helping customers to decide what they need and working with them to use the product as efficiently as possible.

integrated marketing communications (IMC)
Coordination of all promotional activities to produce a unified message that is customer-focused.

personal selling
Promotional presentation made person-to-person to a potential buyer.

SALES TASKS

A salesperson's work can vary significantly from one company or situation to another, but it usually includes three basic tasks: order processing, creative selling, and missionary selling.

Order Processing Receiving and handling an order is **order processing.** The salesperson identifies the customer's needs, points them out, and processes the order. Handling orders efficiently and accurately is critical to satisfying customers' needs. Good salespeople check the quality of the products their customers receive, know their customers' markets, and ensure that their firms can supply products when needed.

order processing
Sales task of receiving and handling an order.

Route sales personnel process orders for such consumer goods as bread, milk, soft drinks, and snack foods. They check a store's stock, report the inventory level to the store manager, and complete the sale. Most sales jobs include at least minor order processing functions. This becomes the primary duty in cases where customers readily identify and acknowledge their needs.

Creative Selling Sales representatives for most business products and some consumer products perform **creative selling,** a persuasive type of promotional presentation. Creative selling promotes a good or service whose benefits are not readily apparent and/or its purchase involves a careful analysis of alternatives. Capital One, the oldest continuously operating credit-card provider in the country, relies on its extensive database of customer information to distinguish its product from its many competitors. By applying mathematical models that the company developed itself to the customer information they already have, Capital One is able to customize its sales efforts on an individual basis, adjusting interest rates, fees, terms, and conditions, and weeding out bad risks. While the average credit-card provider offers only four options, Capital One has thousands.[8]

creative selling
Persuasive presentation to sell a product whose benefits are not readily apparent or whose purchase involves careful analysis of alternatives.

missionary selling
Indirect form of selling in which the sales representative promotes the goodwill of the company and provides technical or operational assistance.

Missionary Selling An indirect form of selling in which the representative promotes goodwill for a company and/or provides technical or operational assistance to the customer is called **missionary selling.** Many businesses that sell technical equipment, such as IBM and Xerox, provide systems specialists who act as consultants to customers. These salespeople work to solve problems and sometimes to help their clients with questions that are not directly related to their employers' products.

One IBM sales rep who gets high marks for his commitment to customers is Terry Brennan. Brennan works to spread the word about IBM's new RISC-chip based workstation. In missionary sales, he explains the new technology of the system to his customers and his vision of how it will work for their companies. As part of his job, he shows customers what steps they need to take over several months to prepare to take on the new system. Brennan has been talking to customers about this product for nearly a year, even though it's still a half year from being introduced. IBM is not even taking orders for the new product yet. Terry's business card reflects his job—his title reads "Evangelist."[9]

A person who sells a highly technical product may do 55 percent missionary selling, 40 percent creative selling, and 5 percent order processing. By contrast, the job of a retail salesperson may be 70 percent order processing, 15 percent creative selling, and 15 percent missionary selling. Marketers often classify sales jobs based on these three sales tasks to evaluate the salesperson's primary task.

SALES PROCESS

The events of the sales process often follow a certain pattern that can be described in seven steps, shown in Figure 16.1: prospecting and qualifying, the approach, the presentation, the demonstration, handling objections, the closing, and the follow-up. Remember the importance of flexibility, though; a good salesperson is not afraid to vary the sales process based on the customer's responses and needs.

FIGURE 16.1 STEPS IN THE SALES PROCESS

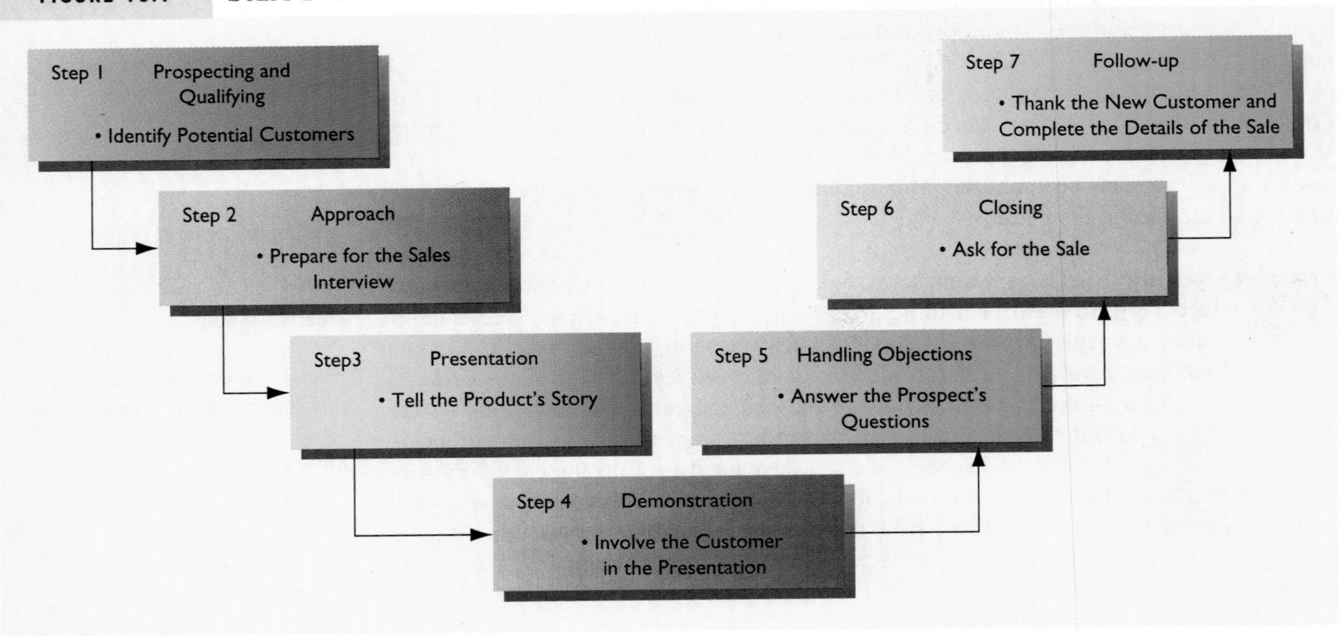

Prospecting and Qualifying In prospecting, salespeople identify potential customers. They may seek new leads from many sources such as previous customers, friends, business associates, neighbors, other sales personnel, and other employees in the firm. Recruiters for the U.S. military, realizing that their usual pool of candidates is shrinking, have decided to target women to fill the ranks of the traditionally male armed forces. They have dedicated $7 million in advertising to attract women and are prospecting for new recruits by placing ads in magazines like *Sassy* and *Seventeen*.[10]

The qualifying process identifies potential customers who have the financial ability and authority to buy. Those who lack the necessary financial resources or who cannot make the purchase decision are not qualified prospects.

The Approach Salespeople should carefully prepare for any approach to potential customers. They should collect and analyze all available information about prospects. Sales representatives should also remember that prospects' first impressions of them often affect those prospects' future attitudes.

Some salespeople employ a hard-sell, direct approach in which they ask aggressively for the sale; others prefer a less direct, soft-sell tactic that focuses on building an image for the product and persuading customers to buy. The choice between hard sell and soft sell can depend on the specific situation. For a one-time sale, perhaps a real estate agent selling a house, the salesperson might want to take a hard-sell approach. For a regular business supplier to a customer who wants to build an ongoing relationship, however, the soft sell will be more effective.

The Presentation At the presentation stage, salespeople transmit their promotional messages. Usually, they describe the major features of the goods or services, highlight their advantages, and cite examples of consumer satisfaction.

Ken Hassen learned early in his company's development that he needed a unique way to get buyers' attention. Ken's company, ProPatch, specializes in private labeling for a variety of accessories sold in bicycle stores. ProPatch serves hundreds of small customers who order products such as repair kits for flat tires that are customized with individual store logos. Hassen wanted to get his products into a major chain, however, and he chose Target Stores. He surveyed bicycle departments in some local Target outlets, taking pictures that showed disorganized shelves without product or variety. Next, Hassen purchased some wire closet organizers and created a display piece on which he hung his various products. He even took a Target brand name, Great Adventure, and made up some sample patch kits.

The presentation got the buyer's attention. When Hassen showed the Target buyer pictures of the stores' bicycle departments, the buyer was in disbelief. He then brought out his display piece and showed the buyer what ProPatch could do for Target. The buyer was so impressed with the presentation and homework that the chain is considering featuring ProPatch products on end-aisle displays as a test in 200 stores.[11]

The Demonstration A demonstration involves the prospect in the presentation. A good demonstration reinforces the message that the salesperson has been communicating, often a critical step in the sales process. Paper manufacturers, for example, produce elaborate booklets to help their salespeople demonstrate different types of paper, paper finishes, and graphic techniques. Such demonstrations allow salespeople to show art directors, designers, printers, and other potential customers what different paper specimens look like after printing. A demonstration ride in a new automobile, for example, gives the salesperson an opportunity to point out special features and strengths, while the customer is able to experience the performance of the vehicle firsthand.

Handling Objections Some salespeople fear prospects' objections because they view the questions as criticism. Instead, salespeople should try to view objections as opportunities to extend presentations and to answer questions. Proper handling of objections allows sales personnel to remove obstacles and to complete sales.

IBM's Terry Brennan made a sales presentation to a rather difficult Midwestern customer. The buyer requested a minicomputer and a personal visit from the division manager by Friday. It was late on Tuesday afternoon and the minicomputer had not yet been built. Brennan spent most of the evening on the telephone with the division manager and the R&D department of IBM. He worked on the problem most of Wednesday. At 4 P.M. Wednesday afternoon, with the backing of his company, Brennan called the customer and asked if he could bring the division manager and the minicomputer to his office on Thursday afternoon. The customer could not refuse. Brennan overcame objections and his efforts paid off—the customer placed a $25 million order for the minicomputer.[12]

The Closing The critical point in selling—the time at which salespeople actually ask prospects to buy—is the closing. To time this move, the seller watches for signals that indicate that a customer is ready to buy. For example, if a couple were to start discussing where their furniture would fit in a home they were inspecting, the real estate agent should see a signal to close the sale.

Salespeople have developed a variety of successful closing techniques over the years. Some of the more popular ones include:

1. The *"If I can show you . . ." technique* The seller first identifies the prospect's major concern in purchasing the good or service and then offers convincing evidence of the offering's ability to resolve it. ("If I can show you how the new heating system will reduce your energy costs by 25 percent, would you be willing to let us install it?")
2. *Alternative-decision technique* The seller poses choices for the prospect, either of which favors the seller. ("Will you take this sweater or that one?")
3. *SRO (standing room only) technique* The seller warns the prospect to conclude a sales agreement immediately because the product may not be available later, or an important feature, such as its price, will soon change.
4. *Silence* The seller can use silence as a closing technique, since discontinuing the sales presentation forces the prospect to take some type of action, either positive or negative.
5. *Extra-inducement close* The seller offers special incentives designed to motivate a favorable buyer response. Extra inducements may include quantity discounts, special servicing arrangements, or layaway options.[13]

The Follow-up The salesperson's actions after the sale may well determine whether the customer will buy again later. After closing, the seller should process the order quickly and efficiently and reassure the customer about the purchase decision. Follow-up is vital to build a long-term working relationship with customers, to make sure that products satisfy them and that they get the service they need. At GM, Pontiac and Buick dealers are keenly aware of the importance of follow-up to long-term customer relationships. Two days after a customer takes home a new car, the salesperson will call to ask if they have any questions. Within 10 days the customer receives a letter from the owner of the dealership thanking him or her for the purchase. After a couple of months, buyers receive an invitation to a new owner's clinic, where a company representative provides information about warranties and other dealership services and even demonstrates how to change a tire and perform other routine car maintenance tasks. The clinic, which lasts about an hour and a half, is family oriented, and dealerships typically provide drinks and snacks for the participants. The expectation is that solid customer-to-dealer relations will lead to return business.[14]

TELEMARKETING

telemarketing
Personal selling conducted entirely by telephone.

Telemarketing is personal selling conducted entirely by telephone. Many firms use this method if it is too difficult or too expensive to have salespeople meet all potential customers in person. A company may use telemarketing all through the sales process, or it may rely on the telephone only for certain stages of the process such as prospecting or follow-up.

Telemarketing is an excellent means of maintaining and servicing smaller accounts while increasing overall productivity. Steven Grossman, president of Massachusetts Envelope Company, figured that his 19-person sales staff spent about 30 percent of its selling time with smaller accounts. Research showed that a salesperson made about four calls each year on accounts with annual sales under $1,000. Each sales call cost Massachusetts Envelope $250, or $1,000 annually.

Management considered discontinuing service to these accounts, but instead of dropping them entirely, Massachusetts Envelope created a telemarketing department and hired two salespeople to handle the phones. The firm created a computerized database to track calls and orders. In its first year, the telemarketing system doubled the firm's sales from small accounts from $400,000 to $800,000. Now, 5 years later, sales are expected to reach $2.5 million, or 10 percent of projected company sales. The average telemarketing call costs Massachusetts Envelope $15. Productivity, sales, and profits have all risen as a result of adding telemarketing to the sales mix.[15]

ADVERTISING

As mentioned earlier in the chapter, the components of nonpersonal selling are advertising, sales promotion, and public relations. Of these, advertising plays the largest role, and many firms find it their most effective method of nonpersonal promotion. **Advertising** is paid, nonpersonal sales communications usually directed at large numbers of potential buyers. While people in the United States often think of advertising as a typically American function, it is now a global activity. In fact, the top ten advertising markets in the world spent $235,500 million in advertising in a recent year. The top five advertisers in the world are Unilever, Procter & Gamble, Nestlé, Fiat SpA, and PSA Peugeot-Citroen. Of these, only P&G is based in the United States. Unilever, the world's largest advertiser, spent over $1.286 billion on advertising in 1 year.[16]

advertising
Nonpersonal sales presentations usually directed at large numbers of potential customers.

Advertising expenditures can vary considerably from industry to industry and company to company. In the nonresidential general contracting industry, for instance, advertising spending amounts to only two-tenths of 1 percent of sales. At the other extreme, the retail mail-order industry spends 14 percent of sales on advertising.

TYPES OF ADVERTISING

The two basic types of ads are product and institutional advertisements. **Product advertising** places messages to sell a good or service. Advertisements for Ivory soap, Days Inn hotels, or the American Automobile Association (AAA) would be classified as product advertising. **Institutional advertising** places messages to promote a concept, idea, or philosophy or the goodwill of an industry, company, organization, or government entity.

product advertising
Nonpersonal selling of a good or service.

institutional advertising
Promotion of a concept, idea, or philosophy or the goodwill of an industry, company, organization, or government entity.

The National Basketball Association uses institutional advertising, placing television ads that feature exciting plays from recent games. At the end of each spot, a celebrity attending a game says enthusiastically, "NBA action—it's FAN-TASTIC!" The league hopes to encourage attendance at the games in each NBA city and viewership of televised match-ups. Individual NBA teams also advertise locally.

A form of institutional advertising that is growing in importance, **advocacy advertising,** promotes a specific viewpoint on a public issue to influence public opinion and the legislative process. Both not-for-profit organizations and businesses use advocacy advertising (sometimes called *cause advertising*). The California Department of Health recently placed ads on billboards to point out the dangers of second-hand smoke. The

advocacy advertising
Advertising that supports a specific viewpoint on a public issue and is designed to influence public opinion or the legislative process.

BUSINESS IN ACTION

TELEPHONE SCAM ARTISTS BEWARE Telemarketing is an effective means of selling goods and services to consumers. Thousands of telemarketing firms function as the selling arms for companies that cannot afford direct sales forces. Other companies utilize telemarketers because of their expertise in particular fields. Telemarketing offers a marketer numerous benefits including one-on-one selling and immediate responses. The telemarketing industry is growing; a recent AT&T study found that telephone sales generate about $280 billion in sales annually. ■ Unfortunately, telemarketing has attracted scam artists who attempt to make a fast buck at the expense of unsuspecting consumers. Fraudulent telemarketers usually promise big prizes to entice consumers to buy very expensive merchandise, real estate, mineral rights, collectibles, unwanted services, and bad investments, among a host of other products. These telemarketers sell products and then take the money and disappear. ■ The consumers most often duped by fraudulent telemarketers are the elderly, the poor, those who speak little to no English, and children. A report by the National Consumers League found that nine out of ten consumers had been contacted by fraudulent telemarketers, and three out of ten had responded to the deceptive offers. Industry analysts estimate that consumers lose between $10 billion and $40 billion in telemarketing scams every year. ■ Until recently, law enforcement officials had little power to stop these scam artists from operating. Because federal rules applied only to transactions with minimum dollar amounts, state officials filed most cases against deceptive telemarketers in state courts. Individual states, however, could not prosecute

campaign, with messages like "Does smoke really stay in the smoking section?" and "Cigarette companies are making a killing off you," advocates a smoke-free environment. Efforts by the department and other organizations helped to persuade lawmakers to pass legislation banning smoking in all public places in the state of California.

The Canadian provinces of Alberta and British Columbia use institutional advertising to promote Western Canada as a tourist destination.

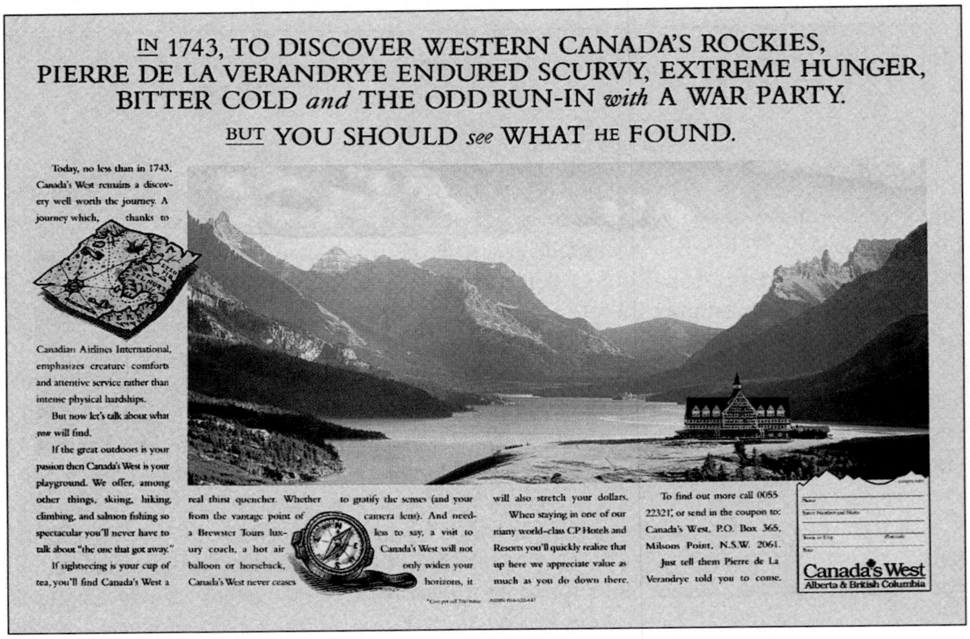

fraudulent telemarketing companies located outside their borders. Federal prosecutors moved very slowly on these cases and took on only the biggest fraud cases. In both situations, a fraudulent telemarketer could simply close up shop at the first sign of trouble and move to another area of the country. ■ Congress finally passed federal legislation protecting consumers from deceptive telemarketers and cracking down on telemarketing fraud. The new legislation targets telemarketers for lawsuits, not prosecution. Private citizens now have the power to file civil lawsuits in federal court if their losses exceed $50,000. State attorneys general can also file lawsuits based on rules developed by the Federal Trade Commission. The rules include a requirement that a telemarketer inform the consumer that the purpose of a call is to sell goods and services, a disclosure about the nature and the price of the goods and services, and restrictions from calling consumers between 9 P.M. and 8 A.M. and repeatedly disturbing individuals with unsolicited calls. ■ The legislation focuses only on deceptive practices, and it omits fraudulent practices. It enables the FTC to stop any telemarketing promotion that deceives consumers. If the term *fraudulent* had appeared in the law, prosecutors would have faced the difficult task of proving that scam artists had a criminal intent to deceive. Instead, in order to obtain restraining orders and damages, the legislation requires only that state officials show that telemarketers' practices had the effect of deceiving consumers. They need not prove criminal intent to deceive. ■ Unfortunately, deceptions by some telemarketers have tarnished the entire industry. Mag Gottlieg, the Direct Marketing Association's director of state government affairs, says, "Honest people pay the price, because everyone becomes wary of doing business over the phone." The federal legislation is welcomed by both consumers and the telemarketing industry as a means of protection. As a follow-up, the FTC must report back to Congress within 5 years on the effect of the law on the industry.

Sources: Tim Triplett, "Telemarketing Law Aims at Big-Money Fraud," *Marketing News,* October 10, 1994, p. 5; "Telemarketing Bill Targets Scams," *Congressional Quarterly,* August 6, 1994, p. 2,248; and Jon Healey, "Crackdown on Phone Fraud Awaits Senate Approval," *Congressional Quarterly,* July 30, 1994, p. 2,131.

QUESTIONS FOR CRITICAL THINKING

1. How can legitimate telemarketers overcome skeptical consumers' objections to telephone sales?
2. What are the pros and cons of relying solely on telemarketing for sales of a good or service?
3. What else can the government do to protect consumers from fraudulent telemarketers?

ADVERTISING AND THE PRODUCT LIFE CYCLE

Both product and institutional advertising can be subdivided into three categories according to its intention to inform, persuade, or remind. A firm uses informative advertising, intended to build initial demand for a product, in the introductory phase of the product life cycle.

When Syntex Corporation and Procter & Gamble introduced Aleve into the saturated $2.4-billion pain reliever market, they launched a huge advertising campaign directed at consumers. The ads informed consumers about Aleve's benefits, claiming that the product was effective for up to 12 hours, more economical, and stronger than competing products.[17]

Persuasive advertising attempts to improve the competitive status of a product, institution, or concept. It is used in the growth and maturity stages of the product life cycle. In Europe, for instance, cereal companies are trying to persuade more consumers to eat their products for breakfast. Continental Europeans prefer bread, cheese, eggs, and meat for their first meal of the day. The French eat only 1.8 pounds of cereal per person per year, compared to the U.S. average of 10.1 pounds per person. Ads of cereal makers such as General Mills and Kellogg's emphasize the benefits that the products bring to busy, cost-conscious families, claiming that cereal is easy to prepare (children can serve themselves), cleanup is quick and easy, and the cost of a meal averages about 20 cents per serving. As a result of such persuasion, cereal consumption in some European countries has risen by 30 percent.[18]

comparative advertising *Persuasive advertising that features direct comparisons between competing goods or services.*

One of the most popular types of persuasive product advertising, **comparative advertising,** compares products directly to their competitors. Many companies have used comparative advertising in recent years. Bristol-Myers Squibb Company has placed comparative ads as part of its newest campaign for Excedrin, claiming that it cures headaches better than market-leader Tylenol. A recent study rates comparative advertisements as very effective. The study found that ads containing comparisons with messages to differentiate advertised brands from competitors scored 21 percent higher than the norm on a persuasion scale. Mark Gleason, vice president of RSC, the company conducting the research, says, "Differentiating your brand from other brands in the category provides the highest likelihood of improving your advertising performance or sales effectiveness."[19] Comparative advertising is especially effective for new products.

Reminder-oriented advertising often appears in the late maturity or decline stages of the product life cycle to remind people of the importance and usefulness of a product, concept, or institution.

ADVERTISING MEDIA

All marketers face the question of how to allocate their advertising budgets. Cost is an important consideration, but they must give equal emphasis to choosing the media best suited for the job. As Table 16.2 demonstrates, all media have their advantages and disadvantages.

Newspapers Newspapers, with 23 percent of total advertising volume, carry the largest share of all advertising media.[20] Because firms can tailor newspaper advertising for individual communities and reach nearly everyone in the area, local advertising commonly appears in newspapers. For other advantages, readers can refer back to these ads, and advertisers can coordinate their messages with other advertising and merchandising efforts. In fact, advertising is considered the third most useful feature in newspapers, after national and local news. A disadvantage comes from the relatively short life span; people usually discard their papers quickly.

Television Television ranks second overall to newspapers, with 22 percent of all advertising volume, but it is the leader in national advertising. Television advertising can be classified as network, national, local, and cable (non-network) ads. TV has the advantage of a significant impact on potential customers and the disadvantage of high cost. Mass coverage, repetition, flexibility, and prestige bring other advantages. Marketers can

TABLE 16.2 ADVANTAGES AND DISADVANTAGES OF ADVERTISING MEDIA

MEDIA	ADVANTAGES	DISADVANTAGES
Newspapers	Tailored to individual communities; readers can refer back to ads	Short life span
Television	Mass coverage; repetition; flexibility; prestige	High cost; temporary message; public distrust; lack of selectivity
Direct mail	Selectivity; intense coverage; speed; flexibility; complete information; personalization	Expensive; consumer resistance; dependent on effective mailing list
Radio	Immediacy; low cost, flexibility; targeted audience; mobility	Short life span; highly fragmented audience
Magazines	Selectivity; quality reproduction; long life; prestige	Lack of flexibility
Outdoor advertising	Communicates simple ideas quickly; promotes local goods and services; repetition	Brief exposure; environmental concerns

now beam their commercials to TVs located in spots like grocery store checkout lines, health clubs, and even schools.

The disadvantages of television as an advertising medium include its high cost, the temporary nature of the message, some public distrust, and lack of selectivity or ability to reach a specific target market without a lot of wasted coverage.

Direct Mail Direct mail is the third-leading advertising medium, with almost 19 percent of total advertising expenditures. Its advantages include selectivity, intense coverage, speed, flexibility, complete information, and personalization. On the negative side, direct mail is very expensive, it depends on effective mailing lists, and it sometimes meets with consumer resistance.

Radio Radio reaches 99 percent of all U.S. households (on average, they own five radios each), making it another important broadcast advertising medium, with 6 percent of total advertising volume. Radio ads can be classified as network, spot, and local advertising. Advantages of radio are its immediacy, low cost, targeted audience selection, flexibility, and mobility. Disadvantages include the short life span of a radio message and its highly fragmented audience.

Magazines Magazines account for about 5 percent of advertising volume. *Modern Maturity,* with almost 23 million subscribers, is the nation's largest magazine measured by paid subscriptions. Advantages of magazines include selectivity, quality reproduction, long life, and prestige.

The main disadvantage of magazines comes from a lack of flexibility as compared to newspapers and broadcast media. However, magazines are taking steps to customize their publications and advertising messages to different regions of the country. One method places local advertising in regional editions of the magazine. Other magazines use wraparounds (half-size covers on top of full-size covers) to highlight articles inside that relate to particular areas; different wraparounds appear in different parts of the country. Tip-ins resembling large Post-It® notes call attention to specific articles of regional interest.

Outdoor Advertising Outdoor advertising like billboards accounts for a little less than 1 percent of total advertising expenditures. Its strength lies in communicating simple ideas quickly. Other advantages are repetition and the ability to promote goods and services available for sale nearby, since restrictions prevent new billboard construction, and outdoor tobacco advertising is down.

Billboard companies are using new technologies to get a bigger piece of the advertising pie. Revere National Corporation is using geographic information systems and computerized market analysis to attract new advertisers to the medium. MapInfo for Windows shows all billboard locations in urban areas. MapInfo, in conjunction with two other programs (MapChart and Prime), analyzes the home ZIP codes of motorists travelling by and determines the consumer demographic and spending data for various areas and products. Revere hopes to almost double its $29 million revenue with this new system.[21]

Outdoor advertising suffers from disadvantages, however. The medium requires brief messages since it doesn't give much time to make a point. Mounting concern for environmental issues is raising opposition to outdoor advertising. Six states and over 1,000 local governments—including cities as large as Houston, San Diego, and St. Louis—have banned billboards or restricted them in some way. While 15,000 new billboards are constructed each year, advertisers are exploring new outdoor media as well, such as moving billboards mounted on trucks and interactive video kiosks in subway stations.[22]

Outdoor advertising in New York City is found on billboards—where MCI promotes its service over AT&T's— and on telephone kiosks. The strength of outdoor advertising lies in communicating simple ideas quickly.

Infomercials Infomercials are gaining popularity with *Fortune* 500 marketers. These 30-minute programs that sell goods or services, once considered fillers for late night or early morning cable television, have gained recognition as effective means of selling products. The 30-minute format allows an advertiser more time to present product benefits, increase awareness, and make an impact on the consumer.

Advertisers also receive immediate responses in the form of sales or inquiries since most infomercials feature 800 numbers. Companies like Braun, Warner Music, GTE, SmithKline Beecham, and Bissell have all experienced success with infomercials. A host of other companies like Johnson & Johnson, Sears, Estée Lauder, Century 21, and Bank of America are now producing or testing them.[23]

Interactive Media Interactive media, introduced in Chapter 10, are increasingly important promotional channels. As described at the beginning of the chapter, marketers' interest in interactive media is rising. Consumers push buttons on their television remote controls or computer keyboards to respond immediately to advertisements. They can view additional ads, obtain further information, print coupons, order products, or answer questions. Most interactive media systems are still in the testing stages. Advertisers are experimenting with a variety of interactive projects, trying to determine advertising's place in the media as well as the potential reach and response by viewers.

Other Media Options Companies can use many other options to advertise their products. About 7 percent of total advertising volume appears in the Yellow Pages of telephone directories.[24] Other media include advertising in movie theaters and on airline movie screens. Soft drinks like Coca-Cola, Pepsi, and Dr. Pepper appear in commercials in movie theaters. Many firms display their advertising messages on trucks, while others use transit advertising, posting their ads in and on public transportation like buses and commuter trains. Another advertising vehicle gaining in popularity, the hot-air balloon, has promoted organizations such as Maxwell House and Eastman Kodak. Airplanes can be hired to trail promotional messages in the sky. More and more marketers are sponsoring blimps to advertise brand images. Brands like Budweiser, Fuji, Gulf Oil, Met Life, and Blockbuster are each paying up to $350,000 per month to advertise on the touring airships.[25] Some companies advertise through computer subscription services such as Prodigy that allow subscribers to place orders on-line. These alternative media can be employed separately or in conjunction with more traditional approaches.

SALES PROMOTION

Sales promotion consists of forms of promotion other than advertising, personal selling, and public relations that increase sales through one-time selling efforts. Traditionally viewed as a supplement to a firm's sales or advertising efforts, sales promotion has emerged as an integral part of the promotional mix.

sales promotion
Form of promotion designed to increase sales through one-time selling efforts such as displays, trade shows, special events, and other methods.

POINT-OF-PURCHASE ADVERTISING

Point-of-purchase (POP) advertising consists of a display or demonstration that promotes a product at a time and place near where consumers can buy it, such as in a retail store. Video advertising on supermarket shopping carts is an example. POP ads can very effectively continue a theme developed by some other aspect of the firm's promotional strategy. Actmedia provides point-of-sale coupon dispensers. Now, the company is testing a point-of-sale device that emits a 10-second promotional message when the consumer presses a button. Manufacturers hope that these point-of-sale gimmicks help to move more product for them.[26]

point-of-purchase (POP) advertising
Sales promotion that displays and demonstrates a product at the place where the actual purchase decision is made.

SPECIALTY ADVERTISING

Take a look around your home. Do you have any item such as a pen, T-shirt, calendar, or calculator imprinted with the name of the business that gave you the item? This is **specialty advertising,** in which a company gives away useful merchandise carrying its name, logo, or business slogan. Because such a product is useful and often personalized with the recipient's name, people tend to keep and use them, giving the advertiser repeated exposure. Originally designed to identify and create goodwill for advertisers, specialty advertising is now used to generate sales leads and develop traffic for stores and trade show exhibitors.

specialty advertising
Sales promotion that gives away useful items imprinted with the donor's name, logo, or message.

TRADE SHOWS

Firms often use **trade shows** to promote goods or services to resellers in their distribution channels. Retailers and wholesalers attend conventions and trade shows where manufacturers exhibit their lines. Such shows are very important in the toy, furniture, and fashion industries. They also are used extensively in international business.

trade show
Exhibition designed to promote goods or services to retailers, wholesalers, international buyers, and other resellers in the distribution channel.

Increasingly, companies attend trade shows less for show-and-tell activities and more as selling opportunities. According to a study by Simmons Market Research Bureau, more than 70 percent of trade show attendees have the authority to purchase products. The average buyer makes purchases in the $31,000 to $78,000 range at a show.[27]

In the past, companies like Beltone Electronics, a hearing-aid manufacturer, used to set up booths merely to talk to passers-by. Today, the company runs a proactive booth. Beltone's trade show representatives now ask visitors to fill out a form that profiles their roles as potential dealers for the company. When a trade show ends, Beltone has a list of truly interested dealers, leading Beltone to increase its participation in trade shows. "Our leads have been unbelievable in terms of the number we generated from interested people," says Michael Maziarek, national recruiting manager. "I can attribute that entirely to trade shows."[28]

OTHER SALES PROMOTION METHODS

Other sales promotion techniques include samples, coupons, premiums, contests, and trading stamps. Most of these methods help firms to introduce new products or encourage consumers to try new brands.

A sample is a free gift of a product distributed by mail, door to door, in a demonstration, or inside packages of other products. Nestlé Beverage Company is attempting to increase awareness for its Taster's Choice coffee brand through sampling. Nestlé recently targeted 6 million households in major metropolitan areas with samples of Taster's Choice French Vanilla, Irish Creme, and Hazelnut instant coffees. The samples came packed inside a plastic bag along with coupons and color ads for the product in the Sunday editions of 70 newspapers around the country. More and more marketers are using this channel to reach consumers in a clutter-free environment. Tom Roberts, regional vice president of sales for Sunflower newspaper groups, says of the sampling, "It's extremely effective. It allows very specific targeting of consumers in certain ZIP codes, going directly to their homes, where people are in a very leisurely mood." Nestlé launched a similar effort for its Carnation Coffeemate Flavors line of nondairy creamers.[29]

A coupon is an advertising clipping or a card included in a package that the customer can redeem for a small price discount. This offer may persuade a customer to try a new or different product. Many retailers, including southern supermarket giant Winn-Dixie and west coast competitors Ralph's, Von's, and Alpha Beta double the face values of manufacturers' coupons.

Consumers in San Diego, California are finding coupons in a new place—the television set. Acu-Trac Services and Cox Enterprises, the cable operator, are testing a service that allows viewers to print coupons in their homes in response to TV commercials. The consumer merely presses a button on the remote control to receive a coupon for an advertised product. The cable company is providing an inexpensive, small printer along with existing cable converters in return for a cut of the redemptions. This CouponSelect system is being tested in 1,000 homes, and the companies plan to reach 1 million homes within a year.[30]

A premium is an item given free or at a reduced price with the purchase of another product. Pizza Hut, the largest pizza chain in the country, found success offering Streetballs as self-liquidating premiums. The custom-designed Rawlings basketballs featuring special graphics and NCAA logos sold for $4.99 to any consumer who purchased a child's meal. The orange version of the ball sold in stores for $17. The premium was a huge success—Pizza Hut sold 3.8 million Streetballs during the promotion.[31]

Trading stamps are similar to premiums in that customers can exchange them for additional merchandise. Historically, they have been used to build loyalty to retailers or suppliers. Minyards, a grocery store in Arlington, Texas offers trading stamps that customers can collect toward the purchase of a set of dishware, which the store displays prominently near the checkout lines.

Contests, sweepstakes, and games offer cash or merchandise as prizes to participating winners. Nestlé's recently teamed its Butterfinger candy bar with Bart Simpson for a whodunit contest. The contest, targeted to consumers 12 to 24 years old, sought to maintain the youth market while increasing purchase frequency. Consumers vied for the $50,000 grand prize by collecting messages from Butterfinger packages featuring Bart Simpson to identify the culprit. Supported with both television and radio ads, the promotion proved very successful; sales increased 51 percent during the promotional period, and the 59,057 entries showed an increased purchase frequency per consumer.[32]

Event sponsorship is a popular form of promotional activity. By sponsoring an event, a marketer gains exposure for a product to the event's audience. The marketer also hopes to associate the product with the image of the event as perceived by its audience. Sponsorship provides a unique promotional opportunity that allows an advertiser to reach a

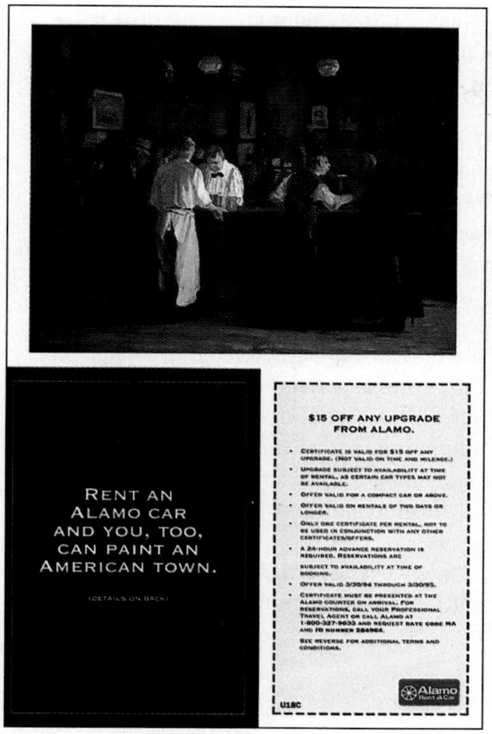

RENT AN
ALAMO CAR
AND YOU, TOO,
CAN PAINT AN
AMERICAN TOWN.
(DETAILS ON BACK)
$15 OFF ANY UPGRADE
FROM ALAMO.
• CERTIFICATE IS VALID FOR $15 OFF ANY UPGRADE. (NOT VALID ON TIME AND MILEAGE.)
• UPGRADE SUBJECT TO AVAILABILITY AT TIME OF RENTAL, AS CERTAIN CAR TYPES MAY NOT BE AVAILABLE.
• OFFER VALID FOR A COMPACT CAR OR ABOVE.
• OFFER VALID ON RENTALS OF TWO DAYS OR LONGER.
• ONLY ONE CERTIFICATE PER RENTAL, NOT TO BE USED IN CONJUNCTION WITH ANY OTHER CERTIFICATES/OFFERS.
• A 24-HOUR ADVANCE RESERVATION IS REQUIRED. RESERVATIONS ARE
SUBJECT TO AVAILABILITY AT TIME OF BOOKING.
• OFFER VALID 3/30/94 THROUGH 3/30/95.
• CERTIFICATE MUST BE PRESENTED AT THE ALAMO COUNTER ON ARRIVAL. FOR RESERVATIONS, CALL YOUR PROFESSIONAL TRAVEL AGENT OR CALL ALAMO AT 1-800-327-9633 AND REQUEST RATE CODE MA AND ID NUMBER 284964.
SEE REVERSE FOR ADDITIONAL TERMS AND CONDITIONS.
U18C
Alamo
Rent A Car

Alamo Rent A Car, Inc. sponsored the exhibition "American Impressionism and Realism," which opened at the Metropolitan Museum of Art in New York, then traveled to Fort Worth's Amon Carter Museum, the Denver Museum of Art, and the Los Angles County Museum of Art. In return for its sponsorship, Alamo was able to put discount car-rental coupons in exhibition brochures and to provide them to shoppers at museum stores. Alamo also created a custom travel guide which directed readers to places shown in the exhibition's paintings.

narrow, but highly desirable audience. Nissan is the main sponsor of the Los Angeles Open golf tournament. The sponsorship brings Nissan name recognition, television spots in the broadcast, ads in the program, signage on the course, premium giveaway opportunities, tickets to the event, and a tent in a prime location for entertaining customers.

PUBLIC RELATIONS

public relations
Organization's communications with its various public audiences.

Public relations refers to an organization's communications with its various public audiences, such as customers, vendors, news media, employees, stockholders, the government, and the general public. Many of these communication efforts serve marketing purposes. For example, Six Flags Theme Parks, a Time Warner Entertainment Company, created the 600-Minute Reading Club for students in the theme parks' local communities. The program, administered through schools, gives each student a tally sheet on which to track a date, the name of a publication, and the amount of time spent reading. Parents or teachers initial to verify each reading session. Any student who reads at least 600 minutes, or 10 hours, during the specified time period receives a free admission ticket to the Six Flags theme park. The 600-Minute Reading Club benefits both Six Flags and the community. The company is supporting and encouraging reading as an activity among youth with its "Read to Succeed" program. Six Flags is also increasing park attendance and thus, sales, since adults who escort the winners to the parks pay for admission. It's a win-win situation for Six Flags and its local communities.[33]

SELECTING A PROMOTIONAL MIX

As you can imagine, developing the right promotional mix is one of the toughest tasks confronting marketers. The following questions provide some general guidelines for allocating promotional efforts and expenditures among personal selling, advertising, sales promotion, and public relations.

1. *What is your target market?* For instance, a manufacturer sells a drill press to the business market, so its strategy must emphasize its sales force. By contrast, selling Scope mouthwash to consumers depends more on an effective advertising campaign.
2. *What is the value of the product?* Most companies cannot afford to emphasize personal selling to market low-priced items like toothpaste, cosmetics, soft drinks, and candy, so they choose advertising instead. Higher-priced items in both business and consumer markets rely more on personal selling. Examples include time-share vacation condominiums and Boeing aircraft.
3. *What time frame is involved?* Marketers usually rely on advertising to precondition customers for sales presentations. An effective and consistent advertising theme may favorably influence a person when a salesperson approaches in a store. Except for self-service situations, however, a salesperson is typically involved in completing an actual transaction. Marketers often expose customers to advertising again after the sale to assure them of the correctness of their selection and to precondition them for repeat purchases.
4. *Should you spend your promotional budget on advertising or personal selling?* Once this decision is made, you need to determine the level of sales promotion and public relations efforts.[34]

PROMOTIONAL STRATEGIES

pushing strategy
Sales-oriented promotional strategy designed to motivate marketing intermediaries to push the product to their customers.

cooperative advertising
Sharing of local advertising costs between the manufacturer and the marketing intermediary.

pulling strategy
Promotional strategy utilizing advertising and sales promotion appeals to generate consumer demand for a product.

The marketer can choose between two promotional strategies: a pushing strategy or a pulling strategy. A **pushing strategy** relies on a sales-oriented campaign to market a product to wholesalers and retailers in the distribution channels. Sales personnel explain to marketing intermediaries why they should carry this particular good or service, usually with support of offers of special discounts and promotional materials. Marketers also provide **cooperative advertising** allowances in which they share the cost of local advertising of the product or line. All of these strategies are designed to motivate wholesalers and retailers to push the good or service to their customers.

Philips Media, an off-shoot of the Dutch electronics giant Philips N.V., has developed an innovative new pushing strategy. They have announced a new multimedia presentation called the Electronic New Release Book, aimed at record retailers. The book, a hybrid CD-ROM and online service catalog containing music, video, and text related to company products, will introduce retailers to 200 new titles every month. Retailers who see something they want to stock can place their orders via an online ordering interface, reducing printing and order processing costs for the retailer and reducing error rates for the distributor.[35]

A **pulling strategy** attempts to generate consumer demand for a product, primarily through advertising and sales promotion appeals. Most advertising targets the ultimate consumer, who then asks the retailer for the good or service, who in turn demands the product from the supplier. The marketer hopes that strong consumer demand will pull the product through the marketing channel by forcing marketing intermediaries to carry it. Power Rangers was a recent example.

Since Saban Entertainment's Power Rangers "morphed" onto television screens over a year ago, kids can't get enough of them. Boys and girls imitate their favorite rangers in schoolyard play. Parents and teachers alike disapprove of the chopping and kicking, but the Power Rangers' popularity continues to grow. Almost any product associated with Power Rangers sells with little or no advertising support. Approximately 300 international licensees put the Power Rangers name and images on everything from nightlights to cookies.

Bandai America, the toy licensee, could not produce enough action figures of the characters to meet the growing demand. The company increased production ten times in an attempt to fill orders. Toys R Us rationed the toys to only one action figure per family and kept the valuable inventory behind a counter rather than on shelves to prevent pilferage. Parents lined up in the middle of the night to ensure that their children would be the lucky recipients of Power Ranger figures when stores received supplies. Other stores established waiting lists, some accounting for 3 months' anticipated advance orders, once again limiting the number of figures sold per person. Power Ranger-mania swept the country. Bandai eventually caught up with backorders and Power Ranger action figures can now be found in some retail outlets. Bandai's accidental pulling strategy, although unplanned, was phenomenally successful.[36]

Most marketing situations require both pushing and pulling strategies, although the emphasis can vary. Consumer products usually depend most on pulling strategies while business products use pushing strategies.

INTERNATIONAL PROMOTIONAL STRATEGY

Cultural sensitivity and good homework are crucial foundations for international promotional strategies. Effective strategies for promoting products to U.S. audiences may not work in other countries due to differences in culture and language.

AVAILABILITY OF MEDIA

Different countries offer different media to advertisers. For instance, in Spain almost 80 percent of the $8.5 billion spent on advertising pays for television ads; in South Korea, however, only about 32 percent is spent on television advertising. Newspapers attract 28 percent of Korea's ad dollars, though, while only 10 percent of Spain's dollars are spent in the same medium. In Germany, magazines receive nearly one-third of all ad expenditures, the highest percentage of any country. In France, almost 17 percent of ad dollars are spent in the cinema. Table 16.3 shows ad spending by medium for the top five global markets.

LAWS AND PRODUCT REGULATIONS

Countries vary in their attitudes toward the amount of time available for TV advertisements. France and Italy limit the profits that the state monopoly systems can make from advertising. U.S. computer manufacturers have sometimes waited up to 18 months to get

TABLE 16.3 COMPARATIVE ADVERTISING EXPENDITURES

COUNTRY	SPENDING ($ BILLIONS)	TELEVISION	NEWSPAPERS	RADIO	MAGAZINES	OUTDOOR	OTHER
1. United States	$134.0	54%*	23%	4%	17%	2%	
2. Japan	30.5	31	22	4	7	7	29%
3. Germany	18.0	35	26	7	31		
4. United Kingdom	14.0	42	51	3		3	1
5. France	9.0	33	17	11	19		20

*This number reflects U.S. expenditures on television worldwide, which is why it differs from the 22% figure given on p. 448 for national expenditures.

STRENGTH IN DIVERSITY

HISPANIC MARKETING SPECIALISTS: ORNELAS & ASSOCIATES Six years ago, Victor Ornelas started his own advertising agency on his dining room table. After holding corporate positions with Levi Strauss, Anheuser Busch, and Seven-Up, Ornelas decided to venture out on his own with start-up capital from cashing in stock options from his last job. He figured that he had enough funds to support his business and family for about 12 months. ■ His first break came by luck. A friend in The Bravo Group, a New York-based Hispanic advertising agency, called Ornelas and asked if he knew anyone with promotions experience within the Hispanic market. Ornelas recommended himself and flew to New York. He sold some marketing ideas, including a campaign for R. J. Reynolds Tobacco, to The Bravo Group for $5,000. With that assignment, Ornelas & Associates was born. ■ Early on, Ornelas struggled to remain independent. Major agencies in the business needed Hispanic divisions to service their clients who targeted the segment. The trend in the industry had seen these large agencies buy up small, Hispanic-oriented shops which would then handle the Hispanic side of the agencies' business. Ornelas didn't want that. He remained independent. ■ Ornelas got his second break 6 months after opening his doors. He was invited to bid on an Anheuser Busch promotion to the Hispanic market by the man who filled his old position at Anheuser Busch. Ornelas & Associates won the $150,000 annual contract to handle Anheuser Busch's Hispanic marketing convention. This was the agency's first major client. ■ Ornelas focused his efforts on expanding his client base. In knocking on larger agencies' doors, he found them unwilling to hire a consultant for their Hispanic business. To succeed, Ornelas needed to be a full-service, Hispanic-oriented agency. This he could not build on his own. "I had client-side experience but I didn't know the agency business," he says. "I felt I needed a big brother to help me kick-start my business." ■ His third break came in 1989 when Ornelas & Associates became affiliated with Tracy-Locke, a $400-million division of the international agency DDB Needham. The agencies share clients, but not ownership. Ornelas maintained 100 percent ownership of his agency. The affiliation was a win–win situation for both agencies. Tracy-Locke needed expertise in marketing to Hispanics for some of its clients such as Pepsi with its major markets in southern California and Texas. Ornelas & Associates needed the backing of a major agency. The strategic affiliation accelerated the new agency's growth. ■ His "Pepsi Man" campaign gained Ornelas recognition and respect within the advertising community. Pepsi was a tough "sell" in the Hispanic community where Coke was entrenched as the dominant leader. Ornelas' campaign used comedian Paul Rodriguez to administer the Pepsi Challenge taste test to Hispanics, increasing awareness of Pepsi in key Hispanic markets. The

airtime on French television, which makes their ads almost useless for introducing new products. Some nations restrict the use of comparative advertising and superlatives. Germany, for instance, forbids the word *best.*

In the United States, many people favor closer regulation of advertising of alcohol and tobacco products. Regulations in other countries for these items vary. France and Switzerland ban TV ads for cigarettes, tobacco products, and alcoholic beverages; the Netherlands bans cigarette and tobacco ads, but permits (and regulates) commercials for alcohol; Great Britain permits (and regulates) ads for alcohol, pipe tobacco, and cigars, but bans cigarette commercials.

AUDIENCE CHARACTERISTICS

Cultural preferences, moral standards, educational levels, language—all of these factors influence how consumers perceive ads. European perfume ads have sometimes been modified, for instance, for display in Saudi Arabia. One French ad showed a man's bare arm being grasped by a woman's hand; the Saudi version clothed the man's arm in a dark suit sleeve and showed the woman's hand just brushing it.[37]

Pepsi Man campaign is one of the largest ad campaigns ever targeted to the Hispanic market. ■ Ornelas & Associates created another successful campaign for Wrangler jeans, whose market positioning was indicated by the slogan "Real cowboys wear Wrangler." Incorporating this tagline proved challenging for the agency since Hispanics don't view Texas-style cowboys the same way. Ornelas created a new "Viva la Tradicion" campaign for Wrangler featuring the original Mexican cowboys of the Southwest, the vaqueros. Wrangler's marketing vice president was very pleased with the campaign. "The ads were extremely successful in creating awareness in the Hispanic market," he said. ■ Since the Pepsi Man campaign, the client list of Ornelas & Associates has grown impressively. In its first year in operation, the firm billed $150,000. Six years later, billings are estimated to reach $25 million. Clients include the Banc One Corporation, the Southland Corporation, Georgia-Pacific, Borden, Inc., the American Heart Association, and the maker of Tabasco Hot Sauce. Ornelas also developed a campaign that doubled Budweiser's share of the Hispanic market in Texas. ■ What makes Ornelas so successful? His love and understanding of the Hispanic culture. Ornelas does not simply take a company's English-language ad and translate it into Spanish. Knowing that the Hispanic community is composed of consumers from many different countries who share a language, Ornelas uses focus groups and quantitative surveys to find out what is relevant to different groups within the segment. His agency then creates a marketing strategy and position and then tests them to see if they hit their marks. ■ Ornelas looks for the same commitment in his employees. He recruits only employees who have a passion for the Hispanic culture. Everyone he hires is both bilingual and bicultural. "There's a spirit here that is lacking in the general market agencies. That's particularly important when it comes to developing campaigns for [Hispanic] consumers," says Ornelas. The owner makes sure that all employees attend computer, time management, and speed reading seminars to ensure proper training for everyone. ■ Ornelas preaches the importance of the Hispanic segment to marketers. He estimates that less than 1 percent of all advertising dollars are spent on the fast-growing Hispanic segment, even though Hispanics comprise about 10 percent of the U.S. population. Hispanics offer a tremendous opportunity to marketers today, but a marketer needs the right media and message to reach this segment. "The whole market has become a paella [a Spanish dish of rice, seafood, meat, and vegetables]," Ornelas says. "Every element is unique and distinct. General market agencies have not become that diverse. They can't walk the bicultural line." Ornelas walks the bicultural line so successfully that he was recently named the *Hispanic Business* Entrepreneur of the Year.

Sources: Maria Zate, "The 1994 *Hispanic Business* Entrepreneur of the Year," *Hispanic Business*, December 1994, p. 29; "Entrepreneur Banks on Hispanic Buying Power," *Northwest Arkansas Times*, December 26, 1994, p. A9; and Kathryn Jones, "A Sharing of Clients, but Not Ownership, Quickens the Growth of a Hispanic-Owned Agency in Dallas, *New York Times*, October 20, 1994, p. D20.

QUESTIONS FOR CRITICAL THINKING

1. Who are Ornelas & Associates' potential clients?
2. Is an agency specializing in marketing to Hispanics too limited in scope?
3. What are the pros and cons of operating as the Hispanic-oriented arm of a large agency versus operating as a small, independent agency focusing on the Hispanic market?

ACHIEVEMENT CHECK SUMMARY

Reread the learning goals that follow, and consider the questions for each goal. Answering these questions will reinforce the most important concepts in the chapter and allow you to check how well you have achieved these learning goals. Where a blank appears before a question, answer with *T* or *F*. Otherwise, circle the letter of the correct answer. An answer key to these questions is found at the end of this chapter.

LEARNING GOAL 16.1: List the objectives of promotion.

1. ___ The objectives of promotional strategy generally include providing information, differentiating a good or service, increasing sales, stabilizing sales, and accentuating the value of a product.
2. ___ Organizations frequently pursue multiple promotional objectives at the same time.

LEARNING GOAL 16.2: Explain the concept of a promotional mix.

1. ___ The promotional mix includes advertising, personal selling, sales promotion, and public relations.
2. ___ Advertising, sales promotion, and public relations are all personal selling techniques.
3. ___ In marketing, promotional strategy and sales promotion mean the same thing.

LEARNING GOAL 16.3: Describe the various personal selling tasks.

1. ___ Personal selling tasks include creative selling, missionary selling, and order processing.

2. ___ Companies that sell highly technical products will typically do some missionary selling.

3. ___ Creative selling is a persuasive type of promotional presentation.

LEARNING GOAL 16.4: Identify the steps in the sales process.

1. ___ Prospecting means finding potential customers.

2. ___ The most important step in the selling process is the close.

3. ___ A good creative salesperson avoids allowing customers to raise objections during the sales process.

LEARNING GOAL 16.5: Describe the different types of advertising.

1. ___ Informative advertising is primarily used to attract stockholders.

2. ___ Comparative advertising can be considered a type of persuasive advertising.

3. ___ Product advertising is a form of public relations.

LEARNING GOAL 16.6: Identify the various advertising media.

1. Total annual advertising expenditures in the United States are highest for: (a) television; (b) magazines; (c) newspapers; (d) radio; (e) direct mail.

2. The advantage of direct mail advertising is: (a) flexibility; (b) personalization; (c) selectivity; (d) speed; (e) all of the above.

3. The highest-cost advertising medium is: (a) television; (b) radio; (c) newspapers; (d) magazines; (e) outdoor advertising.

LEARNING GOAL 16.7: Explain the roles of sales promotion and public relations in promotional strategy.

1. ___ Specialty advertising refers to giveaway items that carry the donor's company name and/or logo.

2. ___ Sales promotion is a promotional technique that includes personal selling and advertising.

3. ___ Public relations efforts are usually aimed at customers, but not at vendors, news media, employees, stockholders, government, or the general public.

LEARNING GOAL 16.8: Identify the factors that influence the selection of a promotional mix.

1. ___ Most firms that sell low-cost items will tend to use personal selling rather than advertising.

2. ___ Sellers of industrial products should normally use advertising rather than personal selling.

3. ___ Advertising is usually needed to precondition a potential customer for a sales presentation.

LEARNING GOAL 16.9: Contrast pushing and pulling promotional strategies.

1. ___ A pushing strategy offers incentives to retailers and other intermediaries to encourage them to aggressively promote the good or service.

2. ___ A strategy designed to generate customer demand is called a pulling strategy.

3. ___ Most marketing situations require either a pushing strategy or a pulling strategy, but not both.

LEARNING GOAL 16.10: Discuss factors that influence international promotion.

1. ___ To use an American advertisement effectively in a foreign market, the advertiser needs only to translate the ad into the foreign language.

2. ___ In all of the top five global advertising markets, expenditures for newspaper advertising exceed those for TV advertising.

3. ___ Some nations restrict the use of comparative advertising.

KEY TERMS

promotional strategy 438
positioning 439
promotional mix 441
integrated marketing communications (IMC) 441
personal selling 441
order processing 441
creative selling 441
missionary selling 442
telemarketing 444
advertising 445
product advertising 445
institutional advertising 445
advocacy advertising 445
comparative advertising 447
sales promotion 451
point-of-purchase (POP) advertising 451
specialty advertising 451
trade show 451
public relations 453
pushing strategy 454
cooperative advertising 454
pulling strategy 454

REVIEW QUESTIONS

1. Not all promotional efforts are aimed at increasing sales. What other goals can promotion accomplish?

2. What promotional mix would be appropriate for each of the following products?
   a. Arc welder
   b. Personal computer
   c. Specialty steel products sold to manufacturers
   d. Landscaping service

3. What is the primary sales task in each of the following occupations?
   a. Office supply salesperson selling to local business firms
   b. Counterhelp at Hardee's
   c. Representative for an outdoor advertising firm
   d. Salesperson representing Dow Chemical

4. Explain the various steps in the sales process. Cite examples of each step.

5. Differentiate among product advertising, institutional advertising, and advocacy, or cause, advertising. Also explain the differences among informative, persuasive, comparative, and reminder-oriented advertising.

6. Which is the most popular advertising medium measured in total advertising volume? How do the other media rank in order of promotional expenditures?

7. What type of sales promotion techniques would you recommend for the following businesses?
   a. Independent insurance agency
   b. Jaguar dealership
   c. Neighborhood restaurant
   d. Hardware wholesaler

8. Should a small company with limited advertising funds consider sponsorship as a viable means of promoting its products? Explain the benefits and drawbacks.

9. What variables should marketers consider when selecting a promotional mix? Explain how each variable influences promotional strategy.

10. Differentiate between pushing and pulling strategies. Under what circumstances should each be employed?

DISCUSSION QUESTIONS

1. Consider the aftermath of the lengthy baseball strike in 1994 to 1995. Some estimates indicated that a substantial percentage of fans would refuse to attend future games. Assuming that you were the commissioner of baseball, what would you have done to get fans back to the ballpark? What aspects of promotional strategy does your plan include? Why?

2. Describe the most effective salesperson you have encountered in the past year. Explain why you think this person is so effective.

3. A 30-second television commercial during the Super Bowl cost $1 million. What type of company should buy this expensive advertising? Why?

4. Describe the best television commercial you have seen in the past year. What made this commercial so memorable, in your opinion?

5. Suppose that you are a business owner who wants to start promoting your consumer products in Latin America. Describe the factors that you should consider in planning your promotional strategy. What cultural differences would you expect to encounter?

SOLUTIONS TO ACHIEVEMENT CHECK SUMMARY

L. G. 16.1: 1. T, 2. T. **L. G. 16.2:** 1. T, 2. F, 3. F. **L. G. 16.3:** 1. T, 2. T, 3. T. **L. G. 16.4:** 1. T, 2. T, 3. F. **L. G. 16.5:** 1. F, 2. T, 3. F. **L. G. 16.6:** 1. c, 2. e, 3. a. **L. G. 16.7:** 1. T, 2. F, 3. F. **L. G. 16.8:** 1. F, 2. F, 3. T. **L. G. 16.9:** 1. T, 2. T, 3. F. **L. G. 16.10:** 1. F, 2. F, 3. T.

TEAM-BUILDING EXERCISE

This exercise has students consider the differences between competitors in a single market and has them work together to devise a simple marketing plan of their own. The exercise will take about 45 minutes. Students will need pen and paper.

1. Your instructor will divide the class into teams of three to five students. Your team will have 15 minutes to develop its competitive grid. You will not need specific knowledge of the different areas to complete the grids. The details can be based on your perceptions of factors such as pricing and decor.

2. After 15 minutes your instructor will announce that it is time to begin work on the next portion of the exercise: planning a marketing strategy for your own restaurant.

3. At the end of the exercise, your instructor will use the chalkboard or an overhead transparency to quickly construct a "master grid" based on the work of the entire class. Which team seems to have the most extensive grid?

VIDEO CASE

DAYTON HUDSON A carefully-reasoned promotional strategy is essential to a company's ultimate ability to win and maintain market share. It provides a specific plan for informing customers about the advantages of its products and for persuading and influencing customers to try them. Dayton Hudson, one of the largest retailers in the United States, required a promotional strategy that would work for Target and Mervyn's (its low- to moderate-income outlets) as well as for its upscale department stores Dayton's, Hudson's, and Marshall Field's. The company also needed policies that would distinguish each of its retail outlets from its competitors.

At the time of this video case, Dayton Hudson had some work to do at Mervyn's, where it planned to target moderate-income customers. The chain's operating income had fallen by 37 percent, and nearly half of its stores were located in California, where a recent recession was still being felt. However, the chain's real problem was declining same-store sales. Something had to be done, so Dayton Hudson made a major effort to improve customer service. It began hustling to get more fashionable attire into Mervyn's stores, reintroducing a women's dresses section after dropping it several years earlier. It also introduced a value pricing strategy, which made it easier for customers to see the discounts they were enjoying. As part of the change, the company found it necessary to replace about 70 percent of the chain's senior management.

As the new chairman and CEO of Dayton Hudson, Robert Ulrich, put it, the primary task for the corporation would now be "creating a consistently positive shopping experience," and he implemented this objective at all of the Dayton Hudson stores. His first goal was to focus on "clarity of offering," which means buying and presenting merchandise so that every store offers dominant assortments, current trends, and a broad selection on a regular basis. Because of customers' increased awareness of global fashions, only the sharpest retailers can regularly satisfy today's intense trend demands. To stay in the forefront, Dayton Hudson relies on constant trend surveillance, quality testing, savvy buying, and strong relationships with vendors who can consistently supply stores according to their requirements. Today's time-pressed customers demand—and Dayton Hudson provides—broad selections within each merchandise category. They make the effort to stock the sizes, colors, finishes, and accessories customers expect. Target, for example, offers a wide range of merchandise in most departments, but particularly in hardlines and health and beauty aids. Mervyn's offers a broader line of fleece and children's selections than other competitors, while the Dayton Hudson department stores typically offer a wide assortment of women's shoes, cosmetics, accessories, ties, and designer-label home fashions and apparel.

Clarity of offering also means making sure that Dayton Hudson stores have key items in stock and that customers can find them easily in the stores. Dayton Hudson has invested significantly in systems to keep shelves and sales floors stocked, and their investment has paid off. At Target, for instance, rain checks on advertised items have declined 72 percent over a five-year period. Once the items are in the stores, Target merchants go out of their

way to display them where the customer is likely to look for them. Target dedicates prominent spaces to seasonal merchandise and various promotional programs, and its merchants are constantly experimenting with exciting presentation methods. In fact, Dayton Hudson tries to do this at all its stores. At Mervyn's, for example, the company has set up "strike points" that captivate browsers, feature merchandise prominently, provide product information, and even demonstrate how to wear the latest styles. The department stores, on the other hand, use decor, floor plan, and fixtures to enhance service and provide specialty retailing ambiance with a wide selection.

Ulrich hopes that, by outperforming competitors in these areas, Dayton Hudson stores will be in a position to benefit further from other promotional efforts. They have run one-day sales at Marshall Field's in order to compete head-to-head with competitors like JCPenney and Barney's, and they are the first major retailer to enter the late-night world of infomercials. The 30-minute program, "Marshall Field's Presents," aired in 30 national markets, expanding the area the company serves five-fold. Whether or not these policies are ultimately successful, the company will have to continually adjust its promotional strategy to the changes in the marketplace.

QUESTIONS

1.
How would the objectives of promotion differ for the various divisions of Dayton Hudson (Target, Mervyn's, department stores—Dayton's, Hudson's, and Marshall Field's)?

2.
Would the above differences result in different promotional mixes for each division? How so?

3.
What advertising media are used by Dayton Hudson? Is the "look and feel" of the promotional message the same for the various divisions? Give examples.

4.
Are the personal selling tasks the same for sales associates in each of the divisions? How do they differ among various departments within a division as well as between divisions?

CAREERS IN BUSINESS

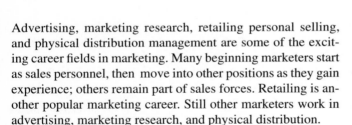

CAREER PROFILE: ED ITHIER IBM, Xerox, Digital. Ed Ithier dreamed of working in sales for one of those blue-chip companies, believing that if he could get a foot in the door, he would be exposed to unlimited career opportunities. ■ For years, he worked hard to achieve his goals, earning a degree in business communications with a concentration in marketing from New Hampshire College. In addition to his college degree, Ithier knew he needed solid business experience to improve his chances of being hired by one of his "dream teams." He took a position as a marketing representative with AIG, a major insurance company, but he never lost sight of his original goal. He continued to look for a job with one of the computer giants. ■ The day finally came when his hard work was rewarded. He landed a position as a sales representative with Xerox. Although his first sales assignment was limited to the company's basic copier models, he believed that his opportunities were only limited by his desire. Within a year, Ithier was promoted to account manager, handling major accounts with the federal government and several Fortune 500 companies. ■ Again, Ithier proved himself to be a valuable asset to Xerox, and a short two years later he was promoted to product specialist. His new job consisted of providing marketing and sales support for Docutech, a digital and network print product division of Xerox. His career was on track, successful, and secure. But Ithier continued to make himself more marketable and knowledgeable about business by attending evening classes until he earned his MBA. ■ As a product specialist, Ithier serves as a consultant working with companies interested in Docutech products. After evaluating the specific needs of a potential customer, he recommends products that best meet those needs. Ithier must determine the best way to connect new products to a company's existing network configuration. Since the equipment requires a significant investment, the most important part of his job is demonstrating the product's benefits to the customer. ■ Drive and determination have led Ithier to set new career goals. He is now working to become a product developer or a marketing specialist in Xerox's education or printing division. While striving for this new goal, Ithier takes advantage of every education or training opportunity Xerox offers him. Ithier is proof that being successful today means continually learning new things to stay abreast of changes. It also means being prepared to take advantage of opportunities when they occur.

Advertising, marketing research, retailing personal selling, and physical distribution management are some of the exciting career fields in marketing. Many beginning marketers start as sales personnel, then move into other positions as they gain experience; others remain part of sales forces. Retailing is another popular marketing career. Still other marketers work in advertising, marketing research, and physical distribution.

Sales is generally considered to have the greatest potential for earnings growth. Brand or product management is next in terms of salary potential, followed by marketing research, advertising, and public relations.

The Bureau of Labor Statistics, which has projected the U.S. employment outlook through 2000, forecasts that job opportunities for wholesale trade salespeople and manufacturers' sales reps will grow faster than the average for all occupations; opportunities for public relations specialists will grow as fast as the average.

MARKETING RESEARCH ANALYSTS

Marketing research is one of the fastest growing fields in business. Marketing research analysts study what consumers will and will not buy. Currently, about 29,000 of them are employed throughout the United States.

Job Description Marketing research analysts use a variety of techniques such as surveys, personal interviews, and test markets to assess consumer perceptions and interests. They try to learn, for example, what consumers think of a company's product and how it is used in the home. These conclusions are then reported to marketing executives, who use them in their decision making. Marketing researchers work in all kinds of businesses, government, not-for-profit organizations, advertising agencies, and marketing research firms.

Career Path Entry-level jobs in marketing research usually involve clerical duties or data collection tasks. Once the individual is established as a marketing research analyst, he or she is assigned specific research projects. Advancement to supervisory positions is possible. Ultimately, the person may become director of marketing research or achieve an even higher management position.

Salary In a recent year the average annual salary of entry-level analysts was $24,100. The salary range of a marketing research director for a large firm is between $100,000 and $150,000.

PUBLIC RELATIONS SPECIALISTS

Public relations jobs are found in businesses, trade associations, government, and other entities such as colleges. The mission of the public relations specialist is to create a favorable image for his or her employer. Currently, some 98,000 public relations specialists are employed in the United States.

Job Description Public relations specialists act as liaisons between their employers and the public. For instance, they send out press releases to newspapers, magazines, radio stations, and television news departments; prepare promotional materials; and write speeches for executives.

Career Path Trainee positions are available in public relations. Senior people are given specific responsibilities depending on their employer and the nature of the task. Supervisory positions are the next level in the public relations career.

Salary In a recent year, the median annual salary for public relations specialists was $32,000. The median pay for experienced public relations specialists and public relations managers was $62,000. Public relations specialists in government jobs made an average of $22,700 for entry-level positions.

ADVERTISING AGENTS

Many jobs are available in advertising. These include copywriter, account executive, artist, media buyer, and production coordinator. Advertising employees can be found in company advertising departments, advertising agencies, and government. More than 250,000 people are currently employed in advertising.

Job Description The entry-level job is often in a specific activity, such as copywriting for an ad agency. Advertising copywriters sell an image of a good or service to the public. They are responsible for the written text of ads that appear in magazines and newspapers and for scripts for radio and television commercials.

Career Path Entry-level positions are available in various phases of advertising. Success in these positions can lead to management positions. For instance, a junior copywriter might advance to senior copywriter and then to chief copywriter. Eventually, the person might become creative director of an advertising agency.

Salary In a recent year, advertising agencies paid the following average salaries: account executive, $34,500, copywriter, $39,400; art director, $37,400; production manager, $34,000; and media buyer, $25,700. Salaries of advertising workers are usually higher in consumer product firms than in industrial product companies.

MANUFACTURERS' SALES REPRESENTATIVES

Manufacturers' sales representatives play key roles in marketing because they work with both retailers and wholesalers. This type of salesperson can be found in both consumer and industrial marketing, working with both technical and nontechnical products. Some 483,900 people are now employed as manufacturers' sales representatives.

Job Description Manufacturers' sales representatives call upon potential customers to explain the features and benefits of their products, answer questions, and offer demonstrations. In addition to making personal contacts with potential customers, manufacturers' sales representatives also investigate customers' credit ratings, report competitive information to the home office, and complete paperwork providing information about their territories, customers, and competitors.

Career Path Most manufacturers provide sales training programs. Such programs usually involve rotation through various parts of the company and on-the-job field experience. Successful completion of the sales training program leads to a regular sales position. Promotion to sales management positions is a typical pattern of career progression.

Salary In a recent year, the median salary for manufacturing sales representatives was $32,000. Actual earnings are a function of such factors as the industry, the company, the individual's experience, and the compensation system used. Experienced manufacturing sales representatives earned an average of $62,000.

WHOLESALE TRADE SALES REPRESENTATIVES

This kind of sales representative works for a wholesaling firm in marketing a line of products to retailers, commercial and industrial firms, and units of government. Currently there are nearly 1.1 million wholesale trade sales representatives in the United States.

Job Description Sales personnel for wholesaling firms make regular calls on their retail, wholesale, or organizational customers. These sellers provide many services to their buyers, including delivery and credit. Some even stock retailers' shelves. Wholesale trade sales representatives also assist their customers with displays, inventory control, and pricing.

Career Path Large wholesale establishments have sales trainee positions that enable applicants to observe experienced personnel and to learn specific sales tasks. Experienced sales representatives are assigned to sales territories. Promotions beyond this level are usually to sales management positions.

Salary Average yearly salaries for wholesale sales workers are about $32,000.

RETAIL BUYERS

Buyers are responsible for choosing the merchandise a store offers its customers. All retailing enterprises have a buyer or a buying function. The type of merchandise a buyer purchases is dictated by the kind of store and its clientele. Some 624,000 people are currently employed as buyers in the retail and wholesale fields, with slower than average growth forecast through 2000.

Job Description A buyer must keep pace with changing consumer needs and tastes as well as the store's competitive strategy. A buyer must also keep abreast of special discounts offered by manufacturers and terms offered by distributors. In addition, a buyer must deal with a store's sales personnel. Feedback from retail sales personnel helps the buyer to stay attuned to consumer preferences.

Career Path Trainees are usually called *assistant buyers.* They support buyers for certain merchandise lines. The step above buyer is usually merchandise manager, a person who directs several buyers.

Salary The salary of buyers varies widely due to the incentive compensation granted by retailing firms. The nature, size, and location of the firm also affect salaries. In a recent year, the median annual salary of buyers was $33,067 with a range up to $56,581.

RETAIL OPERATIONS MANAGERS

Operations managers are responsible for the nonmerchandise-related part of retailing. Many people fail to recognize the behind-the-scenes contributions of these marketers.

Job Description The duties of the operations manager include supervision of receiving, shipping, delivery, service, security, and inventory control departments. Experience in these areas is highly desirable for those people pursuing careers in retailing.

Career Path The first step is to gain experience in one or more activities supervised by the operations manager. A likely stepping stone to an operations manager position is a department head position in an area such as receiving.

Salary Salaries of operations managers vary widely depending upon the individual's experience as well as the nature, size, and location of the store. In a recent year, typical salaries ranged from $18,400 to $23,700.

CAREER DESIGN EXERCISES

BUSINESS WEEK ARTICLE

It is 20 years in the future. As a result of your successful business career, one of the most prominent business magazines in the world has decided to do a story about you! Even better, they will allow you to write the story.

This is your chance to imagine what you want to accomplish in the years ahead. This article is excellent publicity for you, and it has two distinct advantages over advertising: readers will probably find it more believable than an ad, and it is free!

THIS EXERCISE WILL HELP YOU TO:

- Clarify how you might want to participate in the world of business.
- Start to create a picture of your career direction.

HOW TO LOCATE THE EXERCISE

When you see the main menu for Career Design, select "What Do I Want?" Then select "*Business Week* Article."

BILLBOARD

One of the most visible forms of advertising is a billboard. Suppose you had the opportunity to put a message of your choice on the most prominent billboard in town. This brief exercise asks you to create that message.

THIS EXERCISE WILL HELP YOU TO:

- Discover your personal priorities.
- Consider what kinds of activities or businesses in which you might want to become involved.

HOW TO LOCATE THE EXERCISE

When you see the main menu for Career Design, select "What Do I Want?" Then select "Billboard."

CHAPTER 17

INFORMATION FOR BUSINESS DECISIONS

CHAPTER 18

ACCOUNTING

PART V

INFORMATION SYSTEMS AND ACCOUNTING

CHAPTER 17

INFORMATION FOR BUSINESS DECISIONS

LEARNING GOALS

1. Explain the purpose of an information system and how it aids decision making in business.

2. List the major contributions and limitations of computers.

3. Distinguish between computer hardware and software.

4. Distinguish among mainframe computers, minicomputers, and microcomputers.

5. Discuss the role of telecommunications in business.

6. Explain the concept of an information superhighway and its implications for business.

7. Identify the major business applications of computers.

8. Summarize the major computer security issues that affect organizations.

POLYGON NETWORKS At first glance, Dillon, Colorado seems like one of the world's least likely spots to build an on-ramp for the information superhighway. This tiny town of 10,000 located west of Denver on Interstate 70 seems more like a place to buy gas or spend the night at the local Best Western before driving into the nearby Keystone and Breckenridge ski resorts. Despite appearances, Dillon is world headquarters of Polygon Networks, an on-line service that links 1,000 independent jewelers worldwide and allows them to buy and sell merchandise from one another without depending on wholesalers. ■ Polygon is the brainchild of 42-year-old Jacques Voorhees. Founded during the 1970s in New York, the jewelry brokerage firm struggled to earn a profit in the nation's largest, and perhaps most expensive, city. In 1984, Voorhees, his wife, and three children packed up for Colorado. In the move, Polygon abandoned $45.00 per square foot office rental rates for $8.50 per square foot in Dillon. ■ Polygon's corporate headquarters are located above a local bank—one of the few two-story buildings in town. A quick tour through the offices reveals how President Voorhees has harnessed technology to serve his needs and those of his firm's clients. In all, 25 phone lines, 17 modems, a dozen or so personal computers, and two larger mainframes constitute the heart of the operation. Several programmers—typically well-tanned from time on the nearby ski slopes—also make key contributions to the business. Voorhees jokingly points out a unique employee benefit: "One of our key rules is that anyone can take a ski break any time they want." ■ Exactly what services does Polygon provide? To maintain competitive prices and to match inventory to specific customer requests, independent jewelers need systems that give them access to the high-volume purchasing power and other efficiencies of the retail giants. In the past, independents' relatively small purchases forced them to deal with jewelry wholesalers who acted as intermediaries between retailers and jewelry importers and manufacturers. Wholesalers' fees for their services drove up prices, though. Moreover, the retailers often waited through longer response times for their product requests than larger competitors. ■ To improve service, Voorhees created an electronic marketplace called CertNet. Jewelers who subscribe to the network can log onto the system using a personal computer and modem. They can then post requests to buy or sell specific merchandise to be read by other subscribers. Special software automatically searches for availability of requested jewelry, diamonds, or colored stones. In addition to written descriptions of available or requested items, CertNet also displays color photos of merchandise. A subscriber pays an annual fee of $95 for the service, and the list of participants is growing fast. In making sales calls, Voorhees simply plugs in his Austin Computer laptop, logs onto his network from any jewelry store he is visiting, and proceeds to dazzle the startled proprietor with the system's ability to serve retailer needs. ■ Voorhees quickly admits that he is no computer "techie." He simply saw a need in the marketplace and recognized an opportunity to harness computer and communication technology to fill it. "I bought a VAX [mainframe computer] from Digital, and hired a guy to write our own software from scratch. I knew nothing about software." Today, Polygon Networks is both profitable and growing, and the mom-and-pop operation illustrates the use of information technology to solve business problems—even from a tiny Colorado town.[1]

CHAPTER OVERVIEW

Someone once gave the recipe for an effective decision as "90 percent information and 10 percent inspiration." Clearly, obtaining the right information and knowing how to use it are vital to business success.

As the opening story shows, Polygon Networks has prospered by finding new ways to deliver information to small retail businesses all over the world. This chapter will look at how information systems are transforming business and the process of decision making. These systems rely more and more heavily on computers and related technologies to store, access, and manage the information that businesspeople need.

MANAGEMENT INFORMATION SYSTEMS

- What is the sales potential for our brand in Indonesia compared to Malaysia and Thailand?
- If we raise the price for the brand by 2 percent, how will it affect sales in both countries?
- How do our wage rates compare with those of similar firms in Philadelphia?
- What are the storage costs for Model 401?

management information system (MIS)
Organized method of providing information for decision making.

chief information officer (CIO)
Top-management executive responsible for directing a firm's management information system and related computer operations.

Every day in business, people ask questions such as these. An effective information system helps them to find answers. A **management information system (MIS)** is an organized method for providing past, present, and projected information on internal operations as well as external intelligence to support decision making. Large organizations typically assign responsibility for directing the firm's MIS and related computer operations to an executive called the **chief information officer (CIO).** Generally, the CIO reports directly to the firm's CEO.

A company needs information from a variety of sources for almost every activity, whether internal or external. Information can make the difference between staying in business or going broke. Keeping on top of changing consumer demands, competitors' actions, and the latest government regulations will help a firm fine-tune existing products, develop new winners, and market them effectively.

Federal Express created the overnight, small-package delivery industry, attracting major competitors ranging from DHL, Airborne Express, and UPS to the U.S. Postal Service. FedEx has exploited information technology to maintain its industry leadership. Figure 17.1 describes a recent innovation, FedEx Ship.

Overnight shippers expect a lot from a service provider: competitive prices, dependability, ability to track and confirm delivery, flexibility in package pickups, and easy-to-prepare shipping labels. FedEx Ship is designed to meet these expectations through special software that connects the user's computer directly to the FedEx system that stores data on the firm's customers. After a few keystrokes, the FedEx computer creates shipping labels and prints them on the user's own laser printer. The customer makes no telephone calls and spends no time filling out complicated labels; everything is automatic, including billing according to predetermined instructions. Such time and cost savings are intended to enhance customer satisfaction and encourage repeat business.

DATABASES

database
Computer integrated collection of an organization's data resources.

The heart of a management information system is its **database**—a centralized, integrated collection of the organization's data resources. Firms design their databases to meet the particular information processing and retrieval requirements of decision makers. Databases serve as electronic file cabinets, capable of storing massive amounts of data and retrieving it within seconds. Databases also help firms target their direct marketing efforts by finding out more about prospective customers. Kimberly-Clark, maker of Huggies diapers, maintains a database of information on over 10 million new mothers.

FIGURE 17.1

COMBINING INFORMATION AND TECHNOLOGY TO PROVIDE CUSTOMER SATISFACTION

Fingerhut, a catalog retailer with over 13 million customers, relies on its own extensive database to tailor its sales efforts to the particular wants, needs, and habits of its shoppers. First, Fingerhut assembles some 1,400 pieces of information on each household, ranging from past purchases and income to the birthdays and sexes of the children. Statisticians then predict customers' future purchases based on their past histories. Using this information to generate individualized promotions and specialty catalogs, Fingerhut efficiently matches customers to the items they are most likely to buy. For instance, a greeting from Fingerhut to parents before a child's birthday includes information on age-appropriate toys for sale plus the promise of free gifts. It's no surprise that Fingerhut is the fourth-largest mail-order company in the United States.[2]

Online Databases Firms that cannot afford to create and maintain their own databases can subscribe to commercial services that provide fee-for-service databases on

Isabelle Lavoie handles immigration issues for the foreign employees of the dance and circus troupe Cirque du Soleil. The database she created using Microsoft's Access software contains each foreign performer's passport number and expiration date, date and place of birth, social security number, and work permit expiration.

specific topics. In addition to broad-based databases available through such services as Prodigy, CompuServe, Delphi, and GEnie, firms can access specialized commercial databases to meet their own specific needs. If a company is interested in exporting its products to Germany, for instance, it can pay to access ABC der Deutschen Wirtschaft, which carries data on 76,000 manufacturers in Germany. Its listings include such helpful data as each firm's name, address, phone number, products, and number of employees, as well as its industry classification and the names of its bankers.[3]

One in three U.S. households currently owns a personal computer. Similarly, the growth of subscribers to online services is rapidly increasing, with approximately 20 percent of U.S. households using these services. Thousands of new subscribers pay monthly fees to browse news, engage in online chats, shop, and swap e-mail. CompuServe has nearly 2.4 million subscribers worldwide, and Prodigy has 2 million subscribers. Although America Online doubled the number of subscribers to over 1 million in 1994, it is still a distant third. As online services becomes more popular, the top three online service providers are cutting prices, adding features, refining their appearance, and getting ready for tougher competition in the market. Apple Computer now offers its eWorld service, and Ziff-Davis Publishing Co. is launching its own entry. Examples of data and graphics capabilities of three popular online services appear in Figure 17.2.

Software giant Microsoft recently announced its intention to enter the market with its own online service, Microsoft Marvel. This represents a major threat to existing commercial online services because Microsoft can include Marvel software as part of its popular Windows package. Because it faces negligible marketing and set-up costs in comparison with its established competitors, Microsoft will be able to offer its service at a substantially lower price.[4]

computer
Programmable electronic device that can store, retrieve, and process data.

FIGURE 17.2

MENU SCREENS FROM POPULAR ONLINE SERVICE PROVIDERS

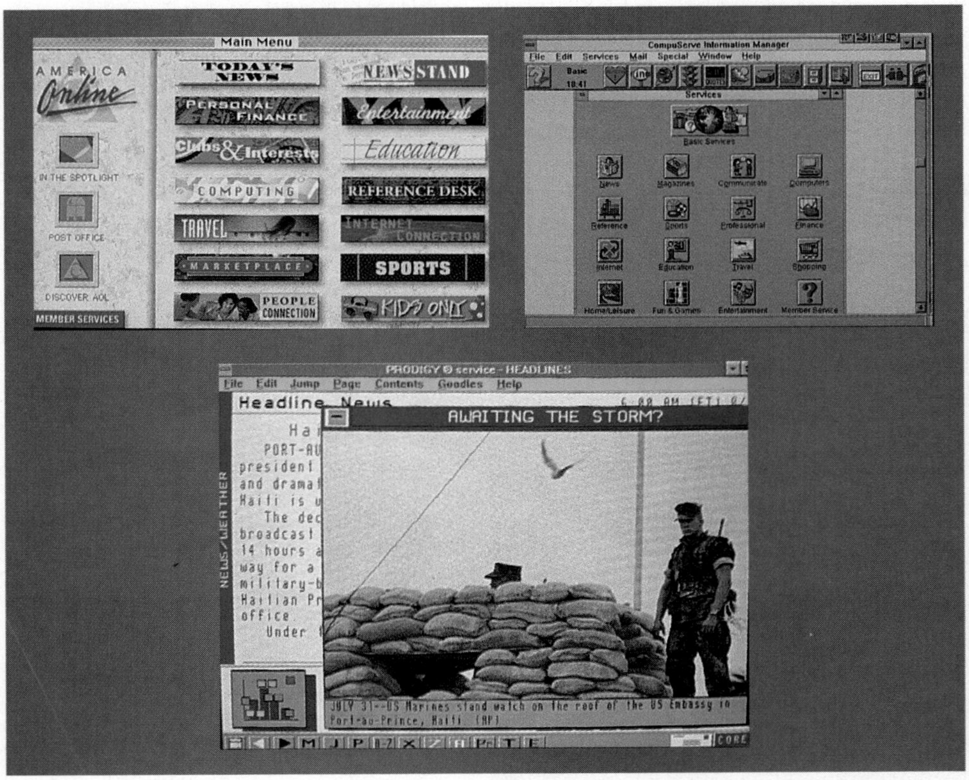

BUSINESS IN ACTION

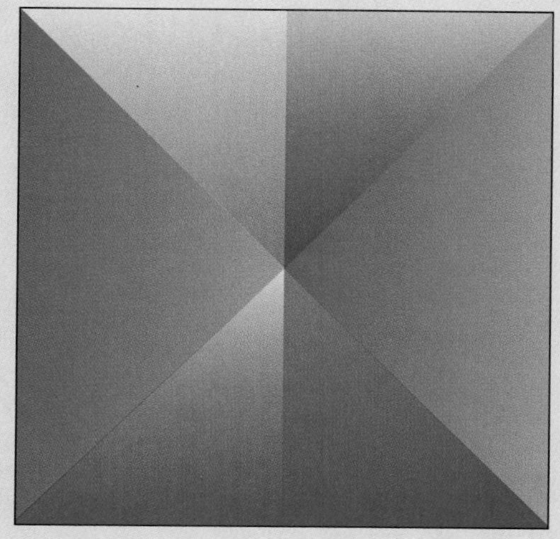

USING DATABASES TO IDENTIFY LOYAL CUSTOMERS Ever wonder why giant drug maker Upjohn spends so much on magazine advertising for its Rogaine hair-growth product? Although Rogaine is viewed as a miracle product by many balding adults, would-be purchasers could not, until this year, buy the product without a doctor's prescription. But the rules changed in 1995 when Rogaine was approved for over-the-counter sales. Since product performance is directly related to daily application, Upjohn marketers have used advertising, direct mail, and telemarketing to create a database of customers who form the core of the firm's business in this market. ■ Upjohn is one of thousands of firms dependent on current, accurate databases as the focal point of their business strategy. Marketers are some of the most frequent business users of databases. What *is* database marketing? According to industry writer Arthur M. Hughes, database marketing is "managing a computerized relational database system that collects relevant data about customers and prospects, which enables us to better service and establish long-term relationships with them." But practitioners offer this working definition: database marketing is an easy way to access and segment information about customers. ■ Manufacturers and retailers are investing heavily in database development to track purchaser behavior and product movement. Databases provide information that keeps customers coming back again and again. Data-collection methods include everything from face-to-face interviews and questionnaires to telephone surveys and retail checkout scanners. Databases are a key to building and maintaining customer loyalty, now seen as crucial to keeping a business alive. One example of this trend is the increase in the number of corporate clubs and loyalty programs, which rose steadily in the early part of the 1990s. From 130 programs in 1992, they grew to 153 in 1993 and 167 in 1994—an increase of 28 percent in two years. ■ Many small businesses routinely gather database information by visiting their rivals, questioning suppliers, socializing with competitors, and subscribing to trade papers for tips. Atlanta chef and restaurant owner Tom Coohill pays for his managers' meals at competitors' establishments to see how and what they are doing. After visiting a computer company down the street, Russ Hebard realized he could capture some of their business by installing a fax machine in his Hoboken, New Jersey, Mail Boxes Etc. franchise—an inexpensive way to offer better service to his customers. ■ Building a database is not always as easy as it sounds. For American Mobile Satellite Corporation, based in Reston, Virginia, creating a database was an arduous and expensive two-year process. For larger organizations, setting up a database may mean hiring a professional database company to install an efficient information gathering and sharing system at a typical cost of $100,000 or more. It is important to remember that databases are not substitutes for traditional business functions—they are a supplement to them. And making data-gathering parameters too general can leave you overwhelmed—with information.

Sources: Quotations from "A Special Background Report on Trends in Industry and Finance," *The Wall Street Journal,* March 9, 1995, p. A1; Jeffrey D. Zbar, "Upjohn Database Rallies Rogaine," *Advertising Age,* January 23, 1995, p. 42; "Using Databases to Seek Out the Brand Loyal Shoppers," *Promo,* February 1995, p. 10; and Martin Everett, "Know Why They Buy," *Sales & Marketing Management,* December 1994, pp. 66–71.

QUESTIONS FOR CRITICAL THINKING

1. What opportunities do databases offer in the areas of promotion and advertising?
2. What types of information do you think Upjohn is tracking in its Rogaine customer database?
3. What are the dangers of relying solely on a database to reach customers?

CONTRIBUTIONS AND LIMITATIONS OF COMPUTERS

English mathematician William Shanks spent one-third of his life computing pi to 707 decimal places, only to discover that he made a mistake at the 528th place! Today, a computer can duplicate Shanks' work without error in less than 5 seconds.

A **computer** is a programmable electronic device that can store, retrieve, and process data. Once considered exotic, these machines have become indispensable to business; 71 percent of the people who work in the finance, insurance, and real estate industries use computers on the job. In all, three of every eight U.S. employees now use computers regularly at work, up from 25 percent a decade ago.[5]

Computers are indispensable tools for the managers of the twenty-first century. Because they are quick sources of needed decision-oriented information, they are as familiar features of the typical manager's desk as the daily appointment book.

Source: © Hewlett-Packard; used by permission.

Computers offer many advantages to businesses. They are fast, accurate, and capable of storing large quantities of information in small spaces. They can make volumes of data available quickly and perform the mechanical, often boring, work of recording and maintaining incoming information. The tremendous speed of computers can save time when correcting problems, implementing solutions, and taking advantage of business opportunities. These machines can perform repetitive tasks, such as adding endless strings of numbers or comparing collected data against established standards, that would soon wear out human beings.

Like any time-saving or labor-saving device, the computer's advantages also bring a number of potential problems. Computer equipment and software designed to meet a firm's particular needs can be expensive. In addition, computers can make disastrous mistakes when programmed incorrectly, as when, a few years ago, a computerized defense system almost tried to shoot down the moon. At about the same time, an amazed magazine subscriber received 700 copies of the same issue in the mail. Computers can also become a crutch rather than a decision-making tool when people rely on them too heavily.

Finally, computers can alienate customers if firms use them so much that they eliminate the human element in customer contact. To overcome consumer resentment toward the typical, depersonalized computer letter, a Charleston, West Virginia hospital uses this message:

> *Hello there. I am the hospital's computer. As yet, no one but me knows that you have not been making regular payments on this account. However, if I have not processed a payment from you within 10 days, I will tell a human, who will resort to other means of collection.*

HARDWARE AND SOFTWARE

hardware
All tangible elements of a computer system.

Computer **hardware** consists of all the tangible elements of the computer system—the input devices, the machines that store and process data and perform the required calculations, and the output devices that present the results to the information user. Computer hardware includes all machinery and electronic gadgets that make up the computer installation.

In order to work, however, hardware requires **software,** which consists of sets of instructions that tell the hardware what to do. Computer languages and computer programs, including both custom-designed and off-the-shelf commercial software packages, are considered software. Over the years, MS-DOS software and its upgrades have remained the most popular choice of businesses. Leading software packages include Microsoft Windows, WordPerfect, Quicken for Windows, and QEMM.[6]

software
Programmed instructions that tell a computer what to do.

MAINFRAMES, MINICOMPUTERS, AND MICROCOMPUTERS

Based on their memory capacities and processing speeds, computers fall into three broad categories: mainframes, minicomputers, and microcomputers. The *mainframe computer* is the largest type of computer system with the greatest amount of storage capacity and the fastest processing speeds. Some observers, noting IBM Corp.'s fall from grace over the past 5 years, argue that mainframes are the dinosaurs of the 21st-century computer industry. After all, IBM, whose name is synonymous with computers and which built most of its fame and revenue base on mainframes, has seen its revenues from that market drop by nearly half since 1990. However, these giant computers are not destined for early extinction, primarily due to their ability to handle dinosaur-sized tasks. In fact, they continue to evolve as people discover new applications for these massive machines.[7]

The increasing popularity of the smaller minicomputers and microcomputers is due to their ever-increasing capabilities to handle many of the functions that mainframes performed 20 years ago. The *minicomputer* is an intermediate-sized computer—more compact and less expensive than a mainframe, but also slower and with less memory. These intermediate computers are often at work in universities, factories, and research labs.

Most people are familiar with the **microcomputer,** the smallest type of computer, since it is so common today in schools, at home, and in business. A microcomputer, typically called a *personal computer* or *PC,* has a *video display monitor* that displays output on a TV-like screen. The boom in home computer sales is also reflected in the growth of online services and the increase in multimedia software on CD-ROM. In business, increasing numbers of computers have given birth to new applications, including online real estate listings and maps, online banking, and electronic bill paying.[8]

microcomputer
Desktop, laptop, and pocket-sized portable computers.

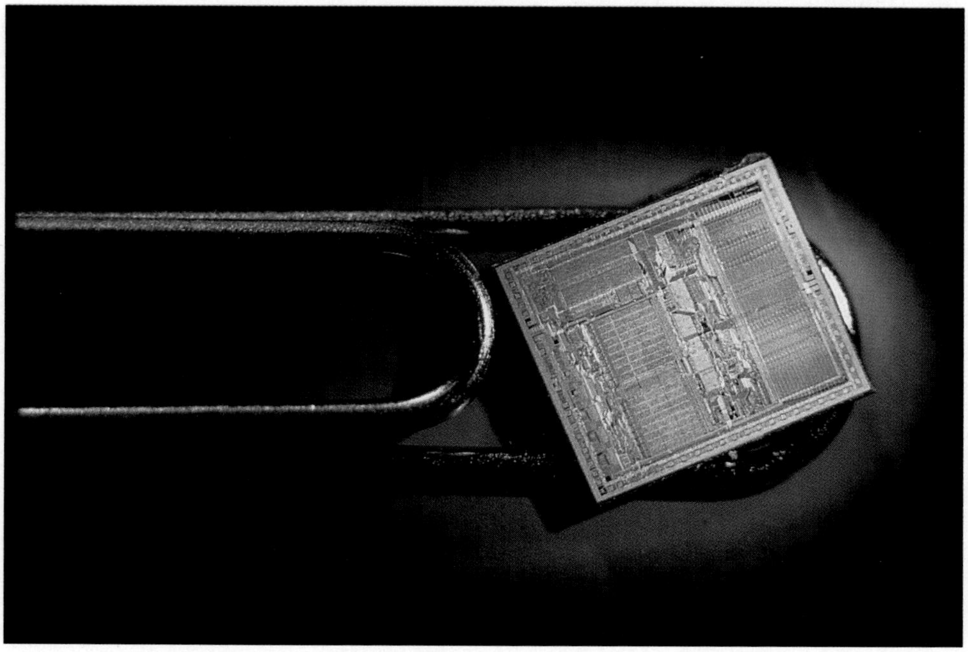

Chips—the miniature brains of the computer.

The distinctions among the three types of computers are blurring due to rapid developments in technology. Today's microcomputers can handle as much work as the huge mainframes of the 1970s. Especially powerful mainframes called *supercomputers* can handle extremely rapid, complex calculations involving thousands of variables. Supercomputers are most commonly used for scientific research.

These advances were made possible by the development of powerful *computer chips*—thin silicon wafers that carry integrated circuits (networks of transistors and electronic circuits). In particular, a *microprocessor* is a fingernail-sized chip that contains an entire central processing unit. Intelligent features of today's new cars, toys, and watches also rely on microprocessors. Additional chips provide instructions and memory to convert the microprocessor into a microcomputer.

As technology continues to improve, computers continue to get smaller. Laptop computers are microcomputers lightweight enough to be easily portable and small enough to be used on a person's lap when no desk is available. Notebook computers are small enough to slip into a briefcase, and palmtops fit in a shirt pocket and run on ordinary AA batteries. Another hot development in miniaturized computers, illustrated in Figure 17.3 is the notepad computer, which can process handwritten letters, numbers, and drawings as input.

The technology of small computers, such as notebooks, lags about 3 years behind microcomputers, but the increasing mobility of American workers makes them popular. Roughly one-third of the people who buy Compaq Computer's notebooks, for example, are replacing desktop machines. Typical of this market is Dallas telephone technician Robert Mears, who recently bought his notebook computer because he does not want to be tied down to his office microcomputer. "I need more portability than that," he says.[9]

The future will produce even smaller PCs. Hewlett-Packard's OmniBook, the first successful subnotebook on the market, has been joined by a color version. Digital Equipment's elegantly designed, 4-pound HiNote Ultra model, just 1.2 inches thick and only as long and as wide as a letter-sized sheet of paper, is also meeting with approval from computer users seeking convenience and mobility.[10]

Industry technologists are developing a credit-card–sized computer that they expect to enable users to access information on office networks from hotel rooms or home.

FIGURE 17.3

NOTEBOOK COMPUTERS: STANDARD EQUIPMENT FOR MOBILE BUSINESSPEOPLE AND BEST-SELLING AUTHOR JOHN GRISHAM

These new technologies lag due to the need for frequent battery recharging and difficulties in upgrading transmission services, but they will soon become the state of the art in personal computing.

TELECOMMUNICATIONS AND THE INFORMATION SUPERHIGHWAY

Information technologies are changing the business world rapidly and in numerous ways. One of the fastest-growing segments of the information industry today, **telecommunications,** includes any system in which data travels over a long or short distance through some type of transmission medium. Besides computers, telecommunications involve such diverse technologies as telephones, television, facsimile (fax) machines, and wireless communications.

telecommunications
Any system in which data travels over a distance through some type of electronic transmission system, typically a telephone line.

These new technologies affect contemporary business in three primary ways. First, the enhanced timeliness and quantity of information makes decision making faster and often more effective. Second, accurate, nonbiased data are available to all interested parties. Finally, since more and more consumers can connect via computers to online services such as travel agents or brokerage houses, the change may potentially eliminate many intermediaries.

Thousands of businesses, both large and small, are changing supplier-buyer relationships by combining computers and communications networks. Information gathered and stored on networks allow retail stores, for example, to analyze customer and sales data and spot trends in their industry. All network members benefit; however, those that are not connected to the network are frequently eliminated from the chain. For example, insurance companies now provide policyholders with 800 numbers to make claims. Such a number may also connect the policyholder with a network repair shop. However, a repair shop that is not on the insurance company's computer network loses access to these customers. When the Globe Glass & Mirror Co. chain created a network for Allstate Corp. in 1990, hundreds of small shops in the $2.3 billion replacement-glass industry found themselves shut out of the market.

In much the same way, retail stores can gather customer data that they can analyze to evaluate sales and spot trends. Accurate, nonbiased information about recorded music sales is now available from an independent source that collects data from 14,000

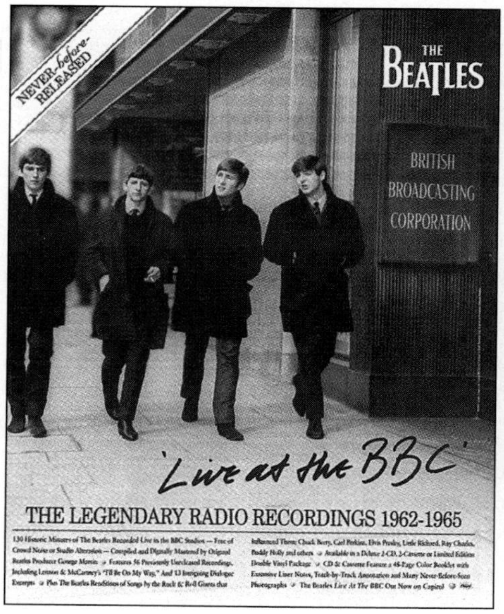

From the Beatles to the Black Crowes, *Billboard* magazine uses information gathered at checkout counters of Camelot Music and 14,000 other retailers to determine what's hot and what's not in its weekly surveys.

FIGURE 17.4 BUILDING NETWORKS FOR THE INFORMATION SUPERHIGHWAY

The information superhighway links networks. Client-server technology provides key guidance toward making this a reality. Rather than directing all computing tasks to a remote mainframe, the network divides tasks between machines. Desktop machines such as personal computers—clients—perform part of the work and computers located throughout the network—servers—do the rest and store information. The goal is to let individual and business clients use personal computers, telephones, and even television sets to retrieve information stored on many large and small servers no matter where they are located.

Servers work hard
Servers are computers on networks that typically run database software containing customer information or parts inventories. They can also manage applications such as electronic mail systems. Servers can be any size, from the personal computer to the biggest mainframe.

The mainframe endures
Client-server computing is heterogeneous, and mainframes are unlikely to disappear. Many different kinds of machines will be linked together. Existing mainframes can often be reconfigured to become very large servers.

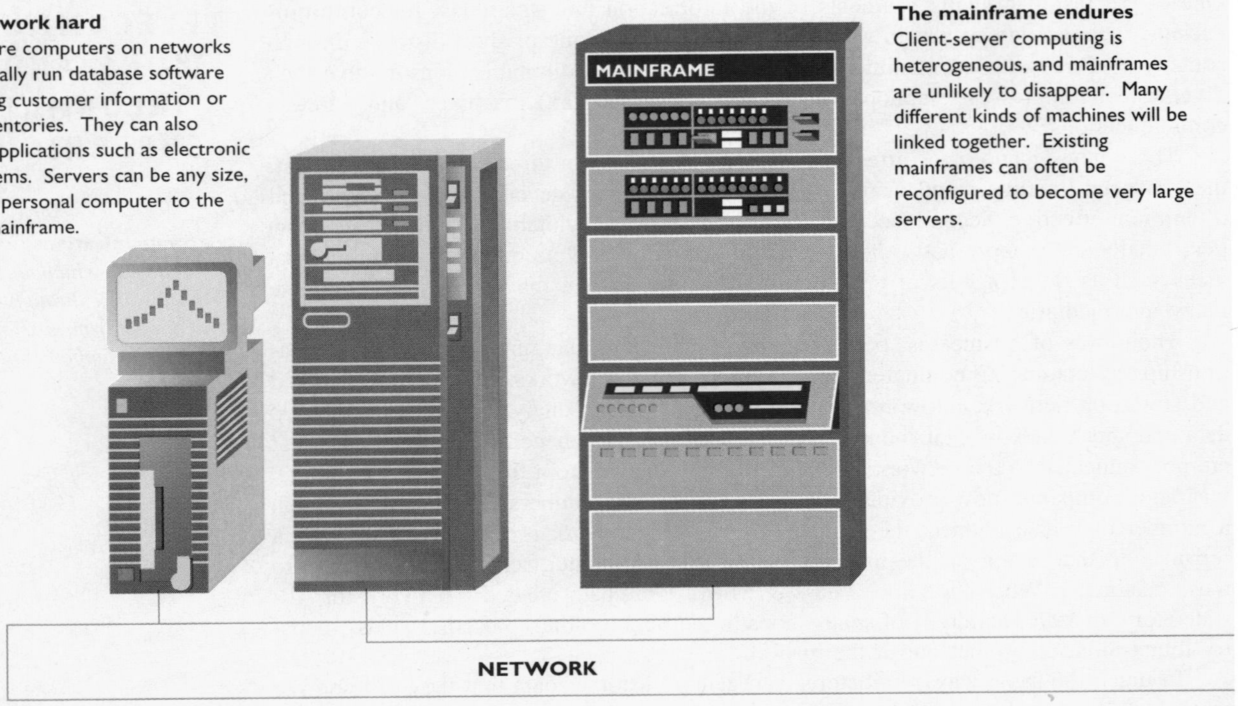

retailers. Among the recent findings, country music is more popular than many record company executives had assumed, and small rap labels such as Priority Records are getting more rack space because the numbers show strong demand. As a result, according to an industry researcher, information technology is "helping make marketplaces operate closer to how classical economic theory says they should," by giving the industry better information on which to act.[11]

The U.S. government recently announced the ambitious goal of merging America's sprawling telecommunications, information, and data networks into a single, enormous pathway accessible to all businesses, not-for-profit organizations, and individual households. This so-called **information superhighway** is viewed as a critical component of the nation's long-term economic competitiveness. Telecommunications media supplied by local cable or telephone companies give a growing number of businesses and residences access to libraries, databases, and teleconferencing, as well as many other services.

information superhighway
Single, enormous network merging telecommunications, information, and data systems that can be assessed by any individual or organization.

The information superhighway affects business in many ways. It reduces the time needed to transmit data and speeds up the pace of work. Some experts suggest, for example, that it will reduce employers' health care costs as much as 20 percent by speeding up medical claims processing. It will overcome geographic barriers by allowing branch offices located in different countries to share information as easily as offices in the same city. Businesspeople can conduct international meetings electronically, rather than having to spend hours and dollars traveling.

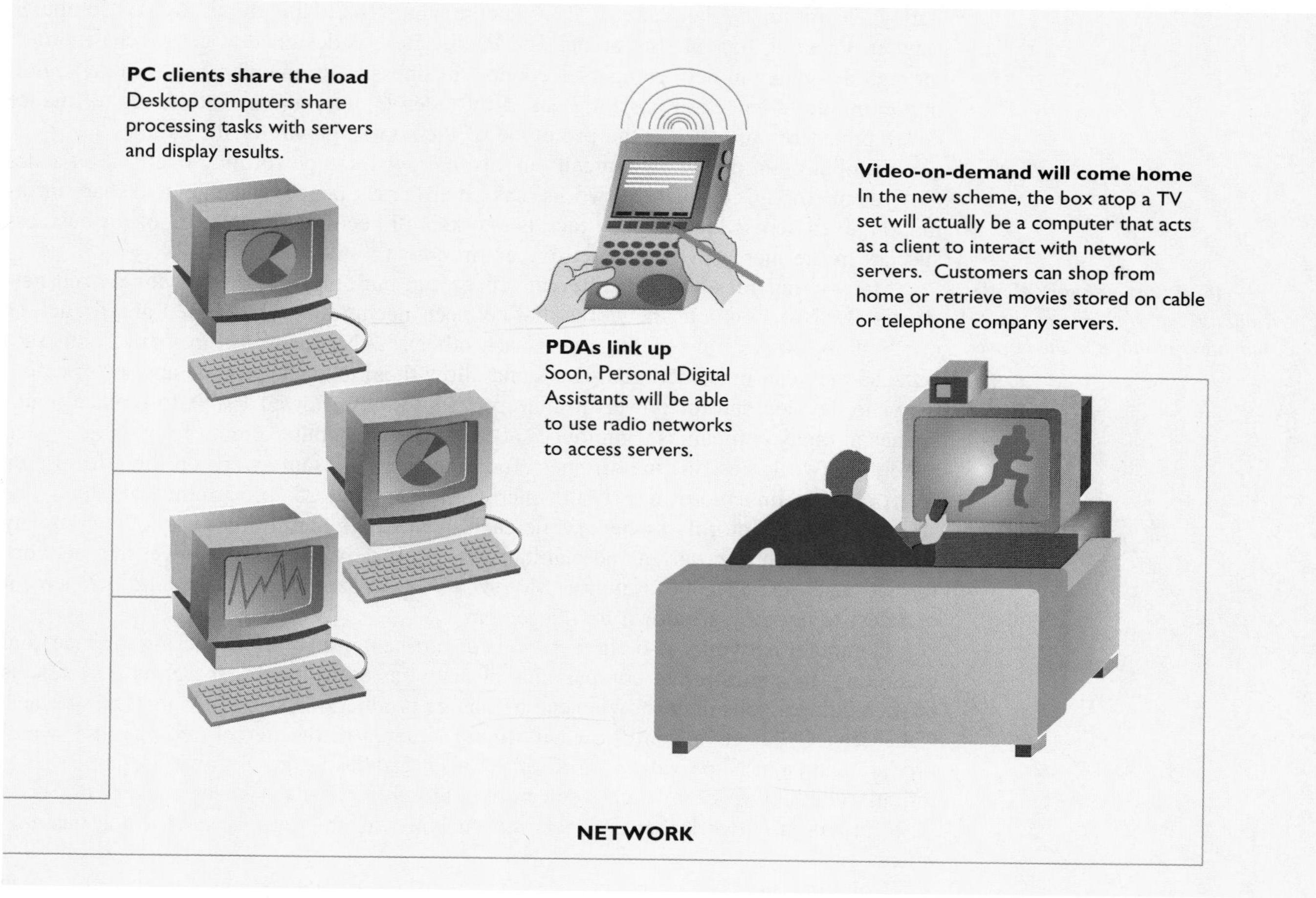

PC clients share the load
Desktop computers share processing tasks with servers and display results.
PDAs link up
Soon, Personal Digital Assistants will be able to use radio networks to access servers.
Video-on-demand will come home
In the new scheme, the box atop a TV set will actually be a computer that acts as a client to interact with network servers. Customers can shop from home or retrieve movies stored on cable or telephone company servers.
NETWORK

An information superhighway will also benefit business relationships by allowing more producers to deal directly with their customers instead of having to go through wholesalers and other intermediaries.[12] By installing order-taking computer terminals in the stockrooms of large hospitals, Baxter Healthcare Corp. has come to dominate the hospital supply business. Besides eliminating the need to place orders through salespeople, the terminals are more convenient to use and produce faster, more efficient service for the hospitals.[13]

As shown in Figure 17.4, the information superhighway originates with video servers linked to mainframe computers. It proceeds through various networks and reaches its final destination in locations as diverse as a home computer or a giant corporation's mainframe.[14]

COMPUTER NETWORKS

The information superhighway will play a greater role in business as it gives access to more and more applications. An important development in this process involves **computer networks,** systems that interconnect numerous computers so they can both function individually and communicate with each other. The network can include one or a combination of mainframes, minicomputers, and microcomputers.

computer network
System in which interconnected computers can both function individually and communicate with each other.

Currently, intercompany computer networks are having their greatest impact in the area of electronic purchasing systems. An estimated 40,000 U.S. companies routinely exchange electronic invoices and other business forms directly from one computer to another in a scheme called *electronic data interchange (EDI).* CommerceNet, a Silicon

Valley electronic marketplace of 20 big companies, including Intel, Apple Computer, Hewlett-Packard, Sun Microsystems, and Pacific Bell, is designed to get purchase orders through the valley to help companies conduct business electronically. The firm's $12 million computer-connection project, backed by federal, state, and private funds to finance development of software, is the prototype of the superhighway of the future.[15]

Computing in the 1980s typically involved one person performing one task on a single system. Today, computer networks make it easier for people to obtain and share information, even across locations. In fact, networks will become a required tool for business success in the increasingly competitive environment.[16]

local area network (LAN)
Computer network that connects machines within a limited area.

Many companies connect different offices and buildings by creating **local area networks (LANs),** computer networks that connect machines within limited areas (such as one building or several buildings near each other). LANs are useful in many businesses because they can link microcomputers and allow them to share printers and information.

The development of powerful microprocessors has allowed LANs to replace mainframes at many companies. Employees at Motorola's computer group, for example, used to rely on two large IBM mainframes. Today they do the same work on three local area networks that link more than 1,000 microcomputers and 25 to 30 minicomputers. The shift has saved Motorola money; while each of the huge mainframes costs the company $30,000 a month to program and maintain, the equivalent computing power in a network format costs just $10,000 a month. Motorola's MIS costs used to consume 3.7 percent of sales; today they are down to 1.2 percent.[17]

Computer networks also allow various departments, such as purchasing, finance, and marketing, to contribute to comparisons of actual sales with sales forecasts. The results of such comparisons may show a need to change production, finance, or marketing plans. Cakebread Cellars is a family owned winery situated in the fiercely competitive wine-producing area of Napa Valley, California. Cakebread has fought for awards, name recognition, and shelf space in a crowded market and won. The key to its success has been its information network that connects the vineyards to the barrel rooms to the business office.[18]

Computer networks have their disadvantages, too. Organizations must carefully plan and control networks. Otherwise, each division might develop its own system that resists efforts to link up with other divisions' systems. Issues of privacy and security also arise. Should everyone in the company be able to access all of the mainframe's data? What about confidential human resource files? Is it safe to give all employees access to the corporation's payroll system? Later, the chapter will examine several of these issues.

HOW COMPUTERS HELP BUSINESS

Computers have changed how people spend their workdays, the skills they need, and the leverage they can bring to their work. Software programs such as ManagePro by Avantos help management to set goals, monitor progress, review personnel and sales performance, and give informal feedback. Roger Corea, vice president for the Northeast region of IDS Financial Services, supervises 15 division vice presidents from his home office in Fairport, New York. Not only does ManagePro help to make Corea better organized and more efficient, but his stress level is a lot lower, too.[19]

Almost every industry has felt the impact of computers and information systems. In addition to fax machines and cellular phones, other important applications include word processing, desktop publishing, decision support systems, spreadsheets, electronic mail, voice processing, multimedia computing, and interactive media.

word processing
Use of computers to write, store, retrieve, edit, and print text materials.

WORD PROCESSING

One of the most popular business applications, **word processing,** uses computers to type, store, retrieve, edit, and print various types of documents. If you have ever used a type-

Networked computers allow film editors in New York and Los Angeles to simultaneously edit a movie. Telecommunications technology from Sprint, combined with computer technology from Silicon Graphics, allows RGA Digital Studios to create a wide area network and edit film at the same time on both coasts.

writer to write a paper, you know the advantages of a personal computer in revising sentences, checking spelling, and correcting mistakes.

Word processing helps a company to handle huge volumes of correspondence, process numerous documents, and personalize form letters. Some firms may use special-purpose computers, called *dedicated word processors,* designed exclusively for this purpose. However, most word processing involves general-purpose computers running special word processing software packages such as AppleWriter, WordPerfect, MacWrite, or WordStar.

DESKTOP PUBLISHING

Another development takes word processing even further. **Desktop publishing** employs a computer system to allow companies to design and produce attractively formatted printed material in-house. Desktop publishing software combines high-quality type, graphics, and layouts to create output that frequently looks as attractive as documents produced by professional publishers and printers. Advanced equipment can scan photos and drawings and duplicate them on the printed page. Firms often use desktop publishing systems to print newsletters, reports, and form letters.

desktop publishing
Software designed to print attractively formatted documents with high-quality type, graphics, and layouts.

Winning Forms, produced by Random House, is a book-disk package designed to work in conjunction with many major software packages, such as Word for Windows, WordPerfect, Lotus 1-2-3, and Quattro Pro. Winning Forms provides templates for many office procedures, including mailing labels, invoices, purchase orders, expense reports, business cards, résumés, and press releases.[20] Advertising and graphic arts departments often use desktop publishing systems to create brochures and marketing materials. A good desktop publishing system can save a company money by allowing it to produce such documents in-house.

Bissett Nursery Corp. stands out in an industry that is not known for state-of-the-art technology. About 10 years ago, the three-generation family business located on Long Island installed a $135,000 IBM System 36, complete with customized software, and the company immediately began to grow faster than ever before. As soon as they analyzed the first computer results, Bissett management recognized that they could now know more about their customers than they had ever dreamed. By simply categorizing information from inquiries, surveys, warranty cards, and actual orders, they compiled detailed information on types of products ordered by geographic location, household, age group, and income level. Bissett used this information to better match offerings to specific customer segments, and it saw its customer base jump from 600 to 7,500.

The firm's next technology-related purchase was a $40,000 desktop-publishing hardware and software system that permitted Bissett to publish its own catalogs aimed at different customer groups. The firm saved enough on the cost of the first issue to pay for the new system. In 1990, Bissett management decided that computer imaging could change the way in which products in the landscaping and nursery business were sold. Within 30 days, Bissett's new imaging system was in operation, complete with a database of landscaping photographs. Not only was Bissett the industry pioneer in computer imaging, but the firm also assisted many of its landscaping and nursery customers in installing their own imaging systems linked to the Bissett system.[21]

DECISION SUPPORT SYSTEMS

decision support system (DSS) *Computer system that quickly provides relevant facts to aid business decision making.*

A **decision support system (DSS)** is a computer system that quickly provides relevant facts to help businesspeople make decisions. It includes software tools that help decision makers to generate the information they need. DSS tools may vary from company to company, but they typically include software that helps people obtain needed information from a database, simulation software that lets employees create computer models to evaluate future company performance under different conditions, and presentation software that lets them create graphs and charts.

SPREADSHEETS

spreadsheet *Computer software that permits businesspeople to manipulate decision variables to determine their effects.*

An electronic **spreadsheet** is the computerized equivalent of an accountant's worksheet. This software package permits businesspeople to manipulate decision variables to determine their impact on such outcomes as profits or sales. Lotus 1-2-3 is a popular spreadsheet software package.

Figure 17.5 demonstrates how a manager uses a spreadsheet to set a price for a proposed product. Assume that the firm will market a proposed new-product entry at $8 per unit. It can produce the product for $4 in variable costs per unit. Total fixed costs of

This ad for Adobe Pagemaker desktop publishing software includes award winning brochures, publications, promotional materials, and company mailers created with the product.

FIGURE 17.5 HOW A SPREADSHEET WORKS

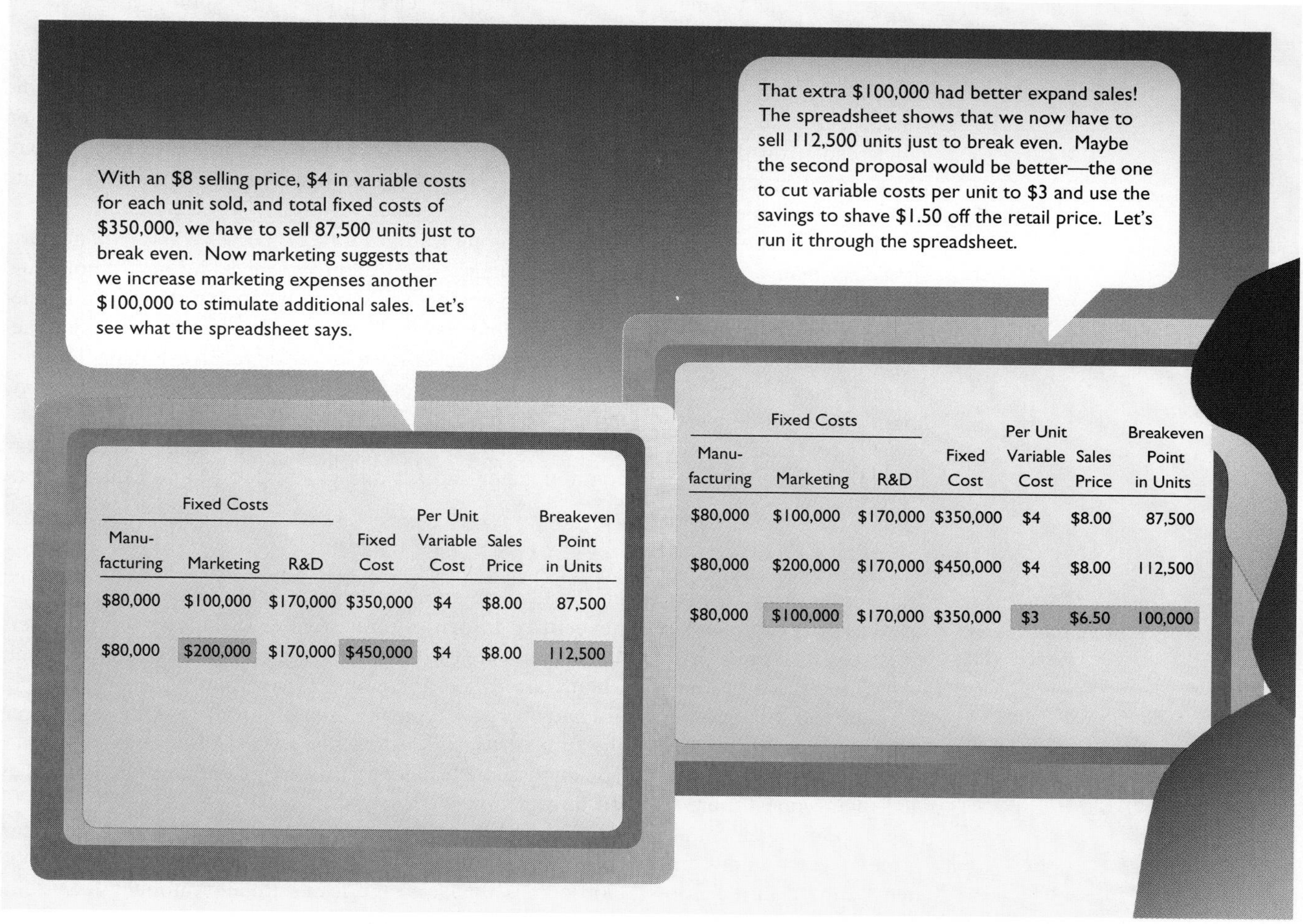

$350,000 include $80,000 for such manufacturing overhead outlays as salaries, general office expenses, rent, utilities, and interest charges; $100,000 for marketing expenditures; and $170,000 for research and development on the product. The spreadsheet calculation, using the basic breakeven model introduced in Chapter 14, reveals that sales of 87,500 units are necessary to cover all costs and break even.

What if the firm's marketing director persuades other members of the group to increase marketing expenditures to $200,000? As the first computer screen shows, the $100,000 increase in marketing expenditures boosts total fixed costs to $450,000, raising the newly calculated breakeven point to 112,500 units. As soon as the analyst changes figures in one or more cells, the computer immediately recalculates all figures. This eliminates the tedious chore of recalculating and revising figures by hand.

The second computer screen demonstrates the impact of a reduction in variable costs to $3.00 by switching to lower-cost materials coupled with a $1.50 reduction in the product's selling price. The new breakeven point is 100,000 units.

This relatively simple example demonstrates the ease with which a manager can use a spreadsheet to analyze alternative decisions. A more complex spreadsheet may stretch across 50 columns, or even wider, but the spreadsheet makes new calculations as fast as the manager can change the variables.

ELECTRONIC MAIL

electronic mail (e-mail) *System for sending and receiving written messages through computers.*

Another popular business use for computers is **electronic mail (e-mail),** a system for sending and receiving written messages from one computer to another via phone lines. To send a message to co-workers, for instance, you would just type in the message, indicate who should receive it, and signal the computer to send it. The computer saves the message in a special file. When your co-workers sign on, they can retrieve the written note, read it on the screen, and dispose of it as they wish—either by printing a hard copy on paper, storing it electronically, forwarding it to other people, answering it with another e-mail message, or just deleting it altogether.

In an average year, more than 16 billion messages travel by e-mail. With the increase in usage, many business cards now include e-mail addresses in addition to phone and fax numbers.[22] Certainly, e-mail can help companies to reduce paper, time wasted in telephone tag, and time necessary to communicate with many different people. Employees must obviously be able to use a computer in order to send or receive e-mail. Furthermore, it may still be more convenient to send long letters on paper, either by fax or by traditional mail delivery.[23] Figure 17.6 illustrates how Sony's Magic Link makes it possible to reach just about anyone in a city of 8 million people. In addition to its e-mail capabilities, the lightweight communicator can fax and page other Magic Link partners.

EXECUTIVE INFORMATION SYSTEMS

executive information system (EIS) *User-friendly, decision-oriented computer system used by senior management.*

Sometimes firms create specialized information systems to address the needs of employees at specific levels. An **executive information system (EIS)** allows top managers to access the firm's primary databases, often by touching the computer screen or pointing with a piece of computer hardware called a *mouse.* EIS software typically produces easy-to-read, full-color graphics and charts. A typical EIS allows users to choose between many kinds of data, such as the firm's financial statements, sales figures, and stock market trends for the company and industry. Managers can start by looking at summaries and then request more detailed information if they wish.

Top management at Kmart, the nation's second-largest retailer behind Wal-Mart, can retrieve an enormous amount of detailed, daily information on sales of any of the 100,000 items carried in the firm's 2,500 outlets thanks to the firm's Retail Automation System.

FIGURE 17.6

COMMUNICATIONS MADE EASY THROUGH E-MAIL

Satellite dishes attached to the tops of all stores transmit daily sales reports to a mainframe at company headquarters. If a company official wants to determine yesterday's sales of the popular Times Indiglo workout watch, the information is available within a matter of seconds. Want to compare per-store sales of the item in Oregon with those in Maryland? A simple query will display the data in a full-color chart on the screen.

EXPERT SYSTEMS

expert system
Computer program that imitates human thinking through the use of "if . . . then" rules.

Expert systems are computer programs that imitate human thinking through complicated sets of "if . . . then" rules. These systems apply human knowledge in specific subject areas in order to solve problems.

Alamo Rent-A-Car Inc. uses an expert system to help employees decide how to price rental cars. The system continually compares Alamo's prices to those of competitors and identifies cases in which Alamo's rates differ. For instance, the demand for rental cars soars every October in Albuquerque, New Mexico when the city hosts international hot-air balloon races. Alamo's expert system signals employees when competitors' prices start rising to meet this peak demand, allowing Alamo to raise its prices, too. The system also catches data-entry errors. By making employees more productive, the system enabled Alamo to keep up with a 25 percent increase in business in 1 year without having to hire additional staff.[24]

Figure 17.7 illustrates an expert system that might be developed based on relevant facts and information regarding misfiring in an auto engine. If you take your car to a repair shop with such a complaint, the mechanic will generally follow some rules to diagnose the problem. The process usually begins by listening to the engine, then checking the distributor and the spark plugs one by one if misfiring is detected. The step-by-step expert system approach solves problems based on "If x, then y" relationships developed from a knowledge base accumulated over years of experience, classes, listening to other mechanics, and reading books and repair manuals.

VOICE PROCESSING

Voice processing technologies use spoken language to send or receive information from a computer, typically over the telephone. For example, automated telephone ordering systems allow customers to order catalog merchandise from some retailers. Montgomery

Top management at Kmart can use the firm's EIS to track sales, inventory levels, and geographic variations in purchase patterns.

FIGURE 17.7 PARTIAL EXPERT SYSTEM FOR AUTO ENGINE REPAIR

IF the engine is misfiring **AND**
IF the plug wires are worn,

THEN turn off the engine, replace the plug wires, turn on the engine, listen again for misfiring cylinders.

IF the engine fires properly, **QUIT.**

IF the engine is misfiring **AND**
IF the distributor cap is cracked,

THEN turn off the engine, replace the distributor cap, turn on the engine, listen again for misfiring cylinders.

IF the engine fires properly, **QUIT.**

IF the engine is misfiring **AND**
IF any spark plug tests faulty,

THEN turn off the engine, replace all spark plugs, turn on the engine, listen again for misfiring cylinders.

IF the engine fires properly, **QUIT.**

IF the engine is misfiring **AND**
IF the fuel filter is clogged,

THEN turn off the engine, replace the filter element, turn on the engine, listen again for misfiring cylinders.

IF the engine fires properly, **QUIT.**

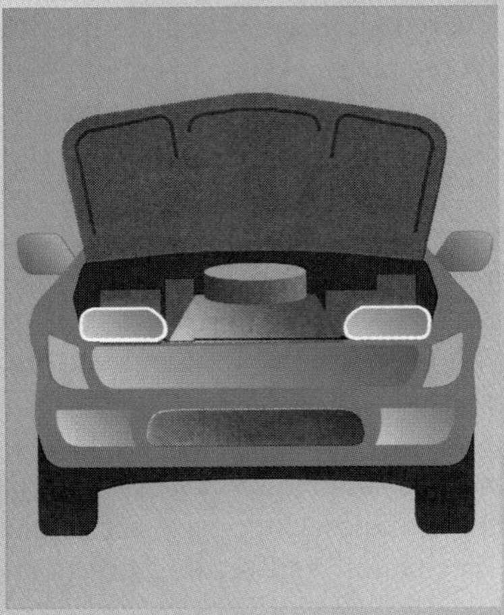

Ward uses voice processing to help a customer find the closest store. The customer calls an 800 phone number and enters a zip code; then a synthesized voice provides the location and phone number of the nearest store.

Voice processing can also improve customer service, while helping companies to keep down their costs. Emerson Electric's In-Sink-Erator Division in Wisconsin offers a toll-free phone line with automated tips on fixing garbage disposals. Says Julie Bezotte, customer service manager, "It's amazing how many people will call at 1, 2, 3 o'clock in the morning." In the past, those calls would have gone unanswered because the company cannot afford to staff 24-hour specialists. The automated service provides a low-cost alternative.[25]

Speech recognition systems that allow computers to interpret and respond to the human voice are still more common in science fiction than in business. At present, no commercially available system can instantly understand a stranger's conversation. Systems first must be trained to recognize specific individuals' voices and speech patterns. However, voice recognition systems such as VoiceAssist can, once trained, convert almost anything a certain speaker says to written text.[26] Table 17.1 lists the most common uses of voice processing in business today, the companies that offer each service, and the current size of the U.S. market.

Voice recognition systems can be an especially valuable boon for the physically challenged. For example, 3 years ago Don Dalton started Micro Overflow Corp., a Naperville, Illinois–based distributorship that adapts computer technology for the disabled. Dalton,

TABLE 17.1 VOICE PROCESSING IN BUSINESS

BUSINESS USES	DESCRIPTION	COMPANIES OFFERING THE SERVICE	SIZE OF THE U.S. MARKET ($ MILLIONS)
Voice-mail equipment	Allows users to record, store, forward, and broadcast voice messages with touch-tone phones	Octel, AT&T, Northern Telecom, Rolm, VMX	$930
Voice-mail service	Instead of buying special equipment to handle voice mail, some companies prefer to use outside services	Local phone companies, service bureaus, Baby Bell holding companies, long-distance carriers	363
Voice response gear	Responding to prerecorded cues, callers can instruct a computer to complete a transaction or recite information by pushing the correct key on a touch-tone phone	AT&T, Syntellect, Inter-Voice, Dytel	406
Audiotex service	Supplies recorded entertainment information over the phone, sometimes with voice response capabilities	Call Interactive, an AT&T-American Express joint venture; Universal Studios, MTV	900
Automatic call distributors	Parcels out incoming calls to operators	Rockwell, AT&T, Rolm, Northern Telecom, Teknekron, Aspect, Solid State Systems	493
Speech recognition	Lets computers interpret and respond to the human voice	AT&T, Texas Instruments, Kurzweil, Dragon, Verbex, Voice Control Systems	100

who is paralyzed from the chest down, runs his computer by voice. Speaking into a microphone in a headset connected to a PC, he can activate all of the computer's functions, type 100 words a minute, and manage the firm's finances and scheduling. Dalton expects sales to top $1 million this year, but another goal is far more important to him. "I want the millions of people who are disabled and unemployed to be working for a living and be happy with themselves."[27]

MULTIMEDIA COMPUTING

multimedia computing
Technologies that facilitate the integration of two or more types of media, such as text, voice, sound, full-motion video, still video, graphics, and/or animation into a single, computer-based application.

Multimedia computing refers to technologies that facilitate the integration of two or more types of media, such as text, voice, sound, full-motion video, still video, graphics, and/or animation into a computer-based application. For example, *Compton's MultiMedia Encyclopedia* is an electronic reference work that includes 15,000 illustrations, many in full color, plus 45 animated sequences, an hour of audio clips of famous speeches and music, and *Webster's Intermediate Dictionary*. Today, 8 percent of U.S. homes have multimedia PCs, one in every three PCs sold includes multimedia capabilities, and it is estimated that by 1997, multimedia will be a $28 billion business.[28]

Figure 17.8 illustrates dramatically how materials from electronic reference sources (on Africa, in this case) can come alive, surrounding the user with vivid colors and patterns, action sequences, and the sounds of the country and animals being studied.

Among the more promising business applications for multimedia computing are employee training and business presentations. Employees at Bethlehem Steel Corp., for

FIGURE 17.8

MULTIMEDIA COMPUTING: COMBINING TEXT, VOICE, GRAPHICS, AND ANIMATION

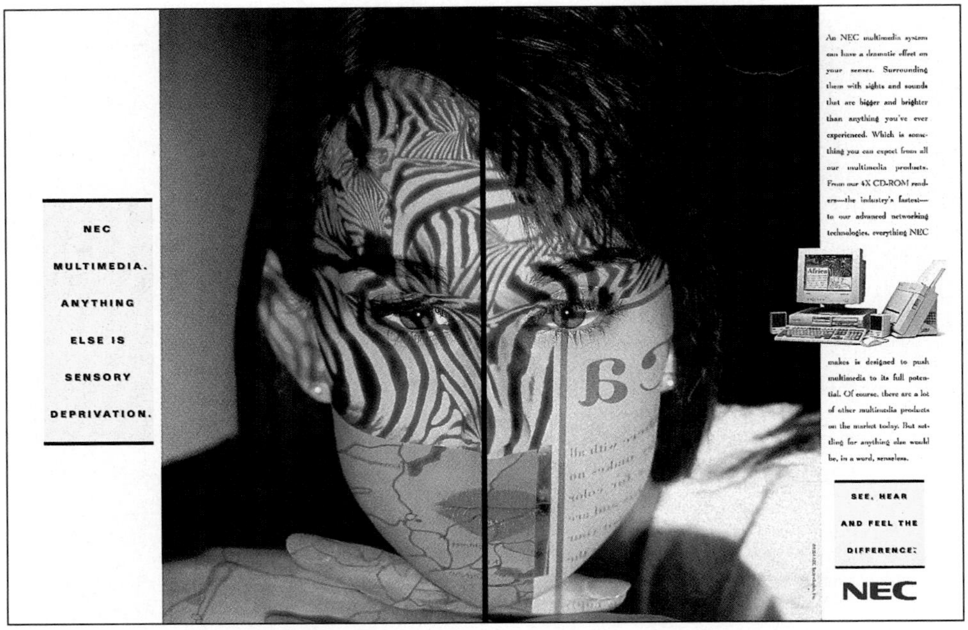

instance, learn new steel production techniques from a video-based multimedia program that shows them how to analyze production, inventory, and sales statistics to control the availability of different types of steel. The multimedia approach has reduced training time at Bethlehem Steel by 20 percent to 40 percent.[29]

Many multimedia applications are programmed on *CD-ROM* (compact disk-read only memory) disks because the spiral-type storage pattern is well suited for retrieving continuous blocks of data, such as converted music or animation sequences. CD-ROMs are also useful because of their durability and large capacity. A single CD-ROM can store 680 megabytes of any kind of data, the equivalent of more than 1,000 floppy disks or a stack of books 10 stories tall.[30]

INTERACTIVE MEDIA AND GROUPWARE

While multimedia computing combines multiple technologies, interactive media focuses more on multiple applications of one technology. *Interactive media* are program applications that allow users to interact with computers to perform several different functions at the same time. For example, computer chip manufacturer Intel and Cable News Network are developing a system that allows the user to view CNN broadcasts in a small window on the computer screen. In addition to simply watching the program, a viewer can retrieve news clips later by subject heading. "Instead of TV being something that happens to you, it can be something you control," says Steven McGeady, vice president of Intel's media delivery lab.[31]

Interactive media will inevitably change the way most people live their lives. A recent study indicates, however, that the largest growth in interactive media will occur in the next few years. Although most U.S. households are equipped with information technology ranging from VCRs and answering machines to personal computers and fax machines, a substantial lack of awareness and interest still inhibits progress of interactive media. Of the 38 percent of survey respondents who were very interested in at least one interactive TV service, the majority—over 56 percent—were between the ages of 18 and 24.[32]

Interactive video allows the TV viewer to select menu options using either a keyboard or a remote control. The science fiction of yesterday's computerized world is closer

Novell is one of many telecommunication companies providing groupware that brings people together through information technologies.

to reality as the television becomes more than an entertainment medium. TV has finally grown to include an increasing number of business and educational applications. Out of 100 million U.S. households, one-third of which own PCs, 7 million people already subscribe to interactive services such as CompuServe, Prodigy, and America Online. CEO Walter Forbes of Stamford, Connecticut-based CUC International shopping service says: "This is virtual-reality inventory. We stock nothing, but we sell everything."[33]

An especially useful interactive medium is **groupware,** computer software that combines and extends the concept of sharing information through a database with a method for moving data between users (e-mail). Groupware is effective as a primary means of collaboration among users. Employees at the accounting and consulting firm Price Waterhouse use Lotus Development Corp.'s Notes groupware to keep in touch with more than 18,000 co-workers in 22 countries. Lotus Notes combines a sophisticated electronic mail system with a huge database of work records and memos. Employees can consult over 1,000 *electronic bulletin boards* (public message centers that appear on computer networks) to learn about and obtain information on a variety of services and industries. They can also give their computers standing orders to locate and retrieve the latest news articles on specific topics.[34]

groupware
Computer software that combines and extends the concept of sharing information through a networked database with a method for moving data between users (e-mail).

INFORMATION SYSTEMS AND SECURITY

As information systems become more important to business, they also become harder to replace. However, natural disasters, power failures, equipment malfunctions, and human error can disrupt even the most sophisticated system. When computers are connected to a network, a problem at any location can affect the entire network. An organization needs to prepare backup plans so it can continue operating if the computer system fails.

While many computer security issues go beyond the scope of this textbook, this section will discuss two important security threats: computer crime and viruses. These threats are so real that the Clinton administration is proposing to require installation of the so-called *Clipper Chip* in telephones, faxes, computer modems, and any other equipment necessary for traveling the information superhighway. The Clipper is a digital scrambler that puts messages and data into a secret code to restrict access to the information to the intended receiver.[35]

A BROADER PURPOSE

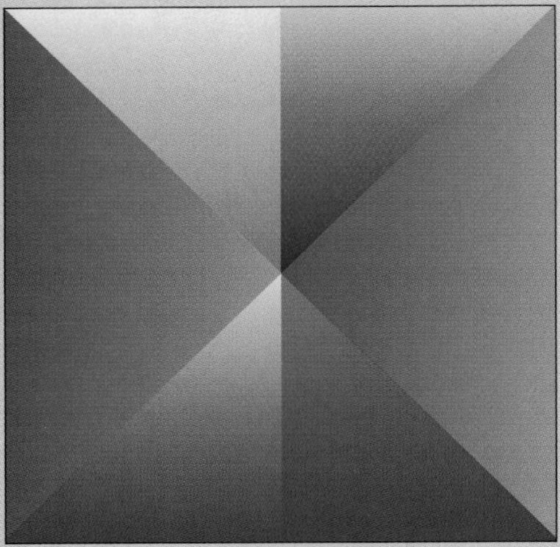

POLICING CYBERSPACE Cybercops and cryptocriminals have brought James Bond-like drama to the Internet. Although no one knows the exact extent of invasion of e-mail privacy and actual white-collar technocrime, it's generally conceded that damages start in the billions of dollars. The big question is how to give information to legitimate users, but still shield it from others to protect it as a valuable asset. ■ Because today's communications systems are so interconnected, it has become almost impossible to restrict access to even the most secret information. As one Internet expert expressed it, "The Internet is nothing like a superhighway. It's an organism." This mass of interconnected information networks allows each one to quickly switch lanes and directions. With 20 million users scattered around the globe, the task of policing activity is a daunting one. As a result, privacy is a concern for millions of e-mail users. As author-cryptographer Bruce Schneier puts it, "Without encryption, e-mail is no more secure than a postcard." ■ Virtually all white-collar crime today involves a computer or telecommunications link. It ranges from the local bike shop bookkeeper who records sales as returned merchandise and then pockets the cash to skilled computer wizards who crack encrypted secret files of businesses and government agencies. ■ Intruders have learned how to penetrate sophisticated barriers and hijack computer systems linked to the Internet, posing a global security threat. Once they gain high-level access to host computers, these high-tech invaders can copy, change, or destroy documents. ■ The new enforcer has a new label: *cybercop*. "The day is coming very fast when every cop will be issued a badge, a gun, and a laptop," says Charles Rinkevich, director of the Federal Law Enforcement Training Center. In addition to handcuffs and bullet-proof vests, these police officers will be armed with modems, cellular phones, and cryptography textbooks. Until better methods of data security and privacy protection are developed, doing business in cyberspace will require sophisticated methods of encryption to thwart code-breakers. ■ The controversy continues as individuals and businesses alike try to find ways to protect and, at the same time, share information. One solution that experts feel is inevitable is that Internet users will be charged for information, much as today's commercial databases serve paying customers. Until then, the problem continues to await a space-age solution. Sources: Vic Sussman, "Policing Cyberspace," *U.S. News & World Report,* January 23, 1995, pp. 55–60; and "Hackers Threaten Internet's Security," *Mobile Press Register,* January 24, 1995, p. 7B.

QUESTIONS FOR CRITICAL THINKING

1. What methods other than charging a fee might protect businesses in cyberspace?
2. Does cyberspace need a specialized police force? Why or why not?
3. Would you send sensitive information about yourself or the company you own through e-mail? Why or why not?

COMPUTER CRIME

Computers can be effective work tools. Unfortunately, they can also be effective tools for criminals. Computer crime falls into three general categories:

1. Data can be changed or invented to produce inaccurate information.
2. Computer programs can be changed to create false information or illegal transactions.
3. Unauthorized people can get access to computer systems for their own illicit benefit.

Every year, U.S. companies lose over one-half billion dollars to computer crime. Often they are reluctant to admit it publicly, fearing the negative image among the public. Table 17.2 describes general controls that organizations can use to protect their information systems.

TABLE 17.2 MEASURES TO PROTECT INFORMATION SYSTEMS

Control	Example
Hardware	Restricting access to machines/terminals; checking for equipment malfunctions
Software	Requiring logs of operating-system activities; restricting unauthorized access to software
Data security	Using passwords; restricting access to terminals to limit access to data files
Operations	Establishing procedures for running computer jobs correctly; establishing backup and recovery procedures for abnormal or disrupted processing
Systems development	Requiring management review and audit of each new information system project for conformity with budget, solution requirements, and quality standards; requiring appropriate technical and business documentation for each system
Management	Establishing formal written policies and procedures; segregating job functions to minimize error and fraud; providing supervision and accountability

COMPUTER VIRUSES

A related problem involves *computer viruses,* programs that secretly attach themselves to other programs and change them or destroy data on a disk. A virus can reproduce by copying itself to other programs stored on the disk. It spreads as the owner of infected software exchanges files with other users, usually by an electronic bulletin board or by trading disks. Viruses can be programmed to remain dormant for a long time, after which the infection suddenly activates itself.

Some viruses result from pranks that get out of hand. One German student sent a Christmas greeting over a computer network that ended up spreading into IBM's international network and within hours attached itself to every mailing list it encountered.

Other viruses involve deliberate crimes. The Michelangelo virus, for example, erases data in computers that are used on March 6, the Italian artist's birthday. In one year, 18.2 percent of major U.S. companies reported systems infected by this virus. It also infected computers in England, the Netherlands, Austria, and South Africa.

To protect against computer viruses, experts recommend the following steps:[36]

- Buy software only in its original shrink-wrapping or sealed container.
- Make backup copies of all new software as soon as you open the package, and store the originals away from the workplace.
- Quarantine each new piece of software by reviewing it carefully on a computer that is not connected to a network.
- Restrict access to data and programs wherever possible.
- Check all programs regularly for changes in the amount of memory they use; any change could be a sign of tampering.
- Use shareware or freeware programs (software that users on a network share with each other) cautiously.

- Develop a plan to immediately remove from the computer system all copies of suspicious programs and related data.

Antivirus programs are also available to help computer users detect and erase computer viruses.[37]

GOING GLOBAL ON THE INFORMATION SUPERHIGHWAY

In the past few years, the information superhighway has grown to more closely resemble an information *air*way, since it now spans the globe. France has swapped nearly all of its old-fashioned telephone switches for new digital ones. Singapore has built a state-of-the-art communications network to encourage international investment. Nippon Telegraph & Telephone Corporation plans to interconnect every Japanese home, school, and business with fiber-optic cables by 2015. Is the United States ready to keep up with the traffic on this global highway?

New technology is expected to merge computers, television, telecommunications, and information systems into a single, interactive information industry, one whose annual revenues could reach a staggering $3.5 trillion worldwide by 2001. President Clinton has included $5 billion in the federal budget over the next few years specifically to develop equipment and software. AT&T, MCI, Sprint, and other telephone companies want to build the information highway and control what people transmit over it. They are focusing on services that generate two-way traffic, such as video phones and long-distance library access—services that can be measured and billed by message units.

Computer companies like IBM and Hewlett-Packard are busy developing file servers to store information and video libraries. Computer software companies such as Microsoft are developing the basic operating systems that will control the flow of information to each home. Entertainment companies are figuring out how to capture some of the $4 billion spent annually on video games, the $12 billion spent on video rentals, and the $70 billion spent on catalog shopping by offering these services in the home.

The U.S. computer industry has moved rapidly into international operations. Compaq, the world's leading producer of personal computers, has opened its first office in

Hong Kong-based AST Computers is a global provider of today's newest technology. The firm began its efforts to ensure that Chinese businesses would be on the information superhighway by donating computers to Chinese schools. Today, nearly one of every three computers purchased in that country is made by AST.

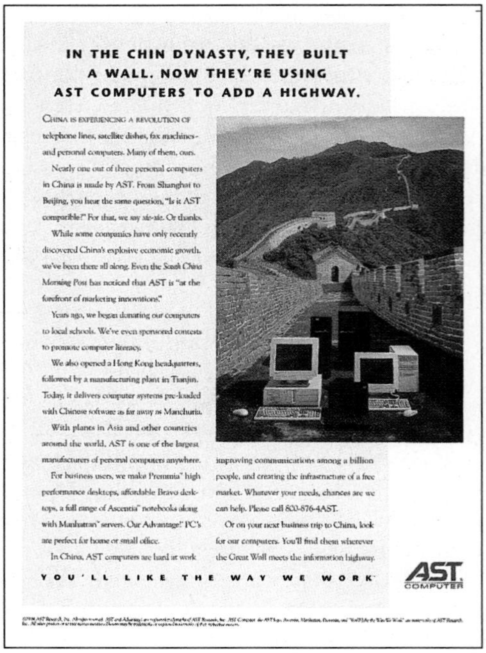

China, and Apple, AST, and IBM have plans to expand operations there, as well. Motorola is perhaps the most international manufacturer in the computer industry. More than 50 years after H-P invented the Handie Talkie for American soldiers to lug through war-torn Europe, portable, wireless, two-way communication is finally becoming a medium for the masses. The Motorola Integrated Radio Service (MIRS) combines all the features of cellular phones, pagers, and two-way radios in a sleek, hand-held device. Another state-of-the-art invention is the Motorola Envoy—a wireless device weighing under 2 pounds that will write and send a fax, retrieve e-mail, interface with online services such as America Online, manage appointments, and keep financial records to mention only a few of its features.

If Motorola continues its current rate of growth, it will generate sales of $270 billion a year by 2013. The company has already gone beyond worldwide status with its sponsorship of Iridium, a $4 billion project to wirelessly interconnect every square mile of the globe via 66 satellites orbiting 420 miles above the earth.[38]

ACHIEVEMENT CHECK SUMMARY

Reread the learning goals that follow, and consider the questions for each goal. Answering these questions will reinforce the most important concepts in the chapter and allow you to check how well you have achieved these learning goals. Where a blank appears before a question, answer with *T* or *F*. Otherwise, circle the letter of the correct answer. An answer key to these questions is found at the end of the chapter.

LEARNING GOAL 17.1: Explain the purpose of an information system and how it aids decision making in business.

1. ___ An information system can turn data inputs into information outputs to support decision making
2. ___ Databases can include data from both internal sources and outside subscription services.
3. ___ Because small firms are better able to track their day-to-day operations, an information system is less critical to them than to large firms.

LEARNING GOAL 17.2: List the major contributions and limitations of computers.

1. All of the following are advantages of computers, *except:* (a) performance of routine, boring tasks; (b) speedy processing of information; (c) seriousness of mistakes made when programmed incorrectly; (d) ability to store and make available large amounts of data.
2. Computers suffer from which of the following limitations? (a) They can alienate customers because they are impersonal. (b) Hardware and software are expensive. (c) They can become crutches rather than tools for effective decision making. (d) All of the above.

LEARNING GOAL 17.3: Distinguish between computer hardware and software.

1. ___ Fax machines, personal computers, and printers are all good examples of software.
2. ___ MS-DOS, Microsoft Windows, and other sets of instructions that tell the computer what to do are known as *software.*

LEARNING GOAL 17.4: Distinguish among mainframe computers, minicomputers, and microcomputers.

1. PCs and laptops are both: (a) miniature computers; (b) microcomputers; (c) minicomputers; (d) macrocomputers; (e) mainframe computers.
2. The largest type of computer system that handles massive amounts of data is known as a: (a) miniature computer; (b) microcomputer; (c) minicomputer; (d) macrocomputer; (e) mainframe computer.

LEARNING GOAL 17.5: Discuss the role of telecommunications in business.

1. ___ Telecommunications systems use telephone lines and other transmission devices to send and receive data.
2. ___ Wireless communication systems and fax machines are not telecommunications devices.
3. ___ While telecommunications systems can link microcomputers and enable them to share information, they do not yet permit microcomputers in different locations to share printers or other output data.

LEARNING GOAL 17.6: Explain the concept of an information superhighway and its implications for business.

1. The information superhighway: (a) is opposed by the U.S. government; (b) will have applications for business, but none for the not-for-profit sector of the economy; (c) will combine telecommunications, information systems, and data networks into a single pathway that will be accessible to all users.
2. It is expected that the information superhighway will help to: (a) reduce the time necessary to transmit data; (b) speed up the

pace of work; (c) overcome geographic and time barriers; (d) all of the above.

LEARNING GOAL 17.7: Identify the major business applications of computers.

1. The computer application that includes typing, storing, retrieving, editing, and printing of documents is: (a) decision support system; (b) word processing software; (c) spreadsheet software; (d) electronic mail.
2. If a manager wants to see how a change in one variable will change the outcome of a calculation, he or she will probably need to use: (a) word processing software; (b) electronic mail; (c) desktop publishing software; (d) spreadsheet software.
3. Technologies that integrate two or more types of media into a computer-based application are known as: (a) multimedia computing; (b) expert systems; (c) voice mail systems; (d) e-mail

LEARNING GOAL 17.8: Summarize the major computer security issues that affect organizations.

1. ___ Organizations need to be prepared with backup plans so they can continue operations if their computer systems fail.
2. ___ When computers are connected to a network a problem at any location can affect the entire network.
3. ___ All computer crime involves the deliberate use of computer viruses.

KEY TERMS

management information system (MIS) 470
chief information officer (CIO) 470
database 470
computer 472
hardware 474
software 475
microcomputer 475
telecommunications 477
information superhighway 478
computer network 479
local area network (LAN) 480
word processing 480
desktop publishing 481
decision support system (DSS) 482
spreadsheet 482
electronic mail (e-mail) 484
executive information system (EIS) 484
expert system 485
multimedia computing 487
groupware 489

REVIEW QUESTIONS

1. Explain the purpose of a management information system and its functions in an organization.

2. What major contributions do computers make? What potential problems are involved with their use? Suggest steps to minimize each of these problems.

3. Categorize each of the following computer system components as either hardware or software and defend your choice:
   a. CD-ROM
   b. Company's customer database
   c. Groupware
   d. Word processing program
   e. Keyboard
   f. Computer instruction manual
   g. Line printer

4. Differentiate among mainframes, minicomputers, and microcomputers.

5. What is telecommunications? Describe its impact on business operations.

6. List at least two computer applications for each of the following areas of business:
   a. Human resources
   b. Marketing
   c. Physical distribution
   d. Production and inventory control
   e. Customer service
   f. Legal
   g. Finance and accounting

7. Explain the term *information superhighway.* Which industries are likely to profit from such a pathway? Which might suffer financially from it?

8. What is multimedia computing? Give several examples.

9. Discuss how groupware might change business procedures and working relationships.

10. Explain why businesspeople need to think about computer security and possible threats to their information systems.

DISCUSSION QUESTIONS

1. Ragnar Vanderhorn, a computer programmer at Tandum Computers, was doing contract work for a San Diego–based software publisher when he accidentally acquired a disk infected with a computer virus. Unsuspecting, he ran the infected disk on his office computer. Later, he reviewed one of the publisher's programs on the same computer and, unknowingly, infected his own company's program. Ragnar returned the program to the publisher, which in turn copied the infected program into its nationwide system. Discuss ways to prevent instances of this nature.

2. Discuss how your college or university uses information systems.

3. Keep a diary for 2 or 3 days recording each time a computer affects your life. Discuss what you learned from the exercise.

4. The Clinton administration wants U.S. companies to begin installing an encryptor—a digital scrambler that puts messages into secret code—in various information system components, including computers, telephones, and fax machines. The encryptor, called the *Clipper Chip,* would make users secure from computer hackers and competitors, who would be unable to crack the code. However, law enforcement agencies, with court orders, would be able to monitor the output of these chips. FBI Director Louis Freeh defends the encryptor concept as a necessity in an age where conventional wiretapping is fast becoming obsolete. However, many U.S. manufacturers claim that this would hurt their sales, especially in fast-growing overseas markets.

Do you feel the government should require U.S. companies to install such a device? Defend your answer.

5. Interview someone who has recently started using a computer at work. Ask this person to compare his or her job before and after the computer was introduced. How has the job changed? Does this employee feel the computer is an asset, a drawback, or both? Why?

SOLUTIONS TO ACHIEVEMENT CHECK SUMMARY

L. G. 17.1: 1. T, 2. T, 3. F **L. G. 17.2:** 1. c, 2. d **L. G. 17.3:** 1. F, 2. T **L. G. 17.4:** 1. b, 2. e **L. G. 17.5:** 1. T, 2. F, 3. F **L. G. 17.6:** 1. c, 2. d **L. G. 17.7:** 1. b, 2. d, 3. a **L. G. 17.8:** 1. T, 2. T, 3. F

VIDEO CASE

UNITED PARCEL SERVICE Fare wars among airlines, taste wars among cold drinks, and price wars among burger chains seem to have become as much a part of the business landscape as the companies themselves. United Parcel Service has been engaged in a fierce delivery-service war with competitors such as DHL, Airborne, and Federal Express for years. Regardless of the industry involved, an important key in winning such wars is information, both about the firm itself and about its competitors.

Current and accurate information is a necessity in every business environment today. Both service companies and goods-producing firms must know the strengths, weaknesses, opportunities, and threats within their own organization, as well as those of competitors. For instance, UPS managers were extremely concerned when FedEx introduced a new PC-based system that lets even its smallest customer print shipping labels, request package pickup, and track delivery without using a telephone. The new system, FedEx Ship, requires only a modem. When Dennis Jones, FedEx Chief Information Officer (CIO), said, "We have to create new technological capabilities so we never become a standing target," everyone at UPS was listening.

UPS countered the new FedEx service by creating an alliance with Prodigy and CompuServe that allows customers to book shipping orders 24 hours a day through their online services. The move was highly effective, since many UPS customers use these two information service providers and are already navigating the information superhighway. This not only held on to former UPS customers, but also attracted new ones.

UPS didn't stop there. Since 1985, the firm has increased the size of its information systems group from 118 to over 4,000 staffers, at the same time increasing allotted funds from $40 million to $200 million annually. In 1993, UPS created the first nationwide mobile data service by placing data collection computers in its 53,000 vehicles. Through efforts like these and with a 10-year, $3 billion technology plan, the firm hopes to strengthen electronic links with its 1.2 million customers.

Although UPS trails rivals DHL and FedEx in global market share, the new focus on technology has allowed the Atlanta-based firm to compete, both in domestic markets and abroad. Its UPS Worldwide Logistics subsidiary faces heavy competition for global distribution, warehousing, and inventory management, but UPS has managed to deliver 3 billion packages a year to 200 countries and territories, and it employs over 303,000 people throughout the world. Priorities in servicing the international market include a new customer automation system and worldwide installation of on-truck computers. A revamped package tracking system will service UPS's 25,000 largest customers. The firm plans to invest $100 million annually for the next few years on customer automation alone. By late 1996, UPS will be able to provide real-time electronic data on each of the 12 million packages it ships daily around the world.

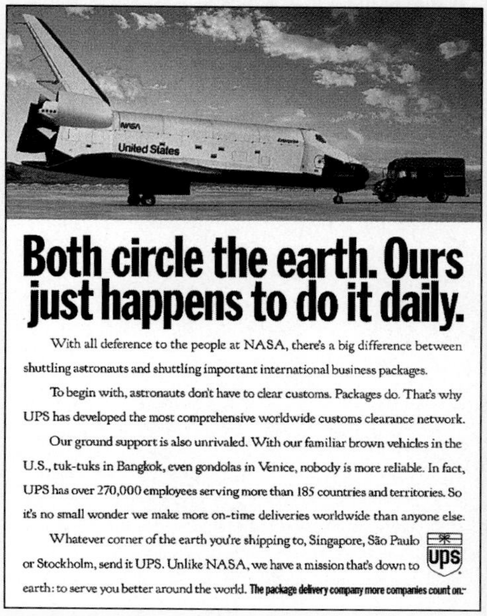

Both circle the earth. Ours just happens to do it daily.
With all deference to the people at NASA, there's a big difference between shuttling astronauts and shuttling important international business packages.
To begin with, astronauts don't have to clear customs. Packages do. That's why UPS has developed the most comprehensive worldwide customs clearance network.
Our ground support is also unrivaled. With our familiar brown vehicles in the U.S., tuk-tuks in Bangkok, even gondolas in Venice, nobody is more reliable. In fact, UPS has over 270,000 employees serving more than 185 countries and territories. So it's no small wonder we make more on-time deliveries worldwide than anyone else.
Whatever corner of the earth you're shipping to, Singapore, São Paulo or Stockholm, send it UPS. Unlike NASA, we have a mission that's down to earth: to serve you better around the world. The package delivery company more companies count on.
UPS

There are 14,648 golf courses nationwide. Guess who delivers to all of them.
Okay, so the pants gave it away. But the bigger story is UPS delivers overnight to every address coast to coast each business day. We also guarantee 10:30 a.m. delivery, and can track your package in seconds. Of course, we do it all very quickly and quietly. Which people at 14,648 clubs really appreciate. For a pick up, call 1-800-PICK-UPS. The package delivery company more companies count on.
UPS

In addition to its new emphasis on technology, UPS has been made aware of the importance of the human element in business. In the past, the firm set on-time delivery as paramount in importance in customer service. Top management at UPS was so focused on shaving seconds off delivery time that package delivery people knew how long it took elevator doors in downtown office buildings to open. Corners were shaved off driver's seats so they could save microseconds when getting in or out of the van. A carefully designed marketing survey on customer quality expectations revealed, however, that many UPS customers faulted the firm for deficiencies. They liked quick, efficient service, but they also wanted human interaction; that is, they wanted to have another human being explain things or answer questions face to face. As a result of this research, UPS allotted each driver an extra 30 minutes a day to talk with customers. Basic communication proved as important as any of the expensive and modern technology systems UPS had implemented.

UPS has no intention of sitting by the roadside as other delivery companies fly by on the information superhighway. As CIO Frank Erbrick puts it, "Nobody in the industry will be able to touch us by the year 2000."

QUESTIONS

1.
How does UPS's information system help it maintain a competitive edge in the package delivery business?

2.
Explain the contribution of telecommunications and the information superhighway in UPS's competitive strategy.

3.
Are factors other than speed and on-time delivery important to UPS customers? What might these factors be and how does UPS deal with them?

4.
Is UPS creating potential security issues by using online services such as CompuServe and Prodigy? What are they and how might UPS resolve them?

LEARNING GOALS

1. Explain the functions of accounting and their importance to the firm's management and to outside parties such as investors, creditors, and government agencies.

2. Identify the three basic business activities that involve accounting.

3. Contrast the roles played by public, private, government, and not-for-profit accountants.

4. Outline the steps in the accounting process.

5. Explain the functions of the balance sheet, income statement, and statement of cash flows, and identify their major components.

6. Discuss how accountants use the major financial ratios to analyze a firm's financial strengths and weaknesses.

7. Explain the role of budgets in business.

8. Explain the impact of exchange rates on international accounting and the importance of uniform financial statements for firms engaged in international business.

ACCOUNTING

CHAPTER 18

STEVEN SPIELBERG Mention the name Steven Spielberg and the average moviegoer thinks of *Jurassic Park* or *E.T., The Extra-Terrestrial* or *Jaws* or *Schindler's List* or *Back to the Future.* In fact, the 46-year-old Phoenix native has directed a mind-boggling 6 of the 15 highest-grossing movies of all time. Despite this success, a combination of creative and accounting savvy has made Spielberg a billionaire. ■ As a young teenager, Spielberg was bitten by the movie bug. He made his first full-length movie, *Firelight,* at age 16 with borrowed funds. Spielberg's father gave him a $400 advance on his allowance, and he actually got his money back when the firm generated $500 in ticket sales at a local theater. ■ That same year, the fledgling director received two pieces of advice that would pay huge dividends over the next 3 decades. While spending the summer in Los Angeles with relatives, he sneaked onto the lot at Universal Studios and managed to finagle an interview with the great director John Ford. Ford escorted the adolescent into his office and showed him his collection of Western art. "When you understand what makes a great Western painting, you'll be a great Western director," Ford said. "And never spend your own money to make a movie. Now get the hell out of here!" ■ Although Spielberg has yet to make a Western, he certainly applied the second bit of advice. By taking the time to understand thoroughly the sources of revenues and the costs associated with making and marketing movies, he managed to develop a system in which he accepted the risk of a box-office failure while he retained partial ownership of blockbuster hits. Fortunately for Spielberg, he has enjoyed more of the latter than the former. ■ The recent hit *Jurassic Park* offers a good example of the revenues and costs involved in a major movie. The megahit generated over $900 million in worldwide ticket sales, of which the studio's share amounted to about 50 percent. *Jurassic Park* proved to be just as successful in the video stores during 1994 and 1995 as domestic video sales and rentals produced approximately $255 million and international video distribution generated another $180 million. Licensing fees from an estimated $1 billion in *Jurassic Park* merchandise, ranging from kids' lunch boxes to T-shirts, produced another $100 million in revenues. TV broadcast rights added a final $50 million. ■ From this revenue, the film's owners had to deduct costs. The film's production costs amounted to about $75 million. Another $60 million went for advertising and the cost of over 1,000 prints. Finally, add distribution fees, interest payments, overhead expenses, and other costs. Spielberg's agreement with the studio required him to put up none of his own money, although he would participate 50–50 in any profits the film generated. ■ The agreement proved to be a great one for both Universal and Spielberg. His estimated take from *Jurassic Park* is a cool $262 million—by far the most an individual has ever earned from a movie. Spielberg is so confident in his businesslike approach to the movie industry that he strongly advocates efforts by other actors and directors to understand the revenues and expenses of moviemaking so they will base their compensation on financial returns instead of demanding exorbitant salaries. ■ "I would love to see [movie] people taking more chances. Forgoing all their salaries and not getting money up front. Taking a piece of the action. Everybody goes out and gambles. And then it becomes kind of like a corporate movie—everyone is a shareholder."[1]

CHAPTER OVERVIEW

Steven Spielberg depends on accounting to determine his financial success in much the same way that he assesses his creative success from receiving the Oscar for *Schindler's List.* Just as high-quality scripts, talented actors, and memorable sets are key tools in his creative success, accounting is a key information tool for Spielberg's business performance. The traditional stereotype views an accountant as a pale, bookish male dressed in a white shirt and narrow tie, seated behind a desk in a small office making notations in a dusty ledger. This image has given way to a picture of contributions illustrated in the following example.

Managers at Kroger, the nation's largest supermarket chain, knew they had a problem. The firm's accounting statements revealed the problem, which stemmed from the decision by discounters like Wal-Mart Stores and Kmart Corp. to build supercenters combining discount supermarkets with traditional discount stores. For every $10 in sales, Kroger earned only $0.08—about half what the typical grocery store expects to earn. Managers knew they had to reverse this result, and they turned to the firm's accounting system to help them decide what to do.

The financial statements reported several revealing facts:

- Stores could earn high profits in areas where the supercenters lag—departments carrying perishables like produce and meat.
- Payroll expenses for corporate staff were three times as high as the typical supermarket chain, indicating too many employees at the Cincinnati headquarters and the need to make staff reductions.
- Such seemingly minor expense reductions as replacing 37-cent cake containers with 25-cent versions would add up to substantial boosts to overall profits.
- Adding scanner technology could improve productivity by speeding up the process of pricing newly received inventory and getting it on the shelves.

Kroger management put this information to use. They reduced corporate staff from 1,400 to 400. Adding scanners reduced operating expenses by $142 million. Additional

Kroger's accounting system identified departments with high profit potential and areas in which competing discount supercenters are relatively weak.

changes produced further savings, and 1995 annual profits soared 43 percent above those of the previous year. As one Kroger employee pointed out, just because Wal-Mart moves next door, it doesn't mean that competition will automatically gobble up profits.[2]

Today's accountants are international businesspeople of both genders and from every ethnic background, equipped with personal computers to track sophisticated information. Never before have they been in such demand. In the United States alone, 1 million men and women list their occupation as accountant, and that number increases by the thousands every year. The availability of jobs and the relatively high starting salaries for talented accounting graduates have made accounting one of the most popular business majors on North American college and university campuses.

Accounting is the process of measuring, interpreting, and communicating financial information to enable others inside and outside the firm to make informed decisions. Like statistics, accounting is a language of business. Both profit-seeking and not-for-profit organizations are involved in business functions such as financing, investing, and operating activities. Accountants gather, record, report, and interpret financial information that describes the status and operation of a firm and aids in decision making. They must accomplish three major tasks: score keeping, calling attention to problems and opportunities, and aiding in decision making.

accounting
Measuring, interpreting, and communicating financial information to support internal and external decision making.

This chapter begins by describing the three basic categories of business activities of all organizations: financing, investing, and operating. It explains the accounting process and then discusses the development of accounting statements from information about financial transactions. It describes methods of interpreting these statements and examines the role of budgets in planning and controlling.

USERS OF ACCOUNTING INFORMATION

While accountants are the primary providers of financial information, many people are users. Who is interested in a firm's accounting information? As Figure 18.1 reveals, the list includes people both inside and outside the firm who rely on this information to help make business decisions. Inside the business, government agency, or not-for-profit organization, managers are the major users of accounting information, which helps them to plan and control daily and long-range operations. Owners of the firm and boards of trustees of not-for-profit groups rely on accounting data to determine how well managers are operating the firm or agency. Union officials use accounting data in contract negotiations, and employees refer to it to monitor productivity and profitability.

Outside the firm, potential investors evaluate accounting information to help them decide whether to invest in the company. Bankers and other current and potential lenders find that it helps them determine a company's credit rating and gives them insight into its financial soundness. The Internal Revenue Service and state tax officials use it to evaluate the company's tax payments for the year. Citizens' groups and government agencies use such information to assess the efficiency of a charitable group, local school system, or a city museum or zoo.

ACCOUNTING AND THE ENVIRONMENTS OF BUSINESS

Accountants play fundamental roles, not only in business, but also in other aspects of society. Their work affects each of the environments of business. Accounting information clearly gives managers important help in dealing with the competitive and economic environments. Accounting makes less obvious contributions to efforts to understand, predict, and react to the technological, regulatory, and social/cultural environments.

Accounting information and interpretation of financial reports affect daily business decisions ranging from adjustments in inventory to employee work schedules. When NationsBank management decided to cut nonsalary expenses by $100 million, the Charlotte-based bank's accounting records identified several likely areas for cost-saving:

FIGURE 18.1 USERS OF ACCOUNTING INFORMATION

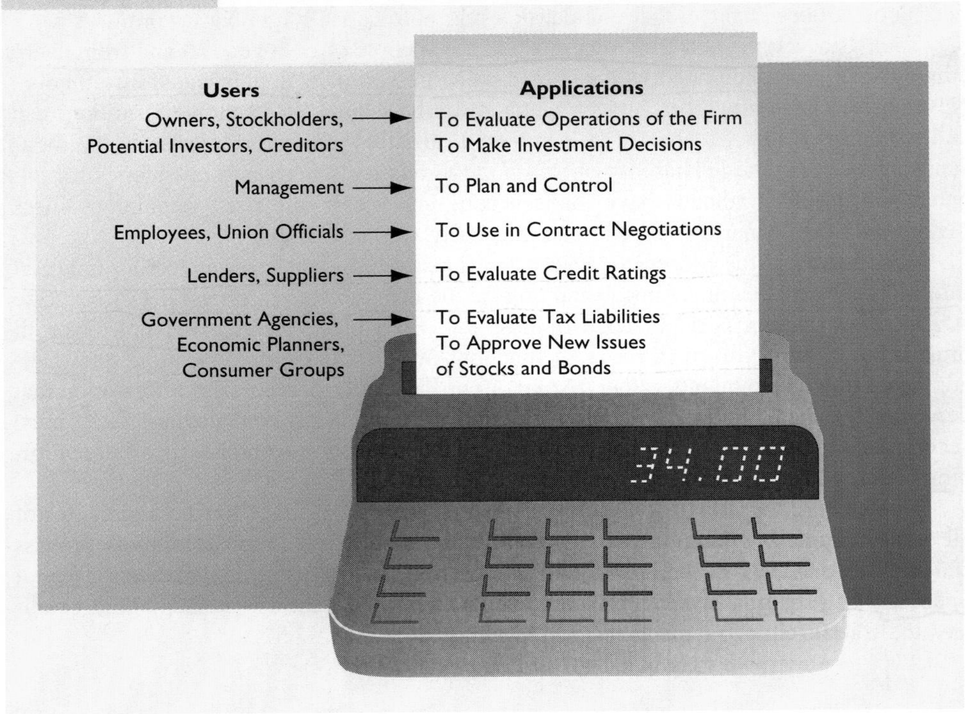

- Annual expenditures of $81 million on travel
- Another $19 million on long-distance phone calls
- Expenses for one copy machine for every 10 employees and $4 million to keep them filled with paper
- An additional $67 million on office supplies, including $200,000 just for Post-It stickers.[3]

On a broader scale, such analyses may lead to decisions such as Kroger's plans to compete profitably in the grocery field by emphasizing high-margin departments and reducing costs. Similar analyses prompted B. F. Goodrich Co., whose name is almost synonymous with tires, to exit the tire business and focus on the less competitive and more profitable chemicals and aerospace industries.[4]

Professional accountants must often provide courts with information in cases involving embezzlement, misrepresentation, fraud, and misuse of funds. In an increasingly automated accounting process, they must be adept in computerized systems and in teaching managers and operative workers how to access this information. Approaching the 21st century, accounting is far different from the bookkeeping stereotype of the past.

BUSINESS ACTIVITIES INVOLVING ACCOUNTING

The natural progression of a business begins with financing, and leads through investing to operating the business. All profit-seeking and not-for-profit organizations perform these three basic activities. Accounting plays a key role in each.

1. *Financing activities* provide necessary funds to start a business and to expand it in the future. The implications of a firm's financial status go beyond the accounting statements. Kroger's $5 billion debt helped it to pay $40 stock dividends, but it also deterred a hostile takeover of the company.

2. *Investing activities* acquire valuable assets to run a business. Kroger invested in scanner technology and automated systems, earning a return of a $142 million reduction in operating costs.
3. *Operating activities* focus on sales of goods and services, but they also must consider expenses as an important part of sound financial management. By substituting a less expensive cake container, Kroger slashed packaging costs by one-third.

For Pentax Corp., financing activities generate funds the firm needs to expand its international operations and compete with such well-known brand names as Minolta and Kodak. Pentax invests these funds in production equipment, raw materials, and research and development activities to produce new products that take advantage of the firm's reputation for high-quality lenses. In addition, the firm seeks the most efficient methods of producing and marketing its output. A current advertising campaign, illustrated by Figure 18.2, uses striking close-up photographs to illustrate the quality, speed, and ease of use of the Pentax IQZoom 115 camera when the family pet goes on a licking rampage.

ACCOUNTING PROFESSIONALS

The 1 million accountants in the United States work in a variety of areas in business firms, government agencies, and not-for-profit organizations; others are self-employed. They are classified as public, private (or management), government, and not-for-profit accountants.

PUBLIC ACCOUNTANTS

A **public accountant** provides accounting services to individuals or business firms for a fee. Most public accounting firms provide four basic services to clients: (1) auditing, or examining, financial records, (2) tax services, (3) consulting services to management, and (4) small-business consulting. Since they are not employees of the firm for which they provide services, public accountants can offer unbiased advice about the firm's financial condition.[5] The six largest public accounting firms, the so-called *Big Six,* are Arthur Andersen, Coopers & Lybrand, Deloitte & Touche, Ernst & Young, KPMG Peat Marwick, and Price Waterhouse.

public accountant
Professional who provides accounting services to other businesses and individuals for a fee.

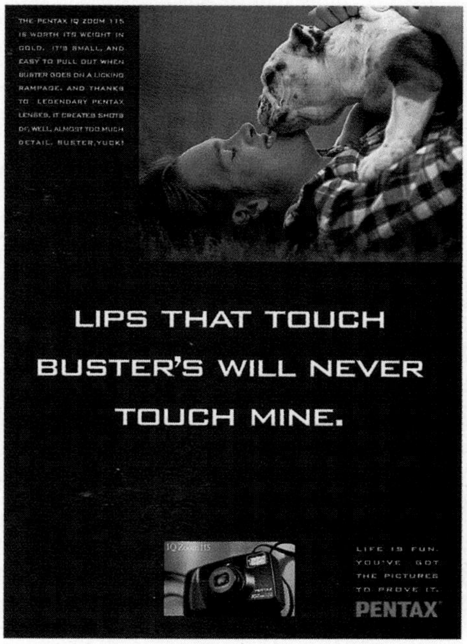

FIGURE 18.2

COMBINING FINANCING, INVESTING, AND OPERATING ACTIVITIES TO PRODUCE SALES SUCCESS FOR PENTAX CAMERAS

STRENGTH IN DIVERSITY

BREAKING THE GLASS CEILING IN ACCOUNTING Although the invisible barrier that seems to keep female managers out of the top jobs in business is generally found throughout industry, it seems even more entrenched in the accounting field. After a decade of efforts to improve the status of women working in accounting, only 1 of every 20 partners in the nation's six largest public accounting firms is a woman. Even so, this represents a major advance when compared with a 1-in-100 proportion that was common as recently as 1982. ■ The tiny percentage of women at the top levels of major accounting firms appears especially surprising, since 50 percent of all entry-level accounting professionals are women. Moreover, about 20 percent of the accountants at the level of manager are women, but the numbers do not carry through to the very top management levels. At least not yet. ■ Deloitte & Touche, the third-largest of the so-called *Big Six* accounting firms, has made the greatest effort to permit women to reap the benefits of their efforts in the form of promotions. The firm hired Ellen P. Gabriel as national director for the newly created Office for the Advancement of Women. She oversaw the creation and operation of workshops and specialized career planning for women. She also implemented flexible work arrangements to meet the needs of both male and female accountants in balancing their careers with personal and family commitments. ■ Besides benefiting employees at Deloitte & Touche, these efforts also strengthen the company as a whole. As Gabriel points out, "With current demographics, these programs will enable us to be more competitive in the future." The new programs are expected to reduce the turnover rate among female managers as well as increase the number of women at the partner (top) level. Of Deloitte's 1,500 partners, 77 are female. Another 80 partners will be selected this year and an estimated 15 percent of them will be women. According to former Bush administration Labor Secretary Lynn Martin, "Because of the high level of women entry-level employees in accounting, I truly believe that opportunities for women may be greater in this profession than elsewhere. Deloitte, without force or pressure, is sincere in wanting to move ahead in this area." ■ Other Big Six firms are moving ahead, too. Ernst & Young now claims 15 percent female managers, while acknowledging that turnover among women is 5 to 10 percent higher than the rate for men. To relieve time pressures that often develop during the hectic tax season from January to April, the firm uses flexible work schedules and provides day-care help for employees. In addition to flextime, Arthur Andersen & Company offers partners in its Atlanta office a special concierge service that assists them in shopping, picking up laundry, and paying bills. The service is intended to alleviate personal and family pressures on both female and male partners. ■ By 2000, more firms will be expected to provide work environments that reflect the changing composition of the work force. That may involve more benefits and services as well as adaptive work scheduling. Accounting is a profession on the leading edge of reaping the benefits of diversity. Source: Gabriel and Martin quotations from Lee Berton, "Deloitte Wants More Women for Top Posts in Accounting," *The Wall Street Journal,* April 18, 1992, p. B1.

QUESTIONS FOR CRITICAL THINKING

1. What other factors may have contributed to the low number of women in partner positions in the accounting field?
2. What other programs could accounting firms offer to help attract and promote female managers?
3. What other industries may be experiencing the same phenomenon?

PRIVATE (OR MANAGEMENT) ACCOUNTANTS

private accountant
Professional employed by a business other than a public accounting firm.

certified public accountant (CPA)
Accountant who has met education and experience requirements and passed a comprehensive examination.

An accountant employed by a business other than a public accounting firm is called a **private accountant.** Private, or management, accountants are responsible for collecting and recording financial transactions and preparing financial statements used by their employers' managers in decision making. In addition to preparing company financial statements, private accountants play major roles in interpreting them.

Certified public accountants (CPAs) have demonstrated their accounting knowledge by meeting state requirements for education and experience and successfully completing a number of rigorous tests in accounting theory and practice, auditing, and law. Other accountants who meet specified educational and experience requirements and pass certification exams carry the title *certified management accountant (CMA)* or *certified internal auditor (CIA)*.

Private accountants frequently specialize in different aspects of accounting. A *cost accountant*, for example, determines the costs of goods and services and helps set their prices. A *tax accountant* works to minimize the taxes a firm must pay and takes charge of the firm's federal, state, county, and city tax returns. An *internal auditor* examines the firm's financial practices to ensure that records are accurate and that company operations comply with federal laws and regulations.

GOVERNMENT AND NOT-FOR-PROFIT ACCOUNTANTS

Federal, state, and local governments also require accounting services. **Government accountants** and those who work for not-for-profit organizations are professional accountants who perform services similar to those of private and public accountants. Instead of emphasizing profit or loss, however, these professionals' reports focus more on determining how efficiently the organization is accomplishing its objectives. Many government agencies employ accountants, including the Environmental Protection Agency, local police and fire departments, the FBI, and the IRS. Not-for-profit organizations such as churches, labor unions, political parties, charities, schools, hospitals, and universities also hire accountants. In fact, this is one of the fastest-growing segments of accounting practice.

government accountant
Professional employed by a government agency or not-for-profit organization.

ACCOUNTING PROCESS

Accounting deals with financial transactions between a firm and its employees, customers, suppliers, owners, bankers, and various government agencies. Weekly payroll checks result in cash outflows to compensate employees. A payment to a supplier results in the receipt of needed materials for the production process. Cash, check, and credit purchases by customers generate funds to cover the costs of operations and earn a profit. Prompt payment of bills preserves the firm's credit rating and its ability to obtain future loans.

The procedural cycle in which accountants convert individual transactions to financial statements is called the **accounting process.** As Figure 18.3 shows, this process involves recording, classifying, and summarizing transactions in order to produce financial statements for the firm's managers and other interested parties.

accounting process
Method of converting information about individual transactions to financial statements.

IMPACT OF COMPUTERS ON THE ACCOUNTING PROCESS

For hundreds of years, accountants recorded, or posted, transactions manually in *journals* and then transferred the information to individual accounts listed in *ledgers*. However, the computer revolution of the 20th century has simplified the accounting systems of thousands of firms, both industrial giants and neighborhood service providers. Fully automated systems developed by firms such as NCR Corporation have eliminated most of the recording, classifying, and summarizing tasks once done by hand. As *point-of-sale terminals* replaced cash registers in stores, they began to perform a number of functions each time a clerk recorded a sale. Not only can such a terminal recall prices from memory and maintain a perpetual inventory count of every item in stock, but it can also automatically perform accounting data entries.

Accounting software programs such as Quicken and Turbo Tax are popular in business today. They facilitate a do-it-once approach to accounting that automatically converts each sale into a journal entry, which is then stored until needed. The system can then provide up-to-date financial statements and financial ratios when needed by decision makers. Integration of computers into accounting in almost every organization requires accountants to be increasingly computer literate.

FIGURE 18.3 ACCOUNTING PROCESS

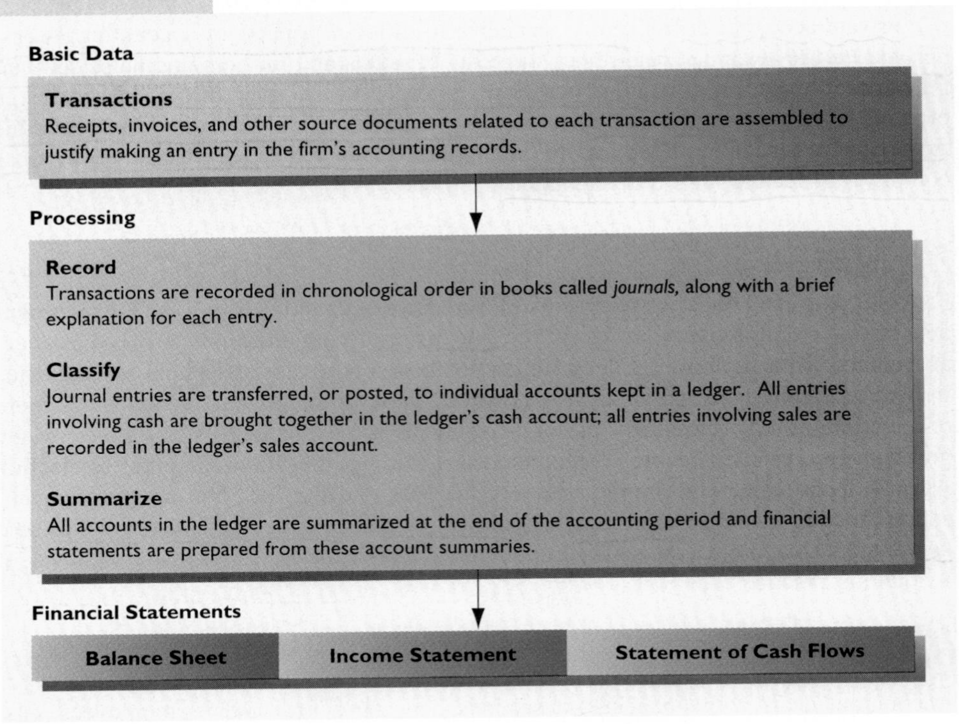
Basic Data
Transactions
Receipts, invoices, and other source documents related to each transaction are assembled to justify making an entry in the firm's accounting records.
Processing
Record
Transactions are recorded in chronological order in books called *journals*, along with a brief explanation for each entry.
Classify
Journal entries are transferred, or posted, to individual accounts kept in a ledger. All entries involving cash are brought together in the ledger's cash account; all entries involving sales are recorded in the ledger's sales account.
Summarize
All accounts in the ledger are summarized at the end of the accounting period and financial statements are prepared from these account summaries.
Financial Statements
Balance Sheet
Income Statement
Statement of Cash Flows

Computers do more than record and organize data for financial statements, however. They help accountants to make sound financial decisions quickly and effectively. In fact, the most important job of the typical private accountant is to communicate this information clearly and effectively to support decision making.

FOUNDATION OF THE ACCOUNTING SYSTEM

In order to ensure that they provide reliable, consistent, and unbiased information to decision makers, accountants follow guidelines or standards known as *generally accepted accounting principles (GAAP)*. These principles set standards that encompass the conventions, rules, and procedures necessary to determine acceptable accounting practices at a particular time. Accountants use GAAP to create uniform financial statements throughout an industry for comparison purposes. GAAP provides the basis for sound decision making.

Three accounting statements form the foundation of the entire accounting system: the balance sheet, the income statement, and the statement of cash flows. Accountants calculate the information in the first two statements based on the accounting equation and a double-entry system. The third statement, the statement of cash flows, focuses specifically on the sources and uses of cash for the firm.

ACCOUNTING EQUATION

asset
Anything of value owned or leased by a business.

Four fundamental terms make up the accounting equation: assets, equities, liabilities, and owners' equity. An **asset** is anything of value owned or leased by a business. Cash, accounts receivable, notes receivable (amounts owed to the business through credit sales), land, buildings, supplies, and marketable securities are all assets.

Using the two computers in his office in Denver, Bill Bodnar, a partner in the CinnaMonster bakery chain, tracks daily sales data from corporate stores using Microsoft's spreadsheet program, Excel, and specially created cash-register polling software. The use of software allows the data to be automatically converted into financial statements, ratios, and graphs.

Although most assets are tangible objects such as machinery, inventories, and buildings, intangible items such as patents and well-known trademarks, like the Jeep name featured in Figure 18.4, can often be some of a firm's most important assets. This is particularly true of computer software firms and biotechnology companies. The publication *Financial World* considers the following brand names to be the world's most valuable trademarks: Coca-Cola, Marlboro, Nescafé, Kodak, and Microsoft.[6]

An **equity** is a claim against the assets of a business. Two major classifications of individuals have equities in a firm: *creditors* (liability holders) and *owners*. A **liability** of a business is anything it owes to creditors, that is, any claim against the firm's assets by a creditor. When the firm makes credit purchases for inventory, land, or machinery, financial statements show the creditors' claims as accounts payable or notes payable. Wages and salaries owed to employees also represent liabilities (known as *wages payable*).

equity
Claim against the assets of a business.

liability
Claim against a firm's assets by a creditor.

FIGURE 18.4

JEEP TRADEMARK: INTANGIBLE ASSET OF CHRYSLER CORPORATION

owners' equity
Claims of the proprietor, partners, or stockholders against the assets of a firm; the excess of assets over liabilities.

Owners' equity represents the investment in the business by its owners and retained earnings that it has not paid out in dividends. Analysts often view a strong owners' equity position as evidence of a firm's financial strength and stability. In fact, insurance giant AIG features its owners' equity strength in its corporate advertising.

Because equities by definition represent the total claims of both owners and creditors against company assets, those assets must equal equities:

$$\text{Assets} = \text{Equities}$$

accounting equation
Basic accounting concept that assets equal liabilities plus owners' equity.

The basic **accounting equation** states that assets equal liabilities plus owners' equity. This equation represents the financial position of any firm at any point in time as:

$$\text{Assets} = \text{Liabilities} + \text{Owners' Equity}$$

Since financing comes from either creditors or owners, the accounting equation also represents the financial structure of a business.

Based on the relationship expressed by the accounting equation, accountants develop two primary accounting statements for every business, large or small: the balance sheet and the income statement. These two statements reflect the current financial position of the firm and the most recent analysis of income, expenses, and profits for interested parties inside and outside the firm. They provide a fundamental basis for planning activities, and they help the firm to attract new investors, secure borrowed funds, and prepare tax returns.

FINANCIAL STATEMENTS

Financial statements provide essential information that managers need to evaluate the *liquidity* of the organization—its ability to meet current obligations and needs by converting assets into cash—along with its *profitability* and *overall financial health.* The balance sheet, income statement, and statement of cash flows provide a basis for management decisions. By interpreting the data provided in these financial statements, analysts can communicate the appropriate information to internal decision makers and to interested parties outside the organization.

BALANCE SHEET

balance sheet
Statement of a firm's financial position on a particular date.

The **balance sheet** shows the financial position of a company on a particular date. It resembles a photograph comparing a firm's assets with its liabilities and owners' equity at a specific moment in time. A firm must prepare balance sheets at regular intervals, since managers and other internal parties are likely to request this information daily, weekly, or at least once a month. On the other hand, external users, such as stockholders or industry analysts, typically use this information less frequently, perhaps every quarter or once a year.

It is helpful to keep the accounting equation in mind as a diagram that is explained by the balance sheet. The balance sheet lists the firm's assets to indicate sources of the firm's strengths—where it gets its money. These assets, shown in descending order by *liquidity* (convertibility to cash), represent the uses that management has made of available funds. On the other side of the equation, liabilities and owners' equity indicate the sources of funds for the firm's assets. Liabilities reflect the claims of creditors—financial institutions or bondholders that have made loans, suppliers that have sold goods and services on credit, and others to be paid, such as federal, state, and local tax officials. Owners' equity represents claims of the owners' (stockholders in a corporation) against the firm's assets, or the excess of all assets over liabilities.

Figure 18.5 shows the balance sheet for The Ski Patrol, a Denver retailer of ski equipment, ski clothing, group ski tours, and ski instruction. The basic accounting equation is illustrated by the three classifications on The Ski Patrol's balance sheet. Total assets must equal the total of the firm's liabilities and owners' equity.

FIGURE 18.5 BALANCE SHEET FOR THE SKI PATROL

1 Current Assets
Cash and other liquid assets that can or will be converted to cash or used within 1 year

2 Fixed Assets
Relatively permanent plant, property, and equipment expected to be used for periods longer than 1 year

3 Current Liabilities
Claims of creditors that are to be repaid within 1 year

4 Long-Term Liabilities
Debts that come due 1 year or more after the date of the balance sheet

5 Owners' Equity
Claims of the proprietor, partners, or stockholders against the assets of a firm; the excess of assets over liabilities

THE **SKI** PATROL
Balance Sheet
as of December 31, 199X

ASSETS		
1 *Current Assets*		
Cash	$ 8,000	
Marketable Securities	30,000	
Accounts Receivable	194,000	
Inventory	124,000	
Total Current Assets		$ 356,000
2 *Fixed Assets* (plant)		
Store Equipment	$ 112,000	
Furniture and Fixtures	40,000	
Total Fixed Assets		$ 152,000
Total Assets		$ 508,000
LIABILITIES AND OWNERS' EQUITY		
3 *Current Liabilities*		
Accounts Payable	$ 82,000	
Current Installments of Long-Term Debt	30,000	
Accrued Expenses	14,000	
Income Taxes Payable	$ 12,000	
Total Current Liabilities		$ 138,000
4 *Long-Term Liabilities*		
Long-Term Notes Payable	$ 60,000	
Total Long-Term Liabilities		$ 60,000
Total Liabilities		$ 198,000
5 *Owners' Equity*		
Common Stock (160,000 shares @ $1)	$ 160,000	
Retained Earnings	150,000	
Total Owners' Equity		$ 310,000
Total Liabilities and Owners' Equity		$ 508,000

INCOME STATEMENT

While the balance sheet reflects a situation at a specific point in time, the income statement is a *flow* statement that reveals the performance of the organization over a specific time period. Resembling a motion picture rather than a snapshot, the **income statement** is a financial record that summarizes a firm's financial performance in terms of revenues, expenses, and profits over a given time period.

income statement
Financial record of a company's revenues, expenses, and profits over a period of time.

The purpose of the income statement is to show the profitability of a firm during a period of time, usually a year, a quarter, or a month. In addition to reporting the firm's profit or loss, it helps decision makers to focus on overall revenues and the costs incurred to generate these revenues. A not-for-profit organization uses this statement to show whether its revenues and contributions will cover the costs of operating it. Finally, the income statement provides much of the basic data needed to calculate numerous financial ratios that managers use in planning and controlling the organization. Figure 18.6 shows a current income statement for The Ski Patrol.

The income statement (sometimes called a *profit and loss* or *P&L statement*) begins with total sales or revenues generated during a year, quarter, or month, and then deducts all of the costs related to producing these revenues. After subtracting all costs—administrative and marketing expenses, costs involved in producing the product, interest, and taxes, for instance—the remaining net income may be distributed to the firm's owners (stockholders, proprietors, or partners) or reinvested in the company as retained earnings. The final figure on the income statement, net income after taxes, is the well-known **bottom line.**

bottom line
Overall profit or loss earned by a firm.

Careful analysis and use of income statement information have enabled home-builder Kaufman and Broad to succeed in a dismal California market. A combination

FIGURE 18.6 INCOME STATEMENT FOR THE SKI PATROL

1 Revenues
Funds received from sales of goods and services and from interest payments, dividends, royalties, and rents (grants and contributions can be revenue sources for not-for-profit firms)

2 Cost of Goods Sold
Cost of merchandise or services that generate the firm's revenue, including a *Purchases* section for retailers and *Cost of Goods Manufactured* for producers

3 Selling Expenses
Advertising, selling, and other expenses incurred in marketing and distributing the firm's output

4 General and Administrative Expenses
Office salaries and supplies, rent, and other operational expenses not directly related to the acquisition, production, or sale of the firm's output

5 Net Income
Profit or loss incurred over a specific period, determined by subtracting all expenses from revenues

THE SKI PATROL
Income Statement
Year Ending December 31, 199X

1 *Revenues*		
Gross Sales	$ 600,000	
Less: Sales Returns and Allowances	16,000	
Net Sales		$ 584,000
2 *Cost of Goods Sold*		
Beginning Inventory	$ 130,000	
Purchases during Year	246,000	
Cost of Goods Available for Sale	376,000	
Less: Ending Inventory	112,000	
Cost of Goods Sold		$ 264,000
Gross Profit		$ 320,000
Operating Expenses		
3 Selling Expenses	$ 150,000	
4 General and Administrative Expenses	96,000	
Total Operating Expenses		$ 246,000
Net Income before Taxes		74,000
Less: Income Taxes		14,000
5 *Net Income*		$ 60,000

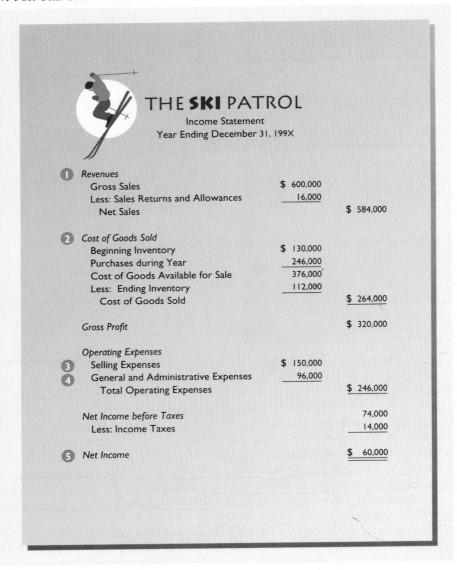

Buying land from distressed California sellers and keeping a tight lid on costs has enabled Kaufman and Broad to lower its average selling price to $161,200 for a single-family home, less than the region's average of about $169,300.

of defense cutbacks, high taxes, and environmental restrictions dropped housing starts from 125,000 annually during the 1980s to 75,000 by the mid-1990s. Besides being the state's largest homebuilder, K&B's market consists largely of first-time homebuyers, a segment that has been especially hard hit. The firm responded to the decline by slashing production costs and purchasing from a small number of suppliers in return for volume discounts. As a result, K&B was able to drive costs down by $4 per square foot within a year following the program's implementation. As Roger Menard, the company's president, points out, "Every dollar [per square foot] saved is $7 million to the bottom line."[7]

STATEMENT OF CASH FLOWS

In addition to the income statement and the balance sheet, most medium-sized and large firms prepare a third accounting statement. Since 1987, every company listed on organized stock exchanges has been required to prepare a statement of cash flows as part of its annual registration information. In addition, major lenders often require this statement of every firm applying for a business loan. As the name indicates, the **statement of cash flows** provides management, as well as investors and creditors, with relevant information about a firm's cash receipts and cash payments during an accounting period. It is sometimes referred to as the *Where Got/Where Gone statement* because it reflects the various sources of cash inflows (funds generated from operations, investments, and sales or purchases of such assets as land, buildings, or equipment) as well as cash expenditures during the period.

statement of cash flows
Statement of a firm's cash receipts and cash payments that presents information on its sources and uses of cash.

Cash flow is the lifeblood of every organization, as the business failure rate clearly demonstrates. Of more than 60,000 businesses that failed during a recent year, three of every five blamed economic factors linked to cash flow for their demise. More recent studies of small and medium-sized companies reveal that one firm in four ranks inability to control cash flow as the firm's primary problem. Proponents of the statement of cash flows hope that its preparation, and scrutiny of it by affected parties, will prevent financial disaster for profitable firms that may otherwise wind up in bankruptcy due to a lack of funds to continue day-to-day operations.

RATIO ANALYSIS

ratio analysis
Use of quantitative measures to evaluate a firm's financial performance.

Accounting professionals do more than prepare financial statements. They are placing ever greater importance on the responsibility of assisting managers in interpreting these documents by comparing the firm's current activities to records from previous periods and to those of other companies in the industry. **Ratio analysis** is one of the most commonly used tools for (1) measuring the firm's liquidity, profitability, and reliance on debt financing, along with the effectiveness of its use of its resources, and (2) permitting comparisons with other firms and with past performance.

Ratios help the manager to interpret actual performance and make comparisons with what should have happened. Comparisons to ratios of similar companies can reflect company performance relative to competitors' results. Industry standards for financial ratios serve as important indicators of problem areas as well as areas of excellence. Comparing ratios for the current accounting period with similar calculations for previous periods can identify trends that might be developing. Ratios can be classified according to their specific purposes.

LIQUIDITY RATIOS

liquidity ratio
Ratio that measures a firm's ability to meet its short-term obligations when they are due.

Liquidity ratios measure a firm's ability to meet its short-term obligations when they are due. Highly liquid firms are less likely to face emergencies in raising needed funds to repay loans. On the other hand, firms with less liquidity may have to resort to high-cost lending sources to meet their maturing obligations or face default.

Small, poorly financed companies often face liquidity crises. When Chicago-based Quality Croutons started business a few years ago with McDonald's as its sole customer, it had no liquidity problem. After all, the fast-food giant follows a pay-in-10-days policy. When the crouton supplier began taking on new customers, however, it learned that not everyone pays bills as quickly. Company owners had to contribute additional operating funds when receipts began to lag by 30 to 45 days.

Two commonly used liquidity ratios are the current ratio and the acid-test ratio. The *current ratio* compares current assets to current liabilities, giving management information about the firm's ability to pay its current debts as they mature.

The current ratio of The Ski Patrol can be computed as follows:

$$\text{Current Ratio} = \frac{\text{Current Assets}}{\text{Current Liabilities}} = \frac{\$356{,}000}{\$138{,}000} = 2.6 \text{ to } 1$$

This means that The Ski Patrol has \$2.60 of current assets for every \$1.00 of current liabilities. In general, a current ratio of 2 to 1 is considered financially satisfactory. Analysts must evaluate this rule of thumb, however, along with other factors such as the nature of the business, the season of the year, and the quality of the company's management. The Ski Patrol's management and other interested parties are likely to compare this ratio of 2.6 to 1 to current ratios from previous operating periods and to industry averages to determine its appropriateness.

The *acid-test* (or quick) *ratio* measures the ability of The Ski Patrol to meet its debt on short notice. It compares *quick assets,* highly liquid current assets, against current liabilities. It excludes inventory or prepaid expenses, considering only cash, marketable securities, and accounts receivable.

The Ski Patrol's current balance sheet lists the following quick assets: cash (\$8,000), marketable securities (\$30,000), and accounts receivable (\$194,000). The firm's acid-test ratio is computed as:

$$\text{Acid-test Ratio} = \frac{\text{Quick Assets}}{\text{Current Liabilities}} = \frac{\$232{,}000}{\$138{,}000} = 1.7 \text{ to } 1$$

Because the traditional rule of thumb for an adequate acid-test ratio is 1 to 1, The Ski Patrol appears to be in a good short-term credit position. However, the same cautions apply as for the current ratio. Analysts should compare the acid-test ratio with industry averages and with ratios from previous operating periods to determine its appropriateness for The Ski Patrol.

PROFITABILITY RATIOS

Profitability ratios measure the firm's overall financial performance in terms of its ability to generate revenues in excess of operating costs and other expenses. These ratios compare earnings with total sales or investments. Over a period of time, these ratios may also reveal the effectiveness of management in operating the business. Three commonly used profitability ratios are earnings per share, return on sales, and return on equity.

profitability ratio
Ratio that measures the overall financial performance of the firm.

$$\text{Earnings per Share} = \frac{\text{Net Income after Taxes}}{\text{Common Shares Outstanding}} = \frac{\$60{,}000}{160{,}000} = \$0.375$$

$$\text{Return on Sales} = \frac{\text{Net Income}}{\text{Net Sales}} = \frac{\$60{,}000}{\$584{,}000} = 10.3 \text{ percent}$$

$$\text{Return on Equity} = \frac{\text{Net Income}}{\text{Total Owners' Equity}} = \frac{\$60{,}000}{\$310{,}000} = 19.4 \text{ percent}$$

All of these ratios reflect positively on the current operations of The Ski Patrol. For example, the return on sales ratio indicates that the firm realized a profit of 10.3 cents for every dollar of sales. Although this ratio varies widely among business firms, The Ski Patrol compares favorably with retailers in general, which average about a 5 percent return on sales. However, analysts should evaluate this ratio, like the other profitability ratios, in relation to profit forecasts, past performance, or more specific industry averages to better interpret the results. Similarly, while the firm's return on equity of almost 20 percent appears to be satisfactory, the degree of risk in the industry affects this judgment.

Profitability ratios such as return on sales are popular indicators of a firm's success in its industry. Although Books-a-Million's 29 superstores seem like a tiny number in

Children and parents attend storytime at a Books-A-Million store. Books-A-Million's success in appealing to a wide audience and keeping those customers satisfied translates into a high 4.6 percent return on sales.

A BROADER PURPOSE

WHY PUBLIC ACCOUNTING FIRMS ARE FIRING THEIR CLIENTS A strange thing has been occurring during the past few years. Major public accounting firms are actually turning down business, particularly auditing work. ■ Auditing traditionally has been a major component of the work performed by these firms. This important societal function aids investors, management, and government, and earns profits for accounting firms, as well. Most medium-sized and large firms and various other organizations that borrow from major lending institutions are required to submit their financial statements for periodic audits by outside CPAs. An auditor provides an official opinion as to whether the firm's financial statements comply with generally accepted accounting principles. Audits are frequently time-consuming and involve considerable cost to the audited firm; on the other hand, they also generate considerable revenues for the accounting firm. ■ A new type of risk has arisen, however: fear of lawsuits. In recent years, accounting firms have paid hundreds of millions of dollars to settle lawsuits brought by investors, the government, and others claiming negligence by auditors. In one such case, Ernst & Young agreed to pay the government $400 million to settle claims that its audits of hundreds of savings and loan associations had been inadequate. Successful lawsuits by tax-shelter investors against Laurence & Horwath forced the large Chicago-based public accounting firm to declare bankruptcy. ■ Public accounting firms concerned about the possibility of auditing malpractice lawsuits are likely to back

comparison with industry giants Barnes & Noble, Kmart's Borders-Walden Group, and Crown Books, the Birmingham-based retailer is succeeding financially by keeping its customers satisfied. Its 4.6 percent return on sales is three times that of Barnes & Noble and Crown and well above Waldenbooks' 2.2 ratio.[8]

LEVERAGE RATIOS

leverage ratio
Ratio that measures a firm's reliance on debt financing in its operations.

The third category of financial ratios, **leverage ratios,** measure a firm's reliance on debt financing. They are particularly interesting to potential investors and lenders. If managers have accepted too much debt to finance the firm's operations, problems may arise in meeting future interest payments and repaying outstanding loans. In addition, both investors and lenders may prefer to deal with a firm whose owners have invested enough of their own money to avoid overreliance on borrowing. The debt to owners' equity ratio answers these questions.

$$\text{Debt to Owners' Equity Ratio} = \frac{\text{Total Liabilities}}{\text{Owners' Equity}} = \frac{\$198{,}000}{\$310{,}000} = 0.64$$

Since a debt-to-equity ratio greater than 1.00 would indicate that the firm would be relying more on debt financing than owners' equity, it is clear that The Ski Patrol's owners have invested considerably more than the total amount of liabilities shown on the firm's balance sheet.

Firms such as RJRNabisco have acquired numerous companies through borrowing, and they often find themselves forced to sell off product lines, and even whole divisions, to reduce the interest costs that accompany heavy reliance on debt. Mobile, Alabama–based Morrison's recently sold its institutional foods subsidiary to improve its away from doing business with small banks, thrifts, and fledgling companies planning initial public offerings (IPOs) of stock. Arthur Andersen CEO Lawrence A. Weinbach echoes these sentiments: "Liability risk has gone so far it's not worth the risk to audit some small companies, real estate ventures, financial services companies, IPOs, and small banks. The risk-reward tradeoff is out of whack." ■ It is important to note that the Big Six and other major public accounting firms are organized as partnerships, so an individual partner can face personal liability for all debts and legal judgments during his or her tenure with the firm. Consequently, many senior partners, worried about successful lawsuits targeting their personal wealth, try to steer their firms away from risk-filled audit assignments. At Deloitte & Touche, top management has put the word out that audits of IPOs must be approved by the head office. Managing Partner J. Michael Cook offers this simple explanation: "Our aversion to risk is greater than our appetite for growth." At KPMG Peat Marwick, the attitude is the same; the firm relies heavily on references from attorneys, bankers, and investors, and conducts background checks before accepting new clients. ■ Even when these firms agree to work with a new client, they may charge more to audit a firm with a higher potential for problems. The result of these higher fees may drive audit customers to seek the services of smaller, local accounting firms. ■ The accounting firms also must confront the problem of recently enacted government regulations for audits of banking and thrift institutions. In addition to normal auditing functions, accountants now have to evaluate management assessments of a bank's internal controls and compliance with laws regulating bank safety and soundness. All of this requires more time and more money. Explains one New Jersey S&L president, "Our auditing costs go up every year because the Office of Thrift Supervision asks for more. I wouldn't want to be having to look for an auditor now, I'll tell you that." Source: Quotations from Kelley Holland and Larry Light, "Big Six Firms Are Firing Clients," *Business Week,* March 1, 1993, pp. 76–77.

QUESTIONS FOR CRITICAL THINKING

1. Does this situation present an opportunity for accounting firms?
2. Should the government relax auditing requirements of financial institutions? Why or why not?
3. What can the accounting industry as a whole do to reverse this trend?

equity position. This placed the firm in a strong position to finance the expansion of its successful casual restaurants, including Ruby Tuesday's, Mozzarella, and Sweetpea's.[9]

ACTIVITY RATIOS

activity ratio
Ratio that measures the effectiveness of the firm's use of its resources.

The final category of financial ratios, **activity ratios,** measure the effectiveness of the firm's use of its resources. The most frequently used activity ratio, the *inventory turnover ratio,* indicates the number of times that merchandise moves through the business.

$$\text{Inventory Turnover Ratio} = \frac{\text{Cost of Goods Sold}}{\text{Average Inventory}} = \frac{\$264{,}000}{\$121{,}000} = 2.2 \text{ times}$$

Average inventory for The Ski Patrol is determined by adding the January 1 beginning inventory of $130,000 and the December 31 ending inventory of $112,000, as shown on the income statement, and dividing by 2. Comparing the 2.2 inventory turnover rate with industry standards gives a measure of efficiency. Retailers such as furniture and jewelry stores average an annual turnover of 1.5 times. A supermarket's turnover rate can be as high as once every 2 weeks.

The four categories of financial ratios relate balance sheet and income statement data to one another and assist management in pinpointing strengths and weaknesses. For large, multiproduct organizations operating in diverse markets, today's sophisticated information systems allow them to update these financial ratios daily or even hourly. Consequently, management must decide on an appropriate review schedule to avoid the costly and time-consuming mistake of overmonitoring.

Recently, Harte & Co. CEO Axel L. Grabowsky concluded that the sheer volume of such information was consuming his working days, leaving him with little time to devote to "the future of business, to new-product development, acquisitions, and to short- and long-term planning."[10] The New York–based manufacturer of plastic sheeting markets products in 12 major categories in numerous domestic and international markets. Grabowsky's current monitoring involves a daily focus on sales, comparing actual sales to forecasts, and weekly reviews of cash flows and profitability and activity ratios. He has concluded that monthly reviews are appropriate for ratios involving production costs, accounts receivable, and sales by major product category, territory, and major customers. However, Grabowsky expects managers from each area to monitor their own operations more frequently and to supply him with detailed explanations for all important variations from budgeted performance within 24 to 48 hours.

BUDGETING

budget
Planning and control tool that reflects expected sales revenues, operating expenses, and cash receipts and outlays.

Although the financial statements discussed in this chapter focus on past results, they are the basis for future planning. A **budget** is a planning and control tool that reflects expected sales revenues, operating expenses, and cash receipts and outlays. It quantifies the firm's plans for a specified future period. Since it requires management to estimate sales, cash inflows and outflows, and costs, it serves as a financial blueprint. The budget becomes the standard against which managers compare actual performance.

Budget preparation is frequently a time-consuming task that involves many people from various departments of the firm. The complexity of the budgeting process varies with the size and complexity of the organization. Giant corporations such as Walt Disney, Intel, and Boeing tend to have extremely complex and sophisticated budgeting systems. Their budgets serve as tools for integrating the numerous divisions of the firm in addition to planning and control tools. Budgeting by both large and small firms resembles household budgeting, however, in that the purpose is to match income and expenses to accomplish objectives and correctly time cash inflows and outflows.

Since the accounting department is the organization's financial nerve center, it provides much of the data for budget development. The overall master, or operating, budget is actually a composite of numerous smaller budgets for individual departments or

FIGURE 18.7

ADVERTISING EXPENDITURES: COMPONENT OF A FIRM'S MARKETING BUDGET

functional areas of the firm. These typically include the production budget, cash budget, capital expenditures budget, advertising budget, and sales budget.

The composite master budget for the division of Panasonic that produces portable CD players and personal stereos includes funds allocated in its marketing budget. The marketing budget, in turn, combines budgets for such functions as transportation, storage, sales, and advertising. The $62,950 cost of the Panasonic stereo ad in *Rolling Stone* shown in Figure 18.7 does not surprise the firm's management; the decision to spend this money was made months earlier, and the cost is reflected in the advertising budget for the current period.

Firms usually establish budgets annually, but they may divide totals into monthly or quarterly amounts for control purposes. Since some activities, such as construction of new manufacturing facilities or long-term purchasing contracts, extend over several years, firms may set longer-term budgets in those cases.

Figure 18.8 shows a sample cash budget for The Ski Patrol. The firm has set a $6,000 minimum cash balance. The cash budget indicates months in which the firm will invest excess funds to earn interest rather than remaining idle. It also indicates periods in which it will need temporary loans to finance operations. Finally, the cash budget produces a tangible standard against which to compare actual cash inflows and outflows.

FIGURE 18.8 SIX-MONTH CASH BUDGET FOR THE SKI PATROL

THE SKI PATROL
16853 Katy Freeway
Houston, Texas 78555

Sample Cash Budget
January–June 199X

	January	February	March	April	May	June
Beginning Monthly Balance	$ 6,000	$ 6,000	$ 6,000	$ 6,000	$ 6,000	$ 6,000
Add: Cash Receipts (collections from customers, interest receipts, and other cash inflows)	4,000	14,000	12,000	10,000	8,000	18,000
Cash Available for Firm's Use	$ 10,000	$ 20,000	$ 18,000	$ 16,000	$ 14,000	$ 24,000
Deduct: Cash Disbursements (for payroll, materials, income taxes, utilities, interest payments, etc.)	10,000	8,000	10,000	12,000	6,000	14,000
Preliminary Monthly Balance	$ -0-	$ 12,000	$ 8,000	$ 4,000	$ 8,000	$ 10,000
Minimum Required Cash Balance	6,000	6,000	6,000	6,000	6,000	6,000
Excess (or Deficiency)	(6,000)	6,000	2,000	(2,000)	2,000	4,000
Short-Term Investment of Excess			2,000		2,000	4,000
Liquidation of Short-Term Investment				2,000		
Short-Term Loan to Cover Deficiency	6,000					
Repayment of Short-Term Loan		6,000				
Ending Monthly Balance	$ 6,000	$ 6,000	$ 6,000	$ 6,000	$ 6,000	$ 6,000

Fashion apparel marketer Benetton has developed an international reputation for its use of provocative, often shocking themes in its advertising. This two-page example, which appeared in *Conde Naste Traveler,* is a collage of faces of the world's people. If the ad is successful in generating sales in the United States, it will result in receipt of U.S. dollars—and an international currency issue for Benetton accountants.

Source: Courtesy Benetton; used by permission.

INTERNATIONAL ACCOUNTING

As organizations become more involved with the global economy, they must adapt their accounting procedures and practices to reflect an international environment. Nestlé, the giant chocolate and food products company, operates throughout the world. A whopping 98 percent of its revenues come from outside Switzerland, its headquarters country. International accounting for this type of firm is primarily concerned with the need to translate financial statements denominated in foreign currencies.

EXCHANGE RATES

As defined in Chapter 3, an *exchange rate* is the rate at which a country's currency can be exchanged for other currencies or gold. Currencies can be treated as goods to be bought and sold. Like the price of any good or service, currency prices change daily according to supply and demand. Exchange rate fluctuations affect accounting entries differently than single-currency transactions do.

Accountants dealing with international transactions must record foreign sales and purchases. The Italian fashion apparel firm Benetton produces and markets clothing and accessories in dozens of countries around the globe. Japanese customers pay in *yen,* Canadian buyers exchange *dollars* for Benetton products, and Spanish shoppers use *pesos.* Each of these currencies can fluctuate in relation to the *lira,* the currency of Benetton's Italian corporate headquarters.

The international firm's consolidated financial statements must reflect any gains or losses due to fluctuations in exchange rates during specific periods of time. Financial statements that cover operations in two or more countries also need to treat fluctuations consistently to allow for comparison.

INTERNATIONAL ACCOUNTING STANDARDS

The International Accounting Standards Committee (IASC) was established in 1973 to promote worldwide consistency in financial reporting practices. The IASC is recognized as the sole source of responsibility and authority to issue pronouncements on international accounting standards. The International Federation of Accountants, formed in 1977, supports the work of the IASC and develops international guidelines for auditing, ethics, education, and management accounting. Every 5 years, an International Congress is held to judge the progress toward achieving consistency in standards. Its objective is to enhance comparability of financial reports between nations and currencies. With the advent of a single European market and the North American trade bloc, the necessity for comparability and uniformity of international accounting standards is becoming widely recognized and will soon be a reality.

ACHIEVEMENT CHECK SUMMARY

Reread the learning goals that follow, and consider the questions for each goal. Answering these questions will reinforce the most important concepts in the chapter and allow you to check how well you have achieved these learning goals. Where a blank appears before a question, answer with *T* or *F*. Otherwise, circle the letter of the correct answer. An answer key to these questions is found at the end of this chapter.

LEARNING GOAL 18.1: Explain the functions of accounting and their importance to the firm's management and to outside parties such as investors, creditors, and government agencies.

1. ___ Accountants measure, interpret, and communicate financial information.
2. ___ If a firm is seeking a loan, it will need to show the potential lender accounting information.
3. ___ Accounting is important in profit-oriented businesses, but it cannot be used to evaluate the performance of not-for-profit organizations.

LEARNING GOAL 18.2: Identify the three basic business activities that involve accounting.

1. ___ Accountants play an important role in the investment decisions of firms acquiring new assets.
2. ___ Accountants produce financial statements that can affect a firm's ability to start or expand a business.
3. ___ While accountants produce information to support financial and investment decisions, they rarely analyze the operational activities of a firm.

LEARNING GOAL 18.3: Contrast the roles played by public, private, government, and not-for-profit accountants.

1. ___ Accountants who own their own accounting firms are known as *private accountants.*
2. ___ Since public accountants involved in an audit do not work for the firm under inspection, their findings are expected to be unbiased.
3. ___ Government and not-for-profit accountants are concerned with how well an organization accomplishes its objectives rather than measuring its profit or loss.

LEARNING GOAL 18.4: Outline the steps in the accounting process.

1. The book used to record day-to-day transactions is the: (a) ledger; (b) budget; (c) journal; (d) balance sheet.
2. Separate accounts to which transactions are posted are entered in the: (a) ledger; (b) budget; (c) journal; (d) balance sheet.
3. The final step in the accounting process is: (a) preparing accounting statements; (b) recording day-to-day transactions; (c) determining which types of ledgers to set up; (d) bringing the owner's equity account up to date.

LEARNING GOAL 18.5: Explain the functions of the balance sheet, income statement, and statement of cash flows, and identify their major components.

1. ___ In the basic accounting equation, assets plus liabilities equal owner's equity.
2. ___ The balance sheet is a summary statement of revenue received and expenses incurred.
3. ___ The statement of cash flows summarizes the cash effects of a firm's operating, investing, and financing activities during a specific accounting period.

LEARNING GOAL 18.6: Discuss how accountants use the major financial ratios to analyze a firm's financial strengths and weaknesses.

1. ___ The four categories of financial ratios relate balance sheet and income statement items to one another to help pinpoint the organization's strengths and weaknesses.
2. ___ Leverage ratios measure the extent to which a firm is using debt financing.
3. ___ The current ratio and acid-test ratio measure the organization's profitability.

LEARNING GOAL 18.7: Explain the role of budgets in business.

1. ___ Only underfinanced organizations need budgets.

2. ___ The budget serves as the standard against which to compare actual performance.
3. ___ In a sense, a budget is a firm's future plan.

LEARNING GOAL 18.8: Explain the impact of exchange rates on international accounting and the importance of uniform financial statements for firms engaged in international business.

1. ___ The IASC sets international accounting standards which are used exclusively in Europe and North America.
2. ___ A firm can earn a profit on an international transaction, but still lose money due to shifts in currency exchange rates.
3. ___ The effects of exchange rate fluctuations on accounting entries differ from the effects of a single currency transaction.

KEY TERMS

accounting 501
public accountant 503
private accountant 504
certified public accountant (CPA) 504
government accountant 505
accounting process 505
asset 506
equity 507
liability 507
owners' equity 508
accounting equation 508
balance sheet 508
income statement 509
bottom line 510
statement of cash flows 511
ratio analysis 512
liquidity ratio 512
profitability ratio 513
leverage ratio 513
activity ratio 514
budget 515

REVIEW QUESTIONS

1. Who are the major users of accounting information?

2. Describe the role that accounting plays in a firm's financing activities, investing activities, and operating activities.

3. Distinguish between public, private, government, and not-for-profit accountants. Why are approximately 50 percent of the nation's certified public accountants employed as private accountants?

4. Explain the steps of the accounting process and the impact of computers on this process.

5. What is meant by the statement, "The balance sheet is a detailed expression of the accounting equation"?

6. Identify the primary purpose of each component of the balance sheet and the income statement. What are the major differences between the balance sheet and the income statement?

7. Identify the four categories of financial ratios discussed in the chapter, and describe specific ratios included in each category.

8. Explain the similarities and differences between budgeting and development of accounting statements.

9. What primary purposes do budgets serve?

10. What financial statements are affected by exchange rates in international accounting? What are the benefits of uniform international financial standards?

DISCUSSION QUESTIONS

1. Many accountants show the values for various items on their firms' income statements in percentages of net sales rather than showing actual figures. What additional insights would this approach make possible?

2. Identify the three types of assets and the two types of liabilities that appear on a typical balance sheet. Categorize the following account titles:

a. Frank Jennings, Capital
b. Mortgage Payable
c. Patent
d. Buildings
e. Common Stock
f. Prepaid Expenses
g. Accounts Payable
h. Marketable Securities

3. Match each of the accounts listed below with the appropriate accounting category. Each account may be included in more than one category.

___ a. Net Sales
___ b. Accounts Receivable
___ c. Advertising Expense
___ d. Common Stock
___ e. Equipment
___ f. Marketable Securities
___ g. Long-Term Notes Payable
___ h. Salaries
___ i. Retained Earnings

1. Current Asset
2. Fixed Asset
3. Current Liability
4. Long-Term Liability
5. Owners' Equity
6. Revenue
7. Expenses

4. Which ratio would provide information on:
a. Ability to meet short-term obligations
b. Ability to pay current debts
c. Ability to pay current debts on short notice
d. Overall financial performance
e. Amount of profits earned for each share of common stock outstanding
f. Net income compared to sales
g. Owners' equity
h. Firm's use of its resources
i. Number of times that merchandise moves through the business
j. Firm's reliance on debt financing
k. Percentage of owners' investments as compared to debt financing

5. At the end of the year, Magellan Company showed the following balances in its accounts:

Land	$ 80,000
Buildings	314,000
Inventory	100,000
Cash	10,000
Accounts Payable	90,000
Marketable Securities	36,000
Retained Earnings	300,000
Common Shares (80,000 shares @ $1)	80,000
Notes Payable	110,000
Equipment	40,000

a. Prepare a balance sheet for the Magellan Company
b. Calculate the current ratio, acid-test ratio, and debt to owners' equity ratio. What conclusions do these ratios suggest?

SOLUTIONS TO ACHIEVEMENT CHECK SUMMARY

L. G. 18.1: 1. T, 2. T, 3. F. **L. G. 18.2:** 1. T, 2. T, 3. F. **L. G. 18.3:** 1. F, 2. T, 3. T. **L. G. 18.4:** 1. c, 2. a, 3. a. **L. G. 18.5:** 1. F, 2. F, 3. T. **L. G. 18.6:** 1. T, 2. T, 3. F. **L. G. 18.7:** 1. F, 2. T, 3. T. **L. G. 18.8:** 1. F, 2. T, 3. T.

TEAM-BUILDING EXERCISE

You are a high-level manager at your company, and you've known for some time now that you need to upgrade your information and accounting systems to retain your competitive edge in the marketplace. You are meeting with an accountant and other managers to evaluate your needs.

1. The instructor will divide the class into teams and hand out a description of your imaginary business along with an imaginary price list for various kinds of computer equipment.

2. Prepare a list of the tasks that the company must perform that could benefit from the use of a computer. When you feel your list is complete, number the items in order of priority.

3. Looking at the imaginary price list, how much will you need to spend to realize all these goals you have identified? Compare that total with the budget you actually have available. How many of the goals/tasks on your list will you actually be able to accomplish within the budget guidelines?

4. Although involved in the initial budgetary process, the company accountant becomes concerned that you might not have enough money to make the investment in new equipment and software after all and asks you to prepare a new balance sheet based on the information in your company description.

5. Still unconvinced, the company accountant requests an income statement and a current leverage ratio for the business.

VIDEO CASE

ARCHWAY COOKIES Despite the "fitness decade" label attached to the 1990s, it is clear that Americans have not abandoned their fondness for sweets. In fact, U.S. consumers spend $25 million a day just buying cookies. Their purchases add up to over $9 billion in annual sales for the cookie industry.

The industry is dominated by Nabisco, which accounts for about one-third of all cookie sales. Keebler is in second place with about 11 percent of the U.S. market, and private-label store brands generate another 13 percent. The second tier of cookie-industry competitors includes Sunshine, Pepperidge Farm, and Archway Cookies. Each of these firms control between four percent and six percent of the domestic cookie market.

The overall cookie market is growing at a snail's pace at only 1 to 2 percent a year. Consequently, firms seeking additional sales must take market share from competitors. And, as costs increase, each firm must increase revenues, expenses, and cash flows to maintain profits. To accomplish this, firms like Archway Cookies rely heavily on accurate accounting data and sales and cost projections.

Archway is a sixty-year-old company, well-known for its fresh-baked "home style" cookies. Headquartered in Battle Creek, Michigan, the firm controls about 4.4 percent of the U.S. cookie market and generates annual sales of $400 million.

Archway's management has taken a multifaceted approach to achieving sales growth and maintaining desired profit levels. The firm has sought to increase sales by continuing to stress quality to maintain its image in the marketplace. It has introduced a line of reduced-fat products to appeal to this small (currently about 5 percent of the total cookie market) but rapidly growing segment of the market. To control costs and aid in decision making, Archway relies on a state-of-the-art accounting system.

Using current, accurate accounting data, Archway managers recently decided to invest in a hand-held computer for each Archway delivery route driver—even though the drivers are independent agents, not company employees. These new computers helped management achieve its objective of having accurate, up-to-the-minute information. Managers can track sales automatically. Orders for future delivery are recorded on the computer by each delivery route driver, then transmitted immediately to the appropriate bakery, where they go into the production schedule. The system also handles customer billing and makes suggestions regarding future delivery routes, based on sales histories and current scheduled deliveries at each stop on the route. The latter service is intended to strengthen the partnership that exists between Archway and its independent route drivers.

Archway uses reports generated by this sales information system to make decisions concerning operating activities. Accounting professionals on the Archway staff are responsible for preparing the reports. The reports often focus on the costs associated with the production and delivery of various lines of Archway cookies. Every four weeks, Archway managers receive and review detailed cost data on each of its over 100 different types of cookies. An income statement is included for each line of cookies so that management can determine whether the line is meeting its sales and profit objectives and if its costs are in line with projections.

Archway's management feels that such close monitoring of sales, costs, and profits are essential because of the extremely thin profit margins that exist in the industry. Consider, for example, a package of cookies carrying a retail price of two dollars. The typical supermarket gross margin for this product is 25 percent, so the retail grocer pays $1.60 and uses the forty-cent difference to cover costs and earn a profit. The Archway delivery person typically receives a 20 percent gross margin, paying the cookie maker $1.33 and reselling the cookies for $1.60. So, for each $2 package of cookies sold, Archway receives $1.33, from which it must pay for ingredients, packaging, human resource expenses, overhead expenses such as utilities, and for a portion of the equipment used in producing the cookies. Any funds remaining after these payments are made are profits.

With relatively small profit margins, a small change in operating expenses can convert a profitable product into a money loser. The recent change in product labeling requirements mandated by the U.S. Food and Drug Administration is a good example. The new, more detailed information requirements resulted in larger labels, pushing the price of each label from about three cents to eight cents. The FDA estimates that it will cost each company around $3,000 per product to relabel. Archway depends on its accounting system to evaluate the impact of such changes on profits and to serve as an early warning system regarding potential problems, so that remedial action can be implemented before a crisis occurs.

QUESTIONS

1.
Refer to the discussion in Figure 18.1 regarding the different users of accounting data. Which of these users are referred to in this case? What kinds of decisions are made on the basis of this data?

2.
How does Archway justify the expenditure of thousands of dollars to supply computers to route delivery personnel who are not company employees?

3.
Every four weeks Archway managers receive separate income statements for each of over 100 different Archway cookie products. Explain how the income statement would be used on a regular basis in planning and controlling operations.

4.
Assume a package of Archway cookies costs $2.00. Identify the different businesses receiving some portion of the two-dollar retail price and the typical amount received by each.

CAREERS IN BUSINESS

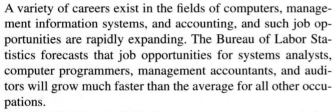

CAREER PROFILE: JESSICA KIM For a while, the American dream seemed more to resemble a nightmare for Jessica Kim. Kim, her husband, and small son moved to the United States from Korea in 1970. Then tragedy struck, when her husband was killed in an automobile accident. Kim faced the daunting task of supporting her child and herself in a new country where people spoke English, a language she barely understood. But she also possessed intelligence, determination, and the motivation to succeed in spite of these challenges. ■ Her first challenge was to master the English language, both written and oral. Kim began a regimen of reading the newspaper daily and learning three new words a day. To provide financial support for her family, she began to pursue job opportunities and succeeded in landing a job in the accounting department at UCLA. While working on campus, she became aware of the large number of nontraditional students and realized that she was not too old to pursue a degree herself. ■ She applied for admission to Los Angeles Pierce College, but was told that classes had already been in session for four weeks. She met with an accounting professor, who explained the difficulty of succeeding in an accounting class after missing so many classes. After convincing the professor that she would invest the time and effort to catch up with reading and homework assignments, she was admitted. Kim was able to complete the program while continuing to work full time and care for her son. ■ Kim then transferred to the California State University at Northridge, where she completed her B.S. degree in accounting. Next, she took the rigorous certified public accountant (CPA) examination and passed every component of the exam on the first attempt, a relatively rare feat. Although she had decided on a career in public accounting, Kim felt that a smaller firm would offer her a better opportunity to learn all aspects of accounting more quickly than would a position at one of the giant Big Six firms. A colleague recommended a local firm, where she was hired immediately following an interview. ■ Hard work and determination paid off for Jessica Kim. She assessed her talents, set goals, planned well, and did everything possible to execute her plan. She remained focused on her goals while overcoming many obstacles. Today, she is a successful accounting professional who believes that if you work diligently, you will be rewarded.

A variety of careers exist in the fields of computers, management information systems, and accounting, and such job opportunities are rapidly expanding. The Bureau of Labor Statistics forecasts that job opportunities for systems analysts, computer programmers, management accountants, and auditors will grow much faster than the average for all other occupations.

Specific jobs available in computers, management information systems, and accounting include systems analysts, computer programmers, management accountants, controllers, auditors, and cost estimators.

SYSTEMS ANALYSTS

Systems analysts are computer experts who plan and develop the computer-based information systems required by an organization. They work in all types of business organizations, governments, and consulting and service firms. Currently, there are some 660,000 systems analysts working in the United States.

Job Description Systems analysts determine what information is needed to solve a problem and how best to obtain it. Once management approves the recommendations, the systems analyst instructs the organization's computer programmers in how to implement the decisions.

Career Path Trainee positions are available in this career. Trainees work under the direction of senior personnel. Additional responsibilities come with experience. Management slots in this field may come later.

Salary In a recent year, experienced analysts earned a median salary of $42,100. Most analysts earn between $25,200 and $65,500 annually. In government, the range of entry-level salaries was $18,300 to $22,700 depending on the academic record of the individual.

COMPUTER PROGRAMMERS

Computer programmers carry out the instructions of systems analysts. Programmers are required in computer installations in both the private and public sectors. Some 570,000 programmers are currently at work in the United States.

Job Description Working with the systems analyst's overall plan, computer programmers write the programs that provide required information. Once these programs are tested and verified, the programmer turns the program over to computer operating personnel.

Career Path Entry-level programmers are assigned basic tasks, while experienced personnel work on more complex assignments. Advancement to supervisory positions is possible in medium- and large-sized firms.

Salary In a recent year, most programmers' earnings ranged between $24,300 and $42,000 with a median salary of $33,000.

MANAGEMENT ACCOUNTANTS

Management accountants work to provide executives with the financial information they need to make decisions. Currently, more than 939,000 accountants are employed throughout the United States. About 60 percent work in the management accounting field.

Job Description Management accountants tend to specialize in specific areas of corporate accounting, such as cost accounting, budgeting, and corporate tax accounting. Regardless of the area, all management accounting practices are designed to provide essential information to corporate decision makers.

Career Path Beginning accountants perform routine tasks in some aspect of management accounting. Responsibilities expand as the person acquires experience. Top positions in management accounting carry titles such as *controller, treasurer,* or *vice president of finance.*

Salary Accounting firms in a recent year offered median salaries of up to $24,700. Accountants with master's degrees earned over $30,000. Certified public accountants averaged $61,900. Experience and performance level dictate future increases. Top corporate accounting executives average $76,000 a year.

CONTROLLERS

Sometimes called a *treasurer* or *vice president of finance,* the controller is the top-level executive in management accounting. Controllers are responsible for a firm's entire accounting and financial function.

Job Description Controllers oversee corporate budgets, cash flow, payroll, accounts receivable, and accounts payable. they are responsible for the business' total flow of funds, both inward and outward. The various accounting departments, such as cost accounting, report to the controller.

Career Path People who want to be controllers must have successful careers in one or more aspects of management accounting. They may then be appointed as assistant controller or division controller. These people report to the corporate controller.

Salary Depending on the size of the company, corporate controllers and other financial managers earn between $44,000 and $129,000.

AUDITORS

Accountants who monitor an organization's internal accounting controls are called *auditors*. These workers are accountants who specialize in auditing procedures in private firms, government, and not-for-profit organizations.

Job Description Auditors evaluate accounting records to determine whether monies are being handled properly and are being correctly recorded by managers and employees. Audit findings are reported to higher levels of management. Consequently, auditors must be thorough and conduct comprehensive accounting reviews.

Career Path Beginning auditors are usually assigned to largely clerical duties such as verifying the accuracy of accounting records. Experienced auditors are placed in charge of specific audits and may have several other auditors reporting to them. Management positions are also available within the auditing department. Successful auditors may also move to other areas of accounting. Many top executives began their career in auditing.

Salary In a recent year, the average salary for internal auditors was $26,500; for more experienced auditors, the average increased to $60,700 and more.

COST ESTIMATORS

Cost estimators project costs and prices for a variety of businesses, from construction and engineering to insurance. An accounting background is helpful. There were 163,000 cost estimators in the United States during a recent year, and job growth is projected to be as fast as the average for all occupations through 2000.

Job Description Estimators prepare specifications for work to be performed and use past records as a guide to current costs, supplemented by changes in the prices charged by various suppliers. They often solicit bids for part or all of some work. Cost estimators project completion dates in addition to prices.

Career Path The career path varies according to the industry in which the work is performed.

Salary Earnings vary according to experience and the industry in which the cost estimator works. In a recent year, cost estimators' starting salaries ranged from $17,000 to $21,000. Highly experienced cost estimators can earn $75,000 or more.

CAREER DESIGN EXERCISES

PEOPLE PREFERENCES

Here is an exercise about which you will probably have some strong feelings. Have you ever thought about how you enjoyed a certain job—or hated one—because of the people at work? In this exercise, you will list all the things you like and dislike about people you have encountered in the workplace. You will even decide which of those characteristics are so important that the next job you take has to have co-workers who possess them.

THIS EXERCISE WILL HELP YOU TO

- Develop a clear picture of exactly what kinds of people you prefer to encounter in your work setting.
- Learn that the people with whom you work can have a significant impact on job satisfaction.

HOW TO LOCATE THE EXERCISE

When you see the main menu for Career Design, select "Who Am I?" Then select "People Preferences."

SETTING GOALS

In Chapter 17 you learned that one of the purposes of an information system is to take data gathered from different sources and put those data in a form that can be used in making decisions. If the information is comprehensive, accurate, and easily retrievable through computers, your decision-making ability will be greatly enhanced. In this exercise you will make some preliminary decisions based on data you have gathered about yourself and your career preferences in previous exercises.

THIS EXERCISE WILL HELP YOU TO

- Gain first-hand experience at using a computerized information system to make decisions.
- Determine the areas of life, both personally and professionally, that are important to you.
- Build specific goals about what you want to accomplish in life.

HOW TO LOCATE THE EXERCISE

When you see the main menu for Career Design, select "What Do I Want?" Then select "Setting Goals."

CHAPTER 19

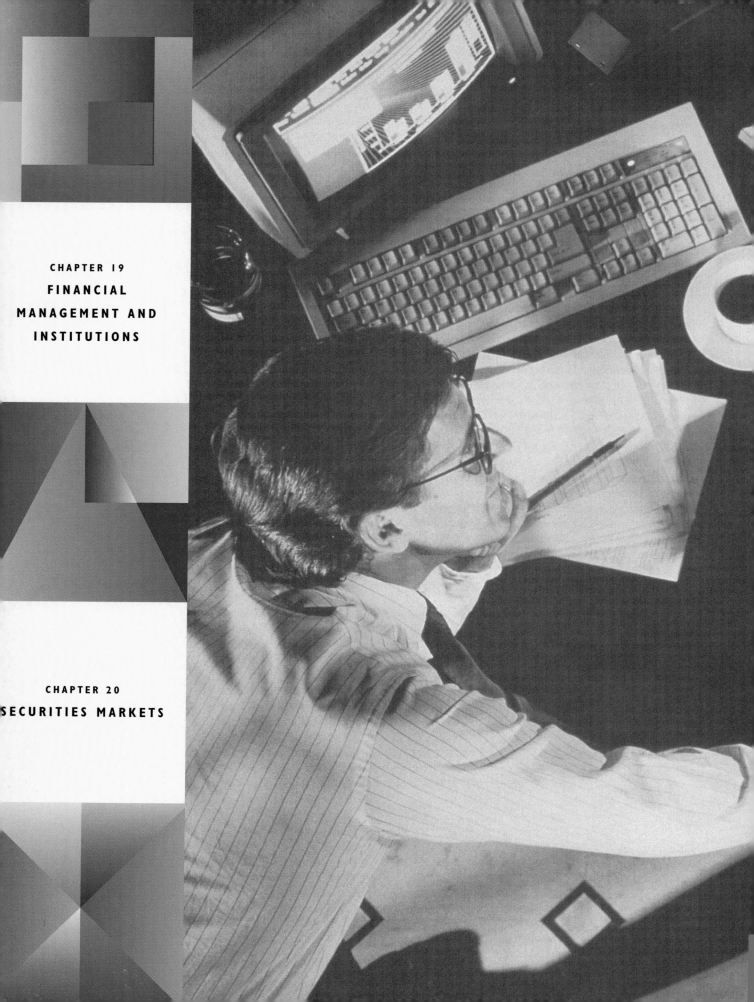

FINANCIAL MANAGEMENT AND INSTITUTIONS

CHAPTER 20

SECURITIES MARKETS

PART VI

FINANCING THE ENTERPRISE

CHAPTER 19

FINANCIAL MANAGEMENT AND INSTITUTIONS

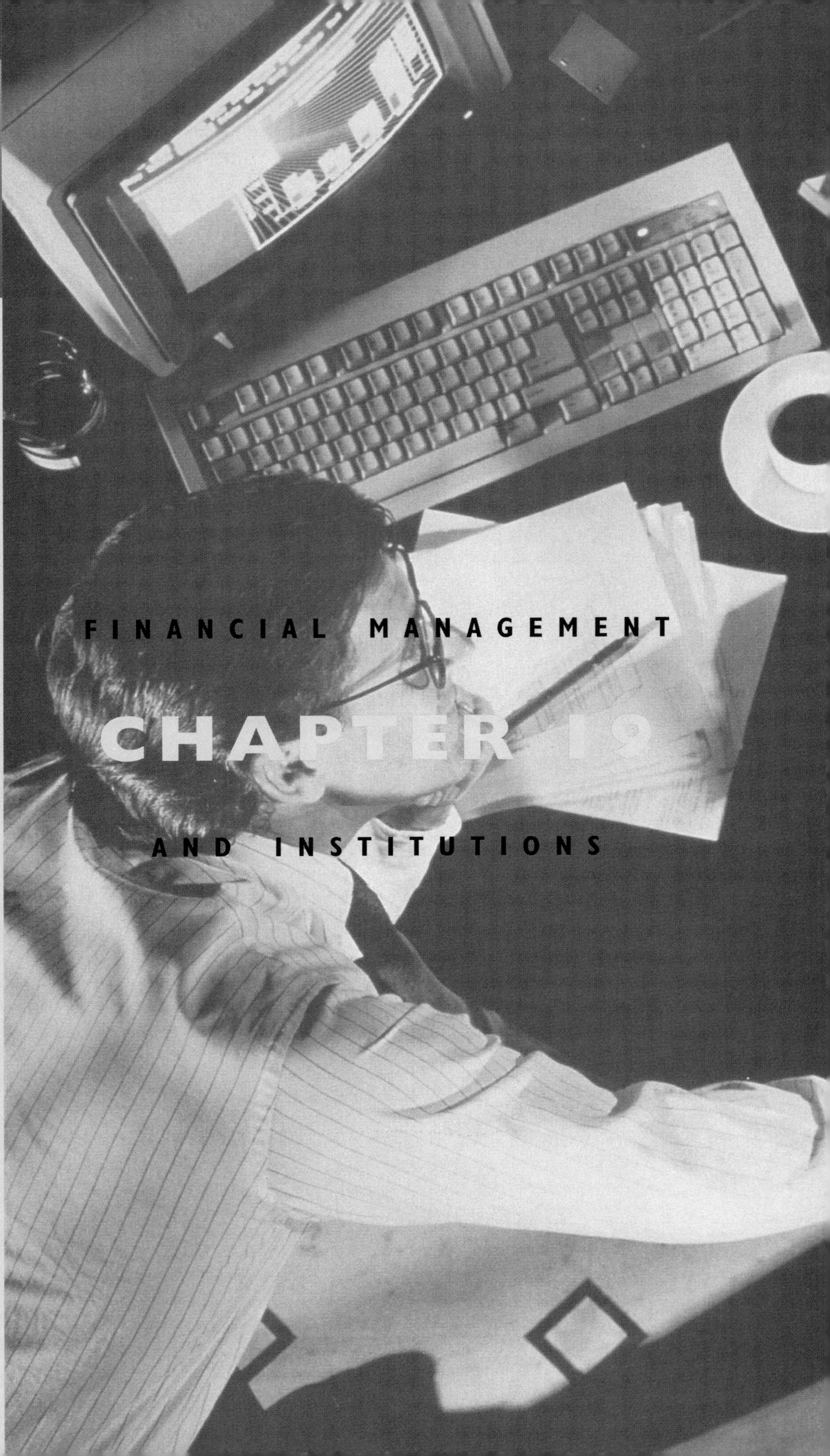

LEARNING GOALS

1. Identify the functions performed by a firm's financial manager.

2. Describe the characteristics of a good form of money, and list the functions of money.

3. Distinguish between money (M1) and near-money (M2).

4. Explain how a firm uses funds.

5. Compare the two major categories of sources of funds.

6. Identify likely sources of short-term and long-term funds.

7. Identify the major categories of financial institutions and the sources and uses of their funds.

8. Explain the functions of the Federal Reserve System and the tools it uses to increase or decrease the money supply.

9. Describe the institutions that regulate bank safety and how they operate.

10. Discuss the U.S. financial system in its global context.

HYDROKINETIC DESIGNS, INC.

David Black had reason to believe that he was living the American dream. His small business, Hydrokinetic Designs, Inc., was flourishing. Sales more than doubled during 1994 to reach the $1 million mark, and a large retail chain contacted him regarding plans to conduct a test market to assess consumer sales of his firm's twin-nozzle shower heads. If the test generated sufficient sales, a 10,000-unit order would follow. ■ Black was all too aware of the dark side of the American dream, though. Like so many fledgling businesses, his Coral Gables, Florida–based firm needed additional funds to invest in parts, finished inventories, employee compensation, and related business expenses. Also, Black's customers typically waited at least 30 days before paying for their purchases, adding to pressures on the firm's cash position. By 1995, the company had over $450,000 tied up in inventory and accounts receivable. Cash was coming in from product sales, but not in sufficient amounts to sustain this growth. Black was beginning to agree with the old warning, "You absolutely can go broke making money." Although the income statement may show the company earning money, the statement of cash flows may report inadequate funds to pay the bills when they are due. ■ Black did what any astute businessperson would do when his firm needed additional funds: he applied for a bank loan. The company founder and CEO was familiar with the so-called three *C*s of credit—capacity, character, and collateral—on which lenders base their judgments of borrowers' ability and willingness to repay loans. He felt confident that his firm met all three criteria. Hydrokinetic Designs' current profitability and its positive sales and earnings projections appeared to satisfy the capacity criterion. Even though the firm had been operating for a relatively short time, it had a strong credit history and Black felt that it would pass the character test. He fully expected potential lenders to demand that he pledge company assets as security in case of a loan default, but he was confident that the firm's inventory and accounts receivable would pass the collateral test. ■ Black was wrong. Not one, but two banks rejected his loan application. In each case, the lender rejected the firm's pledge of collateral, insisting that the debt be secured by fixed assets such as plant and equipment. Unfortunately, Hydrokinetic Designs had no assets that would satisfy the request since it farmed out production to a contract manufacturer. ■ The result is all too familiar to dozens of otherwise highly successful entrepreneurs. Black had to scale back his rapid growth plans while searching for alternative sources of funds. He would have strongly preferred borrowing the needed funds over giving up part ownership in the company to investors, but in his words, "It's still very challenging getting a loan as a small, growing business." ■ Failure to secure the bank loan led him to turn down the retail chain's test-market proposal. Black simply felt that the firm's financial position was not adequate at that time to generate the funds that it would need immediately in the case of a successful test market and a subsequent 10,000-unit order. The inability to secure a bank loan not only forced Black to adjust his financial plan, it also affected the firm's overall business strategy.[1]

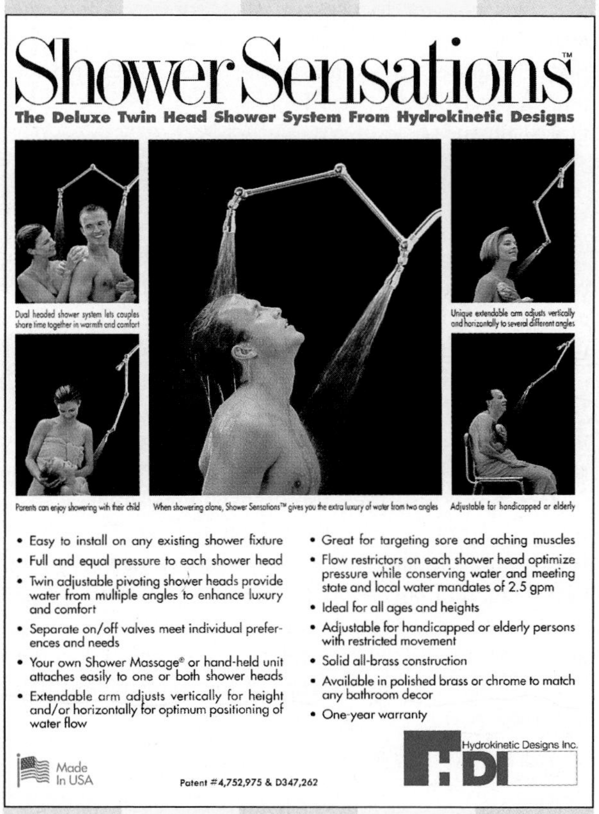

CHAPTER OVERVIEW

This chapter will examine how companies like Hydrokinetic Designs develop and implement financial plans. Earlier, the text discussed two essential functions that a business must perform. First, it must produce a good or service or contract with suppliers to produce it. Second, the firm must market its good or service to prospective customers. A third function is equally important, however: the company must ensure that it has enough money to continue performing its other tasks successfully, both currently and in the future. It must gather adequate funds to buy materials and equipment, pay bills, purchase additional facilities, and compensate employees. This third business function is **finance**—planning, obtaining, and managing the company's use of funds in order to accomplish its objectives most effectively.

finance
Business function of planning, obtaining, and managing a company's use of funds in order to accomplish its objectives most effectively.

Besides meeting expenses, organizational objectives include maximizing the firm's overall value, which is often determined by the value of its common stock. More and more frequently, businesses designate financial managers to be responsible for both meeting expenses and increasing profits for stockholders.

This chapter focuses on such topics as the role of financial managers, why businesses need funds, and the various types and sources of funds. It will discuss how the Federal Reserve System regulates the various institutions that make up the financial system in the United States. Finally, it will examine the role of the U.S. financial system in global business.

ROLE OF THE FINANCIAL MANAGER

In the modern business world, effective financial decisions are increasingly important to organizational success. Businesses are raising the priority of measuring and reducing the costs of conducting business. As a result, **financial managers**—those responsible for developing and implementing the firm's financial plan and for determining the most appropriate sources and uses of funds—are among the most vital people on the corporate scene. Their growing importance is reflected in the number of chief executives promoted from financial management positions. A recent study of major corporations revealed that nearly one in three chief executives had finance or banking backgrounds.

financial manager
Individual in an organization responsible for developing and implementing the firm's financial plan and for determining the most appropriate sources and uses of funds.

Possible job titles for high-ranking financial managers include vice president for finance and chief financial officer (CFO). The way a company manages its money can reduce the frequency or amounts of financing it needs. When it does need money, effective financial management increases the chance of getting it since investors can see how well the company has handled its past finances.[2] In performing their jobs, financial managers continually seek to balance risks with expected financial returns. *Risk* is the uncertainty of gain or loss; *return* is the gain or loss that results from an investment over a specified period.

A heavy reliance on borrowed funds may raise the return on the owners' or stockholders' investment. The financial manager strives to maximize the wealth of the firm's stockholders by striking a balance between the risk of an investment and its potential gain. This balance is called the **risk-return trade-off.** An increase in a firm's cash on hand, for instance, reduces the risk of unexpected cash needs. Cash is not an earning asset, however, and failure to invest surplus funds in an earning asset (such as marketable securities) reduces a firm's potential return or profitability.

risk-return trade-off
Balance between the risk of an investment and its potential gain.

Every financial manager must perform this risk-return balancing act. When John Schnatter started Papa John's International 12 years ago, he quickly realized the importance of balancing risk with return. His first production facility was a broom closet in the back of a Louisville, Kentucky bar. What can a would-be entrepreneur do with financial resources totaling $1,600 in personal savings? Expand, thought Schnatter, and he soon had the makings of a retail chain with three different Louisville outlets.

If he thought it was difficult to operate one tiny outlet with slim cash resources, three stores proved a nightmare. Schnatter decided to stretch his resources by resorting

Making dough by stretching $1,600 in start-up capital to the limit, Papa John's has grown to a 648 outlet, $164 million operation.

to floating checks, a technically illegal practice frowned on by banks, but practiced by most check writers at some point in their lives. "On Fridays," he recalls, "I would figure out what the three or four stores I had were going to do for the weekend and then at 4:05 that afternoon I would start mailing out checks. I never had one bounce. We're a cash business and I could beat the mail." Today, Papa John's 510 franchised and 138 company-owned outlets generate $164 million in systemwide sales and $89 million in total revenues.[3]

FINANCIAL PLAN

Financial managers develop the organization's **financial plan,** a document that specifies the funds it will need for a period of time, the timing of inflows and outflows, and the most appropriate sources and uses of funds. The financial plan is based on *forecasts* of production costs, purchasing, and expected sales activities for the period it covers. Financial managers use these forecasts to determine the specific amounts and timing of expenditures and receipts. The financial plan answers three vital questions:

financial plan
Document that specifies the funds a firm will need for a period of time, the timing of inflows and outflows, and the most appropriate sources and uses of funds.

1. What funds does the firm require during the next period of operations?
2. How will it obtain the necessary funds?
3. When will it need more funds?

A firm receives some funds when it sells goods or services. It needs funds in different amounts at different times, however, and the financial plan must reflect both the amounts and timing of inflows and outflows of funds. A profitable firm may often face a financial squeeze when it needs funds as sales lag, when the volume of its credit sales increases, or when customers make payments slowly. Even though Mike Graham's Frit International is a profitable supplier of frozen shrimp, the Bayou La Batre, Alabama entrepreneur experiences an annual cash-flow timing problem. Every summer he has to pay cash for the 2 million pounds of shrimp his firm freezes every year. His customers take an average of 40 days to pay for their orders, however, many of which occur later in the year. As a result, Graham must secure financing to cover the time between his purchases and ultimate receipts of funds from shrimp sales.[4]

A business experiences cash inflows and outflows similar to those in a household; the members of a household may depend on a weekly or monthly paycheck for funds, but their expenditures vary greatly from one pay period to the next. The financial plan should indicate when the flows of funds entering and leaving the organization will occur and in what amounts.

A good financial plan also involves **financial control,** a process that periodically checks actual revenues, costs, and expenses against forecasts. If reality differs significantly from projected figures, it is important to discover the variation early in order to take corrective action.

financial control
Process that periodically checks actual revenues, costs, and expenses against forecasts.

Steve Shaw and Ric Serrenho, owners of corporate communications firm Visual Concepts Media, discovered firsthand the importance of a good financial manager. When the Connecticut-based company was smaller, Shaw and Serrenho managed everything themselves—marketing, video production, and finance. As the firm began growing rapidly, however, operating costs shot up, and then the IRS conducted a tax audit. The company founders soon realized that they could not maintain financial control and decided to hire Randy LaVigne to develop a financial plan and perform needed financial analyses. LaVigne overhauled the firm's financial system, purchased new financial management software, and taught Shaw and Serrenho how to use the financial reports. He also conducted what-if strategic analyses to answer questions like how much money Visual Concepts Media could save by consolidating its numerous videotape purchases throughout the year into one, annual order. Their financial manager has freed Shaw and Serrenho to concentrate on other aspects of the business. Says Shaw, "[Hiring LaVigne] will save us money and improve our management abilities."[5]

CHARACTERISTICS AND FUNCTIONS OF MONEY

Playwright George Bernard Shaw once said that the *lack* of money is the root of all evil. Many a businessperson would agree, for money is the lubricant of contemporary business. Firms require adequate funds to finance their operations and carry out the plans of management.

CHARACTERISTICS OF MONEY

money
Anything generally accepted as a means of paying for goods and services.

Money is anything generally accepted as a means of paying for goods and services. Most early forms of money had a number of serious disadvantages. For example, a cow is a poor form of money for an owner who wants only a loaf of bread and a bottle of wine. Exchanging money can permit elaborate specialization and provide a general base for purchasing power if the money has certain characteristics. It must be divisible, portable, durable, and difficult to counterfeit, and it should have a stable value.

Divisibility The dollar can be converted into pennies, nickels, dimes, and quarters. The British pound is worth 100 pence; the German deutsche mark can be traded for 100 pfennigs. People can easily exchange these forms of money for products ranging from chewing gum to cars. Today, almost all economic activity is concerned with making and spending money.

Portability Modern paper currency is lightweight, which facilitates the exchange process. Portability is an important characteristic, since the typical dollar bill changes hands 400 times during its lifetime, staying in the average person's pocket or purse less than 2 days.

Durability U.S. dollar bills survive an average of 17 months and can be folded some 4,000 times without tearing. Although coins and paper currency wear out over time, they are replaced easily with new money.

Difficulty in Counterfeiting The distribution of counterfeit money could undermine a nation's monetary system by ruining the value of legitimate money. For this reason, all governments make counterfeiting a serious crime and take elaborate steps to prevent it. A U.S. dollar bill, for instance, contains an interwoven security thread and microprinting on the portrait. The government has plans to redesign paper currency, making bills multicolored, adding a hologram, or using a watermark in order to make counterfeiting even more difficult.[6]

U.S. currency accounts for 80 percent of all counterfeit money intercepted by Interpol, the international police agency. Other nations have incorporated new features into their currencies to make it more difficult to counterfeit. France's new 50-franc note has a watermark while new Canadian currency contains a thin square that changes color when viewed at different angles. Neither can be reproduced by a color copier.

Stability of Value A good money system should have a stable value. If the value of money fluctuates, people become unwilling to trade goods and services for it. Inflation is, therefore, a serious concern for governments. When people fear that money will lose much of its value, they begin to abandon it and look for safer means of storing their wealth. In a period of runaway inflation, where the value of money may decrease 20 percent or more in a single year, people increasingly return to a barter system, exchanging the output of their work for the output of others.

Firms operating in Russia face a similar problem. During the 1980s, the Kama automotive factory, located 600 miles north of Moscow, turned out 150,000 heavy-duty trucks a year, equaling the entire U.S production. The wildly fluctuating ruble drove the firm to adopt the barter tactics of the bazaar. Today, Kama may trade a truck to another firm for sheet metal, electrical parts, or glass components. The new truck may even be involved in a secondhand or thirdhand exchange by purchasers who barter it for needed parts.[7]

A BROADER PURPOSE

"BUDDY, CAN YOU SPARE A MILLION BUCKS?" So you want to be your own boss? Get ready to wipe out your savings, mortgage the house, and borrow from every friend and relative you know with spare cash. After all of this money is gone, you can go out and find new sources of funds. That's what happened to Douglas Pihl and Duane Carlson, founders of NetStar. ■ It all began in 1990 when Pihl invented the gigarouter, a piece of high-performance computer hardware that links electronic workstations and gives them the power of a supercomputer at a fraction of the cost. Pihl and partner Carlson then spent the next 18 months developing a business plan and scraping up $500,000 in seed money for their venture. Although the amount sounds impressive, it was just half of the $1 million the entrepreneurs needed to launch NetStar. They also had to line up additional money for the early years of operation before NetStar began to show profits and positive cash flows. ■ Realizing that their cash needs were far greater than could be extracted from friends, relatives, and business colleagues, the NetStar founders approached a regional brokerage firm in Minneapolis. Within 3 months, the firm had found enough wealthy investors—called *angels*—who agreed to invest a combined $1.35 million in exchange for part ownership of this promising business. By 1995, two more groups of angels had been recruited and the funds raised had grown to $10 million. Says Carlson, "My only regret is that we didn't go to the brokers sooner. We wasted a lot of time at the beginning. When you have a hot product and you know you'll need a given amount of capital to get your business rolling, the main thing is to get on with it." ■ Pihl and Carlson are not exactly novices when it comes to raising money for a new business venture. In fact, they were two of the six co-founders of Lee Data, a highly successful manufacturer of peripherals for IBM computers. Angels who invested in Lee Data realized huge profits when that firm made an initial offering of stock to the general investing public. This track record provided crucial help in enticing investors to ante up the $10 million for an ownership stake in NetStar, a company with no sales and a product that barely existed. ■ Carlson attributes NetStar's success in attracting investors willing to take the necessary financial risk to a combination of a superior product offering, the partners' track record, and their persistence in seeking out investors. As he puts it, "The process is similar to 'cold-calling' in sales. You have to be able to take a lot of rejection." His advice: keep at it; modify your business plan, if necessary; seek out expertise in areas where it is lacking; and work to constantly improve your product. Then keep calling, and calling, and calling. . . .

Source: Carlson quotations from Anne B. Fisher, "Raising Capital for a New Venture," *Fortune*, June 13, 1994, pp. 99–101.

QUESTIONS FOR CRITICAL THINKING

1. What options do entrepreneurs with no track record have in raising funds for a start-up venture?
2. If you had an exceptional new product but were unable to raise funds to start up your own business, what would you do?
3. What percentage of ownership would you be willing to give investors who provided you with seed money for your new venture? Why?

FUNCTIONS OF MONEY

Money performs three basic functions. First, it serves primarily as a medium of exchange—a means of facilitating exchanges and eliminating the need for a barter system. Second, it functions as a unit of account—a common denominator for measuring the value of all goods and services. Finally, money acts as a temporary store of value—a way of keeping accumulated wealth until the owner needs it to make new purchases. Money offers one big advantage as a store of value: It is highly *liquid,* that is, the owner can get access to it and dispose of it quickly and easily. The chief advantage of money is that the owner can keep it immediately available to pay for products or to repay debts.

MONEY SUPPLY AND NEAR-MONEY

The U.S. money supply breaks down into several categories: coins, paper money, traveler's checks, demand deposits (checking accounts), interest-bearing NOW accounts, and credit union share draft accounts. Government reports and business publications often use the term *M1* to refer to the total of these categories of money.

In addition to this money supply, a number of other assets are almost as liquid as cash or checking accounts, but do not serve directly as a medium of exchange. These are known as **near-money.** Time deposits (savings accounts), government bonds, money market mutual funds, and credit cards are considered near-money. These categories of near-money are commonly referred to as *M2*.

near-money
Asset almost as liquid as cash or a checking account, but that cannot serve directly as a medium of exchange.

Film maker Spike Lee resorted to spending near-money when funds dried up while producing an early movie. The ever-resourceful Lee used his VISA card to cover the remaining costs. Michael and Tom Sheehan did the same in raising $300 to start Alpine Computer Systems. Within 8 years, the computer-networking services company was earning the brothers almost $1 million on annual revenues of $9 million.[8]

WHY ORGANIZATIONS NEED FUNDS

Organizations require funds for many reasons, including running day-to-day business operations, paying for inventory, making interest payments on loans, paying dividends to stockholders, and purchasing land, facilities, and equipment. A firm's financial plan identifies the amounts and timing of its specific cash needs. Comparing these needs with expenditures and expected cash receipts from product sales, payments made by credit purchasers, and other sources, the financial manager can determine precisely what additional funds the firm needs at any given time. If inflows exceed cash needs, the financial manager will invest the surplus to earn interest. On the other hand, if inflows do not meet cash needs, the financial manager will seek funds from additional sources.[9] Figure 19.1 illustrates this process.

GENERATING FUNDS FROM EXCESS CASH

Most financial managers choose to invest the majority of their firms' excess cash balances in marketable securities. These financial instruments are often considered near-

FIGURE 19.1 FINANCIAL PLANNING PROCESS

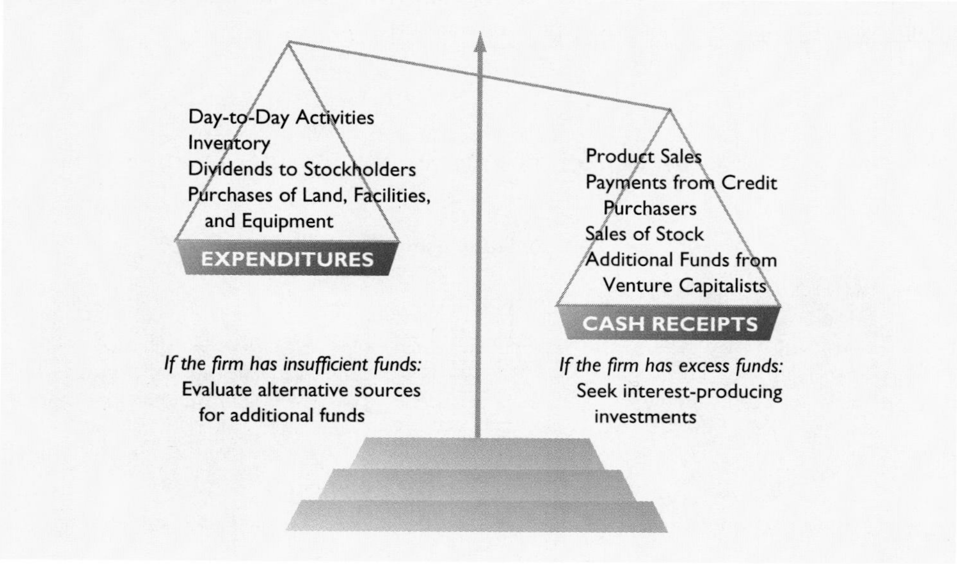

money since they are, by definition, marketable and easy to convert into cash. Three of the most common types of marketable securities are U.S. Treasury bills, commercial paper, and certificates of deposit. *Treasury bills,* one of the most popular kinds of marketable securities, are issued by the U.S. government, so they are considered virtually risk-free and easy to resell. *Commercial paper* is a term for short-term notes issued by major corporations with very high credit standings and backed solely by the reputations of the issuing firms. Commercial paper is riskier than a Treasury bill and lacks a well-developed market for resale prior to maturity, but it pays the purchaser a higher rate of interest. A *certificate of deposit (CD)* is a short-term note issued by a financial institution such as a commercial bank, savings and loan association, or credit union. The sizes and maturity dates of CDs vary considerably and can be tailored to meet the needs of the purchaser. Large CDs in denominations of $100,000 can be purchased for periods as short as 24 hours. At the other extreme, 10-year certificates are available in denominations as low as $100 to $250.

SOURCES OF FUNDS

So far the chapter has focused on half of the definition of finance—the reasons organizations need funds and how they use them. The firm's financial plan must give equal importance to the choice of the best sources of needed funds. Sources of funds fall into two major categories: debt and equity capital. **Debt capital** represents funds obtained through borrowing. **Equity capital** consists of funds provided by the firm's owners when they reinvest earnings, make additional contributions, liquidate assets, issue stock to the general public, or raise contributions from venture capitalists. A firm also obtains equity capital by saving revenues from day-to-day operations and by liquidating some of the firm's assets. These sources are shown in Figure 19.2.

debt capital
Funds obtained through borrowing.

equity capital
Funds provided by the firm's owners when they plow back earnings, liquidate assets, make additional contributions, issue stock to the general public, or raise contributions from venture capitalists.

When Walt Disney Co. executives decided to raise $400 million to rescue their troubled EuroDisney theme park near Paris, they secured the funds from 27-year-old Prince Al-Walid of Saudi Arabia in exchange for 24 percent ownership.[10]

Cash needs vary from one time period to the next, and even an established firm may not generate sufficient funds from operations to cover all costs of a major expansion or a significant investment in new equipment. In such an instance, the financial manager must evaluate the potential benefits and drawbacks of seeking funds by borrowing. As an alternative to borrowing, the firm may raise equity capital in several ways. The financial manager's job includes determining the most cost-effective balance between equity and borrowed funds and the proper blend of short-term and long-term funds. Table 19.1 compares debt capital and equity capital on four criteria.

FIGURE 19.2 DEBT AND EQUITY CAPITAL: TWO BASIC SOURCES OF FUNDS

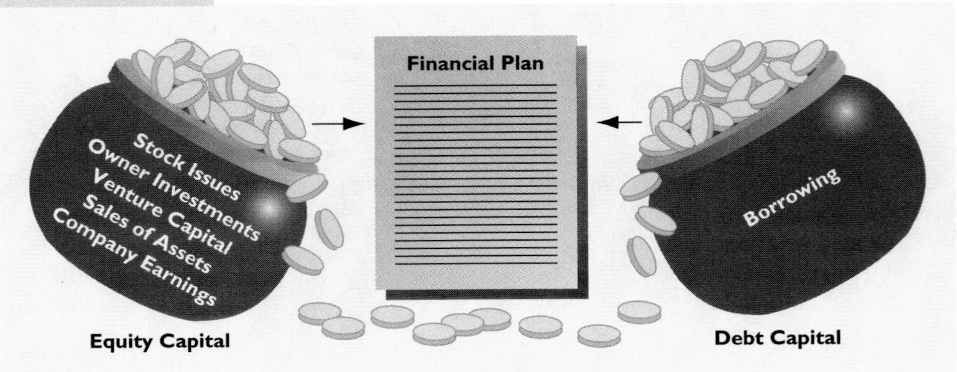

The design for the new DreamWorks SKG movie studio is shown in this computer-generated image. Founders of DreamWorks SKG are film director Steven Spielberg, animated-film executive Jeffrey Katzenberg, and popular music entrepreneur David Geffen, who each put up $33.3 million in equity capital. Microsoft co-founder Paul Allen added $500 million in return for 20 percent equity in the venture. DreamWorks has also secured a $1 billion line of credit from Chemical Bank.

SHORT-TERM SOURCES OF FUNDS

At numerous times throughout the year, an organization may discover that its cash requirements exceed its available funds. Catalog retailers such as Best Products, Service Merchandise, and Gordon Jewelry generate 80 percent of their total annual sales during the Christmas season. A store like Service Merchandise will generate surplus cash for most of the year, but to build up inventory just before the Christmas season, it requires additional funds to finance the stock of merchandise until it is sold. As the firm collects on sales during the Christmas season, it can use the incoming funds to repay the suppliers of the borrowed funds. In these instances, the firm's financial manager will evaluate short-term sources of needed funds. By definition, the firm must repay funds from these sources within 1 year.

TABLE 19.1 COMPARISON OF DEBT AND EQUITY CAPITAL

CRITERION	DEBT	EQUITY
Maturity	Specifies a date by which it must be repaid.	Specifies no maturity date.
Claim on assets	Lenders have prior claims on assets.	Stockholders have claims only after the firm satisfies claims of lenders.
Claim on income	Lenders have prior claim on a fixed amount of interest, which must be paid before dividends can be paid to stockholders. Interest payments are a contractual obligation of the borrowing firm.	Stockholders have a residual claim after all creditors have been paid. Dividends are not a contractual obligation of the firm.
Right to a voice in management	Lenders are creditors, not owners. They have no voice in company affairs unless they do not receive interest payments.	Stockholders are the owners of the company, and most have a voice in the operation of the firm.

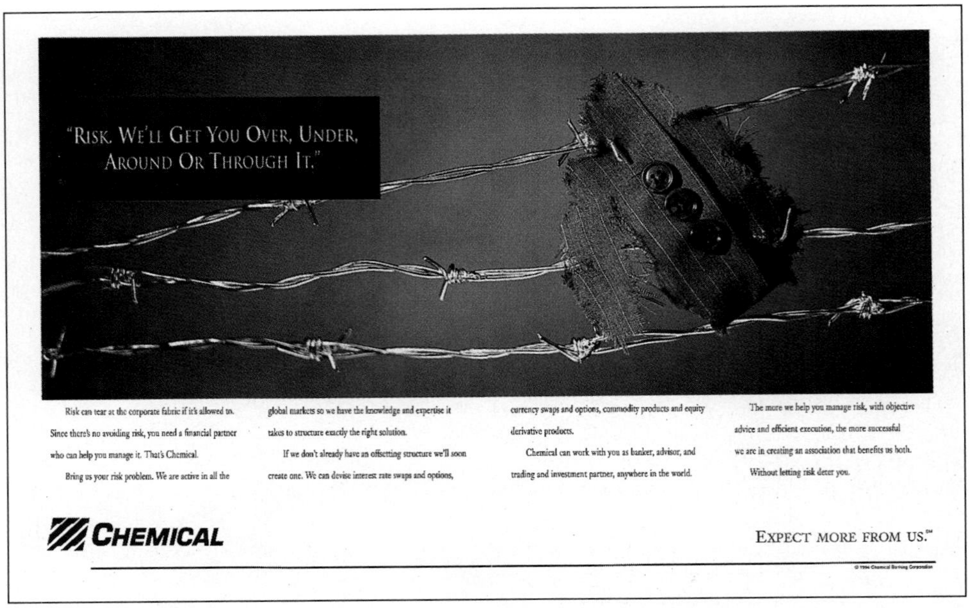

New York–based Chemical Bank attracts business customers by emphasizing its expertise in global markets and its willingness to tailor financial services to meet the needs of individual firms.

The major short-term source is *trade credit,* or open-account purchases from suppliers. A second source is *unsecured bank loans,* for which the business does not pledge any assets as collateral. For another option, *secured short-term loans,* the firm must pledge collateral such as inventory. Large firms with unquestioned financial stability can raise money from a fourth source, by selling *commercial paper.* As mentioned before, commercial paper is typically sold in denominations of $100,000 with a maturity of 30 to 90 days. Issuing commercial paper to raise funds is usually 1 or 2 percent cheaper than borrowing short-term funds from a bank.

LONG-TERM SOURCES OF FUNDS

A firm can use short-term sources of cash to meet current needs for cash or inventory. To acquire another company or make a major purchase such as land, a new plant, and expensive equipment, however, will require funds for a much longer period. Unlike short-term sources, a firm repays long-term sources over a period of 1 year or longer.

A business firm can tap three long-term financing sources. One is long-term loans issued by various financial institutions such as banks, insurance companies, and pension funds. A second source is **bonds**—certificates of indebtedness sold to raise long-term funds for a corporation or government agency. As a third source, it may secure *equity funds* as explained earlier, by selling stock in the company, selling company assets, reinvesting company earnings, or raising additional contributions from venture capitalists or the firm's owners.

bond
Certificate of indebtedness sold to raise long-term funds for a corporation or government agency.

Public Sales of Stocks and Bonds Sales of stocks and bonds represent a major source of funds for corporations. Such a sale provides cash inflows for the issuing firm and either a share in its ownership (for a stock purchaser) or a specified rate of interest and repayment at a stated time (for a bond purchaser). Since stock and bond issues of many corporations are traded on organized securities exchanges, stockholders and bondholders can easily sell their securities. Issuing stock or bonds to finance a corporation is an important decision discussed in more detail in the next chapter.

The strength of the Samsonite balance sheet, like the image of its respected luggage, is enhanced by infusions of equity capital from Apollo Advisors. This large venture capital fund acquired a large share of the firm's ownership shares in exchange for a large infusion of cash.

Attracting Venture Capital The typical business begins operations with an investment of $10,000 or less, but Douglas Pihl and Duane Carlson, founders of computer peripherals maker NetStar, knew they had to raise $10 million to make their firm competitive. Had they conceived a business idea of the $10,000 variety, they could have called the U.S. Small Business Administration at 800-U-ASK SBA and applied for one of the agency's micro loans of up to $25,000. The computer hardware industry is capital-intensive, however, and the partners knew that their capital needs exceeded SBA guidelines, so they turned to venture capital funds and brokerage houses, tapping every source available to them to reach their financial goal.[11]

Venture capital usually comes from outside investors who acquire ownership shares in the business. The venture capitalist may be a corporation, a wealthy individual, a pension fund, or a major endowment fund. In exchange for funds, the venture capitalist receives shares of the corporation's stock at relatively low prices and becomes a part-owner. Apollo Advisors, a major venture capitalist firm, owns substantial shares of companies ranging from Perry Ellis clothing, Converse shoes, Samsonite luggage, and Chi-Chi's restaurants to the Telemundo international Spanish-language TV network.[12] As compensation for taking the risks inherent in any struggling firm, the venture capitalist has the opportunity to earn substantial profits should the firm become successful and issue stock to the general public.

Virtually hundreds of venture capitalists operate in the United States today, and each typically receives dozens of proposals each month from businesses seeking funds. These investors reject most applications; they seek soundly managed firms with unique goods or services in rapidly growing industries. In recent years, venture capitalists have concentrated on such industries as medical technology, computers, and environmental waste management. Often a venture capitalist provides management consulting advice as well as funds.

Leverage Borrowing to raise needed cash allows the firm to benefit from the principle of **leverage,** a technique of increasing the rate of return on an investment by financing it with borrowed funds. The concept of leverage can be related to a physical lever.

leverage
Technique of increasing the rate of return on an investment by financing it with borrowed funds.

Like the fulcrum on which a lever rests, the interest payments on borrowed funds are fixed. The key to managing leverage is ensuring that the company's earnings exceed its interest payments, which increases the leverage on the rate of return on stockholders' investment. Of course, if the company earns less than its interest payments, stockholders will lose money on their original investment.

Table 19.2 shows two identical firms that choose to raise funds in different ways. The Leverage Corp. obtains 90 percent of its funds from lenders who purchase company bonds. The Equity Corp. raises all of its funds through sales of company stock. Each company earns $30,000. Leverage Corp. pays $9,000 in interest to bondholders and earns a 210 percent return for its owners' $10,000 investment; Equity Corp. provides only a 30 percent return on its stockholders' investment of $100,000.

As long as earnings exceed interest payments on borrowed funds, financial leverage will allow a firm to increase the rate of return on its stockholders' investment. However, leverage also works in reverse. If, for example, Equity Corp. earnings drop to $5,000, stockholders earn a 5 percent return on their investment. Because Leverage Corp. must pay its bondholders $9,000 in interest, however, the $5,000 gain actually becomes a $4,000 loss for Leverage stockholders. As a second problem with overreliance on borrowed funds, it reduces management flexibility in future decisions.

Hershey Foods Corp., the Pennsylvania-based candy and pasta company, has very little debt. This fact, combined with a solid track record of steady profits and market leadership, also produces a sterling credit rating for the firm. Consequently, when Hershey decides to borrow funds, its managers encounter little difficulty in securing debt capital at rock-bottom interest rates. With two new plants under construction, Hershey chose to finance them through a $100 million bond issue. The debt carried an annual interest rate at least 1 percentage point less than those paid by competitors with heavier debt burdens.[13]

U.S. FINANCIAL SYSTEM

Traditionally, the U.S. financial system has been composed of two categories of institutions, deposit institutions (which accept deposits from customers or members and provide some form of checking accounts) and nondeposit institutions. Deposit institutions include commercial banks, thrifts (savings and loan associations and savings banks), and credit unions. Nondeposit institutions include insurance companies, pension funds, and consumer and commercial finance companies.

TABLE 19.2 HOW LEVERAGE WORKS

LEVERAGE CORP.		EQUITY CORP.	
Common stock	$ 10,000	Common stock	$100,000
Bonds (at 10% interest)	90,000	Bonds	0
	100,000		100,000
Earnings	30,000	Earnings	30,000
Less bond interest	9,000	Less bond interest	0
	21,000		30,000
Return to stockholders	$\frac{21,000}{\$\ 10,000} = 210\%$	Return to stockholders	$\frac{30,000}{\$100,000} = 30\%$

COMMERCIAL BANKS

Fundamental elements of the U.S. banking system include approximately 12,200 **commercial banks,** profit-making businesses that hold the deposits of individuals, business firms, and not-for-profit organizations in the form of checking or savings accounts and use these funds to make loans to individuals and businesses. They also generate funds from selling certificates of deposit, by borrowing from the Federal Reserve System, and by charging a variety of fees for services. Banks then loan these funds to individuals, business firms, and not-for-profit organizations. By charging higher interest rates to borrowers than they pay to depositors and others who provide funds for lending, the banks generate revenue to cover their operating expenses and earn profits.

commercial bank
Profit-making business that holds deposits of individuals and other businesses in the form of checking or savings balances and uses these funds to make loans to individuals and businesses.

The number of competing banks and their average sizes vary greatly in different countries. More than 12,000 commercial banks, many of them extremely small, operate in the United States as compared with less than 20 giant banks in the United Kingdom. In the half-dozen years since *perestroika,* over 2,500 banks have sprung up in Russia.[14] Figure 19.3 shows how a commercial bank performs its functions.

TYPES AND SERVICES OF COMMERCIAL BANKS

Most U.S. commercial banks are *state banks*—commercial banks chartered by individual states. Approximately one-third of all commercial banks with charters from the federal government are referred to as *national banks.* These tend to be larger institutions, and they hold approximately 60 percent of total commercial bank deposits. While the regulations affecting state and national banks vary slightly, in practice the individual depositor or borrower sees little difference between the two. The five largest U.S. banks are New York–headquartered Citicorp; Chemical Banking Corp. of New York; San Francisco's BankAmerica Corp.; NationsBank of Charlotte, North Carolina; and J. P. Morgan & Co. of New York.

The term *full-service bank* accurately describes the typical commercial bank, which offers dozens of services to its depositors. In addition to a variety of checking and savings accounts and personal and business loans, commercial banks typically offer bank credit cards, safe deposit boxes, tax-deferred individual retirement accounts (IRAs), discount brokerage services, wire transfers (which permit immediate movement of funds by electronic transfers to distant banks), and financial counseling. Most banks provide low-cost traveler's checks and overdraft protection for checking accounts that automatically provides small loans at relatively low interest rates for depositors who write checks exceeding the balances in their accounts.

FIGURE 19.3 OPERATIONS OF A COMMERCIAL BANK

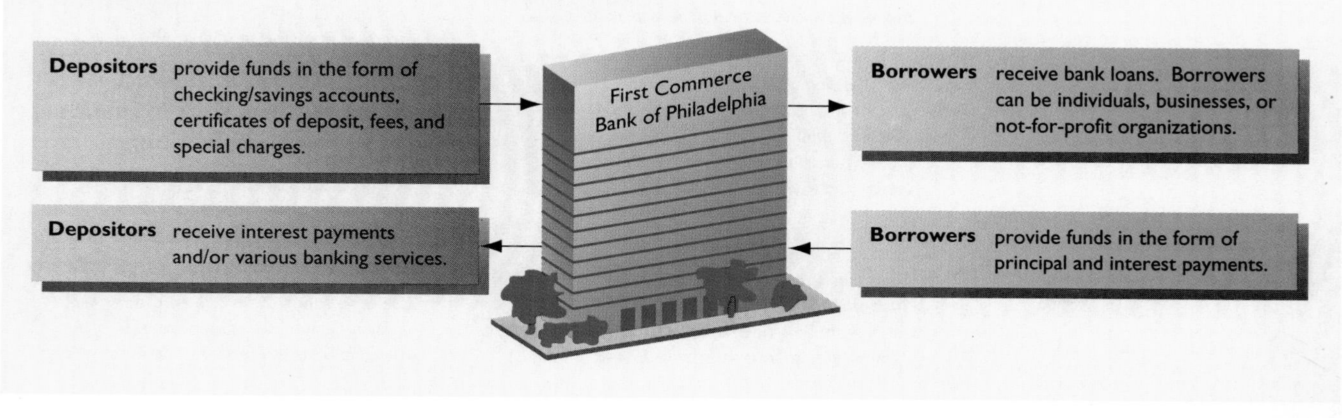

Check processing begins with a check—a document addressed to a bank or other financial institution that gives written, legal authorization to withdraw a specified amount of money from an account and to pay that amount to someone. In Figure 19.4, a purchasing agent for the Sea View Apartments buys a $150 carpet shampoo machine from Sears. The check that pays for the machine authorizes the Georgia National Bank of Savannah, where Sea View has a checking account, to reduce Sea View's balance by $150. The bank pays this sum to Sears to cover the cost of the machine. If both parties have checking accounts at the same bank, check processing is easy; the bank simply increases Sears' balance by $150 and reduces Sea View's balance by the same amount.

However, this purchase was made from a Sears catalog and involves the retailer's Chicago checking account. The Federal Reserve System acts as a collector for most such intercity transactions. It handles a large number of the 180 million checks written every business day. You can trace the route a check has taken by examining the endorsement stamps on the reverse side.

Banks have made themselves more accessible to customers by setting up *automated teller machines (ATMs),* electronic banking machines that permit customers to make

FIGURE 19.4 CHECK'S JOURNEY THROUGH THE FEDERAL RESERVE SYSTEM

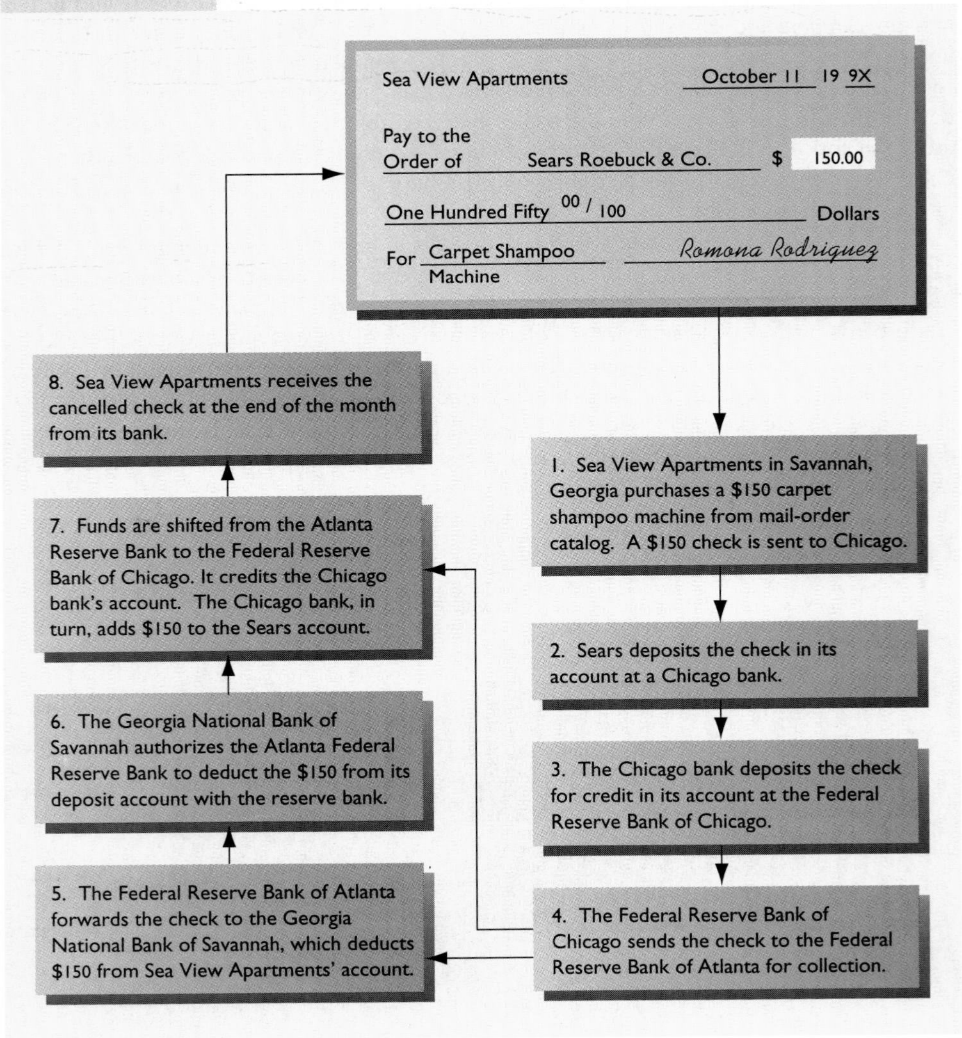
Sea View Apartments
October 11 19 9X
Pay to the Order of Sears Roebuck & Co. $ 150.00
One Hundred Fifty 00/100 Dollars
For Carpet Shampoo Machine
Romona Rodriquez
1. Sea View Apartments in Savannah, Georgia purchases a $150 carpet shampoo machine from mail-order catalog. A $150 check is sent to Chicago.
2. Sears deposits the check in its account at a Chicago bank.
3. The Chicago bank deposits the check for credit in its account at the Federal Reserve Bank of Chicago.
4. The Federal Reserve Bank of Chicago sends the check to the Federal Reserve Bank of Atlanta for collection.
5. The Federal Reserve Bank of Atlanta forwards the check to the Georgia National Bank of Savannah, which deducts $150 from Sea View Apartments' account.
6. The Georgia National Bank of Savannah authorizes the Atlanta Federal Reserve Bank to deduct the $150 from its deposit account with the reserve bank.
7. Funds are shifted from the Atlanta Reserve Bank to the Federal Reserve Bank of Chicago. It credits the Chicago bank's account. The Chicago bank, in turn, adds $150 to the Sears account.
8. Sea View Apartments receives the cancelled check at the end of the month from its bank.

banking transactions on a 24-hour basis by entering personal access codes. In 1980, 20,000 ATMs processed 100 million transactions annually; today, over 87,000 machines handle more than 600 million transactions a year. Network systems now enable ATM users to access their bank accounts from other states and countries. Citibank has programmed its ATMs in 11 different languages to perform foreign currency transactions at branches in a dozen countries.[15]

A growing number of commercial banks have begun to work harder to serve busy depositors through such technological innovations as telephone-based bill-paying systems and electronic funds transfers from one account to another. Figure 19.5 describes Chase PC Banking, a Chase Manhattan Bank service that gives depositors 24-hour access to their accounts. Using a personal computer equipped with a modem, the customer can check account balances, pay bills electronically, transfer funds, review recent transactions, and even receive a detailed history of account activity.

Chase Manhattan Bank is just one of thousands of financial institutions that offer electronic banking through **electronic funds transfer systems (EFTS),** computerized systems for conducting financial transactions electronically. Last year, companies paid more than 35 million invoices electronically, a 59 percent increase over the previous year's total. Although this is still less than 1 percent of the 12 billion checks that U.S. corporations write each year, business use of electronic funds transfer is expected to increase rapidly, for one reason, because EFTS saves money. Estimates place the cost to U.S. firms of printing, mailing, and clearing paper checks at more than $50 billion a year. Another reason for EFTS is the wealth of data that can accompany electronic payments, including invoice numbers, any discounts taken, and which divisions to pay.[16]

electronic funds transfer system (EFTS)
Computerized method for making purchases and paying bills by electronically processing deposits or withdrawals of funds.

THRIFTS: SAVINGS AND LOAN ASSOCIATIONS AND SAVINGS BANKS

Thrift institutions, as savings and loan associations and savings banks are commonly called, offer a variety of banking services such as home mortgages, loans, passbook accounts, time deposits, traveler's checks, consumer leasing, trust services, and credit cards, all at rates competitive with those of commercial banks. A **savings and loan**

savings and loan association (S&L)
Thrift institution that offers savings and checking accounts, using most of its funds to make home mortgage loans.

FIGURE 19.5

SERVING BANKING CUSTOMERS: NEW SERVICES AND INCREASED ACCESSIBILITY

savings bank
State-chartered thrift institution with operations similar to those of savings and loan associations.

association (S&L) is a thrift institution that offers both savings and checking accounts, using most of its funds to make home mortgage loans. **Savings banks,** also known as *mutual savings banks,* are state-chartered banks, concentrated in the New England states, with operations similar to those of S&Ls.

CREDIT UNIONS

credit union
Member-owned financial cooperative that pays interest to depositors, offers share draft (checking) accounts, and makes short-term loans and some home mortgage loans.

A third type of deposit institution, the **credit union,** is a member-owned financial cooperative that pays interest to depositors, offers share draft (checking) accounts, and makes short-term loans and some home mortgage loans. It is typically sponsored by a company, union, or professional or religious group. The nation's 12,800 federally insured credit unions provide consumer loans at competitive rates for their members.[17] They also offer interest-bearing checking accounts (share draft accounts), long-term mortgage loans, life insurance, and financial counseling. While credit unions tend to be relatively small (only

STRENGTH IN DIVERSITY

JESUIT BANKING FOR BOGOTA'S POOR In the past, Ciudad Bolivar's fledgling businesses and households had one source for needed loans: the local loan sharks. That was before Father José María Campoamor, a Jesuit priest, arrived in this slum on the outskirts of Bogota, the capital city of Colombia. His organizing efforts, which began in 1911 as a mixture of business and charity, have evolved into Fundación Social, a full-service financial institution serving the needs of Colombia's poor. ■ Campoamor's initial efforts to establish church programs for local shoemakers, bricklayers, and carpenters made him aware of the severe need for housing. As a solution, he started a credit union owned by the workers. Over the years, Fundación Social has evolved into a diversified financial services company that includes a bank, Caja Social, with almost a million depositors and 126 branches located throughout Colombia. It is the only bank serving the shopkeepers, street vendors, and homemakers of Ciudad Bolivar. ■ Caja Social branches operate in crime-ridden areas like Ciudad Bolivar to cater to the specific banking needs of their clients. An average of 3,000 customers visit a branch each day, avoiding carrying excess cash by depositing and withdrawing as little as $5 at a time. The bank even stays open on Sundays to serve its clients. The average savings account balance at the Ciudad Bolivar branch is $200, and three-fourths of its loans are for less than $2,000 each. ■ Controlled by a Catholic religious order that selects a board of directors, the operation is clearly no charity. In fact, the trade magazine *America Economia* ranks Caja Social as Latin America's most profitable bank with a return on assets of 8 percent. The company functions like any other in Colombia, competing in the marketplace and paying taxes. As bank official Enrique Andrade points out, "The Fundación acts like any private shareholder. We reinvest profits, and we never sacrifice business for charity. We want to stick for the long term." ■ The bank's customers do their part, as well. Even though deposits and loans are relatively small, defaults are almost nonexistent. In Andrade's words, "If they don't borrow from us, they have to go to the loan sharks. So they'll do almost anything to repay on time." ■ Father Campoamor undoubtedly would be pleased at the results of his lifetime efforts. In less than 90 years, his tiny credit union has grown to a large, successful, and sound banking and financial services organization that meets its primary goal of helping Colombia's working poor.

Source: Andrade quotations from Joel Millman, "Jesuit Moneylenders," *Forbes,* August 29, 1994, pp. 56, 58.

QUESTIONS FOR CRITICAL THINKING

1. What other services could Caja Social offer to its clients?
2. Why do you think the loan default rate is almost non-existent at Caja Social?
3. Would this same concept work in poor sections of major U.S. cities?

30 percent have assets of $5 million or more), they serve over 55 million members in every state. Credit unions today have outstanding loans of almost $100 billion.[18]

NONDEPOSIT INSTITUTIONS

Other suppliers and users of funds include insurance companies, pension funds, and consumer and commercial finance companies. An *insurance company* provides financial protection for policyholders in return for premium payments. These firms use the funds generated by premiums to make long-term loans to corporations and commercial real estate mortgage loans and to purchase government bonds. Figure 19.6 illustrates the role played by insurance companies and commercial finance companies in providing long-term financing alternatives for businesses.

A *pension fund* holds and invests a large pool of money set up by a company, union, or not-for-profit organization to provide retirement income for employees or members. Participants in the pension fund may begin to collect monthly allotments upon retiring or upon reaching a certain age. Like insurance companies, pension funds invest in long-term mortgages on commercial property, business loans, and government bonds along with common stock in major firms.

Consumer and commercial finance companies offer short-term loans to borrowers, who pledge tangible items such as inventory, machinery, property, or accounts receivable as security against nonpayment. A *commercial finance company* such as Commercial Credit or CIT supplies short-term funds to businesses, which pledge tangible items such as inventory, machinery, or property as collateral. A *consumer finance company* such as Household Finance plays a similar role in the market for personal loans. Consumer and commercial finance companies obtain funds from sales of bonds and from short-term loans from other firms.

Financial Supermarkets In the late 1990s, some nondeposit institutions are doing just about everything that commercial banks do. The term *financial supermarket* describes a growing number of nonbank corporations that offer wide ranges of financial

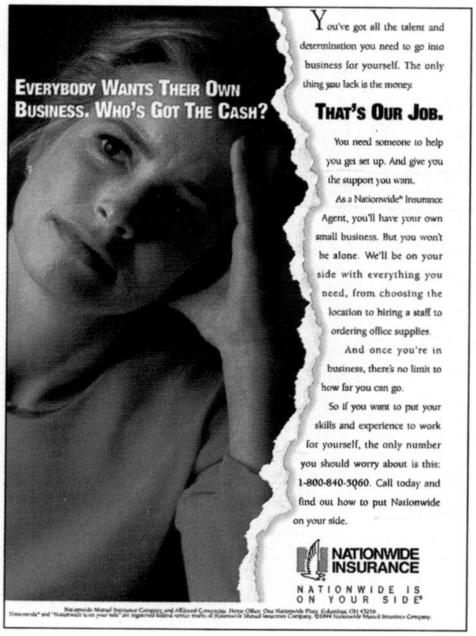

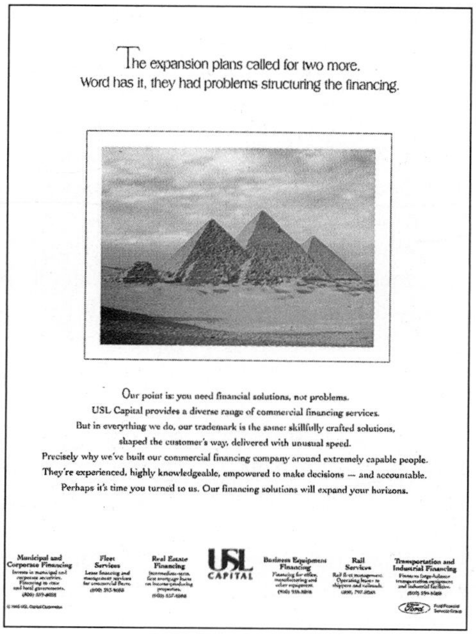

FIGURE 19.6

NONDEPOSIT INSTITUTIONS AS SOURCES OF FUNDS

TABLE 19.3 SOURCES AND USES OF FUNDS FOR FINANCIAL INSTITUTIONS

INSTITUTION	TYPICAL INVESTMENTS	TYPES OF ACCOUNTS OFFERED TO DEPOSITORS	PRIMARY SOURCES OF FUNDS
DEPOSIT INSTITUTIONS			
Commercial bank	Personal loans Business loans Increasingly involved in real estate construction and home mortgage loans	Checking accounts NOW accounts Passbook savings accounts Time deposits Money market deposit accounts	Customer deposits Interest earned on loans
Savings and loan association	Bond purchases Home mortgages Construction loans	Savings accounts NOW accounts Time deposits Money market deposit accounts	Customer deposits Interest earned on loans
Savings bank	Bond purchases Home mortgages Construction loans	Savings accounts NOW accounts Time deposits Money market deposit accounts	Customer deposits Interest earned on loans
Credit union	Short-term consumer loans Increasingly involved in longer-term mortgage loans	Share draft accounts Savings accounts Money market deposit accounts	Deposits by members Interest earned on loans

services, including investments, loans, real estate, and insurance. A good example is GE Capital Services, which serves as both a commercial and consumer finance company. GE Capital insures home mortgages and municipal bonds, supplies the credit behind millions of retail charge cards, and includes an investment bank that has participated in over 100 corporate acquisitions and mergers.[19] Table 19.3 provides a snapshot look at the various sources and uses of funds for deposit and nondeposit institutions.

FEDERAL RESERVE SYSTEM

Federal Reserve System
Network of 12 regional banks that regulates banking in the United States.

Since 1913, a growing number of financial institutions have operated under regulation by the **Federal Reserve System.** The Fed is a network of 12 district banks, controlled by a board of governors, that regulates banking in the United States. In practice, it also acts as a clearinghouse for checks.

While all national banks are required to be members of the Federal Reserve System, membership is optional for state-chartered banks. In all, the Fed oversees approximately 5,500 member banks, and it exercises regulatory powers over all deposit institutions, whether they are Federal Reserve System members or not. All of these institutions must maintain reserves against balances in checking accounts, NOW accounts, and share draft accounts.

The Federal Reserve System's most powerful tool is the *reserve requirement*—the percentage of a bank's checking and savings deposits that it must hold on its premises or on deposit at the local Federal Reserve district bank. By changing the percentage of required reserves, the Fed can affect the amount of money available for making loans. However, changing the reserve requirement is a drastic means of changing the money supply, since even a 1 percent variation in the reserve requirement means a potential fluctuation of billions of dollars in the money supply. Because of this, the Fed relies on other tools more frequently.

INSTITUTION	TYPICAL INVESTMENTS	TYPES OF ACCOUNTS OFFERED TO DEPOSITORS	PRIMARY SOURCES OF FUNDS
NONDEPOSIT INSTITUTIONS			
Insurance company	Corporate long-term loans Mortgages for commercial real estate—major buildings/ shopping centers Government bonds		Premiums paid by policyholders Earnings on investments
Pension fund	Some long-term mortgages on commerical property and business loans Government bonds Corporate securities		Contributions by member employees and employers Earnings on investments
Commercial and/or consumer finance company	Short-term loans to businesses (commerical finance companies) Individual consumer loans (consumer finance companies)		Interest earned on loans Sales of bonds Short-term borrowing from other firms

In a far more common method of influencing the money supply, the Federal Reserve System undertakes *open market operations* by purchasing and selling government securities. If the Fed buys securities, the money it pays enters circulation, increasing the money supply and making more money available to member banks. If the Fed sells government securities, the money generated from these transactions is taken out of circulation, reducing the money supply. Over the years, the Fed has relied increasingly on open market operations as flexible means of expanding and contracting the money supply.[20]

As a third tool to influence the money supply, the Fed can change the *discount rate,* the interest rate it charges on loans to member banks. This tool has often been used in recent years to control the money supply, stimulate economic growth, and match changes in discount rates made by central banks in such nations as Japan and Germany.[21] Even small changes in the discount rate can have large effects on the economy; raising it may motivate bankers to offer fewer new loans, while lowering it can stimulate lending and the economy.[22]

The Federal Reserve System also has the authority to exercise *selective credit controls.* This includes the power to set *margin requirements*—the percentage of the purchase price of a security that an investor must pay in cash in a credit purchase of stock or bonds.

Transactions in international markets affect the U.S. money supply, just as domestic transactions do. On the **foreign exchange market,** purchases and sales of one nation's currency are made for that of another country. Billions of U.S. dollars change hands this way every day. The Fed can lower the exchange value of the dollar by selling dollars and buying foreign currencies; it can raise the dollar's exchange value by doing the opposite, buying dollars and selling foreign currencies. A Fed purchase of a foreign currency has the same effect as buying securities, since it increases the U.S. banking system's reserves. Selling a foreign currency, on the other hand, is like selling securities in that it depletes bank reserves.

foreign exchange market
Market where traders exchange one nation's currency for that of another nation.

Table 19.4 shows several of the tools the Federal Reserve System uses to stimulate or slow the economy.

Changes in currency values are registered on this electronic board. The Fed can lower the exchange value of the dollar by selling dollars and buying yen, German marks, or other foreign currencies. In 1995 the dollar sank to less than 100 yen to the dollar.

BANK SAFETY

Most family histories includes stories of money lost due to bank failures. To increase confidence in the security of financial institutions and to prevent so-called *runs* on banks by depositors seeking to withdraw their balances in times of economic crisis, specialized federal insurance programs have been created for most commercial banks, thrifts, and credit unions. For instance, deposits at all commercial banks that are members of the Federal Reserve System are insured by the **Federal Deposit Insurance Corporation (FDIC).** The FDIC insures depositors' accounts up to a maximum of $100,000 per account and sets requirements for sound banking practices. Deposits at federally insured thrift institutions are covered by the federal Office of Thrift Supervision (OTS) and the Resolution Trust Corporation (RTC). In addition, 88 percent of U.S. credit unions are federally insured by the National Credit Union Share Insurance Fund (NCUSIF).

Federal Deposit Insurance Corporation (FDIC)
Corporation that insures bank depositors' accounts up to a maximum of $100,000 and sets requirements for sound banking practices.

The FDIC's primary guarantee of the safety and soundness of commercial banks and thrifts comes from unannounced inspections of individual institutions at least once a year by its bank examiners. A **bank examiner** is a trained financial analyst who inspects the financial records and management practices of each federally insured financial institution. Other commercial banks are inspected by examiners from the Comptroller of the Currency, the Federal Reserve System, or state regulatory authorities such as state banking commissions. The examination, which may take from a week to several months, evaluates the bank in the following areas: ability of its management; levels and sources of earnings; adequacy of properties pledged to secure loans; capital; and current level of liquidity.

bank examiner
Trained financial analyst who inspects the records and management practices of federally insured financial institutions.

If bank examiners find serious problems in one or more of these areas, they include the bank on a problem list. Regulators view such banks as candidates for failure unless management takes corrective actions immediately, such as arranging for emergency loans or management assistance. Sometimes the government may even replace the bank's directors with new managers. A written examination report typically discusses needed improvements, and regulators express concerns in meetings with the bank's top management and board members. Bank problem lists are confidential, and most depositors are likely to be unaware of such actions. More frequent examinations also take place to evaluate efforts to correct problems.

TABLE 19.4 FEDERAL RESERVE TOOLS

GENERAL TOOL	ACTION	EFFECT ON MONEY SUPPLY	SHORT-TERM EFFECT ON THE ECONOMY
Reserve requirement change	Increase reserve requirements	Reduces money supply	Results in increased interest rates and a slowing of economic activity
	Decrease reserve requirements	Increases money supply	Results in reduced interest rates and an increase in economic activity
Discount rate change	Increase discount rate	Reduces money supply	Results in increased interest rates and a slowing of economic activity
	Decrease discount rate	Increases money supply	Results in reduced interest rates and an increase in economic activity
Open market operation	Purchase government securities	Increases money supply	Results in reduced interest rates and an increase in economic activity
	Sell government securities	Reduces money supply	Results in increased interest rates and a slowing of economic activity
SELECTIVE CREDIT CONTROLS			
Margin requirement change	Increase margin requirements		Reduces credit purchases of securities with a negative impact on securities exchanges and securities prices
	Reduce margin requirements		Increases credit purchases of securities with a positive impact on securities exchanges and on securities prices

Should the problems uncovered during an examination require immediate action, more drastic measures can be taken. If the government cannot locate a satisfactory merger partner or buyer, it may close the institution. In such a case, regulators secure control of the financial records and physical facilities and freeze accounts. They typically do this after business hours on a Friday. By the following Monday, they have either allowed another bank to assume control or have paid off depositors up to the $100,000 deposit insurance limit. Any assets held by the failed institution are sold, and proceeds are divided among creditors and holders of accounts exceeding the $100,000 insurance maximum.

U.S. FINANCIAL SYSTEM: A GLOBAL PERSPECTIVE

Financial services have become a global industry, and it is important to consider the U.S. financial system in its international context. As the headline in Figure 19.7 states, Citibank serves millions of banking customers around the globe with the world's largest branch network. Almost 43 percent of its assets come from outside the United States, and it earns 56 percent of its net annual profits from its foreign operations. Foreign holdings account for 63 percent of the assets of Bankers Trust New York, and the company earns almost 78 percent of its net annual profits from operations abroad. In a typical year, GE Capital earns $150 million outside the United States.

Like the United States, most nations have central banking authorities that control their money supplies. In Germany, it is the Bundesbank, while in the United Kingdom the Bank of England is the central bank. Policy makers at these banks often respond to

FIGURE 19.7

CITIBANK: CAPTURING THE GLOBAL BANKING CUSTOMER

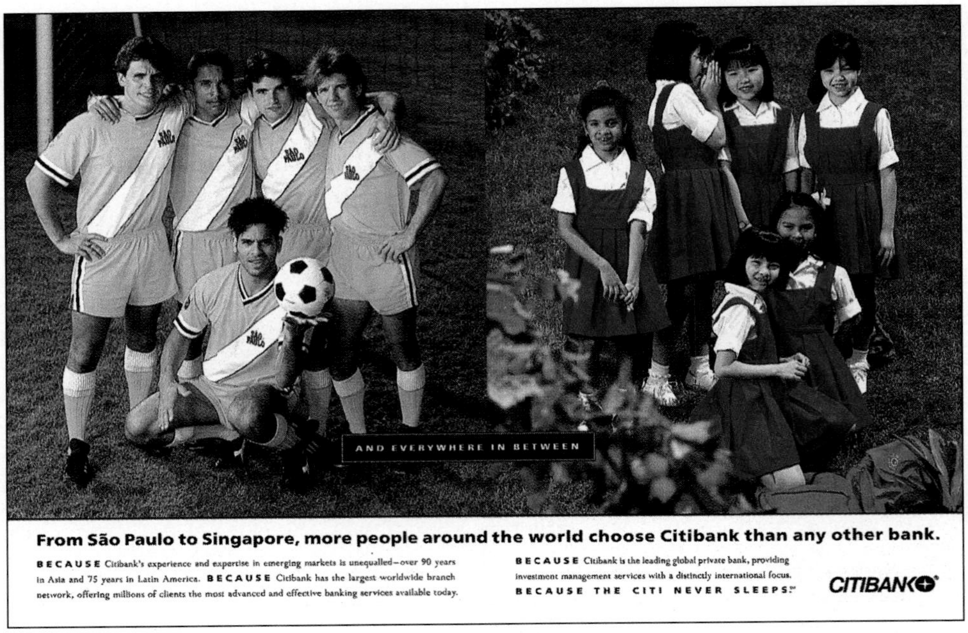

changes in the U.S. financial system by making similar changes in their own systems. When the Fed raised U.S. interest rates recently, interest rates in Japan and Germany also rose. These changes can influence events in countries around the world. Higher U.S. or German interest rates not only increase the cost of borrowing for American and German firms; they also reduce the amount of money available for loans to borrowers in Asia and Latin America.

International banks and financial service firms play important roles in global business. They help to transfer purchasing power from buyers to sellers and from lenders to borrowers. They also provide credit to importers and reduce the risks associated with exchange rates. GE Capital, mentioned earlier in the chapter, is a prime source of funds for companies throughout the world. It is bringing new financial services to Malaysia through a joint venture with that nation's UMW Corporation. Recently, when financial problems at Swedish auto maker Volvo made it difficult for the company to finance a leasing program for its vehicles, GE Capital stepped in to help. Through a joint venture between the two firms, Volvo now offers competitive lease rates for its cars. Without GE Capital, admits Michael Duke, Volvo's car finance operation president, "We would have been pinched. . . . They're the first guys you turn to."[23]

ACHIEVEMENT CHECK SUMMARY

Reread the learning goals that follow, and consider the questions for each goal. Answering these questions will reinforce the most important concepts in the chapter and allow you to check how well you have achieved these learning goals. Where a blank appears before a question, answer with *T* or *F*. Otherwise, circle the letter of the correct answer. An answer key to these questions is found at the end of this chapter.

LEARNING GOAL 19.1: Identify the functions performed by a firm's financial manager.

1. ___ A financial manager seeks to balance financial risks with expected returns.
2. ___ A financial manager is important in a large firm, but not in a small one.
3. ___ A financial manager is responsible for obtaining any needed funds, but plays no role in planning expenditures.

LEARNING GOAL 19.2: Describe the characteristics of a good form of money, and list the functions of money.

1. Money should be: (a) divisible yet durable; (b) portable; (c) stable in value; (d) difficult to counterfeit; (e) all of the above.
2. If you are saving money for a trip after graduation, which function of money are you utilizing? (a) medium of exchange; (b) unit of account; (c) store of value; (d) liquidity; (e) all of the above.
3. Money eliminates the need for a barter system and makes trade easier by serving as a: (a) unit of account; (b) medium of exchange; (c) store of value; (d) all of the above.

LEARNING GOAL 19.3: Distinguish between money (M1) and near-money (M2).

1. ___ A checking account is considered to be money, and is counted as part of M1.
2. ___ Time deposits are classified as near-money and are counted in M2.
3. ___ The forms of near-money counted in M2 can be used directly as a medium of exchange.

LEARNING GOAL 19.4: Explain how a firm uses funds.

1. ___ Firms use funds to finance day-to-day operations, to purchase inventory and long-term assets, and to make payments on loans.
2. ___ Financial managers generally invest excess cash in marketable securities until the funds are needed.
3. ___ The dividends paid to stockholders are not usually counted as expenditures of funds.

LEARNING GOAL 19.5: Compare the two major categories of sources of funds.

1. Sources of equity capital include: (a) owner contributions or stock sold; (b) contributions of venture capitalists; (c) retained earnings; (d) all of the above.
2. Debt capital refers to: (a) owners' investments in the firm; (b) retained earnings; (c) borrowed funds; (d) residual funds; (e) venture capital.
3. Which of the following forms of capital mature? (a) stock; (b) retained earnings; (c) bonds; (d) all of the above.

LEARNING GOAL 19.6: Identify likely sources of short-term and long-term funds.

1. ___ A line of credit is an agreement between a commercial bank and a firm that states the amount of credit the bank will make available to the borrower.
2. ___ A secured loan does not require a borrower to pledge collateral.
3. ___ The three long-term sources of funds are loans repaid over 1 year or longer, bonds, and equity funds.

LEARNING GOAL 19.7: Identify the major categories of financial institutions and the sources and uses of their funds.

1. A profit-making business that holds deposits for individuals and business firms and makes loans to individuals and business firms is a: (a) commercial bank; (b) credit union; (c) commercial finance company; (d) consumer finance company.
2. A form of cooperative that acts as a depository institution and grants loans to its members is a(n): (a) commercial bank; (b) commercial finance company; (c) insurance company; (d) credit union.
3. An institution that offers both savings and checking accounts and that has historically been the major source of home loans is called a: (a) consumer finance company; (b) commercial bank; (c) savings and loan association; (d) credit union.

LEARNING GOAL 19.8: Explain the functions of the Federal Reserve System and the tools it uses to increase or decrease the money supply.

1. ___ The most essential function of the Federal Reserve System is to control the supply of money and credit in order to promote economic growth and a stable dollar.
2. ___ An increase in the reserve requirement or the discount rate will increase the money supply.
3. ___ The Federal Reserve Bank has regulatory powers over all depository institutions, whether or not they are members of the Federal Reserve System.

LEARNING GOAL 19.9: Describe the institutions that regulate bank safety and how they operate.

1. The FDIC insures: (a) deposits at all commercial banks that are members of the Federal Reserve System; (b) depositors' accounts up to a maximum of $100,000 per account; (c) deposits in order to increase confidence in the security of banks; (d) all of the above.

2. Deposits at 80 percent of U.S. credit unions are federally insured by the: (a) FDIC; (b) NCUSIF; (c) OTS; (d) RTC.

3. The primary technique for guaranteeing the soundness of commercial banks and thrifts is: (a) unannounced inspections by bank examiners at least once a year; (b) announcements to depositors when their savings institutions are placed on the "problem list"; (c) closing any bank immediately when problems are discovered; (d) all of the above.

LEARNING GOAL 19.10: Discuss the U.S. financial system in its global context.

1. ___ The United States is the only major nation with a central bank.

2. ___ International banks provide credit to importers and reduce risks associated with exchange rate fluctuations.

3. ___ Each country forms its banking policy independently without regard to policy changes in other countries.

KEY TERMS

finance 532
financial manager 532
risk-return trade-off 532
financial plan 533
financial control 533
money 534
near-money 537
debt capital 538
equity capital 538
bond 540
leverage 541
commercial bank 543
electronic funds transfer system (EFTS) 545
savings and loan association (S&L) 545
savings bank 546
credit union 546
Federal Reserve System 548
foreign exchange market 549
Federal Deposit Insurance Corporation (FDIC) 550
bank examiner 550

REVIEW QUESTIONS

1. Explain the functions performed by a financial manager. What role does forecasting play in these functions?

2. Identify the primary uses of cash in an organization.

3. What are the primary uses of short-term financing? Distinguish between unsecured and secured loans.

4. Distinguish between debt capital and equity capital. What are the primary sources of equity capital?

5. Identify the sources for long-term financing. Explain how borrowed funds produce leverage. What impact does borrowing have on a firm's financial performance?

6. Identify the components of the U.S. money supply. What functions do these components perform?

7. Explain the concept of near-money. Why is it not included as part of the money supply?

8. Explain how to categorize the different types of financial institutions, and identify the primary sources and uses of funds available in each institution.

9. Explain the functions of the Federal Reserve System. Give an example of how the Fed uses each of the following tools to increase the money supply or to stimulate economic activity:
   a. Open market operations
   b. Reserve requirement
   c. Discount rate
   d. Selective credit controls

10. Summarize recent trends and developments in the electronic funds transfer system (EFTS).

DISCUSSION QUESTIONS

1. Miguel Garcia timed the opening of his Sandia Mountain Tours to coincide with Albuquerque's annual International Balloon Festival. Garcia knew from the beginning that his enterprise was undercapitalized, but he hoped to cover his need for funds out of cash flow. Sandia Mountain Tours' annual sales volume grew quickly from $80,000 to $326,000, then to $675,000 and to $750,000. This rapid expansion of business involved the addition of many new services such as overnight and week-long camping trips.

Cash flow was a constant problem and remains so today. Garcia remarked, "There's a limit to bootstrapping. If you wish to remain a mom-and-pop business, bootstrapping will work, but I wanted more than that. Now I know I should have taken more time and put together more capital before jumping in feet first."

Analyze and discuss Sandia Mountain Tours' financial management problems. Do you agree with Garcia's comment on bootstrapping? Why or why not?

2. Gift shops earn 70 percent of their annual volume from just after Thanksgiving through Christmas. Given this simple statistic, chart and then explain the cash inflows and outflows for a new gift shop. When would it be most advisable to open a new gift shop? Discuss.

3. Investigate how one of the following firms was originally financed:
   a. Ben & Jerry's Ice Cream
   b. Gateway Computer
   c. Boston Chicken

d. Snapple (beverages)
e. The Body Shop (cosmetics and skin-care products)

4. Choose a business you would like to start. What short-term and long-term sources of funding would you need? Why? Discuss what business needs are served by each source of funding.

5. Why was the Federal Deposit Insurance Corporation created? Explain its role in protecting the soundness of the banking system. What actions can it take in case of a bank failure?

SOLUTIONS TO ACHIEVEMENT CHECK SUMMARY

L. G. 19.1: 1. T, 2. F, 3. F. **L. G. 19.2:** 1. e, 2. c, 3. d. **L. G. 19.3:** 1. T, 2. T, 3. F. **L. G. 19.4:** 1. T, 2. T, 3. F. **L. G. 19.5:** 1. d, 2. c, 3. c. **L. G. 19.6:** 1. T, 2. F, 3. T. **L. G. 19.7:** 1. a, 2. d, 3. c. **L. G. 19.8:** 1. T, 2. F, 3. T. **L. G. 19.9:** 1. d, 2. b, 3. a. **L. G. 19.10:** 1. F, 2. T, 3. F.

VIDEO CASE

FIRSTBANK CORPORATION Mergers, acquisitions, and the creation of megabanks characterize the banking industry of the late 1990s. As laws prohibiting interstate banking crumble, commercial banking in the United States is beginning to resemble banking in other nations, where a relatively few international banks provide financial services for the entire country. Mergers of previously independent banks and the acquisition of banks in other states are typically followed by name changes, with a more generic name like Nationsbank or Bank One typically replacing the name of the local bank. A few banking institutions have turned this trend into a competitive advantage both by their orientation to the local community and by offering services that the giants are eliminating. That is exactly what Firstbank Corporation has done.

The Michigan-based corporation owns and operates three commercial banks: the Bank of Alma, Firstbank, and 1st Bank. With branches spread over the entire state, Firstbank is able to offer the traditional banking services of checking, savings, and time deposits; trust services; and installment and consumer loans that meet customers' needs for commercial, agricultural, real estate, home improvement, automobile, and personal loans.

Firstbank is not unlike other banks in that it depends on deposits and interest payments on loans to generate revenues. However, in the past three years, income received in the form of loans increased by only 7 percent. During the same period interest on investment securities actually fell 6 percent. Management knew these figures would not spell success in the long run and took decisive measures to increase revenues.

Firstbank management had to decide upon a strategy that would allow a small regional bank to compete successfully with the banking giants. Large banks have resources such as large marketing departments, the ability to handle huge sums of capital, and an international presence that gives them access to customers throughout the world. However, the current trend is for large banks to cut back on services—critical items that local banks can provide their customers. Firstbank management identified several opportunities to retain their loyal customers and, at the same time, attract new ones. Firstbank managers operated on the basic premise that they provide their customers with greater levels of service.

One of the greatest advantages a local bank has is its ability to react more quickly to customers' needs by designing special deposit and loan product offerings. In addition, decision making is generally quicker in small, local banks. A decision to introduce new products, lengthen banking hours, or to make changes in the bank's daily operations might take months in a large national or international bank simply because of the complexity of the organization. In contrast, the same types of decisions might take only a few weeks at a small bank.

Another decided advantage of small banks is that they can build and maintain close relationships with their customers. Because the bank staff, from the bank president to the branch tellers, come from the local community, it is much more likely that they will know their customers personally.

Firstbank Corporation management had to decide upon a strategy that would allow a small regional bank to compete successfully with banking giants.

Firstbank President and CEO John A. McCormack has pointed out that the one constant in banking is change. "Consolidation in the banking industry will most likely continue as larger banks close smaller offices, creating opportunities for community banks. We believe there will be ample opportunity to expand market share and income through acquisition in the next few years." However, expansion means the responsibilities of the bank's financial manager are increased. It becomes critical for forecasts of cash inflows and outflows to be accurate. This is particularly true during times of expansion, since the financial manager must ensure that funds will be readily available when needed, while at the same time making sure that none of the bank's assets are sitting idle.

Faced with expansion opportunities in local markets, Firstbank managers recognized the need for additional funds. In 1993 they made a public offering of 334,058 shares of common stock, which generated $5.5 million in equity capital. Of these funds, $3.2 million was used to repay all outstanding notes payable, $1 million was used to make a capital infusion at its 1st Bank subsidiary, and the remaining $1.3 million was used to acquire additional bank branches.

The stock offering and the focus on customer service at each of the subsidiary banks have allowed Firstbank to grow faster than would have been possible through internal deposit and loan generation alone. In fact, over the past 10 years, assets have grown from $127.3 million to $325 million, and the future looks bright for Firstbank's small local bank network.

QUESTIONS

1.
What are the basic sources and uses of funds for Firstbank?

2.
How can small-town banks compete with banking giants who also have a presence in their marketplace?

3.
Do depositors with accounts in small banks face greater risks than those who have checking accounts at large banks? Explain.

4.
What factors are likely to influence a depositor's decision to have an account in a large bank?

CHAPTER 20

SECURITIES MARKETS

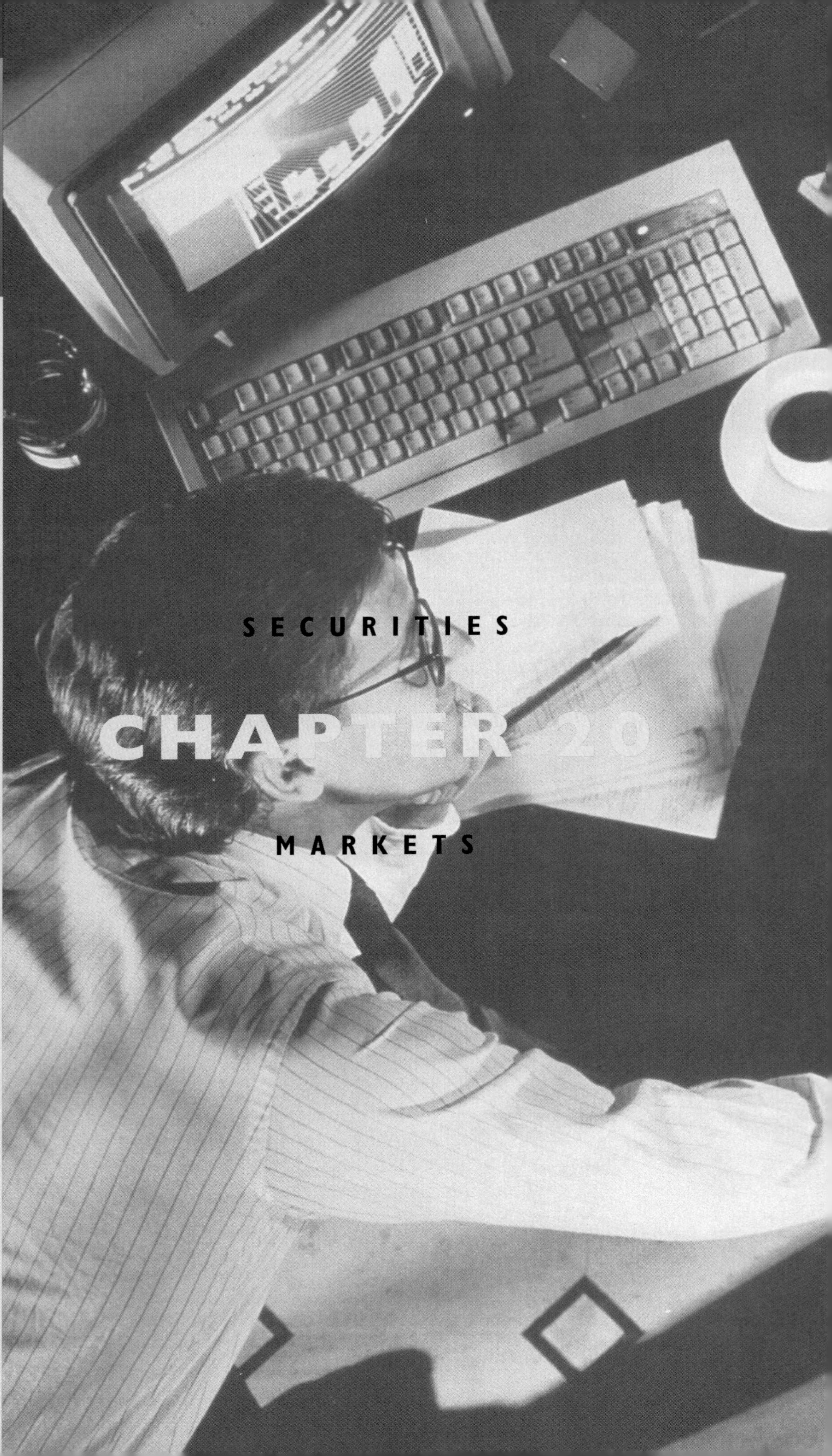

LEARNING GOALS

1. Distinguish between primary markets for securities and secondary markets.

2. Compare common stock, preferred stock, and bonds, and explain why investors might prefer each type of security.

3. Identify the four basic objectives of investors and the types of securities most likely to accomplish each objective.

4. Explain the process of selling or purchasing a security listed on an organized securities exchange.

5. Describe the information in stock, bond, and mutual fund quotations.

6. Explain the role of mutual funds in securities markets.

7. Evaluate the major features of state and federal laws designed to protect investors.

RYKA, INC. Businesses are born in unusual places. Apple Computer was founded in the garage of Steven Jobs' parents; Federal Express evolved from a college term paper written by the firm's CEO, Frederick Smith. The origins of Ryka Inc., the women's athletic shoe company created by Sheri Poe, can be traced to a gym, a need for exercise, aching knees, and a pain in the lower back. ■ Poe had tried high-impact aerobics as a means of overcoming some major health problems. The exercise regimen was working, but her shoes were far from satisfactory. "At that time, women's athletic shoes were poorly made and didn't fit properly. They were basically smaller versions of men's shoes," she explains. Makers of athletic shoes either failed to notice or ignored the differences that needed addressing: women tend to have higher arches and narrower heels than men. ■ Poe also knew that her complaints were not unique. "I talked to other women at my gym. I listened to their conversations. I saw them coming into the dressing room, rubbing their feet and their lower backs." Poe resigned her position as national sales director for a giftware manufacturer, convinced her husband to quit his job as a product designer, and the two started Norwood, Massachusetts-based Ryka in 1987. ■ The decision involved major financial risks for the young couple with two small children. Ryka began operations with only $50,000 in equity capital. Although the concept of athletic shoes made by women for women sounded attractive, $50,000 was only a drop in the bucket of investment capital Ryka would need to take on industry leaders like Nike and Reebok. ■ Poe decided to spread the risk by using other people's money. She would sell shares of Ryka to investors. This proved to be a difficult undertaking for the start-up firm, though. After a series of rejections by Wall Street investment giants, Poe finally found a sympathetic ear in a meeting with a Denver-based investment banker, who was also a woman and a fitness fanatic. The Ryka concept clicked, and the investment banker convinced her firm to handle the stock offering. ■ Even though selling shares of stock reduced Poe's ownership stake, it raised $3 million—enough to launch the venture nationwide. A company in the Far East manufactured the new aerobic shoe, and Poe unveiled it at the 1988 Sporting Goods Manufacturers Association trade show. The shoe was an immediate hit, and she returned to Norwood with orders from Nordstrom, Lady Footlocker, and Athlete's Foot, among others. ■ Although the firm lacked the financial muscle to afford national advertising campaigns on the scale of those of Nike, adidas, and Reebok, Ryka made effective use of grass-roots marketing, especially a discount purchase program to 30,000 fitness instructors who agreed to provide feedback on design. As Poe put it, "There is no better advertising than having an aerobics instructor up there in front of the class wearing your shoes." ■ Sales increased over fourteenfold, from $991,000 in 1988 to $14.4 million by 1994. However, profits proved elusive. Even though Ryka managed to eke out a small profit for the first half of 1994, it never made an annual profit. By 1995, the firm's chronic financing problems were threatening its continued existence. Although Poe had managed to arrange emergency loans through a South Korean financial institution, the 20 percent interest rate charged made most credit card interest rates look attractive. She began to accept the fact that she would have to trade her status as an independent firm in order to grasp a financial lifeline from an established firm. Athletic shoe giant L.A. Gear showed inter-

est in acquiring Ryka, but negotiations fell through in early 1995, leaving Poe to continue her search for long-term funding sources. Her success will determine the future of Ryka. Poe, meanwhile, is learning first-hand the importance of financial security in today's volatile business world.[1]

CHAPTER OVERVIEW

Many entrepreneurs entering business today face daunting challenges in financing their new businesses. Ryka's initial public offering of stock enabled the company to take on established competitors in the rapidly growing athletic-shoe industry. In fact, the small company would not have become a leader in the women's footwear segment of its industry without the inflow of additional funds.

securities
Stock or bond that represents an obligation of the issuer to provide the purchaser an expected or stated return on the investment.

primary market
Market where firms sell new issues of securities publicly for the first time.

The previous chapter discussed two sources of funding for long-term financial needs: debt capital and equity capital. Long-term debt capital takes the form of corporate bonds, U.S. government bonds, and municipal bonds. Equity capital comes from stock—shares of ownership in the corporation. Stocks and bonds are commonly referred to as **securities** because both represent issuers' obligations to provide purchasers with expected or stated returns on the funds invested or loaned.

Stocks and bonds are bought and sold in two kinds of marketplaces. In the **primary market,** firms sell securities initially to the public. In the secondary market, subsequent owners buy and sell previously issued securities.

PRIMARY MARKETS

When a corporation needs capital to expand a plant, develop products, or acquire a smaller firm, or for other business reasons, it may make a stock or bond offering. A stock offering gives investors the opportunity to purchase ownership shares in the firm and to take part in its future growth in exchange for current capital. In another instance, a corporation or a government agency may choose to raise funds by issuing bonds. Announcements of these stock and bond offerings appear daily in such business newspapers as *The Wall Street Journal* in the form of simple, black-and-white announcement ads called *tombstones.* Governments also generate funds in primary markets; the U.S. Treasury sells bonds to finance part of the federal deficit, while city governments issue bonds for various projects such as funding new water systems.

investment banker
Specialist in selling new issues of securities for business and government organizations.

Although a corporation could market its stock or bond issue directly to the public, most large offerings are handled by financial specialists called *investment bankers* or *underwriters.* An **investment banker** is a financial intermediary who specializes in selling new issues of stocks and bonds for business firms and government agencies. Investment bankers usually agree to acquire the total issue from the company or agency and then resell it to other investors. Investment bankers such as Dean Witter Reynolds, A. G. Edwards, First Boston, Morgan Stanley, and Prudential Securities underwrite a securities issue at a discount from the eventual selling price; they keep the difference between what they pay to issuers and what they receive from buyers as compensation for services rendered. Figure 20.1 describes some of the investment services provided by Morgan Stanley for its individual and business investors.

Recently, Morgan Stanley assisted OfficeMax, one of the largest office-products superstores in the United States, in raising $678 million by selling over 35 million shares of stock to the investing public. The investment banker might have acquired the stock for $17 per share and then resold it for $19 per share. In addition to locating buyers for the issue, the underwriter typically advises the issuer on such details as general characteristics of the issue, its pricing, and the timing of the offering. Several investment bankers commonly participate in the underwriting process.

FIGURE 20.1

MORGAN STANLEY & CO.: LEADING INTERNATIONAL INVESTMENT BANKER

SECONDARY MARKETS

Daily news reports of stock and bond trading refer to exchanges in **secondary markets,** where subsequent owners trade previously issued shares of stock and bonds. Such markets offer convenient forms in which buyers and sellers can make exchanges. The issuing corporations receive no proceeds from such transactions, and gains and losses affect only the current and future owners of the securities. The various secondary markets are discussed later in the chapter.

secondary market
Market where subsequent owners trade previously issued shares of stock and bonds.

STOCKS

Stocks represent shares of ownership in a corporation. Although many corporations issue only one type of stock, two types exist: common stock and preferred stock.

COMMON STOCK

The basic form of corporate ownership is embodied in **common stock.** Purchasers of common stock are the true owners of a corporation. In return for their investments, they expect to receive payments in the form of dividends and/or capital gains resulting from increases in the value of their stock.

common stock
Security providing owner voting rights but only a residual claim to company assets.

Holders of common stock vote on major company decisions, such as purchasing other companies or electing members of the firm's board of directors. They benefit from company success, and they risk the loss of their investments if the company fails. In bankruptcy liquidation, claims of creditors and preferred stockholders are paid before those of common stockholders, so holders of common stock are said to have *residual claims* to company assets.

Common stock is sold on either a par value or no-par value basis. *Par value* is the value printed on the stock certificates of some companies. Some states specify par value as the basis for calculating state incorporation taxes. Because par values are highly arbitrary, most corporations now issue no-par value stock. In either case, the total number of shares outstanding represents the total ownership of the firm, and the value of an individual stockholder's investment is based on the number of shares that person owns and the market price of the stock rather than on an arbitrary par value.

Dreyer's Grand ice cream is delivered to a 7-Eleven shop. Dreyer's completed an agreement in 1994 whereby an affiliate of Nestlé USA, Inc. purchased three million shares of common stock. In addition, Dreyer's became the exclusive distributor of Nestlé ice cream novelty products in many markets.

Sometimes confusion arises over two other types of value: market value and book value. *Market value*—the price at which a stock currently sells—is easily determined by referring to the financial page of the daily newspaper. It usually varies from day to day, depending on company earnings and investor expectations about future prospects for the firm and the overall economy. *Book value* is determined by subtracting the company's liabilities and the value of any preferred stock from its assets. Dividing this net figure by the number of shares of common stock that the firm has outstanding gives the book value of each share.

A common stock certificate for Lone Star Steakhouse is shown in Figure 20.2. The certificate specifies the name and address of the registered owner and the number of shares that the certificate represents. It also bears the name of the state in which the firm is incorporated and the signatures of corporate officers.

FIGURE 20.2

LONE STAR STEAKHOUSE COMMON STOCK CERTIFICATE

STRENGTH IN DIVERSITY

SHAREHOLDER REVOLTS IN RUSSIA When one firm's shareholders became completely fed up with delays in converting from military to civilian markets, they proceeded as expected. They voted out the old top management and installed a team of financial experts charged with the task of making the needed changes. The results were immediate. Within 3 months, the firm had secured new contracts equal to all of the previous year's orders. As the leader of the shareholder revolt put it, "Things can change fast if you change the management." ■ Where did these events take place? Not in Detroit or Milwaukee, but in the heart of the former communist citadel, Moscow. The company involved in this change is Yaroslav Rubber Co., a maker of tires and other auto and aircraft parts. Russia's shaky movement toward capitalism during the 1990s has brought privatization of previously state-owned firms. A devastating combination of antiquated production facilities, inexperience in market-driven industries, and a battered Russian economy has thwarted attempts to achieve global competitiveness, though. As a result, a growing number of impatient investors have struggled to oust old-guard Russian managers and replace them with better qualified business leaders. As many as 4,800 Russian chief executives may get the boot within the next 2 years. ■ No one expects current management to go quietly, however. Take a look, for example, at Zil, a well-known dinosaur of a Russian company that has been turning out the same truck model for 30 years. Zil needs an estimated $200 million to finance modernization, but potential investors demand a change in top management before committing the funds. Zil's top managers refuse to go quietly. Instead, they have petitioned the Russian government to stall economic reforms and to replace dissident investors with more "patriotic" ones. The decisions made in the near future will play a crucial role in determining the health of the Russian economy during the next decade. Source: Quotation from Peter Galuszka and Patricia Kranz, "Look Who's Making a Revolution: Shareholders," *Business Week*, February 20, 1995, p. 60.

QUESTIONS FOR CRITICAL THINKING

1. What opportunities do the shareholder revolts pose for Russians?
2. What opportunities do the shareholder revolts pose for countries in the Western hemisphere?
3. Should investors have the power to oust management in businesses in Russia? Why or why not?

PREFERRED STOCK

preferred stock
Security providing owner preferential dividend payments and first claim to company assets after it pays all debts; it seldom confers voting rights.

In addition to common stock, many corporations issue **preferred stock**—stock whose owners receive preference in the payment of dividends. Also, if the company is dissolved, holders of preferred stock have claims on the firm's assets that receive preference over any claim by common stockholders.

In return for this privilege, preferred stockholders usually do not have voting rights. (Even when they have some voting rights, those rights are typically limited to such important proposals as mergers, sales of company property, and dissolution of the company itself.) Although preferred stockholders are granted certain privileges over common stockholders, they are still considered owners of the firm, and their dividend payments are, therefore, not guaranteed.

Firms often issue preferred stock with conversion privileges. This *convertible preferred stock* gives a stockholder the option of converting preferred shares into common shares at some stated price. Owners of AMR's convertible preferred stock currently receive annual dividends equal to 7 percent of their investment, while AMR common stock pays no dividend. They also have the option of converting to common stock at a stated price.[2]

Preferred stock is usually issued to attract conservative investors who want the margin of safety provided by preferential claims over those of common stock. Although preferred stock represents equity capital, many companies consider it a compromise between bonds and common stock.

BONDS

Bondholders are creditors, not owners, of a corporation. Chapter 19 described bonds as sources of long-term debt capital for the corporation and as sources of funds for municipal, state, and federal government units. A bond may be issued in a denomination of $1,000, $5,000, or even $50,000. It indicates a definite rate of interest to be paid to the bondholder and a maturity date on which the issuer will repay the principal of the loan. As creditors, bondholders have claims on issuers' assets before any claims of preferred and common stockholders in the event of liquidation or dissolution. These characteristics are illustrated by the Mobil Corporation bond certificate shown in Figure 20.3.

TYPES OF BONDS

secured bond
Bond backed by a specific pledge of company assets.

The potential bondholder can choose among a variety of bonds. A **secured bond** is backed by a specific pledge of company assets. For instance, mortgage bonds are backed by real and personal property owned by the firm, such as machinery or furniture, and collateral trust bonds are backed by stocks and bonds issued by other companies and owned by the borrowing firm.

Bond purchasers want to balance their financial returns with the risks involved, and bonds backed by pledges of specific assets are less risky than those without such collateral. Consequently, a firm can issue secured bonds at lower interest rates than those for unsecured bonds.

debenture
Bond backed only by the reputation of the issuer.

However, a number of companies do issue these unsecured bonds, called **debentures**—bonds backed only by the reputation of the issuing corporation or government unit. Only governments and major corporations with extremely sound financial reputations, such as auto rental giant Hertz Corp., can find buyers for their debentures.

FIGURE 20.3 MOBIL CORPORATION BOND CERTIFICATE

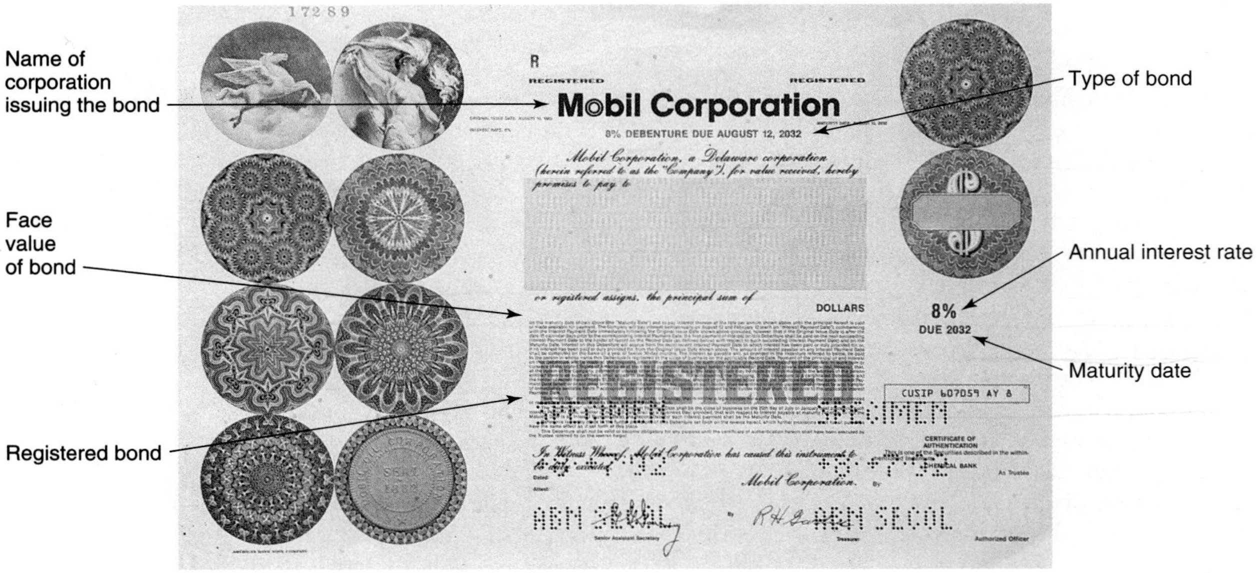

A *government bond* represents funds borrowed by the U.S. government. Because they are backed by the full faith and credit of the U.S. federal government, government bonds are considered the least risky of all debt obligations. A *municipal bond* is a debt issue of a state or political subdivision, such as a county or city. An important feature of municipal bonds is that interest payments are usually exempt from federal income tax and, in most cases, from taxes in the state and locality where the bonds are issued. This attractive feature allows state and local governments to issue these bonds at significantly lower interest rates than those on corporate bonds.

In order to entice more speculative purchasers, corporations sometimes issue convertible bonds. A *convertible bond* gives the bondholder the option of converting it into a specific number of shares of common stock. The number of shares of stock for which the owner can exchange each bond is stated in the *bond indenture*—the legal contract that specifies all provisions of the bond issue. A $1,000 bond might be convertible into 50 shares of common stock. If the common stock is selling at $18 when the bonds are issued, the conversion privilege has no value. If the stock rises in price to $30, however, this conversion privilege has a value of $1,500. Convertible bonds offer lower interest rates than those that lack conversion privileges and, therefore, they can reduce the interest expenses of the issuing firm. Some bond purchasers prefer such bonds, even at lower interest rates, due to the potential for additional gains if the price of the firm's stock increases.[3] Each of the major types of bonds is described briefly in Figure 20.4.

BOND RATINGS

When most people think of investing, they immediately think of the stock market. That is not the only investment arena available, however. Investors seeking safe instruments in which to put their money often choose the bond market.

Two factors determine the price of a bond: its degree of risk and its interest rate. As a creditor of the company, the bondholder has first claim on the firm's assets if it is liquidated. For this reason, bonds are generally less risky than stocks, although not always. To judge the degree of risk in a bond, ask yourself the following questions:

- Will the company or government agency issuing the bond repay the principal when due?
- Will it make the interest payments?
- Is the bond already in default?

FIGURE 20.4 SIX MAJOR TYPES OF BONDS AND THEIR DISTINGUISHING CHARACTERISTICS

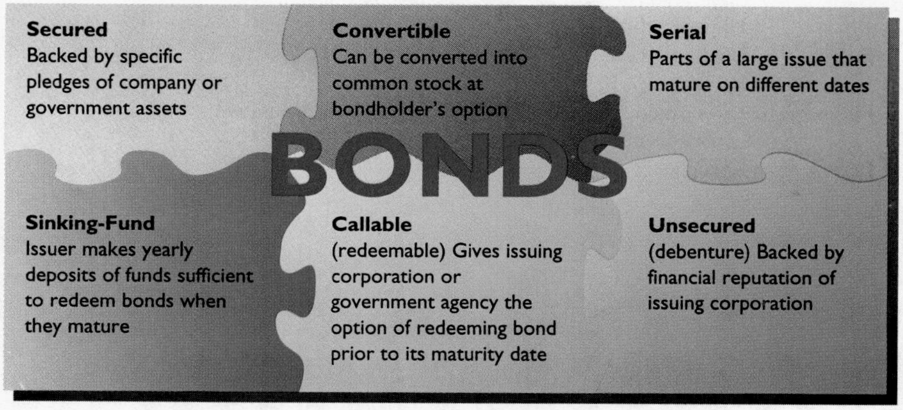

BONDS
Secured
Backed by specific pledges of company or government assets
Convertible
Can be converted into common stock at bondholder's option
Serial
Parts of a large issue that mature on different dates
Sinking-Fund
Issuer makes yearly deposits of funds sufficient to redeem bonds when they mature
Callable
(redeemable) Gives issuing corporation or government agency the option of redeeming bond prior to its maturity date
Unsecured
(debenture) Backed by financial reputation of issuing corporation

In general, the level of risk is reflected in a bond's ratings, from the two bond-rating services, Standard & Poor's (S&P) and Moody's. As Table 20.1 shows, the least risky corporate bonds are rated AAA (S&P) and Aaa (Moody's), and the scales descend to the level of so-called *junk bonds,* and then on to the most speculative issues, usually those in default.

Junk bonds attract investors because they offer high yields in exchange for the risk involved. Typically, a safer bond sells for a higher price. During periods of high interest rates, BB-rated bonds may earn 6 to 7 percent higher interest rates than AAA bonds. Of course, these higher returns also mean higher risk.

The second factor affecting the price of a bond is its interest rate. Other things being equal, a higher interest rate draws a higher price. Everything else usually is not equal, however; two bonds may not be equally risky, or one may tie up money for a longer period than another. Consequently, bond investors must evaluate the trade-offs involved. Another important rule is this: when interest rates rise, bond prices fall. This occurs because holders of older bonds are locked into relatively lower interest rates on their money.

RETIRING BONDS

Because a bond issue matures on a certain date, the issuing corporation must accumulate the necessary funds to repay the principal on the maturity date. The two most common methods of repayment are serial bonds and sinking-fund bonds.

To use the *serial bond* method, a corporation simply issues a large number of bonds that mature on different dates. For example, if a corporation decides to issue $4.5 million in serial bonds for a 30-year period, the maturity dates may be established in such a manner that no bonds mature for the first 15 years. Beginning with the sixteenth year, $300,000 in bonds may mature each year until the bonds are repaid at the end of the 30 years. Serial bonds are often issued by city governments.

TABLE 20.1 MOODY'S AND STANDARD & POOR'S BOND RATINGS

MOODY'S	INTERPRETATION	STANDARD & POOR'S	INTERPRETATION
Aaa	Prime quality	AAA	Bank investment quality
Aa	High grade	AA	
A	Upper medium grade	A	
Baa	Medium grade	BBB	
		BB	
Ba	Lower medium grade or speculative	B	Speculative
B	Speculative	CCC	
		CC	
Caa	From very speculative to near or in default	C	
Ca			
C		DDD	In default (rating indicates the relative salvage value)
		DD	
		D	

A variation of the concept of serial bonds relies on a *sinking fund*. Under this plan, the issuing corporation makes annual deposits of funds to accumulate enough cash to redeem the bonds when they mature. These deposits are held by a *bond trustee*, usually a major bank, with the responsibility of representing bondholders. The deposits must be large enough so that, with accrued interest, they will be sufficient to redeem the bonds at maturity.

A *callable bond* has a provision that allows the issuing corporation to redeem it before its maturity date by paying a premium over the principal of the debt. For instance, a 20-year bond may not be callable for the first 10 years. Between years 11 and 15, it can be called at a premium of perhaps $50, and between years 16 and 20 it can be called at its face value.

Why issue callable bonds? If a corporation issues 30-year bonds paying 14 percent annual interest and interest rates decline to 10 percent, it is paying more interest than it could. In this instance, it may decide to retire the 14 percent bonds and issue new bonds that pay a lower rate of interest. Such actions may be financially sound, even though the firm would incur additional costs in retiring the old bonds and issuing new ones.

SECURITIES PURCHASERS

Two general types of investors, institutional and individual investors, buy securities. An **institutional investor** is an organization that invests its own funds or those it holds in trust for others. This definition covers insurance companies, pension funds, mutual funds, commercial banks, and thrifts, as well as other investors such as not-for-profit organizations and foundations.

institutional investor
Organization that invests its own funds or funds it holds in trust.

Institutional investors buy and sell securities in large quantities, often in blocks of at least 10,000 shares per transaction. Block trading accounts for more than half of the total daily volume on organized securities exchanges, and all of institutional investors' trading accounts for approximately two-thirds of total trading volume. The number of investors who own shares through mutual funds or employers' pension plans is steadily rising, and the firms that manage their funds now control about 40 percent of all U.S. equities.[4]

Over 1,200 institutional investors include General Motors common stock in their investment portfolios. This largest of America's Big Three auto companies, whose Chevrolet trucks are featured in Figure 20.5, has about 750 million shares of common stock outstanding. Institutional investors own about 46 percent of that stock.

Institutional investors have become the most important force in today's securities markets. Since 1980, for example, the percentage of stocks held by individual investors has fallen from 71 percent to 50 percent.[5]

Despite the importance of institutional investors, however, individual investors still play a vital role. About 51 million Americans own stocks, either directly or by investing in stock mutual funds.[6] Furthermore, many institutional investments reflect the demands of individual investors.

In the old stereotype, the typical individual investor was male, average age 55, married, with an annual income of $80,000 or more. These days, however, a growing number of stock market participants are women, and one out of three investors is female. The median age has also declined as younger people have become investors. In fact, one out of nine investors today is under the age of 40. George Salem, banking analyst for Prudential Securities Inc., believes that the growing diversity among individual investors will encourage greater diversity in investment options. These investors, says Salem, "are not going to be satisfied with the three flavors of investments that banks offer. They'll want 50 or 100 flavors."[7]

FIGURE 20.5

GENERAL MOTORS CORP. COMMON STOCK: ROCK SOLID FOR INSTITUTIONAL INVESTORS

INVESTMENT MOTIVATIONS

speculation
Purchasing stocks in anticipation of making large profits quickly.

Why do people and institutions invest? For some, the motivation is **speculation**—the hope of making a large profit on stocks or other securities within short periods of time. Speculation may take the form of acting on a corporate merger rumor or simply purchasing high-risk stocks, such as low-priced penny stocks (so called because they sell for less than $1 per share).

A second motivation is growth. According to the National Association of Investment Clubs, investors who choose growth as a primary goal should invest in fast-growing companies like men's sportswear maker Tommy Hilfiger Corp., featured in Figure 20.6 on page 570. Although the New York–based firm has paid no dividends to its stockholders, the market price of its common shares has shown steady increases prompted by rapidly growing sales and income. By expanding its in-store boutiques in almost 500 department stores, the company has seen its sales increase as much as 50 percent in a single year.

Growth-minded investors are also likely to benefit from stock splits, which typically occur in fast-growing companies such as Wal-Mart. A *stock split* amounts to a recapitalization of a company in which a single share is divided into multiple shares, lowering the price of the stock and making it easier for new investors to buy.

yield
Income received from securities, calculated by dividing dividend or interest income by market price.

As another investment motivation, some people use stocks and bonds to supplement income. The income received from securities investments is called the investor's *return*, or **yield.** Yield on a stock is calculated by dividing dividends by market price. Similarly, the yield on a bond is the amount of interest received divided by its price. The yield from any particular stock or bond varies with the market price and the dividend payments.

Stock investors motivated primarily by income concentrate on the dividends of prospective companies. An investor with enough foresight to purchase 10 shares of General Motors Corp. stock in 1940 for $468 would have received dividend payments of more than $8,000 by the mid-1990s. Because companies pay dividends from their earnings, investors consider a company's past record for paying dividends, its current profitability, and its prospects for future earnings. Purchasers of income stocks are likely to own shares of companies in industries such as banking, insurance, and public utilities.

A BROADER PURPOSE

DERIVATIVES How on earth could affluent Orange County, California, with a population of 2.6 million and a median household income of $47,774, find itself bankrupt? The answer involves sour investments. ■ In seeking more bang for the county's financial buck, Robert L. Citron, the county treasurer, managed to lose $1.5 billion of the $7.4 billion investment fund in his care. When other county officials learned of the stunning loss and realized that they could meet only 60 percent of their budget, they decided to file for protection from creditors under Chapter 9 of the bankruptcy law in Santa Ana Federal Court. Citron, who had been admired for lofty returns on county investments and recently was reelected for a seventh term as treasurer, resigned. ■ The 1980s were good years for Citron. The annual return on his investment fund exceeded 9 percent, double the average return of other California investment pools. Citron's problems began with his decision to seek higher returns for the investment fund by purchasing an exotic type of securities called *derivatives*. Although the name conjures up images of calculus homework, these instruments somewhat resemble an unusual mutual fund. Actually, they allow an investor to take a financial position in a bundle of investments. Developed in the late 1980s and sold by such major financial institutions as Citibank, Bankers Trust, and J. P. Morgan, the values of these securities are *derived* from such underlying investments as collaterized mortgages, options on oil contracts, repurchase agreements, and foreign currencies. ■ Some derivatives are more speculative than others. Orange County's funds went into some of the most exotic varieties called *inverse floaters*. Purchasers of this variety of securities expect interest rates to fall. When this occurs, the inverse floaters soar in value. To Citron's horror, interest rates climbed steadily between 1992 and 1995, and losses mounted. ■ Orange County isn't alone in making such ill-fated investments:

- Odessa College lost $7 million of its $22 million endowment in a single year through similar purchases.
- Charles County, Maryland invested 98 percent of its assets in derivatives and suffered losses of $8.3 million in 1994.
- Cuyahoga County, Ohio lost $137 million when its highly leveraged $1.8 billion fund suffered from a decline in bond prices.
- A 28-year-old trader in the Singapore office of Barings PLC generated derivatives losses of $1 billion, resulting in the collapse of Britain's oldest bank.

Even though the investment decisions were intended to maximize returns in an era of ever-tighter government budgets, hindsight shows that the institutions took far too much risk for their expected returns. Officials in charge of such investments have an overriding obligation to seek safe investments, even at the expense of forgoing greater returns. ■ Tighter restrictions on government officials involved in making such investments are already being enacted. These officials face more frequent and more detailed reporting of investment values, along with descriptions of holdings and investment strategies, to state and local officials and, on request, to the general public. New laws are expected to specify appropriate types of investments and to require regular audits. Business writer Kelley Holland summed up the lesson of the derivatives debacle this way: "Rushing into seemingly miraculous markets is not a recipe for long-term success. In today's financial markets, high-profit products tend to have distressingly short life cycles." Sources: Holland quotation from "Derivatives: Alive, But Oh So Boring," *Business Week,* January 30, 1995, p. 77. See also David J. Lynch and Janet L. Fix, "Global Trades Tax Internal Controls," *USA Today,* February 28, 1995, p. B1; and Carol J. Loomis, "Untangling the Derivatives Mess," *Fortune,* March 20, 1995, pp. 50–68.

QUESTIONS FOR CRITICAL THINKING

1. Should Robert L. Citron and others in similar positions be personally liable for major losses? Why or why not?
2. Should the position of county treasurer be held by a group rather than an individual?
3. What types of investments might have been more appropriate for Orange County's investment funds?

Investors who seek safety as their primary objective are likely to purchase high-quality bonds and preferred stocks. These securities offer substantial protection and are likely to continue paying good returns on the long-term investment.

Most investors pursue more than one investment goal. Investors who emphasize safety of principal may buy preferred stocks, which can also grow in market value. Those who buy growth stocks may choose stocks that pay dividend yields of at least 3 percent in order to receive some short-term returns on their investments. Figure 20.7 provides a

FIGURE 20.6

TOMMY HILFIGER: ATTRACTIVE STOCK FOR GROWTH-ORIENTED INVESTORS

useful guide for evaluating stocks and bonds in terms of the three general long-term investment objectives.

Liquidity and Taxes In addition to these primary investment goals, investors must consider two other factors: liquidity and taxes. Since the prices of securities can vary widely, investors cannot count on making profits whenever they decide to sell. If liquidity (the speed at which assets can be converted to cash) is important, investors should choose securities that tend to remain stable in price.

FIGURE 20.7 LONG-TERM INVESTMENT OBJECTIVES OF SPECIFIC SECURITIES

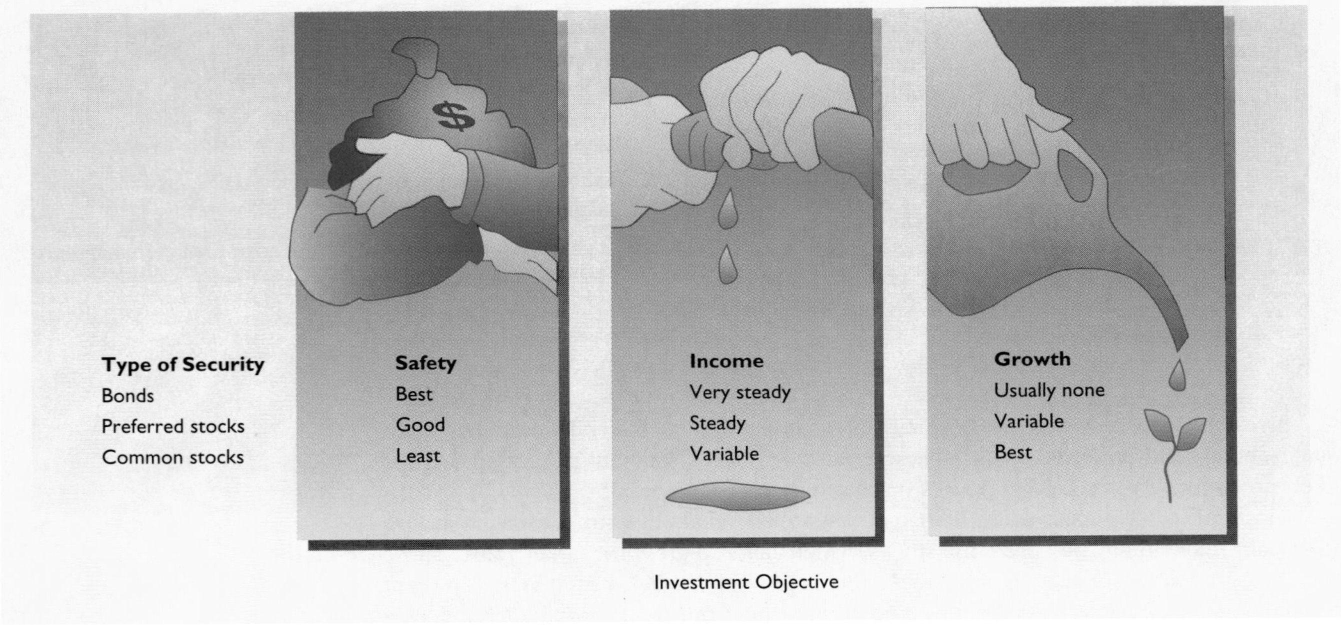
$
Type of Security
Bonds
Preferred stocks
Common stocks
Safety
Best
Good
Least
Income
Very steady
Steady
Variable
Growth
Usually none
Variable
Best
Investment Objective

Taxes can also influence the investment decision. The federal income tax has the greatest impact on investments of any tax; it is levied on investment income and on capital gains (increases in value of assets such as stocks and bonds). Taxes on wealth, such as the federal estate tax or property taxes, can also affect specific types of investments. Some investments, like purchases of gold or antiques, may also be subject to sales taxes.

SECURITIES EXCHANGES AND OTHER SECONDARY MARKETS

Securities exchanges are marketplaces for stocks and bonds. At a **stock exchange,** traders buy and sell stocks and bonds. Although these people trade corporations' securities, those corporations are not directly involved, and they receive no proceeds from the sales. The securities traded at organized exchanges have already been issued by corporations. In these trades, securities change hands between individuals and corporate investors.

stock exchange
Location at which traders buy and sell stocks and bonds.

NEW YORK STOCK EXCHANGE

When investors talk about "the stock market," they are usually referring to the New York Stock Exchange. The *Big Board,* as it is sometimes called, is the largest and best-known of all stock exchanges. Only one out of every 1,000 American corporations qualifies for listing on this exchange, but these firms account for more than 40 percent of the assets held by all U.S. companies. The market value of all trades on the NYSE totals almost $2 billion a year. This includes sales in 2,200 issues of stock and almost 3,000 issues of bonds currently listed on the Big Board. Shares of entertainment giant Walt Disney Co., whose theme park division is advertised in Figure 20.8, are traded there. So, too, are shares of major corporations ranging from IBM and Sears to Alcoa and Wal-Mart Stores.

To do business on the NYSE, a securities firm must be a member. Currently, 2,089 companies are listed as members. Potential members must purchase their seats from current members with the approval of the exchange. Memberships have varied considerably in price, growing from a mere $17,000 each in 1942 to $431,000 in recent years.[8]

FIGURE 20.8

INVESTING IN DISNEY—A BIG BOARD TRANSACTION

AMERICAN STOCK EXCHANGE AND REGIONAL EXCHANGES

The second-largest national exchange operating in the United States is the American Stock Exchange (AMEX). The AMEX, also located in New York, is smaller than the NYSE and handles securities issued by smaller firms with national followings.

To be listed on the AMEX, a firm must meet a number of requirements. These include a minimum of 400,000 shares held by the general public, at least 1,200 shareholders owning 100 or more shares each, and $4 million in tangible assets. These requirements are less stringent than those of the NYSE, which makes the AMEX an attractive seasoning board for firms not ready to be listed on the Big Board. In fact, many of the firms now listed on the NYSE were originally part of the AMEX, and transferred to the Big Board only after achieving larger earnings and asset values.

In addition to the NYSE and AMEX, several regional exchanges operate in the United States. These include the Midwest, Pacific, and Philadelphia exchanges. Originally established to trade the shares of smaller firms operating in limited geographic areas, the regional exchanges now list many major corporations, as well. The largest regional exchange, the Midwest in Chicago, handles about 8 percent of all trades in NYSE-listed stocks.[9] Roughly half of the companies listed on the NYSE are also listed on one or more regional boards.

Even though they serve regional rather than national markets, the Midwest and the Pacific exchanges actually trade more than the AMEX does in total market value. They are still dwarfed, however, by the NYSE and the Tokyo Stock Exchange.

FOREIGN STOCK EXCHANGES

Stock exchanges are not unique to the United States. In fact, the world's oldest board, the Amsterdam Stock Exchange, began operations in 1611. The London Stock Exchange, which lists more than 7,000 securities, traces its beginnings to pre-American Revolution times.

Foreign exchanges are gaining market share of global trading activity. Unlike the NYSE, where overseas listings account for only 5 percent of trades, foreign exchanges actively trade shares from numerous companies around the world. Of the 2,510 securities traded on the Geneva, Switzerland exchange, 257 stocks and 933 bonds are non-Swiss. Some U.S. firms list their securities both at home and abroad. In fact, the London Stock Exchange trades more than 20 million shares daily of NYSE-listed stocks—over 10 percent of the NYSE's own volume. Other American companies prefer to list with foreign exchanges to avoid the Big Board's strict listing requirements.

Overseas securities trading volume is rising three times faster than U.S. trading volume, as stock exchanges in both Europe and Asia grow rapidly. Japan's emergence as an economic giant during the past quarter-century is reflected by the growth of the Tokyo Stock Exchange. The Kawasaki Jet Ski shown in Figure 20.9 is an excellent example of a global product success. Individual and institutional investors attracted to successful products from Kawasaki and other global brand names such as Canon, Hitachi, Nintendo, and Sony frequently purchase shares in their parent companies on the Tokyo Stock Exchange.

GLOBAL SECURITIES TRADING

International stock exchanges are becoming a reality. GLOBEX, an international, 24-hour trading system, links traders to exchanges around the world. It recently received permission to add terminals in Japan. The 12 major exchanges in the European Union are working toward forming one unified exchange. In the process, they will have to overcome significant differences between different nations' business methods. For instance, the stock market in Paris reveals volume and price information within seconds of a trade, while investors in Milan may have to wait until the following day.

FIGURE 20.9

KAWASAKI JET SKI: GLOBAL PRODUCT SUCCESS BY A JAPANESE COMPANY

A big step toward unifying the different markets is Eurolist, a cross-listing of securities issued by over 250 major European companies. While some European firms already list their stock on more than one exchange, this is not cheap to do. One company that trades on six different markets estimates that its annual listing fees total almost $60,000, and the cost of meeting all the different disclosure requirements comes to nearly $1 million a year. Eurolist reduces listing charges to a single fee and allows firms to qualify for listing just by meeting their home countries' requirements.[10]

NASDAQ SYSTEM

In addition to both domestic and foreign stock exchanges, investors can also trade in the *over-the-counter (OTC) market,* an informal method for trading securities through market makers who match customers' buy and sell orders with partners over a computer network. Unlike traditional stock exchanges, the OTC market has no trading floor on which securities are bought and sold. Instead, brokers bring together buyers and sellers by computer, teletype, fax machine, and telephone. Dealers involved in these transactions keep in regular contact with one another, and the prices of the securities they trade are established by supply and demand. Such a dealer "makes a market" by quoting a *bid price* (a price that it will pay for a security) and an *asked price,* or *selling price.* Investors who decide to purchase OTC stocks and bonds contact their brokers, who contact the dealers that handle the security in order to search for the best price. When the investor and a dealer agree on a price, a market is made. Over 500 market-maker firms operate in the OTC market, including such well-known brokerage firms as Merrill Lynch and Goldman Sachs.

At the heart of the OTC market is the **National Association of Securities Dealers Automated Quotation (NASDAQ) system,** a nationwide OTC network. About 4,100 companies, including Ryka Inc., list their securities with NASDAQ. In a typical year, it trades over 48 billion shares with a total market value of $890.8 billion.[11]

National Association of Securities Dealers Automated Quotation (NASDAQ) system
Nationwide, over-the-counter securities trading network.

The NASDAQ system pioneered the use of computers to trade securities. It reports all trades within seconds, providing immediate access to current market information. Also, since stockbrokers have immediate access to bid and asked prices on their desktop quotation machines, they notice little difference between the NASDAQ system and securities trading on national or regional exchanges. However, transactions involving the less actively traded OTC securities are reported less frequently, typically at the end of each trading day.

Many of the firms whose stocks trade on OTC markets have too few shares outstanding to be listed on the NYSE or AMEX. Others have too few stockholders, and still others lack sufficient earnings to qualify for listing. Also, the OTC market includes the shares of most insurance companies and banks and the bonds issued by many city and state government units. A number of major corporations have chosen not to list their stocks and bonds on the national and regional exchanges, opting instead for NASDAQ listings. Well-known firms that are listed on the NASDAQ system include Apple Computer, Cadbury Schweppes, Intel, and Microsoft. Communications giant MCI Telecommunications, whose VideoPhone service is described in Figure 20.10, is also listed there.

MECHANICS OF BUYING AND SELLING SECURITIES

Most securities transactions involve stockbrokers, financial intermediaries who arrange purchases and sales of securities for individual and institutional investors.

PLACING AN ORDER

An investor who wants to purchase Exxon common stock typically contacts his or her stockbroker, who conveys the order to the firm's member at the NYSE. A representative goes directly to the location on the floor of the exchange where Exxon is traded and attempts to make the purchase.

An investor request to buy or sell stock at the current market price is a *market order.* The NYSE member's representative would carry out such an order for Exxon at the best price currently available. An investor may also request to buy or sell stock if and when it reaches a specified price in a *limit order.* In this case, a notation of the limit order is made at the post that handles transactions in the particular stock, and if the price reaches the specified price, the order is filled.

Most stock trades exchange even multiples of 100 shares, called *round lots.* Investor transactions with fewer than 100 shares, called *odd lots*, are grouped together to make

FIGURE 20.10

MAJOR CORPORATIONS LISTED ON THE NASDAQ SYSTEM

up one or more round lots. The stocks are then distributed to the various odd-lot purchasers at completion of the transaction.

Two frequently mentioned stock market terms refer to investor attitudes. As Figure 20.11 illustrates, a **bull** is an investor who expects stock prices to rise. Bulls buy securities in anticipation of increases in market prices. When stock market prices continue to rise, market observers call the trend a *bull market.*

A **bear** is an investor who expects stock prices to decline. Bears are likely to sell their securities in anticipation of falling market prices. When stock market prices continue to fall, market observers call the trend a *bear market.*

bull
Investor who expects stock prices to rise along with a general market trend.

bear
Investor who expects stock prices to decline along with a general market trend.

COSTS OF TRADING

Traders who purchase securities through stockbrokers must pay sales commissions. These fees vary among brokerage firms, generally ranging from 1 to 2 percent of the total value of the stock transaction.

Discount brokerage firms compete with traditional, full-service brokers by offering fewer services and charging lower commissions. For instance, while full-service broker Merrill Lynch might collect a $78 commission for selling 100 shares of stock, discount broker Lombard Institutional Brokerage might charge a $34 commission.[12] Larger purchases through discount brokers save investors more on commissions, since commissions decline as a percentage of the amounts invested as the total costs of those investments rise.

COMPUTERIZED TRADING

Securities traders at NationsBank Corp. need not even speak when placing buy or sell orders, which may range from $15 million to $500 million in any given day. Instead, they log their orders directly onto computers, which execute the trades automatically.

FIGURE 20.11 TWO SPECIES OF INVESTORS

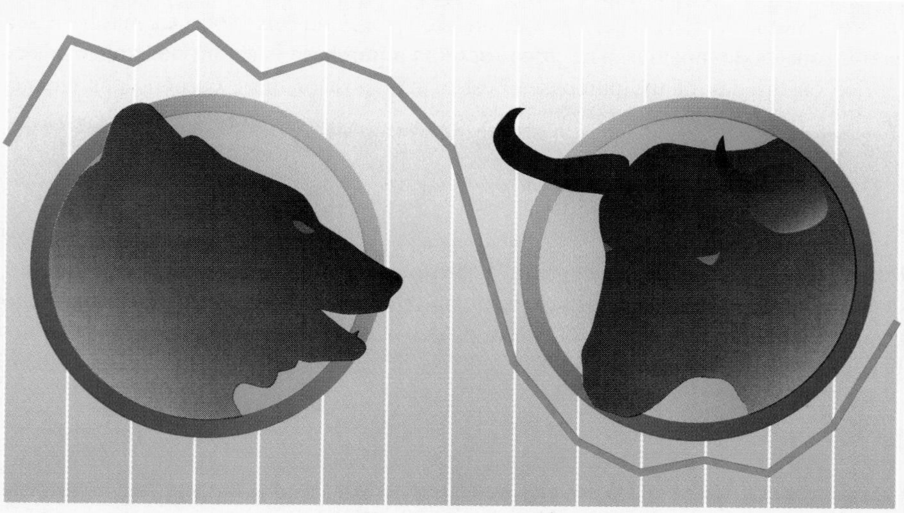

Investor Type	BEAR	BULL
Belief	Stock prices are going to fall.	Stock prices are going to rise.
Investment Strategy	"Sell high, buy low."	"Buy low, sell high."

Perhaps the most useful feature of this system, according to Mary Primm, NationsBank senior vice president, is the direct electronic communication between the computerized trading system and other computer systems at the bank. "The portfolio manager now has the ability to execute a trade electronically by entering it into the system and is assured that the system will automatically update the information to the accounting and custodial systems," she explains.[13]

Computer networks like NationsBank's handle as much as 10 percent of today's stock trading, a percentage that is certain to rise. Electronic systems have revolutionized securities trading by creating vast networks that deliver lightning speed, low overhead, and anonymity. Commissions for trades using such systems average about $0.02 per share, less than half of the typical rate that large institutions pay on traditional trades through stockbrokers. Furthermore, computerized trading operates around the clock, unlike the NYSE, which limits activity to $6\frac{1}{2}$ hours each trading day.[14]

The rise of computerized systems has caused many analysts to question the future of the New York Stock Exchange and its armies of brokers. Since 1980, the NYSE's share of trades in stocks it lists has fallen from 85 percent to 68 percent. Meanwhile, regional exchanges and electronic markets are gaining business. "Pit trading is archaic," says long-time trader Scott Schumer, who now uses the GLOBEX electronic system after spending 17 years at a conventional exchange. "If everything else is done over computer, eventually pit trading will be, too."[15]

FOURTH MARKET

Another reason for the erosion of the NYSE's market share is the rise of the so-called *fourth market,* systems that match buyers with sellers, bypassing both the NASDAQ system and stock exchanges. For example, one privately owned electronic trading firm, Bernard L. Madoff Investment Securities, handles about 10 percent of all trades in NYSE-listed stocks. Other fourth-market systems include Instinet and the Crossing Network, both electronic-trading subsidiaries of Reuters Holdings PLC; Quotron Systems owned by Citicorp; and Dow Jones' Telerate Inc.[16]

A growing number of major corporations offer even more direct systems for purchasing securities. If you would like to acquire common stock in such U.S. industrial giants as Exxon, W. R. Grace, Texaco, and Johnson Controls, you can purchase shares directly from the companies. The price for such a purchase is set at the exchange's closing price on the day of the purchase. Best of all, most of these corporations charge no fees.

READING THE FINANCIAL NEWS

Most major daily newspapers devote at least two or three pages to reporting current financial news. This coverage typically focuses on the previous day's securities transactions. Stocks and bonds traded on the NYSE and AMEX are listed alphabetically in the newspaper, along with information on the volume of sales and the price of each security.

STOCK QUOTATIONS

To read the stock tables in most daily newspapers, you need to understand how to interpret the symbols in the various columns. As Figure 20.12 explains, the symbol in the left-most column is the 52-week indicator. A *U* means that a stock hit its 52-week high during the day. Column 2 gives the stock's highest and lowest trading prices during the previous 52 weeks, and Column 3 shows an abbreviation for the company's name. The next column reports stock footnotes, which provide information about the stock, such as whether it is new, a preferred issue, or in bankruptcy. Column 5 lists the dividend, usu-

FIGURE 20.12

HOW TO READ STOCK TABLES

1	2		3	4	5	6	7	8	9	10		11	12
	52-Week High-Low				Div	Yd	PE	PPE	Vol. (100s)	High	Low	Close	Chg.
	14 5/8	10 3/4	AAR		0.48	3.7	...	656	1391	13 3/8	12 3/4	13 1/8	- 1/8
U	32	25 1/2	ACE	Lt n	0.10e	.4	...	...	1633	26	25 3/4	25 3/4	...
	11 3/4	10 1/2	ACM	In	0.96	8.3	...	...	425	11 5/8	11 1/2	11 5/8	+ 1/8
	10	9	ACM	Op	0.80a	8.3	...	...	107	9 3/4	9 5/8	9 5/8	- 1/8
		9 7/8	ACM	Sc	0.09a	8.6					11	11	

1. **52-WEEK INDICATORS:** U = Hit 52-week high during the day. D = Hit 52-week low.
2. **52-WEEK HIGH/LOW:** Highest and lowest trading prices in the past 52 weeks, adjusted for splits. New issues begin at the date of issue.
3. **STOCK:** The company's name abbreviated. A capital letter usually means a new word. AmExp, for example, is American Express.
4. **STOCK FOOTNOTES:** **n** - new. **pf** - preferred. **rt.** - rights. **s** - stock split, or dividend of more than 20 percent in past 52 weeks. **un** - stock sales in multiple-share units. **v** - trading halted on primary market. **vi** - in bankruptcy or receivership or being reorganized under the Bankruptcy Act, or securities assumed by such companies. **wi** - when issued. **x** - ex-dividend. **xdis** - ex-distribution, paid after stock dividend or split.
5. **DIVIDEND:** Dividends are usually annual payments based on the last quarterly or semiannual declaration. Special or extra dividends or payments are identified in footnotes: **a** - also extra or extras. **b** - annual rate plus stock dividend. **e** - irregular cash dividend. **g** - dividend paid in Canadian money; stock prices in U. S. dollars. **i** - declared or paid after stock dividend or split. **j** - paid this year, dividends omitted, deferred or no action taken at last dividend meeting. **k** - declared or paid this year, an accumulative issue with dividends in arrears. **r** - declared or paid in preceding 12 months plus stock dividend. **t** - paid stock in preceding 12 months, estimated cash value on ex-dividend or ex-distribution date.
6. **YIELD:** Percentage return from a dividend based on the stock's closing price.
7. **PE:** Price-to-earnings ratio, calculated by taking the last closing price of the stock and dividing it by the earnings per share for the latest four quarters.
8. **PPE:** Projected price-to-earnings ratio based on analysts' estimates for the next 12 months.
9. **VOLUME:** Trading volume in 100-share lots. A listing of 2400 means 240,000 shares traded during the day. A figure preceded by a "z" is the actual number of shares traded.
10. **HIGH/LOW:** High and low for the day.
11. **CLOSE:** Closing price.
12. **CHG:** Change in price from the close of the previous trading day.

ally an annual payment based on the last quarterly or semiannual declaration. Column 6 presents the yield, the percentage return from dividends based on the stock's closing price.

Column 7 lists the **price-earnings (P/E) ratio,** the current market price divided by the issuer's annual earnings per share. Next is the projected price-earnings (PP/E) ratio, which is based on analysts' estimates for the next 12 months. The stock's daily trading volume in 100-share lots appears in Column 9, and its highest and lowest prices for the day appear in Column 10. Column 11 gives the closing price for the day, and Column 12 summarizes the stock's change in price from its close on the previous trading day.

price-earnings (P/E) ratio
Stock's current market price divided by the issuer's annual earnings per share.

BOND QUOTATIONS

To learn how to read bond quotations, pick a bond listed in Figure 20.13 and examine the columns of information. Most bonds are issued in denominations of $1,000; thus, bond prices must be read differently from stock prices. The closing price of a bond might read $107\frac{3}{4}$, but this does not mean $107.75. Because bond prices are quoted as percentages of their $1,000 face values, $107\frac{3}{4}$ means $1,077.50.

FIGURE 20.13

1. **BOND:** Abbreviation of company name.
2. **ANNUAL INTEREST RATE:** Annual percentage rate of interest specified on the bond certificate.
3. **MATURITY DATE:** Year in which the bond issuer will repay bondholders the face value of each bond.
4. **YIELD:** Percentage return from interest payment calculated on the basis of the bond's closing price; **cv** indicates a bond that is convertible into shares of common stock at a specified price.
5. **VOLUME:** Number of bonds traded during the day.
6. **CLOSE:** Closing price.
7. **CHG:** Change in the price from the close of the previous trading day.

HOW TO READ BOND TABLES

Bonds (1)(2)(3)	Cur Yld (4)	Vol (5)	Close (6)	Net Chg (7)
PhilEl 11s11	10.2	22	107 3/4	+ 1/4
PhilP 12 1/4	11.2	18	109 5/8	+ 5/8
PhilP 11 1/4 13	10.3	5	108 7/8	+ 1 3/4
PierOn dc 11 1/2 03	11.3	150	101 7/8	...
Pittstn 9.2s04	CV	59	100	– 1/4
PopeTl 6s12	CV	11	88	+ 1
PorG 8 3/4 07	8.7	9	100 1/8	...
PotEl 8 3/8 09	8.3	5	100 5/8	– 5/8
PotEl 9 1/4 16	8.8	9	105	...
PotEl 7s18	CV	15	97 1/2	+ 1/2
viPrmM 6 5/8 11f	CV	30	17 7/8	– 1/8

The notation next to the bond name, such as "11s11," indicates the bonds pay an annual interest rate of 11.0 percent and have a maturity date of 2011. The first figure is the interest rate; the second is the maturity date. Assuming a bond is selling above its original $1,000 face value, the current yield is 10.2 percent, almost a full percentage point less than the 11 percent stated interest rate. Bonds with the notation *CV* are convertible bonds.

The next column indicates the total trading volume during the day. The closing bond price is listed next, followed by the net change in price since the previous day's close.

STOCK MARKET AVERAGES

Dow Jones averages
Averages of stock market activity based on the market prices of 30 industrial, 20 transportation, and 15 utility stocks.

Most daily newscasts report current stock market averages. The most familiar average, the DJIA or Dow Jones Industrial Average, is one of the **Dow Jones averages** (the Dow); however, most people are also familiar with the *Standard & Poor's 500 Index.* Both indexes have been developed to reflect general activity in the stock market.

The Dow actually includes three different indexes based on the market prices of 30 industrial, 20 transportation, and 15 utility stocks. The more broadly based Standard & Poor's 500 Index tracks the market performance of 400 industrial, 40 financial, 40 utility, and 20 transportation stocks.

The Dow Jones Industrial Average has served as a general measure of changes in overall stock prices and a reflection of the U.S. economy since its appearance in 1896. The term *industrial* is a misnomer since the index is composed of both industrial corporations like General Motors, Union Carbide, and Boeing and such nonindustrial firms as American Express, McDonald's, and Sears. The Dow remains the most widely reported barometer of stock market activity, although some financial analysts claim that it overrepresents the market's capital goods and energy sectors, while underrepresenting financial and service firms.[17]

MUTUAL FUNDS

Many investors lack both the time and the knowledge to continually analyze stock market developments. These people may choose another investment option called **mutual funds**—financial organizations that pool investment money from purchasers of their securities and invest the money in diversified portfolios of securities. Investors who buy shares in a mutual fund become part owners of securities issued by a large number of companies, reducing their levels of individual risk. Mutual funds are managed by trained, experienced professionals whose careers are based on success in analyzing the securities markets and specific industries and companies. Figure 20.14 describes services offered to investors by such mutual fund families as Invesco Funds and Janus Funds.

mutual fund
Financial organization that pools investors' money to acquire a diversified portfolio of securities.

The importance of mutual funds as an investment vehicle has increased dramatically since 1981, when they accounted for five percent of a typical U.S. household investment portfolio. Today, mutual funds' portfolio share has grown to 35 percent. Approximately 38 million people in the United States currently own shares in mutual funds. They maintain over 81 million accounts with total assets of $2 trillion.[18]

Reading the mutual fund quotation table shown in Figure 20.15 is relatively simple. The first column lists the fund's net asset value (NAV). Column 2 lists the sales price (the net asset value plus sales charges). The last column shows the change in the fund's asset value from the previous trading session. Footnotes may present additional information, such as whether the fund is a no-load fund, which charges no initial sales fee, or whether a redemption fee or contingent deferred sales load may apply.

LEGAL AND ETHICAL ISSUES IN SECURITIES TRADING

The past two decades will be remembered as one of the most scandal-plagued periods in the history of Wall Street. Jailed insider traders such as Ivan Boesky and junk-bond pioneer Michael Milkin made headlines for months. Financial portfolios filled with junk bonds led to the failures of hundreds of financial institutions. Dozens of corporate giants made drastic financial decisions in attempts to ward off hostile takeovers. These events

FIGURE 20.14

DIVERSIFYING INVESTMENT HOLDINGS WITH PROFESSIONALLY MANAGED MUTUAL FUNDS

FIGURE 20.15

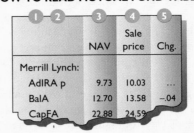

HOW TO READ MUTUAL FUND TABLES

(1) (2)	(3) NAV	(4) Sale price	(5) Chg.
Merrill Lynch:			
AdIRA p	9.73	10.03	...
BalA	12.70	13.58	–.04
CapFA	22.88	24.59	

1. **ISSUER:** Financial organization issuing and managing the mutual fund. Under the Merrill Lynch family of funds are the different funds developed for investors with varying objectives.
2. **FOOTNOTES:** **e** – ex-capital gains distribution; **s** – stock dividend or split; **x** – ex-cash dividend; **f** – previous day's quotation; **(NL)** – no front-end load or sales commission charged; **p** – fund assets are used to pay for costs under special retirement plans; **r** – redemption fee may apply to sellers; **t** – both **p** and **r** apply.
3. **NAV:** Fund's net asset value. Also referred to as *buy.*
4. **SALE PRICE:** Net asset value plus sales charges. NL indicates a no-load fund. Also referred to as *sell.*
5. **CHANGE:** Gain or loss in net asset value from previous session.

created a growing awareness of legal and ethical problems in these areas. Ethical issues in securities trading include illegal bond bids, program trading, insider trading, and abuses of the small-order execution system.

By law, no single company can buy more than 35 percent of the Treasury bonds on the market. However, loose trading practices have allowed some companies to make illegal bond bids, cornering as much as 90 percent of the Treasury notes offered during a single auction and costing traders and investors millions of dollars. The government has announced plans to regulate the $2.2 trillion government securities market more closely in the future.

program trading
Automatic securities transactions using computer systems programmed to issue buy and sell orders in response to price changes exceeding predetermined amounts.

Program trading is a controversial practice in which computer systems are programmed to issue orders to buy or sell securities automatically in response to certain conditions. Program trading started as a type of portfolio insurance that allowed market players to hedge their bets with automatic buy or sell orders whenever their stock prices might reach certain levels. The practice has become controversial since many people blame it for the 1987 stock market crash when the market value of the nation's leading stocks dropped 23 percent in 1 day. In fact, program trading accounted for only 15 percent of that day's trades. However, it can significantly amplify price swings in individual stocks when numerous buy and sell orders reach the market at one time. For this reason, many people have suggested banning program trading.

insider trading
Illegal securities trading by people who try to profit from their access to nonpublic information about a company.

Insider trading refers to illegal securities trades by people who profit from their access to nonpublic information about a company, such as a pending merger or a major oil discovery. While the Securities Exchange Act of 1934 prohibits this practice, analysis of stock trading patterns before major announcements frequently uncovers cases of insider trading. In 1994, for example, suspicious trading preceded one out of three big merger deals.[19]

Clearly, not every stock purchase immediately preceding a merger or major news story about a company involves insider trading. Four examples—two legal and two illegal—are shown in Figure 20.16.

REGULATING SECURITIES TRANSACTIONS

Revelations of unethical practices typically lead to the passage of laws aimed at restricting such practices in the future. Both the federal government and all state governments have enacted legislation regulating sales of securities. State laws typically require that most securities sold in those states be registered with appropriate state officials, usually secretaries of state, and that securities dealers and salespeople renew licenses annually. Interstate sales of securities for the remaining years of the 1990s needed additional protection, though.

Securities Act of 1933 The *Securities Act of 1933,* often called the Truth in Securities Act, is a federal law designed to protect investors by requiring full disclosure of

FIGURE 20.16 INSIDER TRADING: WHAT'S LEGAL AND WHAT ISN'T?

What's legal and what isn't

- A friend tells you that his company is doing very well. You buy stock in the company. That's legal because the information wasn't "material," or important enough to affect investors' decisions.
- You overhear two people saying they heard that Acme Widget Co. is a fabulous buy because a takeover is in the works. You invest in Acme Widget. That's legal—but only if you don't know whether or not the source of the information was an insider such as an officer of the company.
- You're a psychiatrist and your patient mentions her company could face a hostile takeover. You buy its stock. That's illegal because you're "misappropriating" information by breaching your confidential relationship with your patient.
- A high-ranking colleague tells you about an imminent takeover of your company. You don't trade on the information, but you tell a close friend who does. Courts would likely deem that your action was illegal on the grounds that there probably was a quid pro quo.

relevant financial information by any company that sells a new stock or bond issue to the general public. This information requirement mandates two kinds of disclosure: a registration statement containing detailed company information filed with the Securities and Exchange Commission and a condensed version of the registration statement printed in a booklet called a *prospectus,* which must be furnished to each purchaser.

Securities Exchange Act of 1934 The *Securities Exchange Act of 1934* created the Securities and Exchange Commission (SEC) to regulate the national stock exchanges, and it established strict rules for trading on organized exchanges. A 1964 amendment extended the authority of the SEC to the over-the-counter market. All companies with securities listed on the national and regional exchanges or traded over the counter must file registration statements with the SEC and update them annually. The SEC regulates brokerage firms, individual brokers, and dealers selling OTC stocks, and brokers engaged in buying and selling securities must pass an examination.

Other Federal Legislation The *Maloney Act of 1938,* an amendment to the Securities Exchange Act of 1934, authorized self-regulation of OTC securities operations. This led to the creation of the *National Association of Securities Dealers (NASD),* which is responsible for regulating OTC securities businesses. All new brokers and dealers who sell OTC securities must now pass written examinations. The *Investment Company Act of 1940* brought the mutual fund industry under SEC jurisdiction. Mutual funds must register with the SEC. Also, the state and federal laws mentioned protect investors from securities trading abuses and stock price manipulations that occurred before the 1930s.

The *Securities Enforcement Remedies and Penny Stock Reform Act of 1990* expanded the SEC's role in dealing with securities violations. The law created three tiers of fines based on the severity of violations. The first tier imposes a maximum fine of $5,000 for individuals or $50,000 for others to punish an infraction that does not result from a deliberate violation of the securities laws. The second tier imposes a fine of $50,000 to $250,000 for a violation involving fraud, manipulation, or deliberate disregard of the law. The third tier punishes those whose fraud results in substantial losses or risks of loss by other people, imposing a fine of $100,000 to $500,000. The SEC has the right to raise the fines for all three tiers in especially serious cases.[20]

PROTECTING INVESTORS FROM DEALER OR BROKER INSOLVENCY

In 1970, Congress enacted the Securities Investor Protection Act, which created a not-for-profit corporation, the *Securities Investor Protection Corporation (SIPC).* The SIPC insures the accounts of brokerage firm clients for up to cash values of $100,000 in case of dealer or broker insolvency. Losses of securities are insured for up to $500,000. SIPC protection works like the protection that the FDIC provides to bank depositors, but it differs in one important respect; the FDIC is a federal agency, while the SIPC is a membership organization composed of all national securities exchanges and registered brokers. Funding comes through assessments on member firms. Although the SIPC protects investors against financial disasters resulting from a brokerage's bankruptcy, it does not provide protection against market losses caused by price declines.

While the SEC feels that the SIPC is in good shape overall, it is investigating ways to expand the reserves of the insurer. As one possibility, the SIPC could increase its $500 million credit line with the government. For another idea, member brokers could buy Treasury bonds and deposit them with the SIPC to replace some of their annual payments to the fund. In an emergency, the SIPC would be able to cash in the bonds.[21]

Achieving your financial objectives involves not only setting aside funds for investing on a regular basis, but also includes the growing value of these funds as a result of dividends and value appreciation. Compound interest tables show that a $1,000 investment with an annual return of 10 percent will double in less than 8 years.

DEVELOPING A PERSONAL FINANCIAL PLAN

Now that you have studied various types of investment options, you need to apply what you have learned to manage your own money. Here are some tips from the pros for developing a financial plan for the 1990s.[22]

- *Set up a regular savings plan.* Experts advise that you save enough money to live for 6 to 9 months without a salary, if necessary. They also suggest that you save and invest at least 20 percent of your pretax annual salary. This saving can take the form of a retirement plan, savings account, or other investments.
- *Pay off as much as possible of your debt.* Americans are carrying more debt on their credit cards than ever; don't be one of them. Carrying charges on credit cards can cost an average of 19 percent each year in interest.
- *Consider stocks.* Despite the ups and downs of the stock market, many experts still feel that stocks deliver the most profit over the long run. Through the years, stocks have averaged an annual return of 10 percent. While this may not match the profits earned during the booming 1980s, it's still better than the average return on bonds and many other investments.
- *Evaluate bonds.* If you decide to buy bonds, financial advisors suggest devoting 20 to 30 percent of your investment balance to these securities.
- *Shop around.* Do research to identify the best mutual funds and the money managers with the lowest fees.
- *Diversify!* Spread your money around to lower your risk. Says money manager Hutch Vernon, "Being all in stock or all in bonds, you expose yourself to much greater risk than with a balanced portfolio." Joel Isaakson, head of financial planning at New York's Clarfeld & Co., suggests dividing your money among international equity funds and large, medium-sized, and small companies.
- *Look abroad.* Says investment strategist Nimrod Fachler, "The more a country's GDP grows, the better the return for its stocks, and with Europe opening up and the Pacific Rim on fire, overseas nations should grow faster than the United States." Strategists predict that foreign stocks will return about 12.4 percent annually for the rest of this decade.

ACHIEVEMENT CHECK SUMMARY

Reread the learning goals that follow, and consider the questions for each goal. Answering these questions will reinforce the most important concepts in the chapter and allow you to check how well you have achieved these learning goals. Where a blank appears before a question, answer with *T* or *F*. Otherwise, circle the letter of the correct answer. An answer key to these questions is found at the end of this chapter.

LEARNING GOAL 20.1: Distinguish between primary markets for securities and secondary markets.

1. An initial issue of stock or bonds takes place in the: (a) primary market; (b) secondary market; (c) New York Stock Exchange; (d) American Stock Exchange; (e) all of the above.
2. When investors trade securities among themselves, they do so by means of the: (a) primary market; (b) secondary market; (c) Dow Jones Industrial Average; (d) Standard & Poor's rating service.
3. Each time securities are traded on the secondary market, the issuing corporation receives: (a) 100 percent of the selling price; (b) 50 percent of the selling price; (c) 25 percent of the selling price; (d) none of the selling price.

LEARNING GOAL 20.2: Compare common stock, preferred stock, and bonds, and explain why investors might prefer each type of security.

1. The true owners of a corporation: (a) are the common shareholders; (b) have voting rights; (c) have a residual claim to assets; (d) all of the above.
2. Preferred stockholders: (a) have a claim to assets prior to that of common share holders; (b) usually have voting rights; (c) are contributors of debt, not equity capital; (d) all of the above.
3. In the event of a firm's dissolution, the first claim on its assets belongs to: (a) bondholders; (b) preferred stockholders; (c) common stockholders; (d) all investors equally.

LEARNING GOAL 20.3: Identify the four basic objectives of investors and the types of securities most likely to accomplish each objective.

1. A speculator would be most likely to invest in: (a) common stocks or penny stocks; (b) preferred stocks; (c) corporate bonds; (d) government bonds.
2. An investor looking for long-term growth would be most likely to invest in: (a) common stocks; (b) preferred stocks; (c) corporate bonds; (d) government bonds.
3. An investor seeking safety of principal would be most likely to purchase: (a) common stock; (b) preferred stock and bonds; (c) penny stock and bonds; (d) bonds and common stock.

LEARNING GOAL 20.4: Explain the process of selling or purchasing a security listed on an organized security exchange.

1. ___ A market order is an investor request to buy or sell a stock at a specified price.
2. ___ The traditional method of trading securities requires the use of a trained specialist known as a stockbroker.
3. ___ A growing number of investors bypass the traditional exchanges and make their trades through computer networks.

LEARNING GOAL 20.5: Describe the information in stock, bond, and mutual fund quotations.

1. If a stock gained $\frac{5}{8}$ for the day, the price per share increased: (a) \$0.625; (b) \$6.25; (c) \$3.25; (d) \$0.325.
2. If a commercial \$1,000 bond ends the day down $\frac{1}{2}$, it has lost: (a) \$0.05; (b) \$0.50; (c) \$5.00; (d) \$50.00.
3. In a stock quotation, the P/E: (a) indicates the price-to-earnings ratio; (b) is found by dividing today's closing price by the annual earnings per share; (c) is equal to the stock's annual yield; (d) all of the above; (e) a and b only.

LEARNING GOAL 20.6: Explain the role of mutual funds in securities markets.

1. ___ The main advantage of mutual funds is that they prevent investor losses.
2. ___ Mutual funds are professionally managed investment companies that own shares in many different companies.
3. ___ An investor gains greater diversification from buying a share of a mutual fund than from buying an individual stock or bond issue.

LEARNING GOAL 20.7: Evaluate the major features of state and federal laws designed to protect investors.

1. The 1970 Securities Investor Protection Act was created to: (a) protect investors against making bad investment decisions; (b) protect investors against losing their investment principal in the bond market; (c) insure investors' accounts at insolvent brokerage houses; (d) insure brokerage firms against losses when clients do not pay for their stock purchases.
2. The Securities Act of 1933: (a) created the Securities and Exchange Commission; (b) requires full disclosure of financial information by firms selling securities to the public; (c) set the taxation level on each share traded; (d) requires all firms to pay dividends.
3. The Investment Company Act of 1940: (a) set rules for investors; (b) brought mutual funds under the jurisdiction of the Securities and Exchange Commission; (c) set rules for brokers; (d) set rules for the New York Stock Exchange.

KEY TERMS

REVIEW QUESTIONS

1. In what ways does the secondary market differ from the primary market? With which market are investment bankers involved? What role do they play in financial decisions?

2. What is common stock? Explain the alternative methods for evaluating common stock.

3. Explain the major types of bonds issued by corporations and government units. By what primary methods do issuers retire bonds?

4. Identify the four major goals of investors, and suggest an appropriate mix of securities to achieve these goals.

5. Distinguish between the following terms:
   a. Market orders and limit orders
   b. Round lots and odd lots
   c. Bulls and bears

6. How does the New York Stock Exchange operate? Compare the NYSE's operations with those of foreign and international markets and the NASDAQ system.

7. What are stock market averages? How do they affect securities trading? Would you expect the Standard & Poor's Index of 500 stocks to be a better indicator of overall market activity than the Dow Jones Industrial Average?

8. How does an investor place an order for common stock? Explain how computerized trading is revolutionizing the securities industry.

9. Discuss the alternative of purchasing shares in mutual funds as opposed to purchasing stocks and bonds directly.

10. Explain the major laws that affect securities transactions. Include the primary purpose of each law and how it affects individual investors as well as the securities industry.

DISCUSSION QUESTIONS

1. Assume that you just inherited $20,000 from your uncle and his will stipulates that you must invest all the money until you complete your education. Prepare an investment plan for the $20,000 inheritance.

2. Assume that you are an investment counselor with the job of identifying general investment goals for the following individuals, each of whom has adequate current income and about $30,000 to invest. Prepare a short report outlining the proposed investment goals for each person with general suggestions of an appropriate mix of securities:
   a. 56-year-old retired Army officer
   b. 40-year-old divorced mother of two children
   c. 19-year-old college student receiving $200 weekly for the next 10 years in survivors' insurance benefits
   d. 26-year-old unmarried person earning $24,000 annually

3. The chapter notes that the NYSE's market share is slipping. Discuss the domestic and global developments that you feel are related to this trend.

4. How do bond ratings affect bond prices? What impact does a bond's rating have on its yield? How might a bond's rating determine the likely purchasers of a bond?

5. A married couple in their late 20s with two small children and joint earnings of $45,000 have decided to invest in stocks that promise growth with a steady return in the form of dividends. They have narrowed the choice of stocks to five and have assembled the data in the table below from the past 3 years:

Calculate the dividend yield and price-earnings ratio for each stock for each of the 3 years. Based on your analysis of the data and the risks and rewards involved, recommend one of the five stocks for the couple to purchase.

SOLUTIONS TO ACHIEVEMENT CHECK SUMMARY

L. G. 20.1: 1. a, 2. b, 3. d. **L. G. 20.2:** 1. d, 2. a, 3. a. **L. G. 20.3:** 1. a, 2. a, 3. b. **L. G. 20.4:** 1. F, 2. T, 3. T. **L. G. 20.5:** 1. a, 2. c, 3. e. **L. G. 20.6:** 1. F, 2. T, 3. T. **L. G. 20.7:** 1. c, 2. b, 3. b.

	Stock	Average Price per Share	Earnings per Share	Average Dividend per Share
1993	A	$ 60	$ 5.12	$ 2.70
	B	268	13.35	10.00
	C	42	2.17	0.05
	D	6	0.12	0.08
	E	30	3.06	1.70
1994	A	$ 59	$ 7.98	$ 2.80
	B	275	15.94	10.00
	C	45	2.74	0.06
	D	8	0.22	0.10
	E	29	3.20	1.80
1995	A	$ 72	$ 9.00	$ 3.00
	B	320	17.50	10.00
	C	60	3.40	0.10
	D	11	0.80	0.12
	E	42	3.75	2.00

TEAM-BUILDING EXERCISE

The finance section concludes our examination of the three universal functions of any business (production and marketing are the other two). Their importance is illustrated by the fact that senior managers from each function participate in most major decisions affecting the organization. Information plays a vital role in such strategic decisions as mergers, developing new product lines, choosing to subcontract some production to outside firms, or entering new markets. The ultimate decision results from hours, days, and sometimes weeks of interactions among the managers, each of whom has a major stake in the decision. Effective oral and written communication, the ability to work well with others, and negotiation skills are invaluable in these deliberations. This exercise focuses on negotiation.

1. Your instructor will divide the class into teams and distribute a list of tasks to complete, along with some of the materials you will need to complete them.

2. Each team will have different materials but must complete the same tasks. You may bargain for the use of materials and tools in any way that is mutually agreeable. Your instructor will tell you when to begin.

3. The first team to complete all the tasks is the winner and the most successful at negotiation.

VIDEO CASE

RONEY & COMPANY Unless you live in the Midwest, chances are good that you have never heard of Roney & Company. But the firm's name is synonymous with quality service and customer satisfaction to its 70,000 clients in the tri-state area. Headquartered in Detroit and operating 27 branches throughout Indiana, Michigan, and Ohio, Roney's commitment to building and maintaining strong customer relationships has resulted in its position as Michigan's oldest and largest investment securities firm. Roney & Company is organized as a partnership consisting of more than 100 partners and a staff of 575 professionals.

The cornerstone of any business is its ability to build and maintain relationships based on a solid foundation of trust. Since its founding in 1925, Roney's central focus has been on continually evaluating and improving customer service in every department. Many of the firm's clients have conducted their brokerage business with Roney for years. In fact, long-time clients are an important source of new business through referrals. In addition, Roney & Company has improved its service to current clients and added new ones by expanding its services beyond simply buying and selling stocks and bonds.

Like other brokerage firms, Roney & Company is actively involved in the secondary market for securities through the purchase and sale of stocks and bonds for its clientele. The firm has been a member of the New York Stock Exchange longer than any other Michigan-based investment firm. Its extensive database of over 1,000 publicly traded companies is updated quarterly and is available for use by the firm's clients. Roney's bond department and mutual funds department provide expertise for clients interested in these investment vehicles. The firm's securities analysts prepare lists of recommended stocks, bonds, and mutual funds based on different investment criteria, and work with account executives to determine which are most appropriate for individual clients.

Another service provided to Roney clients involves the primary market for securities. Even though the firm is dwarfed in size by giant competitors like Merrill Lynch, First Boston, and Prudential Securities, it is large enough to offer extensive access to financial markets. At the same time, it provides clients with the personalized attention that is the hallmark of successful regional brokerage firms.

Business clients turn to Roney & Company for a variety of financing needs. In some cases, they have decided to "go public" by making an offering of common stock. In other instances, they work with Roney in making a so-called "private placement" of stock with a small group of investors, each of whom invests thousands or even millions in the venture in exchange for a share of ownership. Or a client may want to secure debt financing in the form of a bond issue or complex long-term loan. In all of these situations, Roney has the expertise to compile the needed financial projections, decide upon the structure and placement of a stock or bond offering, and prepare all of the documents required for such offerings. In addition, Roney & Company senior executives counsel clients throughout the entire process. The firm is either involved as the lead underwriter or participant in approximately 100 to 200 offerings a year, each of which raises an average of $5 million to $10 million in debt or equity capital.

Roney & Company also provides specialized services for its clients in the area of mergers and acquisitions. A separate department provides counseling on strategies involving an acquisition, merger, or the sale of such assets as a division, production facility, or product line. Assisting clients in determining the appropriate value of a proposed purchase or sale is an important function of this department.

The firm has also responded to the aging American population by strengthening its services in retirement and estate planning. It offers clients a full range of investment alternatives to meet their unique needs and objectives.

The foundation of a mutually satisfactory customer relationship lies with each employee in every department, from research, corporate finance, and investment planning, to mergers and acquisitions. Roney's competitive advantage results from a combination of its size, the personalized attention it provides for each client, and the comprehensive services each account executive is able to offer its clients. Instead of simply selling *products,* the firm views itself as part of a long-term comprehensive financial relationship in which it can offer the appropriate combination of investment services needed by its clients. Given the number of years most Roney clients have been Roney clients, this relationship is continuing to meet their needs.

QUESTIONS

1.
In the primary market, who would typically be a customer of a firm such as Roney & Company?

2.
What financial products does Roney & Company deal with in the secondary market?

3.
Roney & Company has helped its clients in the placement of more than $1 billion of mutual funds. What are the advantages of holding shares of mutual funds?

4.
At Roney & Company, why are mergers and acquisitions considered to be an important part of a customer's portfolio?

CAREERS IN BUSINESS

CAREER PROFILE: MARY SILVERSTEIN Mary Silverstein entered the University of Alaska as a theater major. In the course of working and going to school, she found she preferred her job to her dream of working in the theater—so much so that she changed her major to pursue a degree in management. ■ Silverstein still doesn't have an official job title. They did away with job titles at Carr-Gottstein Properties, a major financial savings and investment firm headquartered in Alaska, where she is, in effect, a financial analyst. Every Tuesday, she gathers all the data necessary to paint the "big picture" for Mr. Gottstein, who uses it in making major investment decisions. She is responsible for monitoring partnership and executive investment accounts, tracking and analyzing returns on a daily basis, and overseeing the production of an extensive real estate portfolio report. ■ The Carr-Gottstein portfolio that Silverstein manages includes U.S. and foreign partnerships, in addition to investments, stocks, bonds, and mutual funds. Since not all the investments are blue-chip, it is important for her to watch consumer trends as well as the management of the companies in which Carr-Gottstein invests. Using resources such as Reuter's Money Network, CompuServe's online financial services, and several brokers, Silverstein can obtain current information on any of her company's investments until 2:00 P.M. on any given day. ■ Although Silverstein has specific responsibilities, she also shares her investment picks with her boss. Sometimes Mr. Gottstein just laughs, because he and Silverstein have entirely different sets of criteria with which they evaluate investment candidates. Sometimes Silverstein gets to laugh, too, like the time Gottstein ignored her recommendation to invest in a fledgling company called Starbucks Coffee. Soon afterwards, they watched it climb to success. ■ As a working wife and mother, Silverstein was a non-traditional student—something she found advantageous. Silverstein appreciated the support and encouragement of her professors, her family, and her employer, who allowed her the flexibility she needed to accomplish her goals. She took an active role on campus and was the president of the business club. She also sees the immediate benefit of her education in the workplace. For example, after learning how to use a new piece of software in class, Silverstein demonstrated its capabilities to her boss. He not only implemented it, he gave her the additional job responsibility of using it. ■ In more ways than one, Silverstein has shown her adaptability to a changing environment. As she puts it, "If you're open to alternative solutions, willing to learn, and don't take rejection personally, you can sometimes turn an initially negative response around. Never be afraid to ask questions, never be afraid to participate, and never give up."

All businesses and many individuals require financial services. As a result, the area of finance provides lots of career opportunities that are not only exciting and challenging, but also provide excellent advancement possibilities.

Specific jobs in banking, finance, investments, and insurance include bank manager, bank operations officer, credit manager, securities sales representative, actuary, underwriter, claims representative, and insurance agent and broker.

The Bureau of Labor Statistics forecasts that job opportunities for bank officers and managers, insurance agents, and insurance brokers will grow about as fast as the average. Job opportunities will grow much faster than average for securities sales workers, but the demand for such professionals can vary as the economy expands and contracts.

BANK MANAGERS

Bank managers administer the various activities of their units. Currently, about 233,700 bank officers and managers are employed in the United States.

Job Description Bank managers are part of the executive level of the rapidly changing banking industry. They must be familiar with all banking policies, procedures, and practices, and they must keep up with the many changes that occur. Bankers must also be knowledgeable about the legal framework of their industry. The American Bankers Association offers courses to keep banking employees current.

Career Path College-educated candidates usually begin in a management training program. This usually involves rotating among the various bank departments to familiarize candidates with all aspects of banking. Good performance in a junior-level position may lead to an appointment as a bank officer or manager.

Salary In large banks, branch managers earn up to $77,800, depending on the size of the branch and assets of the bank. The average salary is $39,700. In smaller banks, salaries are several thousand dollars lower.

BANK OPERATIONS OFFICERS

The operations officer directs the bank's daily work flow. In a smaller bank, the operations officer is the branch manager. In a large bank, the operations officer handles the teller line and backroom activities and reports to the branch manager.

Job Description The operations officer must be thoroughly trained in bank practices and procedures in order to make decisions about daily work assignments.

Career Path Management trainee positions are available in the banking industry. Successful completion of such a program can lead to appointment as an operations officer, a middle-management position in most banks. Effective performance at this level can lead to an advanced management appointment.

Salary Once the person becomes an operations officer, the salary is usually a function of the bank's size. Annual trainee pay ranges up to $22,800. The head of operations at a large bank averages about $69,300.

CREDIT MANAGERS

Credit managers play a key role on the firm's financial team because they determine whether to grant credit to customers. These people manage the firm's credit function ranging from loan decisions to payment processing to loan payoffs.

Job Description Credit managers set overall credit policy and review the creditworthiness of customers, both businesses and individuals. They also administer the debt collection process.

Career Path Credit managers usually begin as trainees in the credit department. Experienced personnel may advance to management positions in the department. Credit managers are exposed to the entire organization and may eventually reach top management.

Salary Depending on the industry and the size of the bank, analysts may make anywhere from $21,000 to $28,500. Credit managers, like other financial managers, average about $30,400 but some make more than $52,000 a year.

SECURITIES SALES REPRESENTATIVES

Securities sales workers, also known as *registered representatives, account executives,* or *brokers,* link investors to the securities industry. Through securities salespeople, investors buy and sell stocks, bonds, shares in mutual funds, or other financial products. In a recent year, more than 200,000 securities and financial salespeople were employed in the United States.

Job Description Securities sales representatives transmit customer orders to buy and sell securities to the market in which the trade occurs. They also offer clients a range of financial counseling services including advice on purchases of mutual funds, annuities, life insurance, and other investments.

Career Path Before being allowed to work with clients, securities sales reps must pass a series of examinations given by the state, the Securities and Exchange Commission, the exchange on which they will trade, and often the brokerage firm for which they will work. On-the-job training is provided to help workers pass these tests. Once fully qualified, beginning securities sales reps concentrate on building their client contacts. As they gain experience, the number and size of the accounts they handle usually increase. Some experienced reps also take on managerial duties and supervise other salespeople.

Salary While they are being trained, beginning securities salespeople earn minimal salaries. Experienced workers depend on commissions rather than salary. In a recent year, an average securities sales rep earned $78,000, while workers servicing institutional accounts earned $156,000.

ACTUARIES

Actuaries provide the statistical information needed by the insurance industry. They also work in areas such as pension planning.

Job Description Actuaries gather the data needed to determine the risk of losses of various job types and perform the statistical analyses that make such data usable to the insurance industry. They calculate the probability that people will die during the term of their life insurance policy, for example, and calculate the premium necessary for the company to profitably insure them. Some actuaries work for consulting firms or pension funds rather than for insurance companies.

Career Path Advancement in the actuarial industry depends on experience and successfully passing a series of exams given by the actuarial societies, which are broken down by specialty. Depending on the society, there are either nine or ten exams to pass, usually over 5 to 10 years.

Salary The average starting salary for those who had not taken their actuarial exams was $31,800 recently. Those who had taken one exam averaged $34,000 to $38,000. Actuaries who had become associates of the Society of Actuaries earned $46,000 and Fellows of the Society earned $65,500 a year. Fellows with experience earned substantially more.

UNDERWRITERS

Underwriters analyze the risks to which insurance applicants are exposed. In a recent year, there were 100,000 underwriters in the United States. Faster than average employment growth is expected through 2000.

Job Description Underwriters use the information provided by applicants for insurance, in conjunction with statistics provided by actuaries and other specialists, to assess the risk to which the applicant is exposed. They use this information to set the terms of the policy, premiums, and so forth. The underwriter makes sure the company does not assume too much risk (causing it to lose money) but also remains competitive with other insurance firms by not turning down too many policies.

Career Path New underwriters are generally supervised closely and required to take further courses in underwriting. They first work with routine applications and move to more demanding applications as their ability grows. This career ladder extends to supervisory positions or to top management.

Salary In a recent year, median salaries for underwriters of personal lines averaged $25,000, with managers earning, on the average, $61,000. Median salaries of underwriters of commercial lines averaged $28,000, with managers earning, on the average, $61,000.

CLAIMS REPRESENTATIVES

Claims representatives or claims adjusters assess insurance claims and determine how much the applicant will be paid. They study all available evidence about a loss situation and determine the insurance company's liability. Currently, about 142,200 people work as claims representatives throughout the United States.

Job Description Most claims representatives are in property and liability insurance and tend to fall into two classes. Claims adjusters examine physical evidence of loss and witness testimony. Claims examiners investigate questionable claims and work in the field, interviewing experts and witnesses. Both groups determine the validity of a claim, whether the insurance company is liable, and how much of the loss is covered.

Career Path Beginning claims representatives are supervised by senior-level personnel and are usually limited to small claims. As the person gains experience, he or she requires responsibility for larger claims. Supervisory positions in the claims department cap this career.

Salary In a recent year, median salaries of claims representatives averaged $22,360, varying depending on the area of insurance. Senior adjusters earned about $29,000. Similarly, claims examiners earned an average of $29,100.

INSURANCE AGENTS AND BROKERS

It is important to differentiate between insurance agents and brokers. An insurance agent sells insurance for a specific company. A broker is self-employed and represents several companies. Some agents and brokers specialize in certain types of insurance, while others market full lines of insurance products. Recent employment figures show that more than 415,000 insurance agents and brokers are employed in the United States.

Job Description Both agents and brokers evaluate the financial needs of their clients and select insurance coverage that meets their needs. Insurance agents and brokers also answer questions about various types of coverage, assist clients when claims are filed, and act as liaisons between the insured and the insurance company.

Career Path Newly hired agents typically undergo extensive home-office training. Afterward, they spend most of their early careers establishing clientele bases. Insurance brokers undergo a similar training process. Some successful agents advance to sales management positions or to head local or regional offices.

The insurance industry offers various professional certification programs. Completion of such programs is often an important stepping stone in an insurance career.

Salary Independent agents and brokers work on a commission basis. This provides maximum incentive for effective sales performance. In a recent year the median salary of agents and brokers was $30,100, with some earning up to $64,600. Experienced agents and brokers average $50,300 a year. Employees of insurance agencies work on a straight salary, salary plus commission, or salary plus bonus basis.

CAREER DESIGN EXERCISE

PERSONAL FINANCES

As you learned in Chapter 19, one of the responsibilities of a financial manager is to assist the business in determining the amount of money it needs to pursue its goals and then help it raise any needed funds. You experience some of these same responsibilities on a much smaller scale with your own personal finances. First, you determine how much money is needed to pay for your education, housing, food and miscellaneous expenses. Second, you raise the money you need through employment, family, government aid, or other resources.

When you graduate, your goals will certainly change. You will probably have much higher expectations about your standard of living than you do now as a student. It is important to determine exactly what those expectations are and what is required, both financially and professionally, to meet them.

THIS EXERCISE WILL HELP YOU TO

- Determine what level of compensation you will need upon graduation to attain the lifestyle you want.
- Determine whether a given career direction will meet those financial expectations.

HOW TO LOCATE THE EXERCISE

When you see the main menu for Career Design, select "How Do I Get There?" Then select "Personal Finances."

YOUR CAREER

APPENDIX A

IN BUSINESS

INTERVIEW WITH A COMPUTER When Bonnie Dunn applied for a teller's job at Great Western Bank in Chatsworth, California, she found the job interview challenging, to say the least. First, she was tested on her skill in handling money; she had to cash a check for $192.18, including at least three $5 bills and $2 in quarters. She then had to demonstrate her skill in handling people by dealing effectively with two angry bank customers. Finally, the interviewer assessed her sales ability by asking Dunn to cash a check from a competing bank and assessing whether she remembered to extol Great Western's services to this potential customer. ■ Sound difficult? Now imagine going through this interview with a computer doing the interviewing. Like Great Western, several companies are experimenting with such systems. Walt Disney Company, Marriott, and Neiman Marcus use them to hire entry-level employees; shoe retailer Pic 'n Pay uses an electronic system to screen potential sales clerks; American General Life & Accident selects promising insurance agents through computer-assisted interviews. ■ Great Western's system, for example, consists of a 20-minute interactive session in which applicants communicate via a color touch-screen and a microphone. When candidates sit down in front of the machine, a programmed voice welcomes them to the "interactive assessment aid" and warns them, "We'll be keeping track of how long it takes you and how many mistakes you make. Accuracy is more important than speed." While the computer does not understand applicants' spoken comments, it records what they say for later evaluation by a bank staffer. ■ The system tests candidates' poise in tense situations by recording their ability to deal with angry customers who appear on the screen. One customer, for instance, is a touchy young woman who impatiently orders the applicant to cash a $150 check, give her $40 in cash, deposit $65 in her savings account, and put the rest in her checking account, then quickly adds, "No, it has to be $50 in checking because I just wrote a check this morning." If the applicant dares to ask for clarification, the customer's bad mood gets worse. "How many times do I have to tell you?" she snaps. "I thought I wanted $40 in cash but that doesn't matter but I have to put $50 in the checking account and the rest in savings." ■ Later, a bank official listens to the recorded interviews and rates each candidate's performance. Applicants score points for maintaining a friendly tone of voice, apologizing, promising to solve the customer's problem, and suggesting other Great Western services that the customer might find helpful. Points are deducted if the candidate sounds annoyed, asks for clarification too many times, or deposits the wrong amounts of money. ■ Such a system is programmed to detect any hesitation in answering a query, since this could indicate dishonesty. It prompts a human interviewer to delve deeper if it detects a longer-than-average delay in answering a question such as "Have you ever been fired from a job for stealing?" In fact, managers believe that applicants may be more likely to admit past wrongdoing to a computer than to a human interviewer, perhaps because computers seem less judgmental. ■ Can a computer do a better job of screening applicants than a human interviewer? Some people believe that software, no matter how good, simply cannot capture the nuances of human potential. Even Bonnie Dunn, who earned excellent scores in her Great Western interview, has her doubts; computers, she comments, cannot "see how you actually are and get what other qualities you have." ■ Still, many managers claim that computerized interviews are a good way to eliminate unqualified applicants and reduce employee turnover. Frederick Gray, manager of Great Western's Northridge, California branch bank, says that before buying the system, he had to interview at least 12 applicants a month for teller positions. "Four in 10 would be an absolute, total waste of time," he recalls. The computer system now weeds out many of the less-promising candidates, creating a better-qualified applicant pool. Those hired through the system are 26 percent less likely to quit or be fired in their first 90 days on the job. ■ Managers at other companies that use computerized systems also praise the results. Pic 'n Pay, which screens applicants with an electronic, over-the-phone interview program called HR Easy, has seen its annual turnover rate drop from 200 percent to 100 percent, and its annual rate of employee theft fall by 39 percent. Agent turnover at American General Life & Accident dropped from 68 percent to 40 percent after the company instituted its computer-assisted interview program. ■ Richard Garner, Pic 'n Pay's senior vice president of human resources, notes yet another advantage of computerized job interviews: they promote a more culturally diverse work force. Since adopting HR Easy, he finds that the shoe chain's rate of minority hiring has actually risen by 7.9 percent. "Store managers sometimes screen out good people based on preconceived notions or prejudices," says Garner. "But the computer has no prejudices."[1]

IMPORTANCE OF YOUR CAREER DECISION

Selecting a career may be the most important decision you will ever make. This appendix will begin by discussing the best way to approach career decisions and how to prepare for your first **entry-level job,** that is, your first permanent employment after leaving school. It will then look at a range of business careers by profiling five people who are performing very different kinds of jobs. Following each profile, a career section discusses employment opportunities in fields that are related to each major part of the text. In many cases, Bureau of Labor Statistics employment projections to 2000 are also included. You can use these sections as starting points in evaluating your career plans.

entry-level job
First permanent employment after leaving school.

To make those plans, you need to become aware of employment projections and trends. According to the Bureau of Labor Statistics, over the next decade the number of new jobs in every major occupational category will grow. During the same period, the number of American workers ages 25 to 34 will fall by 2.9 million men and almost 1.0 million women. These trends translate into exciting opportunities for those entering the work force. As Alan Reynolds, director of economic research at the Hudson Institute, comments, "Young Americans will be in a strong position to enjoy rapid increases in real incomes over the next 2 decades."[2]

Education will improve your prospects of finding and keeping the right job. Figure A.1 compares the median earnings of three groups of American adults: those who have completed high school, those with bachelor's degrees, and those who hold master's degrees. As you can see, with more education, you are likely to earn more. This trend holds true throughout a person's working life. In 1979, only 47 percent of the nation's best-paid workers (those in the top 10 percent income bracket) had college degrees; today 64 percent of them do.[3]

In addition to taking classes, try to gain related experience, either through a job or participation in campus organizations. Cooperative education programs, internships, or work-study programs can also give you hands-on experience while you pursue your education.

FIGURE A.1 MEDIAN EARNINGS BY AGE AND EDUCATION

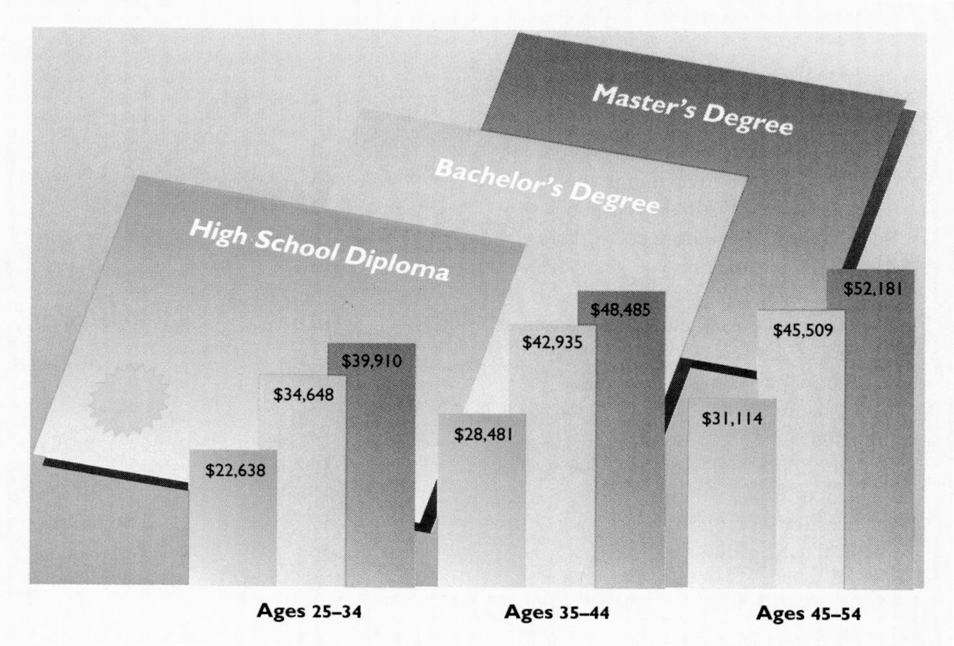

SELF-ASSESSMENT FOR CAREER DEVELOPMENT

You are going to spend a lot of time during your life working, so why not find a job that you enjoy? In order to choose the line of work that suits you best, you must first understand yourself. Self-assessment can be difficult, because it involves answering some tough questions. Remember, however, it does pay off by helping you find a career that will be enjoyable and rewarding.

Not surprisingly, different people have different work-related values. Figure A.2 lists the results of one study that asked U.S. employees to rank the aspects of a job that were most important to them. Most respondents ranked as most important the chance to do something that made them feel good about themselves; other valued job characteristics included the chance to accomplish something worthwhile and the opportunity to learn. These workers ranked the physical environment of a job and its promotional opportunities among the least important aspects.[4]

Take a moment to rank the job factors listed in Figure A.2 as they affect your own job satisfaction. Which are most and least important to you? Be honest with yourself and rank these aspects according to how you really feel, as opposed to how other people might rank them. You can use this self-assessment exercise as a starting point for exploring careers that best meet the needs you identify as important.

A lot of resources offer help in choosing and planning your career. They include school libraries, career guidance and placement offices, counseling centers, and online job search services. You may also wish to talk with graduates from your school who are working in fields that interest you.

informational interview
Session with a company representative designed to get information about a job or occupation.

As another option, you might arrange an **informational interview,** a session with a company representative designed to gather more information about a company or an occupation, rather than to apply for a job. If you are interested in a particular firm, for

FIGURE A.2 MOST IMPORTANT ASPECTS OF A JOB

Aspect of Job	Ranked Importance	Ranked Satisfaction
Chances to do something that makes you feel good about yourself	1	8
Chances to accomplish something worthwhile	2	6
Chances to learn new things	3	10
Opportunity to develop your skills and abilities	4	12
Amount of freedom you have on your job	5	2
Chances you have to do things you do best	6	11
Resources you have to do your job	7	9
Respect you receive from co-workers	8	3
Amount of information you get about your job performance	9	17
Your chances for taking part in making decisions	10	14
Amount of job security you have	11	5
Amount of pay you get	12	16
Way you are treated by co-workers	13	4
Friendliness of co-workers	14	1
Amount of praise you get for a job well done	15	15
Amount of fringe benefits you get	16	7
Chances for promotion	17	18
Physical surroundings of your job	18	13

Note: Data comes from a systematic random sample drawn from 23,008 questionnaires that readers returned.

example, perhaps you could arrange an informational interview with someone who works there to find out what it is really like. If you are curious about a profession, but are not sure it is for you, arrange an informational interview with someone who does that job. Find out what it really involves.

JOB SEARCH GUIDELINES

Once you have chosen a career that seems right for you, get your job search under way. Many others want good, entry-level positions, and you must expect competition. The best first step is to locate available positions that interest you, then be resourceful! Your success depends on gathering as much information as possible. Register at your school's placement office. Establish a placement or credentials file, including letters of recommendation and supporting personal information. Most placement offices send out periodic lists of new job vacancies, so be sure to get your name and address on the mailing list. Become familiar with the process by which your placement office allocates limited interview slots with attractive employers.

PREPARING JOB PLACEMENT MATERIALS

Most placement or credentials files include the following information: (1) letters of recommendation from people who know you—instructors, employers, and others; (2) transcripts of academic work to date; (3) a personal data form to report factual information; and (4) a statement of career goals. The placement office will provide special forms to help you to develop your placement file. Complete these forms neatly and accurately, since employers are extremely interested in your ability to communicate in writing. Keep a copy of the final file for later use in preparing similar information for other employment sources. Check back with the placement office to make sure your file is in order.

Letters of reference are very important. Secure recommendations selectively, and try to include a business instructor in your list of references. Always ask people personally if they will write a letter of recommendation for you. Be prepared to give them brief outlines of your academic preparation along with information concerning your job preferences and career objectives. This will help them to prepare letters and may enable them to respond quickly. Remember, however, that these people are usually busy. Allow them enough time to prepare their reference letters, then follow up on missing ones.

FINDING EMPLOYMENT SOURCES

The next step—identifying specific job openings—involves seeking out additional sources of information on available jobs, such as educational placement offices, private and public employment agencies, and computer services.

Educational Placement Offices Your school placement office is a good place to begin this search, as well. If you have completed formal academic coursework with more than one school, check with placement offices at each school about setting up a placement file. Some colleges have reciprocity agreements that permit students who have completed course work at several schools to establish files with each school's placement office.

Private Employment Agencies Other useful sources to consider are private employment agencies. These firms often specialize in certain types of jobs, performing several services for both employers and job candidates that are not available elsewhere. For example, some private agencies interview, test, and screen job applicants.

A private employment agency usually charges the prospective employer a fee for finding a suitable employee. In some cases, the job seeker is expected to pay a fee. Be sure that you understand the terms of any agreement you sign with a private employment agency.

State Employment Offices For still another source of job leads, check the employment offices of your state government. However, in many states, these public agencies process unemployment compensation along with other related work. Because of the mix of duties, some people view state employment agencies as providing services for semiskilled or unskilled workers. These agencies do list jobs in many professional categories, though.

Computer Services Computer employment services include electronic bulletin boards, job banks, and database services that distribute applicants' resumes on disk to potential employers. Figure A.3 lists phone numbers and prices for several major computer services. Before signing up for a service, find out how many companies subscribe to it; it may be a good idea to use more than one.[5]

Other Sources A variety of other sources can help you to identify job openings. Newspaper employment advertisements, especially Sunday editions of metropolitan newspapers, often prove to be rich sources of job leads. Trade journals or magazines may report this information. College instructors and administrators, community organizations such as the local chamber of commerce, and family and friends can often give direction.

FIGURE A.3

COMPUTER SERVICES THAT CAN HELP WITH YOUR JOB SEARCH

Prodigy
(800) 776–3449.
$14.95 monthly plus $3.60 an hour after first two hours of bulletin-board use.
Speed: up to 9,600 bits.[a]

CompuServ
(800) 848–8199.
$8.95 monthly plus charge for forum use: $4.80 an hour for up to 2,400 bits, $9.60 an hour for 9,600 or 14,400 bits.

America Online
(800) 827–6364.
$9.95 monthly plus $3.50 an hour after first five hours.
Speed: up to 9,600 bits.

Contractors Exchange
(415) 334–0733 voice; (415) 334–7393 modem.
Speed: up to 2,400 bits. Free.

FedWorld
(703) 487–4608 voice; (703) 321-8020 modem.
Speed: up to 9,600 bits. Free.

Internet Through many companies and local universities free or through "gateway" services like Delphi (800/695–4005). One Delphi package costs $10 a month plus $3 a month to access the Internet and $4 an hour after the first four hours. America Online and CompuServe also provide access to the Internet.

Online Career Center
Through Internet.

Help Wanted–USA
Through Internet and America Online.

Online Opportunities (215) 873–2168 voice; (215) 873–7170 modem.
Speed: up to 14,400 bits. Free.
Two months of Help Wanted–USA, $20.

New York Times FasTrak (800) 340–5627.

University ProNet (800) 726–0280.

Career Database (508) 487–2238.

Another approach is to identify all the organizations where you think you might like to work. Mail a letter of inquiry and your résumé to those companies. If possible, direct your mailings to a specific person who has the authority to hire new employees. The letter should ask briefly about employment opportunities in a particular line of work. It should also ask for a personal interview.

WRITING A RÉSUMÉ

Regardless of how you identify job openings, you must learn how to develop and use a **résumé,** a written summary of your personal, educational, and professional achievements. The résumé is a very personal document covering your educational background, work experience, career preferences, major interests, and other personal information. It should also include such basic information as your address and telephone number.

résumé
Written summary of personal, educational, and professional achievements.

The primary purpose of a résumé is to highlight your qualifications for a job, usually on a single page. An attractive layout facilitates the employer's review of your qualifications. Figures A.4, A.5, and A.6 illustrate traditional résumés in chronological, functional, and results-oriented formats.

A job seeker can prepare a résumé in several ways. Some use narrative sentences to explain job duties and career goals; others present information in outline form. A résumé to accompany a placement office credentials file can be quite short. Remember, too, to design it around your own needs and objectives.

If you use a computer service in your job search, you may want to create a résumé that can be scanned and sent electronically to prospective employers. Figure A.7 summarizes tips for creating an effective electronic résumé.

Regardless of which format you choose, write and proofread your résumé carefully. Computerized spell-checking software has not saved many job applicants from submitting résumés filled with spelling errors and misused words. Just ask Robert Half, founder of employment services Robert Half International and Accountemps, who has compiled a list of résumé errors that he calls "Resumania." Among Half's favorite bloopers:

- An applicant listed as one of his strengths an "ability to meet deadlines while maintaining composer."
- Another finished his cover letter with the statement, "Thank you for your consideration. Hope to hear from you shorty."
- A candidate for a secretarial position bragged, "I am a rabid typist."

While some job applicants try to make their résumés distinctive or humorous in order to get noticed, this strategy can backfire. Half recalls one candidate whose résumé was discarded because he claimed: "Extensive background in public accounting. I can also stand on my head!" In another common mistake, some applicants fill their résumés with fancy words just to impress recruiters; Half notes the surprise of an applicant who could not find a job with a résumé that said, "I perform my job with effortless efficiency, effectiveness, efficacy, and expertise."[6]

STUDYING EMPLOYMENT OPPORTUNITIES

You should carefully study the various employment opportunities you have identified. Obviously, you will like some more than others, but you should consider a variety of factors when assessing each job possibility: (1) the actual job responsibilities, (2) industry characteristics, (3) the nature of the company, (4) the geographic location, (5) salary and advancement opportunities, and (6) the job's contribution to your long-run career objectives.

Too many graduates consider only the most striking features of a job, perhaps the location or the salary. However, a comprehensive review of job openings should provide

FIGURE A.4 CHRONOLOGICAL RÉSUMÉ

Beatrice Conner
4256 Pinebluff Lane
Cleveland, Ohio 44120
216–555–3296

OBJECTIVE

Challenging office management position in a results-oriented company where my organizing people skills can be applied; leading to an operations management position.

WORK EXPERIENCE

1991–Present ADM Distribution Enterprises, Cleveland, Ohio

Office Manager of leading regional soft-drink bottler. Coordinating all bookkeeping, correspondence, scheduling of 12-truck fleet to serve 300 customers, promotional mailings and personnel records, including payroll. Installing computerized systems.

1989–1991 Merriweather, Hicks & Bradshaw Attorneys, Columbus, Ohio

Office Supervisor and Executive Secretary for Douglas H. Bradshaw, Managing Partner. Supervising four clerical workers and two paraprofessionals, automating legal research and correspondence functions, improving filing and dictation systems, and assisting in coordinating outside services and relations with other firms and agencies. Promoted three times in 1 year from Secretary to Office Supervisor.

1985–1989 Conner & Sons Custom Coverings, Cleveland, Ohio

Secretary in father's upholstery and awning company. Performing all office functions over the years, running the office when the manager was on vacation.

EDUCATION

Mill Valley High School, Honors, Certificate 1988

McBundy Community College, Office Management, Automated Office Systems, Associate Degree 1990

Telecom Systems, Word Processing Seminar Series, Certificate 1991

PERSONAL

Member of various professional associations; avid reader; enjoy sports such as camping, cycling, scuba diving, skiing; enjoy volunteering in community projects.

a balanced perspective of the overall employment opportunity, including both long-run and short-run factors.

JOB INTERVIEWS

The first objective of your job search is to obtain an appointment for an interview with a prospective employer. Whether you initially interview with a computer, as in the opening story to this appendix, or with a human being, it is important to plan and prepare. You want to enter the interview equipped with a good understanding of the company, its industry, and its competitors. Prepare yourself by researching the following essential information about the company:

FIGURE A.5 FUNCTIONAL RÉSUMÉ

Timothy M. Richards
Two Seaside Drive
Los Angeles, CA 90026
213–555–7092

OBJECTIVE
Joining a cohesive team effort in county government that has a positive impact on the quality of life in constituent communities, particularly in terms of traffic management and control.

EXPERIENCE
Administration
Coordinating multilevel projects within fixed time frames and budget restrictions; maintaining smooth and frequent communications under adverse conditions of competing political party interference; sustaining loyalty throughout.

Planning
Preparing strategic, long-range, and intermediate-range plans using latest computer models; gaining participation and commitment of all key groups in planning processes; establishing reporting points and methods for all milestones in statewide political campaign; integrating planning for financial, strategic actions, capital items, and breaking issues on an ongoing basis.

Problem Solving
Writing position papers for contingencies and for direct appeal in state representative campaign; facilitating 50 discussion groups to reach consensus; contributing to strategy sessions on three campaigns; four months of coordinating community traffic-pattern hearings.

Leadership
Acting as a spokesperson with print and broadcast media and grassroots elements; establishing focus on common issues bringing differing factions together; setting standards and models for operating in various environments.

Traffic Management
Establishing computer-based modeling capability for 10,000 residents in a community traffic control project; assisting in implementing a three-tiered measuring system for tracking in-bound traffic volume in a high-risk neighborhood; submitting three proposals, now under consideration, for traffic reform in targeted communities.

WORK HISTORY	Valley Systems Research Co.
1992–Present	Whittier Community Traffic Study Project
1992	Federal Traffic Studies Grant
1991–1992	Part-time staff of four political campaigns
1986–1991	U. S. Navy Lieutenant
1982–1986	

EDUCATION	UCLA mid-program, M.S. Communications
Currently enrolled	University of Oregon, B.S. Political Science
1990	Loma Linda Junior College, A.S. Journalism
1986	

PERSONAL
Held various leadership positions in school and in community action groups. Special recognition for 5 years' work on city and college task forces. U.S. Navy Reservist.

1. How was the company founded?
2. What is its current position in the industry?
3. What is its financial status?
4. In which markets does it compete?
5. How is the firm organized?
6. Who are its competitors?
7. How many people does it employ?
8. Where are its plants and offices located?

This information is useful in several ways. First, it helps to give you a feeling of confidence during the interview. Second, it can keep you from making an unwise employ-

FIGURE A.6 RESULTS-ORIENTED RÉSUMÉ

T. L. Chambers
3609 N.W. 57th Street
St. Louis, MO 63166
314–555–2394

OBJECTIVE

To apply my expertise as a construction foreman to a management role in an organization seeking improvements in overall production, long-term employee relationships, and the ability to attract top talent from the construction field.

EXPERIENCE

DAL Construction Company, St. Louis, Missouri, 1991–Present
Established automated, on-site recordkeeping system improving communications and morale between field and office, saving 400 work hours per year, and reducing the number of accounting errors by 20 percent. As foreman, developed a crew selected as "first choice crew" by most workers wanting transfers. Completed five housing projects ahead of deadline and under budget.

St. Louis County Housing Authority, St. Louis, Missouri, 1989–1990, Summers
Created friendly, productive atmosphere among workers enabling first on-time job completion in 4 years and one-half of usual materials waste. Initiated pilot materials delivery program with potential savings of 3.5 percent of yearly maintenance budget.

Jackson County Housing Authority, Kansas City, Missouri, 1988
Produced information pamphlet increasing applications for county housing by 22 percent. Introduced labor-management discussion techniques saving jobs and over $21,000 in lost time.

Carnegie Brothers Construction Company, West Palm Beach, Florida, 1986–1987
Introduced expediting methods saving 5 percent of overhead cost on all jobs and attracting a new $1.6 million client. Cut new-worker orientation time in half and on-site accidents by one-fourth through training and modeling desired behavior.

Payton, Durnbell & Associates Architects, Kansas City, Kansas, 1985
Developed and monitored productivity improvements saving 60 percent on information transfer costs for firm's 12 largest jobs.

EDUCATION

1990–1991	Washington University, B.S. English
1988–1989	Central Missouri State University, English

PERSONAL
Highly self-motivated manager. Single and willing to relocate. Avid reader and writer.

ment decision. Third, it can impress an interviewer, who may well try to determine how much an applicant knows about the company as a way of evaluating that person's interest level. A candidate who fails to make the effort to obtain such information often risks elimination from further consideration.

Where do you get this pre-interview information? First, your school placement office or employment agency should have information on prospective employers. Business instructors at your school may also provide tips. Your school or community library should have various references to help you investigate a firm, or you can write directly to a company. Many firms publish career brochures as well as annual reports. Finally, ask friends and relatives for input. They or someone they know may have had experience with the company.

FIGURE A.7 TIPS FOR WRITING AN EFFECTIVE ELECTRONIC RÉSUMÉ

1. Scan from an original résumé printed on a letter-quality printer rather than from a photocopy.
2. Use standard-sized paper ($8^1/_2$ x 11 inches) and don't fold the résumé, since words printed in a crease will not scan well.
3. Print on white or beige paper rather than darker colors to maximize the contrast between letters and background.
4. Use 12-point type or larger; smaller print may not scan correctly.
5. Avoid unusual typefaces, underlining, and decorative graphics.
6. Avoid double columns since scanners read from left to right.
7. Include jargon appropriate to your profession since a computer search of résumés often targets key terms.

Interviewers report two main reasons for poor performance in job interviews. Many job seekers fail due to ineffective communication, either because of inadequate preparation for their interviews or because they lack confidence. Remember that the interviewer will first determine whether you can communicate effectively. You should be specific in answering and asking questions, and you should clearly and positively express your concerns. The questions that interviewers ask most often include the following:

Why do you want this job?
Where do you see yourself 10 years from now?
What are your strengths?
What are your weaknesses?
Why should I hire you?

It is important to know who is doing the interviewing and who will make the final hiring decision. Most people who conduct initial job interviews work in their firms' human resources divisions. These staff workers can make recommendations to line managers about which individuals to employ. Line managers get involved in interviewing later in the hiring process. Some decisions come from human resources personnel together with the immediate supervisor of the prospective employee. More often, immediate supervisors make the decisions alone. Rarely does the human resources department have sole hiring authority.

In a typical format, the interviewer talks little during the interview. This type of **open-ended interview** forces you to talk about yourself and your goals. If you appear unorganized, the interviewer may eliminate you on that basis alone. When faced with this type of situation, be sure to express your thoughts clearly and keep the conversation on target. Talk for about 10 minutes, then ask some specific questions of the interviewer. (Come prepared with questions to ask!) Listen carefully to the responses. Remember that if you prepare for a job interview, it will become a mutual exchange of information.

open-ended interview *Interview designed to force an applicant to talk about personal qualifications and goals.*

A successful first interview will probably lead to an invitation to come back for another interview. Sometimes this will include a request to take a battery of tests. Most students do very well on these tests because they have had plenty of practice in college!

EMPLOYMENT DECISION

By this time, the employer knows a lot about you from your placement file, résumé, and first interview. You should also know a lot about the company. The primary purpose of further interviews is to determine whether you can work effectively within the organization.

If you create a positive impression during your second or later interviews, you may be offered a job. Again, your decision to accept the offer should depend on how well the career opportunity matches your career objectives. Make the best entry-level job decision you can, and learn from it. Learn your job responsibilities as quickly and thoroughly as possible, then start looking for other ways to improve your performance and that of your employer.

NONTRADITIONAL STUDENTS

At one time, colleges and universities seemed to serve a market of mostly 18 to 22 year olds. This was the primary age group that sought to break into the job market. Times have certainly changed.

More people are returning to school to complete degrees, and more people who already have college degrees are returning for more education. These students are often referred to as **nontraditional students.** Although the term covers any student who does not fit into the 18- to 22-year-old age group (the "traditional" clients of higher education), it is actually inaccurate, since older students have become the norm on many campuses. In any case, nontraditional students have two other characteristics: they work, either full-time or part-time, and college is often only one of their daily responsibilities. Many are married, and many, regardless of marital status, have children.

nontraditional student
Any student who does not fall into the 18- to 22-year-old age group.

Most nontraditional students come from one of the following groups:

1. **Displaced homemakers** Full-time homemakers often return to school or join the work force because of divorce or widowhood or for economic reasons.
2. *Military service veterans* Another major segment of nontraditional students enter school after discharge from the military. Many of them lack practical job skills.
3. **Technologically displaced workers** Someone who lost a job to automation or industry cutbacks may return to school. Recently, middle-level and upper-level managers have joined the ranks of displaced workers as their companies have cut costs by eliminating their jobs.[7]
4. *Older, full-time employees* These workers may enter school to seek additional education to enhance career prospects or for personal satisfaction.

displaced homemaker
Homemaker who returns to school or takes a job because of divorce or widowhood or for economic reasons.

technologically displaced worker
Worker who loses a job due to automation or industrial cutbacks.

CHALLENGES FACED BY NONTRADITIONAL STUDENTS

Nontraditional students often face different challenges than younger students. One is scheduling; often older students must juggle the responsibilities of work, school, and family. They may have to study at odd times: during meals, while commuting, or after putting the kids to bed. For another challenge, nontraditional students may be trying to change careers, so they must both learn skills in a different field and work toward breaking into that field with a new job.

Take heart, though. Nontraditional students also have a very important advantage: experience. Even experience in an unrelated field is a plus. Older students know how businesses operate. Often they have developed useful skills in human relations, management, budgeting, and communications. Also, through observing other people's mistakes and living through their own, they have often learned what not to do.

Like other students, nontraditional students need to assess their accomplishments, skills, likes, and dislikes. The same exercises and resources suggested earlier can help both traditional and older students to assess their strengths and determine their career goals.

YOUR CAREER: A LONG-RANGE VIEW

Throughout your career, it is important to stay flexible and continue learning. Challenging new skills will be required of managers and other businesspeople during the next decade. Remain open to unexpected changes and opportunities that can help you to learn and develop new skills. "Don't get into this 1950s 'I am going to stay here forever' mindset," advises executive recruiter Kenneth Kelley. "In the next 20 or 30 years, you may have three different positions." Develop work skills that will transfer easily from one job to the next, such as computer literacy and good communication skills.

Jonathan Webb, for example, earned a bachelor's degree in banking and finance at Morehouse University and obtained an entry-level position as a securities analyst. He wanted to move into a sales position, however, so he took classes in investment banking and began selling securities to institutional investors such as banks and insurance companies. Today Webb is a vice president of regional institutional sales at Shearson Lehman's Chicago division. He appreciates the importance of learning a wide variety of work skills. "At Lehman Bros., if you work as a lending officer, you have to prepare a lot of numbers and sell it internally first so your client outside is not misled," he explains. "You need strong communication and sales skills."[8]

The most important skill to learn may be just that: the ability to learn. James Challenger, an outplacement consultant in Chicago, notes that employers want workers who can collect and analyze both verbal and numerical information. His advice to students is, "Study what you like, and learn to think." Lew Shumaker, manager of college relations for DuPont, emphasizes the importance of flexibility and the talent to function well in a culturally diverse workplace. "Over the past few years 60 percent of our new hires have been women or members of minority groups," says Shumaker. "So we are looking for graduates who have shown that they value those who are different from themselves."[9]

FINAL NOTE—THE AUTHORS' VIEW

We believe that choosing a career is one of the most important decisions you will ever make. Choosing wisely and staying open to new opportunities can help to make it a happy decision, too. Just imagine the satisfaction of getting paid to do something you enjoy!

Do not procrastinate or trust others to make this decision for you. Follow the steps outlined here and in other sources, and make your own decision. Your instructors, parents, friends, and advisors will offer to help in a multitude of ways, but in the end, it is your own decision.

We hope that this textbook has presented a panorama of career options for you. Whatever you decide, be sure it is right for you. As the old saying goes, "You pass this way only once." Enjoy!

KEY TERMS

entry-level job 597
informational interview 598
résumé 601
open-ended interview 605
nontraditional student 606
displaced homemaker 606
technologically displaced worker 606

ASSIGNMENTS

1. Construct your own résumé following the procedures outlined in this appendix. Ask your instructors, friends, relatives, and associates to criticize it. What did you learn from this exercise?

2. Conduct an informational interview with someone in your community who is working in a profession that interests you. (Remember that this person is busy. Call first to request an appointment. The interview should take no more than 15 to 20 minutes; come prepared with questions to ask.) Discuss with the class what you learned from the interview.

3. Discuss how you would answer each of the questions that interviewers most often ask.

4. Choose a partner and take turns interviewing each other for a job in front of the class. (Use the interview questions mentioned in this chapter.) After the interview, ask the class to give you feedback on how you looked and acted during your interview. Would they advise you to do or say anything differently?

5. Discuss what you can do to prepare yourself to become a successful businessperson who possesses the skills necessary to succeed in the next decade.

DISCOVERING YOUR BUSINESS CAREER

"Discovering Your Business Career" takes you through an extensive questionnaire in which you will rate a variety of job-related activities in the field of business from "very appealing" to "very unappealing." Your responses will then be matched to some of the most common business career paths graduating students pursue in management, marketing, information systems, accounting, finance, risk management, and insurance.

After completing the questionnaire, you may select one or more business career opportunities from a menu and view or print a 10–15 page profile which includes some preliminary insights into your degree of interest in that career area. Profiles are practical in that they not only present a detailed picture of actual job responsibilities, but also the academic preparation and skills required to be successful. You are also advised on current compensation levels and associations, directories, books and other relevant information about this career path. Even better, profiles were developed from extensive interviews with top professionals and executives from prominent companies, associations, and consulting firms.

In the same section where you access the current career profile, you'll also be able to play a video on your computer screen which shows examples of actual day-to-day activities performed or interviews with people who are involved in this career.

THIS EXERCISE WILL HELP YOU TO

- Build a clearer picture of some of the major career options in the field of business.
- Discover business careers which match your interests and talents.
- Apply your career insights in choosing a major.

RISK MANAGEMENT

APPENDIX B

AND INSURANCE

Risk is a daily fact of life for both individuals and businesses. Injury or death resulting from the acts of others is a risk that reaches even to the Office of the President of the United States. During 1994, the White House was besieged in separate incidents by a suicidal airplane pilot and by a gunman on foot. The following year, a terrorist's bomb took the lives of 200 men, women, and children in an Oklahoma City Federal building. Risk of property losses, personal injury, or death often results from natural catastrophes. The 1994 Los Angeles-area earthquakes caused billions of dollars in property losses.[1] That same year, floods, drought, and high winds devastated the North Korean rice and corn crops.[2]

Risk affects people's daily lives, too. Although motor vehicle accidents resulting in death declined from 54,633 in 1970 to 40,300 last year, they still represent the fourth leading cause of death in the United States. In a typical year, over 36,000 deaths involving firearms will occur; of these, almost 19,000 are suicides and just over 16,000 are homicides. During the past 4 years, the annual number of murders committed using a firearm in the United States has risen sharply from 10,895 to 15,377.[3]

Companies also face various forms of risk each day. Employees may be injured in job-related accidents. A New Mexico jury awarded 81-year-old Stella Liebeck $2.9 million for third-degree burns she suffered after spilling a cup of McDonald's coffee in her lap. (The trial judge later reduced the amount of the award to less than $1 million.)[4] Intel Corp.'s decision to replace its flawed Pentium computer chip at no cost to any of the 3.3 million purchasers who request it could cost the firm as much as $650 million.[5] Other businesses face risks to their employees in the form of job-related accidents. Changing consumer tastes can turn profits into losses. Employee dishonesty can rob a firm of badly needed revenue.

To fulfill their responsibilities of achieving organizational objectives, managers must understand the types of risks they face and develop methods for dealing with them. One important method of dealing with risk is to shift it to specialized firms called *insurance companies*. This appendix discusses the concept of insurance in an individual firm. It begins by defining the meaning of *risk*.

CONCEPT OF RISK

risk
Uncertainty about loss or injury.

speculative risk
Type of risk involving the chance of either profit or loss.

pure risk
Type of risk involving only the chance of loss.

Risk is uncertainty about loss or injury. The business firm's list of risk-filled decisions is long. A factory or warehouse faces the risk of fire, burglary, water damage, and physical deterioration. Accidents, judgments due to lawsuits, and nonpayment of bills by customers are other risks. Analysts divide risk into two major types: speculative risk and pure risk.

Speculative risk gives the firm or individual the chance of either a profit or a loss. Purchasing shares of stock on the basis of the latest hot tip can result in profits or losses. Expanding operations into a new market may result in higher profits or the loss of invested funds.

Pure risk, on the other hand, involves only the chance of loss. Automobile drivers, for example, always face the risk of accidents. Should they occur, the drivers (and others) may suffer financial and physical loss. If they do not occur, however, no one gains anything. Insurance often helps people to protect against financial loss resulting from pure risk.

RISK MANAGEMENT

Because risk is an unavoidable part of business, managers must find ways of dealing with it. Recognizing it is an important first step. After that, the manager has four methods available for dealing with risk: avoiding it, reducing its frequency and/or severity, self-insuring against it, or shifting the risk to insurance companies.

Risks prowl ceaselessly around every business. Usually, they hunt in packs. Dealing with them piecemeal is ineffective. More often than not, they're linked.
Nowhere is that linkage more intricate than in the airline business. Fuel prices, interest rates, currency swings, load factors, even political pitfalls – each risk has to be examined in light of the others.
Risks hardly ever travel alone.
To bring an element of stability to an industry that changes minute by minute, Bankers Trust has found a way of analyzing the airline business and attaching a monetary value to many of the operational risks it faces. A risk management plan that can turn volatility into profitability.
With our hands at the reins, you'll see which risk will hurt you and which you'll profit by. So risk will do your bidding, not take you unawares.
Bankers Trust
LEAD FROM STRENGTH.

In many instances, firms will use the services of specialized organizations to identify risks and develop plans intended to minimize losses from them. Bankers Trust provides such services to firms in the airline industry as well as other businesses competing in today's global markets.

Source: Bankers Trust; used by permission.

The manager must consider many factors when evaluating the risk of conducting business at home and abroad. These include a nation's economic stability, social and cultural factors (such as language), available technologies, distribution systems, and government regulations. Firms find lower risk in countries with stable economic, social/cultural, technological, and political/legal environments.

AVOIDING RISK

Some firms are willing to take high risks for potentially high rewards, while others are unwilling to risk the potential losses involved in developing new and untried products. Although avoiding risk may ensure profitability, it stifles innovation. As a result, risk-averse companies are rarely leaders in their industries.

REDUCING RISK

Managers can reduce or even eliminate many types of risk by removing hazards or taking preventive measures. Many companies develop safety programs to educate employees about potential hazards and the proper methods of performing certain dangerous tasks. Guard dogs and security guards offer protection from risk for many other firms. Preventive maintenance is yet another way to reduce risk.

All of these actions can reduce the risk involved in business operations, but they cannot eliminate risk entirely. Most major business insurers assist their clients in avoiding or minimizing risk by offering the services of loss-prevention experts to conduct thorough reviews of operations. These safety and health professionals evaluate customers' work environments and recommend procedures and equipment to help firms minimize worker injuries and property losses.

SELF-INSURING AGAINST RISK

Instead of purchasing insurance against certain kinds of pure risk, some multiplant, geographically scattered firms accumulate funds to cover possible losses. Such a

self-insurance fund
Account set up to cover losses due to pure risks.

self-insurance fund is a special fund created by setting aside cash reserves periodically that the firm can draw upon in the event of a financial loss resulting from a pure risk. The firm invests regular payments to the fund in interest-bearing securities, and it charges losses to the fund. Such a fund typically accompanies a risk-reduction program aimed at minimizing losses.

Before the price of business insurance soared during the early years of this decade, self-insurance expenditures accounted for only 25 percent of the total insurance market. Today they amount to over 33 percent. Self-insurance is most useful in cases where a company faces similar risks and the risks are spread over a broad geographic area.

SHIFTING RISK TO AN INSURANCE COMPANY

insurance
Process by which an insurer, in exchange for a fee, agrees to reimburse a firm or individual for losses up to specified limits.

Although a firm can take steps to avoid or reduce risk, the most common method of dealing with it is to shift it to others in the form of **insurance**—the process by which a firm, for a fee, agrees to pay another firm or individual a sum of money stated in a written contract when a loss occurs. The insured party's fee to the insurance company for coverage against losses is called a *premium*. Thus, insurance substitutes a small, known loss—the insurance premium—for a larger, unknown loss that may or may not occur. In the case of life insurance, the loss—death—is a certainty; the main uncertainty is the date when it will occur.

As Figure B.1 points out, it is important for the insurer to understand the customer's business, risk exposure, and insurance needs. Many firms that engage in production and marketing activities in several countries choose to do business with insurance companies like Chubb that maintain global networks of offices and agents.

BASIC INSURANCE CONCEPTS

Insurance companies accumulate premiums to cover eventual losses. The returns from insurance company investments may allow them to reduce premiums, generate profits, or both. By investing accumulated funds, insurance companies represent a major source of long-term financing for other businesses.

FIGURE B.1

SHIFTING RISK TO AN INSURANCE COMPANY

An insurance company is a professional risk taker. For a fee, it accepts risks of loss or damage to businesses and individuals. Three basic principles underlie insurance: the concept of insurable interest, the concept of insurable risks, and the law of large numbers.

INSURABLE INTEREST

In order to purchase insurance, an applicant must demonstrate an **insurable interest** in the property or life of the insured. The policyholder must stand to suffer a loss, financial or otherwise, due to fire, accident, death, or lawsuit. For life insurance, a friend or relative may have an insurable interest despite facing no prospect of financial loss in the event of the insured's death.

insurable interest
Insurance concept that requires a policyholder to stand to suffer loss.

Because top managers are important assets to a firm, it can purchase key executive insurance on their lives. A businessperson cannot collect on insurance to cover damage to the property of competitors in which that person has no insurable interest, nor can an individual citizen purchase an insurance policy on the life of the president of the United States, since he or she lacks an insurable interest.

INSURABLE RISK

Insurable risk refers to the requirements that a risk must meet in order for the insurer to provide protection. Insurers impose five basic requirements on insurable risk:

insurable risk
Risk that meets certain requirements in order for the insurer to provide protection.

1. The likelihood of loss should be predictable.
2. The loss should be financially measurable.
3. The loss should be fortuitous or accidental.
4. The risk should be spread over a wide geographic area.
5. The insurance company has the right to set standards for accepting risks.

LAW OF LARGE NUMBERS

Insurance is based on the law of averages, or statistical probability. Insurance companies have studied the chances of occurrences of deaths, injuries, lawsuits, and all types of hazards. From their investigations, they have developed the **law of large numbers,** a probability calculation of the likelihood of the occurrence of perils, on which they base their premiums. They also use actuarial tables to predict the number of fires, automobile accidents, plane crashes, and deaths that will occur in a given year.

law of large numbers
Probability calculation of the likelihood of occurrence of perils on which insurers base their premiums.

An example can demonstrate how businesspeople can use the law of large numbers to calculate insurance premiums. Previously collected statistical data on a small city with 50,000 homes indicates that the city will experience an average of 500 fires a year, with damages totaling an average of $30,000 per occurrence. What is the minimum annual premium an insurance company would charge to insure a house against fire?

To simplify the calculations, assume that the premiums would not produce profits or cover any of the insurance company's operating expenses. In total, fires in the city would generate claims of $15 million (500 homes damaged × $30,000). If these losses were spread over all 50,000 homes, each homeowner would be charged an annual premium of $300 ($15 million divided by 50,000 homes). In reality, though, the insurance company would set the premium at a higher figure to cover its operating expenses and to earn a reasonable return.

An insurer uses a **mortality table** like the one in Table B.1 to predict the number of people in each age category who will die in a given year. The table data come from past experience with large numbers of male and female policyholders of different ages. After determining the policyholder's expected death rate, the insurer can calculate the premium for a life insurance policy to provide sufficient income to pay death benefits

mortality table
Table with data that predicts the number of persons in each age category who will die in a given year.

TABLE B.1 MORTALITY TABLES AND INSURANCE PREMIUMS

	Expectation of Life in Years					Expected Deaths per 1,000 Alive at Specified Age				
		White		African American			White		African American	
Age	Total	Male	Female	Male	Female	Total	Male	Female	Male	Female
At Birth	74.9	72.3	78.9	64.9	73.4	9.99	9.55	7.47	19.19	16.26
1	74.7	72.0	78.5	65.2	73.6	0.70	0.73	0.55	1.17	0.88
5	70.8	68.1	74.6	61.4	69.8	0.30	0.30	0.23	0.54	0.40
10	65.9	63.2	69.7	56.5	64.9	0.17	0.17	0.13	0.24	0.25
15	61.0	58.3	64.8	51.6	60.0	0.64	0.85	0.38	1.07	0.38
20	56.3	53.6	59.9	47.0	55.1	1.09	1.51	0.51	2.47	0.72
25	51.6	49.0	55.0	42.7	50.4	1.19	1.57	0.52	3.22	1.13
30	46.9	44.4	50.2	38.4	45.7	1.35	1.69	0.61	4.14	1.58
35	42.2	39.8	45.4	34.3	41.1	1.73	2.05	0.82	5.91	2.30
40	37.6	35.2	40.6	30.3	36.6	2.22	2.60	1.21	7.49	3.22
45	33.0	30.7	35.8	26.5	32.2	3.17	3.65	1.95	9.54	4.39
50	28.6	26.3	31.2	22.8	28.0	4.98	5.74	3.26	13.16	6.48
55	24.4	22.2	26.8	19.4	24.0	7.96	9.57	5.37	17.62	9.77
60	20.5	18.4	22.6	16.2	20.3	12.61	15.64	8.63	25.31	15.19
65	16.9	14.9	18.7	13.4	16.9	18.72	23.60	13.17	35.26	21.26

and to cover its own operating expenses. For example, a 30-year-old African-American male would usually pay higher insurance premiums than a 20-year-old African-American male because the number of deaths per thousand increases to 4.14 from 2.47 over the 10-year difference in ages. As the age of the insured increases, the length of expected life decreases and the life insurance premium rises. The same type of calculation sets the premium for an automobile or fire insurance policy. The law of large numbers is the basis of all insurance premium calculations.

MATCHING PREMIUMS TO DIFFERENT DEGREES OF RISK

Although insurance companies use the law of large numbers to design policies, they often divide individuals and industries into different risk categories and attempt to match premiums to risk levels.

An example with which you may be familiar is automobile insurance. Young men often pay higher premiums for automobile insurance than young women pay. While this may seem unfair, insurance statistics show a reason: male drivers are involved in 29 percent more fatal accidents than female drivers. Furthermore, young drivers of both sexes have more than their share of accidents. Drivers under age 21 account for just 7.1 percent of the nation's licensed drivers, but they have 15.0 percent of all fatal accidents. Drivers aged 20 to 24 hold one-tenth of all licenses, but are involved in one of every six accidents.

SOURCES OF INSURANCE

The term **insurance company** includes both private companies, such as Prudential, John Hancock, State Farm, and Travelers, and a number of public agencies that provide insurance coverage for business firms, not-for-profit organizations, and individuals.

PUBLIC INSURANCE COMPANIES

insurance company
Private company or public agency that provides insurance coverage for business firms, not-for-profit organizations, and individuals.

A *public insurance company* is a state or federal government agency established to provide specialized insurance protection for individuals and organizations. It provides protection in such areas as job loss (unemployment insurance), work-related injuries (workers' compensation), and pension plans (Social Security). Public insurance companies also sponsor specialized programs, such as those listed in Figure B.2, ranging from flood insurance to depositor protection at commercial banks.

Unemployment Insurance Every state has an *unemployment insurance* program that assists unemployed workers by providing financial benefits, job counseling, and placement services, typically for a period of 26 to 39 weeks. Compensation amounts vary depending on workers' previous incomes and the states in which they file claims. These insurance programs are funded by payroll taxes paid by employers.

Workers' Compensation Under state laws, employers must provide *workers' compensation insurance* to guarantee payment of wages and salaries, medical care costs, and such rehabilitation services as retraining, job placement, and vocational rehabilitation to employees who are injured on the job. Workers' compensation protects employees in all 50 states and Puerto Rico. Pittsburgh spends more than $20 million a year compensating municipal workers. Nationwide, costs are up 150 percent since 1980. In addition, workers' compensation provides benefits in the form of weekly payments or single, lump-sum payments to survivors of workers who die as a result of work-related injuries. Premiums are based on the company's payroll, the on-the-job hazards to which it exposes workers, and its safety record.[6]

Social Security The federal government is the largest insurer in the United States. Its Social Security program, officially titled *Old-Age, Survivors, Disability, and Health Insurance (OASDHI),* grew out of the Social Security Act of 1935. For over 200 million Americans, their nine-digit Social Security numbers, illustrated in Figure B.3, are almost as familiar as their telephone numbers. In 1965, *Medicare* was added to the OASDHI program to provide a form of health insurance for persons 65 years or older and certain other Social Security recipients. More than nine out of ten U.S. employees and their dependents are eligible for retirement benefits, life insurance, health insurance, and disability income insurance under this program.

FIGURE B.2

OTHER TYPES OF PUBLIC INSURANCE

- **Federal Deposit Insurance Corporation (FDIC)** and **National Credit Union Share Insurance Fund (NCUSIF)** provide insurance protection for deposits in commercial banks and credit unions.
- **Federal Housing Administration (FHA)** provides mortgage insurance to lenders as protection against possible default by home purchasers.
- **National Flood Insurance Association** protects against flooding and mud slides for properties located in flood-prone areas.
- **Federal crime insurance** is available for owners of property located in high-crime areas who might not be able to purchase such insurance from private insurance companies.
- **Federal Crop Insurance Corporation** insures farmers' crops.
- **Pension Benefit Guaranty Corporation** insures the assets of pension plans to prevent loss of retirement benefits for employees should an employer go out of business or declare bankruptcy.

FIGURE B.3

SOCIAL SECURITY: SOURCE OF PUBLIC INSURANCE AND RETIREMENT INCOME

PRIVATE INSURANCE COMPANIES

Much of the insurance in force in the United States and other countries is provided by private insurance companies. These companies are typically categorized by ownership as stock companies and mutual companies. Insurance companies, whether they operate as stock or mutual companies, share the objective of minimizing the premiums necessary to cover operating expenses and to pay for personal or property losses.

Stock Companies A *stock insurance company* operates to earn a profit. Stockholders do not have to be policyholders; they invest funds in the firm by purchasing its stock in order to receive dividends from earnings and/or to benefit from increases in stock prices. The company earns profits from two sources: (1) insurance premiums in excess of claims and operating costs, and (2) earnings from company investments in mortgages, stocks, bonds, and real estate.

Research reveals no clear indication that stock companies charge higher insurance premiums than mutual companies. Stock companies dominate the insurance industry, with the exception of life insurance, which is controlled by mutual insurance companies.

Mutual Companies A *mutual insurance company* is a type of insurance cooperative owned by its policyholders. The mutual company is chartered by the state and governed by a board of directors elected by the policyholders. Prudential Insurance Company of America, the nation's largest insurer, is a mutual company.

Unlike a stock company, a mutual company earns no profits for its owners. As a not-for-profit organization, it returns any surplus funds that remain after it covers operating expenses and claims and establishes necessary reserves to policyholders in the form of dividends or premium reductions.

TYPES OF INSURANCE

Although insurers offer hundreds of policies to individuals and businesses, they fall conveniently into three broad categories: (1) property and liability insurance, (2) health insurance, and (3) life insurance.

PROPERTY AND LIABILITY INSURANCE

As Figure B.4 shows, property and liability insurance defines a general category of insurance that provides protection against a number of perils. **Property losses** are financial losses resulting from interruption of business operations or physical damage to property as a result of fires, accidents, theft, or other destructive events. **Liability losses** are financial losses suffered by business firms or individuals held responsible for property damage or injuries suffered by others.

property loss
Financial loss resulting from interruption of business operations or physical damage to property as a result of a fire, accident, theft, or other destructive event.

liability loss
Financial loss suffered by a business firm or individual held responsible for property damage or injuries suffered by others.

HEALTH INSURANCE

Unfortunately, everyone faces the risk of getting sick or being injured in some way. To guard against this risk, most Americans have some form of **health insurance**—insurance that provides coverage for losses due to sickness or accidents. With soaring costs in health care, this type of insurance has become an important consideration of businesses and individuals in the late 1990s.[7]

health insurance
Insurance that covers losses due to sickness or accidents.

Most businesses and not-for-profit organizations offer health and accident insurance for their employees as part of benefit packages. These *group policies* resemble individual coverage, but are offered at lower premiums.

Private insurance companies, such as Cigna, Nationwide, and Provident Insurance, offer group health packages to employees. The not-for-profit Blue Cross/Blue Shield plans currently insure about 68 million people for another option. Figure B.5 illustrates the coverage included in such group plans.

A **health maintenance organization (HMO)** is a prepaid medical expense plan that provides a comprehensive set of health services and benefits to policyholders, who pay

health maintenance organization (HMO)
Prepaid medical expense plan that provides a comprehensive set of health services and benefits to policyholders, who pay monthly fees.

FIGURE B.4 SOLVING THE PROPERTY AND LIABILITY INSURANCE PUZZLE

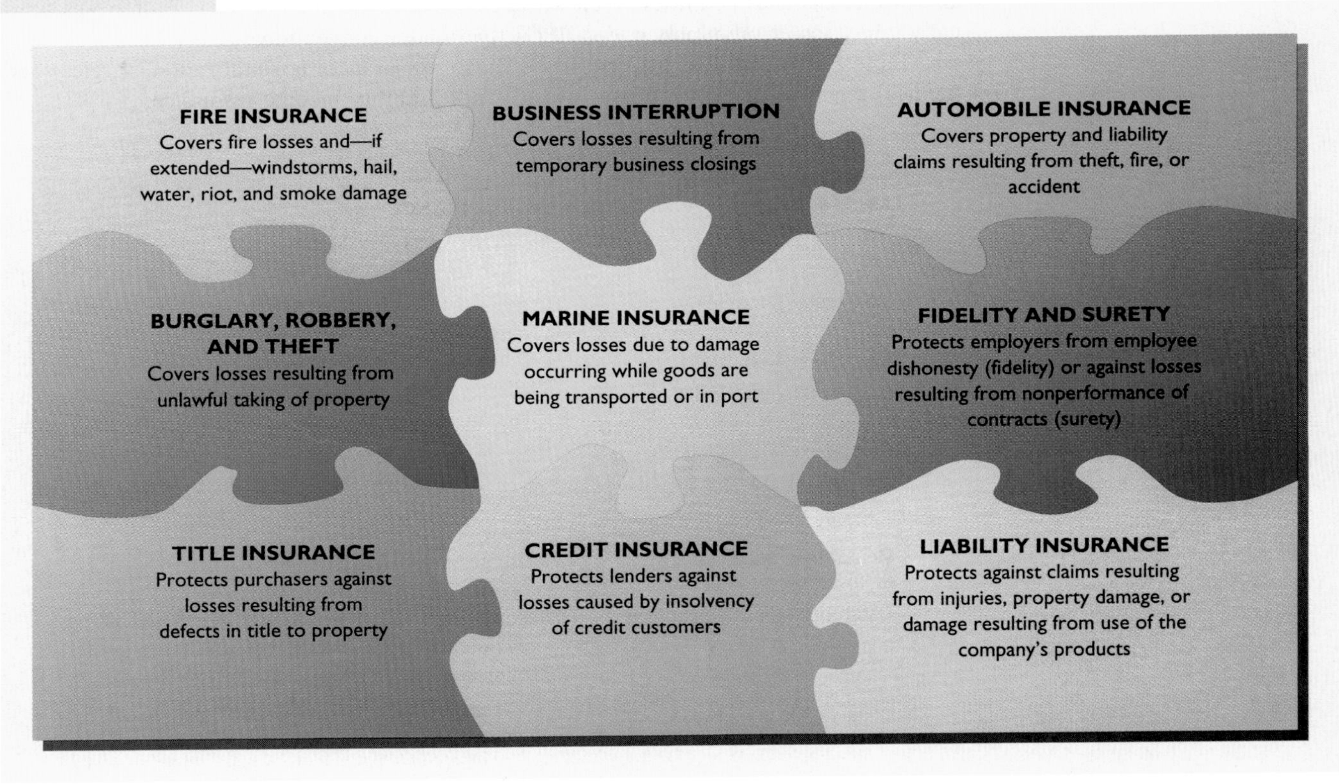
FIRE INSURANCE
Covers fire losses and—if extended—windstorms, hail, water, riot, and smoke damage
BUSINESS INTERRUPTION
Covers losses resulting from temporary business closings
AUTOMOBILE INSURANCE
Covers property and liability claims resulting from theft, fire, or accident
BURGLARY, ROBBERY, AND THEFT
Covers losses resulting from unlawful taking of property
MARINE INSURANCE
Covers losses due to damage occurring while goods are being transported or in port
FIDELITY AND SURETY
Protects employers from employee dishonesty (fidelity) or against losses resulting from nonperformance of contracts (surety)
TITLE INSURANCE
Protects purchasers against losses resulting from defects in title to property
CREDIT INSURANCE
Protects lenders against losses caused by insolvency of credit customers
LIABILITY INSURANCE
Protects against claims resulting from injuries, property damage, or damage resulting from use of the company's products

FIGURE B.5

HEALTH INSURANCE COVERAGE PROVIDED BY BLUE CROSS/ BLUE SHIELD PLANS

monthly fees. It employs its own physicians and health care specialists and often owns hospitals and clinical facilities. Among the largest HMOs are Kaiser Permanente, the Health Insurance Plan of New York, and the Group Health Cooperative of Seattle. Federal law requires employers to offer such plans to employees as alternatives to group insurance plans in areas where HMOs are available.

A *preferred provider organization (PPO)* negotiates reduced prices from hospitals and physicians and then offers their services in packages to employers. Employees typically enjoy lower premiums under *PPOs* than under conventional plans.

Table B.2 shows five major types of health insurance: hospitalization, surgical and medical payments, major medical, dental, and disability income insurance.

TABLE B.2 TYPES OF HEALTH INSURANCE

Hospitalization insurance	Health insurance designed to pay for most hospital costs
Surgical and medical payments insurance	Health insurance designed to pay the costs of surgery, medical specialists, and physicians' care in the hospital during the patient's recovery
Major medical insurance	Health insurance that protects the insured against catastrophic financial losses by covering expenses that exceed the coverage limits of basic policies
Dental insurance	Health insurance designed to pay specified percentages of dental expenses
Disability income insurance	Health insurance designed to protect against loss of income while the insured is disabled as a result of an accident or illness

LIFE INSURANCE

Life insurance differs from all other types of insurance discussed so far because it deals with the risk of a certain event—death. The insurance deals with the uncertainty of when it will occur. Life insurance is a common employee benefit in most firms because its purchase provides financial protection for the family of the policyholder and, in some instances, an additional source of retirement income for employees and their families. The purchase of a life insurance policy creates an immediate estate. Because most households need financial security, some 156 million people—two of every three U.S. citizens—are covered by life insurance.

Table B.3 outlines the provisions of the three major types of life insurance—term, whole life, and endowment insurance—along with some others. A company can choose to offer one type or a combination of them as part of its total benefit package for its employees.

WHAT IS A LIFE WORTH?

When IBM Vice President Don Estridge was killed in a plane crash, a federal jury concluded that his life was worth $7,975,000. The jury based its award on how much the man responsible for IBM's personal computer would have earned over his lifetime. The Estridge case raises the complex question of how much life insurance one should carry.

People can purchase individual life insurance policies for almost any amount. Unlike property and liability insurance, the life insurance purchases are limited only by the amount of premiums that people can afford to pay, provided that the purchasers meet medical qualifications.

The average family has too little insurance to provide true financial security. While life insurance experts recommend that the average adult with family responsibilities should purchase insurance coverage amounting to a minimum of four to five times his or her annual salary, most people have no more than 2 years' protection.

TABLE B.3 Types of Life Insurance

Term insurance	Life insurance that pays a death benefit if the policyholder dies within a specified period of time. (It has no value at the end of that period.)
Credit life insurance	Term life insurance that repays the balance owed on a house or other major credit purchase if the policyholder dies.
Whole life insurance	Life insurance that combines protection and savings for the individual who pays premiums throughout a lifetime. A cash surrender value represents the savings portion of the policy.
Endowment insurance	Life insurance that provides coverage for a specified period, after which the face value is refunded to the policyholder.
Variable life insurance	Hybrid form of whole life insurance in which the policyholder can decide how to invest the cash surrender value.
Universal life insurance	Hybrid form of life insurance combining term insurance with a tax-deferred savings account.

Various government agencies have set widely varying values on a human life. The Department of Transportation and the Federal Aviation Administration say the figure is $1 million. The Consumer Product Safety Commission says it is $2 million. The Occupational Safety and Health Administration values human lives at between $2 million and $5 million each. The Environmental Protection Agency has a still broader range, from $475,000 to $8.3 million.

key executive insurance
Life insurance designed to reimburse an organization for loss of the services of an important executive.

The death of a sole proprietor, partner, or a key executive is likely to result in financial losses to an organization. **Key executive insurance** is life insurance designed to reimburse the organization for the loss of the services of an important executive and to cover the expenses of securing a qualified replacement.

CHALLENGES FACING THE INSURANCE INDUSTRY

One of the principal problems facing the insurance industry today is the soaring cost of medical care. While most Americans enjoy the benefits of top-quality health care, they pay a big price for excellence. Not only are U.S. health-care costs the highest of any industrialized nation measured as a percentage of gross domestic product, but by 2000 they will exceed what the nation currently spends on education, defense, and recreation combined.

In 1994, federal spending on health care for the elderly, poor, disabled, and military veterans amounted to 18½¢ of every dollar spent by the U.S. government. Congressional Budget Office projections show that this will jump to almost 25¢ by the beginning of the next decade.[8] As Figure B.6 shows, federal spending on health care will triple by 2030.

FIGURE B.6 HEALTH-CARE SPENDING AS A PERCENTAGE OF GDP

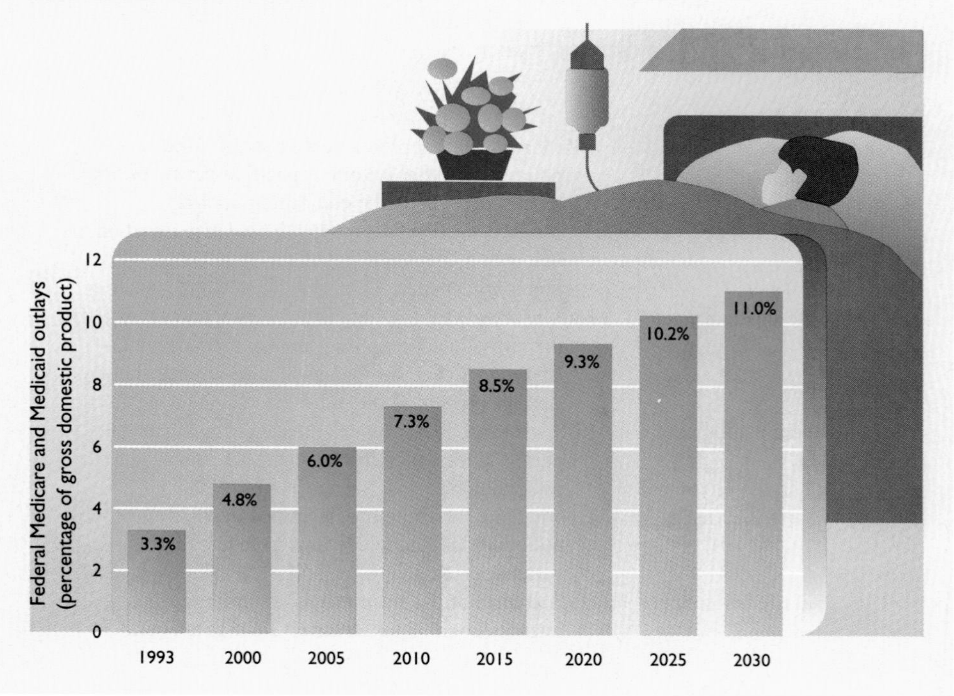

With higher costs come higher premiums, and sometimes less coverage. Moreover, the number of Americans without health insurance coverage has been estimated as high as 37 million people. Despite general agreement that some type of reform is needed to curtail the growth in health-care costs, a solution remains elusive as debate rages over the best way to accomplish this goal. A major factor in the Republican party victories in the 1994 Congressional elections was widespread voter concerns regarding President Clinton's attempts to reform the U.S. health-care system.

Some lawmakers advocate requiring employers to provide health care coverage for all workers. Others suggest requiring companies to pay a percentage of their profits into a government-financed health plan. The Health Insurance Association of America proposes standardizing health insurance premiums by industry and the age mix of companies' employees. All insurers would contribute to a reinsurance system that would foot the bills for serious cases.[9]

HEALTH-CARE REFORM IN THE UNITED STATES

President Clinton's health-care reform proposal targeted five goals. First, it sought to make basic medical coverage available to all Americans. Second, it wanted employers to bear a majority of employees' insurance costs. Third, it recognized the need to keep the federal government out of the medical services business. Fourth, it sought to maintain flexibility so states could customize health programs to meet the needs of their citizens while staying within budget. Finally, the ultimate objective was to control medical costs.

At the center of the proposed health-reform package was managed competition that would have made everyone part of big insurance pools. These pools, representing tens of thousands of citizens each, would then be strong enough to negotiate lower rates and

Major employers such as Johnson & Johnson seek to increase the efficiency of federal programs intended to provide medical, educational, and social services through specialized training programs for program directors.

improved benefits with doctors and hospitals. In exchange for lower rates, employers would have been expected to provide basic coverage for their employees.

Clearly, not everyone was happy at the prospect of a national health-care system. Small businesses maintained that even with lower rates, insurance costs would still run too high to provide coverage for all workers and their dependents.

Big businesses were more likely to support health-care reform, but only if it were implemented nationwide. If states were allowed the flexibility to change some aspects of a federal plan, some corporations could be faced with 50 sets of guidelines on required benefits packages and their respective funding. Any reform to the health-care system is bound to alienate one or more powerful interest groups such as doctors, drug companies, insurance companies, and patients.

EQUAL CARE FOR ALL

Another important health-care issue involves delivering the same quality of care to all U.S. citizens. A recent study found that white Medicare patients are 3½ times more likely to have life-saving heart bypass surgery than are African-American patients. Previous reports have also shown less access to medical care for minorities. Those studies focused on a lack of health-care insurance as the reason, but the difference between surgery rates emphasizes the need to make quality medical care available to everyone who needs it. Perhaps the most surprising statistic in the U.S. insurance debate reports that of the 37 million Americans without insurance, almost 4 million have family incomes over $50,000.[10]

KEY TERMS

risk 612
speculative risk 612
pure risk 612
self-insurance fund 613
insurance 614
insurable interest 615
insurable risk 615
law of large numbers 615
mortality table 615
insurance company 616
property loss 619
liability loss 619
health insurance 619
health maintenance organization (HMO) 619
key executive insurance 622

ASSIGNMENTS

1. Differentiate between speculative and pure risk.

2. Identify and give an example of each of the four methods of dealing with risk.

3. Outline the three basic principles of insurance. What requirements are necessary to have an insurable risk?

4. Define the major types of property and liability, health, and life insurance.

5. What benefits does a group insurance plan bring for an employee? For an employer?

BUSINESS

APPENDIX C

LAW

All management decisions must take into account business law. Some require in-depth planning and review of the law; others involve only simple checks of the legality of proposed actions. Executives learn how to apply legal standards to their decisions in much the same manner as they develop any other business skill: through constant practice and ongoing study. If they lack the experience and judgment to determine the legality of a matter, they should consult attorneys.

law
Standards set by government and society in the form of either legislation or custom.

common law
The body of law arising out of judicial decisions related to the unwritten law the United States inherited from England.

statutory law
Written law that includes state and federal constitutions, legislative enactments, treaties of the federal government, and ordinances of local governments.

international law
The numerous regulations governing international commerce.

Law consists of the standards set by government and society in the form of either legislation or custom. The broad body of principles, regulations, rules, and customs that govern the actions of all members of society, including businesspeople, is derived from several sources. **Common law** refers to the body of law arising out of judicial decisions related to the unwritten law the United States inherited from England. This unwritten law is based on customs and court decisions beginning in early England.

Statutory law, or written law, includes state and federal constitutions, legislative enactments, treaties of the federal government, and ordinances of local governments. Statutes must be drawn precisely and reasonably in order to be constitutional (and thus enforceable), but courts must frequently interpret their intentions and meanings. The court rulings often result in statutory laws being changed or even discarded.

As U.S. investments in foreign countries grow, and as more U.S. firms form joint ventures off-shore, a knowledge of international law becomes crucial. **International law** refers to the numerous regulations that govern international commerce. Companies must be aware of the domestic laws of trading partners, the rules set by the international trading community, and the guidelines established by regional and international organizations.

For example, since 1970 international trade in art and cultural artifacts has been regulated by the guidelines of the United Nations Convention. The U.S. State Department and the International Institute for the Unification of Private Law are negotiating a new agreement, to be known as Unidroit (French for "one law"). Under Unidroit, it will be more difficult to transport art from its native country. Supporters of the new law hope that it will help prevent looting and smuggling of rare art works. Others oppose the law, however, because they fear a negative impact on the multimillion-dollar international art dealing industry.[1]

NATURE OF BUSINESS LAW

business law
The aspects of law that most directly influence and regulate the management of various types of business activity.

judiciary
The branch of government charged with deciding disputes among parties through the application of laws.

In a broad sense, all law is business law because all firms are subject to the entire body of law, just as individuals are. In a narrower sense, however, **business law** consists of those aspects of law that most directly influence and regulate the management of various types of business activity. Specific laws vary widely in their effects from business to business and from industry to industry. Different laws affect small companies and large corporations. The legal interests of the automobile industry, for example, differ from those of real estate developers.

State and local statutes also have varying applications. Some state laws affect all businesses that operate in a particular state. Workers' compensation laws, which govern payments to workers for injuries incurred on the job, are an example. Other state laws apply only to certain firms or business activities. For example, states have specific licensing requirements for businesses like law firms, funeral directors, and hair styling salons. Many local ordinances also deal with specific business activities. For example, regulation of the sizes and types of business signs is commonplace.

COURT SYSTEM

The **judiciary,** or court system, is the branch of government charged with deciding disputes among parties by applying laws. The judiciary consists of several types or levels of courts, each with a specific jurisdiction. Court systems are organized at the federal, state, and local levels. Administrative agencies also perform some limited judicial functions, but these agencies are more properly regarded as belonging to the executive or legislative branches of government.

TRIAL COURTS

At both the federal and state levels, **trial courts**—courts of general jurisdiction—hear wide ranges of cases. Unless a case is assigned by law to another court or to an administrative agency, a court of general jurisdiction will hear it. The majority of cases, both criminal and civil, pass through these courts. Within the federal system, trial courts are known as *U.S. district courts,* and at least one such court operates in each state. In the state court systems, the general jurisdiction courts are usually called *circuit courts,* and most states provide one for each county. Some states call their general jurisdiction courts by other names, such as *superior courts, common pleas courts,* or *district courts.*

trial court
A court of general jurisdiction.

State judiciary systems also include a wide range of courts with lower or more specific jurisdictions. These courts have limited jurisdictions in that they hear only certain sizes or types of cases, as set forth by statute or constitution. In most states, parties can appeal the decisions of the lower courts to the general jurisdiction courts. Examples of lower courts are probate courts (which settle deceased persons' estates) and small claims courts (where people can represent themselves in suits involving limited amounts of damages).

APPELLATE COURTS

Appeals of decisions of general trial courts are heard by **appellate courts.** Both the federal and state systems have appellate courts. An appeal usually is filed when the losing party feels that the case was wrongly decided by the judge or jury. The appeals process allows a higher court to review the case and correct any lower court error complained of by the appellant, the party making the appeal.

appellate court
A process that allows a higher court to review the case and correct any lower-court error.

The federal court's appeals system, together with those of most states, consists of two tiers of courts. The federal courts at the intermediate level, called *U.S. circuit courts of appeal,* hear appeals of decisions from the U.S. district courts. The intermediate level of a state's appellate courts, if any exists, is known as the *court of appeals* or the *district court of appeals* in most states.

Appeals from decisions of the U.S. circuit courts of appeal can go to the nation's highest court, the U.S. Supreme Court. Appeals from state courts of appeal are heard by the highest court in each state, usually called the *state supreme court.* In a state without intermediate appellate courts, the state supreme court hears appeals directly from the trial courts. Parties not satisfied by the verdict of a state supreme court can appeal to the U.S. Supreme Court and may be granted a hearing if they can cite grounds for such an appeal and if the Supreme Court considers the case significant enough to be heard. It is unusual for a case to go all the way to the U.S. Supreme Court; in an average year, the court may hear less than 200 of the thousands of cases that people file with it. One business case that did end up there involved two rival Mexican food restaurant chains in San Antonio. When the Two Pesos chain began building restaurants that were nearly identical to Taco Cabana outlets, Taco Cabana President Richard Cervera sued. The two companies fought the issue all the way to the Supreme Court, which ruled against Two Pesos; its management was told to pay Taco Cabana $3.7 million in damages and to redesign its restaurants. Cervera took the money and then proposed a novel solution; he offered to buy out the Two Pesos chain and assume its debts. The Two Pesos managers accepted his offer and are no doubt glad they did; the Taco Cabana stock they received as part of the deal has risen almost 60 percent since the acquisition.[2]

While the great majority of cases are resolved by the system of courts described here, certain highly specialized cases require particular expertise. Such cases are assigned to special courts by constitutional provisions or statutes. Examples of specialized federal courts are the U.S. Tax Court (for tax cases) and the U.S. Court of Claims (which hears claims against the U.S. government itself). Similar specialized courts operate at the state level.

For example, Delaware's Chancery Court is a 200-year-old institution specializing in corporate governance. Its five chancellors hear about 1,000 cases annually. This tiny court, located in Wilmington's Rodney Square, is important because almost 50 percent of the companies listed on the New York Stock Exchange are incorporated in Delaware. As early as 1913, many firms, attracted by Delaware's low corporate taxes, began relocating from New Jersey. As another draw, Delaware updates its corporate laws regularly. A Corporate Law Council, with members drawn from many of the state's largest law firms, periodically reviews trends in corporate law and recommends changes.

Yet another plus is Delaware's Division of Corporations, which has been quick to adopt new technologies and add extra services. For instance, the division uses a computerized imaging system to store pictures of all documents, even envelopes; it also maintains a 4 P.M.-to-midnight shift to process documents and to assist West Coast companies that need help after the close of business hours on the East Coast.

Perhaps the main reason why many firms choose to incorporate in Delaware, however, is the Chancery Court itself. "The Delaware Chancery Court is a well-respected court," says attorney David King. "The judges are especially conversant in business. . . . A judge is not hearing a divorce or custody case in the morning before moving on to a big takeover case in the afternoon."

A growing trend has seen Chancery Court decisions favor the rights of corporate shareholders. This approach to business law emphasizes a company's obligation to get the best deal possible for those who own stock in it. In some cases, for example, the court has forced company directors to accept the highest bidder in a takeover war, even if they would prefer to sell to another. Several recent takeover verdicts have mandated that managers must choose the most profitable options if it best serves the shareholders' interests.

In other cases, the Chancery Court has mandated that companies must reimburse shareholders who did not receive full value for their money. One case involved Home Shopping Network, which placed a notice on shares warning that their value could decrease, depending on the outcome of pending litigation. As a result, share prices plummeted, and the company repurchased them at a cheaper rate. Bondholders complained, and the court ruled against the company. Another time, Enserch Corporation shareholders claimed that the company had failed to compensate those who exchanged Enserch Exploration Partners stock for Enserch shares; the court ordered Enserch Corporation to pay an extra $3.42 per share.[3]

ADMINISTRATIVE AGENCIES

Administrative agencies, also known as *bureaus, commissions,* or *boards,* decide a variety of cases at all levels of government. They sometimes derive powers and responsibilities from constitutional provisions, but usually state or federal statutes make this determination. Technically, they conduct hearings or inquiries rather than trials. The parties are often represented by attorneys, evidence and testimony are included, and the agency issues legally binding decisions based on government regulations.

Examples of federal administrative agencies are the Federal Trade Commission, the National Labor Relations Board, and the Federal Energy Regulatory Commission. Examples at the state level include public utility commissions and boards that govern the licensing of various trades and professions. Zoning boards, planning commissions, and boards of appeal operate at the city or county level.

MAJOR COMPONENTS OF BUSINESS LAW

The cornerstones of U.S. business law are contract law; sales law; the Uniform Commercial Code; negotiable instruments law; property law; the law of bailment; agency law; tort law; bankruptcy law; patent, trademark, and copyright law; and tax law. The sections that follow set out the key provisions of each of these legal concepts.

CONTRACT LAW

Contract law is important because it affects most aspects of a business operation. It is the legal foundation on which business dealings are conducted. A **contract** is a legally enforceable agreement between two or more parties regarding a specified act or thing.

contract
A legally enforceable agreement between two or more parties regarding a specified act or thing.

CONTRACT REQUIREMENTS

The four elements of an enforceable contract are agreement, consideration, legal and serious purpose, and capacity. The parties must reach agreement about the act or thing specified. In order for such an agreement, or contract, to be valid and legally enforceable, each party must furnish consideration—the value or benefit that a party provides to the others with whom the contract is made. Legal consideration for a contract exists when, for example, A agrees to work for B and B agrees to pay A a specified salary. The contract is just as valid if B actually pays A at the time A agrees to work. Similarly, valid consideration exists even if no promises are exchanged but A works for B and B pays A for the work.

In addition to consideration, an enforceable contract must involve a legal and serious purpose. Agreements made in a joking manner, related to purely social matters, or involving the commission of crimes are not enforceable as legal contracts. An agreement between two competitors to fix the prices for their products is not enforceable as a contract because the subject matter is illegal and carrying out the agreement would violate the law.

The last element of a legally enforceable contract is capacity, the legal ability of a party to enter into agreements. The law does not permit certain persons, such as those judged to be insane, to enter into legally enforceable contracts.

Contracts govern almost all types of business activities. Examples of valid contracts are purchase agreements with suppliers, labor contracts, group insurance policies for employees, franchise agreements, and sales contracts.

BREACH OF CONTRACT

A violation of a valid contract is called a **breach of contract.** The injured party can go to court to enforce the contract provisions and, in some cases, collect **damages**—financial payments to compensate for a loss and related suffering.

breach of contract
A violation of a valid contract.

damages
Financial payments made for a loss and related suffering.

For instance, defense contractors McDonnell-Douglas and General Dynamics Corporation filed suit against the Navy after it canceled its contract for a new bomber, the A-12. The military claimed that the contractors defaulted on the project by falling behind schedule and running up large cost overruns. The companies, for their part, charged that the Pentagon illegally canceled the order after withholding crucial technical information from the development team. They also claimed that Pentagon officials knew that deadlines were unrealistic but told the firms to proceed with the project. The lawsuit, which is expected to take the entire decade to resolve, will probably be the most expensive federal lawsuit of all time; overall litigation costs average $60 million a year.[4]

SALES LAW

sales law
The sale of goods or services for money or on credit.

Sales law governs sales of goods or services for money or on credit. The law of sales derives from contract law, since a sales agreement or sales transaction is a special kind of contract that people enter into millions of times each day. As economic transactions, sales can exchange services or real estate as well as products, but the law of sales is concerned only with transfers of tangible personal property. The law involved with intangible personal property and real estate will be examined later.

Sales law has evolved in a distinct manner. It goes back to ancient English law based largely on the customs of merchants and included a system of merchant courts to resolve disputes. Many of these customs and practices were adopted in the United States as part of common law. Later, the Uniform Commercial Code provided uniformity in all commercial laws, including sales law.

UNIFORM COMMERCIAL CODE (UCC)

The Uniform Commercial Code (UCC) is the basis for commercial law in the United States. It has been adopted by all states except Louisiana, which adopted only part of it.[5] The UCC covers the law of sales as well as other specific areas of commercial law.

Article 2 of the UCC specifies the circumstances under which a buyer and a seller enter into a sales contract. Ordinarily such agreements are based on the express conduct of the parties. The UCC generally requires written agreements for enforceable sales contracts for products worth more than $500. The formation of a sales contract is quite flexible because certain missing terms in a written contract or other ambiguities do not keep the contract from being legally enforceable. A court will look to past dealings, commercial customs, and other standards of reasonableness to evaluate whether a legal contract exists.

A court will also consider these variables when either the buyer or the seller seeks to enforce his or her rights when the other party fails to perform as specified in the contract, performs only partially, or performs in a defective or unsatisfactory way. The UCC's remedies in such cases consist largely of monetary damages awarded to injured parties. The UCC defines the rights of the parties to have the contract specifically performed, to have it terminated, and to reclaim the goods or place a lien—a legal claim—against them.

WARRANTIES

Article 2 of the UCC also sets forth the law of warranties for sales transactions. Products carry two basic types of warranties. An express warranty is a specific representation made by the seller regarding the product, while an implied warranty is one legally imposed on the seller. Generally, unless implied warranties are disclaimed by the seller in writing, they are automatically effective. Other provisions of Article 2 govern the rights of acceptance, rejection, and inspection of products by the buyer; the rights of the parties during manufacture, shipment, delivery, and passing of title to products; the legal significance of sales documents; and the placement of the risk of loss in the event of destruction or damage to the products during manufacture, shipment, or delivery.

NEGOTIABLE INSTRUMENTS

negotiable instruments
Commercial paper that is transferable among individuals and businesses.

The term **negotiable instrument** refers to commercial paper that is transferable among individuals and businesses. The most common example of a negotiable instrument is a check; drafts, certificates of deposit, and notes are also sometimes considered negotiable instruments.

Article 3 of the UCC specifies that a negotiable instrument must be written and must meet several additional conditions:

1. It must be signed by the maker or drawer.
2. It must contain an unconditional promise or order to pay a certain sum of money.
3. It must be payable on demand or at a definite time.
4. It must be payable to order or to bearer.

Checks and other forms of commercial paper are transferred when the payee signs the back of the instrument, a procedure known as *endorsement.* The four kinds of endorsements described by Article 3 of the UCC, shown in Figure C.1, include the following:

1. A blank endorsement consists only of the name of the payee. To make a blank endorsement, the payee need only sign the back of the instrument, which makes the check payable to the bearer. A blank endorsement should not be used for an instrument that moves through the mail.
2. A special endorsement specifies the person to whom the instrument is payable. With this kind of endorsement, only the person whose name appears after "Pay to the order of . . ." can profit from the instrument.
3. A qualified endorsement contains words stating that the endorser is not guaranteeing payment of the instrument. The qualified endorsement of "Without Recourse (signed)" limits the endorser's liability if the instrument is not backed by sufficient funds.
4. A restrictive endorsement limits the negotiability of the instrument. One of the most common restrictive endorsements, "For Deposit Only," is useful if an instrument (usually a check) is lost or stolen, because it means that the instrument can only be deposited to the indicated account; it cannot be cashed.

FIGURE C.1 FOUR KINDS OF ENDORSEMENTS

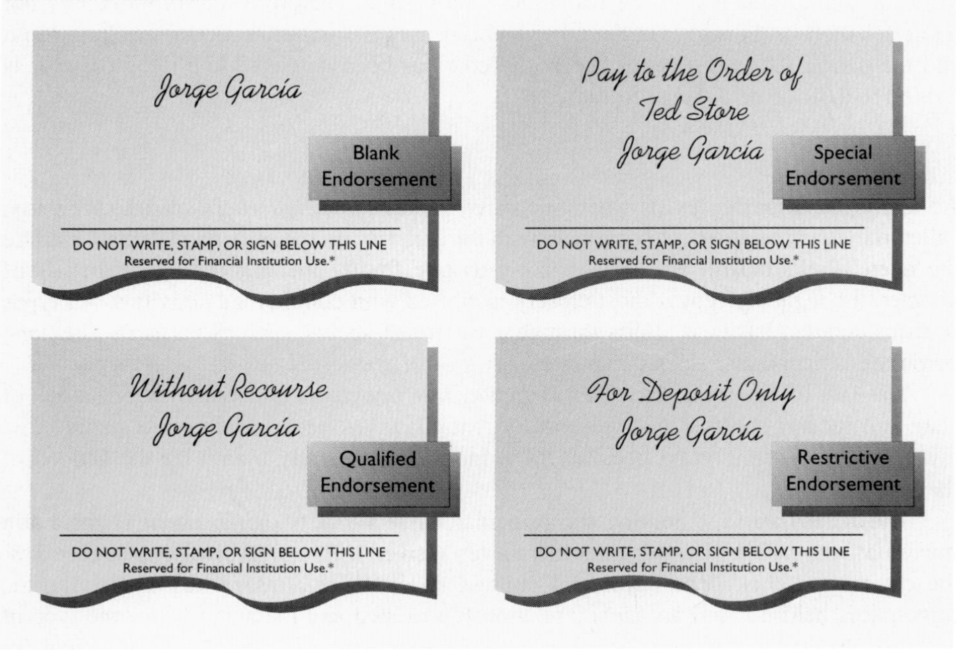

PROPERTY LAW

Property law is a key feature of the private enterprise system. As noted in Chapter 1, property is something for which a person or firm has the unrestricted right of possession or use. Property rights are guaranteed and protected by the U.S. Constitution.

Property can be divided into several categories. Tangible personal property consists of physical things such as equipment, supplies, and delivery vehicles. Intangible personal property is nonphysical property that is most often represented by a document or other written instrument, although it may be as vague and remote as a computer entry. You are probably familiar with certain types of intangible personal property such as checks and money orders. Other, less well-known examples are important to the businesses or individuals who own and use them. Examples are stocks, bonds, Treasury bills, notes, letters of credit, and warehouse receipts. Mortgages are also intangible personal property.

A third category of property is real property, or real estate. Some customs surrounding real property have been formalized in statutes. Case law helps to guide real property owners in their transactions and conduct. All firms have some concern with real estate law because of the need to own or occupy the space or building where they conduct business. Some companies are created to serve these real estate needs. Real estate developers, builders, contractors, brokers, appraisers, mortgage companies, escrow companies, title companies, and architects all deal with various aspects of real property law.

LAW OF BAILMENT

The law of bailment deals with the surrender of personal property by one person to another when the property is to be returned at a later date. The person delivering the property is known as the *bailor,* and the person receiving the property is the *bailee.* Some bailments benefit bailees, others benefit bailors, and still others provide mutual benefits. Most courts now require that all parties practice reasonable care in all bailment situations. The degree of benefit received from the bailment is a factor in court decisions about whether or not parties have met the reasonable care standard.[6]

Rules govern settlement of bailment disputes, which commonly arise in business settings such as hotels, restaurants, banks, and parking lots. The law focuses on actual delivery of an item. For example, a patron in a restaurant who hangs a coat on a hook has made no actual delivery to the restaurant's proprietor. Therefore, the proprietor is not liable for theft or damage. On the other hand, if the restaurant has a coat checking room and the patron receives a claim check, the coat has been delivered and the proprietor is liable for theft of or damage to the coat.

LAW OF AGENCY

agency
A legal relationship whereby one party, called a principal, appoints another party, called the agent, to enter into contracts with third parties in the principal's behalf.

An **agency** relationship exists when one party, called a *principal,* appoints another party, called the *agent,* to enter into contracts with third parties on the principal's behalf.[7] While the agency relationship can be as simple as one family member acting on behalf of another, the legal concept is most closely identified with commercial activities. All types of firms conduct business affairs through a variety of agents, such as partners, directors, corporate officers, and sales personnel.

The law of agency is based on common law principles and case law decisions of state and federal courts. Relatively little agency law has been enacted into statute. The law of agency is important because the principal is generally bound by the actions of the agent.

The legal basis for holding the principal liable for acts of the agent is the Latin maxim of *respondent superior* ("let the master answer"). In a case involving agency law, the court must decide the rights and obligations of the various parties. Generally, the principal is held liable if an agency relationship existed and the agent had some type of authority to do the wrongful act. The agent in such cases is liable to the principal for any damages.

LAW OF TORTS

A **tort** (French for "wrong") refers to a civil wrong inflicted on another person or the person's property.[8] The law of torts is closely related to the law of agency because a business entity, or principal, can be held liable for torts committed by its agents in the course of business dealings. Tort law differs from both criminal and contract law. While criminal law is concerned with crimes against the state or society, tort law deals with compensation for injured persons who are the victims of noncriminal wrongs.

tort
A civil wrong inflicted on other people or their property.

Tort cases can result in considerable judgments. For instance, in 1994, a jury awarded an 81-year-old Albuquerque woman $2.7 million in punitive damages from McDonald's. The woman received third-degree burns when a cup of coffee spilled on her. The judge later reduced the damages to $480,000 in a decision upheld by the New Mexico Supreme Court.[9]

TYPES OF TORTS

A tort may be intentional, or it may be caused by negligence. Assault, slander, libel, and fraud are examples of intentional torts. Businesses can become involved in such cases through the actions of both owners and employees. A security guard who roughly handles a suspected shoplifter and holds the suspect in the manager's office for questioning may be committing a tort if his or her conduct does excessive or otherwise unjustified harm. Under agency law, the store owner can be held liable for any damages or injury caused by the security guard.

The other major group of torts result from negligence. This type of tort is based on carelessness rather than intentional behavior that causes injury to another person. Under agency law, businesses are held liable for the negligence of their employees or agents. The delivery truck driver who kills a pedestrian while delivering goods creates a tort liability for his or her employer if the accident results from negligence.

Product Liability An area of tort law known as **product liability** has been developed by both statutory and case law to hold businesses liable for negligence in the design, manufacture, sale, and/or use of products. Some states have extended the theory of tort law to cover injuries caused by products, regardless of whether the manufacturer is proven negligent. This legal concept is known as *strict product liability.*[10]

product liability
Business liability for negligence in the design, manufacture, sale, and/or use of products.

Some businesspeople feel that the concept of product liability has been carried too far. For example, product liability lawsuits caused many manufacturers of airplanes powered by single piston engines to go out of business. In 1978, U.S. companies made 17,811 light aircraft; 15 years later, they produced 964. Companies have been held liable even for old planes and obsolete designs; the average age of a plane in these suits was 22 years, and Cessna Aircraft was sued for an accident involving a 47-year-old plane of a type it had ceased making.

To protect the general aviation industry, Congress acted to reduce firms' liability exposure and revitalize the industry. The General Aviation Revitalization Act of 1994 excluded from liability claims airplanes and parts over 18 years old. As a result, Cessna plans to start producing small aircraft again, eventually building 2,000 planes a year.[11]

BANKRUPTCY LAW

Bankruptcy, the legal nonpayment of financial obligations, is a common occurrence in contemporary society. The term *bankruptcy* is derived from "banca rotta," or "broken bench," since creditors in medieval Italy would break up the benches of merchants who did not pay their bills.[12]

bankruptcy
The legal nonpayment of financial obligations.

Federal legislation passed in 1918 and revised several times since provides for orderly handling of bankruptcies by the federal court system. The legal process of bankruptcy has two purposes. One is to protect creditors by providing a way to seize and distribute debtors' assets. The second goal, which is almost unique to the United States, is to protect debtors, too, allowing them to start fresh and thus benefiting society in general.[13]

Federal law recognizes two types of bankruptcies. Under voluntary bankruptcy, a person or firm asks to be judged bankrupt because of inability to pay off creditors. Under involuntary bankruptcy, creditors may request that a party be judged bankrupt.

PERSONAL BANKRUPTCIES

Bankruptcy law offers individuals two primary options.[14] Chapter 13 of the bankruptcy law—the wage earner plan—allows a person to set up a 3-year debt repayment plan. (The bankruptcy judge can extend the time to 5 years.) Debtors often end up repaying only a portion of what they owe under Chapter 13. The court considers the bankrupt party's current income in determining the repayment schedule. Chapter 13 is available only if unsecured debts do not exceed $100,000 and secured debts do not exceed $350,000, although Congress may pass legislation to raise these limits.

About 70 percent of all bankruptcies, however, are resolved by the other alternative. Chapter 7 sets out a liquidation plan under which a trustee sells the bankrupt person's assets and divides the proceeds among creditors. Judges can deny the use of Chapter 7, but the initial choice of Chapter 13 does not preclude a later switch to Chapter 7.

Chapter 7 exempts certain property from the claims of creditors:

1. Home equity up to $7,500
2. Motor vehicle equity up to $1,200
3. Amount of $200 on each personal item such as household furnishings, clothes, and books, up to a maximum of $4,000
4. Amount of $500 on personal property
5. Another $400 on any other property
6. Tools of one's trade or prescribed health needs up to $750

Husbands and wives filing jointly can double these amounts. Some states set different allowances than those specified in Chapter 7. Missouri, for example, exempts only $8,000. Florida offers the most liberal exemptions; its homestead law exempts up to 160 acres in rural areas and half an acre in a city. The Sunshine State also exempts all wages, annuities, partnership profits, pension plans, and property owned jointly with a spouse.[15]

A third personal bankruptcy option, Chapter 12, allows farmers with debts up to $1.5 million to set up repayment plans. This supersedes the debt limit set by Chapter 13.

BUSINESS BANKRUPTCIES

Businesses can also go bankrupt. The specific provision under which they do this, Chapter 11, allows a firm to reorganize and develop a plan to repay its debts. Chapter 11 also permits prepackaged bankruptcies, in which companies enter bankruptcy proceedings after obtaining approval of most (as opposed to all) of their creditors. The terms are then imposed on all creditors. Often companies can emerge from prepackaged bankruptcies sooner than those that opt for conventional Chapter 11 bankruptcy proceedings.

Congress is considering revisions to the Chapter 11 code that would streamline the process and make it less expensive. The legislation would also raise the ceiling on personal debts from $350,000 to $1 million, which would make Chapter 11 court-approved repayment plans available to more business owners.[16]

Ironically, declaring bankruptcy under Chapter 11 may keep a bankrupt company in business. Consider the Federated chain of department stores, which filed for bankruptcy after taking on too much debt. The chain's 45,000 creditors were grouped into 77 classes of debt. In 26 months, the company was reorganized into 14 units; 24 of the creditor groups received full payment, and Federated's 80,000 employees kept their jobs.[17]

TRADEMARKS, PATENTS, AND COPYRIGHTS

Trademarks, patents, and copyrights provide legal protection for key business assets by giving a firm the exclusive right to use those assets. A **trademark** consists of words, symbols, or other designations used by firms to identify their products. The Lanham Act (1946) provides for federal registration of trademarks. Intel Corporation, for instance, broadens awareness of its computer chips through its "Intel Inside" logo in advertisements. When competitor Cyrix Corporation parodied the logo by using a similarly shaped logo labeled "Ditto," Intel's lawyers promptly sued Cyrix, its ad agency, and the ad agency's two partners. Ironically, the lawsuit promoted Cyrix far more effectively than its ads did. Indeed, says ad agency owner Frank Priscaro, "We were sort of worried that they wouldn't sue. We never could have generated the publicity and coverage they could generate by suing us. It probably generated $1 million worth of publicity."[18]

trademark
Words, symbols, or other designations used by firms to identify their products.

For another irony, if a product becomes too well-known, this notoriety can create problems; once a trademark becomes part of everyday usage, it loses its protection as a legal trademark. Consider the fate of the terms *aspirin, nylon, kerosene, linoleum,* and *milk of magnesia.* All of them were once the exclusive property of their manufacturers, but they have passed into common language and now anyone can use them. Companies often attempt to forestall this threat by advertising that a term is actually a registered trademark. For example, the National Association of Realtors® promotes its name as a federally registered trademark, and Triangle Publications, Inc., has done the same for its TV GUIDE®.

A **patent** guarantees an inventor exclusive rights to an invention for 17 years. Copyrights and patents have a constitutional basis; the U.S. Constitution specifies that the federal government has the power "to promote the progress of science and useful arts, by securing for limited times to authors and inventors the exclusive rights to their respective writings or discoveries." Patent owners sometimes license others to use their patents for negotiated fees.

patent
Guarantees inventors exclusive rights to their invention for 17 years.

A **copyright** protects written material such as this textbook, designs, cartoon illustrations, photos, computer software, and so on. Copyrights are filed with the Library of Congress. An author or his or her heirs hold exclusive rights to published or unpublished works for the author's lifetime, plus 50 years. Works for hire and anonymous or pseudonymous works receive copyright protection for a period of 75 years from publication or 100 years from creation, whichever is shorter.

copyright
Exclusive rights to written material, either published or unpublished.

As firms do more business overseas, the law regarding trademarks, patents, and copyrights is growing more complex. Despite legal registration and protection in the United States, they may be fair game in other countries. Manufacturers in China have been known to blatantly copy foreign trademarks, brand names, and patents. Shoppers in China can buy Kongalu Corn Strips cereal in a box sporting a rooster reminiscent of the one on Kellogg's Corn Flakes. Also available are Colgate toothpaste in a familiar bright-red package and Cream Style Corn in Del Monte-like green cans. Ray Ban sunglasses are renamed "Ran Bans," and bootleg copies of Madonna albums sell for $1. Brand names sometimes resurface in unexpected ways; one company markets Rambo facial tissues in delicate hues of pink or blue.[19] More legal issues of this type will no doubt develop as business becomes increasingly global.

TAX LAW

A branch of law that affects every business, employee, and consumer in the United States is tax law. **Taxes** are the assessments by which government units raise revenue. Federal, state, and local governments and special taxing authorities all levy taxes.

Federal taxes currently account for about a 20 percent share of the United States gross domestic product (GDP); this figure has fluctuated between 18 and 20 percent since 1960. The share of GDP consumed by state and local taxes has remained stable at roughly 12 percent since the early 1970s.[20]

taxes
The assessments used to raise revenue for government units.

HOW TAXES ARE LEVIED

Some taxes are paid by individuals and some by businesses. Both have decided impacts on contemporary business. Business taxes reduce profits, and personal taxes cut the disposable incomes that individuals can spend on the products of businesses. Governments spend their revenue from taxes to buy industry's goods and services. Governments also act as transfer agents, moving tax revenue to other consumers and transferring Social Security taxes from the working population to retired or disabled persons.

Governments can levy taxes on several different bases: income, sales, business receipts, property, assets, and so on. The type of tax varies from one taxing authority to the other. The individual income tax is the biggest source of revenue for the federal government. Many states rely on sales taxes. In addition to sales taxes, some cities collect taxes on earnings. Finally, community college districts get the bulk of their revenue from real estate or property taxes.

KEY TERMS

law 626
common law 626
statutory law 626
international law 626
business law 626
judiciary 626
trial court 627
appellate court 627
contract 629
breach of contract 629
damages 629
sales law 630
negotiable instrument 630
agency 632
tort 633
product liability 633
bankruptcy 633
trademark 635
patent 635
copyright 635
taxes 635

ASSIGNMENTS

1. U.S. Air Flight 427 crashed while approaching Pittsburgh International Airport on the evening of September 8, 1994, killing all 132 people aboard. Just a few days later the first lawsuit was filed. Arthur Alan Wolk, a Philadelphia lawyer specializing in air crash litigation, predicted that financial settlements could top $200 million. Wolk remarked, "It will be a blockbuster of a case." The only limits on legal claims would involve people flying on international itineraries. Treaties limit damages to $75,000 for international passengers. Families of domestic passengers could expect seven-digit settlements for their losses. However, lawyers working for what are called *contingency fees* would pocket one-third to one-half of the settlements.[21]
   a. Should the law set limits on settlements resulting from domestic air crashes? Why or why not?
   b. Should the law set limits on contingency fees charged by lawyers? Explain your viewpoint.

2. This appendix referred to a case in which defense contractors McDonnell-Douglas and General Dynamics filed suit against the Navy for canceling its contract for the A-12 bomber. The lawsuit appears likely to become the most expensive one that has ever involved the federal government. Attorneys for McDonnell-Douglas and General Dynamics estimate that each company is paying $30 million a year in legal fees. The government has announced that it will not be ready to go to trial for four more years; it has hired a private law firm to provide an estimated $8 million in legal support. The Justice Department has asked Congress for a budget increase to cover the cost of taking hundreds of depositions and reviewing roughly 70 million pages of classified documents. The lawsuit is expected to take the entire decade to resolve, and could result in a total bill of $1.5 billion in legal fees and interest costs.[22] Discuss the implications of this case. Do you feel that these costs are justified? How would you suggest resolving this dispute?

3. Privately owned companies are becoming more common in China. At the same time, the number of bankruptcies in that country has also grown.[23] Explain the relationship, if any, between these two facts. What purpose does bankruptcy law serve? Explain your answer.

4. Managers at U.S. software manufacturer Microsoft estimate that copyright and trademark violations in China cost the company about $30 million a year. The Motion Picture Association states that almost all laser-disk and videotape sales in China involve fakes rather than American-made products. Beijing Jeep Corporation, a joint venture with Chrysler, has found more than 2,000 vehicles that are designed to resemble the Jeep Cherokee.[24] What legal steps, if any, might the U.S. government take to protect trademarks and copyrights in China?

5. United States bankruptcy law permits bankrupt parties to retain a good deal of personal property. Discuss the concept behind this exemption.

NOTES

Chapter 1

1. Francis Williams, "Hong Kong Shrugs off Doubts," *Financial Times,* October 7, 1994, p. 8; David Lindorff, "A Nasty Little Shoving Match in Hong Kong," *Business Week,* October 3, 1994, p. 68; Steven Strasser, "Dreams of an Empire," *Newsweek,* August 8, 1994, pp. 28, 33; Margaret Harris, "Hong Kong's New 1997 Jitters," *World Press Review,* July 1994, pp. 16–17; Gustavo Lombo, "Orient Express," *Forbes,* May 23, 1994, p. 250; Robert Neff, Lynne Curry, and Bruce Einhorn, "Asia's Giants Learn to Waltz," *Business Week,* March 14, 1994, pp. 40–41; Emily MacFarquhar, "A Crucial Test for Reforms," *U.S. News & World Report,* January 24, 1994, p. 56; "It's Already 1997 in Hong Kong," *The Economist,* December 19, 1993, pp. 36–38; Andrew Powell, "Fast Forward," *Harper's Bazaar,* August 1993, p. 102; Joyce Barnathan and Lynne Curry, "Spring Thaw in Hong Kong," *Business Week,* June 14, 1994, p. 49; "The Shape of Things to Come," *The Economist,* June 12, 1993, p. 42; Louis Kraar, "Storm Over Hong Kong," *Fortune,* March 8, 1993, pp. 98–99, 102–104; American Consulate General–Hong Kong, *Hong Kong,* FET 92–49 (October 1992); Kevin Rafferty, "China's Grasp and Hong Kong's Golden Eggs," *Harvard Business Review,* May–June 1991, pp. 54–56, 60, 62–63, 66, 68–69; Emily MacFarquhar, "Will the Last One to Leave Please Turn out the Lights," *U.S. News & World Report,* August 21, 1989, pp. 36–37; and Maria Shao, "The 'Brain Drain' Crimping the Colony," *Business Week,* January 25, 1988, p. 50.
2. George J. Church, "We're #1 and It Hurts," *Time,* October 24, 1994, pp. 50–56.
3. Myron Magnet, "The Productivity Payoff Arrives," *Fortune,* June 27, 1994, pp. 79–84; and Gene Koretz, "Productivity: The U.S. Remains Leader of the Pack," *Business Week,* December 21, 1993, p. 18.
4. Statistics from *Survey of Current Business,* June 1994, p. 14; and *U.S. Industrial Outlook 1994,* pp. 5–2, 35–1.
5. Thomas Stewart, "Managing in a Wired Company," *Fortune,* July 11, 1994, pp. 44–56.
6. Myron Magnet, "The Golden Rule of Business," *Fortune,* February 21, 1994, pp. 60–64.
7. Ibid.
8. Richard L. Daft, *Understanding Management,* (Fort Worth, Tex.: Dryden Press, 1995), pp. 86–87, 525.
9. Michael R. Czinkota, Ilkka A. Ronkainen, and John J. Jarrant, *The Global Marketing Imperative* (Lincolnwood, Ill.: NTC Business Books, 1995), p. 8.
10. Ibid., p. 9
11. William Erickson, "Young Americans Go Abroad to Strike It Rich," *Fortune,* October 17, 1994, pp. 188, 190, 192.
12. "Privatization: A Full Calendar," *Institutional Investor,* June 1994, p. 56; Gil J. Bonwit, "Is There Milk and Honey in the Promised Land? A Profile of Investing in Israel: Silver Anniversary Essays," *Law and Policy in International Business,* January 1994, pp. 491–515.
13. Susan Scherrick, "Your Ticket to the Privatization Party," *Business Week,* April 18, 1994, p. 134.
14. From Samsung's management guide book; quoted in "Other Comments," *Forbes,* October 10, 1994, p. 30.
15. "Workers' New Lament: Too Much Overtime," *U.S. News & World Report,* October 10, 1994, p. 12.

Chapter 2

1. Alex Taylor III, "GM's $11,000,000,000 Turnaround," *Fortune,* October 17, 1994, pp. 54–74; and Judith Dobrzynski, "At GM, a Magna Carta for Directors," *Business Week,* April 4, 1994, p. 37.
2. Patrick J. Welch and Gerry F. Welch, *Economics: Theory and Practice,* 5th ed. (Fort Worth, Tex.: Dryden Press, 1995), p. 3.
3. Lee Smith, "Burned-out Bosses," *Fortune,* July 25, 1994, pp. 44–52.
4. "A New Way to Count the Unemployed," *U.S. News & World Report,* February 14, 1994, p. 6.
5. Vivian Brownstein, "New Threats to the Expansion," *Fortune,* July 25, 1994, pp. 56–64.
6. Thomas Stewart, "Welcome to the Revolution," *Fortune,* December 13, 1993, pp. 66–77.
7. Neil Gross, with John Carey and Joseph Weber, "Who Says Science Has to Pay off Fast?" *Business Week,* March 21, 1994, pp. 110–111.
8. Stratford Sherman, "Are You as Good as the Best in the World?" *Fortune,* December 13, 1993, pp. 95–96.
9. John Carey, with David Woodruff and Peter Coy, "Where's the Juice?" *Business Week,* May 30, 1994, p. 110; and David Woodruff, with Larry Armstrong and John Carey, "Electric Cars," *Business Week,* May 30, 1994, pp. 104–114.
10. Stewart, "Welcome to the Revolution"; and Sherman, "Are You as Good as the Best in the World?"
11. Sherman, "Are You as Good as the Best in the World?"
12. Brian Dumaine, "The Trouble with Teams," *Fortune,* September 5, 1994, pp. 86–92.
13. Stewart, "Welcome to the Revolution."
14. Gross, "Who Says Science Has to Pay off Fast?"
15. Alex Taylor III, "The Auto Industry Meets the New Economy," *Fortune,* September 5, 1994, pp. 52–60.
16. Gross, "Who Says Science Has to Pay off Fast?"

Chapter 3

1. John Stedman, "Baltimore Helps Solidify Smith's U.S. Game Plan," *The Evening Sun,* November 14, 1994, pp. 1c, 5c; Ron Donoho, "A Horse with No Name," *Sales & Marketing Management,* November 1994, p. 16; Randall Lane, "The Market Clears," *Forbes,* October 24, 1994, pp. 228–230; William C. Symonds, "Is the NFL Hearing Footsteps?" *Business Week,* February 14, 1994, p. 71; Richard Hoffer, "South of the Border," *Sports Illustrated,* July 12, 1993, pp. 38–41; and Pat Huckey, "Canadian Players Will Lose CFL Jobs," *The Gazette* (Montreal), January 14, 1993, p. A12.
2. Laura Loro, "PSE&G's TradeLink Assists Companies with Exporting," *Philadelphia Business Journal,* June 24, 1994, p. B3; and "U.S. Sees 20% Increase in Exports by Year 2000," *Atlanta Journal and Constitution,* October 6, 1994, p. E28.
3. James C. Cooper and Kathleen Madigan, "World Growth Is Revving Up the U.S. Export Engine," *Business Week,* September 5, 1994, pp. 23–24; and Richard Lacayo, "America's New Competitive Muscle," *Time,* November 29, 1993, p. 28.
4. Patrick J. Welch and Gerry F. Welch, *Economics: Theory and Practice,* 5th ed. (Fort Worth, Tex.: Dryden Press, 1995), p. 632.
5. Susan Greco, ed., "Hands On: Sales & Marketing," *Inc.,* March 1994, p. 134.
6. Michael R. Czinkota, Ilkka A. Ronkainen, and John T. Tarrant, *The World Marketing Imperative* (Lincolnwood, Ill.: NTC Business Books, 1995), p. 10.
7. Subrata Chakravarty, "For Want of a Lever," *Forbes,* February 14, 1994, p. 18.
8. Amy Borrus and Joyce Barnathan with Bruce Einhorn and Stewart Toy, "China's Gates Swing Open," *Business Week,* June 13, 1994, pp. 52–53.

9. "United States World's Top Debtor Last Year," *Mobile Register,* June 29, 1994, p. 3E.
10. Jolie Solomon, "Mickey's Trip to Trouble," *Newsweek,* February 14, 1994, p. 34.
11. Peter Engardio and Bruce Einhorn, "Rising from the Ashes," *Business Week,* May 23, 1994, pp. 44–46; and Joyce Barnathan, Alex McKinnon, and Doug Harbrecht, "Restitution, Vietnam," *Business Week,* February 14, 1994, pp. 26–27.
12. Michael R. Czinkota and Ilkka Ronkainen, *International Marketing,* 4th ed. (Fort Worth, Tex.: Dryden Press, 1995), pp. 588–590.
13. Ibid., p. 117.
14. "President Signs GATT Legislation—Called Landmark Victory for Free Trade," *DeLoitte & Touche Review,* December 12, 1994, pp. 1–2; Michael Duffy, "Trickery Wins over Trade," *Time,* October 17, 1994, pp. 34–36; Kenneth T. Walsh, David Hage, and Fred Coleman, "Will Politics Still Trip Up World Trade?" *U.S. News & World Report,* September 26, 1994, p. 73; Howard Banks, "Zero-Sum Thinking on GATT," *Forbes,* June 20, 1994, p. 35; Louis S. Richman, "What's Next after GATT's Victory?" *Fortune,* January 10, 1994, pp. 66–70; and Douglas Harbrecht, "GATT: It's Yesterday's Agreement," *Business Week,* December 27, 1993, p. 36.
15. Geoffrey Brewer, "American Businesses Bank On," *Sales & Marketing Management,* April 1994, p. 15.
16. Borrus and Barnathan, "China's Gates Swing Open"; and Richman, "What's Next after GATT's Victory?" p. 66.
17. Richman, "What's Next after GATT's Victory?" p. 66; and "Ahead: A Southbound NAFTA," *U.S. News & World Report,* December 19, 1994, p. 10.
18. Dan McGraw, "Big Business Comes to the Border," *U.S. News & World Report,* October 10, 1994, p. 100; and Mark Memmott, "Exports to Mexico Soar after NAFTA," *USA Today,* May 25, 1994, p. B1.
19. "Leaders of Americas Vow Trade Act by 2005," *Northwest Arkansas Times,* December 11, 1994, p. A7; and "Ahead: A Southbound NAFTA," p. 10.
20. Art Weinstein, "A Primer for Global Marketers," *Marketing News,* June 20, 1994, pp. 4–5; and Allyson Stewart, "Europeans Embrace Tastes of Ethnic Food," *Marketing News,* January 17, 1994, p. 10.
21. Jerry Flint, "One World, One Ford," *Forbes,* June 20, 1994, pp. 40–41.
22. Lacayo, "America's New Competitive Muscle."
23. "Wal-Mart Takes a Few on the Chin," *Northwest Arkansas Times,* April 15, 1994, p. A7; and "Burger Embarrassment," *USA Today,* June 8, 1994, p. 8B.
24. "Ball Teams Interested in Mexico, but Confused," *Northwest Arkansas Times,* March 6, 1994, p. A7.
25. "Starch Wars," *Newsweek,* March 7, 1994, p. 6.
26. Cyndee Miller, "China Emerges as Latest Battleground for Marketing Researchers," *Marketing News,* February 14, 1994, pp. 1–2.
27. "South Africa: Now a Place to Do Business," *U.S. News & World Report,* June 20, 1994, p. 20.

Chapter 4

1. Lisa Gubernick, "Retreat from Victory," *Forbes,* October 24, 1994, p. 14; Lisa Gubernick, "The Third Battle of Bull Run," *Forbes,* October 17, 1994, pp. 67–74; Sallie Hofmeister, "Disney Will Seek a Different Site for Theme Park," *New York Times,* September 30, 1994, pp. A1, A8; and "Virginia's New Battle: Historians vs. Disney," *U.S. News & World Report,* May 23, 1994.
2. Charles Watson, "Managing with Social Integrity: Social Responsibilities of Business as Seen by America's CEOs," *Business Horizons,* July–August 1991, pp. 99–109.
3. Lynn Sharp Paine, "Managing for Organizational Integrity," *Harvard Business Review,* March–April 1994, pp. 106–117.
4. Anastasia Toufexis, "Know What You Eat," *Time,* May 9, 1994, p. 68.
5. Paine, "Managing for Organizational Integrity."
6. Robert McGarvey, "Do the Right Thing," *Entrepreneur,* April 1994, pp. 64–67.
7. Paine, "Managing for Organizational Integrity."
8. Ibid.
9. Joseph Pereira, "Split Personality," *The Wall Street Journal,* May 28, 1993, pp. A1, A4.
10. "Du Pont under Fire," *Chemical Marketing Reporter,* December 21, 1992, p. 7.
11. Geoffrey Smith and Ron Stodghill II, "Are Good Causes Good Marketing?" *Business Week,* March 21, 1994, pp. 64–66.
12. Alicia Mundy, "Blowing Smoke," *ADWEEK Eastern Edition,* April 11, 1994, p. 24.
13. B.E. Pruit & June J. Stein, Health Styles: Decisions for Living Well (Philadelphia: Saunders College Publishing, 1994), pp. 175–182, 20–207.
14. Ibid., pp. 369–371.
15. Ibid., pp. 499–509.
16. Ibid., pp. 514–515.
17. James Jackson, " 'World-Class Litterbugs,' " *Time,* October 18, 1993, p. 80.
18. David Woodruff with Larry Armstrong and John Carey, "Electric Cars," *Business Week,* May 30, 1994, pp. 104–114; David Woodruff with Gail DeGeorge and Gregory Sandler, "The Not-So-Big Wheels Leading the Charge," *Business Week,* May 30, 1994, p. 114.
19. Humphrey Taylor, "N.O.D. Survey of Americans with Disabilities," *Business Week,* May 30, 1994, Special Advertising Section; and "Marriott International," *Business Week,* May 30, 1994, Special Advertising Section.
20. Margie Markarian, "Cultural Evolution," *Sales & Marketing Management,* May 1994, pp. 127–129.
21. Richard Turner, "Disney Hopes Retreat Is Better Part of Public Relations," *The Wall Street Journal,* September 30, 1994, p. B4.
22. Roberta Maynard, "Meet the New Law on Family Leave," *Nation's Business,* April 1993, p. 48.
23. Markarian, "Cultural Evolution."
24. Margaret Jacobs, "Men's Club," *The Wall Street Journal,* June 9, 1994, pp. A1, A8; and Anne Fisher, "Sexual Harassment: What to Do," *Fortune,* August 23, 1993, pp. 84–88.
25. James Aley, "The Pay Gap Narrows, but . . . ," *Fortune,* September 19, 1994, p. 32.
26. Emily MacFarquhar, "The War against Women," *U.S. News & World Report,* March 28, 1994, pp. 42–48.
27. Margaret Jacobs, "Irate Investors Keep Sharp Eye on Attorneys in Smith Barney Suit," *The Wall Street Journal,* September 30, 1994, p. B8.
28. Markarian, "Cultural Evolution."
29. Richard Klonowski, "Foundational Considerations in the Corporate Social Responsibility Debate," *Business Horizons*, July–August 1991, p. 9.

Chapter 5

1. Carla Rapoport, "Nestlé's Brand Building Machine," *Fortune*, September 19, 1994, pp. 147–156.
2. Frank Swertlow, "Money Newsline: A Lesson for You from Burt's Woes," *Money*, Forecast 1995, p. 16.
3. Laura Saunders, "S, C, or Me?" *Forbes*, December 5, 1994, p. 168.
4. "Alternatives for Organizing a New Business," *Deloitte & Touche Review*, May 2, 1994, pp. 7–8.
5. Ibid.
6. Ibid.; and William McCullough, "Limited-Liability Companies," *Business Times*, October 25, 1993, p. 5.
7. Brigid McMenamin, "Help Wanted," *Forbes*, November 2, 1993, p. 186.
8. Judith Dobrzynski, "At GM, a Magna Carta for Directors," *Business Week*, April 4, 1994, p. 37; and Justin Martin, "Directors' Feet to the Fire," *Fortune*, November 29, 1993, p. 10.
9. "Large Wave," *The Wall Street Journal*, August 4, 1994, pp. A1, A4.

10. Anita Sharpe, "This Mr. Fixit Aims to Turn a Mishmash into an Empire," *The Wall Street Journal*, September 8, 1994, pp. B1, B12.
11. "Large Wave."
12. Elyse Tanouye and Greg Steinmetz, "Growth Initiative," *The Wall Street Journal*, August 5, 1994, pp. A1, A10.
13. Del Jones, "Employees Call Shots in Friendly Skies," *USA Today,* July 13, 1994, pp. B1, B2.
14. Del Jones and Julie Schmit, "UAL Plan May Put Industry in New Hands," *USA Today*, December 20, 1993, pp. 1B, 2B.
15. "Where Russia and China Meet," *The Economist*, September 3, 1994, p. 20.
16. "Cooperation in Italian Olive Oil Sector," *Agra Europe*, August 12, 1994, p. N4.

Chapter 6

1. Joel Millman, "From Dakar to Detroit," *Forbes,* September 26, 1994, pp. 86–90; Bernard Drum, "Privatization in Africa," *Columbia Journal of World Business,* Spring 1993, p. 144; and Philip Michelini, "Economic Expansion Spurs a Demand for U.S. Goods," *Business America,* April 6, 1992, p. 40.
2. Brian O'Reilly, "The New Face of Small Business," *Fortune,* May 2, 1994, pp. 82–88.
3. George Gendron, "FYI: Start-Up Fact and Fiction," *Inc.,* October 1994, p. 11.
4. O'Reilly, "The New Face of Small Business."
5. Richard Daft, *Management,* 3d ed. (Fort Worth, Tex.: Dryden Press, 1994), pp. 769–770.
6. Stephanie Mehta, "Working at Home," *The Wall Street Journal,* October 14, 1994, pp. R19, R26.
7. Anne Murphy, "13th Annual *Inc.* 500: A Do-It-Yourself Guide," *Inc. 500 1994*, pp. 17–18.
8. Marianne Sullivan, Administrative Director, Center for Entrepreneurial Leadership, telephone interview, June 1, 1995.
9. Daft, *Management,* pp. 758–761.
10. O'Reilly, "The New Face of Small Business."
11. *Statistical Abstract of the United States: 1994,* 114th ed., Washington, D.C., 1994, p. 549.
12. O'Reilly, "The New Face of Small Business."
13. Martha Mangelsdorf, "Growth in a Declining Market," *Inc. 500 1994*, annual supplement, p. 101.
14. Gene Bylinsky, "Genetics: The Money Rush Is on," *Fortune,* May 30, 1994, pp. 94–108.
15. Rob Norton, "Strategies for the New Export Boom," *Fortune,* August 22, 1994, pp. 124–130.
16. Rahul Jacob, "India Gets Moving," *Fortune,* September 5, 1994, pp. 100–104.
17. Brent Bowers, "No Child's Play," *The Wall Street Journal,* October 14, 1994, p. R18.
18. Jeanne Sadler, "Home Economics 101," *The Wall Street Journal,* October 14, 1994, p. R12.
19. Bowers, "No Child's Play."
20. Mehta, "Working at Home."
21. Udayan Gupta, "Pay As You Go," *The Wall Street Journal,* October 13, 1994, p. R15.
22. Paul Reynolds, "What We Don't Know May Hurt Us," *Inc.,* September 1994, pp. 25–26.
23. "The State of Woman-Owned Start-Ups," *Inc.,* November 1993, p. 34.
24. Michael Cronin, "How to Start an *Inc.* 500 Company: How Much Experience in the Industry Do You Need?" *Inc. 500 1994*, pp. 57–60.
25. "The State of Woman-Owned Start-Ups."
26. Carolyn Brown, "More than Just Window Dressing?" *Black Enterprise,* September 1994, pp. 103–112.
27. "The State of Woman-Owned Start-Ups."
28. Brian Dumaine, "America's Smart Young Entrepreneurs," *Fortune,* March 21, 1994, pp. 34–48.
29. Michael Selz and Udayan Gupta, "Lending Woes Stunt Growth of Small Firms," *The Wall Street Journal,* November 16, 1994, pp. B1, B2.
30. Gupta, "Pay As You Go."
31. Leslie Brokaw, "Minding the Store," *Inc.,* November 1993, pp. 66–75.
32. Peter Henrys, "Look before You Leap," *Business Victoria,* August 1993, p. 5.
33. Brown, "More than Just Window Dressing?"
34. Ibid.
35. Brokaw, "Minding the Store."
36. Brown, "More than Just Window Dressing?"
37. Selz and Gupta, "Lending Woes Stunt Growth of Small Firms."
38. Michael Czinkota and Ilkka Ronkainen, *International Marketing,* 4th ed. (Fort Worth, Tex.: Dryden Press, 1995), pp. 373–378.
39. Henrys, "Look before You Leap."
40. William Echikson, "Young Americans Go Abroad to Strike It Rich," *Fortune,* October 17, 1994, pp. 185–194.
41. Czinkota and Ronkainen, *International Marketing,* p. 386.
42. O'Reilly, "The New Face of Small Business."
43. Richard M. Hodgetts and Donald F. Kuratko, *Effective Small Business Management,* 5th ed. (Fort Worth, Tex.: Dryden Press, 1995), pp. 158–243.
44. PGA of America, *"All about Golf," A Research Study Profiling the Golfer as a Consumer* (Slazenger Panther Press, 1994).

Chapter 7

1. Paul Wiseman and Micheline Maynard, "AT&T Wins Quality Awards," *USA Today*, October 19, 1994, pp. B1, B2; and David Greising, "Quality: How to Make It Pay," *Business Week*, August 8, 1994, pp. 54–59.
2. Douglas MacDonald, "A Conversation with Dr. Val Feigenbaum," *Tenneco Symposium*, Summer 1992, pp. 20–24.
3. Rahul Jacob, "TQM: More than a Dying Fad?" *Fortune,* October 18, 1993, p. 66.
4. Greising, "Quality: How to Make It Pay."
5. Louis Kraar, "Korea Goes for Quality," *Fortune*, April 18, 1994, p. 153; and Stratford Sherman, "Are You as Good as the Best in the World?" *Fortune*, December 13, 1993, pp. 95–96.
6. William Keenan, Jr., "Making the Grade," *Sales & Marketing Management*, March 1994, p. 70.
7. Sherman, "Are You as Good?"
8. Leslie Brokaw, "ISO 9000: Making the Grade," *Inc.*, June 1993, pp. 98–99.
9. Jerry G. Bowles, "Quality '92: Leading the World-Class Company," *Fortune,* Special Supplement, September 21, 1992.
10. Kraar, "Korea Goes for Quality."
11. Brokaw, "ISO 9000."
12. Colleen Barrett, "Coworkers Are Customers, Too," *Sales & Marketing Management*, July 1994, pp. 31–32.
13. William Marbach, "Quality: What Motivates American Workers?" *Business Week*, April 12, 1993, p. 93; and John Waggoner, "AT&T Card Aimed High from Start," *USA Today*, October 15, 1992, pp. B1, B2.
14. Keenan, "Making the Grade."
15. Michael Clements, "Granite Rock: Concrete Improvement," *USA Today*, October 15, 1992, p. B6.
16. "L. L. Summertime," *L. L. Bean 1994 Catalog*, p. 3; Mark Henricks, "Satisfaction Guaranteed," *Entrepreneur*, March 1993, pp. 48–51; and Julie Schmit, "Heavens to Betsy: Now Fliers Can Fax," *USA Today*, May 12, 1993, p. B1.
17. John W. Verity, "The Gold Mine of Data in Customer Service," *Business Week*, March 21, 1994, pp. 113–114.
18. Mark Lewyn, "Teaching Computers to Tell a *G* from a *C,*" *Business Week*, December 7, 1992, pp. 118–119.
19. Verity, "Gold Mine of Data."

20. Stephanie Barlow, "Voice of Reason," *Entrepreneur*, March 1993, p. 52.
21. Rahul Jacob, "TQM: More than a Fad?"
22. Louis E. Boone, *Quotable Business* (New York: Random House, 1992), p. 113.
23. Louis E. Boone and Dianne Wilkins, "The Role of Benchmarking in Total Quality Management," *International Journal of Management*, March 1995, pp. 123–131; Richard Gibson, "Pillsbury's Telephones Ring with Peeves, Praise," *The Wall Street Journal*, April 20, 1994, pp. B1, B8; and Carl Quintanilla and Richard Gibson, "'Do Call Us': More Companies Install 1–800 Phone Lines," *The Wall Street Journal*, April 20, 1994, pp. B1, B8.
24. Julie Schmit, "Ritz-Carlton: Room for Employees," *USA Today*, October 14, 1992, p. B6.
25. Cyndee Miller, "TQM Out; Continuous Process Improvement In," *Marketing News*, May 9, 1994, pp. 5, 20.
26. Pamela Sebastian, "Pleasing Hospital Patients Can Pay Off," *The Wall Street Journal*, May 13, 1993, pp. B1, B6.
27. Richard L. Daft, *Management* (Fort Worth, Tex.: Dryden Press, 1994), p. 636.
28. Michael Hammer, "Reengineering Work: Don't Automate, Obliterate," *Harvard Business Review*, July–August 1990, pp. 104–112.
29. Lynn Coleman, "Total Quality Management Prescribed as Cure for Health Care Ailments," *Marketing News*, May 11, 1992, pp. 5, 8.
30. Rahul Jacob, "TQM: More than a Fad?"
31. Jeff Dewar, "Is 99.9% Good Enough?" *The Competitive Advantage*, (1990), p. 6.
32. Susanne Hatherley, "Benchmarking for the Best Reasons," *Business Victoria*, April 1994, p. 12. See also Neela Banejee, "Firms Analyze Rivals to Help Fix Themselves," *The Wall Street Journal*, May 3, 1994, p. B1.
33. Louis E. Boone and Dianne Wilkins, "Benchmarking at Xerox: A Case Study," *Proceedings of the Academy of Business Administration London International Conference*, June 1994, pp. 569–574.
34. Boone and Wilkins, "Role of Benchmarking."
35. Waggoner, "AT&T Card Aimed High."
36. William Keenan, Jr., "Training for Quality," *Sales & Marketing Management*, March 1994, p. 69.
37. Rahul Jacob, "TQM: More than a Fad?"

Chapter 8

1. "Pact: Sega and Catapult for XBAND," *HFD—The Weekly Home Furnishings Newspaper,* September 12, 1994, p. 8; Cyndee Miller, "Sega vs. Nintendo," *Marketing News,* August 29, 1994, p. 1; Tim O'Brien, "Sega's New Joypolis Expands on High-Tech Theme Park Concept," *Amusement Business,* August 1, 1994, p. 3; and "Sega! It's Blasting beyond Games and Racing to Build a High-Tech Entertainment Empire," *Business Week,* February 21, 1994, pp. 66–72.
2. Kenneth Labich, "Why Companies Fail," *Fortune,* November 14, 1994, pp. 52–68.
3. Louis E. Boone, *Quotable Business* (New York: Random House, 1992), p. 146.
4. Robert Langreth, "Gates & McCaw Propose Launching 840 Satellites," *Popular Science,* July 1994, p. 32; and Mark Lewyn, "He's No Mere Satellite-Gazer," *Business Week,* April 4, 1994, p. 39.
5. Sharon Nelson, "Put Your Purpose in Writing," *Nation's Business,* February 1994, pp. 61–64.
6. Matt Rothman, "Into the Black," *Inc.,* January 1993, pp. 59–65.
7. Stephen R. Grossman, "Why TQM Doesn't Work," *Industry Week,* January 3, 1994, pp. 57, 62.
8. "At L. L. Bean, Quality Starts with People," *Personnel Journal,* January 1994, p. 60.
9. Wilton Woods, "Playing to Thin," *Fortune,* September 5, 1994, p. 107.
10. Marvin W. Tucker and David A. Favis, "Key Ingredients for Successful Implementation of Just-in-Time: A System for All Business Sizes," *Business Horizons,* May–June 1993, pp. 59–65.
11. Bart Ziegler, "Video Conference Calls Change Business," *The Wall Street Journal,* October 12, 1994, pp. B1, B8.
12. Bill Saporito, "And the Winner Is Still . . . Wal-Mart," *Fortune,* May 2, 1994, pp. 62–70.
13. Andy Cohen, "Business Not in the Cards," *Sales & Marketing Management,* November 1994, p. 15.
14. Jim Carlton and Stephen Kreider Yoder, "Humble Pie: Intel to Replace Its Pentium Chip," *The Wall Street Journal,* December 21, 1994, p. B1.
15. Richard Brandt, "Bill Gates's Vision," *Business Week,* June 27, 1994, pp. 56–62.
16. Alan Deutschman, "The Managing Wisdom of High-Tech Superstars," *Fortune,* October 17, 1994, pp. 197–206.
17. John Huey, "The New Post-Heroic Leadership," *Fortune,* February 21, 1994, pp. 42–50.
18. Ibid.
19. "Survey: Boss Reason Most Seek New Jobs," *Mobile Register,* January 2, 1994, p. 7B.
20. Brian Dumaine, "Mr. Learning Organization," *Fortune,* October 17, 1994, p. 147.
21. Brandt, "Bill Gates's Vision"; and Richard Brandt, Julia Flynn, and Amy Cortese, "Microsoft Hits the Gas," *Business Week,* March 21, 1994, pp. 34–35.
22. Richard Daft, *Management,* (Fort Worth: Dryden Press, 1994), pp. 78–100.
23. Brian O'Reilly, "The New Face of Small Business," *Fortune,* May 2, 1994, pp. 82–88.
24. Ibid.

Chapter 9

1. Alan Deutschman, "How H-P Continues to Grow and Grow," *Fortune,* May 18, 1994, pp. 1B, 2B.
2. Lee Smith, "Burned-Out Bosses," *Fortune,* July 25, 1994, pp. 44–52.
3. Brian Dumaine, "Cool Cures for Burnout," *Fortune,* June 20, 1988, pp. 78–84.
4. Brian O'Reilly, "The New Face of Small Business," *Fortune,* May 2, 1994, pp. 82–88.
5. Thomas Stewart, "How to Lead a Revolution," *Fortune,* November 28, 1994, pp. 48–61.
6. Rochelle Sharpe, "Labor Letter: Potty Power," *The Wall Street Journal,* September 13, 1994, p. A1.
7. Wade Lambert, "Have You Ever? New EEOC Guidelines for Job Interviewing Baffle Employers," *The Wall Street Journal,* July 15, 1994, pp. B1, B6; and "How to Comply with the ADA," *Inc.,* August 1994, p. 104.
8. Daniel Benjamin and Tony Horwitz, "German View: You Americans Work Too Hard—and for What?" *The Wall Street Journal,* July 14, 1994, pp. B1, B6.
9. Noel Tichy, "Revolutionize Your Company," *Fortune,* December 13, 1993, pp. 114–118.
10. Toni Mack, "VPs of Planning Need Not Apply," *Forbes,* October 24, 1993, pp. 84–85.
11. Lesley Alderman, "Smart Ways to Maximize Your Company Benefits," *Money,* November 1994, pp. 183–196.
12. Benjamin and Horwitz, "German View"; and "France, Germany Serious about Four-Day Workweek," *Mobile Register,* October 28, 1993, p. 10B.
13. Aaron Bernstein, "Why America Needs Unions but Not the Kind It Has Now," *Business Week,* May 23, 1994, pp. 70–82.
14. Brian Dumaine, "The Trouble with Teams," *Fortune,* September 5, 1994, pp. 86–92.
15. Karen Peterson, "Job Stress, Satisfaction Can Co-Exist," *USA Today,* July 6, 1994, p. D1.
16. Brian O'Reilly, "The New Deal," *Fortune,* June 13, 1994, pp. 44–52.
17. Sue Shellenbarger, "Firms Make the Most of Flexible Scheduling," *The Wall Street Journal,* April 12, 1994, p. B1.

18. Sue Shellenbarger, "Some Thrive, but Many Wilt Working at Home," *The Wall Street Journal,* December 14, 1993, pp. B1, B10.
19. O'Reilly, "New Deal."
20. "Downsizing Often Costly Cut," *Mobile Register,* July 10, 1994, pp. 1F, 2F.
21. Ronald Henkoff, "Getting beyond Downsizing," *Fortune,* January 10, 1994, pp. 58–64.
22. Joann Lublin, "Don't Stop Cutting Staff, Study Suggests," *The Wall Street Journal,* September 27, 1994, p. B1.
23. John A. Byrne, "There Is an Upside to Downsizing," *Business Week,* May 9, 1994, p. 69; and Henkoff, "Getting beyond Downsizing."
24. "Downsizing Often Costly Cut."
25. Lublin, "Don't Stop Cutting. "
26. Henkoff, "Getting beyond Downsizing."
27. Ibid.
28. Richard Knee, "Fujitsu Uses UPS as Hub in Europe," *American Shipper,* December 1993, p. 40.
29. "Services Most Often Outsourced," *Entrepreneur,* May 1994, p. 12.
30. Mark Henricks, "Inside Job," *Entrepreneur,* July 1994, pp. 48–51.
31. Lourdes Lee Valeriano, "Executives Find They're Always on Call as Computer, Fax Supersede Time Zones," *The Wall Street Journal,* August 8, 1991, pp. B1, B3.
32. Walter Kiechel III, "Overscheduled, and Not Loving It," *Fortune,* April 8, 1991, pp. 105–107.
33. O'Reilly, "New Deal."
34. Diane Crispell, "People Patterns: Hispanic Households Outpace White and Black," *The Wall Street Journal,* October 21, 1994, p. B1.
35. May Lord, "Making a Difference and Money, Too," *U.S. News & World Report,* October 31, 1994, pp. 103–105.
36. Rochelle Sharpe, "The Waiting Game," *The Wall Street Journal,* March 29, 1994, pp. A1, A10.
37. Ibid.
38. Faye Rice, "How to Make Diversity Pay," *Fortune,* August 8, 1994, pp. 78–86.
39. Asra Nomani, "Black, Hispanic Women Assert Bias at Work," *The Wall Street Journal,* October 17, 1994, p. B7.
40. Ibid.
41. Michael Mandel, "The New World of Work," *Business Week,* October 17, 1994, p. 85.
42. Robert L. Rose, "Boom Times for Temporary Help Aren't Temporary, Experts Agree," *The Wall Street Journal,* October 25, 1994, p. A1.
43. Mandel, "New World."
44. Ibid.
45. Sue Shellenbarger, "Geriatric Cases," *The Wall Street Journal,* February 16, 1994, pp. A1, A6.
46. Crispell, "People Patterns."
47. Leon Wynter, "Business & Race: Discrimination Follows an Internal Script," *The Wall Street Journal,* October 19, 1994, p. B1.
48. Rice, "Make Diversity Pay."

Chapter 10

1. Brian Dumaine, "Payoff from the New Management," *Fortune,* December 19, 1993, pp. 103–111.
2. James Treece, "Improving the Soul of an Old Machine," *Business Week,* October 25, 1993, pp. 134–136.
3. John A. Byrne, "The Horizontal Corporation," *Business Week,* December 20, 1993, pp. 78–79.
4. Richard Daft, *Management,* 3d ed. (Fort Worth, Tex.: Dryden Press, 1994), pp. 584–591.
5. Brian Dumaine, "The Trouble with Teams," *Fortune,* September 5, 1994, pp. 86–92.
6. William Cook, "The End of the Plain Plane," *U.S. News & World Report,* April 11, 1994, pp. 43–46; and "What Now, Engineer?" *Flight Engineer,* April 20, 1994, p. 3.
7. Alan Farnham, "America's Most Admired Company," *Fortune,* February 7, 1994, pp. 50–54.
8. Daft, *Management,* pp. 591–594.
9. Faye Rice, "How to Make Diversity Pay," *Fortune,* August 8, 1994, pp. 78–86.
10. Ibid.
11. Dumaine, "Payoff from the New Management."
12. Dawn Baskerville, "Why Business Loves Workteams," *Black Enterprise,* April 1993, pp. 85–90.
13. Ibid.
14 Daft, *Management,* pp. 594–596.
15. David Woodruff, "Saturn: Labor's Love Lost?" *Business Week,* February 8, 1993, pp. 122–124.
16. Ibid.
17. Dumaine, "Payoff from the New Management."
18. Ibid.
19. For examples of well-written letters, see Jerry Fisher, "Letter Perfect," *Entrepreneur,* July 1994, pp. 214–216.
20. Philip Elmer-Dewitt, "Bards of the Internet," *Time,* July 4, 1994, pp. 66–67.
21. Andrew Serwer, "Lessons from America's Fastest-Growing Companies," *Fortune,* August 8, 1994, pp. 42–60.
22. See also Ginger Trumfio, "More than Words," *Sales & Marketing Management,* April 1994, p. 55.
23. Louis E. Boone and David L. Kurtz, *Contemporary Business Communication* (Englewood Cliffs, N.J.: Prentice-Hall, 1994), p. 611.
24. Kevin Salwen, "Workplace Friction," *The Wall Street Journal,* July 27, 1993, pp. A1, A7.
25. "The World According to Andy Grove," *Business Week Supplement, The Information Revolution 1994,* pp. 76–78. See also Ginger Trumfio, "The Case for E-Mail," *Sales & Marketing Management,* July 1994, pp. 94–98; and Cheryl J. Goldberg, "Mail Call," *Entrepreneur,* August 1994, pp. 36–39.
26. Suzy Parker, "E-Mail Explosion," *USA Today,* July 19, 1994, p. B1.
27. Serwer, "Lessons from Companies."
28. Daft, *Management,* pp. 568–570.
29. Dumaine, "Payoff from the New Management."
30. Thayer Taylor, "Seeing Is Believing," *Sales & Marketing Management,* March 1994, pp. 47–48.
31. Jack Russell, "U.S. Fast-Food Giants in Japan Slice Prices," *Advertising Age,* June 13, 1994, p. 64.
32. Robert Mamis, "Desk-to-Desk Show-and-Tell," *Inc.,* July 1994, p. 100.
33. Michael Christie, "Slips of the Tongue Result in Classic Marketing Errors," *Advertising Age International,* June 20, 1994, p. 15.
34. Rahul Jacob, "America's Best?" *Fortune,* February 7, 1994, p. 54.
35. "The Infobog, by the Numbers," *Fortune,* July 11, 1994, p. 62.
36. Thomas Stewart, "Managing in a Wired Company," *Fortune,* July 11, 1994, pp. 44–56.
37. Jonathan Berry, "What Is an Ad in the Interactive Future?" *Business Week,* May 2, 1994, p. 103; and Kathy Rebello, "Digital Pioneers," *Business Week,* May 2, 1994, pp. 96–103.
38. John W. Verity and Robert D. Hof, "The Internet: How It Will Change the Way You Do Business," *Business Week,* November 14, 1994, pp. 80–87; and Vic Sussman, "The Internet Will Gain Popularity, Problems," *U.S. News & World Report,* January 2, 1995, p. 76.

Chapter 11

1. "Back in Gear," *Forbes*, August 1, 1994, p. 12; Marjorie Sorge, "Toledo Jeep Enters a New Age," *Ward's Auto World*, October 1993, p. 59; Marjorie Sorge, "We're All Together," *Ward's Auto World*, March 1992, p. 48; and Graham Button, "The Toledo Tale," *Forbes*, September 28, 1992, p. 14.
2. David Hage, "Unions Feel the Heat," *U.S. News & World Report*, January 24, 1994, pp. 57–61.

3. Aaron Bernstein, "Why America Needs Unions but Not the Kind It Has Now," *Business Week*, May 23, 1994, pp. 70–82.
4. Robert Rose, "Unions Hit Corporate-Campaign Trail," *The Wall Street Journal*, March 8, 1993, pp. B1, B2.
5. Robert Rose and Alex Kotlowitz, "Back to Bickering," *The Wall Street Journal*, November 23, 1993, pp. A1, A8.
6. Robert Frank, "Driving Harder," *The Wall Street Journal*, May 23, 1994, pp. A1, A8; Carolyn Hirschman, "Injury Rates at UPS Bring U.S. Citation," *Business First-Columbus*, February 28, 1994, p. 1; "UPS Uses Cellular to Deliver Real-Time Tracking Applications," *Mobile Phone News*, May 2, 1994, p. 3; and Richard Knee, "Fujitsu Uses UPS as Hub in Europe," *American Shipper*, December 1993, p. 40.
7. Gail Schares, "Germany's Mighty Unions Are Being Forced to Bend," *Business Week*, May 1, 1993, p. 52.
8. John Helyar, "Why Can't Athletes and Owners Learn to Play Nice Together?" *The Wall Street Journal*, September 6, 1994, pp. B1, B4; and John Helyar, "Hand in Glove," *The Wall Street Journal*, August 10, 1994, pp. A1, A6.
9. Frank, "Driving Harder"; Hirschman, "Injury Rates at UPS"; "UPS Uses Cellular"; and Knee, "Fujitsu Uses UPS."
10. Hage, "Unions Feel the Heat."
11. Bernstein, "Why America Needs Unions."
12. Thomas Kirkpatrick and Chad Lewis, *Effective Supervision* (Fort Worth, Tex.: Dryden Press, 1995), pp. 314–316.
13. Valerie Reitman and Jathon Sapsford, "Uncharted Course," *The Wall Street Journal*, August 9, 1994, pp. A1, A8.
14. Kenneth Chilton, "Lincoln Electric's Incentive System," *Compensation and Benefits Review*, November–December 1993, p. 21.
15. Richard Daft, *Management*, 3d ed. (Forth Worth, Tex.: Dryden Press, 1994), pp. 537–538.
16. Susan Chandler, "High Spirits, Heavy Weather," *Business Week*, June 13, 1994, pp. 80–82.
17. Bernstein, "Why America Needs Unions"; and Kevin Salwen, "What, Us Worry? Big Unions' Leaders Overlook Bad News, Opt for Status Quo," *The Wall Street Journal*, October 5, 1993, p. B1.
18. "Unions Lose Power, Respect in Argentina," *Mobile Press Register*, March 23, 1994, p. 2E; and Hage, "Unions Feel the Heat."
19. Hage, "Unions Feel the Heat."

Chapter 12

1. Louis Kraar, "Your Next PC Could Be Made in Taiwan," *Fortune*, August 8, 1994, pp. 90–96; Charlene Huang, "Acer Aims at Latin American PC Market," *Electronics*, July 25, 1994, p. 14; "Inside the Box: Taiwan's Computer Industry," *The Economist*, July 9, 1994, p. 65; and Catherine Greenman, "Acer Tackles Ease-of-Use Issue," *HFD—The Weekly Home Furnishings Newspaper*, September 26, 1994, p. 100.
2. Jeffery Rubin, "Industrial Flea Market," *Time*, January 24, 1994, p. 24.
3. Robert Rose, "Plowing Ahead," *The Wall Street Journal*, October 4, 1994, p. A1, A12.
4. David Hage and Linda Grant, "How to Make America Work," *U.S. News & World Report*, December 6, 1993, pp. 48–54.
5. Alex Taylor III, "New Ideas from Europe's Automakers," *Fortune*, December 12, 1994, pp. 159–172.
6. Hage and Grant, "How to Make America Work."
7. Taylor, "New Ideas from Europe's Automakers."
8. Jerry Flint, "The New Zeitgeist at Daimler-Benz," *Forbes*, December 6, 1993, pp. 44–45; and Michael McCarthy, "Unlikely Sites," *The Wall Street Journal*, May 4, 1993, pp. A1, A12.
9. Howard Gleckman. "The Technology Payoff," *Business Week*, June 14, 1993, pp. 57–68.
10. Shawn Tully, "You'll Never Guess Who Really Makes . . ." *Fortune*, October 3, 1994, p. 125.
11. Taylor, "New Ideas from Europe's Automakers."
12. Suzanne Oliver, "Cut Costs, Add a Middleman," *Forbes*, April 25, 1994, p. 135.
13. Ibid.
14. Gleckman, "A Tonic for the Business Cycle," *Business Week*, April 4, 1994, p. 57.
15. James Woolsey, "777," *Air Transport World*, April 1994, p. 23.
16. Robert Rose, "Humming Mills," *The Wall Street Journal*, January 3, 1994, pp. A1, A38.

Chapter 13

1. Laura Koss, "Today's Guests Want Specialized In-Room Amenities," *Hotel & Motel Management*, February 22, 1994, supplement; and Nancy Arnott, "Saved by the Bellman?" *Sales & Marketing Management*, December 1993, pp. 68–73.
2. *1952 Annual Report*, General Electric, p. 21.
3. David Greising, "Quality: How to Make It Pay," *Business Week*, August 8, 1994, pp. 54–59.
4. Marj Charlier, "First Principles: Ailing College Treats Student as Customer, and Soon Is Thriving," *The Wall Street Journal*, July 17, 1991, pp. A1, A10.
5. "They Understand Your Kids," *Fortune*, Autumn/Winter 1993, pp. 29–30.
6. Andrew Tanzer, "All the Music without the Trimming," *Forbes*, February 14, 1994, pp. 43–44.
7. Eileen Fitzpatrick, "Dino-Size Promos for 'Park,'" *Billboard*, June 4, 1994, pp. 1, 134; Marcy Magiera, "Promotional Marketer of the Year," *Advertising Age*, March 21, 1994, pp. S-1, S-8; and Kate Fitzgerald and Marcy Magiera, "'Jurassic Pr.' Blitz: It's (Pre)Historic!" *Advertising Age*, May 17, 1993, pp. 1, 46.
8. Tara Parker-Pope, "Will the British Warm Up to Iced Tea? Some Big Marketers Are Counting on It," *The Wall Street Journal*, August 22, 1994, p. B1.
9. Seth Lubove, "The Last Bastion," *Forbes*, February 14, 1994, pp. 56–58.
10. Linda Himelstein, "Intangible, Yes. Untaxable, No," *Business Week*, March 28, 1994, pp. 34, 36.
11. William M. Bulkeley, "Marketers Mine Their Corporate Databases," *The Wall Street Journal*, June 14, 1993, p. B4.
12. Norton Paley, "Cut Out for Success," *Sales & Marketing Management*, pp. 43–44.
13. Thomas W. Osborne, "An American Mosaic," *Marketing Insights*, June 1989, p. 79.
14. Paley, "Cut Out for Success."
15. Ibid.
16. Michael J. McDermott, "Marketers Pay Attention! Ethnics Comprise 25% of the U.S.," *Brandweek*, July 18, 1994, pp. 26–27; Karen Benezra, "Tactics May Not Translate but Strategies Often Do," *Brandweek*, July 18, 1994, pp. 28–29; and "Surveys Point to Group Differences," *Brandweek*, July 18, 1994, pp. 32–33.
17. Martha Farnsworth Riche, "Psychographics for the 1990s," *American Demographics*, July 1989, pp. 24–26, 30–31, 53–54.
18. Paley, "Cut Out for Success."
19. Rahul Jacob, "Why Some Customers Are More Equal than Others," *Fortune*, September 19, 1994, pp. 215–224.
20. Jacob, "Some Customers More Equal."
21. Michael Slezak, "The Ethnic Makeup Grows," *Supermarket News*, May 2, 1994, pp. 149, 180.
22. Stan Rapp and Thomas L. Collins, *Beyond MaxiMarketing* (New York: McGraw-Hill, 1994); excerpted in "Nestlé Banks on Databases," *Advertising Age*, October 25, 1993, pp. 16, S-7, S-10.
23. Jacob, "Some Customers More Equal."
24. Ibid.
25. Ibid.
26. Ibid.
27. Dom Del Prete, "Latin America Is a Marketer's Dream Come True," *Marketing News*, October 10, 1994, pp. 7–8; and Tim Triplett, "Middle-

Class Mexicans Share Traits with U.S. Counterparts," *Marketing News,* October 10, 1994, p. 8.
28. "Don't Gouge the Customer," *Fortune,* Autumn/Winter 1993, p. 29.
29. Jaffrey D. Zbar, "Blockbuster Database to Fuel Future Expansion," *Advertising Age,* July 18, 1994, p. 26.
30. Keith J. Kelly, "Don't Bank on Classic Image," *Advertising Age,* June 6, 1994, p. 51.
31. Michael Meyer and Dody Tsiantar, "Ninja Turtles, Eat Our Dust," *Newsweek,* August 8, 1994, pp. 34–35.

Chapter 14

1. Tim Triplett, "Cereal Makers Await Reaction to General Mills' Coupon Decision," *Marketing News,* November 7, 1994, p. 1; and Kathleen Deveny and Richard Gibson, "Awash in Coupons? Some Firms Try to Stem the Tide," *The Wall Street Journal,* May 10, 1994, p. B1.
2. *Consumer Reports,* October 1994, p. 644.
3. "Indiana U. Alums Rest Easy," *The Chronicle of Higher Education,* March 30, 1994, p. A6.
4. *1993 Annual Report,* Philip Morris.
5. Nancy Haas, "More Fattening! Tastes Great!" *Newsweek,* February 28, 1994, p. 69.
6. Joshua Levine, "Why 'New' is Old Hat," *Forbes,* July 22, 1991, pp. 302–304.
7. John R. Hayes, "The Spamburger Man," *Forbes,* November 8, 1993, p. 34.
8. Julie Liesse, "Frosted Mini-Wheats: Ad Proposition Powers Success," *Advertising Age,* October 3, 1994, p. S13.
9. Pam Weisz, "Betting the Mint," *Brandweek,* July 18, 1994, p. 1.
10. Julie Liesse, "Lunch Bucket: Hot Category Melts Down into Price Wars," *Advertising Age,* October 3, 1994, p. S2.
11. Pam Weisz, "HBA Companies Are Making Hay with a Little Horse Sense," *Brandweek,* May 16, 1994, p. 32.
12. Adrienne Ward, "Tums—Focus on Secondary Ingredient Pushes Growth," *Advertising Age,* October 3, 1994, p. S3.
13. "Firms Try to Improve Sales with Packaging," *Mobile Register,* July 19, 1994, p. 11B.
14. Weisz, "Betting the Mint."
15. "Attack of the Fighting Brands," *Business Week,* May 2, 1994, p. 125.
16. Ron Harris, "Avon Is Calling, and It's a Jungle out There," *Los Angeles Times,* August 29, 1994, p. A1.
17. *1993 Annual Report,* Black and Decker.
18. Dean Faust, "Does Pepsi Have Too Many Products?" *Business Week,* February 14, 1994, p. 64.
19. Mark Robichaux, "Satellite Dishes Shrink; Cable Starts to Sweat," *The Wall Street Journal,* October 20, 1994, p. B1.
20. Telephone interview with Kathy Jones, administrative assistant, Spectrum Control Inc., October 1991.
21. Telephone Interview with Mary Beth Kraner, Campbell Soup Company, June 2, 1995. Bill Saporito, "Campbell Soup Gets Piping Hot," *Fortune,* September 9, 1991, pp. 142–148.
22. Tim Price, "Giving Customers the Wheel Drives Products and Profits," *Brandweek,* May 23, 1994, p. 20.
23. *1993 Annual Report,* Quaker Oats and Greg W. Prince, "Quaker Getting Up and Going in the Morning," *Beverage World,* January 1995, p. 36.
24. Louis E. Boone and David L. Kurtz, *Contemporary Marketing,* 8th ed. (Fort Worth, Tex.: Dryden Press, 1995), pp. 406–407.
25. Stuart Elliot, "In an Age of Retailing Overkill, New Products Are Fewer and More Focused on Finding Customers," *The Wall Street Journal,* December 30, 1993, p. D16.
26. Elaine Underwood, "Proper ID," *Brandweek,* August 8, 1994, p. 28.
27. Laurel Wentz, "Private Labels on March in Europe Too," *Advertising Age,* May 9, 1994, p. 53.
28. Kellie Krumplitsch, "At Perrier, Focus Is on the Bottle," *Brandweek,* April 25, 1994, p. 20.
29. Adrienne Ward, "Goldschlager: 'Snow Dome' Bottle Turns Golden for Trendy Schnapps," *Advertising Age,* October 3, 1994, p. S15.
30. Michael Czinkota and Ilkka Ronkainen, *International Marketing,* 3rd ed. (Fort Worth, Tex.: Dryden Press, 1994), pp. 273–274, 433–437, 462.
31. Denise Gellene, "Some Foods Give New Label Law the Slip," *Los Angeles Times,* May 6, 1994, p. D3.
32. Czinkota and Ronkainen, *International Marketing,* p. 462.
33. Clifford J. Levy, "A Product Code Leaves the Straight and Narrow," *New York Times,* November 16, 1993, p. D4.
34. Jeanne Whalen, "Chase & Sanborn: Lower Prices Give Buzz to Longtime Coffee Brand," *Advertising Age,* October 3, 1994, p. S15.
35. Gale Eisenstock, "Bullies on the Farm," *Forbes,* July 22, 1991, pp. 84–85.
36. Thomas S. Mulligan, "Room at the Inns," *Los Angeles Times,* June 18, 1994, p. D1.
37. Larry Armstrong, "New from Nissan: Reverse Sticker Shock," *Business Week,* May 23, 1994, p. 27.
38. Michael Parrish, "Thinking Cheaper on Electric Cars," *Los Angeles Times,* June 28, 1994, p. D1.
39. Telephone interview with Buz Fairchild, account executive with Dr. Cookie, Bothell, Washington, October 31, 1991.

Chapter 15

1. Matthew Schifrin, "Middleman's Dilemma," *Forbes,* May 23, 1994, p. 67; and Kathleen Morris, "Beyond Jurassic Park," *Financial World,* June 22, 1993, p. 28.
2. *1993 Annual Report,* Sysco Corp.
3. Jaikumar Vijayan, "Dell Foresakes Retail for Direct Approach," *Computerworld,* July 18, 1994, p. 32.
4. Stephen A. W. Drew and Peter A. C. Smith, "The New Logistics Management: Transportation Organization Learning," *Logistics Information Management* Vol 8(1), 1995, pp. 24–33.
5. Patricia Apodaca, "Speedo Dives into an Ocean of Athleticwear," *Los Angeles Times,* March 15, 1994, p. D2.
6. Schifrin, "Middleman's Dilemma."
7. James M. Clash, "Beer Bash," *Forbes,* December 5, 1994, p. 66.
8. Jeffrey D. Zbar, "Speed and Ease Drive Store of the Future," *Advertising Age,* May 2, 1994, p. S12.
9. Thayer C. Taylor, "Road Warrior: Information-Based Selling," *Sales & Marketing Management,* December 1994, p. 38.
10. Ralph T. King, Jr., "Fritz to Acquire Intertrans Corp. for $210 Million," *The Wall Street Journal,* February 15, 1995, B4 col. 6.
11. Gary McWilliams, "Why NEC Has U.S. Companies 'Shaking in Their Boots,' " *Business Week,* March 26, 1990, pp. 90–92.
12. *McKesson Today: 1993 Annual Report,* McKesson Corp.
13. Valerie Reitman, "Manufacturers Start to Spurn Big Discounters," *The Wall Street Journal,* November 30, 1993, p. B1.
14. Snap-On Tools Corporation, *Annual Report,* December 31, 1990.
15. Telephone interview with Brenda Hayes, Heming Company, June 2, 1995.
16. Telephone interview with Laura Castellano, communications specialist, Global Communications Avon, June 2, 1995. Also "Perfuming the Amazon," *The Economist,* October 22, 1994, p. 74.
17. Thomas McCarroll, "Attention TV Shoppers . . . ," *Time,* July 26, 1993, p. 55.
18. Telephone interview with Audrey Gerber, director of marketing, The Nature Company, June 5, 1995.
19. Mary Hance, "Nashville Challenge: Dollar General Takes Leap of Faith in Low-Income Neighborhood," *Stores,* January 1994, p. 49.
20. Chris Woodyard, "Weeding Out the Frills in the Flower Biz," *Los Angeles Times,* January 9, 1995, p. D2.
21. Darwin Porter, *Frommer's London '95* (New York: Macmillan Travel, 1994), pp. 225–226.
22. Cyndee Miller, "Rediscovering the Inner City," *Marketing News,* January 17, 1994, p. 1.

23. *Forbes,* June 6, 1994, p. 9.
24. Telephone interview with Yolanda Garcia, sales, Fifth Avenue Department Stores, June 2, 1995.
25. Telephone interview with Rita Eisenberg, divisional vice president, Fashion-Special Events & Public Relations, John Wanamaker department store, June 2, 1995.
26. Ronald Henkoff, "Delivering the Goods," *Fortune,* November 28, 1994, p. 64.
27. "Flagship Express Service Launches Nightly Air Freighter Service," *PR Newswire,* June 13, 1991.
28. U.S. Bureau of the Census, *Statistical Abstract of the United States: 1994,* 114th ed. (Washington, D.C.: U.S. Government Printing Office, 1994), p. 622.
29. "Shaw's Supermarkets Ordering Up Products by Computer," *Promo/ Progressive Grocer Special Report,* July 1994, p. S13.
30. Henkoff, "Delivering the Goods."
31. Telephone interview with Joseph Kusso, butcher, Balducci's, New York City, June 2, 1995.

Chapter 16

1. Adrienne Ward Fawcett, "Interactive Awareness Growing," *Advertising Age,* October 3, 1994, p. S1; G. Pascal Zachary, "Advertisers Anticipate Interactive Media as Ingenious Means to Court Consumers," *The Wall Street Journal,* August 17, 1994, p. B1; Debra Aho, "Winn-Dixie, Eckerd Go Interactive," *Advertising Age,* April 18, 1994, p. 16; and Debra Aho, "Ford Hits Canada's Interactive Road," *Advertising Age,* April 18, 1994, p. 18.
2. Leah Rickard, "Growth Spurt for Baby Food," *Advertising Age,* August 1, 1994, p. 26.
3. Julie Liesse, "Ralston Thinks Younger for Chex," *Advertising Age,* January 9, 1995, p. 12.
4. Ira Teinowitz and Nan O'Neal, "Philip Morris? Call Him Dave," *Advertising Age,* November 28, 1994, p. 5.
5. Telephone interview with Don Quinn, lease manager and business manager, Lexus of St. Louis, September 5, 1991.
6. Kate Fitzgerald, "In Live for Integrated Hall of Fame," *Advertising Age,* November 8, 1993, p. S12.
7. U.S. Bureau of the Census, *Statistical Abstract of the United States: 1994,* 114th ed. (Washington, D.C.: U.S. Government Printing Office, 1994), p. 408.
8. Gary H. Anthes, "Customer 'Data Mining' Pays Off," *Computerworld,* May 15, 1995, p. 1, 28. Vol. 29, No. 20.
9. Terry Brennan, personal interview, January 15, 1995.
10. "Here's the Drill," Up Front section, *Business Week,* May 1, 1995, p. 8.
11. Ken Hassen, personal interview, January 10, 1995.
12. Terry Brennan, personal interview, January 15, 1995.
13. Reprinted from Louis E. Boone and David L. Kurtz, *Contemporary Marketing,* 8th ed. (Fort Worth, Tex.: Dryden Press, 1995), p. 654.
14. Telephone interview with Bryan Michael, service relations manager, Pontiac Buick GM, May 24, 1995.
15. Howard Scott, "How to Handle Smaller Accounts," *Nation's Business,* September 1994, p. 48R.
16. "Top Global Markets," *Advertising Age,* March 21, 1994, p. I-11; and Todd Pruzah, "Top Multi-National Marketers—Ad Leader Unilever Sees P&G Close in," *Advertising Age,* December 13, 1993, p. 1.
17. David R. Olmos, "Release of New Pain Reliever Spurs Analgesics Marketing War," *Los Angeles Times,* June 17, 1994, p. D1.
18. Christopher Knowlton, "Europe Cooks Up a Cereal Brawl," *Fortune,* June 3, 1991, pp. 175–178.
19. Leah Rickard, "New Ammo for Comparative Ads," *Advertising Age,* February 14, 1994, p. 26.
20. *Statistical Abstract: 1994,* p. 580.
21. Don Steinberg, "Billboard Ad Company Uses Demographic Software: Integrated Mapping Application Helps Firm Understand Market, Compete for Dollars," *Info World,* March 7, 1994, p. 52.
22. Alexei Barrionuevo, "Fast Track to Revenue," *Los Angeles Times,* March 24, 1993, p. D1; and Adam Bryant, "Advertising," *New York Times,* March 5, 1993, p. D16.
23. Kathy Haley, "Infomercials Lure More Top Marketers," *Advertising Age,* May 9, 1994, p. IN-2.
24. *Statistical Abstract: 1994,* p. 580.
25. William Spain, "Blimps No Longer Just Flights of Fancy," *Advertising Age,* August 1, 1994, p. 27.
26. Ronald Grover, "Big Brother Is Grocery Shopping with You," *Business Week,* March 29, 1993, p. 60.
27. Joseph Conlin, "Beyond the Booth," *Sales & Marketing Management,* November 1994, p. 109.
28. Meg Whittemore, "Trade Shows' Direct Appeal," *Nation's Business,* August 1993, p. 48.
29. Kate Fitzgerald, "Sunday Morning in a Bag," *Advertising Age,* June 6, 1994, p. 30.
30. Mark Robichaux, "Device that Delivers Discount Coupons via TV Screen Is Set by Acu-Trac, Cox," *The Wall Street Journal,* October 4, 1994, p. B9.
31. "Hot Premium Promotions Seven Sure Winners," *PROMO,* May 1994, p. 27.
32. Kellie Krumplitsch, "Promotion Explosion: The Reggie Awards," *Brandweek,* April 4, 1994, p. 29.
33. Current promotional program in local school.
34. This rule is noted in Harold C. Cash and W. J. E. Crissy, "The Salesman's Role in Marketing," *Psychology of Marketing,* vol. 12, Personnel Development Associates.
35. John Evan Frook, "Business-to-business online," Electronic Commerce: Case Studies, *Interactive Age,* March 27, 1995, pp. 19, 23.
36. Kate Fitzgerald, "V.R. Troopers Cast as Hot Holiday Toys," *Advertising Age,* October 3, 1994, p. 3.
37. Michael R. Czinkota and Ilkka A. Ronkainen, *International Marketing,* 4th ed. (Forth Worth, Tex.: Dryden Press, 1995), pp. 128–151.

Chapter 17

1. Voorhees quotations from Jeffrey Young, "Jewel of the Rockies," *Forbes ASAP,* December 5, 1994, pp. 23–24.
2. Jim Bessen, "Riding the Marketing Information Wave," *Harvard Business Review,* September–October 1993, pp. 150–160; and Michael P. Cronin, "Choosing Job-Description Software," *Inc.,* February 1993, p. 30.
3. John F. Dickerson and David S. Jackson, "Hooked Up to the Max," *Time,* September 26, 1994, pp. 58–60.
4. Paul M. Eng, "It's Getting Crowded On Line," *Business Week,* November 7, 1994, pp. 134–136.
5. Lucy Howard and Ned Zeman, "Computerland," *Newsweek,* April 8, 1991.
6. "Top Retail Software," *PC Magazine,* January 11, 1994, p. 31.
7. "Mainframe Comeback?" *Forbes ASAP,* October 1993, pp. 64–73; see also "IBM: There's Many a Slip . . ." *Business Week,* June 27, 1994, pp. 26–27.
8. Keven Maney, "The Home PC Explosion," *USA Today,* January 25, 1995, pp. B1, B2.
9. Kyle Pope, "Changing Work Habits Fuel Popularity of Notebooks," *The Wall Street Journal,* November 11, 1993, pp. B1, B10.
10. Walter S. Mossberg, "Computer Notebooks Get Smaller, Lighter, and Costlier," *The Wall Street Journal,* February 2, 1994, p. B1; Bill Howard, "You'll Love PCMCIA . . . Eventually," *PC Magazine,* November 23, 1993, p. 105; and John R. Quain, "HP's OmniBook: The Ultimate Subnotebook?" *PC Magazine,* July 1993, p. 37.
11. Zachary Schiller and Wendy Zellner, "Making the Middleman an Endangered Species," *Business Week,* June 6, 1994, pp. 114–115.
12. " 'Highway' Paves Path to Information Overload," *Mobile Register,* June 6, 1993, pp. F1, F5; and "How Video on Demand Will Work," *U.S. News & World Report,* December 6, 1993, p. 66.

13. Louis E. Boone and David L. Kurtz, *Management,* 4th ed. (New York: McGraw-Hill, 1992), pp. 504–506.
14. William J. Cook, "Serving Up a New Era in Computing," *U.S. News & World Report,* October 17, 1994, pp. 62–72.
15. John W. Verity, "Truck Lanes for the Info Highway," *Business Week,* April 18, 1994, pp. 112–114; Amy Cortese and Richard Brandt, "Microsoft's Network Wares Still Aren't Connected," *Business Week,* June 27, 1994, pp. 60–61; see also Bart Ziegler, "Building the Highway: New Obstacles, New Solutions," *The Wall Street Journal,* May 18, 1994, pp. B1, B3.
16. Michael J. Miller, "Networked PCs: Nothing Personal?" *PC Magazine,* January 11, 1994, pp. 77–78.
17. Peter Nulty, "When to Murder Your Mainframe," *Fortune,* November 1, 1993, pp. 109–120.
18. Michael S. Malone, "Smart Vineyard," *Forbes ASAP,* October 1993, pp. 31–33.
19. Alison L. Sprout, "Using a PC to Be a Better Boss," *Fortune,* March 7, 1994, p. 107; and Jim Seymour, "Changing the Rules of the Game," *PC Magazine,* January 11, 1994, pp. 97–98.
20. Carol Levin, "Ready-to-Run Résumés, Expense Reports, Newsletters, Flyers," *PC Magazine,* July 1993, p. 71.
21. Donna Fenn, "Picture This," *Inc.,* February 1994, pp. 66–71.
22. Kevin Maney, "No E-Mail? Get with It!" *USA Today,* May 19, 1994, p. 2B.
23. Kenneth Laudon and Jane Laudon, *Business Information Systems,* 2d ed. (Fort Worth, Tex.: Dryden Press, 1993), pp. 241–242; and Owen Edwards, "The Grating Communicator," *Forbes ASAP,* October 25, 1993, pp. 160–161.
24. Paul Desmond, "Alamo Builds Networked Expert System to Set Rates," *Network World,* September 3, 1990, pp. 13–15.
25. Evan Schwartz and Keith Hammonds, "Your New Computer: The Telephone," *Business Week,* June 3, 1991, pp. 126–131; "Here's Looking at Voice Processing," *Network World,* June 17, 1991, pp. 1, 33–40; Chip Johnson, "Telephone Companies Hope Voice Mail Will Make Answering Machines Obsolete," *The Wall Street Journal,* July 23, 1992, pp. B1, B8; and Mary Kathleen Flynn, "Take a Letter, Computer," *PC Magazine,* July 1993, p. 29.
26. Gregg Keizer, "$99 Voice Assist Listens to You," *PC Magazine,* November 23, 1993, p. 48.
27. Timothy O'Brien, "A PC Revolution," *The Wall Street Journal,* October 8, 1993, pp. A1, A9.
28. Bruce Schwartz, "CD-ROMers: Plugged In or Unglued?" *USA Today,* November 14, 1994, pp. D1, D2.
29. Laudon and Laudon, *Business Information Systems,* pp. 131–133.
30. Don Boroughs, "Profits on a Platter," *U.S. News & World Report,* April 2, 1994, pp. 69–72; Schwartz, "CD-ROMers"; David Sullivan, *The New Computer User* (Fort Worth, Tex.: Dryden Press, 1994), pp. 60–70; and Evan Schwartz, "CD-ROM: A Mass Medium at Last," *Business Week,* July 19, 1993, pp. 82–83.
31. Don Clark, "Intel and CNN to Test New Technology to Bring Television to Networks of PCs," *The Wall Street Journal,* April 22, 1994, p. B4.
32. Sam Bradley, "Homes on the Info Highway," *Brandweek,* October 17, 1994, p. 20.
33. Stratford Sherman, "Will the Information Superhighway Be the Death of Retailing?" *Fortune,* April 18, 1994, pp. 98–108.
34. Sullivan, *New Computer User,* pp. 279–285; David Kirkpatrick, "Groupware Goes Boom," *Fortune,* December 27, 1993, pp. 99–106; and Mark Lewyn, "Lotus' Notes Get a Lot of Notice," *Business Week,* March 29, 1993, pp. 84–86.
35. James Aley, "How Not to Help High Tech," *Fortune,* May 16, 1994, pp. 100–101.
36. Laudon and Laudon, *Business Information Systems,* p. 576.
37. Sullivan, *New Computer User,* pp. 331–335.
38. Ronald Henkoff, "Keeping Motorola on a Roll," *Fortune,* April 18, 1994, pp. 67–78.

Chapter 18

1. Ford and Spielberg quotations from Randall Lane, "I Want Gross," *Forbes,* September 26, 1994, pp. 104, 108.
2. Marcia Berss, "Cash Flow Joe," *Forbes,* June 6, 1994, p. 47.
3. Janet Fix, "NationsBank Checks Employee Waste," *USA Today,* June 10, 1994, p. B4.
4. Zachary Schiller, "Goodrich: From Tires to PVC to Chemicals to Aerospace . . ." *Business Week,* July 18, 1994, pp. 86–87.
5. Kelley Holland, Larry Light, and Michele Galen, "Big Six Firms Are Firing Clients," *Business Week,* March 1, 1993, pp. 76–77.
6. Alexandra Ourusoff, "Brands: What's Hot, What's Not," *Financial World,* August 2, 1994, p. 44.
7. Seth Lubove, "Learning from Victoria's Secret," *Forbes,* December 19, 1994, p. 66.
8. William M. Stern, "Southern Fried Reading," *Forbes,* June 20, 1994, pp. 91–92.
9. "Morrisons Sells Institutional Food Division," *Mobile Register,* June 29, 1994, p. B1.
10. Axel L. Grabowsky, "What to Monitor to Stay in Control," *Inc. Magazine's Guide to Small Business Success* (New York: Inc., 1994).

Chapter 19

1. Black quotation from Michael Selz and Udayan Gupta, "Lending Woes Stunt Growth of Small Firms," *The Wall Street Journal,* November 15, 1994, p. A1.
2. Bruce J. Blechman, "Quick Change Artist," *Entrepreneur,* January 1994, pp. 18–21.
3. "Start-ups from Scratch," *Inc.,* September 1994, pp. 76, 77.
4. Monika Guttman, "Fishing for Financing," *U.S. News & World Report,* August 8, 1994, p. 48.
5. Jill Fraser, "Time to Hire a Controller," *Inc.,* May 1994, p. 153.
6. Monika Guttman, "High-Tech Counterfeiting," *U.S. News & World Report,* December 5, 1994, pp. 73–82.
7. "Strategy for Survival," *Time,* December 8, 1991, p. 36.
8. Edward O. Welles, "Bootstrapping for Billions," *Inc.,* September 1994, pp. 78–85.
9. Jill A. Fraser, "Better Returns on Spare Cash," *Inc.,* June 1994, p. 115.
10. John Rossant, "How Disney Snared a Princely Sum," *Business Week,* June 20, 1994, pp. 61–62.
11. Anne B. Fisher, "Raising Capital for a New Venture," *Fortune,* June 13, 1994, pp. 99–101.
12. Matthew Schifrin and Riva Atlas, "Hocus-Pocus," *Forbes,* March 14, 1994, pp. 81–83.
13. Ibid.; and "The Tightwads Are Running the Show Now," *Business Week,* November 4, 1991, p. 114.
14. Adi Ignatius and Neela Banerjee, "Russian Bankers Bring Tricks of the Trade Home after U.S. Visit," *The Wall Street Journal,* May 23, 1994, pp. A1, A10.
15. Margaret Mannix, "Paying the Price of ATM Convenience," *U.S. News & World Report,* July 5, 1993, p. 57; and "ATM Banking: New Prey for Thieves?" *Mobile Register,* June 6, 1993, p. 4F.
16. See Fred Bleakley, "Electronic Payments Now Supplant Checks at Most Large Firms," *The Wall Street Journal,* April 13, 1994, pp. A1, A5; and Thomas McCarroll, "No Checks. No Cash. No Fuss?" *Time,* May 9, 1994, pp. 60–61.
17. Gary Belsky, "Separating the Safe Federal Insurers from the Shaky Ones," *Money,* October 1991, pp. 29–30.
18. *The World Almanac and Book of Facts: 1994* (Mahwah, N.J.: Funk & Wagnalls, 1994), p. 110.
19. Terrence Pare, "GE Monkeys with Its Money Machine," *Fortune,* February 21, 1994, pp. 81–87; and Tim Smart, "GE's Money Machine," *Business Week,* March 8, 1993, pp. 62–67.
20. Beth Belton and Desiree French, "Higher Rates Sideline Some Home Buyers," *USA Today,* June 1, 1994, p. B1.

21. William Meyers et al., "Friendly Fire from the Fed," *U.S. News & World Report,* May 30, 1994, pp. 46–47.
22. Owen Ullman and Dean Foust, "Inside the Fed," *Business Week,* May 2, 1994, pp. 24–27; and Martin Crutsinger, "Interest Rates to Go up Again," *Mobile Register,* May 17, 1994, p. A1.
23. Ullman and Foust, "Inside the Fed"; Pare, "GE Monkeys with Machine"; Smart, "GE's Money Machine"; and William Baumol and Alan Blinder, *Economics,* 6th ed. (Fort Worth, Tex.: Dryden Press, 1994), pp. 926–946.

Chapter 20

1. Poe quotations from Gayle Sata Stodder, "Sole Survivor," *Entrepreneur,* October 1994, pp. 112–117; Mark Maremont and Nanette Byrnes, "Ryka looks like It's on Its Last Legs," *Business Week,* May 15, 1995, p. 48; and Mark Maremont, "Social Conscience for Sale?" *Business Week,* March 20, 1995, p. 38.
2. Antony J. Michels, "The New Appeal of Convertibles," *Fortune,* June 13, 1994, p. 32.
3. Ibid.
4. Rob Norton, "Who Owns This Company, Anyhow?" *Fortune,* July 29, 1991, pp. 131–142.
5. Jeffrey Laderman with Geoffrey Smith, "The Power of Mutual Funds," *Business Week,* January 18, 1993, pp. 62–68.
6. *NYSE Fact Book* (New York: New York Stock Exchange, April 1993), p. 2.
7. Laderman with Smith, "Power of Mutual Funds."
8. *NYSE Fact Book,* p. 8; and Gary Slutsker, "If You Can't Beat 'Em." *Forbes,* January 6, 1992, p. 48.
9. Slutsker, "If You Can't Beat 'Em."
10. Steve Zwick, "GLOBEX Wins, Loses a Few," *Futures: Magazine of Commodities & Options,* May 1993, p. 12.
11. Eric D. Randall, "Scrutinizing NASDAQ," *USA Today,* November 21, 1994, p. 4B.
12. "Advantage Lombard," *The Wall Street Journal,* April 12, 1994, p. C5.
13. Daniel Strachman, "NationsBank's Trading Software Slashes Compliance Costs," *American Banker,* March 28, 1994, p. A4.
14. David Nusbaum, "An Automated Argument," *Futures: Magazine of Commodities & Options,* February 1994, p. 52; and George Anders and Craig Torres, "The New Market," *The Wall Street Journal,* August 28, 1991, pp. A1, A10.
15. Nusbaum, "Automated Argument"; and Slutsker, "If You Can't Beat 'Em."
16. Slutsker, "If You Can't Beat 'Em."
17. Gary Weiss, "What to Do about the Dow," *Business Week,* February 22, 1993, pp. 82–83.
18. Garrison Wells, "Buy, Buy, Hold," *Denver Business Journal,* March 18, 1994, p. 12C.
19. Amy Barrett, "Insider Trading," *Business Week,* December 12, 1994, pp. 70–80.
20. "Washington Briefing," *Deloitte & Touche Review,* October 22, 1990, p. 1.
21. See Leah Nathans Spiro and Michael Schroeder, "Can You Trust Your Broker?" *Business Week,* February 20, 1995, pp. 70–76.
22. Brian Dumaine, "Investing for a New Future," *Fortune,* January 27, 1992, pp. 68–71; and Georgette Jasen and Earl Gottschalk, Jr., "Changing the Mix," *The Wall Street Journal,* February 5, 1992, pp. A1, A5.

Appendix A

1. William Bulkeley, "Replaced by Technology: Job Interviews," *The Wall Street Journal,* August 22, 1994, pp. B1, B4; "Dial a Job Interview," *Chain Store Age Executive with Shopping Center Age,* July 1994, p. 35; Carrie Goerne, "Software 'Interviewers' Screen Job Hopefuls," *Marketing News,* March 2, 1992, p. 14; and Stephen Piontek, " 'Intelligent' System Licks Agent Turnover Problem," *National Underwriter Life & Health—Financial Services Edition,* May 15, 1992, p. 4.
2. Louis Richman, "The New Work Force Builds Itself," *Fortune,* June 27, 1994, pp. 68–76.
3. "Americans' Changing Opportunities," *Money,* December 1993, p. 145.
4. Thomas Kirkpatrick and Chad Lewis, *Effective Supervision* (Fort Worth, Tex.: Dryden Press, 1995), pp. 395–398.
5. Amy Saltzman, "An Electronic Job Hunt," *U.S. News & World Report,* March 28, 1994, pp. 72–75; and Margaret Mannix, "Writing a Computer-Friendly Resume," *U.S. News & World Report,* October 26, 1992, pp. 90–93.
6. C.V.C., "Resumania," *Black Enterprise,* July 1994, p. 48.
7. Stratford Sherman, "Leaders Learn to Heed the Voice within," *Fortune,* August 22, 1994, pp. 92–100.
8. Caryne Browne, "Have I Got a Career for You," *Black Enterprise,* February 1993, pp. 145–152.
9. Richman, "New Work Force"; and Lee Smith, "Landing that First Real Job," *Fortune,* May 16, 1994, pp. 58–60.

Appendix B

1. Nanette Byrnes, "California Insurers Keep Feeling Aftershocks," *Business Week*, September 26, 1994, p. 110.
2. Charles Fenyvesi, "Capitalist Tool," *U.S. News & World Report*, September 12, 1994, p. 30.
3. *The World Almanac and Book of Facts, 1994* (Mahwah, N.J.: Funk & Wagnalls, 1994), pp. 962–963.
4. Linda Himelstein, "Jackpots from Alabama Juries," *Business Week*, November 28, 1994, pp. 83–84.
5. James Kim, "Intel Puts Chips on the Table," *USA Today*, December 21, 1994, pp. 1B, 2B.
6. Kevin Chappell, "Boss, I Feel Lousy. Where's My Check?" *U.S. News & World Report*, July 29, 1991, p. 25.
7. Mark D. Fefer, "Tailored Health Plans Take off," *Fortune*, June 27, 1994, p. 12.
8. Miles Benson, "Slipping down the Health Care Slope," *Mobile Register*, September 18, 1994, p. 1C.
9. Matt Walsh, "Why Ronald Vessey Threw in the Towel," *Forbes*, July 4, 1994, pp. 58–62.
10. Martin Anderson, "The Mystery of the 37 Million Americans without Insurance," *Mobile Register*, May 23, 1993, p. 7C.

Appendix C

1. Alexandra Peers, "Art World Shaken by Nations Seeking to Reclaim Items," *The Wall Street Journal,* June 21, 1994, pp. C1, C18.
2. Christopher Palmeri, "The Great Taco Caper," *Forbes,* December 6, 1993, pp. 106–109.
3. Reinhardt Krause and Carol Haber, "Court Boots TI/Cyrix Suit to Texas Turf," *Electronic News,* March 28, 1994, p. 1; "Delaware Chancery Court Is 'Key' to QVC's Chances of Buying Paramount," *Communications Daily,* November 12, 1993, p. 9; "Delaware Chancery Court," *The Oil and Gas Journal,* January 25, 1993, p. 50; and Michael Armstrong, "Small Wonder Delaware State Is Good Place to Incorporate," *Philadelphia Business Journal,* January 25, 1993, p. 4B.
4. Andy Pasztor, "A-12 Bomber Suit May Be Biggest Ever," *The Wall Street Journal,* July 27, 1994, p. B2.
5. John Allison and Robert A. Prentice, *Business Law: Text and Cases in the Legal Environment* (Fort Worth, Tex.: Dryden Press, 1994), p. 81.
6. Ibid., pp. 301–302.
7. Ibid., pp. 628–629.
8. Ibid., p. 160.
9. "Coffee Appeal," *USA Today,* October 14, 1994, p. 3A.
10. Allison and Prentice, *Business Law,* pp. 447–450.
11. Howard Banks, "Cleared for Take-Off," *Forbes,* September 12, 1994, pp. 116, 118, 122; Adam Bryant, "Aviation Bill Encourages Manufacturers," *New York Times,* September 4, 1994, p. 84; William Stern,"A Wing and a Prayer," *Forbes,* April 25, 1994, pp. 42–43; and Malcolm Forbes,

Jr., "Ending Airborne Ambulance Chasing," *Forbes,* March 14, 1994, p. 26.

12. See, for example, *The New Shorter Oxford English Dictionary,* 4th ed., ed. by Lesley Brown, vol. 1 (Oxford: Oxford University Press, 1993), p. 179.
13. Jonathan Foreman, "The Freedom to Fail," *Audacity,* Winter 1994, pp. 28–37.
14. Some of the information is from Michele Galen, "If Personal Bankruptcy Is Your Only Way Out," *Business Week,* January 21, 1991, pp. 90–91.
15. David Corder, "Harsh Medicine," *Kansas City Business Journal,* May 20, 1994, p. 16; and Rosalind Resnick, "The Deadbeat State," *Forbes,* July 8, 1991, p. 62.
16. Olaf de Senerpont Domis, "Hopes Are High for Bankruptcy Reform," *American Banker,* July 15, 1994, p. 2; Corder, "Harsh Medicine"; and Jim Wise, "Panel Approves Momentous Bankruptcy Code Changes," *Business Credit,* November–December 1993, p. 6.
17. Foreman, "Freedom to Fail."
18. Gerry Khermouch, "Nipping at Intel's Heels, Others Are in the Chips," *Brandweek,* June 6, 1994, pp. 20–22.
19. Marcus Brauchli, "Chinese Flagrantly Copy Trademarks of Foreigners," *The Wall Street Journal,* June 20, 1994, pp. B1, B5.
20. William Baumol and Alan Blinder, *Economics: Principles and Policy,* 6th ed. (Fort Worth, Tex.: Dryden Press 1994), pp. 496–498.
21. Tony Mauro, "Crash Settlements Could Be Staggering," *USA Today,* September 12, 1994, p. 3A.
22. Pasztor, "A-12 Bomber Suit."
23. "Special Article Reviews Results of Bankruptcy Law," *China Intelligence Report,* May 11, 1994.
24. Brauchli, "Chinese Copy Trademarks."

GLOSSARY

accounting Measuring, interpreting, and communicating financial information to support internal and external decision making.

accounting equation Basic accounting concept that assets equal liabilities plus owners' equity.

accounting process Method of converting information about individual transactions to financial statements.

acquisition Procedure in which one firm acquires the property and assumes the obligations of another.

Active Corps of Executives (ACE) SBA program in which volunteer consultants assist people in small business.

activity ratio Ratio that measures the effectiveness of the firm's use of its resources.

adaptive planning Focusing and building on the strengths of the company while remaining flexible to develop opportunities.

adjourning stage Point in team development focused on wrapping up and summarizing the experience and accomplishments of the group before it disbands.

advertising Nonpersonal sales presentations usually directed at large numbers of potential customers.

advocacy advertising Advertising that supports a specific viewpoint on a public issue and is designed to influence public opinion or the legislative process.

affirmative action program Program set up by a business firm to increase employment opportunities for women and minorities.

agency A legal relationship whereby one party, call a principal, appoints another party, call the agent, to enter into contracts with third parties in the principal's behalf.

agency shop Employment policy allowing workers to reject union membership, but requiring them to pay fees equal to union dues.

agents and brokers Independent wholesalers that never take title to the goods they distribute, but may or may not take possession of those goods.

alien corporation Corporation organized in one country that operates in another.

American Federation of Labor (AFL) National union made up of affiliated, individual craft unions.

antitrust laws Laws enacted to preserve the advantages of competition by prohibiting attempts to monopolize markets.

appellate court A process that allows a higher court to review the case and correct any lower-court error.

arbitration Process of bringing an impartial third party into a union-management dispute to render a legally binding decision.

assembly line Manufacturing technique that carries the product past several work stations where workers perform specialized tasks.

asset Anything of value owned or leased by a business.

atmospherics Physical characteristics and amenities that attract customers and help to satisfy their shopping needs.

audience Receiver of verbal, nonverbal, and written messages.

balance of payments Flow of money into and out of a country.

balance of trade Relationship between a country's exports and imports.

balance sheet Statement of a firm's financial position on a particular date.

bank examiner Trained financial analyst who inspects the records and management practices of federally insured financial institutions.

bankruptcy The legal nonpayment of financial obligations.

bargaining zone Range of collective bargaining that defines when a union will strike and when management will close the plant.

bear Investor who expects stock prices to decline along with a general market trend.

benchmarking Setting performance standards by continuously comparing and measuring one's own firm against business leaders.

board of directors Governing body of a corporation whose members are elected by the stockholders.

bond Certificate of indebtedness sold to raise long-term funds for a corporation or government agency.

bottom line Overall profit or loss earned by a firm.

boycott Attempt to keep people from purchasing goods or services from a company as part of a labor dispute.

brand Name, term, sign, symbol, or design that identifies the goods or services of a firm.

brand insistence Degree of brand acceptance at which the consumer will accept no substitute.

brand name Words or letters that identify a firm's offerings.

brand preference Degree of brand acceptance at which the consumer selects one brand over competing brands if the preferred brand is available.

brand recognition Degree of brand acceptance at which the consumer is aware of the brand.

breach of contract A violation of a valid contract.

breakeven analysis Method of determining the minimum sales volume needed at a certain price to cover all costs.

breakeven point Level of sales that will cover all of the company's costs, including both fixed and variable costs.

budget Planning and control tool that reflects expected sales revenues, operating expenses, and cash receipts and outlays.

bull Investor who expects stock prices to rise along with a general market trend.

business All profit-seeking activities and enterprises that provide goods and services that an economic system needs.

business ethics Standards of business conduct and moral values.

business goods Goods purchased for use directly or indirectly in the production of other products for resale. The five categories of business goods are installations, accessory equipment, component parts and materials, raw materials, and supplies.

business incubator Facility that houses start-up firms.

business law The aspects of law that most directly influence and regulate the management of various types of business activity.

business plan A written document that provides an orderly statement of a company's goals, how it intends to achieve its goals, and the standards by which it will measure achievements.

business product Good or service purchased as an input, either directly or indirectly, to production of other goods for resale.

buyer behavior Process by which consumers and business buyers make purchase decisions.

buyer's market Market situation characterized by adequate or even excess supplies.

capital Funds that finance the operations of a business.

capital item Long-lived product whose sales involve large sums of money.

capitalism Economic system founded on the principle that competition among businesses best serves society.

category killer A discount chain that sells only one category of products.

centralized network Communication by team members through a single person to solve problems or make decisions.

certified public accountant (CPA) Accountant who has met education and experience requirements and passed a comprehensive examination.

chain of command Set of relationships that indicates who gives direction to whom and who reports to whom.

channel Medium through which a message sender communicates with an audience.

channel captain Channel member that dominates the activities of a distribution channel.

chief information officer (CIO) Top-management executive responsible for directing a firm's management information system and related computer operations.

closed or closely held corporation A small, often family-owned, corporation with stock in the hands of a few stockholders who control and manage the firm's activities. Stock is generally not available to outsiders.

closed shop Illegal employment policy requiring a firm to hire only current union members.

collective bargaining Negotiation between management and union representatives concerning wages and working conditions.

commercial bank Profit-making business that holds deposits of individuals and other businesses in the form of checking or savings balances and uses these funds to make loans to individuals and businesses.

committee organization Structure in which groups of individuals jointly hold authority and responsibility.

common law The body of law arising out of judicial decisions related to the unwritten law the United States inherited from England.

common market Form of economic integration that maintains a customs union and seeks to bring all trade rules into agreement.

common stock Stock that gives its owners only residual claims to the firm's assets, along with voting rights in corporate decisions.

common stock Security providing owner voting rights but only a residual claim to company assets.

communication Meaningful exchanges of information through messages.

communism Economic theory, developed by Karl Marx, that eliminates private property and provides for common ownership of the means of production.

comparative advertising Persuasive advertising that features direct comparisons between competing goods or services.

competition Battle among businesses for consumer acceptance.

competitive differentiation Any aspect of a company or its performance that makes it more successful than its competitors.

computer Programmable electronic device that can store, retrieve, and process data.

computer network System in which interconnected computers can both function individually and communicate with each other.

computer-aided design (CAD) Interaction between a designer and a computer to conceive a product, facility, or part that meets predetermined specifications.

computer-aided manufacturing (CAM) Computer analysis of CAD output to determine necessary steps to implement the design and electronic transmission of instructions to production equipment to produce the part or product.

computer-integrated manufacturing (CIM) Production system in which computers help workers to design products, control machines, handle materials, and control the production function in an integrated fashion.

conflict Antagonistic interaction in which one party attempts to thwart the intentions or goals of another.

Congress of Industrial Organizations (CIO) National union made up of affiliated, individual industrial unions.

conservation Preservation of declining energy resources.

consumer behavior Buyer behavior of ultimate consumers.

consumer product Good or service purchased by the ultimate consumer for his or her own use.

consumerism Public demand for business to consider consumer wants and needs in making its decisions.

context Every factor that surrounds and affects transmission of a message.

contingency planning Planning to cover problems resulting from a crisis to enable the company to resume operations as quickly and smoothly as possible.

continuous process improvement Constantly studying and adjusting work activities to improve their quality, timeliness, efficiency, and effectiveness.

contract A legally enforceable agreement between two or more parties regarding a specified act of thing.

controlling Evaluating the organization's performance to determine whether it is accomplishing its objectives.

cooling-off period Government-enforced temporary suspension of a threatened strike.

cooperative Organization operated collectively by its owners.

cooperative advertising Sharing of local advertising costs between the manufacturer and the marketing intermediary.

copyright Exclusive rights to written material, either published or unpublished.

corporate culture Value system of an organization.

corporation Legal entity with authority to act and incur liability separate from its owners.

cost-of-living adjustment (COLA) clause Clause in a union contract that protects workers' real income by adjusting wages to reflect changes in the consumer price index; also called an escalator clause.

costs of quality Costs associated with poor quality, such as scrap, rework, and loss of customers.

countertrade International bartering agreement.

craft union Union that organizes skilled workers in a specific craft or trade.

creative selling Persuasive presentation to sell a product whose benefits are not readily apparent or whose purchase involves careful analysis of alternatives.

credit union Member-owned financial cooperative that pays interest to depositors, offers share draft (checking) accounts, and makes short-term loans and some home mortgage loans.

critical path Sequence of operations in a PERT diagram that requires the longest time for completion.

critical success factors Factors that a firm considers most important in gaining competitive advantage and achieving long-term success.

cross-functional team Group of employees from different departments who work on a specific project, such as developing a new product or solving a particular problem.

customer satisfaction Ability of a good or service to meet or exceed a customer's needs and expectations.

customer satisfaction Concept of a good or service pleasing buyers because it meets their emotional needs and quality expectations.

customer service Aspect of a competitive strategy that defines how a firm treats its customers.

customer service standards Specifications for the quality of service that a firm will provide for its customers.

customs union Form of economic integration in which member nations establish a free trade area and impose a uniform tariff structure for trade with nonmember nations.

cycle time Time required to complete a work process or activity.

damages Financial payments made for a loss and related suffering.

database Computer integrated collection of an organization's data resources.

debenture Bond backed only by the reputation of the issuer.

debt capital Funds obtained through borrowing.

decentralized network System in which team members communicate freely among themselves and arrive at decisions together.

decision making Recognizing a problem, identifying it, evaluating alternatives, selecting and implementing an alternative, and following up.

decision support system (DSS) Computer system that quickly provides relevant facts to aid business decision making.

decoding Audience's interpretation of a message.

delegation Act of assigning activities to subordinates.

demand Buyers' willingness and ability to purchase products.

demand curve Graph of the relationship between different prices and the quantity demanded at each price.

departmentalization Subdivision of work activities into units within the organization.

deregulation Elimination of legal restraints on competition.

desktop publishing Software designed to print attractively formatted documents with high-quality type, graphics, and layouts.

devaluation Reduction in value of a country's currency.

dispatching Phase of production control process in which managers instruct each department on what work to do and the time allowed for its completion.

displaced homemaker Homemaker who returns to school or takes a job because of divorce or widowhood or for economic reasons.

distribution channel Path through which goods and services, and title to them, flow from producer to consumer.

divestiture Selling off a corporation's divisions or units.

dividend Payment to stockholders from a corporation's profits.

domestic corporation Corporation that operates in the state in which it is incorporated.

Dow Jones averages Averages of stock market activity based on the market prices of 30 industrial, 20 transportation, and 15 utility stocks.

downsizing Management decision to eliminate layers from the management hierarchy in an effort to reduce costs and improve efficiency.

downward communication Communication from a sender who holds a senior position in an organization to an audience of subordinates.

drop shipper Limited-function merchant wholesaler that takes legal title to the goods it distributes, but never physically handles them.

dual role Role of team members who contribute to the team's task and support members' emotional needs at the same time.

dumping Selling goods abroad at prices lower than those charged in domestic markets.

ecology Study of the relationships between living things and their environments.

economics Social science of allocating scarce resources.

electronic funds transfer system (EFTS) Computerized method for making purchases and paying bills by electronically processing deposits or withdrawals of funds.

electronic mail (e-mail) System for sending and receiving written messages through computers.

embargo Ban on imports or exports of certain products.

emoticons Little faces, also called smileys, constructed with punctuation marks that convey some of a message's emotional content.

employee benefits Employee rewards such as pension plans, insurance, sick-leave pay, and tuition reimbursement that an organization gives, entirely or in part, at its own expense.

employee involvement Practices that motivate employees to perform their jobs better through empowerment, training, and teamwork.

employers' association Organization that encourages cooperative efforts by employers to present a united front in dealing with labor unions.

empowering Giving employees additional decision-making authority and responsibilities.

empowerment Practice of giving employees the authority to make decisions about their work without supervisory approval.

encoding Translation of a message into understandable terms and a form capable of being transmitted through the communication medium selected by the sender.

entrepreneur Risk taker in the private enterprise system.

entrepreneurship Taking risks to set up and operate a business.

entry-level job First permanent employment after leaving school.

environmental impact study Analysis of the impact of a proposed plant location on the quality of life in the surrounding area.

Equal Employment Opportunity Commission (EEOC) Federal commission created to increase job opportunities for women and minorities and to help eliminate job discrimination.

equilibrium price Price at which quantity supplied equals quantity demanded.

equity Claim against the assets of a business.

equity capital Funds provided by the firm's owners when they plow back earnings, liquidate assets, make additional contributions, issue stock to the general public, or raise contributions from venture capitalists.

exchange process Process by which two or more parties trade things of value so that each feels better off after the trade.

exchange rate Rate at which a country's currency can be exchanged for other currencies.

exclusive distribution Market coverage strategy that gives a retailer or wholesaler exclusive rights to sell products in a specific geographic area.

executive information system (EIS) User-friendly, decision-oriented computer system used by senior management.

expense item Inexpensive product, usually consumed within a year.

expert system Computer program that imitates human thinking through the use of "if . . . then" rules.

export management company Firm that performs international marketing services as a commissioned representative or distributor for other companies.

export trading company Trading firm involved in importing, exporting, countertrading, investing, and manufacturing.

exporting Selling domestic goods and services abroad.

external communication Meaningful exchange of information through messages between an organization and its major audiences.

external customer Person or organization that buys or uses another firm's good or service.

factors of production Basic inputs into the private enterprise system, including natural resources, human resources, capital, and entrepreneurship.

Fair Labor Standards Act (1938) Federal law that sets a minimum wage and maximum base work week for workers employed in industries engaged in interstate commerce.

family brand Brand name for several related products or an entire product mix.

family leave Giving employees leaves of absence from work in order to deal with family matters.

featherbedding Requirement to pay workers who do no work.

Federal Deposit Insurance Corporation (FDIC) Corporation that insures bank depositors' accounts up to a maximum of $100,000 and sets requirements for sound banking practices.

Federal Reserve System Network of 12 regional banks that regulates banking in the United States.

federation Association of numerous national and international unions to serve mediation and political functions.

feedback Message returned by the audience to the sender that may cause the sender to alter or cancel an original message.

finance Business function of planning, obtaining, and managing a company's use of funds in order to accomplish its objectives most effectively.

financial control Process that periodically checks actual revenues, costs, and expenses against forecasts.

financial manager Individual in an organization responsible for developing and implementing the firm's financial plan and for determining the most appropriate sources and uses of funds.

financial plan Document that specifies the funds a firm will need for a period of time, the timing of inflows and outflows, and the most appropriate sources and uses of funds.

fiscal policy Government actions to set levels of revenues and expenditures.

fixed cost Cost that remains stable regardless of the production level.

flexible benefit plan System of variable benefits that provides each employee with a specific dollar amount of benefits that the worker can allocate to selected areas of coverage.

flexible manufacturing system (FMS) Facility that allows production methods to be modified quickly when different products are manufactured.

flextime Scheduling system that allows employees to set work hours within constraints specified by the firm.

floating exchange rate Basis of international exchange rates, in which currency traders create a market for the world's currencies based on countries' relative trade and investment prospects.

follow-up Phase of production control process that spots production problems and informs managers of needed adjustments.

forecasting Estimation or prediction of a company's future sales or income over the short term, intermediate term, or long term.

foreign corporation Corporation that operates in a state other than the one in which it is incorporated.

foreign exchange market Market where traders exchange one nation's currency for that of another nation.

foreign production Making goods and supplying services in a foreign country for sale there or in other countries.

form utility Utility created by converting raw materials and other inputs into finished goods and services.

formal communication channel Path for messages that flow within the chain of command or task responsibility structure defined by an organization.

forming stage Orientation period of team development during which team members get to know each other and determine which behaviors the group finds acceptable.

franchisee Small business owner who contracts for the right to sell the goods or services of the supplier (franchisor) in exchange for some payment.

franchising Agreement that specifies the methods by which a dealer can produce and market a supplier's good or service.

franchisor Supplier of a franchise that provides various services in exchange for payments by the franchisee.

free trade area Form of economic integration in which participants agree to trade among themselves without tariffs or trade restrictions.

full-function merchant wholesaler Merchant wholesaler that performs many services in addition to taking legal title to goods it distributes.

General Agreement on Tariffs and Trade (GATT) International accord that has sponsored a series of negotiations on tariffs and trade restrictions.

generic product Nonbranded item with plain packaging and little or no advertising support.

giveback Wage or fringe benefit concession by union members to help an employer to remain competitive.

glass ceiling Invisible barrier that keeps women and minorities from advancing to top management.

global strategy Pursuing a standardized, worldwide product and marketing strategy.

government accountant Professional employed by a government agency or not-for-profit organization.

grapevine Internal channel that transmits information through unofficial, independent sources.

grievance Employee or union complaint that management is violating some provision of the union contract.

gross domestic product (GDP) Sum of all goods and services produced within a nation's boundaries.

groupware Computer software that combines and extends the concept of sharing information through a networked database with a method for moving data between users (e-mail).

hardware All tangible elements of a computer system.

health insurance Insurance that covers losses due to sickness or accidents.

health maintenance organization (HMO) Prepaid medical expense plan that provides a comprehensive set of health services and benefits to policyholders, who pay monthly fees.

high-context culture Communication based not only on the message itself, but also on everything that surrounds it.

home-based work Program in which employees work at home, sometimes linked to their employers by terminals that access central computers.

house brand *See* private brand.

human resource management Process of acquiring, training, developing, motivating, and appraising a sufficient quantity of qualified employees to perform necessary organizational activities, and developing activities and an organizational climate to generate maximum efficiency and worker satisfaction.

human resources Organization's employees.

importing Buying foreign goods, raw materials, and services.

income statement Financial record of a company's revenues, expenses, and profits over a period of time.

individual brand Separate brand name for each product in a line.

industrial distributor Wholesaling intermediary that sells products to business users.

industrial goods *See* business goods.

industrial union Union that organizes workers in a given industry, regardless of their occupation or skill level.

inflation Sustained price increases for all goods and services.

informal communication channel Path for communication outside formally authorized channels without regard for the organization's hierarchy of authority.

information superhighway Single, enormous network merging telecommunications, information, and data systems that can be assessed by any individual or organization.

informational interview Session with a company representative designed to get information about a job or occupation.

injunction Court order prohibiting some union or management practice.

insider trading Illegal securities trading by people who try to profit from their access to nonpublic information about a company.

institutional advertising Promotion of a concept, idea, or philosophy or the goodwill of an industry, company, organization, or government entity.

institutional investor Organization that invests its own funds or funds it holds in trust.

insurable interest Insurance concept that requires a policyholder to stand to suffer loss.

insurable risk Risk that meets certain requirements in order for the insurer to provide protection.

insurance Process by which an insurer, in exchange for a fee, agrees to reimburse a firm or individual for losses up to specified limits.

insurance company Private company or public agency that provides insurance coverage for business firms, not-for-profit organizations, and individuals.

integrated marketing communications (IMC) Coordination of all promotional activities to produce a unified message that is customer focused.

intensive distribution Strategy to achieve market saturation by placing products in every available outlet.

interactive media Program applications that allow users to interact with computers to perform several different functions at the same time.

internal communication System of communication through channels within an organization.

internal customer Employee or department within an organization that depends on the work of other people or departments to perform a job.

international law The numerous regulations governing international commerce.

international union National union with members outside the United States.

Internet All-purpose global network composed of some 48,000 different networks around the globe that, within limits, lets anyone with access to a personal computer send and receive images and data anywhere.

intrapreneurship Entrepreneurial activity within the corporate structure.

inventory control Balancing the costs of holding raw materials, component parts, and finished inventory (which increase with the addition of more inventory) and order-processing costs (which decrease as the quantity ordered increases).

investment banker Specialist in selling new issues of securities for business and government organizations.

ISO 9000 International standards for quality management and quality assurance.

job enrichment Redesigning work to give employees more authority in planning their tasks, deciding how to complete their work, and allowing them to learn related skills or to trade jobs.

joint venture Sharing a foreign operation's costs, risks, and management with a foreign firm or government.

judiciary The branch of government charged with deciding disputes among parties through the application of laws.

just-in-time (JIT) system Management philosophy aimed at improving profits and return on investment by involving workers in the operations process and eliminating waste through cost reductions, inventory reductions, and quality improvements.

keiretsu Japanese term for strategic distribution alliance dominated by single channel members.

key executive insurance Life insurance designed to reimburse an organization for loss of the services of an important executive.

labor union Group of workers who have banded together to achieve common goals in the key areas of wages, hours, and working conditions.

Landrum-Griffin Act (1959) Federal law requiring regularly scheduled elections of union officers by secret ballot and increased regulation of the handling of union funds.

law Standards set by government and society in the form of either legislation or custom.

law of large numbers Probability calculation of the likelihood of occurrence of perils on which insurers base their premiums.

leadership Act of motivating or causing others to perform activities designed to achieve specific objectives.

leading Guiding and motivating employees to accomplish organizational objectives.

leverage Technique of increasing the rate of return on an investment by financing it with borrowed funds.

leverage ratio Ratio that measures a firm's reliance on debt financing in its operations.

liability Claim against a firm's assets by a creditor.

liability loss Financial loss suffered by a business firm or individual held responsible for property damage or injuries suffered by others.

limited liability company (LLC) Company governed by an operating agreement similar to a partnership agreement, with the advantage of limited liability.

limited-function merchant wholesaler Merchant wholesaler that takes legal title to the goods it distributes, but provides few services.

line organization Structure with a direct flow of authority from the chief executive to subordinates.

line-and-staff organization Structure that combines the direct flow of authority of a line organization with staff departments that serve, advise, and support the line departments.

liquidity ratio Ratio that measures a firm's ability to meet its short-term obligations when they are due.

listening Skill of receiving a message and interpreting its genuine meaning by accurately grasping the facts and feelings it conveys.

local area network (LAN) Computer network that connects machines within a limited area.

local union Branch of a national union representing members in a specific area.

lockout Management shutdown of a firm to pressure union members.

loss leader Product offered to consumers at less than cost to attract them to stores in the hope they will buy other merchandise at regular prices.

low-context culture Communication based on explicit written and verbal messages.

macroeconomics Study of the overall operation of an economy.

make, buy, or lease decision Firm's choice among manufacturing, purchasing, or leasing a needed product, component, or material.

management Achievement of organizational objectives through people and other resources.

management development program Training designed to improve the skills and broaden the knowledge of current and potential managers.

management information system (MIS) Organized method of providing information for decision making.

manufacturer's brand *See* national brand.

manufacturing resource planning (MRP II) System that integrates planning data from individual departments to produce a master business plan.

market People with both purchasing power and the ability and authority to buy.

market segmentation Process of dividing a total market into several relatively homogeneous groups.

market share Percentage of a market controlled by a certain company or product.

marketing Planning and executing the conception, pricing, promotion, and distribution of ideas, goods, and services to create exchanges that satisfy individual and organizational objectives.

marketing concept Consumer orientation intended to achieve long-term success.

marketing decision support system (MDSS) Part of an MIS that displays information in useful visual and graphic forms.

marketing information system (MIS) System that combines internal and external data, stores and classifies the data, analyzes and retrieves the data according to decision makers' needs, and produces information that matches users' needs.

marketing intermediary Channel member that operates between the producer and the consumer or business purchaser.

marketing mix Organization's combined product, pricing, distribution, and promotion strategies.

marketing research Collection and evaluation of information to help make marketing decisions.

marketing strategy Studying, analyzing, and selecting a firm's target market and developing a marketing mix to satisfy that market.

mass production Manufacturing goods in large quantities as a result of standardization, specialized labor, and mechanization.

materials handling Movement of goods within a firm's warehouse, terminal, factory, or store.

materials requirement planning (MRP) Computer-based production planning system by which a firm can ensure that it has needed parts and materials available at the right time and place in the correct amounts.

matrix, or project management, organization Structure that brings together specialists from different parts of the organization to work on specific projects.

mechanization Making machines perform work previously done by people.

mediation Process of settling union-management disputes through recommendations of an impartial third party.

merchant wholesaler Independent wholesaler that takes legal title to the goods it distributes.

merger Combination of two or more firms to form one company.

message Written, oral, or nonverbal communication transmitted by a sender to an audience.

microcomputer Desktop, laptop, and pocket-sized portable computers.

microeconomics Study of the economic activities of a firm or individual.

middle management Level of management responsible for developing detailed plans and procedures to implement the general plans devised by top management.

mission statement Written explanation of a company's aims.

missionary selling Indirect form of selling in which the sales representative promotes the goodwill of the company and provides technical or operational assistance.

mixed economy Economic system that mixes government ownership and private enterprise.

monetary policy Government policies and actions to regulate the nation's money supply.

money Anything generally accepted as a means of paying for goods and services.

monopolistic competition Market situation that features firms that differentiate their products from those of competitors.

monopoly Market situation that features no direct competitors.

morale Mental attitude of employees toward their employers and jobs.

mortality table Table with data that predicts the number of persons in each age category who will die in a given year.

motive Inner state that directs an individual toward the goal of satisfying a felt need.

multicultural diversity Racial and cultural blend within a society.

multimedia computing Technologies that facilitate the integration of two or more types of media, such as text, voice, sound, full-motion video, still video, graphics, and/or animation into a single, computer-based application.

multinational corporation Corporation with extensive international operations.

multinational strategy Strategy that treats each national market differently.

mutual fund Financial organization that pools investors' money to acquire a diversified portfolio of securities.

National Association of Securities Dealers Automated Quotation (NASDAQ) system Nationwide, over-the-counter securities trading network.

national brand Brand offered and promoted by a manufacturer.

National Labor Relations Act (1935) *See* Wagner Act.

national union Large labor organization composed of numerous local unions.

natural resources Everything that is useful as a production input in its natural state.

near-money Asset almost as liquid as cash or a checking account, but that cannot serve directly as a medium of exchange.

need Lack of something useful; discrepancy between a desired state and an actual state.

negotiable instruments Commercial paper that is transferable among individuals and businesses.

noise Anything that interferes with a message by distorting its meaning.

nonparticipator role Role of team members who contribute little either to the task or to member's socio-emotional needs.

nontraditional student Any student who does not fall into the 18- to 22-year-old age group.

nonverbal communication Communication transmitted through actions and behaviors.

norming stage Point in team development at which members resolve differences, accept each other, and reach consensus about the roles of the team leader and other participants.

Norris-La Guardia Act (1932) Federal legislation that protects unions by reducing management's ability to obtain court injunctions that halt union activities.

not-for-profit organization Firm whose primary objective is something other than returning a profit to its owners.

objectives Guideposts by which managers define standards that the organization should accomplish in such areas as profitability, customer service, and employee satisfaction.

oligopoly Market situation that features few sellers and substantial entry restrictions.

on-the-job training Training employees for job tasks by allowing them to perform the tasks under the guidance of experienced employees.

open shop Employment policy making union membership and dues voluntary for all workers.

open-ended interview Interview designed to force an applicant to talk about personal qualifications and goals.

operational planning Work standards that guide implementation of tactical plans.

order processing Preparation of an order for shipment. Also, sales task of receiving and handling an order.

organization Structured grouping of people working together to achieve organizational objectives.

organization chart Representation of the authority and responsibility relationships in an organization.

organizational goods *See* business goods.

organizing Management function of blending human and material resources through a formal structure of tasks and authority.

outsourcing Relying on outside specialists to perform functions previously performed by company employees.

owners' equity Claims of the proprietor, partners, or stockholders against the assets of a firm; the excess of assets over liabilities.

parent company Corporation that owns all or a majority of the stock in another corporation (called a subsidiary).

partnership Business operated by two or more people as co-owners.

patent Guarantees inventors exclusive rights to their invention for 17 years.

PDCA cycle Step-by-step process to reduce cycle time by **p**lanning, **d**oing, **c**hecking, and **a**cting.

peer-review board Committee of peer workers and management representatives with the power to make binding decisions to resolve disputes over promotion decisions, dismissals, and other disciplinary actions.

performance appraisal Defining acceptable employee performance levels, evaluating them, then comparing actual and desired performance of individuals to aid in decisions about training, compensation, promotion, transfers, or terminations.

performing stage Phase in team development characterized by problem solving and a focus on task accomplishment.

perpetual inventory Continuously updated listing of items in inventory.

personal selling Promotional presentation made person-to-person to a potential buyer.

PERT (Program Evaluation and Review Technique) Scheduling technique to minimize production delays by coordinating all aspects of the process.

physical distribution Movement of goods from producer to user.

picketing Workers marching at a plant entrance to protest some management practice.

planning Anticipating the future and determining the best courses of action to achieve organizational objectives.

Plant-Closing Notification Act (1988) Federal legislation aimed at assisting employees and cities by requiring employers to give 60 days' notice before a plant closing or mass layoff.

point-of-purchase (POP) advertising Sales promotion that displays and demonstrates a product at the place where the actual purchase decision is made.

pollution Tainting or destroying a natural environment.

positioning Promotional strategy intended to differentiate a good or service from those of competitors in the mind of a prospective buyer.

preferred stock Security providing owner preferential dividend payments and first claim to company assets after it pays all debts; it seldom confers voting rights.

premium Fee paid by an insured party to an insurer for protection against losses.

price Exchange value of a good or service.

price-earnings (P/E) ratio Stock's current market price divided by the issuer's annual earnings per share.

primary boycott Boycott that discourages union members from patronizing a specific firm.

primary market Market where firms sell new issues of securities publicly for the first time.

private accountant Professional employed by a business other than a public accounting firm.

private brand Brand owned by a wholesaler or retailer.

private enterprise system Economic system in which success or failure depends on how well firms match and counter the offerings of competitors.

private property Property that can be owned, used, bought, sold, and bequeathed under the private enterprise system.

privatization Trend to substitute private ownership for public ownership.

problem-solving team Temporary combination of workers who gather to solve a specific problem and then disband.

product Bundle of physical, service, and symbolic attributes designed to satisfy consumer wants.

product advertising Nonpersonal selling of a good or service.

product launch The stage at which a firm offers its new product in the marketplace.

product liability Business liability for negligence in the design, manufacture, sale, and/or use of products.

product life cycle Four stages through which a successful product passes: introduction, growth, maturity, and decline.

product line Series of related products offered by a firm.

product line pricing Offering groups of merchandise at a limited number of prices instead of pricing each item individually.

product mix Assortment of products offered by a firm.

production Application of resources like people and machinery to convert materials into finished goods or services.

production and operations management Managing people and machinery used in converting materials and resources into finished goods and services.

production control Well-defined set of procedures for coordinating people, materials, and machinery to provide maximum production efficiency.

production planning Phase of production control process that determines the amount of resources needed to produce a certain amount of goods or services.

productivity Measure of the efficiency of production.

profit Reward for the businessperson who takes the risks involved in blending people, technology, and information in creating and marketing want-satisfying goods and services that provide customer satisfaction.

profit maximization Pricing strategy in which managers set an increasing level of profitability as an objective.

profitability ratio Ratio that measures the overall financial performance of the firm.

program trading Automatic securities transactions using computer systems programmed to issue buy and sell orders in response to price changes exceeding predetermined amounts.

promotional mix Combination of personal and nonpersonal selling designed to achieve promotional objectives.

promotional strategy Function of informing, persuading, and influencing a consumer decision.

property loss Financial loss resulting from interruption of business operations or physical damage to property as a result of a fire, accident, theft, or other destructive event.

public accountant Professional who provides accounting services to other businesses and individuals for a fee.

public ownership Enterprise owned and operated by a unit or agency of government.

public relations Organization's communications with its various public audiences.

pulling strategy Promotional strategy utilizing advertising and sales promotion appeals to generate consumer demand for a product.

pure competition Market situation that features many firms in an industry so none can individually influence market prices.

pure risk Type of risk involving only the chance of loss.

pushing strategy Sales-oriented promotional strategy designed to motivate marketing intermediaries to push the product to their customers.

quality Degree of excellence or superiority of an organization's goods and services.

quality circle Small group of employees from one work area or department who meet regularly to identify and solve problems.

quality control Measurement of goods and services against established quality standards.

rack jobber Full-function merchant wholesaler that sets up and services a particular section of a retail store.

ratio analysis Use of quantitative measures to evaluate a firm's financial performance.

recession Cyclical economic contraction.

recycling Reprocessing of used materials for reuse.

reengineering Mapping out existing delivery-chain processes in detail and applying technology to key steps to reduce cycle time or errors.

regulated industry Industry in which competition is either limited or eliminated, and government monitoring substitutes for market controls.

relationship marketing Program by a company to develop long-term, cost-effective links with customers.

research and development Scientific process of developing new commercial products.

résumé Written summary of personal, educational, and professional achievements.

retailer Channel member that sells goods and services to individuals for their own use rather than for resale.

right-to-work laws State laws that prohibit compulsory union membership.

risk Uncertainty about loss or injury.

risk-return trade-off Balance between the risk of an investment and its potential gain.

robot Reprogrammable machine capable of performing numerous tasks that require programmed manipulations of materials and tools.

routing Phase of production control process that determines the sequence of work throughout the facility.

sales branch Manufacturer-owned marketing intermediary that stocks a manufacturer's products and processes orders from inventory.

sales law The sale of goods or services for money or on credit.

sales maximization Pricing strategy under which managers set an acceptable minimum level of profitability and then try to maximize sales.

sales office Manufacturer-owned office for salespeople that encourages close local contacts for regular and potential customers.

sales promotion Form of promotion designed to increase sales through one-time selling efforts such as displays, trade shows, special events, and other methods.

savings and loan association (S&L) Thrift institution that offers savings and checking accounts, using most of its funds to make home mortgage loans.

savings bank State-chartered thrift institution with operations similar to those of savings and loan associations.

scheduling Phase of production control process that develops timetables that specify how long each operation in the production process should take and when to perform it.

scrambled merchandising Practice in which retailers carry dissimilar product lines to appeal to consumers seeking one-stop shopping.

secondary boycott Boycott or work stoppage intended to force an employer to cease dealing with another firm.

secondary market Market where subsequent owners trade previously issued shares of stock and bonds.

secured bond Bond backed by a specific pledge of company assets.

securities Stock or bond that represents an obligation of the issuer to provide the purchaser an expected or stated return on the investment.

selective distribution Market coverage strategy that selects a limited number of retailers to distribute products.

self-insurance fund Account set up to cover losses due to pure risks.

self-managed team Group of employees who work with little or no supervision.

self-managed team Work team empowered with authority to make decisions about how to complete its daily work.

seller's market Market situation characterized by product shortages.

sender Participant in a communication who transmits a message to an audience.

Service Corps of Retired Executives (SCORE) SBA program in which retired executives volunteer as consultants to assist small businesses.

services Intangible tasks that satisfy consumers' and business users' needs.

set-aside program Legislation that specifies certain government contracts to allot to small businesses.

sexism Discrimination against members of either sex (primarily a problem for women).

sexual harassment Inappropriate actions of a sexual nature.

small business Business that is independently owned and operated, is not dominant in its field, and meets certain size standards for its income or number of employees.

Small Business Administration (SBA) Principal government agency concerned with small U.S. firms.

Small Business Development Center (SBDC) SBA program in which college faculty members and others assist small businesses through research and consulting activities, charging fees to offset costs.

Small Business Institute (SBI) SBA program in which business students offer consulting services to small businesses.

Small Business Investment Company (SBIC) An investment group that funds small businesses under an SBA license.

social audit Formal examination of a firm's social responsibility performance.

social responsibility Management philosophy that highlights the social and economic effects of managers' decisions.

socialism Economic system that advocates government ownership and operation of all major industries.

socio-emotional role Role played by team members who devote time and energy to providing support for group members' emotional needs and social unity.

software Programmed instructions that tell a computer what to do.

sole proprietorship Ownership and, usually, operation of an organization by one person.

specialization Dividing work into its simplest components so that each worker can concentrate on performing one task.

specialty advertising Sales promotion that gives away useful items imprinted with the donor's name, logo, or message.

speculation Purchasing stocks in anticipation of making large profits quickly.

speculative risk Type of risk involving the chance of either profit or loss.

spreadsheet Computer software that permits businesspeople to manipulate decision variables to determine their effects.

standardization Producing uniform, interchangeable goods and parts.

statement of cash flows Statement of a firm's cash receipts and cash payments that presents information on its sources and uses of cash.

statistical quality control System of locating and measuring quality problems in production processes.

statutory law Written law that includes state and federal constitutions, legislative enactments, treaties of the federal government, and ordinances of local governments.

stock exchange Location at which traders buy and sell stocks and bonds.

stockholder Person who acquires shares of stock in, and therefore owns part of, a corporation.

storming stage Point in team development in which participants' individual personalities begin to emerge as they clarify their roles and expectations.

strategic alliance Long-term partnership of firms designed to improve their overall competitiveness.

strategic business units (SBUs) Related product groupings of businesses within a multiproduct firm with specific managers, resources, objectives, and competitors.

strategic planning Process of determining the primary objectives of an organization, adopting courses of action, and allocating the resources necessary to achieve objectives.

strike Employees' temporary work stoppage until a dispute is settled or a contract signed.

strikebreaker Nonunion worker hired to replace a striking worker.

subsidiary Corporation with all or a majority of its stock owned by another corporation.

supervisory management First-line management responsible for the details of assigning workers to specific jobs and evaluating performance.

supply Sellers' willingness and ability to provide products.

supply curve Graph of the relationship between different prices and the quantity supplied at each price.

SWOT analysis Organized method of assessing a company's internal **s**trengths and **w**eaknesses, and external **o**pportunities and **t**hreats.

tactical planning Planning for short-term implementation of current activities and related resource allocations.

Taft-Hartley Act (1947) Federal law designed to balance the power of unions and management by prohibiting a number of unfair union practices; also known as the Labor-Management Relations Act (LMRA).

target market Group of consumers toward which an organization directs its marketing efforts.

tariff Tax levied against imported products.

task specialist role Role played by team members who devote time and energy to helping the team accomplish its goals.

taxes The assessments use to raise revenue for government units.

team Small group of people with complementary skills who are committed to a common purpose, approach, and set of performance goals.

team cohesiveness Extent to which team members feel attracted to the team and motivated to remain a part of it.

team norm Standard of conduct shared by team members that guides their behavior.

technologically displaced worker Worker who loses a job due to automation or industrial cutbacks.

technology Business application of knowledge based on scientific discoveries, inventions, and innovations.

telecommunications Any system in which data travels over a distance through some type of electronic transmission system, typically a telephone line.

telemarketing Personal selling conducted entirely by telephone.

test marketing Stage in the new-product development process at which the firm sells a product in a limited area.

Theory X Managerial assumption that workers dislike work and must be coerced, controlled, or threatened to motivate them to work.

Theory Y Managerial assumption that workers like work and, under proper conditions, accept and seek out responsibilities to fulfill their social, esteem, and self-actualization needs.

Theory Z Management approach emphasizing employee participation as the key to increased productivity and improved quality of work life.

time management Effective allocation of one's time among different tasks.

top management Highest level of the management hierarchy, staffed by executives who develop long-range plans and interact with the public and outside entities.

tort A civil wrong inflicted on other people or their property.

total quality management (TQM) Company-wide commitment to quality in achieving world-class performance and customer satisfaction as a crucial strategic objective.

trade deficit A unfavorable balance of trade in which a country imports more than it exports.

trade show Exhibition designed to promote goods or services to retailers, wholesalers, international buyers, and other resellers in the distribution channel.

trade surplus A favorable balance of trade in which a country exports more than it imports.

trademark Words, symbols, or other designations used by firms to identify their products, usually with legal protection exclusive to owner.

trial court A court of general jurisdiction.

unemployment Joblessness of people who are looking for work.

union shop Employment policy requiring nonunion workers to join a union that represents a firm's workers within a specified period.

Universal Product Code (UPC) Bar code read by optical scanner in systems that print the name and price of each item on a receipt.

utility Want-satisfying power of a good or service.

variable cost Cost that changes with the production level, such as the costs of labor and raw materials.

venture capitalist Business organization or a group of private individuals that invest in new firms.

vertical marketing system (VMS) Planned distribution channel organized to reduce channel conflict and improve distribution efficiency.

vision Ability to perceive marketplace needs and methods by which an organization can satisfy them.

wage-reopener clause Clause in a union contract that allows contract parties to renegotiate wages at a predetermined date.

Wagner Act (1935) Federal law legalizing collective bargaining and requiring employers to bargain with elected representatives of their employees; also called the National Labor Relations Act.

warehousing Storage of goods.

wheel of retailing Concept of retailing evolution in which new types of retailers gain competitive footholds by emphasizing low prices in exchange for limited services.

wholesaling intermediary Channel member that sells goods primarily to retailers, other wholesalers, or business users.

word processing Use of computers to write, store, retrieve, edit, and print text materials.

work team Mid-1990s style of work in which a small group of people with complementary skills perform the day-to-day work of an organization.

worker buyout Financial incentive designed to encourage older employees to voluntarily retire.

yield Income received from securities, calculated by dividing dividend or interest income by market price.

ACKNOWLEDGMENTS

Photos
xxxii © 1995 Steven Peters/Tony Stone Images
3 © R. Ian Lloyd/Pacific Rim Stock/Westlight
5 Courtesy of Harris Corporation
9 © Will & Deni McIntyre
11 © Ed Kashi
13 © Jeffrey Aaronson/Network Aspen
15 © 1995 Robert Holmgren
18 © Georges De Keerle/Sygma
19 Jan-Peter Boning/Zenit
25 © Cindy Lewis 1995
28 © Atlan/Sygma
32 Courtesy of Knight-Ridder, Inc.
34 © James Schnepf Photography
35 © John S. Abbott
37 © Louis Psyhoyos/MATRIX
38 © Norfolk Southern Corporation
40 © Michael L. Abramson
45 Shreveport Pirates logo is a trademark of the Shreveport Pirates of the Canadian Football League. All rights, title and interest are reserved.
47 © James Schnepf Photography
48 AP/Wide World Photos
50 © Dilip Mehta/Contact
53 © Neil Herndon
55 © Les Stone/Sygma
57 Jean-Pierre Ahmat/Sygma
58 © Steve Liss/Time Magazine
61 Philippe Diedrich/Contact
67 © Charles Nes/The Gamma Liaison Network
70 Wendt World Wide
74 Habitat for Humanity, Lake County, Illinois
77 Courtesy of Knight-Ridder, Inc.
78 © Michael L. Abramson
84 © Richard Schultz
96 © Stewart Cohen/Index Stock
99 Peter Charlesworth/SABA
106 © David Smart
107 © Sal DiMarco/Black Star
109 Courtesy of Pioneer Hi-Bred International, Inc.
110 Courtesy of Western Atlas
112 © James Schnepf Photography
114 Courtesy of Recreational Equipment Inc. (REI)
119 © Lisa Quinones/Black Star
122 David Fields/ONYX
124 T. Michael Keza/Nation's Business
127 © Kevin Mooney/Odyssey Productions
131 © Daniel Cima
132 © John R. Fulton, Jr.
138 © Bart Bartholomew
147 Steven Lewis
151 Courtesy of Allen-Bradley, a Rockwell Automation business
154 Alen McWeeney © 1990
155 © Ed Kashi
157 L. L. Bean
161 © Nina Berman/SIPA-PRESS
163 Rockwell International
164 © 1995 Jose Azel/Aurora & Quanta Productions
167 McDonnell Douglas Corporation photo
171 Rockwell International/David Perry
182 © 1995 Dan Bosler/Tony Stone Images
185 © Alan Levenson
192 © Louis Psyhoyos/MATRIX
195 AP/Wide World Photos
199 Visum/Gotz Georg Linzenmeier
205 © Darryl Heikes/Sygma
209 © 1995 Roger Mastroianni
213 © Lizzie Himmel/Proof
224 © Nina Berman/SIPA-PRESS
228 Insight Magazine/Jon A. Rembold
231 © Don Glentzer
237 © Michael Greenlar
241 © Mitch Kezar
253 © James Schnepf Photography
257 © Robbie McClaran
261 © Scott Goodwin
273 © Bob Hower/Quadrant 1994
274 Tory Westnopski/AP
278 © Jeff Mermelstein
279 Clockwise from upper left: The Louvre; The White House; Delft University; University of California
287 Culver Pictures
294 © Todd Buchanan
299 Bill Swersey/Gamma Liaison
304 © Ameen Howrani
306 John Betancourt
313 © Lincoln Potter/Gamma Liaison
317 © Bankuti/Black Star
319 © Louis Psyhoyos/MATRIX
321 © Louis Psyhoyos/MATRIX
328 Courtesy of Lockheed Martin
330 © Will Panich. Courtesy Baxter International, Inc.
337 © James Schnepf Photography
348 © 1995 Frank Herholt/Tony Stone Images
354 © John S. Abbott
356 © David Woo/Stock Boston
362 © Ann States/SABA
370 © David R. Frazier Photolibrary
372 © Stuart Franklin/Magnum
383 © Tony Freeman/PhotoEdit
393 © 1995 Arthur Meyerson
400 © Paulo Fridman/Sygma
409 © James Schnepf Photography
417 © Mary Beth Camp/MATRIX
422 John Maier, Jr./JB Pictures
428 © Kent Sievers
429 © Michael L. Abramson
430 Fritz Hoffman/JB Pictures
437 Courtesy of Shopper's Express
446 © David R. Frazier Photolibrary
450 Ron Haviv/SABA
453 "McSorley's Bar by John Sloan, oil on canvas, 26 x 32 inches, 1912. © The Detroit Institute of Arts. Gift of the Founders Society, 24.2. Courtesy of Alamo Rent A Car.
466 © The Stock Market/William Taufic 1995
469 © Ray Ng
471 Courtesy of Microsoft Corporation
472 **left** Courtesy of Prodigy Services Company; **right** Courtesy of CompuServe; **bottom** Copyright 1995 America Online; used by permission
475 © Chuck O'Rear/Westlight
482 Courtesy of US Sprint
499 © Nancy Moran/Sygma
500 The Kroger Company
504 © 1995 Steven Peters/Tony Stone Images
507 Courtesy of Miscrosoft Corporation
511 © 1995 Kaufman and Broad Home Corporation
514 © 1995 Peter Cade/Tony Stone Images
516 © Bruce Lankard
531 Courtesy Hydrokinetic Designs Inc.
535 © Steve Wolf
536 Jeffrey Macmillan, U. S. New & World Report
539 © David Strick/Onyx
550 © James Nubile/JB Pictures
559 Cindy Loo/Black Star
561 © Tom Tracy
563 © Robert Wallis/SABA

Figures
10 Adapted from "Americans Are Attracting Foreign Manufacturers," *Time,* October 24, 1994, 53.
33 Adapted from "A New Way to Count the Unemployed," *U.S. News & World Report*, February 14, 1994, 6.
46 Adapted from "Why Overseas? 'Cause That's Where the Sales Are," *Business Week,* January 10, 1994, 62.
86 Adapted from Jim Aley, "The Pay Gap Narrows, But . . .," *Fortune,* September 19, 1994, 32.
111 Adapted from Gary Visgaitis, "USA Snapshots," *USA Today,* July 13, 1994, B1.
121 Reprinted from Charles R. Kuehl and Peggy A. Lambing, *Small Business: Planning and Management* (Ft. Worth, TX: The Dryden Press, 1994), 45.
128 Data from U.S. Small Business Administration, Office of Advocacy, The State of Small Business: A Report of the President, 1992.
129 Adapted from "Hands On: A Manager's Notebook," *Inc.,* September 1990, 130.

130 Adapted from John Hinge, compiler, "Owning the Business," *The Wall Street Journal,* November 22, 1991, R18.
153 John Hillkirk, "On Mission to Revamp Workplace," *USA Today,* October 15, 1990, 4B.
189 Adapted from *1990 General Electric Annual Report,* 3.
198 Adapted from discussion in Ramon J. Aldag and Timothy M. Stearns, *Management* (Cincinnati, OH: South-Western Publishing Co., 1991), 199–201.
208 Adapted from Micheline Maynard, "Evaluations Evolve from Boss," *USA Today,* August 3, 1994, 6B. Copyright 1994, *USA Today.* Reprinted with permission.
221 Adapted from Delbert J. Duncan, Charles F. Phillips, and Stanley C. Hollander, *Modern Retailing Management* (Homewood, IL: Richard D. Irwin, 1972).
231 Christopher Farrell, Paul Magnusson, and Wendy Zellner, "The Scary Math of New Hires," *Business Week,* February 22, 1993, 70–71.
234 "Downsizing Often Costly Cut," *Mobile Register,* July 10, 1994, F1. Statistics from Arthur D. Little, Inc.
236 Adapted from "Out Is In," *Entrepreneur,* May 1994, 12. Statistics from International Facility Management Association.
339 Based on discussion in Thomas Kirkpatrick and Chad Lewis, *Effective Supervision* (Ft. Worth, TX: The Dryden Press, 1995), 376–381.
244 *Business Week,* October 17, 1994, 85. Data from Economic Policy Institute.
256 Artwork by Rodica Prato.
269 David Sullivan, *The New Computer User* (Ft. Worth, TX: The Dryden Press, 1994), 277.
270 From Peter March, ed., *Eye to Eye: How People Interact* (Topsfield, MA: Salem House, 1988), 42.
274 Bob Laird, in Julie Schmidt, "High-Tech Tool Changing the Way Firms Work," USA Today, July 20, 1994, B1. Copyright 1994, USA Today. Reprinted with permission.
297 Adapted from "Germany's Mighty Unions Are Being Forced to Bend," *Business Week,* March 1, 1993, 52. Data from Goldman, Sachs & Co.
308 Adapted from "Why America Needs Unions But Not the Kind It Has Now," *Business Week,* May 23, 1994, 70. Data in left-hand chart from Leo Troy, Rutgers University, Bureau of Labor Statistics; data in right-hand chart from Richard B. Freeman, Harvard University.
316 Adapted from Norman Gaither, Production and *Operations Management: A Problem Solving and Decision Making Approach,* 2d ed., (Ft. Worth, TX: The Dryden Press, 1994).
318 Adapted from *Fortune,* May 21, 1990, 60. © 1990 The Time Inc. Magazine Company. All rights reserved.
323 Adapted from Thomas A. Stewart, "Brace for Japan's Hot New Strategy," *Fortune,* September 21, 1992, p. 63.
324 Adapted from Terence Roth, "German Firms Bemoan Production Costs," *The Wall Street Journal,* January 29, 1992, A6.
329 *Fortune,* April 20, 1992, p. 104.
332 Howard Gleckman, Zachary Schiller, and James B. Treece, "A Tonic for the Business Cycle," *Business Week,* April 4, 1994, 57. Data from the Bureau of Economic Analysis.
366 From Martha Farnsworth Riche, "Psychographics for the 1990s," *American Demographics,* July 1989, 30.
369 Adapted from James F. Engel, Roger D. Blackwell, and Paul Miniard, *Consumer Behavior,* 7th ed. (Ft. Worth, TX: The Dryden Press, 1993).
396 Adapted from Andrew E. Server, "How to Escape a Price War," *Fortune,* June 13, 1994, 83.
480 Adapted from "Team Play," *U.S. News & World Report,* October 17, 1994, 67.
486 Expert system steps based on a discussion in Kenneth C. Laudon, Carol G. Traver, and Jane P. Laudon, *Information Technology Concepts and Issues* (Danvers, MA: Boyd & Fraser, 1995), p. 348,
564 Courtesy Mobile Corporation.
577 *The Dallas Morning News,* April 22, 1994, 5D. Reprinted with permission of *The Dallas Morning News.*
578 *The Dallas Morning News,* April 22, 1994, 5D. Reprinted with permission of *The Dallas Morning News.*
580 *The Dallas Morning News,* April 22, 1994, 8D. Reprinted with permission of *The Dallas Morning News.*
581 Stan Crock, "Insider Trading: There Oughta Be a Law," *Business Week,* December 12, 1994, 82.
597 Adapted from "How You Stand on Income," *Money,* December 1993, 148.
598 Adapted from Patricia Renwick and Edward E. Lawler, "What You Really Want from Your Job," *Psychology Today,* May 1978, 56, as it appeared in Thomas Kirkpatrick and Chad Lewis, *Effective Supervision* (Ft. Worth, TX: The Dryden Press, 1995), 397.
600 Adapted from Amy Saltzman, "An Electronic Job Hunt," *U.S. News & World Report,* March 28, 1994, 74–75.
622 Adapted from the *Mobile Register,* September 18, 1994, 4A. Data from Bipartisan Commission on Entitlement and Tax Reform and Newhouse News Service.

Tables

52 Data from *The World Almanac and Book of Facts 1994* (Mahway, NJ: Funk & Wagnalls, 1994), 184, 188.
103 Adapted from Donald Kuratko and Ray Montagno, "The Intrapreneurial Spirit," *Training and Development Journal,* October 1989, 34.
105 Adapted from Wilton Woods, "The *Fortune* Global 500," *Fortune,* July 27, 1992, 238–246.
126 Jeanne Sadler, "Home Economics 101, *The Wall Street Journal,* October 14, 1994, p. R12.
420 Adapted from "Fortune's Service 500: The 50 Largest Retailers," *Fortune,* May 30, 1994, p.214.
455 "Top Global Markets," *Advertising Age,* March 21, 1994, p. I11.
487 Adapted from "The Voice Processing Business," *Business Week,* June 2, 1991, 128. (Data from Hambrecht & Quist Inc., Market Intelligence-Research Corp., Link Resources, Inc., Northern Business Information, Probe Research Inc.)
491 Adapted from Kenneth C. Laudon and Jane P. Laudon, *Business Information Systems* (Fort Worth, TX: The Dryden Press, 1991), 577.
548 Data from the Federal Reserve System.

Video Cases

22 Matt Krantz, "Independent-Owned Luxury Hotels Are Coming under the Flags of Marriott and Others," *Investor's Business Daily,* May 10, 1995; Bill McDowell, "Czech It Out: E. Europe Courts Conventions," *Crain's Chicago Business,* June 20, 1994; Marriott International, *1993 Annual Report;* and Ernest Beck et al., "Eastern Europe Opens Door to Opportunity," *Crain's Chicago Business,* February 22, 1993.
42 "How Companies Are Easing the Transition to a Virtual Workplace," *Investor's Business Daily, Executive Update,* March 17, 1995; Mickey Williamson, "High-Tech Trainman," *Byte,* December 1994; John A. Byrne, "Hired Guns Packing High-Powered Know-how," *Business Week,* November 18, 1994; "How Ten Leading Consulting Firms Stack Up," *Business Week,* July 25, 1994; and John A. Byrne, "The Craze for Consultants," *Business Week,* July 25, 1994.
64 T. R. Reid, Whirlpool Corporation press release, April 18, 1995; Daniel Howes, "Whitwam's Global Vision Opens the Doors for Whirlpool," *Detroit News,* March 26, 1995; Patrick Oster and John Rossant, "Call It Worldpool," *Business Week,* November 28, 1994; and Whirlpool Corporation, *1994 Annual Report.*
142 "All about Golf," *A Research Study Profiling the Golfer as a Consumer,* PGA of America, 1994.
176 Some information from Wainwright Industries, Inc. application for the 1994 Malcolm Baldrige National Quality Award.
217 Kathy Bush, "No Apple Crunch—New $3 Million Facility Helps Growers Be Competitive," *Grand Rapids Press,* November 25, 1994; Kropf Orchards press release, November 1, 1994; and interview with Roger Welsh.
251 John Schmelter, "Tack on $3 for that Trip to the Bank Teller," *Chicago Tribune,* April 26, 1995 and videos from Paul Hawkins, "Growing a Business" series.
282 Valassis Communications, Inc. 1994 annual report.
310 David Edwards, "1995 Harley-Davidson Bad Boy," *Cycle World,* September 28, 1994; Gail DeGeorge, "Database Marketing—Potent New Tool for Selling," *Business Week,* September 5, 1994; and Kathleen Kerwin and

Deidre A. Depke, "Forget Woodstock—These Folks Are Heading to Spring Hill," *Business Week*, June 26, 1994.
406 Second Chance Film and Video Services, "Second Chance versus the Cop Killers," 1992 video; and Second Chance product brochures.
434 Telephone interview with Barry Chapman, director of human resources, Next Door Food Store and company history fact sheet.
460 Susan Chandler and Laura Zinn, "It's A Wonderful Life for Retailers," *Business Week*, December 26, 1994 and Sandra Jones, "Target Arrives, the Fight Begins: Discounter with Style Will Rattle Market," *Crain's Chicago Business*, March 1, 1994.
496 "The Global 100," *Computer World*, May 1, 1995; "Same Day Service for UPS, FedEx," *Chicago Tribune*, April 12, 1995; David Greising, "Watch Out for Flying Packages," *Business Week*, November 14, 1994; and David Greising, "Quality: How to Make It Pay," *Business Week*, August 8, 1994.
556 FirstBank Corporation 1994 annual report.
588 "Building Business through Relationships," a Roney & Company publication, and "Michigan's Banks, Roney & Company—Colleagues in Finance," *Michigan Banker*, June 1993.

NAME AND COMPANY INDEX

f indicates a figure; *t* indicates a table.

SUBJECT INDEX

Boldfaced page numbers indicate where a key term is introduced; *f* indicates a figure; *t* a table.

INTERNATIONAL INDEX

f indicates a figure; *t* a table.